STRATEGIC MANAGEMENT
FORMULATION, IMPLEMENTATION, AND CONTROL

STRATEGIC MANAGEMENT
FORMULATION, IMPLEMENTATION, AND CONTROL

JOHN A. PEARCE II

School of Business Administration
George Mason University

RICHARD B. ROBINSON, JR.

College of Business Administration
University of South Carolina

Fifth Edition

IRWIN

Burr Ridge, Illinois
Boston, Massachusetts
Sydney, Australia

Senior sponsoring editor: *Craig Beytien*
Developmental editor: *Karen E. Perry/Lara Vergoth*
Marketing manager: *Kurt Messersmith*
Project editor: *Gladys True*
Production manager: *Bette Ittersagen*
Designer: *Heidi J. Baughman*
Art Coordinator: *Mark Malloy*
Art Studio: *Weimer Graphics, Inc.*
Compositor: *Weimer Graphics, Inc.*
Typeface: *10/12 Times Roman*
Printer: *R. R. Donnelley & Sons Company*

Library of Congress Cataloging-in-Publication Data

Pearce, John A.
  Strategic management : formulation, implementation, and control /
John A. Pearce, II, Richard B. Robinson, Jr.—5th ed.
      p.   cm.
  Includes bibliographical references and index.
  ISBN 0-256-11362-9
  1. Strategic planning.   I. Robinson, Richard B. (Richard Braden).
1947-   . II. Title.
HD30.28.P3395   1994
658.4'012—dc20   93–5598

Printed in the United States of America
   4 5 6 7 8 9 0 DO 0 9 8 7 6 5

To
David Donham Pearce, Mark McCartney Pearce,
Katherine Elizabeth Robinson, John Braden Robinson—
for the love, joy, and vitality that they give to our lives.

PREFACE

This fifth edition of our book is the culmination of 15 years of diligent work by many people. It represents our earnest efforts to further improve a book that in its last edition alone was adopted by over 500 colleges and universities and studied by over a quarter of a million students. This preface will provide you with an overview of the content of this newest edition and will give us the opportunity to recognize the many contributors who have aided us in its development.

Strategic Management: Strategy Formulation, Implementation, and Control, 5th edition, provides a thoroughly revised, state-of-the-art treatment of the critical business skills of planning and managing strategic activities. We have organized our treatment of strategic management into 11 chapters, added a critical pedagogical feature that addresses global strategic issues, expanded the number of "real-world" examples, added a totally new and engaging Cohesion Case on Coca-Cola, and further incorporated the work of contemporary scholars into our coverage of strategic management. We feel confident you will find the material to be well organized, laden with current examples, and reflective of new contributions in the strategic management literature while retaining a structure guided by our time-tested and widely accepted model of the strategic management process.

We have selected 35 cases for this edition—all 35 are new! Only one of the cases, a comprehensively updated version of the widely acclaimed "Hazelton Laboratories," pertains to a company studied in our last edition. Our survey of professors confirmed our belief that the most valuable cases review business situations that reflect the realities of today's dynamic, global, and supercompetitive marketplace. For most of us, and certainly for students, there are no classic cases, just old ones.

The cases are grouped into four sections. Eleven cases introduce students to strategic management and the process of strategy formulation, 12 cases place students in the role of implementing basic strategies, 9 cases allow students to experience the challenges of monitoring and controlling implemented strategies, and 2 cases allow you to cover industry analysis and strategic management in an integrated set of information on competitive business situations. We are very excited about the cases selected for this edition—they are contemporary and interesting situations that students will learn from, recognize, and enjoy.

We have prepared a totally new Cohesion Case. Few industries have the worldwide visibility of the soft-drink industry. Our new Cohesion Case from this industry, Coca-Cola focuses on the leader of an industry confronted with the numerous and varied strategic opportunities and challenges. Coca-Cola is large but entrepreneurial, innovative, growing, and cleverly managed. We think that students will find it to be an ideal case to study as they perfect their applications of the text material to actual business situations.

While the Cohesion Case has been recognized by many as one of the unique pedagogical advances in business policy and highlights of this book, we have added a record number of self-teaching aids to this edition. We have a truly comprehensive strategic management teaching package for this edition. It includes Strategic Analyst, which is software that allows students to conduct a computer-based systematic analysis of the strategic options available to a business and do so with built-in linkages to our text. It also includes a set of Lotus templates that are provided free for use by instructors and students. Data from all the cases in the fifth edition are included on these disks.

Other components of our teaching package include a totally revised and enhanced Instructor's Manual, a set of four-color teaching transparencies, and a computerized version of our class-tested, objective question test bank. Each of these components of our teaching package offers the instructor optimal, integrated flexibility in designing and conducting the strategic management course.

Changes to Our Text Material

The literature and research comprising the strategic management field has been developing at a rapid pace in recent years. We have endeavored to create a fifth edition that incorporates major developments in this literature while keeping our focus centered on a straightforward and understandable framework through which students can begin to grasp the complexity of strategic management. Several content areas have been heavily revised:

A three-chapter set on external analysis (Chapters 3, 4, 5) strengthened by application supplements gives our adopters more information on competitive dynamics than is available in any other text. Separate chapters now cover the nature of external environments and industry analysis, environmental forecasting, and the global business setting.

Chapter 5 has been revised to highlight the global issues and strategic management in an international setting.

Organizational culture as a central dimension of strategy implementation receives thorough coverage in Chapter 10. Several useful analytical concepts and techniques that aid identification and management of the strategy-culture interface are incorporated to aid the student in understanding the cultural concept.

A completely new section entitled "Guidelines for Structuring Effective Reward Systems" has been added to Chapter 10. This material provides students who are about to graduate with nine practical guidelines about structuring reward systems that reflect strategic imperatives while helping them deal with the operating reality most of them will soon face.

Major emphasis has been placed on the topic of "strategic control." Three basic types of strategic control and ways to use them are highlighted in this material found in Chapter 11. "Change" and its influence on strategic control have been accorded expanded coverage in Chapter 11 to include a very interesting example developed from John Scully's recent overhaul of Apple's strategic vision.

A completely new section on "The Quality Imperative" has been added to Chapter 11 to help students adapt "quality" coverage in earlier courses into a strategic perspective.

This section emphasizes 10 key practical elements of total quality management as it ties the quality concept into strategic management and strategic control. The section includes a great example in Strategy in Action 11–3 about the 1992 Baldrige Award winner Marlow Industries of Dallas, Texas.

Three supplements accompany our text to increase readers' ability to enhance their competence in the practice of strategic management:

1. A guide to industry information sources follows Chapter 5—Environmental Forecasting. Students will find it most helpful in rapidly orienting them to where and how to get company and industry data.

2. Also following Chapter 5 is a supplement on strategic planning tools and techniques for forecasting. It offers a practical assessment of each of 20 planning aids as well as source information on where detailed how-to materials can be found.

3. A revised guide to financial analysis is provided following Chapter 6—Internal Analysis. It provides perhaps the most thorough and easy-to-use guide to quantitative analysis of financial and operating information available in any strategic management text.

We have updated and improved our Strategy in Action Capsules. The text material contains 34 of these illustration vignettes, 22 of which are new to this edition. Each Strategy in Action provides a contemporary business example of a key chapter topic designed to enhance student interest and aid learning.

New to this edition are Global Strategy in Action Capsules, which provide readers with information on how strategic managers worldwide meet the challenges of global competition. A total of 17 Global Strategy in Action Capsules appear in the text, with at least one of these extended examples provided in every chapter.

Our popular Cohesion Case feature has received considerable attention in this edition. Not only have we prepared a completely new case to illustrate in detail the application of the text material but we also continue to provide Cohesion Case sections at the end of each chapter, which apply chapter material to the Coca-Cola situation. A major theme throughout our revision has been the global economy and its challenge for strategic managers guiding their existing or new firms in the 21st century. The Coca-Cola Company provides perhaps the world's premier "global" company as the setting in which the Cohesion Case places your students to gain a comprehensive, unfolding illustration of strategic management. Coca-Cola has also allowed us to create a video paralleling the Cohesion Case, which reinforces our topical coverage and provides thought-provoking interviews with key Coke executives about strategic management issues.

Our survey of adopters told us that they wanted us to continue to help inform students about what they need to do in preparing a case—and in maintaining a strategic point of view. Therefore, we have included a major section in this edition that is solely intended to aid students in understanding case method pedagogy and to prepare them to analyze a case. The first part of this section provides a thorough and detailed description of the case method format, what to expect in each class session, and how to analyze a case, prepare it for class, and participate in class discussion. The second part offers a short case accompanied by a useful example of former students' analyses and preparation of it.

These two learning aids, combined with the new Cohesion Case illustrating each step of strategic analysis, provide the most thorough package available in any strategy textbook to ensure that students understand and benefit from the case method pedagogy.

In conclusion, we are confident you will find the text material in this edition to be organized, concise, filled with current examples, and consistent with the current theory and practice of strategic management.

Cases in the Fifth Edition

We are very excited about the 35 new cases available in this edition. We are confident that you will find that this case collection does an excellent job of meeting your classroom needs for several reasons.

The collection offers a rich diversity of recognizable domestic, foreign, and international companies and industries. The cases present very current situations. All of the cases involve situations from 1990 to 1993, and all focus on issues in the forefront of strategic management for the 1990s.

Contemporary, recognizable, interest-piquing situations abound: the resurgence of the multinationalized Kentucky Fried Chicken; the reemergence of Apple; the dynamic environment of Blockbuster Entertainment, Southwest Air, and Microsoft; the strategic maneuvering of Philip Morris and Disney; survival strategies in mature defense industries exemplified by Lockheed and Orbital Sciences; TQM at Xerox, an ethical question at IBM; and the explosive growth of global competitor Hazelton Laboratories—all situations our tests have shown stimulate student interest.

The nature of the firms provides varied exposure. We have included 5 small companies in either family or rapid growth phases, 19 companies with international operations, 10 of the largest companies in America, and 2 nonprofit organizations.

In all, adopters have a variety of domestic and international industry settings at different stages of evolution and spanning 15 cases in manufacturing, 13 in services, 4 in food, beer, and wine processing, and 6 in retailing. Different cases cover the basic types of business, companies in market leadership positions, companies falling out of leadership, high-tech companies, exporters, importers, and diversifying companies.

We also have given significant attention to case length. A major effort has been made to ensure that a majority of the cases are short to medium in length.

Finally, we have endeavored to ensure a collection of the cases that are flexible in their course sequencing, yet able to offer exposure to distinct management challenges associated with strategy formulation, implementation, or control. Because our survey found case flexibility to be one of the key concerns of strategic management professors, the cases were assembled with this need foremost in our minds. Overall, we think you will find this case collection interesting and motivating for your students, representative and varied in the application of strategic problems and analytical applications, flexible in terms of course sequencing, and teachable.

Acknowledgments

We have benefited from the help of many people in the evolution of this book over five editions. Students, adopters, colleagues, reviewers, and business contacts have provided hundreds of insightful comments, suggestions, and contributions that have progressively enhanced this book. We are indebted to the researchers, writers, and practicing managers who have accelerated the development of the literature on strategic management.

We are likewise indebted to the talented case researchers who have produced cases used in this book, as well as the growing network of case researchers who are encouraging the revitalization of case research as an important academic endeavor. The discipline of strategic management is eminently more teachable when current well-written and well-researched cases are available. We encourage every opportunity to reinforce proper recognition and reward for first-class case research—it is a major avenue through which top strategic management scholars should be recognized.

The following strategic management scholars have provided the results of their case research in the creation of this fifth edition:

Amy Vernberg Beekman
University of South Carolina

Gary J. Castogiovanni
Louisiana State University

J. Carl Clamp
University of South Carolina

F. Derakhshan
California State University at San Bernardino

Brook Dobni
University of Saskatchewan

Max E. Douglas
Indiana State University

Walter Green
Pan American University

David W. Grigsby
Clemson University

W. Harvey Hegarty
Indiana University

Marilyn M. Helms
University of Tennessee at Chattanooga

Alan Hoffman
Bentley College

Eileen Hogan
George Mason University

Stephen R. Jenner
California State University

James A. Kidney
Southern Connecticut State University

Robert Letovsky
Saint Michael's College

Frank S. Lockwood
University of South Carolina

John Logan
University of South Carolina

Sandra Logan
Newberry College

Patricia P. McDougall
Georgia Institute of Technology

Robert Mookler
St. John's University

Benjamin M. Oviatt
Georgia State University

Keith Robbins
George Mason University

John Seeger
Bentley College

Arthur Sharplin
McNeese State University

Rodney C. Shrader
Georgia State University

F. Bruce Simmons III
The University of Akron

Mark Simon
Georgia State University

Neil Snyder
University of Virginia

George H. Tompson
University of South Carolina

Howard Tu
Memphis State University

Joseph Wolfe
University of Tulsa

We have personally ensured that the dean at each of the case author's respective institutions is aware of the value that his or her case research efforts have added to professionals' ability to teach strategic management.

The development of this book through five editions has been greatly enhanced by the generous commitment of time, energy, and ideas from the following people (we apologize if the affiliation given has changed):

B. Alpert
San Francisco State University

Alan Amason
Mississippi State University

Sonny Aries
University of Toledo

Robert Earl Bolick
Metropolitan State University

Bill Boulton
Auburn University

Jeff Bracker
University of Louisville

Dorothy Brawley
Kennesaw State College

William Burr
University of Oregon

Gene E. Burton
California State University–Fresno

Edgar T. Busch
Western Kentucky University

Gerard A. Cahill

Jim Callahan
University of LaVerne

Jim Carland
Western Carolina University

Richard Castaldi
San Diego State University

Jafor Chowdbury
University of Scranton

Jim Chrisman
University of the Pacific

Earl D. Cooper
Florida Institute of Technology

Louis Coraggio
Troy State University

John P. Cragin
Oklahoma Baptist University

Larry Cummings
Northwestern University

Peter Davis
Memphis State University

William Davis
Auburn University

Julio DeCastro
University of Colorado

Mark Dollinger
Indiana University

Derrick Dsouza
University of North Texas

Norbert Esser
Central Wesleyan College

Forest D. Etheredge
Aurora University

Liam Fahey

Mark Fiegener
Oregon State University

Calvin D. Fowler
Embry-Riddle Aeronautical University

Elizabeth Freeman
Southern Methodist University

Mahmoud A. Gaballa
Mansfield University

Diane Garsombke
University of Maine

Betsy Gatewood
University of Houston

Michael Geringer
Southern Methodist University

Manton C. Gibbs
Indiana University of Pennsylvania

Nicholas A. Glaskowsky, Jr.
University of Miami

Jon Goodman
University of Southern California

Lanny Herron
University of Baltimore

Charles T. Hofer
University of Georgia

Frank Hoy
University of Texas at El Paso

R. H. Gordon
Hofstra University

Peter Goulet
University of Northern Iowa

Daniel E. Hallock
St. Edward's University

Don Hambrick
Columbia University

Barry Hand
Indiana State University

Samuel Hazen
Tarleton State University

Edward A. Hegner
California State University–Sacramento

Marilyn M. Helms
University of Tennessee

D. Higginbotham
University of Missouri

Roger Higgs
Western Carolina University

William H. Hinkle
Johns Hopkins University

Richard Hoffman
College of William and Mary

Gary L. Holman
St. Martin's College

Henry F. House
Auburn University at Montgomery

Warren Huckabay

Tammy G. Hunt
University of North Carolina at Wilmington

John W. Huonker
University of Arizona

C. Boyd Johnson
California State University–Fresno

Troy Jones
University of Central Florida

Jon Kalinowski
Mankato State University

Al Kayloe
Lake Erie College

Kay Keels
Louisiana State University

John D. King
Embry-Riddle Aeronautical University

John B. Knauff
University of St. Thomas

Rose Knotts
University of North Texas

Michael Koshuta
Valparaiso University

Myroslaw Kyj
Widener University of Pennsylvania

Dick LaBarre
Ferris State University

Joseph Leonard
Miami University, Ohio

Benjamin Litt
Lehigh University

Jean M. Lundin
Lake Superior State University

Donald C. Malm
University of Missouri–St. Louis

John Maurer
Wayne State University

Denise Mazur
Aquinas College

Edward McClelland
Roanoke College

Bob McDonald
Central Wesleyan College

Patricia McDougall
Georgia Tech

S. Mehta
San Jose State University

Richard Merner
University of Delaware

Timothy Mescon
Kennesaw State College

Phillip C. Micka
Park College

Cynthia Montgomery
Harvard University

Gary W. Muller
Hofstra University

Terry Munson
Northern Montana College

Stephaine Newell
Bowling Green State University

Michael E. Nix
Trinity College of Vermont

Kenneth Olm
University of Texas at Austin

Benjamin Oviatt
Georgia State University

Joseph Paolillo
University of Mississippi

James W. Pearce
Western Carolina University

Douglas Polley
St. Cloud State University

Mark S. Poulos
St. Edward's University

John R. Pratt
Saint Joseph's College

Oliver Ray Price
West Coast University

John Primus
Golden Gate University

Norris Rath
Shepard College

Paula Rechner
University of Illinois

J. Bruce Regan
University of St. Thomas

F. A. Ricci
Georgetown University

Gary Roberts
Kennesaw State College

Lloyd E. Roberts
Mississippi College

Les Rue
Georgia State University

J. A. Ruslyk
Memphis State University

Jack Scarborough
Barry University

Martin Shapiro
Iona College

Fred Smith
Western Illinois University

Scott Snell
Michigan State University

Coral R. Snodgrass
Canisius College

Rudolph P. Snowadzky
University of Maine

Robert L. Swinth
Montana State University

Melanie Trevino
University of Texas at El Paso

Craig Tunwall
Ithaca College

Elaine M. Tweedy
University of Scranton

Arieh A. Ullman
SUNY at Binghamton

P. Veglahn
James Madison University

George Vozikis
The Citadel

William Waddell
California State University–Los Angeles

Bill Warren
College of William and Mary

Kirby Warren
Columbia University

Steven J. Warren
Rutgers University

Michael White
University of Tulsa

Randy White
Auburn University

Sam E. White
Portland State University

Frank Winfrey
Kent State University

Edward D. Writh, Jr.
Florida Institute of Technology

Robley Wood
Virginia Commonwealth University

John Young
University of Colorado at Denver

Jan Zahrly
Old Dominion University

The valuable ideas, recommendations, and support of these outstanding scholars and teachers have added quality to this book.

Because we are affiliated with two separate universities, we have two sets of co-workers to thank.

The growth and dynamic environment at George Mason University have contributed directly to the development of this edition. Valuable critiques and helpful recommendations have been made by Jack's strategic management colleagues Bill Fulmer, Tracy Kramer, and Keith Robbins. For his gracious support and personal encouragement, we also wish to thank Kees de Kluyver, dean of George Mason University's School of Business Administration. For her excellent administrative and secretarial assistance, we most sincerely appreciate the work of Sondra Patrick.

We are especially grateful to LeRoy Eakin, Jr., and his family for their generous endowment of the Eakin Endowed Chair in Strategic Management at George Mason University that Jack holds. The provisions of the chair have enabled Jack to continue his dual involvements with this book and strategic management research.

The stimulating international environment at the University of South Carolina has contributed to the development of this edition. Thought-provoking discussions with strategy colleagues Alan Bauerschmidt, Carl Clamp, Dan Feldman, Herb Hand, John Logan, Bill Sandberg, Harry Sapienza, and David Schweiger provided many useful ideas and insights. Likewise, we want to thank James F. Kane, dean of the College of Business Administration; James G. Hilton, associate dean; and Susie VanHuss, program director in management, for their interest and support. Our sincere appreciation also goes to Cheryl Fowler and Susie Gossage for their help in preparing this manuscript and in solving endless logistical problems.

In using this text, we hope that you will share our enthusiasm both for the rich subject of strategic management and for the learning approach that we have taken. We value your recommendations and thoughts about our materials. Please write Jack at the Department of Management, School of Business Administration, George Mason University, Fairfax, Virginia 22030, (703-993-1818) or Richard at the College of Business Administration, University of South Carolina, Columbia, South Carolina 29208, (803-777-5961).

We wish you the very best as you advance your knowledge in the exciting and rewarding field of strategic management.

Jack Pearce
Richard Robinson

ABOUT THE AUTHORS

John A. Pearce II, Ph.D., is the holder of the Eakin Endowed Chair in Strategic Management and is a State of Virginia Eminent Scholar in the School of Business Administration at George Mason University.

Professor Pearce has published more than 160 journal articles, invited book chapters, and professional papers in outlets that include the *Academy of Management Executive*, *Academy of Management Journal*, *Academy of Management Review*, *California Management Review*, *Journal of Business Venturing*, *Sloan Management Review*, and the *Strategic Management Journal*. Professor Pearce is also the coauthor or coeditor of 26 texts, proceedings, and supplements for book publishers that include Richard D. Irwin, Inc., McGraw-Hill, Random House, and the Academy of Management.

Elected to more than a dozen offices in national and regional professional associations, Professor Pearce has served as chairman of the Academy of Management's Entrepreneurship Division, Strategic Management and Entrepreneurship track chairman for the Southern Management Association, and Strategy Formulation and Implementation track chairman for the Decision Sciences Institute. He was the president of the Southern Management Association in 1990.

A former Fulbright-Hays Senior Professor in International Management, and an active consultant and executive educator, Professor Pearce specializes in helping executive teams to develop and activate their firms' strategic plans.

Richard B. Robinson, Jr., Ph.D., is Professor of Strategy and Entrepreneurship and is a Business Partnership Foundation Fellow in the College of Business Administration at the University of South Carolina. Professor Robinson recently returned to USC after serving for three years as president and CEO of a rapidly growing hazardous waste management company.

Professor Robinson has published numerous articles and professional papers in preeminent journals and associations dedicated to improving the practice of strategic management and the art of entrepreneurship. He has coauthored 23 texts, proceedings, and supplements for book publishers that include Richard D. Irwin, Inc., McGraw-Hill, Random House, and the Academy of Management.

Professor Robinson is the recipient of several awards in recognition of his work in strategic management and entrepreneurship. Sponsors of these awards include the Heizer

Capital Corporation, the Academy of Management, the Center for Family Business, the National Association of Small Business Investment Companies, the Southern Business Administration Association, the Small Business Administration, the National Venture Capital Association, Beta Gamma Sigma, and the Center for Entrepreneurial Studies at NYU. He also has held offices in the Academy of Management, the Southern Management Association, and the International Council of Small Business.

Professor Robinson has held management positions in companies competing in the restaurant and lodging, pulp and paper, environmental services, and publishing and management development industries. He currently serves as an advisor to several growth-oriented ventures.

CONTENTS

4   The Global Environment: Strategic Considerations for Multinational Firms   106

8 Strategic Analysis and Choice   255

IV   Cases   415

I OVERVIEW OF STRATEGIC MANAGEMENT

The first chapter of this book introduces strategic management, the set of decisions and actions that result in the design and activation of strategies to achieve the objectives of an organization. The chapter provides an overview of the nature, need, benefits, and terminology of strategic management. Subsequent chapters provide greater detail.

The first major section of Chapter 1, "The Nature and Value of Strategic Management," emphasizes the practical value and benefits of strategic management for a firm. It also distinguishes between a firm's strategic decisions and its other planning tasks.

The section stresses the key point that strategic management activities are undertaken at three levels: corporate, business, and functional. The distinctive characteristics of strategic decision making at each of these levels affect the impact of activities at these levels on company operations. Other topics dealt with in this section are the value of formality in strategic management and the alignment of strategy makers in strategy formulation and implementation. The section concludes with a review of the planning research on business, which demonstrates that the use of strategic management processes yields financial and behavioral benefits that justify their costs.

The second major section of Chapter 1 presents a model of the strategic management process. The model, which will serve as an outline for the remainder of the text, describes approaches currently used by strategic planners. Its individual components are carefully defined and explained, as is the process for integrating them into the strategic management process. The section ends with a discussion of the model's practical limitations and the advisability of tailoring the recommendations made to actual business situations.

1

STRATEGIC MANAGEMENT

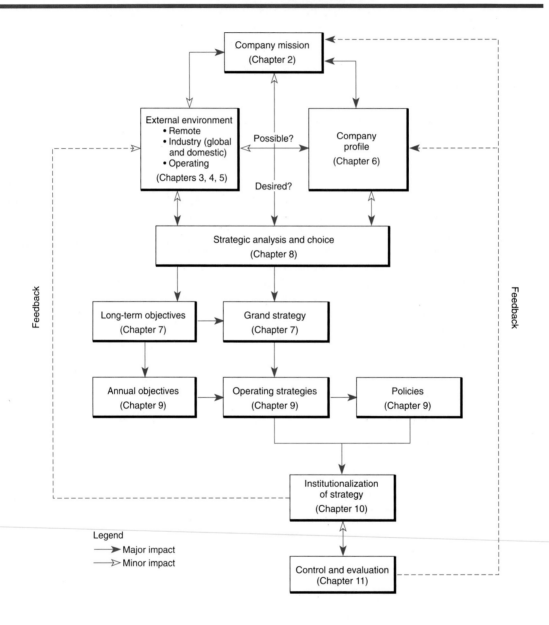

Company mission
(Chapter 2)

External environment
- Remote
- Industry (global and domestic)
- Operating

(Chapters 3, 4, 5)

Possible?

Company profile
(Chapter 6)

Desired?

Strategic analysis and choice
(Chapter 8)

Long-term objectives
(Chapter 7)

Grand strategy
(Chapter 7)

Annual objectives
(Chapter 9)

Operating strategies
(Chapter 9)

Policies
(Chapter 9)

Institutionalization of strategy
(Chapter 10)

Control and evaluation
(Chapter 11)

Feedback

Feedback

Legend
→ Major impact
⇢ Minor impact

THE NATURE AND VALUE OF STRATEGIC MANAGEMENT

Managing activities internal to the firm is only part of the modern executive's responsibilities. The modern executive also must respond to the challenges posed by the firm's immediate and remote external environment. The immediate external environment includes competitors, suppliers, increasingly scarce resources, government agencies and their ever more numerous regulations, and customers whose preferences often shift inexplicably. The remote external environment comprises economic and social conditions, political priorities, and technological developments, all of which must be anticipated, monitored, assessed, and incorporated into the executive's decision making. However, the executive often is compelled to subordinate the demands of the firm's internal activities and external environment to the multiple and often inconsistent requirements of its stakeholders: owners, top managers, employees, communities, customers, and country. To deal effectively with everything that affects the growth and profitability of a firm, executives employ management processes that they feel will position it optimally in its competitive environment by maximizing the anticipation of environmental changes and of unexpected internal and competitive demands.

Broad-scope, large-scale management processes became dramatically more sophisticated after World War II. These processes responded to increases in the size and number of competing firms; to the expanded role of government as a buyer, seller, regulator, and competitor in the free enterprise system; and to greater business involvement in international trade. Perhaps the most significant improvement in management processes came in the 1970s, when "long-range planning," "new venture management," "planning, programming, budgeting," and "business policy" were blended. At the same time, increased emphasis was placed on environmental forecasting and external considerations in formulating and implementing plans. This all-encompassing approach is known as strategic management or strategic planning.[1]

Strategic management is defined as the set of decisions and actions that result in the formulation and implementation of plans designed to achieve a company's objectives. It comprises nine critical tasks:

1. Formulate the company's mission, including broad statements about its purpose, philosophy, and goals.
2. Develop a company profile that reflects its internal conditions and capabilities.
3. Assess the company's external environment, including both the competitive and general contextual factors.
4. Analyze the company's options by matching its resources with the external environment.
5. Identify the most desirable options by evaluating each option in light of the company's mission.
6. Select a set of long-term objectives and grand strategies that will achieve the most desirable options.
7. Develop annual objectives and short-term strategies that are compatible with the selected set of long-term objectives and grand strategies.

---

[1] In this text, the term *strategic management* refers to the broad overall process. To some scholars and practitioners, the term connotes only the formulation phase of total management activities.

8. Implement the strategic choices by means of budgeted resource allocations in which the matching of tasks, people, structures, technologies, and reward systems is emphasized.
9. Evaluate the success of the strategic process as an input for future decision making.

As these nine tasks indicate, strategic management involves the planning, directing, organizing, and controlling of a company's strategy-related decisions and actions. By *strategy*, managers mean their large-scale, future-oriented plans for interacting with the competitive environment to achieve company objectives. A strategy is a company's "game plan." Although that plan does not precisely detail all future deployments (of people, finances, and material), it does provide a framework for managerial decisions. A strategy reflects a company's awareness of how, when, and where it should compete; against whom it should compete; and for what purposes is should compete.

DIMENSIONS OF STRATEGIC DECISIONS

What decisions facing a business are strategic and therefore deserve strategic management attention? Typically, strategic issues have the following dimensions.

Strategic Issues Require Top-Management Decisions Since strategic decisions overarch several areas of a firm's operations, they require top-management involvement. Usually only top management has the perspective needed to understand the broad implications of such decisions and the power to authorize the necessary resource allocations. As top manager of Volvo GM Heavy Truck Corporation, Karl-Erling Trogen, president, wanted to push the company closer to the customer by overarching operations with service and customer relations empowering the work force closest to the customer with greater knowledge and authority. This strategy called for a major commitment to the parts and service end of the business where customer relations was first priority. Trogen's philosophy was to so empower the work force that more operating questions were handled on the line where workers worked directly with customers. He believed that the corporate headquarters should be more focused on strategic issues, such as engineering, production, quality, and marketing.

Strategic Issues Require Large Amounts of the Firm's Resources Strategic decisions involve substantial allocations of people, physical assets, or moneys that either must be redirected from internal sources or secured from outside the firm. They also commit the firm to actions over an extended period. For these reasons, they require substantial resources. Whirlpool Corporation's "Quality Express" product delivery program exemplified a strategy that required a strong financial and personnel commitment from the company. The plan was to deliver products to customers when, where, and how they wanted them. This proprietary service utilized contract logistics strategy to deliver Whirlpool, Kitchen Aid, Roper, and Estate brand appliances to 90 percent of the company's dealer and builder customers within 24 hours and to the other 10 percent within 48 hours. Whirlpool planned to go coast-to-coast with its new system by the end of 1992. In highly competitive service-oriented businesses, achieving and maintaining customer satisfaction frequently involves a commitment from every facet of the organization.

Strategic Issues Often Affect the Firm's Long-Term Prosperity Strategic decisions ostensibly commit the firm for a long time, typically five years; however, the impact of such decisions often lasts much longer. Once a firm has committed itself to a particular strategy, its image and competitive advantages usually are tied to that strategy. Firms become known in certain markets, for certain products, with certain technologies. They would jeopardize their previous gains if they shifted from these markets, products, or technologies by adopting a radically different strategy. Thus, strategic decisions have enduring effects on firms— for better or worse.

Strategic Issues Are Future Oriented Strategic decisions are based on what managers forecast, rather than on what they know. In such decisions, emphasis is placed on the development of projections that will enable the firm to select the most promising strategic options. In the turbulent and competitive free enterprise environment, a firm will succeed only if it takes a proactive (anticipatory) stance toward change.

Strategic Issues Usually Have Multifunctional or Multibusiness Consequences Strategic decisions have complex implications for most areas of the firm. Decisions about such matters as customer mix, competitive emphasis, or organizational structure necessarily involve a number of the firm's strategic business units (SBUs), divisions, or program units. All of these areas will be affected by allocations or reallocations of responsibilities and resources that result from these decisions.

Strategic Issues Require Considering the Firm's External Environment All business firms exist in an open system. They affect and are affected by external conditions that are largely beyond their control. Therefore, to successfully position a firm in competitive situations, its strategic managers must look beyond its operations.[2] They must consider what relevant others (e.g., competitors, customers, suppliers, creditors, government, and labor) are likely to do.[3]

Global Strategy in Action 1–1 tells the strategy of a small but rapidly growing restaurant chain. Notice that even such a brief overview on an entrepreneurial firm covers many of the issues that we described above as critical to the strategic management process.

Three Levels of Strategy

The decision-making hierarchy of a firm typically contains three levels. At the top of this hierarchy is the corporate level, composed principally of a board of directors and the chief executive and administrative officers. They are responsible for the firm's financial performance and for the achievement of nonfinancial goals, such as enhancing the firm's image and fulfilling its social responsibilities. To a large extent, attitudes at the corporate level reflect the concerns of stockholders and society at large. In a multibusiness firm, corporate-level executives determine the businesses in which the firm should be involved. They also

---

[2] R. E. Seiler and K. E. Said, "Problems Encountered in Operationalizing a Company's Strategic Plans," *Managerial Planning*, January–February 1983, pp. 16–20.

[3] M. Allen, "Strategic Management of Consumer Services," *Long Range Planning*, December 1988, pp. 20–25.

B locking the north side of 54th Street between Fifth and Madison avenues each day at lunch-time is a well-dressed but hungry mob. It's crowding the sidewalk outside Bice, the chic Italian eatery that has made itself the Lourdes of pasta.

The airy dining room seats 160 people and serves some 600 meals a day—average check, about $40 per person at lunch, $60 at dinner. Average daily take: $30,000. But even at these prices, the crowds keep coming. Gianfranco Sorrentino, Bice's unflappable maitre d', dispenses choice front tables to Henry Kissinger and Ronald Perelman, shuffling shoppers and Japanese tourists off behind the massive floral arrangement.

What makes Bice (pronounced beechay) different is owner Roberto Ruggeri's notion that it can be cloned worldwide—doing with a $22.00 black risotto with cuttlefish what McDonald's did with the $1.80 Big Mac.

So Bices are popping up everywhere, 14 so far. Branches in Chicago and Beverly Hills opened in 1989; Paris and Palm Beach in 1990; Washington, Atlanta, Miami, and Scottsdale, Arizona, last year. Bice has since sprouted in San Diego and Tokyo. Coming up are new outposts in Aspen, Montreal, Toronto, Mexico City, Caracas, London, and Sydney. The U.S. operations are all wholly owned. The foreign Bices are joint ventures or are licensed to local owners. "I don't know Caracas," Ruggeri says, explaining why he prefers not to entirely own his deals overseas. "You wake up, they shoot, a new government comes in, and I lose my restaurant."

Potential coups aside, Bice looks enviably solid in a notoriously treacherous industry. The New York flagship had revenues of around $10 million last year, a level that only a handful of New York restaurants—like Tavern on the Green and Windows on the World—can beat. Pasta ingredients are

Source: Excerpted from J. Levine, "Where the Maitre d' Outranks the Chef," *Forbes*, June 8, 1992, pp. 70–71.

set objectives and formulate strategies that span the activities and functional areas of these businesses. Corporate-level strategic managers attempt to exploit their firm's distinctive competencies by adopting a portfolio approach to the management of its businesses and by developing long-term plans, typically for a five-year period. A key corporate strategy of Airborne Express's operations involved direct sale to high-volume corporate accounts and developing an expansive network in the international arena. Instead of setting up operations overseas, Airborne's long-term strategy was to form direct associations with national companies within foreign countries to expand and diversify their operations.

Another example of the portfolio approach involved a plan by state-owned Saudi Arabian Oil to spend $1.4 billion in 1991 to build and operate an oil refinery in Korea with its partner, Ssangyong. To implement their program, the Saudis embarked on a new "cut-out-the-middleman" strategy to reduce the role of international oil companies in the processing and selling of Saudi crude oil.

In the middle of the decision-making hierarchy is the business level, composed principally of business and corporate managers. These managers must translate the statements of direction and intent generated at the corporate level into concrete objectives and strategies for individual business divisions, or SBUs. In essence, business-level strategic managers determine how the firm will compete in the selected product-market arena. They

relatively cheap, so New York profit margins are high: 20 percent. Bice's satellite restaurants have revenues of around $3.0 million to $3.5 million, considered hearty performance by the trade. Only one so far is a dud: Scottsdale. Price cuts loom there.

"This is unique," says Clark Wolf, a New York food and restaurant consultant. "No one before has opened the same restaurant of this caliber all over the world."

To finance his growth, Ruggeri sold a half-interest in his company to a Japanese restaurant chain, WDI, for roughly $2 million in 1989—with the provision that he could buy back his stake. He did so last year for about $6 million. The Japanese got back their $2 million in cash and financed the rest in notes. Now Ruggeri is hoping that investors have noticed his success. He says he's contemplating a public offering to raise $15 million for around 30 percent to 40 percent of the company. With that new money he can expand still further.

Ruggeri, 49, an affable, somewhat rumpled Milanese with unruly brown and gray hair, has a simple marketing strategy: predictability and ambience, rather than to-die-for food. Explains Ruggeri: "A customer would rather go to a happy place with exceptional food. I'm giving people comfort, not a peak experience." So at Bice the key job is maitre d', not chef. "Italian cuisine is very simple—any good chef can do it. Personality, you can't teach," says Ruggeri.

The trick in the restaurant trade is to survive when the fickle fashion crowd moves on, as they inevitably do. So Ruggeri makes sure he finds locations close to swank stores like Tiffany and Cartier and to commercial hubs to pull in a diverse clientele. "When the trendies stopped coming, the shopping ladies and business people took over," he says.

strive to identify and secure the most promising market segment within that arena. This segment is the piece of the total market that the firm can claim and defend because of its competitive advantages.

At the bottom of the decision-making hierarchy is the functional level, composed principally of managers of product, geographic, and functional areas. They develop annual objectives and short-term strategies in such areas as production, operations, research and development, finance and accounting, marketing, and human relations. However, their principal responsibility is to implement or execute the firm's strategic plans. Whereas corporate- and business-level managers center their attention on "doing the right things," managers at the functional level center their attention on "doing things right." Thus, they address such issues as the efficiency and effectiveness of production and marketing systems, the quality of customer service, and the success of particular products and services in increasing the firm's market shares.

Figure 1–1 depicts the three levels of strategic management as structured in practice. In alternative 1, the firm is engaged in only one business and the corporate- and business-level responsibilities are concentrated in a single group of directors, officers, and managers. This is the organizational format of most small businesses.

Alternative 2, the classical corporate structure, comprises three fully operative levels: the corporate level, the business level, and the functional level. The approach taken

FIGURE 1–1
Alternative Strategic Management Structures

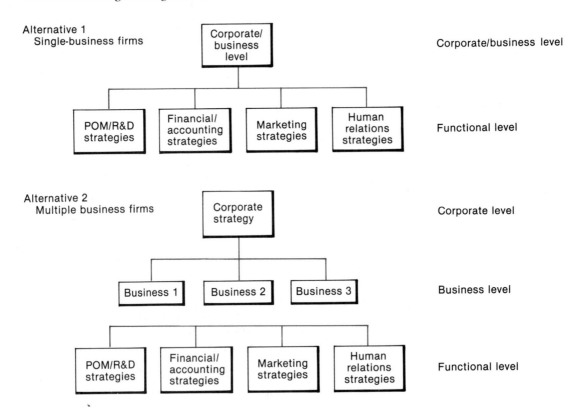

throughout this text assumes the use of alternative 2. Moreover, whenever appropriate, topics are covered from the perspective of each level of strategic management. In this way, the text presents a comprehensive discussion of the strategic management process.

Characteristics of Strategic Management Decisions

The characteristics of strategic management decisions vary with the level of strategic activity considered. As shown in Figure 1–2, decisions at the corporate level tend to be more value oriented, more conceptual, and less concrete than decisions at the business or functional level. For example, at Alcoa, the world's largest aluminum maker, chairman Paul O'Neill planned to make Alcoa one of the nation's most centralized organizations by imposing a dramatic management reorganization that wiped out two layers of management. He found that this effort not only reduced costs but also enabled him to be closer to the front-line operations managers. Corporate-level decisions are often characterized by greater risk, cost, and profit potential; greater need for flexibility; and longer time horizons. Such decisions include the choice of businesses, dividend policies, sources of long-term financing, and priorities for growth.

FIGURE 1–2

Hierarchy of Objectives and Strategies

Ends (What is to be achieved?)	Means (How is it to be achieved?)	Strategic Decision Makers			
		Board of Directors	Corporate Managers	Business Managers	Functional Managers
Mission, including goals and philosophy		✓✓	✓✓	✓	
Long-term objectives	Grand strategy	✓	✓✓	✓✓	
Annual objectives	Short-term strategies and policies		✓	✓✓	✓✓

Note: ✓✓ indicates a principal responsibility; ✓ indicates a secondary responsibility.

Functional-level decisions implement the overall strategy formulated at the corporate and business levels. They involve action-oriented operational issues and are relatively short range and low risk. Functional-level decisions incur only modest costs, because they are dependent on available resources. They usually are adaptable to ongoing activities and, therefore, can be implemented with minimal cooperation. For example, in 1991, Nordstrom and Dillard Department Stores reported first-quarter profits of $26 million, a 95 percent increase over the previous year. They attributed the increased earnings to tighter inventory and operating controls in the parent company. In a second example, the corporate headquarters of Sears, Roebuck & Company spent $60 million in 1992 to automate 6,900 clerical jobs by installing 28,000 computerized cash registers at its 868 stores in the United States. Though this move eliminated many functional level jobs, top management believed that reducing annual operating expenses by at least $50 million was crucial to competitive survival.

Because functional-level decisions are relatively concrete and quantifiable, they receive critical attention and analysis even though their comparative profit potential is low. Common functional-level decisions include decisions on generic versus brand-name labeling, basic versus applied research and development (R&D), high versus low inventory levels, general-purpose versus specific-purpose production equipment, and close versus loose supervision.

Business-level decisions help bridge decisions at the corporate and functional levels. Such decisions are less costly, risky, and potentially profitable than corporate-level decisions, but they are more costly, risky, and potentially profitable than functional-level decisions. Common business-level decisions include decisions on plant location, marketing segmentation and geographic coverage, and distribution channels.

FORMALITY IN STRATEGIC MANAGEMENT

The formality of strategic management systems varies widely among companies. *Formality* refers to the degree to which participants, responsibilities, authority, and discretion in decision making are specified. It is an important consideration in the study of strategic management, because greater formality is usually positively correlated with the cost, comprehensiveness, accuracy, and success of planning.

A number of forces determine how much formality is needed in strategic management. The size of the organization, its predominant management styles, the complexity of its environment, its production process, its problems, and the purpose of its planning system all play a part in determining the appropriate degree of formality.[4]

In particular, formality is associated with the size of the firm and with its stage of development. Methods of evaluating strategic success also are linked to formality. Some firms, especially smaller ones, follow an *entrepreneurial* mode. They are basically under the control of a single individual, and they produce a limited number of products or services. In such firms, strategic evaluation is informal, intuitive, and limited. Very large firms, on the other hand, make strategic evaluation part of a comprehensive, formal planning system, an approach that Henry Mintzberg called the *planning mode*. Mintzberg also identified a third mode (the *adaptive mode*), which he associated with medium-sized firms in relatively stable environments.[5] For firms that follow the adaptive mode, the identification and evaluation of alternative strategies are closely related to existing strategy. It is not unusual to find different modes within the same organization. For example, Exxon might follow an entrepreneurial mode in developing and evaluating the strategy of its solar subsidiary but follow a planning mode in the rest of the company.

The Strategy Makers

The ideal strategic management team includes decision makers from all three company levels (the corporate, business, and functional)—for example, the chief executive officer (CEO), the product managers, and the heads of functional areas. In addition, the team obtains input from company planning staffs, when they exist, and from lower-level managers and supervisors. The latter provide data for strategic decision making and then implement strategies.

Because strategic decisions have a tremendous impact on a company and require large commitments of company resources, top managers must give final approval for strategic action. Figure 1–2 aligns levels of strategic decision makers with the kinds of objectives and strategies for which they are typically responsible.

Planning departments, often headed by a corporate vice president for planning, are common in large corporations. Medium-sized firms often employ at least one full-time staff member to spearhead strategic data-collection efforts. Even in small firms or less progressive larger firms, strategic planning often is spearheaded by an officer or by a group of officers designated as a planning committee.

Precisely what are managers' responsibilities in the strategic planning process at the corporate and business levels? Top management shoulders broad responsibility for all the major elements of strategic planning and management. It develops the major portions of the strategic plan and reviews, and it evaluates and counsels on all other portions. General

---

[4] M. Goold and A. Campbell, "Managing the Diversified Corporation: The Tensions Facing the Chief Executive," *Long Range Planning*, August 1988, pp. 12–24.

[5] H. Mintzberg, "Strategy Making in Three Modes," *California Management Review* 16, no. 2 (1973), pp. 44–53.

managers at the business level typically have principal responsibilities for developing environmental analysis and forecasting, establishing business objectives, and developing business plans prepared by staff groups.

A firm's president or CEO characteristically plays a dominant role in the strategic planning process. In many ways, this situation is desirable. The CEO's principal duty often is defined as giving long-term direction to the firm, and the CEO is ultimately responsible for the firm's success and, therefore, for the success of its strategy. In addition, CEOs are typically strong-willed, company-oriented individuals with high self-esteem. They often resist delegating authority to formulate or approve strategic decisions.

However, when the dominance of the CEO approaches autocracy, the effectiveness of the firm's strategic planning and management processes are likely to be diminished. For this reason, establishing a strategic management system implies that the CEO will allow managers at all levels to participate in the strategic posture of the company.

Benefits of Strategic Management[6]

Using the strategic management approach, managers at all levels of the firm interact in planning and implementing. As a result, the behavioral consequences of strategic management are similar to those of participative decision making. Therefore, an accurate assessment of the impact of strategy formulation on organizational performance requires not only financial evaluation criteria but also nonfinancial evaluation criteria—measures of behavior-based effects. In fact, promoting positive behavioral consequences also enables the firm to achieve its financial goals.[7] However, regardless of the profitability of strategic plans, several behavioral effects of strategic management improve the firm's welfare:

1. Strategy formulation activities enhance the firm's ability to prevent problems. Managers who encourage subordinates' attention to planning are aided in their monitoring and forecasting responsibilities by subordinates who are aware of the needs of strategic planning.

2. Group-based strategic decisions are likely to be drawn from the best available alternatives. The strategic management process results in better decisions because group interaction generates a greater variety of strategies and because forecasts based on the specialized perspectives of group members improve the screening of options.

3. The involvement of employees in strategy formulation improves their understanding of the productivity-reward relationship in every strategic plan and, thus, heightens their motivation.

4. Gaps and overlaps in activities among individuals and groups are reduced as participation in strategy formulation clarifies differences in roles.

5. Resistance to change is reduced. Though the participants in strategy formulation may be no more pleased with their own decisions than they would be with authoritarian decisions, their greater awareness of the parameters that limit the available options makes them more likely to accept those decisions.

---

[6] This section was adapted in part from J. A. Pearce II and W. A. Randolph, "Improving Strategy Formulation Pedagogies by Recognizing Behavioral Aspects," *Exchange*, December 1980, pp. 7–10, with permission of the authors.

[7] A. Langely, "The Roles of Formal Strategic Planning," *Long Range Planning*, June 1988, pp. 400–50.

Risks of Strategic Management

Managers must be trained to guard against three types of unintended negative consequences of involvement in strategy formulation.

First, the time that managers spend on the strategic management process may have a negative impact, thus, on operational responsibilities. Managers must be trained to minimize that impact by scheduling their duties to allow the necessary time for strategic activities.

Second, if the formulators of strategy are not intimately involved in its implementation, they may shirk their individual responsibility for the decisions reached.[8] Thus, strategic managers must be trained to limit their promises to performance that the decision makers and their subordinates can deliver.

Third, strategic managers must be trained to anticipate and respond to the disappointment of participating subordinates over unattained expectations. Subordinates may expect their involvement in even minor phases of total strategy formulation to result in both acceptance of their proposals and an increase in their rewards, or they may expect a solicitation of their input on selected issues to extend to other areas of decision making.

Sensitizing managers to these possible negative consequences and preparing them with effective means of minimizing such consequences will greatly enhance the potential of strategic planning.

Executives' Views of Strategic Management

How do managers and corporate executives view the contribution of strategic management to the success of their firms? To answer this question, a survey was conducted that included over 200 executives from the Fortune 500, Fortune 500 Service, and INC 500 companies.[9] Their responses are summarized in Strategy in Action 1–1.

Overall, these responses indicate that corporate America sees strategic management as instrumental to high performance, evolutionary and perhaps revolutionary in its ever-growing sophistication, action oriented, and cost effective. Clearly, the responding executives view strategic management as critical to their individual and organizational success.

THE STRATEGIC MANAGEMENT PROCESS

Businesses vary in the processes they use to formulate and direct their strategic management activities. Sophisticated planners, such as General Electric, Procter & Gamble, and IBM, have developed more detailed processes than less-formal planners of similar size. Small businesses that rely on the strategy formulation skills and limited time of an entrepreneur typically exhibit more basic planning concerns than those of larger firms in their

---

[8] G. S. Day, "Tough Questions for Developing Strategies," *Journal of Business Strategy*, Winter 1986, pp. 60–68.

[9] V. Ramanujam, J. C. Camillus, and N. Venkatraman, "Trends in Strategic Planning" in *Strategic Planning and Management Handbook*, ed. W. R. King and D. I. Cleland (New York: Van Nostrand Reinhold, 1987), pp. 611–28.

STRATEGY IN ACTION 1–1 EXECUTIVES' GENERAL OPINIONS AND ATTITUDES

Item	Percent of Respondents Indicating		
	Agreement	Neutral	Disagreement
1. Reducing emphasis on strategic planning will be detrimental to our long-term performance.	88.7%	4.9%	6.4%
2. Our plans today reflect implementation concerns.	73.6	16.9	9.5
3. We have improved the sophistication of our strategic planning systems.	70.6	18.6	10.8
4. Our previous approaches to strategic planning are not appropriate today.	64.2	16.2	19.6
5. Today's systems emphasize creativity among managers more than our previous systems did.	62.6	20.2	17.2
6. Our strategic planning systems today are more consistent with our organization's culture.	55.6	30.7	13.7
7. We are more concerned about the evaluation of our strategic planning systems today.	54.0	29.7	16.3
8. There is more participation from lower-level managers in our strategic planning.	56.6	18.0	25.4
9. Our tendency to rely on outside consultants for strategic planning has been on the decrease.	50.8	23.0	26.2
10. Our systems emphasize control more than before.	41.3	33.0	25.7
11. Planning in our company or unit is generally viewed as a luxury today.	15.0	13.0	72.0

Source: Adapted from V. Ramanujam, J. C. Camillus, and N. Venkatraman, "Trends in Strategic Planning," in *Strategic Planning and Management Handbook*, ed. W. R. King and D. I. Cleland (New York: Van Nostrand Reinhold, 1987), p. 619.

industries. Understandably, firms with multiple products, markets, or technologies tend to use more complex strategic management systems. However, despite differences in detail and the degree of formalization, the basic components of the models used to analyze strategic management operations are very similar.[10]

Because of the similarity among the general models of the strategic management process, it is possible to develop an eclectic model representative of the foremost thought in the strategic management area. This model is shown in Figure 1–3. It serves three major functions. First, it depicts the sequence and the relationships of the major components of the strategic management process. Second, it is the outline for this book. This chapter provides a general overview of the strategic management process, and the major components of the model will be the principal theme of subsequent chapters. Notice that the

---

[10] Models by academics that reflect such similarity, typically developed from consulting experience and intended for either business or educational use, include those of Stevenson (1976), Rogers (1975), and King and Cleland (1978). Models recommended for use by small firms—for example, those published by Gilmore (1971) and Steiner (1970)—are almost identical to those recommended for larger firms. Finally, models that describe approaches for accomplishing strategic options contain elements similar to those included in general models; see, for example, Pryor (1964) on mergers, Steiner (1964) on diversification, and TenDam (1986) for governmental agencies. The bibliography at the end of this chapter contains complete citations.

chapters of the text that discuss each of the strategic management process components are shown in each block. Finally, the model offers one approach for analyzing the case studies in this text and, thus, helps the analyst develop strategy formulation skills.

COMPONENTS OF THE STRATEGIC MANAGEMENT MODEL

This section will define and briefly describe the key components of the strategic management model. Each of these components will receive much greater attention in a later chapter. The intention here is simply to introduce them.

Company Mission

The mission of a company is the unique purpose that sets it apart from other companies of its type and identifies the scope of its operations. In short, the mission describes the company's product, market, and technological areas of emphasis in a way that reflects the values and priorities of the strategic decision makers. For example, in 1991, Lee Hun-Hee, the new chairman of the Samsung Group, revamped the company mission by stamping his own brand of management on Samsung. Immediately, Samsung separated Chonju Paper Manufacturing and Shinsegae Department Store from other operations. This corporate act of downscaling reflected a revised management philosophy that favored specialization, thereby changing the direction and scope of the organization.

Company Profile

The company profile depicts the quantity and quality of the company's financial, human, and physical resources. It also assesses the strengths and weaknesses of the company's management and organizational structure. Finally, it contrasts the company's past successes and traditional concerns with the company's current capabilities in an attempt to identify the company's future capabilities.

External Environment

A firm's external environment consists of all the conditions and forces that affect its strategic options and define its competitive situation. The strategic management model shows the external environment as three interactive segments: the operating, industry, and remote environments.

Strategic Analysis and Choice

Simultaneous assessment of the external environment and the company profile enables a firm to identify a range of possibly attractive interactive opportunities. These opportunities are *possible* avenues for investment. However, they must be screened through the criterion of the company mission to generate a set of possible and *desired* opportunities. This screening process results in the selection of options from which a *strategic choice* is made.

The process is meant to provide the combination of long-term objectives and grand strategy that optimally will position the firm in its external environment to achieve the company mission.

Long-Term Objectives

The results that an organization seeks over a multiyear period are its *long-term objectives*.[11] Such objectives typically involve some or all of the following areas: profitability, return on investment, competitive position, technological leadership, productivity, employee relations, public responsibility, and employee development.

Grand Strategy

The comprehensive, general plan of major actions through which a firm intends to achieve its long-term objectives in a dynamic environment is called the *grand strategy*; this *statement of means* indicates how the objectives are to be achieved.[12] Although every grand strategy is, in fact, a unique package of long-term strategies, 14 basic approaches can be identified: concentration, market development, product development, innovation, horizontal integration, vertical integration, joint venture, strategic alliances, consortia, concentric diversification, conglomerate diversification, turnaround, divestiture, and liquidation.

Each of these grand strategies will be covered in detail in Chapter 7.

Annual Objectives

The results that an organization seeks to achieve within a one-year period are *annual objectives* or short-term objectives. Such objectives involve areas similar to those entailed in long-term objectives. The differences between short-term objectives and long-term objectives stem principally from the greater specificity possible and necessary in short-term objectives.

Functional Strategies

Within the general framework of the grand strategy, each business function or division needs a specific and integrative plan of action. Most strategic managers attempt to develop an operating strategy for each related set of annual objectives. Operating strategies are detailed statements of the means that will be used to achieve objectives in the following year.[13]

---

[11] Five years is the normal, but largely arbitrary, time period identified as long term.

[12] J. A. Belohlav and K. Giddens-Ering, "Selecting a Master Strategy," *Journal of Business Strategy*, Winter 1987, pp. 76–82.

[13] B. Powers, "Developing an Operational Plan for Better Performance Results," *Management Solutions*, September 1986, pp. 27–30.

Policies

Policies are broad, precedent-setting decisions that guide or substitute for repetitive managerial decision making. They guide the thinking, decisions, and actions of managers and their subordinates in implementing the organization's strategy. Policies provide guidelines for establishing and controlling the ongoing operating process of the firm in a manner consistent with the firm's strategic objectives. Policies often increase managerial effectiveness by standardizing routine decisions and limit the discretion of managers and subordinates in implementing operation strategies.

The following are examples of the nature and diversity of company policies:

A requirement that managers have purchase requests for items costing more than $500 cosigned by the controller.

The minimum equity position required for all new McDonald's franchises.

The standard formula used to calculate return on investment for the 43 strategic business units of General Electric.

A decision that employees have their annual performance review on the anniversary of their hiring date.

Institutionalizing the Strategy

Annual objectives, functional strategies, and specific policies provide important means of communicating what must be done to implement the firm's overall strategy. By translating long-term intentions into short-term guides to action, they make that strategy operational. But the overall strategy must also be *institutionalized*; that is, it must permeate the day-to-day life of the company if it is to be effectively implemented.[14]

Three organizational elements provide the fundamental, long-term means for institutionalizing the firm's strategy: (1) structure, (2) leadership, (3) culture, and (4) rewards. Successful implementation requires effective management and integration of these three elements to ensure that the strategy "takes hold" in the daily life of the firm.

Control and Evaluation

An implemented strategy must be monitored to determine the extent to which its objectives are achieved.[15] Despite efforts at objectivity, the process of formulating a strategy is largely subjective. Thus, the first substantial test of a strategy comes only after implementation.[16] Strategic managers must watch for early signs of marketplace response to their strategies.

---

[14] R. Wernham, "Bridging the Awful Gap between Strategy and Action," *Long Range Planning*, December 1984, pp. 34–42.

[15] S. P. Scherrer, "From Warning to Crisis: A Turnaround Primer," *Management Review*, September 1988, pp. 30–36; and Don Collier, "How to Implement Strategic Plans," *Journal of Business Strategy* 4, no. 3 (1984), pp. 92–96.

[16] A. F. DeNoble, L. T. Gustafson, and M. Hergert, "Planning for Post-Merger Integration—Eight Lessons for Merger Success," *Long Range Planning*, August 1988, pp. 82–85.

They must also provide monitoring and controlling methods to ensure that their strategic plan is followed.[17]

STRATEGIC MANAGEMENT AS A PROCESS

A *process* is the flow of information through interrelated stages of analysis toward the achievement of an aim. Thus, the strategic management model in Figure 1–3 depicts a process. In the strategic management process, the flow of information involves historical, current, and forecast data on the operations and environment of the business. Managers evaluate these data in light of the values and priorities of influential individuals and groups—often called *stakeholders*—that are vitally interested in the actions of the business. The interrelated stages of the process are the 12 components discussed in the last section. Finally, the aim of the process is the formulation and implementation of strategies that work, achieving the company's long-term mission and near-term objectives.

Viewing strategic management as a process has several important implications. First, a change in any component will affect several or all of the other components. Most of the arrows in the model point two ways, suggesting that the flow of information usually is reciprocal. For example, forces in the external environment may influence the nature of a company's mission, and the company may in turn affect the external environment and heighten competition in its realm of operation. A specific example is a power company that is persuaded, in part by governmental incentives, to include a commitment to the development of energy alternatives in its mission statement. The company then might promise to extend its R&D efforts in the area of coal liquefaction. The external environment has affected the company's mission, and the revised mission signals a competitive condition in the environment.

A second implication of viewing strategic management as a process is that strategy formulation and implementation are sequential. The process begins with development or reevaluation of the company mission. This step is associated with, but essentially followed by, development of a company profile and assessment of the external environment. Then follow, in order, strategic choice, definition of long-term objectives, design of the grand strategy, definition of short-term objectives, design of operating strategies, institutionalization of the strategy, and review and evaluation.

The apparent rigidity of the process, however, must be qualified.

First, a firm's strategic posture may have to be reevaluated in response to changes in any of the principal factors that determine or affect its performance. Entry by a major new competitor, the death of a prominent board member, replacement of the chief executive officer, or a downturn in market responsiveness are among the thousands of changes that can prompt reassessment of a firm's strategic plan. However, no matter where the need for a reassessment originates, the strategic management process begins with the mission statement.

---

[17] A. C. Kelley, "Auditing the Planning Process," *Managerial Planning* 32, no. 4 (January–February 1984), pp. 12–14 and 27; and P. Lorange and D. Murphy, "Consideration in Implementing Strategic Control," *Journal of Business Strategy*, Spring 1984, pp. 27–35.

FIGURE 1–3
Strategic Management Model

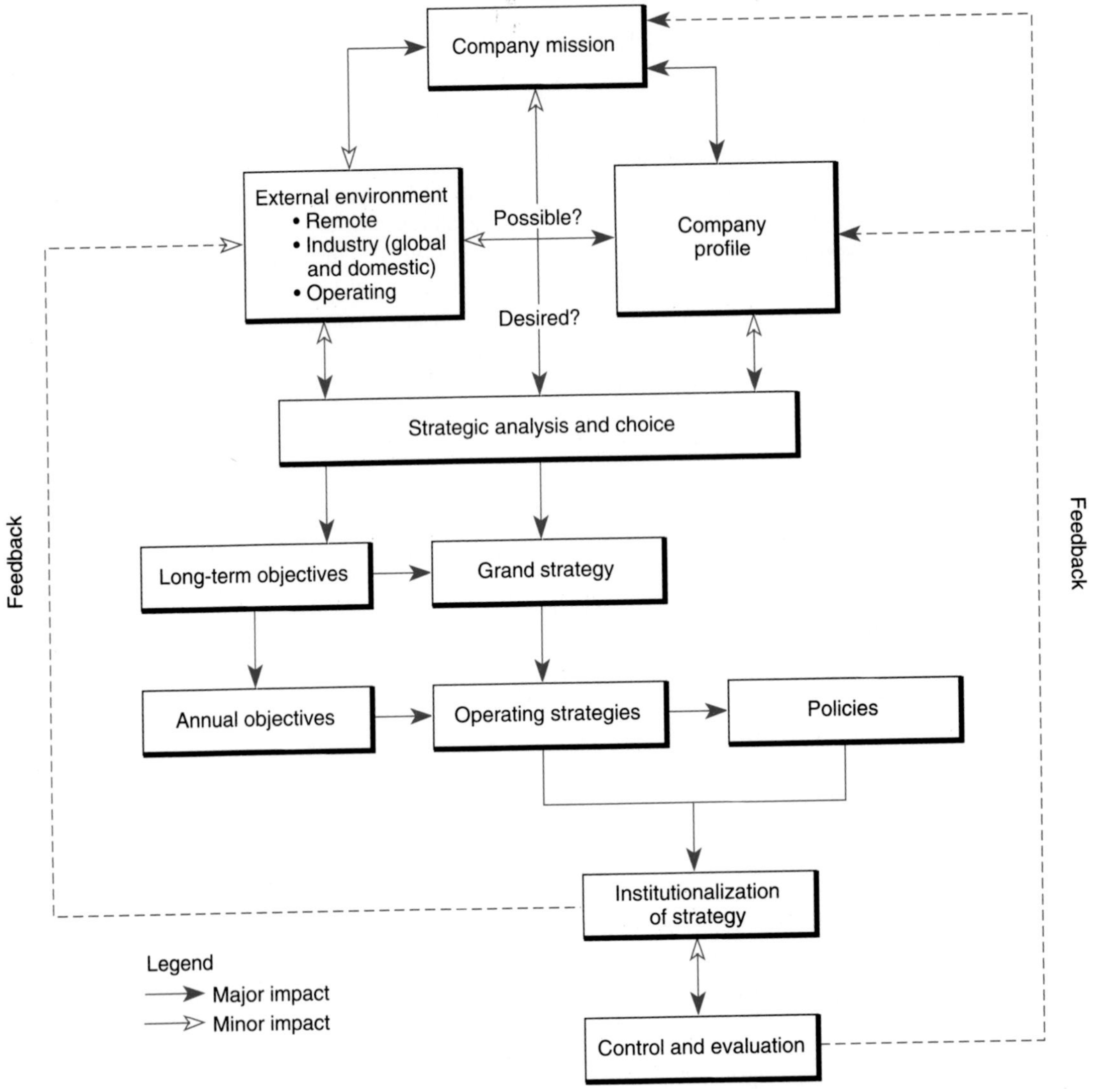

Second, not every component of the strategic management process deserves equal attention each time planning activity takes place. Firms in an extremely stable environment may find that an in-depth assessment is not required every five years.[18] Companies often

---

[18] Formal strategic planning is not necessarily done on a rigid five-year schedule, although this is the most common approach. Some planners advocate planning on an irregular time basis to keep the activity from being overly routine.

are satisfied with their original mission statements even after decades of operation and spend only a minimal amount of time in addressing this subject. In addition, while formal strategic planning may be undertaken only every five years, objectives and strategies usually are updated each year, and rigorous reassessment of the initial stages of strategic planning rarely is undertaken at these times.

A third implication of viewing strategic management as a process is the necessity of feedback from institutionalization, review, and evaluation to the early stages of the process. *Feedback* can be defined as the collection of postimplementation results to enhance future decision making. Therefore, as indicated in Figure 1–3, strategic managers should assess the impact of implemented strategies on external environments. Thus, future planning can reflect any changes precipitated by strategic actions. Strategic managers also should analyze the impact of strategies on the possible need for modifications in the company mission.

A fourth implication of viewing strategic management as a process is the need to regard it as a dynamic system. The term *dynamic* characterizes the constantly changing conditions that affect interrelated and interdependent strategic activities.[19] Managers should recognize that the components of the strategic process are constantly evolving but that formal planning artificially freezes those components, much as an action photograph freezes the movement of a swimmer. Since change is continuous, the dynamic strategic planning process must be monitored constantly for significant shifts in any of its components as a precaution against implementing an obsolete strategy.

Changes in the Process

The strategic management process undergoes continual assessment and subtle updating. Although the elements of the basic strategic management model rarely change, the relative emphasis that each element receives will vary with the decision makers who use the model and with the environments of their companies.

Strategy in Action 1–2 is an update on general trends in strategic management, summarizing the responses of over 200 corporate executives. This update shows there has been an increasing company wide emphasis on and appreciation for the value of strategic management activities. It also provides evidence that practicing managers have given increasing attention to the need for frequent and widespread involvement in the formulation and implementation phases of the strategic management process. Finally, it indicates that, as managers and their firms gain knowledge, experience, skill, and understanding in how to design and manage their planning activities, they become better able to avoid the potential negative consequences of instituting a vigorous strategic management process.

SUMMARY

Strategic management is the set of decisions and actions that result in the formulation and implementation of plans designed to achieve a company's objectives. Because it involves

---

[19] N. Tichy, "The Essentials of Strategic Change Management," *Journal of Business Strategy*, Spring 1983, pp. 55–67.

STRATEGY IN ACTION 1–2 GENERAL TRENDS IN STRATEGIC MANAGEMENT

Item	Percent of Respondents Indicating		
	Increase	No Change	Decrease
1. Overall emphasis on strategic planning systems.	81.2%	7.7%	11.1%
2. Perceived usefulness of strategic planning.	82.0	10.2	7.8
3. Involvement of line managers in strategic planning activities.	75.2	21.4	3.4
4. Time spent by the chief executive in strategic planning.	78.7	17.8	3.5
5. Acceptance of the outputs of the strategic planning exercise by top management.	74.0	20.6	5.4
6. Perceived usefulness of annual planning.	53.9	38.7	7.4
7. Involvement of staff managers in the annual planning exercise.	52.9	39.3	7.8
8. Involvement of the board of directors in strategic planning.	51.4	47.0	1.6
9. Resources provided for strategic planning.	62.9	23.9	13.2
10. Consistency between strategic plans and budgets.	53.4	38.2	8.3

Source: Adapted from V. Ramanujam, J. C. Camillus, and N. Venkatraman, "Trends in Strategic Planning," in *Strategic Planning and Management Handbook*, ed. W. R. King and D. I. Cleland (New York: Van Nostrand Reinhold, 1987), p. 614.

long-term, future-oriented, complex decision making and requires considerable resources, top-management participation is essential.

Strategic management is a three-tier process involving corporate, business, and functional-level planners, and support personnel. At each progressively lower level, strategic activities were shown to be more specific, narrow, short term, and action oriented, with lower risks but fewer opportunities for dramatic impact.

The strategic management model presented in this chapter will serve as the structure for understanding and integrating all the major phases of strategy formulation and implementation. The chapter provided a summary account of these phases, each of which is given extensive individual attention in subsequent chapters.

The chapter stressed that the strategic management process centers on the belief that a firm's mission can be best achieved through a systematic and comprehensive assessment of both its internal capabilities and its external environment. Subsequent evaluation of the firm's opportunities leads, in turn, to the choice of long-term objectives and grand strategies and, ultimately, to annual objectives and operating strategies, which must be implemented, monitored, and controlled.

QUESTIONS FOR DISCUSSION

1. Find a recent copy of *Business Week* and read the "Corporate Strategies" section. Was the main decision discussed strategic? At what level in the organization was the key decision made?

STRATEGY
IN ACTION concluded
1–2

| | Percent of Respondents Indicating | | |
Item	Increase	No Change	Decrease
11. Use of annual plans in monthly performance review.	42.3%	55.6%	2.1%
12. Overall satisfaction with the strategic planning system.	57.4	24.5	18.1
13. Number of planners (i.e., those management personnel whose primary task is planning).	52.9	24.8	22.3
14. Attention to other stakeholders than stockholders.	32.8	63.0	4.2
15. Use of planning committees.	40.9	46.1	13.1
16. Attention to societal issues in planning.	33.2	59.8	7.0
17. The planning horizon (i.e., the number of years considered in the strategic plan).	28.8	56.6	14.6
18. The distance between the CEO and the chief of planning.	13.3	45.1	41.5
19. Threats to the continuation of strategic planning.	12.0	47.0	41.0
20. Resistance to planning in general.	10.2	31.7	58.0

2. In what ways do you think the subject matter in this strategic management-business policy course will differ from that of previous courses you have taken?

3. After graduation, you are not likely to move directly to a top-level management position. In fact, few members of your class will ever reach the top-management level. Why, then, is it important for all business majors to study the field of strategic management?

4. Do you expect outstanding performance in this course to require a great deal of memorization? Why or why not?

5. You undoubtedly have read about individuals who seemingly have given singled-handed direction to their corporations. Is a participative strategic management approach likely to stifle or suppress the contributions of such individuals?

6. Think about the courses you have taken in functional areas, such as marketing, finance, production, personnel, and accounting. What is the importance of each of these areas to the strategic planning process?

7. Discuss with practicing business managers the strategic management models used in their firms. What are the similarities and differences between these models and the one in the text?

8. In what ways do you believe the strategic planning approach of not-for-profit organizations would differ from that of profit-oriented organizations?

9. How do you explain the success of firms that do not use a formal strategic planning process?

10. Think about your postgraduation job search as a strategic decision. How would the strategic management model be helpful to you in identifying and securing the most promising position?

BIBLIOGRAPHY

Adler, P. S.; D. W. McDonald; and F. MacDonald. "Strategic Management of Technical Functions." *Sloan Management Review*, Winter 1992, pp. 19–38.

Allen, M. G. "Strategic Management Hits Its Stride." *Planning Review*, September 1985, pp. 6–9.

Arkam, J. D., and S. S. Cowen. "Strategic Planning for Increased Profit in the Small Business." *Long Range Planning*, December 1990, pp. 63–70.

Blair, J. D., and K. B. Boal. "Strategy Formation Processes in Health Care Organizations: A Context-Specific Examination of Context-Free Strategy Issues." *Journal of Management*, June 1991, pp. 305–44.

Brooker, R. E., Jr. "Orchestrating the Planning Process." *The Journal of Business Strategy.* July–August 1991, pp. 4–9.

Carlson, F. P. "The Long and Short of Strategic Planning." *The Journal of Business Strategy*, May–June 1990, pp. 15–21.

Eastlack, J., Jr., and P. McDonald. "CEO's Role in Corporate Growth." *Harvard Business Review*, May–June 1970, pp. 150–63.

Gilmore, F. "Formulating Strategy in Smaller Companies." *Harvard Business Review*, May–June 1971, pp. 75–85.

Goold, M., and A. Campbell. "Many Best Ways to Make Strategy." *Harvard Business Review*, November–December 1987, pp. 70–76.

Hahn, D. "Strategic Management—Tasks and Challenges in the 1990s." *Long Range Planning*, February 1991, pp. 26–39.

Hax, A. C. "Redefining the Concept of Strategy and the Strategy Formation Process." *Planning Review*, May–June 1990, pp. 34–41.

Hinterhuber, H. H., and W. Popp. "Are You a Strategist or Just a Manager." *Harvard Business Review*, January–February 1992, pp. 105–14.

Hitt, M. A.; R. E. Hoskisson; and J. S. Harrison. "Strategic Competitiveness in the 1990s: Challenges and Opportunities for U.S. Executives." *Academy of Management Executive*, May 1991, pp. 7–22.

King, W. R., and D. I. Cleland. *Strategic Planning and Policy.* New York: Van Nostrand Reinhold, 1987.

Kugla, R. J. "Elements of Effective Corporate Planning." *Long Range Planning*, August 1976, pp. 82–93.

Lorange, P. *Corporate Planning: An Executive Viewpoint.* Englewood Cliffs, N.J.: Prentice Hall, 1980.

Malik, Z., and D. Karger. "Does Long-Range Planning Improve Company Performance?" *Management Review*, September 1975, pp. 27–31.

McKinney, G. W., III. "An Experimental Study of Strategy Formulation Systems." Ph.D. dissertation, Graduate School of Business, Stanford University, 1969.

Meyer, A. D. "What Is Strategy's Distinctive Competence?" *Journal of Management*, December 1991, pp. 821–34.

Mintzberg, H. "Strategy Making in Three Modes." *California Management Review*, Spring 1973, pp. 44–53.

Pearce, J. A., II. "An Executive-Level Perspective on the Strategic Management Process." *California Management Review*, Spring 1982, pp. 39–48.

Pearce, J. A., II, and W. A. Randolph. "Improving Strategy Formulation Pedagogies by Recognizing Behavioral Aspects." *Exchange*, December 1980, pp. 7–10.

Pryor, M. H., Jr. "Anatomy of a Merger." *Michigan Business Review*, July 1964, pp. 28–34.

Rappaport, A. "CFOs and Strategists: Forging a Common Framework." *Harvard Business Review*, May–June 1992, pp. 84–93.

Rogers, D. D. C. *Essentials of Business Policy.* New York: Harper & Row, 1975.

Rue, L., and R. Fulmer. "Is Long-Range Planning Profitable?" *Academy of Management Proceedings*, 1972.

Schonberger, R. J. "Is Strategy Strategic? Impact of Total Quality Management on Strategy." *Academy of Management Executive*, August 1992, pp. 80–97.

Schwaninger, M. "A Practical Approach to Strategy Development." *Long Range Planning*, October 1987, pp. 74–85.

Stagner, R. "Corporate Decision Making." *Journal of Applied Psychology*, February 1969, pp. 1–13.

Stalk, G.; P. Evans; and L. E. Shulman. "Competing on Capabilities: The New Rules of Corporate Strategy." *Harvard Business Review*, March–April 1992, pp. 57–69.

Steiner, G. A. "Why and How to Diversify." *California Management Review*, Summer 1964, pp. 11–18.

———. "The Rise of the Corporate Planner." *Harvard Business Review*, September–October 1970, pp. 133–39.

Stevenson, H. H. "Defining Corporate Strengths and Weaknesses." *Sloan Management Review*, Spring 1976, pp. 51–68.

Stonich, P. J. "Time: The Next Strategic Frontier." *Planing Review*, November–December 1990, pp. 4–7.

TenDam, H. "Strategic Management in a Government Agency." *Long Range Planning*, August 1986, pp. 78–86.

Vancil, R. F. ". . . So You're Going to Have a Planning Department!" *Harvard Business Review*, May–June 1967, pp. 88–96.

Veliyath, R. "Strategic Planning: Balancing Short-Run Performance and Longer Term Prospects." *Long Range Planning*, June 1992, pp. 86–97.

Yon, E. T. "Corporate Strategy and the New Europe." *Academy of Management Executive*, August 1990, pp. 61–65.

CHAPTER 1 COHESION CASE

THE COCA-COLA COMPANY

Celebrating its 110th birthday in 1996, The Coca-Cola Company has become perhaps the world's most well-known company. Behind the world's most ubiquitous trademark is an international corporation—or as Coke's management likes to say: "a truly global business system"—that has many lessons to share with strategic management students. As you prepare for a successful business career in the 21st century, you must be fine-tuning your understanding of how to help your company achieve and sustain global competitiveness while building stockholder value in a social and environmentally responsible manner. This book and this Cohesion Case about Coca-Cola will help you do that.

The Cohesion Case is a set of 11 comprehensive illustrations, one accompanying each chapter in the book, which uses The Coca-Cola Company to illustrate and apply key concepts presented in the chapter. Taken together, they provide a "cohesive" journey through experiences, strategies, and decisions at The Coca-Cola Company that will enhance your understanding of strategic management in today's global marketplace.

The remainder of this introductory section will give you a brief history and overview of The Coca-Cola Company. More complete information about The Coca-Cola Company will be provided in the Cohesion Case Illustrations following each chapter. And there is a wealth of information about The Coca-Cola Company in various company and trade publications, as well as the popular business press, that we encourage you to seek out as a way to enhance your strategic management skills.

HISTORY OF THE COCA-COLA COMPANY

Coca-Cola's origin dates to 1886 when an Atlanta, Georgia, pharmacist, Dr. John S. Pemberton, cooked up the first medicinal syrup extract of "Coca" in a three-legged brass pot in his backyard. Derived as a potential patent medicine, the first glass of the new soda fountain drink went on sale for 5 cents a glass on May 8, 1886, in a Atlanta pharmacy where, by design or accident, carbonated water was blended with the new syrup to produce the drink. Dr. Pemberton sold 25 gallons of the syrup that year, generating approximately $50 in total sales.

Two years later, Atlanta businessman Asa G. Candler bought all rights to Coca-Cola for $2,300. Candler placed major emphasis on promotional activities and quickly expanded distribution of the syrup and registered the Coca-Cola trademark. The bottling of Coca-Cola started in 1894 in Vicksburg, Mississippi, and continued until 1899, when the company granted rights to bottle and sell Coca-Cola in practically the entire continental United States. By 1904, the annual sales for Coca-Cola syrup reached 1 million gallons, and there were 123 plants authorized or licensed to bottle the finished drink.

Ernest Woodruff, an Atlanta banker, led an investor group that bought The Coca-Cola Company from Candler for $25 million in 1919. Robert Woodruff was made president, and the company moved aggressively to expand sales, establishing a foreign sales office and developing a concentrate for the syrup to reduce transportation costs. Shortly after the Woodruff group purchased the company, Coca-Cola stock was sold to the public at $40 per share, helping to lay the capital foundation for its rapid domestic and international expansion. By 1993, consumers in almost 200 countries purchased over 700 million servings daily of soft drinks provided by The Coca-Cola Company.

COCA-COLA'S RECENT HISTORY

The 1960s saw The Coca-Cola Company expand its business focus beyond soft drinks. In rapid succession, Coca-Cola acquired more than 15 different businesses, ranging from food, wine, and soft drinks to film and water treatment. By 1977, The Coca-Cola Company looked something like this:

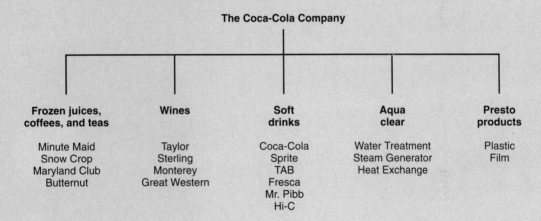

The Coca-Cola Company

Frozen juices, coffees, and teas	Wines	Soft drinks	Aqua clear	Presto products
Minute Maid	Taylor	Coca-Cola	Water Treatment	Plastic
Snow Crop	Sterling	Sprite	Steam Generator	Film
Maryland Club	Monterey	TAB	Heat Exchange	
Butternut	Great Western	Fresca		
		Mr. Pibb		
		Hi-C		

The company reported that, in 1977, 76 percent of total sales ($3.5 billion) and 89 percent of operating profit ($0.6 billion) came from soft drinks. It also reported that 60 percent of worldwide soft-drink volume came from non-U.S. markets. On a companywide basis, sales and profitability looked as follows during that year:

1977 (in millions)

	U.S.	Lat. Am.	Europe and Africa	Canada and Pacific	Total
Net sales	$2,008	$270	$669	$613	$3,556
Operating profit	264	67	189	114	634
Ident'ble assets	1,060	196	414	273	1,943

By 1983, The Coca-Cola Company had become a major player in movie entertainment, acquiring Columbia Pictures. Along the way it sold its wine, water treatment, and plastics businesses. It adopted an aggressive product development effort in soft drinks, with diet, caffeine-free, and citrus soft-drink additions. Introduced one year earlier, Diet Coke became the No. 1 low-calorie beverage in the United States and No. 4 soft drink overall. On a companywide basis, sales and profitability looked as follows during that year:

1983 (in millions)

	U.S.	Lat. Am.	Europe and Africa	Canada and Pacific	Total
Net sales	$4,071	$401	$1,226	$1,131	$6,829
Operating profit	499	69	295	207	993
Ident'ble assets	2,997	421	607	473	4,496

The 10 years that followed saw The Coca-Cola Company make several fundamental changes in its strategic posture, while also accelerating its globalization and achieving some extraordinary results. Having completed the divestiture of Columbia Pictures (to Sony). The Coca-Cola Company of 1994 returned to its roots, operating in only two lines of business:

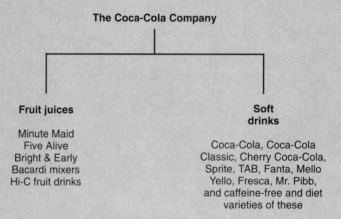

In addition, the company has reversed its traditional approach and aggressively started making major equity investments in bottling facilities owned by bottling franchisees, joint ventures, or company-owned to include creating and selling 51 percent—the largest IPO in U.S. history—of a new publicly traded company (Coca-Cola Enterprises), which buys or invests in Coca-Cola bottling companies worldwide.

As Coca-Cola generously applies itself to help Atlanta be the host to the 1996 Olympics, Coca-Cola's emphasis on globalization is unmistakable. Indeed, Coca-Cola's board chairman and chief executive officer, Robert C. Goizueta, had the following recent remarks about Coca-Cola's global perspective:

> The global marketplace is something people have been writing about for years, and, while it may not be completely here yet, it is a fact that most U.S.-based companies of any size today think and act in international terms. At The Coca-Cola Company, we view ourselves today as an international corporation headquartered in the United States, as opposed to a U.S. company with a sizable international business. Coca-Cola's globalization is unquestioned and long a part of our company. Our attention, therefore, has moved beyond, to what we call "the Coca-Cola system," arguably the only truly global business system in existence today.
>
> The trend toward globalization by U.S.-based companies will continue. Not only do 95 percent of the world's 5+ billion people live outside the United States, but the global climate today is generally favorable for companies disposed to expansion:

E_{NV}

Ext Env
Economic

First, disposable income is rising around the world and, with it, people's ability to purchase more consumer products.

Ext Env

Second, outside the United States and Europe, the world is getting younger, and young people are the most enthusiastic purchasers of many consumer products.

Third, the world's markets are becoming easier to reach. Events in eastern Europe and the former Soviet Union are good examples.

Finally, in many important ways, the world's markets are also becoming more alike. Every corner of the free world is increasingly subjected to intense and similar communications: commercial, cultural, social, and hard news. Thus, people around the world are today connected to each other by brand name consumer products as much as by anything else. Tokyo, London, New York, and Los Angeles resemble each other today far more than they did 25 years ago, in large part because their residents' tastes in consumer products have converged.

Through our advertising and marketing we have encouraged consumers to associate Coca-Cola with their best feelings and memories . . . friends and family. . . joy and laughter. . . sports and music. Through our insistence on product integrity, we have made sure that wherever and whenever they drink a Coke, the product will live up to their expectations.

Through our worldwide business system we have made sure that Coca-Cola is there, so that wherever consumers travel they can always find a point of reference, a friendly reminder of home, regardless of where home may be. And through our efforts to serve our customers and consumers with a passion, they have come to feel passionate about Coca-Cola. . . . It is this deep, heartfelt bond shared by Coca-Cola consumers and the members of the Coca-Cola system around the world that The Coca-Cola Company and its management cherish and value above all else. We cherish it because it is, more than anything else, the true measure of success in the global marketplace.

Goizueta, a Cuban refugee who as a young man worked for a Coke bottler in Cuba until fleeing the country with his family after Castro's rise to power, brings a unique perspective to his insistence on a global perspective. And The Coca-Cola Company has prospered under his leadership. Since becoming CEO in 1980, Goizueta has led Coca-Cola to a virtually unsurpassed level of performance. Compounded annual growth rates for several key indicators through 1992 are shown below:

Compound Annual Growth through 1992

	3 Year (%)	5 Year (%)	10 Year (%)
Operating revenues	13%	11%	9%
Operating income	13	21	12
Pretax income	14	13	12
Net income, continuing operations	16	12	13
EPS	20	15	14
EPS, continuing operations	18	18	15
Dividends	17	13	9
Average return on equity	39	35	28
Share appreciation	53	34	30

At January 1, 1982, Coca-Cola's market value stood at $4.3 billion. Ten years later, it exceeded $53 billion—a 12-fold growth. By any standard, these results were (and still are) truly extraordinary. It is certainly an indication of sound strategic decision making.

The remainder of this book will provide a Cohesion Case discussion at the end of each chapter. Each segment will examine aspects of strategic management at Coca-Cola that should help you understand Coca-Cola's success, while also serving to illustrate the ideas, concepts, and techniques we will present in each chapter of this book. We are excited about being able to "team up" with Coca-Cola to provide you with this unique perspective. And we strongly encourage you to supplement our coverage by obtaining and reviewing past Coca-Cola annual reports and recent business periodicals about the company to broaden your understanding of the company and its willingness to embrace sensible risk-taking and to welcome global change.

II STRATEGY FORMULATION

Strategy formulation guides executives in defining the business their firm is in, the aims it seeks, and the means it will use to accomplish those aims. The approach of strategy formulation is an improvement over that of traditional long-range planning. As discussed in the following seven chapters—about developing a firm's competitive plan of action—strategy formulation combines a future-oriented perspective with concern for the firm's internal and external environments.

The process of strategy formulation begins with definition of the company mission, as discussed in Chapter 2. In that chapter, the purpose of business is defined to reflect the values of a wide variety of interested parties.

Chapter 3 deals with the principal factors in a firm's external environment that strategic managers must assess so they can anticipate and take advantage of future business conditions. It emphasizes the importance to a firm's planning activities of factors in the firm's remote, industry, and operating environments. A key theme of the chapter is the problem of deciding whether to accept environmental constraints or to maneuver around them.

Chapter 4 describes the key differences in strategic planning and implementation among domestic, multinational, and global firms. It gives special attention to the new vision that a firm must communicate in a revised company mission when it multinationalizes.

Chapter 5 focuses on the environmental forecasting approaches currently used by strategic managers in assessing and anticipating changes in the external environment.

Chapter 6 shows how firms evaluate their internal strengths and weaknesses to produce a company profile. Strategic managers use such profiles to target competitive advantages they can emphasize and competitive disadvantages they should correct or minimize.

Chapter 7 examines the types of long-range objectives strategic managers set and specifies the qualities these objectives must have to provide a basis for direction and evaluation. The chapter also examines the 12 grand strategies that firms use to achieve long-range objectives.

Comprehensive approaches to the evaluation of strategic opportunities and to the final strategic decision are the focus of Chapter 8. The chapter shows how a firm's strategic options can be compared in a way that allows selection of the best available option.

2 DEFINING THE COMPANY MISSION

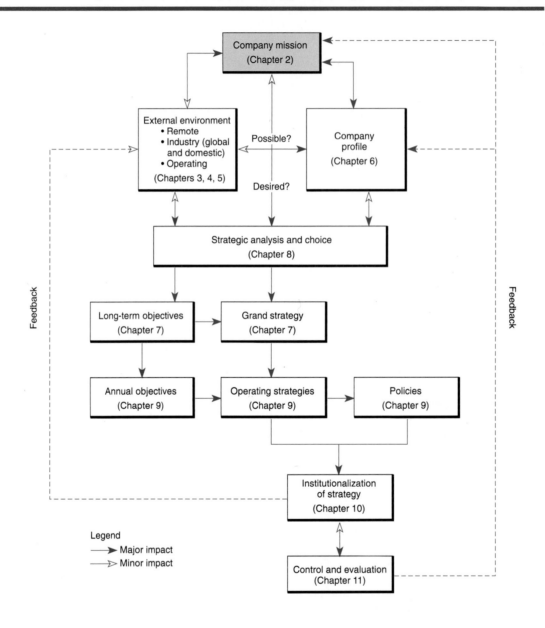

WHAT IS A COMPANY MISSION?

Whether a firm is developing a new business or reformulating direction for an ongoing business, it must determine the basic goals and philosophies that will shape its strategic posture. This fundamental purpose that sets a firm apart from other firms of its type and identifies the scope of its operations in product and market terms is defined as the company mission. As discussed in Chapter 1, the company mission is a broadly framed but enduring statement of a firm's intent. It embodies the business philosophy of the firm's strategic decision makers, implies the image the firm seeks to project, reflects the firm's self-concept, and indicates the firm's principal product or service areas and the primary customer needs the firm will attempt to satisfy. In short, it describes the firm's product, market, and technological areas of emphasis, and it does so in a way that reflects the values and priorities of the firm's strategic decision makers. An excellent example is the company mission statement of Nicor, Inc., shown in Strategy in Action 2–1.

The Need for an Explicit Mission

No external body requires that the company mission be defined, and the process of defining it is time-consuming and tedious. Moreover, it contains broadly outlined or implied objectives and strategies rather than specific directives. Characteristically, it is a statement, not of measurable targets but of attitude, outlook, and orientation.

What is that statement designed to accomplish? According to King and Cleland, the objectives of the company mission are:

1. To ensure unanimity of purpose within the organization.
2. To provide a basis for motivating the use of the organization's resources.
3. To develop a basis, or standard, for allocating organizational resources.
4. To establish a general tone or organizational climate; for example, to suggest a businesslike operation.
5. To serve as a focal point for those who can identify with the organization's purpose and direction and to deter those who cannot do so from participating further in its activities.
6. To facilitate the translation of objectives and goals into a work structure involving the assignment of tasks to responsible elements within the organization.
7. To specify organizational purposes and the translation of these purposes into goals in such a way that cost, time, and performance parameters can be assessed and controlled.[1]

FORMULATING A MISSION

The process of defining the company mission for a specific business can perhaps be best understood by thinking about the business at its inception. The typical business begins with

---

Note: Portions of this chapter are adopted from John A. Pearce II, "The Company Mission as a Strategic Tool," *Sloan Management Review*, Spring 1992, pp. 15–24.

[1] William R. King and David I. Cleland, *Strategic Planning and Policy* (New York: Van Nostrand Reinhold, 1978), p. 124.

PREAMBLE

We, the management of Nicor, Inc., here set forth our belief as to the purpose for which the company is established and the principles under which it should operate. We pledge our effort to the accomplishment of these purposes within these principles.

BASIC PURPOSE

The basic purpose of Nicor, Inc., is to perpetuate an investor-owned company engaging in various phases of the energy business, striving for balance among those phases so as to render needed satisfactory products and services and earn optimum, long-range profits.

WHAT WE DO

The principal business of the company, through its utility subsidiary, is the provision of energy through a pipe system to meet the needs of ultimate consumers. To accomplish its basic purpose,

the beliefs, desires, and aspirations of a single entrepreneur. Such an owner-manager's sense of mission usually is based on the following fundamental beliefs:

1. The product or service of the business can provide benefits at least equal to its price.

2. The product or service can satisfy a customer need of specific market segments that is currently not being met adequately.

3. The technology that is to be used in production will provide a cost- and quality-competitive product or service.

4. With hard work and the support of others, the business can not only survive but also grow and be profitable.

5. The management philosophy of the business will result in a favorable public image and will provide financial and psychological rewards for those who are willing to invest their labor and money in helping the business to succeed.

6. The entrepreneur's self-concept of the business can be communicated to and adopted by employees and stockholders.

As the business grows or is forced by competitive pressures to alter its product–market–technology, redefining the company mission may be necessary. If so, the revised mission statement will contain the same components as the original. It will state the basic type of product or service to be offered, the primary markets or customer groups to be served, and the technology to be used in production or delivery; the firm's fundamental concern for survival through growth and profitability; the firm's managerial philosophy; the public image the firm seeks; and the self-concept those affiliated with the firm should have of it. This chapter will discuss in detail these components. The examples shown in Strategy in Action 2–2 provide insights into how some major corporations handle them.

and to ensure its strength, the company will engage in other energy-related activities, directly or through subsidiaries or in participation with other persons, corporations, firms, or entities.

All activities of the company shall be consistent with its responsibilities to investors, customers, employees, and the public and its concern for the optimum development and utilization of natural resources and for environmental needs.

WHERE WE DO IT

The company's operations shall be primarily in the United States, but no self-imposed or regulatory geographical limitations are placed upon the acquisition, development, processing, transportation, or storage of energy resources, or upon other energy-related ventures in which the company may engage. The company will engage in such activities in any location where, after careful review, it has determined that such activity is in the best interest of its stockholders.

Utility service will be offered in the territory of the company's utility subsidiary to the best of its ability, in accordance with the requirements of regulatory agencies and pursuant to the subsidiary's purposes and principles.

Basic Product or Service; Primary Market; Principal Technology

Three indispensable components of the mission statement are specification of the basic product or service; specification of the primary market; and specification of the principal technology for production or delivery. These components are discussed under one heading because only in combination do they describe the company's business activity. A good example of the three components is to be found in the business plan of ITT Barton, a division of ITT. Under the heading of business mission and area served, the following information is presented:

> The unit's mission is to serve industry and government with quality instruments used for the primary measurement, analysis, and local control of fluid flow, level, pressure, temperature, and fluid properties. This instrumentation includes flow meters, electronic readouts, indicators, recorders, switches, liquid level system, analytical instruments such as titrators, integrators, controllers, transmitters, and various instruments for the measurement of fluid properties (density, viscosity, gravity) used for processing variable sensing, data collecting, control, and transmission. The unit's mission includes fundamental loop-closing control and display devices, when economically justified, but excludes broadline central control room instrumentation, systems design, and turnkey responsibility.
>
> Markets served include instrumentation for oil and gas production, gas transportation, chemical and petrochemical processing, cryogenics, power generation, aerospace, government, and marine, as well as other instrument and equipment manufacturers.

In only 129 words, this segment of the mission statement clearly indicates to all readers—from company employees to casual observers—the basic products, primary markets, and principal technologies of ITT Barton.

STRATEGY   **IDENTIFYING MISSION STATEMENT**
IN ACTION **COMPONENTS: A COMPILATION OF EXCERPTS**
   2–2   **FROM ACTUAL CORPORATE MISSION STATEMENTS**

1. Customer-market

We believe our first responsibility is to the doctors, nurses, and patients, to mothers and all others who use our products and services. (Johnson & Johnson)

To anticipate and meet market needs of farmers, ranchers, and rural communities within North America. (CENEX)

2. Product-service

AMAX's principal products are molybdenum, coal, iron ore, copper, lead, zinc, petroleum and natural gas, potash, phosphates, nickel, tungsten, silver, gold, and magnesium. (AMAX)

3. Geographic domain

We are dedicated to the total success of Corning Glass Works as a worldwide competitor. (Corning Glass)

4. Technology

Control Data is the business of applying microelectronics and computer technology in two general areas: computer-related hardware and computing-enhancing services, which include computation, information, education, and finance. (Control Data)

The common technology in these areas relates to discrete particle coatings. (NASHUA)

5. Concern for survival

In this respect, the company will conduct its operation prudently, and will provide the profits and growth which will assure Hoover's ultimate success. (Hoover Universal)

6. Philosophy

We are committed to improve health care throughout the world. (Baxter Travenol)

We believe human development to be the worthiest of the goals of civilization and independence to be the superior condition for nurturing growth in the capabilities of people. (Sun Company)

7. Self-concept

Hoover Universal is a diversified, multi-industry corporation with strong manufacturing capabilities, entrepreneurial policies, and individual business unit autonomy. (Hoover Universal)

8. Concern for public image

We are responsible to the communities in which we live and work and to the world community as well. (Johnson & Johnson)

Also, we must be responsive to the broader concerns of the public, including especially the general desire for improvement in the quality of life, equal opportunity for all, and the constructive use of natural resources. (Sun Company)

Source: John A Pearce II and F. R. David, "Corporate Mission Statements: The Bottom Line," *Academy of Management Executive*, May 1987, pp. 109–16.

Often the most referenced public statement of a company's selected products and markets appears in "silver bullet" form in the mission statement; for example, "Dayton-Hudson Corporation is a diversified retailing company whose business is to serve the American consumer through the retailing of fashion-oriented quality merchandise."[2] Such an abstract of company direction is particularly helpful to outsiders who value condensed overviews.

---

[2] See W. Ouchi, *Theory Z* (Reading, Mass.: Addison-Wesley Publishing, 1981). Ouchi presents more complete mission statements of three of the companies discussed in this chapter: Dayton-Hudson, Hewlett-Packard, and Intel.

Company Goals: Survival, Growth, Profitability

Three economic goals guide the strategic direction of almost every business organization. Whether the mission statement explicitly states these goals, it reflects the firm's intention to secure *survival* through *growth* and *profitability*.

A firm that is unable to survive will be incapable of satisfying the aims of any of its stakeholders. Unfortunately, the goal of survival, like the goals of growth and profitability, often is taken for granted to such an extent that it is neglected as a principal criterion in strategic decision making. When this happens, the firm may focus on short-term aims at the expense of the long run. Concerns for expediency, a quick fix, or a bargain may displace the assessment of long-term impact. Too often, the result is near-term economic failure owing to a lack of resource synergy and sound business practice. For example, Consolidated Foods, maker of Shasta soft drinks and L'eggs hosiery, sought growth through the acquisition of bargain businesses. However, the erratic sales patterns of its diverse holdings forced it to divest itself of more than four dozen companies. This process cost Consolidated Foods millions of dollars and hampered its growth.

Profitability is the mainstay goal of a business organization. No matter how profit is measured or defined, profit over the long term is the clearest indication of a firm's ability to satisfy the principal claims and desires of employees and stockholders. The key phrase here is "over the long term." Obviously, basing decisions on a short-term concern for profitability would lead to a strategic myopia. Overlooking the enduring concerns of customers, suppliers, creditors, ecologists, and regulatory agents may produce profit in the short term, but, over time, the financial consequences are likely to be detrimental.

The following excerpt from the Hewlett-Packard statement of mission ably expresses the importance of an orientation toward long-term profit:

> To achieve sufficient profit to finance our company growth and to provide the resources we need to achieve our other corporate objectives.
>
> In our economic system, the profit we generate from our operation is the ultimate source of the funds we need to prosper and grow. It is the one absolutely essential measure of our corporate performance over the long term. Only if we continue to meet our profit objective can we achieve our other corporate objectives.

A firm's growth is tied inextricably to its survival and profitability. In this context, the meaning of growth must be broadly defined. Although the product impact market studies (PIMS) have shown that growth in market share is correlated with profitability, other important forms of growth do exist. Growth in the number of markets served, in the variety of products offered, and in the technologies that are used to provide goods or services frequently lead to improvements in a firm's competitive ability. Growth means change, and proactive change is essential in a dynamic business environment.

Hewlett-Packard's mission statement provides an excellent example of corporate regard for growth:

> Objective: To let our growth be limited only by our profits and our ability to develop and produce technical products that satisfy real customer needs.
>
> We do not believe that large size is important for its own sake; however, for at least two basic reasons, continuous growth is essential for us to achieve our other objectives.

In the first place, we serve a rapidly growing and expanding segment of our technological society. To remain static would be to lose ground. We cannot maintain a position of strength and leadership in our field without growth.

In the second place, growth is important in order to attract and hold high-caliber people. These individuals will align their future only with a company that offers them considerable opportunity for personal progress. Opportunities are greater and more challenging in a growing company.

The issue of growth raises a concern about the definition of the company mission. How can a firm's product, market, and technology be specified sufficiently to provide direction without precluding the exercise of unanticipated strategic options? How can a firm so define its mission that it can consider opportunistic diversification while maintaining the parameters that guide its growth decision? Perhaps such questions are best addressed when a firm's mission statement outlines the conditions under which the firm might depart from ongoing operations. General Electric Company's extensive global mission provided the foundation for its GE Appliances (GEA) in Louisville, Kentucky, to grow in spite of the 1990–92 recession. GEA did not see consumer preferences in the world market becoming Americanized. Instead, its expansion goals allowed for flexibility in examining the unique characteristics of individual foreign markets and tailoring strategies to fit them.

The growth philosophy of Dayton-Hudson also embodies this approach:

The stability and quality of the corporation's financial performance will be developed through the profitable execution of our existing businesses, as well as through the acquisition or development of new businesses. Our growth priorities, in order, are as follows:

1. Development of the profitable market preeminence of existing companies in existing markets through new store development or new strategies within existing stores.
2. Expansion of our companies to feasible new markets.
3. Acquisition of other retailing companies that are strategically and financially compatible with Dayton-Hudson.
4. Internal development of new retailing strategies.

Capital allocations to fund the expansion of existing Dayton-Hudson operating companies will be based on each company's return on investment (ROI), in relationship to its ROI objective and its consistency in earnings growth and on the ability of its management to perform up to the forecasts contained in its capital requests. Expansion via acquisition or new venture will occur when the opportunity promises an acceptable rate of long-term growth and profitability, an acceptable degree of risk, and compatibility with Dayton-Hudson's long-term strategy.

Company Philosophy

The statement of a company's philosophy, often called the *company creed*, usually accompanies or appears within the mission statement. It reflects or specifies the basic beliefs, values, aspirations, and philosophical priorities to which strategic decision makers are committed in managing the company. Fortunately, the philosophies vary little from one firm to another. Owners and managers implicitly accept a general, unwritten, yet pervasive code of behavior that governs business actions and permits them to be largely self-regulated. Unfortunately, statements of company philosophy are often so similar and so platitudinous that they read more like public relations handouts than the commitment to values they are meant to be.

Despite the similarity of these statements, the intentions of the strategic managers in developing them do not warrant cynicism. Company executives attempt to provide a distinctive and accurate picture of the firm's managerial outlook. One such statement of company philosophy is that of Dayton-Hudson Corporation. As Strategy in Action 2–3 shows, Dayton-Hudson's board of directors and executives have established especially clear directions for company decision making and action.

Perhaps most noteworthy in the Dayton-Hudson statement is its delineation of responsibility at both the corporate and business levels. In many ways, the statement could serve as a prototype for the three-tier approach to strategic management. This approach implies that the mission statement must address strategic concerns at the corporate, business, and functional levels of the organization. Dayton-Hudson's management philosophy does this by balancing operating autonomy and flexibility on the one hand with corporate input and direction on the other.

Strategy in Action 2–4 provides an example of how General Motors uses a statement of company philosophy to clarify its environmental principles. Strategy in Action 2–5 describes the changes in corporate philosophy that enabled a subsidiary of Johnson & Johnson to achieve an organizational turnaround.

Public Image

Both present and potential customers attribute certain qualities to particular businesses. Gerber and Johnson & Johnson make safe products; Cross Pen makes high-quality writing instruments; Aigner Étienne makes stylish but affordable leather products; Corvettes are power machines; and Izod Lacoste stands for the preppy look. Thus, mission statements should reflect the public's expectations, since this makes achievement of the firm's goals more likely. Gerber's mission statement should not open the possibility for diversification into pesticides, and Cross Pen's should not open the possibility for diversification into $0.59 brand-name disposables.

On the other hand, a negative public image often prompts firms to reemphasize the beneficial aspects of their mission. For example, in response to what it saw as a disturbing trend in public opinion, Dow Chemical undertook an aggressive promotional campaign to fortify its credibility, particularly among "employees and those who live and work in [their] plant communities." Dow described its approach in its annual report:

> All around the world today, Dow people are speaking up. People who care deeply about their company, what it stands for, and how it is viewed by others. People who are immensely proud of their company's performance, yet realistic enough to realize it is the public's perception of that performance that counts in the long run.

Firms seldom address the question of their public image in an intermittent fashion. Although public agitation often stimulates greater attention to this question, firms are concerned about their public image even in the absence of such agitation. The following excerpt from the mission statement of Intel Corporation is an example of this attitude:

> We are sensitive to our *image with our customers and the business community*. Commitments to customers are considered sacred, and we are upset with ourselves when we do not meet our

The corporation will:

Set standards for return on investment (ROI) and earnings growth.

Approve strategic plans.

Allocate capital.

Approve goals.

Monitor, measure, and audit results.

Reward performance.

Allocate management resources.

The operating companies will be accorded the freedom and responsibility:

To manage their own business.

To develop strategic plans and goals that will optimize their growth.

To develop an organization that can ensure consistency of results and optimum growth.

To operate their businesses consistent with the corporation's statement of philosophy.

The corporate staff will provide only those services that are:

Essential to the protection of the corporation.

Needed for the growth of the corporation.

Wanted by operating companies and that provide a significant advantage in quality or cost.

The corporation will insist on:

Uniform accounting practices by type of business.

Prompt disclosure of operating results.

A systematic approach to training and developing people.

Adherence to appropriately high standards of business conduct and civic responsibility in accordance with the corporation's statement of philosophy.

commitments. We strive to demonstrate to the business world on a continuing basis that we are credible in describing the state of the corporation, and that we are well organized and in complete control of all things that determine the numbers.

Company Self-Concept

A major determinant of a firm's success is the extent to which the firm can relate functionally to its external environment. To its proper place in a competitive situation, the firm realistically must evaluate its competitive strengths and weaknesses. This idea—that the firm must know itself—is the essence of the company self-concept. The idea is not commonly integrated into theories of strategic management; its importance for individuals

STRATEGY
IN ACTION **GENERAL MOTORS ENVIRONMENTAL PRINCIPLES**
2–4

As a responsible corporate citizen, General Motors is dedicated to protecting human health, natural resources, and the global environment. This dedication reaches further than compliance with the law to encompass the integration of sound environmental practices into our business decisions.

The following environmental principles provide guidance to General Motors personnel worldwide in the conduct of their daily business practices:

1. We are committed to actions to restore and preserve the environment.
2. We are committed to reducing waste and pollutants, conserving resources, and recycling materials at every stage of the product life cycle.
3. We will continue to participate actively in educating the public regarding environmental conservation.
4. We will continue to pursue vigorously the development and implementation of technologies for minimizing pollutant emissions.
5. We will continue to work with all governmental entities for the development of technically sound and financially responsible environmental laws and regulations.
6. We will continually assess the impact of our plants and products on the environment and the communities in which we live and operate with a goal of continuous improvement.

Source: 1991 General Motors Public Interest Report, p. 23.

has been recognized since ancient times. As one scholar writes, "Man has struggled to understand himself, for how he thinks of himself will influence both what he chooses to do and what he expects from life. Knowing his identity connects him both with his past and with the potentiality of his future."[3]

Both individuals and firms have a crucial need to know themselves. The ability of either to survive in a dynamic and highly competitive environment would be severely limited if they did not understand their impact on others or of others on them.

In some senses, then, firms take on personalities of their own. Much behavior in firms is organizationally based; that is, a firm acts on its members in other ways than their individual interactions. Thus, firms are entities whose personality transcends the personalities of their members. As such, they can set decision-making parameters based on aims different and distinct from the aims of their members. These organizational considerations have pervasive effects.

Organizations do have policies, do and do not condone violence, and may or may not greet you with a smile. They also manufacture goods, administer policies, and protect the citizenry. These are organizational actions and involve properties of organizations, not individuals. They are carried out by individuals, even in the case of computer-produced letters, which are programmed by individuals—but the genesis of the actions remains in the organization.[4]

---

[3] J. Kelly, *Organizational Behavior* (Homewood, Ill.: Richard D. Irwin, 1974), p. 258.

[4] R. H. Hall, *Organizational-Structure and Process* (Englewood Cliffs, N.J.: Prentice Hall, 1972), p. 13.

STRATEGY
IN ACTION   **ORGANIZATIONAL RENEWAL CENTERS ON STRATEGIC COLLABORATION**
2–5

When William Crouse took over as president of Ortho Diagnostic Systems, Inc. (ODSI), he knew this Johnson & Johnson subsidiary was in danger of becoming yet another victim of growth. In its effort to serve its customers and maintain market share, ODSI hit its markets with a dizzying array of products. Its customer base was deep but too wide. Its sales force devoted as much attention to small hospitals as it did to those with greater potential. All of this pointed to a lack of strategic focus, which usually translates into higher operating costs and profit margin deterioration. Clearly, the company needed to change in order to maintain its leadership position in the competitive diagnostic segment of the global healthcare marketplace.

So change it did. The strategy now is more focused, and there's a greater responsiveness to customers and less product-market clutter. Since the transformation began, turnover has been arrested, volume has more than doubled, profits have skyrocketed, and morale has improved.

The turnaround was achieved through a multistep approach to organizational transformation, which began with setting vision and strategy and included diagnosing an organization's structure, systems, culture, and capabilities for strategic fit. The process also included developing action plans and designing a tracking system for monitoring and updating.

When Crouse assumed the presidency, the first thing he did was nothing—except wander down the hallways of the organization, making stops at all levels and functions, soliciting ideas, asking questions, and listening. "I learned about the company and got to know the people by speaking with them about problems and opportunities," he recalls. 'By the end of the first three months, I knew exactly what had to be done."

But Crouse felt that was not enough, so he spent another three months talking with virtually every employee. "I then reported back to them saying, 'This is what you've told me about the company, and here are my conclusions based on what you've told me. This is what I think we should do; now, what do you think?' "

Strategy then evolved from this broadly based, back-and-forth process of questioning and testing conclusions. "Strategy is not only about what you are going to do, it's also about getting

Source: W. A. Schiemann, "Organizational Change: Lessons from a Turnaround," *Management Review*, April 1992, pp. 34–37.

The characteristics of the corporate self-concept have been summarized as follows:

1. It is based on management's perception of the way in which others (society) will respond to the company.
2. It directs the behavior of people employed by the company.
3. It is determined in part by the responses of others to the company.
4. It is incorporated into mission statements that are communicated to individuals inside and outside the company.[5]

Ordinarily, descriptions of the company self-concept per se do not appear in mission statements. Yet such statements often provide strong impressions of the company self-concept. For example, ARCO's environment, health, and safety (EHS) managers were

[5] E. J. Kelley, *Marketing Planning and Competitive Strategy* (Englewood Cliffs, N.J.: Prentice Hall, 1972), p. 5.

STRATEGY IN ACTION 2–5 **concluded**

people to buy in and commit to what's going to happen and having them understand their role in implementation."

The evolutionary approach paid off in terms of the quality of thinking that went into the strategy and the commitment to it down through the ranks. It worked because Crouse was personally involved, and he substituted the top-down textbook approach with a more collaboratively strategy-setting model.

At ODSI, an effort was made to channel people's anxiety over change by focusing their energies on a basic strategic mission. That mission had to meet three criteria: uniqueness (it had to set ODSI apart from competitors); altruism (it had to capture employees' spirit and get them to look beyond themselves); and simplicity (it had to be easily understood, remembered, and enacted). As the business mission states: "ODSI provides customers with fast, simple, accurate means of diagnosing patients and protects the safety of the world's blood supply."

This mission could be accomplished only if everyone remained focused. Crouse's six-month journey through the organization taught him that employees were caught in an activity trap. They were bouncing from one crisis to the next and doing too many things. There were too many customers, too many marginal products, and too many small orders. There was a sense that everyone was looking for silver bullets to solve problems, instead of striving to maintain ODSI's leadership position. To move forward, the company had to go back to the basics.

Although the mission provided a good framework, it needed greater specification. The top-management team developed a business protocol that spelled out how ODSI would conduct business; how it would manage and motivate the work force; new decision-making patterns that pushed responsibility downward; and new structures that promoted teamwork and focus. Developing a clear, specific sense of strategic direction and thinking throughout the organization was key to the ODSI turnaround.

---

adamant about emphasizing the company's position on safety and environmental performance as a part of the mission statement. The challenges facing the ARCO EHS managers in the early 1990s included dealing with concerned environmental groups and a public that has become environmentally aware. They hoped to motivate employees toward safer behavior while reducing emissions and waste. They saw this as a reflection of the company's positive self-image.

The following excerpts from the Intel Corporation mission statement describe the corporate persona that its top management seeks to foster:

> Management is self-critical. The leaders must be capable of recognizing and accepting their mistakes and learning from them.
>
> Open (constructive) confrontation is encouraged at all levels of the corporation and is viewed as a method of problem solving and conflict resolution.
>
> Decision by consensus is the rule. Decisions once made are supported. Position in the organization is not the basis for quality of ideas.

A highly communicative, open management is part of the style.

Management must be ethical. Managing by telling the truth and treating all employees equitably has established credibility that is ethical.

We strive to provide an opportunity for rapid development.

Intel is a results-oriented company. The focus is on substance versus form, quality versus quantity.

We believe in the principle that hard work, high productivity is something to be proud of.

The concept of assumed responsibility is accepted. (If a task needs to be done, assume you have the responsibility to get it done.)

Commitments are long term. If career problems occur at some point, reassignment is a better alternative than termination.

We desire to have all employees involved and participative in their relationship with Intel.

Newest Trends in Mission Components

Recently, two new issues have become so prominent in the strategic planning for organizations that they are increasingly becoming integral parts in the development and revisions of mission statements: sensitivity to consumer wants and concern for quality.

Customers

"The customer is our top priority" is a slogan that would be claimed by the majority of businesses in the United States and abroad. For companies including Caterpillar Tractor, General Electric, and Johnson & Johnson this means analyzing consumer needs before as well as after a sale. The bonus plan at Xerox allows for a 40 percent annual bonus, based on high customer reviews of the service that they receive, and a 20 percent penalty if the feedback is especially bad. For these firms and many others, the overriding concern for the company has become consumer satisfaction.

In addition many U.S. firms maintain extensive product safety programs to help assure consumer satisfaction. RCA, Sears, and 3M boast of such programs. Other firms including Calgon Corporation, Amoco, Mobil Oil, and Whirlpool and Zenith provide toll-free telephone lines to answer customer concerns and complaints.

The focus on customer satisfaction is demonstrated by retailer J. C. Penney in this excerpt from its statement of philosophy: "The Penney Idea is (1) To serve the public as nearly as we can to its complete satisfaction; (2) To expect for the service we render a fair remuneration, and not all the profit the traffic will bear; (3) To do all in our power to pack the customer's dollar full of value, quality, and satisfaction."

Quality

"Quality is job one!" is a rallying point not only for Ford Motor Corporation but for many resurging U.S. businesses as well. Since the 1950s, two U.S. management experts have fostered a worldwide emphasis on quality in manufacturing. W. Edwards Deming and J. M. Juran's messages were first embraced by Japanese managers, whose quality consciousness led to global dominance in several industries including automobile, TV, audio equipment, and electronic components manufacturing. Deming summarizes his approach in 14 now well-known points:

1. Create constancy of purpose.
2. Adopt the new philosophy.
3. Cease dependence on mass inspection to achieve quality.
4. End the practice of awarding business on price tag alone. Instead, minimize total cost, often accomplished by working with a single supplier.
5. Improve constantly the system of production and service.
6. Institute training on the job.
7. Institute leadership.
8. Drive out fear.
9. Break down barriers between departments.
10. Eliminate slogans, exhortations, and numerical targets.
11. Eliminate work standards (quotas) and management by objective.
12. Remove barriers that rob workers, engineers, and managers of their right to pride of workmanship.
13. Institute a vigorous program of education and self-improvement.
14. Put everyone in the company to work to accomplish the transformation.

Beginning in the late 1980s, firms in the United States responded aggressively. The new philosophy is that quality should be the norm. For example, Motorola's 1993 production goal was 60 or fewer defects per every billion components that it manufactures. Managers who emphasize quality have even created their own jargon, as reviewed in Figure 2–1.

OVERSEEING THE STRATEGY MAKERS

Who is responsible for determing the firm's mission? Who is responsible for acquiring and allocating resources so the firm can thoughtfully develop and implement a strategic plan? Who is responsible for monitoring the firm's success in the competitive marketplace to determine whether that plan was well designed and activated? The answer to all of these questions is "strategic decision makers." As you saw in Figure 1–3, most organizations have multiple levels of strategic decision makers; typically, the larger the firm, the more levels it will have. The strategic managers at the highest level are responsible for decisions that affect the entire firm, commit the firm and its resources for the longest periods, and declare the firm's sense of values. In other words, this group of strategic managers is responsible for overseeing the creation and accomplishment of the company mission. The term that describes the group is *board of directors*.

In overseeing the management of a firm, the board of directors operates as the representatives of the firm's stockholders. Elected by the stockholders, the board has these major responsibilities:

1. To establish and update the company mission.
2. To elect the company's top officers, the foremost of whom is the CEO.
3. To establish the compensation levels of the top officers, including their salaries and bonuses.
4. To determine the amount and timing of the dividends paid to stockholders.
5. To set broad company policy on such matters as labor-management relations, product or service lines of business, and employee benefit packages.

FIGURE 2–1
A Glossary of Quality-Speak

Acceptable Quality Level (AQL)
Minimum number of parts that must comply with quality standards, usually stated as a percentage.

Competitive Benchmarking
Rating a company's practices, processes, and products against the world's best, including those in other industries.

Continuous-Improvement Process (CIP)
Searching unceasingly for ever-higher levels of quality by isolating sources of defects. The goal: zero defects. The Japanese call it *Kaizen*.

Control Charts
Statistical plots derived from measuring factory processes, they help detect "process drift," or deviation, before it generates defects. Charts also help spot inherent variations in manufacturing processes that designers must account for to achieve "robust design" (below).

Just-in-Time (JIT)
When suppliers deliver materials and parts at the moment a factory needs them, thus eliminating costly inventories. Quality is paramount: A faulty part delivered at the last minute won't be detected.

Pareto Chart
A bar graph that ranks causes of process variation by the degree of impact on quality.

Poka-Yoke
Making the workplace mistake-proof. A machine fitted with guide rails permits a part to be worked on in just one way.

Quality Function Deployment (QFD)
A system that pays special attention to customer wants. Activities that don't contribute are considered wasteful.

Robust Design
A discipline for making designs "production-proof" by building in tolerances for manufacturing variables that are known to be unavoidable.

Six-Sigma Quality
A statistical measure expressing how close a product comes to its quality goal. One-sigma means 68% of products are acceptable; three-sigma means 99.7%. Six-sigma is 99.999997% perfect: 3.4 defects per million parts.

Statistical Process Control (SPC)
A method of analyzing deviations in production processes during manufacturing.

Statistical Quality Control (SQC)
A method of analyzing measured deviations in manufactured materials, parts, and products.

Taguchi Methods
Statistical techniques developed by Genichi Taguchi, a Japanese consultant, for optimizing design and production. These are used often on "robust design" projects.

Total Quality Control (TQC)
The application of quality principles to all company endeavors, including satisfying internal "customers." Manufacturing engineers, for instance, are customers of the design staff. Also known as *total quality management* (TQM).

Source: Reprinted from October 25, 1991, issue of *Business Week*, by special permission, copyright © 1991 by McGraw-Hill, Inc.

6. To set company objectives and to authorize managers to implement the long-term strategies that the top officers and the board have found agreeable.

7. To mandate company compliance with legal and ethical dictates.

This chapter considers the board of directors because the board's greatest impact on the behavior of a firm results from its determination of the company mission. The philosophy espoused in the mission statement sets the tone by which the firm and all of its employees will be judged. As logical extensions of the mission statement, the firm's objectives and strategies embody the board's view of proper business demeanor. Through its appointment of top executives and its decisions about their compensation, the board reveals its priorities for organizational achievement.

Board Success Factors

A review of writings and research on the behavior of boards discloses that they are judged to be most successful when:[6]

1. They represent the interests of stockholders and carefully monitor the actions of senior executives to promote and protect those interests.[7]

2. They link the firm to influential stakeholders in its external environment, thereby promoting the company mission while ensuring attention to important societal concerns.[8]

3. They are composed of 8 to 12 highly qualified members.

4. They exercise independent and objective thinking in appraising the actions of senior executives and in introducing strategic changes.[9]

5. They pay special attention to their own composition to ensure an appropriate mix of inside and outside directors and the inclusion of minority representatives.[10]

6. They have a well-developed structure; that is, they are organized into appropriate committees to perform specialized tasks (e.g., to review executive compensation and to audit the company's financial transactions).[11]

7. They meet frequently to discuss progress in achieving organizational goals and to provide counsel to executives.[12]

---

[6] S. A. Zahra and J. A. Pearce II, "Boards of Directors and Corporate Financial Performance: A Review and Integrative Model," *Journal of Management* 15 (1989), pp. 291–334.

[7] P. L. Rechner and D. R. Dalton, "Board Composition and Shareholders' Wealth: An Empirical Assessment," *Strategic Management Journal*, in press.

[8] M. S. Mizruchi, "Who Controls Whom?: An Examination of the Relation between Management and Board of Directors in Large American Corporations," *Academy of Management Review*, August 1983, pp. 426–35.

[9] T. M. Jones and L. D. Goldberg, "Governing the Large Corporation: More Arguments for Public Directors," *Academy of Management Review* 7 (1982), pp. 603–11.

[10] I. F. Kesner, "Directors' Characteristics and Committee Membership: An Investigation of Type, Occupation, Tenure, and Gender," *Academy of Management Journal* 31 (1988), pp. 66–84; and J. A. Pearce II, "The Relationship of Internal versus External Orientations to Financial Measures of Strategic Performance," *Strategic Management Journal* 4 (1983), pp. 297–306.

[11] R. Molz, "Managerial Domination of Boards of Directors and Financial Performance," *Journal of Business Research* 16 (1988), pp. 235–50.

[12] A. Tashakori and W. Boulton, "A Look at the Board's Role Planning," *Journal of Business Strategy* 3, no. 3 (1985), pp. 64–70.

8. They evaluate the CEO's performance at least annually to provide guidance on issues of leadership style.[13]

9. They conduct strategy reviews to determine the fit between the firm's strategy and the requirements of its competitive environment. [14]

10. They formulate the ethical codes that are to govern the behavior of the firm's executives and employees.[15]

11. They promote a future-oriented outlook on the company mission by challenging executives to articulate their visions for the firm and for its interface with society.

These criteria can enable board members, CEOs, and stockholders to judge board behavior. The question "What should boards do?" can be answered largely by studying the criteria.

THE STAKEHOLDER APPROACH TO COMPANY RESPONSIBILITY

In defining or redefining the company mission, strategic managers must recognize the legitimate rights of the firm's claimant. These include not only stockholders and employees but also outsiders affected by the firm's actions. Such outsiders commonly include customers, suppliers, governments, unions, competitors, local communities, and the general public. Each of these interest groups has justifiable reasons for expecting (and often for demanding) that the firm satisfy their claims in a responsible manner. In general, stockholders claim appropriate returns on their investment; employees seek broadly defined job satisfactions; customers want what they pay for; suppliers seek dependable buyers; governments want adherence to legislation; unions seek benefits for their members; competitors want fair competition; local communities want the firm to be a responsible citizen; and the general public expects the firm's existence to improve the quality of life.

According to a recent survey of 2,361 directors in 291 of the largest southeastern U.S. companies:

1. Directors perceived the existence of distinct stakeholder groups.
2. Directors have high stakeholder orientations.
3. Directors view some stakeholders differently, depending on their occupation (CEO directors versus non-CEO directors) and type (inside versus outside directors).

The study also found that the perceived stakeholders were, in the order of their importance, customers and government, stockholders, employees, and society. The results clearly indicated that boards of directors no longer believe that the stakeholder is the only constituency to whom they are responsible.

However, when a firm attempts to incorporate the interests of these groups into its mission statement, broad generalizations are insufficient. These steps need to be taken:

---

[13] R. Nader, "Reforming Corporate Governance," *California Management Review*, Winter 1984, pp. 126–32.

[14] J. R. Harrison, "The Strategic Use of Corporate Board Committees," *California Management Review* 30 (1987), pp. 109–25; and J. W. Henke, Jr., "Involving the Board of Directors in Strategic Planning," *Journal of Business Strategy* 7, no. 2 (1986), pp. 87–95.

[15] K. R. Andrews, *The Concept of Corporate Strategy* (Homewood, Ill.: Dow Jones-Irwin, 1987).

1. Identification of the stakeholders.
2. Understanding the stakeholders' specific claims vis-à-vis the firm.
3. Reconciliation of these claims and assignment of priorities to them.
4. Coordination of the claims with other elements of the company mission.

Identification The left-hand column of Figure 2–2 lists the commonly encountered stakeholder groups, to which the executive officer group often is added. Obviously, though, every business faces a slightly different set of stakeholder groups, which vary in number, size, influence, and importance. In defining the company, strategic managers must identify all of the stakeholder groups and weigh their relative rights and their relative ability to affect the firm's success.

Understanding The concerns of the principal stakeholder groups tend to center on the general claims listed in the right-hand column of Figure 2–2. However, strategic decision makers should understand the specific demands of each group. They then will be better able to initiate actions that satisfy these demands.

Reconciliation and Priorities Unfortunately, the claims of various stakeholder groups often conflict. For example, the claims of governments and the general public tend to limit profitability, which is the central claim of most creditors and stockholders. Thus, claims must be reconciled in a mission statement that resolves the competing, conflicting, and contradicting claims of stakeholders. For objectives and strategies to be internally consistent and precisely focused, the statement must display a single-minded, though multidimensional, approach to the firm's aims.

There are hundreds, if not thousands, of claims on any firm—high wages, pure air, job security, product quality, community service, taxes, occupational health and safety regulations, equal employment opportunity regulations, product variety, wide markets, career opportunities, company growth, investment security, high ROI, and many, many more. Although most, perhaps all, of these claims may be desirable ends, they cannot be pursued with equal emphasis. They must be assigned priorities in accordance with the relative emphasis that the firm will give them. That emphasis is reflected in the criteria that the firm uses in its strategic decision making; in the firm's allocation of its human, financial, and physical resources; and in the firm's long-term objectives and strategies.

Coordination with Other Elements The demands of stakeholder groups constitute only one principal set of inputs to the company mission. The other principal sets are the managerial operating philosophy and the determinants of the product-market offering. Those determinants constitute a reality test that the accepted claims must pass. The key question is: How can the firm satisfy its claimants and at the same time optimize its economic success in the marketplace?

Social Responsibility

As indicated in Figure 2–3, the various stakeholders of a firm can be divided into inside stakeholders and outside stakeholders. The insiders are the individuals or groups that are stockholders or employees of the firm. The outsiders are all the other individuals or groups

FIGURE 2–2
A Stakeholder View of Company Responsibility

Stakeholder	Nature of the Claim
Stockholders	Participation in distribution of profits, additional stock offerings, assets on liquidation; vote of stock; inspection of company books; transfer of stock; election of board of directors; and such additional rights as have been established in the contract with the corporation.
Creditors	Legal proportion of interest payments due and return of principal from the investment. Security of pledged assets; relative priority in event of liquidation. Management and owner prerogatives if certain conditions exist with the company (such as default of interest payments).
Employees	Economic, social, and psychological satisfaction in the place of employment. Freedom from arbitrary and capricious behavior on the part of company officials. Share in fringe benefits, freedom to join union and participate in collective bargaining, individual freedom in offering up their services through an employment contract. Adequate working conditions.
Customers	Service provided with the product; technical data to use the product; suitable warranties; spare parts to support the product during use; R&D leading to product improvement; facilitation of credit.
Suppliers	Continuing source of business; timely consummation of trade credit obligations; professional relationship in contracting for, purchasing, and receiving goods and services.
Governments	Taxes (income, property, and so on); adherence to the letter and intent of public policy dealing with the requirements of fair and free competition; discharge of legal obligations of businesspeople (and business organizations); adherence to antitrust laws.
Unions	Recognition as the negotiating agent for employees. Opportunity to perpetuate the union as a participant in the business organization.
Competitors	Observation of the norms for competitive conduct established by society and the industry. Business statesmanship on the part of peers.
Local communities	Place of productive and healthful employment in the community. Participation of company officials in community affairs, provision of regular employment, fair play, reasonable portion of purchases made in the local community, interest in and support of local government, support of cultural and charitable projects.
The general public	Participation in and contribution to society as a whole; creative communications between governmental and business units designed for reciprocal understanding; assumption of fair proportion of the burden of government and society. Fair price for products and advancement of the state-of-the-art technology that the product line involves.

Source: William R. King and David I. Cleland, *Strategic Planning and Policy.* ©1978 by Litton Educational Publishing, Inc., p. 153. Reprinted by permission of Van Nostrand Reinhold Company.

that the firm's actions affect. The extremely large and often amorphous set of outsiders makes the general claim that the firm be socially responsible.[16]

Perhaps the thorniest issues faced in defining a company mission are those that pertain to responsibility. The stakeholder approach offers the clearest perspective on such issues. Broadly stated, outsiders often demand that insiders' claims be subordinated to the greater good of the society; that is, to the greater good of outsiders. They believe that such issues as pollution, the disposal of solid and liquid wastes, and the conservation of natural

---

[16] J. S. Bracker and A. J. Kinicki, "Strategic Management, Plant Closings, and Social Responsibility: An Integrative Process Model," *Employee Responsibilities and Rights Journal* 1, no. 3 (1988), pp. 201–13.

FIGURE 2–3
Inputs to the Development of the Company Mission

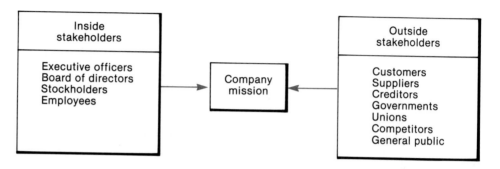

resources should be principal considerations in strategic decision making. Also broadly stated, insiders tend to believe that the competing claims of outsiders should be balanced against one another in a way that protects the company mission. For example, they tend to believe that the need of consumers for a product should be balanced against the water pollution resulting from its production if the firm cannot eliminate that pollution entirely and still remain profitable. Some insiders also argue that the claims of society, as expressed in government regulation, provide tax money that can be used to eliminate water pollution and the like if the general public wants this to be done.

The issues are numerous, complex, and contingent on specific situations. Thus, rigid rules of business conduct cannot deal with them. Each firm *regardless of side* must decide how to meet its perceived social responsibility. While large, well-capitalized companies may have easy access to environmental consultants, this is not an affordable strategy for smaller companies. However, the experience of many small businesses demonstrates that it is feasible to accomplish significant pollution prevention and waste reduction without big expenditures and without hiring consultants. Once a problem area has been identified, a company's line employees frequently can develop a solution. Other important pollution prevention strategies include changing the materials used or redesigning how operations are bid out. Making pollution prevention a social responsibility can be beneficial to smaller companies. Publicly traded firms also can benefit directly from socially responsible strategies, as indicated in Global Strategy in Action 2–1.

Different approaches adopted by different firms reflect differences in competitive position, industry, country, environmental and ecological pressures, and a host of other factors. In other words, they will reflect both situational factors and differing priorities in the acknowledgment of claims. Obviously, winning the loyalty of the growing legions of consumers will require new marketing strategies and new alliances in the 1990s. Many marketers already have discovered these new marketing facts of life by adopting strategies that can be called the "4 e's": (1) make it easy for the consumer to be green, (2) empower consumers with solutions, (3) enlist the support of the consumer, and (4) establish credibility with all publics and help to avoid a backlash.

Despite differences in their approaches, most American firms now try to assure outsiders that they attempt to conduct business in a socially responsible manner. Many firms,

At one time, socially conscious investing was as simple as Just Say No—no investing in companies that produce alcohol, tobacco, or weapons, or are involved in gambling, nuclear energy, or South Africa.

But social investing has matured since arriving in the early 1970s, and it's no longer a cut-and-dried process. "In the past, it has primarily been a boycott movement with social change as a goal," says Amy Domini. "Newer criteria are more about corporate responsibility, and they're more difficult to apply."

Domini, with her husband, Peter Kinder, created the Domini Social Index of 400 socially responsible companies in May 1990. Their Cambridge, Massachusetts, firm screens more than 800 companies for product quality and consumer relations, environmental performance, corporate citizenship, and employee relations, plus the primary screens of South African investment, tobacco, alcohol, and gambling.

Companies on the Domini Social Index are not 1960s holdouts making tie-dye T-shirts or macrame plant hangers. The list includes Wal-Mart, Merck, Coca-Cola, PepsiCo, McDonald's, the Federal National Mortgage, and Sears.

The index should perform on a par with the Standard & Poor's 500 index over the long term, says Domini. But it can be more volatile short term, because it has more small companies than the S&P 500. In 1991, it gained 38 percent, including dividends, versus 30 percent for the S&P 500.

Source: Excerpted from Chris Wloszczyna, "Social Index Lists Responsible Firms," *USA Today*, March 30, 1992, Section 3B. Copyright 1992, USA TODAY. Reprinted with permission.

including Abt Associates, Dow Chemical, Eastern Gas and Fuel Associates, Exxon, and the Bank of America, conduct and publish annual social audits. The Equal Employment Opportunity element of an Exxon social audit and the philanthropy element of an audit published in General Motors Public Interest Report are shown in Strategy in Action 2–6 and Strategy in Action 2–7. Such audits attempt to evaluate a firm from the perspective of social responsibility. Private consultants often conduct them for the firm and offer minimally biased evaluations on what are inherently highly subjective issues.

Guidelines for a Socialiy Responsible Firm

After decades of public debate on the social responsibility of business, the individual firm must still struggle to determine its own orientation. However, public debate and business concern have led to a jelling of perspectives. Sawyer has provided an excellent summary of guidelines for a socially responsible firm that is consistent with the stakeholder approach:

1. The purpose of the business is to make a profit; its managers should strive for the optimal profit that can be achieved over the long run.

2. No true profits can be claimed until business costs are paid. This includes all social costs, as determined by detailed analysis of the social balance between the firm and society.

STRATEGY IN ACTION 2–6   EQUAL EMPLOYMENT OPPORTUNITY/CONTRIBUTION AT EXXON

STEADY PROGRESS FOR WOMEN AND MINORITIES

The percentage of women in Exxon's U.S. work force grew from 25.3 to 25.9 percent, while minority groups increased from 22.5 to 22.9 percent.

At year-end, minorities held 11.4 percent of managerial assignments, compared with 10.3 percent, while minority groups increased from 11.5 to 11.7 percent.

Women employees held 10 percent of managerial posts, compared with 8.9 percent last year, while the women's share of professional jobs rose from 18.9 to 19.5 percent.

The focus on recruitment of minorities and women was expanded through summer jobs, co-op assignments, and scholarships.

EXXON GRANTED $49 MILLION TO NONPROFIT ORGANIZATIONS, INCLUDING $35 MILLION IN THE UNITED STATES

Educational institutions and programs accounted for 59 percent of total U.S. grants. To encourage support for higher education for minority students, the Exxon Education Foundation amended its matching gift program. Employees and annuitants may now make gifts to three organizations with which the donors or their families may have had no prior affiliation. Those educational fits will be matched three-to-one by the Foundation. The three organizations are the United Negro College Fund, the American Indian College Fund, and the Hispanic Association of Colleges and Universities.

A solid grounding in mathematics is a critical asset in many careers in industry. The Exxon Education Foundation began a program in 1988 with these main goals: To foster use of college-level math teaching resources and to address major national math education policy issues.

In its elementary school program, the Foundation's initial 1988 K–3 (kindergarten through third grade) math specialist Planning Grants went to some 50 school districts across America, representing a cross-section of rural, suburban, and inner-city schools. Grantees are now seeking more effective approaches for improving math teaching and learning in these early, formative years.

Of the 24 percent of Exxon's U.S. contributions that were directed to health, welfare, and community service programs, a number addressed problems common to the nation's inner cities. A $50,000 grant was made to the Institute on Black Chemical Abuse in St. Paul, Minnesota, to help develop a national technical assistance, training, and information center.

A $200,000 grant was made to the Environmental and Occupational Health Sciences Institute, a joint program of Rutgers University and the University of Medicine and Dentistry of New Jersey. This grant will contribute to a better understanding of how the environment affects human health.

Source: Exxon 1988 annual report to stockholders.

3. If there are social costs in areas where no objective standards for correction yet exist, managers should generate corrective standards. These standards should be based on the managers' judgment of what ought to exist and should simultaneously encourage individual involvement of firm members in developing necessary social standards.

General Motors is committed to being a socially aware and responsible corporate citizen. It believes that it has an obligation to make reasonable and appropriate contributions to charitable and community organizations and educational institutions.

The Corporation has consistently ranked among the top companies in the United States in terms of dollars contributed. While GM seeks to contribute to worthy local activities in the cities and states in which GM facilities are located, it also works to benefit the nation as a whole.

An important tool in managing GM's contributions is the General Motors Foundation, established in 1976 and funded by the Corporation. As a means to offset fluctuations in charitable and educational contributions which result from economic downturns—times when nonprofit organizations most need support—the Foundation helps GM maintain a consistent response to the needs and challenges of these organizations.

In 1990, combined educational and other charitable contributions from the General Motors Corporation and the General Motors Foundation totaled over $65 million.

With a variety of philanthropic activities being supported at both the plant and corporate levels, it is not possible to list all of them.

Source: 1991 General Motors Public Interest Report, p. 55.

4. Where competitive pressure or economic necessity precludes socially responsible action, the business should recognize that its operation is depleting social capital and, therefore, represents a loss. It should attempt to restore profitable operation through either better management, if the problem is internal, or by advocating corrective legislation, if society is suffering as a result of the way that the rules for business competition have been made.[17]

SUMMARY

Defining the company mission is one of the most often slighted tasks in strategic management. Emphasizing the operational aspects of long-range management activities comes much more easily for most executives. But the critical role of the mission statement repeatedly is demonstrated by failing firms whose short-run actions have been at odds with their long-run purposes.

The principal value of the mission statement is its specification of the firm's ultimate aims. A firm gains a heightened sense of purpose when its board of directors and its top executives address these issues: "What business are we in?" "What customers do we serve?" "Why does this organization exist?" However, the potential contribution of the company mission can be undermined if platitudes or ambiguous generalizations are

[17] G. E. Sawyer, *Business and Society: Managing Corporate Social Impact* (Boston: Houghton Mifflin, 1979), p. 401.

accepted in response to these questions. It is not enough to say that Lever Brothers is in the business of "making anything that cleans anything" or that Polaroid is committed to businesses that deal with "the interaction of light and matter." Only if a firm clearly articulates its long-term intentions can its goals serve as a basis for shared expectations, planning, and performance evaluation.

A mission statement that is developed from this perspective provides managers with a unity of direction transcending individual, parochial, and temporary needs. It promotes a sense of shared expectations among all levels and generations of employees. It consolidates values over time and across individuals and interest groups. It projects a sense of worth and intent that can be identified and assimilated by outside stakeholders; that is, customers, suppliers, competitors, local committees, and the general public. Finally, it asserts the firm's commitment to responsible action in symbiosis with the preservation and protection of the essential claims of insider stakeholders' survival, growth, and profitability.

QUESTIONS FOR DISCUSSION

1. Reread Nicor, Inc.'s mission statement in Strategy in Action 2–1. List five insights into Nicor that you feel you gained from knowing its mission.

2. Locate the mission statement of a company not mentioned in the chapter. Where did you find it? Was it presented as a consolidated statement, or were you forced to assemble it yourself from various publications of the firm? How many of the mission statement elements outlined in this chapter were discussed or revealed in the statement you found?

3. Prepare a two-page typewritten mission statement for your school of business or for a firm selected by your instructor.

4. List five potentially vulnerable areas of a firm without a stated company mission.

5. The partial social audits shown in Strategy in Action 2–6 and 2–7 included only a few of the possible indicators of a firm's social responsibility performance. Name five other potentially valuable indicators and describe how company performance in each could be measured.

6. Define the term *social responsibility*. Find an example of a company action that was legal but not socially responsible. Defend your example on the basis of your definition.

BIBLIOGRAPHY

Board of Directors

Harrison, J. R. "The Strategic Use of Corporate Board Committees." *California Management Review* 30 (1987), pp. 109–25.

Henke, J. W., Jr. "Involving the Board of Directors in Strategic Planning." *Journal of Business Strategy* 7, no. 2 (1986), pp. 87–95.

Kerr, J., and R. A. Bettis. "Boards of Directors, Top Management Compensation, and Shareholder Returns." *Academy of Management Journal* 30 (1987), pp. 645–64.

Kesner, I. F. "Directors' Characteristics and Committee Membership: An Investigation of Type, Occupation Tenure, and Gender." *Academy of Management Journal* 31 (1988), pp. 66–84.

Mizruchi, M. S. "Who Controls Whom?: An Examination of the Relation between Management and Board of Directors in Large American Corporations." *Academy of Management Review* 8, no. 3 (1983), pp. 426–35.

Molz, R. "Managerial Domination of Boards of Directors and Financial Performance." *Journal of Business Research* 16 (1988), pp. 235–50.

Pearce, J. A., II. "The Relationship of Internal versus External Orientations to Financial Measures of Strategic Performance." *Strategic Management Journal* 4 (1983), pp. 297–306.

Rosenstein, J. "Why Don't U.S. Boards Get More Involved in Strategy?" *Long Range Planning*, June 1987, pp. 20–34.

Savage, G. T.; T. W. Nix; C. J. Whitehead; and J. D. Blair. "Strategies for Assessing and Managing Organizational Stakeholders." *Academy of Management Executive*, May 1991, pp. 61–75.

Zahra, S. A., and J. A. Pearce II. "Boards of Directors and Corporate Financial Performance: A Review and Integrative Model." *Journal of Management* 15 (1989), pp. 291–334.

Mission Statments

Ackoff, R. "Mission Statements." *Planning Review*, July–August 1987, pp. 30–32.

Bertodo, R. "Implementing a Strategic Vision." *Long Range Planning*, October 1990, pp. 22–30.

Hunter, J. C. "Managers Must Know the Mission: 'If It Ain't Broke, Don't Fix It.'" *Managerial Planning*, January–February 1985, pp. 18–22.

Ireland, R. D., and M. A. Hitt. "Mission Statements; Importance, Challenge, and Recommendation for Development." *Business Horizons*, May–June 1992, pp. 34–42.

Klemm, M.; S. Sanderson; and G. Luffman. "Mission Statements: Selling Corporate Values to Employees." *Long Range Planning*, June 1991, pp. 73–78.

McGinnis, V. J. "The Mission Statement: A Key Step in Strategic Planning." *Business*, November–December 1981, pp. 39–43.

Osborne, R. L. "Core Value Statements: The Corporate Compass." *Business Horizons*, September–October 1991, pp. 28–34.

Pearce, J. A. II. "The Company Mission as a Strategic Tool." *Sloan Management Review*, Spring 1982, pp. 15–24.

Pearce, J. A. II, and F. R. David. "Corporate Mission Statements: The Bottom Line." *Academy of Management Executive*, May 1987, pp. 109–16.

Pearce, J. A. II; R. B. Robinson, Jr.; and Kendall Roth. "The Company Mission as a Guide to Strategic Action." In *Strategic Planning and Management Handbook*, ed. William R. King and David I. Cleland. New York: Van Nostrand Reinhold, 1987.

Rogers, J. E., Jr. "Adopting and Implementing a Corporate Environmental Charter." *Business Horizons*, March–April 1992, pp. 29–33.

Tregoe, B. B.; J. W. Zimmerman; R. A. Smith; and P. M. Tobia. "The Driving Force." *Planning Review*, March–April 1990, pp. 4–17.

Want, J. H. "Corporate Mission." *Management Review*, August 1986, pp. 46–50.

Social Responsibility and Business Ethics

Aupperle, K.; A. Carroll; and J. Hatfield. "An Empirical Examination of the Relationship between Corporate Social Responsibility and Profitability." *Academy of Management Journal* 28 (1985), pp. 446–63.

Badaracco, J. L., Jr. "Business Ethics: Four Spheres of Executive Responsibility." *California Management Review*, Spring 1992, pp. 64–79.

Bavaria, S. "Corporate Ethics Should Start in the Boardroom." *Business Horizons*, January–February 1991, pp. 9–12.

Bowie, N. "New Directions in Corporate Social Responsibility." *Business Horizons*, July–August 1991, pp. 56–65.

Cadbury, A. "Ethical Managers Make Their Own Rules." *Harvard Business Review*, September–October 1987, pp. 69–73.

Carroll, A. B. "The Pyramid of Corporate Social Responsibility: Toward the Moral Management of Organizational Stakeholders." *Business Horizons*, July–August 1991, pp. 39–48.

Dalton, D. R., and C. M. Daily. "The Constituents of Corporate Responsibility: Separate, But Not Separable, Interests?" *Business Horizons*, July–August 1991, pp. 74–78.

Day, G. S., and L. Fahey. "Putting Strategy into Shareholder Value Analysis." *Harvard Business Review*, March–April 1990, pp. 156–62.

Freeman, R. E., and J. Liedtka. "Corporate Social Responsibility: A Critical Approach." *Business Horizons*, July–August 1991, pp. 92–98.

Gellerman, S. W. "Why 'Good' Managers Make Bad Ethical Choices." *Harvard Business Review*, July–August 1986, pp. 85–90.

Harrington, S. J. "What Corporate America Is Teaching about Ethics." *Academy of Management Executive*, February 1991, pp. 21–30.

Litzinger, W. D., and T. E. Schaefer. "Business Ethics Bogeyman: The Perpetual Paradox." *Business Horizons*, March–April 1987, pp. 16–21.

Wood, D. J. "Social Issues in Management: Theory and Research in Corporate Social Performance." *Journal of Management*, June 1991, pp. 383–406.

———. "Toward Improving Corporate Social Performance." *Business Horizons*, July–August 1991, pp. 66–73.

CHAPTER 2 COHESION CASE

COMPANY MISSION AT THE COCA-COLA COMPANY

At the heart of Coca-Cola, especially in its first 100 years, there has been a commitment to intense marketing and to the preservation of its patented formulas and processes to make its special syrup. The intense secrecy that always has surrounded Coke's formula has long fostered an organizational obsession with secrecy pertaining to other information about Coke and its operations. While reaching almost 40,000 employees working in 135 countries and almost 80,000 stockholders by 1978, Coke's statements of mission and long-term goals or values remained very abbreviated and direct. Excerpts from 1978 company documents show its mission to be a brief description of the business and, later in the document, a reference to very general and typical goals or priorities:

> The Coca-Cola Company is the largest manufacturer and distributor of soft-drink concentrates and syrups in the world. Its product, "Coca-Cola," has been sold in the United States since 1886, is now sold in over 135 countries as well, and is the leading soft-drink product in most of these countries. . . . Through the Foods Division, the Company manufactures and markets Minute Maid and Snow Crop frozen concentrated citrus juices. . . . The Company manufactures and markets still and sparkling wines under the "Taylor" trademark . . . a subsidiary designs and manufactures water treatment systems . . . and a subsidiary is engaged in the manufacture and distribution of plastic film products. . . . Our goal is to continue the strong financial growth trends into the future.

By the mid-1980s, Coke had diversified into movie entertainment, yet its commitment to brevity and secrecy remained, as can be seen in these excerpts from its 1986 mission statements:

> The Coca-Cola Company is the worldwide soft-drink leader, as well as one of the world's leading producers and distributors of filmed entertainment and the leading U.S. marketer of orange juice and juice products. . . . Management's primary objective is to increase shareholder value. To accomplish this objective, The Coca-Cola Company and subsidiaries have developed a comprehensive business strategy that emphasizes improving volume and margins, maximizing long-term cash flow by increasing investments in areas offering attractive returns, divesting low-return assets, and maintaining appropriate financial policies. The Company operates in three markets: soft drinks, entertainment, and food, each of which is consumer oriented and offers attractive rates of returns. In each market, the Company focuses on maximizing unit volume growth, exercising effective asset management, and increasing utilization of its distribution systems. . . . A principal goal for the Soft Drink Business Sector is to increase unit volume at rates in excess of the respective industry rates. . . . Key goals of the Entertainment Business Sector are to leverage its motion picture and television distribution systems and to increase its library of filmed entertainment products. . . . Following a strategy of product and package segmentation, the Foods Business Sector increases unit volume by adding new products into its existing distribution systems.

By the end of the 1980s, Roberto Goizueta had weathered a few storms and enjoyed several successes in Coca-Cola's last 10 years. "New Coke" had caused an unprecedented consumer revolt. The entertainment business was sold to Sony for an impressive gain. An increasing hallmark of Goizueta's leadership was greater openness about the mission and intention of Coca-Cola. In the early 1990s, Goizueta shared the following mission statement in a booklet entitled *Coca-Cola, a Business System toward 2000: Our Mission in the 1990s:*

OUR OPPORTUNITY

Bringing refreshment to a thirsty world is a unique opportunity for our Company . . . and for all of our Coca-Cola associates . . . to create shareholder value. Ours is the only production and distribution business system capable of realizing that opportunity on a global scale. And we are committed to realizing it.

OUR GOAL

With Coca-Cola as the centerpiece, ours is a worldwide system of superior brands and services through which we, our franchisees, and other business partners deliver satisfaction and value to customers and consumers. By doing so, we enhance brand equity on a global basis. As a result, we increase shareholder wealth over time.

Our goal for the 1990s sounds deceptively simple. *It is to expand our global business system, reaching increasing numbers of consumers who will enjoy our brands and products more and more often.*

OUR CHALLENGE

The 1990s promise to be a paradoxical time for our business. Distribution channels will continue to consolidate, while new ones will emerge . . . yet, *customers* will demand more choices, as well as customized service and marketing programs at the lowest possible cost. *Consumers* in developed countries will grow in age and affluence but not in numbers . . . while strong population growth in lesser developed countries means the vitality of these young consumer markets will depend on job creation and expanding economies.

To succeed in this environment we will make *effective use* of our fundamental resources:

- Brands,
- Systems,
- Capital, and, most important,
- People.

Because these resources are already available, one might assume we need only to draw on them for achieving our goal. Nothing could be more wrong. *The challenge of the 1990s will be not only to use these resources but to expand them . . . to adapt them . . . to reconfigure them in constantly changing ways in order to bring about an ever renewed relationship between the Coca-Cola system and the consumers of the world . . . to make the best even better.*

OUR RESOURCES

Brands   Increasing globalization of the communications industry means we can more effectively expose our advertising and other image-building programs through a worldwide brand framework. This places a premium on maintaining our traditional excellence as a premier brand advertiser. Yet, we must remember that it is our franchisee network around the world which will distribute and locally market our brands. To appropriately leverage these brands, we must recognize that we and our franchisees are fundamentally in the business of servicing our customers and meeting the needs, real or perceived, of our consumers.

Tactical decisions regarding the marketing of our products must stay as close to the customer and consumer as possible, within a clear, but flexible, global brand strategy. This is another way of saying that we must think globally but act locally. Thus, intimate knowledge of an account, a channel, or a consumer segment will be required to design specific programs which generate satisfaction and value to that customer or consumer. The Coca-Cola Company does not sell commodities—we will not sell commodities—and we will not cheapen our relationships with customers and consumers.

Coca-Cola, in every form . . . classic, diet, caffeine free, cherry, light . . . is the most widely recognized and esteemed brand in the world. Coca-Cola was, is, and always will be . . . it! It is the centerpiece of our entire refreshment system.

Sprite and Fanta are worldwide brands. They must play a role in our brand strategy. We will continually strive to develop new brands where the opportunity presents itself.

Systems   Moving closer to the consumer both in our own organizational structure and in timely decision-making will be mandated by the global, yet diverse, marketplace of the 1990s.

Structurally, a flatter organization of our Company will be required. Functional groups must be reorganized around business units which focus on market opportunities. And as a company, we must be players, not just cheerleaders or critics.

It will be essential that our franchisees understand this new role we see for ourselves. Our increased equity participation in the Coca-Cola production and distribution network, which may include complete franchise consolidations in some areas of the world, will be carried out *only* whenever it becomes necessary for achieving our goal. A greater involvement in our franchise system will likely necessitate our making investments to help bring about production and distribution capabilities which meet the service demands of customers at the lowest possible cost. This is to ensure a competitive advantage for the entire system.

Entirely new distribution systems may be needed to realize new opportunities in vending and in new and emerging post-mix markets, particularly outside the United States. Joint ventures, in many forms, with our franchisees and suppliers will put our capital directly into building new avenues to reach consumers.

Success in managing these flatter, market-driven structures will depend largely on our information systems. To reach our goal, our information systems—the processes, reports, procedures, and communication linkages that hold the organization together—must lead, rather than trail, developments in the marketplace. Effective and timely information is vital to effective and timely allocation of resources.

Ours is a multilocal business. Its relative state of development varies dramatically from the soft drink frontiers of Asia to the sophisticated markets of North America. Throughout our 103-year history there has been an evolutionary process or cycle of development continuously at work. That cycle, which often evolved over decades in the past, will quicken in astonishing dimensions in the future. By the year 2000, our business system in developing countries must function at levels nearly equal to those seen in today's sophisticated markets. Where lack of hard currency or difficult political realities are constraints to reaching consumers, we must build new strategic alliances and enhance our trading capabilities to overcome constraints.

Capital   Shaping business systems which are close to consumers will require not only the investment of our capital for new assets but more sophisticated management of existing ones. Existing assets will be evaluated as potential resources for meeting our goal. Those assets include not only physical assets but also equity ownership positions, financial capacity, and information systems, as well as creative management of key business relationships.

Capital management is no longer just the process of earning a rate of return above our cost of capital. It is the innovative endeavor of finding more productive uses and new purposes for assets, of trading or leveraging existing assets to meet our goal and to create new strategic alliances.

Our organization has a rich history of effectively allocating resources and of utilizing our financial strength to build value. That will continue. And given our growing experience at managing greater financial leverage, we will periodically evaluate higher leverage ceilings, primarily for investments in our business system or in strategic alliances and, secondarily, in our own shares.

People   Through the years, The Coca-Cola Company has always had an international cadre of individuals. To capture the global soft-drink opportunity in the 1990s, we need more than the right brands, systems, and infrastructure. We need the right people for the 21st century.

We must have people who use facts and knowledge to add something . . . to add value to our customers' businesses. In an age where everyone has basically the same information at the same time, the advantage goes to people who can take information and quickly put it to effective and profitable use. It means having people with what can be called the "mind of the strategist" . . . people who can create a competitive advantage . . . out of common knowledge.

Few are born with such skill. This skill can be developed, however, and should be rewarded. We must recruit and nurture the growth of associates to match the needs of the business. In the 1990s, "internationalists" with multilingual, multicultural capabilities will be the norm. And we must continue to refine our compensation systems to reflect our operating culture and reward value-adding performance.

The responsibility for developing people cannot be delegated to training courses, academic exercises, or professionals in the area of human resources. Those have a role to play but do not constitute an adequate process. *The development of our best people is the personal responsibility of Management.* It requires each manager to see his or her most important responsibility as teaching and developing people. Our charge is that simple—recruiting and training the best talent by the best managers. As that talent grows and develops, they become the next managers capable of and responsible for developing new talent, thus perpetuating a strength.

This process is the link to maintaining the sense of dissatisfaction that has resulted in much of the success we enjoy today. We must continue to cultivate intelligent risk taking and flexible decision making, realizing that, while not every risk taken or decision made brings success, the alternative is complacency and stagnation . . . a stance totally unacceptable to our Company.

OUR REWARDS

The rewards of meeting these challenges and flourishing in a state of rapid change are enormous:

- Satisfied consumers who return again and again to our brands for refreshment.
- Profitable customers who rely on our worldwide brands and services.
- Communities around the world where we are an economic contributor and welcomed guest.
- Successful business partners.
- Shareholders who are building value through the power of the Coca-Cola system.

OUR SHARED VISION

The Coca-Cola system is indeed a special business. One hundred and three years of dedicated effort by literally millions of individuals have combined to create in Coca-Cola a remarkable trademark presence and economic value unchallenged since the dawn of commercial history.

However, any edge we have is fragile. Our journey to the year 2000 requires that our brands, systems, capital, and people grow and change to meet our goal and thus realize our opportunity. To borrow a recent popular phrase, we see 6 billion points of light in a thirsty world—6 billion consumers in the world of the year 2000—all being refreshed as never before by the Coca-Cola system.

That is a wonderful goal we all can share and strive for as we move together—toward 2000.

The evolution of Coca-Cola's use of mission statements from the 1970s to the 1990s displays a consistent commitment to specific, direct statements defining the business of Coca-Cola, while evidencing a move from brevity and secrecy toward greater clarification of values, priorities, and the "Coca-Cola system." Goizueta's elaborate statement of Coke's mission for the 1990s is rather lengthy by comparison to several mission statements excerpted in Chapter 2. But while sensitive to the virtues of brevity, Mr. Goizueta felt a detailed, complete elaboration upon Coke's mission and related components was essential to focusing a diverse, worldwide group of employees and "partners" on the key ingredients for global success in the next century. He felt that providing order and clarity to a detailed "vision" of what the Coca-Cola system is and what it intends to become would provide a framework for future decisions and actions throughout the Coke system to enhance its opportunity for success.

3 THE EXTERNAL ENVIRONMENT

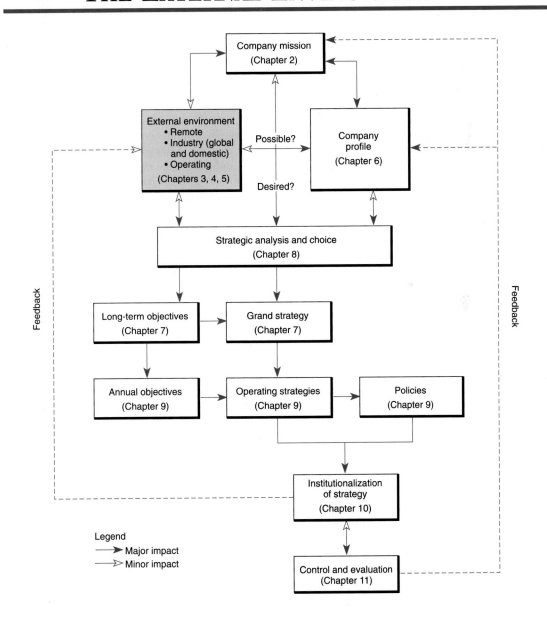

Company mission
(Chapter 2)

External environment
• Remote
• Industry (global and domestic)
• Operating
(Chapters 3, 4, 5)

Possible?

Desired?

Company profile
(Chapter 6)

Strategic analysis and choice
(Chapter 8)

Long-term objectives
(Chapter 7)

Grand strategy
(Chapter 7)

Annual objectives
(Chapter 9)

Operating strategies
(Chapter 9)

Policies
(Chapter 9)

Institutionalization
of strategy
(Chapter 10)

Control and evaluation
(Chapter 11)

Feedback

Feedback

Legend
→ Major impact
⇢ Minor impact

Ahost of external factors influence a firm's choice of direction and action and, ultimately, its organizational structure and internal processes. These factors, which constitute the *external environment,* can be divided into three interrelated subcategories: factors in the *remote* environment, factors in the *industry* environment, and factors in the *operating* environment.[1] This chapter describes the complex necessities involved in formulating strategies that optimize a firm's market opportunities. Figure 3–1 suggests the interrelationship between the firm and its remote, its industry, and its operating environments. In combination, these factors form the basis of the opportunities and threats that a firm faces in its competitive environment.

REMOTE ENVIRONMENT

The remote environment comprises factors that originate beyond, and usually irrespective of, any single firm's operating situation: (1) economic, (2) social, (3) political, (4) technological, and (5) ecological factors. That environment presents firms with opportunities, threats, and constraints; but rarely does a single firm exert any meaningful reciprocal influence. For example, when the economy slows and construction starts to decrease, an individual contractor is likely to suffer a decline in business; but that contractor's success in stimulating local construction activities would be unable to reverse the overall decrease in construction starts. The trade agreements that resulted from improved relations between the United States and China and the United States and Russia are examples of the effects of political factors on individual firms. The agreements provided individual U.S. manufacturers with opportunities to broaden their international operations.

1.   Economic Factors

Economic factors concern the nature and direction of the economy in which a firm operates. Because consumption patterns are affected by the relative affluence of various market segments, in its strategic planning each firm must consider economic trends in the segments that affect its industry. On both the national and international level, it must consider the general availability of credit, the level of disposable income, and the propensity of people to spend. Prime interest rates, inflation rates, and trends in the growth of the gross national product are other economic factors it must consider.

Until recently, the potential impact of international economic forces appeared to be severely restricted and was largely discounted. However, the emergence of new international power brokers has changed the focus of economic environmental forecasting. Among the most prominent of these power brokers are the European Economic Community (EEC, or Common Market), the Organization of Petroleum Exporting Countries (OPEC), and coalitions of developing countries.

The EEC, whose members include most of the West European countries, was established by the Treaty of Rome in 1957. It has eliminated quotas and established a tariff-free

---

[1] Many authors refer to the operating environment as the *task* or *competitive* environment.

FIGURE 3–1
The Firm's External Environment

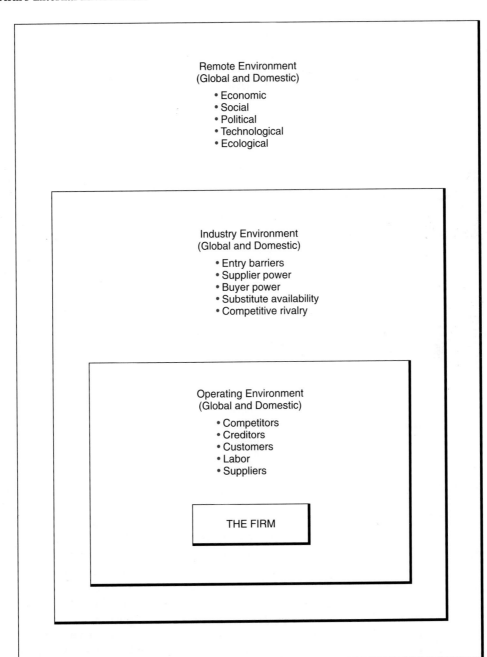

trade area for industrial products among its members. By fostering intra-European economic cooperation, it has helped its member countries compete more effectively in non-European international markets.

Vying with the opening of Eastern European borders to commerce as the most significant marketplace occurrence of the 1990s has been the opening of protected markets by the European Community. Commonly referred to as *EC 92*, the stated goal of this cooperative effort is the elimination of all technical, physical, and fiscal barriers to the conduct of international trade in Europe by 1992. While pragmatists see the EC 92 as a concept and not a deadline, significant progress is being made each year toward the attainment of aims of the collaboration. As of early 1990, 125 of the 265 directives related to 1992 had become EC law.

Much of the excitement over EC 92 stems from the size of the market in Europe, which exceeds 320 million consumers. As Europeans' incomes rise and their tastes become less geocentric, a booming market is expected for consumer goods, from appliances to soft drinks. As evidence of their enthusiasm for the EC 92 marketplace, U.S. companies spent $20.9 billion in 1987 alone to build plants and buy companies in Europe, an amount 28 times greater than their expenditures in 1982.

Among the U.S. firms that invested heavily and early in Europe in the hope of profiting from the EC 92 developments were:

American Express, which projected a 20 percent annual growth rate in Europe in the 1990s owing to weak competition from "mom-and-pop" travel agencies.

AT&T, which completed a five-year, $27 billion deal with Italy's state-owned telephone equipment maker to overhaul the country's aging telephone system.

Federal Express, which was among the early organizers of warehousing and distribution services for European companies. Its $200 million-a-year business in Europe is forecasted to grow 80 percent annually during this decade.

Following the original EEC initiative of economic cooperation, the United States, Canada, Japan, the EEC, and other countries conducted multilateral trade negotiations in 1979 to establish rules for international trade and conduct. Those negotiations had a profound effect on almost every aspect of U.S. business activity.

In terms of impact on the United States, OPEC is at present among the most powerful international economic forces. This cartel includes most of the world's major oil and gas suppliers. Its drastic price increases impeded U.S. recovery from the recession of the early 1970s and fueled inflationary fires throughout the world. Those price increases in particular affected the U.S. automobile industry by raising the fuel costs of automobile users and by giving rise to legislation on engine design and performance standards.

Historically underdeveloped countries recently have assumed a greater role in international commerce as a source of both threats and opportunities. Following OPEC's success, these countries found it economically beneficial to directly confront the established powers. Since 1974, producers of primary commodities in the developing countries have formed or greatly strengthened trade organizations to enforce higher prices and achieve larger real incomes for their members. Even developing countries not desiring or unable to form cartels now exhibit an aggressive attitude in their international economic relations. On the other hand, developing countries offer U.S. firms huge new markets for foodstuffs and capital equipment.

The intense nationalism of the developing countries, with nearly three fourths of the world's population, represents perhaps the greatest challenge our industrialized society and multinational corporations will face in the next two decades. As one Third World expert puts it, "the vastly unequal relationship between the rich and poor nations is fast becoming the central issue of our time."[2]

All of these international forces can affect—for better or worse—the economic well being of the U.S. business community. Consequently, firms must try to forecast the repercussions of major actions taken in both the domestic and international economic arenas. For example, after the second quarter of 1991, some economists and business analysts determined that the United States was recovering from the recession that began during July 1990. Optimistic economists cited increases in industrial production, housing expenditures, and retail sales as signs of better days ahead for U.S. businesses. When the United States entered the fourth quarter of 1991, economists forecasted that recovery was under way and would bode well domestic and international business activity in 1992.

2.   Social Factors

The social factors that affect a firm involve the beliefs, values, attitudes, opinions, and lifestyles of persons in the firm's external environment, as developed from cultural, ecological, demographic, religious, educational, and ethnic conditioning. As social attitudes change, so, too, does the demand for various types of clothing, books, leisure activities, and so on. Like other forces in the remote external environment, social forces are dynamic, with constant change resulting from the efforts of individuals to satisfy their desires and needs by controlling and adapting to environmental factors. Teresa Iglesias-Soloman hoped to benefit from social changes with *Ninos,* a children's catalog written in both English and Spanish. The catalog featured books, videos, and Spanish cultural offerings for English-speaking children who wanted to learn Spanish and for Spanish-speaking children who wanted to learn English. The first edition of *Ninos* was mailed in August 1991. Nino's target market included middle-to-upper income Hispanic parents and a greater number of consumers, educators, bilingual schools, libraries, and purchasing agents. Iglesias-Solomon had reason to be optimistic about the future of *Ninos,* because the Hispanic population was growing five times faster than the general U.S. population.

One of the most profound social changes in recent years has been the entry of large numbers of women into the labor market. This has not only affected the hiring and compensation policies and the resource capabilities of their employers; it also has created or greatly expanded the demand for a wide range of products and services necessitated by their absence from the home. Firms that anticipated or reacted quickly to this social change offered such products and services as convenience foods, microwave ovens, and day-care centers.

A second profound social change has been the accelerating interest of consumers and employees in quality-of-life issues. Evidence of this change is seen in recent contract negotiations. In addition to the traditional demand for increased salaries have been worker

---

[2] R. Steade, "Multinational Corporations and the Changing World Economic Order," *California Management Review,* Winter 1978, p. 5.

demands for such benefits as sabbaticals, flexible hours or four-day workweeks, lump-sum vacation plans, and opportunities for advanced training.

A third profound social change has been the shift in the age distribution of the population. Changing social values and a growing acceptance of improved birth control methods are expected to raise the mean age of the U.S. population, which was 27.9 in 1970, to 34.9 by the end of the 20th century. This trend will have an increasingly unfavorable impact on most producers of predominantly youth-oriented goods and will necessitate a shift in their long-range marketing strategies. Producers of hair- and skin-care preparations already have begun to adjust their research and development to reflect anticipated changes in demand.

A consequence of the changing age distribution of the population has been a sharp increase in the demands made by a growing number of senior citizens. Constrained by fixed incomes, these citizens have demanded that arbitrary and rigid policies on retirement age be modified and have successfully lobbied for tax exemptions and increases in Social Security benefits. Such changes have significantly altered the opportunity-risk equations of many firms—often to the benefit of firms that anticipated the changes.

Translating social change into forecasts of business effects is a difficult process, at best. Nevertheless, informed estimates of the impact of such alterations as geographic shifts in populations and changing work values, ethical standards, and religious orientation only can help a strategizing firm in its attempts to prosper.

3. Political Factors

The direction and stability of political factors is a major consideration for managers on formulating company strategy. Political factors define the legal and regulatory parameters within which firms must operate. Political constraints are placed on firms through fair-trade decisions, antitrust laws, tax programs, minimum wage legislation, pollution and pricing policies, administrative jawboning, and many other actions aimed at protecting employees, consumers, the general public, and the environment. Since such laws and regulations are most commonly restrictive, they tend to reduce the potential profits of firms. However, some political actions are designed to benefit and protect firms. Such actions include patent laws, government subsidies, and product research grants. Thus, political factors either may limit or benefit the firms they influence. For example, when Ethiopian Airlines organized in 1945, it received assistance from TWA and various Ethiopian governments. This support made Ethiopian Airlines one of the most successful members of the African air transport industry. The airline pioneered the hub concept in Africa and arranged its schedules to provide easy connections between many of the continent's countries, as well as between Africa and points in Europe and the Middle East and Asia. Without the political support of the Ethiopian governments, it would have been impossible for the airline to operate.[3]

Political activity also has a significant impact on three governmental functions that influence the remote environment of firms:

Supplier Function   Government decisions regarding the accessibility of private businesses to government-owned natural resources and national stockpiles of agricultural products will affect profoundly the viability of the strategies of some firms.

---

[3] *Air Transport World*, February 1992, pp. 110–12.

Customer Function   Government demand for products and services can create, sustain, enhance, or eliminate many market opportunities. For example, in the same way that the Kennedy Administration's emphasis on landing a man on the moon spawned a demand for thousands of new products, the Carter Administration's emphasis on developing synthetic fuels created a demand for new skills, technologies, and products; and the Reagan Administration's strategic defense initiative (the "Star Wars" defense) sharply accelerated the development of laser technologies.

Entrepreneurial firms often feel such influences especially strongly. For example, in the six months following the August invasion of Kuwait, D. M. Offray & Son, a Chester, New Jersey, bow and ribbon manufacturer, sold about 28,409 miles of yellow ribbon in support of the armed forces. In order to keep up with the demand, the plant manager had to go to a triple-shift, six-day work week.[4]

4.   Technological Factors

The fourth set of factors in the remote environment involves technological change. To avoid obsolescence and promote innovation, a firm must be aware of technological changes that might influence its industry. Creative technological adaptations can suggest possibilities for new products, for improvements in existing products, or in manufacturing and marketing techniques.

A technological breakthrough can have a sudden and dramatic effect on a firm's environment. It may spawn sophisticated new markets and products or significantly shorten the anticipated life of a manufacturing facility. Thus, all firms, and most particularly those in turbulent growth industries, must strive for an understanding both of the existing technological advances and the probable future advances that can affect their products and services. This quasi science of attempting to foresee advancements and estimate their impact on an organization's operations is known as technological forecasting.

Technological forecasting can help protect and improve the profitability of firms in growing industries. It alerts strategic managers to both impending challenges and promising opportunities. As examples: (1) advances in xerography were a key to Xerox's success but caused major difficulties for carbon paper manufacturers and (2) the perfection of transistors changed the nature of competition in the radio and television industry, helping such giants as RCA while seriously weakening smaller firms whose resource commitments required that they continue to base their products on vacuum tubes.

The key to beneficial forecasting of technological advancement lies in accurately predicting future technological capabilities and their probable impacts. A comprehensive analysis of the effect of technological change involves study of the expected impact of new technologies on the remote environment, on the competitive business situation, and on the business-society interface. In recent years, forecasting in the last area has warranted particular attention. For example, as a consequence of increased concern over the environment, firms carefully must investigate the probable effect of technological advances on quality-of-life factors, such as ecology and public safety.

---

[4] *Fortune,* March 11, 1991, p. 14.

5. Ecological Factors

As strategic managers forecast the 1990s, the most prominent factor in the remote environment is often the reciprocal relationship between business and the ecology. The term *ecology* refers to the relationships among human beings and other living things and the air, soil, and water that support them. Threats to our life-supporting ecology caused principally by human activities in an industrial society are commonly referred to as *pollution.*

Air pollution is created by dust particles and gaseous discharges that contaminate the air. Acid rain, or rain contaminated by sulfur dioxide, which can destroy aquatic and plant life, is believed to result from coal-burning factories in 70 percent of all cases. A health-threatening "thermal blanket" is created when the atmosphere traps carbon dioxide emitted from smokestacks in factories burning fossil fuels. This "greenhouse effect" can have disastrous consequences, making the climate unpredictable and raising temperatures. Finally, airborne carcinogens resulting from manufacturing processes have been linked to approximately 20,000 deaths each year.[5] An interesting example of a way in which the free market system can help to reduce air pollution problems is discussed in Strategy in Action 3–1.

Water pollution occurs principally when industrial toxic wastes are dumped or leak into the nation's waterways. Since fewer than 50 percent of all municipal sewer systems are in compliance with Environmental Protection Agency requirements for water safety, contaminated waters represent a substantial present threat to public welfare.

Land pollution is caused by the need to dispose of ever-increasing amounts of waste. Routine, everyday packaging is a major contributor to this problem, as described in Global Strategy in Action 3–1. Land pollution is more dauntingly caused by the disposal of industrial toxic wastes in underground sites. With approximately 90 percent of the annual U.S. output of 500 million metric tons of hazardous industrial wastes being placed in underground dumps, it is evident that land pollution and its resulting endangerment of the ecology have become a major item on the political agenda.

As a major contributor to ecological pollution, business now is being held responsible for eliminating the toxic by-products of its current manufacturing processes and for cleaning up the environmental damage that it did previously. Increasingly, managers are being required by the government or are being expected by the public to incorporate ecological concerns into their decision making.[6] For example, between 1975 and 1992, 3M cut its pollution in half by reformulating products, modifying processes, redesigning production equipment, and recycling by-products. Similarly, steel companies and public utilities have invested billions of dollars in costlier but cleaner-burning fuels and pollution control equipment. The automobile industry has been required to install expensive emission controls in cars. The gasoline industry has been forced to formulate new low-lead and no-lead products. And thousands of companies have found it necessary to direct their R&D resources into the search for ecologically superior products, such as Sears' phosphate-free laundry detergent and Pepsi-Cola's biodegradable plastic soft-drink bottle.

---

[5] "How the EPA Plans to Live with Cancer Risks," *Business Week,* August 8, 1982, p. 84.

[6] P. Kotler, *Marketing Management* (Englewood Cliffs, N.J.: Prentice Hall, 1989), p. 98.

STRATEGY
IN ACTION **COLD CASH FOR OLD CLUNKERS**
3–1

Whaddya bid me for this 1971 Ford? Forget the Blue Book. The value of this beauty depends on how much choking black smoke blasts out of its rusted tailpipe—and the more the better. Thanks to the Bush Administration, there is a thriving free market in dirty old cars: companies that pollute the air buy them, junk them, and earn a "pollution credit" for saving however much smog- and ozone-forming exhaust the cars would have belched out before they died. The company—anything from a utility to a paint factory—subtracts the amount of the credit from the quantity of air pollution they're required to cut under the 1990 Clean Air Act. The idea of this and other market-based approaches to environmental cleanup is to get the most clean for the least green. "Lots of little smokestacks on the highway are equivalent to one big smokestack," says energy-policy analyst Will Schroeer of the U.S. Environmental Protection Agency. "But it will be cheaper to scrap cars than to put emission controls on smokestacks."

Adam Smith would love it. Say a factory must reduce its nitrogen oxide (NO_x) emissions by 130,000 pounds a year. And say it will cost $1 million to do that by installing scrubbers on its smokestacks. If the factory buys 1,000 old cars for an average $700 each, and if each car spews out 130 pounds of NO_x a year, the company will have met its clean-air mandate and saved $300,000 in the bargain. People who sold their old clunkers could buy a cleaner, later-model car. That's how it worked in 1990 in California, when Unocal bought 8,376 pre-1971 cars for $700 apiece. The junked cars accounted for nearly 13 million pounds of emissions per year—as much as the hydrocarbons from 250,000 new cars, one large oil refinery, or all the barbecue lighter fluid used in the Los Angeles basin.

Such "green economics" has become as trendy as recycling newspaper. In 1993, southern California allowed factories to meet clean-air standards by buying pollution credits from companies that had exceeded their mandated emissions cuts. Still, although using market forces to clean up the planet has found support in Congress, the administration, and even among environmental groups, cash-for-clunkers has its detractors. Dan Becker of the Sierra Club calls it "the Cheshire Cat approach. Pollution from the car will continue after the [car] has disappeared"—because the car's "quota" is now coming from the smokestack of the buyer, who can avoid cleaning up his own act. But there is no debate that old cars make a tempting target. The 37.6 million cars that predate 1980 are responsible for 86 percent of the smog-making gases from autos but represent only 38 percent of the fleet; the 5.9 million dirtiest cars cause a whopping 50 percent of all hydrocarbons. Next up for the green marketeers: giving companies pollution credits if they switch to alternative-fuel fleets. Capitalism may turn out to be an environmentalist's friend after all.

Source: Excerpted from S. Begley and M. Hager, "Cold Cash for Old Clunkers," *Newsweek,* April 6, 1992, p. 61.

The increasing attention by companies to protect the environment is evidenced in the attempts by firms to establish proecology policies. One such approach to environmental activism is described in Global Strategy in Action 3–2.

Despite cleanup efforts to date, the job of protecting the ecology will continue to be a top strategic priority—usually because corporate stockholders and executives choose it, increasingly because the public and the government require it. As evidenced by Figure

Packaging is the ultimate symbol of the 20th century's consumer culture. It protects what we buy and raises our standard of living. In developing countries, 30 percent to 50 percent of food shipments are spoiled because of inadequate packaging and distribution systems. In developed countries with more sophisticated packaging, storage, and distribution, only 2 percent to 3 percent are wasted.

Packaging not only protects goods but also conveys information about their contents and preparation or administration, and—in some cases—foils would-be tamperers. It plays a vital and growing role in the global economy.

At the same time, packaging is on the environmental frontline. It is the largest and fastest growing contributor to one of the most troubling environmental problems: garbage.

In the United States, packaging accounted for more than 30 percent of the municipal solid waste stream in 1990. Where is all this packaging going? In this country, most packaging and other waste is buried in landfills. But even with its abundance of open land, America is running out of room for its garbage.

One quarter of the country's municipalities are expected to exhaust their landfill capacity before 1995, and more than half the population lives in regions with less than 10 years of landfill capacity.

Meanwhile, the environmentally sound alternatives to burying garbage—recycling, reuse, and energy recovery—are only just beginning. For the throwaway society, the 1990s are the decade of reckoning.

While packaging is not the only culprit in the solid waste crisis, it is a highly visible component, and one that directly involves consumers. And its short lifetime exacerbates the problem. Although the useful lives of some packages—such as paint cans and reusable canisters—may be as long as several years, the useful lives of others—such as fast-food hamburger wrappers—can be as fleeting as a few minutes.

Fortunately, because of the sheer volume of packaging in the solid waste stream, even relatively small improvements in packaging can make a real difference in the magnitude of the garbage crisis. Packaging, thus, offers a unique opportunity for companies to assume a leadership role in environmental responsibility.

In terms of packaging choices, industry's response to the environmental challenge has so far focused on recycling and source reduction. But the complexity of the issues involved demands a more systemic, integrated approach based on comprehensive analysis and long-term vision as well as innovative solutions.

Among the analytical tools now being deployed is life-cycle analysis. This is a fairly new technique for exploring the environmental implications of a given product decision—in this case, a packaging choice from raw material acquisition through manufacturing, energy consumption, design, and transportation to final use and disposal of the package. Life-cycle thinking is an important step toward understanding the full environmental implications of packaging choices.

Source: Excerpted from E. J. Stilwell and H. B. C. Tibbs, "Packaging for the Environment," *Management Review,* December 1991, p. 48.

3–2, the government has made numerous interventions into the conduct of business for the purpose of bettering the ecology. The consequences of one such attempt are detailed in Strategy in Action 3–2 and 3–3 (*continued on p. 75*).

GLOBAL
STRATEGY IN **TAKING A STEP IN THE RIGHT DIRECTION**
ACTION 3–2

 "The ongoing occurrence of environmental incidents has become unacceptable in the public's mind," says George Pilko, president of Houston-based Pilko & Associates, an environmental consulting firm. That's why companies today are taking a proactive stance when it comes to managing environmental issues. The public just won't tolerate any more Love Canals, Bhopals, or major oil spills. "You've got strong public sentiment, increasingly stringent environmental regulations at the local, state, and federal level, stricter enforcement of existing regulations, and an exponential rise in environmentally oriented lawsuits. It clearly doesn't make sense for companies to continue to operate as they had been up until the late 1980s where they focused in on just remaining in compliance with existing regulations," Pilko adds.

Instead, according to Pilko, companies need to make sure they've got an environmental policy that clearly explains their commitment to being proactive and is communicated clearly to all employees. Companies also should be aware of the effectiveness of their current programs and where they stand relative to their competitors, because "there is a tremendous discrepancy between executives' perception of how they are doing and what is reality." In fact, a recent Pilko & Associates survey of 200 senior executives representing large industrial firms found that 40 percent of the respondents believed their company was doing an excellent job of managing their environmental problems, while only 8 percent thought their competitors were doing an excellent job.

Regardless of perception, however, management of environmental issues must be supported from the top. "Corporate environmental policy is most effectively communicated by the president or CEO," Pilko says. For those CEOs or senior executives interested in getting out the message that they are serious about dealing with the environment, Pilko advises them to ask themselves the following 10 questions:

1. Do you have a clearly articulated environmental policy that has been communicated throughout the company?
2. Have you had an objective, third-party assessment of the effectiveness of your environmental programs?
3. Have you analyzed how your company's environmental performance compares with that of the leading firms in your industry?
4. Does your company view environmental performance not just as a staff function but as the responsibility of all employees?
5. Have you analyzed the potential impact of environmental issues on the future demand for your products and the competitive economics in your industry?
6. Are environmental issues and activities discussed frequently at your board meetings?
7. Do you have a formal system for monitoring proposed regulatory changes and for handling compliance with changing regulations?
8. Do you routinely conduct environmental due-diligence studies on potential acquisitions?
9. Have you successfully budgeted for environmental expenditures, without incurring surprise expenses that materially affected your profitability?
10. Have you identified and quantified environmental liabilities from past operations, and do you have a plan for minimizing those liabilities?

Source: Excerpted from Julie Cohen Mason, "Taking a Step in the Right Direction," *Management Review,* December 1991, p. 23.

Tighter Restrictions on Tailpipe Emissions from Automobiles and Small Light Trucks   The restrictions are phased in over the 1994 through 1996 model years. They require a reduction of about 35 percent in nonmethane HC tailpipe emissions (to 0.25 grams per mile) and 60 percent in NO_x emissions (to 0.4 grams per mile), beginning in 1994. The emission-control requirements would apply for 10 years or 100,000 miles, up from five years or 50,000 miles under current law.

Tailpipe Standards for Light- and Medium-Duty Trucks   Trucks in the 6,000 to 8,500 pounds gross-vehicle-weight range must phase the new California tailpipe standards beginning in the 1996 model year.

Cleaner Fuels for Fleets   Based on noncompliance levels and population, 22 areas must establish a Clean-Fuel Vehicle program. The program applies to commercial fleets of 10 or more vehicles that can be refueled at a central location. Under the program, fleet operators must purchase cars and light trucks that meet emission standards that are more than 80 percent stricter than those for 1991 vehicles, starting with 1998 models. Purchase requirements for heavy-truck fleets (8,500 to 26,000 pounds gross vehicle weight) also are included.

California Pilot Program   Automakers are required to produce Clean-Fuel Vehicles for sale in California. Between 1996 and 1998, the industry annually must sell 150,000 cars and light trucks meeting the lower emission requirements of Clean-Fuel Vehicles. Beginning in 1999, automakers must sell 300,000 a year. These vehicles may run on clean fuels, such as methanol, natural gas, or reformulated gasoline. However, any fuel may be used, provided the Clean-Fuel Vehicle emission requirements are met.

Reformulated Gasoline   Starting in 1995, reformulated gasoline will be required in nine cities that are most out of compliance with federal ozone air quality standards. To qualify as reformulated gasoline, beginning in 1995, volatile organic compounds (VOCs) and toxic emissions will have to decrease by 15 percent, compared with conventional gasoline. In 2000, additional technologically feasible emission reductions must occur.

Low-Temperature CO Provisions   Starting in 1994, cars cannot emit more than 10 grams per mile tested at 20°F. (Exceedances of the ambient CO standard occur most frequently at low temperatures.) This requirement will be phased in at 40 percent of vehicles sold in 1994 MY, 80 percent in 1995 MY, and 100 percent in 1996 MY. Depending on CO air quality, even more stringent levels may be imposed, beginning with MY 2001.

Onboard Diagnostics   Vehicle manufacturers must install systems to alert drivers when an emission-control system has malfunctioned or degraded.

Warranty Provisions   The warranty period for most light-duty vehicle emission-control equipment components is shortened to 2 years/24,000 miles, starting in 1995. The warranty period for major emission-control components (catalytic converter, onboard diagnostics, and the electronic control module) is extended to 8 years/80,000 miles.

Chlorofluorocarbons   Production of stratospheric ozone-depleting chemicals must cease: chlorofluorocarbons (CFCs) and carbon tetrachloride by 2000; methyl chloroform by 2002. Output of hydrochlorofluorocarbons, which are less damaging substitutes for CFCs, will cease by 2030.

Toxic Air Pollutants   The new provisions are intended to reduce emissions of toxic air pollutants from stationary sources by as much as 90 percent by 2003. They list 189 toxic pollutants and require EPA to establish hundreds of categories of industrial and commercial sources of hazardous pollutants (chemical plants, oil refineries, and the like) for the purpose of promulgating standards. Between 1995 and 2003, all except the smallest sources will be required to install the best pollution control equipment available.

Source: Excerpted from the 1991 General Motors Public Interest Report, pp. 24–25, 31.

Variable-Fueled Lumina   Shown here are the many Chevrolet Lumina components unique to a variable-fueled vehicle that can run on any fuel blend ranging from 85% methanol, 15% gasoline, to 100% gasoline.

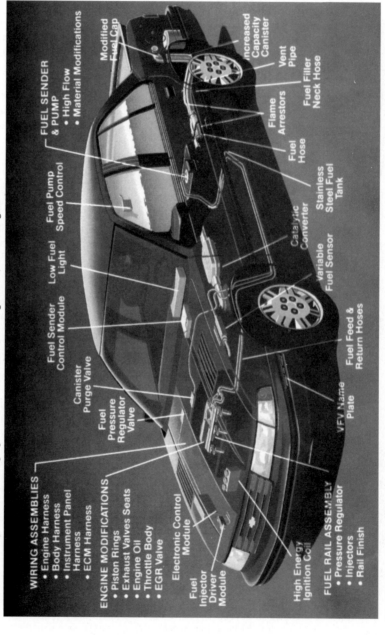

WIRING ASSEMBLIES
- Engine Harness
- Body Harness
- Instrument Panel Harness
- ECM Harness

ENGINE MODIFICATIONS
- Piston Rings
- Exhaust Valves Seats
- Engine Oil
- Throttle Body
- EGR Valve

Electronic Control Module

Fuel Injector Driver Module

High Energy Ignition Coil

FUEL RAIL ASSEMBLY
- Pressure Regulator
- Injectors
- Rail Finish

Fuel Pressure Regulator Valve

Canister Purge Valve

Fuel Sender Control Module

Low Fuel Light

Fuel Pump Speed Control

FUEL SENDER & PUMP
- High Flow
- Material Modifications

Modified Fuel Cap

Increased Capacity Canister

Vent Pipe

Fuel Filler Neck Hose

Flame Arrestors

Fuel Hose

Stainless Steel Fuel Tank

Catalytic Converter

Variable Fuel Sensor

Fuel Feed & Return Hoses

VFV Name Plate

THE EXPERIENCE CURVE AS AN ENTRY BARRIER

In recent years, the experience curve has become widely discussed as a key element of industry structure. According to this concept, unit costs in many manufacturing industries (some dogmatic adherents say in all manufacturing industries) as well as in some service industries decline with "experience," or a particular company's cumulative volume of production. (The experience curve, which encompasses many factors, is a broader concept than the better-known learning curve, which refers to the efficiency achieved over time by workers through much repetition.)

The causes of the decline in unit costs are a combination of elements, including economies of scale, the learning curve for labor, and capital-labor substitution. The cost decline creates a barrier to entry because new competitors with no "experience" face higher costs than established ones, particularly the producer with the largest market share, and have difficulty catching up with the entrenched competitors.

Adherents of the experience curve concept stress the importance of achieving market leadership to maximize this barrier to entry, and they recommend aggressive action to achieve it, such as price cutting in anticipation of falling costs in order to build volume. For the combatant that cannot achieve a healthy market share, the prescription is usually, "Get out."

Is the experience curve an entry barrier on which strategies should be built? The answer is: not in every industry. In fact, in some industries, building a strategy on the experience curve can be potentially disastrous. That costs decline with experience in some industries is not news to corporate executives. The significance of the experience curve for strategy depends on what factors are causing the decline.

A new entrant may well be more efficient than the more experienced competitors; if it has built the newest plant, it will face no disadvantage in having to catch up. The strategic prescription, "You must have the largest, most efficient plant," is a lot different from "You must produce the greatest cumulative output of the item to get your costs down."

Whether a drop in costs with cumulative (not absolute) volume erects an entry barrier also depends on the sources of the decline. If costs go down because of technical advances known generally in the industry or because of the development of improved equipment that can be copied or purchased from equipment suppliers, the experience curve is not an entry barrier at all—in fact, new or less-experienced competitors may actually enjoy a cost advantage over the leaders. Free of the legacy of heavy past investments, the newcomer or less-experienced competitor can purchase or copy the newest and lowest-cost equipment and technology.

If, however, experience can be kept proprietary, the leaders will maintain a cost advantage. But new entrants may require less experience to reduce their costs than the leaders needed. All this suggests that the experience curve can be a shaky entry barrier on which to build a strategy.

While space does not permit a complete treatment here, I want to mention a few other crucial elements in determining the appropriateness of a strategy built on the entry barrier provided by the experience curve:

The height of the barrier depends on how important costs are to competition compared with other areas like marketing, selling, and innovation.

The barrier can be nullified by product or process innovations leading to a substantially new technology and, thereby, creating an entirely new experience curve. New entrants can leapfrog the industry leaders and alight on the new experience curve, to which those leaders may be poorly positioned to jump.

If more than one strong company is building its strategy on the experience curve, the consequences can be nearly fatal. By the time only one rival is left pursuing such a strategy, industry growth may have stopped and the prospects of reaping the spoils of victory long since evaporated.

FIGURE 3–2
Federal Ecological Legislation

CENTERPIECE LEGISLATION
National Environmental Policy Act, 1969 Established Environmental Protection Agency; consolidated federal environmental activities under it. Established Council on Environmental Quality to advise president on environmental policy and to review environmental impact statements.

AIR POLLUTION
Clean Air Act, 1963 Authorized assistance to state and local governments in formulating control programs. Authorized limited federal action in correcting specific pollution problems.
Clean Air Act, Amendments (Motor Vehicle Air Pollution Control Act), 1965 Authorized federal standards for auto exhaust emission. Standards first set for 1968 models.
Air Quality Act, 1967 Authorized federal government to establish air quality control regions and to set maximum permissible pollution levels. Required states and localities to carry out approved control programs or else give way to federal controls.
Clean Air Act Amendments, 1970 Authorized EPA to establish nationwide air pollution standards and to limit the discharge of six principal pollutants into the lower atmosphere. Authorized citizens to take legal action to require EPA to implement its standards against undiscovered offenders.
Clean Air Act Amendments, 1977 Postponed auto emission requirements. Required use of scrubbers in new coal-fired power plants. Directed EPA to establish a system to prevent deterioration of air quality in clean areas.

SOLID WASTE POLLUTION
Solid Waste Disposal Act, 1965 Authorized research and assistance to state and local control programs.
Resource Recovery Act, 1970 Subsidized construction of pilot recycling plants; authorized development of nationwide control programs.
Resource Conservation and Recovery Act, 1976 Directed EPA to regulate hazardous waste management, from generation through disposal.
Surface Mining and Reclamation Act, 1976 Controlled strip mining and restoration of reclaimed land.

WATER POLLUTION
Refuse Act, 1899 Prohibited dumping of debris into navigable waters without a permit. Extended by court decision to industrial discharges.

INDUSTRY ENVIRONMENT

Harvard professor Michael E. Porter's book *Competitive Strategy* propelled the concept of industry environment into the foreground of strategic thought and business planning. The cornerstone of the book is an article from the *Harvard Business Review,* in which Porter explains the five forces that shape competition in an industry. His well-defined analytic framework helps strategic managers to link the impact of remote factors to the resulting effects on a firm's operating environment.

With the special permission of Professor Porter and the *Harvard Business Review,* we present in this section of the chapter the major portion of his seminal article on the industry environment and its impact on strategic management.[7]

---

[7] M. E. Porter, "How Competitive Forces Shape Strategy," *Harvard Business Review,* March–April 1979, pp. 137–45.

FIGURE 3–2 (concluded)

Federal Water Pollution Control Act, 1956 Authorized grants to states for water pollution control. Gave federal government limited authority to correct specific pollution problems.
Water Quality Act, 1965 Provided for adoption of water quality standards by states, subject to federal approval.
Water Quality Improvement Act, 1970 Provided for federal cleanup of oil spills. Strengthened federal authority over water pollution control.
Federal Water Pollution Control Act Amendments, 1972 Authorized EPA to set water quality and effluent standards; provided for enforcement and research.
Safe Drinking Water Act, 1974 Set standards for drinking water quality.
Clean Water Act, 1977 Ordered control of toxic pollutants by 1984 with best available technology economically feasible.

OTHER POINTS
Federal Insecticide, Fungicide and Rodenticide Act, 1947 To protect farmers, prohibited fraudulent claims by salespersons. Required registration of poisonous products.
Federal Insecticide, Fungicide, and Rodenticide Amendments, 1967, 1972 Provided new authority to license users of pesticides.
Pesticide Control Act, 1972 Required all pesticides shipped in interstate commerce to be certified as effective for their stated purposes and harmless to crops, animal feed, animal life, and humans.
Noise Control Act, 1972 Required EPA to set noise standards for major sources of noise and to advise Federal Aviation Administration on standards for airplane noise.
Federal Environmental Pesticide Control Act Amendments, 1975 Set 1977 deadline (not met) for registration, classification, and licensing of many pesticides.
Toxic Substances Control Act, 1976 Required testing of chemicals; authorized EPA to restrict the use of harmful substances.
Comprehensive Environmental Response, Compensation, and Liability Act, 1980 Commonly called "Superfund Act"; created a trust fund (paid for in part by toxic-chemical manufacturers) to clean up hazardous waste sites.

OVERVIEW

The nature and degree of competition in an industry hinge on five forces: the threat of new entrants, the bargaining power of customers, the bargaining power of suppliers, the threat of substitute products or services (where applicable), and the jockeying among current contestants. To establish a strategic agenda for dealing with these contending currents and to grow despite them, a company must understand how they work in its industry and how they affect the company in its particular situation. This chapter will detail how these forces operate and suggest ways of adjusting to them, and, where possible, of taking advantage of them.

HOW COMPETITIVE FORCES SHAPE STRATEGY

The essence of strategy formulation is coping with competition. Yet it is easy to view competition too narrowly and too pessimistically. While one sometimes hears executives complaining to the contrary, intense competition in an industry is neither coincidence nor bad luck.

FIGURE 3–3
Forces Driving Industry Competition

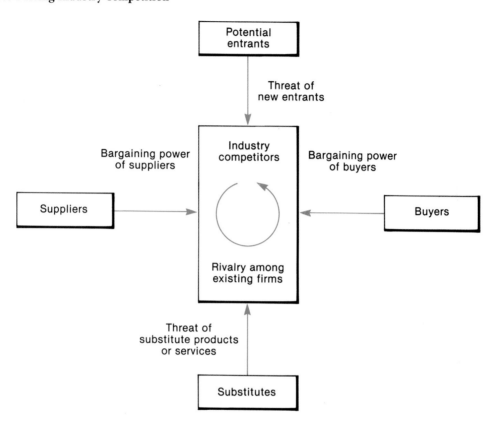

Moreover, in the fight for market share, competition is not manifested only in the other players. Rather, competition in an industry is rooted in its underlying economics, and competitive forces exist that go well beyond the established combatants in a particular industry. Customers, suppliers, potential entrants, and substitute products are all competitors that may be more or less prominent or active depending on the industry.

The state of competition in an industry depends on five basic forces, which are diagramed in Figure 3–3. The collective strength of these forces determines the ultimate profit potential of an industry. It ranges from intense in industries like tires, metal cans, and steel, where no company earns spectacular returns on investment, to mild in industries like oil-field services and equipment, soft drinks, and toiletries, where there is room for quite high returns.

In the economists' "perfectly competitive" industry, jockeying for position is unbridled and entry to the industry very easy. This kind of industry structure, of course, offers the worst prospect for long-run profitability. The weaker the forces collectively, however, the greater the opportunity for superior performance.

Whatever their collective strength, the corporate strategist's goal is to find a position in the industry where his or her company can best defend itself against these forces or can influence them in its favor. The collective strength of the forces may be painfully apparent to all the antagonists; but to cope with them, the strategist must delve below the surface and analyze the sources of competition. For example, what makes the industry vulnerable to entry? What determines the bargaining power of suppliers?

Knowledge of these underlying sources of competitive pressure provides the groundwork for a strategic agenda of action. They highlight the critical strengths and weaknesses of the company, animate the positioning of the company in its industry, clarify the areas where strategic changes may yield the greatest payoff, and highlight the places where industry trends promise to hold the greatest significance as either opportunities or threats.

Understanding these sources also proves to be of help in considering areas for diversification.

CONTENDING FORCES

The strongest competitive force or forces determine the profitability of an industry and so are of greatest importance in strategy formulation. For example, even a company with a strong position in an industry unthreatened by potential entrants will earn low returns if it faces a superior or a lower-cost substitute product—as the leading manufacturers of vacuum tubes and coffee percolators have learned to their sorrow. In such a situation, coping with the substitute product becomes the number one strategic priority.

Different forces take on prominence, of course, in shaping competition in each industry. In the oceangoing tanker industry, the key force is probably the buyers (the major oil companies), while in tires it is powerful OEM buyers coupled with tough competitors. In the steel industry the key forces are foreign competitors and substitute materials.

Every industry has an underlying structure, or a set of fundamental economic and technical characteristics, that gives rise to these competitive forces. The strategist, wanting to position his or her company to cope best with its industry environment or to influence that environment in the company's favor, must learn what makes the environment tick.

This view of competition pertains equally to industries dealing in services and to those selling products. To avoid monotony, I refer to both products and services as *products*. The same general principles apply to all types of business.

A few characteristics are critical to the strength of each competitive force. They will be discussed in this section.

A.   Threat of Entry

New entrants to an industry bring new capacity, the desire to gain market share, and often substantial resources. Companies diversifying through acquisition into the industry from other markets often leverage their resources to cause a shape-up, as Philip Morris did with Miller beer.

The seriousness of the threat of entry depends on the barriers present and on the reaction from existing competitors that the entrant can expect. If barriers to entry are high and a newcomer can expect sharp retaliation from the entrenched competitors, he or she obviously will not pose a serious threat of entering.

There are six major sources of barriers to entry:

1. Economies of Scale   These economies deter entry by forcing the aspirant either to come in on a large scale or to accept a cost disadvantage. Scale economies in production, research, marketing, and service are probably the key barriers to entry in the mainframe computer industry, as Xerox and GE sadly discovered. Economies of scale also can act as hurdles in distribution, utilization of the sales force, financing, and nearly any other part of a business.

2. Product Differentiation   Brand identification creates a barrier by forcing entrants to spend heavily to overcome customer loyalty. Advertising, customer service, being first in the industry, and product differences are among the factors fostering brand identification. It is perhaps the most important entry barrier in soft drinks, over-the-counter drugs, cosmetics, investment banking, and public accounting. To create high fences around their business, brewers couple brand identification with economies of scale in production, distribution, and marketing.

3. Capital Requirements   The need to invest large financial resources in order to compete creates a barrier to entry, particularly if the capital is required for unrecoverable expenditures in up-front advertising or R&D. Capital is necessary not only for fixed facilities but also for customer credit, inventories, and absorbing start-up losses. While major corporations have the financial resources to invade almost any industry, the huge capital requirements in certain fields, such as computer manufacturing and mineral extraction, limit the pool of likely entrants.

4. Cost Disadvantages Independent of Size   Entrenched companies may have cost advantages not available to potential rivals, no matter what their size and attainable economies of scale. These advantages can stem from the effects of the learning curve (and of its first cousin, the experience curve), proprietary technology, access to the best raw materials sources, assets purchased at preinflation prices, government subsidies, or favorable locations. Sometimes cost advantages are enforceable legally, as they are through patents. (For analysis of the much-discussed experience curve as a barrier to entry, see Strategy in Action 3–3.)

5. Access to Distribution Channels   The new boy or girl on the block must, of course, secure distribution of his or her product or service. A new food product, for example, must displace others from the supermarket shelf via price breaks, promotions, intense selling efforts, or some other means. The more limited the wholesale or retail channels are and the more that existing competitors have these tied up, obviously the tougher that entry into the industry will be. Sometimes this barrier is so high that, to surmount it, a new contestant must create its own distribution channels, as Timex did in the watch industry in the 1950s.

6. Government Policy   The government can limit or even foreclose entry to industries, with such controls as license requirements and limits on access to raw materials. Regulated industries like trucking, liquor retailing, and freight forwarding are noticeable examples; more subtle government restrictions operate in fields like ski-area development and coal mining. The government also can play a major indirect role by affecting entry barriers through such controls as air and water pollution standards and safety regulations.

The potential rival's expectations about the reaction of existing competitors also will influence its decision on whether to enter. The company is likely to have second thoughts if incumbents have previously lashed out at new entrants or if:

The incumbents possess substantial resources to fight back, including excess cash and unused borrowing power, productive capacity, or clout with distribution channels and customers.

The incumbents seem likely to cut prices because of a desire to keep market shares or because of industrywide excess capacity.

Industry growth is slow, affecting its ability to absorb the new arrival and probably causing the financial performance of all the parties involved to decline.

B. Powerful Suppliers

Suppliers can exert bargaining power on participants in an industry by raising prices or reducing the quality of purchased goods and services. Powerful suppliers, thereby, can squeeze profitability out of an industry unable to recover cost increases in its own prices. By raising their prices, soft-drink concentrate producers have contributed to the erosion of profitability of bottling companies because the bottlers—facing intense competition from powdered mixes, fruit drinks, and other beverages—have limited freedom to raise their prices accordingly.

The power of each important supplier (or buyer) group depends on a number of characteristics of its market situation and on the relative importance of its sales or purchases to the industry compared with its overall business.

A *supplier* group is powerful if:

1. It is dominated by a few companies and is more concentrated than to the industry it sells.

2. Its product is unique or at least differentiated, or if it has built-up switching costs. Switching costs are fixed costs that buyers face in changing suppliers. These arise because, among other things, a buyer's product specifications tie it to particular suppliers, it has invested heavily in specialized ancillary equipment or in learning how to operate a supplier's equipment (as in computer software), or its production lines are connected to the supplier's manufacturing facilities (as in some manufacturing of beverage containers).

3. It is not obliged to contend with other products for sale to the industry. For instance, the competition between the steel companies and the aluminum companies to sell to the can industry checks the power of each supplier.

4. It poses a credible threat of integrating forward into the industry's business. This provides a check against the industry's ability to improve the terms on which it purchases.

5. The industry is not an important customer of the supplier group. If the industry is an important customer, suppliers' fortunes will be tied closely to the industry, and they will want to protect the industry through reasonable pricing and assistance in activities like R&D and lobbying.

C. Powerful Buyers

Customers likewise can force down prices, demand higher quality or more service, and play competitors off against each other—all at the expense of industry profits.

A *buyer* group is powerful if:

1. It is concentrated or purchases in large volumes. Large-volume buyers are particularly potent forces if heavy fixed costs characterize the industry—as they do in metal containers, corn refining, and bulk chemicals, for example—which raise the stakes to keep capacity filled.

2. The products it purchases from the industry are standard or undifferentiated. The buyers, sure that they always can find alternative suppliers, may play one company against another, as they do in aluminum extrusion.

3. The products it purchases from the industry form a component of its product and represent a significant fraction of its cost. The buyers are likely to shop for a favorable price and purchase selectively. Where the product sold by the industry in question is a small fraction of buyers' costs, buyers are usually much less price sensitive.

4. It earns low profits, which create great incentive to lower its purchasing costs. Highly profitable buyers, however, are generally less price sensitive (i.e., of course, if the item does not represent a large fraction of their costs).

5. The industry's product is unimportant to the quality of the buyers' products or services. Where the quality of the buyers' products is very much affected by the industry's product, buyers are generally less price sensitive. Industries in which this situation exists include oil-field equipment, where a malfunction can lead to large losses, and enclosures for electronic medical and test instruments, where the quality of the enclosure can influence the user's impression about the quality of the equipment inside.

6. The industry's product does not save the buyer money. Where the industry's product or service can pay for itself many times over, the buyer is rarely price sensitive; rather, he or she is interested in quality. This is true in services like investment banking and public accounting, where errors in judgment can be costly and embarrassing, and in businesses like the mapping of oil wells, where an accurate survey can save thousands of dollars in drilling costs.

7. The buyers pose a credible threat of integrating backward to make the industry's product. The Big Three auto producers and major buyers of cars often have used the threat of self-manufacture as a bargaining lever. But sometimes an industry so engenders a threat to buyers that its members may integrate forward.

Most of these sources of buyer power can be attributed to consumers as a group as well as to industrial and commercial buyers; only a modification of the frame of reference is necessary. Consumers tend to be more price sensitive if they are purchasing products that are undifferentiated, expensive relative to their incomes, and of a sort where quality is not particularly important.

The buying power of retailers is determined by the same rules, with one important addition. Retailers can gain significant bargaining power over manufacturers when they can influence consumers' purchasing decisions, as they do in audio components, jewelry, appliances, sporting goods, and other goods.

D. Substitute Products

By placing a ceiling on the prices it can charge, substitute products or services limit the potential of an industry. Unless it can upgrade the quality of the product or differentiate it somehow (as via marketing), the industry will suffer in earnings and possibly in growth.

Manifestly, the more attractive the price-performance trade-off offered by substitute products, the firmer the lid placed on the industry's profit potential. Sugar producers confronted with the large-scale commercialization of high-fructose corn syrup, a sugar substitute, are learning this lesson today.

Substitutes not only limit profits in normal times but also reduce the bonanza an industry can reap in boom times. In 1978, the producers of fiberglass insulation enjoyed unprecedented demand as a result of high energy costs and severe winter weather. But the industry's ability to raise prices was tempered by the plethora of insulation substitutes, including cellulose, rock wool, and styrofoam. These substitutes are bound to become an even stronger force once the current round of plant additions by fiberglass insulation producers has boosted capacity enough to meet demand (and then some).

Substitute products that deserve the most attention strategically are those that *(a)* are subject to trends improving their price-performance trade-off with the industry's product or *(b)* are produced by industries earning high profits. Substitutes often come rapidly into play if some development increases competition in their industries and causes price reduction or performance improvement.

E. Jockeying for Position

Rivalry among existing competitors takes the familiar form of jockeying for position—using tactics like price competition, product introduction, and advertising slugfests. This type of intense rivalry is related to the presence of a number of factors:

1. Competitors are numerous or are roughly equal in size and power. In many U.S. industries in recent years, foreign contenders, of course, have become part of the competitive picture.

2. Industry growth is slow, precipitating fights for market share that involve expansion-minded members.

3. The product or service lacks differentiation or switching costs, which lock in buyers and protect one combatant from raids on its customers by another.

4. Fixed costs are high or the product is perishable, creating strong temptation to cut prices. Many basic materials businesses, like paper and aluminum, suffer from this problem when demand slackens.

5. Capacity normally is augmented in large increments. Such additions, as in the chlorine and vinyl chloride businesses, disrupt the industry's supply-demand balance and often lead to periods of overcapacity and price cutting.

6. Exit barriers are high. Exit barriers, like very specialized assets or management's loyalty to a particular business, keep companies competing even though they may be earning low or even negative returns on investment. Excess capacity remains functioning, and the profitability of the healthy competitors suffers as the sick ones hang on. If the entire industry suffers from overcapacity, it may seek government help—particularly if foreign competition is present.

7. The rivals are diverse in strategies, origins, and "personalities." They have different ideas about how to compete and continually run head-on into each other in the process.

As an industry matures, its growth rate changes, resulting in declining profits and (often) a shakeout. In the booming recreational vehicle industry of the early 1970s, nearly every producer did well; but slow growth since then has eliminated the high returns, except for the strongest members, not to mention many of the weaker companies. The same profit story has been played out in industry after industry—snowmobiles, aerosol packaging, and sports equipment are just a few examples.

An acquisition can introduce a very different personality to an industry, as has been the case with Black & Decker's takeover of McCullough, the producer of chain saws. Technological innovation can boost the level of fixed costs in the production process, as it did in the shift from batch to continuous-line photo finishing in the 1960s.

While a company must live with many of these factors—because they are built into the industry economics—it may have some latitude for improving matters through strategic shifts. For example, it may try to raise buyers' switching costs or increase product differentiation. A focus on selling efforts in the fastest-growing segments of the industry or on market areas with the lowest fixed costs can reduce the impact of industry rivalry. If it is feasible, a company can try to avoid confrontation with competitors having high exit barriers and, thus, can sidestep involvement in bitter price cutting.

INDUSTRY ANALYSIS AND COMPETITIVE ANALYSIS

Designing viable strategies for a firm requires a thorough understanding of the firm's industry and competition. The firm's executives need to address four questions: (1) What are the boundaries of the industry? (2) What is the structure of the industry? (3) Which firms are our competitors? (4) What are the major determinants of competition? The answers to these questions provide a basis for thinking about the appropriate strategies that are open to the firm.

INDUSTRY BOUNDARIES

An industry is a collection of firms that offer similar products or services. By "similar products," we mean products that customers perceive to be substitutable for one another. Consider, for example, the brands of personal computers (PCs) that are now being marketed. The firms that produce these PCs, such as ATT, IBM, Apple, and Compaq, form the nucleus of the microcomputer industry.

Suppose a firm competes in the microcomputer industry. Where do the boundaries of this industry begin and end? Does the industry include desktops? Laptops? These are the kinds of questions that executives face in defining industry boundaries.

Why is a definition of industry boundaries important? First, it helps executives determine the arena in which their firm is competing. A firm competing in the microcomputer industry participates in an environment very different from that of the broader electronics business. The microcomputer industry comprises several related product families, including personal computers, inexpensive computers for home use, and workstations. The unifying characteristic of these product families is the use of a central processing unit (CPU) in a microchip. On the other hand, the electronics industry is far more extensive; it includes computers, radios, supercomputers, superconductors, and many other products.

The microcomputer and electronics industries differ in their volume of sales, their scope (some would consider microcomputers a segment of the electronics industry), their rate of growth, and their competitive makeup. The dominant issues faced by the two industries also are different. Witness, for example, the raging public debate being waged on the future of the "high-definition TV." U.S. policymakers are attempting to ensure domestic control of that segment of the electronics industry. They also are considering ways to stimulate "cutting-edge" research in superconductivity. These efforts are likely to spur innovation and stimulate progress in the electronics industry. In contrast, the same policymakers are attempting to ensure that microcomputer technology does not reach Eastern Bloc countries. These efforts will restrict the scope of international markets for microcomputer producers.

Second, a definition of industry boundaries focuses attention on the firm's competitors. Defining industry boundaries enables the firm to identify its competitors and producers of substitute products. This is critically important to the firm's design of its competitive strategy.

Third, a definition of industry boundaries helps executives determine key factors for success. Survival in the premier segment of the microcomputer industry requires skills that are considerably different from those required in the lower end of the industry. Firms that compete in the premier segment need to be on the cutting edge of technological development and to provide extensive customer support and education. On the other hand, firms that compete in the lower end need to excel in imitating the products introduced by the premier segment, to focus on customer convenience, and to maintain operational efficiency that permits them to charge the lowest market price. Defining industry boundaries enables executives to ask these questions: Do we have the skills it takes to succeed here? If not, what must we do to develop these skills?

Finally, a definition of industry boundaries gives executives another basis on which to evaluate their firm's goals. Executives use that definition to forecast demand for their firm's products and services. Armed with that forecast, they can determine whether those goals are realistic.

Problems in Defining Industry Boundaries

Defining industry boundaries requires both caution and imagination. Caution is necessary because there are no precise rules for this task and because a poor definition will lead to poor planning. Imagination is necessary because industries are dynamic—in every industry, important changes are under way in such key factors as competition, technology, and consumer demand.

Defining industry boundaries is a very difficult task. The difficulty stems from three sources:

1. The evolution of industries over time creates new opportunities and threats. Compare the financial services industry as we know it today with that of the 1970s and 1980s, and then try to imagine how different the industry will be in the year 2000.

2. Industrial evolution creates industries within industries. The electronics industry of the 1960s has been transformed into many "industries"—TV sets, transistor radios, micro- and macrocomputers, supercomputers, superconductors, and so on. Such transformation allows some firms to specialize and others to compete in different, related industries.

3. Industries are becoming global in scope. Consider the civilian aircraft manufacturing industry. For nearly three decades, U.S. firms dominated world production in that industry. But small and large competitors were challenging their dominance by 1990. At that time, Airbus Industries (a consortium of European firms) and Brazilian, Korean, and Japanese firms were actively competing in the industry.

Developing a Realistic Industry Definition

Given the difficulties outlined above, how do executives draw accurate boundaries for an industry? The starting point is a definition of the industry in global terms; that is, in terms that consider the industry's international components as well as its domestic components.

Having developed a preliminary concept of the industry (e.g., computers), executives flush out its current components. This can be done by defining its product segments, as illustrated in Figure 3–4. Executives need to select the scope of their firm's potential market from among these related but distinct areas.

To understand the makeup of the industry, executives adopt a longitudinal perspective. They examine the emergence and evolution of product families. Why did these product families arise? How and why did they change? The answers to such questions provide executives with clues about the factors that drive competition in the industry.

Executives also examine the companies that offer different product families, the overlapping or distinctiveness of customer segments, and the rate of substitutability among product families.

To realistically define their industry, executives need to examine five issues:

1. Which part of the industry corresponds to our firm's goals?
2. What are the key ingredients of success in that part of the industry?
3. Does our firm have the skills needed to compete in that part of the industry? If not, can we build those skills?
4. Will the skills enable us to seize emerging opportunities and deal with future threats?
5. Is our definition of the industry flexible enough to allow necessary adjustments to our business concept as the industry grows?

INDUSTRY STRUCTURE

Defining an industry's boundaries is incomplete without an understanding of its structural attributes. *Structural attributes* are the enduring characteristics that give an industry its distinctive character. Consider the cable television and financial services industries. Both industries are competitive, and both are important for our quality of life. But these industries have very different requirements for success. To succeed in the cable television industry, firms require vertical integration, which helps them lower their operating costs

FIGURE 3–4
Computer Industry Product Segments

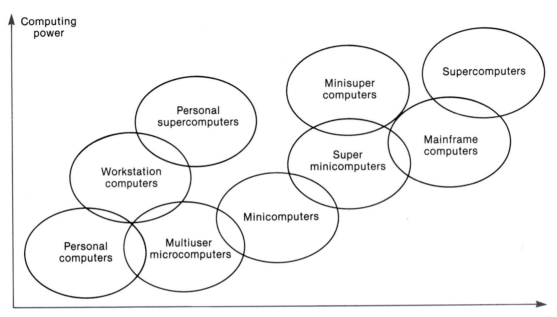

Source: Egil Juliussen and Karen Juliussen, *The Computer Industry Almanac* (New York: Simon & Schuster, 1988), p. 1.11.

and ensures their access to quality programs; technological innovation, to enlarge the scope of their services and deliver them in new ways; and extensive marketing, using appropriate segmentation techniques to locate potentially viable niches. To succeed in the financial services industry, firms need to meet very different requirements, among which are extensive orientation of customers and an extensive capital base.

How can we explain such variations among industries? The answer lies in examining the four variables that industry comprises: (1) concentration, (2) economies of scale, (3) product differentiation, and (4) barriers to entry.

Concentration

This variable refers to the extent to which industry sales are dominated by only a few firms. In a highly concentrated industry (i.e., an industry whose sales are dominated by a handful of companies), the intensity of competition declines over time. High concentration serves as a barrier to entry into an industry, because it enables the firms that hold large market shares to achieve significant economies of scale (e.g., savings in production costs due to increased production quantities) and, thus, to lower their prices to stymie attempts of new firms to enter the market.

The U.S. aircraft manufacturing industry is highly concentrated. In 1988, its concentration ratio—the percent of market share held by the top four firms in the industry—was 67 percent. Competition in the industry has not been vigorous. Firms in the industry have been able to deter entry through proprietary technologies and the formation of strategic alliances (e.g., joint ventures).

Economies of Scale

This variable refers to the savings that companies within an industry achieve due to increased volume. Simply put, when the volume of production increases, the long-range average cost of a unit produced will decline.

Economies of scale result from technological and nontechnological sources. The technological sources are a higher level of mechanization or automation and a greater up-to-dateness of plant and facilities. The nontechnological sources include better managerial coordination of production functions and processes, long-term contractual agreements with suppliers, and enhanced employee performance arising from specialization.

Economies of scale are an important determinant of the intensity of competition in an industry. Firms that enjoy such economies can charge lower prices than their competitors. They also can create barriers to entry by reducing their prices temporarily or permanently to deter new firms from entering the industry.

Product Differentiation

This variable refers to the extent to which customers perceive products or services offered by firms in the industry as different.

The differentiation of products can be real or perceived. The differentiation between Apple's Macintosh and IBM's PS/2 Personal Computer is a prime example of real differentiation. These products differ significantly in their technology and performance. Similarly, the civilian aircraft models produced by Boeing differ markedly from those produced by Airbus. The differences result from the use of different design principles and different construction technologies. For example, the newer Airbus planes follow the principle of "fly by wire," whereas Boeing planes utilize the laws of hydraulics. Thus, in Boeing planes, wings are activated by mechanical handling of different parts of the plane, whereas in the Airbus planes, this is done almost automatically.

Perceived differentiation results from the way in which firms position their products and from their success in persuading customers that their products differ significantly from competing products. Marketing strategies provide the vehicles through which this is done. Witness, for example, the extensive advertising campaigns of the automakers, each of which attempts to convey an image of distinctiveness. BMW ads highlight the excellent engineering of the BMW and its symbolic value as a sign of achievement. Some automakers focus on roominess and durability, which are desirable attributes for the family segment of the automobile market.

Real and perceived differentiations often intensify competition among existing firms. On the other hand, successful differentiation poses a competitive disadvantage for firms that attempt to enter an industry.

Barriers to Entry

As Porter noted earlier in this chapter, barriers to entry are the obstacles that a firm must overcome to enter an industry. The barriers can be tangible or intangible. The tangible barriers include capital requirements, technological know-how, resources, and the laws regulating entry into an industry. The intangible barriers include the reputation of existing firms, the loyalty of consumers to existing brands, and access to the managerial skills required for successful operation in an industry.

Entry barriers both increase and reflect the level of concentration, economies of scale, and product differentiation in an industry, and such increases make it more difficult for new firms to enter the industry. Therefore, when high barrier levels exist in an industry, competition in that industry declines over time.

In summary, analysis of concentration, economies of scale, product differentiation, and barriers to entry in an industry enables a firm's executives to understand the forces that determine competition in an industry and sets the stage for identifying the firm's competitors and how they position themselves in the marketplace.

COMPETITIVE ANALYSIS

Competitive analysis usually has these objectives: (1) to identify current and potential competitors, (2) to identify potential moves by competitors, and (3) to help the firm devise effective competitive strategies.

How to Identify Competitors

In identifying their firm's current and potential competitors, executives consider several important variables:

1. How do other firms define the scope of their market? The more similar the definitions of firms, the more likely the firms will view each other as competitors.

2. How similar are the benefits the customers derive from the products and services that other firms offer? The more similar the benefits of products or services, the higher the level of substitutability between them. High substitutability levels force firms to compete fiercely for customers.

3. How committed are other firms to the industry? Although this question may appear to be far removed from the identification of competitors, it is in fact one of the most important questions that competitive analysis must address, because it sheds light on the long-term intentions and goals. To size up the commitment of potential competitors to the industry, reliable intelligence data are needed. Such data may relate to potential resource commitments (e.g., planned facility expansions).

Common Mistakes in Identifying Competitors

Identifying competitors is a milestone in the development of strategy. But it is a process laden with uncertainty and risk, a process in which executives sometimes make costly mistakes. Examples of these mistakes are:

1. Overemphasizing current and known competitors while giving inadequate attention to potential entrants.

2. Overemphasizing large competitors while ignoring small competitors.

3. Overlooking potential international competitors.

4. Assuming that competitors will continue to behave in the same way they have behaved in the past.

5. Misreading signals that may indicate a shift in the focus of competitors or a refinement of their present strategies or tactics.

6. Overemphasizing competitors' financial resources, market position, and strategies while ignoring their intangible assets, such as a top-management team.

7. Assuming that all of the firms in the industry are subject to the same constraints or are open to the same opportunities.

8. Believing that the purpose of strategy is to outsmart the competition, rather than to satisfy customer needs and expectations.

OPERATING ENVIRONMENT

The operating environment, also called the *competitive* or *task environment,* comprises factors in the competitive situation that affect a firm's success in acquiring needed resources or in profitably marketing its goods and services. Among the most important of these factors are the firm's competitive position, the composition of its customers, its reputation among suppliers and creditors, and its ability to attract capable employees. The operating environment is typically much more subject to the firm's influence or control than the remote environment. Thus, firms can be much more proactive (as opposed to reactive) in dealing with the operating environment than in dealing with the remote environment.

1. Competitive Position

Assessing its competitive position improves a firm's chances of designing strategies that optimize its environmental opportunities.[8] Development of competitor profiles enables a firm to more accurately forecast both its short- and long-term growth and its profit potentials. Although the exact criteria used in constructing a competitor's profile are largely determined by situational factors, the following criteria are often included:

1. Market share
2. Breadth of product line.
3. Effectiveness of sales distribution.
4. Proprietary and key-account advantages.
5. Price competitiveness.
6. Advertising and promotion effectiveness.
7. Location and age of facility.
8. Capacity and productivity.
9. Experience.

---

[8] M. Lauenstein, "The Strategy Audit," *Journal of Business Strategy,* Winter 1984, pp. 87–91.

FIGURE 3–5
Competitor Profile

Key Success Factors	Weight	Rating†	Weighted Score
Market share	0.30	4	1.20
Price competitiveness	0.20	3	0.60
Facilities location	0.20	5	1.00
Raw materials costs	0.10	3	0.30
Caliber of personnel	0.20	1	0.20
	1.00*		3.30

* The total of the weights must always equal 1.00.
† The rating scale suggested is as follows: very strong competitive position (5 points), strong (4), average (3), weak (2), very weak (1).

10. Raw materials costs.
11. Financial position.
12. Relative product quality.
13. R&D advantages-position.
14. Caliber of personnel.
15. General images.[9]

Once appropriate criteria have been selected, they are weighted to reflect their importance to a firm's success. Then the competitor being evaluated is rated on the criteria, the ratings are multiplied by the weight, and the weighted scores are summed to yield a numerical profile of the competitor, as shown in Figure 3–5.

This type of competitor profile is limited by the subjectivity of its criteria selection, weighting, and evaluation approaches. Nevertheless, the process of developing such profiles is of considerable help to a firm in defining its perception of its competitive position. Moreover, comparing the firm's profile with those of its competitors can aid its managers in identifying factors that might make the competitors vulnerable to the strategies the firm might choose to implement.

2. Customer Profiles

Perhaps the most vulnerable result of analyzing the operating environment is the understanding of a firm's customers that this provides.[10] Developing a profile of a firm's present and prospective customers improves the ability of its managers to plan strategic operations,

---

[9] These items were selected from a matrix for assessing competitive position proposed by C. W. Hofer and D. Schendel, *Strategy Formulation: Analytical Concepts* (St. Paul, Minn.: West Publishing, 1978), p. 76.

[10] R. McGill, "Planning for Strategic Performance in Local Government," *Long Range Planning,* October 1988, pp. 77–84.

to anticipate changes in the size of markets, and to reallocate resources so as to support forecast shifts in demand patterns. The traditional approach to segmenting customers is based on customer profiles constructed from geographic, demographic, psychographic, and buyer behavior information, as illustrated in Figure 3–6.

Geographic

It is important to define the geographic area from which customers do or could come. Almost every product or service has some quality that makes it variably attractive to buyers from different locations. Obviously, a Wisconsin manufacturer of snow skis should think twice about investing in a wholesale distribution center in South Carolina. On the other hand, advertising in the *Milwaukee Sun-Times* could significantly expand the geographically defined customer market of a major Myrtle Beach, South Carolina, hotel.

Demographic

Demographic variables most commonly are used to differentiate groups of present or potential customers. Demographic information (e.g., information on sex, age, marital status, income, and occupation) is comparatively easy to collect, quantify, and use in strategic forecasting, and such information is the minimum basis for a customer profile.

Psychographic

Personality and lifestyle variables often are better predictors of customer purchasing behavior than geographic or demographic variables. In such situations, a psychographic study is an important component of the customer profile. Recent advertising campaigns by soft-drink producers—Pepsi-Cola ("the Pepsi generation"), Coca-Cola ("catch the wave"), and 7UP ("America's turning 7UP")—reflect strategic management's attention to the psychographic characteristics of their largest customer segment—physically active, group-oriented nonprofessionals.

Buyer Behavior

Buyer behavior data also can be a component of the customer profile. Such data are used to explain or predict some aspect of customer behavior with regard to a product or service. As Figure 3–6 indicates, information on buyer behavior (e.g., usage rate, benefits sought, and brand loyalty) can provide significant aid in the design of more accurate and profitable strategies.

A second approach to identifying customer groups is by segmenting industrial markets. As shown in Figure 3–7, there is considerable overlap between the variables used to segment individual and industrial consumers, but the definition of the customer differs.

3. Suppliers

Dependable relationships between a firm and its suppliers are essential to the firm's long-term survival and growth. A firm regularly relies on its suppliers for financial support, services, materials, and equipment. In addition, it occasionally is forced to make special requests for such favors as quick delivery, liberal credit terms, or broken-lot orders.

FIGURE 3–6
Major Segmentation Variables for Consumer Markets

Variable	Typical Breakdowns
Geographic	
Region	Pacific, Mountain, West North Central, West South Central, East North Central, East South Central, South Atlantic, Middle Atlantic, New England.
County size	A, B, C, D.
City or SMSA size	Under 5,000; 5,000–20,000; 20,000–50,000; 50,000–100,000; 100,000–250,000; 250,000–500,000; 500,000–1,000,000; 1,000,000–4,000,000; 4,000,000 or over.
Density	Urban, suburban, rural.
Climate	Northern, southern.
Demographic	
Age	Under 6, 6–11, 12–19, 20–34, 35–49, 50–64, 65+.
Sex	Male, female.
Family size	1–2, 3–4, 5+.
Family life cycle	Young, single; young, married, no children; young, married, youngest child under 6; young, married, youngest child 6 or over; older, married, with children; older, married, no children under 18; older, single; other.
Income	Under $10,000; $10,000–$15,000; $15,000–$20,000; $20,000–$25,000; $25,000–$30,000; $30,000–$50,000; $50,000 and over.
Occupation	Professional and technical; managers, officials, and proprietors; clerical, sales; craftspeople, foremen; operatives; farmers; retired; students; housewives; unemployed.
Education	Grade school or less; some high school; high school graduate; some college; college graduate.
Religion	Catholic, Protestant, Jewish, other.
Race	White, Black, Oriental.
Nationality	American, British, French, German, Scandinavian, Italian, Latin American, Middle Eastern, Japanese.
Psychographic	
Social class	Lower lowers, upper lowers, working class, middle class, upper middles, lower uppers, upper uppers.
Lifestyle	Straights, swingers, longhairs.
Personality	Compulsive, gregarious, authoritarian, ambitious.
Behavioral	
Occasions	Regular occasion, special occasion.
Benefits	Quality, service, economy.
User status	Nonuser, ex-user, potential user, first-time user, regular user.
Usage rate	Light user, medium user, heavy user.
Loyalty status	None, medium, strong, absolute.
Readiness stage	Unaware, aware, informed, interested, desirous, intending to buy.
Attitude toward product	Enthusiastic, positive, indifferent, negative, hostile.

SMSA stands for standard metropolitan statistical area.
Source: Philip Kotler, *Marketing Management: Analysis, Planning, Implementation, and Control,* 7th ed., © 1991, p. 269. Reprinted by permission of Prentice Hall, Englewood Cliffs, New Jersey.

FIGURE 3–7
Major Segmentation Variables for Industrial Markets

Demographic
Industry: Which industries that buy this product should we focus on?
Company size: What size companies should we focus on?
Location: What geographical areas should we focus on?

Operating Variables
Technology: What customer technologies should we focus on?
User-nonuser status: Should we focus on heavy, medium, light users or nonusers?
Customer capabilities: Should we focus on customers needing many services or few services?

Purchasing Approaches
Purchasing-function organization: Should we focus on companies with highly centralized or decentralized purchasing organizations?
Power structure: Should we focus on companies that are engineering dominated? financially dominated? other ways dominated?
Nature of existing relationships: Should we focus on companies with which we have strong existing relationships or simply go after the most desirable companies?
General purchase policies: Should we focus on companies that prefer leasing? service contracts? systems purchases? sealed bidding?
Purchasing criteria: Should we focus on companies that are seeking quality? service? price?

Situational Factors
Urgency: Should we focus on companies that need quick and sudden delivery or service?
Specific application: Should we focus on certain applications of our product, rather than all applications?
Size of order: Should we focus on large or small orders?

Perfect Characteristics
Buyer-seller similarity: Should we focus on companies whose people and values are similar to ours?
Attitudes toward risk: Should we focus on risk-taking or risk-avoiding customers?
Loyalty: Should we focus on companies that show high loyalty to their suppliers?

Source: Adapted from Thomas V. Bonoma and Benson P. Shapiro, *Segmenting the Industrial Market* (Lexington, Mass.: Lexington Books, 1983).

Particularly at such times, it is essential for a firm to have had an ongoing relationship with its suppliers.

In assessing a firm's relationships with its suppliers, several factors, other than the strength of that relationship, should be considered. With regard to its competitive position with its suppliers, the firm should address the following questions:

Are the suppliers' prices competitive? Do the suppliers offer attractive quantity discounts?

How costly are their shipping charges? Are the suppliers competitive in terms of production standards?

In terms of deficiency rates? Are the suppliers' abilities, reputations, and services competitive?

Are the suppliers reciprocally dependent on the firm?

4. Creditors

Because the quantity, quality, price, and accessibility of financial, human, and material resources are rarely ideal, assessment of suppliers and creditors is critical to an accurate evaluation of a firm's operating environment. With regard to its competitive position with its creditors, among the most important questions that the firm should address are the following:

Do the creditors fairly value and willingly accept the firm's stock as collateral?

Do the creditors perceive the firm as having an acceptable record of past payment? A strong working capital position? Little or no leverage?

Are the creditors' loan terms compatible with the firm's profitability objectives?

Are the creditors' able to extend the necessary lines of credit?

The answers to these and related questions help a firm forecast the availability of the resources it will need to implement and sustain its competitive strategies.

5. Human Resources: Nature of the Labor Market

A firm's ability to attract and hold capable employees is essential to its success. However, a firm's personnel recruitment and selection alternatives often are influenced by the nature of its operating environment. A firm's access to needed personnel is affected primarily by three factors: the firm's reputation as an employer, local employment rates, and the ready availability of people with the needed skills.

Reputation

A firm's reputation within its operating environment is a major element of its ability to satisfy its personnel needs. A firm is more likely to attract and retain valuable employees if it is seen as permanent in the community, competitive in its compensation package, and concerned with the welfare of its employees, and if it is respected for its product or service and appreciated for its overall contribution to the general welfare.

Employment Rates

The readily available supply of skilled and experienced personnel may vary considerably with the stage of a community's growth. A new manufacturing firm would find it far more difficult to obtain skilled employees in a vigorous industrialized community than in an economically depressed community in which similar firms had recently cut back operations.

Availability

The skills of some people are so specialized that relocation may be necessary to secure the jobs and the compensation that those skills commonly command. People with such skills include oil drillers, chefs, technical specialists, and industry executives. A firm that seeks to hire such a person is said to have broad labor market boundaries; that is, the geographic area within which the firm might reasonably expect to attract qualified candidates is quite large. On the other hand, people with more common skills are less likely to relocate from a considerable distance to achieve modest economic or career advancements. Thus, the labor market boundaries are fairly limited for such occupational groups as unskilled laborers, clerical personnel, and retail clerks.

EMPHASIS ON ENVIRONMENTAL FACTORS

This chapter has described the remote, industry, and operating environments as encompassing five components each. While that description is generally accurate, it may give the false impression that the components are easily identified, mutually exclusive, and equally applicable in all situations. In fact, the forces in the external environment are so dynamic and interactive that the impact of any single element cannot be wholly disassociated from the impact of other elements. For example, are increases in OPEC oil prices the result of economic, political, social, or technological changes? Or are a manufacturer's surprisingly good relations with suppliers a result of competitors', customers', or creditors' activities or of the supplier's own activities? The answer to both questions is probably that a number of forces in the external environment have combined to create the situation. Such is the case in most studies of the environment.

In a recent study involving more than 200 company executives, the respondents were asked to identify key planning issues in terms of their increasing importance to strategic success. As shown in Figure 3–8, domestic competitive trends, customer or end-user preferences, and technological trends were the issues they selected most often.

Strategic managers are frequently frustrated in their attempts to anticipate the environment's changing influences. Different external elements affect different strategies at different times and with varying strengths. The only certainty is that the impact of the remote and operating environment will be uncertain until a strategy is implemented. This leads many managers, particularly in less-powerful or smaller firms to minimize long-term planning, which requires a commitment of resources. Instead, they favor allowing managers to adapt to new pressures from the environment. While such a decision has considerable merit for many firms, there is an associated trade-off, namely that absence of a strong resource and psychological commitment to a proactive strategy effectively bars a firm from assuming a leadership role in its competitive environment.

There is yet another difficulty in assessing the probable impact of remote, industry, and operating environments on the effectiveness of alternative strategies. Assessment of this kind involves collecting information that can be analyzed to disclose predictable effects. Except in rare instances, however, it is virtually impossible for any single firm to anticipate the consequences of a change in the environment; for example, the precise effect on alternative strategies of a 2 percent increase in the national inflation rate, a 1 percent decrease in statewide unemployment, or the entry of a new competitor in a regional market.

Still, assessing the potential impact of changes in the external environment offers a real advantage. It enables decision makers to narrow the range of the available options and to eliminate options that are clearly inconsistent with the forecast opportunities. Environmental assessment seldom identifies the best strategy, but it generally leads to the elimination of all but the most promising options.

FIGURE 3–8
Key Planning Issues

Issue	Percent of Respondents Indicating		
	Increase	No Change	Decrease
1. Competitive (domestic) trends	83.6%	13.5%	2.9%
2. Customer or end-user preferences	69.0	29.1	2.0
3. Technological trends	71.4	25.6	3.0
4. Diversification opportunities	61.7	30.3	8.0
5. Worldwide or global competition	59.4	34.4	6.3
6. Internal capabilities	55.4	40.2	4.4
7. Joint venture opportunities	56.6	36.7	6.6
8. Qualitative data	55.9	38.1	5.9
9. General economic and business conditions	46.4	47.3	6.3
10. Regulatory issues	42.8	51.2	6.0
11. Supplier trends	26.0	69.1	5.0
12. Reasons for past failures	27.6	62.3	10.1
13. Quantitative data	36.8	40.7	22.5
14. Past performance	27.3	51.2	21.5

Source: Adapted from V. Ramanujam, J. C. Camillus, and N. Venkatraman, "Trends in Strategic Planning," in *Strategic Planning and Management Handbook,* ed. W. R. King and D. I. Cleland (New York: Van Nostrand Reinhold, 1987), p. 615.

SUMMARY

A firm's external environment consists of three interrelated sets of factors that play a principal role in determining the opportunities, threats, and constraints that the firm faces. The remote environment comprises factors originating beyond, and usually irrespective of, any single firm's operating situation—economic, social, political, technological, and ecological factors. Factors that more directly influence a firm's prospects originate in the environment of its industry, including entry barriers, competitor rivalry, the availability of substitutes, and the bargaining power of buyers and suppliers. The operating environment comprises factors that influence a firm's immediate competitive situation—competitive position, customer profiles, suppliers, creditors, and the labor market. These three sets of factors provide many of the challenges that a particular firm faces in its attempts to attract or acquire needed resources and to profitably market its goods and services. Environmental assessment is more complicated for multinational corporations (MNCs) than for domestic firms because multinationals must evaluate several environments simultaneously.

Thus, the design of business strategies is based on the conviction that a firm able to anticipate future business conditions will improve its performance and profitability. Despite the uncertainty and dynamic nature of the business environment, an assessment process that narrows, even if it does not precisely define, future expectations is of substantial value to strategic managers.

QUESTIONS FOR DISCUSSION

1. Briefly describe two important recent changes in the remote environment of U.S. business in each of the following areas:

   a. Economic.

   b. Social.

   c. Political.

   d. Technological.

   e. Ecological.

2. Describe two major environmental changes that you expect to have a major impact on the whole-sale food industry in the next 10 years.

3. Develop a competitor profile for your college and of the one geographically closest to it. Next, prepare a brief strategic plan to improve the competitive position of the weaker of the two colleges.

4. Assume the invention of a competitively priced synthetic fuel that could supply 25 percent of U.S. energy needs within 20 years. In what major ways might this change the external environment of U.S. business?

5. With your instructor's help, identify a local firm that has enjoyed great growth in recent years. To what degree and in what ways do you think this firm's success resulted from taking advantage of favorable conditions in its remote, industry, and operating environments?

6. Choose a specific industry and, relying solely on your impressions, evaluate the impact of the five forces that drive competition in that industry.

7. Choose an industry in which you would like to compete. Use the five-forces method of analysis to explain why you find that industry attractive.

8. Many firms neglect industry analysis. When does this hurt them? When does it not?

9. The model below depicts industry analysis as a funnel that focuses on remote-factor analysis to better understand the impact of factors in the operating environment. Do you find this model satisfactory? If not, how would you improve it?

10. Who in a firm should be responsible for industry analysis? Assume that the firm does not have a strategic planning department.

BIBLIOGRAPHY

Aaker, D. A. "Managing Assets and Skills: The Key to a Sustainable Competitive Advantage." *California Management Review,* Winter 1989, pp. 91–106.

Allen, M. G. "Competitive Confrontation in Consumer Services." *Planning Review,* January–February 1989, pp. 4–9.

Bleeke, J. A. "Strategic Choices for Newly Opened Markets." *Harvard Business Review,* September–October 1990, pp. 158–66.

Covin, J. G., and D. P. Slevin. "Strategic Management of Small Firms in Hostile and Benign Environments." *Strategic Management Journal,* January–February 1989, pp. 75–87.

Cowley, R. R. "Market Structure and Business Performance: An Evaluation of Buyer/Seller Power in the PIMS Database." *Strategic Management Journal,* May–June 1988, pp. 271–78.

Fiesinger, E. G. "Dealing with Environmental Regulations and Agencies: An Industry Perspective." *Business Horizons,* March–April 1992, pp. 41–45.

Filho, P. V. "Environmental Analysis for Strategic Planning." *Managerial Planning,* January–February 1985, pp. 23–30.

Ginter, P. M., and W. J. Duncan. "Macroenvironmental Analysis for Strategic Management." *Long Range Planning,* December 1990, pp. 63–70.

Hill, C. W. L. "Differentiation versus Low Cost of Differentiation and Low Cost: A Contingency Framework." *Academy of Management Review,* July 1988, pp. 401–12.

Hooper, T. L., and B. T. Rocca. "Environmental Affairs: Now on the Strategic Agenda." *The Journal of Business Strategy,* May–June 1991, pp. 26–31.

Lieberman, M. B. "The Learning Curve, Technology Barriers to Entry, and Competitive Survival in the Chemical Processing Industries." *Strategic Management Journal,* September–October 1989, pp. 431–47.

MacMillan, I. C. "Controlling Competitive Dynamics by Taking Strategic Initiative." *Academy of Management Executive,* May 1988, pp. 111–18.

Mahmood, S. T., and M. M. Moon. "Competitive Analysis from a Strategic Planning Perspective." *Managerial Planning,* July–August 1984, pp. 37–63.

Mascarenhas, B., and D. A. Aaker. "Mobility Barriers and Strategic Groups." *Strategic Management Journal,* September–October 1989, pp. 475–85.

Mayer, R. "Winning Strategies for Manufacturers in Mature Industries." *Journal of Business Strategy,* Fall 1987, pp. 23–31.

Miles, R. E. "Adapting to Technology and Competition: A New Industrial Relations System for the 21st Century." *California Management Review,* Winter 1989, pp. 9–28.

Miller, D. "Relating Porter's Business Strategies to Environment and Structure: Analysis and Performance Implications." *Academy of Management Journal,* June 1988, pp. 280–308.

Murray, A. I. "A Contingency View of Porter's Generic Strategies." *Academy of Management Review,* July 1988, pp. 390–400.

Ottman, J. A. "Industry's Response to Green Consumerism." *Journal of Business Strategy,* July–August 1992, pp. 3–7.

Peters, T. "Restoring American Competitiveness: Looking for New Models of Organizations." *Academy of Management Executive,* May 1988, pp. 103–9.

Prescott, J. E., and J. H. Grant. "A Manager's Guide for Evaluating Competitive Analysis Techniques." *Interfaces,* May–June 1988, pp. 10–22.

Rafferty, J. "Exit Barriers and Strategic Position in Declining Markets." *Long Range Planning,* April 1987, pp. 86–91.

Reilly, W. K. "Environment, Inc." *Business Horizons,* March–April 1992, pp. 9–11.

Reimann, B. C. "Sustaining the Competitive Advantage." *Planning Review,* March–April 1989, pp. 30–39.

Robertson, T. S., and H. Gatignon. "How Innovators Thwart New Entrants into Their Market." *Planning Review,* September–October 1991, pp. 4–11.

Scherer, F. M. *Industrial Market Structure and Economic Performance.* 2nd ed. Skokie, Ill.: Rand McNally, 1980.

Smith, D. C., and J. Prescott. "Demystifying Competitive Analysis." *Planning Review,* September–October 1987, pp. 8–13.

Svatko, J. E. "Analyzing the Competition." *Small Business Reports,* January 1989, pp. 21–28.

Thomas, L. M. "The Business Community and the Environment: An Important Partnership." *Business Horizons,* March–April 1992, pp. 21–24.

Ulrich, D., and F. Wiersema. "Gaining Strategic and Organizational Capability in a Turbulent Business Environment." *Academy of Management Executive,* May 1988, pp. 115–22.

Vesey, J. T. "The New Competitors: They Think in Terms of 'Speed to Market.'" *Academy of Management Executive,* May 1991, pp. 23–33.

Winsemius, P., and U. Guntram. "Responding to the Environmental Challenge." *Business Horizons,* March–April 1992, pp. 12–20.

Yoffie, D. B. "How an Industry Builds Political Advantage." *Harvard Business Review,* May–June 1988, pp. 82–89.

CHAPTER 3 COHESION CASE

ASSESSING THE EXTERNAL ENVIRONMENT AT THE COCA-COLA COMPANY

Coca-Cola managers place a great deal of emphasis on constant renewal and preparedness of their "worldwide business system." Part of their reasoning eminates from the reality of trying to predict future circumstances in different environmental factors across the thousands of essentially local markets in which they compete throughout the world. Roberto Goizueta addressed this in 1992, when he said:

> Although we cannot foretell the future, we approach it with the premise that in the coming years organizations will be successful to the extent of their effectiveness in managing and coping with change. . . . It is our belief that, in the future, fast change, even chaotic change at times, will pose an equal, if not a greater, challenge. If our premise is correct, then organizations must be sharply focused, flexible, and capable of fast reaction to external forces to succeed in this environment that we foresee.

And a year later, he offered:

> We don't view the future as preordained, but as an infinite series of openings, of possibilities. What is required to succeed in the middle of this uncertainty is what the Greeks called "practical intelligence." Above all else, this "practical intelligence" forces adaptability and teaches constant preparedness. It acknowledges that nothing succeeds quite as planned, and that the model is not the reality. But it also teaches that choice and preparedness can influence the future.

While *preparedness* appears the watchword of Coke management, attention to key environmental factors is evident in Coca-Cola's strategic management perspective. Let's look at a few ways this seems evident.

ECONOMIC

Coca-Cola's products are consumer products, and as such are somewhat sensitive to consumers' disposable income. Coca-Cola's management report two trends that serve to shape its planning related to this factor. First, Coca-Cola consumers view soft drinks as inexpensive pleasure. As such, even in a temporary environment of steady or slightly declining disposable income, Coca-Cola's research suggests that consumers are unlikely to forgo soft drinks. Second, Coca-Cola monitors disposable income in over 200 countries where it sells soft drinks. In 1993, this information suggests that disposable income is generally rising around the world. Coca-Cola interprets this to mean more purchases of consumer products, particularly in countries where consumer product purchasing has been minimal.

Inflation is another economic factor that influences Coca-Cola's success. Asked about this recently, Coca-Cola's CFO offered this comment:

> Inflation is a factor in many markets around the world and consequently impacts the way the company operates. In general, our management believes that we are able to adjust prices to

counteract the effects of increasing costs and generate sufficient cash flow to maintain our productive capacity. In highly inflationary countries, Coca-Cola has benefitted from its net monetary liability position in recent years. This position is viewed as a hedge against the effects of country-specific inflation, since net liabilities would ultimately be paid with devalued currency.

DEMOGRAPHIC/SOCIAL

Consumption of soft drinks has long been inversely correlated with a person's age. In other words, as you age you drink fewer soft drinks, while younger people drink most soft drinks. Coca-Cola subscribes to this basic phenomenon.

The average age of the populations in the United States and most European countries is increasing. Outside the United States and Europe, Coke management observes, *"The world is getting younger and young people are the most enthusiastic purchasers of consumer products."*

TECHNOLOGICAL

Many of us have heard the phrase, "The world is getting smaller and smaller." Ease of travel and increasingly sophisticated, instantaneous worldwide communication capabilities drive this phenomenon. Coca-Cola's management views this phenomenon as favorable:

> As the world has gotten smaller, a "global teenager" has emerged. In Germany and around the world, these teenagers share similar tastes in music, clothing, and consumer brands. With its global scope and the power of the world's most ubiquitous trademark, the Coca-Cola system is uniquely equipped to market to this group.

These are a few of the remote environmental factors that influence Coca-Cola's future and how Coke management views them. Let's now look at some factors within their more immediate "industry environment" and see how Coca-Cola's management views these, too.

RIVALRY

The Coca-Cola Company is rather vague on how it assesses rivals. Recent comments are both brief and generic, such as:

> The commercial beverages industry, of which the soft-drink business is a part, is competitive. The soft-drink business itself is highly competitive. In any parts of the world in which Coca-Cola does business, demand for soft drinks is growing at the expense of other commercial beverages. Advertising and sales promotional programs, product innovation, increased efficiency in production techniques, the introduction of new packaging, new vending and dispensing equipment, and brand and trademark developments and protection are important competitive factors.

Translated, this statement acknowledges that Coke's intense rivalry with Pepsi results in a "rivalry ante" that virtually eliminates other, lesser rivals. That intense rivalry (known as the "cola wars"), unceasing for 20 years, has resulted in an ever-increasing share of a growing market for both Pepsi and Coke at the expense of other players. In the United States alone, they have collectively risen from 60 percent of a 9-billion-gallon market in 1981 to 75 percent of a 14-billion-gallon market in 1991. Maintaining that position requires Coke to be a leader on all the competitive factors mentioned above.

The "front line troops" in the cola wars are Coke and Pepsi bottlers, half of whom are independent bottling franchises. Both companies work incessantly to keep these troops at a fever pitch, because of the critical role these local distributors play—soda moves fast in stores and machines; and, if supplies aren't restocked daily, that firm loses sales. At one recent bottlers' convention, Coke bottlers watched a giant screen where a "Coke" battle tank clanked over a valley, swung its turret while zeroing in on a target, and blew a Pepsi vending machine into a million pieces. The attendees went wild! Similarly, a recent Pepsi bottlers' convention featured a muscle-bound Pepsi bottler who took a sledgehammer and dismantled a Coke machine on stage between regular speakers.

SUPPLIERS

The principal raw material used by the soft-drink industry in the United States is high fructose corn syrup, a form of sugar, which is available from numerous domestic sources. The principal raw material used by the soft-drink industry outside the United States is sucrose. It likewise is available from numerous sources.

Another raw material increasingly used by the soft-drink industry is aspartame, a sweetening agent used in low-calorie soft-drink products. Until January 1993, aspartame was available from just one source—the NutraSweet Company, a subsidiary of the Monsanto Company—in the United States due to its patent, which expired at the end of 1992.

Coke managers have long held "power" over sugar suppliers. They view the recently expired aspartame patent as only enhancing their power relative to suppliers.

BUYERS

Individual consumers are the ultimate buyers of soft drinks. However, Coke and Pepsi's real "buyers" have been local bottlers who are franchised to bottle the companies' products and to whom each company sells its patented syrups or concentrates. While Coke and Pepsi issue their franchise, these bottlers are in effect the "conduit" through which these international cola brands get to local consumers.

Through the early 1980s, Coke's domestic bottlers were typically independent family businesses deriving from franchises issued early in the century. Pepsi had a collection of similar franchises, plus a few large franchisees that owned many locations. Until 1980, Coke and Pepsi were somewhat restricted in owning bottling facilities, which was viewed as a restraint of free trade. Then President Jimmy Carter, a Coke fan, changed that by signing legislation to allow soft-drink companies to own bottling companies or territories, plus upholding the territorial integrity of soft-drink franchises, shortly before he left office.

Prior to this development, Coke "power" relative to its key buyers was weak when compared with Pepsi, which had fewer, larger, better capitalized franchisees. This advantage helped Pepsi grow aggressively until Coca-Cola was legally allowed to "integrate forward," creating simiarly large, modern Coke bottlers.

THREAT OF SUBSTITUTES AND POTENTIAL ENTRANTS

Numerous beverages are available as substitutes for soft drinks. Citrus beverages and fruit juices are the more popular substitutes. Availability of shelf space in retail stores as well as advertising and promotion traditionally have had a significant effect on beverage purchasing behavior. Overall total liquid consumption in the United States in 1991 is shown below, including Coca-Cola's 10 percent share of all liquid consumption.

Total U.S. Liquid Consumption, 1991

Coca-Cola USA

Representing 33 percent of the Company's total sales, more than 3 billion unit cases, Coca-Cola USA posted impressive results, gaining share and volume on an already phenomenal base. Coca-Cola USA now accounts for 41 percent of total U.S. soft drink sales. Coca-Cola USA's gallon sales increased more than 2 percent, and unit case sales increased 2.5 percent, substantially higher than the rest of the industry.

To grasp the sheer size of Coca-Cola USA's growth last year, consider that the division already accounts for 10 percent of America's total liquid consumption. In 1991, the gap between Coca-Cola USA and its nearest competitor expanded to more than our total annual case sales in Brazil, our second-largest international market.

Total Liquid Consumption

- Coca-Cola USA 10%
- Other Carbonated Soft Drinks 15%
- Juice 6%
- Milk 15%
- Coffee 11%
- Beer 12%
- Tap Water 19%
- Other 12%

2.5%

1.1%

1991 Unit Case Sales Growth

Coca-Cola USA   Rest of Industry

Source: Coca-Cola 1991 annual report, p. 43.

The Wall Street Journal, July 27, 1992

Soft-Drink Firms Search for Answers as Volumes Drop

Short-Term Factors Are Cited, but Some Say Colas Have Lost Their Fizz

BY MICHAEL J. MCCARTHY

Staff Reporter of THE WALL STREET JOURNAL

In the annals of soft-drink history, it may come to be called the June Swoon.

For the first time in recent memory, the soda-pop business showed a decline in sales volume—right at the beginning of the all-important summer-selling season.

Industry leaders Coca-Cola Company and PepsiCo., Inc., started off the second quarter with estimated volume increases of about 1 percent to 3 percent in April and May. Then, for reasons soft-drink industry specialists are still trying to sort out, their volume plunged in June, perhaps 2 to 4 percent.

"For this industry, to be down in June is bad: It's like not getting Christmas presents," says Tom Pirko, president of Bevmark, Inc., a beverage consulting company. Adds Roy Burry, an analyst with Kidder Peabody, Inc., "People aren't sure if a down domestic market is the result of the economy, or something more permanent."

Sports and Weather

There is no shortage of explanations for the weakened demand. Chief among them is the nation's limping economic recovery. Then there's sports, followed by pricing: Coke, gambling on its sponsorship of the Summer Olympics to boost sales, has said it shifted advertising spending to the third quarter, and major soft-drink bottlers, or distributors, raised prices a hefty 2.5 percent or more during the quarter. Even

PepsiCo and Coca-Cola by the Numbers

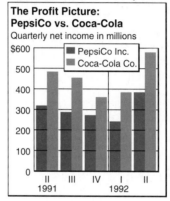

The Profit Picture: PepsiCo vs. Coca-Cola. Quarterly net income in millions.

The Fundamentals		
PepsiCo Inc.	**1991**	**1990**
Revenues ($ billions)	$19.61	$17.80
Net Income ($ millions)	$1.08	$1.08
Earnings per Share	$1.35	$1.35
Coca-Cola Co.	**1991**	**1990**
Revenues ($ billions)	$11.57	$10.24
Net Income ($ millions)	$1.62	$1.38
Earnings per Share	$2.43	$2.04

the weather, unseasonably cool during the period, didn't cooperate.

Reflecting on the quarter, Craig Weatherup, president of Pepsi-Cola North America, says, "I think it's one of the odder phenomenon I've seen in the last 10 years of doing this."

The June decline was enough to hold Pepsi's second-quarter volume growth to less than 1 percent, and to push Coke's down 1 percent. In addition, investors appear to be increasingly cautious about the domestic beverage business. Earlier this month, Dr Pepper/Seven-Up companies withdrew its initial public offering after the company couldn't get the price it sought. Pepsi's stock has been near its 52-week high of $37.125; but it has been

buoyed less by its beverages than by a rebound in the company's Frito-Lay snack-chip subsidiary.

Coca-Cola's stock, which appreciated a torrid 73 percent last year, has been stuck in a slump for several weeks, unable to surpass its 52-week high of $45.125 set in May. (In New York Stock Exchange composite trading Friday, PepsiCo closed at $36.75 a share, up 25 cents, while Coca-Cola closed at $40.50, down 12.5 cents.)

The stock activity and the June volume declines—in an industry accustomed to annual volume growth of 4 to 5 percent during the 1980s—have sparked debate about whether there aren't some discouraging long-term trends at work.

Finally, capital requirements for producing, promoting, and establishing a new soft drink traditionally have been viewed as extremely high. According to industry experts, this makes the likelihood of potential entry by new players quite low, except perhaps in very localized situations that matter little to Coke or Pepsi. Yet, while this view may reflect conventional wisdom, some industry observers question whether a new time is coming, with "new age" beverages selling to well-informed and health-conscious consumers. This issue was

Thin Diets

Diet drinks, the main growth engine of the 1980s, continue to show lackluster sales. Partly as a result, some industry analysts see overall industry growth up only about 2 percent annually for the next few years. The cola flavor—accounting for nearly 70 percent of all soft-drinks sold—appears to be in continuing decline, perhaps having peaked as a proportion of all soft drinks in 1990. And a rush of new competitive beverages seems to be luring consumers away from traditional colas to lower-priced store-brand drinks or to premium-priced, typically fruit-flavored drinks called "New Age" beverages.

From the corner deli to the regional supermarket, retailers are convinced that the consumer of the 1990s is thirsting for alternatives to colas. Last year, a record 1,805 new beverages flooded the market, according to Marketing Intelligence Service, Ltd., a market-research concern. The biggest groups were fruit and fruit-flavored drinks (480), teas (293), and bottled waters (181).

With rising demand for alternative drinks, small beverage companies have begun to make inroads into places that have long been the bastions of the cola giants. Some Arby's, Inc., restaurants, for instance, have started carrying Clearly Canadian flavored waters and Tropicana Twisters, like Orange Passionfruit, in fancy ice chests.

"It's nice to be in this end of the business when trends are like this," says Carl Gillman, vice president of sales and marketing for Snapple Natural Beverage, whose sales through June already doubled last year's total of 12 million cases.

Committing Space

When Kroger Company opened a new store in Smyrna, Tennessee, four weeks ago, it devoted one side of a 48-foot-long aisle to bottled waters and New Age drinks—some 150 different kinds. Responding to changing consumer preferences, Kroger's newer stores are committing space upfront for alternative beverages, says Pat Warden, a Nashville-based buyer for the grocery-store chain. And noting that the Coke and Pepsi price wars of the past few years have hurt Kroger's profit margins on those products, he says, "From a retailer's standpoint, it would not bother us at all to see consumers move from the major brands to the New Age beverages."

Convenience stores and gas stations are another area the new beverages are infiltrating.

The New Age beverage category is small now, estimated to account for about 3 to 5 percent of soft-drink sales. But, by some estimates, that segment is growing 10 to 20 percent annually—and that kind of growth doesn't elude the attention of the major cola companies. Pepsi's Mr. Weatherup blames the second-quarter performance mostly on price increases, but says he believes New Age drinks played a role as well. "The whole New Age, better-for-you phenomenon is out there and [affecting] the business, especially on the diet side," he says. But, without offering specifics, he says he expects Pepsi's volume to rise in the third and fourth quarters, partly as consumers become more accustomed to higher prices.

Need for News

In the past year or so, Coke and Pepsi have stepped up their efforts to capitalize on changing tastes, developing, among other things, new tea drinks and so-called sports drinks aimed at Gatorade's market.

But Mr. Weatherup says he thinks the cola business also needs more of what marketers call news: new products, splashy new advertising and packaging—all stimuli that get consumers thinking about, and buying, colas. Pepsi has recently begun test-marketing a clear, colorless cola called Crystal Pepsi, has changed Pepsi-Cola's logo, and has replaced Pepsi's ad slogan with, "Gotta Have It."

Coca-Cola also has some projects in the works. It is seeking alternatives for its long-running Coca-Cola Classic ad slogan, "Can't Beat the Real Thing." And it has been expanding distribution of Coke II, the renamed, repackaged version of new Coke. It is widely believed that that product will be used as an "attack brand" against Pepsi.

"These companies must come up with new angles on cola," says Mr. Pirko at Bevmark. "The cola excitement is wearing off."

beginning to grab the attention of both Coke and Pepsi in the summer of 1992, when they both were not able to explain a drop in their June 1992 sales. Traditionally, the beginning of summer is the major time for somewhat seasonal sales to experience a welcomed rise of 2 to 4 percent. The above *Wall Street Journal* article lets you see the situation they encountered.

THE GLOBAL ENVIRONMENT: STRATEGIC CONSIDERATIONS FOR MULTINATIONAL FIRMS

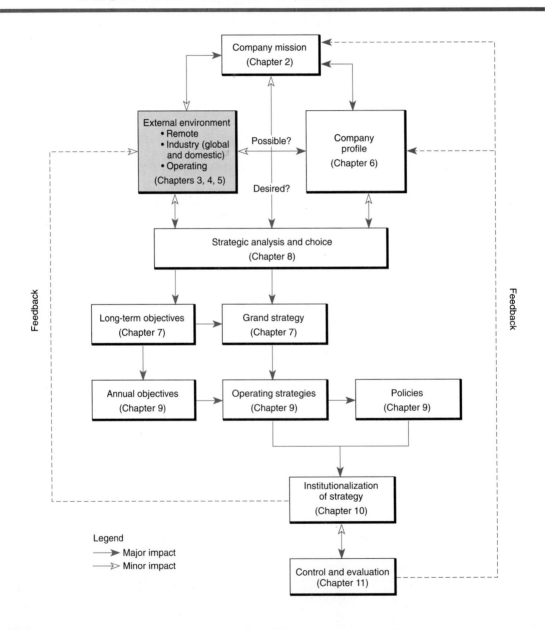

Special complications confront a firm involved in the globalization of its operations. *Globalization* refers to the strategy of approaching worldwide markets with standardized products. Such markets are most commonly created by end consumers that prefer lower-priced, standardized products over higher-priced, customized products and by global corporations that use their worldwide operations to compete in local markets.[1] Global corporations headquartered in one country with subsidiaries in other countries experience difficulties that are understandably associated with operating in several distinctly different competitive arenas.

Awareness of the strategic opportunities faced by global corporations and of the threats posed to them is important to planners in almost every domestic U.S. industry. Among corporations headquartered in the United States that receive more than 50 percent of their annual profits from foreign operations are Citicorp, Coca-Cola, Exxon, Gillette, IBM, Otis Elevator, and Texas Instruments. In fact, the 100 largest U.S. globals earn an average of 37 percent of their operating profits abroad. Equally impressive is the impact of foreign-based globals that operate in the United States. Their "direct foreign investment" in the United States now exceeds $90 billion, with Japanese, German, and French firms leading the way. The extent of this foreign influence is evident in Figure 4–1.

Understanding the myriad and sometimes subtle nuances of competing in global markets or against global corporations rapidly is becoming a required competence of strategic managers. For example, experts in the advertising community contend that Korean companies only recently recognized the importance of making their names known abroad. In the 1980s, there was very little advertising of Korean brands and the country had very few recognizable brands abroad. Korean companies tended to emphasize sales and production more than marketing. The opening of the Korean advertising market in 1991 indicated that Korean firms had acquired a new appreciation for the strategic competencies that are needed to compete globally and created an influx of global firms like Saatchi and Saatchi, J. W. Thompson, Ogilvy and Mather, and Bozell. Many of them established joint ventures or partnerships with Korean agencies. An excellent example of such a strategic approach to globalization by Philip Morris's KGFI is described in Global Strategy in Action 4–1.

Because the growth in the number of global firms continues to overshadow other changes in the competitive environment, this section will focus on the nature, outlook, and operations of global corporations.

DEVELOPMENT OF A GLOBAL CORPORATION

The evolution of a global corporation often entails progressively involved strategy levels. The first level, which often entails export-import activity, has minimal effect on the existing management orientation or on existing product lines. The second level, which can involve foreign licensing and technology transfer, requires little change in management or operation. The third level typically is characterized by direct investment in overseas oper-

---

[1] T. Levitt, "The Globalization of Markets," *Harvard Business Review,* September–October 1982, p. 91; and T. Hout, M. E. Porter, and E. Rudden, "How Global Companies Win Out," *Harvard Business Review,* September–October 1982, pp. 98–108.

FIGURE 4–1
Multinational Corporation Ownership Test

In this test, you go down the alphabet and pick the products that are foreign owned.

A Airwick, Alka-Seltzer antacid, Aim toothpaste.

B Baskin Robbins ice cream, Bactine antiseptic, Ball Park Franks.

C Certain-Teed, Capitol records, Castrol oils.

D Deer Park sparkling water, Dove soap, Dunlop tires.

E ENO antacids, Eureka vacuum cleaners, Ehler spices.

F Four Roses whisky, French's mustard, First Love dolls.

G Good Humor ice cream, Garrard turntables, Grand Trunk Railroad.

H *Humpty Dumpty* magazine, Hires Root Beer, Hills Brothers coffee.

I Imperial margarine, Instant potato mix, Indian Head textiles.

J Juvena cosmetics, Jaeger sportswear, Jade cosmetics.

K Knox gelatine, Kool cigarettes, Keebler cookies.

L Libby's fruits and vegetables, *Look* magazine, Lifebuoy soap.

M Magnavox, Massey-Ferguson tractors, Mr. Coffee.

N Norelco appliances, Nescafé coffee, New Yorker Hotel.

O Ovaltine drink mix, One-a-Day vitamins.

P Panasonic, Pop Shoppes, Pepsodent toothpaste.

Q Nestlé Quik chocolate mix, Quasar television sets, Quadra-Bar sedatives.

R Ray-O-Vac batteries, Rinso, Rona Barrett's gossip magazines.

S Scripto pens, Seven Seas salad dressings, Slazenger tennis balls.

T Tetley tea, Tic Tac breath fresheners, Taster's Choice instant coffee.

U Underwood typewriters, Urise antiseptics, Ultra Tears eye lotion.

V Valium tranquilizers, Vogue pipe tobacco, Vim detergent.

W Wish-Bone salad dressings, Wisk detergent, White Motor trucks.

X Xam clock radios, Xylocaine salves, Xylee plastics.

Y Yardley cosmetics, Yale locks, Yashica cameras.

Z Zesta crackers, Zig-Zag cigarette papers, Zestatabs vitamins.

Answer: All of the companies (A through Z) are foreign owned.

ations, including manufacturing plants. This level requires large capital outlays and the development of global management skills. Although the domestic operations of a firm at this level continue to dominate its policy, such a firm is commonly categorized as a true multinational corporation (MNC). The most involved strategy level is characterized by a substantial increase in foreign investment, with foreign assets comprising a significant portion of total assets. At this level, the firm begins to emerge as a global enterprise with global approaches to production, sales, finance, and control.

Some firms downplay their global nature (to never appear distracted from their domestic operations), whereas others highlight it. For example, General Electric's formal statement of mission and business philosophy includes the following commitment:

> To carry on a diversified, growing, and profitable worldwide manufacturing business in electrical apparatus, appliances, and supplies, and in related materials, products, systems, and services for industry, commerce, agriculture, government, the community, and the home.

A similar global orientation is evident at IBM, which operates in 125 countries, conducts business in 30 languages and more than 100 currencies, and has 23 major manufacturing facilities in 14 countries.

WHY FIRMS GLOBALIZE

The technological advantage once enjoyed by the United States has declined dramatically during the past 30 years. In the late 1950s, over 80 percent of the world's major technological innovations were first introduced in the United States. By 1990, the figure had declined to less than 50 percent. In contrast, France is making impressive advances in electric traction, nuclear power, and aviation. Germany leads in chemicals and pharmaceuticals, precision and heavy machinery, heavy electrical goods, metallurgy, and surface transport equipment. Japan leads in optics, solid-state physics, engineering, chemistry, and process metallurgy. Eastern Europe and the former Soviet Union, the so-called COMECON (Council for Mutual Economic Assistance) countries, generate 30 percent of annual worldwide patent applications. However, the United States can regain some of its lost technological advantage. Through globalization, U.S. firms often can reap benefits from industries and technologies developed abroad. Even a relatively small service firm that possesses a distinct competitive advantage can capitalize on large overseas operations. One such firm that has done this is Domino's Pizza, described in Global Strategy in Action 4–2.

In many situations, global development makes sense as a competitive weapon. Direct penetration of foreign markets can drain vital cash flows from a foreign competitor's domestic operations. The resulting lost opportunities, reduced income, and limited production can impair the competitor's ability to invade U.S. markets. This fact is well understood by the Japanese. As evidence, in 1993 there were 1,500 Japanese owned or operated factories in the United States (up 40 percent since 1989), that employed about 300,000 American workers. More than 75 percent of these plants were in six industries, including electronics, food, and cars.[2] Another case in point is IBM's move to establish a position of strength in the Japanese mainframe computer industry before two key competitors, Fiyitsue and Hitachi, could dominate it. Once IBM had achieved a substantial share of the Japanese market, it worked to deny its Japanese competitors the vital cash and production experience they needed to invade the U.S. market.[3]

---

[2] S. Solo, "Japan's U.S. Plants up 40% in 1990" *Fortune,* April 22, 1991, p. 14.

[3] C. M. Watson, "Counter Competition Abroad to Protect Home Markets," *Harvard Business Review,* January–February 1982, p. 40.

GLOBAL
STRATEGY IN **THE GLOBALIZATION OF PHILIP MORRIS'S KGFI**
ACTION 4–1

Outside of their core Western markets, KGFI's food products have a growing presence in one of the most dynamic business environments in the world—the Asia–Pacific region. Their operations there are expanding rapidly, often aided by links with local manufacturers and distributors.

Japan and Korea, two of the world's fastest-growing economies in the last decade, are important examples. In both countries, local alliances can be crucial to market entry and success. Realizing this fact in the early 1970s, General Foods established joint ventures in both Japan and Korea. In 1993, these joint ventures, combined with Kraft General Foods International's (KGFI) stand-alone operations, generated more than $1 billion in revenues. In the aggregate, their combined food operations in Japan and Korea are larger than many Fortune 500 companies.

Whereas soluble coffee accounts for just over 25 percent of the coffee consumed in U.S. homes, it fills over 70 percent of the cups comsumed in the homes of convenience-minded Japan. Additionally, Japan is the origin of a unique form of packaged coffee—liquid—and a unique channel of distribution—vending machines. Japanese consumers have purchased packaged liquid coffee for years, and in 1993 it amounted to a $5 billion category. Some 2 million vending machines dispense 9 billion cans of liquid coffee annually—an average of 75 cans per person.

Japan offers a culturally unique distribution channel for coffee products—the gift-set market. Many Japanese exchange specially packaged food or beverage assortments at least twice a year to commemorate holidays as well as special personal or business occasions. The gift-set business has helped Maxim products reinforce their quality image; it also will be a launching pad and support vehicle for Carte Noire coffees.

Outside the Ajinomoto General Foods joint venture, KGFI is developing a freestanding food business under the name Kraft Japan. It is building a cheese business with imported Philadelphia Brand cream cheese, the leading cream cheese in the Tokyo metropolitan market,

CONSIDERATIONS PRIOR TO GLOBALIZATION

To begin their globalizing activities, firms are advised to take four steps.[4]

Scan the Global Situation   Scanning includes reading journals and patent reports and checking other printed sources—as well as meeting people at scientific-technical conferences and in-house seminars.

Make Connections with Academia and Research Organizations   Firms active in overseas R&D often pursue work-related projects with foreign academics and sometimes enter into consulting agreements with them.

---

[4] R. Ronstadt and R. Kramer, "Getting the Most out of Innovation Abroad," *Harvard Business Review,* March–April 1982, pp. 94–99.

as well as locally manufactured and licensed Kraft Milk Farm cheese slices. The cheese market is expected to grow approximately 5 percent per year. This is a rapid growth rate for a large food category. In addition to cheese, KGFI also imports Oscar Mayer prepared meats and Jacobs Suchard chocolates.

KGFI's joint venture in Korea, Doug Suh Foods Corporation, is one of the top 10 food companies in the country. Doug Suh manufactures coffees and cereals and has its own distribution network. One of Doug Suh's other businesses in Korea, Post Cereals, is also a strong number two, with a 42 percent category share.

Korea's $400 million coffee market is the fastest-growing major coffee market in the world, expanding at an average annual rate of 14 percent in 1990–91. Growing with the market, Maxim and Maxwell soluble coffees, in both traditional "agglomerate" and freeze-dried forms, account for more than 70 percent of the country's soluble coffee sales. The strength of these brands also brings the company a strong number one position in coffee mix, a mixture of soluble coffee, creamer, and sugar. In addition, its Frima brand leads the market in the nondairy creamer segment.

Beyond Australia, where it has a long-established, wholly owned business, and operations in Japan and Korea, KGFI is targeting many other countries for geographic expansion. In Indonesia, for instance, KGFI has established a rapidly growing cheese business through a licensee and introduced other KGFI products in 1993. In Taiwan, the joint venture company, PremierFoods Corporation, holds a 34 percent share of the soluble coffee market and is aggressively developing a Kraft cheese and Jacobs Suchard import business. KGF Philippines, a wholly owned subsidiary, has a leading position in the cheese and powdered soft drink markets in its country. In the People's Republic of China, the company produces and markets Maxwell House coffees and Tang powdered soft drinks through two successful and rapidly growing joint ventures.

Increase the Firm's Global Visibility   Common methods that firms use to attract global attention include participating in trade fairs, circulating brochures on their products and inventions, and hiring technology acquisition consultants.

Undertake Cooperative Research Projects   Some firms engage in joint research projects with foreign firms to broaden their contacts, reduce expenses, diminish the risk for each partner, or forestall the entry of competitors into their markets.

In a similar vein, external and internal assessments may be conducted before a firm enters global markets.[5] For example, Japanese investors conduct extensive assessments and analyses before selecting a U.S. site for a Japanese-owned firm. They prefer states with strong markets, low unionization rates, and low taxes. In addition, Japanese manufacturing

---

[5] J. Fayweather and A. Kapoor, *Strategy and Negotiation for the International Corporation* (Cambridge, Mass.: Ballinger, 1976).

GLOBAL
STRATEGY IN **THE MULTINATIONALIZATION OF DOMINO'S**
ACTION 4–2

    Domino's Pizza International, adding stores in Japan at an astounding rate of 1 every four weeks, had 10 in operation by mid-October 1987. By the end of 1988, another 16 stores were to be added. A good reason exists for this expansion. Sales in Japan average $25,000 per store each week, compared with an average of $8,000–$8,500 in the United States.

    Domino's works through the Y. Higa Corporation under a licensing agreement to set up pizza franchises. Donald K. Cooper, controller of Domino's Pizza International, has said:

> The key to success is spending a lot of time training the workers. It takes a year and a half for a driver to move up to manager-in-training and eventually become a store manager. Early on, managers-in-training learn how to complete a profit and loss statement every four weeks, and, after six months, they know their inventories and how to run a business.

    Another reason for Domino's success is the attention it gives to standards. The International stores of Domino's Pizza are kept as close to the U.S. version as possible. Employee uniforms, outdoor signs, and logos are the same as those in the United States. Delivery in 30 minutes or $3 off the price is guaranteed no matter where in the world a Domino's is located, and the menu is always kept simple. Each store must limit the number of toppings it offers, and only two pizza sizes are available.

    Domino's operates 200 stores worldwide. It hopes to double that number of stores each year. Cooper said, "Everyone realizes that International is going to be the force in the future."

Source: Adapted from Andrea Chancellor, "Domino's Finds Japanese Sales as Easy as Pie," *Journal of Commerce,* October 13, 1987, p. 1A;   and M. R. Czinkota, P. Rivoli, and I. A. Ronkainen, *International Business* (Hinsdale, Ill.: Dryden Press, 1989).

plants prefer counties characterized by manufacturing conglomeration; low unemployment and poverty rates; and concentrations of educated, productive workers.[6]

    External assessment involves careful examination of critical features of the global environment, particular attention being paid to the status of the host nations in such areas as economic progress, political control, and nationalism. Expansion of industrial facilities, favorable balances of payments, and improvements in technological capabilities over the past decade are gauges of the host nation's economic progress. Political status can be gauged by the host nation's power in and impact on global affairs.

    Internal assessment involves identification of the basic strengths of a firm's operations. These strengths are particularly important in global operations, because they are often the characteristics of a firm that the host nation values most and, thus, offer significant bargaining leverage. The firm's resource strengths and global capabilities must be analyzed. The resources that should be analyzed include, in particular, technical and managerial skills, capital, labor, and raw materials. The global capabilities that should be analyzed include the firm's product delivery and financial management systems.

---

[6] D. Woodward, "Locational Determinants of Japanese Manufacturing Start-Ups in the United States," *Southern Economic Journal,* January 1992, pp. 690–708.

A firm that gives serious consideration to internal and external assessment is Business International Corporation, which recommends that seven broad categories of factors be considered. As shown in Global Strategy in Action 4–3, these categories include economic, political, geographic, labor, tax, capital source, and business factors.

COMPLEXITY OF THE GLOBAL ENVIRONMENT

Global strategic planning is more complex than such purely domestic planning. There are at least five factors that contribute to this increase in complexity:

1. Globals face multiple political, economic, legal, social, and cultural environments as well as various rates of changes within each of them.

2. Interactions between the national and foreign environments are complex, because of national sovereignty issues and widely differing economic and social conditions.

3. Geographic separation, cultural and national differences, and variations in business practices all tend to make communication and control efforts between headquarters and the overseas affiliates difficult.

4. Globals face extreme competition, because of differences in industry structures.

5. Globals are restricted in their selection of competitive strategies by various regional blocs and economic integrations, such as the European Economic Community, the European Free Trade Area, and the Latin American Free Trade Area. Indications of how these factors contribute to the increased complexity of global strategic management are provided in Figure 4–2.

CONTROL PROBLEMS OF THE GLOBAL FIRM

An inherent complicating factor for many global firms is that their financial policies typically are designed to further the goals of the parent company and pay minimal attention to the goals of the host countries. This built-in bias creates conflict between the different parts of the global firm, between the whole firm and its home and host countries, and between the home and host countries themselves. The conflict is accentuated by the use of various schemes to shift earnings from one country to another in order to avoid taxes, minimize risk, or achieve other objectives.

Moreover, different financial environments make normal standards of company behavior concerning the disposition of earnings, sources of finance, and the structure of capital more problematic. Thus, it becomes increasingly difficult to measure the performance of international divisions.

In addition, important differences in measurement and control systems often exist. Fundamental to the concept of planning is a well-conceived, future-oriented approach to decision making that is based on accepted procedures and methods of analysis. Consistent approaches to planning throughout a firm are needed for effective review and evaluation by corporate headquarters. In the global firm, planning is complicated by differences in national attitudes toward work measurement, and by differences in government requirements about disclosure of information.

GLOBAL
STRATEGY IN
ACTION 4–3

CHECKLIST OF FACTORS TO CONSIDER IN CHOOSING A FOREIGN MANUFACTURING SITE

The following considerations were drawn from an 88-point checklist developed by Business International Corporation.

Economic factors:

1. Size of GNP and projected rate of growth.
2. Foreign exchange position.
3. Size of market for the firm's products; rate of growth.
4. Current or prospective membership in a customs union.

Political factors:

5. Form and stability of government.
6. Attitude toward private and foreign investment by government, customers, and competition.
7. Practice of favored versus neutral treatment for state industries.
8. Degree of antiforeign discrimination.

Geographic factors:

9. Efficiency of transport (railways, waterways, highways).
10. Proximity of site to export markets.
11. Availability of local raw materials.
12. Availability of power, water, gas.

Labor factors:

13. Availability of managerial, technical, and office personnel able to speak the language of the parent company.
14. Degree of skill and discipline at all levels.
15. Presence or absence of militant or Communist-dominated unions.
16. Degree and nature of labor voice in management.

Tax factors:

17. Tax-rate trends (corporate and personal income, capital, withholding, turnover, excise, payroll, capital gains, customs, and other indirect and local taxes).
18. Joint tax treaties with home country and others.
19. Duty and tax drawbacks when imported goods are exported.
20. Availability of tariff protection.

Capital source factors:

21. Cost of local borrowing.
22. Local availability of convertible currencies.
23. Modern banking systems.
24. Government credit aids to new businesses.

Business factors:

25. State of marketing and distribution system.
26. Normal profit margins in the firm's industry.
27. Competitive situation in the firm's industry; do cartels exist?
28. Availability of amenities for expatriate executives and their families.

FIGURE 4–2
Differences between U.S. and Multinational Operations That Affect Strategic Management

Factor	U.S. Operations	International Operations
Language	English used almost universally.	Use of local language required in many situations.
Culture	Relatively homogeneous.	Quite diverse, both between countries and within countries.
Politics	Stable and relatively unimportant.	Often volatile and of decisive importance.
Economy	Relatively uniform.	Wide variations among countries and among regions within countries.
Government interference	Minimal and reasonably predictable.	Extensive and subject to rapid change.
Labor	Skilled labor available.	Skilled labor often scarce, requiring training or redesign of production methods.
Financing	Well-developed financial markets.	Poorly developed financial markets; capital flows subject to government control.
Market research	Data easy to collect.	Data difficult and expensive to collect.
Advertising	Many media available; few restrictions.	Media limited; many restrictions; low literacy rates rule out print media in some countries.
Money	U.S. dollar used universally.	Must change from one currency to another; problems created by changing exchange rates and government restrictions.
Transportation/ communication	Among the best in the world.	Often inadequate.
Control	Always a problem, but centralized control will work.	A worse problem—centralized control won't work; must walk a tightrope between overcentralizing and losing control through too much decentralizing.
Contracts	Once signed, are binding on both parties even if one party makes a bad deal.	Can be avoided and renegotiated if one party becomes dissatisfied.
Labor relations	Collective bargaining; layoff of workers easy.	Layoff of workers often not possible; may have a mandatory worker participation in management; workers may seek change through political process rather than collective bargaining.

Source: R. G. Murdick, R. C. Moor, R. H. Eckhouse, and T. W. Zimmerer, *Business Policy: A Framework for Analysis*, adapted from 4th ed. (Columbus, Ohio: Grid, 1984), p. 275.

Although such problems are an aspect of the global environment, rather than a consequence of poor management, they are often most effectively reduced through increased attention to strategic planning. Such planning will aid in coordinating and integrating the firm's direction, objectives, and policies around the world. It enables the firm to anticipate and prepare for change. It facilitates the creation of programs to deal with worldwide development. Finally, it helps the management of overseas affiliates become more actively involved in setting goals and in developing means to more effectively utilize the firm's total resources.

As an example of the need for coordination in global ventures and as evidence that firms can successfully plan for global collaboration (e.g., through rationalized production), consider Figure 4–3. Ford Escort (Europe), the best-selling automobile in the world, has a component manufacturing network that consists of plants in 15 countries.

GLOBAL STRATEGIC PLANNING

It should be evident from the previous sections that the strategic decisions of a firm competing in the global marketplace become increasingly complex. In such a firm, managers cannot view global operations as a set of independent decisions.[7] These managers are faced with trade-off decisions in which multiple products, country environments, resource sourcing options, corporate and subsidiary capabilities, and strategic options must be considered.[8]

A recent trend toward increased activism of stakeholders has added to the complexity of strategic planning for the global firm.[9] *Stakeholder activism* refers to demands placed on the global firm by the foreign environments in which it operates, principally by foreign governments. This section provides a basic framework for the analysis of strategic decisions in this complex setting.

Multidomestic Industries and Global Industries

Michael E. Porter has developed a framework for analyzing the basic strategic alternatives of a firm that competes globally.[10] The starting point of the analysis is an understanding of the industry or industries in which the firm competes. International industries can be ranked along a continuum that ranges from multidomestic to global.

Multidomestic Industries

A multidomestic industry is one in which competition is essentially segmented from country to country. Thus, even if global corporations are in the industry, competition in one country is independent of competition in other countries. Examples of such industries include retailing, insurance, and consumer finance.

---

[7] Y. Wind and S. Douglas, "International Portfolio Analysis and Strategy: The Challenge of the 80s," *Journal of International Business Studies,* Fall 1981, pp. 69–82.

[8] T. H. Naylor, "The International Strategy Matrix," *Columbia Journal of World Business,* Summer 1985, pp. 11–19.

[9] B. S. Chakravarthy and H. V. Perlmutter, "Strategic Planning for a Global Business," *Columbia Journal of World Business,* Summer 1985, pp. 3–10.

[10] Michael E. Porter, "Changing Patterns of International Competition," *California Management Review,* Winter 1986, pp. 9–40.

FIGURE 4–3
The Global Manufacturing Network for the Ford Escort (Europe)

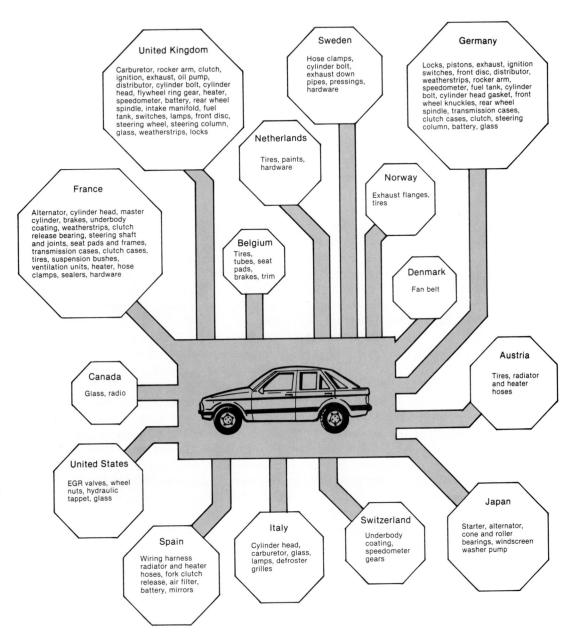

United Kingdom

Carburetor, rocker arm, clutch, ignition, exhaust, oil pump, distributor, cylinder bolt, cylinder head, flywheel ring gear, heater, speedometer, battery, rear wheel spindle, intake manifold, fuel tank, switches, lamps, front disc, steering wheel, steering column, glass, weatherstrips, locks

Sweden

Hose clamps, cylinder bolt, exhaust down pipes, pressings, hardware

Germany

Locks, pistons, exhaust, ignition switches, front disc, distributor, weatherstrips, rocker arm, speedometer, fuel tank, cylinder bolt, cylinder head gasket, front wheel knuckles, rear wheel spindle, transmission cases, clutch cases, clutch, steering column, battery, glass

Netherlands

Tires, paints, hardware

Norway

Exhaust flanges, tires

France

Alternator, cylinder head, master cylinder, brakes, underbody coating, weatherstrips, clutch release bearing, steering shaft and joints, seat pads and frames, transmission cases, clutch cases, tires, suspension bushes, ventilation units, heater, hose clamps, sealers, hardware

Belgium

Tires, tubes, seat pads, brakes, trim

Denmark

Fan belt

Austria

Tires, radiator and heater hoses

Canada

Glass, radio

United States

EGR valves, wheel nuts, hydraulic tappet, glass

Japan

Starter, alternator, cone and roller bearings, windscreen washer pump

Spain

Wiring harness radiator and heater hoses, fork clutch release, air filter, battery, mirrors

Italy

Cylinder head, carburetor, glass, lamps, defroster grilles

Switzerland

Underbody coating, speedometer gears

Note: Final assembly takes place in Halewood (United Kingdom) and Saarlouis (Germany).
Source: Peter Dicken. *Global Shift: Industrial Change in a Turbulent World* (London: Harper & Row, 1986), p. 304.

In a multidomestic industry, a global corporation's subsidiaries should be managed as distinct entities; that is, each subsidiary should be rather autonomous, having the authority to make independent decisions in response to local market conditions. Thus, the global strategy of such an industry is the sum of the strategies developed by subsidiaries operating in different countries. The primary difference between a domestic firm and a global firm competing in a multidomestic industry is that the latter makes decisions related to the countries in which it competes and to how it conducts business abroad.

Factors that increase the degree to which an industry is multidomestic include:[11]

The need for customized products to meet the tastes or preferences of local customers.

Fragmentation of the industry, with many competitors in each national market.

A lack of economies of scale in the functional activities of firms in the industry.

Distribution channels unique to each country.

A low technological dependence of subsidiaries on R&D provided by the global firm.

Global Industries

A global industry is one in which competition crosses national borders. In fact, it occurs on a worldwide basis. In such an industry, a firm's strategic moves in one country can be significantly affected by its competitive position in another country. The very rapidly expanding list of global industries includes commercial aircraft, automobiles, mainframe computers, and electronic consumer equipment. Many authorities are convinced that almost all product-oriented industries soon will be global. As a result, strategic management planning must be global for at least six reasons:

1. *The increased scope of the global management task.*   Growth in the size and complexity of global firms made management virtually impossible without a coordinated plan of action detailing what is expected of whom during a given period. The common practice of management by exception is impossible without such a plan.

2. *The increased globalization of firms.*   Three aspects of global business make global planning necessary: (1) differences among the environmental forces in different countries, (2) greater distances, and (3) the interrelationships of global operations.

3. *The information explosion.*   It has been estimated that the world's stock of knowledge is doubling every 10 years. Without the aid of a formal plan, executives can no longer know all that they must know to solve the complex problems they face. A global planning process provides an ordered means for assembling, analyzing, and distilling the information required for sound decisions.

4. *The increase in global competition.*   Because of the rapid increase in global competition, firms must constantly adjust to changing conditions or lose markets to competitors. The increase in global competition also spurs managements to search for methods of increasing efficiency and economy.

5. *The rapid development of technology.*   Rapid technological development has shortened product life cycles. Strategic management planning is necessary to ensure the replacement of products that are moving into the maturity stage, with fewer sales and

[11] Y. Doz and C. K. Prahalad, "Patterns of Strategic Control within Multinational Corporations," *Journal of International Business Studies,* Fall 1984, pp. 55–72.

declining profits. Planning gives management greater control of all aspects of new product introduction.

6. *Strategic management planning breeds managerial confidence.* Like the motorist with a road map, managers with a plan for reaching their objectives know where they are going. Such a plan breeds confidence, because it spells out every step along the way and assigns responsibility for every task. The plan simplifies the managerial job.

A firm in a global industry must maximize its capabilities through a worldwide strategy. Such a strategy necessitates a high degree of centralized decision making in corporate headquarters so as to permit trade-off decisions across subsidiaries.

Among the factors that made for the creation of a global industry are:

Economies of scale in the functional activities of firms in the industry.

A high level of R&D expenditures on products that require more than one market to recover development costs.

The presence in the industry of predominantly global firms that expect consistency of products and services across markets.

The presence of homogeneous product needs across markets, which reduces the requirement of customizing the product for each market. The presence of a small group of global competitors.

A low level of trade regulation and of regulation regarding foreign direction investment.[12]

The Multinational Challenge

Although industries can be characterized as global or multidomestic, few "pure" cases of either type exist. A global firm competing in a global industry must be responsive, to some degree, to local market conditions. Similarly, a global firm competing in a multidomestic industry cannot totally ignore opportunities to utilize intracorporate resources in competitive positioning. Thus, each global firm must decide which of its corporate functional activities should be performed where and what degree of coordination should exist among them.

Location and Coordination Functional Activities

Typical functional activities of a firm include purchases of input resources, operations, research and development, marketing and sales, and after-sales service. A multinational corporation has a wide range of possible location options for each of these activities and must decide which sets of activities will be performed in how many and which locations. A multinational corporation may have each location perform each activity, or it may center an activity in one location to serve the organization worldwide. For example, research and development centered in one facility may serve the entire organization.

A multinational corporation also must determine the degree to which functional activities are to be coordinated across locations. Such coordination can be extremely low, allowing each location to perform each activity autonomously, or extremely high, tightly

---

[12] G. Harvel and C. K. Prahalad, "Managing Strategic Responsibility in the MNC," *Strategic Management Journal,* October–December 1983, pp. 341–51.

FIGURE 4–4
Location and Coordination Issues by Functional Activity

Functional Activity	Location Issues	Coordination Issues
Operations	Location of production facilities for components.	Networking of international plants.
Marketing	Product line selection. Country (market) selection.	Commonality of brand name worldwide. Coordination of sales to multinaitonal accounts. Similarity of channels and product positioing worldwide. Coordination of pricing in different countries.
Service	Location of service organization	Similarity of service standards and procedures worldwide.
Research and development	Number and location of R&D centers.	Interchange among dispersed R&D centers. Developing products responsive to market needs in many countries. Sequence of product introductions around the world.
Purchasing	Location of the purchasing function.	Managing suppliers located in different countries. Transferring market knowledge. Coordinating purchases of common items.

Source: Adapted from Michael E. Porter. "Changing Patterns of International Competition," *California Management Review,* Winter 1986, p. 18.

linking the functional activities of different locations. Coca-Cola tightly links its R&D and marketing functions worldwide to offer a standardized brand name, concentrate formula, market positioning, and advertising theme. However, its operations function is more autonomous, with the artificial sweetener and packaging differing across locations.[13]

Location and Coordination Issues

Figure 4–4 presents some of the issues related to the critical dimensions of location and coordination in multinational strategic planning. It also shows the functional activities that the firm performs with regard to each of these dimensions. For example, in connection with the service function, a firm must decide where to perform after-sale service and whether to standardize such service.

How a particular firm should address location and coordination issues depends on the nature of its industry and on the type of international strategy that the firm is pursuing. As discussed earlier, an industry can be ranked along a continuum that ranges between multidomestic at one extreme and global at the other. Little coordination of functional

---

[13] J. A. Quelch and E. J. Hoff, "Customizing Global Marketing," *Harvard Business Review,* May–June 1986, pp. 59–68.

FIGURE 4–5
International Strategy Options

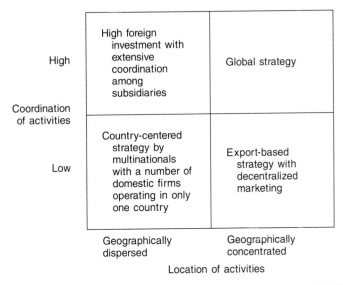

Source: Adapted from Michael E. Porter, "Changing Patterns of International Competition," *California Management Review,* Winter 1986, p. 19.

activities across countries may be necessary in a multidomestic industry, since competition occurs within each country in such an industry. However, as its industry becomes increasingly global, a firm must begin to coordinate an increasing number of functional activities to effectively compete across countries.

International Strategy Options

Figure 4–5 presents the basic multinational strategy options that have been derived from a consideration of the location and coordination dimensions. Low coordination and geographic dispersion of functional activities are implied if a firm is operating in a multidomestic industry and has chosen a country-centered strategy. This allows each subsidiary to closely monitor the local market conditions it faces and to respond freely to these conditions.

High coordination and geographic concentration of functional activities result from the choice of a pure global strategy. Although some functional activities, such as after-sale service, may need to be located in each market, tight control of those activities is necessary to ensure standardized performance worldwide. For example, IBM expects the same high level of marketing support and service for all of its customers, regardless of their location.

Two other strategy options are shown in Figure 4–5. High foreign investment with extensive coordination among subsidiaries would describe the choice of remaining at a particular growth stage, such as that of an exporter. Export-based strategy with decentralized marketing would describe the choice of moving toward globalization, which a multinational firm might make.

GLOBALIZATION OF THE COMPANY MISSION[14]

Few strategic decisions bring about a more radical departure from the existing direction and operations of a firm than the decision to expand globally. Globalization subjects a firm to a radically different set of environmentally determined opportunities, constraints, and risks. To prevent these external factors from dictating the firm's direction, top management must reassess the firm's fundamental purpose, philosophy, and strategic intentions before globalization to ensure their continuation as decision criteria in proactive planning.

Caterpillar Tractor reversed its decline in market share and profitability in part by globalizing its mission. The reversal in 1988–89 can be attributed primarily to the strength of the U.S. dollar, which made Caterpillar's products relatively more expensive in the global market. However, Caterpillar had forecasted the impact of the dollar on its operations in declaring its long-term commitments. Caterpillar's mission states:

1. Caterpillar prefers to locate facilities wherever in the world it is most economically advantageous to do so from a long-term standpoint.
2. Facility operations should be planned with the long term in mind in order to minimize the impact of sudden changes in the local work force and economy.

GLOBALIZATION OF THE MISSION STATEMENT

Expanding across national borders to secure new market or production opportunities initially may be viewed as consistent with the growth objectives outlined in a firm's existing mission statement. However, a firm's direction inherently is altered as globalization occurs. For example, as a firm expands overseas, its operations are physically relocated in foreign operating environments. Since strategic decisions are made in the context of some understanding of the environment, management will absorb information from new sources into its planning processes as the environment becomes pluralistic, with a revised corporate direction as a probable and desirable result. Thus, before reconsidering the firm's strategic choices, management must reassess its mission and institute the required changes as the appropriate environmental information is defined, collected, analyzed, and integrated into existing data bases.

Management also must provide a mission that continues to serve as a basis for evaluating strategic alternatives as this information is incorporated into the firm's decision-making processes. Consider the financial component of Zale Corporation's mission statement from this standpoint:

> Our ultimate responsibility is to our shareholders. Our goal is to earn an optimum return on invested capital through steady profit growth and prudent, aggressive asset management. The attainment of this financial goal, coupled with a record of sound management, represents our approach toward influencing the value placed on our common stock in the market.

From a U.S. perspective, this component seems quite reasonable. In a global context, however, it could be unacceptable. Research has shown that corporate financial goals vary

---

[14] The material in this section is taken from John A. Pearce II and Kendall Roth, "Multinationalization of the Corporate Mission," *Advanced Management Journal*, Summer 1988, pp. 39–44.

in different countries.[15] The clear preference of French, Japanese, and Dutch executives has been to maximize growth in after-tax earnings, and that of Norwegian executives has been to maximize earnings before interest and taxes. In contrast, these executives have assigned a low priority to the maximization of stockholder wealth. Thus, from a global perspective, a mission statement specifying that a firm's ultimate responsibility is to its stockholders may be an inappropriate basis for its financial operating philosophy. This example illustrates the critical need to review and revise the mission statement prior to global expansion so it will maintain its relevance in the new situations confronting the firm.

Components of the Company Mission Revisited

The mission statement must be revised to accommodate the changes in strategic decision making, corporate direction, and strategic alternatives mandated by globalization and must encompass the additional strategic capabilities that will result from globalizing operations. Therefore, each of its basic components needs to be analyzed in light of specific considerations that accompany globalization.

Product or Service, Market, and Technology

The mission statement defines the basic market need that the firm aims to satisfy. This definition is likely to remain essentially intact in the global corporation context, since competencies acquired in the firm's home country can be exploited as competitive advantages when they are transferred to other countries. However, confronted with a multiplicity of contexts, the firm must redefine its primary market to some extent.

The firm could define its market as global, which would necessitate standardization in product and company responses, or it could pursue a "market concept" orientation by focusing on the particular demands of each national market. The mission statement must provide a basis for strategic decision making in this trade-off situation. For example, the directive in Hewlett-Packard's mission statement, "HP customers must feel that they are dealing with one company with common policies and services," implies a standardized approach designed to provide comparable service to all customers. In contrast, Holiday Inn's mission statement reflects the marketing concept: "Basic to almost everything Holiday Inn, Inc., does is its interaction with its market, the consumer, and its consistent capacity to provide what the consumer wants, when, and where it is needed."

Company Goals: Survival, Growth, and Profitability

The mission statement specifies the firm's intention of securing its future through growth and profitability. In the United States, growth and profitability are considered essential to corporate survival. These goals also are acceptable in other countries supportive of the free enterprise system. Following global expansion, however, the firm may operate in countries that are not unequivocally committed to the profit motive. Many countries are committed to

---

[15] A. Stonehill, T. Beekhuisen, R. Wright, L. Remmers, N. Toy, P. Pares, A. Shapiro, D. Egan, and T. Bates, "Financial Goals and Debt Ratio Determinants: A Survey of Practice in Five Countries," *Financial Management*, Autumn 1975, pp. 27–40.

state ownership of industries that they view as critical to domestic prosperity. Austria, France, India, Italy, and Mexico are all good examples. A host country may view social welfare and development goals as taking precedence over the goals of free market capitalism. In developing countries, for example, employment and income distribution goals often take precedence over rapid economic growth.

Moreover, even countries that accept the profit motive may oppose the profit goals of global corporations. In such countries, the flow of global corporation profits often is viewed as unidirectional. At the extreme, the global is seen as a tool for exploiting the host country for the exclusive benefit of the parent company's home country, and its profits are regarded as evidence of corporate atrocities. This means that in a global context, a corporate commitment to profits may increase the risk of failure, rather than help secure survival.

Therefore, the mission statement of a global corporation must reflect the firm's intention of securing its survival through dimensions that extend beyond growth and profitability. A global corporation must develop a corporate philosophy that embodies its belief in a bidirectional flow of benefits among the firm and its multiple environments. The mission statement of Gulf & Western Americas Corporation expresses this view deftly: "We believe that in a developing country, revenue is inseparable from mandatory social responsibility and that a company is an integral part of the local and national community in which its activities are based."[16] This statement maintains a commitment to profitability yet acknowledges the firm's responsibility to the host country.

The growth dimension of the mission statement remains closely tied to survival and profitability even in the global corporation context. Globalization disperses corporate resources and operations. This implies that strategic decision makers are no longer located exclusively at corporate headquarters, and that they are less accessible for participation in collective decision-making processes. To maintain the firm's cohesiveness in these circumstances, some mechanism is required to record its commitment to a unifying purpose. The mission statement can provide such a mechanism. It can provide the global corporation's decision makers with a common guiding thread of understanding and purpose.

Company Philosophy

Within the domestic setting, implicit understandings result in a general uniformity of corporate values and behavior even if a firm's philosophy goes unstated. Few domestic events challenge a firm to properly formulate and implement its implied or expressed philosophy. Globalization, however, is clearly such an event. A corporate philosophy developed from a singular perspective is inadequate for a firm that functions in variant cultures. A firm's values and beliefs are primarily culturally defined, reflecting the general philosophical perspective of the society in which the firm operates. Thus, when a firm extends its operations into another society, it encounters a new set of accepted corporate values and beliefs, which it must assimilate and incorporate into its own.

For example, numerous U.S. global corporations have been subjected to considerable criticism about the policies of their South African, Namibian, and Dominican Republic subsidiaries. In general, violations of corporate social responsibility pertaining to working

---

[16] *See* O. Williams, "Who Cast the First Stone?" *Harvard Business Review* 7, September–October 1984, pp. 151–61.

standards have been alleged, not by coalitions within host countries but by coalitions within the United States, such as the Interfaith Center on Corporate Responsibility. Thus, if a global corporation tailors its values and beliefs to those of interest groups in various host countries, it will generate domestic opposition to which it must respond. Consequently, in adopting a company philosophy, a global corporation must recognize its accountability to such opposition.

Self-Concept

The globalized self-concept of a firm is dependent on management's understanding of the firm's strengths and weaknesses as a competitor in each of its operating arenas. The firm's ability to survive in multiple dynamic and highly competitive environments is severely limited if its management does not understand the impact it has or can have on those environments, and vice versa.

Public Image

Domestically, a firm's public image often is shaped from a marketing viewpoint. That image is managed as a marketing tool whose objective is customer acceptance of the firm's product. Although this consideration remains critical in the global environment, in that environment it must be balanced with consideration of other organizational claimants than the customer. In many countries, the global corporation is a major user of national resources and a major force in socialization processes. Thus, it must broaden its image so as to clearly convey its recognition of the additional internal and external claimants resulting from globalization. The following excerpt from Hewlett-Packard's mission statement exemplifies such an image: "As a corporation operating in many different communities throughout the world, we must assure ourselves that each of these communities is better for our presence. . . . Each community has its particular set of social problems. Our company must help to solve these problems." These words convey an image of Hewlett-Packard's responsiveness to claimants throughout the world.

COMPETITIVE STRATEGIES FOR U.S. FIRMS IN FOREIGN MARKETS[17]

Strategies for firms that are attempting to move toward globalization can be categorized by the degree of complexity of each foreign market being considered and by the diversity in a company's product line. Complexity refers to the number of critical success factors that is required to prosper in a given competitive arena. When a firm must consider many such factors, the requirements of success increase in complexity. Diversity, the second variable in Figure 4–6, refers to the breadth of a firm's business lines. When a company offers many product lines, diversity is high.

---

[17] Material in this section was developed in collaboration with Professors J. Kim DeDee, University of Wisconsin–Oskosh, and Shaker A. Zahra, Georgia State University.

FIGURE 4–6
International Strategy Options

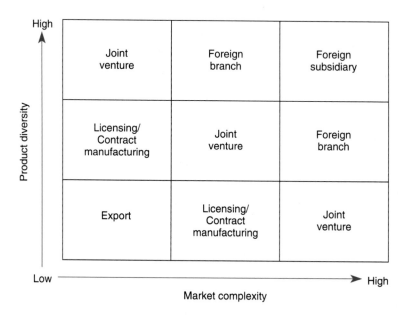

Together, the complexity and diversity dimensions form a continuum of possible strategic choices. Combining these two dimensions highlights many possible actions.

Niche Market Exporting

The primary niche market approach for the company that wants to export is to modify select product performance or measurement characteristics to special foreign demands. Combining product criteria from both the U.S. and the foreign markets can be slow and tedious. There are, however, a number of expansion techniques that provide the U.S. firm with the know-how to exploit opportunities in the new environment. For example, copying product innovations in countries where patent protection is not emphasized and utilizing nonequity contractual arrangements with a foreign partner can assist in rapid product innovation. N. V. Philips and various Japanese competitors, such as Sony and Matsushita, now are working together for common global product standards within their markets. Siemens, with a centralized R&D in electronics, also has been very successful with this approach.

Exporting usually requires minimal capital investment. The organization maintains its quality control standards over production processes and finished goods inventory, and risk to the survival of the firm is typically minimal. Additionally, the U.S. Commerce Department through its Export Now Program and related government agencies lowers the risks to smaller companies by providing export information and marketing advice.

Licensing/Contract Manufacturing

Establishing a contractual arrangement is the next step for U.S. companies wanting to venture beyond exporting but are not ready for an equity position on foreign soil. Licensing involves the transfer of some industrial property right from the U.S. licensor to a motivated licensee. Most tend to be patents, trademarks, or technical know-how that are granted to the licensee for a specified time in return for a royalty and for avoiding tariffs or import quotas. Bell South and U.S. West, with various marketing and service competitive advantages valuable to Europe, have extended a number of licenses to create personal computer networks in the United Kingdom.

Another licensing strategy open to U.S. firms is to contract the manufacturing of its product line to a foreign company to exploit local comparative advantages in technology, materials, or labor.

U.S. firms that use either licensing option will benefit from lowering the risk of entry into the foreign markets. Clearly, alliances of this type are not for everyone. They are used best in companies large enough to have a combination of international strategic activities and for firms with standardized products in narrow margin industries.

Two major problems exist with licensing. One is the possibility that the foreign partner will gain the experience and evolve into a major competitor after the contract expires. The experience of some U.S. electronic firms with Japanese companies shows that licensees gain the potential to become powerful rivals. The other potential problem stems from the control that the licensor forfeits on production, marketing, and general distribution of its products. This loss of control minimizes a company's degrees of freedom as it reevaluates its future options.

Joint Ventures

As the multinational strategies of U.S. firms mature, most will include some form of joint venture (JV) with a target nation firm. AT&T followed this option in its strategy to produce its own personal computer by entering into several joint ventures with European producers to acquire the required technology and position itself for European expansion. Because JVs begin with a mutually agreeable pooling of capital, production or marketing equipment, patents, trademarks, or management expertise, they offer more permanent cooperative relationships than export or contract manufacturing.

Compared to full ownership of the foreign entity, JVs provide a variety of benefits to each partner. U.S. firms without the managerial or financial assets to make a profitable independent impact on the integrated foreign markets can share management tasks and cash requirements often at exchange rates that favor the dollar. The coordination of manufacturing and marketing allows ready access to new markets, intelligence data, and reciprocal flows of technical information.

For example, Siemens, the German electronics firm, has a wide range of strategic alliances throughout Europe to share technology and research developments. For years, Siemens grew by acquisitions, but now, to support its horizontal expansion objectives, it is engaged in joint ventures with companies like Groupe Bull of France, International Computers of Britain, General Electric Company of Britain, IBM, Intel, Philips, and Rolm. Another example is Airbus Industries, which produces wide-body passenger planes for the world market as a direct result of JVs among many companies in Britain, France, Spain, and Germany.

JVs speed up the efforts of U.S. firms to integrate into the political, corporate, and cultural infrastructure of the foreign environment, often with a lower financial commitment than acquiring a foreign subsidiary. General Electric's (GE) 3 percent share in the European lighting market was very weak and below expectations. Significant increases in competition throughout many of their American markets by the European giant, Philips Lighting, forced GE to retaliate by expanding in Europe. GE's first strategy was an attempted joint venture with the Siemens lighting subsidiary, Osram, and with the British electronics firm, Thorn EMI. Negotiations failed over control issues. When recent events in Eastern Europe opened the opportunity for a JV with the Hungarian lighting manufacturer, Tungsram, which was receiving 70 percent of revenues from the West, GE capitalized on it.

Although joint ventures can address many of the requirements of complex markets and diverse product lines, U.S. firms considering either equity- or nonequity-based JVs face many challenges. For example, making full use of the native firm's comparative advantage may involve managerial relationships where no single authority exists to make strategic decisions or solve conflicts. Additionally, dealing with host company management requires the disclosure of proprietary information and the potential loss of control over production and marketing quality standards. Addressing such challenges with well-defined convenants agreeable to all parties is difficult. Equally important is the compatibility of partners and their enduring commitments to mutually supportive goals. Without this compatibility and commitment, a joint venture is critically endangered.

Foreign Branching

A foreign branch is an extension of the company in its foreign market—a separately located strategic business unit directly responsible for fulfilling the operational duties assigned to it by corporate management, including sales, customer service, and physical distribution. Host countries may require that the branch be "domesticated"; that is, have some local managers in middle and upper-level position. The branch most likely will be outside any U.S. legal jurisdiction, liabilities may not be restricted to the assets of the given branch, and business licenses for operations may be of short duration, requiring the company to renew them during changing business regulations.

Foreign Subsidiaries

Foreign subsidiaries are considered by companies that are willing and able to make the highest investment commitment to the foreign market. These companies insist on full ownership for reasons of control and managerial efficiency. Policy decisions about local product lines, expansion, profits, and dividends typically remain with the U.S. senior managers.

Fully owned subsidiaries can be started either from scratch or by acquiring established firms in the host country. U.S. firms can benefit significantly if the acquired company has complementary product lines or an established distribution or service network.

U.S. firms seeking to improve their competitive postures through a foreign subsidiary face a number of risks to their normal mode of operations. First, if the high capital investment is to be rewarded, managers must attain extensive knowledge of the market, the host nation's language, and its business culture. Second, the host country expects both a long-term commitment from the U.S. enterprise and a portion of their nationals to be employed in positions of management or operations. Fortunately, hiring or training foreign managers for leadership positions is commonly a good policy, since they are close to both the market and contacts. This is especially important for smaller firms when markets are regional. Third, changing standards mandated by foreign regulations may eliminate a company's protected market niche. Product design and worker protection liabilities also may extend back to the home office.

The strategies shown in Figure 4–6 are not mutually exclusive. For example, a firm may engage in any number of joint ventures while maintaining an export business. Additionally, there are a number of other strategies that a firm should consider before deciding on its long-term approach to foreign markets. These will be discussed in detail in Chapter 7 under the topic of Grand Strategies. However, the strategies discussed in this chapter provide the most popular starting points for planning the globalization of a firm.

SUMMARY

To understand the strategic planning options available to a corporation, its managers need to recognize that different types of industry-based competition exist. Specifically, they must identify the position of their industry along the global versus multidomestic continuum and then consider the implications of that position for their firm.

The differences between global and multidomestic industries about the location and coordination of functional corporate activities necessitate differences in strategic emphasis. As an industry becomes global, managers of firms within that industry must increase the coordination and concentration of functional activities.

The appendix at the end of this chapter lists many components of the environment with which global corporations must contend. This list is useful in understanding the issues that confront global corporations and in evaluating the thoroughness of global corporation strategies.

As a starting point for global expansion, the firm's mission statement needs to be reviewed and revised. As global operations fundamentally alter the direction and strategic capabilities of a firm, its mission statement, if originally developed from a domestic perspective, must be globalized.

The globalized mission statement provides the firm with a unity of direction that transcends the divergent perspectives of geographically dispersed managers. It provides a basis for strategic decisions in situations where strategic alternatives may appear to conflict. It promotes corporate values and commitments that extend beyond single cultures and satisfies the demands of the firm's internal and external claimants in different countries. Finally, it ensures the survival of the global corporation by asserting the global corporation's legitimacy with respect to support coalitions in a variety of operating environments.

Movement of a firm toward globalization often follows a systematic pattern of development. Commonly, businesses begin their foreign nation involvements progressively through niche market exporting, license-contract manufacturing, joint ventures, foreign branching, and foreign subsidiaries.

QUESTIONS FOR DISCUSSION

1. How does environmental analysis at the domestic level differ from a global analysis?
2. Which factors complicate environmental analysis at the global level? Which factors are making such analysis easier?
3. Do you agree with the suggestion that soon all industries will need to evaluate global environments?
4. Which industries operate almost devoid of global competition? Which inherent immunities do they enjoy?

BIBLIOGRAPHY

Adler, N. J., and S. Bartholomew. "Managing Globally Competent People." *Academy of Management Executive,* August 1992, pp. 52–65.

Allio, R. J. "Formulating Global Strategy." *Planning Review,* March–April 1989, pp. 22–29.

Amsden, A. H. "Private Enterprise: The Issue of Business–Government Control." *Columbia Journal of World Business,* Spring 1988, pp. 37–42.

Bolt, J. f. "Global Competitors: Some Criteria for Success." *Business Horizons,* May–June 1988, pp. 62–72.

Calantone, R. J., and C. A. di Benedetto. "Defensive Marketing in Globally Competitive Industrial Markets." *Columbia Journal of World Business,* Fall 1988, pp. 3–14.

Chankin, W., and R. A. Mauborgne. "Becoming an Effective Global Competitor." *Journal of Business Strategy,* January–February 1988, pp. 33–37.

Copeland, T.; T. Koller; and J. Murrin. "How to Value a Multinational Business." *Planning Review,* May–June 1990, pp. 16–25.

Cox, T., Jr. "The Multicultural Organization." *Academy of Management Executive,* May 1991, pp. 34–47.

Fagan, M. L. "A Guide to Global Sourcing." *The Journal of Business Strategy,* March–April 1991, pp. 21–25.

Franko, L. G. "Global Corporate Competition: Who's Winning, Who's Losing, and the R&D Factor as One Reason Why." *Strategic Management Journal,* September–October 1989, pp. 449–74.

————. "Global Corporate Competition II: Is the Large American Firm an Endangered Species?" *Business Horizons,* November–December 1991, pp. 14–22.

Friedmann, R., and J. Kim. "Political Risk and International Marketing." *Columbia Journal of World Business,* Fall 1988, pp. 63–74.

Garsombke, D. "International Competitors Analysis." *Planning Review,* May–June 1989, pp. 42–47.

Godiwalla, Y. H. "Multinational Planning—Developing a Global Approach." *Long Range Planning,* April 1986, pp. 110–16.

Gomes-Casseres, B. "Joint Ventures in the Face of Global Competition." *Sloan Management Review,* Spring 1989, pp. 17–26.

Heenan, D. A. "Global Strategy: Why the U.S. Government Should Go to Bat for Business." *The Journal of Business Strategy,* March–April 1990, pp. 46–49.

————. "Global Strategy: The End of Centralized Power." *The Journal of Business Strategy,* March–April 1991, pp. 46–49.

Hout, T.; M. E. Porter; and E. Rudden. "How Global Companies Win Out." *Harvard Business Review,* September–October 1982, pp. 98–108.

Hu, Y. S. "Global or Stateless Corporations Are National Firms with International Operations." *California Management Review,* Winter 1992, pp. 107–26.

James, B. "Reducing the Risks of Globalization." *Long Range Planning,* February 1990, pp. 80–88.

Johnston, W. B. "Global Work Force 2000: The New World Labor Market." *Harvard Business Review,* March–April 1991, pp. 115–29.

Kester, W. C. "Global Players, Western Tactics, Japanese Outcomes: The New Japanese Market for Corporate Control." *California Management Review*, Winter 1991, pp. 58–70.

Kim, W. C. "Global Diversification Strategy and Corporate Profit Performance." *Strategic Management Journal*, January–February 1989, pp. 45–57.

Koepfler, E. R. "Strategic Options for Global Market Players." *Journal of Business Strategy*, July–August 1989, pp. 46–50.

Kogut, B. "Designing Global Strategies: Profiting from Operational Flexibility." *Sloan Management Review*, Fall 1985, pp. 27–38.

Kuhn, R. L. "Japanese-American Strategic Alliances." *Journal of Business Strategy*, March–April 1989, pp. 51–53.

Levy, B. "Korean and Taiwanese Firms as International Competitors." *Columbia Journal of World Business*, Spring 1988, pp. 43–51.

Li, J., and S. Guisinger. "How Well Do Foreign Firms Compete in the United States?" *Business Horizons*, November–December 1991, pp. 49–53.

Maruyama, M. "Changing Dimensions in International Business." *Academy of Management Executive*, August 1992, pp. 88–96.

Metzger, R. O., and A. Ginsburg. "Lessons from Japanese Global Acquisitions." *Journal of Business Strategy*, May–June 1989, pp. 32–36.

O'Reilly, A. J. F. "Leading a Global Strategic Charge." *The Journal of Business Strategy*, July–August 1991, pp. 10–13.

Reich, R. B. "Who Is Them?" *Harvard Business Review*, March–April 1991, pp. 77–89.

Reynolds, A. "Competitiveness and the 'Global Capital Shortage.'" *Business Horizons*, November–December 1991, pp. 23–26.

Sera, K. "Corporate Globalization: A New Trend." *Academy of Management Executive*, February 1992, pp. 89–96.

Shanks, D. "Strategic Planning for Global Competition." *Journal of Business Strategy*, Winter 1985, pp. 80–89.

Shetty, Y. K. "Strategies for U.S. Competitiveness: A Survey of Business Leaders." Business Horizons, November–December 1991, pp. 43–48.

Solo, S. "Japan's U.S. Plants up 40% in 1990." *Fortune*, April 22, 1991, p. 14.

Sugiura, H. "How Honda Localizes Its Global Strategy." *Sloan Management Review*, Fall 1990, pp. 77–82.

West, P. "Cross-Cultural Literacy and the Pacific Rim." *Business Horizons*, March–April 1989, pp. 3–17.

Williamson, P. "Successful Strategies for Export." *Long Range Planning*, February 1991, pp. 57–63.

Woodward, D. P. "Locational Determinants of Japanese Manufacturing Start-Ups in the United States." *Southern Economic Journal*, January 1992, pp. 690–708.

Wright, P. "Strategic Management within a World Parameter." *Managerial Planning*, January–February 1985, pp. 33–36.

Yip, G. S., and G. A. Coundouriotis. "Diagnosing Global Strategy Potential: The World Chocolate Confectionery Industry." *Planning Review*, January–February 1991, pp. 4–15.

COMPONENTS OF THE MULTINATIONAL ENVIRONMENT

Multinational firms must operate within an environment that has numerous components. These components include:

I. Government, laws, regulations, and policies of home country (United States, for example).
   A. Monetary and fiscal policies and their effect on price trends, interest rates, economic growth, and stability.
   B. Balance-of-payments policies.
      1. Mandatory controls on direct investment.
      2. Interest equalization tax and other policies.
   C. Commercial policies, especially tariffs, quantitative import restrictions, and voluntary import controls.
   D. Export controls and other restrictions on trade with East European and other Communist nations.
   E. Tax policies and their impact on overseas business.
   F. Antitrust regulations, their administration, and their impact on international business.
   G. Investment guarantees, investment surveys, and other programs to encourage private investments in less-developed countries.
   H. Export-import and government export expansion programs.
   I. Other changes in government policy that affect international business.

II. Key political and legal parameters in foreign countries and their projection.
   A. Type of political and economic system, political philosophy, national ideology.
   B. Major political parties, their philosophies, and their policies.
   C. Stability of the government.
      1. Changes in political parties.
      2. Changes in governments.
   D. Assessment of nationalism and its possible impact on political environment and legislation.
   E. Assessment of political vulnerability.
      1. Possibilities of expropriation.
      2. Unfavorable and discriminatory national legislation and tax laws.
      3. Labor laws and problems.

    F. Favorable political aspects.
1. Tax and other concessions to encourage foreign investments,
2. Credit and other guarantees.

    G. Differences in legal system and commercial law.

    H. Jurisdiction in legal disputes.

    I. Antitrust laws and rules of competition.

    J. Arbitration clauses and their enforcement.

    K. Protection of patients, trademarks, brand names, and other industrial property rights.

III. Key economic parameters and their projection.

    A. Population and its distribution by age groups, density, annual percentage increase, percentage of working age, percentage of total in agriculture, percentage in urban centers.

    B. Level of economic development and industrialization.

    C. Gross national product, gross domestic product, or national income in real terms and also on a per capita basis in recent years and projections over future planning period.

    D. Distribution of personal income.

    E. Measures of price stability and inflation, wholesale price index, consumer price index, other price indexes.

    F. Supply of labor, wage rates.

    G. Balance-of-payments equilibrium or disequilibrium, level of international monetary reserves, and balance-of-payments policies.

    H. Trends in exchange rates, currency stability, evaluation of possibility of depreciation of currency.

    I. Tariffs, quantitative restrictions, export controls, border taxes, exchange controls, state trading, and other entry barriers to foreign trade.

    J. Monetary, fiscal, and tax policies.

    K. Exchange controls and other restrictions on capital movements, repatriation of capital, and remission of earnings.

IV. Business system and structure.

    A. Prevailing business philosophy: mixed capitalism, planned economy, state socialism.

    B. Major types of industry and economic activities.

    C. Numbers, size, and types of firms, including legal forms of business.

    D. Organization: proprietorship, partnerships, limited companies, corporations, cooperatives, state enterprises.

    E. Local ownership patterns: public and privately held corporations, family-owned enterprises.

    F. Domestic and foreign patterns of ownership in major industries.

    G. Business managers available: their education, training, experience, career patterns, attitudes, and reputations.

    H. Business associations and chambers of commerce and their influence.

    I. Business codes, both formal and informal.

    J. Marketing institutions: distributors, agents, wholesalers, retailers, advertising agencies, advertising media, marketing research, and other consultants.

    K. Financial and other business institutions: commercial and investment banks, other financial institutions, capital markets, money markets, foreign exchange dealers, insurance firms, engineering companies.

    L. Managerial processes and practices with respect to planning, administration, operations, accounting, budgeting, control.

V. Social and cultural parameters and their projections.

    A. Literacy and educational levels.

    B. Business, economic, technical, and other specialized education available.

    C. Language and cultural characteristics.

    D. Class structure and mobility.

    E. Religious, racial, and national characteristics.

    F. Degree of urbanization and rural-urban shifts.

    G. Strength of nationalistic sentiment.

    H. Rate of social change.

    I. Impact of nationalism on social and institutional change.

CHAPTER 4 COHESION CASE

THE GLOBAL ENVIRONMENT AND THE COCA-COLA COMPANY

Roberto Goizueta has made it clear that, while Coca-Cola may have its corporate head-quarters in the United States, Coca-Cola is an international corporation, rather than a U.S. company with a sizable international business. Summarizing historical and its own projections through 1994, Table 1 provides Robinson Humphrey's picture of Coca-Cola's sales and operating margins in the 1990s broken out by different areas of the world. By 1995, over 80 percent of Coca-Cola's net revenues from soft drinks will be generated outside the United States, as will a whopping 85 percent of its operating profits from soft drinks. Yes, Coca-Cola is certainly a global company. And as Mr. Goizueta claims, it may well be "the only truly global business system" in the world of the early 1990s.

A look at other aspects of Coca-Cola's experience through 1991 helps to understand the global environment and Coca-Cola. Per capita consumption of Coca-Cola's soft-drink products in selected countries in 1991 is shown on page 137. Domestic per capita consumption is way ahead, while also suggesting the future opportunities in other countries where Coke is already strong. Situations in 12 key countries in 1993 are summarized in the two figures by Coke management on pages 137–138.

Fundamental to global growth of the sales of Coca-Cola's products is the need for local and regional bottlers within each country (over 200 countries by 1994) that will bottle and distribute soft-drink products. Consistent with Figure 4–6 in this chapter, Coca-Cola (low product diversity and high market diversity) has used joint venturing with bottling partners as its major strategy for entering and dominating global markets. The percentage of Coca-Cola's investment in any country's bottler(s) depends on regulations in that country regarding foreign ownership, as well as the capital requirements of prospective bottling partners and the extent to which pecularities exist within the country's retail distribution practices Their resulting ownership of key, worldwide bottling operations by 1993 are shown in the figure, "Worldwide Bottling Investments," on page 139. In just 10 years, Coca-Cola had invested over $2.5 billion in about 41 bottling and canning operations around the world. They ranged from joint ventures to minority positions in public companies to company-owned bottlers. Perhaps more important, this reversed a historical "hands off" approach, allowing Coca-Cola to help capitalize the direct efforts to build retail sales. We will examine this posture more in the Chapter 9 Cohesion Case.

TABLE 1

Revenues	1991	1992	%chg	1993	%chg	1994	%chg
Soft Drinks	$ 9,890.0	$11,249	14%	$12,735	13%	$14,568	14%
US	2,645.2	2,788	5	2,955	6	3,147	7
Int.	7,244.8	8,461	17	9,780	16	11,421	17
Latin Am	1,103.2	1,280	16	1,484	16	1,737	17
EEC	3,338.3	3,872	16	4,647	20	5,623	21
NEA	613.6	703	15	808	15	953	18
Pacific	2,345.8	2,606	11	2,841	9	3,108	9
Foods	1,635.7	1,740	6	1,871	8	2,058	10
Corporate	45.9	48	5	50		55	
Total	$11,571.6	$13,037	13%	$14,656	12%	$16,681	14%

Operating Income	1991	Margin	1992	%chg	Margin	1993	%chg	Margin	1994	%chg	Margin
Soft Drinks	$2,609.8	26.4%	$3,000.0	15%	26.7%	$3,414.7	14%	26.8%	$3,925.6	15%	26.9%
US	468.7	17.7	514	10	18.4	538	5	18.2	573	6	18.2
Int.	2,141.1	29.6	2,486	16	29.4	2,877	16	29.4	3,353	17	29.4
Latin Am	404.6	36.7	469	16	36.7	546	16	36.8	643	18	37.0
EEC	767.3	23.0	929	21	24.0	1,129	22	24.3	1,378	22	24.5
NEA	204.1	33.3	239	17	34.0	272	4	33.7	319	17	33.5
Pacific	777.3	33.1	848	9	32.6	929	10	32.7	1,013	9	32.6
Foods	103.7	6.3	132	28	7.6	157	19	8.4	196	24	9.5
Corporate	(394.5)		(452)			(485)			(543)		
Total	$2,319.0		$2,680.2	16%		$3,086.8	15%		$3,577.9	16%	
Net Interest	($17)		$0			$0			$0		
Equity Income	$40		$75			$85			$98		
Other Income	$41		($10)			$18			$15		
Pretax	$2,383		$2,745			$3,190			$3,691		
Tax Rate	32.1%		31.4%			31.4%			31.4%		
Pfd Dividends	$1										
Net	$1,617		$1,883			$2,188			$2,532		
Share count (mill)	1332		1303			1283			1264		
EPS, continuing operations	$1.22		$1.45			$1.70			$2.00		

Assets	1991	ROA
Soft Drinks	$6,189.3	42.2%
US	$1,447	32.4
Int.	$4,742	45.1
Latin Am	$815	49.7
EEC	$2,558	30.0
NEA	$424	48.2
Pacific	$987	78.7
Foods	$755	13.7
Total		

Source: Robinson Humphrey.

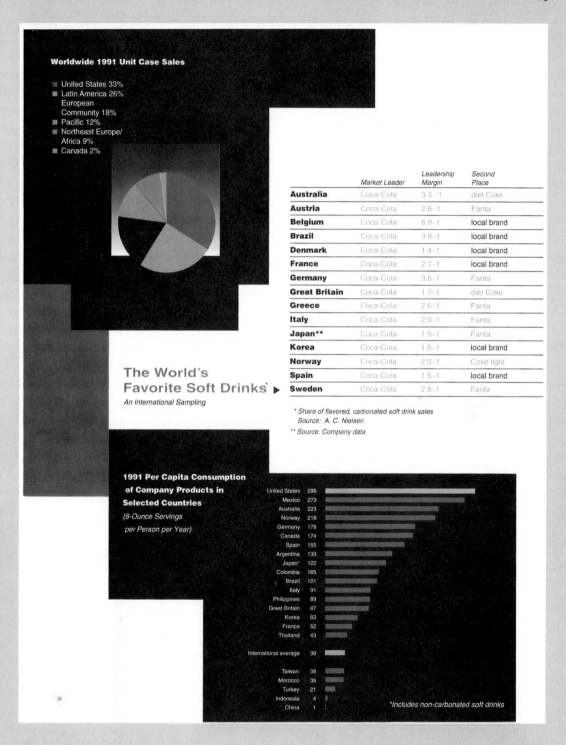

Worldwide 1991 Unit Case Sales

- United States 33%
- Latin America 26%
- European Community 18%
- Pacific 12%
- Northeast Europe/ Africa 9%
- Canada 2%

The World's Favorite Soft Drinks ▶
An International Sampling

	Market Leader	Leadership Margin	Second Place
Australia	Coca-Cola	3.3 –1	diet Coke
Austria	Coca-Cola	2.6–1	Fanta
Belgium	Coca-Cola	6.9–1	local brand
Brazil	Coca-Cola	3.9–1	local brand
Denmark	Coca-Cola	1.4–1	local brand
France	Coca-Cola	2.7–1	local brand
Germany	Coca-Cola	3.5–1	Fanta
Great Britain	Coca-Cola	1.7–1	diet Coke
Greece	Coca-Cola	2.6–1	Fanta
Italy	Coca-Cola	2.0–1	Fanta
Japan**	Coca-Cola	1.5–1	Fanta
Korea	Coca-Cola	1.6–1	local brand
Norway	Coca-Cola	2.0–1	Coke light
Spain	Coca-Cola	1.5–1	local brand
Sweden	Coca-Cola	2.8–1	Fanta

* Share of flavored, carbonated soft drink sales
Source: A. C. Nielsen

** Source: Company data

1991 Per Capita Consumption of Company Products in Selected Countries
(8-Ounce Servings per Person per Year)

United States	296
Mexico	273
Australia	223
Norway	218
Germany	178
Canada	174
Spain	155
Argentina	133
Japan*	122
Colombia	105
Brazil	101
Italy	91
Philippines	89
Great Britain	87
Korea	63
France	52
Thailand	43
International average	39
Taiwan	38
Morocco	35
Turkey	21
Indonesia	4
China	1

*Includes non-carbonated soft drinks

Source: Coca-Cola 1991 annual report, p. 38.

Market Highlights

United States

Most developed market, with great opportunity ahead... key bottle/can growth channels: mass merchandisers, drug store chains, petroleum retailers, warehouse clubs... incremental fountain growth through several new major accounts...share gain of 0.6 points to 41 percent and the largest share advantage ever over our main U.S. competitor...one share point is 74 million unit cases

Germany

Focus on Coca-Cola, Coke light, Sprite and Fanta... bottling efficiencies gained through continued system rationalization...64 bottling entities consolidated into 37 in 1990...incremental growth provided by new eastern German market

Great Britain

Coca-Cola & Schweppes Beverages highly successful joint venture...four-year average unit case growth 22 percent...larger PET packages and can multipacks support volume advances...new production plant planned for southern England

France

Company-owned bottler handles 91 percent of volume... production rationalized...reorganized total sales function to provide national account service...16,000 vending machines and 5,000 post-mix dispensers placed in 1990... aggressive merchandising added 20,000 displays, 700 coolers in 5,000 supermarkets

Australia

Highest per capita consumption in Pacific...86 percent share of cola segment...growth forged by aggressive marketing, expanded availability...vending machines to double to 50,000 by end of decade

Japan

Coca-Cola leads cola segment with 80 percent share... Company products lead world's largest non-carbonated segment...world's highest vending machine per capita... more than 750,000 in place

Philippines

San Miguel joint venture global model since 1981 formation...14 percent average annual unit case growth since 1981...new Santa Rosa superplant helped meet Manila demand...significant post-mix opportunity...three-year average post-mix growth of nearly 25 percent

Norway

Fanta mandarin rollout sparked growth...1.5 lite. returnable/refillable PET launching extended packaging innovation...12 percent Coke light share is among world's highest

Austria

Value pricing strategy and point-of-sale merchandising generated double-digit unit case growth...Sprite light rollout boosted diet segment sales...returnable/refillable PET packaging introduced

Turkey

Company-owned Ankara bottler set growth pace... larger one-way packages, post-mix development, vending placement should drive continued strong growth

Brazil

Solid growth as prices held firm and costs were contained... merchandising and larger packages emphasized...post-mix currently only 7 percent of total volume, representing significant opportunity

Colombia

Larger packages stimulate growth despite overall higher prices...1.5 liter glass bottle introduced...diet Coke relaunched with 100 percent aspartame

Mexico

Per capita consumption second only to U.S....focus on advancing infrastructure, large-size packaging innovation... more than 30,000 coolers/refrigerators placed in 1990... 25 new warehouses opened...new bottling lines commissioned

⑪

Source: Coca-Cola 1990 annual report, p. 11.

Source: Coca-Cola 1991 annual report, p. 36.

5 ENVIRONMENTAL FORECASTING

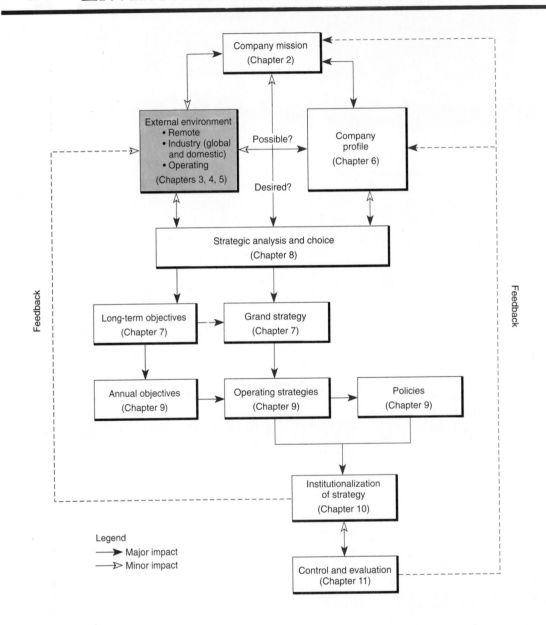

Company mission
(Chapter 2)

External environment
- Remote
- Industry (global and domestic)
- Operating
(Chapters 3, 4, 5)

Possible?

Desired?

Company profile
(Chapter 6)

Strategic analysis and choice
(Chapter 8)

Long-term objectives
(Chapter 7)

Grand strategy
(Chapter 7)

Annual objectives
(Chapter 9)

Operating strategies
(Chapter 9)

Policies
(Chapter 9)

Institutionalization of strategy
(Chapter 10)

Control and evaluation
(Chapter 11)

Feedback

Feedback

Legend
→ Major impact
⇢ Minor impact

IMPORTANCE OF FORECASTING

Change was rapid in the early 1990s, and even greater changes and challenges are forecast for the year 2000. The crucial responsibility for managers will be ensuring their firm's capacity for survival. This will be done by anticipating and adapting to environmental changes in ways that provide new opportunities for growth and profitability. The impact of changes in the remote industry and task environments must be understood and predicted.[1]

Even large firms in established industries will be actively involved in transitions. The $5.5 billion loss in the U.S. auto industry in the early 1980s is a classic example of what can happen when firms fail to place a priority on environmental forecasting. The preceding decade saw a 20 percent penetration of the U.S. new car market by foreign competition, a nation-crippling oil embargo, rapidly climbing fuel prices, and uncertain future supplies of crude oil. Yet the long-range implications of these predictable factors on future auto sales were largely ignored by U.S. automakers. Because it was not open to changes in technology, Detroit was left without viable, fuel-efficient, quality-made alternatives for the American market. On the other hand, Japanese automakers anticipated the future need for fuel efficiency, quality, and service through careful market research and environmental forecasting. As a result, they gained additional market share at Detroit's expense.

In retaliation, American automakers spent $80 billion over a three-year period on product and capital-investment strategies that were meant to recapture their lost market share. They realized that success in strategic decisions rests not solely on dollar amounts but also on anticipation of and preparation for the future.

Accurate forecasting of changing elements in the environment is an essential part of strategic management.[2] Forecasting the business environment for the 1990s led many firms to diversify. For example, USX Corporation (formerly U.S. Steel) purchased Marathon Oil so as to have a profit generator whose proceeds could be used to turn USX into a low-cost steel producer.

Other firms have forecast a need for massive retrenchment. One such firm is IBM, which laid off 40,000 employees in 1991–92 and another 25,000 employees in 1993 to streamline its cost of doing business. Still other firms have cut back in one area of operations to underwrite growth in another. For example, CBS sold its records division to Sony for $2 billion to raise the capital it needed for its planned expansion in television stations in the 1990s.

These and many other examples indicate that strategic managers need to develop skill in predicting significant environmental changes. To aid in the search for future opportunities and constraints, they should take the following steps:

1. Select the environmental variables that are critical to the firm.
2. Select the sources of significant environmental information.

---

[1] S. C. Sufrin and G. S. Odiorne, "The New Strategic Planning Boom: Hope for the Future or a Bureaucratic Exercise?" *Managerial Planning*, January 1985, pp. 4–46; and C. Starry and N. McGaughey, "Growth Industries: Here Today, Gone Tomorrow," *Business Horizons*, July 1988, pp. 69–74.

[2] S. C. Jain, "Environmental Scanning in U.S. Corporations," *Long Range Planning*, April 1984, pp. 117–28; and A. H. Mesch, "Developing an Effective Environmental Assessment Function," *Managerial Planning*, March 1984, pp. 17–22.

3. Evaluate forecasting techniques.
4. Integrate forecast results into the strategic management process.
5. Monitor the critical aspects of managing forecasts.

SELECT CRITICAL ENVIRONMENTAL VARIABLES

Management experts have argued that an important cause of the turbulent business environment is the change in population structure and dynamics. This change, in turn, produced other major changes in the economic, social, and political environments.

Historically, population shifts tended to occur over 40–50 year periods and, therefore, had little relevance to business decisions. During the second half of the 20th century, however, population changes have become radical, erratic, contradictory, and, therefore, of great importance.

For example, the U.S. baby boom between 1945 and the mid-1960s has had and will have a dramatic impact on all parts of society—from maternity wards and schools to the labor force and the marketplace. This population bulge is facing heavy competition for jobs, promotions, and housing, despite a highest-ever educational level. Compounding the problem are the heightened expectations of women and of racial minorities. The lack of high-status jobs to fit these expectations poses a potential impetus for major social and economic changes. In addition, an increasingly aging labor force finds it difficult to give up status, power, and employment when retirement programs are either not financially attractive or not available at the traditional age of 65. (See Figure 5–1 for work force projections through the year 2000.)

Obviously, the demands of these groups will have important effects on social and political changes in terms of lifestyle, consumption patterns, and political decisions. In economic terms, the size and potential affluence of these groups suggest increasing markets for housing, consumer products, and leisure goods and services.

Interestingly, the same shifts in population, life expectancy, and education have occurred in many developed nations. However, developing nations face the opposite population configurations. Although birthrates have declined, high survival rates resulting from medical improvements have created a large population of people who will reach adulthood in the 1990s. Jobs and food are expected to be in short supply. Therefore, many developing countries will face severe social and political instability unless they can find appropriate work for their surplus labor.[3]

The rates of population increase obviously can be of great importance, as indicated by the contrasting effects forecast above. If a growing population has sufficient purchasing power, new markets will be developed to satisfy its needs. However, too much growth in a country with a limited amount of resources or a drastic inequity in their distribution may result in major social and political upheavals that pose substantial risks for businesses.

---

[3] Peter M. Drucker, in *Managing in Turbulent Times* (New York: Harper & Row, 1980), suggests that the practice of production sharing between developed and developing countries can be the economic integration needed by both groups of countries. Production sharing would bring together the abundant labor resources of the developing countries with the management, technology, educated people, markets, and purchasing power of the developed countries.

FIGURE 5–1
The New Work Force

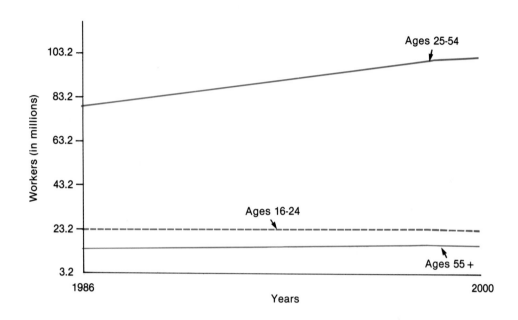

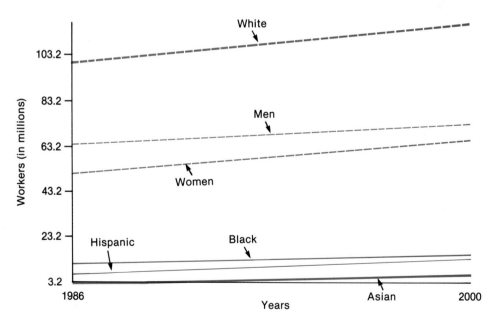

Source: *American Demographics.*

If forecasting were as simple as predicting population trends, strategic managers would only need to examine census data to predict future markets. But economic interpretations are more complex. Population statistics are complicated by migration rates; mobility trends; birth, marriage, and death rates; and racial, ethnic, and religious structures. In addition, resource development and its political use in this interdependent world further confuse the problem—as evidenced by the actions of some of the oil states (e.g., Saudi Arabia, Iraq, Libya, and Kuwait). Changes in political situations, technology, or culture add further complications.

Domestically, the turbulence is no less severe. Continually changing products and services, changing competitors, uncertain government priorities, rapid social change, and major technological innovations all add to the complexity of planning for the future. To grow, to be profitable, and at times even to survive in this turbulent world, a firm needs sensitivity, commitment, and skill in recognizing and predicting these variables that will most profoundly affect its future.

Who Selects the Key Variables?

Although executives or committees in charge of planning may assist in obtaining the forecast data, the responsibility for environmental forecasting usually lies with top management. This is the case at the Sun (Oil) Company, where responsibility for the firm's long-range future is assigned to the chairman and vice chairman of the board of directors. A key duty of the vice chairman is environmental assessment. In this context, environment refers not to air, water, and land but rather to the general business setting created by the economic, technological, political, social, and ecological forces in which Sun plans to operate.

The environmental assessment group consists of Sun's chief economist, a specialist in technological assessment, and a public issues consultant—who all report to the vice president of environmental assessment. The chief economist evaluates and forecasts the state of the economy; the technological assessment specialist covers technology and science; and the public issues consultant concentrates on politics and society.[4]

However, headquarters may lack the capability and proficiency needed to analyze political, economic, and social variables around the world. Therefore, on-the-spot personnel, outside consultants, or company task forces may be assigned to assist in forecasting.

What Variables Should Be Selected?

A list of the key variables that will have make-or-break consequences for the firm must be developed. Some of these variables may have been crucial in the past, and others may be expected to have future importance. This list can be kept manageable by limiting it in the following ways:[5]

1. Include all variables that would have a significant impact although their probability of occurrence is low (e.g., trucking deregulation). Also include highly probable variables

---

[4] E. Weiss, "Future Public Opinion of Business," *Management Review*, March 1978, p. 9.

[5] R. E. Linneman and J. D. Kennell, "Shirt-Sleeve Approach to Long-Range Plans," *Harvard Business Review*, March–April 1977, p. 145.

regardless of their impact (e.g., a minimal price increase by a major supplier). Delete others with little impact and low probabilities.[6]

2. Disregard major disasters, such as nuclear war.

3. When possible, aggregate variables into gross variables (e.g., a bank loan is based more on the dependability of a firm's cash flow than on the flow's component sources).

4. If the value of one variable is based on the value of another, separate the dependent variable for future planning.

Limits of money, time, and forecasting skill prevent a firm from predicting many variables. The task of predicting even a dozen is substantial. Firms often try to select a set of key variables by analyzing the environmental factors in the industry that are most likely to foster sharp growth or decline in the marketplace. For the furniture, appliance, and textiles industries, housing starts are a key variable. Housing starts, in turn, are greatly affected by interest rates.

Figure 5–2 identifies some issues that may have critical impacts on a firm's future success.

SELECT SOURCES OF SIGNIFICANT ENVIRONMENTAL INFORMATION

Before formal forecasting can begin, appropriate sources of environmental information should be identified. Casual gathering of strategic information—through reading, interactions, and meetings—is part of the normal course of executive behavior but is subject to bias and must be balanced with alternative viewpoints. Although *The Wall Street Journal*, *Business Week*, *Fortune*, *Harvard Business Review*, *Forbes*, and other popular trade and scholarly journals are important sources of forecasting information, formal, deliberate, and structured searches are desirable. Appendix 5–A to this chapter lists published sources that strategic managers can use to meet their specific forecasting needs. If the firm can afford the time and expense, it should also gather primary data in such areas as market factors, technological changes, and competitive and supplier strategies.

EVALUATE FORECASTING TECHNIQUES

Debate exists over the accuracy of quantities versus qualitative approaches to forecasting (see Figure 5–3), with most research supporting quantitative models. However, the differences in the predictions derived from these approaches are often minimal. Moreover, subjective or judgmental approaches are often the only practical method of forecasting political, legal, social, and technological trends in the remote external environment. The same is true of several factors in the task environment, especially customer and competitive considerations.

Ultimately, the choice of technique depends not on the environmental factor under review but on such considerations as the nature of the forecast decision, the amount

---

[6] M. A. Stromp, "Questioning Assumptions: One Company's Answer to the Planner's Nemesis," *Planning Review*, September 1986, pp. 10–15.

FIGURE 5–2
Strategic Forecasting Issues

Key Issues in the Remote Environment

Economy

What are the probable future directions of the economies in the firm's regional, national, and international markets? What changes in economic growth, inflation, interest rates, capital availability, credit availability, and consumer purchasing power can be expected? What income differences can be expected between the wealthy upper-middle class, the working class, and the underclass in various regions? What shifts in relative demand for different categories of goods and services can be expected?

Society and demographics

What effects will changes in social values and attitudes regarding childbearing, marriage, lifestyle, work, ethics, sex roles, racial equality, education, retirement, pollution, and energy have on the firm's development? What effects will population changes have on major social and political expectations—at home and abroad? What constraints or opportunities will develop? What pressure groups will increase in power?

Ecology

What natural or pollution-caused disasters threaten the firm's employees, customers, or facilities? How rigorously will existing environmental legislature be enforced? What new federal, state, and local laws will affect the firm, and in what ways?

Politics

What changes in government policy can be expected with regard to industry cooperation, antitrust activities, foreign trade, taxation, depreciation, environmental protection, deregulation, defense, foreign trade barriers, and other important parameters? What success will a new administration have in achieving its stated goals? What effect will that success have on the firm? Will specific international climates be hostile or favorable? Is there a tendency toward instability, corruption, or violence? What is the level of political risk in each foreign market? What other political or legal constraints or supports can be expected in international business (e.g., trade barriers, equity requirements, nationalism, patent protection)?

Technology

What is the current state of the art? How will it change? What pertinent new products or services are likely to become technically feasible in the foreseeable future? What future impact can be expected from technological breakthroughs in related product areas? How will those breakthroughs interface with the other remote considerations, such as economic issues, social values, public safety, regulations, and court interpretations?

Key Issues in the Industry Environment

New entrants

Will new technologies or market demands enable competitors to minimize the impact of traditional economies of scale in the industry? Will consumers accept our claims of product or service differentiation? Will potential new entrants be able to match the capital requirements that currently exist? How permanent are the cost disadvantages (independent of size) in our industry? Will conditions change so that all competitors have equal access to marketing channels? Is government policy toward competition in our industry likely to change?

Bargaining power of suppliers

How stable are the size and composition of our supplier group? Are any suppliers likely to attempt forward integration into our business level? How dependent will our suppliers be in the future? Are substitute suppliers likely to become available? Could we become our own supplier?

FIGURE 5–2 (concluded)

Substitute products or services

Are new substitutes likely? Will they be price competitive? Could we fight off substitutes by price competition? By advertising to sharpen product differentiation? What actions could we take to reduce the potential for having alternative products seen as legitimate substitutes?

Bargaining power of buyers

Can we break free of overcommitment to a few large buyers? How would our buyers react to attempts by us to differentiate our products? What possibilities exist that our buyers might vertically integrate backward? Should we consider forward integration? How can we make the value of our components greater in the products of our buyers?

Rivalry among existing firms

Are major competitors likely to undo the established balance of power in our industry? Is growth in our industry slowing such that competition will become fiercer? What excess capacity exists in our industry? How capable are our major competitors of withstanding intensified price competition? How unique are the objectives and strategies of our major competitors?

Key Issues in the Operating Environment

Competitive position

What strategic moves are expected by existing rivals—inside and outside the United States? What competitive advantage is necessary in selected foreign markets? What will be our competitors' priorities and ability to change? Is the behavior of our competitors predictable?

Customer profiles and market changes

What will our customer regard as needed value? Is marketing research done, or do managers talk to each other to discover what the customer wants? Which customer needs are not being met by existing products? Why? Are R&D activities under way to develop means for fulfilling these needs? What is the status of these activities? What marketing and distribution channels should we use? What do demographic and population changes portend for the size and sales potential of our market? What new market segments or products might develop as a result of these changes? What will be the buying power of our customer groups?

Supplier relationships

What is the likelihood of major cost increases because of dwindling supplies of a needed natural resource? Will sources of supply, especially of energy, be reliable? Are there reasons to expect major changes in the cost or availability of inputs as a result of money, people, or subassembly problems? Which suppliers can be expected to respond to emergency requests?

Creditors

What lines of credit are available to help finance our growth? What changes may occur in our creditworthiness? Are creditors likely to feel comfortable with our strategic plan and performance? What is the stock market likely to feel about our firm? What flexibility would our creditors show toward us during a downturn? Do we have sufficient cash reserves to protect our creditors and our credit rating?

Labor market

Are potential employees with desired skills and abilities available in the geographic areas in which our facilities are located? Are colleges and vocational-technical schools that can aid in meeting our training needs located near our plant or store sites? Are labor relations in our industry conducive to meeting our expanding needs for employees? Are workers whose skills we need shifting toward or away from the geographic location of our facilities?

FIGURE 5–3
Popular Approaches to Forecasting

Technique	Short Description	Cost	Popularity	Complexity	Association with Life-Cycle Stage
Quantitative–Causal models					
Econometric models	Simultaneous systems of multiple regression equations.	High	High	High	Steady state
Single and multiple regression	Variations in dependent variables are explained by variations in one or more independent variables.	High/ medium	High	Medium	Steady state
Times series models	Linear, exponential, S-curve, or other types of projections.	Medium	High	Medium	Steady state
Trend extrapolation	Forecasts obtained by linear or exponential smoothing or averaging of past actual values.	Medium	High	Medium	Steady state
Qualitative or judgmental models					
Sales force estimate	A bottom-up approach aggregating salespersons' forecasts.	Low	High	Low	All stages
Juries of executive opinion	Forecasts jointly prepared by marketing, production, finance, and purchasing executives.	Low	High	Low	Product development
Customer surveys; market research	Learning about intentions of potential customers or plans of businesses.	Medium	Medium	Medium	Market testing and early introduction
Scenario development	Impacts of anticipated conditions imagined by forecasters.	Low	Medium	Low	All stages
Delphi method	Experts guided toward a consensus.	Low	Medium	Medium	Product development
Brainstorming	Idea generation in a noncritical group situation.	Low	Medium	Medium	Product development

and accuracy of available information, the accuracy required, the time available, the importance of the forecast, the cost, and the competence and interpersonal relationships of the managers and forecasters involved.[7] Frequently, assessment of such considerations leads to the selection of a combination of quantitative and qualitative techniques, thereby strengthening the accuracy of the ultimate forecast.[8]

---

[7] S. C. Wheelwright and C. G. Clarke, "Corporate Forecasting: Promise and Reality," *Harvard Business Review*, November–December 1976, p. 42.

[8] R. S. Clark, "The Strategic Planner's Toolbox," *CA Magazine*, July 1987, pp. 24–34.

Techniques Available

Economic Forecasts

At one time, only forecasts of economic variables were used in strategic management. The forecasts were primarily concerned with remote factors, such as general economic conditions, disposable personal income, the consumer price index, wage rates, and productivity. Derived from government and private sources, these economic forecasts served as the framework for industry and company forecasts, which dealt with task-environment concerns, such as sales, market share, and other pertinent economic trends.

Econometric Models

With the advent of sophisticated computers, the government and some wealthy firms contracted with private consulting firms to develop "casual models," especially models involving econometrics. These econometric models utilize complex simultaneous regression equations to relate economic occurrences to areas of corporate activity. They are especially useful when information on casual relationships is available and large changes are anticipated. During the relatively stable decade of the 1970s, econometrics was one of the nation's fastest-growing industries. In the 1980s, however, the three biggest econometric firms—Data Resources (McGraw-Hill), Chase Econometric (Chase Manhattan Bank), and Wharton Econometric Forecasting Associates (Ziff-Davis Publishing)—fell on hard times. The explosion of oil prices, inflation, and the growing interdependence of the world economy created problems that fell beyond the inherent limits of econometric models. And despite enormous technological resources, such models still depend on the often undependable judgment of the model builders.[9]

Two more widely used and less expensive forecasting techniques are *time series models* and *judgmental models*. Time series models attempt to identify patterns based on combinations of historical trends and seasonal and cyclical factors. This technique assumes that the past is a prologue to the future. Time series techniques, such as exponential smoothing and linear projections, are relatively simple, well know, inexpensive, and accurate.

Of the time series models, *trend analysis* models are the most frequently used. Such models assume that the future will be a continuation of the past, following some long-range trend. If sufficient historical data are available, such as annual sales, a trend analysis can be done quickly at a modest cost.

In the trend analysis depicted in Figure 5–4, concern should focus on long-term trends, such as Trend C, which is based on 11 years of fluctuating sales. Trend A, which is based on three excellent years is much too optimistic. Similarly, Trend B, which is based on four bad years, is much too pessimistic.

The major limitation of trend analysis is the assumption that all of the relevant conditions will remain relatively constant. Sudden changes in these conditions falsify trend predictions.

Judgmental models are useful when historical data are unavailable or hard to use. *Sales force estimates* and *juries of executive opinion* are examples of such models. Sales force estimates consolidate salespeople's opinions of customer intentions regarding specific products. These estimates can be relevant if customers respond honestly and their intentions remain consistent. Juries of executive opinion average the estimates made by executives

---

[9] "Where the Big Econometric Models Go Wrong," *Business Week*, March 30, 1981, pp. 70–73.

FIGURE 5–4
Interpretations in Trend Analysis

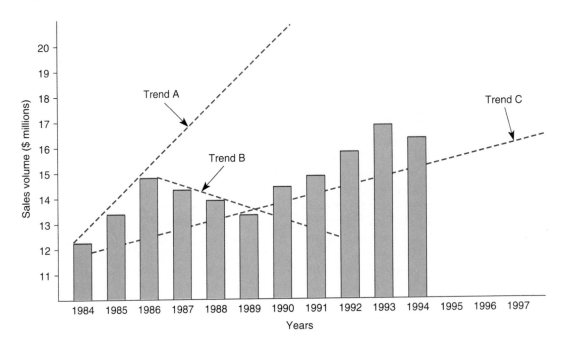

from marketing, production, finance, and purchasing. No elaborate math or statistics are required.

Customer surveys are conducted by means of personal interviews or telephone questionnaires. The questions must be well stated and easily understood. The respondents are a random sample of the relevant population. Custom surveys can provide valuable in-depth information. Although they are often difficult to construct and time-consuming to administer, many marketing research firms use them.

Social Forecasts

If strategic forecasting relies only on economic indictors, social trends that can have a profound impact may be neglected. Some firms have recognized this and identify social trends and underlying attitudes as part of their environmental scanning. Recent social forecasting efforts have involved analysis of such areas as population, housing, Social Security and welfare, health and nutrition, education and training, income, and wealth and expenditures.

A variety of approaches are used in social forecasting, including time series analysis and the judgmental techniques described earlier. However, *scenario development* is probably the most popular approach. Scenarios, the imagined stories that integrate objective and subjective parts of other forecasts, are designed to help prepare strategic managers for alternative possibilities, thus enabling them to develop contingency plans.[10] Because scenarios can be presented in easily understood forms, they often are used in social forecasting. They can be developed by the following process:

1. Prepare the background by assessing the overall social environment under investigation (such as social legislation).
2. Select critical indicators, and search for future events that may affect them (e.g., growing distrust of business).
3. Analyze the reasons for the past behavior of each indicator (e.g., perceived disregard for air and water quality).
4. Forecast each indicator in three scenarios—showing the least-favorable environment, the likely environment, and the most-favorable environment.
5. Write the scenarios from the viewpoint of someone at a given future time.
6. Condense each scenario to a few paragraphs.

Strategy in Action 5–1 presents a scenario that was developed in 1987 for Georgia Power Company. Its purpose was to determine how the future environment might influence the firm's load and energy growth to the year 1995.

With the help of Battelle Columbus Division, a consulting firm, Georgia Power identified five broad areas of influence—the same areas you studied in Chapter 3 as the constituents of the remote external environment. From these areas, 15 key factors were isolated for investigation, of which 5 were judged to be critical to Georgia Power's planning. The scenario in Strategy in Action 5–1 was built on forecasts regarding these five factors. Several Scenarios were developed, of which one presented in Strategy in Action 5–1 shows the greatest economic growth.

Political Forecasts

Some strategic planners want to give political forecasts the same serious consideration that is given to economic forecasts. They believe that business success can be profoundly affected by shifts in a broad range of political factors, such as the size of government budgets, tariffs, tax rates, defense spending, the growth of regulatory bodies, and the extent of business leaders' participation in government planning.

Political forecasts for foreign countries also are important. Political risks in those countries affect firms that are in any way dependent on international subsidiaries, on suppliers for customers, or on critical resources. Increasing worldwide interdependence makes it imperative for firms of all sizes to consider the international political implications of their strategies.

Because of the billions of U.S. dollars lost in the last two decades as a result of revolutions, nationalization, and other manifestations of political instability, multinational firms and consultants have developed a variety of approaches to international forecasting. Some of the better known are:

Haner's Business Environmental Risk Index, which monitors 15 economic and political variables in 42 countries.

---

[10] W. Whipple III, "Evaluating Alternative Strategies Using Scenarios," *Long Range Planning*, June 1989, pp. 82–86.

STRATEGY
IN ACTION   **GEORGIA POWER PLANNING SCENARIOS FOR 1995**
5–1

HIGH ECONOMIC GROWTH SCENARIO

The average annual growth rate of the real U.S. gross national product (GNP) will exceed 3.2 percent between now and the year 2010. This growth rate is about the same as the growth rate of 3.4 percent experienced during the post–World War II era but is greater than the average growth rate for the 1980s. Economic growth in Georgia will exceed that of the nation as a whole by as much as one percentage point. This growth pattern is expected to result from a continuation of the Sunbelt phenomenon that drove Georgia's strong growth over the past two decades. With higher economic growth elsewhere, net migration to Georgia will slow down.

Higher productivity growth and lower real interest rates will be associated with higher U.S. economic growth. Higher productivity growth will occur as the baby boom generation matures and the work experience of its members increases. Interest rates will remain lower as long as inflationary pressures do not reemerge.

The average price of oil in 1985 dollars will remain under $18 per barrel as a result of the transformation of the OPEC-dominated world oil market into a commodity-based market. The surplus of natural gas will diminish, but not until the middle-1990s. Industrial demand for natural gas will dampen, as lower oil prices encourage substitution to oil. Coal prices will increase more slowly. Real electricity prices will decline if the free market energy policy pursued by the Reagan Administration continues. Emissions will remain essentially stable through 1995.

Real U.S. GNP will grow at an annual rate of less than 2.7 percent, a rate lower than the average growth rate experienced so far in the 1980s. This decline will result from a worsening trade imbalance and from large deficit spending that exerts an upward pressure on interest rates. Georgia's personal income growth will exceed that of the United States as a whole by over one percentage point. Higher levels of net migration into Georgia will occur as economic circumstances worsen elsewhere. This will accelerate growth in the state.

The annual increase in U.S. productivity will be less than 1.5 percent, an increase consistent with the slow growth of the 1970s. The low growth rate will result from a decline in demand for most goods and services as the population ages. Taxes will increase to support the aged population. Both higher taxes and higher interest rates will accelerate the shift from a manufacturing to a service economy.

By 1995, oil prices will average over $30 per barrel in 1985 dollars. The current world surplus will erode quickly in the early years as the current strong economic growth increases oil demand. This will cause a return to OPEC price controls. Deregulation will free natural gas prices to adjust rapidly to supply and demand imbalances. Exploration and development will be dampened by the initial lower prices and by inconsistent and unpredictable government energy policy. Real electricity prices will decline. Some acid rain legislation will be passed, but not enough to significantly discourage growth in the utility industry.

Source: D. L. Goldfarb and W. R. Huss, "Building Scenarios for an Electric Utility," *Long Range Planning*, June 1988, pp. 78–85.

Frost and Sullivan's World Political Risks Forecasts, which predict the likelihood of various catastrophes befalling an individual firm.

Probe International's custom reports for specific firms, which examine broad social trends.

The developmental forecasts of Arthur D. Little (ADL), which examine a country's progress from the Stone Age to the computer age. [11]

Of all the approaches in uses, those of ADL may be the most ambitious and sophisticated. With computer assistance, ADL follows the progress of each country by looking at five criteria: social development, technological advancement, abundance of natural resources, level of domestic tranquillity, and type of political system. When a country's development in any one of these areas gets too far ahead of its development in the other areas, tension builds and violence often follows. Using this system, ADL forecast political turbulence in Iran eight years before the U.S. hostage crisis. ADL foresees that uneven development probably will produce similar turmoil in 20 other countries, such as Peru, Chile, Malaysia, and the Philippines. It believes the world is highly predictable if the right questions are asked. Unfortunately, too many executives fail to use the same logic in analyzing political affairs that they use in other strategic areas. Political analysis should be routinely incorporated into economic analyses. Ford, General Motors, PepsiCo, Singer, Du Pont, and United Technologies are among the many firms that follow ADL's advice.

Global Strategy in Action 5–1 provides a guide to political evaluation that is popular among executives who are responsible for international operations. Global Strategy in Action 5–2 presents an actual scenario that was developed to assess political and economic conditions in the Americas in 1992.

Technological Forecasts

Such rapidly developed and revolutionary technological innovations as lasers, nuclear energy, satellites and other communication devices, desalination of water, electric cars, and miracle drugs have prompted many firms to invest in technological forecasts. Knowledge of probable technological development helps strategic managers prepare their firms to benefit from change. Except for econometrics, all of the previously described techniques can be used to make technological forecasts. However, uncertainty of information favors the use of scenarios and two additional forecasting approaches: brainstorming and the Delphi technique.

Brainstorming helps a group generate new ideas and forecasts. With this technique, analysis or criticisms of participants' contributions are postponed so creative thinking is not stifled or restricted. Because there are no interruptions, group members are encouraged to offer original ideas and to build on one another's innovative thoughts. The most promising ideas generated in this way are thoroughly evaluated at a later time.

The *Delphi method* is a systematic procedure for obtaining consensus among a group of experts. This method includes:

1. A detailed survey of opinions of experts, usually obtained through a mail questionnaire.

---

[11] N. Howard, "Doing Business in Unstable Countries," *Dun's Review*, March 1980, pp. 49–55.

GLOBAL
STRATEGY IN **A GUIDE TO POLITICAL EVALUATION**
ACTION 5–1

 The following is an abridged version of the popular Political Agenda Worksheet developed by Probe, a consulting firm that specializes in political analysis, which may serve as a guide for corporate executives initiating their own political evaluations.

EXTERNAL FACTORS AFFECTING SUBJECT COUNTRY

Prospects for foreign conflict.

Relations with border countries.

Regional instabilities.

Alliances with major and regional powers.

Sources of key raw materials.

Major foreign markets.

Policy toward United States.

U.S. policy toward country.

INTERNAL GROUPINGS (POINTS OF POWER)

Government in Power

Key agencies and officials.

Legislative entrenched bureaucracies.

Policies—economic, financial, social, labor, and so on.

Pending legislation.

Attitude toward private sector.

Power networks.

Political Parties (in and out of power)

Policies.

Leading and emerging personalities.

Internal power struggles.

Source: B. Weiner, "What Executives Should Know about Political Risk," *Management Review*, January 1992, p. 21.

2. Anonymous evaluation of the responses by the experts involved.

3. One or more revisions of the experts' answers until convergence has been achieved.

The Delphi method is expensive and time-consuming, but it can be successful in social and political forecasting.

At the end of this chapter, Appendix 5–B briefly describes the 20 most frequently used forecasting approaches and provides references containing more details about their derivation and application.

Sector and area strengths.

Future prospects for retaining or gaining power.

Other Important Groups

Unions and labor movements.

Military, special groups within military.

Families.

Business and financial communities.

Intelligentsia.

Students.

Religious groups.

Media.

Regional and local governments.

Social and environmental activists.

Cultural, linguistic, and ethnic groups.

Separatist movements.

Foreign communities.

Potential competitors and customers.

INTERNAL FACTORS

Power struggles among elites.

Ethnic confrontations.

Regional struggles.

Economic factors affecting stability (consumer inflation, price and wage controls, unemployment, supply shortages, taxation, and so on).

Anti-establishment movements.

INTEGRATE FORECAST RESULTS INTO THE STRATEGIC MANAGEMENT PROCESS

Once the forecasting techniques have been selected and the forecasts made, the results must be integrated into the strategic management process. For example, the economic forecast must be related to analyses of the industry, suppliers, competition, and key resources. Figure 5–5 presents a format for displaying interrelationships between forecast remote environment variables and the influential task environment variables. The resulting predictions become a part of the assumed environment in formulating strategy.

GLOBAL
STRATEGY IN **THE AMERICAS**
ACTION 5–2

I n general, political and economic conditions are likely to be more stable in Central and South
America in 1992 than they have been for several years. The debt crisis has receded as a prime
concern; and while political violence may increase, most regimes are not likely to change during
1992. The biggest headlines will be devoted to the free-trade movements in the region, especially
the North American Free Trade Area (NAFTA).

Some type of free-trade agreement between Mexico and the United States is likely in 1992, but
its economic impact will not be nearly as important as its symbolic significance. Rather than stimulating new trade in Mexico, it will open up new opportunities for joint venture investments. The
most important consequence of such an agreement may well be to sustain political support for President Salinas of Mexico. Other free-trade agreements among South American countries will also
evolve during 1992, but they will have only limited impact on the local economies.

Since Brazil and Argentina together account for 50 percent of all economic activity in South
America, these are the countries to watch closely. Brazil continues to make little headway against
inflation or toward meaningful economic reform. Prospects for improvement are not good while
President Collor battles a recalcitrant congress and the stubbornly independent state governments.

Argentina, on the other hand, has shown significant signs of economic improvement under a new
minister of the economy and President Menem, who has regained much of his earlier popularity. As
more privatization has occurred, the international financial community appears to have talked itself
back into believing in Argentina. Nevertheless, prospects for comprehensive privatization remain
limited, and labor is becoming increasingly opposed to Menem's policies. A new acceleration of
inflation could destroy Menem's chances of implementing the nascent program of far-reaching economic reform now in process.

Source: *Planning Review* 20, no. 2 (March–April 1992), p. 27. Published with permission of The Planning Forum, P.O. Box 70,
Oxford, OH 45056.

It is critical that strategic decision makers understand the assumptions on which environmental forecasts are based. The experience of Itel, a computer-leasing firm, illustrates
the consequences of a failure to understand these assumptions. Itel had been able to lease
200 plug-in computers made by Advance Systems and by Hitachi largely because IBM
could not deliver its newest AT systems. Consequently, Itel bullishly forecast that it would
place 430 of its systems in the following year—despite the rumor that IBM would
announce a new line of aggressively priced systems in the first quarter of that year. Even
Itel's competitors felt that customers would hold off their purchasing decisions until IBM
made the announcement. However, Itel signed long-term purchase contracts with its suppliers and increased its marketing staff by 80 percent. Itel's forecasting mistake and its
failure to examine its sales forecasts in relationship to the actions of competitors and suppliers were nearly disastrous. It slipped close to bankruptcy within less than a year.

Forecasting external events enables a firm to identify its probable requirements for future
success, to formulate or reformulate its basic mission, and to design strategies for achieving
its goals and objectives. If the forecast identifies any gaps or inconsistencies between the

FIGURE 5–5
Task and Remote Environment Impact Matrix

Remote Environments	Task Environments			
	Key Customer Trends	Key Competitor Trends	Key Supplier Trends	Key Labor Market Trends
Economic	*Example:* Trends in inflation and unemployment rates.		*Example:* Annual domestic oil demand and worldwide sulfur demand through the year 2000.	
Social	*Example:* Increasing numbers of single-parent homes.			*Example:* Rising education level of U.S. population.
Political	*Example:* Increasing numbers of punitive damage awards in product liability cases.		*Example:* Possibility of Arab oil boycotts	
Technological		*Example:* Increasing use of superchips and computer-based instru-mentation for synthesizing genes.	*Example:* Use of cobalt 60 gamma irradiation to extend shelf life of perishables.	
Ecological		*Example:* Increased use of biodegradable fast-food packaging.		*Example:* Increasing availability of mature workers with experience in "smokestack" industries.

firm's desired position and its present position, strategic managers can respond with plans and actions. When Apple successfully introduced its new low-priced personal computers in fall 1991, sales climbed 85 percent for the quarter. However, because the firm failed to forecast that sales of the low-price computers would cannibalize the sales of its more expensive models, profits slipped, forcing Apple to lay off 10 percent of its work force, or 1,500 employees.

Dealing with the uncertainty of the future is a major function of strategic managers. The forecasting task requires systematic information gathering coupled with the utilization of a variety of forecasting approaches. A high level of insight also is needed to integrate risks and opportunities in formulating strategy. However, intentional or unintentional delays or the inability to understand certain issues may prevent a firm from using the insights gained in assessing the impact of broad environmental trends. Sensitivity and openness to new and better approaches and opportunities, therefore, are essential.

MONITOR THE CRITICAL ASPECTS OF MANAGING FORECASTS

Although almost all aspects of forecast management may be critical in specific situations, three aspects are critical over the lifetime of a firm.

The first is the identification of the environmental factors that deserve forecasting. Hundreds of factors may affect a firm, but often the most important of these factors are a few of immediate concern, such as sales forecasts and competitive trends. The time and resources needed to completely understand all the environmental factors that might be critical to the success of a strategy are seldom available. Therefore, executives must depend on their collective experience and perception to determine which factors are worth the expense of forecasting.

The second aspect is the selection of reputable, cost-efficient forecasting sources outside the firm that can expand its forecasting database. Strategic managers should identify federal and state government agencies, trade and industry associations, and individuals or other groups that can provide data forecasts at reasonable costs.

The third aspect is the selection of forecasting tasks that are to be done in-house. Given the great credence that often is accorded to formally developed forecasts—despite the inherent uncertainty of the database—the selection of forecasting techniques is indeed critical. A firm beginning its forecasting efforts is well advised to start with less technical methods, such as sales force estimates and the jury of executive opinion, rather than highly sophisticated forecasting techniques, such as econometrics, and to add approaches requiring greater analytic sophistication as its experience and understanding increase. In this way, its managers can learn how to deal with the varied weaknesses and strengths of forecasting techniques.

SUMMARY

Environmental forecasting starts with the identification of critical factors external to the firm that might provide opportunities or pose threats in the future. Both quantitative and qualitative strategic forecasting techniques are used to project the long-range direction and impact of these factors in the remote and task environments. To select the forecasting techniques that are most appropriate for the firm, the strengths and weaknesses of the various techniques must be understood. To offset the potential biases or errors individual techniques involve, employment of more than one technique usually is advisable.

Critical aspects in forecast management include the identification of the environmental factors that deserve forecasting, the selection of forecasting sources outside the firm, and the selection of forecasting tasks that are to be done in-house.

QUESTIONS FOR DISCUSSION

1. Identify five changes in the remote environment that you believe will affect major U.S. industries over the next decade. What forecasting techniques could be used to assess the probable impact of these changes?

2. Construct a matrix with forecasting techniques on the horizontal axis and at least five qualities of forecasting techniques across the vertical axis. Indicate the relative strengths and weaknesses of each technique.

3. Develop three rules of thumb for guiding strategic managers in their use of forecasting.

4. Develop a typewritten two-page forecast of a variable that you believe will affect the prosperity of your business school over the next 10 years.

5. Using prominent business journals, find two examples of firms that either benefited or suffered from environmental forecasts.

6. Describe the background, skills, and abilities of the individual you would hire as the environmental forecaster for a firm with $500 million in annual sales. How would the qualifications of such an individual differ for a much smaller firm? For a much larger firm?

BIBLIOGRAPHY

Allaire, Y., and M. E. Firsirotu. "Coping with Strategic Uncertainty." *Sloan Management Review.* Spring 1989, pp. 7–16.

Ansoff, H. I. "Strategic Management of Technology." *Journal of Business Strategy,* Winter 1987, pp. 40–48.

Barndt, W. D., Jr. "Profiling Rival Decision Makers." *The Journal of Business Strategy,* January–February 1991, pp. 8–11.

Barrett, F. D. "Strategies for the Use of Artificial and Human Intelligence." *Business Quarterly,* Summer 1986, pp. 18–27.

Clark, R. S. "The Strategic Planner's Toolbox." *CA Magazine,* July 1987, pp. 24–34.

Coccari, R. L. "How Quantitative Business Techniques Are Being Used." *Business Horizons,* July 1989, pp. 70–74.

Cohen, B. G. "A New Approach to Strategic Forecasting." *Journal of Business Strategy,* September 1988, pp. 38–42.

Coplin, W. D., and M. K. O'Leary. "1991 World Political Risk Forecast." *Planning Review,* January–February 1991, pp. 16–23.

Czinkota, M. R. "International Information Needs for U.S. Competitiveness." *Business Horizons,* November–December 1991, pp. 86–91.

Daft, R. L.; J. Sormunen; and D. Parks. "Chief Executive Scanning, Environmental Characteristics, and Company Performance: An Empirical Study." *Strategic Management Journal,* March 1988, pp. 123–39.

Drucker, P. M. *Managing in Turbulent Times.* New York: Harper & Row, 1980.

ElSawy, O. A., and T. C. Pauchant. "Triggers, Templates, and Twitches in the Tracking of Emerging Strategic Issues." *Strategic Management Journal,* September 1988, pp. 455–73.

Fahey, L., and W. R. King. "Environmental Scanning for Corporate Planning." *Business Horizons,* August 1977, pp. 61–71.

Fuld, L. "A Recipe for Business Intelligence Success." *The Journal of Business Strategy,* January–February 1991, pp. 12–17.

Fuld, L. M. "Achieving Total Quality through Intelligence." *Long Range Planning,* February 1992, pp. 109–15.

Fulmer, W., and R. Fulmer. "Strategic Group Technique: Involving Managers in Strategic Planning." *Long Range Planning,* April 1990, pp. 79–84.

Gelb, B. D.; M. J. Saxton; G. M. Zinkhan; and N. D. Albers. "Competitive Intelligence: Insights from Executives." *Business Horizons,* January–February 1991, pp. 43–47.

Ghoshal, S., and S. K. Kim. "Building Effective Intelligence Systems for Competitive Advantage." *Sloan Management Review,* Fall 1986, pp. 49–58.

Gilad, B. "U.S. Intelligence System: Model for Corporate Chiefs?" *The Journal of Business Strategy,* May–June 1991, pp. 20–25.

Ginsberg, A. "Measuring and Modeling Changes in Strategy: Theoretical Foundations and Empirical Directions." *Strategic Management Journal*, November 1988, pp. 559–75.

Herring, J. P. "The Role of Intelligence in Formulating Strategy." *The Journal of Business Strategy*, September–October 1992, pp. 54–60.

Howard, N. "Doing Business in Unstable Countries." *Dun's Review*, March 1980, pp. 49–55.

Jain, S. C. "Environmental Scanning in U.S. Corporations." *Long Range Planning*, April 1984, pp. 117–28.

Kahane, A. "Scenarios for Energy: Sustainable World vs. Global Mercantilism." *Long Range Planning*, August 1992, pp. 38–46.

Kast, F. "Scanning the Future Environment: Social Indications." *California Management Review*, Fall 1980, pp. 22–32.

Keiser, B. "Practical Competitor Intelligence." *Planning Review*, September 1987, pp. 14–19.

La Bell, D., and O. J. Krasner. "Selecting Environmental Forecasting Techniques from Business Planning Requirements." *Academy of Management Review*, July 1977, pp. 373–83.

Lederer, A. L., and V. Sethi. "Guidelines for Strategic Information Planning." *The Journal of Business Strategy*, November–December 1991, pp. 38–43.

Madridakis, S., and S. Wheelwright. "Forecasting: Issues and Challenges for Marketing Management." *Journal Marketing*, October 1977, pp. 24–38.

McConkey, D. D. "Planning for Uncertainty." *Business Horizons*, January 1987, pp. 40–45.

Mesch, A. H. "Developing an Effective Environmental Assessment Function." *Managerial Planning*, March 1984, pp. 17–22.

Morris, E. "Vision and Strategy: A Focus for the Future." *Journal of Business Strategy*, Fall 1987, pp. 51–58.

Pant, P. N., and W. H. Starbuck. "Innocents in the Forest: Forecasting and Research Methods." *Yearly Review of Management*, June 1990, pp. 433–60.

Premkumar, G., and W. R. King. "Assessing Strategic Information Systems Planning." *Long Range Planning*, October 1991, pp. 41–58.

Rousch, G. B. "A Program for Sharing Corporate Intelligence." *The Journal of Business Strategy*, January–February 1991, pp. 4–7.

Schnaars, S. P. "How to Develop and Use Scenarios." *Long Range Planning*, February 1987, pp. 105–14.

Starry, C., and N. McGaughey. "Growth Industries: Here Today, Gone Tomorrow." *Business Horizons*, July 1988, pp. 69–74.

Stokke, P. R.; W. K. Ralston; T. A. Boyce; and I. H. Wilson. "Scenario Planning for Norwegian Oil and Gas." *Long Range Planning*, April 1990, pp. 17–26.

Whipple, W., III. "Evaluating Alternative Strategies Using Scenarios." *Long Range Planning*, June 1989, pp. 82–86.

APPENDIX 5–A

SOURCES FOR ENVIRONMENTAL FORECASTS

REMOTE AND INDUSTRY ENVIRONMENTS

A. Economic considerations:
1. *Predicasts* (most complete and up-to-date review of forecasts).
2. National Bureau of Economic Research.
3. *Handbook of Basic Economic Statistics.*
4. *Statistical Abstract of the United States* (also includes industrial, social, and political statistics).
5. Publications by Department of Commerce agencies:
   a. Office of Business Economics (e.g., *Survey of Business*).
   b. Bureau of Economic Analysis (e.g., *Business Conditions Digest*).
   c. Bureau of the Census (e.g., *Survey of Manufacturers* and various reports on population, housing, and industries).
   d. Business and Defense Services Administration (e.g., *United States Industrial Outlook*).
6. Securities and Exchange Commission (various quarterly reports on plant and equipment, financial reports, working capital of corporations).
7. The Conference Board.
8. *Survey of Buying Power.*
9. *Marketing Economic Guide.*
10. *Industrial Arts Index.*
11. U.S. and national chambers of commerce.
12. American Manufacturers Association.
13. *Federal Reserve Bulletin.*
14. *Economic Indicators*, annual report.
15. *Kiplinger Newsletter.*
16. International economic sources:
    a. *Worldcasts.*
    b. Master key index for business international publications.
    c. Department of Commerce.
       (1) Overseas business reports.
       (2) Industry and Trade Administration.

Sources: Adapted with numerous additions from C. R. Goeldner and L. M. Kirks, "Business Facts: Where to Find Them," *MSU Business Topics*, Summer 1976, pp. 23–76, reprinted by permission of the publisher, Division of Research, Graduate School of Business Administration, MSU; F. E. deCarbonnel and R. G. Donance, "Information Source for Planning Decisions," *California Management Review*, Summer 1973, pp. 42–53; and A. B. Nun, R. C. Lenz, Jr., H. W. Landford, and M. J. Cleary, "Data Source for Trend Extrapolation in Technological Forecasting," *Long Range Planning*, February 1972, pp. 72–76.

(3) Bureau of the Census—*Guide to Foreign Trade Statistics.*
17. *Business Periodicals Index.*

B. Social considerations:
1. Public opinion polls.
2. Surveys such as *Social Indicators* and *Social Reporting,* the annals of the American Academy of Political and Social Sciences.
3. Current controls: Social and behavioral sciences.
4. Abstract services and indexes for articles in sociological, psychological, and political journals.
5. Indexes for *The Wall Street Journal, New York Times,* and other newspapers.
6. Bureau of the Census reports on population, housing, manufacturers, selected services, construction, retail trade, wholesale trade, and enterprise statistics.
7. Various reports from such groups as the Brookings Institution and the Ford Foundation.
8. World Bank Atlas (population growth and GNP data).
9. World Bank—World Development Report.

C. Political considerations:
1. *Public Affairs Information Services Bulletin.*
2. CIS Index (Congressional Information Index).
3. Business periodicals.
4. Funk & Scott (regulations by product breakdown).
5. Weekly compilation of presidential documents.
6. *Monthly Catalog of Government Publications.*
7. *Federal Register* (daily announcements of pending regulations).
8. *Code of Federal Regulations* (final listing of regulations).
9. Business International Master Key Index (regulations, tariffs).
10. Various state publications.
11. Various information services (Bureau of National Affairs, Commerce Clearing House, Prentice Hall).

D. Technological considerations:
1. *Applied Science and Technology Index.*
2. *Statistical Abstract of the United States.*
3. Scientific and Technical Information Service.
4. University reports, congressional reports.
5. Department of Defense and military purchasing publishers.
6. Trade journals and industrial reports.
7. Industry contacts, professional meetings.
8. Computer-assisted information searches.
9. National Science Foundation annual report.
10. *Research and Development Directory* patent records.
11. Industry considerations:
    a. *Concentration Ratios in Manufacturing* (Bureau of the Census).
    b. *Input-Output Survey* (productivity ratios).
    c. *Monthly Labor Review* (productivity ratios).

    d. *Quarterly Failure Report* (Dun & Bradstreet).
    e. *Federal Reserve Bulletin* (capacity utilization).
    f. *Report on Industrial Concentration and Product Diversification in the 1,000 Largest Manufacturing Companies* (Federal Trade Commission).
    g. Industry trade publications.
    h. Bureau of Economic Analysis, Department of Commerce (specialization ratios).

INDUSTRY AND OPERATING ENVIRONMENTS

A. Competition and supplier considerations:
1. Target Group Index.
2. U.S. Industrial Outlook.
3. Robert Morris annual statement studies.
4. Troy, Leo Almanac of Business & Industrial Financial Ratios.
5. Census of Enterprise Statistics.
6. Securities and Exchange Commission (10-K reports).
7. Annual reports of specific companies.
8. *Fortune 500 Directory, The Wall Street Journal, Baron's, Forbes, Dun's Review.*
9. Investment services and directories: Moody's, Dun & Bradstreet, Standard & Poor's, Starch Marketing, Funk & Scott Index.
10. Trade association surveys.
11. Industry surveys.
12. Market research surveys.
13. *Country Business Patterns.*
14. *Country and City Data Book.*
15. Industry contacts, professional meetings, salespeople.
16. *NFIB Quarterly Economic Report for Small Business.*

B. Customer profile:
1. *Statistical Abstract of the United States*, first source of statistics.
2. *Statistical Sources* by Paul Wasserman (a subject guide to data—both domestic and international).
3. *American Statistics Index* (Congressional Information Service Guide to statistical publications of U.S. government—monthly).
4. Office to the Department of Commerce:
    a. Bureau of the Census reports on population, housing, and industries.
    b. *U.S. Census of Manufacturers* (statistics by industry, area, and products).
    c. *Survey of Current Business* (analysis of business trends, especially February and July issues).
5. Market research studies (*A Basic Bibliography on Market Review*, compiled by Robert Ferber et al., American Marketing Association).
6. *Current Sources of Marketing Information: A Bibliography of Primary Marketing Data* by Gunther & Goldstein, AMA.

7. *Guide to Consumer Markets*, The Conference Board (provides statistical information with demographic, social, and economic data—annual).
8. *Survey of Buying Power.*
9. *Predicasts* (abstracts of publishing forecasts of all industries, detailed products and end-use data).
10. *Predicasts Basebook* (historical data from 1960 to present, covering subjects ranging from population and GNP to specific products and services; series are coded by Standard Industrial Classifications).
11. *Market Guide* (Individual market surveys of over 1,500 U.S. and Canadian cities; includes population, location, trade areas, banks, principal industries, colleges and universities, department and chain stores, newspapers, retail outlets, and sales).
12. *Country and City Data Book* (includes bank deposits, birth and death rates, business firms, education, employment, income of families, manufacturers, population, savings, wholesale and retail trade).
13. *Yearbook of International Trade Statistics* (UN).
14. *Yearbook of National Accounts Statistics* (UN).
15. *Statistical Yearbook* (UN—covers population, national income, agricultural and industrial production, energy, external trade and transport).
16. *Statistics of (Continents): Sources for Market Research* (includes separate books on Africa, America, Europe).

C. Key natural resources:
1. *Minerals Yearbook, Geological Survey* (Bureau of Mines, Department of the Interior).
2. *Agricultural Abstract* (Department of Agriculture).
3. Statistics of electric utilities and gas pipeline companies (Federal Power Commission).
4. Publications of various institutions: American Petroleum Institute, Atomic Energy Commission, Coal Mining Institute of America, American Steel Institute, and Brookings Institution.

APPENDIX 5–B

STRATEGIC PLANNING FORECASTING TOOLS AND TECHNIQUES

1. **Dialectical Inquiry.**
   Development, evaluation, and synthesis of conflicting points of view by (1) having separate assigned groups use debate format to formulate and refine each point of view and then (2) bringing two groups together for presentation of debate between and synthesis of their points of view.
   R. O. Mason and I. I. Mitroff, *Strategic Assumptions Surfacing and Testing* (New York: John Wiley & Sons, 1981)

2. **Nominal Group Technique.**
   Development, evaluation, and synthesis of individual points of view through an interactive process in a group setting.
   A. L. Delbecq, A. H. Van de Ven, and D. H. Gustafson, *Group Techniques for Program Planning: A Guide to Nominal Group and Delphi Processes* (Glenview, Ill.: Scott, Foresman, 1975).

3. **Delphi Method.**
   Development, evaluation, and synthesis of individual points of view by systematically soliciting and collating judgments on a particular topic through a set of carefully designed sequential questionnaires interspersed with summarized information and feedback of opinions derived from earlier responses.
   A. L. Delbecq, A. H. Van de Ven, and D. H. Gustafson, *Group Techniques for Program Planning: A Guide to Nominal Group and Delphi Processes* (Glenview, Ill.: Scott, Foresman, 1975).

4. **Focus Groups.**
   Bringing together recognized experts and qualified individuals in an organized setting to develop, evaluate, and synthesize their individual points of view on a particular topic.
   D. L. Johnson and A. H. Mendelson, *Using Focus Groups in Marketing Planning* (St. Paul, Minn.: West Publishing, 1982).

5. **Simulation Technique.**
   Computer-based technique for simulating future situations and then predicting the outcome of various courses of action against each of these situations.
   G. D. Craig, "A Simulation System for Corporate Planning," *Long Range Planning*, October 1980, pp. 43–56.

Source: Excerpted with updates from J. Webster, W. Reif, and J. Bracker, "The Manager's Guide to Strategic Planning Tools and Techniques," *Planning Review*, November–December 1989, pp. 4–13, 48.

6. **PIMS Analysis.**

Application of the experiences of a diverse sample of successful and unsuccessful firms.

S. R. Schoeffler, R. D. Buzzell, and D. F. Heaney, "Impact of Strategic Planning on Profit Performance," *Harvard Business Review*, March–April 1974, pp. 137–45.

7. **Market Opportunity Analysis.**

Identification of markets and market factors in the economy and the industry that will affect the demand for and marketing of a product or service.

D. Silverman, "Consultants' Concepts—Field Analysis: A 3–D Look at Opportunities," *Planning Review*, September 1984, pp. 22–24.

8. **Benchmarking.**

Comparative analysis of competitor programs and strategic positions for use as reference points in the formulation of organization objectives.

L. J. Mennon and D. W. Landers, *Advanced Techniques for Strategic Analysis* (Hindsdale, Ill.: Dryden Press, 1987).

9. **Situational Analysis** (SWOT or TOWS).

Systematic development and evaluation of past, present, and future data to identify internal strengths and weaknesses and external threats and opportunities.

H. Weihrich, "The TOWS Matrix—A Tool for Situational Analysis," *Long Range Planning*, April 1982, pp. 54–66.

10. **Critical Success Factors/Strategic Issues Analysis.**

Identification and analysis of a limited number of areas in which high performance will ensure a successful competitive position.

A. C. Boynton and R. W. Zmud, "An Assessment of Critical Success Factors," *Sloan Management Review*, Summer 1984, pp. 17–24.

11. **Product Life Cycle Analysis.**

Analysis of market dynamics in which a product is viewed according to its position within distinct stages of its sales history.

G. S. Day, *Analysis for Strategic Market Decisions* (St. Paul, Minn.: West Publishing, 1986).

12. **Future Studies.**

Development of future situations and factors based on agreement of a group of "experts," often from a variety of functional areas within a firm.

S. W. Edmunds, "The Role of Future Studies in Business Strategic Planning," *Journal of Business Strategy*, Fall 1982, pp. 40–46.

13. **Multiple Scenarios.**

Smoothly unfolding narratives that describe an assumed future expressed through a sequence of time frames and snapshots.

"Scenarios," Special issue topic, *Planning Review*, March–April 1992, pp. 24–27.

14. **SPIRE** (Systematic Procedure for Identification of Relevant Environments).

A computer-assisted, matrix-generating tool for forecasting environmental changes that can have a dramatic impact on operations.

H. Klein and W. Newman, "How to Use SPIRE: A Systematic Procedure for Identifying Relevant Environments for Strategic Planning," *Journal of Business Strategy*, Summer 1980, pp. 32–45.

15. **Environmental Scanning, Forecasting, and Trend Analysis.**
Continuous process, usually computer based, of monitoring external factors, events, situations, and projections of forecasts of trends.

L. Fahey, William R. King, and V. K. Narayanan, "Environmental Scanning and Forecasting in Strategic Planning—The State of the Art," *Long Range Planning*, February 1981, pp. 32–39.

16. **Experience Curves.**
An organizing framework for dynamic analyses of cost and price for a product, a company, or an industry over an extended period.

P. Ghemawat, "Building Strategy on the Experience Curve," *Harvard Business Review*, March–April 1985, pp. 143–49.

17. **Portfolio Classification Analysis.**
Classification and visual display of the present and prospective positions of firms and products according to the attractiveness of the market and the ability of the firms and products to compete within that market.

G. S. Day, *Analysis for Strategic Market Decisions* (St. Paul, Minn.: West Publishing, 1986).

18. **Metagame Analysis.**
Arriving at a strategic direction by thinking through a series of viewpoints on a contemplated strategy in terms of every competitor and every combination of competitive responses.

B. K. Dutta and William R. King, "Metagame Analysis of Competitive Strategy," *Strategic Management Journal*, October 1980, pp. 357–70.

19. **Strategic Gap Analysis.**
Examination of the difference between the extrapolation of current performance levels (e.g., current sales) and the projection of desired performance objectives (e.g., a desired sales level).

H. I. Ansoff, *Corporate Strategy* (New York: McGraw-Hill, 1972).

20. **Sustainable Growth Model.**
Financial analysis of the sales growth rate that is required to meet market share objectives and the degree to which capacity must be expanded to achieve that growth rate.

P. Varadarajan, "The Sustainable Growth Model: A Tool for Evaluating the Financial Feasibility of Market Share Strategies," *Strategic Management Journal*, October 1984, pp. 353–67.

CHAPTER 5 COHESION CASE

FORECASTING AND THE COCA-COLA COMPANY

Coca-Cola's chief executive officer, Roberto Goizueta, communicating with Coke share-holders on February 20, 1992, appeared to suggest that Coke's strategic management process avoids significant emphasis on forecasting when he said:

> As an organization we are not wasting our energy forecasting what the soft-drink industry will be like in the many countries around the world in which we operate. And neither are we spending our time forecasting what the future holds for this company. We will use our resources to construct today the foundation on which OUR future . . . THE FUTURE WE ARE CREATING FOR OURSELVES . . . will be built.

> * * * * *

> We do not want to leave our shareowners with the false impression that this wonderful soft-drink business of The Coca-Cola Company is totally impervious to any and all setbacks. However, we are running this business today at a high efficiency, and we have the attitude and the financial resources, as well as the management team, needed to take care of any negative eventuality which may come our way. So . . . when it does, if we don't completely neutralize it, at the very least, we will minimize its impact.

> On the other hand, and as with everything in life, there will also surely be unexpected positive events in the future of this Company. When they happen, we will quickly put them to work to our advantage. In the past we have demonstrated our system has such capabilities, and we will continue to take advantage of every opportunity in the future.

On the surface, it would appear that Mr. Goizueta places little faith in efforts to forecast future events. A closer reading and review of Coke's management actions suggest otherwise. In other words, Mr. Goizueta is at least in part saying that Coca-Cola is a very focused company. While it serves a myriad of markets worldwide, it has learned some very simple and powerful lessons about the fundamentals of success in the soft-drink business. And it is his belief that Coke's ability to do those things and to adjust those things to changing conditions will perhaps more profoundly influence its success in an unknown future than will reactions generated by any single forecast. According to Mr. Goizueta, successful global marketing of soft-drink products requires certain conditions be in place that require a long time to develop: (1) a company must have, build, or buy a powerful trademark to be a globally successful soft-drink company and (2) that company must have a global business system through which to reach consumers. (3) Such a business system must be able to appeal to cultures as diverse as Switzerland and Swaziland—to tailor products and messages to local markets. And finally, (4) there must be an intangible yet powerful ingredient—a central theme, idea, or symbol—that binds together the business system, the brands, and the consumers into an association with their best feelings and memories each time they drink a Coke. And it is sensitivity to ways that these key conditions can be applied, refined, and expanded that shapes future success at Coke.

While Goizueta eschews forecasts, he recently told *Financial World:*

In the United States, we will be growing 6 percent in volume with double-digit earnings growth. But outside the United States, where we have 9–10 percent volume growth, we will have higher double-digit earnings increases.

Apparently there is keen management interest in charting and projecting soft-drink consumption patterns. An internal company trend analysis of soft-drink consumption during 1991 and the preceding 10 years is shown in the table, "Selected Country Results," from The Coca-Cola Company 1991 Annual Report.

Another area where Coca-Cola management appears sensitive to monitoring are changes in key countries, which have large populations, that support introduction or reintroduction of the "Coca-Cola Business System." Coke management calls this "seeding for the future," as is illustrated regarding India, China, and Indonesia in the excerpt, on page 171, also from the 1991 Annual Report.

Finally, several soft-drink-related facts or trends have appeared in various industry forums that provide Coke management with confirmation of its inclinations or possible "forecasts." Some of these include:

1. While annual per capita soft-drink consumption in the United States is about 770 servings, in markets abroad per capita rates average only 62 servings. In less developed markets, such as India, consumers drink less than three servings a year.

2. In international markets, most soft drinks are sold in single-serve bottles, one at a time. Getting consumers to take home bigger packages means they'll drink more.

3. In the United States, vending machines account for 12 percent of soft-drink sales; but they're still a rarity in many countries.

4. Soft drinks represent about one quarter of all beverages consumed in the United States. That means replacing other beverages or expanding into them represents growth for soft-drink companies.

5. Eastern Europe is developing rapidly as a soft-drink market from a negligible base in 1992. The breakup of the Soviet Union has opened new markets that represent sustained volume growth opportunities.

Summary of

Selected Country Results

Estimated Unit Case Sales[1]
Carbonated Soft Drinks

	Average Annual Growth				1991 Results			
	10 Years		5 Years		Unit Case Growth		Company	
	Company	Industry	Company	Industry	Company	Industry	Share	Per Capita Consumption
Worldwide	6%	5%	6%	5%	5%	3%	43%	54
United States	5	4	4	3	2.5	1.7	41	296
International	7	5	8	6	6	3	44	39
European Community	9	5	11	7	8	1	45	116
France	13	5	16	9	11	1	41	52
Germany	6	5	9	10	19	6	46	178
Great Britain	13	6	14	4	(11)	(10)	32	87
Italy	10	6	8	5	4	4	55	91
Spain	7	5	11	7	6	3	51	155
Pacific[2]	9	7	10	9	4	3	40	18
Australia	7	5	8	6	2	3	56	223
Japan[2]	7	7	9	9	7	6	34	122
Korea	8	10	7	11	(1)	1	49	63
Philippines	12	3	8	5	(1)	(7)	76	89
Thailand	10	9	17	18	3	4	57	43
Northeast Europe/Africa	7	6	8	6	5	4	27	18
Austria	6	6	10	10	12	8	46	141
Nigeria	4	4	8	6	10	3	68	21
Norway	12	7	11	4	8	3	59	218
Switzerland	10	5	8	6	9	11	44	155
Turkey	19	12	17	13	6	14	39	21
Latin America	6	4	6	4	8	6	53	131
Argentina	3	3	(2)	(3)	31	37	62	133
Brazil	8	6	6	4	4	3	60	101
Chile	9	7	16	18	9	6	61	158
Colombia	6	3	3	1	0.4	(2)	43	105
Mexico	5	4	8	7	6	3	53	273

[1]Unit case equals 24 8-ounce drinks. Data include, for the first time, results from the former Soviet Union and China. Excluding those markets, the Company's share of international soft drink sales was 49 percent. [2]Includes Japanese non-carbonated soft drinks

34

the Future

Over the past five years, the Company's international unit case sales have increased at an average annual rate of 8 percent. No countries better exemplify the Company's long-term opportunity to maintain or exceed that sort of growth than the three profiled on this page. **Nearly 45 percent of the more than 5 billion people on earth live in China, India or Indonesia, but the per capita soft drink consumption rates for the countries are only 8, 3 and 6, respectively.** *While explosive short-term growth is unlikely, the potential for tremendous, sustained growth over time is extraordinary, and the Company is taking aggressive actions now to prepare the ground. Set forth below are some of the ways in which we are seeding for the future.*

INDIA

With 860 million people, India is, by far, the largest market in which Company products are not currently produced. That should change in 1993, thanks to the Indian government's approval of a joint venture formed in late 1991.

The Company will not, however, be starting from scratch. During the 1970s, the Coca-Cola system in India comprised 21 bottlers selling more than 32 million unit cases annually and accounting for 60 percent of the country's carbonated soft drink sales. The Company left India in 1977, but the Coca-Cola trademark continues to enjoy strong, positive recognition and recall among consumers.

The immediate task is to re-establish bottling and distribution networks in and around large metropolitan areas. Once up and running, we will be addressing several marketing opportunities, including packaging, where we see tremendous potential for large, multiserve containers.

Last year, the entire Indian carbonated soft drink industry sold only 113 million unit cases, less than the Company sold in Korea, a country with only 5 percent as many people. To say that the opportunity is enormous is an understatement. No market in the world shows greater promise for rapid, sustained growth for years to come.

CHINA

The Company resumed operations in China in 1981 after an absence of 41 years. Since our re-entry, we have invested $75 million in 13 bottling plants and a concentrate plant in Shanghai, which makes it possible for bottlers to purchase concentrate with local currency, a distinct advantage.

Company products have long been acceptable in China — in 1933 the country became the first market outside the United States to post annual sales of more than a million unit cases — and we are continuing to invest as necessary to make them available and affordable to every one of China's 1.2 billion people.

INDONESIA

If there is such a thing as an ideal soft drink market, it probably looks like Indonesia. Fifty-five percent of its 180 million people are under age 25; the average year-round temperature is a humid 80°F; gross national product is growing 6 to 7 percent a year; and the government welcomes foreign investment.

Last year, the Coca-Cola system sold 34 million unit cases of Company products, accounting for 71 percent of all carbonated soft drinks sold in the country. Because we see the potential for a vastly larger market, we have, over the past few years, rationalized our bottling system and entered, directly and indirectly, into three joint ventures that last year posted 87 percent of our system's unit case sales. Since we began making these investments in 1987, unit case sales have grown at a compound annual rate of 15 percent, and the business is well positioned for continued rapid growth in the years to come.

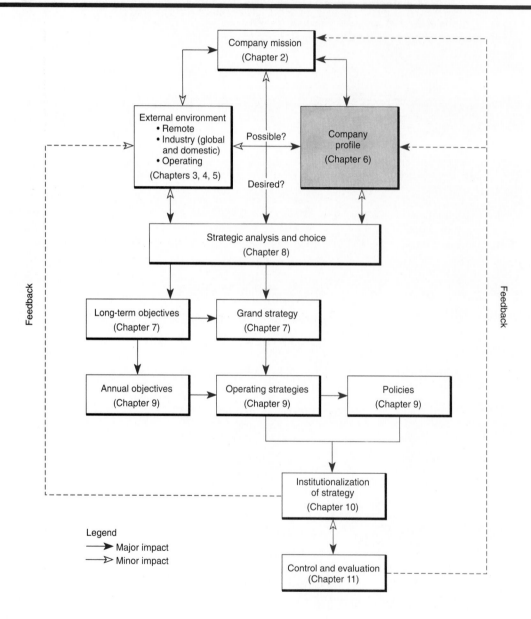

Three ingredients are critical to the success of a strategy. First, the strategy must be *consistent* with conditions in the competitive environment. Specifically, it must take advantage of existing or projected opportunities and minimize the impact of major threats. Second, the strategy must place *realistic* requirements on the firm's internal capabilities. In other words, the firm's pursuit of market opportunities must be based not only on the existence of such opportunities but also on the firm's key internal strengths. Finally, the strategy must be *carefully executed*. The focus of this chapter is on the second ingredient: realistic analysis of the firm's internal capabilities.

The experiences of both large and small firms suggest that thorough internal assessment is critical in developing a successful strategy. To maximize the favorable opportunities in the environment, a firm must base its strategy on a thorough consideration of its internal strengths and weaknesses. The experience of Apple Computer Company illustrates the value of systematic internal analysis in shaping future strategies.

Apple, pioneer of the personal computer, was presented with significant challenges by IBM's meteoric rise in the personal computer market. As the founder of the personal computer industry, Apple had grown rapidly, employing almost 5,000 people by the time IBM entered the industry. These people were divided into product-centered divisions whose significant autonomy and zealous independence reflected the entrepreneurial personality of Steven Jobs, the firm's youthful cofounder. When IBM brought out its PC, Apple ran a full-page ad in *The Wall Street Journal* welcoming IBM into the personal computer market. Apple personnel were confident that their ingenuity, spirit, unique and growing product lines, and strong position in the educational market would keep Apple toe to toe with IBM.

A few years later, Apple was reeling from a series of heavy quarterly losses. Its two early attempts to attract business customers, with the Apple III and Lisa computers, had failed, and its shipments of the Macintosh computer (the product on which it had bet its future) were running at only one eighth of its monthly capacity of 80,000. Jobs was replaced as chairman and CEO of Apple by John Sculley (see Figure 6–1), who sought to realistically identify key internal strengths around which the firm could rebuild its competitive position.

Sculley saw four such strengths—Apple's Macintosh computer, its desktop publishing software and peripherals to go with the Macintosh, its user-friendly product capabilities, and its strong position in the educational market. He devised a careful strategy, centered on these four strengths, which was to introduce successively more powerful high-priced Macs and peripheral (e.g., publishing) products. And addressing what he saw as a major weakness, Sculley reorganized and centralized the firm around functions, rather than the old product-based fiefdoms, which eliminated 20 percent of its overhead and provided greater consistency in the focus of its marketing efforts.

In four years, Apple's profits grew eightfold and its sales tripled to $5.3 billion, making it the first personal computer company to reach the Fortune 100. Continued reassessment of Apple's strengths and weaknesses in light of rapid global changes led Sculley to alter Apple's strategy in the early 1990s to include low-priced Macs, an unprecedented alliance with IBM, and mass merchandising. The results appear promising, with unit sales of Macintosh computers up more than 60 percent—making Macintosh the fastest-growing major computer brand in the United States, Europe, and the Pacific region in the competitive 1990s.

FIGURE 6–1
John Sculley, Apple Chairman and Former CEO

When Apple's strategy was based on emotionally charged feelings among its executives and founders rather than on its objectively assessed strengths and weaknesses, Apple faced a major threat to its survival as a serious player in the personal computer business. But John Sculley has repeatedly focused objectively and intensely on rather limited internal strengths as a basis for a new strategy. Consequently, just as some industry watchers have twice started writing Apple's obituary as a serious player in the personal computer industry, Apple reemerged as a major factor in both the business and educational sectors of the global computer industry. And almost beyond belief for many analysts, IBM enters 1994 as a much weaker industry participant, only now beginning to identify and address several debilitating internal weaknesses.

Internal analysis must identify the strengths and weaknesses on which a firm should base its strategy. When this is done well, a successful strategy is likely to emerge. A firm's managers develop judgments about its key strengths. And based on the match between those strengths and defined or projected market opportunities, the firm's managers ultimately chart its strategic course.

AN OVERVIEW OF INTERNAL ANALYSIS

Managers gauge the "strategic" significance of a firm's internal competences on the basis of the opportunities and threats that are present in the firm's competitive-industry environment. Indeed, the essence of a well-formulated strategy is that it achieves an appropriate match between a firm's opportunities and threats and the firm's strength and weaknesses.

An important foundation for your understanding of internal analysis is an appreciation of the idea of matching internal strengths and weaknesses with environmental opportunities and threats. Appreciating this rather simple idea allows you to see the role of internal analysis in the development of sound strategies. The next section will explain this idea, often defined as SWOT analysis, and the subsequent sections will explain how managers go about the process of internal analysis.

SWOT Analysis

SWOT is an acronym for the internal Strengths and Weaknesses of a firm and the environmental Opportunities and Threats facing that firm. SWOT analysis is a systematic identification of these factors and of the strategy that represents the best match between them. It is based on the assumption that an effective strategy maximizes a firm's strengths and opportunities and minimizes its weaknesses and threats. Accurately applied, this simple assumption has powerful implications for the design of a successful strategy.

Environmental industry analysis (Chapters 3 through 5) provides the information needed to identify opportunities and threats in a firm's environment, the first fundamental focus in SWOT analysis. These can be defined as follows:

Opportunities

An *opportunity is a major favorable situation in a firm's environment.* Key trends are one source of opportunities. Identification of a previously overlooked market segment, changes in competitive or regulatory circumstances, technological changes, and improved buyer or supplier relationships could represent opportunities for the firm.

Threats

A *threat is a major unfavorable situation in a firm's environment.* Threats are key impediments to the firm's current or desired position. The entrance of new competitors, slow market growth, increased bargaining power of key buyers or suppliers, technological changes, and new or revised regulations could represent threats to a firm's success.

Japanese acceptance of superior U.S. technology in personal computers is proving a major opportunity for Apple and IBM. Deregulation of the airline industry was a major opportunity for regional carriers (such as Southwest Airlines) to serve routes previously closed to them. Some traditional carriers (such as United) saw deregulation as a threat to the profitability of their high-traffic routes. So an opportunity for one firm can be a threat to another. Moreover, the same factor can be seen as both an opportunity and a threat. For example, the baby boom generation moving into its prime earning years presents a major opportunity for financial service firms like Merrill Lynch. However, this generation wants convenient inexpensive financial services, which is a major threat to Merrill Lynch's established broker network.[1]

Understanding the key opportunities and threats facing a firm helps its managers identify realistic options from which to choose an appropriate strategy and clarifies the most effective niche for the firm.

The second fundamental focus in SWOT analysis is the identification of internal strengths and weaknesses. These can be defined as follows:

---

[1] "Charles Schwab Corp.," *Forbes,* February 3, 1992, pp. 82–84.

Strengths

A *strength is a resource, skill, or other advantage* relative to competitors and the needs of the markets a firm serves or expects to serve. It is *a distinctive competence* when it gives the firm a comparative advantage in the marketplace. Strengths may exist with regard to financial resources, image, market leadership, buyer-supplier relations, and other factors.

Weaknesses

A *weakness is a limitation or deficiency in resource, skills, and capabilities* that seriously impedes a firm's effective performance. Facilities, financial resources, management capabilities, marketing skills, and brand image can be sources of weaknesses.

The sheer size and level of IBM's customer acceptance proved to be key strengths on which it built its initially successful strategy in the personal computer market. Limited financial capacity was a weakness recognized by Southwest Airlines, which has charted a selective route expansion strategy to build the best profit record in a deregulated airline industry.[2] Global Strategy in Action 6–1 uses the Japanese entry into the U.S. personal computer market to illustrate the basic elements of a SWOT analysis.

SWOT analysis can be used in many ways to aid strategy analysis. The most common way is to use it as a logical framework guiding systematic discussion of a firm's situation and the basic alternatives that the firm might consider. What one manager sees as an opportunity, another may see as a potential threat. Likewise, a strength to one manager may be a weakness to another. Different assessments may reflect underlying power considerations within the firm or differing factual perspectives. The key point is that systematic SWOT analysis ranges across all aspects of a firm's situation. As a result, it provides a dynamic and useful framework for strategic analysis.

A second way in which SWOT analysis can be used to aid strategic analysis is illustrated in Figure 6–2. Key external opportunities and threats are systematically compared with internal strengths and weaknesses in a structured approach. The objective is identification of one of four distinct patterns in the match between a firm's internal and external situations. These patterns are represented by the four cells in Figure 6–2. Cell 1 is the most favorable situation; the firm faces several environmental opportunities and has numerous strengths that encourage pursuit of those opportunities. This situation suggests growth-oriented strategies to exploit the favorable match. Apple's intensive market development strategy in the personal computer market was the result of a favorable match between strengths in reputation and resources and an opportunity for impressive market growth. Cell 4 is the least-favorable situation, with the firm facing major environmental threats from a position of relative weakness. This situation clearly calls for strategies that reduce or redirect involvement in the products or markets examined by means of SWOT analysis. Citicorp's successful turnaround from the verge of insolvency, due to massive defaults on many international loans, is an example of such a strategy in the early 1990s.[3]

In cell 2, a firm with key strengths faces an unfavorable environment. In this situation, strategies would use current strengths to build long-term opportunities in other products-

---

[2] "Striking Gold in the California Skies," *Business Week,* March 30, 1992, p. 48.

[3] "Is the Worst over for Citi?" *Forbes,* May 11, 1992, p. 42.

GLOBAL
STRATEGY IN
ACTION 6–1

USING SWOT ANALYSIS TO UNDERSTAND THE JAPANESE FAILURE IN THE U.S. PERSONAL COMPUTER MARKET

The opportunity was significant: a market for PCs in the United States expected to purchase over 3.5 million units annually through most of the 1990s. The threats were there—IBM and Apple, among others. But after using its manufacturing prowess to corner the market for memory chips in the 1980s, conventional wisdom had it that the Japanese would leverage their advantage in components to beat the United States in personal computers. Besides memory chip strength, Japanese companies also monopolized screen technology and were major suppliers of disk drives. Their conclusion: PCs would go the way of VCRs and become Japanese products in the early 1990s. What happened?

"We've never been able to break into that top tier," admits Richard Miller, marketing VP of the U.S. subsidiary of Japanese computer giant NEC Corporation. While spending over $15 million in each of the last 10 years to lure U.S. consumers, NEC sold only about 260,000 PCs in the United States in 1991. That's less than a fifth as many PCs as were sold by either IBM or Apple. "They were the IBM of Japan, and they thought that in two years they'd be number two here," said Avery More, CEO of a large, Dallas-based computer dealer. "That aspiration crashed against the hard wall of reality."

The *reality* Mr. More refers to includes weaknesses and threats that were not taken into account in the ill-fated Japanese PC invasion. They include:

1. NEC assumed it could sell proprietary Japanese computers when almost all buyers in the United States wanted machines compatible with IBM PCs. "They thought IBM should be NEC-compatible," said Miller.

2. The United States still controls critical pieces of technology, particularly Intel's microprocessors and Microsoft's MS-DOS operating systems. And Intel speeded up its introduction of new processors, making new products obsolete in six to nine months.

3. NEC was first with a notebook computer (Ultralite), but Compaq came out with a laptop that included a floppy drive versus NEC's semiconductor memory cards. "By the time we were shipping, Compaq had a better widget," recalls Miller. "Any remaining momentum was lost because memory chips became scarce. It was ironic. NEC is the largest semiconductor manufacturer in the world, but we couldn't get enough memory chips because NEC Japan had a customer base to worry about."

4. Marketing was as important as product quality. "Product definition is just as crucial as having high-quality components," observed Safi Qureshey, CEO and cofounder of AST Research. "You have to know how to package your components in a viable product."

The bottomline: NEC Japan viewed strengths that had worked in other U.S. forays (semiconductors and VCRs) as applicable in the U.S. PC market. Key threats represented by the product quality and capabilities of IBM and Apple were underestimated; and the critical weaknesses in terms of NEC's operating systems software and its time required for product change were underestimated or undetected.

Source: "The Invasion That Failed," *Forbes*, January 20, 1992, p. 102.

markets. Greyhound, possessing many strengths in intercity bus transportation, still faced an environment dominated by fundamental, long-term threats, such as airline competition and high costs. The result was product development into nonpassenger (freight) services,

FIGURE 6–2
SWOT Analysis Diagram

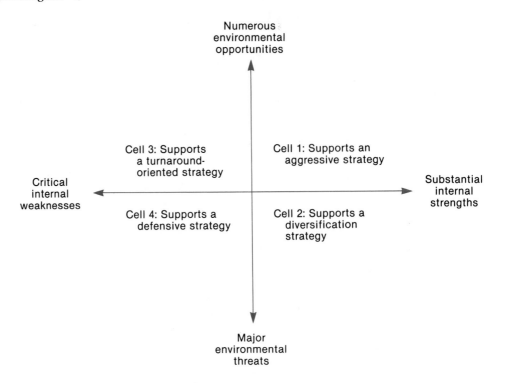

followed by diversification into other businesses (e.g., financial services). A firm in cell 3 faces impressive market opportunity but is constrained by internal weaknesses. The focus of strategy for such a firm is eliminating the internal weaknesses so as to more effectively pursue the market opportunity. Apple's historic 1992 strategic alliance with IBM was an attempt to overcome key weaknesses undergirding its technology-based strategy to pursue global opportunities in the microcomputer industry of the 21st century.

Overall, SWOT analysis highlights the central role that the identification of internal strengths and weaknesses plays in a manager's search for effective strategies. The careful matching of a firm's opportunities and threats with its strengths and weaknesses is the essence of sound strategy formulation.

Although SWOT analysis highlights the role of internal analysis in identifying sound strategies, it does not explain how managers identify internal strengths and weaknesses. The next section explains the process of internal analysis.

VIEWING INTERNAL ANALYSIS AS A PROCESS

Figure 6–3 diagrams the development of a company profile as a four-step process that you should find useful in guiding internal analysis.

FIGURE 6–3
Steps in the Development of a Company Profile*

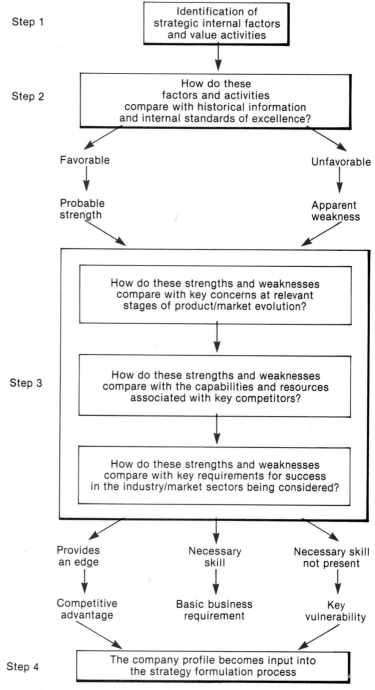

Step 1

Identification of
strategic internal factors
and value activities

Step 2

How do these
factors and activities
compare with historical information
and internal standards of excellence?

Favorable

Unfavorable

Probable
strength

Apparent
weakness

Step 3

How do these strengths and weaknesses
compare with key concerns at relevant
stages of product/market evolution?

How do these strengths and weaknesses
compare with the capabilities and resources
associated with key competitors?

How do these strengths and weaknesses
compare with key requirements for success
in the industry/market sectors being considered?

Provides
an edge

Necessary
skill

Necessary skill
not present

Competitive
advantage

Basic business
requirement

Key
vulnerability

Step 4

The company profile becomes input into
the strategy formulation process

* The work of Leslie Rue and Phyllis Holland, *Strategic Management* (New York: McGraw-Hill, 1989), p. 133, provided an important foundation for the portrayal of these steps.

In step 1, managers examine key aspects of the firm's operation, targeting key areas for further assessment. The areas targeted are those deemed central to the firm's strategic direction. As such, they are called *strategic internal factors.*

In step 2, managers evaluate the firm's status on these factors by comparing their current condition with their past condition. This is where most managers start their planning efforts. How do we compare with last year? Have we improved over the last year? Are we better able to do things this year than we were last year? Does the condition of the strategic internal factors represent a favorable or an unfavorable situation?

The third step is very critical. In this step, managers seek some comparative basis—linked to key industry-market or product-market conditions—against which to more accurately determine whether the condition of a strategic internal factor represents a potential strength or a potential weakness. Managers use three perspectives to do this: (1) the key requirements for success at the relevant stages of product-market evolution, (2) the capabilities of key competitors, and (3) the key requirements for success in the industry-market sectors being considered.

The third step should result in a determination of whether the strategic internal factors are:

   a. Competitive advantages—factors that provide the firm with a competitive edge and are, therefore, factors around which the firm's strategy should be built.
   b. Basic business requirements—factors that are important capabilities of both the firm and its competitors and, therefore, do not represent a potential source of strategic advantage.
   c. Key vulnerabilities—factors on which the firm currently lacks the skill, knowledge, or resources needed to compete effectively. Managers will want to avoid strategies that depend on such factors, and they will usually target these factors as areas requiring remediation.

In the final step, the company profile that results from the earlier steps becomes input into the strategic management process. This input is vital during the early, strategy formulation phase in the strategic management process.

Step 1: Identification of Strategic Internal Factors

What are the firm's specific internal factors? How and where do they originate? How do we decide which of them must be carefully evaluated? These are questions that managers might consider as they identify a firm's key internal factors as strengths or weaknesses and as possible bases for the firm's future strategy.

A Function Approach

Key internal factors are a firm's basic capabilities, limitations, and characteristics. Figure 6–4 lists typical factors of this kind, some of which would be the focus of internal analysis in most firms. The list is broken along functional lines.

Firms are not likely to evaluate all of the factors listed in Figure 6–4 as potential strengths or weaknesses. To develop or revise a strategy, managers would prefer to identify the few factors on which its success is most likely to depend. Equally important, a firm's reliance on particular internal factors will vary by industry, market segment, product life

FIGURE 6–4
Key Internal Factors: Potential Strengths or Weaknesses

Marketing

Firm's products-services: breadth of product line.
Concentration of sales in a few products or to a few customers.
Ability to gather needed information about markets.
Market share or submarket shares.
Product-service mix and expansion potential: life cycle of key products; profit-sales balance in product-service.
Channels of distribution: number, coverage, and control.
Effective sales organization; knowledge of customer needs.
Product-service image, reputation, and quality.
Imaginativeness, efficiency, and effectiveness of sales promotion and advertising.
Pricing strategy and pricing flexibility.
Procedures for digesting market feedback and developing new products, services, or markets.
After-sale service and follow-up.
Goodwill–brand loyalty.

Financial and Accounting

Ability to raise short-term capital.
Ability to raise long-term capital; debt-equity.
Corporate-level resources (multibusiness firm).
Cost of capital relative to that of industry and competitors.
Tax considerations.
Relations with owners, investors, and stockholders.
Leverage position; capacity to utilize alternative financial strategies, such as lease or sale and leaseback.
Cost of entry and barriers to entry.
Price-earnings ratio.
Working capital; flexibility of capital structure.
Effective cost control; ability to reduce cost.
Financial size.
Efficiency and effectiveness of accounting system for cost, budget, and profit planning.

Production, Operations, Technical

Raw materials cost and availability, supplier relationships.
Inventory control systems; inventory turnover.
Location of facilities; layout and utilization of facilities.
Economies of scale.
Technical efficiency of facilities and utilization of capacity.
Effectiveness of subcontracting use.
Degree of vertical integration; value added and profit margin.

cycle, and the firm's current position. Managers are looking for what Chester Barnard calls "the "strategic factors," those internal capabilities that are most critical for success in a particular competitive area. The strategic factors of firms in the oil industry, for example, will be quite different from those of firms in the construction industry or the hospitality industry. Strategic factors also can vary among firms within the same industry. In the mechanical writing industry, for example, the strategies of BIC and Cross, both successful firms, are based on different internal strengths; BIC's on its strength in mass production, extensive advertising, and mass distribution channels; Cross's on high quality, image, and selective distribution channels.

Strategists examine a firm's past performance to isolate key internal contributors to favorable (or unfavorable) results. What did we do well, or poorly, in marketing, operations,

---

FIGURE 6–4   (concluded)

Efficiency and cost-benefit of equipment.
Effectiveness of operation control procedures: design, scheduling, purchasing, quality control, and
  efficiency.
Costs and technological competences relative to those of industry and competitors.
Research and development–technology–innovation.
Patents, trademarks, and similar legal protection.

Personnel

Management personnel.
Employees' skill and morale.
Labor relations costs compared to those of industry and competitors.
Efficiency and effectiveness of personnel policies.
Effectiveness of incentives used to motivate performance.
Ability to level peaks and valleys of employment.
Employee turnover and absenteeism.
Specialized skills.
Experience.

Quality Management

Relationship with suppliers, customers.
Internal practices to enhance quality of products and services.
Procedures for monitoring quality.

Information Systems

Timeliness and accuracy of information about sales, operations, cash, and suppliers.
Relevance of information for tactical decisions.
Information to manage quality issues; customer service.
Ability of people to use the information that is provided.

Organization and General Management

Organizational structure.
Firm's image and prestige.
Firm's record in achieving objectives.
Organization of communication system.
Overall organizational control system (effectiveness and utilization).
Organizational climate; organizational culture.
Use of systematic procedures and techniques in decision making.
Top-management skill, capabilities, and interest.
Strategic planning system.
Intraorganizational synergy (multibusiness firms).

---

and financial management that had a major influence on our past results? Was our sales force effectively organized? Were we in the right channels of distribution? Did we have the financial resources needed to support our past strategy? The same examination can be applied to a firm's current situation, with particular emphasis on changes in the importance of key dimensions over time. For example, heavy advertising, mass production, and mass distribution were strategic internal factors in BIC's initial strategy for ballpoint pens and disposable lighters. With the product life cycle fast reaching maturity, BIC later determined that cost-conscious mass production was a strategic factor, whereas heavy advertising was not.

Analysis of past trends in a firm's sales, costs, and profitability is of major importance in identifying its strategic internal factors. And that identification should be based on a clear picture of the nature of the firm's sales. An anatomy of past sales trends broken down by product lines, channels of distribution, key customers or types of customers, geographic region, and sales approach should be developed in detail. A similar anatomy should be developed on costs and profitability. Detailed investigation of the firm's performance history helps isolate the internal factors that influence its sales, costs, and profitability or their interrelationships. For example, one firm may find that 83 percent of its sales result from 25 percent of its products, and another firm may find that 30 percent of its products (or services) contribute 78 percent of its profitability. On the basis of such results, a firm may determine that certain key internal factors (e.g., experience in particular distribution channels, pricing policies, warehouse location, technology) deserve major attention in the formulation of future strategy.

The identification of strategic internal factors requires an external focus. A strategist's efforts to isolate key internal factors are assisted by analysis of industry conditions and trends and by comparisons with competitors. BIC's identification of mass production and advertising as key internal factors was based as much on analysis of industry and competitive characteristics as on analysis of its own past performance. Changing conditions in an industry can lead to the need to reexamine a firm's internal strengths and weaknesses in light of newly emerging determinants of success in that industry. Furthermore, strategic internal factors are often evaluated in depth because firms are contemplating expansion of products or markets, diversification, and so forth. Clearly, scrutinizing the industry under consideration and potential competitors is a key means of identifying strategic factors if a firm is evaluating its capability to move into an unfamiliar market.

The "Value Chain" Approach

Diagnosing a firm's key strengths and weaknesses is often easier when you adopt a disaggregated view of the firm. Examining the firm across distinct functional areas, as suggested above and in Figure 6–4, is one way to disaggregate the firm for purposes of internal analysis. Another way is to use the "value chain" approach. Developed by Michael Porter in his book *Competitive Advantage,* this approach is a way of systematically viewing the series of activities a firm performs to provide its customers with a product.[4] Figure 6–5 diagrams a typical value chain. The value chain disaggregates a firm into its strategically important activities to understand the behavior of the firm's cost and the firm's existing or potential sources of differentiation. A firm gains competitive advantage by performing these strategically important activities—what we have called *key internal factors*—at a lower cost or better than its competitors.

Every firm can be viewed (disaggregated) as a collection of value activities that are performed to design, produce, market, deliver, and support its product. As portrayed in Figure 6–5, these activities can be grouped into nine basic categories for virtually any firm at the business unit level. Within each category, a firm typically performs a number of discrete activities that may represent key strengths or weaknesses. Service activities, for example, may include such discrete activities as installation, repair, parts distribution, and upgrading—any of which could be a major source of competitive advantage or disadvantage. Through the systematic identification of these activities, managers using the value chain approach can target potential strengths and weaknesses for further evaluation.

---

[4] Michael E. Porter, *Competitive Advantage* (New York: Free Press, 1985).

FIGURE 6–5
A Typical Value Chain

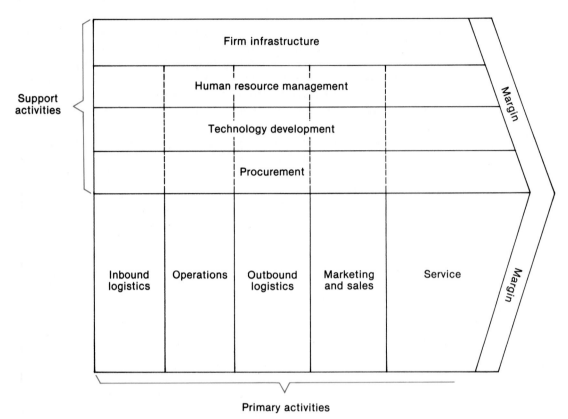

Source: Adapted from Michael E. Porter, *Competitive Advantage* (New York: Free Press, 1985).

The basic categories of activities can be grouped into two broad types. *Primary* activities are those involved in the physical creation, marketing, delivery, and after-sale support of the firm's product or service. Overarching all of these activities are *support* activities, which provide infrastructure or inputs that allow them to take place on an ongoing basis.

Identifying Primary Activities   Identifying primary value activities requires the isolation of activities that are technologically and strategically distinct. Each of the five basic categories of primary activities is divisible into a number of distinct activities, such as the following:[5]

Inbound Logistics   Activities associated with receiving, storing, and disseminating inputs to the product, such as material handling, warehousing, inventory control, vehicle scheduling, and returns to suppliers.

---

[5] Ibid.

Operations   Activities associated with transforming inputs into the final product form, such as machining, packaging, assembly, equipment maintenance, testing, printing, and facility operations.

Outbound Logistics   Activities associated with collecting, storing, and physically distributing the product to buyers, such as finished goods warehousing, material handling, delivery vehicle operation, order processing, and scheduling.

Marketing and Sales   Activities associated with providing a means by which buyers can purchase the product and inducing them to do so, such as advertising, promotion, sales force quoting, channel selection, channel relations, and pricing.

Service   Activities associated with providing service to enhance or maintain the value of the product, such as installation, repair, training, parts supply, and product adjustment.

The primary activities most deserving of further analysis depend on that particular industry. For example, Holiday Inns may be much more concerned about operations activities—it provides its service instantaneously at each location—and marketing-sales activities than about outbound logistics. For a distributor, such as the food distributor PYA, inbound and outbound logistics are the most critical areas. After-sale service is becoming increasingly critical to automotive dealerships. In any firm, however, all of the primary activities are present to some degree and deserve attention in a systematic internal analysis.

Identifying Support Activities   Support value activities arise in one of four categories and can be identified or disaggregated by isolating technologically or strategically distinct activities. Often overlooked as sources of competitive advantage, these four categories can typically be distinguished as follows:[6]

Procurement   Activities involved in obtaining purchased inputs—raw materials, purchased services, machinery, and so on. Procurement stretches across the entire value chain because it supports every activity—every activity uses purchased inputs of some kind. Many discrete procurement activities are typically performed within a firm, often by different people.

Technology Development   Activities involved in designing the product as well as in creating and improving the ways in which the various activities in the value chain are performed. We tend to think of technology in terms of the product or manufacturing process. In fact, every activity a firm performs involves a technology or technologies, which may be mundane or sophisticated, and every firm has a stock of know-how for performing each of these activities. Technology development typically involves a variety of discrete activities, some of which are performed outside the R&D department.

Human Resource Management   Activities necessary to ensure the recruiting, training, and development of personnel. Every activity involves human resources, and thus human resource management activities cut across the entire value chain.

---

[6] Michael E. Porter, "Changing Pattern of International Competition," *California Management Review,* Winter 1986, p. 14.

STRATEGY **THE GAP: SPECTACULAR RETAILING SUCCESS**
IN ACTION **VIA THE VALUE CHAIN APPROACH**
6–1

I n 1992, Melvin Jacobs, chairman of the New York-based Saks Fifth Avenue, observed: "The Gap is a huge success, while retailers around the world are struggling like crazy." Dean Witter analyst Donald Trott says The Gap could hit 2,000 stores and $5 billion in sales by 1995— an impressive accomplishment for what will be its 25th birthday after a one-store start in San Francisco. While The Gap was a 1992 Wall Street darling seeing its stock rise from $4 per share to $52 in three years, president Mickey Drexler says, "We've been doing the same thing for seven or eight years. This company is no overnight success."

What Drexler and founder Donald Fisher did was apply a type of value chain look at specialty retail clothing to identify key value activities around which they could build a long-term competitive advantage. They identified four components of the value chain within which they saw the opportunity to create new, value-added approaches that could become sustained competitive advantages.

1.   PROCUREMENT

Drexler's concept for The Gap was and is: simple, quality, and comfort. Gap's designers are told to design clothes they themselves would wear, to guide their search for merchandise. At an early 1992 meeting in San Francisco, about 30 merchandisers were showing their proposed fall collection for GapKids to Drexler and his staff. The woman in charge of jackets held up a hooded designed coat. After viewing it, Drexler's reaction: "I hate it." A loud cheer among the staff goes up—the New York designers were pushing the item, but The Gap staff found it ugly.

The Gap staff members feel their strong involvement in clothing design choices, rather than the usual reliance of New York or Dallas merchandisers, is a distinct advantage. The Gap designs its own clothes, chooses its own material, and monitors manufacturing so closely that it can keep quality high and costs low.

2.   INBOUND LOGISTICS

The Gap has over 200 quality-control inspectors working inside factories in 40 countries to make sure specifications are met right from the start. Like Wal-Mart, The Gap has computerized, highly automated, carefully located distribution centers serving as hubs directly linked to store groupings. For example, a $75 million automated distribution center opened in 1992 outside

Source: The Gap annual reports, 1991 and 1992; "The Gap," *Business Week,* March 9, 1992, p. 58.

Firm Infrastructure   Such activities as general management, accounting, legal, finance, and strategic planning and all others that are decoupled from specific primary or support activities but are essential to the operation of the entire value chain.

Using the Value Chain in Internal Analysis   The value chain approach provides a useful means for guiding a systematic internal analysis of the firm's existing or potential strengths and weaknesses. By systematically disaggregating a firm into its distinct value activities

STRATEGY
IN ACTION concluded
6–1

Baltimore, allowing The Gap to supply New York City stores daily instead of three times a week. Few in specialty retailing can match this logistical capability.

3. OPERATIONS

Every Gap store is the same—a clean, well-lighted place where harried consumers can shop easily and quickly. Every detail is fussed over, from cleaning the store's floors to rounding the counter corners at GapKids for safety's sake to the detailed instructions on where to display clothes and touching up white walls weekly and polishing wood floors every three days. Already in 700 of the U.S. 1,500 largest malls, it lowers operating cost long term by taking advantage of the 1991–92 recession's impact by locking up sweet-lease deals, moving into downtowns and urban neighborhoods, and opening new stores on the declining main streets of midsized cities. Each of these operational activities ensures higher quality, ease of management, and sustained lower costs.

4. HUMAN RESOURCE MANAGEMENT

In an industry that is low base pay and commission-based, The Gap salespeople receive no commission. But compensation exceeds the industry average. The Gap's COO motivates salespeople with constant contests. The most multiple purchases to the register in one day wins a Gap-logo watch. The Thanksgiving weekend rush saw COO O'Donnell have Pizza Hut and Domino's deliver 15,000 pizzas and 72,000 Pepsis to store personnel on the job. And The Gap's training program is detailed and rigorous before you are free to "work the floor." Again, The Gap pursues policies that differentiate it from current industry practices in a way that adds incremental value—well trained, fairly compensated, highly motivated store personnel, resulting in lower turnover costs and a favorable image for service-leary retail shoppers.

Drexler and Fisher have driven The Gap's success in these and many other ways. But disaggregating specialty clothing retailing into distinct activities in order to better understand their costs and sources of differentiation has led them to design unique approaches (described above) in four strategically important activities that created sustained competitive advantages through lower costs, higher quality, and clear differentiation from all other clothing retailers.

across the nine activity categories, the strategist is able to identify key internal factors for further examination as potential sources of competitive advantage. Strategy in Action 6–1 describes how a value chain analysis helped chart "The Gap's" success in   the 1990s.

Whether using the value chain approach or an examination of functional areas, or both approaches, the strategist's next step in a systematic internal analysis is to compare the firm's status with meaningful standards to determine which of its value activities are strengths or weaknesses. Four sources of meaningful standards for evaluating internal factors and value activities are discussed in the next section.

Steps 2 and 3: Evaluation of Strategic Internal Factors

Identification and evaluation of key internal factors have been separated for discussion, but in practice they are not separate and distinct steps. The objective of internal analysis is to carefully determine a firm's strategic strengths and weaknesses. An internal analysis that generates a long list of resources and capabilities is of little help in strategy formulation. Instead, internal analysis must identify and evaluate a limited number of strengths and weaknesses relative to the opportunities targeted in the firm's current and future competitive environment.

What are potential strengths and weaknesses? A factor is considered a strength if it is a distinctive competence or competitive advantage. It is more than merely what the firm has the competence to do. It is something the firm does (or has the capacity to do) particularly well, relative to the abilities of existing or potential competitors. A distinctive competence (strength) is important, because it gives a firm a comparative advantage in the marketplace. For example, Apple's Macintosh computer and its publishing software were two of its distinctive competences.

A factor is considered a weakness if it is something the firm does poorly or lacks the capacity to do although key competitors have that capacity. IBM's entrenched mainframe computer culture and its large, decentralized sales organization were strengths that have become major weaknesses in its efforts to compete with Apple in the PC industry of the 21st century.

There are four basic perspectives strategists should use in evaluating strategic internal factors: (1) comparison with the firm's past performance, (2) stage of industry evolution, (3) comparison with competitors, and (4) comparison with key success factors in the firm's industry.

Comparison with Past Performance

Strategists use the firm's historical experience as a basis for evaluating internal factors. Managers are most familiar with the internal capabilities and problems of their firm because they have been immersed in its financial, marketing, production, and R&D activities. Not surprisingly, a manager's assessment of whether a certain internal factor—such as production facilities, sales organization, financial capacity, control systems, or key personnel—is a strength or a weakness will be strongly influenced by his or her experience in connection with that factor. In the capital-intensive airline industry, for example, debt capacity is a strategic internal factor. Delta Airlines managers view Delta's debt-equity ratio of less than 0.6, which is comparable to its past debt-equity ratio, as a continued strength, representing significant flexibility for supporting decisions to invest in facilities or equipment. American Airlines managers, on the other hand, view American's much higher 1.8 debt-equity ratio as a growing strength, because it is down 50 percent from its 3.5 level five years earlier.

Although historical experience can provide a relevant evaluation framework, strategists must avoid tunnel vision in making use of it. Japan's NEC, the Japanese IBM, has dominated the Japanese PC market with a 70 percent market share using a proprietary hardware system, much higher screen resolution, powerful distribution channels, and a large software library from third-party vendors. Far from worried, Hajime Ikeda, manager of NEC's planning division, said recently: "We don't hear complaints from our users." But

FIGURE 6–6
Sources of Distinctive Competence at Different Stages of Industry Evolution

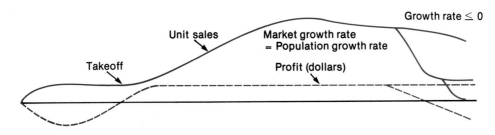

Functional Area	Introduction	Growth	Maturity	Decline
Marketing	Resources/skills to create widespread awareness and find acceptance from customers; advantageous access to distribution	Ability to establish brand recognition, find niche, reduce price, solidify, strong distribution relations, and develop new channels	Skills in aggressively promoting products to new markets and holding existing markets; pricing flexibility; skills in differentiating products and holding customer loyalty	Cost-effective means of efficient access to selected channels and markets; strong customer loyalty or dependence; strong company image
Production operations	Ability to expand capacity effectively, limit number of designs, develop standards	Ability to add product variants, centralize production, or otherwise lower costs; ability to improve product quality; seasonal subcontracting capacity	Ability to improve product and reduce costs; ability to share or reduce capacity; advantageous supplier relationships; subcontracting	Ability to prune product line; cost advantage in production, location or distribution; simplified inventory control; subcontracting or long production runs
Finance	Resources to support high net cash overflow and initial losses; ability to use leverage effectively	Ability to finance rapid expansion, to have net cash outflows but increasing profits; resources to support product improvements	Ability to generate and redistribute increasing net cash inflows; effective cost control systems	Ability to reuse or liquidate unneeded equipment; advantage in cost of facilities; control system accuracy; streamlined management control
Personnel	Flexibility in staffing and training new management; existence of employees with key skills in new products or markets	Existence of and ability to add skilled personnel; motivated and loyal work force	Ability to cost effectively, reduce work force, increase efficiency	Capacity to reduce and reallocate personnel; cost advantage

(continued)

FIGURE 6–6 (concluded)

Functional Area	Introduction	Growth	Maturity	Decline
Engineering and research and development	Ability to make engineering changes, have technical bugs in product and process resolved	Skill in quality and new feature development; ability to start developing successor product	Ability to reduce costs, develop variants, differentiate products	Ability to support other grown areas or to apply product to unique customer needs
Key functional area and strategy focus	Engineering; market penetration	Sales; consumer loyalty; market share	Production efficiency; successor products	Finance; maximum investment recovery

Source: Adapted from Peter Doyle, "The Realities of the Product Life Cycle," *Quarterly Review of Marketing,* Summer 1976, pp. 1–6; Harold Fox, "A Framework for Functional Coordination," *Atlantic Economic Review,* November–December 1973; Charles W. Hofer, *Conceptual Constructs for Formulating Corporate and Business Strategy* (Boston: Intercollegiate Case Clearing House, 1977), p. 7; Philip Kotler, *Marketing Management* (Englewood Cliffs, N. J.: Prentice Hall, 1988); and Charles Wasson, *Dynamic Competitive Strategy and Product Life Cycles* (Austin, Tex.: Austin Press, 1978).

in 1992, the IBM-PC and Macintosh have started filling shelves in Japan's famous consumer electronics district, Akihabara. Hiroki Kamata, president of a Japanese computer research firm, predicts the Japanese PC market will be worth over $15 billion in 1995, with Apple and IBM compatibles each having more market share than NEC because of better technology, software, and the restrictions created by NEC's proprietary technology.[7] Clearly, using only historical experience as a basis for identifying strengths and weaknesses can prove dangerously inaccurate.

Stage of Industry Evolution

The requirements for success in industry segments change over time. Strategists can use these changing requirements, which are associated with different stages of industry evolution, as a framework for identifying and evaluating the firm's strengths and weaknesses.

Figure 6–6 depicts four stages of industry evolution and the typical changes in functional capabilities that are often associated with business success at each of these stages. The early development of a product-market, for example, entails minimal growth in sales, major R&D emphasis, rapid technological change in the product, operating losses, and a need for sufficient resources or slack to support a temporarily unprofitable operation. Success at this introduction stage may be associated with technical skill, with being first in new markets, or with having a marketing advantage that creates widespread awareness. Radio Shack's initial success with its TRS–80 home computer was based in part on its ability to gain widespread exposure and acceptance in the ill-defined home computer market via the large number of existing Radio Shack outlets throughout the country.

The strengths necessary for success change in the growth stage. Rapid growth brings new competitors into the product-market. At this stage, such factors as brand recognition, industry differentiation, and the financial resources to support both heavy marketing

---

[7] "A message for Akihabara," *Forbes,* June 8, 1992, p. 42.

expenses and the effect of price competition on cash flow can be key strengths. IBM entered the personal computer market in the growth stage and was able to rapidly become the market leader with a strategy based on its key strengths in brand awareness and possession of the financial resources needed to support consumer advertising.

As the industry moves through a shakeout phase and into the maturity stage, industry growth continues, but at a decreasing rate. The number of industry segments expands, but technological change in product design slows considerably. As a result, competition usually becomes more intense, and promotional or pricing advantages and differentiation become key internal strengths. Technological change in process design becomes intense as the many competitors seek to provide the product in the most efficient manner. Where R&D was critical in the introduction stage, efficient production is now crucial to continued success in the broader industry segments. Ford's emphasis on quality control and modern, efficient production has helped it prosper in the maturing U.S. auto industry, while General Motors, which pays almost 50 percent more than Ford to produce a comparable car, continues to decline.

When the industry moves into the decline stage, strengths and weaknesses center on cost advantages, superior supplier or customer relationships, and financial control. Competitive advantage can exist at this stage, at least temporarily, if a firm serves gradually shrinking markets that competitors are choosing to leave.

Figure 6–6 is a rather simple model of the stages of industry evolution. These stages can and do vary from the model. What should be borne in mind is that the relative importance of various determinants of success differs across the stages of industry evolution. Thus, the state of that evolution must be considered in internal analysis. Figure 6–6 suggests dimensions that are particularly deserving of in-depth consideration when a company profile is being developed.

Comparison with Competitors

A major focus in determining a firm's strengths and weaknesses is comparison with existing (and potential) competitors. Firms in the same industry often have different marketing skills, financial resources, operating facilities and locations, technical know-how, brand images, levels of integration, managerial talent, and so on. These different internal capabilities can become relative strengths (or weaknesses) depending on the strategy a firm chooses. In choosing a strategy, managers should compare the firm's key internal capabilities with those of its rivals, thereby isolating its key strengths and weaknesses.[8]

In the home appliance industry, for example, Sears and General Electric are major rivals. Sears' principal strength is its retail network. For GE, distribution—through independent franchised dealers—has traditionally been a relative weakness. GE's possession of the financial resources needed to support modernized mass production has enabled it to maintain both cost and technological advantages over its rivals, particularly Sears. This major strength for GE is a relative weakness for Sears, which depends solely on subcon-

---

[8] Michael E. Porter, *Competitive Strategy: Techniques for Analyzing Industries and Competitors* (New York: Free Press, 1980), offers broad, in-depth coverage of numerous techniques for evaluating the strengths and weaknesses of a firm and its competitors. Chapter 7 presents key aspects underlying Professor Porter's analytical approaches.

GLOBAL
STRATEGY IN
ACTION 6–2

SAS USES COMPETITOR COMPARISON TO IDENTIFY ITS STRENGTHS AND WEAKNESSES FOR EUROPE: 1992

For many years, Scandinavian Airline System (SAS) was a premier European airline. Benefiting from International Airline Transportation Association (IATA), a protective European airline industry trade organization, SAS was profitable for 17 straight years. But changes in the global air-

We've got some tough competition. Like the "street fighters" from the rough-and-tumble American domestic

market. Efficient. In shape. Like Delta...

Or European companies which have pursued more consistent and purposeful policies than we have.

And who keep making money, hard times or not.

tracting to produce its Kenmore appliances. On the other hand, maintenance and repair service are important in the appliance industry. Historically, Sears has had strength in this area because it maintains fully staffed service components and spreads the costs of components over numerous departments at each retail location. GE, on the other hand, has had to depend on regional service centers and on local contracting with independent service firms by its independent local dealers.

Among the internal factors that Sears and GE must consider in developing a strategy are distribution network, technological capabilities, operating costs, and service facilities.

GLOBAL STRATEGY IN ACTION 6–2 **concluded**

line industry caused its earnings to plummet in the last few years. When SAS was on the verge of folding, its new CEO undertook an extensive competitor comparison as a basis for finding a strategy to turn it around. The CEO shared the following assessment in an employee pamphlet communicating the firm's new strategy and rationale behind it.

Look at the Differences:

Key figures*	Swissair International	SAS International
Cabin Factor	63.6	59.3
Load Factor	59.2	47.6
Passenger revenue (USD)/RPK	0.09	0.08
Cargo revenue (USD)/RFTK	0.37	0.31
Total revenue (USD)/RTK	0.79	0.73
Operating cost (USD)/ATK	0.45	0.42
Revenue-Cost Relationship (Over 100-profit)	103.5	99.7
Average flight leg/km	1051	967

Delta Has:

40% more revenue tonne-kms per employee

120% more passengers per employee

14% more available tonne-kms per pilot

40% more passenger-kms per cabin attendant

35% more passenger-kms per passenger sales employee

It is difficult to make similar comparisons in the technical and maintenance fields, but even in these areas Delta has a substantially higher productivity than SAS.

* USD—U.S. Dollars, RPK—Revenue Passenger-kilometers, RFTK—Revenue Freight Tonne-kilometers, RTK—Revenue Tonne-kilometers, ATK—Available Tonne-kilometers. Exchange rate: one USD—4.65 Swedish kronor.

Comparison with key competitors can prove useful in ascertaining whether their internal capabilities on these and other factors are strengths or weaknesses. Significant favorable differences (existing or expected) from competitors are potential cornerstones of a firm's strategy. Moreover, through comparison with major competitors, a firm may avoid strategic commitments that it cannot competitively support. Global Strategy in Action 6–2 shows how the Scandinavian Airline System (SAS) used competitor comparison to assess its strengths and weaknesses in the global airline industry.

Comparison with Success Factors in the Industry

Industry analysis (see Chapter 3) involves identifying the factors associated with successful participation in a given industry. As was true for the evaluation methods discussed above, the key determinants of success in an industry may be used to identify a firm's internal strengths and weaknesses. By scrutinizing industry competitors, as well as customer needs, vertical industry structure, channels of distribution, costs, barriers to entry, availability of substitutes, and suppliers, a strategist seeks to determine whether a firm's current internal capabilities represent strengths or weaknesses in new competitive arenas. The discussion in Chapter 3 provides a useful framework—five industry forces—against which to examine a firm's potential strengths and weaknesses. General Cinema Corporation, the largest U.S. movie theater operator, determined that its internal skills in marketing, site analysis, creative financing, and management of geographically dispersed operations were key strengths relative to major success factors in the soft-drink bottling industry. This assessment proved accurate. Within 10 years after it entered the soft-drink bottling industry, General Cinema became the largest franchised bottler of soft drinks in the United States, handling Pepsi, 7UP, Dr Pepper, and Sunkist.

The use of industry-level analysis to evaluate a firm's capacity for success and to help devise future strategy has become a popular technique. The relevance of this technique to comprehensive internal analysis is discussed more fully in the appendix at the end of this chapter.

The final step in internal analysis is to provide its results—the company profile—as input into the strategic management process. That input is vital during the early, strategy-formulation phase of the process.

While this discussion and Figure 6–3 explain internal analysis in a stepwise fashion, it is important to remember that the steps in the process often overlap. Separating the steps helps explain the process of internal analysis, but efforts to distinguish the steps are seldom emphasized in practice because the process is very interactive.

SUMMARY

This chapter has examined the role and nature of internal analysis as part of the strategic management process. The results of an internal analysis, often called the *company profile,* identify a firm's key strengths and weaknesses. Strengths are factors that represent potential competitive advantages in targeted markets; weaknesses are factors that represent potential competitive disadvantages. These strengths and weaknesses are compared with external opportunities and threats as a basis for generating strategic alternatives—a process that is often called *SWOT analysis.*

The process by which managers identify and assess internal capabilities can be conceptualized as three basic steps. Managers first identify strategic internal factors and value activities. They then compare these factors with historical information and internal standards of excellence. Finally, they use stages of industry evolution, key competitors, and industry success factors to segment strengths and weaknesses into a strategic context for input into the strategy formulation process.

When matched with management's environmental analyses and mission priorities, the process of internal analysis provides the critical foundation for strategy formulation. Armed with an accurate, thorough, and timely internal analysis, managers are in a better position to formulate effective strategies. The next chapter describes basic strategy alternatives that any firm may consider.

QUESTIONS FOR DISCUSSION

1. Describe how key internal factors are identified in a firm's strategic management process. Why does such identification appear to be an important part of the strategic management process?

2. Apply the two broad steps of internal analysis to yourself and your career aspirations. What are your major strengths and weaknesses? How might you use your knowledge of these strengths and weaknesses to develop your future career plans?

3. What changes in internal analysis might Japan's NEC have undertaken to avoid its disappointing results when attempting to enter the U.S. PC market? (Refer to Global Strategy in Action 6–1 for background here.)

4. In what ways do the approaches to internal analysis at The Gap (see Strategy in Action 6–1) and Scandinavian Airline Systems (see Global Strategy in Action 6–2) appear to be similar and different?

BIBLIOGRAPHY

Aaker, David A. "Managing Assets and Skills: The Key to a Sustainable Competitive Advantage." *California Management Review,* Winter 1989, pp. 91–106.

Berman, S. J., and R. F. Kautz. "A Sophisticated Tool That Facilitates Strategic Analysis." *Planning Review* 18, no. 4 (1990), pp. 35–39.

Bukszar, Ed, and Terry Connolly. "Hindsight Bias and Strategy Choice." *Academy of Management Journal,* September 1988, p. 828.

Cvitkovic, Emillo. "Profiling Your Competitors." *Planning Review,* May–June 1989, pp. 28–31.

De Geus, A. P. "Planning as Learning." *Harvard Business Review,* March 1988. pp. 70–74.

Fann, G. L., and L. R. Smittzer. "The Use of Information from and about Competitors in Small Business Management." *Entrepreneurship: Theory and Practice,* Summer 1989, pp. 35–46.

Feinman, B. C. "Sustaining the Competitive Market Advantage." *Planning Review,* May 1989, pp. 30–39.

Fifer, R. M. "Cost Bench Marketing Approach: Functions in Value Chain." *Planning Review,* May 1989, pp. 18–27.

Gale, B. T., and R. D. Buzzel. "Market Perceived Quality: Key Strategic Concept." *Planning Review,* March 1989, pp. 6–15.

Hergert, M., and D. Morris. "Accounting Data for Value Chain Analysis." *Strategic Management Journal,* March 1989, pp. 175–88.

Hinterhuber, H. H., and W. Popp. "Are You a Strategist or Just a Manager?" *Harvard Business Review* 70, no. 1 (1992), pp. 105–13.

Kazanjian, Robert K. "Relation of Dominant Problems to Stages of Growth in Technology-Based New Ventures." *Academy of Management Journal,* September 1988, p. 628.

Langley, A. "The Roles of Formal Strategic Planning." *Long Range Planning,* June 1988, pp. 40–50.

Leigh, T. W. "Competitive Assessment in Service Industries." *Planning Review,* January 1989, pp. 10–19.

Morrisey, George L. "Executive Guide to Strategic Thinking." *Executive Excellence* 7, no. 6 (1990), pp. 5–6.

Porter, Michel E. "From Competitive Advantage to Corporate Strategy." *Harvard Business Review,* May–June 1987, p. 43.

Potts, G. W. "Exploit Your Product's Service Life Cycle." *Harvard Business Review,* September 1988, pp. 32–39.

Prahalad, C. K., and G. Hamel. "The Core Competence of the Corporation." *Harvard Business Review* 68, no. 3 (1990), pp. 79–91.

Quinn, J. B. "Strategic Change: Logical Incrementalism." *Sloan Management Review,* Summer 1989, pp. 45–60.

Schmidt, J. A. "The Strategic Review," *Planning Review,* July 1988, pp. 14–19.

Steiner, M. P., and O. Solem. "Factors for Success in Small Manufacturing Firms." *Journal of Small Business Management,* January 1988, pp. 51–56.

Stoner, Charles R. "Distinctive Competence and Competitive Advantage." *Journal of Small Business Management,* April 1987, p. 33.

APPENDIX

USING FINANCIAL ANALYSIS

One of the most important tools for assessing the strength of an organization within its industry is financial analysis. Managers, investors, and creditors all employ some form of this analysis as the beginning point for their financial decision making. Investors use financial analyses in making decisions about whether to buy or sell stock, and creditors use them in deciding whether or not to lend. They provide managers with a measurement of how the company is doing in comparison with its performance in past years and with the performance of competitors in the industry.

Although financial analysis is useful for decision making, some weaknesses should be noted. Any picture that it provides of the company is based on past data. Although trends may be noteworthy, this picture should not automatically be assumed to be applicable to the future. In addition, the analysis is only as good as the accounting procedures that have provided the information. When making comparisons between companies, one should keep in mind the variability of accounting procedures from firm to firm.

There are four basic groups of financial ratios: liquidity, leverage, activity, and profitability.

Depicted in Exhibit 6–1 are the specific ratios calculated for each of the basic groups. Liquidity and leverage ratios represent an assessment of the risk of the firm. Activity and profitability ratios are measures of the return generated by the assets of the firm. The interaction between certain groups of ratios is indicated by arrows.

Typically, two common financial statements are used in financial analyses: the balance sheet and the income statement. Exhibit 6–2 is a balance sheet and Exhibit 6–3 an income statement for the ABC Company. These statements will be used to illustrate the financial analyses.

LIQUIDITY RATIOS

Liquidity ratios are used as indicators of a firm's ability to meet its short-term obligations. These obligations include any current liabilities, including currently maturing long-term debt. Current assets move through a normal cash cycle of inventories—sales—accounts receivable—cash. The firm then uses cash to pay off or reduce its current liabilities. The best-known liquidity ratio is the current ratio: current assets divided by current liabilities. For the ABC Company, the current ratio is calculated as follows:

Prepared by Elizabeth Gatewood, University of Houston. © Elizabeth Gatewood, 1994. Reprinted by permission of Elizabeth Gatewood.

EXHIBIT 6–1
Financial Ratios

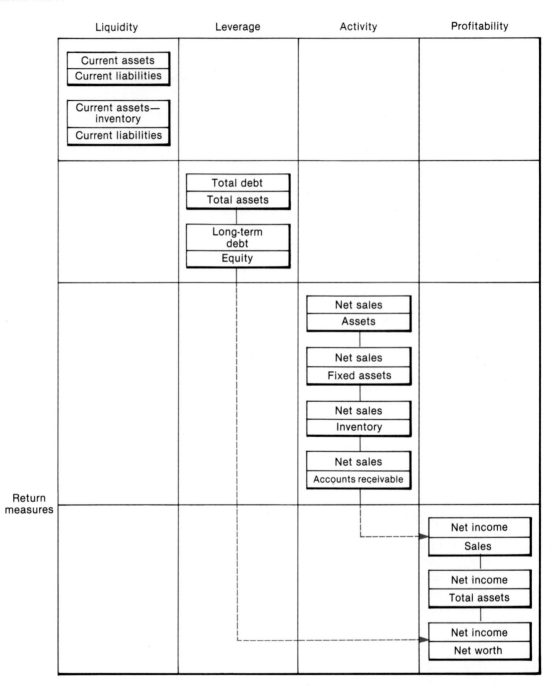

EXHIBIT 6–2

ABC COMPANY
Balance Sheet
As of December 31

		1995		1994
Assets				
Current assets:				
Cash		$ 140,000		$ 115,000
Accounts receivable		1,760,000		1,440,000
Inventory		2,175,000		2,000,000
Prepaid expenses		50,000		63,000
Total current assets		4,125,000		3,618,000
Fixed assets:				
Long-term receivable		1,255,000		1,090,000
Property and plant	$2,037,000		$2,015,000	
Less: Accumulated depreciation	862,000		860.000	
Net property and plant		1,175,000		1,155,000
Other fixed assets		550,000		530,000
Total fixed assets		2,980,000		2,775,000
Total assets		$7,105,000		$6,393,000
Liabilities and Stockholders' Equity				
Current liabilities:				
Accounts payable		$1,325,000		$1,225,000
Bank loans payable		475,000		550,000
Accrued federal taxes		675,000		425,000
Current maturities (long-term debt)		17,500		26,000
Dividends payable		20,000		16,250
Total current liabilities		2,512,500		2,242,250
Long-term liabilities		1,350,000		1,425,000
Total liabilities		3,862,000		3,667,250
Stockholders' equity:				
Common stock (104,046 shares outstanding in 1995; 101,204 shares outstanding in 1994)		44,500		43,300
Additional paid-in capital		568,000		372,450
Retained earnings		2,630,000		2,310,000
Total stockholders' equity		3,242,500		2,725,750
Total liabilities and stockholders' equity		$7,105,000		$6,393,000

EXHIBIT 6–3

ABC COMPANY
Income Statement
For the Years Ending December 31

	1995		1994	
Net sales		$8,250,000		$8,000,000
Cost of goods sold	$5,100,000		$5,000,000	
Administrative expenses	1,750,000		1,680,000	
Other expenses	420,000		390,000	
Total		7,270,000		7,070,000
Earnings before interest and taxes		980,000		930,000
Less: Interest expense		210,000		210,000
Earnings before taxes		770,000		720,000
Less: Federal income taxes		360,000		325,000
Earnings after taxes (net income)		$ 410,000		$ 395,000
Common stock cash dividends		$ 90,000		$ 84,000
Addition to retained earnings		$ 320,000		$ 311,000
Earnings per common share		$ 3.940		$ 3.90
Dividends per common share		$ 0.865		$ 0.83

$$\frac{\text{Current assets}}{\text{Current liabilities}} = \frac{\$4,125,000}{\$2,512,500} = 1.64 \ (1995)$$

$$= \frac{\$3,618,000}{\$2,242,250} = 1.161 \ (1994)$$

Most analysts suggest a current ratio of 2 to 3. A large current ratio is not necessarily a good sign; it may mean that an organization is not making the most efficient use of its assets. The optimum current ratio will vary from industry to industry, with the more volatile industries requiring higher ratios.

Since slow-moving or obsolescent inventories could overstate a firm's ability to meet short-term demands, the quick ratio is sometimes preferred to assess a firm's liquidity. The quick ratio is current assets minus inventories, divided by current liabilities. The quick ratio for the ABC Company is calculated as follows:

$$\frac{\text{Current assets} - \text{Inventories}}{\text{Current liabilities}} = \frac{\$1,950,000}{\$2,512,500} = 0.78 \ (1995)$$

$$= \frac{\$1,618,000}{\$2,242,250} = 0.72 \ (1994)$$

A quick ratio of approximately 1 would be typical for American industries. Although there is less variability in the quick ratio than in the current ratio, stable industries would be able to operate safely with a lower ratio.

LEVERAGE RATIOS

Leverage ratios identify the source of a firm's capital—owners or outside creditors. The term *leverage* refers to the fact that using capital with a fixed interest charge will "amplify" either profits or losses in relation to the equity of holders of common stock. The most commonly used ratio is total debt divided by total assets. Total debt includes current liabilities and long-term liabilities. This ratio is a measure of the percentage of total funds provided by debt. A total debt–total assets ratio higher than 0.5 is usually considered safe only for firms in stable industries.

$$\frac{\text{Total debt}}{\text{Total assets}} = \frac{\$3,862,500}{\$7,105,000} = 0.54 \ (1995)$$

$$= \frac{\$3,667,250}{\$6,393,000} = 0.57 \ (1994)$$

The ratio of long-term debt to equity is a measure of the extent to which sources of long-term financing are provided by creditors. It is computed by dividing long-term debt by the stockholders' equity.

$$\frac{\text{Long-term debt}}{\text{Equity}} = \frac{\$1,350,000}{\$3,242,500} = 0.42 \ (1995)$$

$$= \frac{\$1,425,000}{\$2,725,750} = 0.52 \ (1994)$$

ACTIVITY RATIOS

Activity ratios indicate how effectively a firm is using its resources. By comparing revenues with the resources used to generate them, it is possible to establish an efficiency of operation. The asset turnover ratio indicates how efficiently management is employing total assets. Asset turnover is calculated by dividing sales by total assets. For the ABC Company, asset turnover is calculated as follows:

$$\text{Asset turnover} = \frac{\text{Sales}}{\text{Total assets}} = \frac{\$8,250,000}{\$7,105,000} = 1.16 \ (1995)$$

$$= \frac{\$8,000,000}{\$6,393,000} = 1.25 \ (1994)$$

The ratio of sales to fixed assets is a measure of the turnover on plant and equipment. It is calculated by dividing sales by net fixed assets.

$$\text{Fixed asset turnover} = \frac{\text{Sales}}{\text{Net fixed assets}} = \frac{\$8,250,000}{\$2,980,000} = 2.77 \text{ (1995)}$$

$$= \frac{\$8,000,000}{\$2,775,000} = 2.88 \text{ (1994)}$$

Industry figures for asset turnover will vary with capital-intensive industries, and those requiring large inventories will have much smaller ratios.

Another activity ratio is inventory turnover, estimated by dividing sales by average inventory. The norm for American industries is 9, but whether the ratio for a particular firm is higher or lower normally depends on the product sold. Small, inexpensive items usually turn over at a much higher rate than larger, expensive ones. Since inventories normally are carried at cost, it would be more accurate to use the cost of goods sold in place of sales in the numerator of this ratio. Established compilers of industry ratios, such as Dun & Bradstreet, however, use the ratio of sales to inventory.

$$\text{Inventory turnover} = \frac{\text{Sales}}{\text{Inventory}} = \frac{\$8,250,000}{\$2,175,000} = 3.79 \text{ (1995)}$$

$$= \frac{\$8,000,000}{\$2,000,000} = 4 \text{ (1994)}$$

The accounts receivable turnover is a measure of the average collection period on sales. If the average number of days varies widely from the industry norm, it may be an indication of poor management. A too-low ratio could indicate the loss of sales because of a too restrictive credit policy. If the ratio is too high, too much capital is being tied up in accounts receivable, and management may be increasing the chance of bad debts. Because of varying industry credit policies, a comparison for the firm over time or within an industry is the only useful analysis. Because information on credit sales for other firms generally is unavailable, total sales must be used. Since not all firms have the same percentage of credit sales, there is only approximate comparability among firms.

$$\frac{\text{Accounts}}{\text{receivable turnover}} = \frac{\text{Sales}}{\text{Accounts receivable}} = \frac{\$8,250,000}{\$1,760,000} = 4.69 \text{ (1995)}$$

$$= \frac{\$8,000,000}{\$1,440,000} = 5.56 \text{ (1994)}$$

$$\text{Average collection period} = \frac{360}{\text{Accounts receivable turnover}}$$

$$= \frac{360}{4.69} = 77 \text{ days (1995)}$$

$$= \frac{360}{5.56} = 65 \text{ days (1994)}$$

PROFITABILITY RATIOS

Profitability is the net result of a large number of policies and decisions chosen by an organization's management. Profitability ratios indicate how effectively the total firm is being managed. The profit margin for a firm is calculated by dividing net earnings by sales. This ratio is often called *return on sales* (ROS). There is wide variation among industries, but the average for American firms is approximately 5 percent.

$$\frac{\text{Net earnings}}{\text{Sales}} = \frac{\$410,000}{\$8,250,000} = 0.0497 \text{ (1995)}$$

$$= \frac{\$395,000}{\$8,000,000} = 0.0494 \text{ (1994)}$$

A second useful ratio for evaluating profitability is the return on investment—or *ROI*, as it is frequently called—found by dividing net earnings by total assets. The ABC Company's ROI is calculated as follows:

$$\frac{\text{Net earnings}}{\text{Total assets}} = \frac{\$410,000}{\$7,105,000} = 0.0577 \text{ (1995)}$$

$$= \frac{\$395,000}{\$6,393,000} = 0.0618 \text{ (1994)}$$

The ratio of net earnings to net worth is a measure of the rate of return or profitability of the stockholders' investment. It is calculated by dividing net earnings by net worth, the common stock equity and retained earnings account. ABC Company's return on net worth, also called *ROE,* is calculated as follows:

$$\frac{\text{Net earnings}}{\text{Net worth}} = \frac{\$410,000}{\$3,242,500} = 0.1264 \text{ (1995)}$$

$$= \frac{\$395,000}{\$2,725,750} = 0.1449 \text{ (1994)}$$

It is often difficult to determine causes for lack of profitability. The Du Pont system of financial analysis provides management with clues to the lack of success of a firm. This financial tool brings together activity, profitability, and leverage measures and shows how these ratios interact to determine the overall profitability of the firm. A depiction of the system is set forth in Exhibit 6–4.

The right side of the exhibit develops the turnover ratio. This section breaks down total assets into current assets (cash, marketable securities, accounts receivable, and inventories) and fixed assets. Sales divided by these total assets gives the turnover on assets.

The left side of the exhibit develops the profit margin on sales. The individual expense items plus income taxes are subtracted from sales to produce net profits after taxes. Net profits divided by sales gives the profit margin on sales. When the asset turnover ratio on the right side of Exhibit 6–4 is multiplied by the profit margin on sales developed on the left side of the exhibit, the product is the return on assets (ROI) for the firm. This can be shown by the following formula:

$$\frac{\text{Sales}}{\text{Total assets}} \times \frac{\text{Net earnings}}{\text{Sales}} = \frac{\text{Net earnings}}{\text{Total assets}} = \text{ROI}$$

The last step in the Du Pont analysis is to multiply the rate of return on assets (ROI) by the equity multiplier, which is the ratio of assets to common equity, to obtain the rate of return on equity (ROE). This percentage rate of return, of course, could be calculated

EXHIBIT 6–4
Du Pont's Financial Analysis

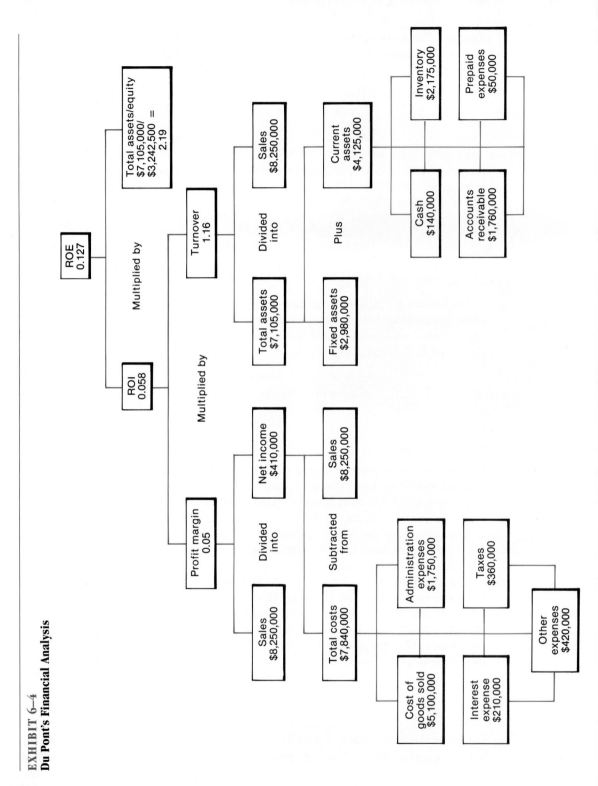

directly by dividing net income by common equity. However, the Du Pont analysis demonstrates how the return on assets and the use of debt interact to determine the return on equity.

The Du Pont system can be used to analyze and improve the performance of a firm. On the left, or profit, side of the exhibit, attempts to increase profits and sales could be investigated. The possibilities of raising prices to improve profits (or lowering prices to improve volume) or seeking new products or markets, for example, could be studied. Cost accountants and production engineers could investigate ways to reduce costs. On the right, or turnover, side, financial officers could analyze the effect of reducing investment in various assets as well as the effect of using alternative financial structures.

There are two basic approaches to using financial ratios. One approach is to evaluate the corporation's performance over several years. Financial ratios are computed for different years, and then an assessment is made about whether there has been an improvement or deterioration over time. Financial ratios also can be computed for projected, pro forma, statements and compared with present and past ratios.

The other approach is to evaluate a firm's financial condition and compare it with the financial conditions of similar firms or with industry averages in the same period. Such a comparison gives insight into the firm's relative financial condition and performance. Financial ratios for industries are provided by Robert Morris Associates, Dun & Bradstreet, and various trade association publications. (Associations and their addresses are listed in the *Encyclopedia of Associations* and in the *Directory of National Trade Associations.*) Information about individual firms is available through *Moody's Manual,* Standard & Poor's manuals and surveys, annual reports to stockholders, and the major brokerage houses.

To the extent possible, accounting data from different companies must be so standardized that companies can be compared or so a specific company can be compared with an industry average. It is important to read any footnotes of financial statements, since various accounting or management practices can have an effect on the financial picture of the company. For example, firms using sale-leaseback methods may have leverage pictures quite different from what is shown as debts or assets on the balance sheet.

ANALYSIS OF THE SOURCES AND USES OF FUNDS

The purpose of this analysis is to determine how the company is using its financial resources from year to year. By comparing balance sheets from one year to the next, one may determine how funds were obtained and how these funds were employed during the year.

To prepare a statement of the sources and uses of funds, it is necessary to (1) classify balance sheet changes that increase and decrease cash, (2) classify from the income statement those factors that increase or decrease cash, and (3) consolidate this information on a sources and uses of funds statement form.

Sources of funds that increase cash are:

1. A net decrease in any other asset than a depreciable fixed asset.
2. A gross decrease in a depreciable fixed asset.
3. A net increase in any liability.

4. Proceeds from the sale of stock.
5. The operation of the company (net income, and depreciation if the company is profitable).

Uses of funds include:

1. A net increase in any other asset than a depreciable fixed asset.
2. A gross increase in depreciable fixed assets.
3. A net decrease in any liability.
4. A retirement or purchase of stock.
5. Payment of cash dividends.

We compute gross changes to depreciable fixed assets by adding depreciation from the income statement for the period to net fixed assets at the end of the period and then subtracting from the total net fixed assets at the beginning of the period. The residual represents the change in depreciable fixed assets for the period.

For the ABC Company, the following change would be calculated:

Net property and plant (1995)	$1,175,000
Depreciation for 1995	+ 80,000
	$1,255,000
Net property and plant (1994)	−1,155,000
	$ 100,000

To avoid double counting, the change in retained earnings is not shown directly in the funds statement. When the funds statement is prepared, this account is replaced by the earnings after taxes, or net income, as a source of funds and dividends paid during the year as a use of funds. The difference between net income and the change in the retained-earnings account will equal the amount of dividends paid during the year. The accompanying sources and uses of funds statement was prepared for the ABC Company.

A funds analysis is useful for determining trends in working-capital positions and for demonstrating how the firm has acquired and employed its funds during some period.

ABC Company
Sources and Uses of Funds Statement
For 1995

Sources:	
Prepaid expenses	$ 13,000
Accounts payable	100,000
Accrued federal taxes	250,000
Dividends payable	3,750
Common stock	1,200
Additional paid-in capital	195,000
Earnings after taxes (net income)	410,000
Depreciation	80,000
Total sources	$1,053,500

ABC Company
Sources and Uses of Funds Statement
For 1995

Uses:

Cash	$ 25,000
Accounts receivable	320,000
Inventory	175,000
Long-term receivables	165,000
Property and plant	100,000
Other fixed assets	20,000
Bank loans payable	75,000
Current maturities of long-term debt	8,500
Long-term liabilities	75,000
Dividends paid	90,000
Total uses	1,053,500

CONCLUSION

It is recommended that you prepare a chart, such as that shown in Exhibit 6–5, so you can develop a useful portrayal of these financial analyses. The chart allows a display of the ratios over time. The "Trend" column could be used to indicate your evaluation of the ratios over time (e.g., "favorable," "neutral," or "unfavorable"). The "Industry Average" column could include recent industry averages on these ratios or those of key competitors. These would provide information to aid interpretation of the analyses. The "Interpretation" column could be used to describe your interpretation of the ratios for this firm. Overall, this chart gives a basic display of the ratios that provides a convenient format for examining the firm's financial condition.

Finally, Exhibit 6–6 is included to provide the quick reference summarizing the calculation and meaning of the ratios discussed earlier.

EXHIBIT 6–5
A Summary of the Financial Position of a Firm

Ratios and Working Capital	1991	1992	1993	1994	1995	Trend	Industry Average	Interpre-tation
Liquidity: Current								
Quick								
Leverage: Debt-assets								
Debt-equity								
Activity: Asset turnover								
Fixed asset ratio								
Inventory turnover								
Accounts receivable turnover								
Average collection period								
Profitability: ROS								
ROI								
ROE								
Working-capital position								

EXHIBIT 6–6
A Summary of Key Financial Ratios

Ratio	Calculation	Meaning
Liquidity ratios:		
Current ratio	$\dfrac{\text{Current assets}}{\text{Current liabilities}}$	The extent to which a firm can meet its short-term obligations.
Quick ratio	$\dfrac{\text{Current assets} - \text{Inventory}}{\text{Current liabilities}}$	The extent to which a firm can meet its short-term obligations without relying on the sale of inventories.
Leverage ratios:		
Debt-to-total-assets ratio	$\dfrac{\text{Total debt}}{\text{Total assets}}$	The percentage of total funds that are provided by creditors.
Debt-to-equity ratio	$\dfrac{\text{Total debt}}{\text{Total stockholders' equity}}$	The percentage of total funds provided by creditors versus the percentage provided by owners.
Long-term-debt-to-equity ratio	$\dfrac{\text{Long-term debt}}{\text{Total stockholders' equity}}$	The balance between debt and equity in a firm's long-term capital structure.
Times-interest-earned ratio	$\dfrac{\text{Profits before interest and taxes}}{\text{Total interest charges}}$	The extent to which earnings can decline without the firm becoming unable to meet is annual interest costs.
Activity ratios:		
Inventory turnover	$\dfrac{\text{Sales}}{\text{Inventory of finished goods}}$	Whether a firm holds excessive stocks of inventories and whether a firm is selling its inventories slowly compared to the industry average.
Fixed assets turnover	$\dfrac{\text{Sales}}{\text{Fixed assets}}$	Sales productivity and plant equipment utilization.
Total assets turnover	$\dfrac{\text{Sales}}{\text{Total assets}}$	Whether a firm is generating a sufficient volume of business for the size of its assets investment.
Accounts receivable turnover	$\dfrac{\text{Annual credit sales}}{\text{Accounts receivable}}$	In percentage terms, the average length of time it takes a firm to collect on credit sales.
Average collection period	$\dfrac{\text{Accounts receivable}}{\text{Total sales/365 days}}$	In days, the average length of time it takes a firm to collect on credit sales.
Profitability ratios:		
Gross profit margin	$\dfrac{\text{Sales} - \text{Cost of goods sold}}{\text{Sales}}$	The total margin available to cover operating expenses and yield a profit.
Operating profit margin	$\dfrac{\text{Earnings before interest and taxes (EBIT)}}{\text{Sales}}$	Profitability without concern for taxes and interest.
Net profit margin	$\dfrac{\text{Net income}}{\text{Sales}}$	After-tax profits per dollar of sales.
Return on total assets (ROA)	$\dfrac{\text{Net income}}{\text{Total assets}}$	After-tax profits per dollar of assets; this ratio is also called *return on investment* (ROI).
Return on stockholders' equity (ROE)	$\dfrac{\text{Net income}}{\text{Total stockholders' equity}}$	After-tax profits per dollar of stockholders' investment in the firm.

EXHIBIT 6–6 (concluded)

Ratio	Calculation	Meaning
Earnings per share (EPS)	$$\frac{\text{Net income}}{\text{Number of shares of common stock outstanding}}$$	Earnings available to the owners of common stock.
Growth ratio:		
Sales	Annual percentage growth in total sales	Firm's growth rate in sales.
Income	Annual percentage growth in profits	Firm's growth rate in profits.
Earnings per share	Annual percentage growth in EPS	Firm's growth rate in EPS.
Dividends per share	Annual percentage growth in dividends per share	Firm's growth rate in dividends per share.
Price-earnings ratio	$$\frac{\text{Market price per share}}{\text{Earnings per share}}$$	Faster-growing and less risky firms tend to have higher price-earnings ratios.

CHAPTER 6 COHESION CASE

INTERNAL ANALYSIS AT THE COCA-COLA COMPANY

A key perspective from which to gauge the strengths and weaknesses at Coca-Cola is via a comparison of key indicators with PepsiCo. Listed below are the net sales, operating incomes, identifiable assets (assets that can be identified with a particular location and business), and capital expenditures for 1989 through 1991.

Key Indicators (in billions)

	Coca-Cola				PepsiCo		
	U.S.	Int.'l	Total	Total+	U.S.	Int.'l	Total
Net sales:							
1991	$2.6	$7.2	$9.8	$11.6	$5.1	$1.7	$6.9
1990	2.5	6.1	8.6	10.2	5.0	1.5	6.5
1989	2.2	4.8	7.0	8.6	4.6	1.2	5.8
Operating income:							
1991	0.469	2.1	2.6	2.7	0.746	0.117	0.863
1990	0.358	1.8	2.2	2.3	0.674	0.094	0.768
1989	0.391	1.5	1.9	2.0	0.578	0.099	0.676
Identifiable assets:							
1991	1.5	4.8	6.3	7.1			6.8
1990	1.7	3.7	5.0	6.1			6.5
1989	1.8	2.8	4.6	5.3			6.2
Capital expenditures:							
1991	0.131	0.546	0.677	0.792			0.426
1990	0.138	0.321	0.459	0.530			0.334
1989	0.136	0.216	0.352	0.413			0.268

Coca-Cola has sustained an overall domestic market share lead versus Pepsi, with 41 percent versus 31 percent. Internationally, Coke is way ahead of Pepsi, and the following chart illustrates that situation:

	1993 Market Leader	Leadership Margin	Second Place
Australia	Coca-Cola	3.3–1	diet Coke
Austria	Coca-Cola	2.6–1	Fanta
Belgium	Coca-Cola	7.3–1	Coke light
Brazil	Coca-Cola	2.7–1	Brazilian brand
Denmark	Coca-Cola	1.7–1	Danish brand
France	Coca-Cola	3.3–1	French brand
Germany	Coca-Cola	3.3–1	Coke light
Great Britain	Coca-Cola	1.3–1	diet Coke
Greece	Coca-Cola	2.6–1	Fanta
Italy	Coca-Cola	2.0–1	Fanta
Japan	Coca-Cola	1.5–1	Fanta
Korea	Coca-Cola	1.5–1	Korea brand
Norway	Coca-Cola	1.9–1	Coke light
Spain	Coca-Cola	2.0–1	Spanish brand
Sweden	Coca-Cola	3.0–1	Fanta

Pepsi's main strength is in the supermarket area, but Coke maintains a virtually equal portion of this market. Pepsi has strong sales through the restaurant chains it owns (Pizza Hut, Kentucky Fried Chicken, Taco Bell) although a recent decision by Burger King to leave Pepsi for Coke, plus McDonald's continued relationship with Coke, seem to confirm Goizueta's long-held policy that Coke will not compete with its customers, such as restaurant chains, by entering their industry. Other financial and operating information as well as key ratios are calculated in the 10-year summary of Coke's financial operations, "Selected Financial Data."

Finally, Coke was weak relative to Pepsi in the early 1980s in terms of the strength of franchisee bottlers. Coke's bottlers, as we mentioned earlier, were second- and third-generation family businesses that had been with Coke from its very early days. Pepsi's franchises, led by what was then the world's largest soft-drink bottler—General Cinema Corporation—had better capitalized and more sophisticated bottlers in many key urban areas in the United States. But Coke recognized this and, over the 1980s, became more aggressively involved with its bottlers, including over $2 billion in investment, which makes its bottling network, particularly abroad, a relative advantage in the 1990s.

Coke likes to assess its strengths and weaknesses against an internal sense of what is required for success in the global soft-drink industry. Drawing from earlier quotes of Goizueta provided in the Chapter 5 Cohesion Case, it appears Coke is exceptionally strong on dimensions it deems key determinants of success. An outside evaluation of Coke's strengths vis-à-vis international markets appears to confirm Coke's perception:

International volume growth [at Coke] has outpaced domestic growth for several years, reflecting the relative immaturity of those markets in terms of soft-drink consumption and, more importantly, The Coca-Cola Company's aggressive efforts to expand distribution and emphasize marketing. While The Coca-Cola Company participates in U.S. bottling activities primarily as an equity investor (albeit a highly involved investor), the international involvement has been varied. In most countries, the preferred avenue has been to establish a joint venture with a strong local business entity, with Coke contributing equity and management expertise. In some markets, notably France and the former East Germany, Coca-Cola has stepped in with direct ownership and investment.

Overall the company's increasing emphasis on bottling investment and support represent a major strength for the company in virtually every market.

Brand loyalty is another major strength for Coca-Cola. In the United States, Coke's mid-1980s debacle—withdrawing regular Coke in favor of New Coke only to have consumers react so negatively that regular Coke, the "Coke Classic," was brought back to head off consumer law suits and other demands—showed Coke the depth of brand loyalty it had engendered. The net result was greater market share and profitability for Coke as it realized the depth of its brand loyalty. The financial data table provided on the following two pages portrays the strong position of the Coke brand abroad, and it suggests a similar brand loyalty in those markets.

Selected Financial Data

Year Ended December 31, (In millions except per share data and ratios)	1992[2,4]	1991[4] (Restated)	1990[4] (Restated)	1989[4] (Restated)
Summary of Operations				
Net operating revenues	$13,074	$11,572	$10,236	$8,622
Cost of goods sold	5,055	4,649	4,208	3,548
Gross profit	8,019	6,923	6,028	5,074
Selling, administrative and general expenses	5,249	4,604	4,076	3,348
Provisions for restructured operations and disinvestment	—	—	—	—
Operating income	2,770	2,319	1,952	1,726
Interest income	164	175	170	205
Interest expense	171	192	231	308
Equity income	65	40[5]	110	75
Other income (deductions)—net	(82)	41	13	66
Income from continuing operations before income taxes and changes in accounting principles	2,746	2,383	2,014	1,764
Income taxes	862	765	632	553
Income from continuing operations before changes in accounting principles	$ 1,884	$ 1,618	$ 1,382	$1,211
Net income	$ 1,664	$ 1,618	$ 1,382	$1,537
Preferred stock dividends	—	1	18	21
Net income available to common share owners	$ 1,664	$ 1,617	$ 1,364	$1,516[6]
Average common shares outstanding[1]	1,317	1,333	1,337	1,384
Per Common Share Data[1]				
Income from continuing operations before changes in accounting principles	$ 1.43	$ 1.21	$ 1.02	$ .86
Net income	1.26	1.21	1.02	1.10[6]
Cash dividends	.56	.48	.40	.34
Market price at December 31	41.88	40.13	23.25	19.31
Balance Sheet Data				
Cash, cash equivalents and current marketable securities	$ 1,063	$ 1,117	$ 1,492	$1,182
Property, plant and equipment—net	3,526	2,890	2,386	2,021
Depreciation	310	254	236	181
Capital expenditures	1,083	792	593	462
Total assets	11,052	10,189	9,245	8,249
Long-term debt	1,120	985	536	549
Total debt	3,208	2,288	2,537	1,980
Share-owners' equity	3,888	4,239	3,662	3,299
Total capital[2]	7,096	6,527	6,199	5,279
Other Key Financial Measures[2]				
Total-debt-to-total-capital	45.2%	35.1%	40.9%	37.5%
Net-debt-to-net-capital	31.9%	19.2%	23.7%	14.7%
Return on common equity	46.4%	41.3%	41.4%	39.4%
Return on capital	29.4%	27.5%	26.8%	26.5%
Economic profit	$ 1,369	$ 1,046	$ 878	$ 821
Dividend payout ratio	44.3%	39.5%	39.2%	31.0%[6]

Adjusted for a two-for-one stock split in 1992, a two-for-one stock split in 1990 and a three-for-one stock split in 1986.
See Glossary on page 70.
In 1992, the Company adopted SFAS No. 106, "Employers' Accounting for Postretirement Benefits Other Than Pensions."
The Company adopted SFAS No. 109, "Accounting for Income Taxes," in 1992 by restating financial statements beginning in 1989.

46   The Coca-Cola Company and Subsidiaries

Source: The Coca-Cola Company 1992 Annual Report, pp. 46–47.

1988	1987	1986	1985	1984	1983	1982
$8,065	$7,658	$6,977	$5,879	$5,442	$5,056	$4,760
3,429	3,633	3,454	2,909	2,738	2,580	2,472
4,636	4,025	3,523	2,970	2,704	2,476	2,288
3,038	2,665	2,446	2,163	1,855	1,648	1,515
—	36	180	—	—	—	—
1,598	1,324	897	807	849	828	773
199	232	154	151	133	90	119
230	297	208	196	128	77	76
92	64	45	52	42	35	25
(33)	40	410	69	13	2	11
1,626	1,363	1,298	883	909	878	852
537	496	471	314	360	374	379
$1,089	$ 867	$ 827	$ 569	$ 549	$ 504	$ 473
$1,045	$ 916	$ 934	$ 722	$ 629	$ 559	$ 512
7	—	—	—	—	—	—
$1,038	$ 916	$ 934	$ 722	$ 629	$ 559	$ 512
1,458	1,509	1,547	1,573	1,587	1,635	1,558
$ .74	$ .57	$ .53	$ .36	$ .35	$ .31	$ .30
.71	.61	.60	.46	.40	.34	.33
.30	.28	.26	.25	.23	.22	.21
11.16	9.53	9.44	7.04	5.20	4.46	4.33
$1,231	$1,489	$ 895	$ 843	$ 768	$ 559	$ 254
1,759	1,602	1,538	1,483	1,284	1,247	1,233
167	152	151	130	119	111	104
387	304	346	412	300	324	273
7,451	8,606	7,675	6,341	5,241	4,540	4,212
761	909	996	801	631	428	423
2,124	2,995	1,848	1,280	1,310	520	493
3,345	3,187	3,479	2,948	2,751	2,912	2,779
5,469	6,182	5,327	4,228	4,061	3,432	3,272
38.8%	48.4%	34.7%	30.3%	32.3%	15.2%	15.1%
18.9%	15.4%	10.9%	15.6%	19.7%	5.6%	13.6%
34.7%	26.0%	25.7%	20.0%	19.4%	17.7%	18.7%
21.3%	18.3%	20.1%	16.8%	16.7%	16.4%	17.9%
$ 748	$ 417	$ 311	$ 269	$ 268	$ 138	$ 61
42.1%	46.0%	43.1%	53.8%	57.9%	65.3%	62.8%

Earnings Per Share
From Continuing Operations
Before Changes in
Accounting
Principles

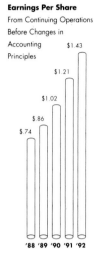

$1.43
$1.21
$1.02
$.86
$.74

'88 '89 '90 '91 '92

Economic Profit
(In millions)

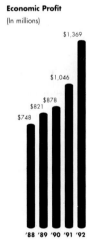

$1,369
$1,046
$878
$821
$748

'88 '89 '90 '91 '92

¹Equity income in 1991 includes a reduction of $44 million related to restructuring charges recorded by Coca-Cola Enterprises Inc.
⁶Net income available to common share owners in 1989 includes after-tax gains of $604 million ($.44 per common share) from the sale of the Company's equity interest in Columbia Pictures Entertainment, Inc. and the Company's bottled water business and the transition effect of $265 million related to the change in accounting for income taxes. Excluding these nonrecurring items, the dividend payout ratio in 1989 was 39.9 percent.

The Coca-Cola Company and Subsidiaries   **47**

7 FORMULATING LONG-TERM OBJECTIVES AND GRAND STRATEGIES

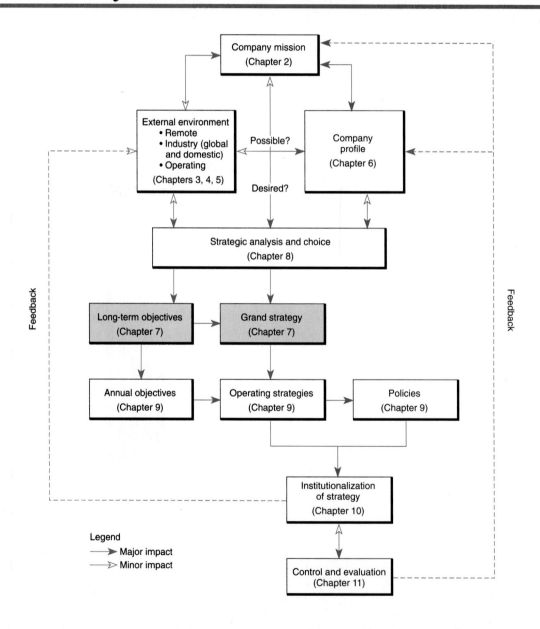

T he company mission was described in Chapter 2 as encompassing the broad aims of the firm. The most specific statement of aims presented in that chapter appeared as the goals of the firm. However, these goals, which commonly dealt with profitability, growth, and survival, were stated without specific targets or time frames. They were always to be pursued but could never be fully attained. They gave a general sense of direction but were not intended to provide specific benchmarks for evaluating the firm's progress in achieving its aims.[1] Providing such benchmarks is the function of objectives.[2]

The first part of this chapter will focus on long-term objectives. These are statements of the results a firm seeks to achieve over a specified period, typically five years. The second part will focus on the formulation of grand strategies. These provide a comprehensive general approach in guiding major actions designed to accomplish the firm's long-term objectives.

The chapter has two major aims: (1) to discuss in detail the concept of long-term objectives, the topics they cover, and the qualities they should exhibit; and (2) to discuss the concept of grand strategies and to describe the 14 principal grand strategy options that are available to firms singly or in combination, including three newly popularized options that are being used to provide the basis for global competitiveness.

LONG-TERM OBJECTIVES

Strategic managers recognize that short-run profit maximization is rarely the best approach to achieving sustained corporate growth and profitability. An often repeated adage states that, if impoverished people are given food, they will eat it and remain impoverished; however, if they are given seeds and tools and shown how to grow crops, they will be able to improve their condition permanently. A parallel choice confronts strategic decision makers:

1. Should they eat the seeds to improve the near-term profit picture and make large dividend payments through cost saving measures such as laying off workers during periods of slack demand, selling off inventories, or cutting back on research and development?
2. Or should they sow the seeds in the effort to reap long-term rewards by reinvesting profits in growth opportunities, committing resources to employee training, or increasing advertising expenditures?

For most strategic managers, the solution is clear—distribute a small amount of profit now but sow most of it to increase the likelihood of a long-term supply. This is the most frequently used rationale in selecting objectives.

---

[1] Max D. Richards, *Setting Strategic Goals and Objectives,* 2nd ed. (St. Paul, Minn.: West Publishing, 1986), p. 22.

[2] Throughout this text, the terms *goals* and *objectives* are each used to convey a special meaning, with goals being the less specific and more encompassing concept. Most authors follow this usage; however, some use the two words interchangeably, while others reverse the usage.

To achieve long-term prosperity, strategic planners commonly establish long-term objectives in seven areas:

Profitability   The ability of any firm to operate in the long run depends on attaining an acceptable level of profits. Strategically managed firms characteristically have a profit objective, usually expressed in earnings per share or return on equity.

Productivity   Strategic managers constantly try to improve the productivity of their systems. Firms that can improve the input-output relationship normally increase profitability. Thus, firms almost always state an objective for productivity. Commonly used productivity objectives are the number of items produced or the number of services rendered per unit of input. However, productivity objectives sometimes are stated in terms of desired cost decreases. For example, objectives may be set for reducing defective items, for customer complaints leading to litigation, or for overtime. Achieving such objectives increases profitability if unit output is maintained.

Competitive Position   One measure of corporate success is relative dominance in the marketplace. Larger firms commonly establish an objective in terms of competitive position, often using total sales or market share as measures of their competitive position. An objective with regard to competitive position may indicate a firm's long-term priorities. For example, Gulf Oil set a five-year objective of moving from third to second place as a producer of high-density polypropylene. Total sales were the measure.

Employee Development   Employees value growth and career opportunities. Providing such opportunities often increases productivity and decreases turnover. Therefore, strategic decision makers frequently include an employee development objective in their long-range plans. For example, PPG has declared an objective of developing highly skilled and flexible employees and, thus, providing steady employment for a reduced number of workers.

Employee Relations   Whether or not they are bound by union contracts, firms actively seek good employee relations. In fact, proactive steps in anticipation of employee needs and expectations are a characteristic concern of strategic managers. Strategic managers believe that productivity is linked to employee loyalty and to perceived management interest in workers' welfare. They, therefore, set objectives to improve employee relations. Among the outgrowths of such objectives are safety programs, worker representation on management committees, and employee stock option plans.

Technological Leadership   Firms must decide whether to lead or follow in the marketplace. Either approach can be successful, but each requires a different strategic posture. Therefore, many firms state an objective with regard to technological leadership. For example, Caterpillar Tractor Company established its early reputation and dominant position in its industry by being in the forefront of technological innovation in the manufacture of large earthmovers. Because of an advanced technological design, Daihatsu Mira became the most popular car in Japan in 1991. The four-seat minicar held a 660cc engine that provided the customer with 30 percent more miles per gallon than any competitor, and it had a 25 percent smaller sales tax.

Public Responsibility   Firms recognize their responsibilities to their customers and to society at large. In fact, many firms seek to exceed the demands made by government. They work not only to develop reputations for fairly priced products and services but also to establish themselves as responsible corporate citizens. For example, they may establish objectives for charitable and educational contributions, minority training, public or political activity, community welfare, or urban renewal. In an attempt to exhibit their sense of public responsibility in the United States, Japanese companies, such as Toyota, Hitachi, and Matsushita, contributed more than $500 million to American educational projects, charities, and nonprofit organizations, a 67 percent increase over the previous year.

Qualities of Long-Term Objectives

What distinguishes a good objective from a bad one? What qualities of an objective improve its chances of being attained? Perhaps these questions are best answered in relation to seven criteria that should be used in preparing long-term objectives: acceptable, flexible, measurable over time, motivating, suitable, understandable, and achievable.

Acceptable   Managers are most likely to pursue objectives that are consistent with their preferences. They may ignore or even obstruct the achievement of objectives that offend them (e.g., promoting a nonnutritional food product) or that they believe to be inappropriate or unfair (e.g., reducing spoilage to offset a disproportionate allocation of fixed overhead). In addition, long-term corporate objectives frequently are designed to be acceptable to groups external to the firm. An example is efforts to abate air pollution that are undertaken at the insistence of the Environmental Protection Agency.

Flexible   Objectives should be adaptable to unforeseen or extraordinary changes in the firm's competitive or environmental forecasts. However, such flexibility usually is increased at the expense of specificity. Moreover, employee confidence may be tempered because adjustment of flexible objectives may affect their jobs. One way of providing flexibility while minimizing its negative effects is to allow for adjustments in the level, rather than in the nature, of objectives. For example, the personnel department objective of providing managerial development training for 15 supervisors per year over the next five-year period might be adjusted by changing the number of people to be trained. In contrast, changing the personnel department's objective of "assisting production supervisors in reducing job-related injuries by 10 percent per year" after three months had gone by would understandably create dissatisfaction.

Measurable   Objectives must clearly and concretely state what will be achieved and when it will be achieved. Thus, objectives should be measurable over time. For example, the objective of "substantially improving our return on investment" would be better stated as "increasing the return on investment on our line of paper products by a minimum of 1 percent a year and a total of 5 percent over the next three years."

Motivating   Studies have shown that people are most productive when objectives are set at a motivating level—one high enough to challenge but not so high as to frustrate or so low as to be easily attained. The problem is that individuals and groups differ in their perceptions of what is high enough. A broad objective that challenges one group frustrates another and minimally interests a third. One valuable recommendation is that objectives be tailored to specific groups. Developing such objectives requires time and effort, but objectives of this kind are more likely to motivate.

Suitable   Objectives must be suited to the broad aims of the firm, which are expressed in its mission statement. Each objective should be a step toward the attainment of overall goals. In fact, objectives that do not coincide with the company mission can subvert the firm's aims. For example, if the mission is growth oriented, the objective of reducing the debt-to-equity ratio to 1.00 would probably be unsuitable and counterproductive.

Understandable   Strategic managers at all levels must understand what is to be achieved. They also must understand the major criteria by which their performance will be evaluated. Thus, objectives must be so stated that they are as understandable to the recipient as they are to the giver. Consider the misunderstandings that might arise over the objective of "increasing the productivity of the credit card department by 20 percent within five years." What does this objective mean? Increase the number of outstanding cards? Increase the use of outstanding cards? Increase the employee workload? Make productivity gains each year? Or hope that the new computer-assisted system, which should improve productivity, is approved by year 5? As this simple example illustrates, objectives must be clear, meaningful, and unambiguous.

Achievable   Finally, objectives must be possible to achieve. This is easier said than done. Turbulence in the remote and operating environments affects a firm's internal operations, creating uncertainty, and limiting the accuracy of the objectives set by strategic management. To illustrate, the wildly fluctuating prime interest rates in 1980 made objective setting extremely difficult for the years 1981 to 1985, particularly in such areas as sales projections for producers of consumer durable goods like General Motors and General Electric.

An especially fine example of long-term objectives is provided in CACI, Inc.'s strategic plan for 1990. Shown in Strategy in Action 7–1 are CACI's major financial objectives for the period. The firm's approach is wholly consistent with the list of desired qualities for long-term objectives. In particular, CACI's objectives are flexible, measurable over time, understandable, and suitable for a high-technology and professional services organization.

GENERIC STRATEGIES

Many planning experts believe that the general philosophy of doing business declared by the firm in the mission statement must be translated into a holistic statement of the firm's strategic orientation before it can be further defined in terms of a specific long-term strategy. In other words, a long-term or grand strategy must be based on a core idea about how the firm can best compete in the marketplace.

The popular term for this core idea is *generic strategy*. From a scheme developed by Michael Porter, many planners believe that any long-term strategy should derive from a firm's attempt to seek a competitive advantage based on one of three generic strategies:

1. Striving for overall low-cost leadership in the industry.

STRATEGY
IN ACTION
7–1

CACI's Long-Term Objectives, 1990

REVENUE

Increase revenue range to $167–$176M or better in FY 90 (FY 90 bookings at $170M).

FY 91: Revenue in the $193–$202M range; bookings at $195–$205M range.

Increase company revenue 15–20 percent per year steadily over next decade.

Consistently increase revenues to $500M per annum by 1997 or earlier. Steady manageable and consistent profitable growth.

PROFITABILITY

Achieve 4 percent NAT or better as an annual corporate target for return on revenues, moving to 5 percent NAT by mid-90s.

Individual departments and divisions must target NAT percentage profits at 50–100 percent above company levels (i.e., 6–8 percent moving to 7.5–10 percent).

SHAREHOLDERS' VALUE

Increase stock price (market value) to $20 per share or better by 1997 (current share basis).

2. Striving to create and market unique products for varied customer groups through *differentiation*.
3. Striving to have special appeal to one or more groups of consumer or industrial buyers, *focusing* on their cost or differentiation concerns.

Advocates of generic strategies believe that each of these options can produce above-average returns for a firm in an industry. However, they are successful for very different reasons.

Low-cost leaders depend on some fairly unique capability to achieve and sustain their low-cost position. Examples of such capabilities are: having secured suppliers of scarce raw materials, being in a dominant market share position, or having a high degree of capitalization. Low-cost producers usually excel at cost reductions and efficiencies. They maximize economies of scale, implement cost-cutting technologies, stress reductions in overhead and in administrative expenses, and use volume sales techniques to propel themselves up the earning curve. The commonly accepted requirements for successful implementation of the low-cost and other two generic strategies are overviewed in Figure 7–1.

A low-cost leader is able to use its cost advantage to charge lower prices or to enjoy higher profit margins. By so doing, the firm effectively can defend itself in price wars, attack competitors on price to gain market share, or, if already dominant in the industry, simply benefit from exceptional returns. As an extreme case, it has been argued that National Can Company, a corporation in an essentially stagnant industry, is able to generate attractive and improving profits by being the low-cost producer.

FIGURE 7–1
Requirements for Generic Competitive Strategies

Generic Strategy	Commonly Required Skills and Resources	Common Organizational Requirements
Overall cost leadership	Sustained capital investment and access to capital. Process engineering skills. Intense supervision of labor. Products designed for ease in manufacture. Low-cost distribution system.	Tight cost control. Frequent, detailed control reports. Structured organization and responsibilities. Incentives based on meeting strict quantitative targets.
Differentiation	Strong marketing abilities. Product engineering. Creative flair. Strong capability in basic research. Corporate reputation for quality or technological leadership. Long tradition in the industry or unique combination of skills drawn from other businesses. Strong cooperation from channels.	Strong coordination among functions in R&D, product development, and marketing. Subjective measurement and incentives instead of quantitative measures. Amenities to attract highly skilled labor, scientists, or creative people
Focus	Combination of the above policies directed at the particular strategic target.	Combination of the above policies directed at the regular strategic target.

Source: Reprinted with permission of the Free Press, a Division of Macmillan, Inc., from *COMPETITIVE STRATEGY: Techniques for Analyzing Industries and Competitors* by Michael E. Porter, pp. 40–41. Copyright © 1980 by The Free Press.

Strategies dependent on differentiation are designed to appeal to customers with a special sensitivity for a particular product attribute. By stressing the attribute above other product qualities, the firm attempts to build customer loyalty. Often such loyalty translates into a firm's ability to charge a premium price for its product. Cross-brand pens, Brooks Brothers suits, Porsche automobiles, and Chivas Regal Scotch whiskey are all examples.

. The product attribute also can be the marketing channels through which it is delivered, its image for excellence, the features it includes, and the service network that supports it. As a result of the importance of these attributes, competitors often face "perceptual" barriers to entry when customers of a successfully differentiated firm fail to see largely identical products as being interchangeable. For example, General Motors hopes that customers will accept "only genuine GM replacement parts."

A focus strategy, whether anchored in a low-cost base or a differentiation base, attempts to attend to the needs of a particular market segment. Likely segments are those that are ignored by marketing appeals to easily accessible markets, to the "typical" customer, or to customers with common applications for the product. A firm pursuing a focus strategy is willing to service isolated geographic areas; to satisfy the needs of customers with special financing, inventory, or servicing problems; or to tailor the product to the somewhat unique demands of the small-to-medium-sized customer. The focusing firms profit from their willingness to serve otherwise ignored or under-appreciated customer segments. The classic

FIGURE 7–2
Risks of the Generic Strategies

Risks of Cost Leadership	Risks of Differentiation	Risks of Focus
Cost leadership is not sustained: • Competitors imitate. • Technology changes. • Other bases for cost leadership erode.	Differentiation is not sustained: • Competitors imitate. • Bases for differentiation become less important to buyers.	The focus strategy is imitated. The target segment becomes structurally unattractive: • Structure erodes. • Demand disappears.
Proximity in differentiation is lost.	Cost proximity is lost.	Broadly targeted competitors overwhelm the segment: • The segment's differences from other segments narrow. • The advantages of a broad line increase.
Cost focusers achieve even lower cost in segments.	Differentiation focusers achieve even greater differentiation in segments.	New focusers subsegment the industry.

Source: Michael E. Porter, *Competitive Advantage: Creating and Sustaining Superior Performance.* Copyright © 1985 by Michael E. Porter. Reprinted with permission of The Free Press, a Division of Macmillan, Inc.

example is cable television. An entire industry was born because of a willingness of cable firms to serve isolated rural locations that were ignored by traditional television services. Brick producers that typically service a radius of less than 100 miles and commuter airlines that serve regional geographic areas are other examples of industries where a focus strategy frequently yields above-average industry profits.

While each of the generic strategies enables a firm to maximize certain competitive advantages, each one also exposes the firm to a number of competitive risks. For example, a low-cost leader fears a new low-cost technology that is being developed by a competitor; a differentiating firm fears imitators; and a focused firm fears invasion by a firm that largely targets customers. As Figure 7–2 suggests, each generic strategy presents the firm with a number of risks.

GRAND STRATEGIES[3]

While the need for firms to develop generic strategies remains an unresolved debate, designers of planning systems agree about the critical role of grand strategies. Grand strategies, often called *master* or *business strategies,* provide basic direction for strategic actions. They are the basis of coordinated and sustained efforts directed toward achieving long-term business objectives.

---

[3] Portions of this section were adapted from John A. Pearce II, "Selecting among Alternative Grand Strategies," *California Management Review,* Spring 1982, pp. 23–31.

The purpose of this section is twofold: (1) to list, describe, and discuss 14 grand strategies that strategic managers should consider and (2) to present approaches to the selection of an optimal grand strategy from the available alternatives.

Grand strategies indicate the time period over which long-range objectives are to be achieved. Thus, a grand strategy can be defined as a comprehensive general approach that guides a firm's major actions.

The 14 principal grand strategies are: concentrated growth, market development, product development, innovation, horizontal integration, vertical integration, concentric diversification, conglomerate diversification, turnaround, divestiture, liquidation, joint ventures, strategic alliances, and consortia. Any one of these strategies could serve as the basis for achieving the major long-term objectives of a single firm. But a firm involved with multiple industries, businesses, product lines, or customer groups—as many firms are— usually combines several grand strategies. For clarity, however, each of the principal grand strategies is described independently in this section, with examples to indicate some of its relative strengths and weaknesses.

Concentrated Growth[4]

Many of the firms that fell victim to merger mania were once mistakenly convinced that the best way to achieve their objectives was to pursue unrelated diversification in the search for financial opportunity and synergy. By rejecting that "conventional wisdom," such firms as Martin-Marietta, Kentucky Fried Chicken, Compaq, Avon, Hyatt Legal Services, and Tenant have demonstrated the advantages of what is increasingly proving to be sound business strategy. A firm that has enjoyed special success through a strategic emphasis on increasing market share through concentration is Chemlawn. With headquarters in Columbus, Ohio, Chemlawn is the North American leader in professional lawn care. Like others in the lawn-care industry, Chemlawn is experiencing a steadily declining customer base. Market analysis shows that the decline is fueled by negative environmental publicity, perceptions of poor customer service, and concern about the price versus the value of the company's services, given the wide array of do-it-yourself alternatives. Chemlawn's approach to increasing market share hinges on addressing quality, price, and value issues; discontinuing products that the public or environmental authorities perceive as unsafe; and improving the quality of its work force.

These firms are just a few of the majority of American firms that pursue a concentrated growth strategy by focusing on a specific product and market combination. Concentrated growth is the strategy of the firm that directs its resources to the profitable growth of a single product, in a single market, with a single dominant technology. The main rationale for this approach, sometimes called a *market penetration* or *concentration strategy,* is that the firm throroughly develops and exploits its expertise in a delimited competitive arena.[5]

---

[4] Portions of this section were adapted from John A. Pearce II and J. Harvey, "Risks and Rewards of a Concentrated Growth Strategy," *Academy of Management Executive,* February 1990, pp. 62–69.

[5] For a more detailed and comprehensive description of alternative business strategies, refer to Pearce, "Selecting among Alternative Grand Strategies."

Rationale for Superior Performance

Why do concentrated growth strategies lead to enhanced performance? A study of product successes and failures across multiple industries suggests several reasons. This study shows that the greatest influences on market success are those characteristic of firms that implement a concentrated growth strategy.[6]

These influences include the ability to assess market needs, knowledge of buyer behavior, customer price sensitivity, and effectiveness of promotion. Further underscoring the importance of concentrated growth-based company skills, the study also shows that these core capabilities are a more important determinant of competitive market success than are the environmental forces faced by the firm. The high success rates of new products also are tied to avoiding situations that require undeveloped skills, such as serving new customers and markets, acquiring new technology, building new channels, developing new promotional abilities, and facing new competition.[7]

A major misconception about the concentrated growth strategy is that the firm practicing it will settle for little or no growth. This is certainly not true for a firm that correctly utilizes the strategy. A firm employing concentrated growth grows by building on its competences, and it achieves a competitive edge by concentrating in the product-market segment it knows best. A firm employing this strategy is aiming for the growth that results from increased productivity, better coverage of its actual product-market segment, and more efficient use of its technology. Strategy in Action 7–2 provides an excellent example of how Hechingers, the home supply chain, is attempting to improve its competitiveness by refocusing its concentration strategy.

Conditions That Favor Concentrated Growth

Specific conditions in the firm's environment are favorable to the concentrated growth strategy. The first is a condition in which the firm's industry is resistant to major technological advancements. This is usually the case in the late growth and maturity stages of the product life cycle and in product-markets where product demand is stable and industry barriers, such as capitalization, are high. Machinery for the paper manufacturing industry, in which the basic technology has not changed for more than a century, is a good example.

An especially favorable condition is one in which the firm's targeted markets are not product saturated. Markets with competitive gaps leave the firm with alternatives for growth, other than taking market share away from competitors. The successful introduction of traveler services by All-State and Amoco demonstrates that even an organization as entrenched and powerful as the AAA could not build a defensible presence in all segments of the automobile club market. Similarly, General Motors attempted to increase its share of the Japanese car market in 1992 with the introduction of its Pontiac Grand AM and Buick Park Avenue. The move was based on GM's knowledge that import auto sales in Japan rose 5.2 percent in 1990, with large cars accounting for most of those sales.

---

[6] Robert G. Cooper, "Identifying Industrial New Product Success: Project NewProd," *Industrial Marketing Management,* April 1979, pp. 124–35.

[7] Robert G. Cooper, "The Impact of New Product Strategies," *Industrial Marketing Management,* October 1983, pp. 243–56.

Hechinger—the company that's helped thousands of weekend do-it-yourselfers with everything from fixing a leaky faucet to building a deck—is kicking up a little dust of its own with the remodeling of its Washington area stores to a new "Home Project Center" format.

In addition to new warehouse-style shelving, the stores cluster products around "project areas" and displays and have more workers on hand to answer questions.

"The most important thing we must do as a retailer . . . is to focus on what the customer wants and give it to them better than anyone else," said John W. Hechinger, Jr., the company's president since 1986. "That's really what's driving us."

"The wave of the present, if not the future, is the warehouse concept," said Neal Kaplan, an analyst at Scott & Stringfellow, a Richmond-based brokerage. "It seems some Hechinger stores aren't really as competitive as they'd like them to be."

Analysts also see Hechinger's rapid move as a "preemptive strike" against expansion by Atlanta-based The Home Depot, Inc., and other specialty hardware retailers, such as Lowes, a North Carolina-based chain that is opening larger "superstores."

The Home Depot, rapidly becoming the dominant company in the nation's $25 billion home improvement products industry, has 200 stores in 18 states and is looking to open its first Washington store in Alexandria next year.

Hechinger expects to convert its two dozen Washington area stores to Home Project Centers by the middle of the decade. In early 1992, the Landover, Maryland–based, company set aside $83 million for the work, which also involves closing or consolidating some stores.

It costs about $6 million to open a new store and about $2 million to convert an older Hechinger to the Home Project Center format. Most of the Washington area stores—in prime locations—will be remodeled.

Hechinger's new centers sell more goods; but operating costs are higher, meaning lower gross margins, according to the company's financial records. In response to competition, the company also cut prices in several markets and started a lowest-price guarantee, which has pared profits.

Analysts say it's important for Hechinger to pick its battles in key markets, in part because of the evolution of the home improvement supplies business. For example, they point to the fact that it's possible to buy a tub of spackle or a hacksaw at a drug store or mulch at the neighborhood grocery.

"We need to be the most flexible, leanest operator in the business," Hechinger said.

Source: Excerpted from "Hechinger Rebuilds Store Concept," by Lloyd Batzler, *The Fairfax Journal Weekly*, December 2, 1992, p. A3.

A third condition that favors concentrated growth exists when the firm's product-markets are sufficiently distinctive to dissuade competitors in adjacent product-markets from trying to invade the firm's segment. John Deere scrapped its plans for growth in the construction machinery business when mighty Caterpillar threatened to enter Deere's mainstay, the farm machinery business, in retaliation. Rather than risk a costly price war on its own turf, Deere scrapped these plans.

A fourth favorable condition exists when the firm's inputs are stable in price and quantity and are available in the amounts and at the times needed. Maryland-based Giant Foods is able to concentrate in the grocery business largely due to its stable long-term arrangements with suppliers of its private-label products. Most of these suppliers are makers of the national brands that compete against the Giant labels. With a high market share and aggressive retail distribution, Giant controls the access of these brands to the consumer. Consequently, its suppliers have considerable incentive to honor verbal agreements, called *bookings*, in which they commit themselves for a one-year period with regard to the price, quality, and timing of their shipments to Giant.

The pursuit of concentrated growth also is favored by a stable market—a market without the seasonal or cyclical swings that would encourage a firm to diversify. Night Owl Security, the District of Columbia market leader in home security services, commits its customers to initial four-year contracts. In a city where affluent consumers tend to be quite transient, the length of this relationship is remarkable. Night Owl's concentrated growth strategy has been reinforced by its success in getting subsequent owners of its customers' homes to extend and renew the security service contracts. In a similar way, Lands' End reinforced its growth strategy in 1992 by asking customers for names and addresses of friends and relatives living overseas who would like to receive Lands' End catalogs.

A firm also can grow while concentrating, if it enjoys competitive advantages based on efficient production or distribution channels. These advantages enable the firm to formulate advantageous pricing policies. More efficient production methods and better handling of distribution also enable the firm to achieve greater economies of scale or, in conjunction with marketing, result in a product that is differentiated in the mind of the consumer. Graniteville Company, a large South Carolina textile manufacturer, enjoyed decades of growth and profitability by adopting a "follower" tactic as part of its concentrated growth strategy. By producing fabrics only after market demand had been well established, and by featuring products that reflected its expertise in adopting manufacturing innovations and in maintaining highly efficient long production runs, Graniteville prospered through concentrated growth.

Finally, the success of market generalists creates conditions favorable to concentrated growth.[8] When generalists succeed by using universal appeals, they avoid making special appeals to particular groups of customers. The net result is that many small pockets are left open in the markets dominated by generalists, and that specialists emerge and thrive in these pockets. For example, hardware store chains, such as Stanbaugh-Thompsons and Hechinger, focus primarily on routine household repair problems and offer solutions that can be easily sold on a self-service, do-it-yourself basis. This approach leaves gaps at both the "semiprofessional" and "neophyte" ends of the market—in terms of the purchaser's skill at household repairs and the extent to which available merchandise matches the requirements of individual homeowners.

Risk and Rewards of Concentrated Growth

Under stable conditions, concentrated growth poses lower risk than any other grand strategy; but, in a changing environment, a firm committed to concentrated growth faces high risks. The greatest risk is that concentrating in a single product-market makes a firm particularly vulnerable to changes in that segment. Slowed growth in the segment would jeopardize the firm because its investment, competitive edge, and technology are deeply

---

[8] Glenn R. Carroll, "The Specialist Strategy," *California Management Review,* Spring 1984, pp. 126–37.

entrenched in a specific offering. It is difficult for the firm to attempt sudden changes if its product is threatened by near-term obsolescence, a faltering market, new substitutes, or changes in technology or customer needs. For example, the manufacturers of IBM clones faced such a problem when IBM adopted the OS/2 operating system for its personal computer line. That change made existing clones out of date.

The concentrating firm's entrenchment in a specific industry makes it particularly susceptible to changes in the economic environment of that industry. For example, Mack Truck, the second-largest truck maker in America, lost $20 million as a result of an 18-month slump in the truck industry.

Entrenchment in a specific product-market tends to make a concentrating firm more adept than competitors at detecting new trends. However, any failure of such a firm to properly forecast major changes in its industry can result in extraordinary losses. Numerous makers of inexpensive digital watches were forced to declare bankruptcy because they failed to anticipate the competition posed by Swatch, Guess, and other trendy watches that emerged from the fashion industry.

A firm pursuing a concentrated growth strategy is vulnerable also to the high opportunity costs that result from remaining in a specific product-market and ignoring other options that could employ the firm's resources more profitably. Overcommitment to a specific technology and product-market can hinder a firm's ability to enter a new or growing product-market that offers more attractive cost-benefit trade-offs. Had Apple Computers maintained its policy of making equipment that did not interface with IBM equipment, it would have missed out on what have proved to be its most profitable strategic opinions.

Concentrated Growth Is Often the Most Viable Option

Examples abound of firms that have enjoyed exceptional returns on the concentrated growth strategy. Such firms as McDonald's, Goodyear, and Apple Computers have used firsthand knowledge and deep involvement with specific product segments to become powerful competitors in their markets. The strategy is associated even more often with successful smaller firms that have steadily and doggedly improved their market position.

The limited additional resources necessary to implement concentrated growth, coupled with the limited risk involved, also make this strategy desirable for a firm with limited funds. For example, through a carefully devised concentrated growth strategy, medium-sized John Deere & Company was able to become a major force in the agricultural machinery business even when competing with such firms as Ford Motor Company. While other firms were trying to exit or diversify from the farm machinery business, Deere spent $2 billion in upgrading its machinery, boosting its efficiency, and engaging in a program to strengthen its dealership system. This concentrated growth strategy enabled it to become the leader in the farm machinery business despite the fact that Ford was more than 10 times its size.

The firm that chooses a concentrated growth strategy directs its resources to the profitable growth of a narrowly defined product and market, focusing on a dominant technology. Firms that remain within their chosen product-market are able to extract the most from their technology and market knowledge and, thus, are able to minimize the risk associated with unrelated diversification. The success of a concentration strategy is founded on the firm's use of superior insights into its technology, product, and customer to obtain a sus-

FIGURE 7–3
Specific Options under the Grand Strategies of Concentration,
Market Development, and Product Development

Concentration (increasing use of present products in present markets):
1. Increasing present customers' rate of use:
   a. Increasing the size of purchase.
   b. Increasing the rate of product obsolescence.
   c. Advertising other uses.
   d. Giving price incentives for increased use.
2. Attracting competitors' customers:
   a. Establishing sharper brand differentiation.
   b. Increasing promotional effort.
   c. Initiating price cuts.
3. Attracting nonusers to buy the product:
   a. Inducing trial use through sampling, price incentives, and so on.
   b. Pricing up or down.
   c. Advertising new uses.

Market development (selling present products in new markets):
1. Opening additional geographic markets:
   a. Regional expansion.
   b. National expansion.
   c. International expansion.
2. Attracting other market segments:
   a. Developing product versions to appeal to other segments.
   b. Entering other channels of distribution.
   c. Advertising in other media.

Product development (developing new products for present markets):
1. Developing new product features:
   a. Adapt (to other ideas, developments).
   b. Modify (change color, motion, sound, odor, form, shape).
   c. Magnify (stronger, longer, thicker, extra value).
   d. Minify (smaller, shorter, lighter).
   e. Substitute (other ingredients, process, power).
   f. Rearrange (other patterns, layout, sequence, components).
   g. Reverse (inside out).
   h. Combine (blend, alloy, assortment, ensemble; combine units, purposes, appeals, ideas).
2. Developing quality variations.
3. Developing additional models and sizes (product proliferation).

Source: Adapted from Philip Kotler. *Marketing Management Analysis, Planning, and Control*, 6th ed., 1987. Reprinted by permission of Prentice Hall, Inc., Englewood Cliffs, N.J.

tainable competitive advantage. Superior performance on these aspects of corporate strategy has been shown to have a substantial positive effect on market success.

A grand strategy of concentrated growth allows for a considerable range of action. Broadly speaking, the firm can attempt to capture a larger market share by increasing the usage rates of present customers, by attracting competitors' customers, or by selling to nonusers. In turn, each of these options suggests more specific options, some of which are listed in the top section of Figure 7–3.

When strategic managers forecast that their current products and their markets will not provide the basis for achieving the company mission, they have two options that involve moderate costs and risk: market development and product development.

Market Development

Market development commonly ranks second only to concentration as the least costly and least risky of the 14 grand strategies. It consists of marketing present products, often with only cosmetic modifications, to customers in related market areas by adding channels of distribution or by changing the content of advertising or promotion. Several specific approaches are listed under this heading in Figure 7–3. Thus, as suggested by the figure, firms that open branch offices in new cities, states, or countries are practicing market development. Likewise, firms are practicing market development if they switch from advertising in trade publications to advertising in newspapers or if they add jobbers to supplement their mail-order sales efforts.

Market development allows firms to practice a form of concentrated growth by identifying new uses for existing products and new demographically, psychographically, or geographically defined markets. Frequently, changes in media selection, promotional appeals, and distribution are used to initiate this approach. Du Pont used market development when it found a new application for Kevlar, an organic material that police, security, and military personnel had used primarily for bulletproofing. Kevlar now is being used to refit and maintain wooden-hulled boats, since it is lighter and stronger than glass fibers and has 11 times the strength of steel.

The medical industry provides other examples of new markets for existing products. The National Institutes of Health's report of a study showing that the use of aspirin may lower the incidence of heart attacks is expected to boost sales in the $2.2 billion analgesic market. It has been predicted that the expansion of this market will lower the market share of non-aspirin brands, such as industry leaders Tylenol and Advil. Product extensions currently planned include Bayer Calendar Pack, 28-day packaging to fit the once-a-day prescription for the prevention of a second heart attack.

Another example is Chesebrough-Ponds, a major producer of health and beauty aids, which decided several years ago to expand its market by repacking its Vaseline Petroleum Jelly in pocket-size squeeze tubes as Vaseline "Lip Therapy." The corporation decided to place a strategic emphasis on market development, because it knew from market studies that its petroleum-jelly customers already were using the product to prevent chapped lips. Company leaders reasoned that their market could be expanded significantly if the product were repackaged to fit conveniently in consumers' pockets and purses.

Product Development

Product development involves the substantial modification of existing products or the creation of new but related products that can be marketed to current customers through established channels. The product development strategy often is adopted either to prolong the life cycle of current products or to take advantage of a favorite reputation or brand name. The idea is to attract satisfied customers to new products as a result of their positive experience with the firm's initial offering. The bottom section in Figure 7–3 lists some of the options available to firms undertaking product development. A revised edition of a college textbook, a new car style, and a second formula of shampoo for oily hair are examples of the product development strategy.

The product development strategy is based on the penetration of existing markets by incorporating product modifications into existing items or by developing new products with a clear connection to the existing product line. The telecommunications industry provides an example of product extension based on product modification. To increase its estimated 8–10 percent share of the $5–$6 billion corporate user market, MCI Communication Corporation extended its direct-dial service to 146 countries, the same as those serviced by AT&T, at lower average rates than those of AT&T. MCI's recent addition of 79 countries to its network underscores its belief in this market, which it expects to grow 15–20 percent annually. Another example of expansions linked to existing lines is Gerber's decision to engage in general merchandise marketing. Gerber's recent introduction included 52 items that ranged from feeding accessories to toys and children's wear. Likewise, Nabisco Brands seeks competitive advantage by placing its strategic emphasis on product development. With headquarters in Parsippany, New Jersey, the company is one of three operating units of RJR Nabisco. It is the leading producer of biscuits, confections, snacks, shredded cereals, and processed fruits and vegetables. To maintain its position as leader, Nabisco pursues a strategy of developing and introducing new products and expanding its existing product line. Spoon Size Shredded Wheat and Ritz Bits crackers are two examples of new products that are variations on existing products.

Innovation

In many industries, it has become increasingly risky not to innovate. Both consumer and industrial markets have come to expect periodic changes and improvements in the products offered. As a result, some firms find it profitable to make innovation their grand strategy. They seek to reap the initially high profits associated with customer acceptance of a new or greatly improved product. Then, rather than face stiffening competition as the basis of profitability shifts from innovation to production or marketing competence, they search for other original or novel ideas. The underlying rationale of the grand strategy of innovation is to create a new product life cycle and, thereby, make similar existing products obsolete. Thus, this strategy differs from the product development strategy of extending an existing product's life cycle. For example, INTEL, a leader in the semiconductor industry, pursues expansion through a strategic emphasis on innovation. With headquarters in California, the company is a designer and manufacturer of semiconductor components and related computers, of microcomputer systems, and of software. It is working on a microprocessor that will give a desktop computer the capability of a mainframe. The innovation strategy pursued at Nippondenso has led to a creative research approach of micronization as described in Global Strategy in Action 7–1.

While most growth-oriented firms appreciate the need to be innovative occasionally, a few firms use it as their fundamental way of relating to their markets. An outstanding example is Polaroid, which heavily promotes each of its new cameras until competitors are able to match its technological innovation; by this time, Polaroid normally is prepared to introduce a dramatically new or improved product. For example, it introduced consumers in quick succession to the Swinger, the SX-70, the One Step, and the Sun Camera 660.

Few innovative ideas prove profitable because the research, development, and premarketing costs of converting a promising idea into a profitable product are extremely high. A

GLOBAL
STRATEGY IN **THE TINIEST TOYOTA**
ACTION 7–1

T he technological edge in the car industry is shifting away from vehicle assemblers to the components makers. They are the ones responsible for such wonders as engine-management chips and antilock braking systems. Now, one of the world's biggest car-components companies, Japan's Nippondenso, has taken the process even further, and built its own car. Although it has yet to make some bits work—such as the engine—the car is still pretty impressive. That is because it is just 4.8mm long.

Nippondenso's microcar is a classic: a replica of the Toyota Model AA, which was developed in 1936 when the Toyota Automatic Loom Works decided to open an automobile division. That division became the third-biggest carmaker in the world. Toyota is Nippondenso's largest shareholder.

It took staff at Nippondenso's basic-research laboratory (one of the first to be opened by a car-parts firm) $2^{1}/_{2}$ months to build the little car. It was assembled from components produced by a number of processes.

Nippondenso now is trying to make the microcar go under its on steam, so to speak. An internal combustion engine is out of the question: too complex to make small enough to fit under the bonnet. Instead, the laboratory has decided to use an environmentally friendly miniaturized electric engine. There is still a problem, though, in supplying the energy. Shrinking the batteries and the necessary electrical connections to fit inside such a small vehicle appear impossible with current technology. So the company plans to supply the engine's energy externally.

The plan is to make what Nippondenso calls an *electromagnetic wave engine*—a tiny device capable of converting the energy contained in microwaves (which would be beamed at the car) into some kind of driving force. The laboratory is coy about the details, but it hopes to put together the components of such an engine within the next two years.

The purpose of all this, of course, is not to build cars for amoebae but to develop micromachining techniques that may be useful in making future products—and not just cars. Nippondenso talks of a self-propelled microcamera that can be driven through human blood vessels, or a microrobot that can repair, from the inside, the small cooling tubes surrounding the core of a nuclear reactor. Toyotas soon could be everywhere.

Source: Excerpted from "The Tiniest Toyota," *The Economist,* July 20, 1991, p. 103.

study by the Booz Allen & Hamilton management research department provides some understanding of the risks. As shown in Figure 7–4, Booz Allen & Hamilton found that less than 2 percent of the innovative projects initially considered by 51 companies eventually reached the marketplace. Specifically, out of every 58 new product ideas: only 12 pass an initial screening test that finds them compatible with the firm's mission and long-term objectives, only 7 remain after an evaluation of their potential, and only 3 survive development attempts. Of the three survivors, two appear to have profit potential after test marketing and only one is commercially successful. In fact, other studies show that the failure rate is far higher. For example, one study found the failure rates for commercial products to be as high as 89 percent.[9]

---

[9] Burt Schorr, "Many New Products Fizzle, Despite Careful Planning, Publicity," *The Wall Street Journal,* April 5, 1961.

FIGURE 7–4
Decay of new Product Ideas (51 Companies)

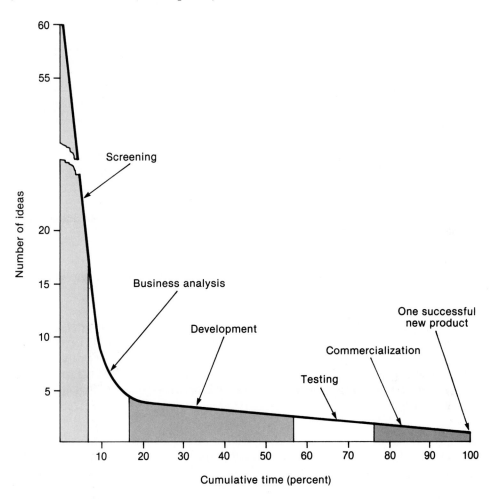

Horizontal Integration

When a firm's long-term strategy is based on growth through the acquisition of one or more similar firms operating at the same stage of the production-marketing chain, its grand strategy is called *horizontal integration*. Such acquisitions eliminate competitors and provide the acquiring firm with access to new markets.[10] One example is Warner-Lambert's acquisition of Parke Davis, which reduced competition in the ethical drugs field for Chilcott Laboratories, a firm that Warner-Lambert previously had acquired. Another example is the long-range acquisition pattern of White Consolidated Industries, which

---

[10] Martin K. Perry and Robert H. Porter, "Oligopoly and the Incentive for Horizontal Merger," *American Economic Review,* March 1985, pp. 219–27.

FIGURE 7–5
Vertical and Horizontal Integrations

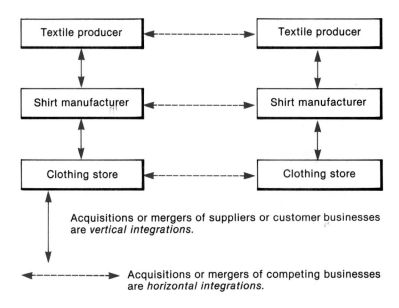

Acquisitions or mergers of suppliers or customer businesses are *vertical integrations.*

Acquisitions or mergers of competing businesses are *horizontal integrations.*

expanded in the refrigerator and freezer market through a grand strategy of horizontal integration, by acquiring Kelvinator Appliance, the Refrigerator Products Division of Bendix Westinghouse Automotive Air Brake, and Frigidaire Appliance from General Motors. More recently, Nike's acquisition in the dress shoes business and N. V. Homes's purchase of Ryan Homes have vividly exemplified the success that horizontal integration strategies can bring.

Vertical Integration

When a firm's grand strategy is to acquire firms that supply it with inputs (such as raw materials) or are a customer for its outputs (such as warehousers for finished products), *vertical integration* is involved. To illustrate, if a shirt manufacturer acquires a textile producer—by purchasing its common stock, buying its assets, or exchanging ownership interests—the strategy is vertical integration. In this case, it is *backward* vertical integration, since the firm acquired operates at an earlier stage of the production-marketing process. If the shirt manufacturer had merged with a clothing store, it would have been *forward* vertical integration—the acquisition of a firm nearer to the ultimate consumer.

Amoco emerged as North America's leader in natural gas reserves and products in 1988 as a result of its acquisition of Dome Petroleum. This backward integration by Amoco was made in support of its downstream businesses in refining and in gas stations, whose profits made the acquisition possible.

Figure 7–5 depicts both horizontal and vertical integration. The principal attractions of a horizontal integration grand strategy are readily apparent. The acquiring firm is able to greatly expand its operations, thereby achieving greater market share, improving economies of scale, and increasing the efficiency of capital use. In addition, these benefits are achieved with only moderately increased risk, since the success of the expansion is principally dependent on proven abilities.

The reasons for choosing a vertical integration grand strategy are more varied and sometimes less obvious.[11] The main reason for backward integration is the desire to increase the dependability of the supply or quality of the raw materials used as production inputs. That desire is particularly great when the number of suppliers is small and the number of competitors is large. In this situation, the vertically integrating firm can better control its costs and, thereby, improve the profit margin of the expanded production-marketing system. Forward integration is a preferred grand strategy if great advantages accrue to stable production. A firm can increase the predictability of demand for its output through forward integration; that is, through ownership of the next stage of its production-marketing chain.

Some increased risks are associated with both types of integration. For horizontally integrated firms, the risks stem from increased commitment to one type of business. For vertically integrated firms, the risks result from the firm's expansion into areas requiring strategic managers to broaden the base of their competences and to assume additional responsibilities.

Concentric Diversification

Grand strategies involving diversification represent distinctive departures from a firm's existing base of operations, typically the acquisition or internal generation (spin-off) of a separate business with synergistic possibilities counterbalancing the strengths and weaknesses of the two businesses. For example, Head Ski initially sought to diversify into summer sporting goods and clothing to offset the seasonality of its "snow" business. However, diversifications occasionally are undertaken as unrelated investments, because of their high profit potential and their otherwise minimal resource demands.

Regardless of the aprroach taken, the motivations of the acquiring firms are the same:

Increase the firm's stock value. In the past, mergers often have led to increases in the stock price or the price-earnings ratio.

Increase the growth rate of the firm.

Make an investment that represents better use of funds than plowing them into internal growth.

Improve the stability of earnings and sales by acquiring firms whose earnings and sales complement the firm's peaks and valleys.

Balance or fill out the product line.

Diversify the product line when the life cycle of current products has peaked.

Acquire a needed resource quickly (e.g., high-quality technology or highly innovative management).

Achieve tax savings by purchasing a firm whose tax losses will offset current or future earnings.

---

[11] Kathryn Rudie Harrigan, "Formulating Vertical Integration Strategies," *Academy of Management Review*, October 1984, pp. 638–52.

Increase efficiency and profitability, especially if there is synergy between the acquiring firm and the acquired firm.[12]

Concentric diversification involves the acquisition of businesses that are related to the acquiring firm in terms of technology, markets, or products. With this grand strategy, the selected new businesses possess a high degree of compatibility with the firm's current businesses. The ideal concentric diversification occurs when the combined company profits increase the strengths and opportunities and decrease the weaknesses and exposure to risk. Thus, the acquiring firm searches for new businesses whose products, markets, distribution channels, technologies, and resource requirements are similar to but not identical with its own, whose acquisition results in synergies but not complete interdependence.

Conglomerate Diversification

Occasionally a firm, particularly a very large one, plans to acquire a business because it represents the most promising investment opportunity available. This grand strategy is commonly known as conglomerate diversification. The principal concern, and often the sole concern, of the acquiring firm is the profit pattern of the venture. Unlike concentric diversification, *conglomerate diversification* gives little concern to creating product-market synergy with existing businesses. What such conglomerate diversifiers as ITT, Textron, American Brands, Litton, U.S. Industries, Fuqua, and I.C. Industries seek is financial synergy. For example, they may seek a balance in their portfolios between current businesses with cyclical sales and acquired businesses with countercyclical sales, between high-cash/low-opportunity and low-cash/high-opportunity businesses, or between debt-free and highly leveraged businesses.

The principal difference between the two types of diversification is that concentric diversification emphasizes some commonality in markets, products, or technology, whereas conglomerate diversification is based principally on profit considerations.

Several of the grand strategies discussed above, including concentric and conglomerate diversification and horizontal and vertical integration, often involve the purchase or acquisition of one firm by another. It is important to know that the majority of such acquisitions fail to produce the desired results for the companies involved. Strategy in Action 7–3 provides seven guidelines that can improve a company's chances of a successful acquisition.

Turnaround

For any one of a large number of reasons, a firm can find itself with declining profits. Among these reasons are economic recessions, production inefficiencies, and innovative breakthroughs by competitors. In many cases, strategic managers believe that such a firm can survive and eventually recover if a concerted effort is made over a period of a few years to fortify its distinctive competences. This grand strategy is known as *turnaround*. It typically is begun through one of two forms of retrenchment, employed singly or in combination:

---

[12] Godfrey Devlin and Mark Bleackley, "Strategic Alliances—Guidelines for Success," *Long Range Planning,* October 1988, pp. 18–23.

1. *Cost reduction.*   Examples include decreasing the work force through employee attrition, leasing rather than purchasing equipment, extending the life of machinery, eliminating elaborate promotional activities, laying off employees, dropping items from a production line, and discontinuing low-margin customers.

2. *Asset reduction.*   Examples include the sale of land, buildings, and equipment not essential to the basic activity of the firm and the elimination of "perks," such as the company airplane and executives' cars.

Interestingly, the turnaround most commonly associated with this approach is in management positions. In a study of 58 large firms, researchers Shendel, Patton, and Riggs found that turnaround almost always was associated with changes in top management.[13] Bringing in new managers was believed to introduce needed new perspectives on the firm's situation, to raise employee morale, and to facilitate drastic actions, such as deep budgetary cuts in established programs.

Strategic management research provides evidence the firms that have used a *turnaround strategy* have successfully confronted decline. The research findings have been assimilated and used as the building blocks for a Model of the Turnaround Process shown in Figure 7–6.[14]

The model begins with a depiction of external and internal factors as causes of a firm's performance downturn. When these factors continue to detrimentally impact the firm, its financial health is threatened. Unchecked decline places the firm in a turnaround situation.

A *turnaround situation* represents absolute and relative-to-industry declining performance of a sufficient magnitude to warrant explicit turnaround actions. Turnaround situations may be the result of years of gradual slowdown or months of sharp decline. In either case, the recovery phase of the turnaround process is likely to be more successful in accomplishing turnaround when it is preceded by planned retrenchment that results in the achievement of near-term financial stabilization. For a declining firm, stabilizing operations and restoring profitability almost always entail strict cost reduction followed by a shrinking back to those segments of the business that have the best prospects of attractive profit margins. The need for retrenchment was shown during the 1990–92 recession when half of all U.S. companies reduced their work forces by an average of 11 percent (especially hard hit were real estate, transportation, and electronic company middle managers).

The immediacy of the resulting threat to company survival posed by the turnaround situation is known as *situation severity.* Severity is the governing factor in estimating the speed with which the retrenchment response will be formulated and activated. When severity is low, a firm has some financial cushion. Stability may be achieved through cost retrenchment alone. When turnaround situation severity is high, a firm must immediately stabilize the decline or bankruptcy is imminent. Cost reductions must be supplemented with more drastic asset reduction measures. Assets targeted for divestiture are those determined to be underproductive. In contrast, more productive resources are protected

---

[13] Other forms of joint ventures (such as leasing, contract manufacturing, and management contracting) offer valuable support strategies. They are not included in the categorization, however, because they seldom are employed as grand strategies.

[14] J. A. Pearce II and D. K. Robbins, "Toward Improved Theory and Research on Business Turnaround," *Journal of Management,* 1993;   D. K. Robbins and J. A. Pearce II, "Turnaround: Recovery and Retrenchment," *Strategic Management Journal* 13, no. 4 (1992), pp. 287–309.

1. *The wrong target.*   This error becomes increasingly visible as time passes after the acquisition, when the acquiror may realize that anticipated synergies just don't exist, that the expanded market just isn't there, or that the acquiror's and target's technologies simply were not complementary.

The first step to avoid such a mistake is for the acquiror and its financial advisors to determine the strategic goals and identify the mission. The product of this strategic review will be specifically identified criteria for the target.

The second step required to identify the right target is to design and carry out an effective due-diligence process to ascertain whether the target indeed has the identified set of qualities selected in the strategic review.

2. *The wrong price.*   Even in a strategic acquisition, paying too much will lead to failure. For a patient strategic acquiror with long-term objectives, overpaying may be less of a problem than for a financial acquiror looking for a quick profit. Nevertheless, overpaying may divert needed acquiror resources and adversely affect the firm's borrowing capacity. In the extreme case, it can lead to continued operating losses and business failure.

The key to avoiding this problem lies in the acquiror's valuation model. The model will incorporate assumptions concerning industry trends and growth patterns developed in the strategic review.

3. *The wrong structure.*   Both financial and strategic acquisitions benefit by the structure chosen. This may include the legal structure chosen for the entities, the geographic jurisdiction chosen for newly created entities, and the capitalization structure selected for the business after the acquisition. The wrong structure may lead to an inability to repatriate earnings (or an ability to do so only at a prohibitive tax cost), regulatory problems that delay or prevent realization of the anticipated benefits, and inefficient pricing of debt and equity securities or a bar to chosen exit strategies due to inflexibility in the chosen legal structure.

The two principal aspects of the acquisition process that can prevent this problem are a comprehensive regulatory compliance review and tax and legal analysis.

4. *The lost deal.*   Lost deals often can be traced to poor communication. A successful strategic acquisition requires agreement upon the strategic vision, both within the acquiring

Source: Excerpted from D. A. Tanner, "Seven Deadly Sins of Strategic Acquisition," *Management Review,* June 1991, pp. 50–53. Reprinted by permission of publisher, from MANAGEMENT REVIEW, June 1991, © 1991. American Management Association, New York. All rights reserved.

from cuts and represent critical elements of the future core business plan of the company (i.e., the intended recovery response).

Turnaround responses among successful firms typically include two stages of strategic activities: retrenchment and the recovery response. *Retrenchment* consists of cost cutting and asset reducing activities. The primary objective of the retrenchment phase is to stabilize the firm's financial condition. Situation severity has been associated with retrenchment responses among successful turnaround firms. Firms in danger of bankruptcy or failure

STRATEGY
IN ACTION **concluded**
7–3

company and between the acquiror and the continuing elements of the target. This should be established in the preliminary negotiations that lead to the letter of intent.

The letter must spell out not only the price to be paid but also many of the relational aspects that will make the strategic acquisition successful. Although an acquiror may justifiably focus on expenses, indemnification, and other logical concerns in the letter of intent, relationship and operational concerns are also important.

5. *Management difficulties.* Lack of attention to management issues may lead to a lost deal. These problems can range from a failure to provide management continuity or clear lines of authority after a merger to incentives that cause management to steer the company in the wrong direction.

The remedy for this problem must be extracted from the initial strategic review. The management compensation structure must be designed with legal and business advisors to help achieve those goals. The financial rewards to management must depend upon the financial and strategic success of the combined entity.

6. *The closing crisis.* Closing crises may stem from unavoidable changed conditions, but most often they result from poor communication. Negotiators sometimes believe that problems swept under the table maintain a deal's momentum and ultimately allow for its consummation. They are sometimes right—and often wrong. Charting a course through an acquisition requires carefully developed skills for every kind of professional—business, accounting, and legal.

7. *The operating transition crisis.* Even the best conceived and executed acquisition will prevent significant transition and postclosing operation issues. Strategic goals cannot be achieved by quick asset sales or other accelerated exit strategies. Management time and energy must be spent to assure that the benefits identified in the strategic review are achieved.

The principal constraints on smooth implementation are usually human: poor interaction of personnel between the two preexisting management structures and resistance to new systems. Problems also may arise from too much attention to the by now well-communicated strategic vision and too little attention to the nuts and bolts of continuing business operations.

(i.e., severe situations) attempt to halt decline through cost and asset reductions. Firms in less severe situations have achieved stability merely through cost retrenchment. However, in either case, for firms facing declining financial performance, the key to successful turnaround rests in the effective and efficient management of the retrenchment process.

The primary causes of the turnaround situation have been associated with the second phase of the turnaround process, the *recovery response*. For firms that declined primarily as a result of external problems, turnaround most often has been achieved through creative new entrepreneurial strategies. For firms that declined primarily as a result of internal problems, turnaround has been most frequently achieved through efficiency strategies.

FIGURE 7–6
A Model of the Turnaround Process

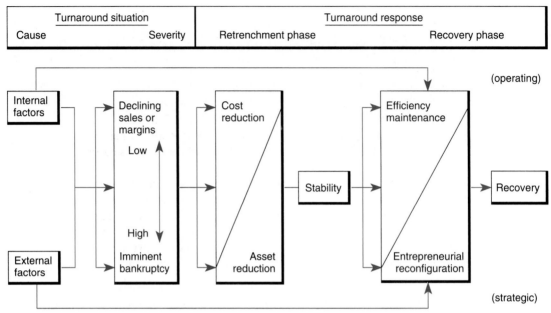

Source: J. A. Pearce II and D. K. Robbins, "Toward Improved Theory and Research on Business Turnaround," *Journal of Management,* 1993.

Recovery is achieved when economic measures indicate that the firm has regained its pre-downturn levels of performance.

Divestiture

A *divestiture strategy* involves the sale of a firm or a major component of a firm. For example, in March 1992, Goodyear Tire and Rubber announced its decision to sell its polyester business to Shell Chemical to cut its $2.6 billion debt. The sale was part of Goodyear's 1991 strategy to bring its debt below $2 billion within 18 months.

When retrenchment fails to accomplish the desired turnaround, as was the Goodyear situation, or when a nonintegrated business activity achieves an unusually high market value, strategic managers often decide to sell the firm. However, because the intent is to find a buyer willing to pay a premium above the value of a going concern's fixed assets, the term *marketing for sale* is often more appropriate. Prospective buyers must be convinced that, because of their skills and resources or because of the firm's synergy with their existing businesses, they will be able to profit from the acquisition.

The reasons for divestiture vary. They often arise because of partial mismatches between the acquired firm and the parent corporation. Some of the mismatched parts cannot be integrated into the corporation's mainstream activities and, thus, must be spun off. A second reason is corporate financial needs. Sometimes the cash flow or financial stability of the corporation as a whole can be greatly improved if businesses with high market value can be sacrificed.[15] The result can be a balancing of equity with long-term risks or of long-term debt payments to optimize the cost of capital.[16] A third, less frequent reason for divestiture is government antitrust action when a firm is believed to monopolize or unfairly dominate a particular market.[17]

Although examples of the divestiture grand strategy are numerous, CBS, Inc., recently provided an outstanding example. From 1986 to 1988, the once diverse entertainment and publishing giant sold its Records Division to Sony, its magazine publishing business to Diamandis Communications, its book publishing operations to Harcourt Brace Jovanovich, and its music publishing operations to SBK Entertainment World. Other firms that recently have pursued this type of grand strategy include Esmark, which divested Swift & Company, and White Motors, which divested White Farm.

The unfortunate but frequent consequence of a firm's failure to achieve turnaround—through a combination of retrenchment, divestiture, and new strategies—is financial bankruptcy. Firms filing for Chapter 11 bankruptcy protection are allowed by federal law to undertake a comprehensive reorganization while being protected from creditor actions. Believed to be in trouble because of serious mismanagement, such firms are allowed to reorganize with "proper management" in the hope they may be able to repay their debts over time and to become profitable operations. One of the hundreds of thousands of troubled businesses that have sought protection under Chapter 11 is Wang, as described in Strategy in Action 7–4.

Liquidation

When liquidation is the grand strategy, the firm typically is sold in parts, only occasionally as a whole—but for its tangible asset value and not as a going concern. In selecting liquidation, the owners and strategic managers of a firm are admitting failure and recognize that this action is likely to result in great hardships to themselves and their employees. For these reasons, liquidation usually is seen as the least attractive of the grand strategies. As a long-term strategy, however, it minimizes the losses of all the firm's stakeholders. Faced with bankruptcy, the liquidating firm usually tries to develop a planned and orderly system that will result in the greatest possible return and cash conversion as the firm slowly relinquishes its market share.

Planned liquidation can be worthwhile. For example, Columbia Corporation, a $130 million diversified firm, liquidated its assets for more cash per share than the market value of its stock.

---

[15] Benjamin Gomes-Casseres, "Joint Ventures in the Face of Global Competition," *Sloan Management Review,* Spring 1989, pp. 17–26.

[16] Christopher Clarke and Francois Gall, "Planned Divestment—A Five-Step Approach," *Long Range Planning,* February 1987, p. 17.

[17] Clark E. Chastain, "Divestiture: Antidote to Merger Mania," *Business Horizons,* November 1987, pp. 43–49.

On the streets of Boston, they're calling it Black Tuesday. The same day that basketball legend Larry Bird said he would end his career with the Boston Celtics, computer giant Wang Laboratories announced it would file for Chapter 11 bankruptcy protection and lay off 5,000 of its 13,000 workers. In many ways, it seemed fitting that Wang, based in Lowell, Massachusetts, and once a heroic player in the computer industry, bowed out during the same 24-hour period as did Boston's beloved hoopster. Like Bird, the 41-year-old industry icon was an old-timer crippled by past injuries that had failed to heal; a pain-racked veteran, it could no longer compete in a world filled with fast-moving rookies. Calling the bankruptcy "a drastic step that I deeply regret," chairman Richard W. Miller said the company, which will continue to operate, had simply "run out of resources."

The announcement was the end of a long, slow slide for the computer maker. Founded by Dr. An Wang, a Harvard-educated Chinese immigrant, Wang Laboratories revolutionized offices around the world with its minicomputers. But as the industry began to shift to personal computers in the mid-1980s, Wang was left behind. Its meteoric growth rates slowed, and earnings fell dramatically. Before the elder Wang's death from esophageal cancer in 1990, he already was preparing bankruptcy papers—but just in case the company rose from the ashes, he named Miller, an experienced turn-around artist, to succeed him.

Since then, Miller has been fighting to stave off the inevitable: The company has talked with more than 40 investors and has bargained with lenders for 56 amendments to its borrowing plan over the last three years. But analysts say Miller wasn't listening to customers—and last week Wang reported an operating loss of $45.4 million for the last fiscal year. "[The company] fell prey to the enormous success of the PC," says Thomas Willmott, a Boston-based computer consultant. "They simply did not react fast enough to compete in the workplace."

Wang could undergo transformation. In any case, the company will emerge from Chapter 11 much changed—if it emerges at all. Miller says, "We're in business today just as we were yesterday." Some analysts are doubtful. Like a wornout basketball player, they say, Wang may finally have benched itself for good.

CORPORATE COMBINATIONS

The 11 grand strategies discussed above, used singly and much more often in combinations, represent the traditional alternatives used by firms in the United States. Recently, three new grand types have gained in popularity; both fit under the broad category of corporate combinations. Although they do not fit the criterion by which executives retain a high degree of control over their operations, these grand strategies deserve special attention and consideration especially by companies that operate in global, dynamic, and technologically driven industries. These three newly popularized grand strategies are joint ventures, strategic alliances, and consortia.

FIGURE 7–7
Joint Ventures in the Oil Pipeline Industry

Pipeline Company (assets in $ millions)	Co-owners	Percent Held by Each
Colonial Pipeline Co. ($480.2)	Amoco	14.3%
	Atlantic Richfield	1.6
	Cities Service	14.0
	Continental	7.5
	Phillips	7.1
	Texaco	14.3
	Gulf	16.8
	Sohio	9.0
	Mobil	11.5
	Union Oil	4.0
Olympic Pipeline Co. ($30.7)	Shell	43.5
	Mobil	29.5
	Texaco	27.0
West Texas Gulf Pipeline Co. ($19.8)	Gulf	57.7
	Cities Service	11.4
	Sun	12.6
	Union Oil	9.0
	Sohio	9.2
Texas–New Mexico Pipeline Co. ($30.5)	Texaco	45.0
	Atlantic Richfield	35.0
	Cities Service	10.0
	Getty	10.0

Source: Testimony of Walter Adams in *Horizontal Integration of the Energy Industry,* hearings before the Subcommittee on Energy of the Joint Economic Committee, 94th Congress, 1st sess. (1975), p. 112.

Joint Ventures

Occasionally two or more capable firms lack a necessary component for success in a particular competitive environment.[18] For example, no single petroleum firm controlled sufficient resources to construct the Alaskan pipeline. Nor was any single firm capable of processing and marketing all of the oil that would flow through the pipeline. The solution was a set of *joint ventures,* which are third commercial companies (children) created and operated for the benefit of the co-owners (parents). As shown in Figure 7–7, these cooperative arrangements could provide both the funds needed to build the pipeline and the processing and marketing capacities needed to profitably handle the oil flow.

The particular form of joint ventures discussed above is *joint ownership.*[19] In recent years, it has become increasingly appealing for domestic firms to join foreign firms by means of this form. For example, Diamond-Star Motors is the result of a joint venture

---

[18] William F. Glueck, *Business Policy and Strategic Management* (New York: McGraw-Hill, 1980), p. 213.
[19] Dan G. Schendel, G. Richard Patton, and James Riggs, "Corporate Turnaround Strategies: A Study of Profit Decline and Recovery," *Journal of General Management* 3 (1976), pp. 3–11.

between a U.S. company, Chrysler Corporation, and Japan's Mitsubishi Motors corporation. Located in Normal, Illinois, Diamond-Star was launched because it offered Chrysler and Mitsubishi a chance to expand on their long-standing relationship in which subcompact cars (as well as Mitsubishi engines and other automotive parts) are imported to the United States and sold under the Dodge and Plymouth names.

The joint venture extends the supplier-consumer relationship and has strategic advantages for both partners. For Chrysler, it presents an opportunity to produce a high-quality car using expertise brought to the venture by Mitsubishi. It also gives Chrysler the chance to try new production techniques and to realize efficiencies by using the work force that was not included under Chrysler's collective bargaining agreement with the United Auto Workers. The agreement offers Mitsubishi the opportunity to produce cars for sale in the United States, without being subjected to the tariffs and restrictions placed on Japanese imports.

As a second example, Bethlehem Steel acquired an interest in a Brazilian mining venture to secure a raw material source. The stimulus for this joint ownership venture was grand strategy, but such is not always the case. Certain countries virtually mandate that foreign firms entering their markets do so on a joint ownership basis. India and Mexico are good examples. The rationale of these countries is that joint ventures minimize the threat of foreign domination and enhance the skills, employment, growth, and profits of local firms.

It should be noted that strategic managers understandably are wary of joint ventures. Admittedly, joint ventures present new opportunities with risks that can be shared. On the other hand, joint ventures often limit the discretion, control, and profit potential of partners, while demanding managerial attention and other resources that might be directed toward the firm's mainstream activities. Nevertheless, increasing globalization in many industries may require greater consideration of the joint venture approach, if historically national firms are to remain viable.[20] Advantages and disadvantages of an international joint venture are highlighted in Global Strategy in Action 7–2.

Strategic Alliances

Strategic alliances are distinguished from joint ventures because the companies involved do not take an equity position in one another. In many instances, strategic alliances are synonymous with licensing agreements. Licensing involves the transfer of some industrial property right from the U.S. licensor to a motivated licensee in a foreign country. Most tend to be patents, trademarks, or technical know-how that are granted to the licensee for a specified time in return for a royalty and for avoiding tariffs or import quotas. Bell South and U.S. West, with various marketing and service competitive advantages valuable to Europe, have extended a number of licenses to create personal computer networks in the United Kingdom (U.K.).

Another licensing strategy open to U.S. firms is to contract the manufacturing of its product line to a foreign company to exploit local comparative advantages in technology, materials, or labor. For example, MIPS Computer Systems has licensed Digital Equipment

---

[20] Richard J. Schmidt, "Corporate Divestiture: Pruning for Higher Profits," *Business Horizons,* May 1987, pp. 26–31.

GLOBAL STRATEGY IN ACTION 7–2   Joint Venture Boosts Siberian Oil Flow

The name White Nights Joint Enterprise plays off the Siberian summer and off the reason U.S. oil companies are here. And while the mission of the first working Russian–U.S. oil venture is simple, the details aren't.

"This is the first arrangement of its kind in all of the oil industry," says Gerald Walston, the Denver oil man who is White Nights' director.

The arrangement he refers to is incremental sharing, which entitles White Nights to all the oil recovered from three fields, above what the Russians had expected to get out, for 25 years.

Varyegan Oil and Gas, the state-owned company that controls the oil, is the Russian partner in White Nights. In exchange for turning its oil fields over to the joint venture, Varyegan gets all the oil up to its production estimates, plus half the oil that comes in addition to that. It also gets 10 percent in royalties.

The U.S. partners, Anglo-Suisse and Philbro Energy Production, split what's left, which is 40 percent of the extra production. They can make their money by shipping their oil out of the country to sell for hard currency.

The venture is pumping ahead of the Russians' estimated production. "Production in all of Russia was down 9.5 percent in 1991. Our fields were up about 40 percent," says Walston.

Anatoly Sivak, director general of Varyegan Oil and Gas, says, "This joint venture will serve as an example. It is the wave of the future."

The reason Sivak turned to the West for help was simple: "The question was how to stop the production decline. For that, we needed money and equipment and technology not available here." Completed wells were sitting idle for lack of parts.

Although the venture has succeeded in boosting production, "We've had some problems," Sivak says.

Anglo-Suisse was designated operator of the venture, and Russian oil people, who have been drilling here since the 1960s, couldn't understand why a U.S. company is running the show.

On top of that resentment were more obvious obstacles: different languages, clashing cultures, huge gaps in economic circumstances among the workers, different drilling techniques, and radically different organizational mindsets.

The Russians, with their five-year plans and strict instructions, "tended to organize and plan down to the last jot and tiddle," says Walston, a graying, unflappable gentleman who appears to keep the joint venture on an even keel via strings of Post-It notes splayed over the top of his desk. "The watchword for us is flexibility," he says.

Source: Excerpted from J. T. Buckley, "Joint Venture Boosts Siberian Oil Flow," *USA Today,* March 12, 1992, section 5B. Copyright 1992, USA TODAY. Reprinted with permission.

Corporation, Texas Instruments, Cypress Semiconductor, and Bipolar Integrated Technology in the United States, and Fujitsu, NEC, and Kubota in Japan to market computers based on its designs in the partner's country.[21]

---

[21] Many of the examples on alliances and consortia came from D. Lei and J. R. Slocum, Jr., "Global Strategic Alliances: Payoffs and Pitfalls," *Organizational Dynamics,* Winter 1991, pp. 44–62.

Service and franchise-based firms—including Anheuser-Busch, Avis, Coca-Cola, Hilton, Hyatt, Holiday Inns, Kentucky Fried Chicken, McDonald's. and Pepsi—have long engaged in licensing arrangements with foreign distributors as a way to enter new markets with standardized products that can benefit from marketing economies.

Consortia, Keiretsus, and Chaebols

Consortia are defined as large interlocking relationships between businesses of an industry. In Japan such consortia are known as *keiretsus,* in South Korea as *chaebols.*

In Europe, consortia projects are increasing in number and in success rates. Examples include The Junior Engineers' and Scientists' Summer Institute, which underwrites cooperative learning and research; The European Strategic Program for Research and Development in Information Technologies, which seeks to enhance European competitiveness in fields related to computer electronics and component manufacturing; and EUREKA, which is a joint program involving scientists and engineers from several European countries to coordinate joint research projects.

A Japanese *keiretsu* is an undertaking involving up to 50 different firms that are joined around a large trading company or bank and are coordinated through interlocking directories and stock exchanges. It is designed to use industry coordination to minimize risks of competition, in part through cost sharing and increased economies of scale. Examples include Sumitomo, Mitsubishi, Mitsui, and Sanwa.

A South Korean *chaebol* resembles a consortia of keiretsu except that they are typically financed through government banking groups and largely are run by professional managers trained by participating firms expressly for the job.

SELECTION OF LONG-TERM OBJECTIVES AND GRAND STRATEGY SETS

At first glance, the Strategic Management Model, which provides the framework for study throughout this book, seems to suggest that strategic choice decision making leads to the sequential selection of long-term objectives and grand strategies. In fact, however, strategic choice is the simultaneous selection of long-range objectives and grand strategies. When strategic planners study their opportunities, they try to determine which are most likely to result in achieving various long-range objectives. Almost simultaneously, they try to forecast whether an available grand strategy can take advantage of preferred opportunities so the tentative objectives can be met. In essence, then, three distinct but highly interdependent choices are being made at one time. Several triads, or sets, of possible decisions are usually considered.

A simplified example of this process is shown in Figure 7–8. In this example, the firm has determined that six strategic choice options are available. These options stem from three interactive opportunities (e.g., West Coast markets) that present little competition. Because each of these interactive opportunities can be approached through different grand strategies—for options 1 and 2, the grand strategies are horizontal integration and market development—each offers the potential for achieving long-range objectives to varying degrees. Thus, a firm rarely can make a strategic choice only on the basis of its preferred opportunities, long-range objectives, or grand strategy. Instead, these three elements must

FIGURE 7–8
A Profile of Strategic Choice Options

	Six Strategic Choice Options					
	1	**2**	**3**	**4**	**5**	**6**
Interactive opportunities	West Coast markets present little competition		Current markets sensitive to price competition		Current industry product lines after too narrow a range of markets	
Appropriate long-range objectives (limited sample): Average 5-year ROI. Company sales by year 5. Risk of negative profits.	15% +50% .30	19% +40% .25	13% +20% .10	17% +0% .15	23% +35% .20	15% +25% .05
Grand strategies	Horizontal integration	Market development	Concentration	Selective retrenchment	Product development	Concentration

be considered simultaneously, because only in combination do they constitute a strategic choice.

In an actual decision situation, the strategic choice would be complicated by a wider variety of interactive opportunities, feasible company objectives, promising grand strategy options, and evaluative criteria. Nevertheless, Figure 7–8 does partially reflect the nature and complexity of the process by which long-term objectives and grand strategies are selected.

In the next chapter, the strategic choice process will be fully explained. However, knowledge of long-term objectives and grand strategies is essential to understanding that process.

SEQUENCE OF OBJECTIVES AND STRATEGY SELECTION

The selection of long-range objectives and grand strategies involves simultaneous, rather than sequential, decisions. While it is true that objectives are needed to prevent the firm's direction and progress from being determined by random forces, it is equally true that objectives can be achieved only if strategies are implemented. In fact, long-term objectives and grand strategies are so interdependent that some business consultants do not distinguish between them. Long-term objectives and grand strategies are still combined under the heading of company strategy in most of the popular business literature and in the thinking of most practicing executives.

However, the distinction has merit. Objectives indicate what strategic managers want but provide few insights about how they will be achieved. Conversely, strategies indicate what types of actions will be taken but do not define what ends will be pursued or what criteria will serve as constraints in refining the strategic plan.

The view of objectives as constraints on strategy formulation, rather than as ends toward which strategies are directed, has been stressed by several prominent management experts.[22] They argued that strategic decisions are designed (1) to satisfy the minimum requirements of different company groups (e.g., the production department's requirement for an increase in inventory capacity on the marketing department's requirement for an increase in the sales force) and (2) to create the synergistic profit potential given these constraints.

Does it matter whether strategic decisions are made to achieve objectives or to satisfy constraints? No, because constraints are themselves objectives. The constraint of increased inventory capacity is a desire (an objective), not a certainty. Likewise, the constraint of an increase in the sales force does not assure that the increase will be achieved, given such factors as other company priorities, labor market conditions, and the firm's profit performance.

SUMMARY

Before learning how strategic decisions are made, it is important to understand the two principal components of any strategic choice; namely, long-term objectives and the grand strategy. The purpose of this chapter was to convey that understanding.

Long-term objectives were defined as the results a firm seeks to achieve over a specified period, typically five years. Seven common long-term objectives were discussed: profitability, productivity, competitive position, employee development, employee relations, technological leadership, and public responsibility. These, or any other long-term objectives, should be acceptable, flexible, measurable over time, motivating, suitable, understandable, and achievable.

Grand strategies were defined as comprehensive approaches guiding the major actions designed to achieve long-term objectives. Fourteen grand strategy options were discussed: concentrated growth, market development, product development, innovation, horizontal integration, vertical integration, concentric diversification, conglomerate diversification, turnaround, divestiture, liquidation, joint ventures, strategic alliances, and consortia.

QUESTIONS FOR DISCUSSION

1. Identify firms in the business community nearest to your college or university that you believe are using each of the 14 grand strategies discussed in this chapter.
2. Identify firms in your business community that appear to rely principally on 1 of the 14 grand strategies. What kind of information did you use to classify the firms?
3. Write a long-term objective for your school of business that exhibits the seven qualities of long-term objectives described in this chapter.
4. Distinguish between the following pairs of grand strategies:

---

[22] See, for example, R. M. Cyert and J. G. March, *A Behavioral Theory of the Firm* (Englewood Cliffs, N.J.: Prentice Hall, 1963);   H. A. Simon, "On the Concept of Organizational Goals," *Administrative Science Quarterly* 9 (1964), pp. 1–22;   and M. D. Richards, *Organizational Goal Structures* (St. Paul, Minn.: West Publishing, 1978).

a. Horizontal and vertical integration.
b. Conglomerate and concentric diversification.
c. Product development and innovation.
d. Joint venture and strategic alliance.

5. Rank each of the 14 grand strategy options discussed in this chapter on the following three scales:

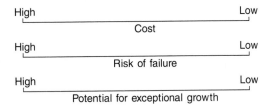

6. Identify firms that use one of the eight specific options shown in Figure 7–1 under the grand strategies of concentration, market development, and product development.

BIBLIOGRAPHY

Anderson, E. "Two Firms, One Frontier: On Assessing Joint Venture Performance." *Sloan Management Review,* Winter 1990, pp. 19–30.

Badaracco, J. L. "Alliances Speed Knowledge Transfer." *Planning Review,* March–April 1991, pp. 10–17.

Bailey, G., and J. Szerdy. "Is There Life after Downsizing?" *Journal of Business Strategy,* January 1988, pp. 8–11.

Bart, C. K. "New Venture Units: Use Them Wisely to Manage Innovation." *Sloan Management Review,* Summer 1988, pp. 35–43.

Bleeke, J., and D. Ernst. "The Way to Win in Cross-Border Alliances." *Harvard Business Review,* November–December 1991, pp. 127–35.

Block, Z. "Damage Control for New Corporate Ventures." *Journal of Business Strategy,* March 1989, pp. 22–28.

Brannen, M. Y. "Culture as the Critical Factor in Implementing Innovation." *Business Horizons,* November–December 1991, pp. 59–67.

Butler, J. E. "Theories of Technological Innovation as Useful Tools for Corporate Strategy." *Strategic Management Journal,* January 1988, pp. 15–29.

Clarke, C. J., and K. Brennan. "Defensive Strategies against Takeovers: Creating Shareholder Value." *Long Range Planning,* February 1990, pp. 95–101.

Clarke, C. J., and E. Gall. "Planned Divestment—A Five-Step Approach." *Long Range Planning,* February 1987, pp. 17–24.

DiPrimio, A. "When Turnaround Management Works." *Journal of Business Strategy,* January 1988, pp. 61–64.

Erickson, T. J.; J. F. Magee; P. A. Roussel; and K. N. Saad. "Managing Technology as a Business Strategy." *Sloan Management Review,* Spring 1990, pp. 73–78.

Ettlie, J. E. "What Makes a Manufacturing Firm Innovative?" *Academy of Management Executive,* November 1990, pp. 7–20.

Evan, W. M., and P. Olk. "R&D Consortia: A New U.S. Organizational Form." *Sloan Management Review,* Spring 1990, pp. 37–46.

Framerman, R. "How to Avoid Technical Traps in Product Development." *Planning Review,* November 1988, pp. 20–27.

Gopinath, C. "Turnaround: Recognizing Decline and Initiating Intervention." *Long Range Planning,* December 1991, pp. 96–101.

Grossi, G. "Promoting Innovation in a Big Business." *Long Range Planning,* February 1990, pp. 41–52.

Harrigan, K. R. "Matching Vertical Integration Strategies to Competitive Conditions." *Strategic Management Journal,* November–December 1986, pp. 535–55.

Haspeslagh, P. C., and D. B. Jemison. "The Challenge of Renewal through Acquisitions." *Planning Review,* March–April 1991, pp. 27–33.

Hughes, G. D. "Managing High-Tech Product Cycles." *Academy of Management Executive,* May 1990, pp. 44–55.

Kanter, R. M. "When Giants Learn Cooperative Strategies." *Planning Review,* January–February 1990, pp. 15–25.

Keller, R., and R. Chinta. "International Technology Transfer: Strategies for Success." *Academy of Management Executive,* May 1990, pp. 33–43.

Kelso, L., and P. Kelso. "Leveraged Buyouts Good and Bad." *Management Review,* November 1987, pp. 28–31.

Kogut, B. "Joint Ventures: Theoretical and Empirical Perspectives." *Strategic Management Journal,* July 1988, pp. 319–32.

Kumpe, T., and P. T. Bolwijn. "Manufacturing: The New Case for Vertical Integration." *Harvard Business Review,* March–April 1988, pp. 75–81.

Lengnick-Hall, C. A. "Innovation and Competitive Advantage: What We Know and What We Need to Learn." *Journal of Management,* June 1992, p. 399.

Leontiades, M. "The Case for Nonspecialized Diversification." *Planning Review,* January–February 1990, pp. 26–33.

Lewis, J. "Using Alliances to Build Market Power." *Planning Review,* September–October 1990, pp. 4–9.

Miller, D. "The Generic Strategy Trap." *The Journal of Business Strategy,* January–February 1992, pp. 37–41.

Morone, J. "Strategic Use of Technology." *California Management Review,* Summer 1989, pp. 91–110.

Nahauandi, A., and A. R. Malekzadeh. "Acculturation in Mergers and Acquisitions." *Academy of Management Review,* January 1988, pp. 79–90.

Newman, W. H. "Focused Joint Ventures in Transforming Economies." *Academy of Management Executive,* February 1992, pp. 67–75.

Nielson, R. P. "Cooperative Strategies." *Planning Review,* March 1986, pp. 16–20.

Paap, J. E. "A Venture Capitalist's Advice for Successful Strategic Alliances." *Planning Review,* September–October 1990, pp. 20–26.

Pearce, J. A., II. "An Executive-Level Perspective on the Strategic Management Process." *California Management Review,* Summer 1981, pp. 39–48.

——————. "Selecting among Alternative Grand Strategies." *California Management Review,* Spring 1982, pp. 23–31.

Pearce, J. A., II, and J. W. Harvey. "Concentrated Growth Strategies." *Academy of Management Executive,* February 1990, pp. 61–68.

Pearce, J. A., II, and D. K. Robbins. "Toward Improved Theory and Research on Business Turnaround." *Journal of Management,* 1993.

——————. "Entrepreneurial Recovery Strategies among Small Market Share Manufacturers." *Journal of Business Venturing,* 1994.

Pearce, J. A., II; D. K. Robbins; E. B. Freeman; and R. B. Robinson, Jr. "The Impact of Grand Strategy and Planning Formality on Financial Performance." *Strategic Management Journal,* March 1987, pp. 125–34.

Peters, T. "Get Innovative or Get Dead." *California Management Review,* Winter 1991, pp. 9–23.

Randall, R. M. "The Coyote and the Bear Form a Strategic Alliance." *Planning Review,* September–October 1990, p. 27.

Reimann, B. C. "Corporate Strategies That Work." *Planning Review,* January–February 1992, pp. 41–46.

Robbins, D. K., and Pearce, J. A., II. "Entrepreneurial Retrenchment among Small Manufacturing Firms." *Journal of Business Venturing,* July 1993, pp. 301–18.

Roberts, E. B., and C. A. Berry. "Entering New Businesses: Selecting Strategies for Success." *Sloan Management Review,* Spring 1985, pp. 3–17.

Rule, E. G., and D. W. Irwin. "Fostering Entrepreneurship: The New Competitive Edge." *Journal of Business Strategy,* May 1988, pp. 44–47.

Schroeder, D. M., and R. Hopley. "Product Development Strategies for High-Tech Industries." *Journal of Business Strategy,* May 1988, pp. 38–43.

Shortell, S. M., and E. J. Zajac. "Internal Corporate Joint Ventures: Development Processes and Performance Outcomes." *Strategic Management Journal,* November 1988, pp. 527–42.

Sutton, R. I., and A. L. Callahan. "The Stigma of Bankruptcy: Spoiled Organizational Image and Its Management." *Academy of Management Journal,* September 1987, pp. 405–36.

Weidenbaum, M., and S. Vogt. "Takeovers and Stockholders: Winners and Losers." *California Management Review,* Summer 1987, pp. 157–68.

Wheelwright, S. C., and W. E. Sasser, Jr. "The New Product Development Map." *Harvard Business Review,* May 1989, pp. 112–25.

Woo, C. Y.; G. E. Willard; and S. M. Beckstead. "Spin-Offs: What Are the Gains?" *Journal of Business Strategy,* March 1989, pp. 29–32.

CHAPTER 7 COHESION CASE

FORMULATING LONG-TERM OBJECTIVES AND GRAND STRATEGIES AT THE COCA-COLA COMPANY

Coca-Cola management sets forth several long-term objectives toward which the company is focused for the next decade. First, they offer a statement about what they call "rewards." In the booklet entitled *Coca-Cola, a Business System toward 2000: Our Mission in the 1990s,* Coke management sets forth the four key rewards it seeks:

- Satisfied consumers who return again and again to our brands for refreshment.
- Profitable customers who rely on our worldwide brands and services.
- Communities around the world where we are an economic contributor and welcomed guest.
- Successful business partners.
- Shareholders who are building value through the power of the Coca-Cola system.

LONG-TERM OBJECTIVES

The company identifies several long-term objectives that support these reward intentions. The first objective most often mentioned is:

Management's primary objective is to maximize shareowner value over time.

The company then indicates that the following objectives help accomplish this overarching objective:

Maximize long-term cash flow by increasing gallon sales, optimizing profit margins, expanding global business systems through investment in areas offering attractive returns.
 The principle objective of bottling investments is to ensure the strongest and most efficient production, distribution, and marketing systems possible, in order to maximize long-term growth in volume, cash flow, and shareowner value of the bottler and the Company.

The Coca-Cola Company pursues several inherent objectives as follows:

Profitability   Double-digit levels annually equal to or exceeding historical levels.

Productivity   Each Coca-Cola facility has as its objective maintenance or improvement of its operating profit margin.

Competitive Position   Coca-Cola seeks to be the market leader in markets in which it competes.

Technological Leadership   Coca-Cola seeks to be the leader in the production and marketing technologies used in the markets in which it competes.

What are the qualities of Coca-Cola's long-term objectives? It would appear Coca-Cola's objectives meet several criteria this chapter has suggested that characterize effective objectives. Specifically, each of these publicly stated Coke objectives appears to be acceptable, flexible, motivating, suitable, reasonable, and achievable.

These objectives all appear deficient in terms of being measurable. None of these publicly stated objectives identifies a quantifiable result to be achieved or a specific time period within which to accomplish those results. Coke officials indicate a preference for stating objectives publicly in broad terms. They prefer to retain key results and timetables for internal consumption only. While this may be quite appropriate, you should nonetheless be able to recognize that objectives without measurable results or measurable timetables within which to accomplish them lose a lot of their value in focusing and directing strategic activities.

COCA-COLA STRATEGIES

Coca-Cola is in the enviable position of being able to pursue numerous strategies. Among generic strategies, Coke is able to pursue low-cost strategies and still enjoy higher profit margins. Its unparalleled trademarks and syrup patent protection offer strong support for differentiation strategies. And the global reality that its success is determined in one local market at a time puts it in the unique posture of needing focus strategies by local geographic markets.

Among grand strategies, Coke has several options available to it. Concentrated growth appears a viable strategy, at least in key major markets like the U.S. market. But given its sizable financial resources, concentrated growth alone may not achieve long-term objectives. Rather, its extraordinary global "system" makes market development a related and potentially advantageous strategy. The many underdeveloped global markets available to Coca-Cola represent attractive targets for Coke's excess resources.

Coke long has been committed to a product development strategy, which creates new but related products that can be marketed to current customers through established channels. Not only does this allow Coke to penetrate existing markets and channels but it preempts new product efforts of weaker competitors.

The diversification strategies, concentric and conglomerate, are available to Coca-Cola given its financial resources and market clout. Since 1975, Coke has included both diversification strategies in the options it has chosen. Coke's move into movie entertainment, water treatment, plastic films, and certain foods were clear diversifications.

Finally, the latter part of the 1980s has seen Coca-Cola seriously consider a forward vertical integration strategy, allowing greater involvement in and control over bottling activity, given the removal of regulatory restrictions on doing so, and combined with the critical role local bottlers play in distributing national brands and the relative strength in this regard of PepsiCo's bottling network.

The global commitments and aspirations of Coca-Cola are another reason forward vertical integration in some form must be considered by the company. Whether this takes the form of joint ventures, strategic alliances, or consortia appears dependent on market and regulatory conditions within each country that Coke targets.

Coke has little need for retrenchment, turnaround, and liquidation strategies. It has a strong position in most of its businesses. Divestiture has been used by Coke when it has chosen to exit a variety of related and unrelated businesses. This strategy was continually considered by Coke's management as it increasingly emphasized the need to focus on soft-drink and clearly related business sectors.

8

STRATEGIC ANALYSIS AND CHOICE

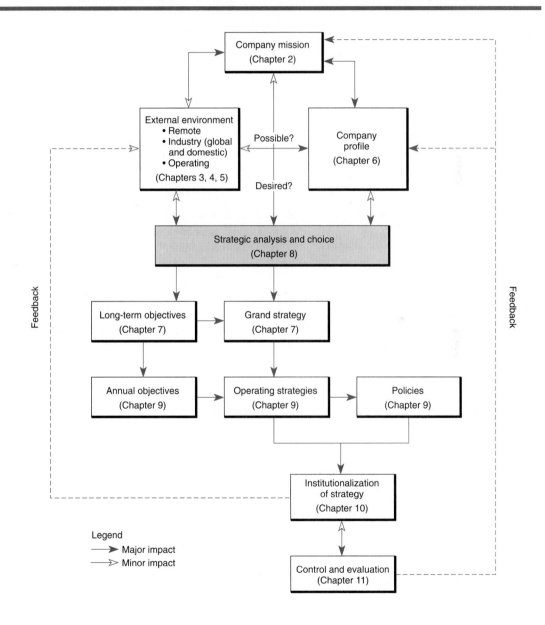

Company mission
(Chapter 2)

External environment
• Remote
• Industry (global and domestic)
• Operating
(Chapters 3, 4, 5)

Possible?

Desired?

Company profile
(Chapter 6)

Strategic analysis and choice
(Chapter 8)

Long-term objectives
(Chapter 7)

Grand strategy
(Chapter 7)

Annual objectives
(Chapter 9)

Operating strategies
(Chapter 9)

Policies
(Chapter 9)

Institutionalization of strategy
(Chapter 10)

Control and evaluation
(Chapter 11)

Feedback

Feedback

Legend
→ Major impact
⇢ Minor impact

Strategic analysis and choice is the step in the strategic management process whereby managers consider alternative strategies and choose those that the firm will pursue. This step usually involves the choice of a corporate-level strategy identifying the business that the firm will be involved in and then the choice of the competitive strategy that each of these businesses will pursue.

Holiday Corporation, a multibusiness firm that included motels (Holiday Inns and Hampton Inns), casino gaming (Harrah's), steamships (Delta), restaurants (Perkins Family Restaurants), and bus lines (Trailways), faced a corporate strategy decision regarding which businesses it should remain in looking toward the 1990s and what level of resources it should commit to each of these businesses. And each of Holiday's businesses requires a choice of strategy. Much the same challenge faces Italy's first family of capitalism, the Agnellis, as they seek to position a portfolio of companies—including Fiat, Perrier, Danone Foods, and Meridiana Airlines—for success in the European Community. In what might appear deceptively simple, McDonald's, the highly successful fast-food chain, faced a corporate strategy decision regarding whether to remain in a single business—the fast-food industry—or to expand into other businesses via vertical integration, horizontal integration, or diversification. With that decision, McDonald's managers had to choose the competitive strategy its single-line business would pursue. At Holiday Corporation, Agnelli, and McDonald's Corporation, strategists had to analyze and choose corporate- and business-level strategies. Such are the decisions that strategists in any firm must face as they chart their firm's future.

This chapter examines the analysis and choice of corporate and business strategies. First, it looks at corporate strategy, examining how corporate managers choose among alternative grand strategies and analyze a diversified portfolio of businesses. Then it turns to analysis and choice among alternative business strategies—to the factors that managers consider in choosing among competitive strategies and to the influence of different types of industries on business strategy choices.

CORPORATE STRATEGY ANALYSIS AND CHOICE

The analysis and choice of corporate strategy varies according to the complexity of the business involvements of the overall firm. For firms that are predominantly in one line of business, such as McDonald's, corporate strategy is concerned with deciding whether to concentrate solely on that line of business or to become involved in other lines of business that are either related or unrelated to it. For firms that are already involved in several lines of business, such as Holiday Inns or Italy's Agnelli family, corporate strategy is concerned with deciding whether to increase or reduce the resources committed to the current lines of business and whether to become involved in other lines that are either related or unrelated to them.

An Evolutionary Perspective

One way to view the analysis and choice of corporate strategy is to look at the typical evolution of corporate strategy in American firms. Figure 8–1 portrays that evolution. Like

FIGURE 8–1
Typical Evolution of Corporate Strategy in American Firms

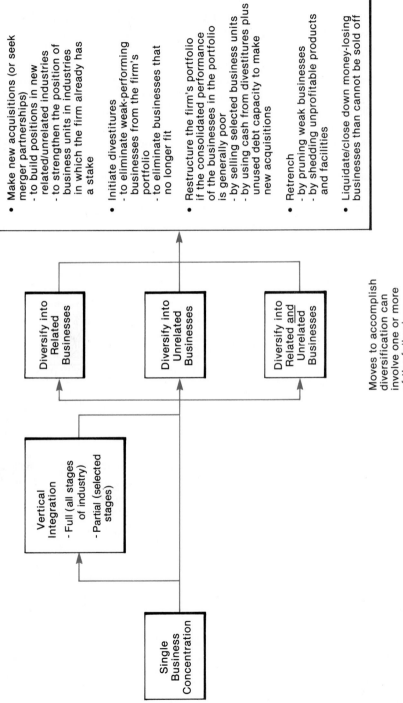

Postdiversification Strategic Alternatives

- Make new acquisitions (or seek merger partnerships)
  - to build positions in new related/unrelated industries
  - to strengthen the position of business units in industries in which the firm already has a stake

- Initiate divestitures
  - to eliminate weak-performing businesses from the firm's portfolio
  - to eliminate businesses that no longer fit

- Restructure the firm's portfolio if the consolidated performance of the businesses in the portfolio is generally poor
  - by selling selected business units
  - by using cash from divestitures plus unused debt capacity to make new acquisitions

- Retrench
  - by pruning weak businesses
  - by shedding unprofitable products and facilities

- Liquidate/close down money-losing businesses than cannot be sold off

Diversify into Related Businesses

Diversify into Unrelated Businesses

Diversify into Related _and_ Unrelated Businesses

Vertical Integration
- Full (all stages of industry)
- Partial (selected stages)

Single Business Concentration

Moves to accomplish diversification can involve one or more of the following:

- Acquisition/merger
- Start-up of own new businesses from scratch
- Joint venture partnerships

Source: Arthur Thompson, Jr., and A. J. Strickland III, *Strategic Management*, 6th ed. (Homewood, Ill.: Richard D. Irwin, 1992), p. 179.

McDonald's, most American firms start by concentrating on a single line of business. This corporate strategy offers compelling advantages. It enhances unity of purpose throughout the firm. It typically is headed by top managers who have come up "through the ranks" and clearly appreciate what makes the firm successful. It makes the firm sensitive to changes in customer needs and industry conditions and, thus, enables it to build strong competitive advantages.

Concentration on a single business also is subject to certain risks. All of the firm's "eggs" are in one industry "basket." As the firm's industry matures, growth becomes more difficult and pressures on profit margins increase. Moreover, technological innovation can rapidly change the industry, as computers changed the typewriter industry and as digital electronics changed the watch industry.

One response to these risks is a corporate strategy of vertical integration. Depending on where the firm's business is concentrated in the product chain, that strategy would have the firm undertake "backward" integration or "forward" integration. Backward integration allows a firm to stabilize its sources of supply previously paid to its suppliers and to absorb the profit margins. Forward integration increases a firm's access to customers, thus enabling it to increase it sales and to acquire the profit margins associated with "downstream" markups. Vertical integration is usually appropriate when downstream or upstream profit margins are attractive, when corporate managers feel comfortable about taking on new areas of business activity, and when it can yield competitive advantages in the pricing or quality areas of the core business.

Related diversification is typically the next move in corporate strategy. As expertise in various aspects of the core business is refined, corporate strategists look for ways to apply that expertise in other businesses or to shore weaknesses by becoming involved in other businesses. Strategy in Action 8–1 describes just such an evolution at PepsiCo. Figure 8–2 provides a typical relatedness checklist that managers might use to pursue a corporate strategy of related diversification.

PepsiCo has become a global consumer products leader in soft drinks, snack foods, and restaurants by exploiting relatedness in distribution, logistics, sales forces, and management know-how. Honda (Japan) has become a global giant exploiting small-engine technology in lawn mowers, boats, and automobiles.

Finally, unrelated diversification occurs in firms whose strategists feel that resources generated by current businesses can be better invested in other business activities. Such firms may engage in unrelated diversification for various reasons: (1) a "cash-rich, opportunity-poor" firm may acquire opportunity-rich, cash-poor businesses; (2) a firm in a seasonal core business may acquire businesses that provide it with counterseasonal financial balance; or (3) a highly leveraged firm may acquire a debt-free business to balance its overall capital structure. ITT is perhaps the best known pioneer of unrelated diversification. Among the many businesses in which it became involved were telephone equipment, Sheraton hotels, Scott lawn products, Wonder Bread, and Hartford Insurance.

The patterns of strategic evolution that researchers have found among American firms provide one perspective on the analysis and choice of corporate strategy. The challenge for corporate strategists using this perspective is to decide when corporate conditions call for movement to a new strategy. The next section provides guidelines that help corporate strategists make such decisions.

CHOOSING AMONG GRAND STRATEGY ALTERNATIVES

Strategists in single-business or dominant-business firms face a choice among 12 grand strategies (described in Chapter 7) as they seek strategy alternatives that offer a stronger fit with a firm's overall situation. This section describes two ways of analyzing this situational fit.

Grand Strategy Selection Matrix

One valuable guide to the selection of a promising grand strategy is the matrix shown in Figure 8–3. The basic idea underlying the matrix is that two variables are of central concern in the selection process: (1) the principal purpose of the grand strategy and (2) the choice of an internal or external emphasis for growth or profitability, or both.

In the past, planners were advised to follow certain rules or prescriptions in their choice of strategies. Now, most experts agree that strategy selection is better guided by the conditions of the planning period and by the company strengths and weaknesses. It should be noted, however, that even the early approaches to strategy selection sought to match a concern over internal versus external growth with a desire to overcome weaknesses or maximize strengths.

The same considerations led to the development of the grand strategy selection matrix. A firm in quadrant I, with "all its eggs in one basket," often views itself as overcommitted to a particular business with limited growth opportunities or high risks. One reasonable solution is *vertical integration,* which enables the firm to reduce risk by reducing uncertainty about inputs or access to customers. Another is *conglomerate diversification,* which provides a profitable investment alternative with diverting management attention from the original business. However, the external approaches to overcoming weaknesses usually result in the most costly grand strategies. Acquiring a second business demands large investments of time and sizable financial resources. Thus, strategic managers considering these approaches must guard against exchanging one set of weaknesses for another.

More conservative approaches to overcoming weaknesses are found in quadrant II. Firms often choose to redirect resources from one internal business activity to another. This approach maintains the firm's commitment to its basic mission, rewards success, and enables further development of proven competitive advantages. The least disruptive of the quadrant II strategies is *retrenchment,* pruning the current activities of a business. If the weaknesses of the business arose from inefficiencies, retrenchment can actually serve as a *turnaround* strategy—that is, the business gains new strength from the streamlining of its operations and the elimination of waste. However, if those weaknesses are a major obstruction to success in the industry and the costs of overcoming them are unaffordable or are not justified by a cost-benefit analysis, then eliminating the business must be considered. Strategy in Action 8–2 describes the extraordinary decision by Holiday Corporation to divest itself of its founding Holiday Inn chain to pursue more profitable opportunities. *Divestiture* offers the best possibility for recouping the firm's investment, but even *liquidation* can be an attractive option if the alternatives are bankruptcy or an unwarranted drain on the firm's resources.

A common business adage states that a firm should build from strength. The premise of this adage is that growth and survival depend on an ability to capture a market share that

---

STRATEGY
IN ACTION **CHOOSING AMONG GRAND STRATEGY ALTERNATIVES AT PEPSICO**
8–1

Twenty-five years ago, PepsiCo was a sleepy and distant second to Coca-Cola in the U.S. soft-drink industry. Soda consumption by the baby boom generation made it easy for PepsiCo to double its sales to almost $1 billion while maintaining a steady ROE in the high teens and a 5 percent return on sales. This profitability allowed the company to generate an additional $40 million in working capital over that needed to operate the company's existing business.

PepsiCo's management team led by Donald Kendall and Andrall Pearson sought to heat up the company's growth, given the predictability of its soft-drink income stream. As they examined alternative grand strategies, they viewed PepsiCo as possessing proven strengths in selling an inexpensive consumable product (Pepsi) to a young, energetic consumer. Their first choice of strategy was one that sought to redirect internal resources (excess cash generated) toward maximizing these strengths. Their conclusion in this regard was a four-part program:

1. Continue to build sales of their Pepsi product in existing outlets. (Concentrated Growth)
2. Expand distribution (and sales) of Pepsi by aggressively pursuing new and different outlets, especially grocery stores and international. (Market Development)
3. Create related but new products like diet drinks to appeal to baby boomers reaching adulthood. (Product Development)
4. Design revolutionary new packaging to reinforce the sales efforts emanating from above. (Innovation—plastics and 32 oz.)

Wisely anticipating that these strategies would continue to generate a growing stream of excess cash, these managers also realized that PepsiCo did not possess other resources (people, experience, and products) necessary to take advantage of related growth opportunities. So PepsiCo had to look externally for the management, experience, and product opportunities that could blend well with and maximize its proven strengths in cola marketing and sales. Their add-on grand strategies to pursue these conclusions were:

5. Acquire 7UP, Mountain Dew, and Mug Rootbeer to expand their product offerings. (Horizontal Integration)
6. Diversify via acquisition into related products including Frito Lay. (Concentric Diversification)

PepsiCo also rationalized the acquisition of Wilson Sporting Goods and United Van Lines as a part of this strategy. Wilson was seen as selling products to the same market—active young people. United complemented PepsiCo's growing transportation network by bringing the expertise to run it efficiently.

Source: PepsiCo, Inc., 1971 and 1991 annual reports.

---

is large enough for essential economies of scale. If a firm believes that this approach will be profitable and prefers an internal emphasis for maximizing strengths, four grand strategies hold considerable promise. As shown in quadrant III, the most common approach is *concentrated growth*; that is, market penetration. The firm that selects this strategy is strongly committed to its current products and markets. It strives to solidify its position by reinvesting resources to fortify its strengths.

STRATEGY
IN ACTION   **concluded**
8–1

PepsiCo's choice of grand strategies generally proved successful. In 10 years net sales had increased sixfold to over $6 billion. Profitability and cash generation ratios remained consistent, meaning even greater excess financial resources to work with. Along the way, Wilson and United were divested, because management saw both businesses to contain several weaknesses not worth (from PepsiCo's perspective) investment to correct. With this overall growth in financial resources, PepsiCo managers concluded the same grand strategies applied that led to the acquisition of Pizza Hut, Kentucky Fried Chicken, and Taco Bell in the early 1980s as a logical concentric diversification.

PepsiCo, now in soft drinks, snack foods, and restaurants, saw its net sales, net income, and cash flow grow at compounded annual rates of 17 percent, 19 percent, and 15 percent, respectively, over the five years preceding 1992. Over this period, operations generated over $10 billion for reinvestment, dividends, or acquisition.

Contributing to and reaping the bounty of this legacy, PepsiCo's colorful chairman and CEO, Wayne Calloway, observed in 1992:

> At PepsiCo, we've increased sales and net income at an exhilarating rate of nearly 15 percent for 26 years. That means we've doubled our business about every five years. But now that we're about $20 billion big, you might well ask, How long can this keep going on? Forever, as far as we're concerned. At least that's our intention.

Mr. Calloway views PepsiCo as being in the fortunate position of maximizing strengths via redirection of internally generated resources in each of its three business sections. Some of the specific strategies he outlines to back up his above assertion are:

1. In many international markets, consumers drink fewer soft drinks in a year than most Americans consume in a week. We're going to change that. [Concentrated Growth]

2. Our (snack food) products are still unavailable to about 70 percent of the world's population. We're changing that. [Market Development]

3. Soft drinks represent about one quarter of all beverages consumed in the United States. That means that three quarters of the beverage market provides opportunity. [Product Development]

4. More than 40 percent of all adults in the United States have a meal delivered from a restaurant at least once a month. We're becoming a front runner in this market segment. [Concentrated Growth]

5. International consumers eat about one sixth the amount of snack chips consumed by their U.S. counterparts, but snacking is becoming more popular every day. [Market and Product Development]

Two alternative approaches are *market development* and *product development*. With these strategies, the firm attempts to broaden its operations. Market development is chosen if the firm's strategic managers feel that its existing products would be well received by new customer groups. Product development is chosen if they feel that the firm's existing customers would be interested in products related to its current lines. Product development also may be based on technological or other competitive advantages. The final alternative for quadrant III firms is *innovation*. When the firm's strengths are in creative product design

FIGURE 8–2
Checklist of Types of Strategic Fit, Their Competitive Advantage Potentials, and the Impediments to Achieving Their Benefits in Related Diversification

Types of Strategic Fit and Opportunities for Sharing	Potential Competitive Advantages	Impediments to Achieving the Benefits of Fit
Market-related strategic fits: Shared sales force activities or shared sales office, or both	• Lower selling costs. • Better market coverage. • Stronger technial advice to buyers. • Enhanced convenience for buyers (can buy from single source). • Improved access to buyers (have more products to sell).	• Buyers have different purchasing habits toward the products. • Different salespersons are more effective in representing the product. • Some products get more attention than others. • Buyers prefer to multiple source rather than single source their purchases.
Shared after-sale service and repair work	• Lower servicing costs. • Better utilization of service personnel (less idle time). • Faster servicing of customer calls.	• Different equipment or different labor skills, or both, are needed to handle repairs. • Buyers may do some in-house repairs.
Shared brand name	• Stronger brand image and company reputation. • Increased buyer confidence in the brand.	• Company reputation is hurt if quality of one product is lower.
Shared advertising and promotional activities	• Lower costs. • Greater clout in purchasing ads.	• Appropriate forms of messages are different. • Appropriate timing of promotions is different.
Common distribution channels	• Lower distribution costs. • Enhanced bargaining power with distributors and retailers to gain shelf space, shelf positioning, stronger push and more dealer attention, and better, profit margins.	• Dealers resist being dominated by a single supplier and turn to multiple sources and lines. • Heavy use of the shared channel erodes willingness of other channels to carry or push the firm's products.
Shared order processing	• Lower order processing costs. • One-stop shopping for buyer enhances service and, thus, differentiation.	• Differences in ordering cycles disrupt order processing economies.
Operating fits: Joint procurement of purchased inputs	• Lower input costs. • Improved input quality. • Improved service from suppliers.	• Input needs are different in terms of quality or other specifications. • Inputs are needed at different plant locations, and centralized purchasing is not responsive to separate needs of each plant.

or unique production technologies, sales can be stimulated by accelerating perceived obsolescence. This is the principle underlying the innovative grand strategy.

Maximizing a firm's strengths by aggressively expanding its base of operations usually requires an external emphasis. The preferred options in such cases are shown in quadrant

FIGURE 8–2 (concluded)

Types of Strategic Fit and Opportunities for Sharing	Potential Competitive Advantages	Impediments to Achieving the Benefits of Fit
Shared manufacturing and assembly facilities	• Lower manufacturing/assembly costs. • Better capacity utilization, because peak demand for one product correlates with valley demand for other. • Bigger scale of operation improves access to better technology and results in better quality.	• Higher changeover costs in shifting from one product to another. • High-cost special tooling or equipment is required to accomodate quality differences or design differences.
Shared inbound or outbound shipping and materials handling	• Lower freight and handling costs. • Better delivery reliability. • More frequent deliveries, such that inventory costs are reduced.	• Input sources or plant locations, or both, are in different geographic areas. • Needs for frequency and reliability of inbound/outbound delivery differ among the business units.
Shared product and process technologies or technology development, or both	• Lower product or process design costs, or both, because of shorter design times and transfers of knowledge from area to area. • More innovative ability, owing to scale of effort and attraction of better R&D personnel.	• Technologies are the same, but the applications in different business units are different enough to prevent much sharing of real value.
Shared administrative support activities	• Lower administrative and operating overhead costs.	• Support activities are not a large proportion of cost, and sharing has little cost impact (and virtually no differentiaiton impact).
Management Fits: Shared management know-how, operating skills, and proprietary information	• Efficient transfer of a distinctive competence—can create cost savings or enhance differentiation. • More effective management as concerns strategy formulation, strategy implementation, and understanding of key success factors.	• Actual transfer of know-how is costly or stretches the key skill personnel too thinly, or both. • Increased risks that proprietary information will leak out.

Sources: Adapted from Michael E. Porter, *Competitive Advantage* (New York: Free Press, 1985) pp. 337–51; and Arthur A. Thompson, Jr., and A. Strickland III, *Strategic Management*, 6th ed. (Homewood, Ill.: Richard D. Irwin, 1992), pp. 167–68.

IV. *Horizontal integration* is attractive because it makes possible a quick increase in output capability. Moreover, in horizontal integration, the skills of the managers of the original business often are critical in converting newly acquired facilities into profitable contributors to the parent firm; this expands a fundamental competitive advantage of the firm—its management.

Concentric diversification is a good second choice for similar reasons. Because the original and newly acquired businesses are related, the distinctive competences of the diversifying firm are likely to facilitate a smooth, synergistic, and profitable expansion.

FIGURE 8–3
Grand Strategy Selection Matrix

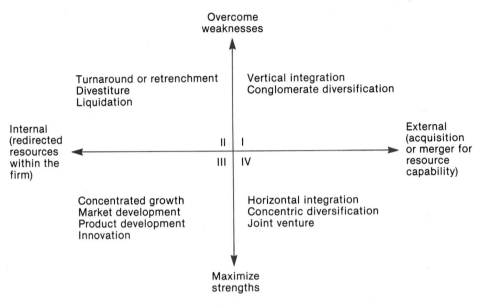

Source: John A. Pearce II, "Selecting among Alternative Grand Strategies," *California Management Review,* Spring 1982, p. 29.

The final alternative for increasing resource capability through external emphasis is a *joint venture.* This alternative allows a firm to extend its strengths into competitive arenas that it would be hesitant to enter alone. A partner's production, technological, financial, or marketing capabilities can reduce the firm's financial investment significantly and increase its probability of success.

Model of Grand Strategy Clusters

A second guide to selecting a promising grand strategy is shown in Figure 8–4. The figure is based on the idea that the situation of a business is defined in terms of the growth rate of the general market and the firm's competitive position in that market. When these factors are considered simultaneously, a business can be broadly categorized in one of four quadrants: (I) strong competitive position in a rapidly growing market, (II) weak position in a rapidly growing market, (III) weak position in a slow-growth market, or (IV) strong position in a slow-growth market. Each of these quadrants suggests a set of promising possibilities for the selection of a grand strategy.

Firms in quadrant I are in excellent strategic position. One obvious grand strategy for such firms is continued concentration on their current business as it is currently defined. Because consumers seem satisfied with the firm's current strategy, shifting notably from it would endanger the firm's established competitive advantages. McDonald's Corporation has followed this approach for 25 years. However, if the firm has resources that exceed the demands of a concentrated growth strategy, it should consider vertical integration. Either

FIGURE 8–4
Model of Grand Strategy Clusters

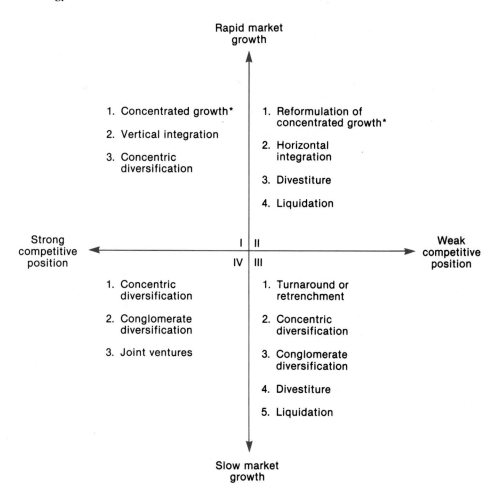

Source: Adapted from R. Christensen, N. A. Berg, and M. S. Salter, *Policy Formulation and Administration* (Homewood, Ill.: Richard D. Irwin, 1976), pp. 16–18.

forward or backward integration helps a firm protect its profit margins and market share by ensuring better access to consumers or material inputs. Finally, to diminish the risks associated with a narrow product or service line, a quadrant I firm might be wise to consider concentric diversification; with this strategy, the firm continues to invest heavily in its basic area of proven ability. Strategy in Action 8–1 describes how PepsiCo, a clear quadrant I firm, has followed these guidelines.

Firms in quadrant II must seriously evaluate their present approach to the marketplace. If a firm has competed long enough to accurately assess the merits of its current grand strategy, it must determine (1) why that strategy is ineffectual and (2) whether it is capable of competing effectively. Depending on the answers to these questions, the firm should

STRATEGY
IN ACTION   **FROM HOLIDAY INNS TO HOLIDAY CORPORATION
8–2   TO THE PROMUS COMPANIES: A STORY OF
              CORPORATE PORTFOLIO MANAGEMENT**

I n 1952, Kemmons Wilson started Holiday Inns to meet what he perceived to be a glaring need for affordable, consistent lodging throughout the United States and ultimately the world. Extraordinarily successful, Holiday Inns became and still is the largest lodging chain in the world, with three times the number of rooms as its nearest competitor. While this story generally is known to most of us, the fact Holiday Inns became a portfolio of businesses that has changed dramatically over the last 15 years is not. Following this latter story is an interesting journey in the application of corporate portfolio analysis.

By 1977, its 25th year, Holiday Inns Corporation was seen as a travel-related company, with several businesses Kemmons Wilson viewed as strategically related. The corporate portfolio looked as follows:

1977: Holiday Inn Corporation

		Revenue	Op. Inc.
A.	Holiday Inns.	$590 mm	$90 mm
B.	Trailways Bus Lines.	$244 mm	$16 mm
C.	Delta Steamships.	$ 80 mm	$17 mm
D.	Products Group:	$144 mm	$ 6 mm
	1. InnKeepers Supply.		
	2. Dohrmann.		
	3. Innkare.		

Over the next five years, Kemmons Wilson would step down to be replaced by his long-time vice chairman and COO, Roy Winegardner. Holiday Inns' board, spurred by their young president, Mike Rose, began to view Holiday Inns as a portfolio of businesses needing significant change. Acting consistently with the strategic suggestions arising from the above portfolio analysis, Trailways, Delta, and the Products Group were divested, raising approximately $280 million. That money, along with new stock and debt, was used to reposition Holiday Inns as a "hospitality company" by acquiring Harrah's and Perkins Restaurants and by seeding two new hospitality ventures.

Source: Holiday Inns Corporation 1977 annual report;   Holiday Corporation 1983 annual report;   The Promus Companies 1992 annual report.

choose one of four grand strategy options: formulation or reformulation of a concentrated growth strategy, horizontal integration, divestiture, or liquidation.

In a rapidly growing market, even a small or relatively weak business often is able to find a profitable niche. Thus, formulation or reformulation of a concentrated growth strategy is usually the first option that should be considered. However, if the firm lacks either a critical competitive element or sufficient economies of scale to achieve competitive cost efficiencies, then a grand strategy that directs its efforts toward horizontal integration is often a desirable alternative. A final pair of options involve deciding to stop competing in the market or product area of the business. A multiproduct firm may conclude that it is most

STRATEGY
IN ACTION   **continued**
8–2

1983: Holiday Corporation

		Revenue	Op. Inc.

A.	Hotel Group:
	  1. Holiday Inns.
	  2. Holiday Inn Crowne
	     Plaza.
		$882 mm	$168 mm

B.	Gaming Group:
	  1. Harrah's Nevada.
	  2. Harrah's Atl. City.
		$592 mm	$116 mm

C.	Perkins Restaurants.	$106 mm	$ 5 mm

D.	New Ventures:
	  1. Hampton Inns.
	  2. Embassy Suites.
		$ 0	$– 8 mm

Mike Rose soon became chairman and CEO of what in 1983 was renamed "Holiday Corporation." He offered these observations at the time:

> We have completed the divestiture of our nonhospitality businesses. The major story for 1983 and the remainder of the decade is execution of our segmentation strategy in the hotel industry and in the casino gaming markets.

What Mr. Rose had done was to restructure Holiday's business portfolio, diverting resources from weak or inconsistent businesses into those with greater future promise. The real question beginning to arise via portfolio analysis was the long-term status of the Holiday Inns chain with its segment, midpriced hotel accommodations, facing increased competition and less demand. By 1992, dramatic change had occurred again.

likely to achieve the goals of its mission if the business is dropped through divestiture. This grand strategy not only eliminates a drain on resources but also may provide funds to promote other business activities. As an option of last resort, a firm may decide to liquidate the business. This means that the business cannot be sold as a going concern and is at best worth only the value of its tangible assets. The decision to liquidate is an undeniable admission of failure by a firm's strategic management and, thus, often is delayed—to the further detriment of the firm.

Strategic managers tend to resist divestiture because it is likely to jeopardize their control of the firm and perhaps even their jobs. Thus, by the time the desirability of divestiture is acknowledged, businesses often deteriorate to the point of failing to attract potential

STRATEGY IN ACTION 8–2 concluded

1992: The Promus Companies

	Revenue	Op. Inc.
A. Gaming Group:	$859 mm	$171 mm
1. Harrah's Atl. City.		
2. Harrah's Lk. Tahoe.		
3. Harrah's Las Vegas.		
4. Harrah's Laughlin.		
5. Harrah's Reno.		
B. Hotel Group:	$167 mm	$ 33 mm
1. Hampton Inns.		
2. Embassy Suites.		
3. Homewood Suites.		

Consistent with the trend predicted and strategic recommendations emanating from the 1983 portfolio analysis, Holiday Corporation's board eventually would sell the Holiday Inns chain to the Bass group for approximately $2.5 billion. Also during this time, the Perkins Restaurant chain was sold at a net loss and Holiday Inn Crowne Suites was sold in a separate transaction. The newly created portfolio of businesses has what was originally the Holiday Inns, now Promus, position with two groups of businesses focused in the faster growing segments of gaming and lodging industries with what Mike Rose called "the leading brands" in each respective segment.

The evolution of Holiday Inns over the last 15 years to include getting out of the Holiday Inns business reflects a corporate portfolio management perspective very consistent with the suggestions of the BCG matrix or industry attractive/business strength matrix approaches. Indeed, so seriously were those suggestions taken to heart that Promus's largest business and the one from which it was founded was "harvested" to raise resources to support more promising business opportunities and building shareholder value.

buyers. The consequences of such delays are financially disastrous for firm owners because the value of a going concern is many times greater than the value of its assets.

Strategic managers who have a business in quadrant III and expect a continuation of slow market growth and a relatively weak competitive position will usually attempt to decrease their resource commitment to that business. Minimal withdrawal is accomplished through retrenchment; this strategy has the side benefits of making resources available for other investments and of motivating employees to increase their operating efficiency. An alternative approach is to divert resources for expansion through investment in other businesses. This approach typically involves either concentric or conglomerate diversification because the firm usually wants to enter more promising arenas of competition than forms of integration or development would allow. The final options for quadrant III businesses are divestiture, if an optimistic buyer can be found, and liquidation.

Quadrant IV businesses (strong competitive position in a slow-growth market) have a basis of strength from which to diversify into more promising growth areas. These businesses have characteristically high cash flow levels and limited internal growth needs. Thus, they are in an excellent position for concentric diversification into ventures that utilize their proven acumen. A second option is conglomerate diversification, which spreads investment risk and does not divert managerial attention from the present business. The final option is joint ventures, which are especially attractive to multinational firms. Through joint ventures, a domestic business can gain competitive advantages in promising new fields while exposing itself to limited risks.

Managing Diversified Corporate Portfolios

When a single- or dominant-business firm is transformed into a collection of numerous businesses across several industries, strategic analysis becomes much more complex. One of the early methods that attempted to aid corporate strategists in this task was the portfolio approach.

The *portfolio approach* involves examining each of the firm's separate "businesses" as elements of its total *portfolio* of business. In a broad sense, corporate strategy is concerned with the generation and allocation of corporate resources. The businesses in the firm's portfolio are, to varying degrees, the generators and recipients of these resources. Thus, the portfolio approach provides a simple, visual way of identifying and evaluating alternative strategies for the generation and allocation of corporate resources.

The BCG Growth/Share Matrix

One of the earliest portfolio approaches to corporate strategic analysis was the growth/share matrix, pioneered by the Boston Consulting Group (BCG) and illustrated in Figure 8–5. This matrix facilitates the strategic analysis of likely "generators" and optimum "users" of corporate resources.

To use the BCG matrix, each of the firm's businesses is plotted according to market growth rate (percentage growth in sales) and relative competitive position (market share). Market growth rate is the projected rate of sales growth for the market being served by a particular business. Usually measured as the percentage increase in a market's sales or unit volume over the two most recent years, this rate serves as an indicator of the relative attractiveness of the markets served by each business in the firm's portfolio of businesses. Relative competitive position usually is expressed as the market share of a business divided by the market share of its largest competitor. Thus, relative competitive position provides a basis for comparing the relative strengths of the businesses in the firm's portfolio in terms of their positions in their respective markets.

The positions of businesses on the BCG matrix are based on their market growth rates and their relative competitive positions. Figure 8–5 represents the BCG matrix for a firm with seven businesses. Each circle represents a business. The size of the circle represents the proportion of corporate revenue generated by that business. The arrows and broken circles represent each business's future position in the corporate portfolio as anticipated in strategic planning analysis.

Market growth rates are frequently separated into "high" and "low" areas by an arbitrary 10 percent growth line. The dividing point between "high" and "low" competitive positions usually is set between 1.0 and 1.5, since any amount above 1.0 signifies

FIGURE 8–5

FIGURE 8–5
BCG's Growth/Share Matrix

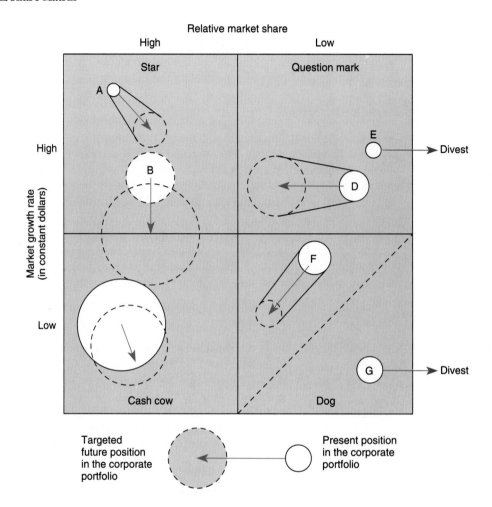

a market share greater than that of the largest competitor. The positions of businesses on the BCG matrix will be in one of four cells, with differing implications for their role in corporate-level strategy.

High-Growth/High Competitive Position

The *stars,* as the BCG matrix labeled them, are businesses in rapidly growing markets with large market shares. These businesses represent the best long-run opportunities (growth and profitability) in the firm's portfolio. They require substantial investment to maintain (and expand) their dominant position in a growing market. This investment requirement is often in excess of the funds that they can generate internally. Therefore, these businesses are often short-term, priority consumers of corporate resources.

Low-Growth/High Competitive Position

Cash cows are businesses with a high market share in low-growth markets or industries. Because of their strong positions and their minimal reinvestment requirements, these businesses often generate cash in excess of their needs. Therefore, they are selectively "milked" as a source of corporate resources for deployment elsewhere (to stars and question marks). Cash cows are yesterday's stars and the current foundation of corporate portfolios. They provide the cash needed to pay corporate overhead and dividends and provide debt capacity. They are managed to maintain their strong market share while generating excess resources for corporatewide use.

Low-Growth/Low Competitive Position

The BCG matrix calls businesses with low market share and low market growth the *dogs* in the firm's portfolio. These businesses are in saturated, mature markets with intense competition and low profit margins. Because of their weak position, they are managed for short-term cash flow (through ruthless cost cutting, for example) to supplement corporate-level resource needs. According to the original BCG prescription, they are divested or liquidated once this short-term harvesting has been maximized.

Recent studies have questioned the notion that all *dogs* should be destined for divestiture/liquidation.[1] The thrust of these studies is that *well-managed dogs* turn out to be positive, highly reliable resource generators (though far less resource rich than cows). These dogs, according to the studies, combine a narrow business focus, emphasis on high product quality and moderate prices, strenuous cost cutting and cost control, and limited advertising. (We will examine this situation later in the chapter.) While suggesting that well-managed dogs can be useful components of a business portfolio, the studies warn that ineffective dogs should still be considered prime candidates for harvesting, divestiture, or liquidation.

High-Growth/Low Competitive Position

Question marks are businesses whose high growth rate gives them considerable appeal but whose low market share makes their profit potential uncertain. Question marks are cash guzzlers because their rapid growth results in high cash needs, while their small market share results in low cash generation. At the corporate level, the concern is to identify the question marks that would increase their market share and move into the star group if extra corporate resources were devoted to them. Where this long-run shift from question mark to star is unlikely, the BCG matrix suggests divesting the question mark and repositioning its resources more effectively in the remainder of the corporate portfolio.

The BCG matrix was a useful initial development in the portfolio approach to corporate-level strategy. Its goal is to determine the corporate strategy that best provides a balanced portfolio of business units. The ideal BCG portfolio would have the largest sales in cash cows and stars, with only a few question marks and very few dogs (the last with favorable cash flow).

---

[1] Carolyn Y. Woo and Arnold C. Cooper, "Strategies of Effective Low-Market-Share Business," *Harvard Business Review,* November–December 1982, pp. 106–13; Donald Hambrick and Ian MacMillan, "Dogs," *Boardroom Reports,* October 15, 1981, pp. 5–6.

The BCG matrix makes two major contributions to corporate strategic choice: it assigns a specific role or mission to each business unit, and it portrays multiple business units as components of an overall corporate strategy. As a result of its simultaneous focus on comparative growth and share positions, the premise of corporate strategy becomes exploitation of competitive advantage to maximize the generation and use of corporate resources.

Although the BCG matrix may yield useful insights in developing a corporate portfolio strategy, strategists must recognize its limitations:

1. Since clearly defining a *market* is often difficult, accurately measuring *share* and *growth rate* can be a problem. This creates a potential for distortion or manipulation.

2. Dividing the matrix into four cells based on a *high/low* classification scheme is somewhat simplistic. It does not recognize markets with *average* growth rates or businesses with *average* market shares.

3. Contrary to the premises of the BCG matrix, the relationship between market share and profitability—the *experience curve* effect—varies across industries and market segments. In some industries, a large market share creates major advantages in unit costs; in others, it does not. Furthermore, some firms with low market share generate superior profitability and cash flow through careful strategies based on differentiation, innovation, or market segmentation. Mercedes-Benz and Polaroid are two examples.

4. The BCG matrix is not particularly helpful in comparing relative investment opportunities across the business units in the corporate portfolio. For example, is every star better than a cash cow? On what basis should one question mark be built into a star and another divested?[2]

5. Strategic evaluation of a set of businesses requires examination of more than relative market share and market growth. The attractiveness of an industry may increase not only because of its growth rate but also because of technological, seasonal, competitive, or other considerations. Likewise, the value of a business within a corporate portfolio is often linked to considerations other than market share.[3]

6. The four colorful classifications in the BCG matrix somewhat oversimplify the types of businesses in a corporate portfolio. Likewise, the simple strategic missions recommended by the BCG matrix often don't reflect the diversity of options available, as shown earlier in the discussion of dogs.[4]

A fundamental deficiency of the BCG approach was its emphasis on market share as the central determinant of the relative position of each business. In essence, its prescription for every business was as follows: Higher market share leads to higher accumulated volume, which leads to lower unit cost and higher profitability.

---

[2] Derek F. Abell and John S. Hammond, *Strategic Market Planning* (Englewood Cliffs, N.J.: Prentice Hall, 1979), p. 212.

[3] For an interesting elaboration of this point, see Walter E. Ketchell III, "Oh Where Oh Where Has My Little Dog Gone? Or My Cash Cow? Or My Star?" *Fortune,* November 2, 1981, pp. 148–52. A discussion of the uses and limits of portfolio planning, including coverage of companies and industries in terms of portfolio usage, is found in P. Haspelslagh's "Portfolio Planning: Uses and Limits," *Harvard Business Review.* March–April 1982, pp. 58–73.

[4] Anil K. Gupta and V. Govindarajan, "Build, Hold, Harvest: Converting Strategic Intentions into Reality," *Journal of Business Strategy,* March 1984, pp. 34–47.

FIGURE 8–6
Underlying Relationship between ROI and Market Share in the New BCG Matrix

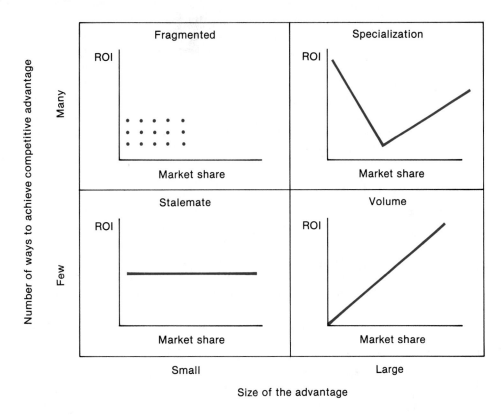

A new approach proposed by the Boston Consulting Group for the 1990s is a matrix with two dimensions: the size of a business's competitive advantage and the number of ways in which that advantage can be achieved. The matrix, shown in Figure 8–6, recognizes four categories of businesses: Volume, Stalemate, Fragmented, and Specialization.

1. Only in the volume businesses are the previous strategies of market-share leadership and cost reduction still meaningful. In this category, a close association between market share and profitability still can be observed. A typical example of such businesses would be the American automakers prior to the emergence of foreign competitors.

2. The stalemate businesses are in industries where profitability is low for all competitors and unrelated to the size of the business. The difference between the most profitable and the least profitable business is relatively small. The American steelmakers provide an illustration of businesses in this category.

3. The profitability of businesses in the fragmented category is uncorrelated with market share. There are poor and good performers among both large and small businesses. The performance of businesses in this category depends on how they exploit the very many ways in which they can achieve competitive advantage. A typical example of such businesses would be restaurants.

4. Finally, the specialization category shows that the most attractive profitability may be enjoyed by the smallest businesses if they are able to distinguish themselves among their competitors by pursuing a focused strategy. The Japanese automakers pursued that strategy to enter the American automobile industry.

In this matrix, the horizontal axis, pertaining to the size of the advantage, is definitely linked to the barriers of entry, because it is only with high entry barriers that a business can sustain a long-term defensible advantage over its competitors. Likewise, the number of ways to achieve advantages seems to be strongly linked to the issue of differentiation. At the extremes of the differentiation range, we encounter the commodity and specialty products. The overall contribution of the new BCG matrix is its recognition that requirements for business success vary across industry settings and that a strategy based solely on gaining market share is not always effective in building a high return on investment.

The Industry Attractiveness/Business Strength Matrix

General Electric popularized a nine-cell planning grid (Figure 8–7), an adaptation of the BCG approach, that attempted to overcome some of the limitations mentioned above. First, the GE grid uses multiple factors to assess industry attractiveness and business strength, rather than the single measures (market share and market growth, respectively) employed in the BCG matrix. Second, GE expanded the matrix from four cells to nine—replacing the high/low axes with high/medium/low axes to make finer distinctions among business portfolio positions.

To use the Industry Attractiveness/Business Strength Matrix, each of the firm's businesses is rated on multiple strategic factors within each axis of the matrix, such as those suggested in Figure 8–8. The position of a business within the matrix is then calculated by "subjectively" quantifying the two dimensions of the matrix.

To measure the attractiveness of an industry, the strategist first selects the factors that contribute to it. Each attractiveness factor is then assigned a weight that reflects its perceived importance relative to the others. Favorable to unfavorable future conditions for those factors are forecast and rated, based on some scale (a 0–to–1 scale is illustrated in Figure 8–9). A weighted composite score is then obtained for the overall attractiveness of an industry, as shown in Figure 8–9.

To assess business strength, a similar procedure is followed. Factors are selected, and weights are assigned to them, and then the business is rated on those dimensions, as illustrated in Figure 8–9.

These examples illustrate how one business within a corporate portfolio might be assessed using the Industry Attractiveness/Business Strength Matrix. It is important to remember that what factors should be included or excluded, as well as how they should be rated and weighted, is primarily a matter of managerial judgment and that several managers usually are involved in the planning process. The result of the ratings is a high, medium, or low classification for both the projected strength of the business and the projected attractiveness of the industry, as shown in Figure 8–9.

Depending on the location of a business within the matrix, one of the following strategic approaches is suggested: (1) invest to grow, (2) invest selectively and manage for earnings, or (3) harvest or divest for resources. The resource allocation decisions remain quite similar to those of the BCG approach.

FIGURE 8–7
The GE Nine-Cell Planning Grid

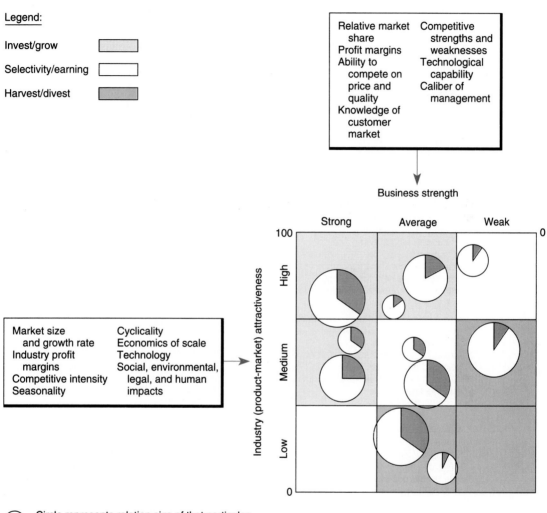

Legend:

Invest/grow

Selectivity/earning

Harvest/divest

Relative market share	Competitive strengths and weaknesses
Profit margins	
Ability to compete on price and quality	Technological capability
Knowledge of customer market	Caliber of management

Business strength

Market size and growth rate	Cyclicality
Industry profit margins	Economics of scale
Competitive intensity	Technology
Seasonality	Social, environmental, legal, and human impacts

Circle represents relation size of that particular industry segment in terms of annual sales volume.

Pie wedge represents the firm's market share as defined by sales volume within that industry segment.

Although the strategic recommendations generated by the Industry Attractiveness/Business Strength Matrix are similar to those generated by the BCG matrix, the Industry Attractiveness/Business Strength Matrix improves on the BCG matrix in three fundamental ways. First, the terminology associated with the Industry Attractiveness/Business Strength Matrix is preferable because it is less offensive and more understandable. Second, the multiple measures associated with each dimension of the business strength matrix tap many

FIGURE 8–8
Factors Contributing to Industry Attractiveness and Business Strength

Industry Attractiveness	Business Strength
Market Factors	
Size (dollars, units, or both).	Your share (in equivalent terms).
Size of key segments.	Your share of key segments.
Growth rate per year:	Your annual growth rate:
Total	Total.
Segments.	Segment.
Diversity of market.	Diversity of your participation.
Sensitivity to price, service features, and external factors.	Your influence on the market.
	Lags or leads in your sales.
Cyclicality.	Bargaining power of your suppliers.
Seasonality.	Bargaining power of your customers.
Bargaining power of upstream suppliers.	
Bargaining power of downstream suppliers.	
Competition	
Types of competitors.	Where you fit, how you compare in terms of
Degree of concentration.	products, marketing capability, service,
Changes in type and mix.	production strength, financial strength,
Entries and exits.	management.
Changes in share.	Segments you have entered or left.
Substitution by new technology.	Your relative share change.
Degrees and types of integration.	Your vulnerability to new technology.
	Your own level of integration.
Financial and Economic Factors	
Contribution margins.	Your margins.
Leveraging factors, such as economies of scale and experience.	Your scale and experience.
Barriers to entry or exit (both financial and nonfinancial).	Barriers to your entry or exit (both financial and nonfinancial).
Capacity utilization.	Your capacity utilization.
Technological Factors	
Maturity and volatility.	Your ability to cope with change.
Complexity.	Depths of your skills.
Differentiation.	Types of your technological skills.
Patents and copyrights.	Your patent protection.
Manufacturing process technology required.	Your manufacturing technology.
Sociopolitical Factors in Your Environment	
Social attitudes and trends.	Your company's responsiveness and flexibility.
Laws and government agency regulations.	Your company's ability to cope.
Influence with pressure groups and government representatives.	Your company's aggressiveness.
Human factors, such as unionization and community acceptance.	Your company's relationships.

Source: Derek F. Abell and John S. Hammond, *Strategic Market Planning: Problems and Analytical Approaches.* © 1979, p. 214. Reprinted by permission of Prentice Hall, Inc., Englewood Cliffs, New Jersey.

FIGURE 8–9
An Illustration of Industry Attractiveness and Business Strength Computations

	Weight	Rating (1–5)	Value
Industry Attractiveness:			
Overall market size	0.20	4.00	0.80
Annual market growth rate	0.20	5.00	1.00
Historical profit margin	0.15	4.00	0.60
Competitive intensity	0.15	2.00	0.30
Technological requirements	0.15	3.00	0.45
Inflationary vulnerability	0.05	3.00	0.15
Energy requirements	0.05	2.00	0.10
Environmental impact	0.05	1.00	0.05
Social/political/legal	Must be acceptable		
	1.00		3.45
Business strength:			
Market share	0.10	4.00	0.40
Share growth	0.15	4.00	0.60
Product quality	0.10	4.00	0.40
Brand reputation	0.10	5.00	0.50
Distribution network	0.05	4.00	0.20
Promotional effectiveness	0.05	5.00	0.25
Productive capacity	0.05	3.00	0.15
Productive efficiency	0.05	2.00	0.10
Unit costs	0.15	3.00	0.45
Material supplies	0.05	5.00	0.25
R&D performance	0.10	4.00	0.20
Managerial personnel	0.05	4.00	0.20
	1.00		4.30

Source: Philip Kotler, *Marketing Management: Analysis, Planning, and Control,* 5th ed. Copyright © 1984, p. 56. Reprinted by permission of Prentice Hall, Inc., Englewood Cliffs, New Jersey. Slightly modified from La Rue T. Hormer, *Strategic Management* (Englewood Cliffs, N.J.: Prentice Hall, 1982), p. 310.

factors relevant to business strength and market attractiveness besides market share and market growth. And this, in turn, makes for broader assessment during the planning process, bringing to light considerations of importance in both strategy formulation and strategy implementation. Strategy in Action 8–2 illustrates the matrix approach as acted on at Holiday Inns over the last 15 years.

One criticism of the portfolio approaches is their static quality—they portray businesses as they exist at one point in time, rather than as they evolve over time. To overcome this problem and better identify "developing winners" or "potential losers," Hofer proposed a 15-cell matrix like that shown in Figure 8–10.[5] As before, the circles represent industry size and wedges represent market share. Referring to Figure 8–10, business A appears to be a *developing winner;* business C, a *potential loser;* business E, an *established winner;* Business F, a *cash cow;* and business G, a loser or a dog. The value of Hofer's life-cycle matrix lies in the story it tells about the distribution of the firm's businesses across the stages of industry evolution.

---

[5] Charles W. Hofer, "Conceptual Constructs for Formulating Corporate and Business Strategies" (Boston: Harvard Case Services, #9–378–754, 1977), p. 3.

FIGURE 8–10
The Life-Cycle Portfolio Matrix

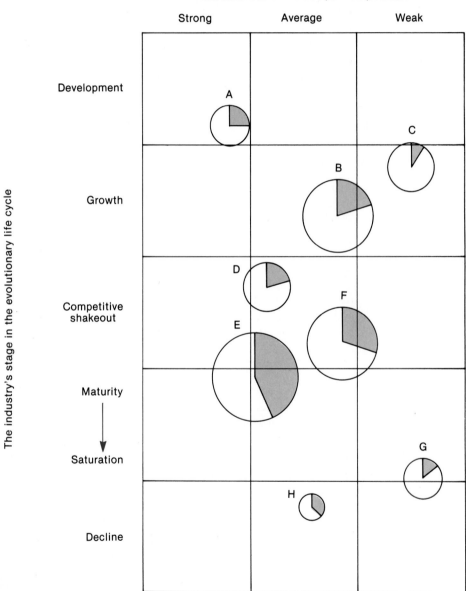

Source: Adapted from Charles W. Hofer, "Conceptual Constructs for Formulating Corporate and Business Strategies" (Boston: Harvard Case Services, #9–378–754, 1977), p. 3.

Beyond the Portfolio Matrix

Constructing business portfolio matrixes can be a useful first step in appraising the strategic situation of a diversified firm. But at best it merely provides a basis for further discussion of corporate strategy and the allocation of corporate resources. Corporate strategists must become thoroughly aware of the status of each business unit and of the industry conditions that give rise to the expectations of its managers. Hofer and Schendel have summarized the types of awareness that corporate strategists must pursue to complete the task of evaluating corporate strategy alternatives:

1. Constructing a summary profile of the industry and competitive environment of each business unit.

2. Appraising the strength and competitive position of each business unit. Understanding how each business unit ranks against its rivals on the key factors for competitive success affords corporate managers a basis for judging its chances for real success in its industry.

3. Identifying the external opportunities, threats, and strategic issues peculiar to each business unit.

4. Determining how much corporate financial support is needed to fund each unit's business strategy and what corporate skills and resources could be deployed to boost the competitive strength of the various business units.

5. Comparing the relative attractiveness of the businesses in the corporate portfolio. This includes not only industry attractiveness/business strength comparisons but also comparisons of the businesses on various historical and projected performance measures—sales growth, profit margins, return on investment, and the like.

6. Checking the corporate portfolio to ascertain whether the mix of businesses is adequately "balanced"—not too many losers or question marks, not so many mature businesses that corporate growth will be slow, enough cash producers to support the stars and the developing winners, enough dependable profit performers, and so on.[6]

EVALUATING AND CHOOSING BUSINESS-LEVEL STRATEGY[7]

Chapter 7 identified three generic strategies from which business strategists choose one overriding competitive orientation—low cost, differentiation, or focus. This section examines key factors that business strategists must consider as they choose among these generic strategies. Managers must first determine whether their business possesses the requirements of each strategy—skills, resources, and organizational assets. Second, they must carefully weigh the risks associated with each strategy. Finally, they must consider the requirements for strategic success emanating from the type of industry in which the business competes.

---

[6] Charles W. Hofer and Dan G. Schendel, *Strategy Formulation: Analytical Concepts* (St. Paul, Minn.: West Publishing, 1978) pp. 84–93; and Arthur A. Thompson, Jr., and A. A. Strickland III, *Strategic Management,* 6th ed. (Homewood, Ill: Richard D. Irwin, 1992), pp. 281–82.

[7] This section is based on Michael E. Porter, *Competitive Strategy* (New York: Free Press, 1980), chap. 2; and Michael Porter, *Competitive Advantage* (New York: Free Press, 1985), chap. 3.

FIGURE 8–11
Skill, Resource, and Organizational Requirements of the Three Generic Business Strategies

Generic Strategy	Commonly Required Skills and Resources	Common Organizational Requirements
Overall cost leadership	Sustained capital investment and access to capital. Process engineering skills. Intense supervision of labor. Products designed for ease in manufacture. Low-cost distribution system.	Tight cost control. Frequent, detailed control reports. Structured organization and responsibilities. Incentives based on meeting strict quantitative targets.
Differentiation	Strong marketing abilities. Product engineering. Creative flair. Strong capability in basic research. Corporate reputation for quality or technological leadership. Long tradition in the industry or unique combination of skills drawn from other businesses. Strong cooperation from channels.	Strong coordination among functions in R&D, product development, and marketing. Subjective measurement and incentives instead of quantitative measures. Amenitites to attract highly skilled labor, scientists, or creative people.
Focus	Combination of the above policies directed at the particular strategic target.	Combination of the above policies directed at the particular strategic target.

Source: Michael E. Porter, *Competitive Strategy* (New York: Free Press, 1980), pp. 40–41.

Requirements for the Success of Each Generic Strategy

Strategists choosing among the three generic strategies must be confident that the business possesses the basic requirements necessary to pursue a particular strategy. Figure 8–11 summarizes these requirements for each of the generic strategies in two categories: (1) skills and resources needed to make the strategy work and (2) organizational requirements necessary to implement the strategy.

The low-cost leader strategy requires a sustainable cost advantage. Businesses pursuing the low-cost leader strategy must be capable of providing products or services similar to their competitors at a distinct price advantage over those competitors. Through the skills or resources identified in Figure 8–11, a business must either be able to accomplish one or more steps in its value chain (see Chapter 6)—procuring raw materials, processing them into products, marketing the products, and distributing the products—in a more cost-effective manner than that of its competitors or it must be able to reconfigure its value chain so as to achieve a cost advantage. Global Strategy in Action 8–1 shows how the highly successful GM-Europe is revamping itself to create a sustainable cost advantage in the rapidly changing European automobile industry.

The business strategy of differentiation requires that the business have sustainable advantages that allow it to provide buyers with something uniquely valuable to them. A successful differentiation strategy allows the business to provide a product or service of perceived higher value to buyers at a differentiation cost below the value premium to the buyers. Differentiation usually arises from one or more activities in the value chain that create a unique value important to buyers. Perrier's control of a carbonated water spring in France, Stouffer's frozen food packaging and sauce technology, Apple's highly integrated chip designs in its Macintosh computers, American Greeting Card's automated inventory system for retailers, and Federal Express's customer service capabilities are all examples of sustainable advantages around which successful differentiation strategies have been built. A business can achieve differentiation by performing its existing value activities or reconfiguring in some unique way. And the sustainability of that differentiation will depend on two things—a continuation of its high perceived value to buyers and a lack of imitation by competitors.

A focus strategy must be able to achieve a cost or differentiation advantage targeted to a niche market that is a distinct subset of the overall market served by the industry of which the business is a part. For this strategy to work, the business must possess the required skills and organizational capacity, and a distinct subgroup of buyers must be identified. Wendy's implemented a highly successful focus strategy by targeting young adults and selling fresh-meat hamburgers in pleasing surroundings that created high perceived value at a sustainable premium above its costs.

To make an informed choice among the generic strategies, strategists must be sensitive to the risks inherent in each of them. Figure 8–12 summarizes the key risks that must be considered. The concern central to all of these risks is whether the business will be able to sustain the cost or differentiation advantage on which its strategy is based. Thus, before choosing the generic strategy, strategists must determine the likelihood of these risks.

GENERIC INDUSTRY ENVIRONMENTS AND STRATEGIC CHOICES[8]

The analysis and choice of business strategies can be enhanced by taking industry conditions into account. Chapters 3 through 5 discussed ways to do this in detail. The purpose of this section is to summarize business strategy concepts that increase the likelihood of generating competitive advantage in five "generic" industry settings. The success that business strategists experience in their analysis and choice of a business strategy will be enhanced if they apply these concepts during that process.

Strategy in Fragmented Industries[9]

A fragmented industry is one in which no firm has a significant market share and can strongly influence industry outcomes. Fragmented industries are found in many areas of the economy and are common in such areas as professional services, retailing, distribution, wood and metal fabrication, and agricultural products.

A number of strategic alternatives for coping with a fragmented industry should be considered when business strategy alternatives are being examined. These are specific

---

[8] This section benefits from the ideas of Porter, *Competitive Strategy,* chap. 11.

[9] Ibid., chap. 9.

GM-EUROPE ADOPTS A LOW-COST LEADERSHIP STRATEGY TO COMPETE WITH THE JAPANESE

While GM's North American operations have been sputtering, GM-Europe has enjoyed huge success and hefty profits for five straight years. It has run rings around Ford-Europe. It has done so well, in fact, that its former chief, John Smith, was recently brought back to Detroit to become the parent company's new president.

But what's most unexpected is that, despite all its success, GM-Europe is running scared. There's good reason. Although the Japanese automakers aren't a major factor in Europe in 1992—a market share of about 12 percent is only one third that for North America—that's about to change. Nissan Motor will begin building 270,000 cars a year in northern England by late 1993. Early 1993 will see Toyota and Honda open their plants in southern England. The inevitable outcome is price pressure, and Louis Hughes, GM-Europe's 43-year-old president, is worried.

"Our net profit margins are about 5 percent, the best in Europe," he says. "But European car prices are higher than those in the United States. If we were to sell at U.S. price levels, we'd be losing money." So Mr. Hughes is telling his troops they must cut costs. But GM-Europe isn't doing what its U.S. parent did in the 1980s when it poured billions into high-tech manufacturing that failed miserably. Instead, GM-Europe is completely overhauling the way it develops and manufactures cars. It is adopting the Japanese "lean" production methods that slash inventory, factory space, equipment, and employees.

At GM-Europe's 1992 senior management conclave in Paris, each of the 180 attendees got a fake $1,000 bill encased in lucite—representing the company's estimate of its per-car cost disadvantage against Japanese rivals and its cost-cutting target for each car. Before they came to the meeting, all the senior managers had to work on a factory floor for one full week.

Cost cutting, shifting to a low-cost leadership strategy, is a tough cut in a company that has been rolling along in high gear. That's where a GM assembly plant in Eisenach, in what used to be East Germany, comes in. Starting up in late 1992 around the skeleton of a never-used Wartburg plant, the plant helps explain GM-Europe's decision to pursue a low-cost leadership strategy.

While workers in GM's existing European plants are hesitant to change, those in eastern Germany are more malleable—casting off Communism and adopting a whole new way of life. To GM, this willingness to change spells opportunity. "If we can take a work force in a former Communist country and make it the most efficient in Europe," Mr. Hughes says, "it will send an incredibly strong signal to our organization." That signal accompanies other recent moves by GM-Europe that Louis Ross, Ford-Europe's president, "thought were impossible":

Source: Excerpted from "Gearing Up: Worried by Japanese, Thriving GM-Europe Vows to Get Leaner," *The Wall Street Journal,* July 27, 1992, p. A1. Reprinted by permission of THE WALL STREET JOURNAL, © 1992 Dow Jones & Company, Inc. All Rights Reserved Worldwide.

approaches to the pursuit of the low-cost, differentiation, or focus strategies discussed above.

Tightly Managed Decentralization

Fragmented industries are characterized by a need for intense local coordination, a local management orientation, high personal service, and local autonomy. Recently, however,

GM-Europe began running its plants round the clock, maximizing the use of costly machinery.

In a shrewd internal move, GM-Europe shifted its European headquarters out of Germany to Zurich, settling in a low-slung suburban building that can't hold more than 200 people. The move cut bureaucracy and escaped the German old-boy network at Opel's headquarters, which remains in a Frankfurt suburb.

At the same time, then-president John Smith picked an aggressive Spaniard, J. Ignacio Lopez de Arriortua, to shake up GM's cozy relationship with parts suppliers.

GM-Europe launched a series of sleek new models to belie the German slogan, "Every yokel drives an Opel."

It created a "strategy board," a group of 15 top executives, that had broad authority to act promptly on virtually any important issue. For example, the strategy board dispatched teams to set up dealerships in any town larger than 10,000 people when the former East Germany became awash in deutsche marks upon the 1990 monetary union with West Germany. The company had the first commercial ever to appear in East Germany, and it published 1 million copies of a book explaining to eastern Germans how to buy a car. Opel quickly became No. 1 in eastern Germany and has stayed there.

GM-Europe's new Eisenach plant will soon turn out 150,000 Opel Astras a year with 2,000 workers. That's 75 percent more cars per worker than either of Opel's other two German plants. The difference lies in the fact that the Eisenach facility resembles the most modern factories in Japan—clean and brightly lit, delivery trucks that unload parts just a few meters from the assembly line, and so forth. Hundreds of such details are expected to add up to huge efficiencies.

GM-Europe executives are cautiously optimistic that they possess the skills, resources, and organizational requirements necessary to support a cost leadership strategy. They view the industry as one headed into maturity, with success most likely associated with process innovation, cost reduction, and international expansion—all elements GM-Europe sees itself as possessing or committed to. Perhaps Tom LaSorda (no relation to the L.A. Dodgers' manager), who came from a G.M. joint venture with Suzuki in Canada to head the Eisenach plant at age 34, said it best: "When you get into this system [low cost/quality sensitive production] and live with it for a while, you become a disciple. And then you can't go back."

successful firms in such industries have introduced a high degree of professionalism into the operations of local managers.

"Formula" Facilities

This alternative, related to the previous one, introduces standardized, efficient, low-cost facilities at multiple locations. Thus, the firm gradually builds a low-cost advantage over localized competitors. Fast-food and motel chains have applied this approach with considerable success.

FIGURE 8–12
Risks Associated with the Generic Business Strategies

Risks with Low-Cost Leadership

Technological change that nullifies past investments or learning.
Low-cost learning by industry newcomers or followers, through imitation or through their ability to invest in state-of-the-art facilities.
Inability to make required product or marketing changes because of the attention placed on cost.
Inflation in costs that narrows the ability of the business to maintain enough of a price differential to offset competitors' brand images or other approaches to differentiation.

Risks with Differentiation

The cost differential between low-cost competitors and the differentiated business becomes too great for differentiation to hold brand loyalty. Buyers thus sacrifice some of the features, services, or image possessed by the differentiated business for large cost savings.
Buyers' need for the differentiating factor falls. This can occur as buyers become more sophisticated.
Imitation narrows perceived differentiation, a common occurrence as industries mature.

Risks with Focus

The cost differential between broad-range competitors and the focused business widens to eliminate the cost advantages of serving a narrow target or to offset the differentiation achieved by focus.
The differences between the products or services desired by the strategic target and those desired by the market as a whole narrow.
Competitors find submarkets *within* the strategic target and outfocus the focuser.

Source: Michael E. Porter, *Competitive Strategy* (New York: Free Press, 1980), pp. 45–46.

Increased Value Added

The products or services of some fragmented industries are difficult to differentiate. In this case, an effective strategy may be to add value by providing more service with the sale or by engaging in some product assembly that is of additional value to the customer.

Specialization

Focus strategies that creatively segment the market can enable firms to cope with fragmentation. Specialization can be pursued by:

Product Type   The firm builds expertise focusing on a narrow range of products or services.

Customer Type   The firm becomes intimately familiar with and serves the needs of a narrow customer segment.

Type of Order   The firm handles only certain kinds of orders, such as small orders, custom orders, or quick turnaround orders.

Geographic Area   The firm blankets or concentrates on a single area.

Although specialization in one or more of these ways can be the basis for a sound focus strategy in a fragmented industry, each of these types of specialization risks limiting the firm's potential sales volume.

Bare Bones/No Frills

Given the intense competition and low margins in fragmented industries, a "bare bones" posture—low overhead, minimum wage employees, tight cost control—may build a sustainable cost advantage in such industries.

Strategy in Emerging Industries[10]

Emerging industries are new formed or re-formed industries that typically are created by technological innovation, newly emerging customer needs, or other economic or sociological changes. Among the emerging industries of the last two decades have been the personal computer, fiber optic, video game, solar heating, and cellular telephone industries.

From the standpoint of strategy formulation, the essential characteristic of an emerging industry is that there are no "rules of the game." The absence of rules presents both a risk and an opportunity—a wise strategy positions the firm to favorably shape the emerging industry's rules.

Business strategies must be shaped to accommodate the following characteristics of markets in emerging industries.[11]

Technologies that are mostly proprietary to the pioneering firms and technological uncertainty about how product standardization will unfold.

Competitor uncertainty because of inadequate information about competitors, buyers, and the timing of demand.

High initial costs but steep cost declines as the experience curve takes effect.

Few entry barriers, which often spurs the formation of many new firms.

First-time buyers requiring initial inducement to purchase and customers confused by the availability of a number of nonstandard products.

Inability to obtain raw materials and components until suppliers gear up to meet the industry's needs.

Need for high-risk capital because of the industry's uncertainty prospects.

For success in this industry setting, business strategies require one or more of these features:

1. The ability to *shape the industry's structure* based on the timing of entry, reputation, success in related industries or technologies, and role in industry associations.
2. The ability to *rapidly improve product quality* and performance features.
3. *Advantageous relationships* with key suppliers and promising distribution channels.
4. The ability to *establish the firm's technology as the dominant one* before technological uncertainty decreases.
5. The early acquisition of *a core group of loyal customers* and then the expansion of that customer base through model changes, alternative pricing, and advertising.
6. The ability to *forecast future competitors* and the strategies they are likely to employ.

---

[10] Ibid., chap. 10.

[11] Ibid., pp. 216–21.

A firm that has had repeated successes with business in emerging industries is 3M Corporation. In each of the last 20 years, over 25 percent of 3M's annual sales have come from products that did not exist 5 years earlier.[12] Start-up companies enhance their success by having experienced entrepreneurs at the helm, a knowledgeable management team and board of directors, and patient sources of venture capital.

Strategy in the Transition to Industry Maturity[13]

As an industry evolves, it rate of growth eventually declines. This "transition to maturity" is accompanied by several changes in its competitive environment:

Competition for market share becomes more intense as firms in the industry are forced to achieve sales growth at one another's expense.

Firms in the industry selling increasingly to experienced, repeat buyers that are now making choices among known alternatives.

Competition becomes more oriented to cost and service as knowledgeable buyers expect similar price and product features.

Industry capacity "tops out" as sales growth ceases to cover up poorly planned expansions.

New products and new applications are harder to come by.

International competition increases as cost pressures lead to overseas production advantages.

Profitability falls, often permanently, as a result of pressure to lower prices and the increased costs of holding or building market share.

These changes necessitate a fundamental strategic reassessment. Strategy elements of successful firms in maturing industries often include:

1. *Pruning the product line* by dropping unprofitable product models, sizes, and options from the firm's product mix.
2. *Emphasis on process innovation* that permits low-cost product design, manufacturing methods, and distribution synergy.
3. *Emphasis on cost reduction* through exerting pressure on suppliers for lower prices, switching to cheaper components, introducing operational efficiencies, and lowering administrative and sales overhead.
4. *Careful buyer selection* to focus on buyers that are less aggressive, more closely tied to the firm, and able to buy more from the firm.
5. *Horizontal integration* to acquire rival firms whose weaknesses can be used to gain a bargain price and are correctable by the acquiring firms.
6. *International expansion* to markets where attractive growth and limited competition still exist and the opportunity for lower-cost manufacturing can influence both domestic and international costs.

---

[12] Masters of Innovation," *Business Week,* April 10, 1989, p. 56.

[13] This section benefits from the ideas of Porter, *Competitive Strategy,* chap. 11.

Business strategists in maturing industries must avoid several pitfalls. First, they must make a clear choice among the three generic strategies and avoid a middle-ground approach, which would confuse both knowledgeable buyers and the firm's personnel. Second, they must avoid sacrificing market share too quickly for short-term profit. Finally, they must avoid waiting too long to respond to price reductions, retaining unneeded excess capacity, engaging in sporadic or irrational efforts to boost sales, and placing their hopes on "new" products, rather than aggressively selling existing products.

Strategies for Mature and Declining Industries[14]

Declining industries are those that make products or services for which demand is growing slower than demand in the economy as a whole or is actually declining. This slow growth or decline in demand is caused by technological substitution (such as the substitution of electronic calculators for slide rules), demographic shifts (such as the increase in the number of older people and the decrease in the number of children), and shifts in needs (such as the decreased need for red meat).

Firms in a declining industry should choose strategies that emphasize one or more of the following themes:

1. *Focus* on segments within the industry that offer a chance for higher growth or a higher return.
2. *Emphasize product innovation and quality improvement,* where this can be done cost effectively, to differentiate the firm from rivals and to spur growth.
3. *Emphasize production and distribution efficiency* by streamlining production, closing marginal productions facilities and costly distribution outlets, and adding effective new facilities and outlets.
4. *Gradually harvest the business*—generate cash by cutting down on maintenance, reducing models, and shrinking channels and make no new investment.

Strategists who incorporate one or more of these themes into the strategy of their business can anticipate relative success, particularly where the industry's decline is slow and smooth and some profitable niches remain. At the same time, three pitfalls must be avoided: (1) being overly optimistic about the prospects for a revival of the industry, (2) getting trapped in a profitless war of attrition, and (3) harvesting from a weak position.

Strategies in Global Industries[15]

A global industry is one that comprises firms whose competitive positions in major geographic or national markets are fundamentally affected by their overall global competitive positions. To avoid strategic disadvantages, firms in global industries are virtually required to compete on a worldwide basis. Oil, steel, automobiles, apparel, motorcycles, televisions, and computers are examples of global industries.

Global industries have four unique strategy-shaping features:

---

[14] Ibid., chap. 12.

[15] Ibid., chap. 13.

Differences in prices and costs from country to country due to currency exchange, fluctuations, differences in wage and inflation rates, and other economic factors.

Differences in buyer needs across different countries.

Differences in competitors and ways of competing from country to country.

Differences in trade rules and governmental regulations across different countries.

These unique features and the global competition of global industries require that two fundamental components be addressed in the business strategy: *(a)* the approach used to gain global market coverage and *(b)* the generic competitive strategy.

Three basic options can be used to pursue global market coverage:

1. *License* foreign firms to produce and distribute the firm's products.
2. *Maintain a domestic production base* and export products to foreign countries.
3. *Establish foreign-based plants and distribution* to compete directly in the markets of one or more foreign countries.

Along with the market coverage decision, strategists must scrutinize the condition of the global industry features identified earlier to choose among four generic global competitive strategies:

1. *Broad-line global competition*—directed at competing worldwide in the full product line of the industry, often with plants in many countries, to achieve differentiation or an overall low-cost position.
2. *Global focus* strategy—targeting a particular segment of the industry for competition on a worldwide basis.
3. *National focus* strategy—taking advantage of differences in national markets that give the firm an edge over global competitors on a nation-by-nation basis.
4. *Protected niche* strategy—seeking out countries in which governmental restraints exclude or inhibit global competitors or allow concessions, or both, that are advantageous to localized firms.

Competing in global industries is an increasing reality for many U.S. firms. Strategists must carefully match their skills and resources with global industry structure and conditions in selecting the most appropriate strategy option.

In conclusion, the analysis and choice of business strategy involves three basic considerations. First, strategists must recognize that their overall choice revolves around three generic options and that once one of them has been chosen, it will require total, consistent commitment. Second, strategists must carefully weigh the skills, resources, organizational requirements, and risks associated with each generic business strategy. Finally, strategists must consider the unique influence that the generic industry environment most similar to the firm's situation will have on the desired features of the generic strategy they choose.

BEHAVIORAL CONSIDERATIONS AFFECTING STRATEGIC CHOICE

Strategic choice is a decision. At both the corporate and business levels, that decision determines the future strategy of the firm.

After alternative strategies have been examined, a strategic choice is made. This is a decision to adopt one of those strategies. If the examination identified a clearly superior strategy or if the current strategy will clearly meet future company objectives, then the decision is relatively simple. Such clarity is the exception, however, meaning that the decision often is judgmental and difficult. After comprehensive strategy examination, strategic decision makers often are confronted with several viable alternatives rather than the luxury of a clear-cut choice. Under these circumstances, several factors influence the strategic choice. Some of the more important are:

1. Role of past strategy.
2. Degree of the firm's external dependence.
3. Attitudes toward risk.
4. Internal political considerations.
5. Timing.
6. Competitive reaction.

Role of Past Strategy

Current strategists are often the architects of past strategies. If they have invested substantial time, resources, and interest in those strategies, they logically would be more comfortable with a choice that closely parallels them or represents only incremental alterations to them.

Such familiarity with and commitment to past strategy permeates the entire firm. Thus, lower-level managers reinforce the top managers' inclination toward continuity with past strategy during the choice process. In one study, during the planning process, lower-level managers suggested strategic choices that were consistent with current strategy and likely to be accepted while withholding suggestions with less probability of approval.[16]

Research by Henry Mintzberg suggests that past strategy strongly influences current strategic choice.[17] The older and more successful a strategy has been, the harder it is to replace. Similarly, once a strategy has been initiated, it is very difficult to change because organizational momentum keeps it going. Strategy in Action 8–2 illustrates just this situation at Holiday Inns.

Mintzberg's work and research by Barry Staw found that, even as a strategy begins to fail due to changing conditions, strategists often increase their commitment to it.[18] Thus, firms may replace top executives when performance has been inadequate for an extended period because replacing these executives lessens the influence of unsuccessful past strategy on future strategic choice.

---

[16] Eugene Carter, "The Behavioral Theory of the Firm and Top-Level Corporate Decisions," *Administrative Science Quarterly* 16, no. 4 (1971), pp. 413–28.

[17] Henry Mintzberg, "Research on Strategy Making," *Proceedings of the Academy of Management* (Minneapolis, 1972).

[18] Barry M. Staw, "Knee-Deep in the Big Muddy: A Study of Escalating Commitment to a Chosen Course of Action," *Organizational Behavior and Human Performance,* June 1976, pp. 27–44;   Mintzberg, "Research on Strategy Making."

Degree of the Firm's External Dependence

A comprehensive strategy is meant to effectively guide a firm's performance in its external environment. Owners, suppliers, customers, government, competitors, and unions are elements in that environment, as elaborated on in Chapters 3 through 5. A major constraint on strategic choice is the power of environmental elements over this decision. If a firm is highly dependent on one or more environmental elements, its strategic alternatives and its ultimate strategic choice must accommodate that dependence. The greater a firm's external dependence, the lower its range and flexibility in strategic choice.

For many years, Whirlpool sold most of its major appliance output to one customer—Sears. With its massive retail coverage and its access to alternative suppliers, Sears was a major external dependence for Whirlpool. Whirlpool's strategic alternatives and ultimate choice of strategy were limited and strongly influenced by Sears's demands. Whirlpool carefully narrowed its grand strategy and important related decisions in areas such as research and development, pricing, distribution, and product design with its critical dependence on Sears in mind.

Progressive firms in the 1990s are accepting external dependencies as a more positive reality—perhaps a source of competitive advantage. In the push for higher, more consistent quality, these firms seek to view key suppliers and customers as "partners" in strategic and operating decisions. More on this in Chapter 11.

Attitudes toward Risk

Attitudes toward risk exert considerable influence on strategic choice. Where attitudes favor risk, the range of the strategic choices expands and high-risk strategies are acceptable and desirable. Where management is risk averse, the range of strategic choices is limited and risky alternatives are eliminated before strategic choices are made. Past strategy exerts far more influence on the strategic choices of risk-averse managers.

Industry volatility influences the propensity of managers toward risk. Top managers in highly volatile industries absorb and operate with greater amounts of risk than do their counterparts in stable industries. Therefore, top managers in volatile industries consider a broader, more diverse range of strategies in the strategic choice process.

Industry evolution is another determinant of managerial propensity toward risk. A firm in the early stages of the product-market cycle must operate with considerably greater risk and uncertainty than a firm in the later stages of that cycle.

In making a strategic choice, risk-oriented managers lean toward opportunistic strategies with higher payoffs. They are drawn to offensive strategies based on innovation, company strengths, and operating potential. Risk-averse managers lean toward safe, conservative strategies with reasonable, highly probable returns. They are drawn to defensive strategies that minimize a firm's weaknesses, external threats, and the uncertainty associated with innovation-based strategies.

A recent study of the relationship between SBU performance and the willingness of SBU managers to take risks found a link between risk taking and strategic choice. Looking first at SBUs that had been assigned build or star strategic missions within a corporate portfolio, it found that the general managers of the higher-performing SBUs were *more willing to take risks* than their counterparts in the lower-performing SBUs. Looking next at SBUs that had been assigned harvest missions, it found that the general managers of the high-performing SBUs were *less willing to take risks* than the general managers of the lower performing SBUs.[19]

This study supports the idea that managers make different decisions depending on their willingness to take risks. The study suggests that being either risk prone or risk averse is not inherently good or bad; rather, the risk orientation-effectiveness relationship depends on the strategic mission of the SBU.

Internal Political Considerations

Power/political factors influence strategic choice. The use of power to further individual or group interest is common in organizational life. An early study by Ross Stagner found that strategic decisions in business organizations were frequently settled by power, rather than by analytical maximization procedures.[20]

A major source of power in most firms is the chief executive officer (CEO). In smaller firms, the CEO is consistently the dominant force in strategic choice, and this is also often true in large firms, particularly those with a strong or dominant CEO. When the CEO begins to favor a particular choice, it is often selected unanimously.

Another power source that influences strategic choice, particularly in larger firms, is the *coalition* phenomenon.[21] In large firms, subunits and individuals (particularly key managers) have reason to support some alternatives and oppose others. Mutual interest draws certain groups together in coalitions to enhance their position on major strategic issues. These coalitions, particularly the more powerful ones (often called *dominant coalitions*), exert considerable influence on the strategic choice process. Numerous studies confirm the frequent use of power and coalitions in strategic decision making. Interestingly, one study found that managers occasionally tried to hide their preference for judgmental/political bargaining over systematic analysis and that when politics was a factor, it slowed decision making.[22]

Figure 8–13 illustrates the focus of political action across the phases of strategic decision making. It shows that the *content* of strategic decisions and the *processes* of arriving at such decisions are politically intertwined. Each phase in the process of strategic choice presents an opportunity for political action intended to influence the outcome. The challenge for strategists lies in recognizing and managing this political influence. If strategic choice processes are not carefully overseen, managers can bias the content of

---

[19] Gupta and Govindarajan, "Build, Hold, Harvest."

[20] Ross Stagner, "Corporate Decision Making," *Journal of Applied Psychology* 53, no. 1 (1969), pp. 1–13.

[21] Richard M. Cyert and James G. March, *A Behavioral Theory of the Firm* (Englewood Cliffs, N.J.: Prentice Hall, 1963).

[22] See, for example, Henry Mintzberg, D. Raisinghani, and Andre Theoret, "The Structure of Unstructured Decision Process," *Administrative Science Quarterly,* June 1976, pp. 246–75; and William Guth, "Toward a Social System Theory of Corporate Strategy," *Journal of Business,* July 1976, pp. 374–88.

FIGURE 8–13
Political Activities in Phases of Strategic Decision Making

Phases of Strategic Decision-Making	Focus of Political Action	Examples of Political Activity

Identification and diagnosis of strategic issues	Control of:
	  Issues to be discussed.
	  Cause-and-effect
	  relationships to be examined.
		Control agenda.
		Interpretation of past events and future trends.

Narrowing the alternative strategies for serious consideration	Control of alternatives.	Mobilization:
		  Coalition formation.
		  Resource commitment for
		  information search.

Examining and choosing the strategy	Control of choice.	Selective advocacy of criteria. Search and representaiton of information to justify choice.
Initiating implementation of the strategy	Interaction between winners and losers.	Winners attempt to "sell" or co-opt losers. Losers attempt to thwart decisions and trigger fresh strategic issues.
Designing procedures for the evaluation of results	Representing oneself as successful.	Selective advocacy of criteria.

Source: Adapted from Liam Fahey and V. K. Naroyanan, "The Politics of Strategic Decision Making," in *The Strategic Management Handbook,* ed. Kenneth J. Albert (New York: McGraw-Hill, 1983), p. 21-20.

strategic decisions in the direction of their own interests.[23] For example, selecting the criteria used to compare alternative strategies or collecting and appraising information regarding those criteria may be particularly susceptible to political influence. This possibility must be recognized and, where necessary, "managed" to avoid dysfunctional political bias. Relying on different sources to collect and appraise information might serve this purpose.

Rather than simply being denoted as "bad" or "inefficient," organizational politics must be viewed as an inevitable dimension of organizational decision making that strategic management must accommodate. Some authors argue that politics is a key ingredient in the "glue" that holds an organization together. Formal and informal negotiating and bargaining between individuals, subunits, and coalitions are indispensable mechanisms for organizational coordination.[24] Accommodating these mechanisms in the choice of strategy will result in greater commitment and more realistic strategy. The costs of doing so, however, are likely to be increased time spent on decision making and incremental (as opposed to drastic) change.

---

[23] Liam Fahey and V. K. Naroyanan, "The Politics of Strategic Decision Making," in *The Strategic Management Handbook,* ed. Kenneth J. Albert (New York: McGraw-Hill, 1983), p. 21-18.

[24] Ibid.

Timing

The time issue can have considerable influence on strategic choice. Research by Peter Wright indicates that managers put greater weight on negative than on positive information and prefer defensive strategies.[25]

Another aspect of the time issue is the timing of a strategic decision. A good strategy may be disastrous if it is undertaken at the wrong time. The sudden outbreak of the Gulf War in 1991 proved disastrous for many small U.S. retailers who had expanded inventories for Spring 1991. And the sudden end of the war proved equally problematic for small military suppliers of products like Patriot missiles and body bags who had geared up for considerably increased demand.

Competitive Reaction

In weighing strategic choices, top management frequently incorporates perceptions of likely competitor reactions to those choices. For example, if it chooses an aggressive strategy directly challenging a key competitor, that competitor can be expected to mount an aggressive counterstrategy. In weighing strategic choices, top management must consider the probable impact of such reactions on the success of the chosen strategy.

The beer industry provides a good illustration. In the early 1970s, Anheuser-Busch dominated the industry, and Miller Brewing Company, recently acquired by Philip Morris, was a weak and declining competitor. Miller's management decided to adopt an expensive advertising-oriented strategy that challenged the big three (Anheuser-Busch, Pabst, and Schlitz) head-on because it assumed that their reaction would be delayed due to Miller's current declining status in the industry. This assumption proved correct, and Miller was able to reverse its trend in market share before Anheuser-Busch countered with an equally intense advertising strategy.

Miller's management took another approach in its next major strategic decision. In the mid-1970s, it introduced (and heavily advertised) a low-calorie beer—Miller Lite. Other industry members had introduced such products without much success. Miller chose a strategy that did not directly challenge its key competitors and was not expected to elicit immediate counterattacks from them. This choice proved highly successful, because Miller was able to establish a dominant share of the low-calorie beer market before those competitors decided to react. In this case, as in the preceding case, expectations regarding the reactions of competitors were a key determinant in the strategic choice made by Miller's management.

SUMMARY

This chapter has examined several considerations in strategic analysis and choice. The first concern of strategic analysis and choice is with an overall corporate strategy that answers the questions of what businesses to be in and what basic brand strategy to adopt. To understand the evolving role of corporate strategy, it is important to recognize how firms

---

[25] Peter Wright, "The Harassed Decision Maker," *Journal of Applied Psychology* 59, no. 5 (1974), pp. 555–61.

typically evolve from single-business to multibusiness operations. When a firm moves from a single-business or dominant-business posture to a multibusiness posture, its managers usually choose among 12 grand strategies. As single-business firms become multibusiness firms, they also use a portfolio-type approach to their corporate strategy.

At the business level, strategic analysis and choice are concerned with the competitive posture of a single business. Strategists must choose among three generic strategies. This choice is accomplished by matching the skill, resource, and organizational requirements of each strategy with the capabilities of the business. In choosing the generic strategy most appropriate to their business, strategists also must consider five generic industry environments.

Strategic analysis often limits alternatives to several viable strategic choices. The luxury of making what is obviously the best strategic choice are seldom available. Nonetheless, a choice must be made. Strategic choice is influenced by several factors that are outside the realm of purely analytic consideration, such as propensity for risk, past strategy, and coalitions.

The strategic management process does not end with the choice of corporate- and business-level strategies. Functional strategies and organizational systems and processes to initiate and control daily activities in a manner consistent with those must be identified and implemented. The next part of this book examines the implementation phase of the strategic management process.

QUESTIONS FOR DISCUSSION

1. How does strategic analysis at the corporate level differ from strategic analysis at the business level? How are they related?

2. When would multi-industry firms find the portfolio approach to strategy evaluation useful?

3. Explain the role of a tool facilitating strategic choice within the grand strategy selection matrix and the model of grand strategy clusters of corporate strategy.

4. Define each of the generic business strategies, and explain their skills, resource, and organizational requirements.

5. Select two generic industry environments and state the strategic alternatives that are most likely to succeed in them.

6. What role does politics play in the development and evaluation of alternative strategies? Please explain.

7. Explain and illustrate the role of three behavioral considerations in strategy examination and choice.

BIBLIOGRAPHY

Aaker, A. David, and Robert Jacobson. "The Role of Risk in Explaining Differences in Profitability." *Academy of Management Journal,* June 1987, p. 227

Acar, W.; A. J. Melcher; and K. E. Aupperle. "The Implementation of Innovative Strategies." *International Journal of Technology Management* [Switzerland] 4, no. 6 (1989), pp. 631–51.

Allaire, Yvon, and Michaela E. Firsirotu. "Coping with Strategic Uncertainty." *Sloan Management Review,* Spring 1987, p. 7.

Bart, K. Christopher. "Implementing 'Growth' and 'Harvest' Product Strategies." *California Management Review,* Summer 1987, p. 139.

Barwise, Patrick; Paul R. Marsh; and Robin Wensley. "Must Finance and Strategy Clash?" *Harvard Business Review,* September–October 1989, p. 85.

Berman, S. J., and R. F. Kautz. "Complete! A Sophisticated Tool That Facilitates Strategic Analysis." *Planning Review* 18, no. 4 (1990), pp. 35–39.

Bitner, Larry N., and Judith D. Powell. "Expansion Planning for Small Retail Firms." *Journal of Small Business Management,* April 1987, p. 47.

Chaganti, Rajeswararao, and Vijay Mahajan. "Profitable Small Business Strategies under Different Types of Competition." *Entrepreneurship: Theory and Practice,* Spring 1989, p. 21.

Cohen, B. G. "A New Approach to Strategic Forecasting." *Journal of Business Strategy,* September–October 1988, pp. 38–42.

Cravens, David W. "Gaining Strategic Marketing Advantage." *Business Horizons,* September–October 1988, p. 44.

Dess, Gregory G., and Nancy K. Orizer. "Environment, Structure, and Consensus in Strategy Formulation." *Academy of Management Review,* April 1987, p. 313.

Eisenhardt, K. M. "Speed and Strategic Choice: How Managers Accelerate Decision Making." *California Management Review* 32, no. 3 (1990), pp. 39–54.

Eynn, P. J. "Avoid the Seven Deadly Sins of Strategic Risk Analysis." *Journal of Business Strategy,"* September 1988, pp. 18–23.

Fry, J. N., and P. J. Killing. "Vision-Check." *Business Quarterly* [Canada] 54, no. 2 (1989), pp. 64–69.

Fulmer, William E., and Jack Goodwin. "Differentiation: Begin with the Consumer." *Business Horizons,* September–October 1988, p. 55.

Ginter, P. M.; W. J. Duncan; L. E. Swayne; and A. G. Shelfer. "When Merger Means Death: Organizational Euthanasia and Strategic Choice." *Organizational Dynamics* 20, no. 3 (1992), pp. 21–33.

Govindarajan, Vijay. "A Contingency Approach to Strategy Selection at the Business Unit Level." *Academy of Management Journal,* December 1988, p. 828.

Hamilton, W. F.; J. Vila; and M. D. Dibner. "Patterns of Strategic Choice in Emerging Firms." *California Management Review* 32, no. 3 (1990), pp. 73–86.

Henderson, Bruce D. "The Origin of Strategy." *Harvard Business Review,* November–December 1989, p. 139.

Hill, Charles W. L., and Robert E. Hoskisson. "Strategy and Structure in the Multi-Product Firm." *Academy of Management Review,* April 1987, p. 331.

Hoskinson, Robert E. "Multidivisional Structure and Performance: The Contingency of Diversification Strategy." *Academy of Management Journal,* December 1987, p. 621.

Jones, T., and G. Seiler. "The Rapidly Growing Pump Company: Marketing for Competitive Advantage." *Planning Review,* May–June 1988, pp. 30–35.

Kennedy, C., "Planning Global Strategies for 3M." *Long Range Planning,* February 1988, pp. 9–17.

Krubasik, E. G. "Customize Your Product Development." *Harvard Business Review,* September–October 1988, pp. 46–53.

Lado, A. A.; N. G. Boyd; and P. Wright. "A Competency-Based Model of Sustainable Competitive Advantage: Toward a Conceptual Integration." *Journal of Management* 18, no. 1 (1992), 77–91.

Mason, David H., and Robert G. Wilson. "Future-Mapping: A New Approach to Managing Strategic Uncertainty." *Planning Review,* May–June 1987, p. 20.

McConkey, Dale D. "Planning in a Changing Environment." *Business Horizons,* September–October 1988, p. 64.

Pelham, A. M., and D. E. Clayson. "Receptivity to Strategic Planning Tools." *Journal of Small Business Management,* January 1988, pp. 43–50.

Schofield, M., and D. Arnold. "Strategies for Mature Businesses." *Long Range Planning,* October 1988, p. 69–76.

Schrage, Michael. "A Japanese Firm Rethinks Globalization: Interview with Yoshihisa Tabuchi." *Harvard Business Review,* July–August 1989, p. 70.

Stalk, G. "Time—The Next Source of Competitive Advantage." *Harvard Business Review,* July–August 1988, pp. 41–53.

—————.; P. Evans; and L. E. Shulman. "Competing on Capabilities: The New Rules of Corporate Strategy." *Harvard Business Review* 70, no. 2 (1992), pp. 57–69.

Ulrich David. "Tie the Corporate Knot: Gaining Complete Customer Commitment." *Sloan Management Review,* Summer 1987, p. 139.

Varadarajan, P. R. "Product Portfolio Analysis and Market Share Objectives: An Exposition of Certain Underlying Relationships." *Journal of the Academy of Marketing Science,* 18, no. 1 (1990), pp. 17–29.

—————.; T. Clark; and W. M. Pride. "Controlling the Uncontrollable: Managing Your Market Environment." *Sloan Management Review* 33, no. 2 (1992), pp. 39–47.

CHAPTER 8 COHESION CASE

STRATEGIC ANALYSIS AND CHOICE AT THE COCA-COLA COMPANY

A historical synopsis is useful to illustrate the "evolutionary perspective" on strategic choice at Coca-Cola. Consistent with our Figure 8–1, Coca-Cola focused its efforts on Single Business Concentration for an extended time. Through the 1960s, The Coca-Cola Company focused on market development and product development in its core business—soft drinks. This focus on a single business concentration built Coke a domestic dominance and a growing dominance in selected overseas markets it gradually entered. Facing some regulatory restrictions from vertically integrating into bottling—as well as hesitance to aggressively commit to such a capital intensive arena when it "controlled" these businesses through franchising the rights to bottle Coke and other soft drinks—Coke found itself with a "cash cow" in the early 1970s.

Similar to other large U.S. companies, The Coca-Cola Company chose to pursue diversification as a way to spread its risks and opportunities. It principally chose the acquisition approach, entering over 15 diverse businesses already described in the Cohesion Case at the end of Chapter 1. By the early 1980s, Coke's management found itself facing increased losses to a rejuvenated PepsiCo, with weaknesses in its bottling franchise network relative to Pepsi's, and gradual maturation of the domestic market while facing rapidly expanding market opportunities abroad. While Coke remained financially strong, it found itself needing resources to respond to challenges and opportunities facing its core business at home and abroad. So Coke gradually divested itself of most of its nonbeverage businesses, culminating in the divestiture of Columbia Pictures, which alone generated $1.3 billion for investment in Coca-Cola's beverage-related businesses. Each of these shifts in strategy at Coke including its mid-1990s refocus on its core business, soft drinks,* and soft-drink bottling (vertical integration forward) is consistent with the evolutionary pattern suggested in Figure 8–1 of Chapter 8.

Another way to visualize strategic analysis and choice at Coke centers around the basic notion that strategists seek strategy alternatives offering a strong "fit" with a firm's overall situation. Two approaches—the Grand Strategy Selection Matrix and the Model of Grand Strategy Clusters—suggest sets of strategic alternatives associated with different strategic situations. Applying the first approach, Coca-Cola has long been in the situation of maximizing several strengths, while also preferring to emphasize "internally" generated growth. The Grand Strategy Selection Matrix would suggest concentrated growth, market development, product development, and innovation. These strategies are just what Coca-Cola has emphasized in its core soft-drink business, which it has returned to even more in the 1990s. Coke seeks first to hold and expand current market positions; then expand into new, particularly international as well as previously underemphasized outlets (e.g., restaurants, airlines); and also gradually add new product versions or those preferred in key local markets.

---

*Along with its citrus beverage business.

At the same time, Coca-Cola's management watched with some apprehension during the late 1970s as Pepsi's increasingly concentrated bottling network was out-distributing and out-marketing Coke's independent (franchised) bottlers in many local domestic markets. Pepsi's fewer, newer, and larger franchise bottlers were able to bring extra resources and professional management of marketing activities to bear in markets where they competed with smaller and usually older family-business franchises of Coca-Cola in the United States and in selected European countries. Applying the Grand Strategy Selection Matrix to overcome this relative "weakness," Coca-Cola had to look outside the company (externally) toward its existing bottling franchise network and seek to overcome a critical weakness—a situation wherein the matrix suggests a vertical integration strategy. Coca-Cola's analysis and choice reached the same conclusion—integrate forward into soft drink bottling. To pursue this capital intensive strategy, Coke decided to sell Columbia Pictures (net $1.3 billion) as well as create and take Coca-Cola Enterprises (CCE—a bottling franchise company) public to raise another source of funds. Coke remained a 49 percent owner and used CCE to buy old Coke bottling franchises in the United States and abroad so it could create bigger, more modern, and aggressive distributors-marketers of Coca-Cola's soft drinks in each local market. This allowed Coke to neutralize Pepsi's previous advantage in key markets.

The Model of Grand Strategy Clusters would focus on the market growth and strength of Coke's competitive position. The conclusion suggested by that model as portrayed in Figure 8–4 would have Coca-Cola's management following concentrated growth (includes market and product development), vertical integration, and, perhaps, concentric diversification when the success of the other strategies starts to fade. Indeed, this set of grand strategies is very similar to those suggested by the Model of Grand Startegy Clusters and appears to be the basic grand strategies Coca-Cola's management has charted toward the 21st century.

As we described at the end of Chapter 1, Coca-Cola was a multibusiness company in the 1970s and early 1980s. Strategic analysis and choice during this period could be aided by a matrix approach similar to the industry attractive–business strength matrix. A selective assessment of some of Coke's businesses at the time would look something like:

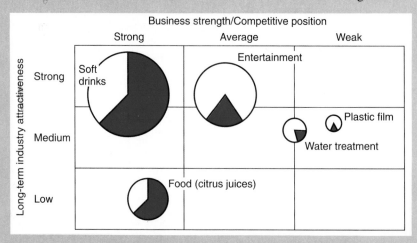

This assessment would suggest increased investment in soft drinks, harvesting water treatment and plastic films, selective investment and managing the juice business for cash generation, and investment to grow entertainment or harvesting the attractive opportunity if the company couldn't financially support the opportunity represented by both this business and soft drinks.

Strategic analysis and choice of Coca-Cola's generic strategy toward the 21st century is an important element we must consider to appreciate this perspective on strategic management and to understand fundamentals behind Coke's key strategic decisions. Coca-Cola's management under the new leadership of Roberto Goizueta set a new tone within The Coca-Cola Company of the 1980s. Some analysts have likened it to waking a sleeping giant. Regardless of the analogy you choose, it is abundantly clear that Coca-Cola reinvigorated the "Cola Wars" with aggressive behavior toward competitors and toward proving its uniqueness in every market it served throughout the world. If you refer back to Figure 8–11, you will see the commonly required skills, resources, and organizational requirements of the three basic generic business strategies. Coca-Cola has long possessed most of those required by a differentiation strategy—strong marketing abilities, product engineering, reputation for quality, a long tradition in the industry, and a strong coordination among R&D, product development, and marketing. The decisions made by Roberto Goizueta and his management team at that time and followed today seek to build Coke's success on differentiating it from every other source of refreshment in the world.

Finally, Coke's decision to focus on soft drinks, expand control of its primary distribution channel, and aggressively expand internationally is consistent with an industry that is in a transition to maturity in the United States, while the global market is rapidly emerging as a stable (for the sale of soft drinks) modern setting worldwide. And Coca-Cola's industry analysis shows that the main threats to industry profitability come from buyer power (bottlers), rivalry (Pepsi), and, perhaps, substitutes. Suppliers and potential entrants offer little concern. Coke is very strong relative to suppliers, and the capital requirement of serious entry is high. So Coca-Cola's differentiation strategy, combined with its swift, aggressive program of vertical integration acquiring bottlers or major interests in them, is a logical strategy to deal with rivalry and substitutes on the one hand and buyer power on the other. Coca-Cola's strategic decision to sell Columbia Pictures to Sony, whereby Coke netted $1.3 billion, was a clear decision to redirect substantial resources toward an aggressive vertical integration strategy suggested by the industry analysis as well as the other approaches outlined earlier.

III STRATEGY/IMPLEMENTATION

The last section of this book examines what is often called the *action phase* of the strategic management process: implementation of the chosen strategy. Up to this point, three phases of that process have been covered—strategy formulation, analysis of alternative strategies, and strategic choice. Although important, these phases alone cannot ensure success. To ensure success, the strategy must be translated into carefully implemented action. This means that:

1. The strategy must be translated into guidelines for the daily activities of the firm's members.
2. The strategy and the firm must become one—that is, the strategy must be reflected in the way the firm organizes its activities and in the firm's values, beliefs, and tone.
3. In implementing the strategy, the firm's managers must direct and control actions and outcomes and adjust to change.

The three remaining chapters discuss these issues.

Organizational action is successfully initiated in three interrelated steps:

1. Identification of measurable, mutually determined *annual objectives.*
2. Development of specific *functional strategies.*
3. Development and communication of concise *policies* to guide decisions.

Annual objectives guide implementation by converting long-term objectives into short-term goods. Functional strategies translate the firm's grand strategy into action plans for its units. Policies provide operating managers and their subordinates with specific guidelines for executing strategies. Chapter 9 examines how to operationalize a strategy through the use of annual objectives, functional strategies, and policies.

To be effectively implemented, a strategy must be institutionalized—it must permeate the firm's day-to-day life. Chapter 10 discusses four organizational elements that provide fundamental, long-term means for institutionalizing the firm's strategy:

1. The firm's *structure.*
2. The *leadership* provided by the firm's CEO and key managers.
3. The fit between the strategy and the firm's *culture.*
4. The firm's *reward systems.*

Since the firm's strategy is implemented in a changing environment, successful implementation requires that execution be controlled and evaluated. The control and evaluation process must include at least these dimensions:

1. *Strategic controls* that "steer" execution of the strategy.
2. *Operations control systems* that monitor performance, evaluate deviations, and initiate corrective action.

Chapter 11 examines the dimensions of the control and evaluation process. It explains the essence of change as an ever-present force driving the need for strategic control. And the chapter concludes with a look at the global "quality imperative," which is redefining the essence of control into the 21st century.

Implementation is "where the action is." It is the arena that most students enter at the start of their business careers. It is the strategic phase in which staying close to the customer, achieving competitive advantage, and pursuing excellence become realities. The chapters in this part will help you understand how this is done.

IMPLEMENTING STRATEGY THROUGH THE BUSINESS FUNCTIONS

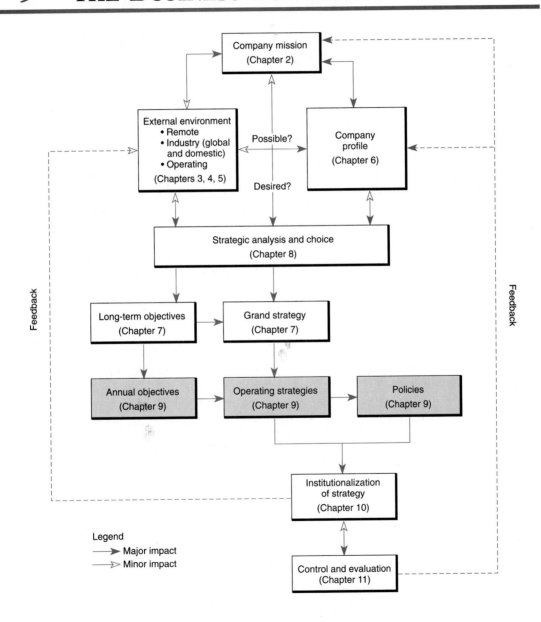

Even after the grand strategies have been determined and the long-term objectives set, the strategic management process is far from complete. Strategic managers now move into a critical new phase of that process—translating strategic thought into organizational action. In the words of two well-worn phrases, they move from "planning their work" to "working their plan" as they shift their focus from strategy formulation to strategy implementation. This shifting gives rise to three interrelated concerns:

1. Identifying measurable, mutually determined annual objectives.
2. Developing specific functional strategies.
3. Communicating concise policies to guide decisions.

Annual objectives translate long-range aspirations into this year's targets. If well developed, these objectives provide clarity, a powerful motivator and facilitator of effective strategy implementation. This chapter shows how to develop annual objectives that maximize implementation-related payoffs.

Functional strategies translate grand strategy at the level of the firm as a whole into activities for the firm's units. Operating managers participate in the development of these strategies, and their participation, in turn, helps clarify what their units are expected to do in implementing the grand strategy.

Policies are specific guides for operating managers and their subordinates. Although often misunderstood and misused, policies can be powerful tools for strategy implementation if they are clearly linked to functional strategies and long-term objectives. This chapter explains how to use policies in the implementation and control of the firm's strategies.

ANNUAL OBJECTIVES

Chapter 7 dealt with the importance of long-term objectives as benchmarks for corporate strategies. Such objectives as market share, return on investment (ROI), return on equity (ROE), stock price, and new market penetration provide guidance in assessing the ultimate effectiveness of a chosen grand strategy. While objectives of this kind clarify the long-range purposes of a grand strategy and the bases for judging its success, they are less useful in guiding the daily operating activities that implement a grand strategy. Short-term (usually annual) objectives provide key mechanisms to aid managers in guiding such activities toward the accomplishment of the firm's long-term objectives.[1] Accomplishing these objectives adds up to successful execution of the firm's long-term plan.

Qualities of Effective Annual Objectives

Annual objectives are specific, measurable statements of what organization units are expected to contribute to the accomplishment of the firm's grand strategy. Problems in the

---

[1] An *annual* time frame is the most popular short-term planning horizon in most firms. Short-term objectives, particularly for a key project, program, or activity, may involve a shorter time horizon (e.g., a three- or six-month horizon). The discussion in this section accommodates such shorter horizons.

implementation of grand strategies often stem from ill-conceived or poorly stated annual objectives. The contribution of these objectives will be maximized if they possess certain basic qualities.

Link to Long-Term Objectives

Each annual objective must be clearly linked to one or more long-term objectives of the firm's grand strategy. To accomplish this, it is important to understand the three basic ways in which annual objectives differ from long-term objectives:

1. *Time frame.* Long-term objectives are usually focused five years or more into the future. Annual objectives are more immediate, usually involving one year or less.

2. *Specificity.* Long-term objectives are broadly stated companywide ends. Annual objectives are very specific and are directly linked to a project or to a functional area or a unit of the firm.

3. *Measurement.* Although both long-term and annual objectives are quantifiable, long-term objectives are stated in broad, relative terms (e.g., 20 percent market share), where as annual objectives are stated in absolute terms (e.g., a 15 percent increase in sales in the next year).

Annual objectives add breadth and specificity in identifying *what* must be accomplished to achieve long-term objectives. For example, Wal-Mart's top management recently set forth "to obtain 40 percent market share in five years" as a long-term objective.[2] Achieving that objective can be greatly enhanced if a series of specific annual objectives identify what must be accomplished each year in order to do so. If Wal-Mart's market share is now 25 percent, then one likely annual objective might be "to have each regional office achieve a minimum 3 percent increase in market share in the next year." "Open two regional distribution centers in the Southwest in 1994" might be an annual objective that Wal-Mart's marketing and distribution managers consider essential if the firm is to achieve a 40 percent market share in five years. "Conclude arrangements for a $1 billion line of credit at 0.25 percent above prime in 1994" might be an annual objective of Wal-Mart's financial managers to support the operation of new distribution centers and the purchase of increased inventory in reaching the firm's long-term objective.

The link between short-term and long-term objectives should resemble cascades through the firm from basic long-term objectives to specific annual objectives in key operation areas. Thus, long-term objectives are segmented and reduced to annual objectives. The cascading effect has the added advantage of providing a clear reference for communication and negotiation, which may be necessary to integrate and coordinate objectives and activities at the operating level.[3]

Integrated and Coordinated Objectives and Activities

As the objective-setting cascades through the firm, it should force discussions and negotiations among operating managers with often conflicting priorities. Consider the example in Figure 9–1. The priorities of the marketing function easily can conflict with those of the

---

[2] George Stalle, Phillip Evans, and L. E. Shulman, "Competing on Capabilities: The New Rules of Corporate Strategy," *Harvard Business Review,* March–April 1992, p. 58.

[3] Lawrence G. Hrebiniak and William F. Joyce, *Implementing Strategy* (New York: Macmillan, 1984), p. 110.

FIGURE 9–1
The Role of Short-Term Objectives in the Integration/Coordination of Activities in a Manufacturing Firm

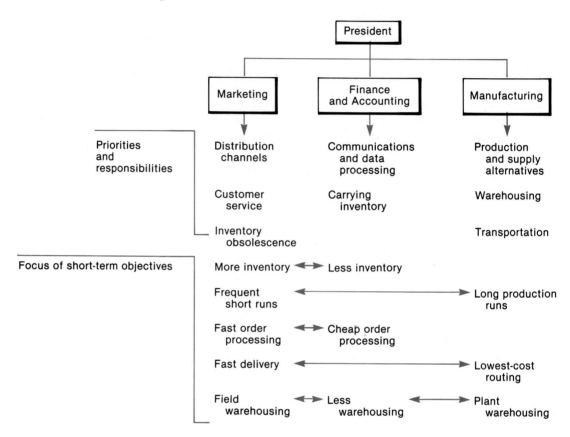

manufacturing or finance/accounting function. As a result of these priorities, manufacturing managers might set annual efficiency objectives that only long production runs and plant warehousing can accomplish; whereas marketing managers might set customer convenience objectives that are better served by frequent, short production runs and field warehousing. Unless annual objectives are integrated and coordinated, each operating unit might pursue activities that detract from the success of other operating units and this might result in the failure of the long-term objectives (and the grand strategy). Thus, the setting of annual objectives must be viewed as a focal point for resolving conflicts between organizational units that might impede strategic performance.

Measurable Objectives

Annual objectives are more consistent when they clearly state *what* is to be accomplished, *when* it will be accomplished, and *how* its accomplishment will be *measured*. These objectives then can be used to monitor both the effectiveness of each operating unit and the

FIGURE 9–2
Operationalizing Measurable Annual Objectives

Examples of Deficient Annual Objectives	Examples of Annual Objectives with Measurable Criteria for Performance
To improve morale in the division (plant, department, etc.)	To reduce turnover (absenteeism, number of rejects, etc.) among sales managers by 10 percent by January 1, 1995. *Assumption:* Morale is related to measurable outcomes (i.e., high and low morale are associated with different results).
To improve support of the sales effort	To reduce the time lapse between order data and delivery by 8 percent (two days) by June 1, 1995. To reduce the cost of goods produced by 6 percent to support a product price decrease of 2 percent by December 1, 1995. To increase the rate of before- or on-schedule delivery by 5 percent by June 1, 1995.
To develop a terminal vision of the SAP computer program	To develop a terminal version of SAP capable of processing X bits of information in time Y at cost not to exceed Z per 1,000 bits by December 1, 1995. *Assumption:* There is virtually an infinite number of "terminal" or operational versions. Greater detail or specificity defines the objective more precisely.
To enhance or improve the training effort	To increase the number of individuals capable of performing X operation in manufacturing by 20 percent by April 15, 1995. To increase the number of functional heads capable of assuming general management responsibility at the division level by 10 percent by July 15, 1995. To provide sales training to X number of individuals, resulting in an average increase in sales of 4 percent within six months after the training session.
To improve the firm's image	To conduct a public opinion poll using random samples in the five largest U.S. metropolitan markets to determine average scores on 10 dimensions of corporate responsibility by May 15, 1995. To increase our score on those dimensions by an average of 7.5 percent by May 1, 1996.

Source: Adapted from Laurence G. Hrebiniak and William F. Joyce, *Implementing Strategy* (New York: Macmillan, 1984), p. 116.

collective progress of all operating units toward the firm's long-term objectives. Figure 9–2 illustrates several effective and ineffective annual objectives. Measurable objectives make misunderstanding less likely among the interdependent operating managers who must implement the grand strategy. It is far easier to quantify the objectives of *line* units (e.g., production) than of certain *staff* areas (e.g., personnel). Difficulties in quantifying objectives often can be overdone by initially focusing on *measurable activity* and then identifying *measurable outcomes.*

Priorities

Although all annual objectives are important, some deserve priority because of a timing consideration or their particular impact on a strategy's success. If such priorities are not established, conflicting assumptions about the relative importance of annual objectives may inhibit progress toward strategic effectiveness.[4] Facing the most rapid, dramatic decline in profitability of any major computer manufacturer as it confronted relentless lower pricing by Dell Computer and AST, Compaq Computer formulated a retrenchment strategy with several important annual objectives in pricing, product design, distribution, and financial condition. But its highest priority was to dramatically lower overhead and production costs so as to satisfy the difficult challenge of dramatically lowering prices while also restoring profitability.[5]

Priorities are established in various ways. A simple *ranking* may be based on discussion and negotiation during the planning process. However, this does not necessarily communicate the real difference in the importance of objectives, so such terms as *primary, top,* and *secondary* may be used to indicate priority. Some firms assign *weights* (e.g., 0–100 percent) to establish and communicate the relative priority of objectives. Whatever the method, recognizing priorities is an important dimension in the implementing action of annual objectives.

The qualities of good objectives discussed in Chapter 7—acceptable, flexible, suitable, motivating, understandable, and achievable—also apply to annual objectives. They will not be discussed again here, but the reader should review the discussion in Chapter 7 to appreciate these qualities common to all good objectives.

Benefits of Annual Objectives

One benefit of annual objectives is that they give operating personnel a better understanding of their role in the firm's mission. "Achieve $2.5 million in 1994 sales in the Chicago territory," "Develop an OSHA-approved safety program for handling acids at all Georgia Pacific plants in 1994," and "Reduce Ryder Truck's average age of accounts receivable to 31 days by the end of 1994" are examples of how annual objectives clarify the role of particular personnel in their firm's broader mission. Such *clarity of purpose* can be a major force in effectively mobilizing a firm's "people assets."[6] Strategy in Action 9–1 illustrates how annual objectives and short-term strategies were used to reverse the decline of the National Basketball Association (NBA).

A second benefit of annual objectives comes from the process of developing them. If the managers responsible for the accomplishment of the annual objectives have participated in their development, these objectives provide valid basis for addressing and accommodating conflicting concerns that might interfere with strategic effectiveness. Meetings to set annual objectives become the forum for raising and resolving conflicts between strategic intentions and operating realities.

---

[4] Ibid., p. 119.

[5] "Identity Crisis," *Forbes,* May 25, 1992, p. 82.

[6] Extensive literature supports the value of objective setting in achieving desired performance. See, for example, Karl Albrecht, *Successful Management by Objectives* (Englewood Cliffs, N. J.: Prentice Hall, 1978); Thomas J. Peters and Robert H. Waterman, Jr., *In Search of Excellence* (New York: Harper & Row, 1982); and Charles Garfield, *Second to None: How Our Smartest Companies Put People First* (Homewood, Ill.: Business One Irwin, 1992).

STRATEGY **ANNUAL OBJECTIVES AND FUNCTIONAL STRATEGIES AT THE**
IN ACTION **NATIONAL BASKETBALL ASSOCIATION**
9–1

By the mid-1980s, a safe bet around sport circles was that the NBA would not survive to the 1990s. Of the NBA's 23 teams, 16 were losing money; the NBA's TV ratings were dropping; and buyers of "for sale" NBA franchises were nowhere to be found. In 1987 NBA commissioner David J. Stern identified three annual objectives and five functional strategies to turn the situation around.

Annual Objectives for the NBA

Stern set three objectives for 1988:

1. Gross league revenues will be $325 million.
2. All 23 teams will generate a profit.
3. The NBA's TV ratings will increase by 10 percent.

Functional Strategies for the NBA

Stern used five functional strategies to accomplish these objectives:

1. *Stop overspending for players.* Selected NBA teams had courted bankruptcy by overspending for players. The new salary strategy set a salary pool beyond which a team could not (normally) spend. The figure was arrived at by apportioning 53 percent of total NBA revenues equally among the 23 teams.
2. *Recruit businesspersons to buy sagging franchises.* Stern took charge of targeting and recruiting successful businesspeople to acquire problem NBA franchises. He felt such owners would understand, appreciate, and restore financial sanity to these franchises.
3. *Reduce overexposure on TV.* In 1984, over 200 NBA games were televised nationally on cable and network TV. This avalanche of games depressed NBA ratings, which reduced its advertising rates and revenues. Stern reduced the number of televised games to 55 regular season games and 20 playoff games. This strategy raised NBA ratings and increased its revenues.
4. *Institute a league MIS system.* An MIS system was developed that offered each team an item-by-item revenue-and-expense comparison with other teams and the NBA averages.
5. *Institute an antidrug program.* The NBA took the forefront among professional sports in fighting the drug problem. It developed a comprehensive drug program for its athletes that generated sizable goodwill toward the NBA.

Source: Based on "Basketball: Business Is Booming," *Business Week*, October 28, 1986.

A third benefit of annual objectives is that they provide *a basis for strategic control.* The control of strategy will be examined in detail in Chapter 11; but it is important to recognize here that annual objectives provide a clear, measurable basis for developing budgets, schedules, trigger points, and other mechanisms for controlling the implementation of strategy.

A fourth benefit of annual objectives is their *motivational payoffs.* Annual objectives that clarify personal and group roles in a firm's strategies and are also measurable, realistic, and challenging can be powerful motivators of managerial performance—particularly when these objectives are linked to the firm's reward structure.

Although annual objectives are a powerful tool for implementing a firm's strategy, other tools are necessary. Successful implementation also requires functional strategies, the *means* to accomplish the annual objectives.

DEVELOPING FUNCTIONAL STRATEGIES

Functional strategies are the short-term activities that each functional area *within* a firm must undertake in order to implement the grand strategy. Such strategies must be developed in the key areas of marketing, finance, production/operations, R&D, and human resource management. They must be consistent with the long-term objectives and the grand strategy. They help implement the grand strategy by organizing and activating specific units of the firm (marketing, finance, production, and the like) to pursue that strategy in daily activities. In a sense, functional strategies translate thought (grand strategy) into action designed to accomplish specific annual objectives. For every major unit of a company, functional strategies identify and coordinate actions that support the grand strategy and help accomplish annual objectives. Strategy in Action 9–1 illustrates key functional strategies that were used to implement the NBA's turnaround in the late 1980s.

Figure 9–3 illustrates the important role of functional strategies in implementing corporate and business strategy. The corporate strategy defined General Cinema Corporation's general posture in the broad economy. The business strategy outlined the competitive posture of its operations in the movie theater industry. To increase the likelihood that these strategies would be successful, more specific strategies were needed for the firm's operating components. These functional strategies clarified the business strategy, giving specific, short-term guidance to operating managers. Figure 9–3 shows possible functional strategies in the areas of marketing, operations, and finance. Additional functional strategies were necessary, most notably in the personnel area.

Differences between Grand and Functional Strategies

To better understand the role of functional strategies within the strategic management process, they must be differentiated from grand strategies. Three basic characteristics differentiate functional strategies from grand strategies:

1. Time horizon covered.
2. Specificity.
3. Participants in strategy development.

Time Horizon

Functional strategies identify activities that are to be undertaken now or in the immediate future. Grand strategies focus on the firm's posture three to five years out. Japan's NEC, for example, might implement a spring 1994 marketing strategy of increasing price discounts and sales bonuses in its U.S. subsidiary to reduce excess laptop inventory. This functional strategy focuses on immediate activities, whereas NEC's grand strategy focuses on its world-wide market posture as a full-line computer manufacturer in 1998.

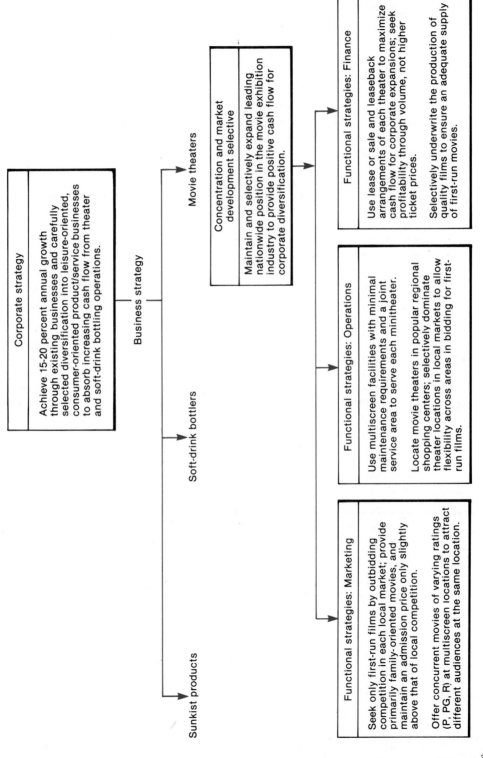

**LESSONS FROM GERMANY'S MIDSIZE GIANTS:
FIVE KEY FUNCTIONAL STRATEGIES**

everal of Germany's small and midsized companies, known as the *Mittelstand,* offer an inconspicuous source of wisdom on global competitiveness through key functional strategies. While German companies like Mercedes-Benz, Siemens, Bosch, and Bayer are better known, companies like Krones, Korber/Hauni, Weinig, Webasto, and TetraWerke have world market shares in the range of 70 to 90 percent and, combined, account for the bulk of Germany's considerable trade surplus. Quite a feat when you consider Germany has been the world's largest exporter every year since 1986.

Why are they so successful? The answer appears to lie in a common business strategy and several key functional strategies used to implement the business strategy. According to Hermann Simon, professor of business administration at Johannes Gutenberg University in Mainz, Germany, their common business strategy is to focus narrowly on a particular market niche that requires technical expertise, and to direct all of their resources toward maintaining the top position in the niche on a worldwide basis. As one Mittelstand executive put it: "If you are small, your front of attack has to be narrow. You'd better focus your business. And if you are focused, you have to find customers for your specialty all over the world in order to recoup your R&D investment." While this business strategy is clear enough, Professor Simon finds the roots of its success in a common set of functional strategies that can be grouped in five basic areas:

1. *Make a strong commitment to global expansion in the form of investment and people.* Thirty-nine Mittelstand companies recently studied by Simon had 354 foreign sales, service, or manufacturing subsidiaries—about 10 per company—a high number for companies of their size (average $303 million in sales). They typically maintain full control over foreign subsidiaries, and have unusually long tenures (over 10 years) for Mittelstand executives running those operations.

2. *Focus resources to ensure superiority in areas customers value most.* Mittelstand companies place a priority on three factors: product quality, closeness to the customer, and service. They create strong service networks wherever they do business. Weinig, world leader in automatic molders, is a good example. Weinig Japan has a service branch on each of Japan's four main islands, with plans to open three additional offices soon, with Japanese service engineers trained for one full year in Germany with additional training each subsequent year in Germany. The sales manager for Weinig

Source: Hermann Simon, "Lessons from Germany's Midsize Giants," *Harvard Business Review,* March–April 1992, pp. 115–23.

The shorter time horizon of functional strategies is critical to the successful implementation of a grand strategy for two reasons. First, it focuses the attention of functional managers on what needs to be done *now* to make the grand strategy work. Second, it allows functional managers to adjust to changing current conditions.

Specificity

Functional strategies are more specific than grand strategies. Grand strategies provide general direction. Functional strategies identify the specific activities that are to be

Japan described it best: "We offer German products [meaning precision quality] and Japanese service. That's our secret."

3. *A balanced emphasis on technology and market knowledge.* While 81 percent of large company managers tended to see their company as either more market or technology driven, Professor Simon's research found 75 percent of all Mittelstand companies said market and technology are equally important. When technology dominates, they believe, engineers become remote from customers and customers suffer. When marketers focusing on customers are solely at the helm, however, technology suffers. So Mittelstand companies have direct contact between nonmarketing people and customers more than twice as often as large companies. It's often hard to separate service, operations, and R&D people—the division of labor that characterizes larger German companies does not prevail among the Mittelstand. Mittelstand facilities are located close to customers. And Mittelstand CEOs see customer contact as their primary responsibility, even when it requires incessant travel.

4. *Rely on "inhouse" capabilities, not "outside" sources.* Mittelstand companies trust their own capabilities. They believe they can enter new markets and solve manufacturing and R&D problems on their own and that doing so strengthens their product knowledge and preserves their top competitive position. With the exception of Japan (where joint ventures and partnerships often are used), Mittelstand companies enter foreign markets alone, rather than cooperate with domestic companies. Mittelstand are staunchly independent in manufacturing and R&D—solving their own problems, doing their own research, and sometimes even providing their own materials or components—which they believe deepens their manufacturing and R&D capabilities. The firms pursue "make," rather than "buy," even sacrificing some economies of scale (and cost) with the belief that quality is more important.

5. *Foster close relationships between managers and workers.* The typical single Mittelstand is located in a small town or village, rather than in a big city. The rural locations create interdependence between employer and employee. Top managers tend to have closer relationships with employees than is seen in large companies. Mittelstand companies actively involve workers in the business—90 percent offered incentives for workers that contributed new ideas, 60 percent had quality circles, and 40 percent had profit-sharing programs.

undertaken in each functional area and thus show operating managers *how* they are expected to pursue annual objectives.

Figure 9–3 illustrates the difference in the specificity of grand and functional strategies. General Cinema's grand strategy gave its movie theater division broad direction on how to pursue a concentration and selective market development strategy. Two functional strategies in the marketing area give managers specific direction on what types of movies (first-run, primarily family-oriented, P, PG, R) should be shown and what pricing strategy (competitive in the local area) should be followed.

Specificity in functional strategies contributes to successful implementation for several reasons. First, it adds substance, completeness, and meaning to what a specific unit of the firm must do. The existence of specific functional strategies helps ensure that managers know what needs to be done and can focus on accomplishing results.[7] Second, specific functional strategies clarify for top management how functional managers intend to accomplish the grand strategy. This increases top management's confidence in and sense of control over the grand strategy. Third, specific functional strategies facilitate coordination among operating units *within* the firm by clarifying areas of interdependence and potential conflict.

Participants

Different people participate in strategy development at the functional and business levels. Business strategy is the responsibility of the general manager of a business unit. That manager typically delegates the development of functional strategy to subordinates charged with running the operating areas of the business. The manager of a business unit must establish long-term objectives and a strategy that corporate management feels contributes to corporate-level goals. Similarly, key operating managers must establish annual objectives and operating strategies that contribute to business-level goals. Just as business strategies and objectives are approved through negotiation between corporate managers and business managers, so, too, are annual objectives and functional strategies approved through negotiation between business managers and operating managers.

Involving operating managers in the development of functional strategies improves their understanding of what must be done to achieve annual objectives and, thus, contributes to successful implementation. It also helps ensure that developed strategies reflect the reality of the day-to-day operating arenas. And perhaps most important, it can increase the commitment of operating managers to the strategies developed.

The next several sections will highlight the key elements that should receive attention in the functional strategies of the various functional areas.

Functional Strategies in Production/Operations

Production/operations management is the core function of any organization. That function converts inputs (raw materials, supplies, machines, and people) into value-enhanced output. The POM function is most easily associated with manufacturing firms, but it also applies to all other types of businesses (service and retail firms, for example). Global Strategy in Action 9–1 identifies some key POM strategies that have made several smaller German companies worldwide leaders.

The functional strategies of production/operations management (POM) must be coordinated with the functional strategies of marketing if the firm is to succeed. Careful coordination of POM strategy with components of financial strategy (such as capital budgeting and investment decisions) and of personnel strategy is also necessary. Figure 9–4 illustrates the importance of such coordination by showing the different POM concerns that arise

---

[7] While a company typically has one grand strategy, it should have a functional strategy for each major subunit and several operating strategies within the subunit. For example, a business may specify distinct pricing, promotion, and distribution strategies as well as an overall strategy to guide marketing operations.

FIGURE 9–4
Concerns Associated with Different Elements of a POM Strategy

Possible Elements of Strategy	Concomitant Conditions That May Affect or Place Demands on the Operations Activities
1. Compete as low-cost provider of goods or services	Broadens market. Requires longer production runs and fewer product changes. Requires special-purpose equipment and facilities.
2. Compete as high-quality provider	Often possible to obtain more profit per unit, and perhaps more total profit from a smaller volume of sales. Requires more quality-assurance effort and higher operating cost. Requires more precise equipment, which is more expensive. Requires highly skilled workers, necessitating higher wages and greater training efforts.
3. Stress customer service	Requires broader development of servicepeople and service parts and equipment. Requires rapid response to customer needs or changes in customer tastes, rapid and accurate information system, careful coordination. Requires a higher inventory investment.
4. Provide rapid and frequent introduction of new products	Requires versatile equipment and people. Has higher research and development costs. Has high retraining costs and high tooling and changeover costs. Provides lower volumes for each product and fewer opportunities for improvements due to the learning curve.
5. Strive for absolute growth	Requires accepting some projects or products with lower marginal value which reduces ROI. Diverts talents to areas of weakness instead of concentrating on strengths.
6. Seek vertical integration	Enables firm to control more of the process. May not have economies of scale at some stages of process. May require high capital investment as well as technology and skills beyond those currently available within the firm.

when different marketing/financial/personnel strategies are required as elements of the grand strategy.

The functional strategies of POM must guide decisions regarding (1) the basic nature of the firm's POM system, seeking an optimum balance between investment input and production/operations output and (2) location, facilities design, and process planning on a short-term basis. Figure 9–5 illustrates these concerns by highlighting key decision areas in which the POM strategies should provide guidance.

The facilities and equipment component of POM strategy involves decisions regarding plant location, size, equipment replacement, and facilities utilization that should be consistent with grand strategy and other operating strategies. In the mobile home industry, for example, the facilities and equipment strategy of Winnebago was to locate one large centralized, highly integrated production center (in Iowa) near its raw materials. On the other

FIGURE 9–4   (concluded)

Possible Elements of Strategy	Concomitant Conditions That May Affect or Place Demands on the Operations Activities
7. Maintain reserve capacity for flexibility	Provides ability to meet peak demands and quickly implement some contingency plans if forecasts are too low.
	Requires capital investment in idle capacity.
	Provides capability to grow during the lead time normally required for expansion.
8. Consolidate process (centralize)	Can result in economies of scale.
	Permits location near one major customer or supplier.
	Vulnerability—entire operation can be halted by one strike, fire, or flood.
9. Disperse processing of service	Permits location near several market territories.
	Requires more complex coordination network, perhaps expensive data transmission, and duplication of some personnel and equipment at each location.
	If each location produces one product in the line, then other products still must be transported to be available at all locations.
	If each location specializes in a type of component for all products, the company is vulnerable to strike, fire, flood, etc.
	If each location provides the total product line, then economies of scale may not be realized.
10. Stress the use of mechanization, automation, robots	Requires high capital investment.
	Reduces flexibility.
	May affect labor relations.
	Makes maintenance more crucial.

hand, Fleetwood, Inc., a California-based competitor, located dispersed, decentralized production facilities near markets and emphasized maximum equipment life and less-integrated, labor-intensive production processes. Both firms are leaders in the mobile home industry.

The purchasing component of POM strategy should address such questions as the following: Are the cost advantages of using only a few suppliers outweighed by the risk of overdependence? What criteria (e.g., payment requirements) should be used in selecting vendors? Which vendors can provide "just-in-time" inventory and how can the business provide it to our customers? How can operations be supported by the volume and delivery requirements of purchases?

The planning and control component of POM strategy provides guidelines for ongoing production operations. These guidelines are intended to match production/operations resources to long-range, overall demand. The planning and control component often dictates whether production/operations will be demand oriented, inventory oriented, or subcontracting oriented. POM strategy may have to ensure that production/operations processes are geared to a cyclical or seasonal demand pattern. A bathing suit manufacturer, for example, would seek to maximize inventories in the early spring. If demand is less

FIGURE 9–5
Key Functional Strategies in POM

Functional Strategy	Typical Questions That the Functional Strategy Should Answer
Facilities and equipment	How centralized should the facilities be? (One big facility or several small facilities?)
	How integrated should the separate processes be?
	To what extent should further mechanization or automation be pursued?
	Should size and capacity be oriented toward peak or normal operating levels?
Purchasing	How many sources are needed?
	How should suppliers be selected, and how should relationships with suppliers be managed over time?
	What level of forward buying (hedging) is appropriate?
Operations planning and control	Should work be scheduled to order or to stock?
	What level of inventory is appropriate?
	How should inventory be used (FIFO/LIFO), controlled, and replenished?
	What are the key foci for control efforts (quality, labor cost, downtime, product use, other)?
	Should maintenance efforts be oriented to prevention or to breakdown?
	What emphasis should be placed on job specialization? Plant safety? The use of standards?

cyclical, POM strategy may aim at a steady level of production and inventories. Given unpredictable fluctuations in demand, idle capacity and excess capital investment may be avoided by using subcontractors to handle sudden increases.

Functional Strategies in Marketing

The role of the marketing function is to achieve the firm's objectives by bringing about the profitable sale of products/services in target markets. Functional marketing strategies should guide marketing managers in determining who will sell what, where, to whom, in what quantity, and how. These strategies typically entail four components: products, price, place, and promotion. Figure 9–6 illustrates the types of questions that the strategies must address in terms of these four components. Global Strategy in Action 9–1 shows how selected German companies have made this a cornerstone of their success.

The functional strategy for the *product component* of the marketing function should clearly identify the customer needs that the products/services are intended to meet. This strategy should provide a comprehensive statement of the product/service concept and of the target markets that the firm is seeking to serve. Such a statement fosters consistency and continuity in the daily activity of the marketing function.

The functional strategy for the *place component* identifies where, when, and by whom the products/services are to be offered for sale. The primary concern here is the channels of distribution—the combination of marketing institutions through which the products/services flow to the final user. This component of marketing strategy guides decisions

FIGURE 9–6
Key Functional Strategies in Marketing

Functional Strategy	Typical Questions That the Functional Strategy Should Answer
Product (or service)	Which products do we emphasize?
	Which products/services contribute most to profitability?
	What product/service image do we seek to project?
	What consumer needs does the product/service seek to meet?
	What changes should be influencing our customer orientation?
Price	Are we competing primarily on price?
	Can we offer discounts or other pricing modifications?
	Are our pricing policies standard nationally, or is there regional control?
	What price segments are we targeting (high, medium, low, and so on)?
	What is the gross profit margin?
	Do we emphasize cost/demand or competition-oriented pricing?
Place	What level of market coverage is necessary?
	Are there priority geographic areas?
	What are the key channels of distribution?
	What are the channel objectives, structure, and management?
	Should the marketing managers change their degree of reliance on distributors, sales reps, and direct selling?
	What sales organization do we want?
	Is the sales force organized around territory, market, or product?
Promotion	What are the key promotion priorities and approaches?
	Which advertising/communication priorities and approaches are linked to different products, markets, and territories?
	Which media would be most consistent with the total marketing strategy?

regarding channels (e.g., single versus multiple channels) to ensure consistency with the total marketing effort.

The functional strategy for the *promotion component* defines how the firm will communicate with the target markets. This strategy should provide marketing managers with basic guides for the use and mix of advertising, personal selling, sales promotion, and media selection. It must be consistent with the other components of the marketing strategy, and, due to its cost requirements, it should be closely integrated with the financial strategy.

The functional strategy for the *price component* is perhaps the single most important consideration in marketing. That strategy directly influences demand and supply, profitability, consumer perception, and regulatory response. The approach to pricing strategy may be cost oriented, market oriented, or competition (industry) oriented. With a cost-oriented approach, pricing decisions center on the total cost and usually involve an acceptable markup or target price ranges. With a market-oriented approach, pricing based on consumer demand (e.g., gasoline pricing in a deregulated oil industry). With a competition-oriented approach, pricing decisions center on those of the firm's competitors. The discount pricing that occurred in the U.S. airline industry in 1992, with several domestic and foreign airlines following American Airlines' discount pricing initiatives, is an example of competition-oriented pricing. While one of these orientations may predominate in

FIGURE 9-7
Key Functional Strategies in Finance

Key Functional Strategy	Typical Questions That the Functional Strategy Should Answer
Capital Acquisition	What is an acceptable cost of capital?
	What is the desired proportion of short- and long-term debt? Preferred and common equity?
	What balance is desired between internal and external funding?
	What risk and ownership restrictions are appropriate?
	What level and forms of leasing should be used?
Capital allocation	What are the priorities for capital allocation projects?
	On what basis should the final selection of projects be made?
	What level of capital allocation can be made by operating managers without higher approval?
Dividend and working capital management	What portion of earnings should be paid out as dividends?
	How important is dividend stability?
	Are things other than cash appropriate as dividends?
	What are the cash flow requirements? The minimum and maximum cash balances?
	How liberal/conservative should the credit policies be?
	What limits, payment terms, and collection procedures are necessary?
	What payment timing and procedure should be followed?

a firm's pricing strategy, that strategy is always influenced to some degree by the other orientations.

Functional Strategies in Finance and Accounting

While most functional strategies guide implementation in the immediate future, the time frame for functional strategies in the area of finance varies, because these strategies direct the use of financial resources in support of the business strategy, long-term goals, and annual objectives. Functional financial strategies with longer time perspectives guide financial managers in long-term capital investment, debt financing, dividend allocation, and leveraging. Functional financial strategies designed to manage working capital and short-term assets have a more immediate focus. Figure 9-7 highlights some key questions that functional financial strategies must answer.

Capital acquisition usually is guided by long-term financial strategies, since priorities in capital acquisition usually change infrequently over time. The desired level of debt versus equity versus internal long-term financing of business activities is a common issue in capital acquisition strategy. For example, Delta Airlines has a long-standing functional strategy that seeks to minimize the level of debt in proportion to equity and to fund capital needs internally, whereas General Cinema Corporation has a long-standing functional strategy of expanding its theater and soft-drink bottling facilities through long-term leasing. The debt-to-equity ratios of these two firms are approximately 0.50 and 2.0, respectively. Both firms have had similar records of steady profitable growth over the last 20 years, yet they represent two very different functional strategies for capital acquisition.

Capital allocation, like capital acquisition, is a functional financial strategy of major importance. Growth-oriented grand strategies generally require numerous major investments in facilities, projects, acquisitions, and people. Since it is usually neither possible nor desirable to make these investments immediately, the capital allocation strategy sets priorities and timing for them. This also helps manage conflicting priorities for capital resources among operating managers.

Retrenchment or stability often requires a financial strategy that focuses on the reallocation of existing capital resources. This could necessitate pruning product lines and reallocating production facilities or personnel. Under the best of circumstances, the overlapping careers and aspirations of key operating managers create a politically charged organizational setting. With retrenchment, a functional strategy that clearly delineates capital allocation priorities becomes particularly important for effective implementation in such a setting.

Capital allocation strategy frequently defines the level of capital expenditure that is to be delegated to operating managers. If a firm is pursuing a strategy of rapid growth, timely responses to an evolving market may be facilitated by flexibility in making capital expenditures at the operating level. On the other hand, if a firm is pursuing a strategy of retrenchment, it may carefully control capital expenditures at the operating level.

Dividend management is an integral part of a firm's financing. Lower dividends increase the internal funds available for growth, and internal financing reduces the need for external, often debt, financing. However, stable dividends often enhance the market price of a firm's stock. Therefore, the strategy guiding dividend management must support the firm's posture toward equity markets.

Working capital is critical to the daily operation of firms, and the working capital requirements of a firm are influenced by seasonal and cyclical fluctuations, the size of the firm, and the pattern of the firm's receipts and disbursements. The working capital component of financial strategy must be built on accurate projections of cash flow and must provide cash management guidelines for conserving and rebuilding the cash balances required for daily operation.

Functional Strategies in Research and Development

With the increasing rate of technological change in most competitive industries, research and development (R&D) has assumed a key functional role in many firms. In the technology-intensive computer and pharmaceutical industries, for example, firms typically spend between 4 and 6 percent of their sales dollars on R&D. In other industries, such as the hotel/motel and construction industries, R&D spending is less than 1 percent of sales. Thus, functional R&D strategies may be more critical instruments of the business strategy in some industries than in others.

Figure 9–8 illustrates the types of questions addressed by functional R&D strategies. First, R&D strategy should clarify whether basic research or product development research will be emphasized. Several major oil companies now have solar energy subsidiaries in which basic research is emphasized, while the smaller oil companies emphasize product development research.

Directly related to the choice of emphasis between basic research and product development is the time horizon for R&D efforts. Should these efforts be focused on the near

FIGURE 9–8
Key Functional Strategies in R&D

R&D Decision Area	Typical Questions That the Functional Strategy Should Answer
Basic research versus product and process development	To what extent should innovation and breakthrough research be emphasized? In relation to the emphasis on product development, refinement, and modification?
	What critical operating processes need R&D attention?
	What new projects are necessary to support growth?
Time horizon	Is the emphasis short term or long term?
	Which orientation best supports the business strategy? The marketing and production strategy?
Organizational fit	Should R&D be done in-house or contracted out?
	Should R&D be centralized or decentralized?
	What should be the relationship between the R&D units and product managers? Marketing managers? Production managers?
Basic R&D posture	Should the firm maintain an offensive posture, seeking to lead innovation in its industry?
	Should the firm adopt a defensive posture, responding to the innovations of its competitors?

term or the long term? The solar energy subsidiaries of the major oil companies have long-term perspectives, while the smaller oil companies want to establish a competitive niche in the growing solar industry.

Functional R&D strategies should also guide organization of the R&D function. For example, should R&D work be conducted solely within the firm, or should portions of that work be contracted out? A closely related issue is whether R&D should be centralized or decentralized. What emphasis should be placed on process R&D versus product R&D?

Decisions on all of the above questions are influenced by the firm's R&D posture, which can be offensive or defensive, or both. If that posture is offensive, as is true for small high-technology firms, the firm will emphasize technological innovation and new product development as the basis for its future success. This orientation entails high risks (and high payoffs) and demands considerable technological skill, forecasting expertise, and the ability to quickly transform innovations into commercial products.

A defensive R&D posture emphasizes product modification and the ability to copy or acquire new technology. Converse Shoes is a good example of a firm with such an R&D posture. Faced with the massive R&D budgets of Nike and Reebok, Converse placed R&D emphasis on bolstering the product life cycle of its prime products (particularly canvas shoes).

Large companies with some degree of technological leadership often use a combination of offensive and defensive R&D strategy. GE in the electrical industry, IBM in the computer industry, and Du Pont in the chemical industry all have a defensive R&D posture for currently available products *and* an offensive R&D posture in basic, long-term research. Global Strategy in Action 9–1 describes the R&D orientation of some of Germany's most successful companies.

FIGURE 9–9
Key Functional Strategies in HRM

Functional Strategy	Typical Questions That the Functional Strategy Should Answer
Recruitment, selection, and orientation	What key human resources are needed to support the chosen strategy? How do we recruit these human resources? How sophisticated should our selection process be? How should we introduce new employees to the organization?
Career development and training	What are our future human resource needs? How can we prepare our people to meet these needs? How can we help our people develop?
Compensation	What levels of pay are appropriate for the tasks we require? How can we motivate and retain good people? How should we interpret our payment, incentive, benefit, and seniority policies?
Evaluation, discipline, and control	How often should we evaluate our people? Formally or informally? What disciplinary steps should we take to deal with poor performance or inappropriate behavior? In what ways should we "control" individual and group performance?
Labor relations and equal opportunity requirements	How can we maximize labor-management cooperation? How do our personnel practices affect women/minorities? Should we have hiring policies?

Functional Strategies in Human Resource Management (HRM)

The strategic importance of functional strategies in HRM has become more widely accepted in recent years. Germany's "Mittelstand" companies have found success via HRM strategies described in Global Strategy in Action 9–1. HRM management aids in accomplishing the grand strategy by ensuring the development of managerial talent and competent employees and the presence of systems to manage compensation of regulatory concerns. Functional HRM strategies should guide the effective utilization of human resources to achieve both the firm's annual objectives and employees' satisfaction and development. These strategies involve the areas shown in Figure 9–9. The recruitment, selection, and orientation component of functional personal strategies should establish the basic parameters for bringing new people into a firm and adapting them to "the way things are done" in the firm. The career development and training component should guide the actions that personnel takes to meet the future human resources needs of the grand strategy. Merrill Lynch, a major brokerage firm whose long-term corporate strategy is to become a diversified financial service institution, has moved into such areas as investment banking, consumer credit, and venture capital. In support of its long-term objectives, it has incorporated extensive early-career training and ongoing career development programs to meet its expanding need for personnel with multiple competences.

Larger organizations need functional HRM strategies that guide decisions regarding labor relations, EEOC requirements, and employee compensation, discipline, and control.

To summarize, functional strategies specify how each major activity of a firm contributes to the implementation of the firm's grand strategy. The specificity of functional strategies and the involvement of operating managers in their development help ensure understanding of and commitment to the chosen strategy. A related step in implementing that strategy is the development of policies that guide and control the decisions of operating managers and their subordinates.

DEVELOPING AND COMMUNICATING CONCISE POLICIES

Policies are directives designed to guide the thinking, decisions, and actions of managers and their subordinates in implementing a firm's strategy. Policies provide guidelines for establishing and controlling ongoing operations in a manner consistent with the firm's strategic objectives. Often referred to as *standard operating procedures,* policies increase managerial effectiveness by standardizing many routine decisions and controlling the discretion of managers and subordinates in implementing functional strategies. Logically, policies should be derived from functional strategies (and, in some instances, from corporate or business strategies) with the key purpose of aiding strategy execution.[8] Strategy in Action 9–2 illustrates selected policies of several well-known firms.

The Purpose of Policies

Policies communicate specific guides to decisions. They are designed to control and reinforce the implementation of functional strategies and the grand strategy, and they do this in several ways.

1. *Policies establish indirect control over independent action* by clearly stating how things are to be done *now.* By limiting discretion, policies in effect control decisions and the conduct of activities without direct intervention by top management.

2. *Policies promote uniform handling of similar activities.* This facilitates the coordination of work tasks and helps reduce friction arising from favoritism, discrimination, and the disparate handling of common functions.

3. *Policies ensure quicker decisions* by standardizing answers to previously answered questions that otherwise would recur and be pushed up the management hierarchy again and again.

4. *Policies institutionalize basic aspects of organization behavior.* This minimizes conflicting practices and establishes consistent patterns of action in attempts to make the strategy work.

---

[8] The term *policy* has various definitions in management literature. Some authors and practitioners equate policy with strategy. Others do this inadvertently by using "policy" as a synonym for company mission, purpose, or culture. Still other authors and practitioners differentiate policy in terms of "levels" associated respectively with purpose, mission, and strategy. "Our policy is to make a positive contribution to the communities and societies we live in" and "our policy is not to diversify out of the hamburger business" are two examples of the breadth of what some call policies. This book defines *policy* much more narrowly as specific guides to managerial action and decisions in the implementation of strategy. This definition permits a sharper distinction between the formulation and implementation of functional strategies. And, of even greater importance, it focuses the tangible value of the policy concept where it can be most useful—as a key administrative tool to enhance effective implementation and execution of strategy.

3M Corporation has a *personnel policy,* called the *15 percent rule,* that allows virtually any employee to spend up to 15 percent of the workweek on anything that he or she wants to, as long as it's product related.

(This policy supports 3M's corporate strategy of being a highly innovative manufacturer, with each division required to have a quarter of its annual sales come from products introduced within the past five years.)

Wendy's has a *purchasing policy* that gives local store managers the authority to buy fresh meat and produce locally, rather than from regionally designated or company-owned sources.

(This policy supports Wendy's functional strategy of having fresh, unfrozen hamburgers daily.)

General Cinema has a *financial policy* that requires annual capital investment in movie theaters not to exceed annual depreciation.

(By seeing that capital investment is no greater than depreciation, this policy supports General Cinema's financial strategy of maximizing cash flow—in this case, all profit—to its growth areas. The policy also reinforces General Cinema's financial strategy of leasing as much as possible.)

IBM had a *marketing policy* of not giving free IBM personal computers (PCs) to any person or organization.

(This policy attempted to support IBM's image strategy by maintaining its image as a professional, high-value, service business as it sought to dominate the PC market.)

Crown, Cork, and Seal Company has an *R&D policy* of not investing any financial or people resources in basic research.

(This policy supports Crown, Cork, and Seal's functional strategy, which emphasizes customer services, not technical leadership.)

NationsBank of South Carolina has an *operating policy* that requires annual renewal of the financial statement of all personal borrowers.

(This policy supports NationsBank's financial strategy, which seeks to maintain a loan-to-loss ratio below the industry norm.)

5. *Policies reduce uncertainty in repetitive and day-to-day decision making,* thereby providing a necessary foundation for coordinated, efficient efforts.

6. *Policies counteract resistance to or rejection of chosen strategies by organization members.* When major strategic change is undertaken, unambiguous operating policies clarify what is expected and facilitate acceptance, particularly when operating managers participate in policy development.

7. *Policies offer predetermined answers to routine problems.* This greatly expedites dealing with both ordinary and extraordinary problems—with the former, by referring to these answers; with the latter, by giving managers more time to cope with them.

8. *Policies afford managers a mechanism for avoiding hasty and ill-conceived decisions in changing operations.* Prevailing policy can always be used as a reason for not

yielding to emotion-based, expedient, or temporarily valid arguments for altering procedures and practices.[9]

Policies may be written and formal or unwritten and informal. Informal, unwritten policies are usually associated with a strategic need for competitive secrecy. Some policies of this kind, such as "promotion from within," are widely known (or expected) by employees and implicitly sanctioned by management. Managers and employees often like the latitude "granted" by unwritten and informal policies. However, such policies may detract from the long-term success of a strategy. Formal, written policies have at least seven advantages:

1. They require managers to think through the policy's meaning, content, and intended use.
2. They reduce misunderstanding.
3. They make equitable and consistent treatment of problems more likely.
4. They ensure unalterable transmission of policies.
5. They communicate the authorization or sanction of policies more clearly.
6. They supply a convenient and authoritative reference.
7. They systematically enhance indirect control and organizationwide coordination of the key purposes of policies.[10]

The strategic significance of policies can vary. At one extreme are such policies as travel reimbursement procedures, which are really work rules and may not be linked to the implementation of a strategy. At the other extreme are organizationwide policies that are virtually functional strategies, such as Wendy's requirement that every location invest 1 percent of its gross revenue in local advertising.

Policies can be externally imposed or internally derived. Policies regarding equal employment practices are often developed in compliance with external (government) requirements, and policies regarding leasing or depreciation may be strongly influenced by current tax regulations.

Regardless of the origin, formality, and nature of policies, the key point to bear in mind is the valuable role that they can play in strategy implementation. Existing policies should be reviewed periodically so as to ensure their guidance and control of operating activities in a manner consistent with current business and functional strategies. Lotus Development Corporation (Lotus 1–2–3) recently halted a policy forcing customers to destroy spreadsheet programs from competing software makers. Aimed at preventing unauthorized use of 1–2–3 software, Lotus found it was creating major problems for some customers. Communicating specific policies will help overcome resistance to strategic change and foster commitment to successful strategy implementation.

---

[9] These eight points are adapted from related discussion by Richard H. Buskirk, *Business and Administrative Policy* (New York: John Wiley & Sons, 1971), pp. 145–55;　Milton J. Alexander, *Business Strategy and Policy* (Atlanta: University Publications, 1983), chap. 3.

[10] Adapted from Robert G. Murdick, R. Carl Moor, Richard H. Eckhouse, and Thomas W. Zimmerer, *Business Policy: A Framework for Analysis* (Columbus, Ohio: Grid, 1984), p. 65.

SUMMARY

The first concern in the implementation of a grand strategy is to translate that strategy into action throughout the organization. This chapter discussed three important tools for accomplishing this: annual objectives, functional strategies, and policies.

Annual objectives are derived from long-term objectives, which they translate into current targets. They differ from long-term objectives in time frame, specificity, and measurement. To be effective in strategy implementation, they must be integrated and coordinated. They also must be consistent, measurable, and prioritized.

Functional strategies are derived from the business strategy. They identify the specific, immediate actions that must be taken in key functional areas to implement the grand strategy.

Policies provide another means for directing and controlling behavior, decisions, and actions at the firm's operating levels in a manner consistent with its business and functional strategies. Effective policies channel actions, behavior, decisions, and practices to promote strategic accomplishment.

Annual objectives, functional strategies, and policies represent only the start of the strategy implementation. The strategy must be institutionalized—must permeate the firm. The next chapter examines this phase of strategy implementation.

QUESTIONS FOR DISCUSSION

1. How does the concept "Translate thought into action" bear on the relationship between grand strategy and operating strategy? Between long-term and short-term objectives?
2. How do functional strategies differ from corporate and business strategies?
3. What key concerns must functional strategies address in marketing? Finance? POM? Personnel?
4. How do policies aid strategy implementation? Illustrate your answer.
5. Illustrate a policy, an objective, and a functional strategy in your personal career strategy.
6. Why are annual objectives needed when long-term objectives are already available?

BIBLIOGRAPHY

Allio, R. J. "Formulating Global Strategy." *Planning Review,* March –April 1989, pp. 22–29.

Boag, David A., and Ali Dastmalchian. "Market Vulnerability and the Design and Management of the Marketing Function in Small Firms." *Journal of Small Business Management,* October 1988, p. 37.

Charalambides, L. C. "Designing Communication Support Systems for Strategic Planning." *Long Range Planning,* December 1988, pp. 93–100.

Coates, N. "The Globalization of the Motor Vehicle Manufacturing Industry." *Planning Review,* January–February 1989, pp. 34–39.

David, F. R. "How Companies Define Their Mission." *Long Range Planning,* February 1989, pp. 90–97.

Freund, Y. P. "Critical Success Factors." *Planning Review,* March–April 1988, pp. 20–23.

Fulmer, William E. "Human Resource Management: The Right Hand of Strategy Implementation." *Human Resource Planning* 13, no. 1 (1990), pp. 1–11.

Garavan, Thomas N. "Strategic Human Resource Development." *International Journal of Manpower* 12, no. 6 (1991), pp. 21–34.

Giles, William D. "Making Strategy Work." *Long Range Planning* 24, no. 5 (1991), pp. 75–91.

"Inside Met Life's Growth Strategy." Interview with CEO J. Creedon. *Journal of Business Strategy,* January–February 1988, pp. 23–27.

Kazanjian, N., and Jay Golbraith. *Strategy Implementation: Structure, Systems, and Process* (St. Paul, Minn.: West Publishing, 1986).

Marucheck, Ann; Ronald Pannesi; and Carl Anderson. "An Exploratory Study of the Manufacturing Strategy Process in Practice." *Journal of Operations Management* 9, no. 1, pp. 101–23.

Miller, J. G., and W. Hayslip. "Implementing Manufacturing Strategic Planning." *Planning Review,* July–August 1989, pp. 22–29.

Nielson, Richard P. "Cooperative Strategy in Marketing." *Business Horizons,* July–August 1987, p. 61.

Ohmae, K. "Getting Back to Strategy." *Harvard Business Review,* September–October 1988, pp. 149–56.

Peterson, R. T. "An Analysis of New Product Ideas." *Journal of Small Business Management,* April 1988, pp. 25–31.

Randolph, W. A., and B. Z. Posner. "What Every Manager Needs to Know about Project Management." *Sloan Management Review,* Summer 1988, pp. 65–74.

Roth, Kendall; David M. Schweiger; and Allen J. Morrison. "Global Strategy Implementation at the Business Unit Level: Operational Capabilities and Administrative Mechanisms." *Journal of International Business Studies* 22, no. 3 (1991), pp. 369–402.

Shank, J. K., and V. Govindarajan. "Making Strategy Explicit in Cost Analysis." *Sloan Management Review,* Spring 1988, pp. 19–30.

Stern, Joel. "Think Cash and Risk—Forget ESP." *Planning Review,* January–February 1988, p. 6.

Stonich, Paul. *Implementing Strategy: Making Strategy Happen.* (New York: Ballinger, 1982).

Wheelwright, S., and N. S. Langowitz. "Plus Development Corporation: Joint Venturing a Breakthrough Product." *Planning Review,* July–August 1989, pp. 6–21.

"Winning Turnaround Strategies at Black and Decker." Interview with Marketing Executive G. DiCamillo. *Journal of Business Strategy,* March 1988, pp. 30–33.

Wright, Norman B. "The Driving Force: An Action-Oriented Solution to Strategy Implementation." *Canadian Business Quarterly* 54, no. 1 (1989), pp. 51–54, 66.

CHAPTER 9 COHESION CASE

IMPLEMENTING STRATEGY THROUGH THE BUSINESS FUNCTIONS AT THE COCA-COLA COMPANY

Management at The Coca-Cola Company feels that detailed functional strategies are essential if their grand strategies of concentrated growth, market development, product development, and vertical integration are to differentiate Coca-Cola and achieve global success. One way to get a sense of the managers' commitment to these strategies—and at the same time illustrate the importance of functional strategies as vehicles for implementing corporate and business strategies in any firm—is to look at what Coke management calls its "global business system." As a way of introduction, let's look at a few things they say about their "system":

> A successful global company must have a global business system through which to reach consumers. In our case, the system comprises not only the Company itself, but a worldwide network of employees, bottling partners, vendors, and customers. This system is made up of dedicated people working long and hard to sell products they believe in. . . . Such a system must do much more than just deliver products. In order to appeal to cultures as diverse as those in Switzerland and Swaziland, it must also tailor products and messages to local markets. . . . Graphically, this system can best be represented as an inverted triangle or pyramid comprising many levels, of which the Company is only the base. The following figure [on page 329] depicts this incomparable global system, which builds from 650,000 employees through more than 8 million customers to satisfy the thirst of the world's more than 5 billion consumers. And most important, the system is growing and expanding every day. As impressive as the numbers in the figure are, by the time you read them, they will have been surpassed.

This "figure" mentioned above hints at numerous functional activities that reinforce effective implementation of Coke's overall strategies. Some of those include the following.

HUMAN RESOURCE MANAGEMENT

Coke provides attractive compensation; places a major emphasis on employee training and indoctrination into "the Coke way" so that employees worldwide share a similar understanding of and appreciation for what the product stands for and seeks to be in the consumers' mind. Coke places a lot of emphasis on having its people "think globally, but act locally; respond daily to competitive situations; serve customers and consumers with a passion." Coke has a very loyal workforce, minimal turnover, and a strong tendency to promote from within.

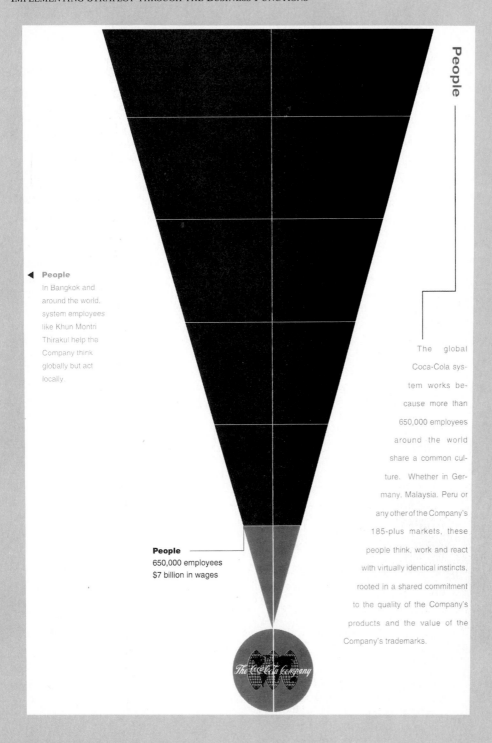

People

People

In Bangkok and around the world, system employees like Khun Montri Thirakul help the Company think globally but act locally.

People
650,000 employees
$7 billion in wages

The global Coca-Cola system works because more than 650,000 employees around the world share a common culture. Whether in Germany, Malaysia, Peru or any other of the Company's 185-plus markets, these people think, work and react with virtually identical instincts, rooted in a shared commitment to the quality of the Company's products and the value of the Company's trademarks.

The Coca-Cola Company

MARKETING

Perhaps the best way to get a sense of Coca-Cola's marketing strategies for implementing its overall grand strategies on a worldwide basis is to see how Ira Herbert, Coke's chief marketing officer, answered recent questions about Coke's global marketing strategy. Let's look at some questions and Herbert's answers:

Q: Does the company follow a global marketing strategy?
A: Yes, we do. But we say, "Think Globally, Act Locally." Essentially, in the vast majority of the world, we pursue a basic marketing strategy for Coca-Cola, which we then extend by adapting it to local conditions and to specific tactics that might be more appropriate for each geographic venue. . . . The execution of a strategy should always be localized.

Q: Concerning the company's global marketing strategy, does Coca-Cola sell its products in a similar way? For example, in Atlanta as well as in Argentina or Australia?
A: In a similar way—yes. In exactly the same way—no. For example, there are differences in packaging that are important to a particular country or to a particular geographic location. There are differences in distribution and differences in media. Some countries don't allow commercials on television, for example. As a result of these differences, certain aspects of a marketing plan need to be adapted to a specific environment.

Q: What are some cultural considerations in marketing that Coca-Cola's management must be aware of in its marketing mix?
A: The thrust of our business is to increase the number of times that Coca-Cola is consumed during the day and to expand our age group appeal. So our marketing efforts attempt to ensure that a soft drink, specifically Coca-Cola, becomes a part of their lives. . . . For example, we have to know how Coca-Cola is used with food. In Argentina, for example, a high percentage of our product is consumed with food; in other countries, it is not. Rather, in those locations, it is strictly a refreshment beverage.

Relative to product, in some parts of the world, the use of a sugar-containing soft drink is important to generate calories and energy. Diet is not important. Yet in other markets, like the United States, Australia, the United Kingdom, and Canada, the opposite is true. Indeed, we have a number of products that are tailored to a specific country or to a specific geography. For example, in Brazil, we make a product called Guarana Tai. In northern Latin America, we make another product called Fanta-Kolita, which is a cream soda type of drink. Those products, like even Mello-Yello, are not marketed globally. We only market three products in a global manner: Coca-Cola, Sprite, and Fanta.

The stiffer challenges facing Coca-Cola in the U.S. market, namely Pepsi, have led Coke to adapt much more aggressive marketing strategies and tactics than it did in the 1980s. Specifically, it's relying less on feel-good image ads, which have long characterized Coke. Efforts on behalf of Mello-Yello coordinated with Tom Cruise's movie, *Days of Thunder*—as well as joint promotions about the Super Bowl, fast-food chains, and selected grocery chains—are but a few of the newly aggressive domestic efforts to implement Coca-Cola's global strategy. Said Coke president Donald Keough, "Great ads can take Coke only so far. The consumer has gotten the message. Better selling right where the cola meets the consumer—means closer relationships with retailers, bolder merchandising, cheaper prices, and faster delivery."

OPERATIONS

Coca-Cola has followed a strategy of increased ownership of bottling operations worldwide as a way to make its operations more efficient and also to improve product availability as well as marketing focus. In some cases, investments represent minority shares in the bottling company, wherein Coca-Cola is able to help focus and improve sales and marketing programs, assist in the development of effective business and information systems, and lend operating expertise. In other situations, like East Germany, Coke seeks 100 percent or at least controlling ownership so a modern soft-drink business can be established quickly. Finally, situations where the current bottler is not competitive with current competition or systemwide sales standards, Coke frequently moves in to acquire the franchise and quickly turn the situation around. The major bottlers in the United Kingdom and France have been bought out by Coca-Cola because of frustration with their nonaggressive approach. The result has been a 25 to 35 percent annual increase in sales, compared with stable or single-digit growth each of the 10 years prior to Coke's taking over.

Another operating strategy that Coke has implemented to help its new approach is to seek total automation of distribution activities. Consider Coca-Cola Enterprises, the U.S. bottling company in which Coca-Cola holds a 49 percent interest. It has 1,800 salespeople selling over 150 products to 560,000 outlets along 6,500 routes, delivering over 2.5 million cases daily. Those salespeople now carry handheld computer terminals, which unload orders to a central dispatch computer, which decodes addresses and allows CCE dispatchers to experiment with alternate routes, and, in one third the time previously spent, create routes for the next day that have dropped distance traveled by 8 percent, total hours spent on delivery by 13 percent, and the number of vehicles and delivery people needed by 14 percent.

Over the last 10 years, Coca-Cola has moved to a regional operating strategy with centralized concentrate production facilities (e.g., France, Ireland, and Puerto Rico) that reduces manufacturing costs. That is followed by pooled purchasing across all bottlers in that region. Finally, pooled regional marketing at the bottler level is thought to offer a cost effective way to enhance marketing and promotional activities.

FINANCE

A few of Coca-Cola's financial strategies and policies employed to implement its strategy for the 1990s are:

1. Strong earnings growth has enabled the company to reduce its dividend payout ratio while increasing the cash dividend per common share every year since 1961—a common stock dividend payout ratio of approximately 40 percent of earnings available to common share owners.

2. The company receives approximately 80 percent of operating income from outside the United States. So the company closely monitors currency fluctuations and engages in various hedging activities to minimize potential losses on cash flows denominated in foreign currencies.

3. Coca-Cola uses relatively low amounts of debt to lower its overall cost of capital. The company has established a net-debt-to-net-capital ratio ceiling of 35 percent.

INTERNATIONAL MARKETS

One of the things Coca-Cola management emphasizes about functional strategies is that it must be adjusted or altered to adapt to local conditions that will certainly vary across so many diverse international settings. Coca-Cola's management illustrates this with its descriptions of key functional strategies it is emphasizing in selected countries around the world.

European Community Group

In 1991, Coke light became Europe's number three selling soft drink, behind Coca-Cola and Fanta. Despite adverse economic conditions in Great Britain, where gallon sales were down, overall gallon sales in the EC Group rose 6 percent. Two concentrate megaplants are now serving a vastly more efficient network of approximately 100 bottlers, less than half the number of just 10 years ago, and many Company departments have been reorganized to function on a pan-European basis.

**European Community
1991 Unit Case Sales**

- Germany 34%
- Great Britain 12%
- Spain 15%
- Italy 13%
- France 7%
- Benelux 9%
- Other 10%

Germany 13 manufacturing and distribution facilities operating in eastern Germany...two years after entering eastern Germany, sales reached 71 million unit cases...restructuring in western Germany resulted in further consolidation

Spain Comprehensive marketing programs implemented to capitalize on Summer Olympics and Seville's Expo '92

Italy Coca-Cola light reintroduced... strong bottler system initiated aggressive marketing programs... continued acquisition and consolidation of Company-owned bottling operations in the north

France Aggressive pricing and merchandising programs expanded market leadership nearly 4 points...emphasis on relationships with key retail customers improved in-store presence... intensified focus on cold drink market

Growth Rate
1991 vs. 1990

	Gallon Sales	Unit Case Sales
Germany	17%	19%
Great Britain	(9)%	(11)%
Spain	(2)%	6%
Italy	4%	4%
France	10%	11%
Benelux	8%	9%
Other	3%	4%
Total	6%	8%

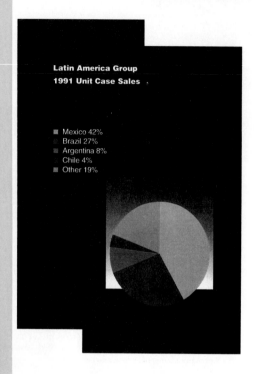

Latin America Group

Latin America Group
1991 Unit Case Sales

- Mexico 42%
- Brazil 27%
- Argentina 8%
- Chile 4%
- Other 19%

Gallon sales for the Latin America Group rose 8 percent, thanks in part to falling trade barriers and government deregulation, which permitted the introduction of larger package sizes. Larger packages were introduced in Guatemala, Colombia, Paraguay, Chile and Mexico. And in Brazil and Argentina, the 1.5-liter PET bottle is quickly becoming the most popular package. Mexico became the first country outside the United States to sell more than 1 billion unit cases in a year.

Growth Rate
1991 vs.1990

	Gallon Sales	Unit Case Sales
Mexico	7%	6%
Brazil	4%	4%
Argentina	31%	31%
Chile	11%	9%
Other	9%	9%
Total	8%	8%

Mexico Larger refillable glass and 1.5-liter PET packages launched...Sprite launched in key markets...significant investments in production and distribution infrastructure

Brazil Four new production facilities opened, four more planned for 1992... larger cups and 2,200 additional dispensers helped increase post-mix volume

Argentina Diet Coke reformulated and relaunched...cans introduced in key markets...larger package sizes helped drive 31 percent unit case sales increase

Chile Diet Coke unit case sales up 29 percent...340 additional post-mix units placed...cans launched in Santiago and other key markets...key account management system implemented for large customers

42

NEA Group

The Northeast Europe/Africa (NEA) Group registered excellent unit case sales growth in most major markets. This growth, however, was partly offset by the effects of recession and civil disturbances in some markets, principally in Africa. Overall, the NEA Group achieved a 5 percent increase in unit case sales and a 3 percent increase in gallon sales, as bottlers in Africa reduced concentrate inventories. During the year, important groundwork was laid for future growth in East Central Europe and the Middle East. The dynamic geopolitical environment and the move toward market economies bode well for the NEA Group.

Nigeria Double-digit unit case growth...larger packages and thousands of new coolers driving volume...new concentrate plant opened, permitting reduction in bottler's inventory levels, which moderated gallon sales growth

Norway New PET packaging contributed strongly to solid growth...Coke light reached 14 percent share, highest in world

Turkey Company-owned Ankara bottler set pace with 50 percent unit case growth...new Company-owned plant opened in Trabzon, contributing to overall solid growth

Austria Coke, Fanta, Sprite and each of their light versions all gained ground, propelling double-digit unit case growth...new PET packaging

Growth Rate
1991 vs.1990

	Gallon Sales	Unit Case Sales
Africa Division	(2)%	2%
East Central European Division	12%	9%
Middle East Division	27%	11%
Nordic and Northern Eurasia Division	(14)%	6%
Total	3%	5%

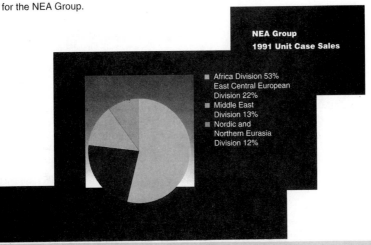

NEA Group
1991 Unit Case Sales

■ Africa Division 53%
East Central European Division 22%
■ Middle East Division 13%
■ Nordic and Northern Eurasia Division 12%

41

Pacific Group

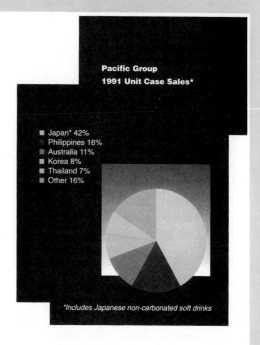

**Pacific Group
1991 Unit Case Sales***

- Japan* 42%
- Philippines 16%
- Australia 11%
- Korea 8%
- Thailand 7%
- Other 16%

*Includes Japanese non-carbonated soft drinks

Fueled by continued strong momentum in Japan, overall gallon sales increased 4 percent, despite several natural disasters in the region. Significant investments in soft drink production and distribution equipment are building a foundation for future growth in premier markets like Japan and Australia and in largely untapped markets like Indonesia and China.

Growth Rate
1991 vs.1990

	Gallon Sales	Unit Case Sales
Japan*	7%	7%
Philippines	0%	(1)%
Australia	1%	2%
Korea	1%	(1)%
Thailand	3%	3%
Other	3%	7%
Total*	4%	4%

*Includes Japanese non-carbonated soft drinks

Japan Coca-Cola light unit case sales increased 35 percent...Georgia Ice Coffee and Cafe Au Lait Premium successfully launched... Betacarotene-enriched soft drink VegitaBeta and Bonaqua flavored water test marketed

Philippines Sprite position enhanced through launch of 1-liter package... pre-sell delivery program implemented, increasing distribution efficiencies... Company products accounted for 76 percent of industry soft drink sales

Thailand More than 100 million unit cases sold...strong Fanta and Sprite unit case sales helped secure Company market leadership...strong post-mix growth

Australia Lift and diet Lift launched... 12-pack cans rolled out... new Skysurfer commercial immensely successful... cold drink equipment placements increased by 34 percent

China Shanghai, Nanjing, Hangzhou and Tianjin plants sparked 64 percent unit case sales increase... cold drink availability increased... post-mix sales nearly doubled... joint venture bottling plant opened on Hainan Island

10 IMPLEMENTING STRATEGY THROUGH STRUCTURE, LEADERSHIP, CULTURE, AND REWARDS

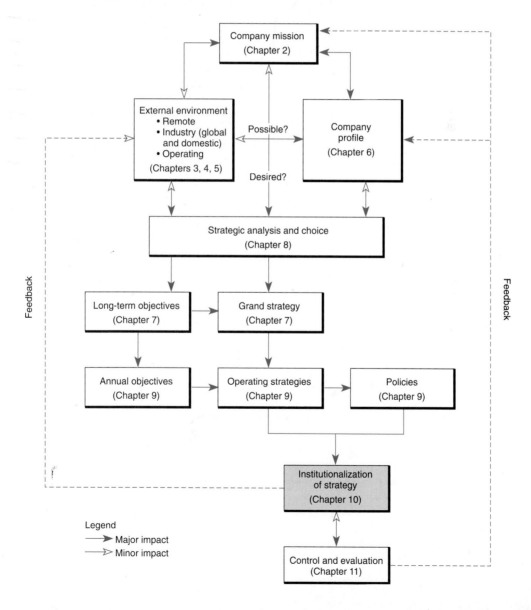

Say "IBM" to European or Japanese executives, and they are still likely to nod knowingly and respectfully. Technologically powerful, active in more than 130 countries, the world's eighth-largest industrial corporation has traditionally been emblematic of America's hopes for winning on the rugged fields of global competition. Yet IBM faltered as it moved toward the 1990s. Accustomed to an annual sales growth exceeding 10 percent, IBM experienced a revenue decrease approaching $5 billion in both 1991 and 1992 and lost almost $8 billion after taxes over these two years.[1]

John Akers, IBM's former chairman and CEO, responded to the situation with candor. "We took our eye off the ball," he observed. "We decided to be careful instead of aggressive, and we were trying to solve some problems that were more IBM's than the customer's." He concluded that IBM's strategy of product development for the 1990s was basically sound, that IBM's fundamental problems lay in the way its 340,000 people (down to 280,000 by 1993) were organized.[2]

Akers set out to remedy those problems by reinventing the firm. To reorganize IBM's bureaucratic management structure into a structure designed to address customer needs, he divided IBM into seven autonomous business units and into an eighth unit that handled marketing for all of the others. He systematically pushed responsibility down the ranks by putting the firm's fate in the hands of the general managers of these autonomous business units. Sales had been the sole route to the top at IBM, but Akers added many top executives with strong technological backgrounds. This, he believed, would change IBM's longtime practice of telling customers what it thought was good for them to one in which technologically capable executives listened to customers and became problem solvers. To sanction this new "culture," he took the unprecedented step of having several key customers participate in IBM's annual strategic planning conferences. And finally, Akers changed IBM's reward system, in which bonuses had been based on sales of existing products, to emphasize the varied challenges facing each of the autonomous business units.[3]

The IBM situation shows that a firm must be properly *organized for action* if its strategy is to be successful. Although annual objectives, functional strategies, and specific policies provide important means of communicating what must be done to implement the firm's strategy, more is needed to implement that strategy successfully. To be successfully implemented, the strategy must permeate the firm's day-to-day life. Four organization elements provide the fundamental, long-term means for doing this: (1) structure, (2) leadership, (3) culture, and (4) rewards.

IBM's John Akers focused on these four elements as he prepared IBM for global competitiveness in the 21st century. He revamped IBM's *organizational structure,* allowing autonomous business units to position the firm close to appropriate customer groups. He brought in a new type of *leadership,* giving technical people greater access to top positions. He sought to transform IBM's inwardly focused *culture* into a customer-driven culture. And he revised IBM's *reward systems* to reinforce these strategic changes.

---

[1] IBM 1992 annual report, p. 30.

[2] IBM 1991 annual report, pp. 4, 6;   and "The New IBM." *Business Week,* December 16, 1991, pp. 112–18.

[3] "IBM," *Business Week,* June 17, 1991, pp. 26, 30.

FIGURE 10–1
McKinsey 7–S Framework

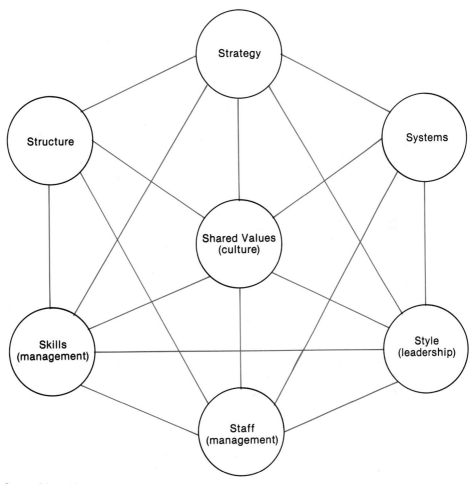

Source: Adapted from Thomas J. Peters and Robert H. Waterman, Jr., *In Search of Excellence* (New York: Harper & Row, 1982), p. 11.

Akers's early success was mixed. As a result, he relinquished the CEO post in 1993. He was replaced by Lou Gerstner, previously RJR-Nabisco CEO and, before that, American Express CEO. Gerstner is the first "outsider" and "noncomputer industry" person to lead IBM.

Gerstner appears to believe that the basic IBM product development strategy is sound and that these four organization elements are where IBM needs to revitalize itself. He further appears committed to continue Akers's structural changes toward decentralization and reward systems more aligned with new products and services. But while agreeing with Akers's structural and reward changes, Gerstner and the board committee that hired him feel that Akers, a lifelong IBM insider, never initiated the cultural and leadership changes necessary to truly revitalize IBM.

These topics received considerable attention from executives, authors, and researchers during the last decade as they sought to understand the reasons behind the superior performance among the "best" American companies. *In Search of Excellence* is perhaps the best known of these efforts. It offered a framework identifying the key factors found in the research of authors Tom Peters and Robert Waterman to best explain superior performance. That framework, known as the McKinsey 7–S Framework, is provided in Figure 10–1. This framework provides a useful visualization of the key components managers must consider in making sure a strategy permeates the day-to-day life of the firm.

Once the strategy has been designed, the McKinsey Framework suggests that managers focus on six components to ensure effective execution: structure, systems, shared values (culture), skills, style, and staff. This chapter organizes these six components into four basic elements through which managers can implement strategy. The first is *structure*—the basic way the firm's different activities are organized. Second is leadership, encompassing the need to establish an effective *style* as well as the necessary *staff* and *skills* to execute the strategy. The third element is culture—the *shared values* that create the norms of individual behavior and the tone of the organization. The final elements are the *systems* for rewarding performance as well as monitoring and controlling organizational action. Reward systems are examined in this chapter, while a discussion of systems for monitoring and controlling organizational action is reserved for Chapter 11.

This chapter has these major aims as it introduces you to these four elements: (1) to examine the advantages and disadvantages of structural alternatives and their role in strategy implementation; (2) to discuss the leadership dimensions that are important in strategy implementation; (3) to explain how the organizational culture influences organizational life and to examine ways of managing the strategy-culture relationship; and (4) to show how reward systems can reinforce strategic intent.

STRUCTURING AN EFFECTIVE ORGANIZATION

Successful strategy implementation depends in large part on the firm's primary organizational structure. Structure helps identify the firm's key activities and the manner in which they will be coordinated to achieve the firm's strategic purpose. The preceding IBM example referred to a change from a highly centralized, functional structure to a highly decentralized, strategic business unit structure that IBM's top managers viewed as more consistent with the firm's product development strategy.

A primary organizational structure comprises the firm's major elements, components, or differentiated units. Such a structure portrays how key tasks and activities have been divided to achieve efficiency and effectiveness.

The primary structure is not the only means for getting "organized" to implement the strategy. Reward systems, coordination terms, planning procedures, alliances, information, and budgetary systems are among the other means that often become necessary. However, it is through the primary structure that strategists attempt to position the firm so as to execute its strategy in a manner that balances internal efficiency and overall effectiveness.

FIGURE 10–2
Functional Organization Structures

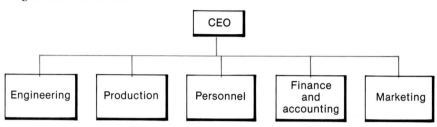

A process-oriented functional structure (an electronics distributor):

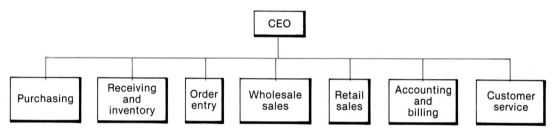

Strategic Advantages	Strategic Disadvantages
1. Achieves efficiency through specialization.	1. Promotes narrow specialization and functional rivalry or conflict.
2. Develops functional expertise.	2. Creates difficulties in functional coordination and interfunctional decision making.
3. Differentiates and delegates day-to-day operating decisions.	
4. Retains centralized control of strategic decisions.	3. Limits development of general managers.
5. Tightly links structure to strategy by designating key activities as separate units.	4. Has a strong potential for interfunctional conflict—priority placed on functional areas, not the entire business.

Primary Organizational Structures and Their Strategy-Related Pros and Cons

Matching the structure to the strategy is a fundamental task of company strategists. To understand how that task is handled, we first must review the five basic primary structures. We will then turn to guidelines for matching structure to strategy.

The five basic primary structures are: (1) functional organization, (2) geographic organization, (3) divisional organization, (4) strategic business units, and (5) matrix organization. Each of these structures has advantages and disadvantages that strategists must consider when choosing an organization form.

Functional Organizational Structure

Functional structures predominate in firms with a single or narrow product focus. Such firms require well-defined skills and areas of specialization to build competitive advantages in providing their products or services. Dividing tasks into functional specialties enables the personnel of these firms to concentrate on only one aspect of the necessary work. This allows use of the latest technical skills and develops a high level of efficiency.

Product, customer, or technology considerations determine the identity of the parts in a functional structure. A hotel business might be organized around housekeeping (maids), the front desk, maintenance, restaurant operations, reservations and sales, accounting, and personnel. An equipment manufacturer might be organized around production, engineering/quality control, purchasing, marketing, personnel, and finance/accounting. Two examples of functional organizations are illustrated in Figure 10–2.

The strategic challenge presented by the functional structure is effective coordination of the functional units. The narrow technical expertise achieved through specialization can lead to limited perspectives and to differences in the priorities of the functional units. Specialists may see the firm's strategic issues primarily as "marketing" problems or "production" problems. The potential conflict among functional units makes the coordinating role of the chief executive critical. Integrating devices (such as project teams or planning committees) are frequently used in functionally organized firms to enhance coordination and to facilitate understanding across functional areas.

Geographic Organizational Structure

Firms often grow by expanding the sale of their products or services to new geographic areas. In these areas, they frequently encounter differences that necessitate different approaches in producing, providing, or selling their products or services. Structuring by geographic areas is usually required to accommodate these differences. Thus, Holiday Inns is organized by regions of the world because of differences among nations in the laws, customs, and economies affecting the lodging industry. And even within its U.S. organization, Holiday Inns is organized geographically because of regional differences in traveling requirements, lodging regulations, and customer mix.

The key strategic advantage of geographic organizational structures is responsiveness to local market conditions. Figure 10–3 illustrates a typical geographic organizational structure and itemizes the strategic advantages and disadvantages of such structures.

Divisional Organizational Structure

When a firm diversifies its product/service lines, utilizes unrelated market channels, or begins to serve heterogeneous customer groups, a functional structure rapidly becomes inadequate. If a functional structure is retained under these circumstances, production managers may have to oversee the production of numerous and varied products or services, marketing managers may have to create sales programs for vastly different products or sell through vastly different distribution channels, and top management may be confronted with excessive coordination demands. A new organizational structure is often necessary to meet the increased coordination and decision-making requirements that result from increased diversity and size, and the divisional organizational structure is the form often chosen.

For many years, Ford and General Motors have used divisional structures organized by product groups. Manufacturers often organize sales into divisions based on differences in distribution channels.

A divisional structure allows corporate management to delegate authority for the strategic management of distinct business entities—the divisions. This expedites decision

FIGURE 10–3
A Geographic Organizational Structure

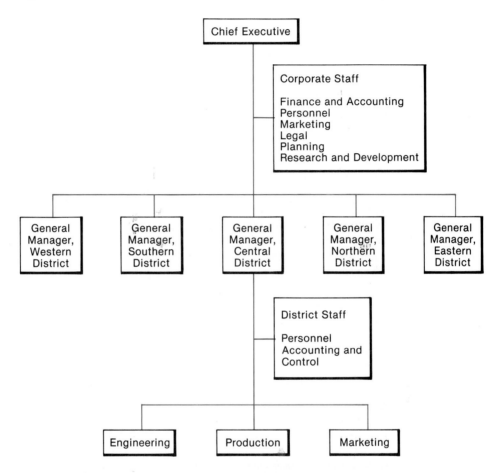

Strategic Advantages

1. Allows tailoring of strategy to needs of each geographic market.
2. Delegates profit/loss responsibility to lowest strategic level.
3. Improves functional coordination within the target market.
4. Takes advantage of economies of local operations.
5. Provides excellent training grounds for higher-level general managers.

Strategic Disadvantages

1. Poses problem of deciding whether headquarters should impose geographic uniformity or geographic diversity should be allowed.
2. Makes it more difficult to maintain consistent company image/reputation from area to area.
3. Adds layer of management to run the geographic units.
4. Can result in duplication of staff services at headquarters and district levels.

Source: Arthur A. Thompson, Jr., and A. J. Strickland III, *Strategic Management: Concepts and Cases* (Homewood, Ill.: 1987, Richard D. Irwin), p. 208.

making in response to varied competitive environments and enables corporate management to concentrate on corporate-level strategic decisions. The divisions usually are given profit responsibility, which facilitates accurate assessment of profit and loss.

Figure 10–4 illustrates a divisional organizational structure and specifies the strategic advantages and disadvantages of such structures.

Strategic Business Units

Some firms encounter difficulty in evaluating and controlling the operations of their divisions as the diversity, size, and number of these units continue to increase. Under these conditions, a firm may add another layer of management to improve strategy implementation, to promote synergy, and to gain greater control over the firm's diverse business interests. This can be accomplished by creating groups that combine various divisions (or parts of some divisions) in terms of common strategic elements. These groups, commonly called *strategic business units* (SBUs), usually are based on the independent product-market segments served by the firm. Figure 10–5 illustrates an SBU organizational structure.

As companies grow, they often adopt a new structure from among the alternatives we have described as a way to help them manage complexity brought on by growth. The SBU structure's main value appears to be that it provides a way for the largest companies to regain focus in different parts of their business that was central to earlier success yet lost in the complexity and size that success brought the company. IBM adopted the SBU approach in 1992 by creating 14 distinct SBUs, or "Baby Blues," out of the formerly highly centralized structure. Five of these IBM SBUs are geographically distinct SBUs that provide marketing, services, and support for their customers in five global regions. IBM also created nine distinct manufacturing and development (M&D) SBUs that have worldwide responsibility for product development, manufacturing, and delivery of their own distinct product lines. IBM's former CEO, John Akers, had these early 1992 comments:

> As we begin 1992, we have set into motion comprehensive changes that are redefining IBM from a single, centralized company into a network of more competitive businesses. Our manufacturing and development businesses and our marketing and service companies will be increasingly free-standing; each more independent, fast, and focused on the markets it serves; responsive to its customers and accountable for its results. At the same time, these businesses and companies will remain linked and able to draw upon the full range of IBM's technological and financial resources.
>
> Putting a premium on autonomy will unleash the full creativity of our people to achieve greater speed, agility, and ingenuity in delivering the right products, services, and solutions. In countries around the world, the value we bring to customers will come increasingly from our marketing and services companies. They will focus more on market selection and consulting services and will combine the best product and service offerings from IBM and, as appropriate, from other companies to provide integrated solutions that are truly tailored to customer needs. IBM's manufacturing and development businesses will optimize product manufacturing, as well as development, on a worldwide basis. As they become increasingly autonomous, these M&D businesses will sell their products not only to IBM marketing and services companies but also to other manufacturers.[4]

---

[4] IBM 1991 annual report, pp. 3–6.

FIGURE 10–4
Divisional Organization Structure

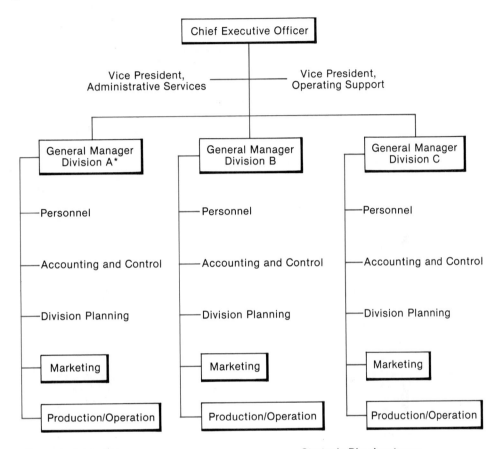

Strategic Advantages

1. Forces coordination and necessary authority down to the appropriate level for rapid response.
2. Places strategy development and implementation in closer proximity to the unique environments of the divisions.
3. Frees chief executive officer for broader strategic decision making.
4. Sharply focuses accountability for performance.
5. Retains functional specializaiton within each division.
6. Provides good training grounds for strategic managers.

Strategic Disadvantages

1. Fosters potentially dysfunctional competition for corporate-level resources.
2. Presents the problem of determining how much authority should be given to division managers.
3. Creates a potential for policy inconsistencies among divisions.
4. Presents the problem of distributing corporate overhead costs in a way that's acceptable to division managers with profit responsibility.

FIGURE 10–5
Strategic Business Unit Organizational Structure

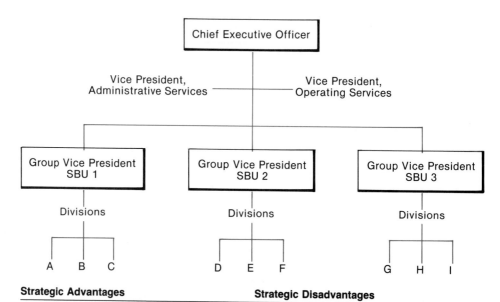

Strategic Advantages

1. Improves coordination between divisions with similar strategic concerns and product-market environments.
2. Tightens the strategic management and control of large, diverse business enterprises.
3. Facilitates distinct and in-depth business planning at the corporate and business levels.
4. Channels accountability to distinct business units.

Strategic Disadvantages

1. Places another layer of management between the divisions and corporate management.
2. May increase dysfunctional competition for corporate resources.
3. May present difficulties in defining the role of the group vice president.
4. May present difficulties in defining how much autonomy should be given to the group vice presidents and division managers.

Matrix Organization

In large companies, increased diversity leads to numerous product and project efforts of major strategic significance. The result is a need for an organizational form that provides skills and resources where and when they are most vital. The matrix organization has been used increasingly to meet this need. Among the firms that now use some form of matrix organization are Citicorp, Matsushita, Unilever, Shell Oil, Dow Chemical, and Texas Instruments.

The matrix organization provides dual channels of authority, performance responsibility, evaluation, and control, as shown in Figure 10–6. Essentially, subordinates are assigned both to a basic functional area and to a project or product manager. The matrix form is intended to make the best use of talented people within a firm by combining the advantages of functional specialization and product-project specialization.

The matrix structure also increases the number of middle managers who exercise general management responsibilities (through the project manager role) and, thus, broaden

FIGURE 10–6
Matrix Organizational Structure

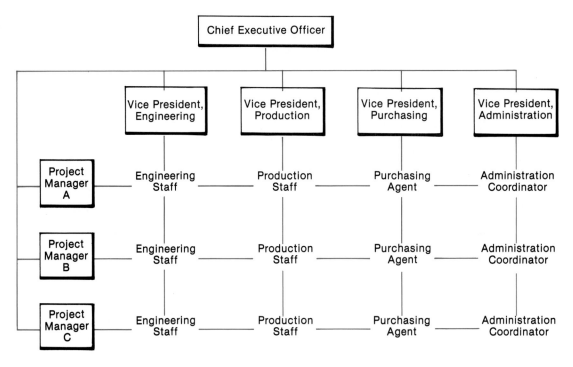

Strategic Advantages

1. Accommodates a wide variety of project-oriented business activity.
2. Provides good training grounds for strategic managers.
3. Maximizes efficient use of functional managers.
4. Fosters creativity and multiple sources of diversity.
5. Gives middle management broader exposure to strategic issues.

Strategic Disadvantages

1. May result in confusion and contradictory policies.
2. Necessitates tremendous horizontal and vertical coordination.
3. Can proliferate information logjams and excess reporting.
4. Can trigger turf battles and loss of accountability.

their exposure to organizationwide strategic concerns. In this way, the matrix structure overcomes a key deficiency of functional organizations while retaining the advantages of functional specialization.

Although the matrix structure is easy to design, it is difficult to implement. Dual chains of command challenge fundamental organizational orientations. Negotiating shared responsibilities, the use of resources, and priorities can create misunderstanding or confusion among subordinates. These problems are heightened in an international context with the complications introduced by distance, language, time, and culture.

To avoid the deficiencies that might arise from a permanent matrix structure, some firms are accomplishing particular strategic tasks, by means of a "temporary" or "flexible" *overlay structure.* This approach, used recently by such firms as NEC, Matsushita, Phillips, and Unilever, is meant to take *temporary* advantage of a matrix-type team while preserving an underlying divisional structure.[5] Thus, the basic idea of the matrix structure—*to simplify and amplify the focus of resources on a narrow but strategically important product, project, or market*—appears to be an important structural alternative for large, diverse organizations.

Choosing an Effective Organizational Structure[6]

Which organizational structure is best? Considerable research has been done on this question, and the collective answer is that this depends on the strategy of the firm. Since the structural design ties together key activities and resources of the firm, it must be closely aligned with the demands of the firm's strategy.

Alfred Chandler conducted a landmark study of structural choice as a function of strategy.[7] In examining 20 large corporations over an extended period, Chandler found a common strategy-structure sequence:

1. The choice of a new strategy.
2. Administrative problems and a decline in performance.
3. A shift to an organizational structure more in line with the strategy's needs.
4. Improved profitability and strategy execution.

The logic underlying this sequence was that firms changed their growth strategy in response to environmental changes but that the new strategy created administrative problems that resulted in a decline in performance. These problems arose because the existing structure was ineffective in organizing and coordinating the activities required by the new strategy. To resolve the problems and improve performance, the structure was redesigned. Chandler implied that a failure to redesign structure would eventually cause a decline in performance. Strategy in Action 10–1 presents a description of the evolving organizational structure at Procter & Gamble. The description, offered by John Smale, P&G's recently retired chairman and CEO, vividly illustrates Chandler's findings.

Chandler also observed a common sequence of evolution in strategy and structure among American firms. The sequence reflected their increasing scope. Most firms began as simple functional units operating at a single site (e.g., a plant, a warehouse, or a sales office) and within a single industry. The initial growth strategy of such firms was *volume expansion,* which created a need for an administrative office to manage the increased volume. The next growth strategy was *geographic expansion,* which required multiple field units, still performing the same function but in different locations. Administrative problems with regard to standardization, specialization, and interunit coordination then

---

[5] Christopher A. Bartlett and Sumantra Ghoshal, "Matrix Management: Not a Structure, a Frame of Mind," *Harvard Business Review* 68, no. 4 (1990), pp. 138–45.

[6] This section benefited from ideas and unpublished material shared with the authors by Professor David Schweiger, University of South Carolina.

[7] Alfred D. Chandler, *Strategy and Structure* (Cambridge, Mass.: MIT Press, 1962).

gave rise to the need for geographic units and for a central administrative unit to oversee them. *Vertical integration* was usually the next growth strategy. Firms remained within the same industry but performed additional functions. Problems associated with the flow of information and materials among the various functions led to the functional organization, in which staff personnel developed forecasts and schedules that facilitated overall coordination.

The final growth strategy was *product diversification.* Firms entered other industries in which they could use their existing resources. Problems in managing diverse product divisions and evaluating their capital investment proposals led to the multidivisional structure in which similar activities were grouped. Separate divisions handled independent products and were responsible for short-run operating decisions. General managers (i.e., group managers) at a central office were responsible for long-term strategic decisions. These managers had to relate divisional decisions and performance to strategic direction and to balance divisional autonomy against central control.

Larry Wrigley built on Chandler's work by examining how a firm's degree of diversification from its core business affected its choice of structure. He identified four growth strategies: (1) *single-product businesses;* (2) *single dominant businesses,* with one business accounting for 70–95 percent of sales; (3) *related diversified businesses* based on a common distribution channel or technology, with more than 30 percent of sales outside the primary business; and (4) *unrelated diversified businesses,* with more than 30 percent of sales outside the primary business.[8]

Wrigley's major finding was that greater diversity led to greater divisionalization. Specifically, single-product businesses used a functional structure; related and unrelated businesses used a divisionalized structure; and single dominant businesses used a functional structure in the dominant business and a divisional structure in the remaining businesses.

Richard Rumelt extended Chandler's and Wrigley's work by using a more detailed classification scheme.[9] His findings generally confirmed those of Chandler and Wrigley. The greater the diversity in a firm's businesses, the greater was the likelihood that the firm would employ a multidivisional structure. Rumelt also found that from 1949 to 1969 the use of the single-product and single dominant business strategies declined and the use of the multidivisional strategy increased. Finally, Rumelt's research suggested that the fit between strategy and structure affected performance. Table 10–1 summarizes the strategy-structure recommendations emanating from this stream of research.

More recent research has extended our understanding of the strategy-structure fit.[10] This research continues to suggest that, in smaller firms with a single product or product line, the functional structure significantly outperforms the multidivisional structure. In larger firms, however, the roles of corporate- and lower-level staffs significantly affect performance. The greater the diversity among a firm's businesses, the more desirable it is to

---

[8] Larry Wrigley, *Divisional Autonomy and Diversification,* doctoral dissertation, Harvard Business School, 1970.

[9] Richard Rumelt, *Diversification Strategy and Performance, Strategic Management Journal* 3 (January–February 1982), pp. 359–69;   Richard Rumelt, *Strategy, Structure and Economic Performance* (Boston: HBS Press, 1986).

[10] D. A. Nathanson and J. S. Cassano, "Organization, Diversity, and Performance," *Wharton's Magazine* 6 (1982), pp. 19–26;   and Bartlett and Ghoshal, "Matrix Arrangement."

STRATEGY **PROCTER & GAMBLE'S RETIRING CEO**
IN ACTION **TALKS ABOUT P&G'S EVOLVING**
   10–1   **ORGANIZATIONAL STRUCTURE**

John Smale, recently retired as P&G's chairman and CEO, made the following remarks about P&G's changing organizational structure a year before retiring:

> Many students take notice of *Fortune* magazine's ranking of the 500 largest industrial corporations in the United States, which show Procter & Gamble advancing over the last few years to the 15th position on that list.
>
> While we have no objectives with respect to Procter & Gamble's position on such lists, it underscores the point that Procter & Gamble is a very large business which grows ever larger.
>
> Procter & Gamble has always planned for growth. In that planning, there is perhaps nothing more fundamental than sound organizational structuring.
>
> Recently, in a move to position P&G for strengthened performance, three major changes were made in the way we are organized to manage our U.S. consumer business—first, a move to management of this business on a strategic business unit basis; second, the combination of our manufacturing, engineering, purchasing, and distribution functions into a simple product supply function; and, finally, the initial steps of restructuring our sales organization. I want to tell you about the first, our move to SBUs.
>
> Some history will be helpful. At the end of the Second World War, P&G's business in the United States was based on five product categories—toilet soaps, laundry detergents, hard surface cleaners, shortening, and shampoo.
>
> In the decade that followed the war, P&G's energy was importantly directed toward the growth of its business within these categories, particularly the laundry category. But by 1955, P&G had entered new businesses—dentifrice, peanut butter, and home permanent waves among them—and was looking to even more growth through more product diversity in the future.
>
> In order to prepare itself to manage a broader-based consumer goods business, P&G then created the *division organizational structure*—centering profit responsibility with the divisions. It is that concept which we followed until a year ago, when core profit center responsibility within P&G was moved a notch down from the division level. This was done with the creation of strategic business units.
>
> Why this change?
>
> The fundamental reason is simply the growth in the size and complexity of our business, which has in turn created the need for sharper focus on each of the business categories in which P&G is competing.

Source: Adapted from Procter & Gamble, *Annual Meeting of Stockholders,* October 11, 1988.

have strong, decentralized staffs within the businesses (or divisions); with less diversity, firms having strong staffs at higher organizational levels are more effective. In other words, the greater the diversity among the businesses in multibusiness firms, the greater is the necessary degree of decentralization and self-containment. This need has only been heightened by the rapid globalization among many countries. On the other hand, where the diversity among a firm's businesses is low and the interdependence of these businesses is high, more integration at the corporate level is needed.

Four significant conclusions can be drawn from this research:[11]

1. *A single-product firm or single dominant business firm should employ a functional structure.* This structure allows for strong task focus through an emphasis on special-

---

[11] V. R. Galbraith and R. K. Kazanjian, *Strategy Implementation: Structure, Systems & Processes* (St. Paul, Minn.: West Publishing, 1986).

STRATEGY
IN ACTION **concluded**
10–1

When P&G divisionalized its structure in 1955, we were engaged in 10 categories in our U.S. consumer goods business.

That number had grown to 26 categories by 1980.

But in the first nine years of the 1980s, our rate of entry into new businesses accelerated. Seventeen additional categories of business have been entered since 1980.

Growth in the number of categories in which P&G competes had, of course, been accommodated over the years by expanding the number of divisions.

Our divisions themselves, however, had grown over the years to the point that some are larger than P&G's total U.S. business was when the divisional structure was established. Also, the volume in several of our business categories surpasses the volume of some of our original divisions.

But quite apart from any measure based on the size of our business units, growth in the diversity of our businesses has multiplied the amount of change that needs to be effectively managed somewhere in P&G at any given instant.

All of this led to the decision to manage the U.S. business by SBUs and to locate core profit center responsibility at the SBU management level.

The move to strategic business units has been accomplished, by and large, without adding people or layers to the organization. Rather, our previous structures have been rearranged to create business units—each headed by a general manager—with product supply and financial analysis resources.

These SBU teams are lean. They bring sharp focus to each of P&G's varied businesses, and we are already beginning to see the results.

There is a common thread to all of our organization changes. They are designed to simplify what we do—to flatten our organization, to drive decisions and responsibility for those decisions down in the organization, to bring increased focus to each of our businesses, and to move closer to our customers.

And in the final analysis, the moves that have been taken over the last year to restructure Procter & Gamble's organization and governance will strengthen our ability to continue the growth that has been characteristic of this company since its inception 151 years ago.

---

ization and efficiency, while providing opportunity for adequate controls through centralized review and decision making.

2. *A firm in several lines of business that are somehow related should employ a multidivisional structure.* Closely related divisions should be combined into groups within this structure. When synergies (i.e., shared or linked activities) are possible within such a group, the appropriate location for staff influence and decision making is at the group level, with a lesser role for corporate-level staff. The greater the degree of diversity across the firm's businesses, the greater should be the extent to which the power of staff and decision-making authority is lodged within the divisions.

3. *A firm in several unrelated lines of business should be organized into strategic business units.* Although the strategic business unit structure resembles the multidivisional structure, there are significant differences between the two. With a strategic business unit structure, finance, accounting, planning, legal, and related activities should be centralized at the corporate office. Since there are no synergies across the firm's businesses, the cor-

TABLE 10–1
Choosing a Primary Structure to Fit Different Strategies

Strategic Conditions, Product and Market Factors, and Other Key Variables	Strategies	Primary Structure
I. Commodity-type products. Small numbers of products and services. High degree of production and market relatedness. Need to focus on efficiency criteria, cost reduction, or economies of scale.	Volume expansion (horizontal growth). Geographic expansion.	Functional organization (process specialization). Geographic organization with central administration.
II. As in I above, plus high stability or low demand volatility for products. Prospect of adding new products with high production or technological relatedness. High proportion of potential new productive capacity being absorbed by existing or new products.	As in I above, plus vertical integration.	As in I above, plus more sophisticated functional structures (usually special coordination teams, planning councils, and staff coordination roles).
III. Large numbers of products or services. Low production relatedness. Low market relatedness. Excess productive capacity (distinctive competence). Slack resources. Need to reduce coordination costs.	Product diversification.	Multidivisional organization (purpose specialization by product, customer, or geography). Strategic business units (discrete units, highly self-contained).
IV. Need for dual focus—products and functions. Scarcity of resources, with opportunity for cross-fertilization or synergy across products or projects. High uncertainty, complexity, and interdependence, increasing need to process information and make decisions more efficiently.	As in I, II, or III above.	Matrix organization.

Source: Adapted from L. G. Hrebiniak and W. F. Joyce, *Implementing Strategy* (New York: Macmillan, 1984), pp. 88–89.

porate office serves largely as a capital allocation and control mechanism. Otherwise, its major decisions involve acquisitions and divestitures. All operational and business-level strategic plans are delegated to the strategic business units.

4. *Early achievement of a strategy-structure fit can be a competitive advantage.* A competitive advantage is obtained by the first firm among competitors to achieve an

appropriate strategy-structure fit. That advantage will disappear as the firm's competitors also attain such a fit. Moreover, if the firm alters its strategy, its structure must obviously change as well. Otherwise, a loss of fit will lead to a competitive disadvantage for the firm.

The description in Strategy in Action 10–1 of Procter & Gamble's organizational structures over a 50-year period provides a good illustration of these conclusions.

ORGANIZATIONAL LEADERSHIP

Organizational structure provides the overall framework for strategy implementation, but an appropriate organizational structure is not in itself sufficient to ensure successful implementation. Within the organizational structure, individuals, groups, and units are the mechanisms of organizational action. And the effectiveness of that action is a major determinant of successful implementation. Three basic factors encourage or discourage effective action—leadership, culture, and rewards.[12] This section examines leadership as a key element of strategy implementation; the next section explains the role of organizational culture; and a final section considers the importance of reward systems.

Leadership, a seemingly vague and esoteric concept, is an essential element of effective strategy implementation. In this regard, two leadership issues are of fundamental importance: (1) the role of the chief executive officer (CEO) and (2) the assignment of key managers.

Role of the CEO

The chief executive officer is a key catalyst in strategic management. This individual is most closely identified with and ultimately accountable for a strategy's success. CEOs spend up to 80 percent of their time in developing and guiding strategy.

The CEO's role in strategy implementation is both *symbolic* and *substantive*. First, the CEO is a symbol of the new strategy. This individual's actions and the perceived seriousness of his or her commitment to the chosen strategy, particularly if that strategy represents a major change, significantly influence the intensity of subordinate managers' commitment to implementation. Bill Gates' highly visible role as spokesperson for Microsoft in business magazines, user organizations, Microsoft facilities, and before securities analysts is intended to provide a strong symbol of the workability of continued aggressive strategy and expectations into the 21st century.

Second, the personal goals and values of the CEO strongly influence the firm's mission, strategy, and key long-term objectives. To the extent that the CEO invests time and effort in the chosen strategy, he or she represents an important source for clarification, guidance, and adjustment during implementation.

Major changes in strategy often are preceded or quickly followed by a change in CEO. This suggests that different strategies require different CEOs. Roy Clymer's resignation as

---

[12] Leadership and organizational culture are interdependent phenomena. Each aspect of leadership ultimately helps shape organizational culture. Conversely, the prevailing organizational culture can profoundly influence a leader's effectiveness. The richness of this interdependence will become apparent. The topics are addressed in separate sections because it is important to develop an appreciation of the role of each in strategy implementation.

GLOBAL STRATEGY IN ACTION 10–1	SIEMENS' NEW MANAGEMENT GENERATION: EUROPE'S HIGH-TECH HOPE

With France's Groupe Bull and Italy's Olivetti in trouble and Britain's ICL recently sold to the Japanese, Germany's electronic giant, Siemens, "must stay strong for the good of Europe," says Groupe Bull chairman Francis Lorentz. But with $46 billion in revenue and 402,000 employees last year, Siemens earned only $1.1 billion in 1991 profit—mostly by investing its $11.3 billion in cash. Realizing its challenge, Siemens' board has approved a drastic management reorientation and reorganization designed by CEO Karlheinz Kaske, 64, two years ago to whip Siemens into shape.

Kaske is scheduled to retire in one year, due to mandatory retirement rules, with this change effort barely underway. So a 51-year-old lawyer and economist—and former German tennis champion, Heinrich von Pierer—has been catapulted from his responsibility as Siemens' energy chief to the top of Germany's electronics giant in the midst of a dramatic transformation of the company. Von Pierer is the tip of an iceberg that represents a broad transformation underway in Siemens and other German companies as they prepare for the realities of global competition in the 21st century. A recent story about von Pierer helps illustrate this change:

> The bus plunged ahead aimlessly in the darkness of a forest near the German-Czech border. As an aide struggled to read a map, the dinner outing for Siemens managers and several reporters was turning into a fiasco. Taking charge, [then] energy chief von Pierer marched to the front, fired the fumbling aide, and guided the bus to the restaurant. Onlookers were stunned: Von Pierer's swift punishment broke sharply with tradition at paternalistic Siemens. Next morning, he rehired the man. But the message was clear: Von Pierer was breaking the mold.*

CEO von Pierer is well aware that he is at the cutting edge of a new generation of managers taking the reins of power at Siemens. A key tenet for these younger managers is that status quo, lethargy, and hierarchy are out, and that entrepreneurship is in. This is Kaske's legacy to von Pierer.

Billions spent on acquisitions and new technologies was how Kaske started attacking Siemens' lack of competitiveness. But he also started "the chosen 500" as a way to transform Siemens' old management structure, which required younger managers to wait years before moving up Siemens' ranks. Desiring to break Siemens into smaller, market responsive units headed by risk-taking manag-

---

* "The New Generation at Siemens," *Business Week,* March 9, 1992, p. 46.
Source: Based on the article "The New Generation at Siemens," *Business Week,* March 9, 1992, pp. 46–48.

CEO of Holiday Inns clearly illustrates this point. Holiday Inns's executive group was convinced that casinos provided a key growth area for the firm. Clymer chose to resign because a move into this area was not consistent with his personal values and with his perception of what Holiday Inns should be. Rod Canion, founder, CEO, and early architect of Compaq Computer's early success selling quality and features, not price, was forced to resign as Compaq adopted a radical turnaround strategy to sell low-priced computers in 1992. Research has concluded that a successful turnaround strategy "will require almost without exception either a change in top management or a substantial change in the behavior of the existing management team."[13] Global Strategy in Action 10–1 describes such a change at

---

[13] Charles W. Hofer, "Turnaround Strategies," *Journal of Business Strategy,* January–February 1980, p. 25.

ers, Kaske put 500 young managers on a fast track so they could assume senior positions by age 35 to 45, instead of Siemens' usual 50 to 60. Most of these chosen 500 are in their late 20s and 30s, although a few in their 40s made the list, which included von Pierer.

Von Pierer's success to date is attributed to his being at once tough and likeable. He had a reputation for dodging the Siemens' bureaucracy as he rose to success in Siemens' power-engineering group. Von Pierer reportedly circumvented the chain of command, called lower-level managers into his office to get information, and regularly refused to adhere to the power structure.

Joining the chosen 500 at Siemens starts with persuading your immediate boss to recommend you for Siemens' management training boot camp outside Munich. There you spend one week in an intensive involvement with peers: role playing, solving case studies, and taking a battery of psychological tests. The best performers make the first cut.

For the next 5 to 10 years, the scrutiny continues. Performance results, retesting, and decisions are scrutinized. The better performers experience a whirlwind career, moving from plum job assignments in different countries and divisions on a regular basis. Compensation starts at $60,000, with 30 percent annual raises for excellent performance.

Some boot camp grads already are acting like the chosen and are driving hard to change Siemens—just what Kaske and von Pierer want. Markus Kirchgeorg, 29, who is aiming to be among the chosen, said: "You need to find people you work well with and establish a critical mass for change. And not only people on the same level."

Wolfram Martinsen, 50, almost quit Siemens while lost in the energy-and-auto division's hierarchy. Now, as head of an autonomous transportation unit, he has turned Siemens into a major force in the world market for high-speed trains. He did it by acquiring eight companies in two years, including Duewag Corporation in California. Pointing out that neither the acquisitions nor the quick strategic change would have occurred under Siemens' former structure, Martinsen said: "I'm the entrepreneur now." That's just the type of management change Siemens wants to permeate the company.

Siemens in Germany. Clearly, successful strategy implementation is directly linked to the characteristics, orientation, and actions of the CEO.

Assignment of Key Managers

A major concern of top management in implementing a strategy, particularly if it involves a major change, is that the right managers be in the right positions for the new strategy. Of all the means for ensuring successful implementation, this is the one that CEOs mention first. Confidence in the individuals occupying pivotal managerial positions is directly correlated with top-management expectations that a strategy can be successfully executed.

This confidence is based on the answers to two fundamental questions:

1. Which persons hold the leadership positions that are especially critical to execution of the strategy?

2. Do these persons have the characteristics needed to ensure effective implementation of the strategy?

Although it is impossible to specify the characteristics that are most important in this context, they probably include (1) ability and education, (2) previous track record and experience, and (3) personality and temperament. An individual's suitability on these counts, combined with top managers' gut feelings about the individual, provides the basis for top management's confidence in the individual.

Recently, numerous studies have attempted to match "preferred" managerial characteristics with different grand strategies.[14] These studies are meant to capsulize, for example, the behavioral characteristics appropriate for a manager responsible for implementing an "invest to grow" strategy in contrast to those appropriate for a manager implementing a "harvest" strategy. One of the studies found that three managerial characteristics—years of experience in marketing/sales, willingness to take risks, and tolerance for ambiguity—positively related to managerial effectiveness for divisions pursuing a build strategy and negatively related to managerial effectiveness for divisions being harvested. Despite widespread theoretical discussion of this idea, a study comprising a broad sample of firms failed to find a single firm that matched managerial characteristics to strategic mission in a formal manner. However, the study did find several firms that addressed such considerations as an informal, intuitive manner.[15] The following comment summarizes these findings:

> Despite the near unanimity of belief that, for effective implementation, different strategies require different skills . . . many corporate executives avoid too rigid an approach to matching managerial characteristics and strategy [for three reasons]: (1) exposure to and experience at managing different kinds of strategies and businesses is viewed as an essential component of managerial development: (2) too rigid a differentiation is viewed as much more likely to result in some managers being typecast as "good builders" and some others as "good harvesters," thereby creating motivational problems for the latter; and (3) a "perfect match" between managerial characteristics and strategy is viewed as more likely to result in overcommitment [or] self-fulfilling prophecies (a harvester becoming only a harvester) as compared with a situation where there was some mismatch.[16]

One practical consideration in making key managerial assignments when implementing strategy is whether to utilize current (or promotable) executives or bring in new personnel. This is obviously a difficult, sensitive, and strategic issue. Figure 10–7 highlights the key advantages and disadvantages of these alternatives.

---

[14] See, for example, M. Gerstein and H. Reisman, "Strategic Selection: Matching Managers to Business Conditions," *Sloan Management Review* 24 (1983), pp. 33–49; V. Govindarajan, "Implementing Competitive Strategies at the Business Unit Level: Implications of Matching Managers to Strategies," *Strategic Management Journal* 10 (1989), pp. 251–69; A. Gupta, "Matching Managers to Strategies: Point and Counterpoint," *Human Resource Management* 25 (1986), pp. 215–34; A. Szilagyi and D. Schweiger, "Matching Manager to Strategies: A Review and Suggested Framework," *Academy of Management Review* 6, pp. 577–87; and "Wanted, a Manager to Fit Each Strategy," *Business Week,* February 25, 1980, p. 166.

[15] Anil K. Gupta and V. Govindarajan, "Build, Hold, Harvest: Converting Strategic Intentions into Reality," *Journal of Business Strategy,* Winter 1984, p. 41; and Peter Lorange, "The Human Resources Dimension in the Strategic Planning Process" (Cambridge, Mass.: Sloan School, MIT, 1983, mimeographed), p. 13.

[16] Gupta and Govindarajan, "Build, Hold, Harvest," p. 41.

FIGURE 10–7
Using Existing Executives versus Bringing in Outsiders in Managerial Assignments to Implement a New Strategy

	Advantages	Disadvantages
Using existing executives to implement a new strategy	Existing executives already know key people, practices, and conditions.	Existing executives are less adaptable to major strategic changes because of their knowledge, attitudes, and values.
	Personal qualities of existing executives are better known and understood by associates.	Past commitments of existing executives hamper the hard decisions required in executing a new strategy.
	Existing executives have established relationships with peers, subordinates, suppliers, buyers, and the like.	Existing executives have less ability to become inspired and credibly convey the need for change.
	Use of existing executives symbolizes organizational commitment to individual careers.	
Bringing in outsiders to implement a new strategy	Outsiders may already believe in and have "lived" the new strategy.	Bringing in outsiders often is costly in terms of both compensation and "learning-to-work-together" time.
	Outsiders are unencumbered by internal commitments to people.	Candidates suitable in all respects (i.e., exact experience) may not be available, leading to compromise choices.
	Outsiders come to the new assignment with heightened commitment and enthusiasm.	Uncertainty exists in selecting the right outsiders to bring in.
	Bringing in outsiders can send powerful signals throughout the organization that change is expected.	"Morale costs" are incurred when an outsider takes a job that several insiders want.
		The "what to do with poor ol' Fred" problem arises when outsiders are brought in.

Sources: Adapted from Boris Yavitz and William H. Newman, *Strategy in Action* (New York: Free Press, 1982), chap. 10;   and Paul J. Stonich, *Implementing Strategy* (Cambridge, Mass.: Ballinger, 1982), chap. 4.

ORGANIZATIONAL CULTURE

Organizational culture is the set of important assumptions (often unstated) that members of an organization share in common. Every organization has its own culture. An organization's culture is similar to an individual's personality—an intangible yet ever-present theme that provides meaning, direction, and the basis for action. In much the same way as personality influences the behavior of an individual, the shared assumptions (beliefs and values) among a firm's members influence opinions and actions within that firm.

Shared Assumptions: Internalized Beliefs and Values that Organizational Members Hold in Common

A member of an organization can simply be aware of the organization's beliefs and values without sharing them in a personally significant way. Those beliefs and values have more personal meaning if the member views them as a guide to appropriate behavior in the organization and, therefore, complies with them. The member becomes fundamentally committed to the beliefs and values when he or she internalizes them; that is, comes to hold them as personal beliefs and values. In this case, the corresponding behavior is *intrinsically rewarding* for the member—the member derives personal satisfaction from his or her actions in the organization because those actions are congruent with corresponding personal beliefs and values. *Assumptions become shared assumptions through internalization among an organization's individual members.* And those shared, internalized beliefs and values shape the content and account for the strength of an organization's culture.

Understanding the relevance of an organization's culture to strategic success is facilitated by examples from a classic series of reports on America's best-managed companies initiated by Peters and Waterman.[17] Some examples include:[18]

> **The cultures of excellent companies are seen in key themes that guide members' behavior and orientation.** At Xerox, the key themes include respect for the individual and services to the customer. At Procter & Gamble (P&G), the overarching value is product quality. McDonald's uncompromising emphasis on QSCV—quality, service, cleanliness, and value—through meticulous attention to detail is legendary. Delta Airlines is driven by the "family feeling" theme, which builds a team spirit and nurtures each employee's cooperative attitude toward others, cheerful outlook toward life, and pride in a job well done. Du Pont's safety orientation—a report of every accident must be on the chairman's desk within 24 hours—has resulted in a safety record that was 17 times better than the chemical industry average and 68 times better than the all-manufacturing average.
>
> **Companies with strong cultures are enthusiastic collectors and tellers of stories, anecdotes, and legends in support of basic beliefs.** Frito-Lay's zealous emphasis on customer service is reflected in frequent stories about potato chip route salesmen who have slogged through sleet, mud, hail, snow, and rain to uphold the 99.5 percent service level to customers in which the entire company takes great pride. Milliken (a textile leader) holds "sharing" rallies once every quarter at which teams from all over the company swap success stories and ideas. Typically, more than 100 teams make five-minute presentations over a two-day period. Every rally is designed around a major theme, such as quality, cost reduction, or customer service. No criticisms are allowed, and awards are given to reinforce this institutionalized approach to storytelling. L. L. Bean tells customers service stories; 3M tells innovation stories; P&G, Johnson & Johnson, IBM, and Maytag tell quality stories. These stories are very important in developing an organizational culture, because organization members identify strongly with them and come to share the beliefs and values they support.

---

[17] Thomas J. Peters and Robert H. Waterman, Jr., *In Search of Excellence* (New York: Harper & Row, 1982); and Thomas J. Peters and Nancy Austin, *A Passion for Excellence* (New York: Random House, 1985).

[18] Adapted from Peters and Waterman, *In Search of Excellence,* pp. xxi, 73–78, 280–86; Peters and Austin, *A Passion for Excellence,* pp. 279–86; and Arthur A. Thompson, Jr., and A. A. Strickland III, *Strategic Management,* 6th ed. (Homewood, Ill.: Richard D. Irwin, 1992), pp. 260–61.

Companies with strong cultures are clear on what their beliefs and values need to be and take the process of shaping those beliefs and values very seriously. Most important, the values these companies espouse undergird the strategies they employ. For example, McDonald's has a yearly contest to determine the best hamburger cooker in its chain. First, there is a competition to determine the best hamburger cooker in each store; next, the store winners compete in regional championships; finally, the regional winners compete in the "All-American" contest. The winners, who are widely publicized throughout the company, get trophies and All-American patches to wear on their McDonald's uniforms.

The most typical beliefs that shape organizational culture include (1) a belief in being the best (or, as at GE, "better than the best"); (2) a belief in superior quality and service; (3) a belief in the importance of people as individuals and a faith in their ability to make a strong contribution; (4) a belief in the importance of the details of execution, the nuts and bolts of doing the job well; (5) a belief that customers should reign supreme; (6) a belief in inspiring people to do their best, whatever their ability; (7) a belief in the importance of informal communication; and (8) a belief that growth and profits are essential to a company's well-being. Every company implements these beliefs differently (to fit its particular situation), and every company's values are the handiwork of one or two legendary figures in leadership positions. Accordingly, every company has a distinct culture that it believes no other company can copy successfully. And in companies with strong cultures, managers and workers either accept the norms of the culture or opt out from the culture and leave the company.

The stronger a company's culture and the more that culture is directed toward customers and markets, the less the company uses policy manuals, organization charts, and detailed rules and procedures to enforce discipline and norms. The reason is that the guiding values inherent in the culture convey in crystal-clear fashion what everybody is supposed to do in most situations. Poorly performing companies often have strong cultures. However, their cultures are dysfunctional, being focused on internal politics or operating by the numbers as opposed to emphasizing customers and the people who make and sell the product.

Content of Culture

The content of a firm's culture ultimately derives from three sources. First, the influence of the business environment in general and the industry in particular is an important determinant of shared assumptions. For example, firms in industries characterized by rapid technological change, such as computer and electronics firms, normally have cultures that strongly value innovation. At high-technology firms, such as Apple, GE, and 3M, top executives deliberately make "champions" out of individuals who believe so strongly in their ideas that they take it upon themselves to hurdle the bureaucracy, maneuver their projects through the system, and turn them into improved services, new products, or even new businesses. In these firms, "product champions" are given high visibility, room to push their ideas, and strong executive support. Champions whose ideas prove out are usually handsomely rewarded; those whose ideas don't pan out still have secure jobs and are given chances to try again.[19]

---

[19] Peters and Waterman, *In Search of Excellence,* p. 240;   and Thompson and Strickland, *Strategic Management,* p. 260.

Second, founders, leaders, and employees bring a pattern of assumptions with them when they join a firm. Such assumptions often depend on the experiences of these individuals in the cultures of the national, regional, ethnic, religious, occupational, and professional communities from which they came.[20] For example, some firms with otherwise low-paying jobs upgrade the importance and status of individual employees by referring to them as cast members (Disney), crew members (McDonald's), or associates (Wal-Mart and J. C. Penney). Such firms as Tupperware and McDonald's actively seek out reasons and opportunities for giving pins, buttons, badges, and medals to honor good showings by average performers—the idea being to show appreciation and help give a boost to the "middle 60 percent" of the work force.

Third, shared assumptions are molded by the actual experiences that people in the firm have had in working out solutions to the basic problems it encounters. Consider the example of the manager of a New York area sales office who rented the Meadowlands Stadium (home field of the New York Giants) for an evening. On that evening, all the salesmen of the New York office were assembled at the stadium and were asked to run one at a time through the player's tunnel onto the field. As each emerged, the electronic scoreboard flashed his name to those gathered in the stands—executives from corporate headquarters, employees from the sales office, family, and friends—so they could cheer loudly in honor of his sales accomplishments. The firm involved was IBM. The action was intended to reaffirm IBM's commitment to satisfy the need of individuals to be part of something great and to reiterate IBM's concern for championing individual accomplishment as IBM's problem-solving approach.[21]

The above examples help demonstrate the pervasive impact of organizational culture. As a consequence, managing culture to successfully implement a strategy is a critical issue—an issue that is easy to state yet exceedingly difficult to manage. The critical issue that must be managed is ensuring that the culture "fits" with the implementation requirements of the chosen strategy.

Managing the Strategy-Culture Relationship

Managers find it difficult to think through the relationship between a firm's culture and the critical factors on which strategy depends. They quickly recognize, however, that key components of the firm—structure, staff, systems, people, style—influence the ways in which key managerial tasks are executed and how critical management relationships are formed. And implementation of a new strategy is largely concerned with adjustments in these com-

---

[20] Differing backgrounds, often referred to as *cultural diversity,* is something that most managers will certainly see more of, both because of the growing cultural diversity domestically and the obvious diversification of cultural backgrounds that result from global acquisitions and mergers. For example, Harold Epps, manager of DEC's computer keyboard plant in Boston, manages 350 employees representing 44 countries of origin and 19 languages. Useful reading on cultural diversity can be found in David Jamieson and Julie O'Mara, *Managing Workforce 2000: Gaining the Diversity Advantage* (San Francisco: Josey-Bass, 1991), and R. R. Thomas, *Beyond Race and Gender: Unleashing the Power of Your Total Workforce by Managing Diversity* (New York: AMACOM Books, 1991). To get an informative appreciation of the global scene, see Rosabeth Moss Kanter, "Transcending Business Boundaries: 12,000 World Managers View Change," *Harvard Business Review* 69, no. 6 (1991), pp. 151–64.

[21] Peters and Austin, *A Passion for Excellence,* p. 305; and Thompson and Strickland, *Strategic Management,* p. 261.

FIGURE 10–8
Managing the Strategy-Culture Relationship

		High	Low
Many	Changes in key organizational factors that are necessary to implement the new strategy	Link changes to basic mission and fundamental organizaitonal norms. **1**	Reformulate strategy or prepare carefully for long-term, difficult change. **4**
Few		**2** Synergistic—focus on reinforcing culture.	**3** Manage around the culture.

Potential compatibility of changes
with existing culture

ponents to accommodate the perceived needs of the strategy. Consequently, managing the strategy-culture relationship requires sensitivity to the interaction between the changes necessary to implement the new strategy and the compatibility or "fit" between those changes and the firm's culture. Figure 10–8 provides a simple framework for managing the strategy-culture relationship by identifying four basic situations a firm might face.

Link to Mission

A firm in cell 1 is faced with a situation in which implementing a new strategy requires several changes in structure, systems, managerial assignments, operating procedures, or other fundamental aspects of the firm. However, most of the changes are potentially compatible with the existing organizational culture. Firms in this situation usually have a tradition of effective performance and are either seeking to take advantage of a major opportunity or are attempting to redirect major product-market operations consistent with proven core capabilities. Such firms are in a very promising position: they can pursue a strategy requiring major changes but still benefit from the power of cultural reinforcement.

Four basic considerations should be emphasized by firms seeking to manage a strategy-culture relationship in this context. First, *key changes should be visibly linked to the basic company mission.* Since the company mission provides a broad official foundation for the organizational culture, top executives should use all available internal and external forums to reinforce the message that the changes are inextricably linked to it. Second, *emphasis should be placed on the use of existing personnel* where possible to fill positions created to implement the new strategy. Existing personnel embody the shared values and norms that help ensure cultural compatibility as major changes are implemented. Third, *care should be taken if adjustments in the reward system are needed.* These adjustments should be consistent with the current reward system. If, for example, a new product-market thrust requires significant changes in the way sales are made, and, therefore, in incentive compensation, common themes (e.g., incentive oriented) should be emphasized. In this way, current and future reward approaches are related and the changes in the reward system are justified (encourage development of less familiar markets). Fourth, *key attention should be paid to the changes that are least compatible with the current culture,* so current norms are not disrupted. For example, a firm may choose to subcontract an important step in a production process because that step would be incompatible with the current culture.

IBM's strategy in entering the personal computer market is an illustration. Serving this radically different market required numerous organizational changes. To maintain maximum compatibility with its existing culture while doing so, IBM went to considerable public and internal effort to link its new PCs with its long-standing mission. Numerous messages relating the PCs to IBM's tradition of top-quality service appeared on television and in magazines, and every IBM manager was given a PC. Where feasible, IBM personnel were used to fill the new positions created to implement the strategy. But because the PC's production requirements were not compatible with IBM's current operations, virtually all manufacturing of the PC was subcontracted.

Maximize Synergy

A firm in cell 2 needs only a few organizational changes to implement its new strategy, and those changes are potentially quite compatible with its current culture. A firm in this situation should emphasize two broad themes: (1) *take advantage of the situation to reinforce and solidify the current culture* and (2) *use this time of relative stability to remove organizational roadblocks to the desired culture.* Holiday Inns's move into casino gambling required a few major organizational changes. Holiday Inns saw casinos as resort locations requiring lodging, dining, and gambling/entertainment services. It only had to incorporate gambling/entertainment expertise into its management team, which was already capable of managing the lodging and dining requirements of casino (or any other) resort locations. It successfully inculcated this single major change by selling the change internally as completely compatible with its mission of providing high-quality accommodations for business and leisure travelers. The resignation of Roy Clymer, its CEO, removed an organizational roadblock, legitimizing a culture that placed its highest priority on quality service to the middle-to-upper-income business traveler, rather than a culture that placed its highest priority on family-oriented service. The latter priority was fast disappearing from Holiday Inns's culture, with the encouragement of most of the firm's top management, but its disappearance had not yet been fully sanctioned because of Clymer's personal beliefs. His voluntary departure helped solidify the new values that top management wanted.

Manage around the Culture

A firm in cell 3 must make a few major organizational changes to implement its new strategy, but these changes are potentially inconsistent with the firm's current organizational culture. The critical question for a firm in this situation is whether it can make the changes with a reasonable chance of success.

A firm can manage around the culture in various ways: create a separate firm or division; use task forces, teams, or program coordinators; subcontract; bring in an outsider; or sell out. These are a few of the available options, but the key idea is to create a method of achieving the change desired that avoids confronting the incompatible cultural norms. As cultural resistance diminishes, the change may be absorbed into the firm.

In the 1970s, Rich's was a highly successful, quality-oriented department store chain that served higher-income customers in several southeastern locations. With Wal-Mart stores and Kmart experiencing rapid growth in the sale of mid- to low-priced merchandise,

Rich's decided to serve this market as well. Finding such merchandise inconsistent with the successful values and norms of its traditional business, it created a separate business called *Richway* to tap this growth area in retailing. Through a new store network, it was able to *manage around its culture*. Both Rich's and Richway have since flourished, though their cultures are radically different in some respects.

Reformulate the Strategy

A firm in cell 4 faces the most difficult challenge in managing the strategy-culture relationship. To implement its new strategy, such a firm must make organizational changes that are incompatible with its current, usually entrenched, values and norms. A firm in this situation faces the complex, expensive, and often long-term challenge of changing its culture.[22] According to numerous consultants on organizational culture, it is a challenge that borders on impossible.[23] Strategy in Action 10–2 describes the challenge faced by Robert Daniell, CEO of United Technologies, as he attempted to change the culture of his firm.

When a strategy requires massive organizational change and engenders cultural resistance, a firm should determine whether reformulation of the strategy is appropriate. Are all of the organizational changes really necessary? Is there any real expectation that the changes will be acceptable and successful? If the answer to these questions is no, the firm should reformulate its strategic plan so as to make it more consistent with established organizational norms and practices.

Merrill Lynch faced the challenge of strategy-culture incompatibility in the last decade. Seeking to remain number one in the newly deregulated financial services industry, it chose to pursue a product development strategy in its brokerage business. Under this strategy, Merrill Lynch would sell a broader range of investment products to a more diverse customer base and would integrate other financial services, such as real estate sales, into the Merrill Lynch organization. The new strategy could succeed only if Merrill Lynch's traditionally service-oriented brokerage network became sales and marketing oriented. Initial efforts to implement the strategy generated substantial resistance from Merrill Lynch's highly successful brokerage network. The strategy was fundamentally inconsistent with long-standing cultural norms at Merrill Lynch that emphasized personalized service and very close broker-client relationships. Merrill Lynch ultimately divested its real estate operation, reintroduced specialists that supported broker/retailers, and refocused its brokers more narrowly on basic client investment needs.

REWARD SYSTEMS: MOTIVATING STRATEGY EXECUTION

The execution of strategy ultimately depends on individual organizational members, particularly key managers. And motivating and rewarding good performance by individuals and organizational units are key ingredients in effective strategy implementation. If strategy

---

[22] T. H. Fitzgerald, "Can Change in Organizational Culture Really Be Managed?" *Organizational Dynamics* 17, no. 2 (1988), pp. 9–15.

[23] "The Corporate Culture Vultures," *Fortune*, October 17, 1983, p. 6.

STRATEGY **TRANSFORMING ORGANIZATIONAL CULTURE**
IN ACTION **AT UNITED TECHNOLOGIES**
10–2

I t was with some urgency that Robert F. Daniell, the newly appointed CEO of United Technologies Corporation, summoned his top executives. Just weeks after taking the reins from Harry J. Gray, Daniell called a management powwow at the Jupiter Beach Hilton in Florida. The subject? UTC's shaky future. Customers of its Pratt & Whitney jet engines, outraged by lousy service, were defecting in droves to archrival General Electric Company. Market shares at UTC's once dominant Otis elevator unit and Carrier air-conditioning company were evaporating. Profits had hit a 13-year low. "Things had to change," says Daniell.

Unlike the iron-fisted Gray, however, Daniell did not lecture at management meetings. Instead, a Boston consultant moderated a roiling discussion in which managers put forth their remedies: dump divisions wholesale, diversify, pump up research-and-development spending. "Just the fact that we went through all of that yelling and screaming was unusual," says one executive who attended. After two days, Daniell and his team decided to remake UTC—to level its autocratic structure and bring more of its 186,800 employees into the decision-making process. *The ultimate goal: To get UTC's haughty culture to take marching orders from its customers.*

Worker empowerment. Team building. Getting close to your customer. While a lot of companies are just starting to talk about such methods, Bob Daniell is already proving that they can work wonders on the bottom line. The changes are nowhere more apparent than at jet-engine maker Pratt & Whitney, which pulls in more than half of UTC's operating profit. Orders have increased eightfold, to nearly $8 billion, since 1987.

When Daniell finally became CEO, he inherited a divided, argumentative management. Executives were too frightened to admit mistakes, and they directed their staffs like armies. All the way down the line, staffers refused to take responsibility for errors.

At the same time, Daniell was working on a long-term goal: changing Pratt's by-the-book structure. Dictatorial management and a Byzantine approval process made employees feel powerless. Take the case of an airplane builder who wants to mount an engine a fraction of a millimeter closer

Source: "Changes at United Technologies," *Forbes,* August 28, 1989, pp. 42–46.

accomplishment is a top priority, then the reward system must be clearly and tightly linked to strategic performance. Motivating and controlling managerial personnel in the execution of strategy are accomplished through a firm's reward mechanisms—compensation, raises, bonuses, stock options, incentives, benefits, promotions, demotions, recognition, praise, criticism, more (or less) responsibility, group norms, performance appraisal, tension, and fear. These mechanisms can be positive and negative, short run and long run.

There Is No One Perfect Reward System

A firm's reward system should align the actions and objectives of individuals and units with the objectives and needs of the firm's strategy. And reward systems, like strategies, vary greatly across different firms. For example, Harold Geneen, former CEO of ITT, purportedly used an interesting combination of money (compensation and incentives), tension (strict accountability for results), and fear to reward individual managers' efforts toward strategy implementation. According to one author:

STRATEGY
IN ACTION **concluded**
10–2

to the wing than the blueprint specifies. Normally, a good engineer at Pratt could just eyeball the blueprint and give the customer the nod for such a change. But until Pratt changed the system in February 1988, the request would wind through nine departments, including a committee that met only once a week.

Now, the design engineer makes the decision and only needs to get three signatures. Says Garvey: "It's all part of quality—taking responsibility." As a result, average response time has gone from 82 days to 10, and the request backlog has shrunk from 1,900 cases to fewer than 100.

Daniell went further with this campaign to improve service. He increased the number of service representatives in the field by nearly 70 percent—despite 30 percent staff cuts in the rest of the company.

Overall, Daniell's effort to change the culture is based on four approaches:

Flatten the hierarchy. Daniell leveled a Byzantine corporate structure by cutting many layers of decision making. At Pratt & Whitney, for instance, he cut eight levels of management to as few as four.

Empower your workers. Managers pushed decision making down. For instance, field representatives at Pratt & Whitney now make multimillion-dollar decisions about reimbursing customers on warranty claims. Before, they would have to wait for approvals from numerous layers above.

Get close to your customers. This is Daniell's battle cry. Worker empowerment helps, but the imperative goes even further than that. For instance, Pratt & Whitney lends some of its top engineers to customers for a year—and pays their salaries.

Train, train, train. Daniell uses training to revamp the corporate culture. More than 5,000 senior and middle managers are getting at least 40 hours of classroom work. In some classes, customers are brought in for gripe sessions and a problem-solving team gathered from many different departments must come up with solutions.

Geneen provided his managers with enough incentives to make them tolerate the system. Salaries all the way through ITT are higher than average—Geneen reckoned 10 percent higher—so few people could leave without taking a drop. As one employee put it: "We're all paid just a bit more than we think we're worth." At the very top, where the demands are greatest, the salaries and stock options were sufficient to compensate for the rigors. As someone said, "He's got them by their limousines."

Having bound his men to him with chains of gold, Geneen induced the tension that drives the machine. "The key to the system," one of his men explained, "was the profit forecast. Once the forecast had been gone over, revised, and agreed on, the managing director had a personal commitment to Geneen to carry it out. That's how he produced the tension on which success depended." The tension goes through the company, inducing ambition, perhaps exhilaration, but always with some sense of fear: what happens if the target is missed?[24]

---

[24] Anthony Sampson, *The Sovereign State of ITT* (New York: Stein & Day, 1973), p. 132.

BIC Pen Company took a different approach. Its reward structure involved incentive systems, wide latitude for operating managers, and clearly specified objectives to motivate and control individual initiative. All employees were invited to participate in a stock purchase plan whereby up to 10 percent of their salary could be used to purchase stock at a 10 percent discount from the market price. Functional managers were given wide rein in operational decisions while being held strictly accountable for results. The director of manufacturing, for example, was free to spend up to $500,000 for a cost-saving machine as long as profit margin objectives are maintained. Commenting on his approach to rewarding executives, Robert Adler, BIC's president, said:

> We have a unique bonus system, which I'm sure the Harvard Business School would think is crazy. Each year I take a percentage of profits before tax and give 40 percent to sales, 40 percent to manufacturing, and 20 percent to the treasurer to be divided up among executives in each area. Each department head keeps some for himself and gives the rest away. We never want bonuses to be thought of as salaries because they would lose their effect. So we change the bonus day each year so that it always comes as a pleasant surprise, something to look forward to.[25]

These two examples illustrate several generalizations about the use of rewards and sanctions to control individuals, particularly managers, in strategy execution. Financial incentives are important reward mechanisms. They are particularly useful in encouraging managerial success when they are directly linked to specific activities and results. Intrinsic, nonfinancial rewards, such as flexibility and autonomy in the job and visible control over performance, are important managerial motivators. And negative sanctions, such as the withholding of financial and intrinsic rewards or the tensions emanating from possible consequences of substandard performance, are necessary ingredients in encouraging managers' efforts.

Timing Is an Important Consideration in Reward Systems

The time horizon on which rewards and sanctions are based is a major consideration in linking them to strategically important activities and results. Numerous authors and business leaders have expressed concern about incentive systems based on short-term (typically annual) performance. They fear that short-term reward structures can result in actions and decisions that undermine the long-term position of firms. A marketing director whose rewards are based on the cost effectiveness of the sales generated by the marketing staff might place significantly greater emphasis on established distribution channels than on "inefficient" nurturing and development of new channels. A reward system based on maximizing current profitability can shortchange the future in terms of current investments (in time, people, and money) in the areas from which the primary return is intended to come.[26] If the firm's grand strategy is growth through horizontal integration of current products into new channels and markets, and the company distributes 40 percent of annual profit as its

[25] C. R. Christensen, K. R. Andrews, and J. L. Bower, *Business Policy: Text and Cases* (Homewood, Ill.: Richard D. Irwin, 1978), p. 318.

[26] William R. King and David I. Cleland, *Strategic Planning and Policy* (New York: Van Nostrand Reinhold, 1978), p. 364.

main bonus program, the reward structure may be directing the marketing director's efforts in ways that thwart the ultimate success of the strategy. And the marketing director, having performed notably within the current reward structure, may have moved on to other responsibilities or another company before the shortcomings emerge.

Short-term executive incentive schemes typically focus on last year's (or last quarter's) profits. In terms of promoting a new strategy, this exclusive concentration on the bottom line has four weaknesses:

1. It is backward looking. Reported results reflect past events and, to some extent, past strategy.
2. The focus is short term, though many of the recorded transactions have effects over longer periods.
3. Strategic gains or losses are not considered due to, among other things, basic accounting methods.
4. Investment of time and money in future strategy can have a negative impact. Since such outlays and efforts are usually intermingled with other expenses, a manager can improve his or her bonus by *not* preparing for the future.[27]

Although incentive systems can easily encourage short-run thinking and neglect the longer term, there is real danger in hastily condemning short-term measures. It is a mistake to conclude that short-term concerns are not important or that they are necessarily counterproductive to the strategic needs of the organization. Long-term versus short-term incentive priorities should vary depending on the time focus of the strategy, as illustrated in Figure 10–9. In an effectively implemented strategy, short-term aims support, and are critical to, the attainment of long-term strategic objectives. The real problem is not the short- versus long-term concerns of management but the failure to achieve consistency between long- and short-term plans and objectives in the reward system.[28] Once timing considerations are addressed, there are other critical ingredients in designing appropriate rewards and incentives.

Guidelines for Structuring Effective Reward Systems

Regardless of the short- or long-term strategic considerations, managers face additional challenges in structuring rewards in a manner that energizes every person in their organization. One success story in meeting this challenge has been Nucor Corporation. Described in Strategy in Action 10–3, Nucor's reward system is largely credited with driving the success of its strategy in a U.S. steel industry where experts have said the United States has "lost its comparative advantage, can no longer compete in world markets, and should exit the business altogether." Managers at every level within Nucor, and any other business, can improve the effectiveness of their reward system by following these nine guidelines:

1. **Link rewards *tightly* to the strategic plan.** As the earlier discussion pointed out, rewards linked to a firm's strategy logically enhance its chance of success. Linking rewards to the accomplishment of key objectives, milestones, completion of key projects,

---

[27] B. Yavitz and W. H. Newman, *Strategy in Action* (New York: Free Press, 1982), p. 207.

[28] Lawrence G. Hrebiniak and William F. Joyce, *Implementing Strategy* (New York: Macmillan, 1984), pp. 204–9.

FIGURE 10–9
Perceived Importance of Various Performance Dimensions in Determination of SBU General Manager's Incentive Bonus

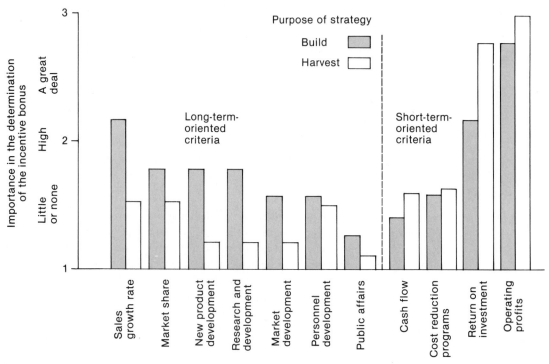

Source: Anil K. Gupta and V. Govindarajan, "Build, Hold, Harvest: Converting Strategic Intentions into Reality," *Journal of Business Strategy,* Winter 1984, p. 43.

or actions that sustain competitive advantage (like Nucor's high productivity) keeps people energized and focused on the right things and on doing them right.

2. **Use variable incentives and make them a major part of everyone's compensation.** If a significant portion of a person's compensation (usually 25 to 60 percent) varies with successful execution of his or her responsibilities, then a person should be very attentive to do them well. Nucor did this with low base pay and virtually open-ended bonus capability. AT&T has introduced "internal venturing," whereby employees with approved new product ideas can forgo a part of their compensation as a "co-investment" in their own internal venture and receive up to eight times that investment if the venture is successful within five years. This guideline obviously can backfire on any manager if the incentive is not fair, not understood, and not consistent with the next guideline.

3. **Rewards and incentives must be linked to an individual's job and the outcomes the individual can personally effect.** People are more accepting of incentive compensation when they control what needs to be done to accomplish the outcomes that earn them the incentive. While easier for salespeople to visualize than for production or administrative personnel, effective managers strive to introduce this guideline in all areas

of the company. Team bonuses are one way this is done. Employee participation in designing the rewards is another.

4. **Reward performance and value to success, rather than to position in the hierarchy.** While seniority has its place, and positions of responsibility in a management hierarchy often correlate with contribution to results, progressive managers increasingly are recognizing the importance of structuring incentives and compensation to reward the key skills or expertise necessary for a strategy to be successful. In the rapidly growing environmental and bio-engineering industries, several companies have compensation and bonus programs under which technical personnel can earn significantly more than managers of their units or managers at higher levels in the organization. The reason is simple. The skills those people possess are essential to successful strategic outcomes.

5. **Reward everyone and be sensitive to discrepancies between the top and bottom of the organization.** A successful strategy requires energized, cooperative effort from every organization member. Incentive-based reward systems should reflect this by including programs wherein every member participates in some fashion. And while varying skills, levels of responsibility, and roles must be recognized with significantly different incentive amounts, inexplicably high rewards at high executive levels with little or none at the lowest level can erode confidence and commitment. A major controversy has arisen in the United States over CEO compensation as a result of extraordinary bonuses accruing to selected executives in the auto industry and others while their companies were losing billions, massive layoffs were commonplace, and their highly successful Japanese and German counterparts were much more modestly compensated.[29] In smaller firms the discrepancy usually arises in perks or special founding-family compensation. But whether the reward involves cash, stock, options, perks, or other benefits, a reward system designed to incentivize everyone in the organization to share in strategic success (or a lack thereof) will be more effective long term.

6. **Be scrupulously fair, accurate, and informative.** Related to the previous guideline, reward systems that are perceived to be fair work better than those that are not. Where incentives are linked to work teams, groups, or units, fairness among individuals' contribution and reward often will be an issue facing operating-level managers. Accurate measurement of the outcomes triggering rewards, timing considerations, and amounts paid play a key role in perceived fairness. Complete openness in sharing information about "how we're doing," so participants can see clearly the reasons behind compensation results, is another important way to reinforce fairness.

7. **Reward generously when successful; minimally when not.** Reward systems that reinforce success do just that. Systems that provide similar rewards (or a lack thereof) whether successful or not can send the message that extra effort doesn't matter. Food Lion

---

[29] The issue of CEO compensation is a complex, highly charged issue. Some people question the high compensation and bonus package accruing to executives like Lee Iacocca (Chrysler), Steve Ross (Time-Warner), Mike Eisner (Disney), and Roberto Goizueta (Coke) to name a few. Others strongly defend their high compensation, pointing to the rise in market value of their respective firm's stock since they took control. For thoughtful analyses of this issue, see Andrew R. Brownstein and Morris J. Panner, "Who Should Set CEO Pay? The Press? Congress? Shareholders?" *Harvard Business Review* 70, no. 3 (1992), pp. 28–39; and "CEO Pay: How Much Is Enough?" *Harvard Business Review* 70, no. 4 (1992), pp. 130–39. For practical guidelines on handling executive pay in an atmosphere of increased public scrutiny, see John D. McMillan, "Executive Pay a New Way," *HRMagazine* 37, no. 6 (1992), pp. 46–48, 194.

STRATEGY
IN ACTION   **Nucor's Secret to Success: A Logical Reward System**
   10–3

> T he last 10 years have seen most analysts write off the U.S. steel industry as outdated, inefficient, and no match for Japan, Taiwan, and Europe. But they should come down to Charlotte, North Carolina. In an industry where the giants are hemorrhaging red ink, closing plants, and diversifying, midsized Nucor Corporation is an unprecedented success. Nucor is taking market share *away* from Japan and Taiwan!
>
> Nucor is the low-cost producer, combining outfront technology with innovative incentive systems. The results are globally competitive steel products, highly productive steel mills, and a well-paid work force.
>
> Nucor's reward system is based on four principles: (1) earnings according to productivity, (2) job security for proper performance, (3) fair and consistent treatment, and (4) easy and direct avenues of appeal. Nucor believes that "money is the best motivator." The compensation system is incentive oriented, with those incentives tied directly to productivity. Base salaries are low; but incentives can easily add 50 to 100 percent of base salary to total compensation, with no upper limit. All employees have a significant part of their compensation based around productivity. All incentive systems are designed around groups, not individuals. This applies to everyone, from production workers to clerks and secretaries to senior officers.
>
> In the production incentive program, groups range from 25 to 35 people who are working as a team on some complete task. There are nine production bonus groups in Nucor's typical minimill— three each in melting and casting (M&C), rolling, and finishing and shipping. The M&C group begins with a base goal of 12 tons of good billets per hour; above this, every person in the group gets a 4 percent bonus for every ton per hour produced. If over a week they average 30 tons per hour—which is considered low—they earn a 72 percent bonus [4 x (30 – 12)] for that week. The multiplier affects all pay—overtime and regular. In the joist production line, bonuses are based on 90 percent of the historical time it takes to make a particular product. If during the week a group makes the product at 40 percent less than standard time, its members receive a 40 percent bonus— with the *next* paycheck.

Sources: Nucor Corporation 1991 annual report;   R. L. Kuhn, *Creativity and Strategy in Midsize Firms* (Englewood Cliffs: Prentice Hall, 1989), pp. 252–58.

has butchers and cashiers, while Wal-Mart has greeters and cashiers that have seen their small stock incentives valued at a few thousand dollars 20 years ago make them worth in excess of $2 million today. IBM's former chairman John Akers answered a stockholder's question about his compensation by pointing out that his 1992 compensation package was cut 60 percent as a result of 1991 results. Nucor's management took 40 to 70 percent cuts and employees 20 to 25 percent cuts (via shorter work weeks) during the recession-induced reduction in demand for steel. Whether long term or short term, incentive compensation linked to results provide appropriate reinforcement of the need to formulate and implement good strategies effectively, regardless of organizational level.

8. **Don't underestimate the value of a rewarding and motivational environment.** While cash, stock, and perks get people's attention, a motivating environment is a very important part of a sound reward system. Increased responsibility, autonomy, participation in decision making, recognition, and opportunity for growth are long-advocated and

STRATEGY
IN ACTION **concluded**
10–3

Managerial bonuses are based on return on assets. Top managers have no employment contracts, nor do they receive guaranteed or discretionary bonuses, profit sharing, pension plans, or other executive perks (no company cars, planes, country club memberships, executive dining rooms, or reserve parking). Base salaries are set at 75 percent of what executives earn in comparable positions in other companies. If the company produces below par (9 percent return on equity), that's all they get. For every pretax dollar above this base, 5 percent goes into an officers' pool that is divided according to salary. For example, if return on equity goes to 24 percent, which it has, Nucor executives receive up to 270 percent of their base in cash and an additional 180 percent in stock.

All Nucor employees receive the same insurance, holidays, and vacations. Everyone, including the CEO, flies coach. There is a profit-sharing plan for all nonexecutive employees. Nucor provides a scholarship of $2,000 per year for four years of college or vocational training for every child of every employee. (When the children graduate, many come to work for Nucor.) The company has not laid off a single employee for more than 20 years. Ken Iverson, Nucor's president, confessed he was proud to be the lowest compensated Fortune 500 CEO in the recession of the early 1980s. Why? During that period, to avoid layoffs, Nucor had to cut back to four- or even three-and-a-half-day workweeks, which cut employee pay 20 to 25 percent below normal. But few complained: they knew that department heads were cut more (35 to 40 percent) and officers even more (60 to 70 percent). Iverson calls it our "Share the Pain" program. If a company isn't successful, the reasons are irrelevant. Management should take the biggest cut because they are the most responsible.

Can Nucor's incentive compensation be applied to other companies and industries? There are limitations. Two elements are necessary: (1) it must make sense to break out small groups of people who work as a team on a particular function and (2) that particular function must be both self-contained and measurable.

proven "rewards" that motivate most people. Significant attention to creating ways to structure these elements into an individual and work team environment can provide any manager with a powerful tool for motivating strategy execution.

9. **Be open to changing the reward systems.** Strategies and tactics change. Situations change. Organization members come and go or encounter different needs. Certain aspects of a reward system prove inappropriate or counterproductive. These and other reasons should keep managers looking at reward systems as evolving, rather than permanent, indefinitely. Tempered with the need to avoid confusion and any sense of unfairness, a thoughtful change in reward systems can be an effective management option.

Following these guidelines in structuring reward systems will not guarantee successful strategy implementation. But a system so designed will make a big difference, particularly at operating levels of the company. For decisions on incentive compensations, salary increases, promotions, and key assignments, as well as perks, praise and recognition are operational managers' foremost attention-getting and commitment-generating devices.

SUMMARY

This chapter examined the idea that a key aspect of implementing a strategy is the *institutionalization* of the strategy so it permeates daily decisions and actions in a manner consistent with long-term strategic success. Four fundamental elements must be managed to "fit" a strategy if the strategy is to be effectively institutionalized: *organizational structure, leadership, culture,* and *rewards.*

Five fundamental organizational structures were examined, and the advantages and disadvantages of each were identified. Institutionalizing a strategy requires a good strategy-structure fit. This chapter dealt with how this requirement often is overlooked until performance becomes inadequate and then indicated the conditions under which the various structures would be appropriate.

Organizational leadership is essential to effective strategy implementation. The CEO plays a critical role in this regard. Assignment of key managers, particularly within the top-management team, is an important aspect of organizational leadership. Deciding whether to promote insiders or hire outsiders is often a central leadership issue in strategy implementation. This chapter showed how this decision could be made in a manner that would best institutionalize the new strategy.

In recent years, organizational culture has been recognized as a pervasive influence on organizational life. Organizational culture, which is the shared beliefs and values of an organization's members, may be a major help or hindrance to strategy implementation. This chapter discussed an approach to managing the strategy-culture fit. It identified four fundamentally different strategy-culture situations and provided recommendations for managing the strategy-culture fit in each of these situations.

The reward system is a key ingredient in motivating managers to execute a firm's strategy. Firms should emphasize incentive systems that ensure adequate attention to strategic thrusts. This usually requires a concerted effort to emphasize long-term strategic performance as well as short-term measures of performance. In addition to timing, nine key guidelines must be accommodated to have an effective reward system.

QUESTIONS FOR DISCUSSION

1. What key structural considerations must be incorporated into strategy implementation? Why does structural change often lag a change in strategy?

2. Which organizational structure is most appropriate for successful strategy implementation? Explain how state of development affects your answer.

3. Why is leadership an important element in strategy implementation? Find an example in a major business periodical of the CEO's key role in strategy implementation.

4. Under what conditions would it be more appropriate to fill a key management position with someone from outside the firm when a qualified insider is available?

5. What is organizational culture? Why is it important? Explain two different situations a firm might face in managing the strategy-culture relationship.

6. How would you vary an incentive system for a growth-oriented versus a harvest-oriented business?

7. Why do strategists prefer reward systems similar to the one shown in Figure 10–9? What are the advantages and disadvantages of such a system?

8. What do you anticipate your first management job may be? Outline a reward system for your employees based on the guidelines provided at the end of this chapter.

BIBLIOGRAPHY

Bailey, G., and J. Szerdy. "Is There Life after Downsizing?" *Journal of Business Strategy,* January 1988, pp. 8–11.

Barney, J. B. "Organizational Culture: Can It Be a Source of Sustained Competitive Advantage?" *Academy of Management Review,* July 1986, p. 656.

Block, Barbara. "Creating a Culture All Employees Can Accept." *Management Review,* July 1989, p. 41.

Botterill, M. "Changing Corporate Culture." *Management Services* (UK) 34, no. 6 (1990), pp. 14–18.

Bower, Joseph Lyon, and Martha Wagner Weinberg. "Statecraft, Strategy, and Corporate Leadership." *California Management Review,* Winter 1988, p. 107.

Byles, C. M., and R. J. Keating. "Strength of Organizational Culture and Performance: Strategic Implications." *Journal of Business Strategy,* Spring 1989, pp. 45–55.

Chapman, P. "Changing the Corporate Culture of Rank Xerox." *Long Range Planning,* April 1988, pp. 23–28.

Chingos, P. T., and V. J. Elliott. "Using Incentives to Foster Business Unit Results." *Bottomline* 8, no. 3 (1991), pp. 15–19.

Cowherd, D. M., and R. H. Luchs. "Linking Organization Structures and Processes to Business Strategy." *Long Range Planning,* October 1988, pp. 47–53.

"Cultural Transition at AT&T." *Sloan Management Review,* Fall 1983, pp. 15–26.

Daft, R. L.; J. Sormunen; and D. Parks. "Chief Executive Scanning." *Strategic Management Journal,* March 1988, pp. 123–40.

Drake, Bruce H., and Eileen Drake. "Ethical and Legal Aspects of Managing Corporate Cultures." *California Management Review,* Winter 1988, p. 107.

Fitzgerald, T. H. "Can Change in Organizational Culture Really Be Managed?" *Organizational Dynamics* 17, no. 2 (1988), pp. 5–15.

Forman, R. "Strategic Planning and the Chief Executive." *Long Range Planning,* August 1988, pp. 57–64.

Fredrickson, James W.; Donald C. Hambrick; and Sara Bawmrin. "A Model of CEO Dismissal." *Academy of Management Review,* April 1988, p. 255.

Freund, York P. "Critical Success Factors." *Planning Review,* July–August 1988, p. 20.

Gomez-Mejia, Luis R.; Henri Tose; and Timothy Hinkin. "Managerial Control, Performance, and Executive Compensation." *Academy of Management Journal,* March 1987, p. 51.

Gomez-Mejia, L. R., and T. Welbourne. "Compensation Strategies in a Global Context." *Human Resource Planning* 14, no. 1 (1991), pp. 29–41.

Gupta, Anil K. "SBU Strategies, Corporate-SBU Relations, and SBU Effectiveness in Strategy Implementation." *Academy of Management Journal,* September 1987, p. 477.

Hinterhuber, H. H., and W. Popp. "Are You a Strategist or Just a Manager?" *Harvard Business Review* 70, no. 1 (1992), pp. 105–14.

Hosking, D. M. "Organizing, Leadership and Skillful Process." *Journal of Management Studies,* March 1988, pp. 147–66.

Johnson, G. "Managing Strategic Change—Strategy, Culture, and Action." *Long Range Planning* 25, no. 1 (1992), pp. 28–36.

Kim, W. C., and R. A. Mauborgne. "Parables of Leadership." *Harvard Business Review* 70, no. 4 (1992), pp. 123–28.

Koch, D. L., and D. W. Steinhauser. "Changing the Corporate Culture." *Datamotion,* October 1983, pp. 247–52.

Larson, Erik W., and David H. Gobeli. "Matrix Management: Contradictions and Insights." *California Management Review,* Summer 1987, p. 126.

Lei, D.; J. Slocum; and R. Slater. "Global Strategy and Reward Systems: The Key Roles of Management Development and Corporate Culture." *Organizational Dynamics* 19, no. 2 (1990), pp. 27–41.

Lewis, P. "Performance Related Pay: Pretexts and Pitfalls." *Employee Relations* (U.K.) 13, no. 1 (1991), pp. 12–16.

Liden, Robert C., and Terence R. Mitchell. "Ingratiatory Behavior in Organizational Settings." *Academy of Management Review,* October 1988, p. 572.

Main, John G., and John Thackray. "The Logic of Restructuring." *Planning Review,* May–June 1987, p. 5.

Meindl, James R., and Sanford B. Ehrlich. "The Romance of Leadership and Evaluation of Organizational Performance." *Academy of Management Journal,* March 1987, p. 91.

Miller, Danny. "Strategy Making and Structure: Analysis and Implications for Performance." *Academy of Management Journal,* March 1987, p. 7.

Nichols, Don. "Bottom-Up Strategies." *Management Review,* December 1989, p. 44.

Putz, B. J. "Productivity Improvement: Changing Values, Beliefs, and Assumptions." *SAM Advanced Management Journal* 56, no. 4 (1991), pp. 9–12.

Reed, R., and M. Reed. "CEO Experience and Diversification Strategy Fit." *Journal of Management Studies,* March 1988, pp. 251–70.

Reimann, Bernard C., and Yoash Wiener. "Corporate Culture: Avoiding the Elitist Trap." *Business Horizons,* March–April 1988, p. 36.

Saffold, Guy S., III. "Culture Traits, Strength, and Settings." *Academy of Management Review,* October 1988, p. 546.

Schneier, C. E. "Capitalizing on Performance Management, Recognition, and Rewards Systems." *Compensation and Benefit Review* 21, no. 2 (1989), pp. 20–30.

Spector, Bert A. "From Bogged-Down to Fired-Up: Inspiring Organizational Change." *Sloan Management Review,* Summer 1989, p. 29.

Spohn, A. G. "The Relationship of Reward Systems and Employee Performance." *Compensation and Benefits Management* 6, no. 2 (1990), pp. 128–32.

Stone, N. "Building Corporate Character." *Harvard Business Review* 70, no. 2 (1992), pp. 94–104.

"Strategic Leaders and Leadership." *Strategic Management Journal,* special issue, Summer 1989.

Vancil, Richard F. "A Look at CEO Succession." *Harvard Business Review,* March–April 1987, p. 107.

Vincent, D. R. "Understanding Organization Power." *Journal of Business Strategy,* March 1988, pp. 40–44.

Wagner, John A., III, and Richard Z. Gooding. "Shared Influence and Organizational Behavior: A Meta-Analysis of Situational Variables Expected to Moderate Participation-Outcome Relationships." *Academy of Management Review,* September 1987, p. 524.

Webber, Alvin M. "The CEO Is the Company." *Harvard Business Review,* January–February 1987, p. 114.

—————. "Consensus, Continuity, and Common Sense." *Harvard Business Review* 68, no. 4 (1990), pp. 115–23.

Zabriskie, N., and A. Huellmantel. "Implementing Strategies for Human Resources." *Long Range Planning,* April 1989, pp. 70–77.

Zaleznik, A. "Managers and Leaders: Are They Different?" *Harvard Business Review* 70, no. 2 (1992), pp. 126–35.

Zemke, R. "Rewards and Recognition: Yes, They Really Work." *Training* 25, no. 1 (1988), pp. 48–53.

CHAPTER 10 COHESION CASE

IMPLEMENTING STRATEGY THROUGH STRUCTURE, LEADERSHIP, CULTURE, AND REWARDS AT THE COCA-COLA COMPANY

STRUCTURE

The Coca-Cola Company had the following basic structure at the beginning of the 1980s:

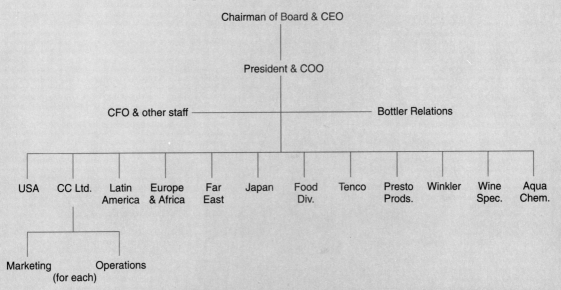

The figure suggests Coke was a rather decentralized company with relatively autonomous operating units based on both the product-service of the business and geographic location. This facilitated local decision making and aided Coke's rapid advance in international markets.

By the mid-1980s, Roberto Goizueta had completed significant restructuring and consolidation of Coca-Cola to allow for decentralized decision making while also retaining more centralized control. The following figure shows Coke's structure by 1984. According to Goizueta:

> To operate more effectively in today's business environment and more sharply focus management's attention on the expansion opportunities within the industries in which they operate, we have regrouped the Company's various units into four business sectors. . . . Each of our four business sectors is operating according to a well-defined plan. Each is moving forward in line with a broad strategy to capitalize on its superior positioning and expertise, while drawing from complementary corporate resources that bind the sectors into a single, powerful enterprise.

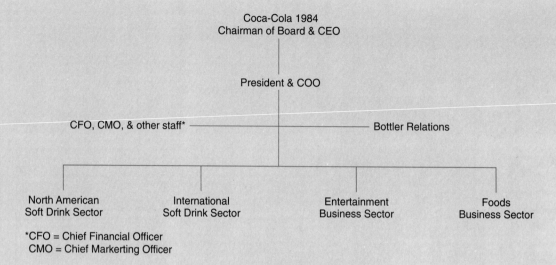

Coca-Cola 1984
Chairman of Board & CEO

President & COO

CFO, CMO, & other staff* ————————————— Bottler Relations

| North American Soft Drink Sector | International Soft Drink Sector | Entertainment Business Sector | Foods Business Sector |

*CFO = Chief Financial Officer
 CMO = Chief Markerting Officer

By 1993, the structure looked as follows:

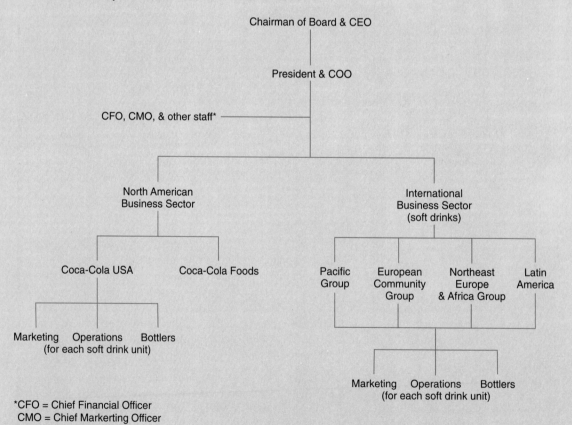

Chairman of Board & CEO

President & COO

CFO, CMO, & other staff* ——————————

North American Business Sector

International Business Sector (soft drinks)

Coca-Cola USA   Coca-Cola Foods

Pacific Group   European Community Group   Northeast Europe & Africa Group   Latin America

Marketing   Operations   Bottlers
(for each soft drink unit)

Marketing   Operations   Bottlers
(for each soft drink unit)

*CFO = Chief Financial Officer
 CMO = Chief Markerting Officer

The Coke structure of the mid-1990s reflected subtle but key adjustments designed to implement its key strategies more effectively. First, it had essentially two lines of business—soft drinks and foods (citrus juices). Second, it operated in two broad arenas—domestic (United States) and international. Goizueta's management team felt geographic focus was the most logical and fundamental organizing dimension to implement an international emphasized strategy. Then, in the case of the United States, the team's preference was to place the two main U.S. businesses (soft drinks and foods) within the U.S. geographic organization. Perhaps synergies involving deliveries to many retail outlets could be better supported or conflicts overcome by having these two "under one roof."

A second dimension of this new organization kept bottling relations and overall marketing support as a corporate function, while giving each unit control of operations and day-to-day marketing and distribution. This allowed corporate control of broad themes, resources, and guidelines, while also allowing significant autonomy within each basic geographic sector. It also allowed for greater coordination of resources across international markets—an essential ingredient if Coke's aggressive international growth posture was to be maintained or indeed accelerated. Overall, the changes reflected in this structure points to Coca-Cola's major emphasis on international development and aggressive marketing adapted to local markets.

LEADERSHIP

Coca-Cola has many incidents of leadership selection that appear well coordinated with its strategies and changing strategic needs. Let's look at a few examples.

First, and perhaps most notable, was the selection of Roberto Goizueta as CEO and soon thereafter chairman in 1980. As we have briefly described earlier, Goizueta is Cuban by birth. His family owned a sugar refinery, which had made them wealthy. After finishing school in Cuba, Roberto chose to start to work for a major Coke bottler in Cuba, rather than join his family's business. Soon thereafter, Fidel Castro's rebellion took control of the island nation and, stripped of their sugar business, the Goizueta family left Cuba for the United States. Roberto Goizueta soon joined his family and went to work for a Florida bottler partially owned by the parent company. His background was in engineering and chemistry, which aided his rise within the organization, quickly turning into a position in Atlanta. From there he became a star in operations and rose quickly to the executive V.P. level.

When Paul Austin decided to step down in 1978, Coke had embarked on a serious effort to grow its international sales. While facing some lingering doubt as a rather conservative group, Coke's board was impressed with Roberto Goizueta's ability to articulate what Coke stood for and certainly was aware of the positive message it would convey to its budding international partners, employees, and investors. His appointment also reinforced Coke's long-standing policy of promotion from within, while sending a clear message to domestic personnel that it was serious about its long-term international commitment.

Goizueta has set a precedence of expecting managers to bring results-oriented commitment and dedication to their assignments at Coke. When results miss expectations, he is quick to move to support his managers and their ideas for improvement—or to change managers where their ideas engender a lack of confidence. In 1989, Coca-Cola USA—

the big domestic arm selling Coke syrups and concentrates—was steadily losing modest market share to Pepsi in selected outlets. Goizueta's reaction was to suddenly bring in then 61-year-old Ira Herbert out of headquarters staff obscurity and put him in charge of this subsidiary. Herbert, marketing guru during Coca-Cola's very successful "Coke is it" and "It's the real thing" campaigns, insisted that he had not been called in "to pull the cart out of a ditch." Business writers thought otherwise. By 1992, Herbert had returned to staff duties and pending retirement, with Coca-Cola USA now leading Pepsi in every distribution outlet, including Pepsi's powerful grocery store channel. The lesson we see from this is the decisive decision to adjust leadership to the growth demands and aggressive marketing posture inherent in Coke's strategy for the 1990s. Rather than just talk about what it will take, Goizueta communicated his total commitment and expectation of the same from others by this action.

A third story related to leadership, Coke's aggressive move into eastern Germany with the fall of the Berlin Wall, is also a good illustration of Coke's current culture created to encourage aggressive growth efforts throughout its worldwide system. A brief description follows in the "Culture" section below.

CULTURE

The culture Goizueta has pushed throughout the worldwide Coca-Cola system is to build an organization of people with initiative, commitment, understanding of how to make Coke forever remain the true pause that refreshes; people who take unabashed pleasure in [and are rewarded for] their efforts. He feels this must be the very foundation of Coke's worldwide business system. An interesting way to illustrate this culture is to look at Coke's reaction to the sudden fall of the Berlin Wall as the decade of the 1990s was about to begin.

The Berlin Wall was daily being destroyed in 1991 as millions watched on worldwide TV. Coke's Chairman Roberto Goizueta and president Don Keough worried that a large, fast push into eastern Germany—with its ill-suited market structure—might become a colossal failure. But Horst Muller and Heinz Weizorek pressed their argument and quickly succeeded in changing the minds of Coke's top brass, especially Goizueta. The two Germans argued that monetary union would come faster than most people expected, which in turn would make doing business in eastern Germany much easier. They also saw economic advantages via tax breaks and investment assistance going to those companies and investors that moved quickly into a decrepit East Germany once it opened to the West. Also, they were aware of pent-up demand among East Germans, who consumed colas as frequently as their West German counterparts but were forced to drink poor-quality sodas provided by state-run factories.

Horst Muller, the new head of Coca-Cola's East German operations, first asked himself how to find sales reps in a country that has never had any. He needed people to handle store merchandising, order-taking, and delivery. The dilemma for Muller, or one of many, was that East Germans lived in a culture where "selling" was a completely foreign idea.

Muller's choice was to scrutinize his 2,000+ employees in East Germany, most of whom worked at six old bottling plants Coca-Cola had bought from East Germany just weeks earlier. With the aid of his West German managers, Muller picked out the most friendly and engaging clerks, factory workers, and technicians from the old East German work force and sent them off to West Germany (and the United States) for a special version of Coke's sales personnel training programs. They returned in 30 days as obsessed market ambassadors and hustlers for Coca-Cola.

German personnel used "anything with wheels" to get their product and vending machines and other items into any outlet that would sell it. They jury-rigged the old East German bottling plants to keep up with demand and worked long hours, resulting in a dominant cola position in East Germany by the end of 1993—even before Pepsi had been seriously able to attempt to compete. And at the heart of this success was again a "can-do culture" found throughout the Coca-Cola worldwide business system.

Within one year, Coke had taken East Germany by storm and sold over 75 million cases in a territory where none were sold the previous year. Sales topped 100 million cases in 1992. Since Muller started, Coke has invested $500 million in eastern Germany, and Germany has become Coke's largest market in the European Community, which in turn generated more operating profits than the U.S. market since 1990. Indeed, it appears that Coke will usurp Pepsi's previous advantage in most of Eastern Europe and the old Soviet Union based on its aggressive move into East Germany from its strong position in West Germany.

The East German experience conveys just the type of "culture" Goizueta seeks for Coca-Cola worldwide—people with initiative, commitment, and understanding of how to dominate markets and people who take great pleasure in their work effort.

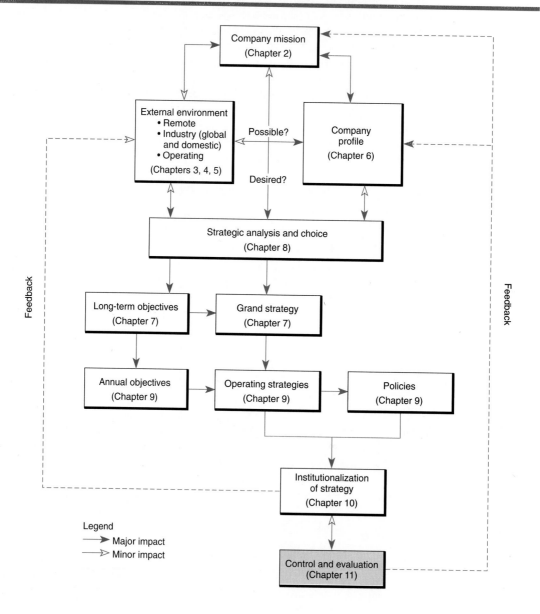

Strategies are forward looking, designed to be accomplished several years into the future, and based on management assumptions about numerous events that have not yet occurred. How should managers control a strategy? The traditional approach to control compares actual results against a standard. After work is done, the manager evaluates it and then uses that evaluation as input to control further work. Although this approach has its place, it is inappropriate as a means for controlling a strategy. The full execution of a strategy often takes five or more years, during which many changes occur that have major ramifications for the strategy's ultimate success. Consequently, the traditional approaches to control must be replaced by an approach that recognizes the unique control needs of long-term strategies.

Strategic control is concerned with tracking a strategy as it is being implemented, detecting problems or changes in its underlying premises, and making necessary adjustments. In contrast to postaction control, strategic control is concerned with guiding action in behalf of the strategy as that action is taking place and when the end result is still several years off. Managers responsible for the success of a strategy typically are concerned with two sets of questions:

1. Are we moving in the proper direction? Are key things falling into place? Are our assumptions about major trends and changes correct? Are we doing the critical things that need to be done? Should we adjust or abort the strategy?
2. How are we performing? Are objectives and schedules being met? Are costs, revenues, and cash flows matching projections? Do we need to make operational changes

Strategic controls, augmented by certain operational controls, are designed to answer these questions.

ESTABLISHING STRATEGIC CONTROLS

The control of strategy can be characterized as a form of "steering control."[1] Ordinarily, a good deal of time elapses between the initial implementation of a strategy and achievement of its intended results. During that time, investments are made and numerous projects and actions are undertaken to implement the strategy. Also, during that time, changes are taking place in both the environmental situation and the firm's internal situation. Strategic controls are necessary to steer the firm through these events. They must provide the basis for adapting the firm's actions and directions in implementing its strategy to these developments and changes.

Prudential Insurance Company provides a useful example of the proactive, steering nature of strategic control. Several years ago, Prudential adopted a long-term market development strategy, in which it sought to attain the top position in the life insurance industry by differentiating its level of service from those of its competitors. It decided to achieve a differential service advantage by establishing regional home offices. Exercising strategic control, its managers used the experience of the first regional offices to reproject the overall expenses and income associated with this strategy. The predicted expenses were so high

---

[1] B. Yavitz and W. H. Newman, *Strategy in Action* (New York: Free Press, 1982), p. 207.

that the original schedule for establishing other regional offices had to be modified. And on the basis of other early feedback, the restructuring of the services performed at Prudential's corporate headquarters was sharply revised. Thus, the steering control (or strategic control) exercised by Prudential managers significantly altered the firm's strategy. In this case, the major objectives of the strategy remained in place; in other cases, strategic control has led to changes in the major strategic objectives.

The four basic types of strategic control are:

1. Premise control.
2. Implementation control.
3. Strategic surveillance.
4. Special alert control.

The nature of these four types is summarized in Figure 11–1.

Premise Control

Every strategy is based on certain planning premises—assumptions or predictions. *Premise control is designed to check systematically and continuously whether the premises on which the strategy is based are still valid.* If a vital premise is no longer valid, the strategy may have to be changed. The sooner an invalid premise can be recognized and rejected, the better are the chances that an acceptable shift in the strategy can be devised.

Which Premises Should Be Monitored?

Planning premises are primarily concerned with environmental and industry factors. These are described next.

Environmental Factors   Although a firm has little or no control over environmental factors, these factors exercise considerable influence over the success of its strategy, and strategies usually are based on key premises about them. Inflation, technology, interest rates, regulation, and demographic/social changes are examples of such factors.

EPA regulations and federal laws concerning the handling, use, and disposal of toxic chemicals have a major effect on the strategy of Velsicol Chemical Company, a market leader in pesticide chemicals sold to farmers and exterminators. So Velsicol's management makes and constantly updates premises about future regulatory actions.

Industry Factors   The performance of the firms in a given industry is affected by industry factors. These differ among industries, and a firm should be aware of the factors that influence success in its particular industry. Competitors, suppliers, product substitutes, and barriers to entry are a few of the industry factors about which strategic assumptions are made.

The strategies guiding the sales of IBM's minicomputer series (S–36, S–38, AS–400) were based in part on assumptions about two competitors—Wang and DEC.[2] Wang's continuing financial difficulties and DEC's product miscues have caused IBM executives to adjust their ministrategy based on a revised premise about the strength of Wang and DEC.[3]

---

[2] IBM annual report, 1991.

[3] "Recreating DEC," *Forbes*, March 30, 1992, p. 124.

FIGURE 11–1
Four Types of Strategic Control

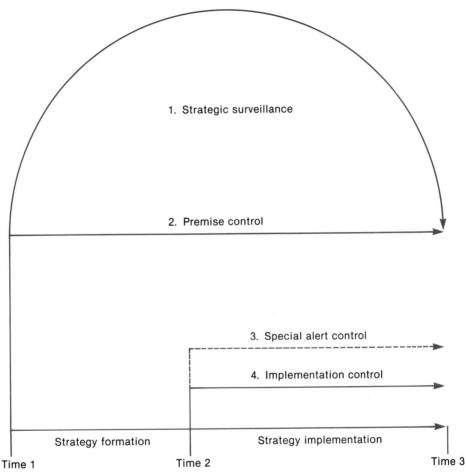

Source: Adapted from G. Schreyogg and H. Steinmann, "Strategic Control: A New Perspective," *Academy of Management Review* 12, no. 1 (1987), p. 96.

Strategies are often based on numerous premises, some major and some minor, about environmental and industry variables. Tracking all of these premises is unnecessarily expensive and time consuming. Managers must select premises whose change (*a*) is likely and (*b*) would have a major impact on the firm and its strategy.

How Are Premise Controls Enacted?

A strategy's key premises should be identified and recorded during the planning process. Responsibility for monitoring those premises should be assigned to the persons or departments that are qualified sources of information. To illustrate, members of the sales force might be assigned to monitor the expected price policy of major competitors and the finance department might be assigned to monitor interest rate trends. The required amount of monitoring effort varies for different premises; to avoid information overload, emphasis should be placed on the monitoring of key premises. These premises should be updated (and new predictions should be made) on the basis of updated information. Finally, key areas within the firm, or key aspects of the strategy that would be significantly affected by changes in certain premises, should be preidentified so adjustments necessitated by revisions in those premises can be determined and initiated. For example, senior marketing executives should be alerted to changes in competitors' pricing policies so these executives can determine whether revised pricing, product repositioning, or other strategy adjustments are necessary.

Implementation Control

Strategy implementation takes place as series of steps, programs, investments, and moves that occur over an extended time. Special programs are undertaken. Functional areas initiate strategy-related activities. Key people are added or reassigned. Resources are mobilized. In other words, managers implement strategy by converting broad plans into the concrete, incremental actions and results of specific units and individuals.

Implementation control is the type of strategic control that must be exercised as those events unfold. *Implementation control is designed to assess whether the overall strategy should be changed in light of the results associated with the incremental actions that implement the overall strategy.* Prudential's updating of cost and revenue projections based on early experiences with regional home offices is an example of implementation control. The two basic types of implementation control are (1) monitoring strategic thrusts and (2) milestone reviews.

Monitoring Strategic Thrusts

As a means of implementing broad strategies, narrow strategic projects often are undertaken—projects that represent part of what needs to be done if the overall strategy is to be accomplished. These strategic thrusts provide managers with information that helps them to determine whether the overall strategy is progressing as planned or needs to be adjusted.

Although the utility of strategic thrusts seems readily apparent, it is not always easy to use them for control purposes. It may be difficult to interpret early experience or to evaluate the overall strategy in light of such experience. One approach is to agree early in the planning process on which thrusts or which phases of thrusts are critical factors in the success of the strategy. Managers responsible for these implementation controls will single them out from other activities and observe them frequently. Another approach is to use stop/go assessments that are linked to a series of meaningful thresholds (time, costs, research and development, success, and so forth) associated with particular thrusts. A program of regional development via company-owned inns in the Rocky Mountain area was a monitoring thrust that Days Inn used to test its strategy of becoming a nationwide motel chain. Problems in meeting time targets and unexpectedly large capital needs led Days Inn's executives to abandon the overall strategy and eventually sell the firm.

Milestone Reviews

Managers often attempt to identify significant milestones that will be reached during the time a strategy is being implemented. These milestones may be critical events, major resource allocations, or simply the passage of a certain amount of time. The milestone reviews that then take place usually involve a full-scale reassessment of the strategy and of the advisability of continuing or refocusing the firm's direction.

A useful example of implementation control based on milestone review is offered by Boeing's product development strategy of entering the supersonic transport (SST) airplane market. Boeing had invested millions of dollars and years of scarce engineering talent during the first phase of its SST venture, and competition from the British/French Concorde effort was intense. Since the next phase represented a billion-dollar decision, Boeing's management established the initiation of the phase as a milestone. The milestone reviews greatly increased the estimates of production costs; predicted relatively few passengers and rising fuel costs, thus raising the estimated operating costs; and noted that the Concorde, unlike Boeing, had the benefit of massive government subsidies. These factors led Boeing's management to scrap its SST strategy in spite of high sunk costs, pride, and patriotism. Only an objective, full-scale strategy reassessment could have led to such a decision.

In this example, a milestone review occurred at a major resource allocation decision point. Milestone reviews may also occur concurrent when a major step in a strategy's implementation is being taken or when a key uncertainty is resolved. Managers even may set an arbitrary period, say two years, as a milestone review point. Whatever the basis for selecting that point, the critical purpose of a milestone review is to thoroughly scrutinize the firm's strategy so as to control the strategy's future.

Strategic Surveillance

By their nature, premise control and implementation control are focused controls; strategic surveillance, however, is unfocused. *Strategic surveillance is designed to monitor a broad range of events inside and outside the firm that are likely to affect the course of its strategy.*[4] The basic idea behind strategic surveillance is that important yet unanticipated information may be uncovered by a general monitoring of multiple information sources.

Strategic surveillance must be kept as unfocused as possible. It should be a loose "environmental scanning" activity. Trade magazines, *The Wall Street Journal,* trade conferences, conversations, and intended and unintended observations are all subjects of strategic surveillance. Despite its looseness, strategic surveillance provides an ongoing, broad-based vigilance in all daily operations that may uncover information relevant to the firm's strategy. Citicorp benefited significantly from a Peruvian manager's strategic surveillance of political speeches by Peru's former president, as discussed in Strategy in Action 11–1.

---

[4] G. Schreyogg and H. Steinmann, "Strategic Control: A New Perspective," *Academy of Management Review* 12, no. 1 (1987), p. 101.

STRATEGY
IN ACTION **EXAMPLES OF STRATEGIC CONTROLS**
  11–1

PREMISE CONTROL AT LOTUS DEVELOPMENT CORPORATION

Lotus Development Corporation in Massachusetts rode the PC revolution to spectacular success in the 1980s with its spreadsheet software product, Lotus 1-2-3. Because of the ease with which software could be copied (without payment to the developing company), Lotus emerged as an aggressive pursuer of any attempts to use unauthorized (not paid for) copies of its 1-2-3 software. As a part of this effort, Lotus held strong to a policy forcing customers to destroy spreadsheet programs from competing software makers in return for the license to load 1-2-3 onto a computer.

This policy evolved from Lotus's broader strategy to give big discounts to customers who were buying upgraded versions of Lotus 1-2-3 or other Lotus products. The premise underlying this strategy and the policies related to it was that Lotus wanted to keep customers from using the bargain prices to buy programs for computers that did not already have the 1-2-3 software. In other words, if you had developed numerous spreadsheets using other software, you had to destroy that software and related spreadsheets before you could load 1-2-3 on that computer if the 1-2-3 was purchased at a heavily discounted price. Lotus's premise was that multistation users, in return for heavily discounted prices, would gladly remove competing software and related spreadsheets, and so on.

Ongoing customer and market research aimed in part at monitoring these premises ultimately caused Lotus to change this part of its strategy in 1992 because the premise was seen as no longer valid. Paul McNulty, director of marketing for the Lotus 1-2-3 spreadsheet program, said the Cambridge-based company was trying to prevent the unauthorized use of its computer software. "We were surprised with the response," he said. "We have created some problems for some of our customers." So Lotus reversed itself and dropped the policy because its fundamental premise about customer priorities was no longer valid.

IMPLEMENTATION CONTROL AT DAYS INN

When Days Inn pioneered the budget segment of the lodging industry, its strategy placed primary emphasis on company-owned facilities and it insisted on maintaining a roughly 3-to-1 company-owned/franchise ratio. This ratio ensured the parent company's total control over standards, rates, and so forth.

As other firms moved into the budget segment, Days Inn saw the need to expand rapidly throughout the United States and, therefore, reversed its conservative franchise posture. This reversal would rapidly accelerate its ability to open new locations. Longtime executives, concerned about potential loss of control over local standards, instituted *implementation controls* requiring both franchise evaluation and annual milestone reviews. Two years into the program, Days Inn executives

Source: Adapted from "Lotus Reverses Policy," *Greenville News,* April 23, 1992, p. D3; conversations with selected Days Inn executives; "Is the Worst over for Citi?" *Forbes,* May 11, 1992; P. F. Drucker, "The Emerging Theory of Manufacturing," *Harvard Business Review* 68, no. 3 (1990), pp. 94–111; and "How Companies Prepare for the Worst," *Business Week,* December 23, 1985, p. 74.

Special Alert Control

Another type of strategic control, really a subset of the other three, is special alert control. *A special alert control is the thorough, and often rapid, reconsideration of the firm's strategy because of a sudden, unexpected event.* A political coup in the Middle East, an

STRATEGY
IN ACTION **concluded**
11–1

were convinced that a high franchise-to-company ratio was manageable, and so they accelerated the growth of franchising by doubling the franchise sales department.

STRATEGIC SURVEILLANCE AT CITICORP

Citicorp has been pursuing an aggressive product development strategy intended to achieve an annual earnings growth of 15 percent while it becomes an institution capable of supplying clients with any kind of financial service anywhere in the world. A major obstacle to the achievement of this earnings growth is Citicorp's exposure to default because of its extensive earlier loans to troubled Third World countries. Citicorp is sensitive to the wide variety of predictions about impending Third World defaults.

Citicorp's long-range plan assumes an annual 10 percent default on its Third World loans over any five-year period. Yet it maintains active *strategic surveillance control* by having each of its international branches monitor daily announcements from key governments and from inside contacts for signs of changes in a host country's financial environment. When that surveillance detects a potential problem, management attempts to adjust Citicorp's posture. For example, when Peru's former president, Alan Garcia, stated that his country would not pay interest on its debt as scheduled, Citicorp raised its annual default charge to 20 percent of its $100 million Peruvian exposure.

SPECIAL ALERT CONTROL AT UNITED AIRLINES

The sudden impact of an airline crash can be devastating to a major airline. United Airlines has made elaborate preparations to deal with this contingency. Its executive vice president, James M. Guyette, heads a crisis team that is permanently prepared to respond. Members of the team carry beepers and are always on call. If United's Chicago headquarters receives word that a plane has crashed, for example, they can be in a "war room" within an hour to direct the response. Beds are set up nearby so team members can catch a few winks; while they sleep, alternates take their places.

Members of the team have been carefully screened through simulated crisis drills. "The point is to weed out those who don't hold up well under stress." says Guyette. Although the team was established to handle flight disasters, it has since assumed an expanded role. The crisis team was activated when American Airlines launched a fare war. And according to Guyette, "We're brainstorming about how we would be affected by everything from a competitor who had a serious problem to a crisis involving a hijacking or taking a United employee hostage."

outside firm's sudden acquisition of a leading competitor, an unexpected product difficulty, such as the poisoned Tylenol capsules—events of these kinds can drastically alter the firm's strategy.

Such an event should trigger an immediate and intense reassessment of the firm's strategy and its current strategic situation. In many firms, crisis teams handle the firm's initial response to unforeseen events that may have an immediate effect on its strategy.

TABLE 11–1

Characteristics of the Four Types of Strategic Control

Basic Characteristics	Types of Strategic Control			
	Premise Control	Implementation Control	Strategic Surveillance	Special Alert Control
Objects of control	Planning premises and projections	Key strategic thrusts and milestones	Potential threats and opportunities related to the strategy	Occurrence of recognizable but unlikely events
Degree of focusing	High	High	Low	High
Data acquisition:				
Formalization	Medium	High	Low	High
Centralization	Low	Medium	Low	High
Use with:				
Environmental factors	Yes	Seldom	Yes	Yes
Industry factors	Yes	Seldom	Yes	Yes
Strategy-specific factors	No	Yes	Seldom	Yes
Company-specific factors	No	Yes	Seldom	Seldom

Source: Adapted from G. Schreyogg and H. Steinmann, "Strategic Control: A New Perspective," *Academy of Management Review* 12, no. 1 (1987), pp. 91–103.

Increasingly, firms have developed contingency plans along with crisis teams to respond to circumstances such as those illustrated in Strategy in Action 11–1.

Table 11–1 summarizes the major characteristics of the four types of strategic control. Unlike operational controls, which are concerned with the control of action, strategic controls are designed to continuously and proactively question the basic direction and appropriateness of a strategy. Each type of strategic control shares a common purpose: to assess whether the strategic direction should be altered in light of unfolding events. Many of us have heard the axiom, "The only thing that is constant is change itself." Organizations face the constancy of change from endless sources within and without the organization, all occurring at an ever accelerating pace. There is very little that organizations can do to directly control those many sources of change. Yet, with performance and long-term survival at stake, better organizations adopt and regularly refine strategic controls as a way to deal with pervasive change. Apple Computer's chairman and former CEO John Sculley's recent explanation of the reasons behind Apple's dramatic strategic changes in the early 1990s serves to illustrate the pervasive, dramatic character of change and the essence of strategic control as a means to deal with it:

> Everywhere we look the computer industry is changing. Customers are changing; they're more knowledgeable about technology and, as a result, are demanding more from their investment in computers. Technology is changing, offering customers new capabilities but requiring

that they deal with greater complexity, especially when it comes to integrating networks of computers. And the economics of the industry—prices, margins, and expense levels—are changing.

The ground rules of our industry are being rewritten, forcing computer companies everywhere to rethink their strategies. New opportunities exist, but only for those poised to take advantage of them. The companies that succeed in the long run will be those with the courage and the ability to quickly transform their businesses to capitalize on change.[5]

Both operational and strategic controls are needed to manage the strategic process effectively. The next section examines the key types of operational control systems that are used to aid the strategic management process.

OPERATIONAL CONTROL SYSTEMS

Operational control systems guide, monitor, and evaluate progress in meeting annual objectives. While strategic controls attempt to steer the company over an extended period (usually five years or more), operational controls provide postaction evaluation and control over short periods—usually from one month to one year. To be effective, operational control systems must take four steps common to all postaction controls:

1. Set standards of performance.
2. Measure actual performance.
3. Identify deviations from standards set.
4. Initiate corrective action.

Three types of operational control system are *budgets, schedules,* and *key success factors.* The nature and use of these three types of systems are described in the next sections.

Budgets

The budgetary process was the forerunner of strategic planning. A budget is a resource allocation plan that helps managers coordinate operations and facilitates managerial control of performance. Budgets themselves do not control anything. They simply set standards against which action can be measured. They also provide a basis for negotiating short-term resource requirements to implement strategy at the operating level. Figure 11–2 represents a typical budgeting system for a manufacturing business.

Most firms employ at least three budgets as a part of their planning and control activities. Three examples follow.

1. *Profit and loss (P&L) budgets* are perhaps the most common. These budgets serve as the basis to monitor sales on a monthly or more frequent basis, as well as to monitor expense categories on a comparable time frame against what has actually occurred. Sales and expense numbers often are subdivided by department, location, product lines, and other relevant subunits to more closely project and monitor organizational activities.

---

[5] Apple Computer, Inc., annual report, 1992, p. 2.

FIGURE 11–2

A Typical Budgeting System for Controlling Strategy Implementation

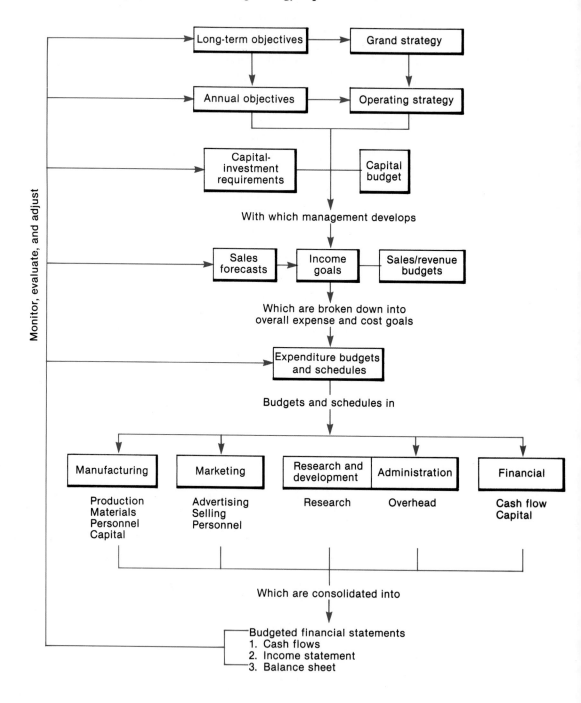

2. *Capital budgets* usually are developed to show the timing of specific expenditures for plant, equipment, machinery, inventories, and other capital items needed during the budget period.

3. *Cash flow budgets* forecast receipt and disbursement of cash during the budget period. They tie together P&L expectations, capital expenditures, collection of receivables, expense payments, and borrowing needs to show just where the life blood of any business, cash, will come from and go to each month.

A typical budgeting system also includes a beginning and projected (ending) balance sheet. The budgeting system serves as an important and early indicator about the effectiveness of a firm's strategy by serving as a frame of reference against which to examine month-to-month results in the execution of that strategy. The budgeting system (see Figure 11–2) provides an integrated picture of the firm's operation as a whole.[6]

Scheduling

Timing is often a key factor in the success of a strategy. Scheduling considerations in allocating time-constrained resources and sequencing interdependent activities often determine the success of strategy implementation. Scheduling offers a mechanism with which to plan for, monitor, and control these dependencies.[7] For example, a firm committed to a vertical integration strategy must carefully absorb expanded operations into its existing core. Such absorption, given either forward or backward integration, will require numerous changes in the operational practices of the firm's organizational units. A good illustration is Coors Brewery's decision to integrate backward by producing its own beer cans. A comprehensive two-year schedule of actions and targets for incorporating the manufacture of beer cans and bottles into the product chain contributed to the success of this strategy. Purchasing, production scheduling, machinery, and production systems were but a few of the critical operating areas that Coors's scheduling efforts were meant to accommodate and coordinate.

Key Success Factors

One useful way to effect operational control is to focus on "key success factors." These factors identify the performance areas that are of greatest importance in implementing the company's strategies and, therefore, must receive continuous management attention. Key success factors focused on internal performance include (1) improved productivity, (2) high employee morale, (3) improved product-service quality, (4) increased earnings per share, (5) growth in market share, and (6) completion of new facilities. Global Strategy in Action 11–1 illustrates the key success factors that Citicorp's management monitored to control its turnaround strategy in the 1990s.

---

[6] For a more thorough discussion of budgeting as a dynamic tool in strategic and operational control, see these references: Robert S. Kaplan and David P. Norton, "The Balanced Scorecard—Measures That Drive Performance," *Harvard Business Review* 70, no. 1 (1992), pp. 71–79; *Coopers and Lybrand Guide to Growing Your Business,* call 212-259-2244; and Brian Milling, *Cash Flow Problem Solver* (New York: Sourcebooks, 1992), call 708-961-2161.

[7] A useful primer on scheduling considerations in strategic project planning is provided by Steven Wheelwright and Kim Clark in "Creating Project Plans to Focus Project Development," *Harvard Business Review* 70, no. 2 (1992), pp. 70–82; and Steven Wheelwright and Kim Clark *Revolutionizing Product Development: Quantum Leaps in Speed, Efficiency, and Quality* (New York: The Free Press, 1992).

Each key success factor must have measurable performance indicators. Lotus Corporation management, for example, having identified product quality, customer service, employee morale, and competition as the key determinants of success in the firm's strategy of rapidly expanding its software offerings, then specified three indicators to monitor and control each of these key success factors, as shown in Figure 11–3.

Key success factors succinctly communicate the critical elements for which operational managers are responsible. These factors require the successful performance of several key individuals and, thus, can be a foundation for teamwork among managers in meeting the firm's strategic objectives.

Budgeting, scheduling, and monitoring key success factors are important means of controlling strategy implementation at the operational level. Common to all of these operational control systems is the need to establish measurable standards and to monitor performance against those standards. The next section examines how to accomplish this.

USING OPERATIONAL CONTROL SYSTEMS: MONITORING PERFORMANCE AND EVALUATING DEVIATIONS

Operational control systems require performance standards. As the strategy is implemented, timely information on deviations from these standards must be obtained so the causes of the deviations can be determined and corrective action taken.

Figure 11–4 illustrates a simplified report that links the current status of key performance indicators to a firm's strategy. These indicators represent progress after two years of a five-year strategy intended to differentiate the firm as a customer-service-oriented provider of high-quality products. Management's concern is to compare *progress to date* with *expected progress*. The *current deviation* is of particular interest, because it provides a basis for examining *suggested actions* (usually suggested by subordinate managers) and for finalizing decisions on changes or adjustments in the firm's operations.

From Figure 11–4, it appears that the firm is maintaining control of its cost structure. Indeed, it is ahead of schedule on reducing overhead. The firm is well ahead of its delivery cycle target, while slightly below its target service-to-sales personnel ratio. Its product returns look OK, although product performance versus specification is below standard. Sales per employee and expansion of the product line are ahead of schedule. The absenteeism rate in the service area is on target, but the turnover rate is higher than that targeted. Competitors appear to be introducing products more rapidly than expected.

After deviations and their causes have been identified, the implications of the deviations for the ultimate success of the strategy must be considered. For example, the rapid product-line expansion indicated in Figure 11–4 may have been a response to the increased rate of competitors' product expansion. At the same time, product performance is still low; and, while the installation cycle is slightly above standard (improving customer service), the ratio of service to sales personnel is below the targeted ratio. Contributing to this substandard ratio (and perhaps reflecting a lack of organizational commitment to customer service) is the exceptionally high turnover in customer service personnel. The rapid reduction in indirect overhead costs might mean that administration integration of customer service and product development requirements has been cut back too quickly.

| GLOBAL STRATEGY IN ACTION 11–1 | **STRATEGIC SUCCESS FACTORS IN CITICORP'S TURNAROUND IN THE 1990S** |

Citicorp, the largest U.S. bank holding company, had been viewed with great skepticism in the early 1990s. Representative John Dingell (Democrat—Michigan) called the bank "technically insolvent" in early 1992. Speculators had shorted 14 million share, 4 percent of the stock outstanding, at $8 per share in early 1992 (the stock sold for over $40 per share two years earlier).

John Reed, Citicorp's besieged chairman, continued to follow a turnaround strategy, the success of which was being monitored by several key strategic success factors. His post-1992 status appeared contingent on the success of Citicorp's strategies. Those factors, and their status in 1992, are summarized below:

1. Generate a profit each quarter in 1992 and beyond, regardless of the write-offs necessary to deal with bad foreign loans.

The first quarter, in 1992, Citicorp showed a small profit of 37 cents per share, owing to the sale of some property, but encouraging in light of $1 billion in loan write-offs.

2. Maintain a capital ratio over the 4 percent required by federal regulators.

Selling $1 billion in convertible preferred stock, and having a profitable first quarter 1992, Citicorp capital ratio was 4.06 percent of assets in April 1992.

3. Achieve profitably while aggressively writing off bad loans.

Citicorp missed this factor in 1991 (a loss of $457 million, or $1.89 per share) but achieved it in the first quarter 1992 (37 cents per share). Analyst note: *"The 1991 loss was not so shocking when you consider that Citicorp wrote off $3.9 billion in provisions for loan losses. Excluding the costs of nonperforming loans, Citicorp earned $1.5 billion—perhaps $3.40 per fully diluted share—on $15 billion in revenue."*

4. Maintain a profitable, dominant position in global consumer banking.

Citicorp's global consumer banking, 62 percent of total revenues, generated a net profit of $549 million in 1991—even after a provision for $2 billion in consumer credit losses. As a stand-alone operation, its global consumer banking could be worth $9 billion, nearly one third more than 1992 market capitalization of $6.2 billion.

5. Maintain Citicorp's No. 1 status in international banking.

Citicorp surpassed any other bank in terms of presence and services in 1992, with 2,054 consumer and corporate banking outlets in 91 countries outside the United States. Japanese banks like Dai-Ichi and Sumitomo are bigger but have far less global presence.

In mid-1992, John Reed predicted that Citicorp's earnings would be solidly in the black by year's end. Much of Wall Street lacks faith in Reed's predictions. If Reed managed to produce $1.90 in earnings per share in 1992, analyst Frank De-Santis of Donaldson, Lufkin & Jenrette predicts Reed will survive.

So you, as the student using this book, should look up current information on Citicorp to see if John Reed is still chairman, and if the strategic success factors indicate where that outcome was determined.

Source: "Is the Worst over for Citicorp?" *Forbes,* May 11, 1992, p. 36.

FIGURE 11–3
Key Success Factors at Lotus Corporation

Key Success Factor	Measurable Performance Indicator
1. Product quality	*a.* Performance data versus specification.
	b. Percentage of product returns.
	c. Number of customer complaints.
2. Customer service	*a.* Delevery cycle in days.
	b. Percentage of orders shipped complete.
	c. Field service delays.
3. Employee morale	*a.* Trends in employee attitude survey.
	b. Absenteeism versus plan.
	c. Employee turnover trends.
4. Competition	*a.* Number of firms competing directly.
	b. Number of new products introduced.
	c. Percentage of bids awarded versus the standard.

This information presents operations managers with several options. They may attribute the deviations primarily to internal discrepancies. In that case, they can scale priorities up or down. For example, they might place more emphasis on retaining customer service personnel and less emphasis on overhead reduction and new product development. On the other hand, they might decide to continue as planned in the face of increasing competition and to accept or gradually improve the customer service situation. Another possibility is reformulating the strategy or a component of the strategy in the face of rapidly increasing competition. For example, the firm might decide to emphasize more standardized or lower-priced products to overcome customer service problems and take advantage of an apparently ambitious sales force.

This is but one of many possible interpretations of Figure 11–4. The important point here is the critical need to monitor progress against standards and to give serious in-depth attention to both the causes of observed deviations and the most appropriate responses to them.

Such evaluations are appropriate for a firm's organizational subunits, product groups, and operating units. Budgets, schedules, and other operating control systems with performance targets and standards linked to the strategic plan deserve this type of attention in detecting and evaluating deviations. The evaluations are usually quarterly but may even be monthly. The operating manager typically reviews year-to-date progress against budgeted figures. After the deviations have been evaluated, slight adjustments may be made to keep progress, expenditure, or other factors in line with the strategy's programmed needs. In the unusual event of extreme deviations—generally because of unforeseen changes—management is alerted to the possible need for revising the budget, reconsidering certain functional plans related to budgeted expenditures, or examining the units concerned and the effectiveness of their managers.

An acceptable level of deviation should be allowed; otherwise, the control process will become an administrative overload. Standards should not be regarded as absolute, because

FIGURE 11–4
Monitoring and Evaluating Performance Deviations

Key Success Factors	Objective, Assumption or Budget	Forecast Performance at This Time	Current Performance	Current Deviation	Analysis
Cost control: Ratio of indirect overhead costs to direct field and labor costs	10%	15%	12%	+3 (ahead)	Are we moving too fast, or is there more unnecessary overhead than was originally thought?
Gross profit	39%	40%	40%	0%	
Customer service: Installation cycle in days	2.5 days	3.2 days	2.7 days	+0.5 (ahead)	Can this progress be maintained?
Ratio of service to sales personnel	3.2	2.7	2.1	−0.6 (behind)	Why are we behind here? How can we maintain the installation-cycle progress?
Product quality: Percentage of products returned	1.0%	2.0%	2.1%	−0.1% (behind)	Why are we behind here? What are the ramifications for other operations?
Product performance versus specification	100%	92%	80%	−12% (behind)	
Marketing: Monthly sales per employee	$12,500	$11,500	$12,100	+$600 (ahead)	Good progress. Is it creating any problems to support?
Expansion of product line	6	3	5	+2 products (ahead)	Are the products ready? Are the perfect standards met?
Employee morale in service area: Absenteeism rate	2.5%	3.0%	3.0%	(on target)	
Turnover rate	5%	10%	15%	−8% (behind)	Looks like a problem! Why are we so far behind?
Competition: New product introductions (average number)	6	3	6	−3 (behind)	Did we underestimate timing? What are the implications for our basic assumptions?

the estimates used to formulate them typically are based on historical data, which, by definition, are after the fact. Furthermore, absolute standards (keep equipment busy 100 percent of the time or meet 100 percent of quota) make no provision for variability. Standards are also often derived from averages, which, by definition, ignore variability. These difficulties suggest the need to define acceptable *ranges* of deviation in budgetary figures or key indicators of strategic success. This approach helps in avoiding administrative difficulties, in recognizing measurement variability, in delegating more realistic authority for short-term decisions to operating managers, and in improving motivation.

Some firms use trigger points for the clarification of standards, particularly in monitoring key success factors. A *trigger point* is a level of deviation of a key indicator or figure (such as a competitor's actions or a critical cost category) that management identifies in the planning process as representing either a major threat or an unusual opportunity. When that point is reached, management immediately is altered (triggered) to consider necessary adjustments in the firm's strategy. Strategy in Action 11–2 describes one such approach to control. Some firms take this idea a major step forward and develop one or more *contingency plans* that are to be implemented when predetermined trigger points are reached. These contingency plans redirect priorities and actions so rapidly that valuable reaction time is not wasted on administrative assessment of the extreme deviation.

Correcting deviations in performance brings the entire management task into focus. Managers can correct such deviations by changing measures or plans. They also can eliminate poor performance by changing how things are done, by hiring or retraining workers, by changing job assignments, and so on. Correcting deviations, therefore, can involve all of the functions, tasks, and responsibilities of operations managers. Operational control systems are intended to provide essential feedback so managers can make the decisions and adjustments necessary to implement the current strategy. Companies worldwide increasingly view this activity as part of a pervasive commitment to quality, often called *total quality management* (TQM), which is seen as essential to strategic success into the 21st century.

THE QUALITY IMPERATIVE

The initials TQM have become the most popular abbreviation in business management literature since MBO.[8] TQM stands for Total Quality Management, an umbrella term for the quality programs that have been implemented in many U.S. businesses in the last decade. TQM was first implemented in several large U.S. manufacturers in the face of the overwhelming success of Japanese and German competitors. Japanese manufacturers embraced the quality messages of Americans W. Edward Deming and J. M. Juran following World War II, and by the 1970s Japanese products had acquired unquestioned reputations for superior high quality.

---

[8] This section draws on total quality management ideas found in the following: G. Stalk, P. Evans, and L. E. Shulman, "Competing on Capabilities: The New Rules of Corporate Strategy," *Harvard Business Review,* March–April 1992, pp. 57–69;   M. Barrier, "Small Firms Put Quality First," *Nation's Business,* May 1992, pp. 22–31;   *Total Quality,* Ernst & Young, SCORE Retrieval File no. A49003, 1991;   and Mary Walton, *The Deming Management Method* (New York: Perigee Books, 1986).

STRATEGY
IN ACTION **OPERATIONAL CONTROLS AT WESTINGHOUSE ELECTRIC**
11–2

Wall Street can't forgive Westinghouse Electric Corporation its sins of the past. A bad bet on uranium prices threatened to sink the company in the mid-1970s. It was driven out of the appliance business. There were 1970s losses from low-income housing, its mail-order business, and other silly diversification moves. The company grabbed the market lead in nuclear power plants and then watched orders disappear in 1978. Even one of its biggest acquisitions in the early 1920s, robotmaker Unimation, was a bust.

What does the 102-year-old company now do? Defense electronics, power generation, broadcasting, finance, and soda bottling, among other things. A curious combination (though clearly it works), the legacy of decades of diversification.

Durable Westinghouse is one of only 22 companies to appear in the 1917 and 1987 *Forbes* lists of 100 largest U.S. corporations. Its work force is down to 117,000 from a 1974 high of 199,000, and productivity gains have been running 6 percent–plus a year. From 1985 to 1987, while divestitures kept sales flat, net profit rose 22 percent, to $739 million, and primary earnings per share shot up 45 percent, to $5.12, as the company bought back stock.

Westinghouse has a simple view: If a division performs, keep it; if not, dump it. Why does it hang on to such remnants of 1960s and 1970s diversification as land development and soda bottling? (It is the largest 7UP bottler in the country.) Simple. They're highly profitable.

Westinghouse managers have three basic annual targets that provide operational control: 8.5 percent annual growth in revenue, double-digit per share annual earnings gains, and an ROE of 18 percent to 21 percent.

A division that misses these targets for two years becomes a candidate for divestiture. In this way, corporate strategists maintain operational control over the long-term prospects for the overall company.

Source: "What's a Westinghouse?" *Forbes,* April 4, 1988, p. 34.

Growing numbers of U.S. manufacturers have attempted to change this imbalance with their own quality programs, and the practice has spread to large retail and service companies as well. Increasingly, smaller companies that supply big TQM companies have adopted quality programs, often because big companies have required small suppliers to adopt quality programs of their own. Strategy in Action 11–3 describes the quality program in one such company, Dallas-based Marlow Industries, a recent winner of the Malcolm Baldrige National Quality Award.

TQM is viewed as virtually a new organizational culture and way of thinking. It is built around an intense focus on customer satisfaction; on accurate measurement of every critical variable in a business's operation; on continuous improvement of products, services, and processes; and on work relationships based on trust and teamwork. One useful explanation of the quality imperative suggests 10 essential elements of implementing total quality management, as follows:[9]

---

[9] Ideas about these 10 elements are based in part on excellent work by the firm Ernst and Young, in *Total Quality*, Ernst & Young, SCORE Retrieval File no. A49003, 1991.

STRATEGY **DO OR DIE: MARLOW INDUSTRIES ADOPTS**
IN ACTION **TOTAL QUALITY MANAGEMENT**
11–3

Congress created the Baldrige Award in 1987 to recognize U.S. firms with outstanding records of quality improvement and quality management. Marlow Industries, the Dallas-based firm that was the 1992 small-business winner of the Malcolm Baldrige National Quality Award, is one of those companies that adopted TQM under pressure from its customers.

There's a simple reason for such customer pressure: When an appliance maker is trying to produce defect-free products, it cannot tolerate defects in the parts provided by its small suppliers.

Marlow, with 160 employees, is the smallest business yet to win the award. Only three small firms have ever won, out of 125 that have applied. Marlow makes thermoelectric coolers—small solid-state devices used to spot cooling in critical applications for telecommunications, aerospace, and the military. Most of Marlow's products are custom made for customers who impose their own quality requirements on their suppliers. Marlow had to come up with comprehensive quality systems that would meet all of those requirements.

That might sound like an intimidating task for so small a company, but Marlow successfully introduced profound changes in the way it operates. For example, about two years ago Marlow broke up its quality-assurance department, assigning product inspectors to "minifactories"—self-contained units, made up of approximately 15 people each. Today, according to Chris Witzke, Marlow's COO, the inspectors "look after the quality systems, set training standards, do audits—but they're not in the product-inspection business."

In other words, Marlow switched from product inspection to process control—from catching and correcting defects at the end of the process to monitoring the process itself, so defects do not occur. It was not easy to adopt TQM at Marlow. Raymond Marlow, founder and president of Marlow, said "You've got to have patience, because it takes a couple of years" before employees can work together smoothly in problem-solving teams. While the transition is taking place, Marlow says, top management must display "consistency of purpose. You have to keep the quality thing moving."

Measurement was critical at Marlow. "If you measure something," said Chris Witzke, "it improves." Simply posting measurements—putting up a chart showing how well departments are

Source: Excerpted from "Small Firms Put Quality First," *Nation's Business,* May 1992, pp. 22–31.

1. **Define "quality."** Rather than be left to individual interpretation, company personnel should have a clear definition of what quality means in the job, department, and throughout the company. It should be developed from your customer's perspective and communicated as a written policy.

2. **Develop a customer orientation.** Quality is what the customer says it is. Don't rely on secondary information—talk to your customers directly. Also recognize your "internal" customers. Usually less than 20 percent of company employees come into contact with external customers, while the other 80 percent serve internal customers—other units with real performance expectations.

3. **Focus on the company's business processes.** Break down every minute step in the process of providing the company's product or service and look at ways to improve it, rather than focusing simply on the finished product or service.

---

doing at turning in their time cards on schedule, for instance—can sometimes solve a problem. But deciding what to measure is not always easy. Marlow devoted a full year to developing statistical process controls. "We really dedicated ourselves to understanding our processes and finding the key variables," Witzke said. "All this stuff used to be black art. Now it's science." Marlow at one time measured 52 variables in a plating process—but had constant problems anyway. Now it measures only 14 variables (including seven new ones), and the problems have disappeared. Measurements sometimes can reveal things about a business that no one would have suspected if the measurements hadn't been made. When Marlow began subjecting employee turnover to Pareto analysis, it discovered that a 90-day probationary period was contributing to turnover by encouraging supervisors to make marginal hires. Once the supervisors understood the cost of that turnover, they tightened their hiring practices. At Marlow, decisions on what should be measured usually have followed surveys of "internal customers" so what was important could be measured.

As any TQM company would be expected to do, Marlow measures its suppliers' performances—and it also tells them how they're doing. "It's amazing how quick a reaction you can get just from sending out a letter saying, 'Hey, your supplier index has dropped to 1.1,'" said Marlow's Witzke. One of Marlow's minifactories, responding to just such a review, came up with a "service guarantee" for its internal customers. Posted prominently in a hall at the plant, the guarantee promises replacement of any unsatisfactory part within 24 hours. After that guarantee went up, Witzke said, "it wasn't long before they started popping up in other places. That's the ideal situation—where management doesn't have to spend all of its time making things happen."

Marlow does a lot of in-house training, in both work skills and quality techniques—the average employee spent almost 50 hours in training last year—and the training helps managers as well as employees. Said Witzke: "By the time you've taught a course three or four times, you begin to believe it."

When a quality program is working, Witzke says—when customers are happy, products are defect-free, deliveries are on time—"all of a sudden you've got 30 percent more staff than you thought you had," because employees are spending less time correcting problems.

---

4. **Develop customer and supplier partnerships.** Organizations have a destructive tendency to view suppliers and even customers adversarially. It is better to understand the horizontal flow of a business—outside suppliers to internal suppliers/customers (a company's various departments) to external customers. This view suggests suppliers are partners in meeting customer needs, and customers are partners by providing input so the company and suppliers can meet and exceed those expectations.

5. **Take a preventive approach.** Many organizations reward "fire fighters," not "fire preventers," and identify errors after the work is done. Management, instead, should be rewarded for being prevention oriented and seeking to eliminate nonvalue-added work.

6. **Adopt an error-free attitude.** Instill an attitude that "good enough" is not good enough anymore. "Error free" should become each individual's performance standard, with managers taking every opportunity to demonstrate and communicate the importance of this imperative.

7. **Get the facts first.** TQM companies make decisions based on facts, not on opinions. Accurate measurement, often using readily available statistical techniques, of every critical variable in a business's operation—and using those measurements to trace problems to their roots and eliminate their causes—is a better way.

8. **Encourage every manager and employee to participate.** Employee participation, empowerment, participative decision making, and extensive training in quality techniques, in statistical techniques, and in measurement tools are the ingredients TQM companies employ to support and instill a commitment to quality.

9. **Create an atmosphere of total involvement.** Quality management cannot be the job of a few managers or of one department. TQM cannot be achieved unless all areas of the organization apply quality concepts simultaneously.

10. **Strive for continuous improvement.** Stephen Yearout, director of Ernst & Young's Quality Management Center, recently observed that, "In the '80s, meeting your customers' expectations would distinguish you from your competitors. The '90s will require you to anticipate customer expectations and deliver quality service faster than the competition." Quality is not a one-time program of competitive response, for it creates a new standard to measure up to. Organizations quickly find that continually improving quality in their products and services is not just good business, it's a necessity for long-term survival.

The quality initiative and strategic control are two sides of the same "coin"—attention to factors that, in themselves, or because of change impacting them, influence the long-term success and survival of an organization. So it is not surprising, in the face of increasing global competition, that the quality initiative has evolved as a prominent factor that strategic-thinking managers are instilling in the way their organizations do business in the 1990s and beyond.

SUMMARY

Two fundamental perspectives—strategic control and operational control—provide the basis for designing strategy control systems. Strategic controls are intended to steer the company toward its long-term strategic goals. Premise controls, implementation controls, strategic surveillance, and special alert controls are types of strategic control. All four types are designed to meet top-management's needs to track the strategy as it is being implemented, to detect underlying problems, and to make necessary adjustments. These strategic controls are linked to the environmental assumptions and the key operating requirements necessary for successful strategy implementation. Ever-present forces of change fuel the need for and focus of strategic control.

Operational control systems identify the performance standards associated with allocation and use of the firm's financial, physical, and human resources in pursuit of its strategy. Budgets, schedules, and key success factors are the primary means of operational control.

Operational control systems require systematic evaluation of performance against predetermined standards or targets. A critical concern here is identification and evaluation of performance deviations, with careful attention paid to determining the underlying reasons and strategic implications for observed deviations before management reacts. Some firms use trigger points and contingency plans in this process.

The "quality imperative" that has redefined global competitiveness is an important arena in which companies are reshaping their strategic and operational control orientation.

QUESTIONS FOR DISCUSSION

1. Distinguish strategic control from operating control. Give an example of each.
2. Select a business whose strategy is familiar to you. Identify what you think are the key premises of the strategy. Then select the key indicators that you would use to monitor each of these premises.
3. Explain the differences between implementation controls, strategic surveillance, and special alerts. Give an example of each.
4. Why are budgets, schedules, and key success factors essential to operations control and evaluation?
5. What are key considerations in monitoring deviations from performance standards?
6. What are five key elements of quality management? How is the quality imperative related to strategic and operational control?

BIBLIOGRAPHY

Asch, D. "Strategic Control: A Problem Looking for a Solution." *Long Range Planning* 25, no. 2 (1992), pp. 97–104.

Baysinger, B., and R. E. Hoskisson. "The Composition of Boards of Directors and Strategic Control: Effects on Corporate Strategy." *Academy of Management Review* 15, no. 1 (1990), pp. 72–87.

Boeker, Warren. "Strategic Change: The Effects of Founding and History." *Academy of Management Journal,* September 1989, p. 489.

Bungay, S., and M. Goold. "Creating a Strategic Control System." *Long Range Planning* 24, no. 3 (1991), pp. 32–39.

Cowen, S. S., and J. K. Middaugh. "Designing an Effective Financial Planning and Control System." *Long Range Planning,* December 1988, pp. 83–92.

Duchessi, P., and J. Hobbs. "Implementing a Manufacturing Planning and Control System." *California Management Review,* Spring 1989, pp. 75–90.

Finkin, E. F. "Expense Control in Sales and Marketing." *Journal of Business Strategy,* May 1988, pp. 52–55.

Goold, M. "Strategic Control in the Decentralized Firm." *Sloan Management Review* 32, no. 2 (1991), pp. 69–81.

Goold, M., and J. J. Quinn. "The Paradox of Strategic Control." *Strategic Management Journal* 11, no. 1 (1990), pp. 43–57.

Gundy, T., and D. King. "Using Strategic Planning to Drive Strategic Change." *Long Range Planning* 25, no. 1 (1992), pp. 100–09.

Gupta, A. K., and V. Govindarajan. "Knowledge Flows and the Structure of Control within Multinational Corporations." *Academy of Management Review* 16, no. 4 (1991), pp. 768–92.

Harrison, E. F. "Strategic Control at the CEO Level." *Long Range Planning* 24, no. 6 (1991), pp. 78–87.

Hill, C. W. L. "Corporate Control Type, Strategy, Size and Financial Performance." *Journal of Management Studies,* September 1988, pp. 403–18.

Johnson, G. N. "Managing Strategic Change: Strategy, Culture and Action." *Long Range Planning* 25, no. 1 (1992), pp. 28–36.

Kellinghusen, G., and K. Wiebbenhorst. "Strategic Control for Improved Performance." *Long Range Planning* 25, no. 3 (1992), pp. 30–37.

Kelly, D., and T. L. Amburgey. "Organizational Inertia and Momentum: A Dynamic Model of Strategic Change." *Academy of Management Journal* 34, no. 3 (1991), pp. 591–612.

King, E. M.; W. Norvell; and D. Deines. "Budgeting: A Strategic Managerial Tool." *Journal of Business Strategy,* Fall 1988, pp. 69–75.

Klein, Howard J. "An Integrated Control Theory Model of Work Motivation." *Academy of Management Review,* April 1989, p. 50.

Murphy, T. "Pay for Performance—An Instrument of Strategy." *Long Range Planning,* August 1989, pp. 40–45.

Norburn, D., and S. Birley. "The Top Management Team and Corporate Performance." *Strategic Management Journal,* May 1988, pp. 225–38.

Odiorne, George S. "Measuring the Unmeasurable: Setting Standards for Management Performance." *Business Horizons,* July–August 1987, p. 69.

Reichheld, F. F., and W. E. Sasser. "Zero Defects: Quality Comes to Services." *Harvard Business Review* 68, no. 3 (1990), pp. 94–111.

Rogers, T. J. "No Excuses Management." *Harvard Business Review* 68, no. 4 (1990), pp. 105–13.

Ross, Joel, and David Georgoff. "A Survey of Productivity and Quality Issues in Manufacturing: The State of the Industry." *Industrial Management* 33, no. 1 (1991), pp. 3–5, 22–25.

Taguchi, G., and D. Clausing. "Robust Quality." *Harvard Business Review* 68, no. 1 (1990), pp. 65–75.

Zahra, S. "Increasing the Board's Involvement in Strategy." *Long Range Planning* 23, no. 6 (1990), pp. 10–16.

Zent, Charles H. "Using Shareholder Value to Design Business Unit Manager Incentive Plans." *Planning Review,* March–April 1988, p. 40.

CHAPTER 11 COHESION CASE

STRATEGIC CONTROL AT THE COCA-COLA COMPANY

Fundamental to Coca-Cola's strategic control in its soft-drink business is daily monitoring of "unit case sales" in each of the thousands of markets Coke serves around the world. The following table of "Selected Country Results" illustrates Coke doing this in selected countries on an annual basis. The same scrutiny is applied to all markets, sales territories, routes, and customers (stores selling or disbursing soft drinks) on a weekly basis throughout the Coca-Cola system.

A second critical strategic variable monitored by Coke management is the sales volume or market share attained by independently owned as well as company-owned (full or partially) bottling franchises worldwide. You will recall that a major element of Coke's strategy for the 1990s has been its decision to vertically integrate forward into bottling as necessary to ensure accelerated access to consumers. And where Coke already has established long-time franchisees in place, Coke is aggressively monitoring and evaluating their sales results, choosing quickly when necessary to buy out underperforming franchises. This has been true even in international markets, where some international business experts consider such a move, usually accompanied with inserting an American manager in charge, as being too aggressive. Yet Coke has pushed forward and done so successfully, most notably in Great Britain and France. Recent comments by Coke management on this activity include:

Summary of

Selected Country Results

Estimated Unit Case Sales[1]
Carbonated Soft Drinks

| | Average Annual Growth | | | | 1991 Results | | | |
| | 10 Years | | 5 Years | | Unit Case Growth | | Company | |
	Company	Industry	Company	Industry	Company	Industry	Share	Per Capita Consumption
Worldwide	6%	5%	6%	5%	5%	3%	43%	54
United States	5	4	4	3	2.5	1.7	41	296
International	7	5	8	6	6	3	44	39
European Community	9	5	11	7	8	1	45	116
France	13	5	16	9	11	1	41	52
Germany	6	5	9	10	19	6	46	178
Great Britain	13	6	14	4	(11)	(10)	32	87
Italy	10	6	8	5	4	4	55	91
Spain	7	5	11	7	6	3	51	155
Pacific[2]	9	7	10	9	4	3	40	18
Australia	7	5	8	6	2	3	56	223
Japan[2]	7	7	9	9	7	6	34	122
Korea	8	10	7	11	(1)	1	49	63
Philippines	12	3	8	5	(1)	(7)	76	89
Thailand	10	9	17	18	3	4	57	43
Northeast Europe/Africa	7	6	8	6	5	4	27	18
Austria	6	6	10	10	12	8	46	141
Nigeria	4	4	8	6	10	3	68	21
Norway	12	7	11	4	8	3	59	218
Switzerland	10	5	8	6	9	11	44	155
Turkey	19	12	17	13	6	14	39	21
Latin America	6	4	6	4	8	6	53	131
Argentina	3	3	(2)	(3)	31	37	62	133
Brazil	8	6	6	4	4	3	60	101
Chile	9	7	16	18	9	6	61	158
Colombia	6	3	3	1	0.4	(2)	43	105
Mexico	5	4	8	7	6	3	53	273

[1]Unit case equals 24 8-ounce drinks. Data include, for the first time, results from the former Soviet Union and China. Excluding those markets, the Company's share of international soft drink sales was 49 percent. [2]Includes Japanese non-carbonated soft drinks

Source: The Coca-Cola Company, 1991 Annual Report, p. 34.

Bottling Investments

Region	Year of Investment	Company Ownership (%)	Share (%)		Annual Unit Case Sales Growth (%)
			Before	1990	
Philippines	1981	30%	31%	71%	14%
Taiwan	1985	35	10	48	52
Great Britain	1986	49	21	32	22
Indonesia	1987	29	58	72	18
Netherlands	1988	30	24	28	16
France	1989	100	32	37	24
Australia	1989	51	52	54	9

Our accelerated growth rate of the past five years [1985–90] would seem to indicate that we are doing business differently than before, and we are. Without question, the biggest difference is our willingness to do whatever is advisable to grow our concentrate and syrup business around the world. In large measure, around the world we are able to maximize profitable growth with the traditional bottler system. Sometimes, however, the practical action is taking significant equity positions in important components of our global bottling network. Taking ownership positions in approximately 60 different bottling, canning, and distribution operations around the world and, often, assuming management responsibility has been a way to ensure ourselves of working with bottling partners who share our commitment to reinvestment in, and profitable growth of, the business.

The results speak for themselves. The accompanying table illustrates the success we have had in a number of individual markets [and also serves to show the focus of a key aspect of Coke's strategic control system].

Another element of Coca-Cola's strategic control centers around the basic goal the company seeks to accomplish. Speaking to business analysts, Roberto Goizueta put it simply: "Management doesn't get paid to make the shareholders comfortable. We get paid to make the shareholders rich." So fundamental strategic control at Coca-Cola monitors the market valuation of Coke and continuously tries to evaluate strategies, assumptions, and actions in light of their effect on this situation. Through the 1980s and early 1990s, the feedback has been extremely encouraging, as shown in the graph on the next page.

Perhaps the best-known example of this willingness to react quickly is Coke's reaction to the consumers' reception to New Coke in the mid-1980s. After extensive market tests showed Pepsi's slightly sweeter Pepsi was preferred in blind taste tests to traditional Coke, and after still further ruminations, Goizueta's relatively new management team introduced New Coke in an extraordinarily expensive promotional and distribution blitz while also having it take the place of Coke's traditional beverage. Coke was quickly caught by surprise in the consumer rebellion by loyal Coke drinkers who adamantly refused to let the old Coke die. While Coke management had invested millions in this new move—literally changing distribution practices, promotional material, and the like nationwide in 1985—it quickly readjusted its strategy, apologized for its decision, brought back a new "Coke Classic," and ended up with more shelf space in grocery stores (Pepsi's stronghold) as retailers allowed Coke to keep both New Coke & Coke Classic (as well as other brands) for sale. Even with

For our Company, the year 1991 could be characterized by the words **challenging** and **rewarding**. It was **challenging** because of the harsh economic conditions which prevailed in several of our most important markets, *e.g.*, Australia, Canada, the United States and the United Kingdom. Balancing those economic negatives, however, were the strong free market economies emerging in Latin America with their resulting positive impact on our business; the new markets evolving in eastern Europe; and the continued strong showing of our soft drink business in the Pacific Rim countries. In addition, we achieved share gains relative to the competition in most countries where soft drink industry growth was affected by the local economies.

1991 was especially **rewarding** because our Company, together with the global Coca-Cola system, demonstrated an extraordinary capability to adapt to local market conditions so as to derive the greatest benefits for our soft drink business. This pragmatic adaptability is largely responsible for our Company's ability to continue to produce consistent and reliable profitable growth.

Last year our share price gained nearly 73 percent, almost three times the increase of the S&P 500. Adding the annual dividend of 96 cents per share to the stock price appreciation gave the owners of this Company a total return of 75 percent on their investment. The annualized total return over the past five and 10 years, assuming reinvestment of dividends, has been 37 percent and 34 percent, respectively.

In 1991 the market value of The Coca-Cola Company **increased** by more than $22 billion, an amount $6 billion greater than our Company's **total** market value at January 1, 1989. **In other words, last year, in terms of market capitalization, we created the equivalent of another company larger than The Coca-Cola Company was less than three years ago.**

At year-end 1991, our Company was the sixth-largest public company in the U.S. in terms of market value, worth over $53 billion. This market value is more than three times what it was three years ago, and more than 12 times what it was 10 years ago, back on January 1, 1982, when it stood at $4.3 billion. Stated differently, **$49 billion of additional wealth**

Total Return

Appreciation plus reinvested dividends on $100 investment on 12/31/81. From 1982 to 1991, the Company's common stock outperformed the S&P 500 by approximately 4-to-1 and the Dow Jones Industrial Average by approximately 5-to-1.

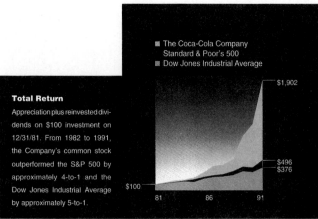

■ The Coca-Cola Company
  Standard & Poor's 500
■ Dow Jones Industrial Average

$1,902
$496
$376
$100
81   86   91

Source: The Coca-Cola Company 1991 Annual Report, p. 2.

the huge mistake, Coke management's rapid response (strategic control) resulted in yet another record year, in terms of sales and profitability, as well as a valuable lesson in and reinforcement of consumer loyalty to the Coke brand.

A final illustration of strategic control at Coca-Cola, which takes place in the international arena, serves to illustrate the importance Coke places on two underpinnings of its unprecedented worldwide consumer franchise—its well-known trademark and the formulas for its soft-drink syrup. It takes place in India, the world's second-largest consumer market, with just under 1 billion people.[1]

> The Coca-Cola Company came to India in the early 1950s when it set up four bottling operations in Bombay, Calcutta, Delhi, and Kanpur. Initially, the plants used imported concentrates for the soft drink. In 1958, the company received permission to set up a facility that would make the concentrates in India from imported raw materials. By 1970, Coca-Cola had 22 bottling plants in India, 45 percent of India's soft-drink market, and a sizable export business as well.
>
> However, when the Indian government began to take a closer look at Coca-Cola's operations, it found that when repatriated profits and raw material imports were taken into account, the company's operation was consuming India's precious foreign exchange, rather than earning it.
>
> There were a series of early skirmishes between the government and the company over import licenses and export credits in the mid-1970s, as Coca-Cola's exports, which once had been substantial, evaporated.
>
> As one high-level Indian official remarked in 1977, "The activities of Coca-Cola Company in India during the last 25 years furnish a classic example of how a multinational corporation operating in a low-priority, high-profit area in a developing country attains runaway growth and, in the absence of alertness on the part of the government concerned, can stifle the weaker indigenous industry in the process."
>
> Because Coca-Cola was engaged in a low-priority industry, not requiring sophisticated technology and with little export potential, the Indian government directed the company to comply with regulations that applied to other such firms. Specifically, it was directed to reduce foreign equity to 40 percent. Most foreign-owned operations that were requested to do so complied with this directive and brought Indian investors into their ownership structure. Coca-Cola, however, refused.
>
> A major factor in the decision hinged on another aspect of the Indian law, which required the company to transfer technical knowledge to any Indian-owned successor. This would have required the company to reveal the proprietary secret recipe for its soft drink concentrate.
>
> Thus, by the late 1970s, Coca-Cola faced a situation that pitted the corporation's strategic and operational policy against the development policies of the Indian government. Ultimately, it chose to sacrifice a lucrative Indian subsidiary—one with pretax profit margins between 55 percent and 60 percent and an estimated return on investment of more than 800 percent— rather than bend to the policies of a foreign government.
>
> In a strategic move of its own, the Indian government had begun to develop a cola substitute in the early 1970s. By the time Coca-Cola declared it would not comply with the government order and would leave India in 1978, Indian authorities were in a position to convert Coca-Cola bottling operations to the production of a domestically developed substitute,

---

[1] Anant R. Negandi and Peter A. Donhowe, "It's Time to Explore New Global Trade Options," *The Journal of Business Strategy,* January/February 1989, p. 29.

thereby preventing plant closings and 20,000 layoffs that would have otherwise followed an abrupt withdrawal by Coca-Cola.

Coke's decision in this situation was criticized by some and admired by others. From the company's point of view, it preferred to forgo a major investment in bottling activity, rather than give up what management considered a central strategic advantage: Coke's technological know-how and secret syrup formulas. And as we saw earlier in this cohesion case, Coke continued to monitor that situation and, in 1993, has found the Indian government willing to allow Coke to reenter the Indian market on a joint venture basis without having to compromise its formulas.

GUIDE TO STRATEGIC MANAGEMENT CASE ANALYSIS

THE CASE METHOD

Case analysis is a proven educational method that is especially effective in a strategic management course. The case method complements and enhances the text material and your professor's lectures by focusing attention on what a firm has done or should do in an actual business situation. Use of the case method in the strategic management course offers you an opportunity to develop and refine analytical skills. It also can provide exciting experience by allowing you to assume the role of the key decision maker for the organizations you will study.

When assuming the role of the general manager of the organization being studied, you will need to consider all aspects of the business. In addition to drawing on your knowledge of marketing, finance, management, production, and economics, you will be applying the strategic management concepts taught in this course.

The cases in this book are accounts of real business situations involving a variety of firms in a variety of industries. To make these opportunities as realistic as possible, the cases include a variety of quantitative and qualitative information in both the presentation of the situation and the exhibits. As the key decision maker, you will need to determine which information is important, given the circumstances described in the case. Keep in mind that the results of analyzing one firm will not necessarily be appropriate for another since every firm is faced with a different set of circumstances.

PREPARING FOR CASE DISCUSSION

The case method requires an approach to class preparation that differs from the typical lecture course. In the typical lecture course, you can still benefit from each class session even if you did not prepare, by listening carefully to the professor's lecture. This approach will not work in a course using the case method. For such a case course, proper preparation is essential.

Suggestions for Effective Preparation

1. *Allow adequate time in preparing a case.* Many of the cases in this text involve complex issues that are often not apparent without careful reading and purposeful reflection on the information in the cases.

2. *Read each case twice.* Because many of these cases involve complex decision making, you should read each case at least twice. Your first reading should give you an overview of the firm's unique circumstances and the issues confronting the firm. Your second reading allows you to concentrate on what you feel are the most critical issues and to understand what information in the case is most important. Make limited notes identifying key points during your first reading. During your second reading, you can add details to your original notes and revise them as necessary.

This guide was developed by John A. Pearce II, Richard B. Robinson, Jr., and William R. Bayer.

3. *Focus on the key strategic issue in each case.* Each time you read a case you should concentrate on identifying the key issue. In some of the cases, the key issue will be identified by the case writer in the introduction. In other cases, you might not grasp the key strategic issue until you have read the case several times. (Remember that not every piece of information in a case is equally important.)

4. *Do not overlook exhibits.* The exhibits in these cases should be considered an integral part of the information for the case. They are not just "window dressing." In fact, for many cases you will need to analyze financial statements, evaluate organizational charts, and understand the firm's products, all of which are presented in the form of exhibits.

5. *Adopt the appropriate time frame.* It is critical that you assume the appropriate time frame for each case you read. If the case ends in 1985, that year should become the present for you as you work on that case. Making a decision for a case that ends in 1985 by using data you could not have had until 1986 defeats the purpose of the case method. For the same reason, although it is recommended that you do outside reading on each firm and industry, you should not read material written after the case ended unless your professor instructs you to do so.

6. *Draw on all of your knowledge of business.* As the key decision maker for the organization being studied, you will need to consider all aspects of the business and industry. Do not confine yourself to strategic management concepts presented in this course. You will need to determine if the key strategic issue revolves around a theory you have learned in a functional area, such as marketing, production, finance, or economics, or in the strategic management course.

PARTICIPATING IN CLASS

Because the strategic management course uses the case method, the success and value of the course depend on class discussion. The success and value of the class discussion, in turn, rely on the roles both you and your professor perform. Following are aspects of your role and your professor's, which, if kept in mind, will enhance the value and excitement of this course.

The Student as Active Learner

The case method requires your active participation. This means your role is no longer one of sitting and listening.

1. *Attend class regularly.* Not only is your grade likely to depend on your involvement in class discussions, but the benefit you derive from this course is directly related to your involvement in and understanding of the discussions.

2. *Be prepared for class.* The need for adequate preparation already has been discussed. You will benefit more from the discussions, will understand and participate in the exchange of ideas, and will avoid the embarrassment of being called on when not prepared. By all means, bring your book to class. Not only is there a good chance you will need to refer to a specific exhibit or passage from the case, you may need to refresh your memory of the case (particularly if you made notes in the margins while reading).

3. *Participate in the discussion.* Attending class and being prepared are not enough; you need to express your views in class. You can participate in a number of ways: by addressing a question asked by your professor, by disagreeing with your professor or your classmates (by all means, be tactful), by building on an idea expressed by a classmate, or by simply asking a relevant question.

4. *Participate wisely.* Although you do not want to be one of those students who never raises his or her hand, you also should be sensitive to the fact that others in your class will want to express themselves. You have probably already had experience with a student who attempts to dominate each class discussion. A student who invariably tries to dominate the class discussion breeds resentment.

5. *Keep a broad perspective.* By definition, the strategic management course deals with the issues facing general managers or business owners. As already mentioned, you need to consider all aspects of the business, not just one particular functional area.

6. *Pay attention to the topic being discussed.* Focus your attention on the topic being discussed. When a new topic is introduced, do not attempt to immediately introduce another topic for discussion. Do not feel you have to have something to say on every topic covered.

Your Professor as Discussion Leader

Your professor is a discussion leader. As such, he or she will attempt to stimulate the class as a whole to share insights, observations, and thoughts about the case. Your professor will not necessarily respond to every comment you or your classmates make. Part of the value of the case method is to get you and your classmates to assume this role as the course progresses.

The professor in a strategic management case course performs several roles:

1. *Maintaining focus.* Because multiple complex issues need to be explored, your professor may want to maintain the focus of the class discussion on one issue at a time. He or she may ask you to hold your comment on another issue until a previous issue is exhausted. Do not interpret this response to mean your point is unimportant; your professor is simply indicating there will be a more appropriate time to pursue that particular comment.

2. *Getting students involved.* Do not be surprised if your professor asks for input from volunteers and nonvolunteers alike. The value of the class discussion increases as more people share their comments.

3. *Facilitating comprehension of strategic management concepts.* Some professors prefer to lecture on strategic management concepts on a "need-to-know" basis. In this scenario, a lecture on a particular topic will be followed by an assignment to work on a case that deals with that particular topic. Other professors will have the class work through a case or two before lecturing on a topic to give the class a feel for the value of the topic being covered and for the type of information needed to work on cases. Still other professors prefer to cover all of the theory in the beginning of the course, thereby allowing uninterrupted case discussion in the remaining weeks of the term. All three of these approaches are valid.

4. *Playing devil's advocate.* At times your professor may appear to be contradicting many of the comments or observations being made. At other times your professor may adopt a position that does not immediately make sense, given the circumstances of the case. At other times your professor may seem to be equivocating. These are all examples of how your professor might be playing devil's advocate. Sometimes the professor's goal is to expose alternative viewpoints. Sometimes he or she may be testing your resolve on a particular point. Be prepared to support your position with evidence from the case.

ASSIGNMENTS

Written Assignments

Written analyses are a critical part of any strategic management course. In fact, professors typically put more weight on written analyses than on exams or quizzes. Each professor has a preferred format for these written analyses, but a number of general guidelines will prove helpful to you in your written assignments.

1. *Analyze.* Avoid merely repeating the facts presented in the case. Analyze the issues involved in the case and build logically toward your recommendations.

2. *Use headings or labels.*   Using headings or labels throughout your written analysis will help your reader follow your analysis and recommendations. For example, when you are analyzing the weaknesses of the firm in the case, include the heading Weaknesses. Note the headings in the sample case analysis that follows.

3. *Discuss alternatives.*   Follow the proper strategic management sequence by (1) identifying alternatives, (2) evaluating each alternative, and (3) recommending the alternative you think is best.

4. *Use topic sentences.*   You can help your reader more easily evaluate your analysis by putting the topic sentence first in each paragraph and following with statements directly supporting the topic sentence.

5. *Be specific in your recommendations.*   Develop specific recommendations logically and be sure your recommendations are well defended by your analysis. Avoid using generalizations, clichés, and ambiguous statements. Remember that any number of answers are possible, and so your professor is most concerned about how your reasoning led to your recommendations and how well you develop and support your ideas.

6. *Do not overlook implementation.*   Many good analyses receive poor evaluations because they do not include a discussion of implementation. Your analysis will be much stronger when you discuss how your recommendation can be implemented. Include some of the specific actions needed to achieve the objectives you are proposing.

7. *Specifically state your assumptions.*   Cases, like all real business situations, involve incomplete information. Therefore, it is important that you clearly state any assumptions you make in your analysis. Do not assume your professor will be able to fill in the missing points.

Oral Presentations

Your professor is also quite likely to ask you and your classmates to make oral presentations on a particular case. Oral presentations usually are done by groups of students. In these groups, each member will typically be responsible for one aspect of the overall case. Keep the following suggestions in mind when you are faced with an oral presentation:

1. *Use your own words.*   Avoid memorizing a presentation. The best approach is to prepare an outline of the key points you want to cover. Do not be afraid to have the outline in front of you during your presentation, but do not just read the outline.

2. *Rehearse your presentation.*   Do not assume you can simply read the outline you have prepared or that the right words will come to you when you are in front of the class making your presentation. Take the time to practice your speech, and be sure to rehearse the entire presentation with your group.

3. *Use visual aids.*   The adage "a picture is worth a thousand words" contains quite a bit of truth. The people in your audience will more quickly and thoroughly understand your key points—and will retain them longer—if you can use visual aids. Think of ways you and your team members can use the blackboard in the classroom; a graph, chart, or exhibit on a large posterboard; or, if you will have a number of these visual aids, a flip chart.

4. *Be prepared to handle questions.*   You probably will be asked questions by your classmates. If questions are asked during your presentation, try to address those that require clarification. Tactfully postpone more elaborate questions until you have completed the formal phase of your presentation. During your rehearsal, try to anticipate the types of questions that you might be asked.

Working as a Team Member

Many professors assign students to groups or teams for analyzing cases. This adds more realism to the course, since most strategic decisions in business are addressed by a group of key managers. If you are a member of a group assigned to analyze a case, keep in mind that your performance is tied to the performance of the other group members, and vice versa. The following are some suggestions to help you be an effective team member:

1. *Be sure the division of labor is equitable.* It is not always easy to decide how the workload can be divided equitably, since it is not always obvious how much work needs to be done. Try breaking down the case into the distinct parts that need to be analyzed to determine if having a different person assume responsibility for each part is equitable. All team members should read and analyze the entire case, but different team members can be assigned primary responsibility for each major aspect of the analysis. Each team member with primary responsibility for a major aspect of the analysis also will be the logical choice to write that portion of the written analysis or to present it orally in class.

2. *Communicate with other team members.* This is particularly important if you encounter problems with your portion of the analysis. Since, by definition, the team members are dependent on each other, it is critical that you communicate openly and honestly with each other. It, therefore, is essential that your team members discuss problems, such as some members not doing their fair share of work or members insisting that their point of view dominate the team's report.

3. *Work as a team.* Since a group's output should reflect a combined effort, the whole group should be involved in each part of the analysis, even if different individuals assume primary responsibility for different parts of the analysis. Avoid having the marketing major do the marketing portion of the analysis, the production major handle the production issues, and so forth. This will both hamper the group's aggregate analysis and do all of the team members a disservice by not giving each member exposure to decision making involving the other functional areas. The strategic management course provides an opportunity to look at all aspects of the business situation, to develop the ability to see the big picture, and to integrate the various functional areas.

4. *Plan and structure team meetings.* When working with a group on case analysis, it is impossible to achieve the team's goals and objectives without meeting outside of class. As soon as the team is formed, establish mutually convenient times for regular meetings, and be sure to keep this time available each week. Be punctual in going to the meetings, and manage the meetings so they end at a predetermined time. Plan several shorter meetings, as opposed to one longer session right before the case is due. (This, by the way, is another way realism is introduced in the strategic management course. Planning and managing your time is essential in business, and working with others to achieve a common set of goals is a critical part of life in the business world.)

SUMMARY

The strategic management course is your opportunity to assume the role of a key decision maker in a business organization. The case method is an excellent way to add excitement and realism to the course. To get the most out of the course and the case method, you need to be an active participant in the entire process.

The case method offers you the opportunity to develop your analytical skills and to understand the interrelationships of the various functional areas of business; it also enables you to develop valuable skills in time management, group problem solving, creativity, organization of thoughts and ideas, and human interaction. All of these skills will prove immensely valuable when you enter the job market and begin your career.

CASES

A STRATEGY FORMULATION

SOUTHWEST AIRLINES

1 Herb Kelleher is dancing in the airplane aisle. It's 8:30 A.M. and he is already bumming cigarettes, cavorting with flight attendants to the music of *Flash Dance*, and sipping a screwdriver. The plane lunges left, then right, as its pilot instructs passengers to sway with the movement. Welcome to the zany world of Southwest Airlines.[1]

2 As Southwest Airline's chief executive officer, Mr. Kelleher finds the image of a maverick very much to his liking. As he recalls, "If we hadn't been mavericks back in 1967 when we started doodling about an intrastate airline, air travel might still be out of reach for millions of people. Instead of using low-fare flights to reach business meetings a couple of hundred miles away in less than an hour, you might have found yourself driving four or five hours to the destination because air travel was too expensive. That's the impact that Southwest is proud to have made upon the airline industry."

3 In 1967, Roland King hired Herb Kelleher, an up-and-coming attorney in San Antonio, to assist in the dismantling of his small commuter air service. The two met one afternoon to discuss a new business venture—one that sounded like King's old business, but with a slight twist. Instead of flying to small towns, King envisioned service to the three largest cities in Texas, offering low fares, convenient schedules, and a no-frills approach quite different from the standards of established airlines. Using a bar napkin to further explain, he drew a triangle and labeled the corners: Dallas, Houston, and San Antonio. The young attorney questioned King's judgment, but after some homework decided that he, too, was willing to give it a try.

This case was prepared by Russell Teasley and Richard Robinson, University of South Carolina.

[1] *Dallas Morning News*, April 7, 1985.

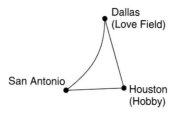

4   In November 1967, with $500,000 of newly acquired seed capital, Kelleher filed an application with Texas Aeronautics Commission (TAC), asking permission for the proposed airline to serve Dallas, Houston, and San Antonio. During that era, the aviation industry was highly regulated, and starting new airlines or adding routes required proof that such service was needed and that it would be used by the public. "Air Southwest" was granted approval on the merit of its request. However, Braniff, Trans Texas, and Continental quickly challenged TAC's approval and produced a restraining order that banned delivery of Southwest's operating certificate. The bitter legal battle that followed lasted three years. Southwest lost its appeal in local courts and in the State Court of Civil Appeal. Finally, Kelleher won a series of decisions in the Texas State Court that allowed Southwest to begin service with a fleet of three planes. Finally, on June 18, 1971, the first Southwest Air flight took off from Love Field in Dallas headed for Houston.

5   Southwest had won the first battle, but its legal ordeals were far from over. In 1972, the Dallas/Fort Worth Regional Airport Board sued Southwest, hoping to inhibit its operations at Love Field, Dallas's downtown airport. Southwest's fight to remain at Love Field lasted for five years, and the case finally was settled in its favor during January 1977. In a separate legal skirmish, Kelleher campaigned all the way to Washington to establish interstate traffic routes for the airline. Flights from its downtown airfield headquarters were restricted to intrastate flights. However, his aggressive actions resulted in the passing of federal legislation called the Wright Amendment, 1979, which authorized limited interstate service from Love Field to states adjacent to Texas. This granted Southwest interstate routing but limited it to direct destinations no further than one state away.

6   Ironically, these legal ramifications reinforced some key components of Southwest's competitive strategy. For example, in 1973, the battle to keep Love Field drained Southwest (financially) and forced it to sell one of its four operating jets. Management, however, figured the company could still maintain its same routes with three planes and stay on schedule if the aircraft's turnaround ground times were limited to 10 minutes. Competitors were amazed as they watched Southwest's ground crews service and turn around jets in less than 10 minutes. Rapid turnarounds remain a key part of Southwest's low-cost strategy because of the associated efficiency and low-cost operations.

7   Stemming from its determination to remain at the downtown Dallas field, Southwest earned the critical advantage of convenience for Dallas-bound or departing business people. It continues to utilize downtown airports wherever possible. Although the Wright Amendment restricted Southwest's capacity to compete as an interstate airline, it also forced the company to concentrate on short-haul service: frequent and direct flights. This short-haul strategy is now another key component of Southwest's competitive strategy everywhere that it flies.

8   The 1970s witnessed numerous events that set lasting directions for Southwest's future. In 1973, after only two years of operation, the company experienced its first profitable year. Its common stock was listed on the American Stock Exchange in October 1975, with the ticker symbol "LUV," and the company completed that year with a record load, exceeding 1.1 million passengers. Between 1975 and 1977, the "LUV Line" expanded its web of intrastate service with new destinations to Harligan, Corpus Christi, Austin, Midland Odessa, Lubbock, and El Paso. In 1978, Lamar Muse resigned as CEO, and Herb Kelleher quickly evolved as the new CEO. In the same year, deregulation restructured the U.S. airlines industry, and shortly thereafter Southwest opened its first interstate service to New Orleans, Louisiana.

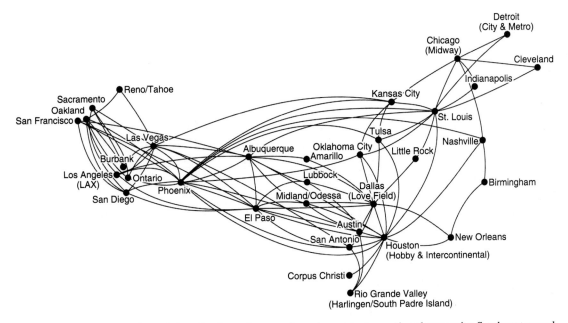

9   Since deregulation, Southwest has experienced consistent growth and prosperity. Southwest served cities in 15 of the United States, extending from Cleveland, Ohio, to San Francisco, California, by early 1992. It was the seventh largest U.S. carrier, with reported earnings in 1991 of $1.31 billion and 2.6 percent of the nation's air travel market. The company has substantially increased traffic in every route it has opened, and it has spawned economic growth in every downtown airport it has served (estimates credit Hobby Field's reopening with annual benefits of over $1.9 billion to the Houston area economy). In 1992, the U.S. airline industry was decimated by nearly three years of steep losses and was operating with about $7.5 billion of industry red ink. Southwest, however, continued to remain profitable, as it has for all but the first 2 of its 21 operating years. Within the industry, the company has experienced unprecedented success. Exhibit 1 provides a 10-year summary of Southwest's financial and operating accomplishments.

STRATEGY

10   Southwest consistently has favored a low-cost focus strategy since its first flight. The airline is the industry's standard of cheap air travel, typically offering the lowest fares on any of its routes and forcing cheaper rates from competitors whenever it enters a new territory. Believing there was price elasticity in the airline industry, its management felt there were a lot of people who wanted to fly but couldn't because ticket costs were too high. In response, the airline has managed to offer fares averaging only 60–70 percent of those charged by other carriers on similar routes. It has maintained the low-cost strategy and has targeted travelers desiring convenient high-frequency travel between relatively close cities. According to Kelleher, "You can innovate by not doing anything (new) if it's a conscious decision. When other airlines set up hub-and-spoke systems, we continued what we had always been doing. As a consequence, we wound up with a unique market niche: we are the world's only short-haul, high frequency, point-to-point carrier. Everything about the airline has been adapted to serving that market segment in the most efficient and economical way possible."

11   To support low costs, an airline must operate with peak efficiency. From Southwest's point of view, this means keeping its fleet in the air working, rather than spending time on the ground. To shorten

EXHIBIT 1
Southwest Airlines Company 10-Year Summary
Selected Consolidated Financial Data (in thousands except per share amounts)

	1991	1990	1989
Operating revenues:			
Passenger	$1,267,897	$1,144,421	$ 973,568
Freight	26,428	22,196	18,771
Other	19,280	20,142	22,713
Total operating revenues	1,313,605	1,186,759	1,015,052
Operating expenses (see Exhibit 2)	1,250,669	1,104,880	917,426
Operating income	62,936	81,879	97,626
Other expense (income), net	19,096	7,126[1]	(13,356)[2]
Income before income taxes	43,840	74,753	110,982
Provision for income taxes	16,921	27,670	39,424
Net income	$ 26,919	$ 47,083	$ 71,558
Net income per common and common equivalent share	$0.63	$1.10	$1.58
Cash dividends per common share	$ 0.1000	$ 0.0967	$ 0.0933
Total assets (see Exhibit 2)	$1,837,291	$1,471,138	$1,415,096
Long-term debt (see Exhibit 2)	$ 617,016	$ 326,956	$ 354,147
Stockholders' equity (see Exhibit 2)	$ 628,521	$ 604,851	$ 587,316
Consolidated Financial Ratios			
Return on average total assets	1.6%	3.3%	5.2%
Return on average stockholders' equity	4.4%	7.9%	12.4%
Debt as a percentage of invested capital	49.5%	35.1%	37.6%

total trip time and maximize each plane's air time, Southwest maintains the industry's fastest on-ground turnaround (unloading, reboarding, and departing the gate) times, sometimes as short as eight and a half minutes. This enables the airline to offer more flights with fewer planes. Not only is its aircraft fleet the youngest and most fuel-efficient in the industry, the fleet is also standardized (utilizing only two types of airplanes), permitting efficiencies in maintenance, training, and spares. Furthermore, Southwest's employees are highly motivated and efficient, creating cost savings both in air and on ground. Selected Southwest operating statistics for 1982–1991 are summarized in Exhibit 1.

12   Southwest steadily has maintained the lowest cost structure in the industry. For example, in 1989, Southwest limited its expenses to only 6.8 cents per available seat mile, compared with an industry average of 10 cents. Its low-cost structure translates directly into affordable ticket prices and makes the airline a brutal fare war opponent for other airlines. In 1988, Southwest endured $19 flights from Phoenix to Los Angeles as part of a long-standing price war with American West Airlines and eventually drove American West out of this route. During that period it maintained rock-bottom prices on all its other routes as well (round-trip tickets between Houston and Dallas, at that time, were a mere $38). Southwest's operating expenses for 1987–1991 are summarized in Exhibit 2. A comprehensive sampling of industrywide operating statistics are included in Exhibit 3.

EXHIBIT 1 (continued)

1988	1987	1986	1985[7]	1984	1983	1982
$ 828,343	$ 751,649	$ 742,287	$ 656,689	$519,106	$433,388	$317,996
14,433	13,428	13,621	13,643	12,115	10,357	9,469
17,658	13,251	12,882	9,340	4,727	4,491	3,724
860,434	778,328	768,790	679,672	535,948	448,236	331,189
774,454	747,881	679,827	601,148	467,451	379,738	291,964
85,980	30,447[4]	88,963	78,524	68,497	68,498	39,225
620[3]	1,374[5]	23,517[6]	17,740	649	4,927	(5,165)[8]
85,360	29,073	65,446	60,784	67,848	63,571	44,390
27,408	8,918	15,411	13,506	18,124	22,704	10,386
$ 57,952	$ 20,155	$ 50,035	$ 47,278	$ 49,724	$ 40,867	$ 34,004
$1.23	$0.42	$1.03	$1.03	$1.13	$0.93	$0.85
$ 0.0883	$0.0867	$0.0867	$0.0867	$0.0867	$0.0867	$0.0867
$1,308,389	$1,042,640	$1,061,419	$1,002,403	$646,244	$587,258	$420,542
$ 369,541	$ 251,130	$ 339,069	$ 381,308	$153,314	$158,701	$106,306
$ 567,375	$ 514,278	$ 511,850	$ 466,004	$361,768	$314,556	$240,627
5.1%	1.9%	4.8%	5.6%	8.1%	8.1%	9.6%
10.8%	4.0%	10.3%	11.4%	14.7%	14.2%	16.7%
39.4%	32.8%	39.8%	45%	29.8%	33.5%	30.6%

13   Although Southwest's service is distinctly low-cost, it caters to a distinct market niche. It is a "no-frills" short-haul carrier that does not serve meals on most of its flights, contending that its customers prefer the low fares to typical airline cuisine. Southwest does not arrange connections with other airlines, and passengers must transport their own baggage to recheck them onto connecting airlines. Reserved seating is nonexistent at Southwest, because passengers are seated in the order of their ticket purchases, which are executed at the flight gates. During its early years, Southwest did not use travel agents or a massive (usually leased) reservation system to book its flights.[2] In Southwest's view, computerized reservations systems run up tremendous overhead, and it eliminates premium seating well before departure time. Reserved seating also slows down airplanes during loading, increasing their precious turnaround times.

14   The airline is a "short-haul" carrier, capitalizing on direct routes between major metropolitan areas, with an average flight time of 55 minutes. The short-haul concept, combined with low cost

---

[2] Travel agents typically receive a 10 percent "commission" from airlines for tickets purchased through them. Southwest now uses travel agents, but sill handles all reservations "in house" rather than subscribe to expensive outside reservation systems.

EXHIBIT 1   (continued)

	1991	1990	1989
Consolidated Operating Statistics			
Revenue passengers carried	22,669,942	19,830,941	17,958,263
RPMs (000s)[9]	11,296,183	9,958,940	9,281,992
AMSs (000s)[10]	18,491,003	16,411,115	14,796,732
Load factor	61.1%	60.7%	62.7%
Average length of passenger haul	498	502	517
Trips flown	382,752	338,108	304,673
Average passenger fare	$55.93	$57.71	$54.21
Passenger revenue per RPM	11.22¢	11.49¢	10.49¢
Operating revenue per ASM	7.10¢	7.23¢	6.86¢
Operating expenses per ASM	6.76¢	6.73¢	6.20¢
Fuel cost per gallon (average)	65.69¢	77.89¢	59.46¢
Number of employees at yearend	9,778	8,620	7,760
Size of fleet at yearend[11]	124	106	94
Aircraft utilization[12]	10:48	11:03	10:50

[1] Includes $2.6 million gains on sales of aircraft and $3.1 million from the sale of certain financial assets.

[2] Includes $10.8 million gains on sales of aircraft, $5.9 million from the sale of certain financial assets, and $2.3 million from the settlement of a contingency.

[3] Includes $5.6 million gains on sales of aircraft and $3.6 million from the sale of certain financial assets.

[4] Includes TranStar's results through June 30, 1987.

[5] Includes $10.1 million net gains from the discontinuance of TranStar's operations and $4.3 million from the sale of certain financial assets.

[6] Includes a gain of $4 million from the sale of aircraft delivery positions.

[7] Includes the accounts of TranStar since June 30, 1985.

[8] Includes a gain from the sale of tax benefits relating to three aircraft of $11 million.

[9] Revenue passenger miles.

[10] Available seat miles.

[11] Includes leased aircraft: 33 subject to long-term leases and 23 subject to short-term leases expiring over the next one to three years.

[12] Average hours and minutes per plane per day.

and convenience, was intended to put Southwest's service in direct competition with the automobile as a viable means of transportation. If one can fly between two points in less time and for less expense than driving an automobile, then that person is very likely to leave the car in the garage. In conjunction with the short-haul concept, Southwest's service pattern is point-to-point, as opposed to the hub-and-spoke patterns incorporated by most major carriers. Its goal is to fly people directly to where they want to go, rather than through hubs, and to do so in less time and with less cost than possible in an automobile.

15   Another Southwest feature is the high frequency of flights between any two points. Believing that frequency equates customer convenience, the company lets people fly when they want to fly and not when an airline wants them to fly. For example, Southwest provides the Dallas–Houston route with over 80 flights per day, making it the most heavily served market in the world by any single carrier.

EXHIBIT 1 (concluded)

1988	1987	1986	1985[7]	1984	1983	1982
14,876,582	13,503,242	13,637,515	12,651,239	10,697,544	9,511,000	7,965,554
7,676,257	7,789,376	7,388,401	5,971,400	4,669,435	3,893,821	3,022,142
13,309,044	13,331,055	12,574,484	9,884,526	7,983,093	6,324,224	4,907,945
57.7%	58.4%	58.8%	60.4%	58.5%	61.6%	61.6%
516	577	542	472	436	409	379
274,859	270,559	262,082	230,227	200,124	175,421	140,030
$55.68	$55.66	$54.43	$51.91	$48.53	$45.57	$39.92
10.79¢	9.65¢	10.05¢	11.00¢	11.12¢	11.13¢	10.52¢
6.47¢	5.84¢	6.11¢	6.88¢	6.71¢	7.09¢	6.75¢
5.82¢	5.61¢	5.41¢	6.08¢	5.86¢	6.00¢	5.95¢
51.37¢	54.31¢	51.42¢	78.17¢	82.44¢	85.92¢	94.51¢
6,467	5,765	5,819	5,271	3,934	3,462	2.913
85	75	79	70	54	46	37
10:47	10:59	11:06	11:13	11:28	—	—

The result, Kelleher claims, is that Southwest tends to breed air traffic, with traffic typically doubling on any route within 12 months after his airline begins its service there. The airline's frequent-flyer program is clearly structured to reward travelers for the number of flights they take, rather than their accumulated mileage.

16 Southwest hopes businesspeople will equate their routes with the convenience afforded by a corporate-owned aircraft. According to Kelleher, "You want to leave early—we'll have a flight to get you there at noon. You get through early—we'll have an early flight back. Your meeting runs late— we'll have a late flight back and you can still get home when you're finished." Although this type of scheduling gives Southwest the highest no-show rate of any airline in the nation, management is not particularly worried about it nor finds it detrimental to the bottom line.

17 To provide additional convenience, Southwest constantly battles tardy departures and strives for a goal of 90 percent on-time schedules. When Kelleher noticed departing passengers dawdling at the airplane's forward closets, he promptly had the forward closets removed from all Southwest's planes. The airline has maintained such high scheduling standards that Department of Transportation statistics have frequently recognized the airline as best in the industry for average on-time performance. It also has consistently maintained an over 99 percent average of flight completion performance (flights that actually arrive at their scheduled destinations). Southwest's unprecedented reputation for fast airport turnarounds is built on the performance typified in Exhibit 4.

18 To compete with automobiles, Southwest realizes that it's not just time in the air that people consider, it's the time it takes to get to the airport, to park the car, and actually to get on the airplane. To further reduce this total travel time, the company serves close-in municipal airports wherever possible. Smaller municipal terminals mean shorter drives to the airport, shorter walks from the parking lot to the ticket counter, and fewer marathon runs to the departure gate. Southwest incorporates quick-ticketing procedures, utilizing cash registers and vending machines, which help reduce ticket purchases to as little as ten seconds. The tickets themselves resemble sales receipt slips, rather than

EXHIBIT 2
Five-Year Consolidated Statement of Expenses (in thousands except per share amounts)

	Years Ended December 31				
	1991	1990	1989	1988	1987
Operating expenses:					
Salaries, wages, and benefits	$ 407,961	$ 357,357	$301,066	$255,046	$222,461
Fuel and oil	225,463	242,001	168,579	130,321	140,334
Maintenance materials and repairs	97,598	82,887	75,842	54,208	59,469
Agency commissions	81,245	72,084	61,362	53,063	47,444
Aircraft rentals	49,171	26,085	21,636	22,629	22,001
Landing fees and other rentals	83,177	61,167	51,902	40,441	38,860
Depreciation	86,202	79,429	72,343	66,169	65,484
Other operating expenses	219,852	183,870	164,696	152,577	151,828
Total operating expenses	1,250,669	1,104,880	917,426	774,454	747,881
Operating income	62,936	81,879	97,626	85,980	30,447
Other expenses (income):					
Interest expense	43,939	32,001	33,496	29,209	30,682
Capitalized interest	(15,301)	(13,738)	(10,227)	(9,279)	(8,066)
Interest income	(10,631)	(7,595)	(16,637)	(10,970)	(7,028)
Net gains on disposals of TranStar assets less provision for operating losses during shut-down period	—	—	—	—	(10,181)
Nonoperating losses (gains), net	1,089	(3,542)	(19,988)	(8,340)	(4,033)
Total other expenses (income)	19,096	7,126	(13,356)	620	1,374

the higher-cost folders used by other airlines. To insure speedy baggage handling, Southwest has adopted the standard to deliver baggage from aircraft to baggage claim areas within eight minutes.

19   Southwest's management team retains an offensive, competitive posture. They search out markets that are overpriced and underserved, then move in with considerable force. For example, on its top 75 routes, Southwest has captured more than 50 percent of the traffic, while the next carrier averages only 10 percent. "We attack a city with a lot of lights, which is another form of aggression in the airlines industry," states Kelleher, "We won't go in with just one or two flights. We'll go in with 10 or 12. That eats up a lot of airplane capacity, so you can't open a lot of cities. Call it guerrilla warfare against bigger opponents. You hit them with everything you've got in one or two places instead of trying to fight them everywhere."

20   Southwest's management meets competitive and environmental threats head-on, sometimes engaging in court battles and price wars to secure its position. Southwest more than once has faced losing its access to downtown airfields because of excessive noise pollution. Its most serious standoff was in Dallas, where an influential community group was determined to end its in-town service. Kelleher did not hesitate to confront complainants, in court, with the massive economic benefits accruing from his transportation activities at Love Field. His arguments convinced the jury and his airline was allowed to continue its Love Field service. While fare wars frequently have besieged the airline industry, Southwest's low-cost structure, profitability, and aggressive posture have allowed it to consistently outlast and outmaneuver its opponents.

EXHIBIT 3

Domestic operating statistics of the major U.S. airlines

Year	American	America-West	Continental	Delta	Eastern	Northwest	Pan-American	South-west	Trans World	United	USAir	Total all majors
Seat-miles flown (millions)												
1991	104,616	19,460	48,742	94,350	...	48,847	9,042	18,440	29,684	88,092	56,470	518,911
1990	102,864	18,139	48,385	87,748	25,299	47,210	12,157	16,456	33,942	86,085	58,014	536,300
1989	98,638	13,523	47,107	82,440	15,489	44,372	11,670	14,788	35,246	82,758	40,652	500,772
1988	88,620	11,994	53,343	79,719	41,126	39,349	10,331	13,370	35,024	84,240	28,234	506,691
1987	77,724	10,318	54,626	71,504	50,156	41,499	8,217	11,457	33,566	86,246	20,014	488,549
Revenue passenger-miles flown (millions)												
1991	63,667	12,637	30,122	56,566	...	30,724	5,473	11,274	18,090	56,579	32,880	318,624
1990	63,242	11,063	28,266	50,879	15,380	29,522	7,294	9,972	19,990	54,968	34,542	325,119
1989	62,767	7,802	28,427	52,392	9,589	27,015	7,146	9,279	20,943	54,149	24,878	312,626
1988	55,928	6,950	31,386	45,899	25,418	24,303	6,553	7,711	20,987	56,532	17,315	310,562
1987	49,497	5,786	33,179	39,672	32,773	25,653	5,265	6,750	20,805	56,032	13,072	301,092
Revenue passengers carried (millions)												
1991	67.31	16.78	31.62	70.52	...	35.28	5.32	25.21	17.80	55.61	55.05	381.28
1990	66.38	15.57	30.10	62.67	20.59	35.11	7.43	22.06	20.20	52.56	59.52	382.19
1989	67.04	13.30	30.18	65.40	13.07	33.63	7.73	20.24	21.10	51.19	44.35	383.73
1988	60.10	12.65	33.57	57.70	32.47	31.51	6.78	16.84	21.34	53.28	32.47	385.62
1987	52.13	11.23	37.29	52.70	41.27	33.53	5.51	14.21	21.45	52.74	24.77	374.63
Revenue per passenger-mile (cents)												
+1991	12.93	10.25	11.72	13.75	...	12.78	13.60	10.82	11.48	12.21	16.90	13.10
1990	12.86	11.14	12.48	14.21	11.66	13.24	11.65	11.48	12.34	12.71	16.37	13.20
1989	12.27	11.84	12.04	13.91	11.71	13.02	11.98	10.49	12.10	12.18	15.83	12.93
1988	11.92	10.52	10.61	13.52	12.00	12.54	10.94	10.74	11.47	10.86	15.33	12.23
1987	11.06	9.66	9.34	13.10	11.02	11.73	9.97	10.02	11.02	10.10	14.91	11.35
Passenger load factor (percent)												
1991	60.86	64.94	61.80	59.95	...	62.90	60.53	61.14	60.94	64.23	58.22	61.40
1990	61.48	60.99	58.42	57.98	60.79	62.53	60.00	60.60	58.90	63.85	59.54	60.62
1989	63.63	57.69	60.34	63.55	61.91	60.88	61.24	62.75	59.42	65.43	61.20	62.43
1988	63.11	57.94	58.84	57.58	61.81	61.76	63.43	57.68	59.92	67.11	61.33	61.29
1987	63.68	56.07	60.74	55.48	65.34	61.82	64.08	58.92	61.98	64.97	65.31	61.63
Passenger revenues (mil.$)												
+1991	8,231	1,295	3,531	7,780	457	3,925	744	1,220	2,077	6,907	5,558	41,726
1990	8,130	1,232	3,529	7,228	1,793	3,909	850	1,144	2,466	6,986	5,655	42,923
1989	7,702	923	3,422	7,285	1,123	3,516	856	974	2,533	6,593	3,937	40,410
1988	6,669	731	3,330	6,205	3,049	3,049	717	828	2,406	6,137	2,654	37,983
1987	5,476	559	3,100	5,198	3,612	3,009	525	676	2,292	5,662	1,949	34,161
Operating revenues (mil.$)												
+1991	9,309	1,394	4,031	8,268	522	4,330	818	1,264	2,494	7,850	5,878	51,941
1990	9,203	1,322	4,036	7,697	2,022	4,298	946	1,187	2,878	7,946	5,960	53,332
1989	8,670	998	3,896	7,780	1,295	3,944	957	1,015	2,918	7,463	4,160	49,669
1988	7,548	781	3,682	6,684	3,423	3,395	804	860	2,777	7,006	2,803	46,432
1987	6,369	577	3,404	5,638	4,054	3,328	625	699	2,668	6,500	2,070	41,884
Operating expenses (mil.$)												
+1991	8,642	1,496	4,428	8,549	700	4,378	1,116	1,228	2,777	8,209	6,439	52,057
1990	9,100	1,353	4,227	7,873	2,524	4,430	1,226	1,105	3,012	7,980	6,522	54,212
1989	7,962	950	3,772	7,103	1,961	3,886	1,074	918	2,908	7,161	4,400	47,927
1988	6,753	763	3,769	6,243	3,610	3,376	986	774	2,665	6,545	2,659	44,046
1987	5,886	612	3,459	5,255	3,988	3,256	885	657	2,589	6,403	1,807	40,175
Operating margins (Operating revenues/expenses)												
+1991	107.73	93.13	91.03	96.72	...	98.89	73.29	102.94	89.81	95.62	91.29	99.78
1990	101.13	97.66	95.49	97.76	80.09	97.02	77.16	107.38	95.54	99.58	91.38	98.38
1989	108.90	105.06	103.28	109.54	66.04	101.47	89.05	110.63	100.34	104.22	94.56	103.64
1988	111.76	102.38	97.70	107.06	94.82	100.55	81.60	111.12	104.23	107.04	105.40	105.42
1987	108.20	94.22	98.39	107.29	101.66	102.22	70.66	106.28	103.06	101.51	114.58	104.25
Net operating income (mil.$)												
+1991	668	-103	-397	-281	...	-49	-298	36	-283	-359	-561	-116
1990	103	-32	-191	-176	-503	-132	-280	82	-134	-34	-562	-880
1989	709	48	124	677	-666	57	-118	98	10	302	-239	1,742
1988	794	18	-87	441	-187	19	-181	86	113	461	144	2,387
1987	483	-35	-56	383	66	72	-260	41	79	97	263	1,709
Net income (mil.$)												
+1991	-252.54	-205.76	-1,550.43	-215.95	-701.03	10.27	-301.85	13.50	-86.33	-175.25	-488.59	-3,510.90
1990	-39.68	-76.70	-1,217.69	-118.97	-1,313.79	-27.22	-346.83	47.08	-220.65	72.88	-410.27	-3,182.72
1989	412.29	12.80	-55.82	466.89	-681.14	115.90	-143.41	71.39	-178.96	245.64	-145.13	493.21
1988	450.31	-12.25	-309.79	285.84	-290.08	48.47	-188.85	57.40	116.24	425.92	76.17	1,015.74
1987	224.74	-45.68	-304.22	201.27	-143.09	63.57	-287.74	19.69	-3.91	21.62	164.11	150.35

+Twelve months ending September. *Includes data for cargo carriers, and is adjusted to include airlines newly qualifying as Majors.
Source: Department of Transportation.

EXHIBIT 4
Anatomy of a 15-Minute Turnaround

7:55	Ground crew chat around gate position.
8:03:30	Ground crew alerted, move to their vehicles.
8:04	Plane begins to pull into gate; crew moves toward plane.
8:04:30	Plane stops; jetway telescopes out; baggage door opens.
8:06:30	Baggage unloaded; refueling and other servicing underway.
8:07	Passengers off plane.
8:08	Boarding call; baggage loading, refueling complete.
8:10	Boarding complete; most of ground crew leaves.
8:15	Jetway retracts.
8:15:30	Pushback from gate.
8:18	Push-back tractor disengages; plane leaves for runway.

On a recent weekday a Southwest Airlines flight arrived at New Orleans from Houston. The scheduled arrival time was 8:00 A.M., and departure for Birmingham, Alabama, was 8:15 A.M. *Forbes* clocked the turnaround, half-minute by half-minute.

Source: "Hit 'em Hardest with the Mostest," *Forbes*, September 16, 1991.

PROMOTIONS

21   Southwest promotions have employed a variety of creative approaches to attract passengers. The company initiated its first garish marketing campaign in 1971. Southwest was billed as "Love" airlines, flying from Love Field, serving "love potions" (drinks), "love bites" (peanuts), and hiring "lovely" stewardesses. Thinly clad in hot pants and Southwest colors, stewardesses frequently were pictured in the public press, including the cover of *Esquire* and of a Budapest newspaper. The love campaign emphasized Southwest as a fun and caring alternative for regional flyers. "If it hadn't been for the power of that campaign," reflects Kelleher, "it's possible that Southwest might not have survived its early years."

22   Another promotion was the direct response to an aggressive 1973 price war waged against Southwest. To compete head-on in Southwest's primary market, Braniff discounted its Dallas–Houston fare to $13, which was exactly one half Southwest's normal $26 fare. Southwest retaliated by running the advertisement, "We're not going to lose you for a lousy $13, so you can fly Southwest for $13, too." But Southwest also offered an alternative: "Or, pay $26 and we'll give you a free bottle of Smirnoff vodka, Canadian whiskey, or Wild Turkey bourbon." For about two months, claimed Kelleher, Southwest was one of the biggest liquor distributors in the state of Texas. Forty-five percent of the people flying that route purchased tickets on company accounts and were thrilled to have their company cover the flight cost while taking home free bottles of whiskey. Before closing the campaign, Southwest offered ice buckets as well. Braniff's calculated assault backfired as a result of Southwest's promotion.

23   Other promotions have included "West Fly One, Get One," in which customers flying to any western city on certain days were awarded round-trip tickets to any Southwest destination. The "Sweetheart Pass" awarded free companion trips for any travelers flying three round-trip flights between November 1989 and Valentine's Day 1990. Southwest's frequent-flyer club offers a variety of bonus awards, including free round trips for every eight round trips flown in one year, and, for every 50 round trips flown in a year, a pass is awarded allowing companions to fly free for a year.

24   Some promotions have approached the realm of outrageous. For example, Southwest celebrated its status as official airlines of the Texas and California Sea Worlds by painting three of its Boeing 737s in the distinctive black-and-white markings of Shamu, Sea World's killer whale. Another of its aircraft is painted as an unfurling Texas flag. A 30-second television ad retorted to America West Airline's charge that Southwest passengers were embarrassed to fly on its no-frills flights with "plain" planes. Kelleher appeared on the ad with a brown paper bag over his head as the "Unknown Flyer." His comment: "If you are embarrassed to fly the airline with the fewest customer complaints in the country and with the most convenient schedules to the cities it serves, Southwest will give you this bag." He then lifts the bag from his head and offers it to anyone flying Southwest so they can "hold all the money you'll save by flying with us." The final scene shows Kelleher in a shower of money, grinning at the camera.

CULTURE/KELLEHER

25   Corporate culture at Southwest and the persona of Herb Kelleher are closely intertwined. When asked what was his favorite hobby, Kelleher replied, "My hobby is Southwest Airlines; it really is. There is a lot of talk about stress; but if your vocation is also your avocation, then none of those things apply. I'd much rather spend an evening sitting around talking to some of our people [Southwest's people] than making a trip to Paris." The airline literally epitomizes Kelleher's personality: his irreverence, his spontaneity, his zaniness, his depthless energy, and, most of all, his competitiveness. The airline he helped found and now runs is a direct extension of that personality—Kelleher himself even stars in the company's offbeat commercials.

26   Three themes underlie Southwest's culture: love, fun, and efficiency. Kelleher regards the over 9,000 employees of Southwest as his "lovely and loving family." This feeling is sanctioned among all employees and is especially encouraged in relationships with Southwest customers. For example, a Dallas flight attendant received a company award for befriending Kisha, an 18-month-old customer on route from Amarillo to Dallas for a kidney transplant. During Kisha's hospitalization, Burgess, the flight attendant, ran errands for Kisha's parents, including washing and ironing their clothes. Kelleher beamed while presenting Burgess the award as he described how she had hired a sitter to care for her two children so she could help Kisha.

27   To support a "loving, family" culture, Kelleher knows as many employees by name as possible, and he insists that they refer to him as "Herb" or "Herbie." Herb tells people, at the company's weekly Friday afternoon barbecue, "We've got as many as six members of the family working for us. Why, some of our employees have been married to one employee, divorced, and married to two, maybe three others." Employees respond to this warmth with loyalty and dedication. When fuel costs skyrocketed during Iraq's invasion of Kuwait, employees initiated a "Fuel from the Heart" program. As participants, about a third of the 8,600 employees took voluntary deductions from their pay checks to buy aviation fuel for the airline. Kelleher has successfully used his personality to charm workers, earn their trust, and breed leaders throughout the entire organization.

28   When decorating the new corporate headquarters in Dallas, management declined fancy corporate art for company and employee photographs, print ads, and mannequins dressed in the Southwest uniforms donned over the years. Most of the photographs were from company parties and award ceremonies. The memorabilia is displayed so that a walk through the building displays a 20-year history of the Southwest "family."

29   Community service is part of the company's employee motivation program, because management perceives it to foster a sense of camaraderie. Employees participate in various community service projects, which include cooking dinner once a month at a local Ronald McDonald house, volunteering for Junior Olympics events, and hosting a day at the Muscular Dystrophy Camp. The company is recognized at these events and participant photos are printed in the company newsletter.

30   Southwest continually encourages its employees to have fun while working at Southwest Air. Kelleher, a frequent Elvis and Roy Orbison impersonator, wants employees to have a meaningful experience at work. At one company picnic before 4,000 workers, he wore a dress, bonnet, and bloomers while singing "Tea for Two" in a duet with his vice president of ground operations. Such behavior is not unusual. The "Southwest Experience" has included flight attendants wearing anything from baggy shorts and wild-print shirts to reindeer or Easter bunny outfits. Safety instructions have been announced in rap, Christmas carols sung over the PA system, and the wrong time announced on purpose. One might have heard the captain announce, "As soon as y'all set both cheeks on your seat, we can get this old bird moving."

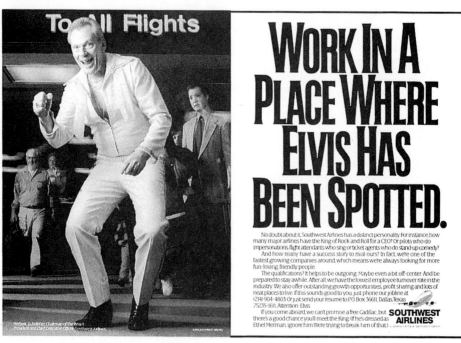

Source: 1990 annual report, Southwest Airlines.

31   The philosophy behind this fun focus is that humor rubs off on people. If people are having a good time, they will be back, or want to stay, whether they are customer or employee. In either case, value is created for the airline. As described by the boss, Uncle Herb, "A lot of people think you're not really serious about your business unless you act serious. At Southwest, we understand that it's not necessary to be uptight in order to do something well. We call it professionalism worn lightly. Fun is a stimulant to people. They enjoy their work more and work more productively." For the customer, he says, "What's important is that a customer should get off the plane feeling good: 'I didn't just get from A to B. I had one of the most pleasant experiences I ever had and I'll be back for that reason.'"

32   Southwest runs company contests simply for the fun of it, and prizes might include cash or travel passes. Typical contests are a Halloween costume contest, a Thanksgiving poem contest, or a design contest for the newsletter cover. Each year the company parking lot is converted to an annual chili cook-off celebration. All these factors create an unusual, enjoyable, yet highly productive culture at the airlines.

33   "Management by fooling around" is the principle adopted by Kelleher to run his airline. For him, that might mean doing a rap video promoting the airline, or it might mean working hands-on with mechanics, baggage handlers, and ticket agents at Love Field, most of whom he knows by name. Or it might mean his wearing jungle-print pajamas or a leprechaun suit on business flights to Houston, and commenting on his employees, "I love their irreverence." Beyond his own commitment to fooling around, he requires that every quarter, every Southwest manager take at least one day to work at some other job—as a gate agent, baggage handler, flight attendant, or even janitor.

34   Every month Kelleher personally hands out "Winning Spirit" awards to employees selected by fellow workers for exemplary performance. For example, one employee was awarded two free airline tickets and a boss's bear hug for returning to a customer a lost purse that contained $800 and several credit cards. This philosophy supports the value that management places on individuality among its workers at all levels of the company. According to Kelleher, individuality produces leadership.

35   To stay in touch with customers, Kelleher and his vice president for administration, Colleen Barret, personally read as many as two hundred letters a week from customers. Kelleher and most employees make it regular practice to interact with customers throughout their exposure to Southwest.

HUMAN RESOURCE MANAGEMENT

36   Underlying Southwest's operational capabilities is an employee relations philosophy aimed at closely linking each employee with the company's short- and long-term goals. Its management feels that mission-oriented employees are more productive. Employees are asked to put out more effort in return for higher pay, yet their efforts go beyond a straight work-harder-for-more-money arrangement. Their efficiency and commitment allow Southwest to hold down overall costs while paying higher wages. Top management devotes a large part of its time to fostering productive attitudes among employees and to emphasizing direct contact between management and employees. "The front office is there to support the troops, not vice versa," says Kelleher. "We want to know what they need and then supply it."

37   Southwest's primary employee benefit is its profit-sharing plan, which, as of 1991, contained about $121 million. Employees collect from this fund only when they leave the company. A stock-option plan allows employees to acquire stock at 90 percent of market value via payroll deductions. Other perks include unlimited space-available travel for employees and their families, a flexible health benefit plan, and a 401(k) retirement plan.

38   When a poorly performing year besieged Southwest, the first people to reflect the losses were its corporate officers. "If there's going to be a downside, you should share it," reflects Kelleher. "When we were experiencing hard times [unprofitable year], I went to the board and told them I wanted to cut my salary. I cut all officers' bonuses 10 percent, mine 20 percent." Other employees are moved by such initiatives. When asked about the high productivity of his employees (analysts consider them the most productive in the industry, enabling the airline to minimize its costs), Kelleher replied, "They are that way, because they know we aren't trying to milk them for the bottom line."

39   Southwest looks for special people to staff its vacant positions. "We draft great attitudes," according to Kelleher. "If you don't have a good attitude, we don't want you no matter how skilled you are. We can change skill levels through training. We can't change attitudes. We are fanatics about hiring the right people. We want to give them the latitude to be individuals on their job. We want them to be good-natured and have a good-humored approach to life and to have fun doing their job." In an effort to match employee personalities to those of its customers, Southwest invites its most-frequent flyers to both interview and participate in the screening of potential new employees.

40   Unlike many of the airlines created under deregulation, Southwest's employees are unionized. By maintaining a favorable relationship with the unions, management has been able to negotiate flexible work rules for its employees. Relationships throughout the company are cooperative and people take pride in their organization. For example, since cleaning crews come on board only at the end of each day, flight attendants and pilots often pick up trash left on planes. Employees perceive their airline as an ongoing institution, so they're thinking about its longevity, not its next week.

41   Even though Southwest's work force is 90 percent unionized, its employees own 11 percent of the company, the highest percentage of any major airline. As of 1991, the average employee age was 34 (among the lowest in the industry), and the average pay was $42,000 per employee (among the industry's highest). Annual turnover was a mere 7 percent (the industry's lowest), and 80 percent of promotions came from within. In 1990, 62,000 people applied for jobs at Southwest. Only 1,400 were hired, based on their ability, among other things, to work hard, to have fun, and to be a part of the company's extended family. Employees are consistently aware of their stake in the efficient operations of the company, as evidenced in its rapid turnarounds and high productivity levels.

42   To encourage top-notch performance, management has incorporated employee involvement programs. These programs utilize a suggestion system and a variety of incentives, including cash, merchandise, and travel passes. In 1987, the "Together We Make It Great Program" was initiated. In this program, employees work in seven-member teams to create money-saving ideas. These ideas then are studied by a middle- and upper-level management committee, which then forwards the best ideas to departmental managers for approval or disapproval. The committee can override any manager's disapproval; and, even if an idea is not used, the team gets a letter explaining why. The most effective suggestions are printed in the company's newsletter, *Luv Lines*.

43   If an idea is accepted, employee teams receive points, based on the savings that result from the idea. The first year, those whose ideas saved the most money were allowed to trade their points for merchandise in a St. Louis warehouse operated by the incentive firm Maritz, Inc. In years following, winning teams received cash awards, ranging from $150 to $5,000, depending on how much money was saved by the idea. Employees providing ideas that saved company time or made a work process easier, but did not directly save money, were awarded travel passes.

44   Another incentive system is the "Black Bag" program, which encourages baggage handlers to reduce the amount of money having to be spent on lost and damaged luggage. Baggage stations that are at least 15 percent below budget each month receive cash incentives for every employee group working the station. Although each station can spend the money any way it pleases, stations typically spend the money on parties, luncheons, or dinners.

45   Outstanding employees are formally recognized at periodic awards ceremonies. All workers from baggage handlers to ticket agents can participate in the programs and be eligible for awards. At the annual award's banquet, employees are recognized for length of service and awarded plaques for outstanding service to the company or community. The winner of the Founder's Award, Southwest's most prestigious annual award, receives $1,000 cash. Southwest's monthly in-flight magazine, *Spirit*, runs a "Star of the Month" column featuring an outstanding employee chosen from peer nominations and customer recommendations. Management chooses the best examples from its customer mail each month and prints them in the company newsletter, and awards outstanding performers two travel passes, a Winning Spirit pin, and a certificate signed by the president.

46   Management is particularly fond of its pilots and solicits their participation in the evaluation of new aircraft. Kelleher believes that pilots bring technical expertise and pragmatic experience to an evaluation. "You want to make sure that an airplane is acceptable to your pilots in sort of a spiritual way because, if they don't like it, it might not fly as well as it should," says Kelleher. "There has got to be a feeling, I think, between the pilot and the airplane like there is between the cowboy and the horse. I wanted to be sure that our pilots were comfortable with the 737–300s. We not only seek the pilot's input on equipment, we seek the pilot's advice on a whole range of questions."

47   Pilots always have been paid on a per-trip basis, rather than hourly. This increases their awareness that the airline must be productive in order to exist. It also is an incentive for them to move things along as fast as possible, consistent with safety regulations. As key members of the airlines industry's first profit-sharing plan, many have benefited handsomely. They know that productivity is the key to maintaining Southwest's low-cost, low-fare niche. The pay-per-trip system gives the pilot a great deal of responsibility and, to a certain extent, the means to control his or her own income.

48   Southwest won first place in a 1990 Business Insurance Employee Benefits Communication Awards competition for its unique implementation of a flexible benefits insurance program. In order to lower the $13 million spent on health care during 1989, the company opted for a new flexible benefits program, which could save 6 percent of these costs if employee enrollment in the program was 40 percent of the work force or above. Southwest reached that goal within 15 months after the program's implementation kickoff, a remarkable feat. This was done through a series of newspaper and morning news show parodies. Southwest employees found the format less intimidating than typical insurance company booklets that people normally receive but do not read. In conjunction, a humorous 35-minute video on Benefits Plus was aired continuously in high-employee-traffic areas throughout its widely dispersed, 31-city work force. The method was a widely acclaimed success, and the resulting employee participation unprecedented.

FINANCIAL STRATEGY

49   In 1989, Southwest catapulted from a regional to a national carrier, as defined within Department of Transportation categories. To achieve this distinction, its operating revenues exceeded $1 billion for the year. This represents a post-deregulation (since 1978) revenue growth of over $900 million. The airline has coupled their continued growth with an uncanny ability to minimize operating costs. It also has consistently maintained one of the industry's strongest balance sheets (see Exhibit 5), with a 1990 debt-to-equity ratio of 0.65, compared to an industry average of almost 3.75. During the same year, a Salomon Brothers analyst rated Southwest's financial status the industry's strongest, with the exception of Delta Airlines. Both low-cost and favorable debt structures play key roles in Southwest's financial strength.

50   Southwest's low-cost capacity is the core of its financial strategy. Full utilization and standardization of its fleet (in 1992, on a typical day Southwest planes are in the air 11 hours versus an industry average of 8 hours), no-frills operations, and a work force dedicated to low cost and service uniquely position the airline as the industry's premier bargain. Its low-cost operations allowed Southwest to maintain normal passenger traffic while the 1989–91 recession severely deteriorated much of its competitors' business. Its low-cost structure has allowed Southwest to endure and to conquer rivals in ferocious and long-lasting price wars.

51   Southwest frequently employs an aggressive aircraft leasing policy that has helped maintain a favorable reserve of cash and liquid resources. This reserve along with an outstanding debt position has assisted Southwest's survival during adverse economic environments while enhancing its competitive position within the industry. For example, Southwest has been able to expand assertively as circumstances have presented themselves. As new routes and gate facilities became available, the company was able to seize them quickly while other debt-strapped, less-liquid competitors lost these opportunities.

FUTURE

52   In 1989, the Texas Turnpike Authority created the Texas High-Speed Rail Authority. Its purpose is to review private sector applications for financing, constructing, operating, and maintaining high-speed rail facilities between several major cities in Texas. Since then, at least two major joint ventures have expressed interest in developing these projects. In 1993, a new U.S. political administration took office, and backed a platform that included the creation of high-speed railroad infrastructures between various business centers throughout the United States. The availability of public funding to construct high-speed rail links suddenly became a real possibility.

EXHIBIT 5
Five-Year Consolidated Balance Sheet (in thousands except share and per share amounts)

	December 31				
	1991	1990	1989	1988	1987
Assets					
Current assets:					
Cash and cash equivalents	$ 260,856	$ 87,507	$ 146,364	$ 209,983	$ 142,734
Accounts receivable	47,507	43,887	37,951	37,045	44,116
Inventories of parts and supplies, at cost.	23,036	15,460	12,484	8,790	7,693
Prepaid expenses and other current assets	8,602	10,973	7,079	9,211	6,577
Total current assets.	340,001	157,827	203,878	265,029	201,120
Property and equipment, at cost:					
Flight equipment	1,551,519	1,369,324	1,255,076	1,126,474	858,713
Ground property and equipment.	218,522	194,118	164,362	124,840	106,465
Deposits on flight equipment purchase contracts	182,932	153,201	137,956	109,742	134,726
	1,952,973	1,716,643	1,557,394	1,361,056	1,099,904
Less allowance for depreciation.	458,779	406,106	353,137	325,088	275,546
Total	1,494,194	1,310,537	1,204,257	1,035,968	824,358
Other assets	3,096	2,774	6,961	7,392	17,162
Total assets	$1,837,291	$1,471,138	$1,415,096	$1,308,389	$1,042,640

53   A marketing study commissioned by the Texas High-Speed Rail Association concluded that, if the rail tickets were priced competitively with airline fares, a high-speed system in Texas would attract 4 million passengers in its first year (probably 1997) and increase to 9.8 million by 2015. Kelleher's response to all this: "What the hell, bring on the trains. Horse---t. If that's the case, I'll just buy some 757s and double the number of seats between Houston and Dallas. The whole thing is just so ludicrous!"

54   In 1986, Kelleher faced, in front of the Dallas City Council, a citizen's action committee that was determined to drive Southwest from its base of operations at Love Field. The committee's anger stemmed from the obtrusive noise pollution created by Southwest's fleet of jets operating within a heavily congested residential area. Nearly 30,000 people live in housing sections near Love Field that are subjected to unacceptable levels (by federal standards) of aircraft noise. The potential effects include auditory problems, increased blood pressure, narrowed attention spans, and aggravation to the "victims." Kelleher based his counter-argument on the economic prosperity that the reopened airport afforded the city, and it won the council's support.

55   Operating in and out of congested populations poses a threat to Southwest's future, particularly where alternative airports exist outside city limits, and particularly as pollution to American citizens becomes a more potent issue. Furthermore, close-in operations are a key element of Southwest's strategy. To a large extent court decisions are based on past precedents and so far Southwest has remained within the statutory bounds of precedent. The odds of precedent changing on this thorny issue is anybody's guess.

56   Although Southwest has operated within its niche relatively competition-free, its success has attracted the attention of competitors. Attempts to enter this niche have been rather fruitless for other

EXHIBIT 5 (concluded)

	December 31				
	1991	1990	1989	1988	1987
Liabilities and Stockholders' Equity					
Current liabilities:					
Accounts payable	$ 54,970	$ 51,172	$ 47,986	$ 35,286	$ 26,877
Accrued liabilities	155,895	112,296	94,816	76,165	56,993
Air traffic liability.	42,069	38,562	32,938	27,059	11,540
Income taxes payable	377	9,716	3,990	4,408	7,230
Current maturities of long-term debt	6,583	13,612	16,168	9,986	9,743
Total current liabilities	259,894	225,358	195,898	152,904	112,383
Long-term debt less current maturities	617,016	326,956	354,147	369,541	251,130
Deferred income taxes	105,757	109,273	118,395	101,374	85,918
Deferred gains from sale and leaseback of aircraft.	222,818	202,002	157,030	115,314	77,668
Other deferred liabilities	3,285	2,698	2,310	1,881	1,263
Stockholders' equity:					
Common stock, $1.00 par value: 200 million shares authorized.	42,438	42,412	32,254	32,254	32,254
Capital in excess of par value.	81,987	81,447	175,170	175,170	175,170
Retained earnings.	507,259	484,559	441,591	374,211	320,402
	631,684	608,418	649,015	581,635	527,826
Less treasury stock, at cost	3,163	3,567	61,699	14,260	13,548
Total stockholders' equity	628,521	604,851	587,316	567,375	514,278
Total liabilities and stockholders' equity	$1,837,291	$1,471,138	$1,415,096	$1,308,389	$1,042,640

airlines, and Southwest's continued outstanding performance may well depend on its competitors' inability or lack of desire to crack that niche.

57　　The airline industry of the 1990s will witness growing internationalization. Analysts predict that the growth of international travel will exceed that of U.S. domestic travel during that decade. New destinations will open in the United States for foreign carriers, and in foreign nations for U.S. carriers. Many airlines will develop global systems as the incidence of multinational alliances increases. In the period from 1986 through 1991, the international revenue passenger miles of several U.S. carriers grew significantly: Delta's increased 448 percent, American's 263 percent, United's 220 percent, and Northwest's 88 percent.[3] In the United States, foreign entities may now own up to 49 percent of a U.S. airline but are still not allowed to control more than a 25 percent voting interest. In a related area, Southwest is well-located to capitalize on air transportation needs generated by the expanding economic development in Mexico. And passage of the proposed NAFTA agreement should signal a growing traffic flow between selected U.S. and Mexican destinations.

---

[3] Standard & Poor's *Industry Outlook*, October 1992.

CASE 2

THE VIRGINIA WINE INDUSTRY AND
THE CASE OF MEREDYTH VINEYARDS

U.S. WINE INDUSTRY

1   The domestic market for alcoholic beverages began to decline in the early 1980s in the wake of national awareness of the ill effects of alcohol and of a national crackdown on driving while under the
influence of alcohol. In response, wine was repositioned in the marketplace as a food item to be enjoyed at lunch, dinner, and when entertaining. The market for domestic wines showed signs of a turnaround by the middle of the decade. Premium wines, positioned as a light, low-alcohol product, grew
to command a 45 percent share of the domestic wine market in the 1980s.

2   New levels of national consumption, improved international market standings, and increasing domestic sales all brightened the future of the American wine industry. U.S. wine consumption was up
70 percent in the 1980s. Domestic wines composed 58.3 percent of all wines consumed worldwide
in those 10 years, and 83 percent of the national wine market.

3   As of 1990, there were 42 wine producing states in the United States. In Exhibit 1, national production is broken down into the seven largest wine producing states by their production volume. According to a study done by the National Wine Coalition, total annual U.S. retail wine sales exceeded
$12 billion and total wine consumption exceeded 212.1 million cases.

4   Wine production in the United States contributed to the financial health of the nation. In 1988,
$3.1 billion in wages were paid to employees in the industry, including winemakers, sales representa-
tives, wholesalers, and tour guides. The wine industry also consumed $6 billion in goods and services,
including advertising and supplies (bottles, labels, and corks). Overall, the nation's wine industry contributed $1.5 billion in state and local taxes.

VIRGINIA FARM WINE INDUSTRY

Importance of the Wine Industry to Virginia

5   In 1990, the Commonwealth of Virginia was the seventh largest wine producing state in the nation.
Virginia's wine industry was valued at over $37 million. As the national market for domestic wine
sales improved, Virginia placed its emphasis on marketing and producing premium wines to meet the
demand for varietals. Its sales campaigns were based on the production of traditional and premium
wines.

6   Virginia produced popular varietals, such as Chardonnay, Cabernet Sauvignon, and Riesling, as
its top selections. The breakdown of total grape production by variety is shown in Exhibit 2.

This case was prepared by John A. Pearce II of George Mason University, and by Kristin Orebaugh Long, Nancy Raynor, and
Andrew Spell. Development of this case was made possible by a grant from the Funds for Excellence Program of the State Council
of Higher Education for Virginia.

EXHIBIT 1
1988 State Production (in thousands of gallons)

Rank	Production
1. California	345,073.0
2. New York	25,787.7
3. Washington	3,040.7
4. Virginia*	2,589.5
5. Oregon	1,004.1
6. Ohio	693.1
7. Pennsylvania	389.5

*These figures are from the most recent study done in 1988. As of January 1989, the Richmond-based Wild Irish Rose producer moved out of Virginia, thus making the Virginia farm wine production level 375 gallons. This lowers Virginia's rank to seventh, right behind Pennsylvania.

Source: A study performed by the National Wine Coalition.

7   Wine production is broken into two categories: commercial wine and farm wine. Commercial wine is wine produced from grapes of any source and cannot be classified as the wine of a certain state. To be defined as farm wine, the Virginia Winegrowers Advisory Board's (VWAB) Report to the Governor says that wine must come from a "winery that produces and bottles wine that is made from at least 75 percent fruit from Virginia, and 51 percent of the fruit must be from land the winery owns or leases."[1] A wine meeting these criteria may put the name Virginia on its label.

8   Wines are further classified as either premium or nonpremium. Premium wines are defined as those that retail for $5.75 or more per bottle. Farm wines often are referred to as premium wines even though some may actually sell for slightly less than $5.75 per bottle. Production figures by state are not broken down into farm and commercial categories.

9   Virginia farm wineries offer many financial incentives over their commercial counterparts. Farm wineries are taxed as agricultural entities, whereas commercial wineries must pay the significantly higher taxes associated with commercial entities. While out-of-state grapes are less expensive to purchase, the tax incentives and the poorer quality of imported grapes make farm wine production attractive.

10   The poorer quality of non-Virginia grapes can be attributed to either of two factors. First, grapes shipped fresh from other states often arrive damaged due to inferior packaging methods and extensive transit time. Second, flash-frozen chunks of mash grapes shipped from out of state contain reduced acid levels and elevated pH. The result is a low-grade juice that produces a poorer quality wine.

11   Virginia legislators were supportive of the farm wine industry for several reasons, including the prestige, agricultural diversity, and tourism diversity afforded by the product. These motives often overlapped. First, the industry was widely viewed as exciting, novel, and romantic. In Richmond, the state capital, the farm wine industry was seen as an upmarket industry that was good for the state's prestige.

12   Second, Virginia wanted to maintain its status as a state with a strong agricultural base. Agriculturally, Virginia was know primarily for the production of tobacco, beef, dairy products, and apples.

---

[1] Virginia Winegrowers Advisory Board, *Virginia Wine/Grape Fact Sheet*, 1990, p. 56.

EXHIBIT 2

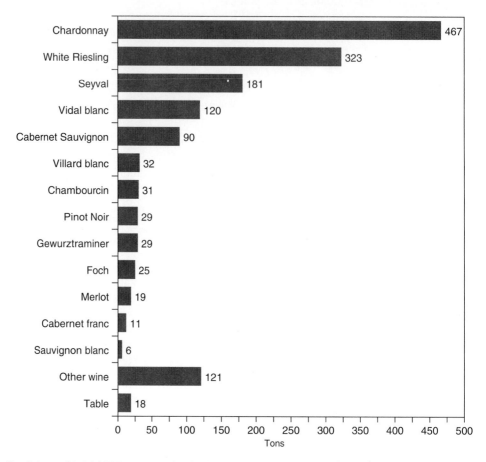

Breakdown of total 1987 grape production by variety. Data are based on responses from 69 of 107 independent grape growers and 23 of 33 wineries. Total reported production in 1987 was 1,502 tons.

In 1987, the governor of Virginia urged state farmers to adopt a "demand-side strategy" that might require them to seek new crops whose markets were expanding. One such market was grapes, "Virginia's newest and most glamorous crop."

13   The objective of state legislation in supporting the wine industry was to promote land use within the state. Wine was treated as an agricultural product, not as an alcoholic beverage. The farm wine industry stimulated the use of land for agriculture, as opposed to development. A repeated claim was that "the objective is to keep the state from looking like one big parking lot."

14   Third, state tourist attractions had been criticized as lacking in certain areas. According to a *Better Homes and Gardens* survey of readers, Virginia may not always provide the ideal vacation. The state ranked low in the categories of variety, beaches, and romantic atmosphere. Wineries filled a niche in the state's tourism package, providing a varied, scenic, and romantic gateway. Tourist-based businesses, such as bed-and-breakfasts, country inns, guest houses, and restaurants, also reap the benefits of increased Virginia state wine production and promotions. Tours of Virginia vineyards,

EXHIBIT 3
Distribution of Virginia Grape Acreage, by County, April 1987

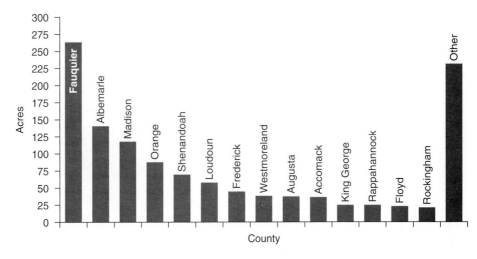

when promoted in coordination with bed-and-breakfasts and inns, provided an increase in the number of tourists visiting from all over the mid-Atlantic region.

Industry History

15 Thomas Jefferson, touted as the father of American wine, pioneered wine production in Charlottesville, Virginia, in the 1700s. Virginia came to be a wine growing state of international acclaim until the 1850s. The many Civil War battles fought within the state destroyed most of the progress that viticulturists had made. In addition, the Prohibition Era of the 1920s devastated what remained of the industry. For half a century, the industry lay dormant.

16 The modern farm wine industry was in a new infancy, and it was not until the 1970s that the wine industry was revived in the commonwealth. By 1979, six wineries were in operation. State wine production accelerated, so, by 1991, 42 wineries were in operation.

17 The state contained five designated grape-growing regions, or viticultural areas, approved by the Federal Bureau of Alcohol, Tobacco, and Firearms: Monticello, Northern Fork George Washington Birthplace, Shenandoah Valley, Rocky Knob, and the North Fork of the Roanoke.

Growing Grapes in Virginia

18 Due to the youth of the wine industry in Virginia, grape growers were inexperienced in comparison to the European and California wineries, which often had been in the industry for generations. For a breakdown of grape acreage by county, see Exhibit 3.

19 While grapes were seen as a substantial cash crop for the state, a great deal of cash is needed to enter the grape market, and vines require three to five years to initially produce fruit suitable for use in wine production. An initial investment of $10,000 per acre, not including the price of the land, is required to set up a new vineyard. The average yield per acre is between two and a half and three tons of grapes, with an average market price in 1988 of $1,200 per ton. Average 1988 operating costs were $1,000 per acre.

EXHIBIT 4
Variables Affecting Grape Cultivation

Soil type, drainage, and depth.	Frost and heat pockets.
Soil nutrients.	Annual rainfall.
Soil texture.	Wind.
Soil temperature.	Proximity to other growth.
Soil replant status.	Drainage.
Soil pH.	Specific type of organic matter.
Solar radiation.	Slope.

Source: Cox, 1985.

20   Virginia growers were low on the learning curve in comparison to the more established growers in Europe and California. Grape growing is an art learned only through experience. Many region-specific variables affect the cultivation of grapes. A list of the most important variables can be found in Exhibit 4. Differing climates and terrains create different growing situations, each with its own set of problems and benefits.

21   For example, California's warm and dry climate afforded a unique set of grape-growing conditions, compared with other states including Virginia, where growers were still developing the cultivation techniques needed to build the richest harvest possible in a moist and varied temperature climate. Unfortunately, technology from other areas could not always be transferred to Virginia growers.

22   Three broad categories of grapes, called *cultivars*, were grown in Virginia. Vinifera was the most popular, followed by French and American hybrids. The statewide breakdown of cultivars by acreage is shown in Exhibit 5. Acreage is further broken down into specific varieties in Exhibit 6.

State Support of the Industry

23   Larry Fox of *The Washington Post* wrote, "If Virginia is the biggest wine-producing state in the area, it's because of strong support and promotion. In Virginia the wineries are new, big, and well-publicized. Across the border in Maryland, Annapolis's support for wineries is comparatively non-existent, and the wineries there are fewer and their output is smaller."[2]

24   The state's goal was to make wine production a profitable venture. Industry incentives were first offered by the state in 1980, with the enactment of the Farm Winery Law (House Bill No. 1280), which required wineries to be licensed by the state. An initial incentive was to offer a state alcoholic beverage tax break on wine manufactured under a state farm winery license. This made the in-state wines less expensive than the wines produced elsewhere.

25   Second, farm wineries were allowed to act as both wholesale distributors and retailers. Other alcoholic beverages are required to be sold through independent wholesalers. Farm wineries were given the option to act as their own wholesalers, interacting directly with retail outlets. This was important to the industry, not only because the middle man was eliminated, again making wine production more profitable, but because most wineries were at that time very small and had difficulty attracting wholesalers who would carry their products.

---

[2] L. Fox, "The Area's Wineries Are Made for Touring—With Taste," *The Washington Post*, June 12, 1987, pp. WE 52–54.

EXHIBIT 5
Composition of Virginia Grape Acreage by Grapevine Species, April 1987

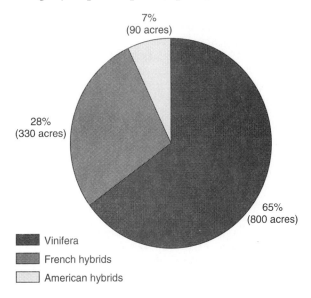

7%
(90 acres)

28%
(330 acres)

65%
(800 acres)

■ Vinifera
▨ French hybrids
☐ American hybrids

EXHIBIT 6
Composition of Virginia Grapevine Acreage by Cultivar: April 1987
Total Acreage = 1,220 acres

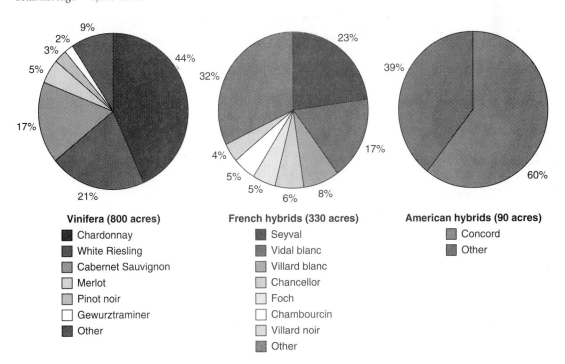

Vinifera (800 acres)
■ Chardonnay
■ White Riesling
▨ Cabernet Sauvignon
☐ Merlot
▨ Pinot noir
☐ Gewurztraminer
▨ Other

French hybrids (330 acres)
■ Seyval
▨ Vidal blanc
▨ Villard blanc
☐ Chancellor
▨ Foch
☐ Chambourcin
▨ Villard noir
▨ Other

American hybrids (90 acres)
▨ Concord
▨ Other

26   State-run alcoholic beverage (ABC) stores expanded their Virginia wine inventory on a permanent basis and began statewide in-store promotion of these wines. ABC stores were, at the time, a very important sales channel. Only in-state wines are sold in these outlets. In 1983, Virginia wine sales accounted for 7.6 percent of all ABC sales. The small wineries especially benefited from this effort. Because private distributors were reluctant to carry newer wines from small vineyards, this provided an avenue that placed these wines on retail shelves.

27   In 1984, $190,000 in state funds was allocated for the creation of three industry personnel positions, as well as the development of state-run wine lab facilities. The Virginia Department of Agriculture and Consumer Services (VDACS) employed a wine marketing specialist, and Virginia Polytechnic Institute and State University employed a state ecologist. A state viticulturist was based in Winchester at the Fruit Research Lab.

28   The growing sentiment in Richmond was that the state needed to emphasize the quality of state wines. Promotional programs would be wasted if the state failed to produce quality wines. A grapevine certification program was launched, as well as a "Wine Country" tour campaign.

29   Another $140,000 was allocated in 1985 for the establishment of the Virginia Winegrowers Advisory Board to "encourage the increased productivity of all phases of grape and wine production in Virginia and to provide for continuing orderly growth by sponsoring and encouraging research, education, and marketing of Virginia wine."

30   Legislators again supported the industry in 1988 by allocating $185,000 for the Virginia Wine Marketing Program. Funds were used to expand existing marketing and promotions and to develop new programs, such as the Virginia Governor's Cup Wine Competition. Governor Charles Robb declared August 1989 as the first Virginia Farm Winery month, offering state-supported promotional campaigns aimed at arousing interest in the state wine industry. The "We Have It Made in Virginia" campaign of that same year spotlighted state wines along with many other state-produced products in retail stores.

31   Wine sales increased dramatically during each August until the campaign was switched to the month of October. Since then, sales have moved accordingly, with August sales returning to normal, while October sales rose. See Exhibit 7 for the currently monthly distribution of sales.

32   State programs had made obvious progress by 1989. Virginia wines had been honored with many national and international awards. Exhibit 8 shows some of the awards won by state wines. Virginia wines also were served at the National Democratic Convention and at the Presidential Summit on Education. A new position was created at VDACS to assist in both marketing and educational development for the wine industry. A survey of Virginia wine industry members showed that they believed the increased quality of state wines was directly related to state-supported research and extension services. State support continued to help growers advance along the learning curve.

MEREDYTH VINEYARDS

Company History

33   In 1971, Archie Smith, Jr., began to fulfill a dream of converting his Middleburg, Virginia, beef cattle farm into a winery. Falling prices for livestock and rising land prices threatened the future of his 209-acre Fauquier County farm. In 1972, with the help of his son, Archie Smith III, who operated the business on a day-to-day basis, he planted 56 acres of vinifera grapevines and established Meredyth Vineyards. The exact location of the winery is shown in Exhibit 9.

34   The Smiths cultivated the grape crop until their first crush, the extraction of grape juice by pressing, in 1975. The farmland consisted of over 200 acres, but, due to the delicate nature of grape growing, much of the terrain is unsuitable for planting. By 1990, Meredyth was producing 15,000 cases of wine per year.

EXHIBIT 7
1989 Virginia Farm Wine Sales Share of All Wine Sales in State (figures in cases)

Month	Total Va. Wine Sales	Va. Farm Wine Sales	Share (%)
January	272,024	3,776	1.38%
February	279,212	3,716	1.33
March	353,254	5,271	1.49
April	299,239	6,723	2.25
May	354,478	7,806	2.20
June	334,832	9,458	2.82
July	292,281	7,194	2.46
August	324,877	9,084	2.80
September	310,704	9,133	2.94
October	348,645	12,760	3.66
November	436,818	9,088	2.08
December	470,474	6,524	1.81
Total	4,076,838	90,523	2.27%

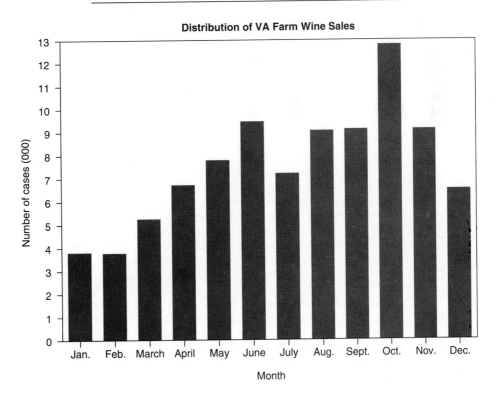

Distribution of VA Farm Wine Sales

EXHIBIT 8
Major Virginia Wine Awards

1983	First annual Governor's Cup Award given in Virginia competition; Virginia placed second to New York in number of awards won at Wineries Unlimited Eastern Wine Competition.
1984	Virginia wine wins gold medal at 8th International Wine Competition in Milan, Italy.
1985	Virginia Chardonnay wins a bronze in the International Wine & Spirits competition in London.
1986	Virginia Chardonnay receives Gold in 33rd International Viticulture and Wine Growing Fair in Ljubljaha, Yugoslavia.
1987	Virginia Reisling is served on Lufthansa Airlines International flights, and three Virginia wines received gold and silver awards at the Atlanta International Wine Competition.
1988	Virginia Seyval given to Soviet Premier Mikhail Gorbachev by President Ronald Reagan at the Moscow summit in May.
1989	Virginia Chardonnays are judged and awarded praise from national press and wine and food critics in attendance at the 2nd Annual Virginia Governor's Cup Wine Competition and Awards Banquet in Williamsburg.

35   The Meredyth production facility consisted of a 5,000-square-foot winery located on the Smith property. All production took place on the premises. Grapes first were destemmed and then crushed. Once the grape juice had been extracted, it was allowed to ferment in large holding tanks. Impurities settled to the bottom and were filtered out at several stages during the fermentation process. Once the fermentation process was complete, the wine was transferred to aging casks. While many other wineries used stainless steel casks, Meredyth used only oak to age its wine. Oak adds a distinctive character to fine wines that stainless steel lacks. Tests were performed throughout the process to ensure the proper levels of tannin and acidity.

36   Wines, principally described by the type of grape used in the production, are called *varietal* wines. To carry a varietal name, such as Chardonnay, a wine must be made with at least 75 percent of a particular grape type. Unlike French wines, which take their names from the region in which the grapes are grown, most American wines are designated as varietal wines. European in origin, vinifera grapes are the standard wine grapes, from which many of the world's "premium" wines are made. Most American farm wines are made from grapes grown on vinifera vines that have been grafted to American roots. Major American varieties include Concord and Delaware.

37   Meredyth offered one such American varietal, the white wine made from the Delaware grape. The rest of its line was made of vinifera varietals, such as their popular Seyval Blanc and Chardonnay, as well as an award-winning Reisling and the generic October Harvest. Red wines included de Chaunac, Cabernet Sauvignon, Villard Noir, and Harvest Red. Premium red, white, and blush wines were also offered. Due to production limitations, not all varietals could be produced in a given year, and crops needed to be rotated.

38   With a variable production cost of $24 to $30, a case of wine sold to a wholesaler or through ABC stores for $45, allowing for a gross margin of $15 to $21.

39   The average case sold for $84 at the winery retail outlet. The gross margin for these sales ranged from $54 to $60. Meredyth sold 60 percent of its inventory at the lower margin and 40 percent at the higher margin. Its gross margin was approximately $500,000 in 1990.

EXHIBIT 9

Tour
Meredyth Vineyards

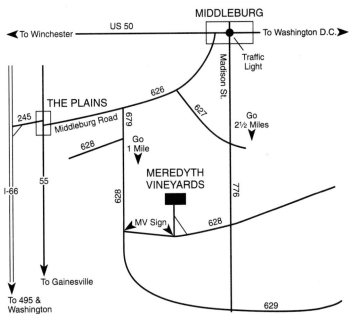

No charge for small groups.
Large groups: $1 per person, by appointment

Closed Christmas, Easter, Thanksgiving
and New Year's Day

TOURS seven days a week, 10 to 4.

Meredyth Vineyards

P.O. Box 347, Middleburg, Virginia 22117
(703) 687-6277 or
Washington Metro 478-1835

Printed in U.S.A. 5/87

State Issues Affecting Meredyth

40   Meredyth sought to become a national competitor, but it was hampered by the infancy of the Virginia farm wine industry. Demand for Meredyth wine was outstripping supply. External capital was needed to finance an increase in capacity. Potential creditors, however, were reluctant to invest in the fledgling industry.

41   Meredyth, one of the six largest wineries in Virginia, was one of those most affected by the limitations of doing business in the state. Most state efforts to boost the wine industry had been aimed at helping smaller wineries through the start-up phase, and many small wineries had begun production as a result. However, the state's wine industry, as a whole, had not had time to build the needed credibility with the creditors to finance growth beyond the start-up phase. Meredyth was ready to expand but unable to finance its growth.

42   Of the 42 states wineries in operation, only 10 produced more than 10,000 gallons annually, and only 6 others, including Meredyth, produced more than 20,000 gallons per year. The remaining 26 state wineries each produced less than 8,000 gallons per year. While newer and smaller wineries concentrated on becoming established and on learning trade techniques, Meredyth was focusing on expanding its operations.

43   Limiting Meredyth's expansion efforts were the youth of the industry itself, the lack of strong wholesale distributor relationships, and the competition for a limited state grape supply.

44   Virginia wines were comparatively new on the market. California wineries, such as Beeaulieu Vineyards and Robert Mondavi, had long been recognized as producers of premium table wine and had established strong market positions. A positive image was associated with California wines, in general.

45   Virginia wines, on the other hand, had not had time to develop strong reputations. In general, Virginia wines were not perceived as being of equal quality to the more well known California wines, even though they have beaten those wines in competitions (Exhibit 8).

46   The Virginia Farm Winery Law of 1980 was created to provide industry incentives to farm wineries. Two main incentives were offered. First, the law allowed farm wineries to act as their own wholesale distributors to independent retail outlets. Second, the law allowed farm wineries to set up retail operations on premises, at their own individual wineries. By comparison, beer, hard liquor, and commercial wine producers were required to utilize independent distributors to market their products. Nonfarm wine production facilities cannot legally retail directly to consumers, even on their own premises.

47   Allowing farm wineries to operate their own retail outlets at the vineyards became a profitable sales channel. According to statistics compiled by the ABC, farm wineries reported that, in 1989, an aggregate of 57 percent of all sales occurred at the vineyards.

48   The wholesale distributor function permitted by the law benefits fledgling wineries by granting them access to retail sales channels that might not otherwise be available to their products. Young wineries often lack the inventory needed to supply retail outlets on a regular basis. Premium wines that are new to the market often are sold in small quantities, sometimes less than a case at a time, to retailers.

49   Retailers generally are unwilling to purchase large quantities of unproven wines; thus, independent wholesalers are not motivated to carry such wines. If farm wineries did not have the option of selling directly to independent retail outlets, their wines might not be carried in these stores at all.

50   Distributor relationships become more important to wineries as they begin to grow. Smith found this to be the case at Meredyth. While many younger and smaller wineries sell most of their inventory at their own retail operations, Meredyth expanded by increasing sales at a growing number of independent retail outlets. Meredyth sold 40 percent of its inventory at the winery (compared with a 57 percent state average), and 50 percent through various retail outlets (compared with a state average of

EXHIBIT 10

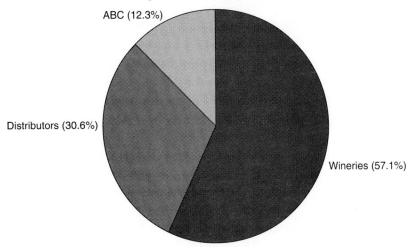

Average market share by sales channel

ABC (12.3%)

Distributors (30.6%)

Wineries (57.1%)

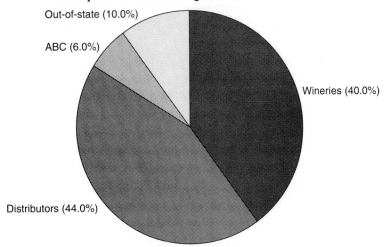

Meredyth's % of sales through various sales channels

Out-of-state (10.0%)

ABC (6.0%)

Wineries (40.0%)

Distributors (44.0%)

43 percent). These figures include both ABC and independent retailers. Exhibit 10 contains both industry and Meredyth breakdowns of sales by distribution channel.

51   The task of developing strong working relationships with distributors is a difficult one. Smith feels that due to its youth, "To a certain extent, the wholesale community looks askance at the VA wine industry. They still think of it as sort of hobby type industry."

52   Having to deal directly with numerous retailers creates an additional workload for vintners. Unlike beer, which can be sold straight off the truck with no prior sales order, wine cannot be peddled. It must be ordered by retail outlets prior to delivery. This increases the required number of retail interfaces. For example, if each retailer carries a half case of Meredyth wine at a time, and a total of 28,000 cases are sold through these outlets annually, 112,000 interfaces are required. The wholesaler, whether independent or working directly for Meredyth, must contact each retailer, first to draw up an invoice and again to make delivery.

53   The above scenario is not an unreasonable one. It would be costly and cumbersome for a Meredyth sales representative to make every sales call himself or herself. Due to the economies of scale, independent distributors are better suited to wholesale Meredyth's products. Each distributor has an area of operation in which he or she supplied retailers with a full line of products, of which Meredyth is but a fraction.

54   Virginia wines must be made from at least 75 percent state-grown grapes. As demand for Virginia wines grows, a problem is created for the vineyards when the price of the limited state grape supply is driven up sharply. Therefore, Virginia grapes command a premium price in the marketplace. In 1988, for example, the price of a ton of Virginia grapes averaged $1,200. In the same year, California grapes averaged $150 a ton. While this $150 figure understates the value of premium California grapes, they are comparatively less expensive than premium Virginia grapes.

55   The limited state grape supply drives up prices for outside grapes that Meredyth must purchase, since it lacks the crop capacity to provide all of the grapes needed for winemaking from its own vineyards. The state average for grape production in 1990 was approximately three tons per acre. Meredyth averaged four and a half tons per acre.

56   Smith attributes his relative success to a greater investment in his crops than is the industry average: "There is nothing magical about our success; it just takes more work and more money per acre to get a good yield." While the average amount spent annually on an acre of grapes was approximately $1,000, Meredyth spent $1,500 per year on operating costs.

57   This added investment was spent on extra pesticides and on a process called *leaf pulling*. The removal of unproductive stems after budding, as opposed to simply pruning before budding, allows productive buds more ventilation space. This process greatly increased the yield of Smith's acreage. While Meredyth performed better in this area than most of its competitors, it was still forced to buy grapes from other state growers to keep pace with demand.

Meredyth's Current Strategies

58   Meredyth's first priority has been to build product quality. Smith feels that promotional efforts will come to nothing without quality wines. Its second priority is on marketing efforts geared toward building awareness. Smith feels that, as the awareness of Virginia wines grows, Meredyth will be a forerunner in the industry.

59   Meredyth has advanced farther along the learning curve than most of its in-state competitors. The quality of its wines rivals that of premier European and California wines. Meredyth wines have won over 150 honors and awards in both national and international competitions. These awards include gold medals at the Homestead, the Eastern International Wine Competition, the Atlanta International Wine Festival, and the International Wine Review.

60   Getting people to taste its wine is a challenge to Meredyth. Once wine drinkers actually taste these wines, the quality becomes apparent. Attracting tourists to the Meredyth vineyard is a key strategy.

61   Smith found that tours of the vineyard were his most valuable sales tool. Sales figures indicated that 40 percent of sales occur at the vineyard retail outlet. A tour guide offered an informative trip through the production facility, and free samples of the vineyard's offerings for that particular year.

Tourists were encouraged to bring picnic lunches and make a day of the event. Smith believed that customers who tasted and enjoyed the wines at the vineyard would continue to buy them at their local stores and restaurants.

62   Meredyth also had other marketing programs. Private functions, such as wedding receptions, were held on the vineyard grounds, as well as business meetings, buffets, brunches, and luncheons. Smith traveled to the northern Virginia area to display his line at winemakers' dinners. These events, often held at popular restaurants, featured a different Meredyth wine with each part of a five-course meal.

63   Special public events also were held at the vineyard, including concerts, candlelight dinners, special theme tastings, fairs, festivals, holiday parties, and murder mystery theater presentations. Meredyth also special-labeled wines for restaurants and large private functions.

64   These programs all were aimed at getting potential customers to sample Meredyth wines. Smith also found that word-of-mouth advertising was of vital importance in attracting tourists. Visitors often made the trip to the vineyard on the recommendation of friends. To keep the interest of existing customers, Smith published a Meredyth newsletter, and he sent brochures to those who had expressed an interest in the winery. Schedules of events were dropped into purchases made at the vineyard's retail outlet. All of these actions were directed at promoting customer growth and loyalty.

65   Meredyth developed several strategies to deal with distribution problems. Smith communicated two messages to his distributors. First, that distributors were an integral part of the wine industry; and second, that there was money to be made by the independent wholesalers. For example, in 1989, 28,000 cases of Virginia wines were sold at $45 a case, with an average markup of 33 percent. This represented some $420,000 of markup profits for the wholesaler. As the industry grows, the profit potential grows as well.

66   Smith also believed it vital for the wineries to understand the basic wholesaling process. The wineries needed to be aware of the significant commitments of time and resources needed to gain the continued support of their wholesalers. Wineries needed to acquaint themselves with the wholesale pricing system, to understand the wholesalers' situation and provide them with the necessary support.

67   Meredyth employed a full-time sales representative to manage vineyard sales. Only four other farm wineries used full-time sales representatives to market through wholesalers.

68   These factors interacted to create a problem of restricted capacity for Meredyth. Smith was forced to purchase grapes at market price to achieve the desired production levels of certain varieties of the farm wines. The long-term goal of Meredyth was to expand acreage and production capacity. Smith hoped to attract investors who were willing to purchase an interest in Meredyth Vineyards. The goal of expansion was tied to the need to enhance the wholesale distributor relationship by offering a consistent product line.

CASE 3

SPLATTERBALL ADVENTURE GAMES, INC.

1   Splatterball Adventure Games, Inc., conducts paintball games in the Chattanooga, Tennessee, area. The company also maintains a store located in East Ridge, Tennessee, approximately five miles outside the Chattanooga city limits. The playing field location for the game is in Apison, Tennessee, approximately 20 miles from Chattanooga.

2   As of 1992, Splatterball has one principal, Mr. Doug Gray, who runs all aspects of the business, including monitoring the games, conducting sales, bookkeeping, and gun repair.

WHAT IS PAINTBALL?

3   Paintball became popular nationally in the early 1980s and includes both amateur and professional players in the sport. The development of the professional player occurred in the late 1980s. Like other sports, professional status is obtained when players earn money for playing paintball. In the case of paintball, money is earned by winning tournaments. Some of these tournaments have first-place prizes as high as $30,000 for a 10-member team. For a team to be designated as a professional team, three fifths of the members must be professional players.

4   Paintball is played mainly in the United States. Mr. Gray estimates there are approximately 300 fields across the United States. There are some fields located around the world. It is difficult to know exactly how many fields exist outside the United States because many are located in countries that consider the guns used in paintball to be illegal.

5   The development of the sport also has led to the development of a standard of governing. Although several different governing organizations exist, the most prevalent is the International Paintball Player's Associations (IPPA). This organization was set up to create tournament and field guidelines. It also monitors any pending legislation that may be harmful to the industry and attempts to bring together the participants in paintball to prevent any adverse actions.

6   There are several variations in the way paintball is played. These variations depend on the location of the field, the type of field, and the field operator. However, because tournaments usually follow the IPPA rules, these are the guidelines most commonly followed in field operations.

7   There is some standard equipment for all players. Comfortable clothing and shoes for running through the obstacles are required. Many people choose to wear camouflage, although it is not necessary. All players must wear protective eye goggles whenever on the field. Also required are the guns, carbon dioxide tanks, and paintballs. All of the equipment, with the exception of the clothing, can be bought or rented from the field operator.

8   Additional equipment used by regular players include semiautomatic guns, gun cleaners, replacement parts for guns, vests, and speedloaders. This equipment is allowed in tournament play and is used

This case was prepared by Beth Jack and Marilyn M. Helms, University of Tennessee at Chattanooga, School of Business Administration.

to increase the playing ability of the players. It can be ordered from vendors across the country or purchased from paintball specialty stores.

9   Games usually are played in densely wooded areas. This gives players obstacles to hide behind and adds to the difficulty of the game. The games can be played in backyards; however, there usually are not enough obstacles for effective play. Paintball is not played in parks unless prior approval is received from park managers. The paint used in the paintball is water-based, but it still leaves marks on trees and other obstacles until there is enough rain to wash away the paint. The paint used is environmentally safe. Also, the plastic casing around the paintball will be left behind.

10   The object of paintball is to capture the opponent's flag and return it to your own flag station. The flags remain at the flag stations until a member of the opposing team captures it. These flag stations are simply a small area from which a flag is hung from a tree or sometimes it is a pole placed in the clearing. The area around the flag station varies from field to field. In some cases there will be a natural barrier from which a player can defend the station. In other cases it is wide and open and must be defended from its perimeter. If the person who has captured the flag is shot while carrying the flag, the flag is considered "dead." That individual must return the flag to its original station and it then must be recaptured by another team member. It cannot simply be transferred to another teammate.

11   There are two main differences in tournament play and casual play. In casual play, the team returning the captured flag to its own station wins the game. However, in tournament play, teams advance through round-robin brackets in a point system. Points are awarded for the number of opposing players shot, for first flag pulled, and for returning the flag to one's own flag station. There are point penalties for safety violations, foul or abusive language, and physical contact during a game. The maximum number of points awarded is 100.

12   Each member of the team carries a carbon-dioxide-based gun that shoots the paintball. The original guns were pressed plastic with few moving parts. The carbon dioxide came in small metal tubes that were pierced when inserted into the gun and would shoot approximately 20 to 30 rounds of paintballs. The guns now used have become more complicated, with more moving parts. These guns are made of metal and often more closely resemble real guns. Manufacturers have begun the introduction of new types of guns, such as semiautomatics. The carbon dioxide used in the guns can be obtained in refillable tanks and can be used for an entire game.

13   The paintballs are about the size of a marble. They originally were made of oil-based paint enclosed in a thin plastic shell. This quickly changed because, once this paint dried on clothing, it was extremely difficult to remove. The paintballs now are water based so the paint can easily be washed out. They come in a wide variety of colors. However, most fields avoid using red, so injuries are not mistaken for paint. The manufacturing process for the paintball is constantly being improved so a more uniform ball can be made for better accuracy.

14   Professional teams have developed from 15-member teams to 10 and 5 members. This development occurred so games could be played under a 45-minute time limit.

15   Amateur games, usually played on weekends, are not as strict about time limits or the number of members on a team. Usually, the field operator will split up individuals to form two to four teams, depending on the number of people at the field. They try not to allow more than 25 players on a team, if possible. Games usually are limited to one hour, although amateur games tend to end within 30 minutes.

16   The typical paintball player is male. Some females play as amateurs and a few are on professional teams. The average professional player is 22 to 35 years old; the average casual player is 18 to 30. Players come from a wide variety of backgrounds, including professional managers, physicians, blue-collar workers, and students.

17   Tournaments are sponsored year-round in the United States. A tournament circuit has games in San Francisco and Chicago and two in Nashville. The most prestigious tournament takes place every

October in Nashville. This tournament, the International Masters Tournament, is the biggest of its kind, with a 64-team field and a $30,000 first prize. This tournament lasts five days and includes both 5-member and 10-member team competitions. This tournament usually includes at least two British teams every year. The top eight finishers of this tournament are able to get sponsorship from manufacturers of paintball equipment. This tournament is also a chance for vendors to display their new products and innovations to the players.

HISTORY OF SPLATTERBALL ADVENTURE GAMES, INC.

18   Splatterball Adventure Games, Inc., is located in Chattanooga and runs local paintball games. Also, it has a store that sells some paintball supplies and repairs guns. It is through this store that many of the games are scheduled.

19   The owner of Splatterball, Doug Gray, began his involvement with the sport of paintball in 1981. He was a member of a small team based in Chattanooga. Shortly after joining, the team moved to Nashville when the field they were using was sold and was no longer available for their use. Many of the players lived in Nashville at that time, so they decided to open a field in Nashville, rather than look for a new field in Chattanooga. The team in Nashville became known as the Nashville Ridgerunners. Mr. Gray is still an active member of the Nashville Ridgerunners Professional Paintball Team.

20   Because there was no longer a field in Chattanooga, Mr. Gray drove two hours to Nashville almost every weekend to play the sport. It was during these trips he decided to open a field of his own in Chattanooga so he could practice closer to home.

21   Mr. Gray began to get his friends and acquaintances to go to Nashville with him to generate interest. Eventually, he was able to get enough people interested in paintball to support his field in Chattanooga.

22   Mr. Gray leased a parcel of land approximately 20 miles southeast of Chattanooga. According to Mr. Gray, "Since this was more of a hobby than business, I decided to run the operations from my home." He bought some of the plastic guns to use for rentals so he could continue to bring in new players to his field.

23   During this time, the field in Nashville became very successful at organizing paintball tournaments. Many tournaments were organized to bring in teams from the southeast region. Mr. Gray worked closely with the Nashville field in setting up his own field. His close ties enabled him to obtain many of his supplies at volume discount prices, as well as to gain other advantages that would otherwise have been denied to him as an independent.

24   Mr. Gray's business continued to grow as paintball began to receive more attention nationally. Businesses and groups began to schedule games for their members only. As his business expanded, Mr. Gray began to carry more rental equipment and supplies for the part-time player.

25   Eventually the business grew so large it became difficult to manage from his home. The rental equipment took up so much room that he decided it was time to establish a center of operations. However, to make this feasible, Mr. Gray needed an infusion of capital for the store lease, furniture lease, and the addition of even more equipment. He figured the total cost would run approximately $7,500. At this time he took in one partner and incorporated the business, with each partner owning 500 shares of stock.

26   Unfortunately, the partnership was not successful. Both partners had differing ideas on how the income should be distributed. Mr. Gray wanted most of the money reinvested in the business for further growth. However, his partner decided he wanted his capital infusion paid back immediately. After one year the partnership was dissolved, through Mr. Gray's purchase of his partner's 500 shares of stock for $11,000. The original investment was $10,000 and his partner had received approximately $1,200 in capital withdrawals when the repurchase was made.

THE SITUATION IN 1992

27   As of 1992, Mr. Gray is the sole stockholder of Splatterball, and he has decided to reevaluate what he is trying to accomplish. What is the future of Splatterball? Where is he trying to go with the business? How does he get there?

28   The business itself is quickly becoming a full-time operation. The hours of operation of the store are currently 11 A.M. to 3 P.M., Monday through Friday. It is open only on weekends if no games are being played at the field. Mr. Gray would like to increase the hours of operation but currently is not in the position to do so. Mr. Gray has full-time job as a computer programmer and he works 4:00 P.M. to 12:15 A.M., Monday through Friday. Eventually he would like to leave this position and have the business as his main source of income.

29   The store does bring some walk-in business, often from people who play the game on their own land. Mr. Gray offers a gun repair service on the premises. He is able to sell guns, supplies, and trade magazines at the store. Most of Splatterball's income is derived from the games. The field is available all year, but games are scheduled in advance, especially during the winter months. With scheduling, the proper amount of supplies can be ordered and the appropriate number of field judges can be obtained. Splatterball only keeps 100 rental guns in stock, so, if extremely large groups play, Mr. Gray has to borrow guns from another field. He has worked out an agreement with a field in Atlanta, in which each field makes guns available to the other at no charge.

30   Splatterball has its own professional and amateur teams that play regularly at the Splatterball field and in national tournaments. These teams were started in 1990 and have no sponsorship. There is no fee to become a member, and each member is responsible for all tournament entry fees and supplies. Mr. Gray relies heavily on his professional team members to give their support in running the store and in officiating games when they are not playing. Their compensation is in the form of discounts on supplies and gun repairs. New members are recruited from individuals playing the game with a group who have decided that they would like to play on a regular basis. These individuals will generally play with the team for six months before becoming a team member.

31   Currently, almost all of the games are scheduled on Saturday and Sunday mornings and afternoons. Groups schedule the field for an entire day. It also is possible for Mr. Gray to run the games during the week before 2 o'clock. Splatterball continues to run walk-on games on weekends, enabling individuals to try paintball without having to find other players to make up two teams. In addition to the typical player, Mr. Gray has some school groups that regularly rent the field for an entire day.

32   Mr. Gray's business background includes several years of college courses and his own trial-and-error experience when he first started Splatterball. He has taken a small business management course at a local junior college, but feels that he learned the most about management from starting the business. When asked about his management style, Mr. Gray says, "Currently I am doer out of necessity, but I am delegator by nature. I am great at long-range planning, and I need to be careful not to forget the small daily details that keep me in business."

THE COMPETITION

33   Splatterball's competition is primarily from the amusement industry and other paintball fields. Movies, music, and sport hunting are just three examples of the competition. Also, because of the great deal of physical activity involved, Mr. Gray feels he competes for the physical fitness dollar as well.

34   Competition between the paintball fields is actually very friendly. The closest fields to Chattanooga are in Atlanta, Knoxville, and Nashville. Each of these fields is approximately a two-hour drive from Chattanooga. Because no fields are close by, Mr. Gray does not compete directly with them for

local players. Instead, he has worked out arrangements with many of them, enabling each of them to host all of the participating regional teams in a league play. This league has 10 teams from Chattanooga, Nashville. Atlanta, and Birmingham. Ten times a year, all the teams meet at different fields to play each other. This was set up to give each of the teams a chance to play different types of fields with a higher level of competition. Although a trophy is awarded to the team accumulating the most points at the end of a calendar year, the main purpose of this league is to provide a higher level of practice for the major tournaments.

35   Most of the fields in this league are about the same size as Mr. Gray's, with the exception of the Nashville field. The Nashville field is able to handle approximately three to four times the size of the Splatterball field. Also, the Nashville field has an agreement with a local campground to use the campground for major tournaments in the spring and the fall. Because it is privately held, the exact earnings are unknown but are estimated to be around $1 million annually, including field operations, store operations, and tournaments.

36   In competing with the physical fitness sector, Splatterball actually has been able to work in cooperation with different programs. The game has been included as an activity in an intensive six-week fitness program in Chattanooga. This program is used to build self-confidence as well as physical fitness.

37   Splatterball also competes with the hobby/entertainment industry in general. Often it can be heard around the field that someone played that weekend instead of hunting or buying some personal item.

COSTS

38   The cost of playing Splatterball depends on the experience of the player. The novice player generally will have lower costs, because each rents the equipment. Mr. Gray typically charges a $22.52 flat field fee, which includes the $12.00 gun rental, 40 rounds of paint, and one small tank of carbon dioxide. Novice players generally shoot less than more experienced players and often do not have to purchase extra paint. The typical charge is $1.08 for one tube of paint (eight rounds).

39   The experienced player tends to incur much higher costs, so most will purchase their own guns, which will start at about $150. Also, there is the purchase of camouflage and other extra equipment to maintain the performance of their equipment. It is not uncommon for an experienced player to shoot up to 30 tubes of paint per game. Since most play a minimum of three 45-minute games, this will add up quickly.

40   The players who are part of a team often will have expenses on top of those incurred by the experienced player. Many own several guns in case of gun failure. These failures usually are due to wear on parts and do not occur regularly; but if a gun fails during a tournament, then the team is short a player. Also, there are the high entrance fees for tournaments, which can be as much as $200 per member.

FINANCIAL SITUATION

41   Splatterball Adventure Games, Inc., actually has a very "loose" accounting system. However, Mr. Gray recently has had an offer of free accounting services for 100 shares of stock. (Mr. Gray owns 1,000 shares of the 1,500 shares; 500 shares are retained by the business.)

42   Exhibits 1 and 2 show the current financial statements for the firm. The largest debt is Mr. Gray's repayment of the $11,000 loan used to repurchase the stock from his former partner. Other expenses, such as supplies, usually can be matched directly to the sales, since most supplies are received within two days of use. This helps eliminate spoilage of the supplies. The paintballs have a shelf life of several months, but they do tend to become soft. The sooner they are used, the better they perform.

EXHIBIT 1

**Income Statement
For the Quarter Ending
December 31, 1991**

Income:

Sales	$ 7,107.00
Net sales.................	7,107.00

Cost of goods sold:

Total cost of goods sold	0.00
Gross profit	7,107.00

Expenses:

Advertising	2,195.00
Auto expense...............	15.22
Bank service charges	22.50
Bank wire transfer fees	18.00
Casual labor	175.00
Dues & subscriptions...........	58.00
Entertainment................	173.28
Entry fees	278.00
Miscellaneous expense	190.10
Office expense...............	377.69
Paint & CO2 supplies	6,280.71
Postage...................	10.24
Rent	100.00
Field supplies...............	1,204.97
Telephone	111.88
Uniforms	128.56
Total expenses	11,339.15
Net operating income	(4,232.15)

Other income:

Interest income...............	13.00
Total other income	13.00

Other expenses:

Total other expenses	0.00
Income before taxes	(4,219.15)
Net income	$(4,219.15)

EXHIBIT 2

Balance Sheet
December 31, 1991

Assets

Current assets:

Cash	$(1,777.58)	
Inventory	260.99	
Total current assets		$(1,516.59)

Fixed assets:

Office equipment	189.95	
Paint guns	8,539.10	
Field equipment	2,592.25	
Total fixed assets.		11,321.30

Other assets:

Total other assets		0.00
Total assets.		$9,804.71

Liabilities & Equity

Current liabilities:

Accounts payable	$ 1,145.00	
Notes payable	11,363.26	
Sales tax payable	515.60	
Total current liabilities		$13,023.86

Long-term liabilities:

Total long-term liabilities		0.00
Total liabilities		$13.023.86

Stockholders' equity:

Common stock	1,000.00	
Current earnings	(4,219.15)	
Total equity		(3,219.15)
Total liabilities & equity		$ 9,804.71

43   Mr. Gray also has had an offer from two of the members of his team to work for 150 shares of stock each in the business. These players have helped Mr. Gray run Splatterball for two years. Neither would invest any money at this time but, instead, would reinvest their share of the profits plus provide free services. They would be able to assist in running the games and working in the store to increase its hours of operation. Both are experienced in gun repair and would be able to assist in this aspect of the business as well. One is a computer programmer with a college degree, who assists in the management of his family's convenience store. The other individual is an accountant, who will contribute free accounting and tax services to Splatterball. Both individuals would be able to work during the

hours when Mr. Gray is at his full-time job. This is currently under consideration with the attorneys in regards to fair value and distribution of future income through dividends or through salaries.

LEGAL ENVIRONMENT

44   The current legal environment is of great concern to Splatterball. Although every player signs a waiver form (see Exhibit 3) each time he or she plays, these waivers have not been tested through a lawsuit. Mr. Gray has had several attorneys review his form and has always received approval.

Injuries are one of the main concerns for Mr. Gray. Last year a new player was hit in the eye with a paintball and lost his vision. This player had taken off his goggles, even though he had been instructed not to and had signed the waiver stating he would wear the goggles at all times. In this particular instance, the Splatterball company was very lucky, because a spectator had just taken a picture of the injured player not wearing the required safety goggles. This picture prevented a lawsuit for negligence. However, the potential legal problems were brought to the forefront by this incident.

45   The entire paintball industry has worked very hard to promote safe usage practices both on and off the fields. *Paintball Sports Magazine* has published several articles regarding the usage of guns off the field. Tournaments impose penalties against teams whenever a player is found not to be wearing goggles. Off the field, barrels are required to have plugs in them so, if they accidentally are shot, the paintball breaks in the gun. Field operators also monitor how hard the guns are shooting the paintball. They chronograph the guns to ensure the guns do not shoot so hard they injure a player who is shot. Even though the guns are carefully monitored, being hit by a paintball will hurt. If shot from a very close range it will leave a bruise and occasionally a small welt. This welt, although painful, usually disappears within two days with no special attention required.

46   Most fields, including Splatterball, and all tournaments discourage shooting other players in the head. They have simply ruled that head shots do not count as "kills" or points. If a player is hit in the head, he or she may call a judge to help wipe off the paint. The judge will declare the player neutral until the paint is wiped off and then puts the player back into the game.

47   Whenever new players come out to the field, they are given instructions before the game begins. The field operator will walk over the field with the new player(s) to point out the boundaries and the flag stations. The field operator also points out any areas that players may want to avoid because of potential injury.

48   The entire industry also has worked together about concerns on equipment. There have been attempts in several states, most notably California, where there are several major fields, to ban the sale of toys that closely resemble guns. This is due to the very publicized shooting of children, because someone thought they had real guns. Because the newer guns closely resemble real guns, the industry is notably concerned.

49   Teams, field operators, and suppliers have worked together to keep paintball games as safe as possible. Because of the nature of the sport, sometimes there are injuries; but the people involved know that, when care and caution are used, most of these injuries can be avoided. These same people also have worked very hard to keep the sport legal in all states through letter-writing campaigns and lobbying.

THE FUTURE

50   Mr. Gray eventually would like to turn Splatterball into his full-time job. Currently, he works evenings to supplement his income. He stated, "If I could create a larger demand in the off season, I could depend on Splatterball as my sole source of income."

EXHIBIT 3
Application to Play
Waiver of Liability and Assumption of Risk

1. I, the undersigned wish to play the Splatterball Adventure game. I recognize and understand that playing the game involves running certain risks. Those risks include, but are not limited to, the risk of injury relating from the impact of the paint pellets used in the Game. Injuries resulting from possible malfunction of equipment used in the Game and injuries resulting from tripping or falling over obstacles in the Game playing field. In addition, I recognize that the exertion of playing the game could result in injury or death.

2. Despite these and other risks, and fully understanding such risks, I wish to play the Game and hereby assume the risks of playing the Game. I also hereby hold harmless Splatterball Adventure Game, Inc., hereafter called the Sponsors, and John Felts (landowner) and indemnify them against any and all claims, actions, suits, procedures, costs, expenses (including attorney's fees and expenses), damages and liabilities arising out of, connected with, or resulting from my playing the Game, including without limitation, those resulting from the manufacture, selection, delivery, possession, use or operation of such equipment. I hereby release the Sponsors from any and all such liability, and I understand that this release shall be binding upon my estate, my heirs, my representatives and assigns. I hereby certify to the Sponsors that I am in good health and do not suffer from a heart condition or other ailment which could be exacerbated by the exertion involved in playing the Game.

3. I hereby promise to play the Game only in accordance with the rules of the Game as set forth by the Sponsors. In particular, I agree:

   a. to wear safety goggles at all times when I am on the playing field or at the target area, even after I have been marked with paint or the game is over and to keep the goggles snug by pulling the straps tight; I understand that serious eye injury, including loss of eyesight, could occur if the safety goggles are not on when marking pistols may be discharged anywhere near me. Should my safety goggles fog up or for any reason be such that I cannot see through them properly, I will ask someone near me, on the playing field or in the target area, to lead me out of the area I am into to one where all marking pistols are on "SAFETY". Only then will I remove my safety goggles to clean them. I understand that any "safety goggle" is subject to fogging up or getting dirty and that if I am anywhere near a marking pistol as it discharges, and my "safety goggles" are not properly on, I may get seriously and permanently injured;

   b. to avoid any physical contact or fighting with other players;

   c. to stay within the boundaries of the playing field and not to chase or run after anyone over ledges or mountainous terrain; and

   d. to keep the marking pistol I am using on "safety" (the no-shoot position) in the staging area at all times, in the target area while not shooting and on the playing field before and after each game, to aim or point the pistol at another person ONLY during an active game and never to wave or brandish the pistol about in the staging area or the target area.

   e. to avoid pointing at or shooting at the head of any player at any time.

51　　Because of his expansion, the addition of shareholders to ease the financial burden is another consideration of Mr. Gray's. It would enable Splatterball to run more games, especially during the week.

52　　There is no real marketing strategy in place for Splatterball and Mr. Gray feels it is needed. Although Mr. Gray had some informational brochures printed for distribution, the main source of new business comes from word-of-mouth advertising. Mr. Gray would like to implement a strategy that will not deplete too much of his personal financial resources yet will enable him to work full time in his hobby.

EXHIBIT 3   (concluded)

4. For safety reasons I agree to use only equipment and/or supplies provided to me by the Sponsors while playing the game or in the target area. Written permission of the Sponsors is necessary should I elect to use other equipment or supplies. If I have chosen not to use the goggles or marking pistol available from the Sponsors, I hereby certify that the goggles or marking pistol, which I have chosen to use, are at least as safe as the Sponsor's form claims arising out of any additional risk resulting from my use of goggles or marking pistol other than those available from the Sponsors.

5. I agree to ask the Sponsor for clarification of any rule or safety procedure, for further instruction as regard anything that I don't understand about the equipment and supplies as regards anything else that may effect the safety of or playing of the Game.

6. I have read this waiver of liability and assumption of risk carefully, and understand that by signing below, I am agreeing, on behalf of myself, my estate, my heirs, representatives and assigns not to sue the Splatterball Adventure Games, Inc., or to hold them or their insurors liable for any injury including death, resulting from my playing the Game, I intend to be fully bound by this Agreement.

By virtue of my signature, I acknowledge and agree to all terms and conditions set forth on this form.

XSignature ————————————————

Date Signed ————————————————

Is this your first visit to our field? YES ( ) NO ( )

PLEASE PRINT CLEARLY:

Name ————————————————————————

Address ————————————————————————

City ——————— State ————— Zip ————— Daytime Phone —————

CASE 4

AKRON ZOOLOGICAL PARK 1992

AKRON ZOOLOGICAL PARK

1   As custodians of our wildlife heritage and animal preservation efforts, zoos remain an important educational and recreational resource. This case serves to illustrate the efforts made by the local zoo community in response to changes in consumer preferences, general price levels, governmental priorities, and international ownership of the rubber industry. The zoo's history, mission, relationship to its area competitors, administration, organization, and financial status are presented. The zoo has lowered its per visitor operating costs and increased its annual attendance. It has embarked on a building program and engages in strategic planning. As a recognition of its achievements as an outstanding microzoo, it has recently been awarded its accreditation by the American Association of Zoological Parks and Aquariums.

AKRON ZOOLOGICAL PARK 1991

Background

2   Zoos are perceived as custodians of our cultural wildlife heritage and as educators of the skills of conservation. Zoos can collectively maintain about 1,500 species of rare and endangered birds and animals. This represents less than one half of 1 percent of the species that are expected to become extinct during the next 10 years. Zoos are strategically placed to inform and to educate the public. More people annually visit zoos than enter all U.S. national parks. More people attend North American zoological facilities and programs than the combined number of persons who attend professional football, basketball, baseball, and hockey games. Zoos have remained a strong attraction for the people of the United States.

3   Collectively, during 1991, member institutions of the American Association of Zoological Parks and Aquariums had 105,903,570 visitors; over $799 million in operating budgets; $441,842,396 in combined capital improvements; 4,241,869 support organization members; over 25,633 acres in parklands; and more than 493,620 specimens from among mammals, birds, reptiles, amphibians, fish, and invertebrates. Zoological parks, aquariums, and botanical gardens come in all sizes. For example, the largest institution had 4 million visitors and an annual operating budget of $54 million. The smallest institution had 3,500 visitors. Another had a $100,000 budget.

This case was prepared by Professor F. Bruce Simmons III, the University of Akron, College of Business Administration.

The cooperation and assistance of the Akron Zoological Park is acknowledged and appreciated. Copyright © 1992.

4   Approximately 38 percent of A.A.Z.P.A. member institutions had annual operating budgets of less than $1 million. However, 17 percent had budgets in excess of $6 million. The association, at its annual 1989 meeting, awarded membership to the Akron Zoological Park. This recognition established that the zoo is one of the best 160 institutions in the Western Hemisphere.

5   During the late 1970s in Akron, changes in consumer preferences for radial automobile tires, the internationalization of the rubber industry, the economic ravages of rapidly increasing general price levels, and changes in governmental priorities almost resulted in the permanent closing of the Akron Children's Zoo. Sagging attendance and a low level of family memberships did not help matters. Faced with the uncertain prospect of continuing its zoo operations, the city of Akron sought to reduce, or eliminate, its financial commitment. As a response, the Akron Zoological Park was organized as an eleemosynary corporation under Section 501(c)3 of the Internal Revenue Code. The board of trustees contracted with the city to operate the zoo.

6   During the 1980s, the major employers in the Akron area were buffeted by the winds of change. For example, Firestone was purchased by Bridgestone, General Tire changed its name and sold off its broadcasting affiliates and its tire operations, Michelin acquired the combined Uniroyal–Goodrich company, and Goodyear had to sell several of its divisions to fend off an attempted takeover. In the 1980s and 1990s, many area corporations are pursuing the strategies of delayering, destaffing, and operating under the just-in-time manufacturing philosophy.

7   Although the zoo made it through these turbulent and difficult times, its president and CEO remains mindful that yesterday's achievements do not guarantee tomorrow's survival. Under the guidance of this CEO, the zoo expanded its operations and facilities, increased its annual attendance, and received A.A.Z.P.A. accreditation. To keep the zoo open and financially solvent, the CEO believes she needs to develop more animal exhibits, restroom facilities, parking spaces, and community outreach programs. Yet, she must balance the costs of this approach with the flows of operating revenues. The zoo CEO is currently searching for a course of action to follow. What would you recommend? If you advise adding employees, exhibits, or events, how would you obtain the funds to build, operate, and employ them?

History

8   Residents of Akron, like people in many other cities, created their zoo by donating animals to their city. Earlier this century, two brown bears were given to the city of Akron. The city fathers constructed an appropriate facility in a neighborhood park. Subsequently, other individuals established a Museum of Natural History near the Perkins Park bears. In 1953, both facilities were combined to create the Akron Children's Zoo. By the late 1970s, the city's ability and willingness to satisfactorily husband its animals was questioned. The future of the zoo as a community resource and its continuing operation were in grave danger. In response to this turmoil, the trustees of the Akron Zoological Park contracted with the city to manage and operate the zoo.

9   While contemplating the future direction of the zoo, and mindful of the severe financial constraints, the zoo's trustees decided to restrict their animal husbandry to North, South, and Central America birds, animals, and reptiles. The old Mother Goose exhibits were eliminated. They were replaced by more natural and native animal environments. These animal exhibits contain the zoo's collection of 183 specimens, which represent 66 different species of birds, reptiles, and animals.

10   During the past several years, the zoo has expanded its operations. Although it continues to follow the Western Hemisphere exhibits policy, the zoo opened an animal clinic, renovated its "petting zoo" barnyard, and constructed a gift shop, an alpaca exhibit, a concessions area, a reptile building, and a North American River Otter exhibit. New maintenance facilities and educational display areas were built. Also, the zoo has completed phase one of its educational signs installation.

Purpose

11 The mission of the Akron Zoological Park is to manage its resources for the recreation and education of the people of Akron and of surrounding communities and to promote the conservation of wildlife. To be successful, the Akron Zoological Park must maintain its image as a quality place where its visitors desire to spend their time. It seeks to keep the animal exhibits clean and neat so they are easy for all to see and enjoy. Flowers and plants abound. As resources become available for construction and continuing operations, it adds new exhibits and new activities. For example, the park's attendance increased from 63,034 people in 1986 to its record of 133,762 people in 1988. As a unique institution, the Akron Zoological Park presents a balanced program of education, recreation, conservation, and scientific activities.

Operating Season

12 Due to its northern climate, the zoo conducts its open season from mid-April until mid-October. Except for Halloween and the winter holidays, the zoo is closed for the winter months. It reopens for one week during Halloween. For the month of December, it is decked out in excess of 150,000 yuletide lights. Its operating season is shorter than many of its local competitors. Also, it is totally dependent on the largess of nature. For the 1990 year, the Akron area experienced its wettest weather in its recorded history. More than 57 inches of rain and snow were received. New Orleans; San Juan, Puerto Rico; Miami, Florida; and Mobile, Alabama, are among the lush locales that generally have this type of wet weather. This 1990 weather far exceeded the spring 1989 record precipitation. Additionally, in the month of December 1989, local records were broken for the coldest temperature on this date, the lowest windchill factors, and the most snow. Due to this record of extreme cold and snow, several evenings of the Holiday Lights were cancelled. Attendance at this event in 1988 was over 48,000 patrons. In December 1989, the Holiday Lights' attendance did not exceed 21,000 people. Weather influences zoo admissions.

13 The variations in weather also affect crop yields and the prices of fresh animal foods. A drought in 1988 and too much rain in 1989 and 1990 impacted the costs of feeding the animals. Weather can cause variations in the cost of animal feed.

14 In less extreme climatic circumstances, the zoo may be able to achieve its target attendance goal. Although its surrounding community suffered a declining population level, from 524,472 people in 1980 to 514,990 people in 1990, the zoo seeks to attract an annual attendance equal to 40 percent of its community. This goal may be too ambitious. The target audience for any zoological park tends to be young children and their parents. The Akron zoo's community contains a high percentage (approximately two fifths) of senior citizens. As indicated in Exhibit 1, since the zoo has become better known as an innovative community resource, the annual attendance has doubled.

Membership

15 Membership in the Akron Zoological Park is available to all. Becoming a zoo member means one has an unlimited no-charge admission to the zoo grounds during the operating season, plus reciprocal admission at over 130 other zoological parks, aquariums, and botanical gardens. Members receive a quarterly newsletter and invitations to members-only events. There exist differing types of memberships. They include: family, grandparents, donor, patron, zookeeper, safari leader, and director's club. Each type of membership reflects different levels of financial support for zoo activities. As indicated in Exhibit 2, during the past several years the number of memberships has increased. As the variety and number of activities have increased, membership and attendance more than doubled.

EXHIBIT 1
Annual Attendance

Year	Total	Admission Fee		
		Adult	**Child**	**Group**
1992	117,874	$4.00	$2.50	$1.50
1991	125,363	3.00	2.00	1.50
1990	126,853	3.00	2.00	1.50
1989	108,363	2.50	1.50	1.00
1988	133,762	2.50	1.50	1.00
1987	95,504	2.00	1.00	0.50
1986	63,034	1.50	0.75	0.50
1985	63,853	1.50	0.75	0.50
1984	61,417	1.50	0.75	0.50
1983	53,353	1.50	0.75	0.50

Source: Akron Zoological Park.

EXHIBIT 2
Annual Memberships

Year	Total
1992	2,021
1991	1,825
1990	1,365
1989	1,100
1988	1,158
1987	1,200
1986	1,036
1985	1,295
1984	986
1983	492
1982	437
1981	312

Source: Akron Zoological
Park.

16   Providing good customer service to the zoo's clientele pays dividends. Part of customer service is providing exciting events at the zoo. As indicated in Exhibit 3, during 1991, the zoo promoted several newsworthy and special events. These events serve to attract community media recognition. In return, this community attention increases annual memberships.

EXHIBIT 3
Special Events in 1992

Activity	Month
Snow Bowl	January
Spring Fling	April
Earth Day Observance	April
Super Saturday & Keep Akron Beautiful	May
Beastly Black & White Blast	May
Akron Zoo Day at the Cleveland Stadium	May
Sunday Sundae: Zoobilation	June
Recycle with Ohio Zoos	June
Nature Train	June
Zoo Camp	June
Reptile Day	July
Nocturnal Golf Classic	August
Spots & Stripes Celebration.	August
Member's Night	September
Boo at the Zoo	October
Annual Bird Seed Sale	October
Downtown Yule Display	November
Holiday Lights Celebration	December
Zoorific birth parties	May through September

Source: Akron Zoological Park.

Edzoocators

17   This unpaid volunteer group began in the 1970s. These volunteers have no responsibility for the direct operations of the zoo. In 1983, the zoo created the position of education curator. One aspect of this position is to coordinate this group's educational activities. As volunteers, members of this group are trained to provide on-site and off-grounds educational programs using the zoo's birds, reptiles, and animals. They provide guided tours of the zoo grounds, give presentations at local schools, provide a speakers' bureau, and appear on radio and television programs. They also receive free admission to the zoo grounds.

Outreach Programs

18   To take the zoo's services to those who are not able to visit the zoo's location, two zoomobile programs exist. The fur, feathers, and scales and the rain forest offerings provide the opportunity for people to learn about the zoo's conservation mission and its animals in a personal way. These individuals are taught to respect the animal and to preserve its dignity. For a nominal fee, plus gas mileage if located outside the city, the zoo's educational services are available for citizens groups, day care centers, schools, and other community organizations. If you are not able to travel to the zoo, it can come to you. If you can visit the grounds, the zoo offers a summer day zoocamp program and the opportunity for your child to celebrate a zoorific birthday party. Also, the zoo established a highly popular and

well-known teen volunteer program. Young adults between the ages of 14 and 18 years are trained and permitted to handle the animals while working one or two days per week at the zoo.

Advertising

19   Akron and Summit County are situated just south of Cleveland, Ohio. Cleveland is a major metropolitan area. It has television stations that are affiliated with all four major networks. It has three independent and one public broadcasting station. In contrast, Akron has one affiliate, one independent, and one public broadcasting station. Since many people view Cleveland television broadcasts, the local residents are generally more conversant about Cleveland events than they are about Akron's.

20   To gain media exposure in this market, the zoo must create media events. It must develop exciting activities that pass the threshold as newsworthy. Unlike the Cleveland MetroParks Zoo, the Akron zoo does not possess access to sufficient funds to permit it to advertise on commercial television. Budgetary pressures do not permit advertising expenditures. The zoo remains totally dependent on public service announcements, on the zoo's public television series, and on press coverage of the activities at the zoo.

Promotional Programs

21   The zoo creates newsworthy activities and conducts several promotions. For example, in the spring when the animals give birth to their young, the zoo conducts a contest to name the new arrivals. To create the opportunity for members of the community to learn firsthand about the animals within the zoo's collection, the zoo sponsors an annual expedition. In the past, these expeditions have taken participants to the Amazon of Peru, the forests of Belize, the sea turtles and rain forests of Costa Rica, and the Galapagos Islands of Ecuador. In July 1992, the zoo offers its members the opportunity to travel to Kenya. The local press has been quite supportive in reporting these globe-trotting activities. In Exhibit 3, the scheduled 1992 events are listed. These events have served to generate media attention. Many activities are but a few years old. They are a strong reason that zoo attendance increased.

Safety

22   In the event of an animal escape, zoo employees have a written procedure to follow for the recapture of the animal. As a good citizen, the zoo management, through its risk management and safety audit program, aims to ensure a safe environment for the visitor, employee, and the animals that inhabit the zoo. The zoo management remains committed to improving the quality of its exhibits and the habitats of their animals. For example, in conformance with A.A.Z.P.A.'s Code of Professional Ethics mandatory standards, exhibit animals are marked with identifying numbers. This animal marking system facilitates the proper care and security of the animal, bird, or reptile. Animal acquisition and disposal, breeding cooperation, and research for the health and preservation of endangered species is coordinated with other zoos. Cooperative research with colleges and universities is performed within written policy guidelines. As part of its strong commitment to customer service, the personnel of the zoo constantly strive to adhere to high standards of safety and professional conduct.

Administration

23   The president and CEO of the zoo is Patricia Simmons. She believes that her main function is to ensure the fiscal and conservational integrity of the zoo. She strives to maintain and improve the zoo's excellent customer service. A zoo employee for seven years, her contributions have resulted in increases in her operational authority and various promotions. She possesses a diverse background.

Her training and education are in fishery administration, fund-raising, fine arts, and management. She possesses a graduate degree in arts management. A community organization, Leadership Akron, honored her contributions by enrolling her in its 1989 class. On April 17, 1989, the trustees adopted the business corporation structure of governance and elected Mrs. Simmons as the president and CEO. Mrs. Simmons holds a seat and a vote on the board of trustees and is a member of the executive committee.

24   The board of trustees oversees the policies of the zoo and sets the guidelines for memberships and promotional activities. The board sees that all financial statements are audited by independent public accountants. Each trustee is elected to serve a three-year term. There are currently 24 trustees. The executive committee consists of the president & CEO plus the five elected trustee officers and the chairs of three standing board committees. The officers, who are elected annually and have a limit on the number of years in office, are the chairman of the board, two vice chairmen, a secretary, and a treasurer. The three standing committees are planning and finance, promotion and sales, and animal care and education. The board has quarterly and annual meetings.

Organization

25   The director of zoo operations, Mr. Pat Barnhardt, is provided via a grant with the city of Akron. He supervises the animal curator and the keeping staff as well as the maintenance and security crews. When his father was the Akron park's superintendent, he learned firsthand, as a volunteer, about the daily aspects of zoo operations.

26   The employees of the zoo are nonunion and noncivil service. As depicted in Exhibit 4, there are 20 full-time zoo employees. The education curator is responsible for the informational activities and coordinates the efforts of the volunteer groups. The public relations person seeks to obtain recognition for zoo events in the local media. The business manager supervises the accounting procedures and the daily commercial operations.

27   It is the zoo's policy that hiring, promotion, and employee transfer are based strictly on individual merit without favoritism or discrimination. A strong antinepotism policy is in place. For example, should an applicant for employment be under the direct supervision or within the same department as a relative, the zoo will not hire the relative of the employee.

Other Area Nonprofit Institutions

28   With greater competition for private gifts and grants, with the decline in the availability of donations due to changes in federal taxation law, and with weather-related gate receipts from clientele patronage, the zoo must consider the actions of its competitors. The Akron Zoological Park must successfully compete for resources within its community. Four other museums currently exist. They are the Historical Society, Hale Farm and Village, the Art Museum, and Stan Hywet Hall and Gardens. A brief description of each institution is provided in Exhibit 5. The most recent addition to the local museums is the National Inventors' Hall of Fame. Its organizers have announced an intention to raise $40 million from the community to construct a physical facility. Funds that are raised for this endeavor will necessarily not be available for other community institutions. When coupled with local universities' fund-raising activities, the competition for the community's resources and their allocation will be very intense.

29   A survey of current admission prices and operating statistics is given in Exhibit 6. The other institutions charge higher fees and have different sources of funding. For example, the historical society receives its funding from the county government. The zoo's admission pricing policy serves to keep it sensitive to other attractions.

EXHIBIT 4
Administrative Structure

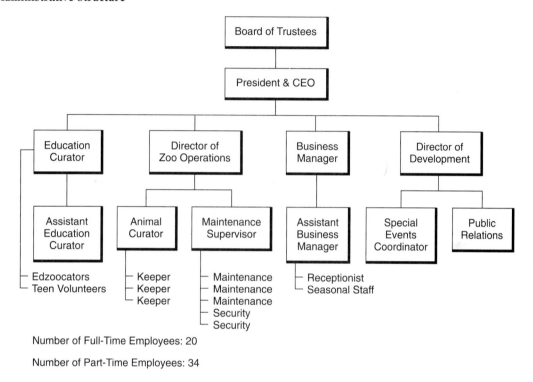

Number of Full-Time Employees: 20

Number of Part-Time Employees: 34

Source: Akron Zoological Park.

EXHIBIT 5
Brief Description of Competitors

Institution	Description
Historical Society	Consists of the General Simon Perkins Mansion and the abolitionist John Brown's home. The mansion, built in 1837, is 15 rooms of 19th-century items. Located near the zoo.
Invention Center	Hall of Fame for holders of U.S. patents. Soliciting funds from community to construct a permanent site.
Hale Farm & Village	A living history museum, with authentic renovated buildings and costumed guides, that depicts rural life in mid-19th century northeast Ohio.
Art Museum	The major exhibition of modern art between New York state and Chicago. It houses the E.C. Shaw collection and contains the finest art from 1850 to the present.
Stan Hywet Hall	An English country manor with 65 rooms that once was a self-sufficient estate of 3,000 acres. It is decorated with treasures collected from around the world.

Source: Akron Summit Visitors and Convention Bureau.

EXHIBIT 6

Summit County Museums
1992 Operating Statistics

Institution	Operating Budget	Visitors	Open Hours	Membership
Historical Society	$ 240,000	2,839	1,144	900
Zoological Park	798,650	117,784	1,467	2,021
National Invention Center	750,000	—	—	7,000
Hale Farm and Village	900,000	90,000	1,350	1,600
Art Museum	1,000,000	67,225	2,345	1,300
Stan Hywet Hall & Gardens . . .	1,200,000	56,800	2,100	2,000

Survey of Pricing
1992 Admission Fees

Institution	Admission Fee		
	Adult	Child	Group
Historical Society	$ 3.00	$ 2.00	$ 2.00
Zoological Park	4.00	2.50	1.50
National Invention Center . . . . . . Not yet open.			
Hale Farm and Village	7.50	4.50	1.00 off
Art Museum . . . . There is no charge.			
Stan Hywet Hall & Garden	6.00	3.50	0.50/1.00 off
Cleveland Zoo.	5.00	2.00	1.75
Sea World of Ohio	19.50	16.50	15.50

Source: Telephone survey.

Financial status

30   The zoo's ability to survive remains a function of its gate receipts, memberships, creative special events, donations, and its many volunteers. Nearly 75 percent of all operating funds are generated from zoo events and activities. During four of the past five years, excluding the grant contracted for with the city, the zoo received an average of $124,000 in donative grants. During the same period, membership sales increased by a net 144 percent, ticket and merchandise sales increased by more than 78 percent.

31   Financing its activities remains an important consideration to zoo management. The zoo has looked into alternate sources of financing. It has explored the feasibility in placing before the voters a property tax levy to sustain zoo operations. Also, the zoo has discussed with the other area nonprofit organizations the possibility of a joint tax levy. These other institutions receive funding from other sources and believe that they must not join with the zoo in a joint effort because their access to these other funds would be placed in serious jeopardy. The zoo has been left alone in its struggle for fiscal integrity. Recently, a committee of the regional chamber of commerce (A.R.D.B.) studied the financial feasibility of merging the zoo with the county MetroPark system. Since the executive management desires to reduce the uncertainty and to secure a more reliable source of operating revenues, it supplied

EXHIBIT 7

Combined Balance Sheet
As of December 31, 1990

	Unrestricted Fund	Restricted Fund	Plant Fund	Total
Assets				
Cash	$197,055	$109,363	$105,145	$ 411,563
Inventories	26,498	0	0	26,498
Accounts receivable	2,776	0	17,892	2,776
Other assets	1,000	0	0	1,000
Total current assets	227,329	109,363	105,145	441,837
Buildings & equipment............	0	0	936,251	936,251
Less accumulated depreciation	0	0	308,371	308,371
Total fixed assets	0	0	627,880	627,880
Total assets	$227,329	$109,363	$733,025	$1,069,717
Liabilities				
Accounts payable	$ 35,674	0	$ 1,695	$ 37,369
Accrued payroll	4,242	0	0	4,242
Accrued payroll taxes	7,686	0	0	7,686
Accrued bonus	20,000	0	0	20,000
Deferred membership	15,155	0	0	15,155
Deferred income	9,403	0	0	9,403
Deferred restricted contributions	0	$109,363	103,450	212,813
Total liabilities..................	$ 92,160	$109,363	$105,145	$306,668
Fund Equities				
Fund balance	$ 89,875	0	$627,880	$ 717,755
Board restricted	45,294	0	0	45,294
Total fund equities	$135,169	0	$627,880	$ 763,049
Total liabilities and fund equities	$227,329	$109,363	$733,025	$1,069,717

Source: Akron Zoological Park.

whatever information the committee requested. At this time, the committee report has not been made public.

32　　　Audited financial statements for Akron Zoological Park are provided in Exhibits 7 through 12. Since nonprofit accounting is somewhat different from conventional business accounting practices, a brief description of the accounts is necessary. The unrestricted fund accounts for all revenues and expenditures that are not accounted for in other funds. The unrestricted expenditures for each calendar year are financed principally by admissions, donations, memberships, concessions, and a grant from the city of Akron. The restricted fund accounts for all grants and other revenue that are designated for

EXHIBIT 8

Combined Balance Sheet
As of December 31, 1989

	Unrestricted Fund	Restricted Fund	Plant Fund	Total
Assets				
Cash	$138,303	$1,938	$160,739	$300,980
Inventories	26,203	0	0	26,203
Accounts receivable.............	4,213	0	17,892	22,105
Other assets	824	0	0	824
Total current assets	169,543	1,938	178,631	350,112
Buildings & equipment	0	0	843,142	843,142
Less accumulated depreciation	0	0	250,167	250,167
Total fixed assets.............	0	0	592,975	592,975
Total assets	$169,543	$1,938	$771,606	$943,087
Liabilities				
Accounts payable	$ 25,828	0	$ 36,745	$ 6,573
Accrued payroll................	2,808	0	0	2,808
Accrued payroll taxes	6,745	0	0	6,745
Deferred membership............	14,055	0	0	14,055
Deferred income	8,779	0	0	8,779
Deferred restricted contributions	0	$1,938	141,886	143,824
Total liabilities	$ 58,215	$1,938	$178,631	$238,784
Fund Equities				
Fund balance	$ 54,686	0	$592,975	$647,661
Board restricted	56,642	0	0	56,642
Total fund equities.............	$111,328	0	592,975	704,303
Total liabilities and fund equities	$169,543	$1,938	$771,606	$943,087

Source: Akron Zoological Park.

specific uses by their benefactors. The plant fund accounts for all the acquisition and deletion of building and equipment plus related depreciation. Land is leased from the city of Akron for nominal consideration. Depreciation is straight line over an applicable 5- to 20-year period. Buildings typically represent approximately 80 percent of the amount. Deferred membership income is recognized at the time of receipt but is amortized to operations over the one-year membership period. Deferred restricted contributions are recognized at the time of receipt and are recorded in operations when the expenditure for the specific purpose is made. Inventories are stated at the lower of FIFO cost or market. Contributed utilities and benefits are provided by the city of Akron. The city supplies the utilities to the zoo and provides the salary and benefits of one city worker.

EXHIBIT 9

Combined Balance Sheet
As of December 31, 1988

	Unrestricted Fund	Restricted Fund	Plant Fund	Total
Assets				
Cash	$197,519	$4,514	$113,480	$315,513
Inventories	9,088	0	0	9,088
Accounts receivable	4,166	0	12,920	17,086
Other assets	824	0	0	824
Total current assets	211,597	4,514	126,400	342,511
Buildings & equipment	0	0	734,724	734,724
Less accumulated depreciation	0	0	198,941	198,941
Total fixed assets	0	0	535,783	535,783
Total assets	$211,597	$4,514	$662,183	$878,294
Liabilities				
Accounts payable	$ 22,571	0	$ 12,920	$ 35,491
Accrued payroll	2,202	0	0	2,202
Accrued payroll taxes	5,981	0	0	5,981
Deferred membership	17,082	0	0	17,082
Deferred income	10,668	0	0	10,668
Deferred restricted contributions	0	$4,514	113,480	117,994
Total liabilities	$ 58,504	$4,514	$126,400	$189,418
Fund Equities				
Fund balance	$ 55,573	0	$535,783	$591,356
Board restricted	97,520	0	0	97,520
Total fund equities	$153,093	0	$535,783	$688,876
Total liabilities and fund equities	$211,597	$4,514	$662,183	$878,294

Source: Akron Zoological Park.

33   Along with the skyrocketing increases in veterinary and trash disposal costs, the rapid escalation in health and liability insurances also are a major concern. The availability of health care insurance is not guaranteed. Few insurance companies are interested in writing a policy for an employer with but 17 employees. The few who are interested want to select only a few employees and leave the others without insurance. Should the zoo have one employee who is deemed to be a high risk by the issuing company, there may be no insurance available for any employee. The dilemma remains: how to obtain health insurance for all employees at an affordable rate.

34   As the costs of fringe benefits increase, the salary level available for the employee cannot rise. This places the dedicated zoo employee at a distinct financial disadvantage relative to an employee at the city of Akron. The city's wages are among the highest for municipal employees in the state of Ohio.

EXHIBIT 10

Combined Balance Sheet
As of December 31, 1987

	Unrestricted Fund	Restricted Fund	Plant Fund	Total
Assets				
Cash	$70,657	$6,021	$119,728	$196,406
Inventories	4,611	0	0	4,611
Accounts receivable	2,330	0	0	2,330
Other assets	824	0	0	824
Total current assets	78,422	6,021	119,728	204,171
Buildings & equipment	0	0	661,947	661,947
Less accumulated depreciation	0	0	154,098	154,098
Total fixed assets	0	0	507,849	507,849
Total assets	$78,422	$6,021	$627,577	$712,020
Liabilities				
Accounts payable	$19,766	0	$ 3,677	4 23,443
Accrued payroll	1,325	0	0	1,325
Accrued payroll taxes	5,286	0	0	5,286
Deferred membership	5,229	0	0	5,229
Deferred income	4,840	0	0	4,840
Deferred restricted contributions	0	$6,021	116,051	122,072
Total liabilities	$36,446	$6,021	$119,728	$162,195
Fund Equities				
Fund balance	19,455	0	507,849	527,304
Board restricted	22,521	0	0	22,521
Total fund equities	$41,976	0	$507,849	$549,825
Total liabilities and fund equities	$78,422	$6,021	$627,577	$712,020

Source: Akron Zoological Park.

By contrast, the basic wage at the zoo is the legally prescribed minimum wage. Recent increases in the federal minimum wage have significantly raised annual wage costs. One half of the employees received a pay raise from the enactment of this recent legislation. Without corresponding increases in revenue, the zoo could become a victim of this legislation.

35   Although it possesses federal nonprofit status, the zoo must seek to ensure that its sources of income equal or exceed its operating and physical plant costs. Its continued existence and its promotion of wildlife conservation remain totally dependent on its ability to generate revenues and to reduce its expenses.

EXHIBIT 11

Combined Balance Sheet
As of December 31, 1986

	Unrestricted Fund	Restricted Fund	Plant Fund	Total
Assets				
Cash	$64,654	$12,171	$242,892	$319,717
Inventories	6,242	0	0	6,242
Accounts receivable	4,247	1,000	0	5,247
Due from unrestricted fund	0	7,718	0	7,718
Other assets	824	0	0	824
Total current assets	$75,967	$20,889	$242,892	$339,748
Buildings & equipment	0	0	$416,996	$416,996
Less accumulated depreciation	0	0	119,602	119,602
Total fixed assets	0	0	297,394	297,394
Total assets	$75,967	$20,889	$540,286	$637,142
Liabilities				
Accounts payable	$ 2,351	$11,579	0	$13,930
Accrued payroll	1,910	0	0	1,910
Accrued payroll taxes	4,549	0	0	4,549
Deferred membership	3,915	0	0	3,915
Deferred income	0	0	0	0
Deferred restricted contributions	7,718	9,310	$242,892	259,920
Total liabilities	$20,443	$20,889	$242,892	$284,224
Fund Equities				
Fund balance	$20,524	0	$297,394	$317,918
Board restricted	35,000	0	0	35,000
Total fund equities	$55,524	0	$297,394	$352,918
Total liabilities and fund equities	$75,967	$20,889	$540,286	$637,142

Source: Akron Zoological Park.

Admissions Policy

36   The park is open to all persons who follow the general admission rules. These rules are printed on the visitor's brochure. All visitors must wear a shirt and shoes. No alcoholic beverages are permitted. The zoo reserves the right to remove visitors who prove to be unruly, or those who harass the animals, feed the animals, enter into the exhibit areas, or litter the park.

EXHIBIT 12

Statement of Support, Revenue, Expenses, and Changes in Fund Balances
For the Years Ended December 31, 1991, 1990, 1989, 1988, 1987, and 1986

	Operating Funds					
	1991	1990	1989	1988	1987	1986
Support and revenue:						
City of Akron Grant	$200,000	$180,000	$180,000	$175,000	$165,000	$160,000
City Services in kind	124,915	58,597	55,367	51,160	49,722	50,398
Donations	111,640	152,289	155,143	227,102	311,263	201,842
Admissions	198,505	167,307	109,523	113,840	71,725	47,297
Concessions.	87,441	76,788	55,177	54,419	41,054	42,297
Memberships	48,736	38,800	27,247	24,666	15,891	26,502
Interest	31,124	32,112	22,291	15,634	13,768	13,901
Total revenue.	802,361	705,893	604,748	661,821	668,423	542,857
Expenses:						
Program:						
Animal collections	131,057	133,819	127,410	113,037	113,897	118,789
Buildings & grounds	289,746	233,121	189,763	169,870	161,605	141,914
Cost of concessions	25,124	13,489	14,267	14,434	13,888	26,336
Education	39,117	26,510	28,509	22,699	25,169	23,277
Strategic planning	0	0	3,838	0	0	0
Total expenses	485,044	406,939	363,787	320,040	314,559	310,316
Supporting:						
Administration.	242,610	228,391	206,217	175,426	131,327	95,629
Promotion	57,816	8,277	15,795	23,903	23,130	17,534
Legal and accounting	4,200	3,540	3,522	3,401	2,500	26,073
Total supporting.	304,626	240,208	225,534	202,730	156,957	139,236
Total expenditures	789,670	647,147	589,427	522,770	471,516	449,552
Excess of support & revenue over expenses	12,691	58,746	15,427	139,051	196,907	93,305
Operating fund balance: Beginning of year	763,044	704,303	688,876	549,825	352,918	259,613
Operating fund balance: End of year	$775,740	$763,049	$704,303	$688,876	$549,825	$352,918

Source: Akron Zoological Park [Auditors: Deloitte & Touche].

Master Plan

37 The zoo is located in Perkins Park. The shade trees serve to keep the grounds relatively free from the harsh effects of the sun. The zoo consists of 25 acres and stretches across two plateaus. Between the upper and lower level is a comparatively steep natural incline. This incline runs throughout the middle of the zoo. The current master grounds plan is shown in Exhibit 13. It was created in 1983. Nationally,

EXHIBIT 12 (concluded)

**Combined Balance Sheet
as of December 31, 1991**

	Unrestricted Fund	Restricted Fund	Plant Fund	Total
Assets				
Cash	$153,560	$114,538	$ 119,931	$ 388,029
Inventories	18,188	0	0	18,188
Accounts receivable	4,283	0	0	4,283
Prepaid expenses	2,935	0	0	2,935
Other assets	1,000	0	0	1,000
Total Current Assets	$179,966	$114,538	$ 119,931	$ 414,435
Buildings & equipment	0	0	1,024,483	1,024,483
Less accumulated depreciation	0	0	367,601	367,601
Total fixed assets	0	0	656,882	656,882
Total Assets	$179,966	$114,538	$ 776,813	$1,071,317
Liabilities				
Accounts Payable	$ 10,014	$ 0	$ 0	$ 10,014
Accrued payroll & payroll taxes	28,790	0	0	28,790
Deferred membership	11,092	0	0	11,092
Deferred income	11,212	0	0	11,212
Deferred restricted contributions	0	114,538	119,931	234,469
Total Liabilities	$ 61,108	$114,538	$ 119,931	$ 295,577
Fund equities				
Fund balances	94,136	0	656,882	751,018
Board designated	24,722	0	0	24,722
Total Fund Equities	$118,858	0	$ 696,882	$ 775,740
Total Liabilities and Fund Equities . . .	$179,966	$114,538	$ 776,813	$1,071,317

EXHIBIT 13
Master Plan

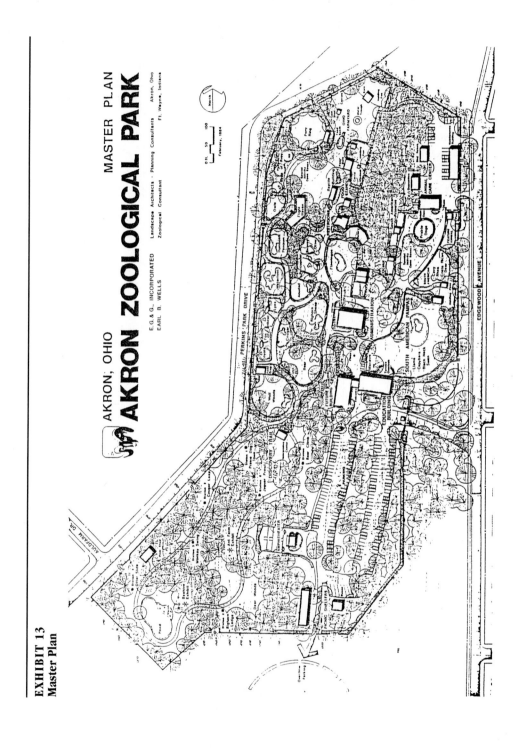

AKRON, OHIO   MASTER PLAN

AKRON ZOOLOGICAL PARK

E.G. & G., INCORPORATED   Landscape Architects · Planning Consultants   Akron, Ohio
EARL B. WELLS   Zoological Consultant   Ft. Wayne, Indiana

zoos are responding to rapid changes in accreditation requirements. Since the Akron zoo is now an accredited institution, it, too, must change. The terrain hinders the access to the grounds for the handicapped and disabled. Also, to improve zoo access, a higher quality of washroom facilities is necessary.

38   To continue to provide great customer service, the zoo also will need to expand its parking area. On days of special events when the crowds number near 3,000 people or more, the parking space is inadequate. The zoo does have some space within its fenced perimeter where it can expand parking. However, the zoo is in Perkins Park. By expanding into this park, the zoo could double its size. Yet this presents a dilemma. To expand and to construct new exhibits will increase admissions, but it will require increases in both capital and operating funds. Without additional parking and concession areas the zoo will not be able to increase its gate receipts. Further, extra exhibits can mean that customers will remain longer in the zoo and are likely to purchase more concessions and souvenirs. Continued pursuit of its educational and recreational objectives can become a financial burden. Failure to follow its expansion strategy is risking organizational decline and acceptance of the uncertainty of present financing. Zoo executive management will not accept a secondary community status.

Survey Report on the Zoo

39   The zoo contracted with the local university to conduct a study of zoo clientele. Telephone surveys were made the last week of September 1989. Interviewers received 757 usable responses. In general, those people who patronize zoos have a positive overall evaluation of the facility. They favorably rate its cleanliness, safety, convenience, and animal displays. Approximately one half of the respondents avail themselves the opportunity to use the Akron zoo. The zoo satisfies the current customs in terms of features and facilities.

40   However, nearly two fifths of the people interviewed report never going to a zoo. The results of this survey are reviewed in Exhibit 14. The basic reasons given for not attending a zoo are a "dislike of zoos," "no time for a visit," "lacking in transportation," "the children are grown," and simply "I do not have an answer."

41   When asked about the zoo, many people responded that it is too small. Seventy-five percent of its patrons and two thirds of the general public expressed concern at the relative smallness of the facility. The respondents offered suggestions for five additional facilities they would like the zoo to construct. These requests include "more exhibits for the children with visitor involvement," "a railroad," "bring back the black bears," and to "add more small cats and monkeys."

42   To better understand the needs of its customers, the survey asked whether the respondents visited any other attractions in the area during 1989. The responses indicated that the zoo's clientele attended five other area institutions. These were the Cleveland Zoo, Sea World, Stan Hywet Hall and Gardens, Hale Farm and Village, and Geauga Lake Park Amusements. Three fifths who attend the Akron Zoological Park also visit these competing facilities.

43   Zoos, aquariums, and botanical gardens are evolving from their origins in the museum community. They are caretakers of life in an age of extinction. They focus on life and its diversity. The employees and board members are concerned with the zoo's future viability, prosperity, and perspective. What recommendations would you make to enable the zoo to continue its operations?

EXHIBIT 14
Akron Zoological Park

Visitor Survey: Primary Competitors, December 1989

Other attractions Visited in 1989	Percent
Cleveland Zoo	51.8%
Sea World	45.2
Stan Hywet Hall and Gardens.	41.2
Hale Farm and Village	32.2
Geauga Lake Park Amusements	31.2

Visitor Survey: Reasons Not to Attend, December 1989

Multiple Reasons Given	Percent
Do not like zoos	16.3%
Transportation problems	6.1
Not personally able	16.7
Lack of time.	27.2
No interest	13.6
Kids are grown	12.2
Unsafe urban neighborhood	2.4
New to area	1.7
Unable to supply an answer	12.0

Visitor Survey: Preferred New Projects, December 1989

New Projects	Response Ranking
Build exhibits for children	First (tie)
Bring back the bears	Second
Addition of small cats to collection	Third
More monkeys.	Fourth
Addition of a railroad	First (tie)

Source: The University of Akron Survey Research Center Project Report.

CASE 5

THE WALT DISNEY COMPANY

HISTORY OF THE COMPANY

1   Walt Elias Disney, the creative genius and founder of what is today an international entertainment conglomerate, was born in 1901 into a struggling midwestern farm family. Fueled by clever concepts and an innovative spark, young Walt worked as a cartoonist for a Kansas City newspaper and created animated shorts for local movie theaters. However, when his early business ventures failed, the 21-year-old dreamer left for Hollywood.

2   Once in Los Angeles, Walt went into business with his older brother Roy, who was recovering from a bout with tuberculosis. Although Roy's only exposure to business had entailed a short stint as a bank teller, he had a better grasp of numbers than Walt. Together they formed the "Disney Brothers" and immediately began work on their first series of shorts. From the beginning, it was Walt who handled the production of cartoons while Roy was relegated to the secondary, but necessary, role of arranging the financing for Disney Brothers animation. Inspired by the moderate success of their first series, entitled *Alice in Cartoonland,* the brothers next created *Oswald the Rabbit.* However, disaster struck when a New York distributor stole the series along with all of its animators.

3   Disappointed but not defeated, the Disneys renewed their search for concepts and animators. It was Walt who developed the idea for Disney's earliest character, Mickey Mouse. Ironically, New York distributors were uninterested in *Plane Crazy,* the first silent short to spotlight the mouse that would become one of Disney's most endearing and timeless characters. Nonetheless, the brothers persevered and featured Mickey in a new film the following year. In the enormously successful *Steamboat Willie,* the Disney Brothers were the first production company to employ sound in an animated short. Walt alone had provided the inspiration for the studio's first major hit, and it came as no surprise when he renamed the company "Walt Disney Productions."

The Studio of Walt Disney Productions

4   Under Walt's control, the new studio was characterized by attention to detail and constant striving for improvement and innovation, even during times of financial difficulty. Studio animators were trained at an elaborate art school and, thereafter, were encouraged to experiment with lavish cartoons and new techniques at any expense.

5   Disney quickly became the leading studio in innovative animation. For example, the studio pioneered the use of full color and of synchronized sound in cartoons. In 1937, Disney produced *Snow White,* the first full-length animated film ever released. The movie also featured the use of a revolutionary multiplane camera, which produced the illusion of depth in the figures on screen. The studio had a similar commitment to innovation in its true-life adventure movies. In preparation for the films,

This case was prepared by Neil H. Snyder, Ralph A. Beeton Professor of Free Enterprise, University of Virginia; George H. Tompson, University of South Carolina; and Joanna Blattberg, University of Virginia School of Law.

Walt required naturalist cameramen and artists to study the anatomy and locomotion of animals in their natural habitat.

6   The single-minded pursuit of quality and innovation in the studio meant, however, that during the early years Disney operated on borrowed money. On the brink of bankruptcy, the company's leaders responded to crisis with flexibility. To alleviate the burden of bank loans, Disney went public in 1940. It was during these early financial difficulties that Disney first implemented its cross-promotional efforts by licensing Mickey Mouse and other cartoon characters. Creative business planning coupled with quality products pulled Disney out of debt. The studio was in full swing by 1964, when it grossed over $45 million after the release of its first animated and live action musical, *Mary Poppins*.

Disneyland

7   Shortly after the formation of the family business, Walt had begun to develop his dream of building an amusement park for the enjoyment of "honest American" families. For over 20 years he worked on the concept as a hobby until he had produced a sketch for the theme park in 1952. Roy, however, would invest only $10,000 of Disney Studio money in the risky project. Determined to realize his vision, Walt came up with the rest of the capital he needed by borrowing on his life insurance policy.

8   The goal at Disneyland was to ensure that guests enjoyed an educational and friendly escape. To that end, the attention to detail and quality was as apparent at the theme park as it was in the studio. Walt spared no expense in demanding that the rides be authentic and the audio-animatronic figures as lifelike as possible. Disney characters at the park were required to undergo days of training and indoctrination before appearing in public to entertain guests. Characters such as Mickey Mouse, Pluto, and Donald Duck also were featured in a successful weekly television show, "Disneyland," that promoted the theme park as well as Disney-licensed consumer products. The gross revenues from Disneyland during its first year totaled $10 million and accounted for roughly one third of overall sales at Disney.

DISNEY UNDER NEW MANAGEMENT: THE TROIKA

9   Over the years the division of labor between the creative "Walt men" and the financial "Roy men" intensified and often resulted in severe disagreements, generally over whether to invest company money in risky new ventures. After a decade of feuding, the brothers reconciled their differences before Walt died of lung cancer in 1966. Although Walt had neglected to designate a succession plan, 73-year-old Roy was the obvious successor.

10   The management team that emerged promptly replaced the autocratic style of Walt's leadership with a committee-rule approach. Roy, previously president of Disney, became the chairman of a new "Troika." The former executive vice president of administration, Don Tatum, moved into the position of president. Tatum, a quiet and intelligent Oxford-educated man, had risen under the direction of Roy through the ranks of Disney's financial side. On the other hand, Card Walker, who left his position as head of marketing to become executive vice president in charge of operations, was clearly an impulsive and outgoing "Walt man." Walker had first worked at Disney as a mail-room messenger in 1938, then with Walt as a cameraman on *Fantasia*. Later, as he rose through the marketing division, Walker had become one of Walt's closest confidantes.

Walt Disney World

11   Under the reign of Roy, Tatum, and Walker, gross revenues at Walt Disney Productions grew dramatically, more than doubling over six years. The completion of Walt Disney World, a dream on which Walt had begun to focus a few years before his death, accounted for one source of the growth in revenues. The complex, which included rides, themed attractions, restaurants, and shops, was built in 1971 on 29,000 acres of land just outside Orlando, Florida. The futuristic

park, featuring "castmembers" and "guests" rather than employees and guests, was an immediate success.

12   To accommodate guests of the park, Disney later developed eight resort hotels, a complex of houses and villas, and a camping and recreational facility. The company went on to build the Disney Village Marketplace, which serviced guests at the resort with a blend of shopping, dining, clubhouse, conference center, and entertainment facilities.

13   Roy died within a year of the opening of Walt Disney World. Until that point, either Walt or Roy had overseen every aspect of the operation of the family business. It was unclear whether the company could produce leaders capable of leading Disney into the 1970s with the innovation and imagination that had characterized Disney from the start.

DISNEY PRODUCTIONS IN TRANSITION

14   In the aftermath of Roy's death, Walker moved into the position of president. Four years later he made it clear that he was in control at Disney when he added to his title of president that of chief executive officer. Walker viewed himself as a corporate heir entrusted with the founder's legacy and, accordingly, insisted on a rather rigid adherence to traditional Disney formulas. According to top executives at Disney, the company's mission was to nurture the imaginations of children around the world as well as to celebrate American values. Under Walker's direction, the studio delivered predictable and wholesome entertainment that generated increasing revenues for several years.

15   However, by 1979, the studio's market share of the motion picture industry had fallen to a mere 4 percent. One explanation was that, while American moviegoers had changed, particularly in their taste for more violent films, Disney insisted on adherence to old formulas. Without the leadership of Walt, company executives resisted engaging in uncertain and imaginative ventures. Moreover, Disney routinely lost top projects because of an unwillingness to pay the huge salaries that had become customary in the movie industry.

16   These changes in the film division troubled Roy E. Disney, who was Roy Disney's son, a principal shareholder, and a member of the executive committee. Roy was disturbed by the deferential philosophy that had come to prevail in the film division, as well as by the back seat that the studio had been taking in the company's other projects. He believed that, instead of producing silly comedies and sequels, the studio should concentrate on producing updated versions of the inventive, high-quality films that had been central to its successes of the past. However, the widespread belief at the studio was that Roy was "the idiot nephew." Frustrated by the lack of response to his suggestions, Roy resigned in 1977.

17   Internal discord at the company continued into 1980, when Walker, without the consent of the board, selected Ron Miller for the position of president and chief operating officer. Several years after his marriage to Walt's daughter, Diane, Miller had been invited by his father-in-law to join the company's studio operations. Miller immediately abandoned his position as tight end for the Los Angeles Rams and began his career as a second assistant director. Though unassertive and inexperienced, Miller received special attention and training from Walt as he moved up the ranks of Disney's production division. When Miller became head of production in 1976, critics attributed his success to his close ties with Walt, who had no sons of his own.

18   Though Miller may indeed have lacked the experience necessary to direct corporate strategy, by the 1970s he had nonetheless realized that Disney's approach to film-making was outdated. Finally out from under his father-in-law's shadow, Miller attempted to implement changes at the company. He directed Thomas Wilhite, Disney's publicity director, to take control of creative development in the studio. Wilhite's first priority would be to broaden the appeal of the Disney brand of family entertainment. However, Wilhite's tenure as head of the new film operations was unfruitful, and foreseeably so; although he had been exposed to the film industry through Disney's marketing department, he had

never before produced films. His contemporary movies, marketed toward a more mature audience, were opposed by Walker and were poorly received by moviegoers.

19   To make matters worse, the company had taken on a huge amount of debt to finance construction work at the Environmental Prototype Community of Tomorrow. EPCOT would be divided into two themed areas. Pavilions in Future World would dramatize significant historical trends and explore resulting energy, health, communication, and cultural issues. World Showcase exhibits, on the other hand, would feature exhibits that surveyed cultural traditions and accomplishments of foreign nations.

20   Disney was determined to open EPCOT by 1982, but costs had risen unexpectedly because of design difficulties and labor shortages. Moreover, the sharp rise in gas prices in the 1970s and the downturn in the economy in the early 1980s led to falling attendance at Disneyland and Walt Disney World.

21   Faced with mounting problems, Disney's leaders failed to implement the flexible business plans that had characterized the company's recovery from hard financial times under Walt's guidance. To preserve Disney's friendly reputation, Walker refused to increase ticket prices for admission to theme parks and rejected proposals that advertising be permitted. At the same time, Disney management scaled back on necessary upkeep at the aging theme parks.

Disney under Miller and Watson

22   Before retiring in 1982, Walker, whose confidence in Miller had dwindled, appointed Ray Watson as vice chairman. Watson was an architect with extensive experience in real estate development, resulting from years of converting farmland into planned communities. Watson's background in real estate, coupled with his creative training as an architect, made him especially valuable to Walt. He had worked as a consultant to Disney on real estate development issues for several decades and clearly understood the Disney culture.

23   As newly appointed vice chairman, Watson inherited a company plagued by a falling stock price. Though rich with Florida real estate, massive theme park complexes, and a treasury of cartoons and classic films, Disney had failed to exploit its assets. Dwindling confidence among the investment community in the Disney management team pushed the company into crisis by 1984.

24   The possibility of a hostile takeover was too great to ignore when the board noted unusually heavy trading of Disney stock in March. By the end of that month, Watson learned that Saul Steinberg, one of America's most aggressive corporate raiders, had been acquiring Disney stock for several weeks. Not surprisingly, many Americans viewed the threat of a takeover as unpatriotic. One journalist in Hollywood wrote that:

25   while Steinberg and his ilk are making millions by threatening to tear down what took years to build, Disney and other creative institutions still are developing ideas, tangible products—and jobs. Steinberg apparently thought nothing of dissolving an American original, a monument to ingenuity and quality.

26   To prevent a Steinberg takeover, the company began to strengthen its position through mergers and acquisitions. Disney first bought Arvida, a solid real estate and development company specializing in resorts and apartment buildings in Florida. Disney next acquired Gibson, a greeting card company. Watson believed that the acquisitions made solid business sense, not only because they reduced Steinberg's stake in Disney from 12.1 to 11.1 percent but also because ownership of Arvida would facilitate aggressive development of the Disney's Orlando property.

27   Of course, the acquisitions diluted Roy Disney's holdings in the company as well. In response, Roy and a group of his business allies known as the "brain trust" hired Drexel Burnham Lambert junk bond guru Michael Milken to structure the financing for a takeover battle. However, the brain trust backed down when they realized that the risky venture, if successful, would result in the dismemberment of the company. Milken then took the same package to Steinberg, who eagerly accepted and publicly announced his tender offer on June 8, 1984. Instead of a self-tender, proxy fight, or direct

appeal to shareholders, Disney's managers responded with a strategy that would most effectively keep the company intact: they paid "greenmail" and bought back Steinberg's stock at a premium.

28   Although Disney had survived the attempts by corporate raiders, its management team was in desperate need of revitalization as its stock continued to fall steadily. In the aftermath of the takeover attempt, stockholders, members of both factions of the Disney family, and potential investors showed little confidence in Disney's management. The company had preserved its independence, but many in the investment community questioned the propriety of the greenmail payment since Disney had not offered to buy the shares of other stockholders at the same premium that Steinberg had received.

29   The Gibson deal was another source of criticism, particularly from Roy Disney and his lawyer and financial advisor, Stan Gold. When the board refused to respond to pressure to bail out on the deal, Roy and Gold approached the company with a request to be incorporated into the management team. After the managers rejected the proposal, Roy initiated a lawsuit against the board on the grounds that Disney's acquisition of Gibson had not been in the best interests of its shareholders. In addition, Gold threatened to bring the Gibson issue before the shareholders for a vote.

30   Disney found itself once again in a vulnerable position. Disney's management team was widely perceived to be weak, ineffectual, and divided. A shareholder vote against Gibson would exacerbate heightening skepticism about management's ability to perform. Despite the release of *Splash,* the Studio's most successful film ever, and the improved earnings that resulted from the hit movie, the financial industry remained unenthusiastic about Disney's ability to bounce back in the wake of the takeover attempts.

31   To ward off the pending law suit, stabilize the company, and harmonize the two factions of the Disney family, Watson agreed to appease Roy. First, Watson gave him three board seats, which went to Roy Disney, Gold, and advertising executive Peter Dailey, Roy's brother-in-law. Before dropping the suit, Roy demanded that Walker and Tatum be forced off the executive committee—Roy apparently wanted revenge for the decades he had spent with the company in vain.

32   Once back on the board of directors, Roy focused on the rejuvenation of the film division, which he saw as the company's most important asset. This would mean an increase in production and a search for a new creative leader. Gold agreed that the studio should be restored to primacy under a creative, high-powered management team.

33   The search for new leadership coincided with widespread critique of Miller's leadership. Financial analysts blamed the decline of the film division, the greenmail maneuver, and the Gibson deal on weak leadership by Miller, who was becoming increasingly dispensable. In a memorandum dated July 28, Watson wrote that "Disney's primary support historically comes from the Disney family and the institutional investors. Today that support is at best precarious." Watson went on to write that institutional investors viewed Disney as "a rudderless boat caught in a violent storm" and concluded that the company needed "to resolve the [Ron Miller] issue as soon as possible. Perceived lack of leadership hurts all alternatives." The board soon agreed that a decisive change in management was needed to send a clear message to Wall Street that the company was ready to begin rebuilding; Ron Miller was an easy scapegoat for the problems that had been plaguing the company during his tenure. On September 7, the board unanimously voted to ask for Miller's resignation.

REVIVAL UNDER TEAM DISNEY

Eisner and Wells Join Disney

34   In the wake of Miller's resentful resignation, Watson faced the ominous task of configuring a new executive management team that would appease the board, both branches of the Disney family, and the shareholders. Gold argued that the most suitable leaders for a creative institution like Disney were

"creative crazies." Watson was inclined to agree, at least to the extent that Disney's chief executive ought to be a "Walt man." In the meantime, Michael Eisner, president of Paramount Pictures Corporation, and Peter Wells, a consultant to Warner Brothers, had decided to campaign for the Disney job as a team: Eisner as chairman and chief executive and Wells as president and chief operating officer.

35   Eisner was born into an established New York family and was raised amid the affluence of Park Avenue. His father, a Harvard-trained attorney who had served as an executive housing official under Eisenhower, believed not only in the value of the dollar but also of discipline, culture, and formality. Eisner's exposure to the world of arts and entertainment was cultivated—his family attended the theater to celebrate every special occasion.

36   Like Walt, Eisner was a man driven by ideas. After several futile attempts to act while a student at Dennison University, in 1963 Eisner got his first show business job with NBC. At the network, he worked as an usher, clerk, and traffic reporter for the radio station. Eisner's big break came when he was hired by Barry Diller at ABC, then in third place among the three major networks. Eisner took charge of Saturday morning programming and captured the top position within three years. He then was given responsibility for the prime time schedule at ABC, and again under his guidance ABC became the top-ranked network.

37   In 1976, Eisner left ABC to begin work at Paramount Pictures, where he again joined forces with Barry Diller. The two creative executives spent eight years at Paramount, during which time the studio produced a remarkable string of box office hits. Eisner, it turned out, had the common touch: a natural aptitude for pop programming through simple storytelling techniques. Like Walt, he had a creative flair as well as the ability to recognize mass appeal. In fact, Eisner was widely perceived as one of the most creative executives in Hollywood.

38   On the other hand, Wells, who was detail oriented and pragmatic, had the business sense to translate Eisner's concepts into profitable realities. Wells was bred in a blue-collar family, and, from an early age, he learned the importance of hard work and commitment from his father, a navy commander. Wells was a dedicated student who graduated Phi Beta Kappa from Pomona College, studied as a Rhodes Scholar at Oxford, and edited the law review at Stanford Law School. Upon graduation from Stanford, he went to work for the entertainment law firm, Gang, Tyre & Brown, where he was eventually made a partner.

39   Wells left the legal profession to take over Warner Brothers' West Coast business operations in 1969. Within eight years he became co-chief executive and president of Warner Brothers. After running the business side of the company for five years, Wells unexpectedly left his job to pursue a lifelong dream of climbing the tallest mountain on each of the seven continents. Unfortunately, just before reaching the top of the seventh mountain, Mount Everest, he was forced to turn back because of a severe storm. When he returned he was given a position as consultant to Warner Brothers, where he remained until 1984.

40   Eisner and Wells were an attractive and suitable combination for the task of resurrecting Disney, particularly because of their resemblance to the founding brothers. When campaigning for the position, Eisner reasoned with one of Disney's largest shareholders: "It's going to take a creative person to run this company. . . . Look at the history of America's companies. They have always gotten into trouble when the creative people are replaced by the managers." Wells was the perfect counterpart to Eisner. He once said to Ray Watson: "I love the business of business."

41   The Disney board had finally found a high-powered team of executives to update the business while maintaining its traditional commitment to quality and innovation. Perhaps to underscore such high expectations, the two executives were offered uncharacteristically attractive compensation packages. In addition to signing and performance bonuses and options and portfolios, Eisner and Wells would receive $750,000 and $400,000 a year, respectively. The signing of the contracts marked the beginning of Disney's return to prominence in the entertainment industry.

Studio Leadership

42   Eisner and Wells began by assembling a group of talented executives from the entertainment and financial industries. To lure the best, they secured a promise from the board to approve higher salaries and bonuses than ever before. That commitment proved worthwhile when, only a week after Eisner had taken over, Disney signed Paramount executive Jeffrey Katzenberg as president of the studio.

43   Like Eisner, Katzenberg grew up on Park Avenue. The son of a stockbroker, he developed an interest in politics at an early age and dropped out of New York University after two years to become a full-time member of Mayor John Lindsay's staff. Through his political connections, Katzenberg eventually met Barry Diller, who hired him as an assistant at Paramount in 1975.

44   In Hollywood, Katzenberg was known as the "golden retriever," because of his uncanny aptitude for sniffing out directors and agents with hot scripts. Renowned for his tough negotiating and relentless work ethic, Katzenberg routinely arrived at work before 7 A.M., even on holidays and weekends. He advanced quickly through Paramount's marketing division, television network, and eventually productions, where he became Eisner's closest confidante. It, therefore, came as no surprise when Katzenberg joined Disney only a week after Eisner.

Finance Department

45   The 1984 fiasco had revealed weaknesses not only in the studio but in the company's finance department as well. Eisner was well aware that any public company in the 1980s operated in a more threatening investment environment. It would no longer be enough for Disney's leaders to simply provide wholesome family entertainment. To remain competitive, Disney's leaders needed to confidently promote the company image to investors. In a maneuver symbolic of Disney's new approach to the investment community, at the 1986 annual meeting the name Walt Disney Productions was dropped in favor of The Walt Disney Company.

46   Unlike Ron Miller, Eisner and Wells had the wherewithal to cultivate Wall Street's support, and they sought a new chief financial officer who could structure the necessary creative financial deals. Gary Wilson, CFO at Marriott for 12 years, was the strongest candidate for the position. Under Wilson's leadership, Marriott had grown dramatically, its revenues increasing over five times in just a decade. To inspire that growth, Wilson had pioneered the pattern of raising funds through limited partnerships, then selling off the hotels to investors while retaining the revenue-generating contracts for Marriott. To lure Wilson, Disney offered the Marriott executive an immense compensation package complete with stock options. Wilson accepted and became the highest paid CFO in the industry.

Emphasis on Group Creativity

47   In addition to bringing in top-flight executives from the entertainment and financial industries, Eisner began to change the management style at Disney. He placed a greater emphasis on group encounter meetings to more efficiently generate ideas for movie scripts and creative business strategies. Typically, a group of the company's most creative talents would meet on Sunday mornings to brainstorm. During the meetings, which came to be known as "gong shows," a head executive would require each attendant to offer a new idea. Those which fell below group standards would be rejected with a gong.

48   By infusing the company with new executives, a fresh approach to the investment community, and a highly creative format for generating new ideas, Disney's leaders had positioned the company to expand its studio, theme park complexes, and consumer product divisions into the 1990s.

THE WALT DISNEY STUDIOS

49   Katzenberg, who had epitomized the work ethic at Paramount, revamped the management culture at Disney and infused the leadership team with dozens of Paramount executives. Among the new Team Disney members were Helene Hahn, who took over the legal affairs department for the film division; Bill Mechanic, previously in charge of Paramount's pay television; and Ricardo Mestres, one of Katzenberg's most impressive production assistants. Katzenberg's relentless work ethic became the model for these and other studio executives, who were expected to arrive early, stay late, and work weekends.

50   Furthermore, innovative financing was essential to the studio's turnaround. In producing its films, Disney not only showed restraint and efficiency but also proved that its retreat from creative corporate structures had merely been temporary. Significantly, the studio began to rely heavily on investors to fund its film projects. The company, thereby, was able to increase output while relinquishing neither control nor high returns.

Updated Film Division

51   During Ron Miller's tenure, Disney had created a second label, Touchstone Pictures, under which Disney could produce racier movies that were preferred by American audiences. Katzenberg began his reign at the studio by exploiting the new label; he signed a deal for Disney's first R-rated film, *Down and Out in Beverly Hills,* which was released in December 1985. The film quickly replaced *Splash* as Disney's most successful movie and marked the beginning of the studio's ascent to the top of the industry.

52   Critics of Disney's more daring approach to film making charged that the movies, though highly successful, were losing the unique Disney flavor and had come to resemble the ordinary films routinely turned out by the other major studios. Supporters, on the other hand, argued that Disney's new direction was in fact more consistent with the company's fundamental commitment to creativity and innovation. By any account, the film division had become a profitable and resourceful division of the company.

53   However, Eisner was not satisfied. In a drive to create new products, he encouraged the film division to begin work on new Disney characters. Before long, animators had come up with an idea that developed into the central character of Disney's next live action animated film. Innovative and fast-paced, *Who Framed Roger Rabbit* was an immense success for the studio. Similarly, Disney's next character, featured in *The Little Mermaid,* was reminiscent of the Disney classics and was heavily promoted in the consumer product as well as the theme park industry. Under the leadership of Eisner and Katzenberg, Disney was once again turning out fresh and marketable products.

54   The studio's insistence on long hours, good scripts, and fresh ideas paid off. By late 1988, Disney was making and marketing traditional family-oriented films as well as 12 films per year under the Touchstone label. Eisner and Katzenberg wanted to increase the number of movies it was producing, but they knew that studios that grew too large inevitably sacrificed quality. As a result, they launched Hollywood Pictures, a third Disney film unit that, like Touchstone, would produce light adult entertainment with simple story lines and tight budgets.

55   Disney's overall film division has produced a steady stream of successful films, featuring top talent, strong writing, and original formats. Moreover, Touchstone Pictures also has done well at the international box office; in particular, Disney made millions with its successful 1991 international release of *Pretty Woman,* which was even more popular with foreign than American moviegoers.

56   That year, Walt Disney Pictures produced another major success, *Beauty and the Beast.* Eisner compared the immensely successful *Beauty and the Beast* with *Snow White,* in that each classic was a wellspring for consumer products, videos, and theme park rides. Katzenberg called the musical, whose star is uncharacteristically sophisticated and spunky, the Disney animation team's "greatest ar-tistic achievement." *Beauty and the Beast* had the most successful opening weekend for an animated film of all time, grossing $9.6 million.

Film Slump and the Studio's Response

57   Notwithstanding the success of *Beauty and the Beast,* Disney had its first noticeable film slump in 1991. Eisner justified the studio's problems by reference to the downturn in America's economy and to industrywide falling box office revenues. It seems that Disney, third in total box office in 1991, was not immune to the trend towards skyrocketing production costs and resulting decreases in overall profitability.

58   Katzenberg responded to the slump by cutting back on the costs involved in making and marketing Disney films. In a 1991 memorandum to his staff, Katzenberg wrote: "We have slowly drifted away from our original vision of how to run a movie business." He went on to articulate the studio's revised mission: to return to "the kind of modest, story-driven movies we tended to make in our salad days."

59   The studio begain to implement the policy of producing films with tight budgets and correspond-ingly reasonable returns, rather than hit-or-miss blockbusters like *Dick Tracy* that cost over $100 mil-lion to make and market. At Hollywood Pictures, the average film budget was cut from $20 million to $15 million. The overall strategy is to avoid making expensive flops by sticking to budgets that fall below Disney's average budget in previous years as well as below the industry averages.

Diversification Strategy: Home Videos

60   Under Katzenberg, the studio has pursued a strategy of diversification, with a steady expansion into home video, network, cable and syndicated television, and radio. Disney distributes home video ver-sions of its studio releases into domestic and foreign markets. Since 1988, Disney Video has captured and maintained the largest market share in the domestic home video industry. In addition to releasing mainstream feature films on video, the company has been squeezing value out of its previously un-derexploited library of animated classics. Over 500,000 copies of the videocassette *Pinocchio* were sold within one year of its release, making it one of the industry's most successful videos. Classic Dis-ney animated films subsequently released and skillfully marketed in home video have included *101 Dalmations, The Jungle Book,* and *Fantasia.*

61   Disney's video division has benefited from a revival of wholesome family entertainment. The car-toon videocassettes are especially popular with the postwar generation that grew up with Disney and is now having children of its own. Much of Disney Video's success over the last several years can also be credited to "sell-through titles," which are sold at low prices to encourage purchase, rather than rental, by consumers.

Network Television and KCAL-TV

62   Not surprisingly in view of Eisner's background in television programming, Disney has been remark-ably successful in the network TV industry. Under the labels Touchstone Television and Walt Disney Television, Disney produces TV programs that it distributes to the major networks and other broad-casters. The TV division has made an aggressive drive to distribute half-hour situation comedies for prime-time broadcast and its Saturday morning animated cartoon series. In 1991, Disney placed a total of 12 programs, more than any other Hollywood studio, on the major networks. Among its successes are "Golden Girls," "Empty Nest," "Home Improvement," and "Blossom."

63   Disney also has been successful in the international syndicated television market. A series of pro-grams, known as Disney Clubs, airs segments before 50 million viewers. The programs, produced in

Italy, Venezuela, and Australia, serve generally to promote the Disney spirit and specifically to advertise Euro Disneyland. In addition, 135 million viewers from Poland, Czechoslovakia, Hungary, and what was once the Soviet Union watch top-ranked "Walt Disney Presents," the only American show that appears in all four Eastern European markets.

64 Disney also earns revenues from advertising sales tied to its independent radio station. KCAL, which broadcasts in southern California, offers news, entertainment, and sports.

Disney Cable Channel

65 The company's pay television programming service has 6 million subscribers nationwide. While other cable channels are struggling to maintain their market share, since 1984 Disney has seen a 300 percent increase in the number of subscribers to its pay-cable services. Disney attributes the success of its cable division to its varied programming, a blend that offers educational, dramatic, comedy, adventure, and documentary programs for children, teenagers, and adults.

Emphasis on Expansion

66 Disney is eager to accelerate its distribution of television shows and movies. Manic deal-making is expected to continue, but Katzenberg has made it clear that efficiency and restraint will continue to be important values at the studio. Furthermore, studio management has suggested that an evolving hands-off policy will lead to more autonomy for Disney executives and a more dynamic creative process.

67 Although it has been rumored that Eisner is considering the addition of a second cable channel, he has said that an expensive acquisition is not Disney's mission:

68 It's not to be the biggest, to have the most toys, to own things writers think are important and sexy like networks, cable companies, satellites and countries. Our mission is to grow our own. We can have a nice respectable 20 percent without having to impress anybody.

69 Nonetheless, there also has been some speculation that, given the expected reform of federal antitrust regulations, Disney will seriously consider a merger with a major television network, which would provide Disney with a powerful distribution network for its already strong programming.

WALT DISNEY ATTRACTIONS: THEME PARK AND RESORT COMPLEXES

Tokyo Disneyland

70 Expansion of theme parks and resorts under Team Disney has emphasized the increasing importance and attractiveness of foreign markets. The company capitalized on the prospects for growth abroad by opening its first international theme park, Tokyo Disneyland. Disney and Oriental Land, a Japanese corporation, came together in 1979 to establish the theme park in Tokyo. Under the terms of their agreement, Oriental Land would pay for construction and provide the land, while Disney would receive royalties on the revenues generated: 10 percent of ticket sales, 5 percent of concession sales, and 10 percent of corporate sponsorship agreements.

71 Tokyo Disneyland, located on a 600-acre landfill in Tokyo Bay, opened in April 1983. The park, which features traditional Disney rides, restaurants, shops, and entertainment, also showcases Japanese cultural traditions. More than 10 million people visited the park during its first year in operation. From the start, attendance at Tokyo Disneyland threatened to surpass that at Disneyland, and it has continued to climb, setting records along the way. The park had its most successful year in 1991 with a record 16 million guests. Indeed, the success of Tokyo Disneyland has proven that Disney's brand of family entertainment is marketable worldwide.

Euro Disneyland

72　Eight years before Eisner joined Disney, the theme park division had begun to study the population and demographic projections of Europe, following Card Walker's suggestion that the company look into building a resort complex on the Continent. Although Ray Watson supported the idea, the project was put on the back burner while the company was defending itself against corporate raiders.

73　　By 1984, there was an inviting European market for Disney theme parks and products. An estimated 2 million Europeans visited American theme parks annually. Furthermore, roughly 25 percent of Disney trinkets, magazines, and T-shirts were sold in Europe. In September, Eisner and Wells enthusiastically endorsed a search for a European theme park site. Disney officials selected Marne-la-Vallee, France, mainly because of its demographic advantages. The theme park would be located 20 miles east of Paris, which has a population of 10 million people. Paris, in turn, is well located in relation to major European population centers; 68 million people are within four hours by car, and 300 million within two hours by plane.

74　　Eisner and Wells believed that Disney had sacrificed too many profits in negotiating the Tokyo deal and were determined to retain control as well as a healthy share of the profits generated by the new European park. But they also wanted to minimize its risk by sharing costs with a maximum number of participants. To do so, the company would have to rely on a new corporate structure. In yet another innovative financing maneuver directed by Gary Wilson, Disney set up a French version of a limited partnership to be managed by Euro Disneyland, a publicly held French company in which Disney now owns a 49 percent equity interest.

75　　The complex is expected to generate substantial licensing royalties and management fees for Disney. As with the Tokyo project, Disney is entitled to 10 percent of ticket sales and 5 percent of merchandise and food sales. Furthermore, just as in Wilson's Marriott schemes, Disney will manage the complex. Under a 30-year agreement, in exchange for running the park Disney will receive 3 percent of the profits for five years and 6 percent during each subsequent year.

76　　From a tax standpoint, the deal that was ultimately negotiated with the French government is extremely favorable to Disney. Disney will have to pay only 7.0 percent tax on the cost of goods sold, rather than the 18.6 percent that other French companies pay. Also, the buildings will be depreciated over 10 instead of the usual 20 years. Moreover, the host country is committed to a major expansion of its roads as well as its commuter rail line. Finally, the French government agreed to lend the project 40 percent of the cost of the project, roughly $1.2 billion.

77　　Construction of Euro Disneyland began in 1988, and the $3.6 billion theme park was scheduled to open on April 12, 1992. Euro Disneyland is an ultra-modern version of Disney's Magic Kingdom with a European flair. In the 1991 annual report, Eisner calls Euro Disneyland "the most wonderful project we have ever done. . . . [a] theme park jewel, a creative extension of Walt's first park utilizing new technology." The rides were built by Walt Disney Imagineering, a group of design specialists, writers, artists, and engineers that design Disney attractions worldwide. To ensure smooth operation, the Imagineers have built indoor arcades to connect the 29 attractions.

78　　Disney applied its Orlando strategy to Euro Disney by providing lodging for guests of all income levels. The park is surrounded by six hotels with distinctly American themes and by a campground with 414 cabins. For further entertainment, the park contains Festival Disney, a complex of shops, restaurants, discotheques, and a 27-hole golf course. Finally, Wells has referred to Euro Disneyland as the linchpin for Disney's other divisions. Long-term plans for Euro Disney include building 15 additional hotels with 13,000 additional rooms.

Other Development Projects

79　In addition to building theme parks and resorts abroad, Disney has improved its existing complexes and embarked on new projects. First, however, Disney streamlined its operations by selling Arvida, the real estate company it had purchased during the 1984 crisis. By 1986, Disney's real estate division had begun to reassess its acquisition of Arvida. Eisner in particular thought that Disney should develop only its own hotels. He also worried that Arvida's Florida land was a liability, considering the volatile and increasingly soft real estate market. In 1987, Disney sold Arvida to JMB Realty Corporation in a move that reflected the company's financial flexibility and willingness to shed assets that no longer suited its long-term plans.

80   In 1989, Disney added to the Walt Disney World Complex the Disney–MGM Studios Theme Park and an accompanying production facility. The park contains themed attractions, backstage tours, restaurants, and shops based on Hollywood's golden age of the 1930s and 1940s. Next, the company built three new resort hotels with 2,222 rooms and 51,000 square feet of conference space to its already existing accommodations. Disney also has begun to develop more moderately priced accommodations, including one 2,048 room resort, at Walt Disney World.

81   Finally, in 1991, the Disney Development Company, which plans new projects related to properties in California, Florida, and Europe, introduced the Disney Vacation Club. Under the unique plan, members pay a fee, purchase a real estate interest in Walt Disney World vacation accommodations, and, thereby, acquire the right to stay at vacation resorts around the world.

Disney's Response to Falling Attendance

82   While 1991 was a good year for Disney's moderately priced hotels (which averaged 94 percent occupancy rate), Disney's theme park and resort division showed decreases in overall revenues and profits. Wells and Eisner attributed the 1991 fall in profits to the recession, to lower levels of domestic and international travel, resulting from the Persian Gulf War, and to the cost of additional Walt Disney World hotels and attractions. Even though 1991 operating profits fell 23 percent from 1990, Eisner explained, Disney's operations are healthy in comparison to an overall decline in performance by other hotel operators in the travel and leisure industry.

83   Team Disney management addressed the problem of falling attendance at its theme parks in a cautious but effective and resourceful manner. First, the company departed from former policy and raised ticket prices. The cost was raised in small increments to avoid negative publicity. As a result, instead of tarnishing Disney's friendly image and, thus, exacerbating the decline in attendance, the strategy led to soaring revenues. However, critics contend that ticket prices cannot be acceptably increased beyond the $33 that it now costs for a one-day adult ticket to Walt Disney World.

84   Furthermore, management called for the creation of new theme park attractions that would appeal to teenagers. The new attractions designed by the Imagineering team include *Captain Eo*, a 3-D short produced by George Lucas, directed by Francis Ford Coppola, and starring Michael Jackson. The successful 12-minute film became a permanent addition to Disneyland and EPCOT.

85   Third, management also sought to augment attendance by aggressively investing in advertising campaigns. Eisner, wearing Mickey Mouse ears, has appeared in advertisements to encourage the use of Walt Disney World for business conventions. In another break with tradition, Disney began discounting. Guests at the Disney–MGM Studios in Orlando receive free videos of *Fantasia,* while visitors holding $25 receipts from Vons Grocery Store in southern California gain free admission to Disneyland.

Future Expansion of Theme Parks Complexes

86   The theme park division will remain the central focus at Disney. At a 1990 press conference, Eisner announced Team Disney's intent to "do nothing less than reinvent the Disney theme park experience." Imagineers continue to work on revolutionary high-tech rides. To ensure continued creativity, Eisner has also encouraged Team Disney executives to develop the Disney Institute, a think tank in Orlando, and The Workplace, an entertainment and educational facility focusing on manufacturing plants.

87   Disney anticipates the construction of several new theme parks, including one each in southern California, in Florida, and in Japan. Disney Imagineers have drawn up plans for an Anaheim theme park which, like EPCOT Center, will feature exhibits from around the world and corporate-sponsored pavilions. The new theme park, expected to be six times as large as Disneyland, will be Disney's first project of this scale to be built in an existing urban area. With the exception of building time-share resort villas near its California amusement parks, the company has been lobbying to amend a California law that regulates such resorts.

88   Likewise, in 1990, Disney announced plans to build Dream City on 5,200 acres just southwest of Walt Disney World. The high-tech city, which is expected to cost more than $2.5 billion and take 25 years to complete, will consist of 15,000 apartments, 6,300 mid-priced homes, an upscale shopping mall, museums, and commercial high-rise office buildings.

89   In October 1990, Eisner and Wells also made a proposal to Oriental Land to build a new theme park similar to MGM Studios next to Tokyo Disneyland. Analysts have predicted that Disney might seek an equity position in the new park, rather than simply an entitlement to royalties.

HOLLYWOOD RECORDS

90   With the formation of Hollywood Records in 1991, Disney entered the mainstream music business, a $25 billion a year industry characterized by low overhead and comparatively high rewards. Disney's participation in the popular music business is guided by a pursuit of both fresh talent as well as more established and expensive groups like Queen.

91   In furtherance of its goal to become a major competitor in the worldwide pop music business, Hollywood Records opened an office in Great Britain. Disney executives anticipate a dramatic expansion of the international music industry, and, as a result, Hollywood Records entered licensing agreements in Germany, Italy, Spain, Scandinavia, Japan, Australia, and New Zealand.

WALT DISNEY CONSUMER PRODUCTS

92   The sale of consumer products in both domestic and foreign markets not only generates significant revenues for the company but also promotes Disney resorts, theme parks, and characters. In addition, Disney receives major media exposure for its ventures through tie-ins with companies like Mattel and Nestlé.

Disney Stores

93   Disney has 123 retail stores, including four successful international divisions. The stores, most of which can be found in shopping malls and retail complexes, promote Disney's other businesses and carry Disney-related merchandise. Specialty retail products include Disney Babies infant products, Baby Mickey & Company infant apparel, merchandise drawn from animated characters, and Mattel toys. In spite of increasing competition from other entertainment giants like Time Warner, Inc., and a depressed retail environment, same-store sales show a steady increase.

94   Disney intends to set up and operate 100 stores in Japan, the first of which is expected to open in May 1992. The chain will sell toys, games, and clothing, and possibly food inspired by Disney characters. Based on soaring profits at Tokyo Disneyland, executives in the Consumer Products Division estimate 50 billion yen per year in sales.

Licensing

95   The company licenses the name "Walt Disney" as well as its characters, literary and visual properties, and music to consumer manufacturers, publishers, and retailers around the world. In particular, Disney-licensed products enjoy great popularity in Japan, the world's second-largest toy market.

96   Royalties generally are based on a fixed percentage of the retail or wholesale selling price of the product bearing a Disney trademark. Disney oversees the development, approval, and generation of licensed products featuring classic and newly created characters. Licensed merchandise includes toys, apparel, watches, and housewares. Books, magazines, and comic strips are examples of licensed publications. The company also licenses software products for video machines and educational products, such as teaching aids.

Publications and *Discover* Magazine

97   Disney built on its extensive experience in licensing by starting a new publishing venture, Hyperion Press, which offers trade books for adults. Under Walt Disney Publications, the company publishes books, comics, and magazines for children in the United States and Italy.

98   In addition, in September 1991, Disney bought the rights from Family Media to *Discover,* a family-oriented science magazine. The acquisition broadened Disney's focus on science and marked the company's entry into the general-interest magazine business. Disney plans to redesign and update the packaging of the science magazine and may go on to publish a children's version. According to Eisner, Disney may buy more magazines, but only those with a family-oriented image. Executives in the publishing unit anticipate building a profitable, vertically integrated publishing company.

Music and Audio

99   Disney has long been a participant in the children's music business. In fact, Walt Disney Records is the largest children's label in the world. The bulk of revenues in the music and audio division is from the domestic retail sales of audio cassettes and records.

Mattel Alliance

100   Disney has recently announced plans to enter a long-term agreement with Mattel, Inc., under which the latter will sponsor attractions and develop toys to be sold in special retail stores at Disney parks. The companies also expect to concentrate on foreign markets and to expand their toy-licensing pact, sales from which topped $200 million in 1991. Wells pointed to the enormous potential for growth in Europe to explain a heightening interest in the international market:

101   More of Mattel's growth, like our own, will be coming from the international market, rather than the more mature domestic market. . . . If you look at projections, the enormity of growth in Europe exceeds that of any other geographic section in the world.

102   Thus, the Mattel alliance underscores Disney's commitment to its merchandising operations in international markets.

103   Despite a recession in the domestic retail market, Disney's Consumer Products Division showed an increase in overall profits in 1991. Retail sales, consistently strong in the European market, reached $2 billion in 1991. The success is in large part due to increasingly popular Disney stores and outstanding merchandise and publishing sales in Asia and Europe.

104   Eisner, referring to the 1990s as the "Disney Decade," has said that only "a lack of continued creativity and nerve can impede us as we move into the 90s." Indeed, management has pledged to continue a strategy of diversification, expansion of foreign projects, commitment to excellence and innovation, and concentration on theme parks as a wellspring for Disney's other services and products in an increasingly globalized economy.

105   Exhibit 1 is a financial review of The Walt Disney Company that was obtained from the company's 1991 annual report.

EXHIBIT 1
The Walt Disney Company 1991 Financial Review

OBJECTIVES

The Walt Disney Company has several strategic and financial objectives that guide management decision-making in creating value for its shareholders. The overriding objective is to sustain Disney as the world's premier entertainment company from a creative, strategic and financial standpoint.

The Company's financial objectives are to achieve 20% earnings growth over any five-year period and, through profitable reinvestment of cash flow, 20% annual return on stockholders' equity. The Company met its earnings objective for the five-year period ending with 1991, achieving a 25% compound annual EPS growth from continuing operations. The Company fell short, however, of its ROE objective in 1991, with lower earnings resulting in a return on equity of 17% for the year. The decline in earnings experienced in 1991, if coupled with a continued weak economy in 1992, would make it difficult for the Company to achieve its EPS objective in the short term. However, on a going-forward basis from 1991, the Company continues to view 20% earnings growth over future five-year periods and 20% annual return on equity as realistic financial objectives.

RETURN ON EQUITY

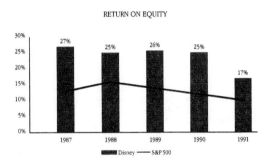

Another objective is to maintain and build upon the integrity of the Disney name and franchise. The Disney "brand" is an asset of considerable value which the Company continues to enhance and protect.

And finally, it is the Company's goal to accomplish all of the above while preserving the basic Disney values – quality, imagination, guest service – which have enabled The Walt Disney Company to entertain billions of people around the world for decades.

STOCK PRICE PERFORMANCE

On September 30, 1991, the Company's stock closed at $114 on the New York Stock Exchange. As shown on the following chart, long-term investors in Disney stock have experienced returns superior to those generated by the market. Over the last five years, the annualized return on Disney stock was a full eight percentage points higher than the S&P 500. A hypothetical investment of $1000 in Disney stock in fiscal year 1987, including dividends paid, would have been worth $2,669 as of September 30, 1991.

Source: 1991 annual report.

EXHIBIT 1 (continued)

FINANCIAL REVIEW

RETURN ON DISNEY COMMON STOCK VERSUS S&P 500

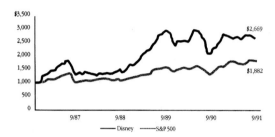

STOCK REPURCHASES

It has been The Walt Disney Company's practice to increase shareholder value by repurchasing Disney stock at attractive levels when the Company's excess cash or debt capacity enables it to do so efficiently. Since the adoption of a program to repurchase shares was approved by the Board of Directors early in fiscal year 1985, Disney has repurchased 13 million shares at an aggregate cost of $780 million, an average price of $60 per share. If valued on September 30, 1991, at the NYSE closing price, these shares would have a market valuation of approximately $1.5 billion.

DEBT RATING

Currently, Disney's long-term Moody's/Standard & Poor's senior unsecured debt ratings are Aa3/A+. Over the long term, Disney's objective is to maintain an A or better credit rating. With this in mind, the Company will strive to maintain conservative levels of leverage in relation to its ability to service its debt.

INTEREST COVERAGE RATIO

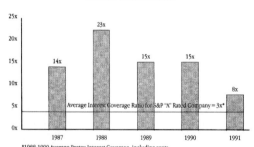

*1988-1990 Average Pretax Interest Coverage, including rents.

CASH FLOW AND CAPITAL SPENDING

As shown by the chart below, Disney continues to have strong cash generating capabilities. Even in difficult economic times, it was able to generate a record $1.5 billion in cash flow from operations in 1991, achieving a five-year annualized growth rate of 18%.

CASH FLOW FROM OPERATIONS
(in Millions)

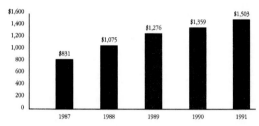

Disney puts its capital to work both in existing businesses and new projects, thereby creating long-term value and contributing to future growth. Approximately $70 million of total 1991 capital spending was incurred to ensure that theme park and other assets remain well maintained, fresh and state-of-the-art. The rest of the spending was investment in existing businesses and new projects.

CAPITAL SPENDING
(in Millions)

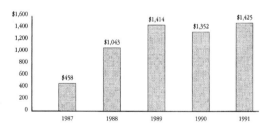

As the bulk of this spending is discretionary, The Walt Disney Company has generated substantial free cash flow in each of the last five years.

EXHIBIT 1   (continued)

FINANCIAL REVIEW

NEW PROJECTS

All Disney projects are carefully analyzed and are expected to make a positive contribution on a net present value basis against a risk-adjusted discount rate. New projects developed since 1987, such as the hotel build-out at Walt Disney World Resorts, the self-distribution of home video product and The Disney Stores, contributed over $1.7 billion (or over 28%) of fiscal 1991 revenues, having grown from virtually zero five years ago.

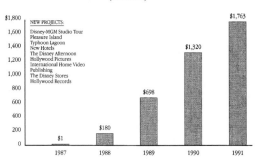

ANNUAL REVENUES GENERATED BY NEW PROJECTS
(In Millions)

RECENT FINANCINGS

Innovative financings create value for the Company by reducing the potential volatility of its earnings. Consistent with the philosophy of allowing partners to share in the upside from film successes, while helping to limit the downside, Disney closed Touchwood Pacific Partners I, L.P., in fiscal year 1991. Touchwood raised $600 million for Walt Disney, Touchstone and Hollywood Pictures film production, with $420 million in non-recourse debt financing provided by a consortium of banks and $180 million in limited partnership units raised largely from Japanese institutions. Since 1985, the Company has raised over $1.5 billion in funds for film financing.

INTERNATIONAL

Over the last several years, The Walt Disney Company's business has become increasingly global, with approximately 22% of fiscal year 1991 revenues coming from foreign sources.

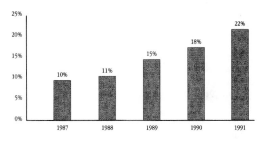

TOTAL REVENUE CONTRIBUTION BY
INTERNATIONAL OPERATIONS

While Disney products are well-recognized and sought after worldwide, the Company believes it has substantial room for increased penetration in international markets. Therefore, future overseas business represents a key growth opportunity. The demand for Disney products is expected to be especially strong in Europe over the next several years, fueled by the opening of Euro Disney in April, 1992, and expanded film and television activity.

International expansion has made foreign exchange management increasingly important to the Company. Disney monitors and manages its economic exposure to foreign currency fluctuations within a five-year planning horizon, and seeks to minimize the impact of changes in exchange rates on the Company's financial performance.

EXHIBIT 1   (continued)

CONSOLIDATED STATEMENT OF INCOME

(In millions, except per share data)

Year ended September 30	1991	1990	1989
Revenues			
Theme parks and resorts	**$2,864.7**	$3,019.6	$2,595.4
Filmed entertainment	**2,593.7**	2,250.3	1,587.6
Consumer products	**724.0**	573.8	411.3
	6,182.4	5,843.7	4,594.3
Costs and Expenses			
Theme parks and resorts	**2,247.7**	2,130.3	1,810.0
Filmed entertainment	**2,275.6**	1,937.3	1,331.1
Consumer products	**494.2**	350.6	224.2
	5,017.5	4,418.2	3,365.3
Operating Income			
Theme parks and resorts	**617.0**	889.3	785.4
Filmed entertainment	**318.1**	313.0	256.5
Consumer products	**229.8**	223.2	187.1
	1,164.9	1,425.5	1,229.0
Corporate Activities			
General and administrative expenses	**160.8**	138.5	119.6
Interest expense	**105.0**	43.1	23.9
Investment and interest income	**(119.4)**	(80.8)	(67.4)
	146.4	100.8	76.1
Income Before Income Taxes	**1,018.5**	1,324.7	1,152.9
Income taxes	**381.9**	500.7	449.6
Net Income	**$ 636.6**	$ 824.0	$ 703.3
Earnings Per Share	**$ 4.78**	$ 6.00	$ 5.10
Average Number of Common and Common Equivalent Shares Outstanding	**133.2**	137.2	138.0

See Notes to Consolidated Financial Statements

EXHIBIT 1   (continued)

CONSOLIDATED BALANCE SHEET

(In millions)

September 30	1991	1990
Assets		
Cash and cash equivalents	$ **886.1**	$ 819.8
Marketable securities	**782.4**	588.1
Receivables	**1,128.2**	851.5
Merchandise inventories	**311.6**	269.2
Film and television costs	**596.9**	641.1
Theme parks, resorts and other property, at cost		
Attractions, buildings and equipment	**5,628.1**	4,654.6
Accumulated depreciation	**(1,667.8)**	(1,405.1)
	3,960.3	3,249.5
Projects in progress	**540.9**	594.0
Land	**70.4**	67.0
	4,571.6	3,910.5
Other assets	**1,151.7**	942.1
	$9,428.5	$8,022.3
Liabilities and Stockholders' Equity		
Accounts payable and other accrued liabilities	**$1,433.8**	$1,158.1
Income taxes payable	**296.2**	200.3
Borrowings	**2,213.8**	1,584.6
Unearned royalty and other advances	**859.5**	841.9
Deferred income taxes	**753.9**	748.8
Stockholders' equity		
Preferred stock, $.10 par value		
Authorized — 5.0 million shares		
Issued — none		
Common stock, $.10 par value		
Authorized-300.0 million shares		
Issued — 137.2 million shares and 136.8 million shares	**549.7**	502.8
Retained earnings	**3,950.5**	3,401.1
Cumulative translation adjustments	**35.2**	67.7
	4,535.4	3,971.6
Less treasury stock, at cost — 7.0 million shares and 5.0 million shares	**664.1**	483.0
	3,871.3	3,488.6
	$9,428.5	$8,022.3

See Notes to Consolidated Financial Statements

EXHIBIT 1 (continued)

CONSOLIDATED STATEMENT OF CASH FLOWS

Year ended September 30	1991	1990	1989
Cash Provided by Operations Before Income Taxes	**$1,764.5**	$1,780.3	$1,688.8
Income taxes paid	**(261.2)**	(421.4)	(413.2)
	1,503.3	1,358.9	1,275.6
Investing Activities			
Theme parks, resorts and other property, net	**924.6**	716.3	749.6
Film and television costs	**486.8**	533.0	426.7
Acquisitions	**13.8**	103.1	237.3
Marketable securities, net	**194.3**	(74.2)	(6.3)
Euro Disney and other	**113.4**	(96.3)	321.9
	1,732.9	1,181.9	1,729.2
Financing Activities			
Borrowings	**641.9**	965.0	452.3
Reduction of borrowings	**(124.6)**	(255.9)	(27.2)
Repurchases of common stock	**(181.1)**	(427.5)	(14.4)
Cash dividends	**(87.2)**	(74.1)	(61.8)
Other	**46.9**	54.5	57.5
	295.9	262.0	406.4
Increase (Decrease) in Cash and Cash Equivalents	**66.3**	439.0	(47.2)
Cash and Cash Equivalents, Beginning of Year	**819.8**	380.8	428.0
Cash and Cash Equivalents, End of Year	**$ 886.1**	$ 819.8	$ 380.8

The difference between Income Before Income Taxes as shown on the Consolidated Statement of Income and Cash Provided By Operations Before Income Taxes is explained as follows.

	1991	1990	1989
Income Before Income Taxes	**$1,018.5**	$1,324.7	$1,152.9
Charges to Income Not Requiring Cash Outlays:			
Depreciation	**263.5**	203.1	191.5
Amortization of film and television costs	**531.0**	335.2	272.1
Other	**29.7**	(36.7)	24.1
Changes in:			
Receivables	**(266.8)**	(166.2)	(131.4)
Merchandise inventories	**(42.4)**	(44.9)	(64.4)
Prepaid expenses	**(46.9)**	(64.1)	(15.0)
Accounts payable and other accrued liabilities	**280.1**	300.0	169.6
Unearned royalty and other advances	**(2.2)**	(70.8)	89.4
	746.0	455.6	535.9
Cash Provided by Operations Before Income Taxes	**$1,764.5**	$1,780.3	$1,688.8
Supplemental Cash Flow Information:			
Interest paid	**$ 69.8**	$ 67.3	$ 66.9

See Notes to Consolidated Financial Statements

EXHIBIT 1 (continued)

12 BUSINESS SEGMENTS

	1991	1990	1989
Capital Expenditures			
Theme parks and resorts	$ 790.1	$ 519.8	$ 665.4
Filmed entertainment	50.1	39.5	27.2
Consumer products	35.5	34.3	21.6
Corporate	48.9	122.7	35.4
	$ 924.6	$ 716.3	$ 749.6
Depreciation Expense			
Theme parks and resorts	$ 213.2	$ 177.4	$ 172.4
Filmed entertainment	23.9	12.9	12.2
Consumer products	12.4	5.8	3.1
Corporate	14.0	7.0	3.8
	$ 263.5	$ 203.1	$ 191.5
Identifiable Assets			
Theme parks and resorts	$5,165.7	$4,420.3	$4,066.9
Filmed entertainment	1,878.2	1,672.8	1,252.1
Consumer products	351.4	236.4	193.1
Corporate	2,033.2	1,692.8	1,145.1
	$9,428.5	$8,022.3	$6,657.2
Supplemental Revenue Data			
Theme Parks and Resorts			
Admissions	$1,093.0	$1,179.9	$1,021.7
Merchandise, food and beverage	1,048.0	1,113.5	1,019.5
Filmed Entertainment			
Theatrical product	1,776.9	1,545.7	1,090.1
Export revenues	1,267.1	938.8	653.3

EXHIBIT 1   (concluded)

Five-Year Summary

SELECTED FINANCIAL DATA

(In millions, except per share and other data)

	1991	1990	1989	1988	1987
Statement of Income					
Revenues	$6,182.4	$5,843.7	$4,594.3	$3,438.2	$2,876.8
Operating income	1,164.9	1,425.5	1,229.0	884.8	776.8
Interest expense	105.0	43.1	23.9	5.8	29.1
Income from continuing operations	636.6	824.0	703.3	522.0	392.3
Net income	636.6	824.0	703.3	522.0	444.7
Per Share					
Net income					
Continuing operations	$4.78	$6.00	$5.10	$3.80	$2.85
Total	4.78	6.00	5.10	3.80	3.23
Cash dividends	.67	.555	.46	.38	.32
Balance Sheet					
Total assets	$9,428.5	$8,022.3	$6,657.2	$5,108.9	$3,806.3
Borrowings	2,213.8	1,584.6	860.6	435.5	584.5
Stockholders' equity	3,871.3	3,488.6	3,044.0	2,359.3	1,845.4
Statement of Cash Flows					
Cash flow from operations	$1,503.3	$1,358.9	$1,275.6	$1,075.4*	$830.6
Investing activities	(1,732.9)	(1,181.9)	(1,729.2)	(1,909.5)	(506.8)
Financing activities	295.9	262.0	406.4	(245.8)	44.7
Other Data					
Stockholders at year-end	189,000	175,000	143,000	124,000	101,000
Employees at year-end	58,000	52,000	47,000	39,000	31,000

* Excludes $722.6 million unearned royalty advances.

CASE 6

FEDERATED DEPARTMENT STORES, INC.

INTRODUCTION

1   In February 1992, Federated Department Stores emerged from bankruptcy after more than two years of complex negotiations with lenders, bondholders, suppliers, and stockholders. Federated's bankruptcy documents listed over 50,000 creditors, who made aggregate claims of $90 billion.[1] Despite the relatively short bankruptcy period, Federated still faces an uphill battle to formulate a strategy that will return the department store conglomerate to profitability.

2   Federated's mission was simple, according to Allen I. Questrom, chairman and CEO: "This is not a complicated business. You have to have what the customer wants and take care of them while they are in the store."[2] Despite his optimism, Questrom and Federated face at least three challenges: unfavorable demographic trends and macroeconomic conditions, the trend among consumers toward specialty stores, and a highly leveraged balance sheet.

FEDERATED'S BACKGROUND

3   Federated's genesis was a result of the LBO craze of the 1980s. Canadian real estate developer Robert Campeau planned to develop $10 billion in retailing properties and decided that department stores would be his first step. In September 1986, Campeau offered $66 per share to purchase the sixth largest U.S. department store chain, Allied Stores, Inc. When his offer was rejected, Campeau bought huge blocks of the stock on the open market. Finally, on Halloween 1987, Campeau purchased the remaining stock at a price of $3.6 billion ($67/share), financed almost entirely by debt. In November 1987, Allied released financial statements for the previous nine months. Free cash flow for the period was about $100 million, but interest expenses were $244 million.

4   One year later, Campeau focused his guns on Federated Department Stores, which was suffering from falling profit margins but was three times larger than Allied. May's Department Stores also was interested in acquiring Federated. And, in a bidding war, Campeau initially offered $47 per share but eventually was driven up to $73.50. On April Fool's Day 1988, Campeau acquired Federated for a total price of $6.5 billion.

This case was prepared by George H. Tompson, University of South Carolina.

[1] *Business Week*, February 10, 1992, p. 126.

[2] *Business Week*, February 19, 1990, p. 40.

FEDERATED'S COMPETITIVE POSITION

5   Allen Questrom is well known in the department store industry. For 23 years he had risen through the ranks at Federated, only to leave so he could head the Dallas-based chain of Neiman-Marcus. During bankruptcy, Federated's board convinced Questrom to return to Federated in hopes that he could devise a strategy similar to the one that he used to revitalize Neiman-Marcus, Rich's, and Bullock's. According to *Business Week*:

6   At Neiman-Marcus, for example, Questrom increased the sales force by 10 percent, added more designer labels to the profitable men's and women's apparel sections, and frequently phoned dissatisfied customers himself to offer them gift certificates. At Bullock's, he cut corporate jobs and hired more salespeople at higher commissions.[3]

7   To achieve the same success at Federated, Questrom faces three major problems. First is the broad and lingering effect of the early 1990s recession in the United States. The recession continues to hinder consumer spending. Beginning in mid-1989, two measures of the U.S. consumers' outlook fell dramatically to their lowest levels in years. Both the Consumer Confidence Index (CCI) and the Index of Consumer Sentiment (ICS) measure two aspects of consumers' perceptions of the economy. The first part of the measures asks respondents to compare their current financial situations with their past financial conditions. The second part gathers data on consumers' expectations about economic conditions in the future. Except for an increase during the Persian Gulf War, U.S. consumers have become increasingly pessimistic about the economic conditions in the country (see Figure 1). With the Democratic victory in the White House in November 1992, both measures of consumer sentiment rebounded slightly. Continuing uncertainty about President William Clinton's fiscal policy has prevented both the economy and consumer confidence from recovering fully.

8   Also affecting consumer spending habits will be "changing priorities among baby boomers, the increasing population of older Americans, and a declining number of household formations."[4] The free spending era of yuppies and conspicuous consumption has ended. In conjunction with the faltering economy, these changing spending habits already have had an impact on how consumers are spending their disposable income. Figure 2 demonstrates that consumers are spending a smaller and smaller portion of their disposable income at national department store chains.

9   A second problem faced by Federated is particular to the department store industry. As a group, the conventional mall-based national department store chains recently have been battered by specialty stores. Figure 3 shows the trend in the ratio of national department store sales to four categories of specialty store sales. Apparel and accessory stores (e.g., Accessory Lady), discount department stores (e.g., Price Club, Sam's), electronics and appliance stores (e.g., Circuit City), and general merchandise stores (e.g., Target) all have shown large sales increases relative to national department stores. Successful specialty stores have customarily identified a retailing niche and have developed distinctive competencies around a particular customer need. In general, the result has been that the department stores have been marginally successful at many aspects of retailing while the specialty stores have been exceptionally successful at one or two aspects of retailing (e.g., inventory control, low cost, merchandise turnover, attention to fashion trends). While the consumer preference toward specialty retailers already has started, industry experts do not see a return to the old status quo. According to Carl Steidtmann, chief economist for Management Horizons, the specialty store concept is here to stay: "The future of retailing is going to look nothing like the past. New Wave retailers are creating new rules, roles, and relationships that tradition-bound or debt-burdened retailers will find hard to follow."[5]

---

[3] Ibid.

[4] Standard & Poor's *Industry Outlook*, June 4, 1992.

[5] As quoted in S&P's *Industry Outlook*, June 4, 1992, p. R81.

FIGURE 1
Measures of Consumer Outlook

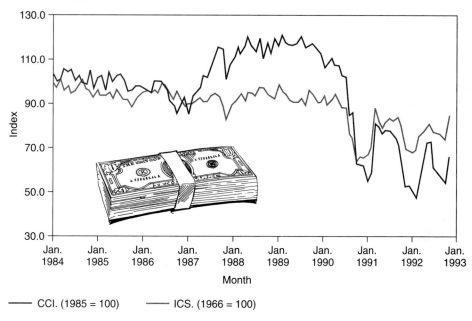

CCI measures consumer opinion about current and future business and employment conditions.

ICS is a broader measure that includes assessment of interest rates.

10   Among the specialty retailers are discounters, warehouse clubs, category specialists, and specialty apparel retailers. A good example of exploiting a niche is how both The Gap and The Limited maintain a staff of fashion designers on the payroll. The stores sell private label products that were created by the designers on staff. The result is that both stores have a backward integration advantage not available to conventional retailers. The Limited often receives deliveries on merchandise that was ordered only four weeks previously, while at May's Department Stores (currently one of the best-performing national department stores), the lag time usually is closer to six months.[6] Among other specialty retailers (e.g., Banana Republic, Pep Boys), the general recipe for success is similar: be the industry leader in a narrow aspect of retailing.

11   The third problem faced by Federated is internal. The reorganization plan allowed Federated to discharge approximately $5.0 billion in debt and preferred stock obligations; but, despite this reduction, the company still carries $3.2 billion in long-term debt. Exhibit 1 shows the consolidated balance sheet of Federated and Exhibit 2 shows the income statement. In Exhibit 3, industry norms for various financial measures are presented.

12   Allen Questrom looks to chart Federated's strategy for 1993 and beyond in a manner that deals with these three fundamental challenges plus prepares Federated to face the other challenges that will inevitably emerge. After the initial takeovers of Allied and Federated, Campeau's parent firm controlled 35 subsidiaries. Campeau sold such familiar names as Brooks Brothers, Ann Taylor, and

---

[6] Ibid., p. R84.

FIGURE 2
U.S. Department Store Sales as a Percent of Disposable Personal Income

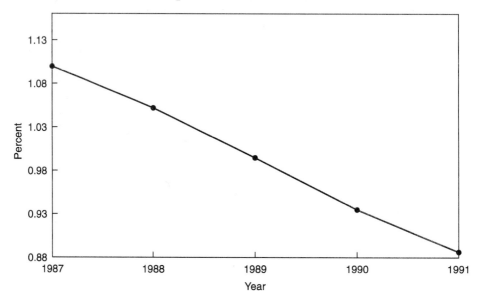

FIGURE 3
Ratio of Specialty Store Sales to Department Store Sales

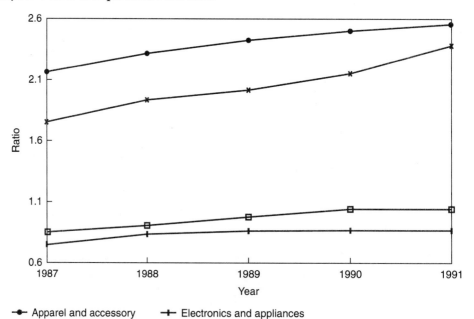

EXHIBIT 1
Balance Sheet
Annual Assets (in thousands)

	Fiscal Year Ending			
	02/01/92	02/02/91	02/03/90	01/28/89
Cash	$1,002,482	$ 453,560	$ 285,249	$ 310,326
Receivables	1,515,378	1,629,219	1,017,721	971,467
Inventories	1,209,961	1,335,008	973,433	975,534
Other current assets	113,342	N.A.	N.A.	25,000
Total current assets	3,841,163	3,417,787	2,276,403	2,282,327
Prop., plant, & equip.	2,499,700	2,749,867	2,089,837	2,173,460
Net prop. & equip.	2,499,700	2,749,867	2,089,837	2,173,460
Other noncur. assets	420,575	815,779	806,674	814,781
Intangibles	375,244	1,856,914	1,284,665	2,460,934
Deposits & oth. asset	364,463	309,709	114,610	181,280
Total assets	7,501,145	9,150,056	6,572,189	7,912,782

Foley's to reduce Federated Department Stores, Inc., to a more manageable level. Federated's eight divisions are concentrated mainly along the eastern seaboard and looked as follows in 1991:

	Location	Number	1991 Sales (in millions)
Abraham & Strauss:	NE U.S.	15	$ 819.5
Bloomingdale's:	eastern and southern U.S.	15	1,074.0
Bon Marché:	NW U.S.	39	720.4
Burdines:	Florida	46	1,255.0
Jordan Marsh:	NE U.S.	20	565.7
Lazarus:	Midwest	40	934.8
Rich's:	SE U.S.	23	817.7
Stern's:	NE U.S.	22	669.3

13   Figure 4 contrasts the trends between department store sales and population for various regions of the United States.

14   Based on meetings with Federated's executives and board members, Questrom has narrowed the number of strategic options that he is willing to consider. The first option is a plan of geographical consolidation that could offer cost savings at the corporate level. Under this option, Questrom must consider two facts: the Bon Marché chain is geographically secluded from the majority of Federated's stores and, among the rest of the corporation's chains, the geographical overlap is both a blessing and a curse. Due to the seclusion of Bon Marché, it is difficult to capture operating and information synergies between Bon Marché and any of the other chains. For example, Stern's, Jordan Marsh, and Abraham & Strauss can share information about the market in which they compete and can take advantage of volume-based price advantages in shipping and purchasing activities. The second

EXHIBIT 1   (concluded)
Annual Liabilities (in thousands)

	Fiscal Year Ending			
	02/01/92	02/02/91	02/03/90	01/28/89
Notes payable.................	$ 771,605	$ 309,268	$ 136,216	$1,554,803
Accounts Payable	1,111,011	897,249	389,133	740,749
Income taxes	34,735	254,233	70,847	275,637
Total current liab...............	1,917,351	1,460,750	596,196	2,571,189
Deferred charges/inc.............	746,627	1,192,053	1,098,227	1,074,252
Long-term debt	3,176,687	1,004,000	1,204,000	3,020,888
Other long-term liab.	206,348	6,534,003	3,980,756	116,597
Total liabilities	6,047,013	10,190,806	6,879,179	6,782,926
Preferred stock	N.A.	357,778	N.A.	N.A.
Common stock net	N.A.	N.A.	N.A.	1
Capital surplus	1,454,132	−1,398,527	−306,989	1,286,173
Retained earnings	N.A.	N.A.	N.A.	−156,317
Shareholders' equity	1,454,132	−1,040,749	−306,989	1,442,491
Tot. liab. & net worth	7,501,145	9,150,057	6,572,190	8,225,417

N.A. means not available.

important fact regarding the locations of Federated's chains addresses this competitive overlap issue. While resource and information sharing can be the source of cost savings, cannibalism may overshadow any synergistic advantages. Because the subsidiaries of Federated compete in many of the same markets in the large eastern seaboard cities, Questrom is concerned that gains made by one chain may be at the expense of another chain. So he must consider a geographical reorganization to cut costs and relieve intersubsidiary competition.

15   A second option is to design and implement an information system that will allow Federated's subsidiaries to communicate seamlessly with each other and with suppliers. Questrom recognizes the advantages that Dillard's and May's Department Stores have acquired and has gathered the following information from a task force studying this option: the system would cost roughly $60 million and will require that all of Federated's vendors conform to some information practices that will be used by Federated's system. In return, Federated will have automated replenishment of merchandise, tighter inventory control, and clearer information about sales trends throughout the corporation.

16   The third option being considered by Questrom is the most familiar to him and the least radical of the three. When he was hired to oversee the turnaround at the Neiman-Marcus Group, Questrom made a simple but uncompromising commitment to customer satisfaction. Rather than cutting the sales staff, he cut positions out of middle management and *increased* the sales staff so a customer would never search for assistance and would rarely need to wait to pay for merchandise. Implementing such a change at Federated would require moderate corporate restructuring and a larger and better-trained sales staff throughout the corporation.

EXHIBIT 2
Annual Income (in thousands)

	Fiscal Year Ending			
	02/01/92	**02/02/91**	**02/03/90**	**01/28/89**
Net sales.	$6,932,323	$7,141,983	$7,577,586	$3,571,692
Cost of goods.	4,964,471	5,172,892	5,447,121	2,553,966
Gross profit	1,967,852	1,969,091	2,130,465	1,017,726
Sell., gen., & admin. exp.	1,700,880	1,833,918	1,881,017	789,470
Inc. bef. dep. & amort.	266,972	135,173	249,448	228,256
Nonoperating inc.	−1,612,676	−43,447	−1,102,035	59,283
Interest expense	504,257	639,527	914,557	445,644
Income before tax	−1,849,961	−547,801	−1,767,144	−158,105
Prov. for inc. taxes	−613,989	−276,355	6,783	−1,787
Net inc. bef. ex. items	−1,235,972	−271,446	−1,773,927	−156,318
Ex. items & disc. ops.	2,072,364	N.A.	N.A.	N.A.
Net income	836,392	−271,446	−1,773,927	−156,318

N.A. means not available.

17   In Federated's *Corporate Fact Book 1992*, the management philosophy is stated as: "Federated clearly recognizes that the customer is paramount, and that all actions and strategies must be directed toward providing an enhanced merchandising offering and better service to targeted consumers through dynamic department stores." An analyst that follows Federated had the following comment when she heard Questrom refer to this philosophy in a recent presentation to a meeting of financial analysts: "Devising a management philosophy or mission is important, but what is crucial at Federated now is crafting the strategy that will allow the company to accomplish that mission."

EXHIBIT 3
Industry Comparisons
Average Results of Selected Performance Measures

Retail Industry	Net Income ($ millions)			Return on Assets (%)			Current Ratio			Debt/Total Capital		
	1989	1990	1991	1989	1990	1991	1989	1990	1991	1989	1990	1991
Department stores	$206	$199.7	$163	5.2%	5.8%	4.7%	2.6	3.1	3.3	56.0	57.0	73.8
General merchandise	795	766.4	791	6.9	6.4	5.3	1.9	1.9	2.0	29.5	32.0	36.3
Discount dept. stores	-34	-158	-82	5.0	8.5	N.A.	1.8	2.5	2.6	26.2	27.0	30.2
Specialty chains	199	216.8	235	11.3	9.2	9.9	2.1	2.0	2.1	18.5	17.1	18.0
Catalogue retailers	8.9	-38.5	31.7	9.2	6.2	9.4	1.6	2.7	1.5	55.3	46.0	57.0

N.A. means not available.

FIGURE 4
Department Store Sales and Population

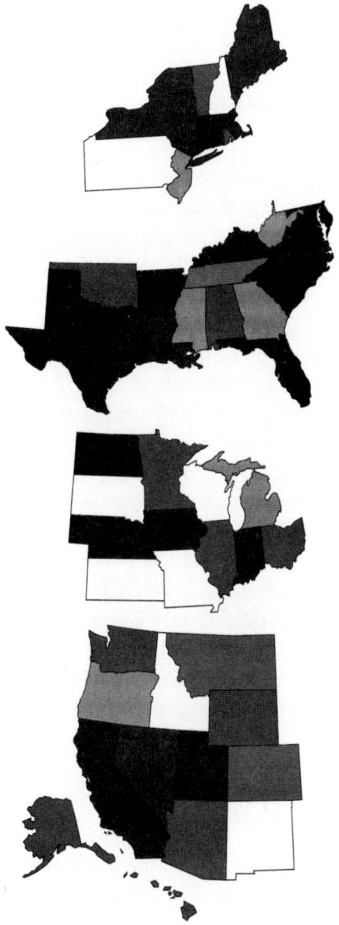

Department Store Sales ($000,000s)				Population (000s)		
1989	**1990**	**1991**		**1970**	**1980**	**1990**
31,496	31,320	31,487		49,061	49,135	50,809
61,478	61,154	64,201		62,812	75,372	85,446
47,604	47,381	36,494		56,589	56,866	59,669
35,433	35,241	36,494		34,838	43,172	52,786

CASE 7

SYSTEMATICS, INC.

1   After experiencing dramatic growth by providing financial services to both American and foreign banks since its formation in Little Rock, Arkansas, in 1968, Systematics, Inc., now faces many internally and externally generated problems and opportunities. Since it was acquired by ALLTEL Corporation in May 1990 for $528 million in stock, Systematics has suddenly obtained access to a vast amount of capital that it can use to pursue additional growth avenues. For its part, ALLTEL expects its average annual five-year growth rate of 10.0 percent to be greatly enhanced by Systematics' 21.1 percent rate while simultaneously capturing various operating and technological synergies.

2   In the face of this pressure for profits and growth, John Steuri, president and chief executive officer of Systematics, must deal with several violent changes occurring in the banking industry. Some describe a general sickliness associated with America's banking institutions. In recent years, profit performance has been low or negative, much of the banking public has low confidence in the system's strength and integrity, and massive consolidations and mergers have been completed in attempts either to seek safety in size or to obtain various operating economies or portfolio diversifications. These problems have affected Systematics, which is a major supplier of software and other financial services to over 800 banks in 45 states and nearly 20 countries.

3   How Systematics should respond to these pressures has divided its management team. Many feel the company should stick to the banking industry, which has been the source of its past successes. Other executives feel they must capitalize on ALLTEL's strengths as a telephone holding company that has diversified into cellular telephone and other communications services.

THE BANK FINANCIAL SERVICES INDUSTRY

4   In 1980, the *ABA Banking Journal* sensed the development of a new trend in bank operations management. Given that an average-sized bank devotes about 8 percent of its expenses to data processing (DP), various economies should be realized by a bank if this work could be "farmed out" to a more efficient data processor. Five forces seem to be driving this development:

5   1. The scarcity and high price of technical talent—many banks find it difficult to attract and hold DP personnel. Rather than creating their own programs, many banks must buy off-the-shelf software or contract outside technical labor.

6   2. Pressure for more sophisticated applications—as technological capabilities increase banks, as well as their customers, wish to realize the cost and convenience advantages these technologies can bring to an operation.

7   3. Greater competition from bank saturation or industry deregulation—competition is fierce between the savings and loan banks versus commercial banks and credit unions. Small banks are attempting to match the services provided by the larger banks, while the larger banks are attempting to prevail by providing the best services available.

This case was prepared by Joseph Wolfe, Management and Marketing Department, College of Business Administration, University of Tulsa, based on a graduate student research project conducted by Robert Knapp.

TABLE 1
Source of Bank Data Processing Services

Bank Size (assets in millions of dollars)	In-House (%)		Outside (%)	
	1978	1984	1978	1984
Very large (over $1,000)	95.0%	96.0%	5.0%	4.0%
Large ($500 to $1,000)	92.0	94.0	8.0	6.0
Medium ($100 to $500)	79.0	72.0	20.0	28.0
Small (under $100)	9.0	12.0	56.0	68.0

Source: *Input*, Palo Alto, California.

8   4. Pressure for profits—as various markets converge and growth cannot come from increased revenues, banks must find profit sources through operating efficiencies.

9   5. Changes in the capabilities of those offering financial services to the banking industry—computer service companies have grown in their size and in their financial stability; thus they have become dependable suppliers of DP skills and applications. Many service organizations have created software and possess technical talent that can only be duplicated by individual banks at a very high cost.

10   It has been estimated that, by 1994, this trend will result in the doubling of the industry to one with sales of over $2.6 billion, or an annual growth rate of over 17.0 percent per year. Table 1 suggests this growth has occurred mainly amongst the smaller institutions, although various industry experts feel the trend may spread to the larger banks once they succumb to the natural pressures building within the industry.

11   A bank's data processing system helps in the delivery of many bank services:

12   1. *Basic operations.* This entails keeping track of teller operations, handling demand and time-deposit accounting, and processing installment and mortgage loan applications and payments.

13   2. *Trust services.* These manage the various investments contained in customers' trust portfolios.

14   3. *Financial analysis.* This poses "what-if" questions to aid in the selection and balancing of investment portfolios owned by either bank customers or the bank itself.

15   4. *Automated customer services.* These handle the accounting and electronic operations of the bank's automated teller machines.

16   5. *Specialized services.* These services vary from bank to bank, based on the clientele it wishes to cultivate and special needs associated with that clientele. Once this audience is identified, the operations associated with this group are automated through computer support.

17   Banks historically have attempted to solve their data processing needs in three ways. Some have done all the work themselves, from programming to computer operations with in-house personnel. This has been difficult to do even by the largest banks. Most banks use what is called a *double approach.* They employ outside services for their routine DP work, while using in-house personnel to handle their unique or critical needs. A third approach has been to completely rely on third-party consulting firms to perform all DP work. These firms range from general accounting firms to specialized DP management consulting companies.

18   Just as competition within the banking industry has increased, competition between those servicing the industry also has increased. More than 640 vendors supply the industry, and these vendors differ regarding their product strategies. Some can satisfy all a bank's data processing needs, while

others offer a more limited variety of products or services. Those products and services are the following:

19   1. *Software packages.*   These are preprogrammed computer programs purchased by the bank, rather than having the bank create its own programs with in-house personnel. The DP servicer's range of participation can vary from merely selling the software off the shelf to installing and customizing the product (within its own preprogrammed limitations) to meet the bank's specific needs.

20   2. *Remote computing services.*   These are mainframe computer time-sharing operations in which banks use on-line computing through an off-site computer via office terminals in a real time mode.

21   3. *Remote batch processing.*   This is a slower data processing method, which involves the bank entering data on-site and sending it to a central computer that will process the data overnight and re-distribute the information the following day.

22   4. *Turnkey purchase.*   This method does not entail the direct purchase of equipment or software by the bank but, instead, has the vendor select the equipment, program it, and get it up and running, while providing on-going maintenance once the bank itself has taken custody of the operation.

23   5. *Facilities management.*   This is the most comprehensive set of services a vendor can provide. In this method the vendor assumes full responsibility for hiring and training operators, installing and running the computer, programming all bank computer applications, and delivering results according to the basic contract in force between the bank and the facilities management supplier.

24   Figure 1 outlines the products and services offered by several firms in the information technology industry, while Figure 2 outlines the characteristics of some of the industry's major competitors. Among the top 10 suppliers, 7 sell applications software, 9 offer data processing services of some kind, and 3 offer facilities management. In 1990, the aggregate revenues for these firms were $3.7 billion. This was a 32 percent increase over the prior year, although this increase was less than the 50 percent increment that occurred between 1987 to 1988.

25   Given the banking industry's rather bleak profit situation, a strong cost control trend has exerted itself. As observed by Frank Martire, chairman of Citicorp Information Resources, a devilish dilemma exists within the industry:

26   What we hear—and we talk regularly to a couple of hundred bankers across the country—is cost control, and it's not different by size of bank or location—it's across the country. If banks can delay investments, they're going to do it, but intelligent banks with real foresight are not going to try to control costs so much that it harms service to the customer. They still want to position the right product or right service for a recovery, which will come in 1993 or '94.

27   Accordingly, banks have begun to look more intensely at the financial service industry's offerings. Extreme concentration has been placed on maximizing short-term efficiency combined with major long-term technological improvements. Many feel this will lead to an increase in banking's search for alliances and technology partners to aid in sharing the costs and risks of technological advancement during the period of severe cost control.

SYSTEMATICS, INC.

28   Systematics, Inc., was founded by Walter Smiley after having been a systems engineer for IBM and an eight-year data processing manager for the First National Bank of Fayetteville, Arkansas. By 1977, its sales had grown to $13.3 million after having begun as an eight-person company just nine years before. In 1980, the company began to market software packages to banks, other than the one it was servicing in Fayetteville, and by 1981 its sales had reached $36.3 million. Shortly after that, Systematics began to service international customers, and Smiley began to voluntarily take on a less-dominant role within the company.

FIGURE 1
Products and Services Offered by Selected Bank Vendors

Vendor	1989 Revenu (in millions)	Products and Services
Electronic Data Systems (Plano, Texas)	$900.0	Applications software. Turnkey systems. Local batch processing. Remote noninteractive processing. Interactive processing. Facilities management. Custom programming. Consulting. Education and training.
First Financial Management (Atlanta, Georgia)	741.0	Applications software. Turnkey systems. Local batch processing. Remote noninteractive processing. Interactive processing. Custom programming. Consulting. Education and training.
Systematics (Little Rock, Arkansas)	224.7	Applications software. Remote noninteractive processing. Interactive processing. Turnkey systems. Facilities management. Custom programming. Consulting.
Mellon Information Services (Pittsburgh, Pennsylvania)	170.9	Applications software. Interactive processing.
NCR (Dayton, Ohio)	168.1	Applications software. Interactive processing. Custom programming. Consulting. Education and training.
SunGard Data Systems (Wayne, Pennsylvania)	125.0	Applications software. Interactive processing.
Citicorp Information Resources (Stamford, Connecticut)	104.0	Turnkey systems. Interactive processing. Facilities management. Custom programming.
Unisys (Detroit)	99.9	Applications software. Consulting.
BISYS (Houston)	54.2	Facilities management. Custom programming. Consulting.
The Kirchman Corporation (Orlando, Florida)	54.0	Applications software. Local batch processing. Education and training.
National Computer Systems (Eden Prairie, Minnesota)	38.4	Turnkey systems.
Financial Information Trust (West Des Moines, Iowa)	31.1	Interactive processing.

Source: Adapted from "America's Top Fifty Banking Software Products," *Banking Software Review*, Autumn 1990, pp. 28–31.

FIGURE 2
Company Sketches

Electronic Data Systems (EDS). This company has been providing services, in general, for more than 25 years to all 50 states and 27 countries. It attempts to create solutions through its 2,000 employees that best accomplish the individual financial institution's goals while still maintaining EDS's unique corporate personality. EDS offers an almost complete line of services, including such others as systems integration and communications facilities management. Because of its size it can process more than 3 billion instructions per second, 24 hours a day, 365 days a year. It can transmit voice, data, and video around the world using terrestrial, satellite, microwave, and fiber optic technology.

IBM Corporation. IBM brings its image of reliability plus its dominance of the mainframe computer to the financial services industry. It is a prime contractor in many banks, but daily operations are subcontracted to a third-party vendor. IBM's marketing strategy involves tailoring each contract to the customer's individual requirements; it refuses to use the term *facilities management,* as it implies an off-the-shelf approach that IBM rejects.

Software Alliance. Software Alliance markets its UNIX-based Total Banking Solution to small to medium-sized banks while it markets its Marshall & Isley Integrated Banking System to larger banks. The company's software interfaces with all IBM compatible computers. Rather than developing its own applications, Software Alliance obtains the marketing rights from successful software developers. After obtaining these rights, it targets banks with up to $750 million in assets and a second group of those with assets ranging from $2 billion to $200 billion.

Newtrend Miser2. Founded in 1977, this company's software consists of over 40 deposit, loan, customer service, financial control, management support, and EFT/ATM applications—all operating on Unisys hardware. Newtrend's components are not sold individually. Customers purchase an integrated core system to which modules are added as needed. The company is well known for individually customizing its integrated system, which is available through in-house use, a service bureau, or facilities management.

The Kirchman Corporation. Kirchman claims over 6,000 clients, and it allocates approximately 20 percent of its gross revenues to research and development. The company operates solely on IBM machines designed for single or multibank environments. Its newest product is called *Dimension Software,* which is an integrated system for small to medium-sized banks.

---

29 In August 1988, John Steuri took over Smiley's position as Systematics' CEO. Steuri was himself a 24-year IBM veteran, beginning as a sales representative in Topeka, Kansas, and ultimately headed an IBM marketing force of 9,000 people doing more than $6 billion worth of business a year. Systematics was an attractive opportunity for him when he left IBM at the age of 49 with an attractive early-out package.

30 The qualities I admired in IBM were evident in Systematics. It was a well-run, focused, growth-oriented company with a commitment to customer service. Systematics also was still small enough that I felt I had a chance to be a part of a real entrepreneurial enterprise.

31 Sales have continued to grow and many expect, as shown in Table 2, that its revenue prospects are very bright. Table 3 displays the income from operations obtained by Systematics. See Figures 3 and 4 for financial information. Industry experts feel the firm's strengths lie in the integrated, IBM-based COBOL software it possesses, as well as in its reputation for quality service. The software addresses a wide range of applications, including deposits, loans, profitability analysis, branch automation, electronic funds transfer, and marketing. Its newest product is entitled Extended Application Architecture (EAA), and it allows banks to migrate to new technologies, such as regional databases, in an orderly

TABLE 2
Systematics, Inc., Actual and Forecasted Revenues (in millions)

Year	Revenues
1985	$ 95.9
1986	122.6
1987	141.6
1988	179.5
1989	206.8
1990	254.8
1991	305.5
1992	365.0
1993	440.0

Note: Revenues after 1991 are Yankee Group estimates.
Sources: 10-K reports and the Yankee Group, 1991.

TABLE 3
Systematics, Inc., Operating Income (in millions)

Year	Operating Income
1985	$15.0
1986	17.0
1987	20.0
1988	28.0
1989	32.0
1990	34.0

Source: Company stockholder reports.

manner when it becomes cost effective. Systematics also has begun to offer an advanced loan system that was created with the EAA. This is a comprehensive loan servicing system that allows users to introduce new loan products with little programming support. It also offers many debt management features not offered by other systems.

32 Systematics delivers its products three ways, depending on the size of the bank being serviced. First, it provides facilities management and data processing services for 390 American and foreign bank clients. Second, it sells its applications software to financial institutions for their in-house use. Third, it sells turnkey operations, consisting of mid-range systems and applications software through an IBM remarketing agreement.

33 Approximately 75 percent of its revenues are derived from facilities management. In December 1990, Systematics signed a 10-year service contract valued at between $350 million and $500 million with the City National Bank of Beverly Hills, California, and another contract to operate First New Hampshire Bank's data processing center was announced in February 1991. As of January 1991, Systematics had over 80 on-site financial management agreements. Table 4 presents a summary of the company's past and forecasted activity in the area of facilities management.

FIGURE 3
Systematics, Inc., Income Statements, 1987–89 (in thousands)

	1989	1988	1987
Net sales	$206,786	$179,474	$141,577
Cost of goods sold	153,223	133,262	105,053
Gross profit	53,563	46,212	36,524
R&D expenditures.	9,476	9,064	7,741
Selling and general administration expenses	15,056	14,070	11,895
Interest expense	517	621	514
Operating income	28,514	22,457	16,374
Nonoperating income	1,702	2,425	3,164
Pretax income.	30,216	24,882	19,538
Taxes	11,352	9,458	9,376
Net income.	$ 18,864	$ 15,424	$ 10,162

Note: Fiscal year ends May 31.
Source: 10-K reports.

TABLE 4
Actual and Forecasted Facilities Management Contracts

Activity	1984	1985	1986	1987	1988	1989	1990	1991	1992	1993
New contracts added	4	6	6	12	16	13	12	14	15	16
Contract expirations due to:										
Client mergers and consolidations	1	2	4	6	2	4	2	3	4	6
In-house conversions with Systematics software	0	0	0	1	1	0	0	1	1	2
Year-end contracts in effect	39	43	45	50	63	72	82	92	102	110
Contracts renewed	6	8	10	5	5	7	8	6	8	12

Notes: Activities are for fiscal years ending May 31. Data after 1990 are Yankee Group estimates.
Sources: Systematics, Inc., and the Yankee Group, 1991.

34   To some degree the banking industry's generally poor financial condition, plus the closing or consolidation of smaller banks, which are an important target group for Systematics, has had an effect on the company's thinking. Steuri, however, saw a silver lining in this cloud.

35   Everyone knows there is a general malaise in the financial sector. Granted, that hurts our software sales, which accounted for only 10 to 12 percent of our business last year. There is another side though. If they turn their data processing over to us, we can help them. We can reduce their costs at least 10 to 15 percent and put money on their bottom line real fast.

FIGURE 4
Systematics, Inc., Balance Sheets, 1987–89 (in thousands)

	1989	1988	1987
Cash.	$ 2,858	$ 4,931	$ 879
Marketable securities	32,477	22,013	37,704
Receivables	26,569	20,536	20,083
Other current assets	3,941	1,123	1,156
Total current assets	65,845	48,603	59,822
Property, land, and equipment	108,313	95,855	80,078
Accumulated depreciation	51,788	44,683	34,243
Net property and equipment	56,525	51,172	45,835
Other noncurrent assets	5,635	5,635	—
Deposits and other assets	4,768	1,658	1,848
Total assets	132,773	107,068	107,505
Notes payable	1,456	9,366	1,010
Accounts payable	15,272	8,812	4,003
Accrued expenses	12,052	10,237	7,035
Income taxes	1,446	910	2,296
Other current liabilities.	12,427	5,407	5,015
Total current liabilities.	42,653	34,732	19,359
Deferred charges	7,109	6,443	8,936
Long-term debt.	5,626	2,911	3,777
Other long-term liabilities	—	—	5,631
Total liabilities	55,388	44,086	37,703
Net common stock	278	276	272
Capital surplus	28,876	26,655	24,917
Retained earnings.	51,860	37,399	45,656
Treasury stock	3,629	1,348	1,043
Shareholders' equity.	77,385	62,982	69,802
Total liabilities and net worth	$132,773	$107,068	$107,505

Note: Fiscal year ends May 31.
Source: 10-K reports.

36   Despite the industry's doldrums, Systematics met its 12-month goal for facilities management contracts within the first nine months of the 1990 fiscal year. In fact, Steuri has said, "There have been occasions when our sales reps have been sent home for a week or two so we would not sign more contracts than we could service."

TABLE 5
ALLTELL 1990 Sales and Operating Income by Business Segment (in thousands)

Business Segment	Sales	Operating Income
Telephone	$818,150	$290,032
Systematics	254,806	34,159
Product distribution	331,565	22,507
Cellular systems	42,272	2,227
Other	126,992	14,965

Note: Fiscal year ending December 31, 1990.
Source: 10-K report.

ALLTEL ENTERS THE PICTURE

37   With the acquisition of Systematics, Inc., by another Little Rock company, ALLTEL became a $1.57 billion operation, with diversified interests in cellular telephone systems, natural gas service, air traffic control voice switching and control systems, signal data converters, encrypted voice communications systems, and high resolution color graphic display systems. Table 5 shows that Systematics would garner about 16 percent of ALLTEL's total sales but would contribute more than that percentage to its operating income. Accordingly, Joe Ford, ALLTEL's president and CEO, called this acquisition "one of the most significant of our strategic moves." Various industry observers are more skeptical about the acquisition and its long-term benefits to either company. James Stork, a security analyst for Duff & Phelps, Inc., stated:

38   There are really no strategic reasons or synergies [here]. We do not view this as a strategic acquisition, although data processing and telecommunications may be converging, it is difficult to see how the combination of these two companies will result in much in the way of synergy over the next five years. We get the impression that ALLTEL acquired Systematics simply because it became available, and ALLTEL felt it could increase its consolidated growth potential for a reasonable price.

39   Both John Steuri and Joe Ford have begun to rise to the occasion. Steuri says, "We foresee some potential synergies as the communications and computer industries continue to converge." Because there are about 1,300 telephone companies currently competing in the United States, he felt they could be approached by the same sales pitch used when they recruited banks and savings and loan institutions: "Let us do your data processing for you. We can do it cheaper and more efficiently than you can do it in-house."

40   In this quest for synergies between the two companies, Systematics completed a deal in March 1991 to acquire C-TEC Corporation's cellular telephone billing and information system, and ALLTEL turned its cellular data processing operation over to Systematics. ALLTEL also has begun to sell off various operations not related to telecommunications and information processing. It sold its natural gas distribution systems in Nevada and California to Southwest Gas Corporation for $16 million in June 1991, and it is attempting to sell off its Ocean Technology, Inc., subsidiary as well as its alternate energy investments.

41   Although moves are being made to make this a successful acquisition for ALLTEL, and John Steuri feels pressure is being placed on him to help his new parent corporation realize its own growth goals, he thinks numerous diverse factors need to be considered. Admittedly, the banking industry is in a state of turmoil, but Systematics' business strengths lie within that industry. What path or paths should Systematics pursue? Should the company attempt to ride out the banking industry's storm while possibly incurring the wrath of ALLTEL's management for failing to move ahead with applications in the telecommunications industry? Could Systematics attempt to fill other product-services niches in the banking industry despite the awesome size of its major competitors? Does Systematics have any other options?

CASE 8

BLOCKBUSTER ENTERTAINMENT CORPORATION

INTRODUCTION

1   Seated at his desk in a rented two-story stucco executive office building in downtown Fort Lauderdale, Florida, H. Wayne Huizenga prepared to announce record revenues and net income for his chain of Blockbuster Video stores. His mid-April 1992 announcement would attribute those results to "increasing market penetration, gains in same-store revenue, and continued emphasis on cost control and increased productivity."[1] As Blockbuster Entertainment Corporation's chairman of the board and chief executive officer, he also prepared to announce that it was now possible to pay a cash dividend to the company's 8,000 stockholders—something that had not been done before.

2   At the end of 1991, having achieved a 13 percent share of market, the company announced that its goal was to reach a 20 percent share of the U.S. home video market and to have 3,000 Blockbuster Video stores operating in North America by 1995.[2] In some of its most mature markets, such as Atlanta, Chicago, Dallas, Detroit, and south Florida, that would mean market shares well in excess of 30 percent. Such a high share of market has been rare in specialty retailing. However, Blockbuster was the only U.S. video rental chain operating on a nationwide basis. Its next largest competitor was a regional chain, less than one 10th its size.

EXTERNAL CHALLENGES AND OPPORTUNITIES

3   As Huizenga optimistically pondered the company's strategic situation over the next five to seven years, several interesting external challenges and opportunities were lurking on the horizon:

4   With a higher market share than all of its 300 closest competitors combined, how much further could the company's market penetration grow?

Could any significant technological changes in home entertainment alter the video rental industry's attractiveness?

What were the future implications of Philips Electronics N.V.'s recent investment in Blockbuster stock?

This case was prepared by Dr. James A. Kidney, Management Department, School of Business, Southern Connecticut State University. Distributed by the North American Case Research Association.

[1] Corporate news release dated April 21, 1992.

[2] The total population of video rental stores operating throughout the United States ranged between 25,000 and 29,000, and turnover of individual store locations was quite high during the late 1980s and early 1990s.

COMPANY HISTORY

5   David P. Cook, a 31-year-old Texas entrepreneur, founded the company in December 1982 as Cook Data Services, Inc., a provider of software and computer services to the oil and gas industries. Facing a sagging market for such services, Cook decided to switch over to a new, rapidly growing niche in specialty retailing—video rental stores. Cook's first store was opened during 1985, and the present corporate name was adopted one year later. From the outset, Cook recognized that an innovative superstore concept would draw many customers away from typical mom-and-pop rental stores, and that well-designed computerized information systems would be advantageous for inventory planning and control as well as for customer information.

6   The typical mom-and-pop store had a spartan, nondescript atmosphere; short hours; a selection of fewer than 3,000 titles, stressing recent hits; and empty boxes to be brought to a clerk who would have to find appropriate tapes—provided they were then in stock. Many mom-and-pops obtained significant rental revenues from X-rated videos, and that occasionally created an unwholesome image.

7   In comparison, Cook's idea was to have a family-oriented atmosphere, with an extensive selection of children's videos, longer and more convenient hours, improved layout, quality service, faster check-in/check-out, state-of-the-art real-time computer information systems, and a thoroughly trained professional staff.

ATTRACTING HUIZENGA'S ATTENTION

8   After only two years of operation, Blockbuster's latent potential attracted the attention of Huizenga. By that time, Cook owned 8 stores and franchised 11 more in the Dallas area. Huizenga, then 48 years old, was restless, looking for a way to come back from early retirement, after having successfully made a small fortune from several companies.

9   Huizenga's previous experience had been in building businesses in a variety of dissimilar industries, such as trash bin rentals and garbage hauling, dry cleaning, lawn care, portable toilet rentals, water cooler rentals, and sale of bottled water. His most notable success was Waste Management, Inc., which he had honed into the world's largest waste collection and disposal company.

10   There was a common denominator running throughout his past entrepreneurial ventures. Each had rendered relatively basic services, had repeat customers, required little employee training, earned a steady cash flow, and was able to expand within an industry filled with small undercapitalized competitors. Usually, the fragmented industries he entered were ripe for consolidation, because greater firm size led to economies of scale in marketing, distribution, computerized information systems, and potential clout in purchasing products and services.

EXPANSION AND ACQUISITION OF STORE LOCATIONS

11   During 1987, Huizenga and a couple of close business associates bought out Blockbuster's founders and franchise holders for $18 million, and soon thereafter they began acquiring small regional chains, such as Southern Video Partnership and Movies to Go. To help him run the new business, Huizenga hired several former upper-level managers from McDonald's Corporation. His upper-management group adopted the view that Blockbuster's target audience should be very similar to McDonald's broad-based restaurant clientele. Thus, Blockbuster's national expansion of its retail business was based on McDonald's well-established growth philosophy, namely: blitz major markets, add stores quickly, use franchising to speed the process of obtaining managerial talent and operating capital, and never admit that the market is saturated.

12   Facing a rapid rise in VCR ownership, management tried to combine careful planning with opportunistic risk taking. An aggressive acquisition program was financed by new equity capital to avoid burdensome long-term debt. Over the following four years, additional regional chains, such as Video Library, Inc., Major Video Corporation, Oklahoma Entertainment, Inc., Vector Video, Inc., Video Superstores Venture L.P., and Erol's, Inc., were eagerly gobbled up.

13   A major international thrust was launched in early 1992, with the acquisition of Cityvision PLC, the largest home video retailer in the United Kingdom. Operating under the "Ritz" name and enjoying a 20 percent share of market, this firm had roughly 800 small stores and was considered to be an underperformer.

14   Around the same time, several Blockbuster Video stores were opened in Japan in a joint venture with Fujita & Company, a retailer running over 800 McDonald's restaurants and holding a stake in Toys-"R"-Us Japan, Ltd. Jointly they hoped to open 1,000 stores over the next 10 years.

15   Describing the hectic and occasionally disorganized rush to add store locations, Huizenga explained, "We felt we had to go fast because we had nothing proprietary. We had to get the locations in each area before somebody else moved in. It was a mistake, but it turned out okay. We have the locations, the people are trained, and the customers are ours. Now if somebody else comes in, they have to take it away from us."[3]

BLOCKBUSTER VIDEO'S PROFILE AS OF 1992

16   Blockbuster Video was a membership-only club, serving more than 29 million members worldwide who rented more than 1 million of the company's videocassettes daily. Without incurring any membership fees, patrons were provided with bar-coded membership cards that allowed for speedy computerized check-out from the issuing store. Cards sometimes were honored at other locations in the chain, as well. By requiring personal photo identification and an application for membership, rather than dealing with anonymous walk-ins, the rental store was able to secure an extra measure of control over tapes that left the premises. A major credit card also had to be presented, so the store could charge members for lost or damaged inventory.

17   The typical Blockbuster Video store was located in a free-standing building of approximately 6,000 square feet (560 square meters) and was open from 10 A.M. to midnight, 7 days per week, 365 days per year. The atmosphere was bright and wholesome. Aisles were clearly marked and divided into more than 30 categories to distribute customer traffic and encourage browsing. Video boxes with tapes inside were openly displayed within easy reach. Similar categories were placed adjacent to one another, thereby increasing the potential for increased rentals. Blockbuster's superstores typically carried a comprehensive selection of 10,000 prerecorded videocassettes, consisting of more than 8,000 titles. The strongest months for video store rentals tended to be December through March and June through August, with Hollywood's release schedule being a crucial variable.

18   Blockbuster Video stores proudly claimed to offer "More Movies Than Anyone in the World." Additionally, their relatively weak, fragmented rivals seldom were able to match Blockbuster's advertising clout and wide array of attractions, such as computer-driven movie selection aids; a three-evening rental policy; an attractive overnight pricing policy for new hit releases, which improved turnover and in-stock positions; a state-of-the-art management information system, which tracked rentals and market trends; microwave popcorn and other snack foods; promotional tie-ins with Domino's Pizza, Pepsi-Cola, Pizza Hut, Subway, USAir, and Universal Studios; drop-off boxes for fast returns; and publicity from an annual Blockbuster Bowl football game. Nevertheless, some competitors clearly

---

[3] *The New York Times Business World Magazine*, June 9, 1991.

EXHIBIT 1
Number of Blockbuster Video Stores, by Ownership Type

Date	Company	Franchised	Total
December 31, 1985 . . .	1	0	1
December 31, 1986 . . .	19	0	19
December 31, 1987 . . .	112	126	238
December 31, 1988 . . .	341	248	589
December 31, 1989 . . .	561	518	1,079
December 31, 1990 . . .	787	795	1,582
December 31, 1991 . . .	1,025	1,003	2,028
March 31, 1992	1,805	1,024	2,829

Note: The surge in company stores during the first quarter of 1992 is attributable to the Cityvision PLC acquisition.
Sources: Blockbuster's 1991 Annual Report and 1992 press releases.

differentiated themselves from Blockbuster by offering lower prices, reservations, home delivery, or hard-core adult videos.

19   As of March 31, 1992, there were 2,829 Blockbuster Video stores worldwide, up from 19 just five years earlier (Exhibit 1).

LOCATIONS AND OPERATIONS

20   By the first quarter of 1992, 68 percent of Blockbuster's stores were located in 46 of America's 50 states, with the remaining 32 percent located in Austria, Australia, Canada, Chile, Guam, Japan, Mexico, Puerto Rico, Spain, the United Kingdom, and Venezuela. Nearly all of the company's retail, distribution, and administrative facilities were rented under noncancellable operating leases, which in most cases contained renewal options. Blockbuster employed approximately 12,500 individuals.

21   Historically, there had tended to be a 50–50 balance between company-owned and franchised locations. Although franchising remained beneficial in foreign countries, where local partners made it easier to conduct business, franchising in the United States became less essential once the company had an ample cash flow and employed many competent people who could help manage ongoing growth.

22   The usual initial investment (i.e., franchise fee, inventory, equipment, and start-up capital) for a franchised location ranged from $700,000 to $1 million. Annual operating costs per location fell in the $400,000 to $500,000 range. Franchisees were provided extensive guidelines for site selection, store design, and product selection, as well as for customer service and management training programs. In addition, the company furnished national and local advertising and promotional programs for the entire system. Franchisees paid royalties and other fees for those services and also routinely paid Blockbuster Entertainment for videocassette inventories, computer hardware, and software.

23   For a typical Blockbuster Video store, cash flow payback on initial store investment occurred rapidly—generally in under three years. The average new store attained monthly revenues of $70,000 within 12 months of opening date.

24   Systemwide revenues, for company-owned and franchise-owned operations combined, as well as other selected financial data are shown in Exhibit 2.

EXHIBIT 2
Selected Annual Financial Data (dollars in millions except stock and per share data)

	1991	1990	1989	1988	1987
Income Data					
Systemwide revenue	$1,520	$1,133	$663	$284	$ 98
Company revenue	868	633	402	136	43
Operating costs & expenses	714	514	326	110	37
Operating income	154	119	76	26	6
Net income	94	69	44	17	3
Depreciation & amortization	189	124	76	22	5
Cash flow	283	193	120	39	8
Balance Sheet Data					
Total assets	$804	$608	$417	$235	$105
Cash & cash equivalents	48	49	40	9	7
Current assets	163	116	93	39	27
Current liabilities	164	110	83	49	17
Long-term debt	134	169	118	39	22
Shareholders' equity	483	315	208	124	59
Per Share Data					
Earnings per share	$0.56	$0.42	$ 0.28	$0.12	$0.04
Tangible book value	2.35	1.65	1.18	0.75	0.41
Stock price—high	15.12	13.37	10.81	6.25	2.63
Stock price—low	7.75	6.75	4.87	1.06	0.75
Common Stock and Equivalents (millions)					
Average shares outstanding	168	162	155	142	75

Notes: Systemwide revenues include franchise store revenues, while company revenues do not. Operating costs and expenses include depreciation and amortization. Cash flow is net income plus depreciation and amortization. Tangible book value excludes cost of purchased businesses in excess of market value of tangible assets acquired (unamortized goodwill).

Sources: Blockbuster's 1991 Annual Report and Standard & Poor's Stock Report.

SOURCES OF REVENUES

25   During 1991, 5 percent of company revenues were derived from franchise royalties and fees, 20 percent from product sales mainly to franchisees, and 75 percent from rentals. Other than low-priced used products, outright sales of home videos never were emphasized prior to late 1991, because the largest sellers were highly competitive national discount chains like Wal-Mart and Kmart. As a growing portion of consumer spending went toward videocassette and laser disc purchases, it became logical for video rental stores to begin taking the sell-through market more seriously.

26   Mr. Joseph Baczko, who headed the highly successful International Division of Toys-"R"-Us, Inc., for eight years, was hired in 1991 as Blockbuster's new president and chief operating officer. To carry

EXHIBIT 3
Estimated and Projected Annual U.S. Movie Revenues, by Viewing Method (dollars in billions)

Viewing Method	1990	1995	2000
Home video	$10.3	$15.2	$19.3
Movie theater	5.1	6.9	7.4
Pay cable (premium channels)	5.1	6.2	7.6
Pay-per-view	0.1	0.5	2.0
Total	$20.6	$28.8	$36.3

Source: Blockbuster's 1991 Annual Report.

out a process of "retailizing," as well as internationalizing the company, he brought several executives with significant retailing experience into the firm. Promotional and display efforts to stimulate sell-through transactions got added emphasis under Baczko's direction. Given his background in toys, he was interested in treating child-oriented movies, such as *Batman, Bambi, The Little Mermaid*, and *101 Dalmatians*, mainly as sell-through, rather than rental, products. Blockbuster's stores also began renting Nintendo and Sega Genesis video game products.

INDUSTRY ENVIRONMENT

27 Rentals and sales of home videos in the United States amounted to a mere $700 million in 1982. By 1991, domestic revenue for the video rental industry reached $11 billion, and Americans were spending more than twice as much to watch movies at home as they did to watch them in movie theaters. Within the marketplace for prerecorded videocassettes, movies accounted for more than 80 percent of rental revenues and at least 50 percent of dollars spent on purchases. Blockbuster Entertainment estimated that the U.S. video rental market for movies would reach $19.3 billion by the turn of the century (Exhibit 3).

28 In 1980, the percentage of U.S. households owning at least one television set reached 98 percent and remained at that level thereafter. By 1995, there were expected to be almost 100 million households in the United States, and 98 percent of them were likely to own at least one color TV set. Blockbuster Entertainment expected 91 percent of those TV-owning households also to own VCRs (Exhibit 4), with more than 35 percent of them owning at least two machines.

29 VCR ownership in Europe also was growing rapidly, with household penetration rates in individual countries lagging behind the United States anywhere from two to five years. Total 1991 worldwide spending for home video rental and sales was $21.2 billion (Exhibit 5). Licensing, sale, and rental practices differed from one product/market to another, and in some countries most of the television viewing population remained unaware that movie videos could be rented instead of being purchased.

MOVIE PRODUCTION AND DISTRIBUTION

30 Approximately 390 to 450 new feature films were released annually in the United States. Eight of the largest distributors accounted for more than 90 percent of movie theater film rentals in the United States and Canada. Most of them, such as Paramount, Universal, Warner, Fox, Columbia, and Disney,

EXHIBIT 4

Estimated and projected VCR and cable TV penetration among U.S. TV-owning households (millions of TV-owning households, percent with VCRs, percent with cable TV, and percent with additional pay-per-view or pay cable services, by year).

Year	No. of TV-Owning Households	Percent with		
		VCR	Cable	Pay Cable
1980 . . .	76	1%	20%	7%
1981 . . .	78	3	22	10
1982 . . .	82	6	30	16
1983 . . .	83	10	34	19
1984 . . .	84	17	39	24
1985 . . .	85	30	43	26
1986 . . .	86	42	46	27
1987 . . .	87	53	48	26
1988 . . .	89	62	49	27
1989 . . .	90	68	53	29
1990 . . .	92	72	56	29
1991 . . .	92	77	58	30
1992 . . .	93	82	61	31
1993 . . .	95	86	64	32
1994 . . .	96	89	67	34
1995 . . .	97	91	70	36

Note: From 1982 through 1995, it's assumed that 98 percent of all U.S. households own televisions.

Sources: Blockbuster's 1991 Annual Report, the *Universal Almanac*, and author's estimates.

had been in business for more than 50 years. The leading producers and distributors of videos were usually subsidiaries of large companies that owned other leisure-time businesses. Large distributors also had prime access to international channels for distributing American-made films in foreign countries. Musical, cultural, educational, exercise programs, instructional, and documentary videos tended to be handled by smaller distributors.

31   The time span from the point when work began on a new movie to the point when its revenue stream was largely realized often was five years or longer. Over that period, producers and distributors attempted to play out their products in a manner that gave them an optimum revenue stream.

32   By 1991, home video had become a major ancillary source of revenue for movie studios. For example, *Nothing but Trouble* (directed by Dan Aykroyd, 1991) grossed $8.5 billion in box office receipts. The studio's share was roughly 50 percent. When released on videocassette, the same movie earned an additional $9.6 million in revenue for the studio.[4]

---

[4] Source: Blockbuster Entertainment 1991 Annual Report.

EXHIBIT 5

Estimated population, home video spending, VCR penetration, and basic cable penetration by country, as of 1991.

Country	Population (millions)	Video Spending ($ billions)	VCRs (% of households)	Cable (% of households)
Australia	17	$ 0.7	70%	0%
Canada	27	1.2	65	69
France	56	0.7	40	10
Germany.	79	0.7	46	32
Italy	58	0.6	38	1
Japan.	124	2.6	70	20
United Kingdom	57	1.4	70	2
United States	250	11.0	75	55
Others	4,732	2.3	N.A.	N.A.
Worldwide total	5,400	$21.2	N.A.	N.A.

Note: N.A. means not available.

Sources: Blockbuster's 1991 Annual Report, *This Business of Television*, and 1992 *World Almanac*.

33 The sequence of each film's release depended on the nature of individual deals made by the distributor. Domestic release usually occurred somewhat ahead of international release. A typical major studio's U.S. release tended to be rolled out in the following illustrative manner:

34 Theatrical showings: January through April 1992.

Home video: mid-summer 1992.

Airline: mid-summer 1992.

Pay-per-view: late-summer or fall 1992.

Pay cable (premium channels): winter 1992–93.

35 If attractively priced, popular movies developed for young children were likely to achieve a sell-through market of 1.5 million or more copies. Movies that had been adult hits at the box office within the latest year were the ones most in demand for rentals, and 100,000 to 500,000 copies of them generally were sold, mostly to video rental stores. Assuming a $3 charge per rental, it normally took anywhere from 13 to 19 rentals to recover a store's initial investment in a hit movie tape.

36 Distributors set high initial suggested retail prices (roughly $80 to $100 on box office hits) for videotaped films they expected consumers to rent and set low prices (roughly $20 to $30) for those they expected consumers to buy. Each videocassette costs distributors about $2 to manufacture and $2 to market. Wholesale prices paid by Blockbuster were generally 55 to 65 percent of suggested retail prices.

WHOLESALERS

37   Despite the fact that movies were the mainstay of the home video business, Blockbuster Entertainment traditionally purchased its movie rental inventory from wholesalers, rather than from film distributors. Having achieved nationwide scope, the company could decide to bypass regional wholesalers and purchase its movies more economically direct from motion picture distributors.

TECHNOLOGICAL THREATS

38   During the decade from 1982 through 1991, Americans purchased 1.2 billion prerecorded and 2.2 billion blank videocassettes. They also built up a $32 billion investment in VCR equipment. This burgeoning consumer commitment to VCR technology seemed to assure long-range demand for videocassettes. Nevertheless, the ease of duplicating and pirating videocassettes was a matter of some concern to movie producers. As laser discs began to attract a modest following, rentals and sales of video discs were being added to many video store's product offering.

39   No one knew precisely when new types of home entertainment might begin to undermine home videotape viewing. Cable television was expected to become a more and more serious threat. Even though three out of five TV-owning households subscribed to cable service as of 1991, only one third of those subscribers had access to movies on pay cable (e.g., HBO, Showtime, Cinemax, The Disney Channel, The Movie Channel), or pay-per-view channels.

40   Employing addressable technology, pay-per-view service allowed customers to call in and have a movie, concert, or sporting event broadcast on their TV for a fee. Being transaction-based, pay-per-view depended upon impulse buying. It was sold by direct mailings, advertisements, bill stuffers, and 24-hour "barker" promotional channels.

41   In 1992, sporting events generated almost twice as much pay-per-view business as other alternatives. As pay-per-view's market potential continued to develop, the summer of 1996 was regarded as an important psychological turning point. Cable operators were seeking the broadcasting rights for live coverage of the Olympic Games in Atlanta, Georgia, hoping that such coverage would significantly boost the number of new subscribers for pay-per-view services.

42   While viewers had to watch pay-per-view at a scheduled time, this service certainly provided greater convenience than having to make two round trips to a video store. The competitive threat was moderated by the fact that most new movies were released on videocassettes before they appeared on pay-per-view services or pay cable. However, that disparity could disappear rapidly, if movie distributors were enticed by cable's potential for licensing and revenue-sharing arrangements.

INTERACTIVE TELEVISION

43   Over the long term, advances in satellite and cable television technology and entry of regional telephone companies into the electronic home delivery arena were other potential concerns within the U.S. market. With new developments in fiber optics and digital signal compression, expansion to 500 channels could become feasible for video delivery systems. Thus, there was a possibility that video-on-demand could become a reality on cable or telephone systems by the mid 1990s.

44   Anticipating major advances in communications, IBM and Time Warner Corporation had begun discussing ways to combine data processing and transmitting expertise with cable TV systems, TV shows, and movies. IBM believed interactive television eventually would encroach on a wide array of existing entertainment and information product/markets, including catalog shopping, broadcast and

cable advertising, home video, information services, theater, video games, electronic messaging, video-conferencing, photography, records, tapes, and CDs. Furthermore, the Federal Communications Commission (FCC) had allocated a portion of the broadcast spectrum to interactive television and intended to award licenses to investors who could serve large markets.

NERVOUS INVESTORS

45 Had the video rental market remained extremely fragmented, it might not have become so large and well established. Some industry watchers predicted that Blockbuster's success in becoming a high-quality specialty retail chain might impair the development of innovative competing technologies for accessing home entertainment.

46 Recognizing that other forms of retailing were withstanding competition from television, Baczko made the following point: "Home shopping has not taken the store away, and pay-per-view is not going to do so to video. I don't think you can ever beat a retailing environment."[5]

47 Nevertheless, newspaper reports of questionable depreciation accounting practices, of bankruptcy filings by sizable video retailers, and of media hype of future electronic home delivery systems, from time to time, stirred predictions of impending disaster for the video rental industry. Consequently, Blockbuster's common stock attracted speculators and short sellers, and the market price per share plunged every so often as frightened investors hastily bailed out to take profits or stop losses. For example, the price per share reached a high of $15.125 and a low of $7.750 on the New York Stock Exchange during the first half of 1991.

STRATEGIC ALLIANCE WITH PHILIPS ELECTRONICS

48 During 1992, an intriguing strategic alliance began to emerge between Blockbuster Entertainment Corporation and Philips Electronics, N.V. Headquartered in the Netherlands, Philips was the world's second-largest consumer electronics company after Japan's Matsushita Electric Industrial Company. Philips' decision to purchase 13 million newly issued common shares (nearly 7.2 percent of share outstanding) suggested that the two companies might be heading toward a close working relationship.[6]

49 In 1991, consumer products accounted for 47 percent of Philips' $33 billion in sales revenues. The early 1990s found the United States, Canada, Australia, the United Kingdom, and Japan all experiencing economic downturns and declining consumer confidence. Stagnant demand and bloody price wars were curbing profits throughout the consumer electronics industry. Battered by stagnant demand and stiff price competition from its Japanese competitors, Philips reported a $3 billion loss in 1990. Philips' new president, Jan D. Timmer, was struggling to slash the payroll, close inefficient plants, and divest unprofitable operations. A streamlining and restructuring process initiated by Timmer provided a $210 million profit on sales of $33 billion in 1991. Recent sales data are shown in Exhibit 6.

50 Some analysts, suspecting that Huizenga might be ready to move to another new venture, speculated that Philips might be interested in acquiring a controlling interest in Blockbuster Entertainment Corporation. Others expressed doubts that outright ownership and management of a captive group of rental stores would serve Philips' best interest.

51 Having pioneered such consumer electronics products as the videocassette recorder, audio compact disc, digital compact cassette, and high definition television, Philips had long been a superior

---

[5] *The New York Times*, February 21, 1992.

[6] These funds have been used by Blockbuster to help pay for the Cityvision PLC acquisition.

EXHIBIT 6
Philips Electronics N.V.
Net Sales by Product Sector and Geographic Area (millions of guilders)

	1991	1990
Product Sector		
Lighting	7,351	7,026
Consumer products	26,861	25,856
Professional products and systems	12,510	12,400
Components and semiconductors	7,844	7,953
Miscellaneous	2,420	2,529
Net sales	56,986	55,764
Geographic Area		
Netherlands	3,206	3,604
Rest of Europe	30,433	30,366
U.S.A. and Canada	12,833	11,819
Latin America	3,142	3,361
Africa	730	772
Asia	5,565	4,770
Australia and New Zealand	1,077	1,072
Net sales	56,986	55,764

Note: On December 31, 1991 and 1990, respectively, one U.S. dollar equaled 1.71 and 1.69 Dutch guilders.
Source: Philips' 1991 Annual Report.

technological leader. Marketing agility and competitive pricing had never been Philips' strengths. Philips conceivably might be aiming for a reliable international retail base for rapid, broad distribution of future hardware and software products.

52 Philips owned 51 percent of Super Club Holding & Finance S.A., a poorly performing music and video retail chain. With store locations in Europe and the United States, Super Club might benefit from a tie-in with Blockbuster. Philips also owned 80 percent of Polygram, one of the three largest music publishing, production, marketing, and distribution companies in the world, and a major European manufacturer of compact discs. Recognizing the increasingly complementary natures of the audio and video fields, Polygram had begun producing and distributing filmed entertainment, as part of its strategy to become a multicultural, global entertainment company.

PHILIPS' MULTIMEDIA SYSTEMS

53 Potentially even more relevant were Philips' plans for a new Imagination Machine. Philips had developed a new Compact Disk Interactive (CD-I) entertainment system, which could turn the family TV into a terminal through which one could play regular music CDs, view photo CD disks, and interact

with programs, rather than just watch them. Touted as the "VCR of the 21st century," Philips' Imagination Machine was one of the products that Timmer was counting on heavily to revive depressed earnings. Blending text, full-motion video, and stereo-quality sound, it called up sports statistics during live broadcasts, displayed digital snapshots, played karaoke sing-along discs, used Nintendo's new games, and played movies and music videos. While CD-I had been promoted primarily to the consumer market, it also was highly suited to the educational market.

54   Philips utilized a special format for its CD-ROM, which was supported by several other electronics firms as well. Commodore, Apple, Toshiba, and Tandy were offering multimedia equipment with different CD formats. Sony and Panasonic (Matsushita) had not yet revealed the type of standard they might support. Having witnessed the VHS/Beta wars of the late 1970s, Philips recognized the need to insure that its CD-I standard won out over its rivals. Ultimately, the availability of appealing multimedia software would help determine which compact disc standard would dominate.

POTENTIAL NEW UNDERTAKINGS

55   As Blockbuster entered numerous foreign markets, its employees started to acquire increasing familiarity with markets for movies and home entertainment within many different cultures and political jurisdictions. Blockbuster's increasing knowledge of ways to formalize and expand global rental markets could help foster widespread acceptance of the rental concept for expensive multimedia CDs, such as encyclopedias, music libraries, and games. Blockbuster, thus, could become a leading worldwide distributor of a new generation of home entertainment products, perhaps selling and renting Philips' Imagination Machines and CDs.

56   Reacting to investor skepticism a year earlier, Huizenga had optimistically asserted, "We have the best locations in town. We've got a plain vanilla box. We can sell shoes there if we want to. Maybe we'll build a music store that's green and white. We could call it Chartbusters."[7] Such remarks indicate that someday Blockbuster Entertainment Corporation could be attracted to retailing opportunities elsewhere within the diverse, yet more and more intertwined, marketplace for home entertainment products.

---

[7] *The New York Times Business World Magazine*, June 9, 1991.

CASE 9

AMERICAN MANAGEMENT SYSTEMS, INC.— DEFENSE GROUP

INTRODUCTION

1   American Management Systems—Defense Group (AMSDG), a subsidiary of American Management Systems, Inc. (AMS), served the information needs of the defense industry. Although AMSDG had exhibited strong and consistent revenue growth from 1985 to 1988, 1989 found AMS chairman of the board, Charles Rossotti, analyzing AMS's major revenue division because AMSDG had the corporation's only revenue decline in that year.

2   The decade of the 1980s witnessed volatile growth in the number of technological and software consulting firms serving the defense industry. Through the use of computers, the value of information had matured, and every agency within the government wanted to take advantage of the efficiencies its proper use offered.

3   Although the bulk of the government's spending was for weapons production and other forms of military hardware, information management was a component of every defense program. With the large defense expenditures of the Reagan years and the increasing importance of information management, firms with an expertise in information processing readily obtained government contracts. In fact, industry consultants agreed that the demand for information management, within both the government and commercial sectors, was so strong that firms offering services in this area succeeded in spite of themselves. In reality, many consulting firms had difficulty keeping pace with the growth of the industry. As a result, it was not uncommon for competing firms to experience problems with internal control and strategic focus.

4   By the end of the decade, the Reagan Administration's military buildup had peaked. The democratic revolution occurring in Eastern Europe and the political reforms in the Soviet Union provided unexpected opportunities for major reductions of the defense budget in the 1990s. Eastern Europe's transition away from Communism created a climate where the United States could work with the Soviet Union toward global security. Consequently, the need to build U.S. defenses against the Soviet superpower was diminished.

5   Business analysts preparing market projections for the defense industry in the 1990s were concerned about the shrinking number of new program opportunities contained in their long-range forecasts. In fiscal year 1989–90, the federal government approved a 25 percent decrease for U.S. Army, Navy, Air Force, and Department of Defense (DOD) agency budgets over the next five years. Further cuts were contemplated as the Soviet threat diminished and Congress attempted to get the federal deficit under control.

6   The budget cuts had a number of adverse effects on defense contractors. Budgetary constraints would keep new military programs on the drawing board for indefinite periods, postponing a source of revenue for contractors and increasing overhead costs as the period to develop those contract pro-

This case was prepared by John A. Pearce II of the School of Business Administration at George Mason University and by Kelly S. Nix. Development of this case was made possible by a grant from the Funds for Excellence Program of the State Council of Higher Education for Virginia.

posals was extended. Additionally, some established] programs were susceptible to modification or cancellation, resulting in the narrowing or complete withdrawal of anticipated sources of revenue.

7   Pentagon policies forced contractors to take on a larger share of the financial burden and the risk associated with system development. Further, the government program to eliminate contract abuses resulted in reduced profit margins and a shift toward fixed-price contracts. Fixed-price contracts forced contractors to develop system discipline and stay within development parameters. Understandably, a certain amount of flexibility was build into each contract proposal, but the competitive nature of the industry caused profit margins to narrow. Often, the tremendous investment required to compete in the industry undercut the profitability of those firms that received even major programs. Companies were beginning to question whether the rewards from the military market justified the necessary investments.

8   The attrition rate for companies in the defense industry was devastating. As many as 40 percent of the defense consulting firms active in the market in 1985 had gone out of business by 1989. Firms particularly at risk were large companies with very specific markets, and smaller companies who went into business with a single large contract. The larger companies, with the vast majority of their business falling outside the area of consulting, lacked the incentive to sink resources into the defense industry, where it was increasingly difficult to turn a profit. The smaller companies did not possess the broad range of skills necessary to compete successfully in the declining and highly competitive market.

COMPANY BACKGROUND

9   American Management Systems, Inc. (AMS), founded in Arlington, Virginia, in 1970, was one of the many computer systems consulting firms that rose to capitalize on the information revolution. The founders, Ivan Selin, Charles Rossotti, Franc Nicolai, Pat Gross, and Jan Lodal were experienced computer personnel who came from the Defense Department. Members of former Secretary of Defense Robert S. McNamara's "Whiz Kids," they helped implement the "system integration" approach to defense management. In addition to experience, their backgrounds included impressive educational credentials. The five founders held among them two doctorates and eight master's degrees, three of which were MBAs from Harvard, Stanford, and Cornell. Collectively, the five had a total of 23 years of postgraduate education.

10   Selin and Rossotti's original concept of the firm was to develop a viable business serving information management needs by marketing the five founders as a highly educated group with a proven track record at DOD. They intended to build on the techniques and concepts the group acquired at DOD in the application of computers to manage information for large organizations. Rossotti envisioned their role as that of consultants providing the link between management and their respective computer operations. The company's original client base was comprised of large computer users, but, as computer services became an integral component of most companies' competitive strategy, AMS began to service smaller clients, providing them with customized software service.

11   In the 1970s, the company grew and diversified into the nation's 40th largest computer services and supply company, with company revenues increasing from $500,000 to almost $60 million. The firm's growth had been facilitated by a strategy that encouraged a diversified skills base. This enabled the company to reach a large number of clients in a wide range of industries. In 1979, AMS went public at $18 a share, and the company's stock quickly rose to as much as $40 per share. However, in 1981, all segments of business faltered, resulting in company losses during the first nine months of that year. Although revenues were increasing, profit margins were declining. As a result, the company shifted its marketing strategies away from software packaging for small clients and back to its original focus on large computer users, such as banks, telephone companies, and governments.

EXHIBIT 1
AMS's Reveune History (in millions)

1989	$225,000
1988	213,000
1987	174,000
1986	135,000
1985	112,000
1984	97,000
1983	79,000
1982	69,000
1981	65,000
1980	58,000

12   Exhibit 1 diagrams the company's explosive growth in revenues throughout the 1980s. With 1989 revenues of $225 million, AMS had completed its 20th consecutive year of growth. However, earnings declined slightly from $7.4 million to $5.8 million. This coincided with a leadership change at AMS. Ivan Selin was chairman of the board until March of 1989, when he became U.S. Undersecretary of State for Management. Charles Rossotti, who had been the president of the company since its founding and its chief executive officer since 1981, became Selin's successor. The 1989 earnings decline was traced to an operating loss of $506,000 in the first and second quarters; this was the company's first loss since 1981. Rossotti attributed the drop in profit to dwindling defense business revenues, which declined by 20 percent, putting pressure on firms to narrow their margins. Rapid growth in the third and fourth quarter of companywide operations helped turn these figures into a $5.8 million net income for the year. Exhibit 2 highlights the company's troubled 1989 financial performance. Exhibit 3 provides a comparison of revenues earned across AMS's client markets. Exhibit 4 provides a five-year financial summary for the AMS Corporation.

BUSINESS DIVISONS

13   AMS was split into 14 business divisons (AMSDG is shown as "Defense Agency" on Exhibit 5), some of which were functionally oriented and some of which were client oriented. Exhibit 5 depicts AMS's organizational structure. The divisions operated autonomously, yet they were able to team with other divisions for specific projects, or trade experience and personnel when the situation required. The company's target markets were financial service institutions, insurance companies, federal agencies, aerospace firms, state and local governments, colleges and universities, energy industry clients, and telecommunication firms. AMS's client base as of January 1, 1990, broke down as follows:

Federal government	29%
State and local governments	23
Financial institutions	21
Other	13
Telecommunications firms	8
Energy firms	6
Total	100%

14   The company provided a full range of products and services to its clients through its extensive skill base. AMS's professional staff included experts in application design, hardware, systems software,

EXHIBIT 2
1989 Financial Highlights (in thousands except per share data)

	1st Half		2nd Half	
	1988	1989	1988	1989
For the Year				
Services and products revenues	$174,998	$ 90,746	$ 99,313	$190,059
Total revenues	213,305	107,715	117,588	225,303
Client project expenses	127,536	64,174	64,236	128,410
Other operating expenses	65,260	37,383	38,284	75,667
Corporate expenses	8,899	5,955	5,876	11,831
Total operating expenses	201,695	107,512	108,396	215,908
Income from operations	11,610	203	9,192	9,395
Other (income) expenses	1,118	1,054	(1,136)	(82)
Income before income taxes	10,492	(851)	10,328	9,477
Income taxes	3,104	(345)	3,595	3,250
Net income	7,388	(506)	6,733	6,227
Dividends on Series B preferred stock and amortization of issuance costs			448	448
Net income to common shareholders	$ 7,388	$ (506)	$ 6,285	$ 5,779
Net income per common share	$ 0.71	$ (0.05)	$ 0.61	$ 0.56
Weighted average shares and equivalents	10,388	10,434	10,347	10,391
At Year End				
Total assets	$102,858			$124,290
Working capital	29,581			48,990
Common stock, retained earnings, and other stockholders' equity	43,778			48,095

systems engineering, systems application architecture, database management systems, communications, office automation, local area networks, document imaging technology expert systems, software quality management, and other aspects of systems technology.

AMS DEFENSE GROUP

15   Where Ivan Selin had been a strong advocate for building a defense-oriented business, which in 1989 represented 29 percent of the company's total service and product revenues, Rossotti was anxious to see the firm diversify into a variety of industries so the company would not depend on any one business sector for the vast percentage of its revenues.

16   Specifically, Rossotti was not pleased with the operating performance of AMSDG. He was anxious to identify and effect operating and market orientation changes that would turn around the division as well as offer opportunities for new growth by serving nondefense customers. The people that Rossotti started with in the division included 380 individuals employed in 14 different business sectors. This

EXHIBIT 3
Revenues by Market
Year Ended December 31 (in thousands)

	1985	1986	1987	1988	1989
Services and products revenues:					
Financial services institutions	$ 15,323	$ 23,605	$ 31,857	$ 37,155	$ 40,590
Federal government agencies and aerospace companies	32,227	39,516	51,542	62,022	54,603
State and local governments and universities	19,177	24,831	27,578	32,148	44,253
Energy industry clients	7,249	4,339	5,876	9,108	11,557
Telecommunications firms	3,098	4,389	6,873	11,254	15,024
Other corporate clients	11,377	11,056	21,445	23,311	24,032
Total services and products revenues	88,451	107,736	145,171	174,998	190,059
Reimbursed expenses revenues	23,766	27,785	29,137	38,307	35,244
Total revenues	$112,217	$135,521	$174,308	$213,305	$225,303

group had specialists in financial management, logistics and maintenance, human resources, program management, intelligence, digital imaging, expert systems, and software quality engineering.

17   AMSDG had achieved particular success in the defense arena, where its financial management software had captured over 90 percent of an expanding market. The group realized similar defense industry success with digital imaging and information engineering services.

18   Exhibit 6 depicts AMSDG's organizational structure. Each box represents a program within the division that was operated as an independent profit center. Each program manager controlled, and was accountable for, his or her own portion of the group's business. However, budget projections were submitted to and approved by the division manager.

19   Under Selin, AMSDG was to meet the information management needs of the defense industry. Rossotti was pleased to note the group had since expanded its client base to include federal and commercial clients that were in need of the AMSDG services. However, when Rossotti became chairman, 70 percent of AMSDG's revenues were attributable to DOD alone. Although the group was not solely dependent upon defense revenues, Rossotti noted that the defense budget reductions experienced in the late 1980s had a direct effect on the group's bottom line.

20   In 1989, AMSDG experienced an $8 million decline in revenues, and, with declining profits, missed its target ROA. In fact, from a peak of 26 percent of AMS revenues in the first quarter of 1988, AMSDG's revenues declined to a low of 13 percent of the company's revenues in the fourth quarter of 1989. A breakdown of the five-year history of the revenues attributable to defense sector business was as follows:

1985	$30.9M
1986	42.0M
1987	47.8M
1988	47.0M
1989	39.0M

In addition, although the group's revenues were affected by changes occurring throughout the defense industry, long-time AMSDG employees voiced the suspicion that personnel policies were at the root of the division's declining profits.

EXHIBIT 4
Five-Year Financial Summary
Year Ended December 31 (in thousands except per share data)

	1985	1986	1987	1988	1989
Operating Results					
Services and products revenues	$ 88,451	$107,736	$145,171	$174,998	$190,059
Total revenues	112,217	135,521	174,308	213,305	225,303
Client project expenses.	65,351	79,710	99,241	127,536	128,410
Other operating expenses	32,665	37,391	52,233	65,260	75,667
Corporate expenses	6,934	8,181	9,418	8,899	11,831
Total operating expenses	104,950	125,282	160,892	201,695	215,908
Income from operations	7,267	10,239	13,416	11,610	9,395
Other (income) expenses	731	106	371	1,118	(82)
Income before income taxes	6,536	10,133	13,045	10,492	9,477
Income taxes	2,816	4,902	5,463	3,104	3,250
Net income	3,720	5,231	7,582	7,388	6,227
Dividends on Series B preferred stock and amortization of issuance costs					448
Net income to common shareholders	$ 3,720	$ 5,231	$ 7,582	$ 7,388	$ 5,779
Per Common Share Data					
Net income per common share	$ 0.37	$ 0.51	$ 0.73	$ 0.71	$ 0.56
Financial Position					
Total assets	$ 49,609	$ 66,200	$ 82,891	$102,858	$124,290
Fixed assets, net	12,190	11,339	11,840	13,947	14,614
Working capital	15,670	13,653	21,762	29,581	48,990
Common stock, retained earnings, and other stockholders' equity	22,690	26,293	34,467	43,778	48,095

21   In 1990, considering declining company profits in the face of the company revenue growth, Rossotti concluded that the operations of the AMSDG division were not being performed efficiently, and that primarily AMSDG's poor performance was affecting companywide profit margins. He decided to dedicate 1991 to turning AMSDG around. AMSDG's personnel policies and strategic direction were to receive special attention. Rossotti further decided that a failure to achieve turnaround in the division would result in its reorganization in 1992. Only those business units within AMSDG that could prove their profitability would remain.

PERSONNEL POLICIES

22   Many military personnel left the armed services and found management positions in consulting firms that conducted business with the federal government. The individuals brought to their jobs a wealth

EXHIBIT 5
AMS Organization

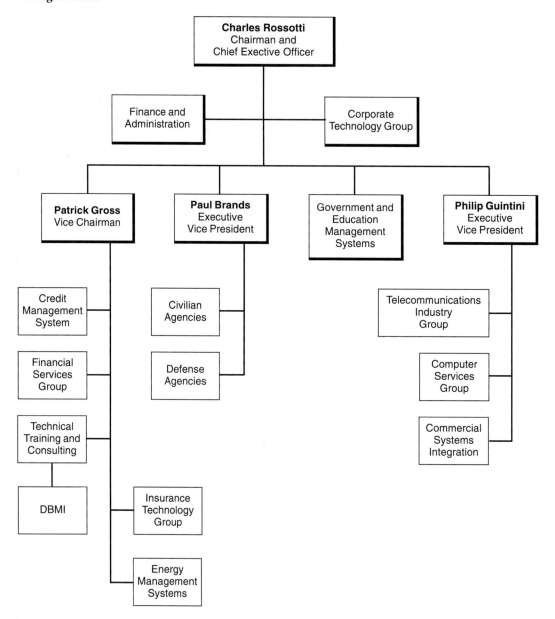

EXHIBIT 6
AMSDG Organization

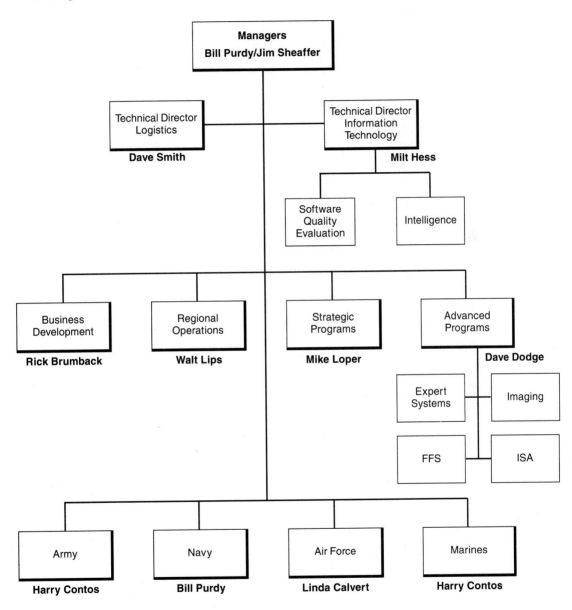

of knowledge about the defense industry, as well as an invaluable network of business contacts. The technical expertise required of the consulting industry was left to the lower-echelon employees.

23   In the 1970s and early 1980s, client connections played an integral part in the process of awarding military contracts. In the latter half of the 1980s, conflict of interest laws were enacted to promote a more equitable public procurement system, and contracts awarded by the government under the new

legal environment were based on merit. The awarding of contracts based on favoritism became illegal. Consequently, the advantages of hiring former military personnel were reduced.

24   An AMSDG manager noted, "After the laws changed, we found ourselves with an imbalance of skills in middle management. The former military personnel that made up a considerable portion of middle management had knowledge of the defense industry, but unable to use their contacts, and lacked the marketing skills necessary to compete in the new environment." Therefore, managers needed to identify opportunities before they committed time and expense to participating in public bidding wars. They had to identify, develop, and present their ideas from an entirely different perspective and utilize tools and techniquest not previously required.

25   Said another manager, "We also suffered from productivity problems within our professional staff. Experiencing high growth in a competitive industry, we found it difficult to operate efficiently while satisfying personnel requirements concerning avoiding layoffs. Consequently, individuals who failed to perform satisfactorily still continued to work for the group. With the high demand for personnel, individuals evaluated as marginal performers were kept on because their short-term services were needed."

26   Consequently, in periods of relatively low growth, AMSDG suffered the cost of increased overhead. Salary costs in most service industries were billed directly to company clients. When personnel were not working on a client project, or were performing tasks specifically for the company's use, their salaries were paid out of the company's overhead expense account. On the other hand, with the funding constraints and budget volatility of the defense industry, other firms reduced their overhead costs by hiring and firing personnel as contracts were started and completed.

27   The size and diversity of AMSDG's business base, as well as the diversity of the entire company, allowed the group a degree of flexibility in its personnel policy that most firms working in the defense industry did not enjoy. AMSDG placed great importance on building relationships with its employees, and it shifted personnel among units when there was a temporary surplus in one area or a deficit in another.

28   Because of lost contracts, contract cancellations, and funding postponements in early 1989, AMSDG had to relocate more individuals than the division had positions to absorb over the short term. All but 10 group employees were retained during the interim. However, the situation caused AMSDG's expenses to far exceed its revenues in the first half of that year.

STRATEGIC DIRECTION

29   Rossotti knew that the AMSDG vice presidents had called a meeting of their top marketing specialists to discuss the group's future in the defense industry. The vice presidents needed to analyze the division's performance figures and management policies to devise a workable and profitable scheme for future growth. With increasing revenues and declining profits, Rossotti noted 1989's performance figures proved that the company's profit margins were narrowing. However, he felt the cause of AMSDG's failure to better contribute to company profits was unclear. Was AMSDG not utilizing its resources efficiently? Or was the group simply competing in an industry whose profits were being eroded by the heightened competition of a shrinking market?

30   Management needed to evaluate its personnel resources to determine the group's current strengths. If AMSDG was not maximizing the use of its resources, there were a number of options for improving the group's performance. Following the industry's example, AMSDG could increase and decrease its personnel base as contracts were begun or completed. This approach insured that unnecessary overhead costs due to nonbillable personnel would be kept to a minimum. However, in so doing, the group ran the risk of losing extremely valuable employees.

31   Many experts in the service sector argued that a firm's greatest resource was its employees. Since client connections could no longer be utilized, AMSDG felt that it was increasingly important to create

a personal relationship with potential clients by selling them on the capabilities of its employees. Such an approach would be difficult, if not impossible, if the group had to wait to hire a project staff until after a contract was received.

32   AMS, as a whole, had never practiced the use of layoffs. Employees were likely to interpret such a move as a precedent for future practice. In a climate of uncertainty, they were likely to protect themselves by pursuing avenues that provided greater job security. Those avenues could include finding other positions within the company or exploring opportunities outside the company. The latter option presented the expenses associated with replacing those individuals who left the company when their skills were subsequently required by a new contract.

33   A reduction in the work force, by whatever means, might allow the group to get its cost structure under control. Most lower-level employees had similar educations in business, systems engineering, computer science, and management information systems, and they could easily be replaced in times of need. However, a small percentage of individuals masterminded the development of marketable products and services. These individuals were the backbone of the company and were necessary not only to create opportunities, but to oversee their evolution. If AMSDG enacted a layoff policy in an effort to control costs, it must do so in a way that did not threaten these key personnel.

34   Where marketing and management skills once had provided a distinctive competitive advantage over competitors in the defense industry, such skills were now a fundamental requirement in the new business environment and an absolute necessity in the commercial sector. AMSDG executives recognized that the group was badly in need of marketing expertise. In the past, they had relied on middle management to market the group's services, but these individuals were skilled in computer-oriented services and had no formal training in marketing.

35   The vice presidents wondered whether marketing skills should be taught to middle management, or whether new personnel with marketing skills should be hired instead. Top management was considering the initiation of a new training program, which each member of the business group would be required to attend. The program would include courses geared toward market awareness and general marketing skills, as well as the more traditional writing seminars and software development classes.

36   On the other hand, AMSDG also was considering the merits of hiring an in-house marketing and business development group trained to identify and promote specific opportunities. Top executives, though, wondered if AMSDG's growth potential was large enough to justify the cost of such a group. The marketing group's sole responsibility would be to cultivate new business, allowing the present personnel to concentrate on doing what they had been trained to do.

37   In addition to these personnel problems, top management needed to focus on a strategic direction. Over the next few years, the attrition rate of consulting firms in the defense industry was expected to rise as the defense budget declined. However, there would always be a need for defense work, and the Washington, D.C., area probably could expect to receive the majority of such work. With a strong presence in the defense industry in 1989, AMSDG stood a good chance of not only rebuilding its existing business but capturing a wealth of new business as its competitors left the stage.

38   Alternatively, the opportunities available in the commercial sector could not be ignored. The potential for continued growth in markets now currently at risk for losing funding was quite attractive for AMSDG. The group had successfully worked in the commercial sector in the past, and it had a number of existing products, formerly utilized in the defense arena, with possible commercial applications.

39   Should the group's commercial business be expanded, AMSDG ran the risk of having to compete with other divisions within the company. Such a situation actually would cannibalize existing revenue, rather than add to the company's overall revenue base. Because AMSDG was initially a client-based group that had been allowed to expand across other divisions' functional boundaries, the pursuit of further opportunities in the commercial environment could create structural problems for the company as a whole. Whatever direction Rossotti chose to pursue, he needed to consider what was best for the company as a whole, while maximizing the long-term potential of AMSDG.

CASE 10

THE GREAT WESTERN BREWING COMPANY LIMITED (A)

INTRODUCTION

1   It was a chilly afternoon that November of 1991. Peter McCann, president of Great Western Brewing Company, was gazing out the window at the snow drifting across the street of downtown Saskatoon, Saskatchewan. The release of the company's third brand, Great Western Gold, was only days away, and he wondered if the next few months would produce the planned gains in market share.

2   He knew that the long-term viability of the new operation depended on a lot of cooperation between people and events, and a little bit of good luck. Since the employee takeover deal of one year ago, it had been a roller coaster ride for everyone at the brewery. The young company had gone from a stunning 22 percent of Saskatchewan market share one month after start-up to the present low of 10 percent. McCann knew that the work required to keep the operation solvent was just beginning. The novelty of the original brand launches was wearing off, and Great Western was going to have to hold its own against its major competitors, Labatt Breweries and Molson Breweries.

BACKGROUND

3   In recent years, the brewing industry had seen a shift toward increasingly efficient use of resources. Mergers were being used to achieve increased efficiency and strengthen corporate competitiveness necessary to tap the vast United States beer market. It was as a result of this situation that the Great Western Brewing Company was born.

4   On January 18, 1989, the merger of Molson Breweries of Canada and the North American operations of Elders IXL, an Australian company that owned Carling O'Keefe, was announced. The implications of this announcement were significant. In total, 1,400 jobs were to be cut and seven plants closed across Canada over three years. After the merger the new corporation would have assets of $2.3 billion and annual production capacity of 12.6 million hectolitres (hLs) of beer.[1] The Carling O'Keefe facility in Saskatoon was one of the seven Canadian breweries scheduled to be closed.

5   For the employees of the Saskatoon Carling O'Keefe brewery, the announcement came as a shock. Their only comfort was the package of special early retirement programs, enhanced severance benefits, and career counseling to minimize the impacts of the merger. Approximately 40 of the 70 Saskatoon workers were going to be laid off when Molson moved all of its Saskatchewan production to Regina.

This case was prepared by B. Allen, R. Maguire, S. Oliver, C. Yeung, and Y. Zhu under the direction of Professor Brooke Dobni and Professor Rein Lepnurm.

[1] A hectolitre (hL) = 100 litres = 22 imperial gallons = 24.4 dozen bottles (12 ounce) of beer.

6   With an uncertain future, a group of employees considered the idea of buying the brewery from Carling and operating it themselves. Greg Kitz, a 14-year employee with the plant, prepared a package to solicit investor interest in buying the facility. This effort was unsuccessful, so the employees were left with only one option, an employee buyout.

7   The buyout was a high risk venture and the employees who were committed to the project must have considered their other options. They could try to find another job and start over. This probably would be the most difficult option, with approximately 1,000 people per month leaving Saskatchewan to look for better opportunities elsewhere. Several employees took jobs that were offered at Molson's Regina brewery. But a few brave, committed employees took the severance packages, worth on average $20,000, and the chance of a lifetime.

8   An employee association was formed with 23 out of the total of approximately 70 full-time employees from the Carling O'Keefe plant scheduled to close. The goal of the association was, on consummation of a deal with Carling O'Keefe, to buy out the brewery and go into the brewing industry themselves. In the end, only 15 of those 23 would remain with the project.

9   The group of 15 workers needed a leader to champion their cause, bringing expertise and credibility to the venture. Peter McCann was attracted by the challenge. McCann had spent his entire career, over 30 years, in the brewing industry, working in breweries and malt plants throughout the world. He held a BSc in brewing science from Heriot-Watt University in Edinburgh, Scotland, as well as management diplomas from England and the University of Western Ontario. In the months that followed, the Carling facility was sold to 16 investors and the Great Western Brewing Company was formed. McCann assumed the position of chief operating officer, in addition to becoming the 16th shareholder.

10   The group of 16 now formed a cohesive unit determined to turn the plant into a successful regional brewery. Each person invested what was, for most, a life savings, between $50,000 and $100,000 each. Their commitment amounted to 25 percent of the purchase price of approximately $5 million. The Saskatchewan Economic Diversification Corporation (SEDCO) invested the other 75 percent of the initial investment price. A chartered bank provided an operationg loan of $450,000.

STRATEGY

11   Peter McCann never had to dwell on what strategy to follow in the marketplace. The beer industry had become an intuitive part of McCann's career as a brewmaster. Great Western's strategy was to position itself as the "Saskatchewan" brewer, by maximizing Saskatchewan content and having a high community profile. It was projected that, if Great Western could get 10 percent of the Saskatchewan market share within the first year, the company would break even.

12   The Canadian brewing industry is characterized as a market containing a number of highly successful and competent brewing companies. Each brewer is capable of producing a high-quality beer, but the key to success in the industry is to create product differentiation at competitive prices in efforts to sustain market share. The Great Western product line was no different than its competition. The launch of regular and light products gave Great Western differentiated mainstream products to compete against the industry leaders. What Great Western had, though, was a product that appealed to the internal values of people in Saskatchewan. The success of Great Western's product line hinged on the loyalty of the Saskatchewan consumer to locally produced products.

13   In the early period of Great Western's operations, McCann had become convinced that the survival of Great Western would be closely linked to the success of its marketing initiatives. Great Western would have to build its product line and promote its beer as a product for people who were committed to the province and who wanted to share in the success of an underdog in its fight against the big breweries with their megaplants in the east. It would be essential for consumers to forsake their traditional brands and try Great Western. Once they tried Great Western, it was equally important to keep them buying.

14   According to Doug Sargeant, vice president of marketing of Great Western Brewery, the Saskatoon media were very supportive at the time of the new brewery's launch. They helped sell the company to the people of Saskatchewan lock, stock, and barrel. Everyone in the province seemed to be trying Great Western, and the brewery had to struggle to keep adequate supplies of beer in the liquor stores. Even the local restaurants and bars, which had been cautious about stocking Great Western, were placing orders after a few weeks as the public in Regina and Saskatoon demanded a Great Western product with their meals.

15   Now, almost two years after Great Western hit the market, people were still drinking "Saskatchewan's Own," but sales were down. The honeymoon was over and the local press was not providing its liberal doses of Great Western promotion. The company was at an important crossroad in ensuring its survival. With a reduced but stable market share, Great Western had carved out its niche in the Saskatchewan marketplace. In the future, Great Western had to decide whether it should be content as a regional brewery or if it should expand its horizons and carve out similar niches in the neighboring provinces of Alberta and Manitoba. Moreover, given the present underutilized plant capacity,[2] the American market was also an attractive opportunity.

16   McCann knew that the introduction of Great Western Gold marked a change in strategy of the company. Great Western's first two brands were positioned head-to-head with the market share leaders, Labatt's Blue and Molson Canadian. Great Western had to establish a presence in this segment to survive. Having done this, the brewery could now look at niche opportunities, either by introducing brands that were not available in Saskatchewan or by attacking the weakly defended, low market share brands of other brewers. It was anticipated by McCann that the major breweries would not be likely to react strongly to the latter strategy as the brands targeted offer very low margins. The incremental sales achieved by Great Western, on the other hand, would significantly improve the financial position by allowing the company to allocate fixed costs over a larger production base.

CANADIAN BREWING INDUSTRY—MARKET OVERVIEW

17   The Canadian brewing industry is characterized by comprehensive regulation and declining beer consumption (see Exhibit 1). From 1975 to 1988, the Canadian adult population grew by about 25 percent while beer sales only increased by 10 percent. This resulted in a per capita consumption erosion of approximately 11 percent. This shift in consumer demand away from beer products was prompted by several factors, including increased health and safety consciousness, changing age demographics, and greater taxation of beer in relation to other beverages. By 1989, there was yet no indication of any significant reversal in these trends. In fact, volume was expected to remain static or to decline slightly over the next five years.

18   Brand loyalty toward beer products generally has weakened over the past 10 years, and brewers in Canada have been forced to also sell beer on the basis of image and fashion. This can be partially attributable to the spillover of American marketing campaigns into the Canadian media, resulting from infiltration of American cable television on the Canadian airways. Further, a number of marketing and licensing agreements between Canadian and U.S. breweries were negotiated during this period.

19   As an example of this consumer fickleness toward brand loyalty, in 1983, when Carling O'Keefe broke with tradition and introduced Miller High Life and Miller Lite in tall bottles, the company was able to capture an incremental 9 percent of the total Canadian market. This share came at the expense of other Canadian brands and, in fact, cannibalized some of Carling's traditional brands. Later, the

---

[2] Even at 10 percent of Saskatchewan market share, Great Western was producing 55,000 hLs annually. Total annual capacity of Great Western was 262,000 hLs.

EXHIBIT 1
Consumption of Beer, Spirits, and Wine in Canada (litres per capita)

Selected Years	Beer	Spirits	Wine
1975	85.92	7.82	5.90
1979*	84.00	8.32	8.22
1980*	86.79	8.03	8.41
1981*	86.09	8.35	8.98
1982	85.34	8.12	9.19
1983	83.54	7.64	9.43
1984	83.50	7.05	9.45
1985	82.52	6.72	9.78
1986†	82.13	6.55	10.20
1987	81.87	6.34	9.97
1988	83.11	6.30	10.31
1989	81.83	6.13	9.87
1990	80.62	5.82	9.47

* Consumption figures reflect the effect of strikes in the brewing industry in Western Canada.

† Consumption figures reflect the effect of strikes in the brewing industry in Alberta, Ontario, and New-foundland.

Source: Brewers Association of Canada, Annual Statistical Bulletin, 1990.

twist-off cap introduced by Labatt in 1984 was said to have added about 1.5 to 3 percent to its total market share.

20   Domestic beer sales in Canada in 1990 was 20,092,150 hectolitres. Despite stagnant beer sales, price increases have caused the value of beer shipments to increase 13.7 percent. The value of beer sold in the fiscal year 1990 was $8.9 billion.[3] Saskatchewan, however, was only estimated to have 549,200 hectolitres of sales.

21   Competitive threats to the Canadian beer industry include foreign imports, impending GATT rulings, interprovincial trade barriers, continued consumer movement toward healthier lifestyles, sin taxes imposed by the federal government, and the share of belly concept. The *belly concept* implies there is only a finite quantity of liquid a person will consume and, unless the population increases, the market size will be stagnant. Beer producers, therefore, must compete with other beverages.

22   Among brewery products, bottled beer is the biggest seller, with 79.2 percent of total value of beer shipments. In Canada in 1988, bottled beer sales increased by 22.1 percent. Canned beer had 13.6 percent of the total value of beer shipments and saw a strong increase of 26 percent in 1988. Import beers are relatively low in significance, with 2.2 percent of total beer sales in 1988. However, import sales activity is expected to increase over the long term under the terms and conditions of the Free Trade Agreement (FTA).[4] The long-term influences of the proposed North American Free Trade Agreement (NAFTA) are speculative at present, but the potential exists for further erosion of the domestic protection of the provincial brewing industries in Canada.

23   The threat of free trade and abolishment of interprovincial beer sale regulations are real concerns for Canadian brewers. Yet it may not be as much a threat to Great Western as it is to Labatt and

[3] Consumer expenditure includes purchase of beer for home and on-premise consumption. Source: Brewers Association of Canada, "1990 Annual Statistical Bulletin," 1990, p. 36.

[4] Reference: Beverage and Tobacco Products Industries, Statistics Canada, Catalogue 32-251 Annual, 1988.

EXHIBIT 2
Sales of Beer by Province (hLs) and per Capita Consumption (hLs) 1990

Month	Manitoba	Saskatchewan	Alberta	Total
January	50,168	34,910	93,694	178,772
February	58,130	34,022	101,086	193,238
March	41,656	40,715	123,769	206,140
April	59,549	42,540	124,738	226,827
May	66,991	50,825	154,991	272,807
June	69,637	61,168	155,899	286,704
July	77,824	63,851	163,971	305,646
August	70,170	57,262	164,256	291,688
September	50,553	39,445	113,598	203,596
October	56,620	42,914	122,284	221,818
November	52,207	39,506	116,216	207,929
December	62,969	42,045	126,504	231,518
Total	716,474	549,203	1,561,006	2,286,683
Per capita consumption	0.710	0.549	0.634	

Source: The Brewers Association of Canada, Annual Report, 1990.

Molson. "If interprovincial barriers come down, we can see lots of brewing plants being shut down," Sargeant says. When asked whether such shutdowns could create more employee takeovers like the Great Western scenario, Sargeant said it would probably never happen again. "Molson obviously underestimated the threat Great Western could pose to them when they sold their Saskatoon plant to its employees. This oversight must have been costly to Molson."

24   In an effort to improve the competitive advantages of Canadian brewers in an ever increasingly global marketplace, interprovincial trade barriers are being reviewed and reciprocal sales agreements are being negotiated between provinces to give brewers access to new markets.

THE SASKATCHEWAN SITUATION

25   Beer consumption in Saskatchewan has been declining moderately since 1982. Parallel consumption patterns have been observed across Canada. At present Saskatchewan has the lowest per capita beer consumption of any province (see Exhibit 2).

26   Within Saskatchewan, the Saskatchewan Liquor Board has the authority to market all beers in the province. All other Canadian provinces have similar liquor boards and liquor authorities that control the retail liquor stores and the licensing of off-sale establishments. These organizations enjoy considerable power of the retailing of beer through supply management of sales establishments. Pricing authority also ensures continued provincial revenues and controlled competition within the industry.

27   American beer has been licensed for sale in Canada for many years. Prices were established by liquor boards in each province. In 1990, Saskatchewan became one of the first provinces to be "totally GATT fair." Under the General Agreement on Tariffs and Trade (GATT), Saskatchewan was required to open its borders to foreign brew. Saskatchewan Liquor Board argued their prices were in accordance with GATT in so far as American products had access to the market. Pricing differences were attributed to distribution costs incurred by the liquor board (see Exhibit 3).

28   Molson and Labatt distribute their products through their own distribution company, the Saskatchewan Brewers' Association (SBA). Great Western has a contract with SBA for beer distribu-

EXHIBIT 3
Saskatchewan Beer Prices, Select Brands—1990

	Beer Prices (per dozen including deposit where applicable			
	Sask.	Alta.	B.C.	Man.
Milwaukee's Best (I) (cans)	$16.00	$10.10	N.A.	$13.40
Old Milwaukee (I) (cans)	16.40	10.20	9.30	13.30
Pabst Blue Ribbon (I) (cans)	16.40	N.A.	13.40	13.70
Michelob (I) (bottles)	18.70	14.40	14.00	18.00
Labatt's Blue (D) (cans)	13.80	13.50	12.05	13.80

Notes:
1. (I) = Import.
   (D) = Domestic.
2. Labatt's Blue is considered a good proxy for domestic beer in terms of domestic beer prices due to its substantial market share.
3. Prices effective in October 1990.
N.A. means not available.
Source: *Saskatoon Star-Phoenix*, October 12, 1990.

tion on a fee-for-service basis. Other brewers, such as American brewers, must either negotiate a deal with the Saskatchewan Brewers' Association, pay the liquor board handling charges, or establish their own distribution channel in the province. With the tight control over the distribution channel, Saskatchewan brewers feel less threatened about the implications of GATT and free trade in the brewing industry.

NATIONAL AND INTERNATIONAL PRESSURES FOR DEREGULATION

29   National pressures for deregulation have been increasing since a 1987 conference in Toronto, where an endorsement in principle was made to achieve a general reduction or elimination of interprovincial trade barriers, including those relating to beer. In response to this, an interprovincial panel on liquor board marketing practices was appointed, but, as yet, the panel had not reached a consensus on action to be taken.

30   The international pressures are evolving from two sources. In 1987, a General Agreement on Tariffs and Trade panel sided with the European Community (EC) ruling that Canada's listing, marketing, and pricing practices for alcoholic beverages violated its obligations as a GATT member. Intense negotiation around this issue resulted in an agreement that required Canada to open its market to beer imported from EC member states and to remove discriminatory pricing practices.

31   Second, when the Canada–U.S. Free Trade Agreement (FTA) talks began in the mid 1980s, the Canadian brewers lobbied for an exemption. In October 1987, these efforts paid off as both the Canadian and U.S. negotiators recognized that the industry needed time to readjust. The exemption allowed Canada to continue to limit access by U.S. brands to distribution channels with quotas and higher taxes on U.S. beer.

32   The exclusion from the FTA and the Canadian government's willingness to agree to industry adjustment was seen by industry analysts as a window of opportunity for Canadian brewers to accomplish three things: (1) satisfy GATT that the beer market will be opened, (2) provide Canadians

with more competitive and possibly lower priced beer products, and (3) give the industry time to gear up for the inevitable competition with U.S. firms 5 to 10 years down the road.[5]

33   Clearly, Canadian brewers had the most to gain from this exemption as, on average, 11.0 percent of annual Canadian production is exported to the United States, while conversely, only 0.2 percent of U.S. production is imported into Canada.

INDUSTRY PLAYERS

Megabrewers

34   Up until the merger of Molson with Carling O'Keefe Breweries of Canada Limited (Carling), the Canadian brewing industry was dominated by three firms: Labatt with a 42 percent market share, Molson at 31.6 percent of market, and Carling with a 19.6 percent share.

35   Since the brewing industry was capital intensive and economies of scale were critical for profitability, the barriers to entry were high. This had led to a concentration of sales, and, by 1990, two players dominated the Canadian beer industry. These conventional brewers were John Labatt Breweries of Canada (Labatt) and Molson Breweries of Canada Limited (Molson) with combined estimated brewing capacities of 14,000,000 hLs and 12,600,000 hLs, respectively.

36   Great Western has identified Molson and Labatt as its primary competition in Canada. Great Western has launched brands that compete head to head with Molson Canadian and Labatt Blue products. The following is information on these megabrewers.

Molson Breweries of Canada

37   Molson Breweries was founded by John Molson in 1786, and, in 1989, was North America's oldest continuing brewer. Until 1955, Molson was primarily a regional brewer, serving the Quebec market. By the early 1960s, the company had expanded its brewing business and had plants in most Canadian provinces. By late 1980s, Molson Breweries was part of TCML, a diversified Canadian multinational corporation with more than 11,000 employees and revenues of $2.4 billion.

38   In 1988, Elders IXL, based in Australia and recent acquirees of Carling O'Keefe, approached TCML about a possible merger of their respective Canadian brewing operations. Further negotiations laid the groundwork for an eventual 50/50 partnership. The merged entity was seen by Molson as an important factor in a North American strategy that would require a strong and efficient infrastructure to battle the mammoth American brewers, primarily Anheuser-Busch, Miller Brewing Company, the Stroh Brewing Company, G. Heileman Brewing Company, and Adolph Coors Company.

39   The merged entity was called Molson Breweries, with the stronger Molson products as the core brands, therefore ensuring preservation of the Molson name.

Labatt Breweries of Canada

40   Labatt's brewing operation is part of John Labatt, Ltd., a diversified food and beverage company with business in three main sectors, brewing, agriculture, and packaged foods.

41   Labatt's dominant market share can be traced back to several events that occurred over the past decade. In 1979, after realization that profitability could be sustained only through market share improvement and not overall market growth, Labatt made the first move to the so-called brand and pack-

---

[5] *The Toronto Globe and Mail*, November 12, 1987.

aging wars that characterized the 1980s. In 1989, Labatt produced 31 different brands and operated 12 breweries in nine provinces and spent over $36 million in advertising. Labatt's leading brand, Blue, was sold in all provinces and had an estimated 18 percent national share.

42   Labatt has close marketing and licensing agreement ties with Anheuser-Busch, and, like the American firm, focused its brand development through sports and community events. Labatt also owns 45 percent of the Toronto Blue Jays.

Regional Brewers

43   During the late 1970s and throughout the 1980s, regional brewers, such as Amstel, Northern Breweries, and most recently the Great Western Brewing Company, emerged as regional brewers. Regional brewers produce over 25,000 hLs but considerably under 1 million hLs. The product is generally targeted for a local market, or region.

44   Great Western, as a regional brewer with production levels of over 55,000 hLs, is sandwiched between microbrewers and the megabrewers of Labatt and Molson, with competition coming from both sides. Most recently, the regional brewers have become aggressive in their marketing strategies in efforts to capture market share. The establishment of minimum price levels by regulation has helped this cause by eliminating any efforts of price wars. Great Western has had to carefully position itself to maintain a steady pressure on mainstream markets and to develop desired niches not in the mainstream market.

Microbrewers, Brew Pubs, and Home Brewers

45   Microbrewers are local companies producing under 25,000 hLs for their immediate markets, such as Brick, Upper Canada, Connors, and Big Rock. Exhibit 4 provides an indication of the growing number of profitable microbrewers in the Canadian market that target small market niches.

Brew Pubs

46   In addition, two new sectors emerged in the 1980s, brew pubs and home brewers. Brew pubs are licensed establishments that brew their own products for on-premise consumption. The last 10 years in Canada have seen the emergence of brew pub establishments. Like English pubs, they provide a place for community gathering and socialization. Beer is brewed and consumed on premise and the capacity for production is very limited. These establishments are an increasingly popular alternative to the bar scene.

Home Brewers

47   The home brewer brews his or her beer from a prepackaged kit for personal consumption. This industry has been growing dramatically in recent years, as evidenced by the growing number of brewing supply retailers locating in small to large centers. While little formal research has been gathered to quantify the size of this market, it is estimated that 1 percent of the adult beer drinking population has entered the home brewing industry. Those who have entered this market universally indicate they do so to save money.[6] Those who remain involved in home brewing indicate they enjoy the taste of their beer and, therefore, continue in their personal brewing efforts.

---

[6] Approximately 53 cents on every dollar in beer sales is taxes.

EXHIBIT 4
1988 Taxable Production Canadian Microbrewers

Company Name	City, Province	Production (hLs)
The Upper Canada Brewing Co., Ltd.	Toronto, Ontario	20,603
Big Rock Brewing, Ltd.	Calgary, Alberta	17,618
Horseshoe Bay Brewery & Troller Pub	Horseshoe Bay, B.C.	15,500
Okanagan Spring Brewery	Vernon, B.C.	11,443
Connors Brewing Co., Ltd., No. 1	Missisauga, Ontario	10,000
Island Pacific Brewing Co.	Victoria, B.C.	10,000
Granville Island Brewing Co.	Vancouver, B.C.	9,800
Highland Breweries, Ltd.	Sydney, N.S.	6,070
Creemore Springs Brewery	Creemore, Ontario	4,685
G.M.T. Brewery	Montreal, Quebec	4,000
Bavarian Specialties (Canada), Ltd.	Riverview, N.B.	3,000
Missawippi Brewing Co., Inc.	Lennoxville, Quebec	3,000
Shaftebury Brewing Co., Ltd.	Vancouver, B.C.	3,000
Wellington County Brewery, Ltd.	Guelph, Ontario	2,260
Canadian Heritage Brewing Co., Ltd.	Richmond, B.C.	2,045
The Ottawa Valley Brewing Co., Inc.	Nepean, Ontario	2,000
Halton County Brewery	Burlington, Ontario	1,818
Great Lakes Brewing Co.	Brampton, Ontario	500
Sculler Brewing Co., Ltd.	St. Catherines, Ontario	195
Golden Lion Brewing Co.	Lennoxville, Quebec	N.A.
G. A. Miller Brewing Co.	Thunder Bay, Ontario	N.A.
Nanton Interbrew, Ltd.	Nanton, Alberta	N.A.
Les Brasseurs du Nord	St. Jerome, Quebec	N.A.
Conners Brewing Co. (Don Valley)	North York, Ontario	N.A.
Island Brewery, Ltd.	Charlottetown, P.E.I.	N.A.
The Simcoe Brewing Co.	Newmarket, Ontario	N.A.
Wheatley Brewery	Wheatley, Ontario	N.A.
York Brewery	Brampton, Ontario	N.A.

THE GREAT WESTERN BREWING COMPANY—OPERATIONS OVERVIEW

Marketing

48   The key success factors for Great Western beer in Saskatchewan, identified by Sargeant, are its image of being a local brewer using Saskatchewan-produced grain as its main raw material and supporting local community events. This successful local image gave Great Western its initial 22 percent of the Saskatchewan beer market share.

49   The phenomenal success at the beginning gave Great Western much publicity in the local media. The coverage provided Great Western with free advertising. Sargeant readily appreciated "the media was very kind to us, generally reporting the success side of the company. At times such reports could be misleading; the public could overestimate the success of the company."

50   Sargeant believes that there are two groups of people with differing perceptions of the company. One group thinks that the company is now strong enough to stand on its own feet. People in

this group have been influenced by the media to overestimate the success of the company. The company risks losing the support of these people, because they no longer perceive it as a fledgling local brewer that needs continued support from Saskatchewan consumers. The other group consists of people who understand the real situation at Great Western. The initial break-even sales target was projected to be 5 to 6 percent of the market, with 26 employees. The phenomenal success brought the employment level at Great Western up to 45 people. The company now needs at least 8 percent of the market to break even, while its actual market share fluctuates between 9 and 11 percent.

51   Contrary to the industry norm of heavy television advertising and sponsorship, Great Western has never spent any money on television advertising. Ninety-nine percent of its advertising is done through radio and the rest through newspapers and magazines. Great Western gets the lower local rate, rather than the national rate, on radio commercials, about $2,000 for a three-week program consisting of 35 to 45 commercial spots. The commercials alternate between stations to improve a hit ratio, catching more people's attention. One quarter page in the local newspaper, the *Saskatoon Star-Phoenix*, costs $1,000. "Radio is the best medium for advertising," Sargeant argues, "because when people hear commercials on radio it does not bother them or force them to switch channels as television commercials do. It has the best retention rate on people who listen to radio regularly. People reading newspapers may simply skip over the ad, but people listening to radio just cannot do so unless they shut off the radio." Total marketing cost for a brand of beer at Great Western is about $1 per dozen beers. About half of that cost is spent on media advertising.

52   At this time, Great Western has only two brands on the market, regular and light. The company plans to push out two more brands, following the release of Great Western Gold. Another light beer is being considered with a very low (3.2 percent) alcohol content and a malt beer is in the planning stages. As Sargeant explained, "We are only producing at one third of our capacity now and any increase of production will reduce our unit cost. New brands usually attract new segments of the market and bring in extra sales, while the cost of launching a new brand is minimal apart from its start-up costs." Such set-up costs are usually low except for draft beer.

53   The pricing of beer is restricted by regulations set by the Saskatchewan Liquor Board. The same type of beer of different brands is set at basically the same price, so competition occurs mainly in cutting unit production costs, rather than on the basis of price. Regulation also forces the brewers to compete on the basis of product differentiation, supporting marketing efforts aimed at brand loyalty. Exhibit 5 gives the Saskatchewan Liquor Board regulated beer prices in 1990.

54   Great Western Gold is not just another brand to be added to the existing line of Great Western brands. It carries the hopes of the company to regain its lost market share. Gold is a malt liquor with 6.5 percent alcohol content. "Unfortunately, alcohol still sells beer," Sargeant says. "There are still a lot of people who are very sensitive to what they get for their money. Since prices for Gold and regular beers are much the same, many price-conscious beer drinkers would prefer to have Gold simply for its extra alcohol content. In the current market, there is only one brand, the O'Keefe Extra Old Stock, that has an alcohol content higher than the regular 5 percent. It has 6 percent alcohol and 2 percent of the market share. It will be significant to us if we can get half of that."

55   Great Western also wanted to use Gold to target the younger adult drinkers. These younger drinkers are more price conscious and do not care as much about supporting locals as their elders do. Great Western wants to focus on these younger drinkers because brand loyalty for beer is believed to develop around the age of 25 or 26.

56   To effectively reach these markets, the company has launched its promotions for the Gold brand to get quick results. Heavy advertising has been used on both radio and newspapers; however, television advertising is still avoided. Direct mail, end of aisle displays, posters, and enter-and-win sweepstake draws also have been used. There is even a sweepstakes draw for three pieces of real gold worth over $500 each as the prizes. Sales representatives go to bars and restaurants to promote the new brand with special promotional packages.

EXHIBIT 5
Saskatchewan Liquor Board Retail Prices, August 1990

Regular and light brands (bottles):
    6 pack $6.60 including $0.60 deposit
    12 pack $12.70 including $1.20 deposit
    24 pack $24.80 including $2.40 deposit

Price or generic brands (bottles):
    12 pack $12.45 including $1.20 deposit

Canned beer (all brands):
    6 pack $6.90 including $0.30 deposit
    12 pack $13.80 including $0.60 deposit
    24 pack $27.60 including $1.20 deposit

57   Great Western has seven sales representatives throughout the province. The market that needs the most personal selling attention and promotions is the local pubs and bars. "We just can't leave our beer to the pubs and hope it will sell by itself. Today's beer drinkers at the pubs do not have much loyalty to any brands of beer. It's up to the reps to push our beer to the bartenders and managers," Sargeant asserts. The "value-added" promotional strategies the company has used regularly include scratch-and-win cards, free tickets to sports events and concerts, and free key chains put in each case of beer.

58   The subject of social responsibility for brewers is a sensitive issue. Great Western spends a lot of time promoting responsible drinking and reinforcing in people not to "drink and drive." "It's contradictory to our interest in promoting our sales," as Sargeant admits, "but we also want people to be safe and healthy so that they can drink more of our beer. We are certainly not telling them not to drink at all. We are simply telling them not to drink and drive at the same time."

59   Demand for beer is largely seasonal and is greatly affected by the weather. Hot weather sells more beer, so the summer months of May to August are the peak periods, with over 40 percent of annual sales occurring during the period. It drops sharply in September and does not begin to pick up until February. Sargeant recognizes that he has only 32 days to sell the bulk of their beer, the 16 summer weekends (recall Exhibit 2).

60   While its priority is still the Saskatchewan market, Great Western also is constantly searching for new market developments. With the newly installed canning line facility, Sargeant wonders if it is now feasible to ship canned beers to the neighboring provinces of Manitoba and Alberta, since transportation costs for canned beer are less than for bottled beer. The Manitoba and Alberta markets combined are more than four times the Saskatchewan market. If Great Western can get 1 percent of these markets, it would be equivalent to increasing its Saskatchewan market share by 4 percent.

61   The United States market has been another natural target for Great Western to look for expansion. Great Western has made efforts to obtain the licensing rights to produce a Chinese brand beer, Qingdao (pronounced *chingdow*) beer. Qingdao is a well-known Chinese beer that has achieved significant market acceptance in the United States with its direct imports from China. The Chinese brewing company has shown great interests in the deal, and the two sides have discussed the matter in detail and exchanged plant visits at the senior-management level. However, problems still exist, because a United States company currently holds the exclusive distribution rights for the Qingdao brand in the United States. Further, Great Western also would have to provide several employment positions for its Chinese counterpart as part of the attempted agreement. Sargeant was aware that the Qingdao beer is well known for drawing mineral water directly from the Laoshan Mountain spring, a key success factor for the brand name. It was questionable how the market (especially the

ethnic Chinese market) would react once they discovered that the beer is no longer directly imported from China but brewed under license in Canada.

An Employee-Owned Company

62   "People are the key," according to Gib Henderson. "Our people are willing to work for a little less money and are always eager to help out wherever there is work to be done. It allows us to operate at a lower cost and react quickly to changes." Each of the 16 people who came together to reopen the brewery had a large stake in the operation both personally and financially. The distribution of share-holdings ranges from 2.3 to 9.9 percent, with no one person able to control more than 10 percent of shares outstanding.

63   The commitment of the group and its experience were significant assets to the project. Between the 16 people, they had combined brewing experience of over 300 years. However, this experience was mainly in production and operations, not management of an entire brewery.

64   In an attempt to keep costs low, the group was willing to take voluntary pay and benefits cuts of approximately 25 to 30 percent. The impact of the labor cost reduction on operating costs would be significant, providing the brewery with an advantage over the national brewers.

65   McCann and representatives of the United Food and Commercial Workers Union negotiated a two-year contract under which all full-time employees would receive $15.50 per hour. This represented approximately 80 percent of the wage paid by Carling O'Keefe and other major competitors. A part-time employee and workers on a 130-day probation would receive $7.75 per hour. Employee benefits were also reduced from the Carling O'Keefe level of 25 percent of base pay to 15 percent of base pay. The specific benefits to be allocated were to be agreed upon by the employees.

66   Initial staffing requirements of 26 people were based on market share estimates of 5 to 10 percent and production requirements of 30,000 to 50,000 hLs in the first year of operation. However, the early success of the company allowed Great Western to expand to its current total staff level of 45 people, including the 16 shareholders.

67   Having 15 shareholders, who are also unionized members of the bargaining unit, has a tremendous impact on the operations of the business. John O'Connor is a shareholder, head of the Brewery Work-ers Local Union, and a shipping clerk or "whatever position needs to be filled on any particular day." O'Connor claims that he does not have a conflict of interest in the dual role she plays. "Negotiations," he states, "were relaxed and informal. McCann and I sat down for two days, discussed the situation, and came to an agreement. It's as simple as that. We treat our employees fairly. They have a vested interest in the success of this company. In return, we get their loyalty. Since we began operations, there has not been one sick day taken. I think that says a lot."

68   Great Western's organizational structure is innovative and nontraditional in the sense that the orga-nization is hierarchical in design but functions upon bottom-up approvals (see Exhibit 6). Employees, owners, and management gather weekly to discuss issues related to weekly and monthly market positions, in addition to planning upcoming promotional activities. Through common interests, shared focus, and cooperation, the employees, owners, and management approach problems in a coordinated manner in which consensus is reached prior to an organizational commitment. Problems are brought into the open before they become serious, and resolutions are reached as a result of negotiations. This process is not always easy or expedient, but the decisions reached are understood by all and implemented.

69   Twenty-nine of the 45 employees are, however, nonshareholders and their interests and morale are affected by different factors. Great Western prides itself in providing a dynamic work environment. The family atmosphere and approach extends to the nonshareholders. Everyone is on a first name basis and it is not uncommon for part-time positions to be filled by family members of the investors. An open door policy is maintained and management regularly solicits the advice of all employees for promotion and product launch recommendations.

EXHIBIT 6
Great Western Organizational Dynamics

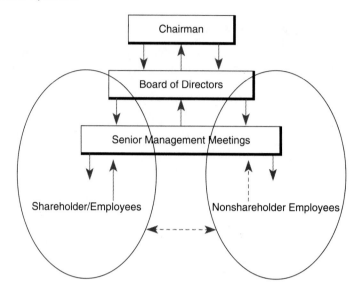

Top Down Decision Making and Bottom Up Approvals

Facilities

70   The Great Western building opened in 1928 under the name Hub City Brewing Company. A large portion of the original equipment is still in use at the brewery; however, the equipment has been upgraded to keep pace with new technology, and new buildings have been added as required.

71   The plant occupies a full city block (approximately 11,000 square metres, or 2.6 acres) in downtown Saskatoon. The brewery's buildings occupy about 65 percent of the site, with the remainder being used for parking, building access roads, and a private garden area. The older buildings, which house the office, brewing equipment, aging cellars, and bottling plant, are constructed from brick. The newer buildings, which include the warehouse and cold storage cellar, are insulated steel frame construction with steel cladding. All of the buildings are in good condition and have been projected to serve the needs of the new operation for at least 20 years.

Production

72   As McCann says, "Production operations at Great Western is one of the company's strong points. Our people have the experience required to make a quality beer." Although the brewery is old, it is well equipped with the tools required to produce high-quality beer.

73   The actual brewing equipment is constructed mainly from stainless steel, and includes: a malt and corn storage area, malt mill, brewing syrup tank, cereal cooker, mash mixer, lauder tun, brew kettle, wort cooler, 27 fermentation tanks, beer filters, 18 primary storage tanks, 14 secondary storage tanks, and 6 packaging tanks.

74   As is typical of breweries, Great Western brews beer in batches. One brew will produce 180 hLs, or 4,300 dozen beer, and takes about 28 days from start to finish, including aging time. Several brews can be prepared in parallel, since most of the 28 days is spent in fermentation and aging tanks. Up to 34 brews can be produced in a five-day period, which sets the present capacity of the brewery at about

260,000 hLs per year. While under the management of the previous owners, equipment for diluting beer with water before final packaging was installed and used to increase capacity by another 20 percent. It is unlikely that this technique will be used by Great Western, because doing so would violate the culture of a company which takes great pride in the quality of the finished product.

75   The smallest batch that can be produced using the present brewing equipment is 140 hLs (3,300 dozen). This batch size is suitable for small-scale test marketing of new brands.

76   The brewery has both a bottling line and a canning line. The bottling line is capable of filling 350 bottles per minute. The maximum bottling capacity is roughly 350,000 hLs per year, based on three shifts and allowing for downtime. Some of the equipment is quite old and downtime is increasing. To complicate matters, replacement parts are no longer stocked and must be manufactured in-house by resident millwrights.

77   The canning line, which was installed in the summer of 1990, is capable of operating at a maximum of 400 cans per minute, which is a limitation imposed by the capacity of the pasteurizer. The equipment was purchased used, but it was completely reconditioned by brewery mechanics and is expected to last for several years.

78   Great Western is not presently equipped to handle draught beer. In early 1988, the Saskatchewan brewing industry switched from "Peerless" kegs to new "Sankey" kegs. Peerless and Sankey are both brand names for beer kegging systems. Beer that is sold unpasteurized in bulk containers, usually 12 gallons, is called *draft beer* and is sold "on tap" in bars and restaurants to be dispensed from kegs. The Peerless keg was the industry standard for many years. Recently, the improved design of the Sankey keg has almost completely replaced the Peerless keg, because there is less wasted product left in the keg when it is emptied and because it is better suited to automatic washing and filling. Gib Henderson, VP of operations, estimates that it would cost $500,000 to install the equipment required to process Sankey kegs, including the cost of the kegs themselves.

79   Great Western normally maintains five working days of stock, with warehousing done on-site. The warehouse has sufficient storage for finished product ready to ship, as well as for empty bottles, cartons, and pallets. The working capacity of the warehouse is 250,000 dozen bottles.

80   Raw materials are stored in various locations on the site. Malt barley is stored in tanks and silos near the brew-house. Other brewing materials, such as hops, do not require much space and are stored near their point of consumption in quantities sufficient for six months to one year of production. The brewery has a secure supply of high-quality raw materials. Most raw materials are bought from local Saskatchewan suppliers. Hops do not grow in Saskatchewan and must be imported from British Columbia, Washington, or England. Historically, there has been no problem with hop supplies. The majority of the raw material cost is driven by commodity products. As such, Great Western does not pay a penalty relative to their competitors for low-volume purchases.

81   An abundant supply of water is critical for any brewery. Not only is it used in the product itself, but it is also required to carry out the rigorous cleaning program required to ensure sterility during brewing. Great Western uses the city of Saskatoon water supply. Water consumed in making the beer is triple filtered to remove all traces of chlorine and bacteria and is treated to adjust the chemical balance to make it suitable for brewing.

Quality Control

82   Quality control in the brewing industry is critical. In the case of a small regional brewery, it takes on even more importance, because a single batch of "off" beer could cost the company a significant percentage of market share. As such, Great Western places considerable emphasis on quality control. First in the quality control program is the pride that the employees have in their product. The company has a very strong culture to produce nothing but the best it can. Careful attention is paid to the choice of raw materials, and a careful "hand-crafted" brewing process is used. No compromises are made in the interest of saving cost at the expense of quality.

83   This attention to quality and pride in the product is not as highly developed in all breweries. Great Western uses traditional European brewing methods, which place the emphasis of the operation on the quality and taste of the finished product, rather than on the most efficient and cost-effective method. This results in a better beer; but it is being sold to an unappreciative market, because Saskatchewan consumers in general do not understand or appreciate the difference in the taste, quality, or tradition associated with European methods of brewing beer. "Beer is beer" is the attitude of most consumers, and that explains the industry norm of heavy advertising to influence consumer preference by establishing preferable images.

84   As a final line of defense, a well-equipped quality control lab staffed by an experienced chemist ensures that the finished product meets both Great Western and regulatory specifications throughout the process.

Production Scheduling

85   Since Great Western operates at approximately one third of capacity, creative scheduling is used to make the most of time and people. Changeover from bottles to cans or between bottle sizes is time consuming and is normally only done during scheduled downtime between production runs. In any single seven-hour shift, it is not practical to package more than four brands, which means that the minimum economic quantity for packaging is about 3,000 dozen.

86   Bottling runs are scheduled to allow the line to run for full shifts to minimize set-up times. The bottling line will run two to five days a week, as needed to meet demand. The rest of the time is used to do equipment maintenance, housekeeping duties, or operation upgrades. As an example, the canning line was installed during downtime with the help of the packaging line workers. This allowed the line to be quickly installed, kept the crew busy, and provided first-hand training that allowed those individuals to operate and troubleshoot the line once it was operational.

Scales of Operation and Overhead

87   One of the problems that Gib Henderson knows Great Western must address is the present underutilization of capacity. Great Western's total annual capacity is 262,000 hLs, a far cry from the 1990 production of 55,000 hLs. "The brewery is capable of producing enough beer to supply 50 percent of the demand in the Saskatchewan market. This underutilization leads to inefficient operations with frequent set-up changes and low labor utilization. When you are operating at just above break-even, incremental sales are critical. It allows you to reduce the impact of overhead costs," says Henderson. "We also need to find other products to allow us to use some of our capacity. Our overhead costs are disproportionately high." Several options have been explored by Great Western, including producing bottled water, packaging juices or carbonated drinks, leasing out warehouse space, and others, but as yet none of these options have been aggressively pursued. The focus of the effort has been on survival in the beer market.

88   One other problem has been the stability of demand for the product. It has been very difficult to manage the operation while demand for the product has experienced wide fluctuations. The estimated cost structure for production at Great Western is detailed in Exhibit 7.

Production Support for Differentiated and Niche Products

89   The flexibility of the labor force, the low-cost marketing program, and the ability of the equipment to handle quite small batch sizes allow Great Western's operations to quickly and easily accommodate small-run niche products. This production flexibility allows the company to experiment with new brands and to pursue opportunities with a small window, such as "seasonal" brews released to coincide

EXHIBIT 7
Great Western Brewing Company Limited, Estimated Cost of Production ($) per hL (24.4 dozen = 1 hL)

Brewing costs:	
Wages/salaries	3.52
Benefits	0.53
Vacation pay	0.21
Malt	5.00
Hops	0.45
Adjunct	1.50
Supplies	1.60
Total brewed costs	12.80
Bottling costs:	
Wages/salaries	8.11
Benefits	1.22
Vacation pay	0.49
Bottles	16.88
Cost of bottle loss	0.60
Crowns	1.20
Labels	1.20
Cartons	8.00
Supplies	1.00
Bottle amortization	1.13
Total packaging cost	39.83
Total cost of production	52.63 = $2.19/dozen
Excise tax (per hL)	27.98 = $1.14/dozen

with special occasions. However, there are only six packaging tanks at the brewery. This means Great Western cannot package more than six different brands on the same shift. It is not uncommon for some brewers to package several brands from one type of brew. Beer is brewed overstrength. The high-alcohol beer is packaged first, then the brew is progressively "cut" with water to produce regular and low-alcohol brands. Since Great Western does not "cut" its beer, it is restricted to 6 brands, rather than 12, 18, or more brands, by the limited availability of packaging tank space.

Distribution

90   All beer brewed in the province is distributed by the Saskatchewan Brewers Association (SBA), a company jointly owned by Labatt and Molson. SBA has warehouses in seven centers across the province. The warehouses receive bulk loads from the breweries. Local distribution is done daily from the warehouses to licenses on an order basis. The warehouses also manage the return of empties to the breweries. Beer is distributed to over 1,600 licensed outlets in Saskatchewan, which include liquor board stores, hotels, bars and night clubs, restaurants, and special-occasion events.

91   Orders are placed from the warehouse to breweries by computer. Stock levels usually are kept at about two weeks' supply, but fluctuate with unexpected demand. Both stock level and sales by brand are reported to the brewery weekly. The breweries also are provided with weekly gross sales quantities, by brewery, for the province. This provides quick and accurate market feedback to the breweries.

92   SBA operates on a user-pay, not-for-profit basis. Distribution costs are approximately $1 per dozen. Great Western, however, has to pay a markup, since it is provided with full goods distributions and sorting returns on a fee-for-services basis. The rates charged, therefore, are higher than rates charged to Molson and Labatt.

Finance

93   The Great Western Brewing Company Limited has earned remarkable profits in the first 10 months of its operation. Net income before taxes was projected to be $250,000 for the first 10 months ending October 31, 1990. This only represented nine months of actual sales revenue. The products were priced competitively with Labatt and Molson, even though Great Western does not share similar economies of scale. From January to March, the company had been getting started and was heavily involved in product development and quality testing.

94   Cash flow in the brewing industry is unique. Retail outlets pay the liquor board two days before they receive their products. This cash availability means that cash flow can be easily monitored and predicted.

95   The finance department at Great Western consists of the manager of finance, an accounting graduate from the University of Saskatchewan, and an accounting clerk. A computerized financial control system is in use and performance reports are monitored on a daily basis. A standard costing system is used to manage variances.

96   Great Western is highly leveraged. Over 75 percent of assets are financed by debt. The major creditor is SEDCO (Saskatchewan Economic Development Corporation), owned by the government of Saskatchewan. Two types of loans were provided by SEDCO. A $300,000 participating loan, which has no scheduled principal, and interest payments and repayments are based on the profitability of Great Western. Twenty-five percent of net cash flow must be repaid every year to retire the participating loans. Second, a mortgage loan has a five-year maturity and a fixed 12.5 percent interest rate with scheduled principal and interest payments.

97   The remaining 25 percent of Great Western's assets are financed through equity. The 16 shareholders chose a structure that could take advantage of provincial investment tax credits for personal income tax purposes.

THE CROSSROADS

98   McCann was now at a crossroads. He did not have all the answers regarding the future. One thing was certain, however, that some tough decisions were required if Great Western was to remain competitive. McCann knew that the key success factors for a regional brewer were tight control of production costs, broad public product acceptance, flexible operations to respond to changing consumer needs, brand association, and the maintenance of close associations with local market.

99   As McCann pondered, he wondered if the company should just focus its limited resources on its home market in Saskatchewan in the hope of regaining some of the initial 22 percent market share that it enjoyed just a few months ago. What strategic advantages would it have and how can the product be differentiated once it goes beyond the Saskatchewan border? Would it not be just another brand of the dozens that are already on the market? How can Great Western sustain such expansions with its current working capital situation? Can Great Western survive on its Saskatchewan market alone, or does it have to become a big player in the market just to survive? Was the American threat as big as it looked, and what about the other regional and larger microbrewers in Canada? Who will be its competition, anyway? After all, it has proved to them that the smaller brewers can compete against the giants with the help of regulation.

100   McCann walked into the hospitality room of Great Western where the shareholders had assembled for their Friday morning meeting. The conversation settled down as Peter cleared his throat. "The monthly figures are in, and Gold seems to be stealing market share, about 1 percent of the total market," he announced. Applause broke out as the room basked in the achievement of the launch. McCann continued. "We think that 2 percent market share is achievable. The bad news is our total market share continues to erode for our other brands. I am open for suggestions on where we go from here."

APPENDIX 1

Estimated Total Sales of Canadian Produced and Packaged Beer in Canada, 1990, hLs

Month	Draught (A)	Bottles (B)	Cans (C)	Subtotal (A + B)	Total (A + B + C)
January	139,361	870,424	191,287	1,061,711	1,201,072
February	140,965	921,656	192,587	1,114,243	1,255,208
March	165,586	1,092,413	238,110	1,330,523	1,496,109
April	160,469	1,170,657	264,668	1,435,325	1,595,794
May	174,456	1,346,857	334,568	1,681,425	1,855,881
June	175,492	1,468,672	421,148	1,889,820	2,065,312
July	175,527	1,436,462	475,920	1,912,382	2,087,909
August.	191,791	1,455,967	480,771	1,936,738	2,128,529
September	144,365	1,055,790	303,282	1,359,072	1,503,437
October.	168,091	1,126,054	278,759	1,404,813	1,572,904
November	162,052	1,115,860	247,938	1,636,798	1,525,850
December	150,316	1,369,507	284,321	1,653,828	1,804,144
Total	1,948,471	14,430,319	3,713,359	18,143,678	20,092,149

Source: Brewers Association of Canada, annual report, 1990.

APPENDIX 2

Brands Available in Saskatchewan, August 1991

Labatt	Carling	Molson
Blue	Fosters Lager	Canadian
50 Ale	Colt 45*	Coors
Budweiser	Miller High Life	Coors Lite
Bud Lite	Miller Lite	Bohemian*
Schooner	Old Vienna	Molson Golden
Labatt's Lite	Old Vienna Lite	Molson Light
Guiness	Trilight	Pilsner
Labatt Dry	Extra Old Stock	
Beer*	Calgary Lager	

* "Low-price" brand.

APPENDIX 3

World's Major Beer Producers' Production (000s hLs)

Country	1989	1988	1987
United States	233,619	232,265	229,297
Fed. Rep. Germany	93,017	92,493	92,602
U.S.S.R.	66,000	55,800	50,700
Japan	60,500	57,894	54,922
United Kingdom	60,015	60,155	59,897
China	60,000	55,000	50,000
Brazil	55,000	47,800	47,500
Mexico	39,131	34,534	29,157
Spain	27,337	26,579	25,842
Dem. Rep. Germany	24,800	24,400	25,000
Czechoslovakia	22,770	22,670	22,228
Canada	22,710	23,149	23,114
France	20,927	20,113	19,894
South Africa	18,680	18,340	18,000
Australia	18,700	19,500	18,765

Source: The Brewers Association of Canada, annual report, 1990.

APPENDIX 4

Total 1988 United States Import Beer Market (volume* share)

	Volume Share (%)	Changes
Corona	16.1%	+0.3
Heineken	13.9	−1.0
Molson	11.6	−0.8
Labatt's	7.1	+2.7
Becks	4.8	−0.3
Moosehead	4.4	−0.5
St. Pauli Girl	3.3	−0.5
Foster's Lager	3.2	+0.3
Molson Light	2.5	0.0
Dos Equis	2.4	−0.5
All Others	30.5	+0.1

*Volume expressed in 288-oz. equivalent units.
Source: InfoScan.

APPENDIX 5

Total 1988 United States Beer Market (dollar share)

	Volume* Share (%)	Dollar Share (%)
Low calorie/light	34.2%	34.2%
Premium	31.5	33.4
Popular price	24.3	18.2
Imports	4.8	8.0
Super premium	3.2	4.1
Malt liquor	1.1	1.1
Low/nonalcoholic	0.9	0.9

*Volume expressed in 288-oz. equivalent units.

Source: InfoScan.

APPENDIX 6

Comparative Income Statements, 1990 ($000s)

	Labatt	Molson	Great Western
Gross sales	$5,274,000	$2,549,957	$8,306
Operating costs and expenses:			
Cost of sales, selling, and administration	4,283,000	1,871,980	7,605
Depreciation and amortization	134,000	56,847	295
Net interest expense.	33,000	25,784	283
Operating income before income taxes	824,000	595,346	123
Income taxes	72,000	59,809	43
Net income	752,000	535,537	80

Notes:

1. Labatt's fiscal year end is April 30; Molson's is March 31; and Great Western's is December 31.

2. Only 32.15% of Labatt's gross revenue, but 75.32% of operating income before income taxes, were from brewing activities.

3. 53.83% of Molson's gross revenue and 77.31% of operating income before income taxes were from brewing activities.

4. Information regarding Labatt and Molson is from the 1990 annual reports of the respective companies.

APPENDIX 7

Comparative Balance Sheets, 1990 ($000s)

	Labatt	Molson	Great Western
Assets			
Current assets:			
Cash and accounts receivable	$ 718,000	$ 491,996	$ 910
Inventories	397,000	255,025	1,064
Other current assets.	69,000	65,131	61
Total current assets	1,184,000	812,152	2,035
Noncurrent assets:			
Property, plant, and equipment.	1,181,000	538,749	4,787
Other noncurrent assets	581,000	491,016	0
Total noncurrent assets	1,762,000	1,134,202	4,787
Total assets	$2,946,000	$1,841,917	$6,822
Liabilities			
Current liabilities:			
Accounts payable and accrued liabilities.	$ 557,000	$ 305,267	$1,194
Current portion of long-term debt	26,000	37,996	394
Other current liabilities	45,000	49,202	0
Total current liabilities.	628,000	392,465	1,588
Long-term liabilities:			
Long-term debt	544,000	252,960	3,471
Other long-term liabilities.	130,000	270,749	269
Total long-term liabilities	674,000	523,709	3,740
Total liabilities	$1,302,000	$ 916,174	$5,328
Shareholders' Equity			
Convertible debentures	$ 277,000	0	0
Share capital	595,000	$ 145,907	$1,263
Retained earnings	801,000	801,645	231
Cumulative translation adjustment	(29,000)	(21,809)	0
Total shareholders' equity	1,644,000	925,743	1,494
Total liabilities and S/E.	$2,946,000	$1,841,917	$6,822

APPENDIX 8

Comparative Statistics (1990)

	Molson	Labatt	Great Western
Net sales ($'000)	$2,549,957	$5,274,000	$ 8,306
Net income ($'000)	117,911	169,000	231
Number of employees	13,900	16,000	45
Net sales per employee	183,450	339,000	184,578
Profit per employee	12,036	14,438	6,089
Total assets per employee	132,512	184,125	151,622

Notes:

1. Profit per employee was calculated using income before taxes.

2. Great Western's net sales and net income are estimates.

Source: From the 1990 annual reports of the respective companies.

APPENDIX 9

Canadian Market Shares, 1972–1988

Canadian Market Shares

	72	73	74	75	76	77	78	79	80	81	82	83	84	85	86	87	88
Labatt	33.9	36.9	35.9	36.6	37.6	38.4	38.6	36.6	36.5	34.9	36.7	36.3	34.6	38.0	39.1	40.3	41.9
MBC	29.2	30.5	31.6	33.5	33.6	33.9	34.1	36.2	35.9	35.1	35.8	34.7	31.5	30.6	29.8	31.5	31.6
Carling	30.6	28.3	26.1	25.3	24.9	24.1	23.2	22.7	23.2	22.8	23.1	24.3	28.2	25.0	22.8	22.0	19.6
Other	5.3	4.0	6.1	4.2	3.3	2.9	3.2	3.5	3.5	3.8	2.9	3.6	4.2	4.8	4.5	4.7	4.7
Imports	0.3	0.3	0.3	0.4	0.6	0.7	0.9	1.0	0.9	3.4	1.5	1.1	1.5	1.6	3.8	1.5	2.2
Total	100.0	100.0	100.0	100.0	100.0	100.0	100.0	100.0	100.0	100.0	100.0	100.0	100.0	100.0	100.0	100.0	100.0

Sources: TMCL, Brewers Association of Canada, and Statistics Canada.

APPENDIX 10

Provincial Market Share Data at November 30, 1989

	Percentage Share			Percentage of
	Molson	Carling	Labatt	Canada Sales
Newfoundland	19%	28%	53%	2.3%
Nova Scotia	—	—	82	3.0
Prince Edward Island	2	—	53	0.4
New Brunswick	—	—	43	2.3
Quebec	33	31	36	26.1
Ontario	40	15	41	39.6
Manitoba	14	29	57	3.9
Saskatchewan	40	23	37	2.9
Alberta	42	20	29	8.2
British Columbia	26	22	44	10.9
NWT/Yukon	—	—	—	0.3
Total				100.0%

Sources: Molson, Labatt Breweries.

APPENDIX 11

Great Western Brewing Company Limited, Pro Forma Income Statements ($'000s)

	1991	1992	1993	1994
Sales	$8,306	$10,902	$11,447	$12,019
Cost of goods sold	4,074	5,339	5,543	5,753
Distribution and freight	934	1,375	1,589	1,825
Total cost of goods sold	5,008	6,714	7,132	7,577
Gross profit	3,298	4,188	4,314	4,442
Overhead expenses:				
Engineering	415	561	572	584
Brewing	80	108	116	122
Marketing	651	880	943	990
Quality control	28	38	41	43
Administration	430	564	576	587
Salaries and Benefits	1,288	1,327	1,353	1,380
Interest	283	243	209	180
Out of province marketing	0	250	268	281
Total overhead expenses	3,175	3,971	4,077	4,166
Net operating income	123	216	237	275
Other income	151	70	72	75
Net income before taxes	274	286	309	350
Income taxes	79	84	93	109
Net income	$ 195	$ 203	$ 217	$ 242

Assumptions:
1. 5 percent growth in sales every year.
2. 1991 sales figure has been adjusted by 27.5 percent over 1990 figures to reflect 12 months' operations and inflation.
3. 3 percent inflation in 1991, and 2 percent thereafter.
4. 1.5 percent decrease in COGS each year because of increasing utilization of plant.
5. 1 percent increase in distribution and freight each year because of increasing out of province distribution.
6. Interest payment decreases because of amortization of loan.
7. 25 percent tax rate for the first $200,000 profit, and 39 percent on the additional profits.

CASE 11

PHILIP MORRIS COMPANIES

---

1 Philip Morris (PM) is best known as a manufacturer and marketer of cigarettes. In fact, PM is the largest cigarette company in the United States, with a 42 percent share of the $70 billion industry.[1] However, over the past 30 years the company has been pursuing such a systematic diversification strategy that, in addition to cigarettes, the company now ranks as the second largest beer brewer in the United States and the second largest food processing company in the world.[2] The company's brands include Clark Chewing Gum, Louis Kemp Seafood, Miller, Miller Lite, Lowenbrau, Jell-O, Oscar Mayer, Sealtest, Maxwell House, Oroweat Baked Goods, Light Touch Desserts, and Marlboro, Virginia Slims, Bucks, Benson & Hedges, Merit, and Parliament (see Table 1).

2 Philip Morris Companies was incorporated in Virginia on March 1, 1985, as the holding company for the diverse businesses of Philip Morris, Inc.[3] Today, the company is the largest private employer in Richmond.[4,5] The company's ambition has been and remains to be the most successful consumer packaged goods company in the world.[6]

3 This ambition is reflected in the company's mission statement presented in its 1991 annual report to shareholders: "We are a global consumer products company, manufacturing and marketing tobacco, food, and beer brands around the world. Our broad-based operations generate strong and growing returns for investors by answering consumer needs with low-priced, high-volume, quality products. We are committed to the highest standards of ethics and fairness in all of our activities and operations."

4 Current CEO Michael Miles (the first nonsmoking CEO at Philip Morris in 145 years) describes the company's strategy for meeting its goal as developing new products to meet emerging consumer trends, expanding geographically, and manufacturing and marketing globally.[7] The strategy appears to be working, as PM remains the largest and most profitable consumer products company in the world. In 1990, Philip Morris had risen to seventh on *Fortune*'s list of largest U.S. manufacturers, with sales approaching $50 billion.[8]

This case was prepared by Keith Robbins of the School of Business Administration at George Mason University. Development of this case was made possible by a grant from the Funds for Excellence Program of the State Council of Higher Education in Virginia.

[1] Standard & Poor's, *Industry Survey,* 1992.

[2] P. Sellers, "Can He Keep Philip Morris Growing?" *Fortune* 125, no. 7 (1992), pp. 86–92.

[3] Moody's *Industrial Manual,* 1991.

[4] "The Forbes 500 Ranking," *Forbes* 149, no. 9 (April 29, 1992), pp. 190–396.

[5] "The Fortune 500 Largest Industrial Corporations," *Fortune* 125, no. 8, 1991.

[6] PM, annual report, 1991.

[7] Ibid.

[8] "The Fortune 500."

TABLE 1
PM Brands

Cigarettes: *Philip Morris U.S.A., Philip Morris International*
Marlboro Brands
Virginia Slims
Benson & Hedges
Merit
Parliament

Beer: *The Miller Brewing Company*
Miller Lite
Miller High Life
Milwaukee's Best
Lowenbrau
Sharp's

Food: *Kraft General Foods, Kraft International, General Foods International*
Kraft Cheeses
Maxwell House Coffees
Louis Rich Turkey
Oscar Mayer Luncheon Meats, Hot Dogs, and Bacon
Louis Kemp Seafood Products
Post Cereals
Jell-O Brand Gelatin
Kool-Aid
Sealtest Dairy Products
Breyers Dairy Products
Light 'n Lively Dairy Products

Financial: *Philip Morris Capital Corporation*
Major equipment leasing programs for customers and suppliers

A HISTORY OF DIVERSIFICATION VIA ACQUISITION

5   The company has a distinct heritage among U.S. tobacco companies; it is the only major company that was not formed when the Supreme Court broke up the James Duke American Tobacco Trust in 1912.[9] Since its inception in England, Philip Morris has emphasized growth through acquisitions (see Exhibit 1). The success of Philip Morris in growing the purchased companies into industry leaders is legendary.

6   In 1957, Philip Morris was sixth and last in the U.S. cigarette market. Under the leadership of Joseph F. Cullman III and by emphasizing the Marlboro brand, the company climbed to first place by the end of 1983. In 1970, it bought Miller Brewing, which at the time ranked seventh among U.S. brewers. By 1977, the company had leapfrogged up to second place behind Anheuser-Busch.[10]

7   Philip Morris has been able to fund its numerous acquisitions through its high-margin tobacco products, which continue to contribute a disproportionate share of corporate earnings. According to U.S. Labor Department statistics, retail tobacco prices have increased on average 10 percent over the past 11 years. This rate of increase exceeds that of any other product, including hospital rooms and

---

[9] R. Levering, M. Moskowitz, and M. Katz, *The 100 Best Companies to Work for in America* (Reading, Mass.: Addison-Wesley, 1984).

[10] Ibid.

EXHIBIT 1
PM's History of Acquisitions

June 1944:	Purchased cigarette-producing assets from Axton-Fisher Tobacco Company, Louisville, Kentucky, for $8.9 million cash.
Feb. 1945:	Acquired 99% interest in Benson & Hedges through common stock exchange on a share-for-share basis.
Dec. 1959:	Acquired an interest in C.A. Tabacalera Nacional Venezuela.
Dec. 1963:	Acquired a substantial interest in Fabriques de Tabac Reunies, S.A., Swiss cigarette manufacturer and licensee.
April 1967:	Acquired an interest in Kwara Tobacco Company, Ilorin, Nigeria.
June 1969:	Purchased 53% interest in Miller Brewing Company for $130 million.
Jan. 1970:	Acquired control of Mission Viejo, Cal., new city and land developer for $20 million.
Feb. 1977:	Acquired Wisconsin Tissue Mills, Menasha, Wis., for 314 thousand shares of common stock.
Feb. 1977:	Purchased 97% of common stock of The Seven-Up Company, a soft-drink extract manufacturer, for $520 million.
June 1978:	Purchased the international cigarette business of Liggett Group, Inc., (consisting of rights to sell L&M, Lark, Chesterfield, Eve, and Decade outside of United States) for $45 million.
Nov. 1985:	Purchased General Foods Corporation for $5.6 billion.
Dec. 1988:	Acquired, through merger with a subsidiary, Kraft, Inc., for approximately $12.9 billion.
Aug. 1990:	Acquired Swiss-based coffee and confectionery company Jacobs Suchard AG for $4.1 billion.

Source: Moody's *Industrial Manual*, 1991.

prescription drugs, over this period.[11,12] Cigarette manufacturers have found demand for tobacco to be price inelastic—smokers do not seem to decrease consumption despite price increases.

8   The acquisition spree has been motivated by the company's desire to lessen its dependence on tobacco. Many senior executives openly express concern about the company's heavy dependence on tobacco.[13] Thus, the central issue facing management at Philip Morris is the careful selection of the correct portfolio of consumer packaged goods that will allow the company to protect and build upon global operations. This mixture of businesses must smooth the transition away from tobacco dependence to avoid adverse consequences in an increasingly hostile environment.

INDUSTRY SEGMENTS

9   Philip Morris's significant industry segments consist of tobacco products, food products, beer, and financial services, including real estate. Operating revenues and operating profits for each of the segments over the past three years are detailed in Table 2.

---

[11] J. Dagnoli, "Philip Morris Keeps Smoking," *Advertising Age* 61, no. 48 (1990), p. 20.

[12] E. Giltenan, "Profits Keep Rollin' in . . . ," *Forbes* 146, no. 1 (1992), pp. 152–53.

[13] Sellers, "Can He Keep."

10   The company's dependence on tobacco is evidenced by the fact that tobacco revenues account for 41 percent of the company's revenue and 68 percent of its income, though this dependence has lessened somewhat recently. Tobacco's profits represented 72 percent of the company's operating income in 1989. Food products accounted for approximately 27 percent of the company's operating profit in 1990, compared with 23 percent in 1989. In 1990, beer accounted for 7 percent of company revenues and 4 percent of income from operations.[14]

Tobacco Products

11   Philip Morris U.S.A. is responsible for the manufacture, marketing, and sale of tobacco products in the United States (including military sales), and Philip Morris International is responsible for the manufacture, marketing, and sale of such products outside the United States and for tobacco product exports from the United States.

Domestic Tobacco

12   Philip Morris sold 220.5 billion units of cigarettes in 1990, an increase of 1 billion units over 1989. Industry sales decreased 0.3 percent in 1990, compared to 1989. Over the past three years, Philip Morris has increased its sales and market share in the United States even though industry revenues have declined:

Year	Industry (billions of units)	Philip Morris	Market Share (%)
1990	522.1	220.5	42.2%
1989	523.9	219.5	41.9
1988	558.1	219.3	39.3

Source: Wheat, First Securities, Inc.

13   The major industry rivals in domestic tobacco are American Brands; RJR Nabisco, Inc.; B.A.T. Industries (parent of Brown and Williamson); Loews Corporation (parent of Lorillard); and the Liggett Group. The tobacco companies typically are operated as a subsidiary of diverse parent corporations. American Brands, in addition to its Pall Mall and Carlton cigarettes, markets Titleist golf balls, Jim Beam whiskey, and Master Locks. RJR Nabisco, in addition to its Winston, Salem, and Camel cigarettes, markets Oreos cookies, Planter's Peanuts, Del Monte Fruits, and Grey Poupon mustard. Loews Corporation, in addition to its Newport, Kent, and True cigarettes, owns CNA Financial Services, Inc.; Loew's theaters and hotels; and the Bulova Watch Company.

14   Philip Morris is the overwhelming leader in domestic market share, achieving 1.5 times the sales of its closest rival, RJR Nabisco (see Table 3).

15   The Maxwell Consumer Report issued by Wheat, First Securities, Inc., has ranked Philip Morris U.S.A. as the leading cigarette company in the United States market since 1983. The company's best-selling brands are Marlboro, Benson & Hedges, Merit, Virginia Slims, and Cambridge. Philip Morris produces 4 of the top 10 selling brands in the United States, including best-selling Marlboro, which garnered 26 percent of the market in 1990 (see Table 4).

---

[14] Moody's *Industrial Manual,* 1990, 1991, and 1992.

TABLE 2
Company Income and Revenue Contribution by Industry Segment
(in millions of dollars)

	1990	1989	1988
Operating revenues:			
Tobacco	$21,090 (41%)	$17,849 (40%)	$16,576 (53%)
Food	26,085 (51)	22,373 (51)	10,898 (35)
Beer	3,534 (7)	3,342 (7)	3,177 (10)
Financial services	460 (1)	516 (2)	622 (2)
Total operating revenues	51,169	44,080	31,273
Operating profit:			
Tobacco	5,596 (67%)	5,063 (72%)	3,846 (84%)
Food	2,205 (27)	1,580 (23)	392 (9)
Beer	285 (4)	226 (3)	190 (4)
Financial services	196 (2)	172 (2)	162 (3)
Total operating revenues	8,282	7,041	4,590

TABLE 3
Domestic Cigarette Producers' Market Shares (percentage of industry units sold)

Company	1990	1989	1988	1987
Philip Morris	42.0%	42.2%	39.3%	37.8%
Reynolds	28.9	28.7	31.8	32.5
Brown & Williamson.	10.8	11.4	10.9	11.0
Lorillard	7.8	7.1	8.2	8.2
American	6.8	7.0	7.0	6.9
Liggett.	3.7	3.4	2.8	3.6

Source: Standard & Poor's *Industry Surveys,* 1991.

Cigarette Industry Segments

16   **Premium and Discount Brands**   Philip Morris premium brands consist of top 10 performers Marlboro, Benson & Hedges, Merit, and Virginia Slims. In the summer of 1991, PM spent a record $60 million to advertise Marlboro Medium, the first spinoff from the Marlboro brand in 20 years.[15] According to Marlboro VP Nancy Brennan Lund, the brand's 26 percent domestic market share should increase, though its volume probably will not.

---

[15] Sellers, "Can He Keep."

TABLE 4
Top 10 Domestic Cigarette Brands, 1990

Rank	Brand	Company	Units (billions)	Mkt. Share
1 . .	Marlboro	Philip Morris	135.6	26%
2 . .	Winston	Reynolds	46.4	9
3 . .	Salem	Reynolds	32.0	6
4 . .	Kool	Brown & Williamson	32.0	6
5 . .	Newport	Lorillard	25.1	5
6 . .	Camel	Reynolds	21.2	4
7 . .	Benson & Hedges	Philip Morris	20.5	4
8 . .	Merit	Philip Morris	20.3	4
9 . .	Doral	Reynolds	19.2	4
10 . .	Virginia Slims	Philip Morris	16.8	3

Sources: Moody's, Standard & Poor's.

17   A growing industry segment consists of the discount brands. After initially rejecting the idea of selling less-profitable brands, Philip Morris decided to enter the discount segment in 1985. This was prompted by the realization that many of its customers were switching to cheap cigarettes.[16,17] By 1991, Philip Morris became the market leader in the low-priced segment. Now, 17 percent of PM's U.S.A. sales are discount brands, such as Cambridge, Alpine, Bristol, and Bucks.

18   Industrywide discount brand sales have risen from 11 percent of sales in 1989 to 25 percent today and are expected to double again over the coming five years. Although Philip Morris is performing well in the discount segment, it is unable to put its formidable advertising might behind these brands for fear of cannibalizing its higher-margin premium brands. Recently tobacco companies have raised prices on the discount brands—last year PM increased its prices by 20 percent on the discount brands.

19   According to industry analysts,[18,19,20] William Campbell, CEO of Philip Morris U.S.A., is determined to compete in every major cigarette category. The result is that the company now produces low-profit generic cigarettes. Generics, sometimes referred to as *black and whites,* are sold in places like Wal-Mart bearing such names as Best Buy, Basic, and Gridlock: The Commuter's Cigarette—a California brand. Campbell's predominant goal is to increase PM's domestic market share a point a year.

20   **Low Tar**   The low tar segment of the market consists of cigarettes delivering 15 milligrams (mg) or less of "tar" per cigarette. In 1990 and 1989, this market accounted for 57.4 percent and 55.5 percent of U.S. industry sales, respectively.[21,22] Philip Morris's low tar brands comprised 42.1 percent of the

---

[16] C. Leinster, "Is Bigger Better for Philip Morris?" *Fortune* 119, no. 10 (1989), pp. 66–68+.

[17] A. Farnham, "From Soup to Nuts," *Fortune* 119, no. 1 (1989), pp. 43–47.

[18] S. Chakravraty, "Philip Morris Is Still Hungry," *Forbes* 145, no. 7 (1990).

[19] J. Dagnoli, "CEO Miles Sees International Growth for Philip Morris," *Advertising Age* April 8, 1991.

[20] Sellers, "Can He Keep."

[21] Moody's *Industrial Manual,* 1990 and 1991.

[22] S&P's *Industry Surveys,* 1990 and 1991.

low tar market in 1990 and 42.8 percent in 1989. The low tar market includes a subsegment referred to as *ultra-low tar* that consists of brands that deliver 6 mg. or less of tar per cigarette. Ultra-low tar brands accounted for 11.3 percent of industry sales in 1990, compared with 10.8 percent in 1989. Philip Morris's ultra-low tar brands garnered 32.9 percent of this market in 1990 and 33.4 percent in 1989.

21   The low tar and ultra-low tar segments are growing, whereas the industry is in general decline. Philip Morris must ensure that its brands competing in these segments are able to achieve market share positions at least commensurate with its non-low tar cigarettes. This is currently not the case in the rapidly expanding ultra-low tar category, where Philip Morris lost market share during 1990.

International Tobacco

22   Worldwide tobacco industry sales have been growing at approximately 2 percent per year for the past several years. The United States exported $5 billion of tobacco products in 1990.[23] Philip Morris International's share of this market was 7.6 percent in 1990, compared with 6.7 percent in 1989. Marlboro is the leader. Its sales increased 13.2 percent in 1990. Its 206.9 billion units accounted for over 4.3 percent of the non-United States cigarette market. In particular, Philip Morris International has strong market share positions in Argentina, Australia, Finland, France, Germany, Hong Kong, Italy, Mexico, Saudi Arabia, and Switzerland, holding at least a 15 percent market share position in each.

23   Philip Morris is the leading cigarette exporter. Total cigarette exports to 111 foreign countries in 1990 were valued at $4.75 billion. The leading destinations were Asian (58 percent) and European (38 percent) countries. Two factors were primarily responsible for the growth in international sales: the lowering of trade barriers in Japan, Taiwan, and South Korea, and the weakened dollar.[24]

24   The market for cigarettes outside the United States in 1980 was 3.9 trillion units, with only 40 percent open to Western companies. Currently, international (non-U.S.) consumption stands at 4.9 trillion cigarettes a year, and Western companies now can deal with 95 percent of this market. PM sold 640 billion, or 11.6 percent of the world's cigarettes last year. That places PM second behind the Chinese government (1.5 trillion) in terms of total cigarette sales.

25   It is interesting that the company's global perspective largely resulted from its inability to penetrate domestic markets. When it was No. 6 among U.S. tobacco companies during the '50s, PM was the first U.S. manufacturer to begin selling its products in duty-free shops in foreign countries. It focused on those countries most frequented by U.S. travelers. Because many of these markets were closed to imports, the company was forced to license the sale of its cigarettes in the areas. The company reasoned that foreign-domestic managers could best oversee these foreign operations. As a result of this early emphasis on international operations, PM's management is more globally diverse than most: Miles and Mayer are Americans, Maxwell is a Scot, Campbell is Canadian, David Dangoor (PM U.S.A. marketing head) is Iranian. Two of the three bosses Miles vied with for the CEO position are Australian; the third is German.[25]

26   Though many foreign markets recently have opened access to U.S. firms, many protectionist policies are mitigating penetration. Many governments control prices, levy huge taxes, and even market state-owned brands (Taiwanese government's Long Life cigarettes; Japan's Dean cigarettes). Last year in Hong Kong, a 200 percent tax increase on imported cigarettes effectively doubled the price of a pack of Marlboros and cut PM's sales by 80 percent. The government later cut the tax in half after Philip Morris International employees and friends gathered 75,000 signatures.

---

[23] M. Levin, "U.S. Tobacco Firms Push Easily into Asian Markets," *Marketing News* 25, no. 2 (January 21, 1991), pp. 2, 14.

[24] Sellers, "Can He Keep."

[25] Ibid.

27   In Italy, the company was implicated in a government investigation of cigarette imports that illegally avoided Italian taxes. Consequently, Italy imposed a one-month ban on Marlboro, Merit, and Muratti, a popular local blend.

28   International tobacco's profit margins are half those of the United States. These margins are improving—they rose 24 percent in 1991 on a 14 percent increase in revenues. In the European community, sales volume has risen 25 percent during the past three years. PM management views Turkey as the "gateway to the east," particularly the former Soviet Union and Central Asia. PM recently broke ground on a $400 million cigarette factory there.[26]

29   In 1990, PM bought three deteriorating East German factories that churn out the leading local cigarette, F6. Last year, PM shipped 22 billion cigarettes to the former Soviet Union.[27]

Food

30   CEO Miles was formerly head of Kraft General Foods (KGF), which was formed after PM bought Kraft. He was instrumental in the successful implementation of Hamish Maxwell's diversification strategy. Miles's promotion to chief executive helped ease the tension between PM and General Foods that had existed since the latter's hostile takeover. Miles's insight into the food business permitted him to ignore pessimistic forecasts for traditionally strong brands, such as Maxwell House and Post. Many insiders felt that these brands could expect, at best, marginal increases in volume. Miles reemphasized growth and, as a consequence, sales of such leading products as Kool-Aid, Jell-O, and Grape Nuts cereal are expanding again.[28,29] Operating profits in General Foods exceeded $700 million in 1991, versus $433 million in 1989.

31   Kraft's cheese division has not fared as well. Sales have stagnated. Analysts blame this on Miles's continued price hikes in the face of stable prices for private label cheeses. During 1991, Kraft began cutting prices in an attempt to regain lost market share from the private labels. However, the retailers—who profit quite nicely off their own private label brands—were naturally reluctant to pass the cuts on down to the consumers.[30] The division experienced a shortfall of $125 million between anticipated and realized cheese profits. The problems of the cheese division also have resulted from increased health consciousness among consumers. Cheese products are notoriously high in saturated fat and cholesterol. As more consumers become sensitive to nutritional guidelines espoused by leading health agencies, overall demand for cheese likely will continue to decline. Kraft's products in general and cheese products in particular typically are not purchased by health conscious consumers due to their high fat content.

32   Richard Mayer, president and CEO of KGF, has two primary ideas for stimulating the food division: (1) to get market research and computer people working in teams with brand managers to make better use of scanner-generated sales data and (2) to distribute all KGF products within a particular region from a single warehouse location to serve customers better.[31] Presently, grocers buy 10 percent of all their grocery items from KGF but draw from many warehouses. These strategies should help KGF respond more expeditiously to market trends and competitors' moves.

---

[26] Moody's *Industrial Manual,* 1992.

[27] PM, annual reports, 1991 and 1992.

[28] Dagnoli, "CEO Miles Sees."

[29] Sellers, "Can He Keep."

[30] Ibid.

[31] Dagnoli, "CEO Miles Sees."

PHILIP MORRIS AS AN EMPLOYER

33   Philip Morris consistently is ranked as one of the more progressive employers in the United States. Levering, Moskowitz, and Katz included PM among their listing of *The 100 Best Companies to Work for in America.*

34   According to James Bowling, director of public relations and public affairs, caring about its employees is what distinguishes Philip Morris: ". . . everybody bought tobacco competitively at auction; manufactured cigarettes in Kentucky, Virginia, and North Carolina; used essentially the same machinery; paid the same union wages; and sold through the same wholesalers and retailers. Therefore, they said that, if there is going to be a difference, it will have to be in the people. As simplistic and corny as that seems, it has been the guiding principle here since that day. We have always tried to treat our people better—by being the first or among the first with amenities and working pleasantries."

35   One survey of senior managers conducted by an independent auditor, showed very high satisfaction with the company. The benefits package includes long- and short-term disability compensation. Employees automatically are insured for twice their annual salary, and there is a survivor income benefit that, in the event of employee death, would start paying, after four years, 25 percent of last base pay to surviving spouses every month plus 5 percent of your last base pay to each surviving child. There is an employee stock ownership plan and employees who smoke—and the majority do—are entitled to one free carton of cigarettes per week.[32]

36   Philip Morris was one of the first companies to employ blacks in sales positions. One out of every four persons who works for the company is a minority-group member—and minorities hold 14 percent of positions classified as "officials and managers."[33]

37   The Richmond cigarette factory is a futuristic plant completed in 1974 at cost of over $200 million—at the time the largest capital investment in the company's history. The plant boasts of parquet floors and floor-to-ceiling windows overlooking elaborate ornamental gardens.[34]

1991 PERFORMANCE AND FUTURE PROSPECTS

38   Philip Morris currently sells more than 3,000 items. The value of the shares of stock outstanding reached $74 billion in December 1991 (trading at $75 per share) exceeding the value of all other U.S. companies except Exxon. Among the 1991 highlights: revenues increased 10 percent to $56.5 billion; operating income grew 14 percent to $9.9 billion; unit sales increased nearly 200 million in the United States over 1990, whereas U.S. industry volume decreased by 13 billion units.

39   Despite many bright spots, particularly in fat-free products, beverages, and breakfast cereals, overall results in North American food businesses were lower than expected. Volume in the brewing business grew 0.4 percent despite a doubling of the federal excise tax at the beginning of the year. Performance in 1991 allowed the company to increase dividends by 22.1 percent to an annualized rate of $2.10 per share, the 24th consecutive year of dividend increases.[35]

40   According to Miles, the company will throw off free cash of more than $21 billion. This is the excess after capital expenditures, dividends, and taxes—and Philip Morris can use it either to pay for acquisitions or to buy back stock, or both. The company currently realizes $15 billion annually from

---

[32] Levering et al., *The 100 Best.*

[33] PM, annual report, 1991.

[34] Levering et al., *The 100 Best.*

[35] PM, annual report, 1992.

TABLE 5
Philip Morris Companies, Inc: Consolidated Income (in millions of dollars)

	1991	1990	1989	1988	1987
Operating revenues.	$56,458	$51,169	$44,080	$31,273	$27,650
Cost of sales	25,612	24,430	21,868	13,565	12,183
Excise taxes on products	8,394	6,846	5,748	5,882	5,416
Gross profit	22,452	19,893	16,464	11,826	10,051
Marketing, admin., & research.	13,331	11,499	9,290	7,304	5,956
Amortization of goodwill	499	448	385	125	105
Operating income	8,622	7,946	6,789	4,397	3,990
Interest & other debt expense.	1,651	1,635	1,731	670	646
Earnings before income taxes	6,971	6,311	5,058	3,727	3,344
Provision for income taxes	3,044	2,771	2,112	1,663	1,502
Earnings before cumulative effect of acct. change	3,927	3,540	2,946	2,064	1,842
Cumulative effect of acct. change for income taxes	921			273	
Net earnings	3,006	3,540	2,946	2,337	1,842
Retained earnings (B.O.Y.)	10,960	9,079	7,833	6,437	5,344
Common dividends	(1,765)	(1,432)	(1,159)	(941)	(749)
Four-for-one stock split			(478)		
Exercise of stock options	(172)	(218)	(63)		
Other	(9)	(9)			
Retained earnings (E.O.Y.)	12,038	10,960	9,079	7,833	6,437

international operations (more than Coca-Cola, PepsiCo, and Kellogg combined). Marlboro is especially strong internationally in Asia, Eastern Europe, and the former Soviet Union.[36]

41   As portrayed in the company's consolidated income statement (Table 5), Philip Morris U.S.A.'s sales went up 9 percent to $9.4 billion in 1991, and operating profits rose even faster to reach $4.8 billion. Operating margin rose a fabulous 51 percent, up from 42 percent seven years ago. Philip Morris's gains in market share are impressive, too—43.3 percent of total U.S. cigarette sales today, versus 35.9 percent in 1985.

42   The primary objective at Philip Morris traditionally has been to achieve 20 percent annual earnings growth. Hamish Maxwell hit the mark each of the last five years, but Miles is facing a more maleficent marketplace.

43   The company is in a very solid financial position as it remains one of the more liquid U.S. companies. It often is referred to as the "King of Cash" (see Table 6).

---

[36] Sellers, "Can He Keep."

TABLE 6

Comparative Consolidated Balance Sheet
As of December 31
(in millions of dollars)

	1991	1990	1989	1988	1987
Assets					
Consumer products:					
Cash & equivalents	$ 126	$ 146	$ 118	$ 168	$ 90
Receivables, net	4,121	4,101	2,956	2,222	2,065
Inventories	7,445	7,153	5,751	5,384	4,154
Other current assets	902	967	555	377	245
Total current assets	12,594	12,367	9,380	8,151	6,554
Property, plant, & equipment	15,281	14,281	12,357	11,932	9,398
Less accum. depreciation	5,335	4,677	3,400	3,284	2,816
Property account net.	9,946	9,604	8,951	8,648	6,582
Other assets	20,306	20,712	17,251	16,992	5,411
Total consumer products assets	42,846	42,683	35,588	33,791	18,547
Total financial & real estate assets	4,538	3,886	3,440	3,169	2,890
Total assets	$47,384	$46,569	$39,028	$36,960	$21,437
Liabilities					
Total current liabilities	11,824	11,360	8,943	7,969	5,164
Total consumer products liabilities	31,344	31,460	26,108	26,664	12,234
Total financial & real estate assets	3,528	3,162	2,849	2,617	2,330
Stockholders' Equity					
Common stock ($1, par)		935	935	240	240
Additional paid-in capital				252	272
Earnings reinvested in business		10,960	9,079	7,833	6,437
Currency translation adj.		561	143	117	146
Net stockholders' equity	12,512	11,344	9,871	8,208	6,803
Total	$47,384	$45,956	$38,828	$37,489	$21,367

THREATS TO PHILIP MORRIS'S TRADITIONAL LEVEL OF PERFORMANCE

The Declining American Cigarette Industry

44   Domestic cigarettes contributed $4.8 billion in operating income last year, roughly half the corporate total. But the American cigarette industry is declining 2 to 3 percent per year. Additionally, the trend is toward budget brands with smaller profit margins and away from premium products, such as Marlboro, Merit, Virginia Slims, and Benson & Hedges. According to industry analysts, the bargain brands—including those marketed by Philip Morris—pose more of a threat to the 20 percent target than the product liability litigation now pending Supreme Court review.[37]

Slowing Processed Food Sales

45 Recession intensifies price elasticity, so shoppers are moving toward less-costly private label brands. Increasing consumer awareness of ingredients has invited comparison between the private labels and national brands, such as Kraft General Foods (KGF). In many cases, there is no substantive difference. KGF's North American revenues rose only 1 percent last year. Excluding special charges, operating income increased a disappointing 8 percent.

Antismoking Litigation and Legislation

46 Investors remain concerned about tobacco's legal status. This hinges on a Supreme Court ruling expected during the summer of 1992. The court will decide whether the federally mandated warning labels on cigarette packs—required since 1966—insulate tobacco companies from liability claims in state courts.

SMOKING AND HEALTH RELATED ISSUES

47 Since 1964, the Surgeon General of the United States and the Secretary of Health and Human Services have released reports alleging a correlation between cigarette smoking and numerous physical maladies, including cancer, heart disease, and chronic diseases of the respiratory system. Recent reports continue to emphasize the health warnings from the earlier studies and additionally focus on the addictive nature of smoking and the demographics of smokers. In particular, the prevalence and growth rates of smoking among women and African-Americans have received much publicity.[38]

48 Federal law requires marketers of cigarettes in the United States to include one of four warnings on a rotating basis on cigarette packages and advertisements:

49 SURGEON GENERAL'S WARNING: Smoking Causes Lung Cancer, Heart Disease, Emphysema, and May Complicate Pregnancy.

SURGEON GENERAL'S WARNING: Quitting Smoking Now Greatly Reduces Serious Risk to Your Health.

SURGEON GENERAL'S WARNING: Smoking by Pregnant Women May Result in Fetal Injury, Premature Birth, and Low Birth Weight.

SURGEON GENERAL'S WARNING: Cigarette Smoke Contains Carbon Monoxide.

50 In addition to the warnings, federal regulations require that cigarettes sold in the United States disclose the average tar and nicotine deliveries per cigarette.

51 A more recent concern has been the alleged health risks to nonsmokers from what is most often referred to as *passive smoking* or *environmental tobacco smoke* (ETS). In 1986, the U.S. Surgeon General issued a report claiming that nonsmokers were at increased risk of lung cancer and respiratory illness due to ETS. The Environmental Protection Agency is currently at work on a report detailing the risks of ETS. The findings concerning ETS have been instrumental in the passage of legislation that restricts or bans cigarette smoking in public places and places of employment.

[37] S&P's *Industry Survey,* 1992.

[38] Ibid.

52   Television and radio advertising of cigarettes has been prohibited in the United States since 1971. Since this time, regulatory agencies have acted to further restrict or prohibit smoking in certain public places, on buses, trains, and airplanes, and in places of employment.

53   Such restrictions are not exclusive to the United States. Many foreign countries have restricted or prohibited cigarette advertising and promotion, increased taxes on cigarettes, and openly campaigned against smoking. Thailand, Hong Kong, France, Italy, and Portugal all have implemented cigarette advertising bans. This virtually precludes successful introduction of new brands in these countries. The European Economic Community (EEC) is contemplating a ban on tobacco advertising in newspapers, magazines, and billboards.[39] More recently, the Asian Consultancy on Tobacco Control, a 14-nation consortium, has been formed to combat smoking in this region. Thus, some countries have tighter restrictions than the United States.

LITIGATION

54   Approximately 50 court cases are pending, wherein plaintiffs are seeking damages from leading United States cigarette manufacturers. The litigation involves alleged cancer and other health maladies directly resulting from cigarette smoking. Philip Morris was a defendant in 23 actions pending as of March 1, 1991, compared with 24 at the same point in 1990 and with 32 in 1989. The number of court cases appears to have stabilized.

55   Philip Morris's primary defense tactic has been based on seeking a preemption of liability based on the Federal Cigarette Labeling and Advertising Act. Five federal courts have ruled that the cigarette labeling act does protect cigarette manufacturers from some liability claims. Conversely, the Supreme Court of New Jersey and one of the Texas appellate courts ruled that the cigarette labeling act does not limit the liability of the cigarette manufacturers. The discrepancy in lower court rulings is scheduled to be resolved during the summer of 1992 when the Supreme Court reviews the case of *Cipollone* v. *Liggett Group Inc., et al.*

56   As with any court case the outcome is uncertain. A finding in favor of the plaintiff would have the effect of denying preemption of liability on the basis of the existence of the cigarette warning labels. This could entice additional litigation against cigarette manufacturers. Philip Morris remains confident that, even in this worst-case scenario, the lawsuits will not pose a substantive threat to its overall financial health.

THE COMPANY'S POSITION

57   No tobacco company has never lost a liability case or paid a penny to settle; juries thus far have ruled that smokers have been adequately warned cigarettes can ruin their health. According to John McMillin of Prudential Securities: "A Supreme Court ruling against the industry has limited downside for the stock because worries have already pulled down the price. A tobacco victory could mean the end of major litigation risk and take Philip Morris's stock up 15 to 20 percent."

58   Tobacco use is one of the most widely discussed health issues around the world. The company's position was stated by CEO Miles in a letter to shareholders in 1992: "Given the general availability of information concerning the health issue, we regard smoking as a voluntary lifestyle decision that need not be subjected to new marketing or use restrictions."

59   He added: "While we believe that consumers are aware of the claimed health risks of smoking, nonetheless in February 1992 we took actions to begin placing the U.S. Surgeon General's health

---

[39] P. Engardio, "Asia: A New Front in the War on Smoking," *Business Week* (Industrial/Technical Edition), no. 3201 (February 25, 1991), p. 66.

warning on all our cigarette packages worldwide where warnings are not currently required. This initiative applies to brands manufactured in the United States for export, as well as to those produced overseas by our affiliates and affected licensees. We are taking these steps because the lack of warning on a relatively small number of packages—approximately 10 percent of our volume—has become an issue out of proportion to its importance."

60   Continuing, Miles stated: "Moreover in the United States we are acting to increase awareness and enforcement of minimum age purchase restrictions on our tobacco products through multimillion-dollar programs involving advertising, trade relations, and family education."

FUTURE PROSPECTS

61   According to Miles, the company has no plans to diversify outside of packaged goods. Since acquisition opportunities in tobacco are limited, most analysts predict a major food acquisition, probably in Western Europe within the coming year or so. In 1990, PM bought one of Europe's largest coffee and chocolate companies, Jacobs Suchard, well known for Tablerone candy bars. The $4.1 billion deal made PM the third-largest food marketer in Europe, behind Nestlé and Unilever. The company's European revenues today are approaching $10 billion in food. Nestlé has about $15 billion in European sales but, with acquisitions, PM figures it will grow faster.

62   There is much speculation centered on acquisition targets. One is rumored to be H. J. Heinze, a European powerhouse. PepsiCo is not considered a likely target but Cadberry Schweppes is. Another suspected target is Paris-based BSN, which would help PM penetrate the lucrative French cheese market with its Velveeta, Cracker Barrel, and Kraft Natural brands.

63   For Miles to meet the company's goals, PM must reach $85 billion in sales by 1995, with net income of $9 billion.[40] The future of the tobacco industry, particularly domestically, is cloudy. With numerous product liability lawsuits pending and increasing antismoking sentiments, PM must face the increasingly realistic possibility that cigarette smokers will become virtually nonexistent. As pessimistic as this may sound, a more threatening though less-likely scenario exists: cigarette manufacturing could be banned by the FDA. Within the coming five years, Miles must reposition the firm so it may withstand the effects of declining tobacco income.

---

[40] Sellers, "Can He Keep."

CASE 12

CADBURY SCHWEPPES, PLC

1 All large [food] companies have broken out of their product boundaries. They are no longer the bread, beer, meat, milk, or confectionery companies they were a relatively short time ago—they are food and drink companies.

—Sir Adrian Cadbury, chairman (retired), Cadbury Schweppes, PLC[1]

2 In the early 1990s, Cadbury Schweppes, PLC, embodied the archetypical modern food conglomerate. With extensive international operations in confectionery products and soft drinks, the company maintained a diversified global presence. Although Cadbury had enjoyed a relatively stable competitive environment through much of the company's history, contemporary developments in the international arena presented Cadbury management with many different and critical challenges.

THE HISTORY OF CADBURY

3 The company began in 1831, when John Cadbury began processing cocoa and chocolate in the United Kingdom (U.K.) to be used in beverages. In 1847, the company became Cadbury Brothers, and, in 1866, it enjoyed its first major achievement when the second generation of Cadburys found a better way to process cocoa. By using an imported cocoa press to remove unpalatable cocoa butter from the company's hot cocoa drink mix, instead of adding large quantities of sweeteners, Cadbury capitalized on a growing public concern for adulterated food.

4 The company further prospered when it later found that cocoa butter could be used in recipes for edible chocolates. In 1905, Cadbury introduced Cadbury Dairy Milk (CDM) as a challenge to Swiss firms' virtual monopoly in British milk chocolate sales. A year later, the firm scored another success with the introduction of a new hot chocolate drink mix, Bournville Cocoa. These two brands provided much of the impetus for Cadbury's early prosperity.[2]

5 Cadbury faced rather benign competition throughout many of the firm's early years. In fact, at one point, Cadbury provided inputs for the U.K. operations of the American firm, Mars, Inc.[3] Cadbury also formed trade associations with its U.K. counterparts, J. S. Fry and Rowntree & Company, for the purpose of, among other things, reducing uncertainty in cocoa prices. The company later merged financial interests with J. S. Fry but spurned offers to consolidate with Rowntree in 1921 and 1930.[4]

This case was prepared by Franz T. Lohrke, James Combs, and Gary Castrogiovanni, Louisiana State University Department of Management, College of Business Administration.

[1] C. Smith, Child, J., & M. Rowlinson, *Reshaping Work: The Cadbury Experience.* (Cambridge: Cambridge University Press, 1990), p. 9.

[2] G. Jones. "The Chocolate Multinationals: Cadbury, Fry, and Rowntree 1918–1939," in *British Multinationals: Origins, Management and Performance*, ed. G. Jones (Brookfield, Vt.: Gower Publishing, 1986), pp. 96–118.

[3] Smith, *Reshaping Work.*

[4] Jones, "The Chocolate Multinationals."

FIGURE 1
Cadbury's Foreign Direct Investment

1914–1918	1921	1930	1933	1937	1939–1945
World War I	Australia	New Zealand	Ireland	South Africa	World War II

Source: G. Jones, "The Chocolate Multinationals," in *British Multinationals*, ed. G. Jones (Brookfield, Vt.: Gower Publishing, 1986), pp. 96–118.

6 Facing growing protectionist threats in overseas markets following World War I, Cadbury began manufacturing outside the U.K., primarily in Commonwealth countries (see Figure 1). This international growth was also prompted by increasing competition. For example, by 1932 Cadbury management considered the Swiss company, Nestlé, as the primary competitor in the international arena.[5]

7 In 1969, Cadbury merged with Schweppes, the worldwide maker of soft drinks and mixers. The merger offered both companies an array of advantages, both defensive and offensive. First, both companies faced potential takeover threats from larger firms, so the merger placed the new company in a better defensive posture to ward off unwanted suitors. On the offensive side, the marriage allowed the new company to compete better on a worldwide scale.

8 Cadbury had invested primarily in Commonwealth countries, and Schweppes had branched out into Europe and North America, so the new company enjoyed greater geographic dispersion. The increased international presence also allowed the company to defray product development costs over a wider geographic base. Furthermore, the new company enjoyed greater bargaining power from suppliers. For example, following the merger, Cadbury Schweppes became the largest U.K. purchaser of sugar.[6]

9 The British confectionery companies historically pursued a different strategy than their American counterparts. While U.S. companies, such as Mars, manufactured narrow product lines and employed centralized production, Cadbury maintained 237 confectionery products until World War II forced the company to scale back to 29. While faced with a lack of intense competition, Cadbury's brand proliferation strategy could be undertaken. As rivalry heated up in the mid-1970s, though, Cadbury's share of the U.K. chocolate market fell from 31.1 percent to 26.2 between 1975 and 1977. Management then began to realize that the lower-cost American-style strategy of rationalized product lines and centralized production provided the only viable means to compete.[7]

10 Cadbury had long been famous for its unique management style. "Cadburyism" drew influence from the founders' Quaker heritage, providing for worker welfare and harmonious community relations. Following Cadbury's reorientation toward core products and rationalized production, though, the company's old management style underwent a transformation. Confectionery manufacturing personnel were reduced from 8,565 to 4,508 between 1978 and 1985.[8] In the process, management's traditional close relationship with workers, which had been built through years of maintaining employment stability, began to erode as worker reduction became a professed goal of Cadbury executives.

---

[5] Ibid.

[6] Smith, *Reshaping Work*.

[7] J. Child and C. Smith. "The Context and Process of Organizational Transformation—Cadbury Limited in Its Sector," *Journal of Management Studies* 24 (1987), pp. 565–93.

[8] Ibid.

TABLE 1
Assorted Major Brand Names of Cadbury Schweppes and Its Confectionery Competition

Cadbury Schweppes:
Cadbury Dairy Milk (CDM)	Whole Nut
Milk Tray	Roses
Crunchie	Fruit and Nut
Whispa	Trebor

Nestlé:
Nestlé Crunch bar	Polo
KitKat	Quality Street
Smarties	Yorkie
After Eight	Aero
Rolo	Black Magic
Dairy Box	Fruit Pastilles
Butterfinger	Baby Ruth

M&M/Mars, Inc.:
Mars Bar	Galaxy
Twix	Maltesers
Bounty	Milky Way
M&Ms	Snickers

Hershey:
Hershey bars	Reese's Peanut Butter Cup
Hershey Kisses	Reese's Pieces
Mounds	Almond Joy

Philip Morris:
- Milka
- Toblerone
- E. J. Brach candy

THE ENVIRONMENT

11   As is the case with several products in the food industry, many of Cadbury's product lines enjoyed very long product life cycles. (See Table 1 for assorted confectionery products of Cadbury and its rivals.) Food and beverage companies derived substantial benefit from their long-established products, such as Cadbury's CDM bar, and the occasional new product introductions required little in the way of technological investment. The food companies, therefore, competed primarily by seeking cost reduction through process improvements, such as automation, by finding alternative inputs to replace expensive cocoa, and by introducing creative packaging and marketing.[9]

12   Successful new product introductions remained sporadic, and many of the most successful confectionery products, such as Mars Bar and Rowntree's KitKat, had been around since the 1930s.[10] Some unsatisfied demanded seemed to persist, however, as was evidenced by Rowntree's successful 1976 launch of its Yorkie bar, Mars's profitable introduction of Twix a few years later, Cadbury's notable 1984 launch in the U.K. of its Whispa bar, and Hershey's 1988 introduction of Bar None.[11]

13   Nevertheless, new brand introductions required immense investments in development and marketing costs, with only limited possibilities for success. For instance, various research suggests that

---

[9] Ibid.

[10] P. Tisdall. "Chocolate Soldiers Clash," *Marketing,* July 29, 1982, pp. 30–34.

[11] J. Weber. "Why Hershey Is Smacking Its Lips," *Business Week,* October 30, 1989, p. 140.

approximately 60 percent of new food product introductions have been withdrawn inside of five years, and this figure may be an underestimate.[12] Consequently, established brands with customer loyalty represented crucial assets for food and beverage companies.

MODERN CADBURY SCHWEPPES

14   Expansion was key to Cadbury's plans to improve its international position. Chief executive officer Dominic Cadbury commented, "If you're not operating in terms of world market share, you're unlikely to have the investment needed to support your brands."[13] In 1986, Cadbury shared third place in the world with Rowntree and Hershey, each having approximately 5 percent of the market. Nestlé held second place with about 7.5 percent, while Mars dominated internationally with approximately 13 percent.[14]

15   To generate its necessary worldwide expansion, Cadbury had two primary markets in which to gain positions. Enjoying a dominant position in its home market, the company realized that the United States and the remaining countries of the European Economic Community (those besides the United Kingdom) provided critical markets for a worldwide standing. According to Jerry Organ, director of International Confectionery, "Rightly or wrongly . . . we decided to tackle the United States first."[15] Earlier, Cadbury had taken steps toward competing more vigorously in the United States by acquiring Peter Paul in 1978. By 1980, however, the company still controlled only about 3.5 percent of the U.S. confectionery market, far eclipsed by its bigger rivals, Hershey and Mars.

16   Cadbury did not have sufficient size to employ the sales force of its competitors. The company, therefore, had to rely on food brokers to push products to wholesalers, which left the firm far removed from the consumer. Further, the company easily could be outspent in advertising by its two larger rivals.[16]

17   To compound problems, the company also committed two marketing blunders in the U.S. market. When Cadbury introduced Whispa, the company's marketing success of the decade in the U.K., management did not realize that distribution channels in the United States were longer than in the United Kingdom. Consequently, the candy bars aged seven to nine months by the time they reached test markets in New England, and consumers reacted accordingly.

18   The company's second mistake occurred following an effort to standardize its candy bar size across countries. When Cadbury first introduced its CDM bar in the United States, the bar commanded a higher price than its U.S. rivals. Since CDM also was larger than U.S. competitors' regular bars, consumers were willing to pay a little extra. When Cadbury reduced the size, management discovered that, given the choice between CDM and American confectionery products of equal size and price, U.S. consumers usually chose the more familiar American products.[17] According to one former Cadbury executive, "What happened in the United States was a gigantic, gargantuan cock-up, and the fact that London [Cadbury headquarters] did not know what was happening is a sheer disgrace."[18]

---

[12] Smith, *Reshaping Work.*

[13] A. Borrus, J. Sassen, and M. A. Harris. "Why Cadbury Schweppes Looks Sweet to the Raiders," *Business Week,* January 13, 1986, pp. 132–33.

[14] A. van de Vliet. "Bittersweet at Cadbury," *Management Today,* March 1986, pp. 44–45.

[15] Ibid., p. 45.

[16] Borrus, Sassen, and Harris, "Why Cadbury Schweppes."

[17] van de Vliet, "Bittersweet."

[18] K. Gofton. "Has Cadbury Got His Finger on the Button?" *Marketing,* July 31, 1986, pp. 20–25.

TABLE 2
Top Five Soft-Drink Companies in United States (percent of total market)

	1986	1987	1988	1989	1990
Coca-Cola, Co.	39.8%	39.9%	39.8%	40.0%	40.4%
Classic	19.1	19.8	19.9	19.5	19.4
Diet Coke	7.2	7.7	8.1	8.8	9.1
Sprite	3.6	3.6	3.6	3.6	3.6
PepsiCo	30.6	30.8	31.3	31.7	31.8
Pepsi-Cola	18.6	18.6	18.4	17.8	17.3
Diet Pepsi	4.4	4.8	5.2	5.7	6.2
Mountain Dew	3.0	3.3	3.4	3.6	3.8
Dr Pepper	4.8	5.0	5.3	5.6	5.8
Dr Pepper	3.9	4.0	4.3	4.6	4.8
Diet Dr Pepper	0.4	0.4	0.4	0.4	0.4
Seven-Up	5.0	5.1	4.7	4.3	4.0
7UP	3.5	3.4	3.1	3.0	2.9
Diet 7UP	1.4	1.0	1.0	0.9	0.9
Cadbury Schweppes	4.2	3.7	3.5	3.1	3.2
Canada Dry	1.4	1.4	1.4	1.3	1.2
Sunkist	0.9	0.7	0.7	0.7	0.7
Schweppes prod.	0.5	0.5	0.5	0.6	0.6
Crush	1.4	1.0	0.8	0.6	0.6
Total market share of top five	84.5	84.5	84.5	84.6	85.2

Source: "Food, Beverages, and Tobacco," *Standard & Poor's Industry Surveys,* June 27, 1991, pp. F23–27.

19   Not all the news from the other side of the Atlantic was bad for the U.K. company, however. Although Peter Paul/Cadbury only commanded a small slice of the market, some products, such as Coconut Mounds and York Peppermint Patties, dominated their segments. Cadbury's Creme Eggs also enjoyed seasonal success. Moreover, the company's acquisition of Canada Dry from R. J. Reynolds provided Cadbury Schweppes with a strong position in the carbonated mixers market in the United States and many other countries. (See Table 2 for U.S. market shares.) For example, although Cadbury Schweppes only commanded about a 3 percent market share in the $43 billion U.S. soft-drink industry, the company sold Canada Dry, the No. 1 ginger ale and club soda in the United States, and Schweppes, the leading tonic water in the American market.[19] Additionally, the cola giants, Coca-Cola and PepsiCo, did not (as yet) vigorously market products in segments dominated by Cadbury Schweppes. Overall, though, the company faced an uphill struggle in many segments of the U.S. market.

20   In an effort to remedy some of the company's problems in the U.S. confectionery market, Cadbury decided to sell its manufacturing assets to Hershey in 1988, catapulting the Pennsylvania company to the dominant position in the U.S. market (see Table 3). Cadbury also granted Hershey licenses to

---

[19] P. Winters. "Cadbury Schweppes' Plan: Skirt Cola Giants," *Advertising Age,* August 13, 1990, pp. 22–23.

TABLE 3
Top Five Companies in the $8 Billion U.S. Confectionery Market (percent of total market)

1980		1988	
Company	Market Share	Company	Market Share
Mars	17.0%	Hershey	20.5%
Hershey	15.3	Mars	18.5
Nabisco	7.1	Jacobs Suchard	6.7
E. J. Brach	6.4	Nestlé	6.7
Peter Paul/Cadbury	3.5	Leaf	5.6

Source: J. Weber, "Why Hershey Is Smacking Its Lips," *Business Week,* October 30, 1989, p. 140.

manufacture and sell its Peter Paul products, including Mounds, Almond Joy, and York Peppermint Patties. Under this arrangement, Cadbury gained the benefit of Hershey's marketing muscle behind the Peter Paul products.[20]

21   Cadbury faced additional challenges to building market share in the European Economic Community (EEC). Schweppes' beverages enjoyed success on the Continent,[21] but Europe's confectionery industry proved difficult to break into since the market remained dominated by family-owned firms and suffered from overcapacity.[22] Successful expansion in the EEC, however, was crucial to Cadbury's remaining a dominant player in the worldwide food and beverage industries.

CONTEMPORARY CHALLENGES

22   The 1990s brought about radical shifts in the industries in which Cadbury Schweppes competed. First, corporate leaders (and stock markets) discovered that food and beverage enterprises with established brand names were not mundane investments offering only lackluster financial returns. Purchasing popular brands or taking over companies that had portfolios full of well-known products often provided a safer and more economical avenue for growth than attempting to develop entirely new products. In 1985, for instance, Philip Morris acquired General Foods for $5.75 billion, approximately three times book value, while R. J. Reynolds laid out $4.9 billion for Nabisco Brands.[23]

23   These attempts to acquire popular brands also were dictated by dramatic industrywide changes, which altered the nature of competition faced by the international food and beverage enterprises. First, the push by the 12 countries of the European Economic Community to remove trade barriers among the member nations by 1992 had sparked a buying frenzy of European food companies with established brand names (see Table 4 for a comparison of the North American and EEC markets). Many non-European companies feared that the EEC eventually would increase tariff barriers for products from outside the community, which could have effectively closed foreign companies out of the market. This anticipation of "Fortress Europe" sent companies without EEC operations scurrying to acquire European enterprises.

24   Second, the common perception that only the largest companies in most industries would survive in Europe, as well as internationally, contributed to the takeover hysteria. To become big quickly,

---

[20] R. L. Swarns and B. Toran. "Hershey to Buy U.S. Business from Cadbury," *The Wall Street Journal,* July 25, 1988, p. 30.

[21] Borrus, Sassen, and Harris, "Why Cadbury Schweppes."

[22] van de Vliet, "Bittersweet."

[23] Ibid.

TABLE 4
The United States and the European Economic Community (EEC)

	U.S.	EEC
Population	243.8 million	323.6 million
Gross national product (GNP) (in 1987 $U.S.)	$4.436 trillion	$3.782 trillion
Per capita GNP	$18,200	$11,690
Inflation	3.7%	3.1%
Unemployment	6.1%	11.0%

Note: EEC members include the United Kingdom (England, Scotland, Wales, Northern Ireland), Ireland, Denmark, Germany, France, Belgium, the Netherlands, Luxembourg, Portugal, Spain, Italy, and Greece.
Source: K. E. House, "The 90s and Beyond: The U.S. Stands to Retain Its Global Leadership," *The Wall Street Journal,* January 23, 1989, p. A8.

companies began to aggressively acquire rival food companies. For example, Nestlé scored a major victory in July 1988 when it outbid its Swiss counterpart, Jacob Suchard, to acquire Cadbury's longtime U.K. competitor, Rowntree. In the process, Nestlé moved from a minor status in the EEC confectionery market into a first place duel with Mars. In the U.K. market, Nestlé's acquisition positioned the company in a second-place battle with Mars and within striking distance of first-place Cadbury.[24] In January 1992, Nestlé also attempted to continue its acquisition binge by launching a hostile takeover bid for the French mineral water company, Source Perrier.

25   Other major food conglomerates, such as Phillip Morris (U.S.) and Unilever Group (U.K./Netherlands), also were rumored to be on the prowl for acquisitions in Europe.[25] These heavyweights not only presented medium-sized food and beverage companies, like Cadbury, with increased competition in the marketplace, they also represented potential bidders in any acquisitions attempted by Cadbury. This increased competition threatened to drive up acquisition prices through cutthroat bidding for popular brand names. In fact, as the takeover battles became more heated, stock market analysts speculated that Cadbury and other medium-sized companies could find themselves targets of acquisition attempts.[26] (See Table 5.)

26   The European food and beverage industries were undergoing other changes along with the acquisition binges. At the end of the food and beverage distribution pipeline, for example, many European supermarkets also were consolidating. In April 1990, eight EEC grocery chains formed an alliance to combine buying power and promote house brands. As these supermarket companies combined forces, they greatly enhanced their bargaining power against the food and beverage companies. This increased power threatened future profits of food and beverage companies, since the grocery chains' ability to demand price concessions from the companies was enhanced by the stores' consolidation. Furthermore, since supermarkets only wanted to carry the top two or three brands for each product type, food and beverage companies faced the option of acquiring popular brands or risking lost shelf space in stores.[27]

---

[24] "The Nestlé–Rowntree Deal: Bitter Battle, Sweet Result," *Mergers and Acquisitions,* September/October 1989, pp. 66–67.

[25] E. S. Browning and M. Studer. "Nestlé and Indosuez Launch Hostile Bid for Perrier in Contest with Agnellis," *The Wall Street Journal,* January 21, 1992, p. A3.

[26] Ibid.

[27] J. Templeman and R. A. Melcher. "Supermarket Darwinism: The Survival of the Fattest," *Business Week,* July 9, 1990, p. 42.

TABLE 5
Food Sales—Europe (including the United Kingdom)

Nestlé	$15.1 billion
Unilever	12.2
Philip Morris*	8.0
BSN	7.8
Mars	4.1
Cadbury Schweppes	3.1

* Includes Jacobs Suchard.
Source: J. Templeman and R. A. Melcher, "Supermarket Darwinism: The Survival of the Fattest," *Business Week*, July 9, 1990, p. 42.

TABLE 6
Cadbury Schweppes' 1990 Worldwide Sales (in £ million*)

Region	Total Sales	Confectionery	Beverages
United Kingdom	£1,476.0	£715.4	£760.6
Continental Europe	638.0	195.6	442.4
Americas	403.7	18.3	373.5
Pacific Rim.	495.5†	N.A.	N.A.
Africa and other	132.9	91.2	38.8

* 1 £ = $1.93.
† Sales primarily in Australia and New Zealand.
N.A. means not available.
Note: Total sales will not always equal confectionery plus beverages. In the United States (Americas region), for example, Cadbury Schweppes also generated sales from its Mott's subsidiary.
Sources: Compact Disclosure; *The Wall Street Journal,* various issues.

27   In response to these massive changes in the industry, Cadbury also began acquiring name brand products and searching for strategic alliances. In 1986, for example, the company decided to end its bottling agreement with Pepsi to form a joint venture with Coke in the United Kingdom.[28] In 1990, Cadbury purchased the European soft-drink operations of Source Perrier,[29]and, in 1991, the company formed a joint venture with Appolinarus Brunnen AG, a German bottler of sparkling water.

28   With the competitive environment heating up, Cadbury management faced a number of crucial questions. Could the company continue to compete independently against the food and beverage mega-corporations that were forming or should Cadbury merge with another company before being faced with a hostile takeover attempt? Did Cadbury have the resources to acquire more brand names or should management continue to investigate the joint venture route? Should the company reduce emphasis on Europe and, instead, attempt to exploit new opportunities in the underdeveloped Asian market? Whatever Cadbury Schweppes management decided to do, it had to move quickly. The choices of popular name brand food and beverage products on the table were being cleared away fast. (See Table 6 and appendix.)

---

[28] Gofton, "Has Cadbury Got His Finger."

[29] Templeman and Melcher, "Supermarket Darwinism."

APPENDIX

TABLE 7
Financials

Balance Sheet
(in thousands, sterling)

	Fiscal Year Ending		
	12/29/90	12/30/89	12/31/88
Assets			
Cash	£ 62,600	£ 57,400	£ 41,300
Marketable securities	118,000	33,300	200,700
Receivables	554,100	548,200	434,500
Inventories	328,200	334,800	253,400
Total current assets	1,062,900	973,700	929,900
Net prop., plant, equip.	978,800	822,500	602,200
Other long-term assets	320,700	332,600	20,700
Total assets	£2,362,400	£2,128,800	£1,552,800
Liabilities			
Notes payable	£ 60,100	£ 57,400	£ 92,200
Accounts payable	272,100	263,900	409,500
Current capital leases	76,200	76,300	21,900
Accrued expenses	320,900	305,900	52,100
Income taxes	78,200	95,800	81,800
Other current liab.	154,700	143,600	118,800
Total current liab.	962,200	942,900	776,300
Long-term debt	407,900	381,400	124,700
Other long-term liab.	108,400	124,000	74,600
Total liabilities	£1,478,500	£1,448,300	£ 975,600
Shareholders' Equity			
Preferred stock	£ 300	N.A.	£ 3,300
Net common stock	174,400	£ 173,600	150,400
Capital surplus	95,800	36,700	33,000
Retained earnings	115,800	167,600	88,800
Miscellaneous	381,600	217,400	210,500
Total shareholders' eq.	767,900	595,300	486,000
Minority interest	116,000	85,200	91,200
Tot. liab. & net worth	£2,362,400	£2,128,800	£1,552,800
1 £ =	$1.93	$1.61	$1.81

Income Statement
(in thousands, sterling)

	Fiscal Year Ending		
	12/29/90	12/30/89	12/31/88
Net sales	£3,146,100	£2,766,700	£2,381,600
Cost of goods sold	1,738,400	1,596,900	1,365,000
Gross profit	£1,407,700	£1,179,800	£1,016,600
Sell., gen., & admin. exp..	£1,074,700	£ 907,500	£ 787,800
Income before int. and tax	333,000	272,300	228,800
Nonoperating inc.	3,800	3,100	4,400
Interest expense	57,200	31,100	17,500
Income before taxes	279,600	234,300	215,700
Taxes and misc. expenses	100,020	85,500	75,200
Income before ex. items	179,580	157,800	140,500
Extraordinary items	N.A.	15,200	28,400
Net Income.	£ 179,400	£ 164,000	£ 168,900
1 £ =.	$1.93	$1.61	$1.81

N.A. means not applicable.
Sources: Compact Disclosure; *The Wall Street Journal,* various issues.

Case 13

PWH CORPORATION

INTRODUCTION

1   Technological advances coupled with sweeping demographic and sociological trends have dramatically altered a number of once-stable industries, such as automobile manufacturing, food retailing, and investment banking. Perhaps nowhere have these factors combined to transform an industry as substantively as in health care services. Whereas once there were hospitals and doctors' offices, now there are HMOs and PPOs, urgent care and continuous care, wellness centers and health fairs, and birthing centers and trauma centers. The array of specialized services offered by the modern health care organization directly reflects the changing nature of modern society.

2   Over the course of its 27-year existence, PWH Corporation and its affiliates illustrate the shifting nature of health care services. Today PWH's array of services contribute to its mission:

3   We are dedicated to protecting the health of our community. Our family of organizations offers your family the keys to a better quality of life. We do more than diagnose and cure illness—we help you to develop a lifestyle that promotes well-being.[1]

4   PWH corporation and its primary subsidiary, Prince William Hospital Corporation, are located in the city of Manassas in Prince William County in northern Virginia (see Figure 1). Prince William County is approximately 25 miles southwest of Washington, D.C.; 50 miles southwest of Baltimore, Maryland; and 80 miles north of Richmond, Virginia. The hospital is located on State Route 234 on a campus of approximately 55 acres. The facility is approximately three miles south of Interstate Route 66, a main east-west artery into Washington that provides easy access to the hospital.

THE DEVELOPMENT OF PRINCE WILLIAM HOSPITAL CORPORATION

5   The hospital got its start in 1959 when the Manassas Kiwanis Club took on itself to determine whether Prince William County had the population and interest to support the building of a hospital. In the meantime, members of the Kiwanis began to recruit physicians, mostly internists and surgeons, to come into the area on the assurance that a hospital was imminent.

6   As things progressed there was a need to raise money through an ongoing hospital association. The unanimous choice to head the association was civic leader Caton Merchant, founder the Merchant Tire Company.

7   It was estimated that $1.5 million would be needed to get the project off the ground. A federal program would provide matching funds, so the association needed to raise $750,000. Merchant set

This case was prepared by Keith Robbins of the School of Business Administration at George Mason University. Development of this case was made possible by a grant from the Funds of Excellence Program of the State Council of Higher Education for Virginia.

[1] PWH annual report, 1989

FIGURE 1
Location of Prince William Hospital and PWH Corporation

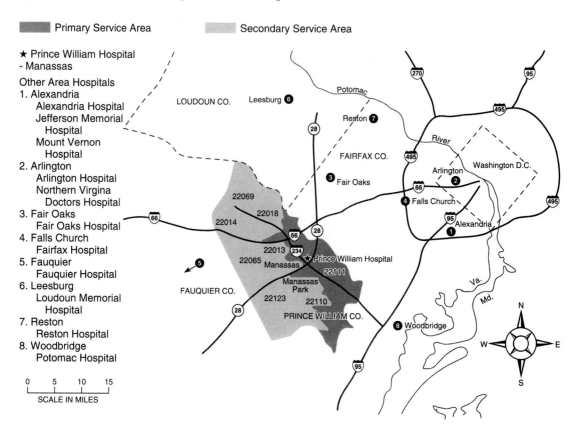

out to visit his personal acquaintances in the community, asking for donations of between $10,000 and $25,000. In return, they were given a room to dedicate as they chose.

8   At this time the hospital association hired the consulting firm of Sanger and Beale out of Richmond. Dr. Sanger was the chancellor of the Medical College of Virginia and Walter Beale was the director of Norfolk General Hospital. The consultants reported an urgent need for at least a 60-bed facility to serve the rapidly growing community, and they provided guidance in terms of forming a board of directors and structuring the administration of the proposed hospital. Thus, the founding of the hospital was due to the cooperative efforts of individuals, businesses, and civic organizations, all of whom contributed time and money to the project. Ultimately, the city of Manassas donated the 16 acres on which the hospital opened in June of 1964.

9   The hospital board hired its first administrator from North Carolina. He came in and oversaw construction of the hospital and its opening on June 26, 1964. Sadly, the administrator died six weeks after the hospital was opened.

10   Caton Merchant continued as the driving force behind the hospital association and hired the hospital's second administrator, I. B. Heinemann, from Roanoke. The Manassas-born Heinemann quickly gained a reputation as a skilled administrator. His knowledge of the community, along with sound fiscal policies, ensured that the hospital was operated from a strong financial base.

11   Heinemann spearheaded the effort to obtain accreditation, which he felt was essential in attaining public acceptance of the new hospital. Prince William Hospital applied for accreditation from the Joint Commission on Accreditation of Hospitals on March 10, 1966. The joint commission is comprised of four national medical and hospital organizations: the American College of Physicians, the American College of Surgeons, the American Hospital Association, and the American Medical Association.

12   Accreditation involved inspection of the hospital's physical plant, housekeeping, pharmacy, emergency room, dietary services, laboratory, and emergency power system. Each were described as in "excellent working order." Accreditation was received on January 26, 1967. Heinemann resigned once accreditation was received.

13   E. L. Derring was interviewed for the vacated position at this time by Caton Merchant. Derring was employed as an associate administrator at Roanoke Memorial Hospitals, running their rehabilitation center. According to Derring, he was a "little fish in a big pond" and decided to accept the job and become a big fish in a small pond. On February 23, 1967, Derring accepted the position at a financial sacrifice to get the opportunity to prove himself as a hospital administrator.

14   The hospital opened originally with 60 beds, 20 physicians, and 100 employees. Of the 60 beds, 40 were medical and surgical and 20 were obstetrics (OB). Though the consultants had determined an urgent need for at least this number of beds, the hospital was consistently operating at a mere 40 percent occupancy. Derring attributed the low occupancy rate to his belief that a lot of people still were not sure of this "country hospital" and, therefore, were going into Washington or Fairfax County for their treatment.

15   The crucial supplier of patients to hospitals is physicians. Derring pondered the nature of the occupancy problem for a month. He had inherited what he found to be a well-run and orderly hospital, but the food was not pleasing and the nursing was terrible. Even more disturbing was the poor relationship between the medical staff and hospital management.

16   At this point, Derring made appointments with each of his 20 physicians, got in his personal automobile, and visited them at their homes or offices. He asked them what they wanted from the hospital. Their responses were remarkably consistent; they all wanted the same things: cleanliness, good food, good nursing, an anesthesiologist M.D., and a cystology room.

17   He struck a bargain with the physicians: if they could help increase patient occupancy, then he would have the financial capability to provide these hoped-for changes. In one month's time, hospital occupancy jumped from 40 percent to 85 percent and then in rapid succession to 100 percent and eventually 120 percent, which meant that the hospital literally had patients out in the hallway. At this point, according to Derring, the hospital encountered a situation of diminishing returns. The additional revenues were eroded by the additional costs associated with an overburdened system.

18   Within one year after Derring's arrival it was evident that the hospital needed to expand to meet increasing demand. This scenario has been played out many times over the years, as evidenced by the steady growth in the hospital's physical facility.

19   The hospital's latest expansion, a $22 million construction program now nearing completion, is enabling Prince William Hospital to update and expand a wide range of services. Already finished are a new Addiction Treatment Center, a Birthing Center, and a critical care unit, as well as new operating rooms. The pediatric unit and psychiatric center have been moved into expanded quarters in the new wing.

20   The bulk of the expansion effort will be allocated to a new five-story medical health care center. It will contain the new main entrance, admissions, and registration. The hospital's business office, physicians' offices, and outpatient services also will be in the building. PWH Corporation, the parent company, will be located on the top floor, along with a conference center for meetings and educational programs. The structure will increase the hospital's profile, since it will be visible from quite a distance. Grand opening is scheduled for fall 1991.

21   Table 1 contains a five-year summary of Prince William Hospital Corporation's income statement. The statements show a steady increase in revenues over the period. This, combined with the fact that Prince William is recognized as the cost leader in northern Virginia, allows the corporation to continually reinvest in upgraded services for its clients.

PWH AFFILIATED BUSINESSES

22   PWH Corporation was formed in 1984 as the holding corporation for its affiliates, including Prince William Hospital Corporation. The reorganization was spurred by Caton Merchant's untimely death in August of 1983. Until this time, Merchant had served as president and Derring as executive vice president.

23   Originally, 10 corporations were under the PWH Corporate umbrella: the hospital, the nursing home, the retirement facility, home health program, the foundation, two credit bureaus, a durable medical equipment company that had under it a health fair store in the mall, and a physician billing company that has since gone out of business. Derring was in charge of running all 10 companies but, after a board of directors retreat for planning in 1986, it became evident that, because of the now diverse functions of the holding company, Derring needed to spend more of his time at that level.

24   Derring became president and CEO of the holding company and oversaw operations of the various boards. Kenneth Swenson, who had served as assistant administrator of the hospital since 1974, was named president of the hospital, Harley Tabak was appointed as president of the nursing home and retirement community (Long Term Care Corporation), and Garnett C. Ball was designated senior vice president of the holding company, PWH Corporation (see Exhibit 1).

25   Today, PWH Corporation is comprised of nine companies, the hospital being the flagship and accountable for 75 percent of the revenues. Among the smaller affiliates some make money; others are marginal losers. The corporation grossed $72 million in its most recently completed fiscal year. With 1,200 employees in all companies, PWH is the third-largest employer in the county after the county government itself and IBM. The hospital has 180 physicians on its staff.

26   In addition to the hospital there are five other not-for-profit, nonstock Virginia business affiliates: Long Term Care Corporation, PWH Home Health Care, Inc., PWH Foundation, PWH Personal Care Corporation, PWH Child Care Center, Inc., and Medical Collection Bureau, Inc. Under the PWH corporate umbrella is a for-profit holding company, Fiscal Corporation, Ltd., that is comprised of two for-profit table corporations: Creative Collection Bureau, Inc., and PWH Medical Supply, Inc. (see Figure 2).

27   Through the years PWH Corporation, in responding to the health needs of the community that it services, has evolved into much more than a hospital. The corporation now operates a nursing home, a retirement home, a child care center, and a medical equipment company. It has entered joint ventures with other health care organizations to provide urgent care facilities and liability or malpractice insurance coverage. But perhaps the most dramatic departure from the past is evidenced by the corporation's current emphasis on the prevention side of health care. The following sections will detail the circumstances and decision-making processes that accompanied the corporation's diversification.

LONG-TERM CARE

28   When Prince William bought the nursing home in 1979, few hospitals in Virginia—or the nation—owned long-term care facilities. Manassas Manor, however, had a serious licensing problem with the Virginia Department of Health and the community turned to its hospital for help.

29   According to Derring, "The privately operated nursing home in Manassas was run so badly that the health department wanted to shut it down. I had a friend who was a licensor of nursing homes for the state. He explained the situation and the need for these patients and thus we acquired the nursing home."

30   The facility was bought and renamed Annaburg Manor and so remained available to area residents. Today, Annaburg Manor offers extended care for older adults and for any patient disabled by injury or illness. The facility houses the only ward in northern Virginia dedicated to the care of patients having Alzheimer's disease.

31   The 54-bed unit is secured via locked doors and elevators. The patients are free to roam the hallways as they choose, but they wear electronic bracelets that trigger an alarm if they try to leave the ward. Alzheimer's patients often become disoriented and lose their sense of reality; therefore, Annaburg offers an environmental stimulation support group.

32   According to the Alzheimer's Disease and Related Disorders Association, 1 in every 100 people 65 years or older suffers from Alzheimer's. The debilitating affliction slowly deteriorates the nervous system and leaves its victim helpless. The chances of developing the disease increase with age—it strikes on average 20 of every 100 Americans over the age of 85. According to ADRDA, Alzheimer's is the fourth leading killer of Americans.

33   Caton Merchant House personal care apartments were opened on the Annaburg Manor campus in 1986. The 78-unit facility represents PWH's response to the housing needs of older adults. Residents occupy a private apartment and are provided with optional nursing support, daily meals, and other services. This arrangement is suitable for those individuals who do not require nursing home care but who are unable to live independently.

34   "Caton Merchant home is for folks in their 80s not ready to go into a nursing home," says Derring. "Perhaps they forget to take their medicine or have trouble with the dosage; Caton Merchant House provides this service. They have an emergency pull cord if they get in trouble. They are provided three meals a day. These people typically don't care to bother with cooking or preparing food for themselves."

35   The retirement home industry has grown in response to the inability of many of today's households to support an extended family. Derring says that today most families are dual-career, requiring two incomes to support their preferred lifestyle given today's cost of living; "They can't afford to give up one income source to stay at home and care for an elderly relative."

36   According to Derring, Annaburg Manor stays completely filled all the time. Caton Merchant House averages 60 to 65 percent occupancy, which he expects to increase steadily to full capacity in the coming years.

37   When PWH made the decision to purchase the nursing home, the next issue to be resolved was the hiring of an administrator. Derring called a friend at an Alexandria, Virginia, nursing home and asked for his recommendation. His recommendation, it turned out, was sitting in his office at the time of Derring's call in the person of then 22-year-old Harley Tabak.

38   According to Derring, it was quite a stroke of good fortune, for Tabak has "put Annaburg Manor on the map and was the driving force behind the decision to expand the business to include a retirement home."

39   Also, "Harley Tabak is an outstanding man in the industry in the state, as demonstrated by his status as immediate past president of the State Nursing Home Association of the state of Virginia," says Derring. "He runs a very tight organization. He gives quality care to all the residents, which stems from the fact that he has personal compassion for them." This compassion was strengthened by the fact that Tabak's grandfather, a cancer victim, spent the last three months of his life at Annaburg Manor.

40   Says Tabak, "I learned a lot about what a nursing home looks like through the eyes of a family member, as opposed to what it looks like to a staff member. I became much more empathetic to the

TABLE 1
Prince William Hospital Corporation
Revenue and Expense Summaries for the Years Ended September 30, 1984, 1985, 1986, 1987, and 1988, and for the Five Months Ended February 28, 1988 and 1989

	For the Years Ended September 30					For the Five Months Ended February 28	
	1984	1985	1986	1987	1988	1988	1989
Operating revenues:							
Revenue	$28,533,584	$27,222,702	$32,201,787	$37,136,440	$42,962,589	$17,654,830	$18,868,731
Reductions of revenue*	4,567,690	4,006,298	5,883,828	7,163,618	9,610,584	4,150,065	3,770,646
Net patient service revenue . .	23,965,894	23,216,404	26,317,959	29,972,822	33,352,005	13,504,765	15,098,085
Other operating revenues . . .	597,391	698,391	408,238	559,417	450,855	194,158	155,234
Total	24,563,285	23,914,795	26,726,197	30,532,239	33,802,860	13,698,923	15,253,319
Other expenses:							
Nursing	7,437,001	7,035,915	8,340,122	10,556,619	13,406,996	5,312,901	6,110,646
Other professional services . .	6,481,467	5,510,931	6,173,698	6,729,932	7,516,898	3,003,996	3,500,285
General services	3,044,983	2,987,267	3,077,852	3,340,214	3,825,548	1,434,162	1,556,321
Fiscal services	1,522,453	1,384,619	1,614,256	1,574,353	1,735,668	696,301	828,805
Administrative services . . .	2,932,272	3,137,468	3,403,401	3,794,061	4,230,168	1,680,383	1,751,976
Interest	140,764	156,839	254,858	241,260	215,552	95,061	84,470
Depreciation.	1,081,980	1,145,208	1,229,489	1,394,770	1,633,503	658,241	735,861
Total	22,640,920	21,358,247	24,093,676	27,631,209	32,564,333	12,881,045	14,568,364
Excess of operating revenues over operating expenses—Hospital . . .	1,922,365	2,556,548	2,632,521	2,901,030	1,238,527	817,878	684,955

Nonoperating revenue:							
Unrestricted gifts	89,339	64,327	141,828	116,466	241,793	229,870	167,872
Income on investments:							
Limited by agreement with third-party payors	312,079	363,529	499,388	473,051	742,218	241,488	265,674
Limited by board for future operations and improvements	6,038	10,817	14,019	22,384	52,724	17,064	23,416
Other		6,311					
Other	407,456	444,984	655,235	611,901	1,036,735	488,422	456,962
Excess of revenue over expenses—Hospital	2,329,821	3,001,532	3,287,756	3,512,931	2,275,262	1,306,300	1,141,917
Income from Nursing Home Division†	433,991						
Excess of revenues over expenses	$ 2,763,812	$ 3,001,532	$ 3,287,756	$ 3,512,931	$ 2,275,262	$ 1,306,300	$ 1,141,917

*In 1988, the corporation experienced a significant increase in uncollectible patient accounts. As a result of this, management elected to increase the provision for uncollectible accounts by $865,000 at year end. A pro rata portion of this adjustment is included in the February 28, 1988, period; for the February 28, 1989, period, a favorable Medicare cost report settlement for a prior year amounting to $202,864 is recorded.
†For the year ended September 30, 1984, the corporation's activities included an acute care hospital and a nursing home. Effective October 1, 1984, under a plan of reorganization, the nursing home operation became a separate corporate entity, with the corporation leasing the nursing home facility to the new corporate entity. The income from Nursing Home Division shown above represents the net revenues and expenses of the Nursing Home Division.

EXHIBIT 1
Management of PWH Corporation and Major Affiliates

Elwyn Lanier Derring, president and chief executive officer, PWH Corporation (61).   Mr. Derring has been associated with the hospital and PWH Corporation since 1967. He served for 21 years and administrator and chief executive officer of the hospital before assuming his current responsibilities in 1988. Mr. Derring earned a BS degree in business administration from Virginia Commonwealth University in 1953 and a master's degree in hospital administration from the Medical College of Virginia in 1958. Before joining the hospital, Mr. Derring served as an associate director at Roanoke Memorial Hospital, prior to which he was an administrative resident and assistant administrator at Richmond Memorial Hospital. He is past president of the Virginia Hospital Association and recently has completed a six-year term as the Virginia delegate to the American Hospital Association. Mr. Derring is a member of the board of directors of the Virginia Hospital Insurance Reciprocal and a fellow of the American College of Healthcare Executives.

Kenneth B. Swenson, president/administrator and chief executive officer, Prince William Hospital Corporation (45).   Mr. Swenson has been associated with the hospital since 1972. His service began as assistant administrator, with his responsibilities and title progressing to his current position. Mr. Swenson has a bachelor of science degree from the University of Evansville (1970) and a master's degree in health care administration from Georgia State University (1972). He served as a sergeant in the U.S. Army during the war in Vietnam. Prior to his service at the hospital, Mr. Swenson served as administrative resident at Roanoke Memorial Hospital. Mr. Swenson is a member of the American College Health Care Executives and the board of directors of Voluntary Hospitals of America. He is also a member of the Virginia Hospital Association and is a past president of the District of Columbia/Maryland/Virginia Hospital Association. Mr. Swenson served as the chairman for the 1988 Prince William County United Way campaign. He is currently chairman of the executive committee of the Prince William United Way. He is also chairman of the regional policy council of the Virginia Hospital Association and a member of the board of directors of the Virginia Insurance Reciprocal.

Harley L. Tabak, president and chief executive officer, Long Term Care Corporation and PWH Personal Care Corporation (35).   Mr. Tabak has been associated with the hospital and PWH Corporation since 1979. He has a bachelor of arts in religious studies from Franklin and Marshal College (1976) and a master of arts in health care administration from George Washington University (1979). He has published many professional papers and has served as an expert witness in court proceedings dealing with nursing home administration. Mr. Tabak is a past president of the Virginia Health Care Association and is a member of the American Hospital Association and a certified fellow of the American College of Health Care Administrators.

family members' plight. We don't know how these patients were when they didn't have these problems. We see them as how they are, not as how they used to be before the stroke, before the cancer."

41   With the first baby boomers turning 65 in 2010, housing and health care for older adults will become increasingly important. PWH Corporation is leading the way—as did the hospital that bought a nursing home in 1979.

CHILD CARE

42   The child care center originally was conceived to deal with the child care needs of PWH Corporation employees. "We did two internal surveys that showed we could fill it with just our own employees' children; but when we opened, it didn't turn out that way," says Derring. "Consequently we decided to open it to the public. Now, we can accommodate at any one time 125 children. It is making money; not a lot, but it is in the black. It is the only accredited child care center in the area. This is quite an advantage. It is well run. Presently our patrons are 60 percent PWH employees and 40 percent general public."

FIGURE 2
PWH Corporation Corporate Structure

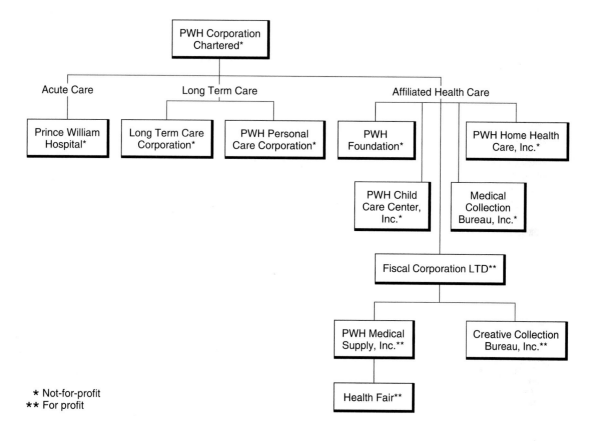

★ Not-for-profit
★★ For profit

43   Derring added, "We are looking into the possibility of expanding this service to accommodate an additional 40 children and to provide an expanded learning center or classroom. Much of the facility's recreational space has been filled with overflow beds to accommodate expanding demand."

44   According to Derring, the child care center presently has a waiting list of over 100 children. The facility is located directly behind the hospital.

HEALTH FAIR

45   The health fair, located in Manassas Mall, offers books, audio and video tapes, self-care products, and children's items—all related to health and wellness. The health fair is a for-profit operation that is way in the red.

46   The health fair emphasized the preventive side of health care, including weight control, stop smoking, and proper nutrition. Derring says this is a very underdeveloped dimension of health care; "most people do not think in terms of preventive maintenance."

47   The store has been a boon for public relations. Unfortunately, if the health fair doesn't show signs of improving in the near future, PWH may consider closing it due to losses, says Derring.

TABLE 2

Combining Statement of Income
For the Year Ended September 30, 1990

	Combined	PWH Corporation	PWH Foundation, Inc.	Prince William Corporation
Gross revenue	$69,587,462		$ 225	$57,388,690
Reductions of revenue	18,206,868			15,961,400
Net revenue	51,380,594		225	41,427,290
Other operating revenue	620,219			555,044
Total operating revenue	52,000,813		225	41,982,334
Operating expenses:				
Salaries and wages.	25,164,895		31,219	19,277,308
Supplies and other expenses	20,995,205	$3,225	30,443	17,332,206
Provision for depreciation	2,483,226	785	360	1,966,120
Total operating expenses	48,643,326	4,010	62,022	38,575,534
Income from operations.	3,357,487	(4,010)	(61,767)	3,406,800
Nonoperating revenues:				
Contributions (net).	153,231		11,896	149,337
Income on investments:				
Fund depreciation	819,716			753,356
Funds for future operations and improvements	154,887			85,631
Other.		573	4,103	
Total nonoperating revenue	1,127,834	573	15,999	988,324
Excess (deficit) of revenue over expenses	$ 4,485,321	$(3,437)	$45,768	$ 4,395,124

*Medical Collection Bureau, Inc., contributed $40,000 to Prince William Hospital Corporation. Had this contribution not been made, Medical Collection Inc., would have had an excess of revenue over expenses of $11,038.

A BRIEF DESCRIPTION OF OTHER AFFILIATED CORPORATIONS

48   PWH Home Health Care, Inc., is a service offering private duty nursing, personal care, and rehabilitation services to patients in their own home or in the hospital setting.

49   Medical Collection Bureau, Inc., was formed to serve as a collection agency to service charged-off patient accounts. The for-profit holding company is Fiscal Corporation, L.T.D., which controls through stock ownership the Creative Collection Bureau, Inc. (CCB), and PWH Medical Supply, Inc. CCB operates as a collection agency serving private businesses. PWH Medical Supply was formed as a medical equipment and supply company to rent medical equipment and to provide disposable medical supplies necessary for patient recuperation or rehabilitation.

50   The PWH Foundation is responsible for fund-raising and promoting the overall organization and its needs. Over $200,000 has been raised in just over a year since its inception, mostly by way of

Long Term Care Corporation	PWH Personal Care Corporation	PWH Home Health Service, Inc.	Medical Collection Bureau, Inc.	PWH Child Care Center, Inc.	Creative Collection Bureau, Inc.	PWH Medical Supply, Inc.
$9,197,195	$1,142,615	$294,847	$494,167	$437,418	$195,519	$585,329
2,187,994						57,474
7,009,201	1,142,615	294,847	494,167	437,418	195,519	527,855
122,862						100,000
7,132,063	1,142,615	294,847	494,167	437,418	195,519	627,855
4,379,862	261,329	238,796	282,192	303,940	92,595	189,755
2,495,501	85,218	45,279	194,211	131,219	88,268	615,566
26,883	154,777	827	8,551	4,891	3,700	33,151
6,902,246	1,201,324	284,902	484,954	440,050	184,563	838,472
229,817	(58,709)	9,945	9,213	(2,632)	10,956	(210,617)
30,958			(40,000)*			
66,360						
69,256						
	1,788	1,266	1,825	1,675	1,913	426
166,574	1,788	1,266	(38,175)	1,675	1,913	426
$ 396,391	$ (56,921)	$11,211	$ (28,962)	$ (957)	$ 12,869	$(210,191)

$1,000 or $10,000 contributions. An affiliated group is known as Friends of the Foundation. This is a group designed for younger individuals with social functions for a $25 per year subscriber fee.

51   Table 2 contains consolidated and separate 1990 income statements for PWH Corporation and its affiliates. The hospital accounts for 82 percent ($57 million) of the corporation's $69 million revenues. It is approximately six times larger than Long Term Care, which is the second leading revenue producer, at $9 million.

SERVICES AND SERVICE-CAPACITY PLANNING

52   PWH Corporation clearly faces an increasingly complex external environment. General environmental factors, such as shifting demographics, increasing emphasis by society on wellness, and economic fluctuations, can have a profound impact on the demand for health care service. Competitive environmental factors, such as increasing costs from suppliers of insurance and medicine, substitute

services, such as urgent care facilities, and the emergence of both profit and not-for-profit specialized services facilities, to name a few, have dramatically altered the structure of the health care service industry.

53   In the past, PWH has responded to marketplace opportunities in an ad-hoc or piecemeal fashion. The results have been largely successful. However, due to increasing environmental complexity, the corporation has formed a task force to implement a systematic and integrative strategic planning effort.

54   Says Derring, "We are trying to develop a system that promotes coordination of efforts so that we can consolidate the planning effort into a cohesive, ongoing strategic planning effort from the corporate perspective. We are in the middle of developing this process."

55   The development of the planning program is being done by the members of the holding company staff and by board members with a special emphasis on equal representation of the various companies comprising the corporation. The planning program will place special emphasis on the hospital and long-term care businesses, since they account for the overwhelming proportion of PWH's revenues.

FORECAST ASSUMPTIONS

56   This financial forecast presents PWH Corporation's expectations for the forecast period. Accordingly, the forecast reflects management's judgment, as of the date of this feasibility study, of the expected conditions and its expected course of action. The assumptions disclosed herein are those that the management of Prince William Hospital Corporation (hereafter referred to as the Hospital) believe are significant to the forecast. There will usually be differences between forecasted and actual results, because events and circumstances frequently do not occur as expected, and those differences may be material.

HOSPITAL BED COMPLEMENT

57   The current registered bed complement and the registered bed complement on completion of the latest expansion of the Hospital are presented as follows:

	Hospital Bed Complement	
Service	**Current Licensed Beds**	**Forecasted Licensed Beds**
Medical/surgical	114	105
Obstetrics	14	14
Pediatrics	8	8
Psychiatric	12	12
Alcohol/chemical dependency	19	31
Total beds	170	170
Nursery bassinets	16	20
Total beds and bassinets	186	190

58   Prince William Hospital is a general acute care hospital offering a full-range of services, including CT scan and nuclear medicine. In addition, the Hospital has received the certificate of need approval for a mobile magnetic resonance imaging (MRI) unit, as a joint venture with Fauquier Hospital and Mary Washington Hospital.

ANALYSIS OF DEMAND FOR HEALTH CARE SERVICES

59   A forecast of Hospital utilization has been prepared by Hospital management and tested for reasonableness to provide guidance for strategic planning. The results of this utilization forecast are summarized as follows:

	Actual			
	1986	**1987**	**1988**	**1988**
Available beds	170	170	170	170
Bassinets	16	16	16	16
Admissions	6,609	6,900	7,068	7,352
Patient days.	41,405	40,967	40,190	40,235
Average length of stay.	6.26	5.93	5.69	5.47
Emergency room visits	30,103	32,422	34,005	36,219
Outpatient visits	24,818	27,915	31,000	35,927
Home health visits	N.A.	N.A.	3,015	9,662

	Forecasted				
	1989	**1990**	**1991**	**1992**	**1993**
Available beds	170	170	170	170	170
Bassinets	16	16	20	20	20
Admissions.	7,608	7,877	8,151	8,367	8,586
Patient days	40,499	42,078	44,322	45,600	46,848
Average length of stay	5.32	5.34	5.44	5.45	5.46
Emergency room visits	37,949	39,345	40,763	41,790	42,816
Outpatient visits	38,750	41,369	43,498	45,038	46,605
Home health visits.	9,636	9,603	9,754	9,999	10,245

60   Inpatient and outpatient utilization, as indicated on the table above, are forecasted to increase during the forecast period.

INPATIENT UTILIZATION

61   Medical/surgical and critical care admissions have been forecasted to increase from 1989 to 1993. This is due in part to the increasing service area population (13.3 percent) for the medical/surgical population group. In addition, the Medicare population (age group 65+) is forecasted by National Planning Data Corporation (NPDC) to increase by 44.9 percent from 1988 to 1993, which represents an increase of 1,935 persons.

62   Over the past several years, medical/surgical use rates at the Hospital have decreased from 74.69 admissions per 1,000 population in 1985 to 72.57 admissions per 1,000 population in 1988. The 1988 use rate of 72.57 is up from the 1987 use rate of 71 per 1,000 population. Use rates are calculated by dividing the admissions to a particular service of the Hospital by the appropriate service area population and multiplying the result by 1,000. The result is the admissions use rate per 1,000 total population. The use rate for medical/surgical care is anticipated to increase 1.2 percent during the forecast period.

63   This assumption is supported by many factors. Management believes that this increase will be due primarily to the strategic location of the Hospital. It is very near a fast-growing area of Prince William County and increases are expected to continue throughout the forecast period. In addition, the service area population during the forecast period will experience shifting demographics, whereby the over-65 population will become much larger.

64   The over-65 age group historically utilizes a hospital much more than other age groups. The Hospital will experience increase in its Medicare admissions above historical levels due to this fact. Last, the state of Virginia estimates that usage of medical/surgical specialties in hospitals in northern Virginia will increase over the historical levels. This is partly due to the expected increase in population and also is due to the state's forecasted increase of medical/surgical utilization.

65   The average length of stay (ALOS) for medical/surgical patients declined at the Hospital during the years 1985 through 1987. In 1988, the average length of stay for medical/surgical patients increased slightly. The average length of stay is forecasted to increase slightly through the forecasted period. This assumption follows previous assumptions related to forecasted increase of Medicare admissions. These patients are older and normally are more seriously ill patients and require more care and longer periods of recovery. Lengths of stay related to these patients are higher than other age groups. With the increase in the over-65 patient mix and a stable length of stay for the other age groups, Hospital's ALOS will increase slightly during the forecasted period.

66   Total medical/surgical patient days at the Hospital, the product of admissions and the average length of stay, have remained stable over the past several years. During the forecast period, medical/surgical patient days are projected to increase by 12.8 percent. This increase is due mainly to the increasing population and to a relatively stable average length of stay.

67   Obstetric admissions have been forecasted to increase during the forecast period. This appears likely due to the increase in the service area population of females age 15 to 44, from 23,462 in 1988 to 24,424 in 1993, an increase of 4.1 percent. Additionally, several young physicians specializing in obstetrics/gynecology have joined the medical staff in recent years, and their practice should continue to mature. The obstetrics/gynecology use rate has increased in each of the last four years, and it is forecasted to continue to increase slightly over present levels.

68   The ALOS for obstetric/gynecology patients has declined in each of the past four years (from 2.88 days in 1985 to 2.35 days in 1988). The ALOS is expected to further decrease but not less than two days. Management believes that it is unlikely that the Hospital will be able to decrease the obstetric/gynecology length of stay below such level. A stable ALOS, coupled with increasing admissions, results in increasing patient days during the forecast period.

69   Pediatric utilization, in terms of admissions, is forecasted to increase during the forecast period. The increase is driven by population growth of 14.5 percent in the service area age group of 0 to 14 years. The pediatric use rate has been stable over the past four years, and it is expected to remain stable during the forecast period. The pediatric average length of stay has declined in each of the past four years and is forecasted to decline further. Patient days are forecasted to increase slightly during the period, because the growth in admissions outweighs the decline in the average length of stay.

70   Psychiatric admissions are forecasted to increase significantly during the forecast period. The rate of increase, however, is less than the historical rate of increase in psychiatric admissions at the Hospital. The continued increase can be attributed to population growth, enhanced community awareness of the Hospital's program, and continued maturing physician practices.

71   The use rate for psychiatric admissions has increased dramatically over the past four years. The forecasted use rate is estimated to continue to increase, but at a decreasing rate. The ALOS for psychiatric admissions has declined in each of the past four years. The forecasted ALOS continues to decrease early in the forecast period and then stabilizes later in the period. The increasing level of

admissions, coupled with a declining ALOS, results in a slight increase in psychiatric patient days during the forecast period.

72   The addiction treatment center (ATC) admissions are forecasted to increase significantly during the forecast period. The increase is attributable to several factors, including the increased scope of the program to include adolescents, an increase in the bed complement of the unit, the enhanced facility upon completion of the project, the continued maturing of physician practices, enhanced community program awareness, and population growth.

73   ALOS for ATC patients has been relatively stable and is forecasted to remain stable during the forecast period. Total patient days for the unit are forecasted to increase, due to increasing admissions coupled with a stable ALOS.

74   Nursery admissions are forecasted to increase during the forecast period as a result of the increase in forecasted obstetric admissions. The average length of stay for nursery patients has been relatively stable, and it is forecasted to remain stable during the forecast period. Patient days in the nursery are forecasted to increase during the forecast period as a result of the increase in nursery admissions.

OUTPATIENT UTILIZATION

75   Emergency room visits have increased each of the past four years; they are forecasted to continue to increase during the forecast period. The rate of increase during the forecast period is less than the historical rate of increase. The emergency room use rate has increased each of the last four years, and it is forecasted to continue to increase at a decreasing rate. Coupled with an increasing population in the service area, this results in continued growth in emergency room volume.

76   Outpatient visits are forecasted to increase during the forecast period. The increase can be attributed to increasing outpatient use rate, increasing service area population, and an enhanced capability to provide outpatient services upon completion of the project.

77   Inpatient ancillary volumes, based on relatively stable intensity levels, are forecasted to:

1. Continue to increase in the areas of surgical procedures, respiratory treatments, laboratory tests, EKGs, EEGs, nuclear medicine procedures, physical therapy treatments, occupational therapy treatments, radiology examinations, and CT scans.
2. Be stable in the areas of cardiac rehabilitation treatments, pulmonary rehabilitation treatments, and speech therapy treatments.

78   Outpatient ancillary volumes, based on relatively stable intensity levels, are forecasted to:

1. Continue to increase in the areas of surgical procedures, respiratory treatments, laboratory tests, EKGs, EEGs, nuclear medicine procedures, cardiac rehabilitation treatments, pulmonary rehabilitation treatments, physical therapy treatments, radiology examinations, and CT scans.
2. Be stable in the areas of speech therapy and occupational therapy treatments.

79   As support for the utilization forecasts, analyses have been prepared and consideration given to the following critical success factors:

Hospital history, physical condition, and programs.

Service area definition and description.

Service area population trends, demographic information, and economic characteristics.

Area hospitals and competitive factors.

Areawide bed need.

Virginia Department of Health Planning.

District Eight market share.

Analysis of medical staff composition.

Medical staff recruitment.

Alternative delivery system activity.

Medical staff support for the Hospital and its programs.

Historical utilization levels and use rates.

80   The results of these analyses are presented in the following service area environmental assessment.

SERVICE AREA POPULATION TRENDS: DEMOGRAPHIC AND ECONOMIC

Hospital Service Area Definition and Description

81   In Virginia, cities and counties are not overlapping units of government. The Hospital facility is located in the city of Manassas (the City). The City and the adjacent City of Manassas Park are surrounded on three sides by Prince William County. The Hospital is located on Route 234, a major route in the county approximately three miles south of Interstate 66. The City is located approximately 30 miles west of Washington, D.C.

82   Determination of the relevant service area for the Hospital was made by analyzing historical admissions by zip code of patient residence.

83   The primary service area of the Hospital was determined to be zip code areas 22110 and 22111, composed primarily of the City of Manassas and the City of Manassas Park. This area has consistently accounted for approximately two thirds of Hospital's admissions.

84   The secondary service area of the Hospital was determined to be the area defined by the following zip codes:

22013 Bristow.

22014 Broad Run.

22018 Catharpin.

22065 Gainesville.

22069 Haymarket.

22123 Nokesville.

85   These zip code areas lie contiguously to the west of the identified primary service area and have historically accounted for approximately 13 percent of the Hospital's admissions. The primary and secondary service area, when combined, determine the Hospital's total service area.

86   Information pertaining to historical hospital admissions from the primary and secondary service area is presented in the following table:

Historical Percentage of Admissions

Zip Code	Community	For the 12 Months Ending September 30			
		1985	1986	1987	1988
Primary Service Area:					
22110	North Manassas	49.0%	49.8%	49.8%	51.1%
22111	South Manassas	16.8	17.8	17.1	15.9
Total primary service area		65.8%	67.6%	66.9%	67.0%

Historical Percentage of Admissions

		For the 12 Months Ending September 30			
Zip Code	**Community**	**1985**	**1986**	**1987**	**1988**
Secondary service area:					
22013	Bristow	1.2%	1.2%	1.0%	1.2%
22014	Broad Run	0.3	0.6	0.5	0.5
22018	Catharpin	0.6	0.4	0.5	0.5
22065	Gainesville	3.1	3.3	3.3	2.8
22069	Haymarket	2.8	2.9	2.8	3.1
22123	Nokesville	5.3	4.5	4.9	4.9
Total secondary service area		13.3%	12.9%	13.0%	13.0%
All other admissions		20.9%	19.5%	20.1%	20.0%
Total.		100.0%	100.0%	100.0%	100.0%

Source: Hospital records.

Population Trends

87   The total service area has experienced one of the most rapid population growth rates in the nation for the past quarter century. According to estimates prepared by the National Planning Data Corporation, the primary service area population is currently estimated to be 72,747. This represents a 31.3 percent increase from 1980. By 1993, the population of the primary service area is expected to be 83,598, an additional 14.9 percent increase over present levels. Additionally, according to NPDC, the secondary service area population currently is estimated to be 18,359. This represents at 15.3 percent increase from 1980. By 1993, the population of the secondary service area is expected to be 19,910, an additional increase of 8.45 percent over present levels.

Demographic Information

88   From 1988 to 1993, the elderly population in the primary and secondary service areas, age 65 and over, is expected to increase 40.5 percent from 4,796 to 6,731. In 1980, this age group represented 4.2 percent of the total population; in 1988, 5.3 percent; and, in 1993, this age group is expected to represent 6.5 percent of the total population. These changes are expected to leave an impact on the Hospital's future utilization. During the same time period, the female population age 15 to 44 is expected to increase 4.1 percent from 23,462 to 24,424.

89   The following tables summarize the historical and anticipated population changes in the primary and secondary services areas:

Demographic Information
Primary and Secondary Service Area

Age Group	1990 Census	1988 Estimate	1980–1988 Percent Inc. (Dec.)	1993 Forecasted	1988–1993 Percent Inc. (Dec.)
0–14	20,038	23,059	15.1%	26,392	14.5%
15–64	48,287	63,251	31.0	70,385	11.3
65 and over	2,989	4,796	60.5	6,731	40.4
Total population	71,314	91,106	27.8	103,508	13.6
Female 15–44	19,209	23,462	22.1	24,424	4.1

Source: National Planning Data Corporation (NPDC).

Economic Characteristics

90 The following analyses relate to factors that affect the economic stability of the City of Manassas and Prince William County, including the majority of the Hospital's service area. The economic characteristics of the service area impacts upon the ability of the area to hold and attract residents to a community. Furthermore, the economic composition of the service area affects the financial payor mix of the Hospital.

91 According to the Virginia Employment Commission, 43,623 jobs were within Prince William County as of March 31, 1987. Many industries have located in the county. The major private and public employers in Prince William County and the greater Manassas area include:

Firm	Product or Service	Number of Employees
IBM Corporation*	Semiconductor components	5,000
Prince William Public Schools	Public education	4,820
Prince William County	County government	2,093
Federal Government (DoD)	USMC base, Quantico	1,420
Atlantic Research Corporation	Missile propellants	1,230
Prince William Hospital*	Health care	922
Potomac Hospital	Health care	700
Continental Telephone*	Telephone utility	582
Northern Virginia Community College (NOVA)	Higher education	514
Virginia Electric Power Co.	Electric utility	372
Atlas Machine and Iron Work	Metallurgy	300
No. Va. Electric Coop.	Electric utility	268
Atlantic Foods.	Food distribution	200
Dynapac	Communications	200
Herndon Lumber & Millworks	Wood products	200
Treasure Chest Advertising	Advertising	200

*Located within the cities of Manassas or Manassas Park, or both.
Source: Department of Economic Development.

92   The county has extensive and diversified transportation facilities and is served by over 13 truck-lines, two rail lines, two commercial airports within 25 miles, a municipal airport in the city of Manassas, two major Interstates (I–95 and I–66), and a port facility within 30 miles.

93   Until recently, Prince William County was primarily a residential county with strategically located shopping areas. Now local commerce is expanding, with retail sales increasing 86 percent between 1983 and 1986, from $539 million to over $1 billion. In 1986, over 1 billion square feet of retail space was under construction.

94   An important measure of economic stability in any community is the unemployment rate. The unemployment situation as of December 1988 is illustrated in the following table:

Labor Force Information
Unemployment Rates

Prince William County		City of Manassas	Prince William* County	Va.	U.S.
Labor Force	Unemployed				
104,117†	2,099	1.9%	1.8%	4.1%	5.0%

*Prince William County Chamber of Commerce.
†The number of employees that commute from outside of Prince William County to inside the county is approximately 8,790 persons. Conversely, the number of employees that commute from Prince William County to outside the county is approximately 51,228 persons.
Source: Virginia Employment Commission.

95   Prince William Hospital is the only hospital located in the Hospital's defined primary and secondary service ares. Other hospitals that may be considered as competitors due to their geographic location and the types of services offered include:

	Approximate Miles from Primary Service Area
Alexandria Hospital Alexandria, Virginia	40 miles
Arlington Hospital Arlington, Virginia	40
Fair Oaks Hospital Fair Oaks, Virginia	15
Fairfax Hospital Falls Church, Virginia	20
Fauquier Hospital Warrenton, Virginia	25
Jefferson Memorial Hospital Alexandria, Virginia	40
Loudoun Memorial Hospital Leesburg, Virginia	25
Mount Vernon Hospital Alexandria, Virginia	30
Northern Virginia Doctors Hospital Arlington, Virginia	38
Potomac Hospital Woodbridge, Virginia	18
Reston Hospital Reston, Virginia	20

96   The following tables present the licensed bed complement and the select 1985, 1986, and 1987 comparative data for Prince William Hospital and the hospitals listed above as compiled by Health Care Investment Analysts, Inc., which is an on-line data and analytical service that compiles financial, utilization, and market share data on over 4,500 hospitals in the United States.

THE STRATEGIC PLANNING TASK FORCE

97   The Strategic Planning Task Force was chartered and tasked by the board of PWH Corporation with the responsibility of undertaking "thoughtful analysis of the current health care environment in western Prince William County as well as those health care services and related strategies appropriate for the future."[2]

98   The task force set forth after a review and acceptance of the mission statement and primary objectives.

99   The mission of PWH Corporation is to marshal, manage, and maintain the resources, both human and capital, necessary to guarantee that all citizens have available to them a continuum of quality, cost-effective health services to include physical, mental, and social health well being.

100   To accomplish this mission, the following goals and objectives must be pursued:

In the years to come the PWH Corporation must maintain and enhance its financial integrity in order to ensure access to vital resources.

It is essential that every effort be made to enhance community awareness and support.

New business ventures must be financially sound, and the corporation's position of health care leadership must be maintained.

101   The task force must combine the information from the general external environmental analysis with the major forces in the competitive environment to identify the key issues facing the firms in the coming years. The end result of their work will be a five-year plan, detailing the actions that will be taken by PWH Corporation so it may meet its obligations as set forth in the company mission.

102   The company has responded to the needs of its service area in recent years, as evidenced by the expanding diversity of its businesses. The durable medical products company was founded in response to the emerging trend toward home health. PWH has joined InterNet, which is a PPO that covers the District of Columbia, southern Maryland, and northern Virginia. It is tied in with INNOVA, which is the Fairfax County Hospital System.

103   Derring says that InterNet has just bought a capital area preferred provider unit that has a lot of physicians in it. "We're all a part of that. So we're stepping into this area in a big way. However, this does not preclude us from negotiating with HMOs and PPOs individually. We are also doing that."

104   PWH also has an urgent care center in Centreville that it jointly operates with INNOVA. "It [the urgent care center] was in the red for several years but now it's making money and doing very well for both parties," says Derring. But he does not anticipate additional urgent care facilities in the near future. "The urgent care centers were a trend at one time—they're not anymore. We need to consider developing group practices of doctors and locating them in certain areas. We have identified several potential areas where this need exists, such as Manassas Park, Independent Hill, Nokesville, and the Haymarket/Gainesville area."

105   The company has pondered the idea of a wellness center on campus. The company performed a feasibility study of the idea that, according to Derring, was inconclusive. "With the commuter population and the time required, it was decided that there would not be a sufficient customer base," says Derring.

---

[2] PWH Corporation Records.

106   Another issue that was given considerable review but ultimately rejected was to invest in a major retirement village. Both projects are open for further consideration in the future.

107   PWH currently is reviewing the feasibility of investing in a radiation treatment cancer center. Discussion has taken place with INNOVA about a possible joint venture for the cancer center.

108   These are but a few of the issues that face PWH Corporation as it plans for its second quarter century of operation. The Strategic Planning Task Force is being asked to formulate responses for addressing these and other health-related needs for the residents of Prince William County.

CASE 14

LOCKHEED CORPORATION

1   By 1990, the Lockheed Corporation was a national institution and had been one for many decades. Its pioneering efforts in the fields of aviation and space were legendary. In fact, Lockheed's contributions during times of war and peace suggest that it was an instrument of national security as well as a profit-seeking enterprise.

2   A business it was, however, and, like other aerospace companies, it had experienced dramatic boom-to-bust cycles due primarily to shifts in government expenditures. The U.S. government, and principally the Department of Defense (DOD), were the corporation's major customers by far. Their political and military strategies had been principal determinants of Lockheed's corporate strategy.

3   At the end of the 1980s, Lockheed found itself in a crisis of uncertainty. It had survived the post-Vietnam cutbacks, several contracting scandals, a disastrous attempt to get back into the civilian sector, and the changing tides of defense policy. It then had healed and profited through the initiatives of the Reagan Administration. Headquartered in Calabasis, California, having its airplane-related component in Burbank and its space-related component a few hundred miles north in Sunnyvale, Lockheed prospered in the graces of a Californian president devoted to matching global military threats. Sales doubled from 1983 to 1988. At the close of the decade, however, world events seemed to conspire against its business once again—the Soviet hegemony was crumbling in metaphor as the Berlin wall crumbled in fact. The Defense Department, based on Secretary of Defense Richard Cheney's voluntary proposal in 1989, was poised to cut spending by about $180 billion and reduce the overall size of the armed forces by 25 percent in just a few years. Naturally, these events caused a severe political and military reassessment of programs under development, and companies like Lockheed suddenly found themselves poised to become big losers.

4   The Lockheed posture was not a slave to the situation, though. Dan Tellep, corporate veteran for over three decades, became CEO at the end of 1988 and was a Renaissance-man type of executive. He doted on innovation and encouraged nontraditional thinking. His proudest achievement had been to garner sales of $1 billion in space station and Star Wars contracts. For four years he ran the Lockheed Missiles and Space Company and was the driving force behind the D-5 missile program, which the House Armed Services Committee chairman dubbed as the "best-managed program I've seen." Though Tellep admitted to knowing nothing about airplanes (perhaps the proudest part of the Lockheed legacy), corporatewide changes in strategy certainly seemed imminent.

A LIVING HISTORY

5   From the corporation's initiation to World War II, Lockheed's technical accomplishments were impressive, but the business aspect sometimes stumbled. The Lockheed founders were Allan and Malcolm Loughhead who, in 1912, built one airplane as part of a business that lasted only one year. Later, the Loughhead Aircraft Manufacturing Company existed in Santa Barbara, California, from 1916 to 1921, and resurfaced in 1926 as the Lockheed Aircraft Company. In 1929, Lockheed became a di-

This case was prepared by Robert N. McGrath, Franz Lohrke, and Gary J. Castrogiovanni, Louisiana State University Department of Management, College of Business Administration.

FIGURE 1

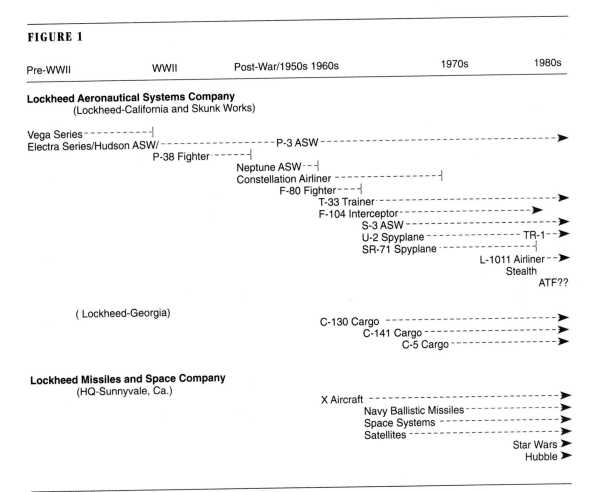

Note: Lines represent approximate operational life of product.

vision of the Detroit Aircraft Corporation in 1929. When that firm went bankrupt in 1931, Lockheed went into receivership. It resurrected itself in 1932 and had since operated continuously.

6   Though business results were cyclical, contributions to history were steady and significant (see Figure 1). The Vega line of aircraft boasted endurance and speed accomplishments in aviation's halcyon era. Wiley Post's *Winnie Mae* was a Vega. Charles Lindbergh broke records in a Vega. It was in 1933 that a young engineer named Clarence "Kelly" Johnson contributed to the design of a series to be known as Electra. Amelia Earheart flew an Electra. Howard Hughes set his round-the-world record in an Electra. Neville Chamberlain flew to Hitler in an Electra. A follow-on series called Orion was the mainstay airliner of the day, and Lodestar, Ventura, and Harpoon models were almost as common. Despite the Great Depression, Lockheed did a steady civilian business and assets grew to $3 million in 1936.

7   With World War II things changed. A bomber derivative of the Electra named the Hudson was ordered and was the largest order ever placed with an aircraft company—$25 million. Kelly Johnson designed the P-38 Lightning, one of the greatest fighters ever built and feared as the "forked tailed devil" by the Japanese. More than 10,000 were produced, which is more than any other craft ever

produced by Lockheed. Employment in 1939 was at 7,300—a 15-fold increase in well under a decade. By 1941, employment was at 50,000—a 100-fold leap. At the time Pearl Harbor was bombed, Lockheed was the biggest aircraft company in the country. During the war, it produced 19,297 airplanes, and employment peaked at 93,000. From 1939 to 1943, sales went from $35.3 million to $697.4 million, net income from $442,111 to $8.2 million. Clearly, government business was smart business.

8   Contributing quietly during the war years was the advent of the Lockheed "Skunk Works." In 1944, Kelly Johnson assembled a 128-man team and produced one of the first jet aircraft, FROM SCRATCH—in 139 days! That incredible accomplishment coined the term *Skunk Works* (because of the odor of a revolutionary epoxy) and started a string of innovations and management miracles that never stopped.

9   With war's end, hard lessons were learned. The air force canceled 600 Lockheed contracts and 42,000 purchase orders, worth over $1 billion. By September 1945, employment was at 35,000, and, by 1947, 14,000. Sales in 1946 were $112.7 million, down 87 percent from 1943. Net income fell to a $2.5 million loss. Fortunately, the company survived by selling 5,691 F-80s (the first production jet fighter) over the next 16 years, and 5,691 T-33 jet trainers, which became a worldwide mainstay for decades. Also of critical importance was the sale of 856 Constellation airliners, modified into everything from the Pan Am and TWA flagships to Air Force One.

10   During this era, Lockheed also established a firm foothold in the narrow area of maritime patrol aircraft and antisubmarine warfare (ASW) technology. Between 1946 and 1962, a total of 1,052 Neptune aircraft were built for many countries, giving Lockheed unrivaled expertise in the maritime patrol niche. Then, building on the Electra design, the new Orion was produced, eventually becoming the standard maritime patrol aircraft through at least the end of the century. Lockheed's prowess in ASW also produced the ungainly Viking, a carrier-based aircraft that took the ASW mission to new levels of aviation technology. Though a narrow business, ASW technology provided a steady cash flow, which was to be instrumental in saving the corporation during hard times ahead.

11   In 1954, Lockheed again demonstrated its technological prowess by introducing the F-104 Starfighter, the first Mach-2 aircraft, known as the "missile with a man in it." Over 2,500 were sold to many air forces. Another of Kelly Johnson's masterpieces, in 1958 it set an altitude record the same day it won the prestigious Collier Trophy for the year's greatest achievement in aviation. It was so "hot" that even NASA bought versions to train astronauts and do exotic performance tests.

12   It is difficult to underestimate the importance of the Skunk Works during this period, and especially of Kelly Johnson up to his retirement in 1975. His leadership, born of technical genius, may be the most significant single contribution to aviation ever. In addition to the projects mentioned, the Skunk Works produced the U-2 spy plane, famed not only because of its use in Cold War crises but also because of its technical capabilities. It was eventually replaced by the TR-1, so remarkably similar that it stood as testimony to the original design. Perhaps the most mysterious project, though, was the Mach-3 (and up) SR-71 Blackbird. This spy plane, with a theoretically unlimited (and never divulged) top speed, holds all speed records. Every detail of the airplane had to be invented to withstand high-speed/high-altitude rigors, such as oil that gets so hot it is solid until the plane warms up, and titanium skin that expands so much from the heat at those speeds that it is porous at ground conditions. Its advanced state was still unmatched even at its retirement after almost 30 years. (Only arrays of satellites could do more.) The SR-71 became "the" symbol of Lockheed excellence. Additionally, the Skunk Works produced the F-117 stealth fighter, secretly operational for the better part of a decade before the Northrop stealth bomber even flew as prototype. It is hard to imagine what would have happened to Lockheed without the Skunk Works and Kelly Johnson.

13   While technological limits were pushed, Lockheed was strong in other areas of aviation as well. In 1951, a simple contract to take the B-29 bomber production line out of mothballs for the Korean War effort evolved into one of the strongest businesses Lockheed ever had. At a plant in Georgia, the U.S. Air Force subsequently contracted Lockheed to build a new, rugged cargo aircraft. This was to

be the C-130 Hercules, which was designed so well that over 30 distinct derivatives were sold for at least as many purposes in over 45 countries. Production was almost continuously sold out for at least 40 years. This established a tradition of heavy aircraft, for next came the C-141 Starlifter, the air force's workhorse airlifter. The next step was to build the C-5 Galaxy, which was for years to be the largest airplane in the world, holding outsize and gross-weight cargo records for many years.

14   Ironically, the C-5 program almost crippled the company. Although the air force agreed to buy the plane, the rival Boeing 747 was successfully marketed commercially, killing hopes for volume efficiencies. Also, the technical problems of building a plane so big and yet so versatile were costly. Overruns inspired the Pentagon to cancel 31 of the 115 originally ordered. Corporate losses in 1970 were $187.8 million, the worst in Lockheed's history. The value of common stock dropped almost in half. In the end, $250 million was written off. Eventually, though, the C-5A established such a good technical reputation that 50 follow-on C-5B versions were ordered, worth $6.6 billion.

15   Confident in its success with big airplanes, Lockheed decided to reenter the civilian sector in the late 1960s. It had not produced an airliner since the mid-40s—the Constellation. Nevertheless, Lockheed saw an unmistakable market for at least 300 250-passenger airliners and invested over $1 billion in the development of the L-1011 TriStar. Unfortunately, McDonnell-Douglas saw the same opportunity, and eventually the L-1011 split the market with the DC-10. Nevertheless, Lockheed continued. Part of its strategy was to contract Rolls-Royce as its engine manufacturer, hoping for inroads to subsequent European markets. Rolls-Royce went bankrupt in the meantime, though, and efforts to save the engine manufacturer for the sake of the TriStar almost destroyed Lockheed financially. Because of Lockheed's importance for national defense, Congress saw fit to guarantee a $250 million line of credit. Though the government eventually profited by $30 million from that guarantee agreement, negative publicity gave Lockheed a scandalous reputation. After the L-1011 write-off in 1981, net income began to increase again. From $207.3 million in 1982 it tripled in three years to $401.0 million while sales increased from $5.6 billion to $9.5 billion. Predictably, TriStar demonstrated technical superiority, establishing records in the civilian aviation industry and admiration for Lockheed.

16   Of equal technical excellence, Lockheed established itself as a leader in the missiles and space segment of the aerospace industry. In the 50s, Kelly Johnson again proved his genius by participating in the development of a series of "X" (for experimental) aircraft, which were the pioneers into ranges of air and near-space necessary for further exploration. From this experience, Lockheed was to produce the Polaris, Poseidon, and Trident missiles, which in concert constituted the entire U.S. Navy submarine-launched ballistic missile capability. These programs in themselves were models of managerial acumen, achieving results ahead of schedule and pioneering organizational techniques. Involvement with the national space programs developed into steady, understated, but vital business as well.

PRESENT BUSINESS ENVIRONMENT

17   As mentioned, the Reagan Administration brought in a new era for defense contractors, raising real spending 55 percent during the first five years. Reagan's advocacy of the stealth bomber, the "Star Wars" concept of nuclear deterrence, and a 600-ship navy are examples of the expansion. Defense spending peaked in 1985, though, and from that point until the end of the decade the defense industry outlook eroded at an increasing rate. It became predicted that, by 1995, defense spending would fail by 13.6 percent to $261 billion, and to $225 billion by 2000. Military aerospace and missiles were expected to drop at least 10 percent a year, mostly by canceling new programs. By 1990, up to 1 million defense-related jobs might be lost. Lockheed was extremely vulnerable to these forces.

18   By the mid-80s, public opinion and burgeoning defense budgets had influenced a fairly strict policy of "fixed price." This term is almost self-explanatory. A contract stipulated (in voluminous detail) a product was to be delivered and one price was to be paid for it. Again, almost all front-end risk had been shifted to the contractor, for major contracts always needed some level of engineering

development and R&D. A strategy of winning business by bidding low became popular, though it was frequently financially ruinous to do so. In concept, fixed price might be good free-market economics, but in practice it threatened to undermine national security by driving out important players, reducing incentives for innovation, and discouraging participation in defense contracting itself.

19   The hostility of this environment became exacerbated by other issues. A policy of separating development and production awards, with no guarantee that a production contract would be awarded, aggravated the risks of development. Further, the loser of a contract competition often won second-source contracts. In other words, in the interest of national security, the government frequently contracted a second company for a major product as a back-up source. This player, usually the runner-up in the original competition, was frequently *given* the results of developmental work expensively performed by the "winner." Runners-up were winners in their own way, deterring unique technological risk.

20   Additionally, the DOD adopted policies of *(a)* requiring contractors to pay for tooling and test equipment, *(b)* demanding long-term warranties, *(c)* establishing strict guidelines for calculating allowable profits, and *(d)* making progress payments more frugal. Finally, a policy of criminal liability took effect. Periodic accusations of fraud and abuse induced a trend of pursuing criminal action against not only contractors but their employees. Many veteran players simply opted out of this environment. Risks were just too severe.

21   The geopolitical scene and the Secretary Cheney reduction plan also made the industry consider major restructuring. A 25 percent reduction in force, massive base closings, the crumbling Soviet bloc, and a serious domestic economic agenda made prospects for enormously expensive new systems increasingly speculative. Obviously, the major companies would be pursuing fewer programs. Even within existing (already fielded) systems, costly technological upgrades would be competing for scarce resources. On the other hand, an equally likely possibility would be for the DOD to pursue upgrades as cheaper alternatives to buying new systems. It was impossible to predict which would be sacrificed to finance what. The advanced tactical fighter program, for example, undergoing fierce competition between a Lockheed-led team and a Northrop-led team and still in R&D, might be scrapped in favor of upgrading existing fleets of F-15 or F-16 fighters, or both, or producing enhanced derivatives. Or a limited number of advanced fighters might be bought as a short-term budget compromise, destroying economies of scale. Any acquisition combination was possible, and no one could make an accurate prediction.

22   In the industry, long-range marketing and operating strategies began to emerge. Principally, industry wisdom emphasized reorganizing production and operations, securing subcontracting work, upgrading existing programs, and diversifying into stronger growth areas in order to maintain a business base on which to compete for future programs. However, most past efforts to diversify out of this industry had been catastrophic. After Vietnam, Grumman had tried its hand at subway cars. McDonnell had forayed into computer services. Hundreds of millions were lost. There were some success stories, but horror stories were the rule. One explanation is that defense contractors build huge bureaucracies to serve the Pentagon, while commercial companies must stay flexible. It is not uncommon for a defense contract to take five times as long as a civilian program. Also, defense contractors build to specifications, with minimal risk. Technical prowess is valued over cost control. Fixed-price concepts, common in the civilian sector, wreaked havoc in the defense sector.

23   However, the lure of the civilian sector was powerful. Operating profits in that industry in 1988 alone were $2.5 to $3.0 billion. The demands there were huge and long-term. World traffic was expected to grow at a rate of 5.4 percent through 2005. Generally favorable economic conditions and airline deregulation, favorable tourism policies, and a favorable investment climate sustained a buying spree augmented by concerns of airlines about aging fleets and a trend toward larger aircraft. The key elements for market share were affordable equipment and low operating and maintenance costs. As such, major steps toward advanced technology or all-new aircraft programs were avoided. Long-range market prospects were for $516 billion by 2005, including a $96 billion backlog and

a $420 billion open market (comprising $125 billion for replacements, and $295 billion for aircraft to accommodate growth). There was little doubt that civilian aviation had a bright future in almost every segment.

24   In strategic defense, the environment was somewhat different again. Arms limitations talks notwithstanding, there was little or no evidence that Soviet economic troubles were impacting their growth in strategic capability: missiles, submarines, military adventurism in space, and the like. To balance the threat, American strategic funding had grown faster in real terms than that for conventional forces, absorbing about 15 percent of the defense budget. Despite the need for balance, the administration was forced by economics to take a gradualist approach to new systems and modernizations. Three major modernization programs were expected to consume the lion's share of the strategic budget: the navy's Trident 2 D-5 missile (a Lockheed product), Rockwell's B-2 bomber, and a replacement for the aging intercontinental ballistic missile force, all many years into development. Despite its cost of $35 billion, the Trident missile seemed to be the most politically secure. The Northrop B-2 stealth bomber, in the prototype stage, was in the severest doubt. The future of the strategic defense initiative (Star Wars) was almost totally unpredictable.

LOCKHEED'S POSITION

Organization

25   By the end of the 1980s, Lockheed was organized into five major business groups (see Figure 2). The largest was the Aeronautical Systems Company (LASC), with about half of the corporation's employment of over 90,000 people, and headquartered in Burbank. Most of the rest of the company was employed at Marietta, Georgia, just outside Atlanta.

26   Activities in California included production of the P-3 Orion antisubmarine aircraft and the TR-1 reconnaissance aircraft. Production of these aircraft would be completed soon. There was a good deal of service-support business related to the S-3 Viking carrier-based ASW aircraft and the L-1011 TriStar. The Advanced Development Projects (Skunk Works) office was also part of this organization, having recently delivered the last of about 50 F-117 stealth fighters. The Skunk Works was also currently developing the F-22 advanced tactical fighter (ATF).

27   In Georgia, ongoing activities included the production of the last C-5Bs under contract, steady but modest production of the venerable C-130 transport, and almost continuous modernization-support projects for existing fleets of C-141, C-130, and C-5 transports.

28   Niche and service-oriented components of LASC included the Lockheed Aeromod Center in Greenville, South Carolina, the Murdock Engineering Company in Irving, Texas, Lockheed Support Systems in Arlington, Texas, and Lockheed Aircraft Services in Ontario, California.

29   While LASC was essentially half the corporation, the other half was essentially the Lockheed Missiles and Space Company (LMSC). Headquartered in Sunnyvale, California, its principal activities included the development and production of all U.S. Navy fleet ballistic missiles, and development-production of spacecraft and space systems for NASA and the U.S. Air Force. The list of projects was long, and included the D-5 Trident missile, advanced observation satellites, information retrieval systems, advanced materials (e.g., space shuttle exterior silica tiles and lithium batteries), physical sciences research (e.g., atomic and molecular physics, astronomy, nuclear physics, nuclear weapons effects, plasma physics, and reentry physics), ground vehicles, ocean systems (deep-diving vehicles), ocean mining (and vehicles), advanced tactical systems (radiometric area correlation guidance, airfield destruction, offensive suppression systems), extensive Star Wars R&D (accredited with "major" breakthroughs), remotely piloted vehicles, and the pride-and-joy Hubble telescope. (With resolution up to 10 times better than any earth-based telescope, the Hubble would allow a view into 350 times more of the universe than ever seen before and revolutionize our understandings through an array of sensors

FIGURE 2
Organizational Chart (case-simplified)

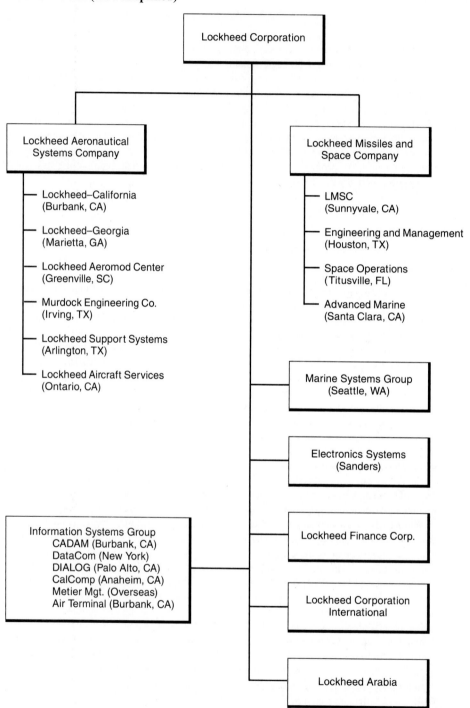

unprecedented in technological capacity.) Futuristic possibilities included a rejuvenated idea for a supersonic transport, a role in the hypersonic national aerospace plane, and liquid hydrogen aircraft fuel.

30   Components of LMSC included the Engineering and Management Service Company in Houston, the Space Operations Company in Titusville, Florida, and Advanced Marine Systems in Santa Clara, California.

31   Lockheed's Information Systems Group (the corporation's smallest) included CADAM (computer-aided design and manufacturing) in Burbank, DataCom Systems of New York City, DIALOG Information Services of Palo Alto, CalComp of Anaheim, Metier Management Systems (five computer companies with offices in the Far East and Europe), and Lockheed Air Terminal, established in 1941 to manage the company-owned Burbank Airport. (The airport was eventually sold, but Lockheed stayed in the airport management business.)

32   The Marine Systems Group, headquartered in Seattle, concerned itself with ship designs, engineering, construction, overhaul, repair, and logistical support. It employed about 1 percent of Lockheed's work force.

33   The Electronics Systems Group was formed in 1986, with the acquisition of Sanders Associates, Inc. It developed and manufactured advanced electronic systems for both military and civilian applications.

34   Unassigned to company groups were the Lockheed Finance Corporation, formed to help customers finance business with Lockheed; Lockheed Corporation International, which provided marketing and support services for all of Lockheed worldwide; and Lockheed-Arabia, a joint venture concerned with a broad spectrum of basic aviation needs.

POSTURING FOR THE '90S

35   At the end of the 1980s, Lockheed found itself on a knife's edge. The Pentagon supplied 77 percent of its business. Though the corporation had its highest earnings ever in 1988 ($624 million), this was due to a beneficent receivables schedule and was not completely representative. Earnings in 1989 were $2 million on $9.9 billion in sales. Some of the reasons for this situation struck right at the heart of the Lockheed identity. (For Lockheed financial information and the effects of Pentagon cutbacks, of competition, and of aerospace market forecasts, see the exhibits in the Appendix.)

36   One was the paucity of business in LASC. Except for the F-117 stealth fighter, no new aircraft types had been introduced since 1972. All business was either ongoing or derivative (Skunk Works rumors aside). This stood in stark contrast to the decades before, when, on average, one new type was introduced every year.

37   The legacy of Lockheed's "heavies" had been broken. The contract for the next generation of cargo aircraft, the C-17, was awarded to McDonnell-Douglas. (To add insult to injury, Lockheed's poor performance as a subcontractor for C-17 wing parts caused that business to be canceled, about $1 billion in revenue.) Delivery of the last C-5Bs occurred in 1989. Production of the C-5B had accounted for 20 percent of corporate sales of $11.2 billion in 1986. In 1987, it accounted for $2.0 billion, $1.2 billion in 1988, and $0.2 billion in 1989. Production of the C-130 was steady but short term, averaging production of 36 aircraft a year. Solid revenues were expected for modifications of all types of transports for years, but no new models were on the horizon.

38   Though the last delivery of the P-3 Orion ASW aircraft also was imminent, that business was expected to continue with the development of its replacement, the P-7. However, in 1989, Lockheed suddenly announced that the P-7 program was $300 million over budget, virtually wiping out the profit made elsewhere in the corporation (mostly in LMSC). Because of technical insufficiencies, schedule delays, eroding performance promises, and the world and budget scenes, the U.S. navy poised itself to cancel the $5 billion program outright. If the navy did so, it would be the largest cancellation ever in DOD history.

39 Not much else was left in LASC beside the possibility of the advanced tactical fighter. About $1 billion was being invested in the R&D stage to chase about $100 billion in future contracts, spread over the life of the system and across the winning consortium of companies. Within a year, Lockheed's ATF was scheduled to fly as prototype and would compete with the Northrop competitor for the entire procurement package. Analysts were undecided about which was more likely to win, and strategic reassessments and budget constraints were threatening major portions (if not all) of the eventual buy.

40 On the other hand, in LMSC Lockheed was on contract for $5.3 billion worth of 52 D-1 missiles, and an extrapolation predicted $20 billion more in the 1990s. Star Wars projects were generating about $300 million a year in revenue, but politics made that business unpredictable.

41 On balance, stockholders were not happy; despite a booming stock market, their average total return in the last three years had fallen 1.9 percent. The collective market value of the seven "purest" defense contractors had fallen 23 percent in three years. The tradition of underbidding early to get business, save jobs, keep the production lines rolling, and position for the next big program was serving employees but not investors.

42 Lockheed became a takeover target. Dallas investor and turnaround artist Harold Simmons owned 19 percent of common stock and was not happy with his paper losses of about $100 million. Though he had never taken over an aerospace firm before, his record was outstanding. It seemed that he wanted to take over Lockheed, boost profits, and help raise stockholder's value. He openly vowed to invest heavily in the aerospace and defense segments and sell other assets. He embarked on a proxy fight to elect his own cadre of 15 directors.

43 CEO Tellep had entirely different ideas. In late 1988, he set up a division in Washington, D.C., to stay close to emerging defense computer and electronics demands. The idea was to replace the shrinking aircraft business by growing electronics from the present 40 percent of total volume to 60 percent. Not only would Lockheed chase modest programs, like fire-control systems for tactical weapons, but giant contracts as well. He planned to transfer Lockheed's experience with computer-controlled weapons and space systems to a potential $1.5 billion contract to network U.S. Air Force computer systems, and a similar $2 billion project for the Treasury Department. Facing competition from IBM, Honeywell, EDS, Computer Sciences, and other veterans, he hired a former vice president of Computer Sciences Corporation and the former assistant defense secretary for the Pentagon's "Command, Control, Communications, and Intelligence" strategy. Though the Sanders acquisition in 1986 had produced disappointing results so far, it was expected to be a key player in efforts like this.

44 In April of 1989, a major restructuring plan was inaugurated. It was intended to focus on Lockheed's core business of aircraft, missiles, space, and electronics, while growing in such markets as government services and ASW. Some details of the plan included:

45 The phasing out of the information Systems Group and the sale of CalComp, CADAM, Metier, and Lockheed DataPlan, which had combined revenues in 1988 of $589 million.

46 Establishment of a technology services group to capitalize on modernization and maintenance needs.

47 Formation of an ASW office in Washington, headed by a retired navy vice admiral.

48 Pursuit of a role as a subcontractor for the final assembly of McDonnell-Douglas's new airliner, the MD-11, to offset the vacuum left by the C-5B program completion. As well, Fokker (of Germany) was approached for similar subcontracting work.

49 Establishment of an employee stock ownership plan with 17 percent total corporate ownership.

50 Acceleration of a general LASC migration from Burbank to sites in Palmdale and in Rye Canyon, California, and the move of the Skunk Works to Palmdale.

51 Rumors of massive layoffs.

52 The aggressive lobbying of employees by Harold Simmons, however, grew as Wall Street's opinion of Lockheed continued to deteriorate. Tellep was forced to all but abandon his restructuring plan.

APPENDIX

EXHIBIT 1
Lockheed's Balance Sheet (in millions except book value)

	1990	1989
Assets		
Cash and equivalent	$ 372	$ 86
Accounts receivable	1,880	1,786
Inventories	1,187	1,266
Other current assets	139	260
Total current assets	3,578	3,398
Prop., plt., & equip. at cost	4,064	4,053
Less accum. depr. & amort.	2,205	2,150
Net property	1,859	1,903
Excess of purc. price over fair asset val.	858	895
Other noncurrent assets	565	596
Total assets	$6,860	$6,792
Liabilities		
Short-term borrows	$ 40	$ 19
Accounts payable	778	732
Salaries and wages.	317	326
Inc. tax, primarily defer.	230	728
Customers' advs. in excess of rel. costs	439	228
Curr. portion of long-term debt	25	22
Other current liabilities.	793	840
Total current liabilities	2,622	2,895
Long-term debt.	1,929	1,835
Common stock	70	70
Additional cap.	707	707
Retained earnings.	2,322	2,103
Treasury shares, at cost.	(328)	(328)
Guarantee of ESOP obligs..	(472)	(490)
Total shareholders' equity	2,299	2,062
Total liabilities.	$6,850	$6,792
Net current assets	$ 956	$ 503
Book value	$22.98	$18.47

Source: Lockheed, *Moody's Industrial Manual*, 1991.

EXHIBIT 2
Business Segment Sales and Profits (in thousands)

	12/31/90	12/31/89
Sales		
Missiles and space	$5,116,000	$4,780,000
Aeronautical systems	2,329,000	2,572,000
Technical services	1,550,000	1,432,000
Electronics	963,000	1,107,000
Total	9,958,000	9,891,000
Costs and expenses	9,397,000	9,838,000
Profits		
Missiles and space	$ 379,000	$ 368,000
Aeronautical systems	96,000	(377,000)
Technical services	58,000	36,000
Electronics	28,000	26,000
Total	561,000	53,000

Source: Lockheed, *Moody's Industrial Manual,* 1991.

EXHIBIT 3
The Top 10 Defense Suppliers
Projected 1990 Revenues and Percent of Sales

Company and Products	1990 Est. Rev. from Govt. Sales (in billions)	Percent of Total Sales
McDonnell Douglas airplanes, missiles, helicopters, electronics, space	$10.2	67%
Lockheed airplanes, missiles, electronics, space	9.0	91
General Dynamics airplanes, submarines, tanks, missiles, space, electronics	8.6	87
General Electric engines, electronics	8.2	18
Boeing airplanes, helicopters, missiles, space	5.6	20
Martin Marietta missiles, electronics, space	5.4	90
Rockwell International electronics	5.3	44
General Motors (Hughes) electronics, space, missiles	5.2	4
United Technologies engines, helicopters	5.2	24
Northrop airplanes, missiles, electronics	4.6	88

Source: *Fortune,* August 27, 1990.

EXHIBIT 4
U.S. Aerospace Industry Market Forecast
Sales in Billions of Current Dollars

	1988	1989	1990	1991
Grand total—aerospace	$126	$140	$155	$170
Military aircraft	38	40	41	44
Missiles	14	15	16	17
Space	27	28	32	37
Commercial air transport	23	31	37	42
Business flying	2	2	3	3
Avionics	37	39	43	47
Military computers	22	25	30	34
Engines/parts—military	7	8	9	9
Engines/parts—civil	6	7	9	11
Flight simulators/trainers	1	2	2	3

Source: *Aviation Week and Space Technology,* March 20, 1989.

EXHIBIT 5
Employment Effects of Pentagon Cutbacks

	Est. Number of Workers Employed		
Professions Hit Hardest	**1988**	**1991**	**1994**
Communications equipment	349,600	261,400	213,400
Guided missiles	134,900	122,600	105,000
Shipbuilding/repair	102,300	79,400	61,700

Source: *Business Week,* July 2, 1990.

REFERENCES

"Aircraft Upgrades Will Be Critical to Maintaining Tactical Defenses." *Aviation Week and Space Technology,* March 14, 1988, pp. 38–41.

Anderson, R. A. *A Look at Lockheed.* Princeton, N.J.: Princeton University Press, 1983.

"Budget Realities Forcing Tough Strategic Choices." *Aviation Week and Space Technology,* March 20, 1989, pp. 49–51.

"Commercial Airframe Makers Take Conservative Approach." *Aviation Week and Space Technology,* March 20, 1989, pp. 197–198.

"Congress Saddled with Years of Tough Defense Positions." *Aviation Week and Space Technology,* March 14, 1988, pp. 63–67.

"Contractors Must Adapt to Survive under New U.S. Acquisitions Policies." *Aviation Week and Space Technology,* March 20, 1989, pp. 76–79.

"Declining Military Aircraft Sales Weather Aerospace Market Forecast." *Aviation Week and Space Technology,* March 14, 1988, pp. 75–76.

"Defense Acquisition Policies Hinder Contractors' Ability to Innovate." *Aviation Week and Space Technology,* March 14, 1988, pp. 69–71.

"Defense Budget Actions Delayed by Administration's Slow Start." *Aviation Week and Space Technology,* March 20, 1989, p. 65.

"Defense Cuts Will Trim Aerospace Firms' Earnings, Despite Civil Gains." *Aviation Week and Space Technology,* March 20, 1989, pp. 82–83.

"Defense Firms Re-Order Programs, Operations to Survive Lean Years." *Aviation Week and Space Technology,* May 30, 1988, pp. 59–64.

"Defenseless Against Cutbacks." *Business Week,* January 14, 1991, p. 69.

"Growth Trends: Air Transport, 1979–1991." *Aviation Week and Space Technology,* March 20, 1989, p. 193.

"Growth Trends: U.S. Aerospace Industry." *Aviation Week and Space Technology,* March 20, 1989, pp. 38–39.

"Growth Trends: U.S. Military Aircraft, 1979–1991." *Aviation Week and Space Technology.* March 20, 1989, p. 45.

"Growth Trends: U.S. Space Sales, 1979–1991." *Aviation Week and Space Technology,* March 20, 1989, p. 105.

"Harold Simmons Is Playing a Crafty War Game." *Business Week,* March 12, 1990, p. 40.

"If Simmons Boards Lockheed, Can He Fly It?" *Business Week,* April 2, 1990, pp. 77–78.

"Lockheed Dons New Armour to Keep the Raiders at Bay." *Business Week,* April 17, 1989, pp. 20–21.

"Lockheed Implements Restructuring to Focus on Primary Business." *Aviation Week and Space Technology,* April 10, 1989, p. 31.

Lockheed. *Moody's Industrial Manual,* 1991.

Lockheed. *Standard and Poor's Industrial Manual,* 1991.

"Lockheed's Lesson: It's Open Season on Yes-Man Boards." *Business Week,* April 16, 1990, p. 25.

"Lockheed's New Top Gun Comes out Blazing." *Business Week,* September 5, 1988, pp. 75, 88.

"Market Focus." *Aviation Week and Space Technology,* March 14, 1988, p. 243.

"Oh, What a Difference a Year Makes." *Business Week,* February 25, 1991, p. 37.

"Tactical Aircraft Producers Face Diminishing Returns." *Aviation Week and Space Technology,* February 22, 1989, p. 34.

"The Arms Makers' Next Battle." *Fortune,* August 27, 1990, pp. 84–88.

"The $75 Billion Question: Whose Fighter Will Win?" *Business Week,* April 8, 1991, pp. 64–65.

"U.S. Armed Forces Vary Means of Coping with Tight Budgets." *Aviation Week and Space Technology,* March 20, 1989, pp. 52–53.

"Who Pays for Peace?" *Business Week,* July 2, 1990, pp. 64–70.

Yenne, W. *Lockheed.* New York: Crown Publishers, 1987.

CASE 15

KENTUCKY FRIED CHICKEN CORPORATION

1   During the 1960s and 1970s, Kentucky Fried Chicken Corporation (KFC) pursued an aggressive strategy of restaurant expansion, quickly establishing itself as one of the largest fast food restaurant chains in the United States (see Exhibit 1). KFC was also one of the first U.S. fast-food restaurant chains to expand overseas. By 1990, restaurants located outside of the United States were generating over 50 percent of KFC's total sales. KFC now operates in 58 foreign countries and is the largest fast-food restaurant chain outside of the United States.

2   Japan, Australia, and the United Kingdom (U.K.) accounted for the greatest share of KFC's international expansion during the 1970s and 1980s. However, as KFC entered the 1990s, a number of other international markets offered significant opportunities for growth. China, with a population of over 1 billion, and Europe, with a population roughly equal to the United States, offered such opportunities. However, Latin America also offered a unique opportunity because of the size of its markets, its common language and culture, and its geographical proximity to the United States. KFC already had established successful subsidiaries in Mexico an Puerto Rico and now operates franchises in 20 other Latin American countries.

3   As Mexico continued to struggle with economic and currency problems, a debate ensued within KFC management regarding further expansion in Mexico. Bob Briggs, vice president of international finance, opposed further expansion in Mexico until economic stability could be established in that country. Instead, Briggs supported expansion in other areas of the world. On the other hand, Guillermo Heredia, vice president of Latin America, believed that KFC had an opportunity to make significant market share gains in Mexico by expanding now. Heredia argued strongly that another competitor—namely McDonald's—was expanding in Mexico and KFC's past market share gains easily could be lost if it failed to follow through with its planned growth strategy in Mexico.

COMPANY HISTORY

4   Fast-food franchising was still in its infancy in 1954 when Harland Sanders began his travels across the United States to speak with prospective franchisees about his "Colonel Sanders Recipe Kentucky Fried Chicken." By 1960, "Colonel" Sanders had granted KFC franchises to over 200 take-home retail outlets and restaurants across the United States. He also had succeeded in establishing a number of franchises in Canada. By 1963, the number of KFC franchises had risen to over 300 and revenues had reached $500,000.

5   By 1964, at the age of 74, the Colonel had tired of running the day-to-day operations of his business and was eager to concentrate on public relations issues. Therefore, he sought out potential buyers, eventually deciding to sell the business to two Louisville businessmen—Jack Massey and John Young Brown, Jr.—for $2 million. Massey was named chairman of the board and Brown, who would later become governor of Kentucky, was named president. The Colonel stayed on as a public relations man and goodwill ambassador for the company.

This case was prepared by Jeffrey A. Krug and W. Harvey Hegarty, Graduate School of Business, Indiana University.

EXHIBIT 1
Leading U.S. Fast-Food Chains

Chain	Parent	U.S. Sales ($m) 1988	1989	1989 Units
McDonald's	McDonald's	$11,380	$12,012	8,270
Burger King	Grand Metropolitan	4,840	5,110	5,361
Pizza Hut	PepsiCo, Inc.	2,800	3,100	6,050
Hardee's	Imasco, Ltd.	2,810	3,040	3,327
KFC	PepsiCo, Inc.	2,900	3,000	4,997
Wendy's	Wendy's International	2,720	2,830	3,490
Domino's Pizza	Domino's Pizza	2,300	2,600	5,008
Dairy Queen	Dairy Queen	1,859	2,068	4,700
Taco Bell	PepsiCo, Inc.	1,600	1,840	3,080
Denny's	TW Holdings	1,227	1,300	1,300
Arby's	DWG Corporation	1,100	1,300	2,158
Red Lobster	General Mills	1,050	1,200	1,000
Little Caesars	Little Caesars	908	1,200	2,747
Big Boy	Elias Bros.	1,030	1,040	1,030
Dunkin' Donuts	Allied-Lyons	880	1,014	1,925
Jack in the Box	Foodmaker, Inc.	775	875	1,031
Shoney's	Shoney's, Inc.	779	860	704
Subway	Doctors Associates	583	805	3,440
Sizzler	Collins Foods	749	846	628
Long John Silver's	Jerrico, Inc.	753	785	1,525
Ponderosa	Metromedia Co.	696	710	720
Roy Rogers	Imasco, Ltd.	575	620	660
Bonanza	Metromedia Co.	571	620	652
Friendly	Tennessee Restaurants	564	590	848
Popeyes	Biscuit Investments	447	590	1,030
Baskin-Robbins	Allied-Lyons	502	524	2,600
Western Sizzlin'	Western Sizzlin'	488	500	550
Carl's Jr.	Carl Karcher Enterprises	399	481	482
Golden Corral	Investors Management	456	465	501
Bennigan's	S&A Restaurant Corporation	455	459	222
Perkins	Tennessee Restaurants	375	450	370
Chi-Chi's	Foodmaker, Inc.	431	422	203
Total		$49,002	$53,256	70,609

Source: S&P's 1990 *Industry Surveys.*

6   During the next five years, Massey and Brown concentrated on growing KFC's franchise system across the United States. In 1966, they took KFC public and the company was listed on the New York Stock Exchange. By the late 1960s, a strong foothold had been established in the United States, and Massey and Brown turned their attention to international markets. In 1969, a joint venture was signed with Mitsuoishi Shoji Kaisha, Ltd., in Japan, and the rights to operate 14 existing KFC franchises in England were acquired. Subsidiaries also were established in Hong Kong, South Africa, Australia, New Zealand, and Mexico. By 1971, KFC had 2,450 franchises and 600 company-owned restaurants worldwide and was operating in 48 countries.

Heublein, Inc.

7   In 1971, KFC entered negotiations with Heublein, Inc., to discuss a possible merger. The decision to seek a merger candidate was driven partially by Brown's desire to pursue other interests, including a political career (Brown was elected governor of Kentucky in 1977). On April 10, Heublein announced that an agreement had been reached. Shareholders approved the merger on May 27, and KFC was merged into a subsidiary of Heublein.

8   Heublein was in the business of producing vodka, mixed cocktails, dry gin, cordials, beer, and other alcoholic beverages. It was also the exclusive distributor of a variety of imported alcoholic beverages. Heublein had little experience in the restaurant business. Conflicts quickly erupted between Colonel Sanders, who continued to act in a public relations capacity, and Heublein management. In particular, Colonel Sanders became increasingly distraught over quality control issues and restaurant cleanliness. By 1977, new store openings had slowed to about 20 per year (in 1989, KFC opened a new restaurant on average every two days). Stores were not being remodeled and service quality was declining.

9   In 1977, Heublein sent in a new management team to redirect KFC's strategy. Richard P. Mayer, who later became chairman and chief executive officer, was part of this team (Mayer remained with KFC until 1989, when he left to become president of General Foods USA). A "back-to-basics" strategy was immediately implemented. New unit construction was discontinued until existing stores could be upgraded and operating problems eliminated. Stores were refurbished, an emphasis was placed on cleanliness and service, marginal products were eliminated, and product consistency was reestablished. By 1982, KFC had succeeded in establishing a successful strategic focus and again was aggressively building new units.

R. J. Reynolds Industries, Inc.

10   On October 12, 1982, R. J. Reynolds Industries, Inc. (RJR), announced that it would merge Heublein into a wholly owned subsidiary. The merger with Heublein represented part of RJR's overall corporate strategy of diversifying into unrelated businesses. RJR's objective was to reduce its dependence on the tobacco industry, which had driven RJR sales since its founding in North Carolina in 1875. Sales of cigarettes and tobacco products, while profitable, were declining because of reduced consumption in the United States, due mainly to the increased awareness among Americans regarding the negative health consequences of smoking.

11   RJR's diversification strategy included the acquisition of a variety of companies in the energy, transportation, and food and restaurant industries. RJR had no more experience in the restaurant business than did Heublein when Heublein purchased KFC in 1971. However, RJR decided to take a hands-off approach to managing KFC. Whereas Heublein had installed its own top management at KFC headquarters, RJR left KFC management largely intact, believing that existing KFC managers were better qualified to operate KFC's businesses than were its own managers. By doing so, RJR avoided many of the operating problems that Heublein had experienced during its management of

EXHIBIT 2
PepsiCo, Inc.—1989 Operating Results (dollars in millions)

	Soft Drinks	Snack Foods	Restaurants	Total
Net sales	$5,776.7	$4,215.0	$5,250.7	$15,242.4
Operating profit	690.1	820.9	421.2	1,932.2
Percent net sales	11.9%	19.5%	8.0%	12.7%
Assets	$6,241.9	$3,366.4	$3,095.2	$12,703.5
Capital spending	267.8	257.9	424.6	959.5*

* Includes corporate spending of $9.2 million.

KFC. This strategy paid off for RJR, as KFC continued to expand aggressively and profitably under RJR's ownership.

12   In 1985, RJR acquired Nabisco Corporation for $4.9 billion. Nabisco sold a variety of well-known cookies, crackers, cereals, confectioneries, snacks, and other grocery products. In October 1986, Kentucky Fried Chicken was sold to PepsiCo, Inc.

PEPSICO, INC.

Corporate Strategy

13   PepsiCo, Inc. (PepsiCo), was first incorporated in Delaware in 1919 as Loft, Inc. In 1938, Loft acquired the Pepsi-Cola Company, a manufacturer of soft drinks and soft-drink concentrates. Pepsi-Cola's traditional business had been the sale of its soft-drink concentrates to licensed independent and company-owned bottlers, which manufacture, sell, and distribute Pepsi-Cola soft drinks. Today, Pepsi-Cola's best known trademarks are Pepsi-Cola, Diet Pepsi, Mountain Dew, and Slice. Shortly after its acquisition of Pepsi-Cola, Loft changed its name to Pepsi-Cola Company. On June 30, 1965, Pepsi-Cola Company acquired Frito-Lay, Inc., for 3 million shares, thereby creating one of the largest consumer companies in the United States. At that time, the present name of PepsiCo, Inc., was adopted. Frito-Lay manufactures and sells a variety of snack foods. Its best-known trademarks are Fritos brand Corn Chips, Lay's and Ruffles brand Potato Chips, Doritos and Tostitos Chips, and Chee-Tos brand Cheese Flavored Snacks. In 1989, 66 percent of PepsiCo's net sales were generated by its soft-drink and snack-food businesses (see Exhibit 2).

14   Beginning in the late 1960s, PepsiCo began an aggressive acquisition program. Initially, PepsiCo pursued an acquisition strategy similar to that pursued by RJR during the 1980s: buying a number of companies in areas unrelated to its major businesses. For example, North American Van Lines was acquired in June 1968. Wilson Sporting Goods was merged into the company in 1972 and Lee Way Motor Freight was acquired in 1976. However, success in operating these businesses failed to live up to expectations, mainly because the management skills required to operate these businesses lay outside of PepsiCo's expertise.

15   In 1984, then-chairman and chief executive officer Don Kendall decided to restructure PepsiCo's operations. Most important, PepsiCo would divest those businesses that did not support PepsiCo's consumer product orientation. PepsiCo sold Lee Way Motor Freight in 1984. In 1985, Wilson Sporting Goods and North American Van Lines were sold. Additionally, PepsiCo's foreign bottling operations were sold to local business people, who better understood the cultural and business conditions

EXHIBIT 3
PepsiCo., Inc.—Principal Divisions

Executive offices: Purchase, New York

Soft-Drink Segment	Snack-Food Segment	Restaurants
PepsiCo Worldwide Beverages Somers, New York	PepsiCo Worldwide Foods Plano, Texas	Kentucky Fried Chicken Louisville, Kentucky
Pepsi-Cola Co. Somers, New York	Frito-Lay, Inc. Dallas Texas	Pizza Hut, Inc. Wichita, Kansas
Pepsi-Cola Int'l Somers, New York	PepsiCo Foods Int'l Dallas, Texas	Taco Bell Corporation Irvine, California
		PepsiCo Food Service Purchase, New York

operating in their respective countries. Last, Kendall reorganized PepsiCo along three lines: soft drinks, snack foods, and restaurants (see Exhibit 3). All future investment would be directed at strengthening PepsiCo's performance in these three related areas.

Restaurant Business and Acquisition of Kentucky Fried Chicken

16   PepsiCo first entered the restaurant business in 1977 when it acquired Pizza Hut's 3,200-unit restaurant system. Taco Bell was merged into a division of PepsiCo in 1978. The restaurant business complemented PepsiCo's consumer product orientation. The marketing of fast food followed much of the same patterns as the marketing of soft drinks and snack foods. Therefore, PepsiCo's management skills easily could be transferred among its three business segments. This was compatible with PepsiCo's practice of frequently moving managers among its business units as a way of developing future top executives. PepsiCo's restaurant chains also provided an additional outlet for the sale of Pepsi soft-drink products. In addition, Pepsi soft drinks and fast-food products could be marketed together in the same television and radio segments, thereby providing higher returns for each advertising dollar.

17   To complete its diversification into the restaurant segment, PepsiCo purchased Kentucky Fried Chicken Corporation from RJR Nabisco in 1986 in $841 million. The acquisition of KFC gave PepsiCo the leading market share in three of the four largest and fastest-growing segments within the U.S. quick-service industry. At the end of 1989, Pizza Hut held a 32 percent share of the $10 billion U.S. pizza segment, Taco Bell held 54 percent of the $3.7 billion Mexican food segment, and KFC held 51 percent of the $5.9 billion U.S. chicken segment. In an analysis of PepsiCo's restaurant business in 1989, Shearson Lehman Hutton analyst Caroline Levy commented that "on balance, PepsiCo's restaurants are clearly outperforming the industry and most of the major chains." (See Exhibits 2 and 4 for business segment financial data and restaurant count.)

18   PepsiCo's success during the last decade can be seen by its upward trend in *Fortune* magazine's annual survey of "America's Most Admired Corporations." For the 1990 survey, *Fortune* polled 8,000 executives, directors, and financial analysts, who were asked to rate the largest companies in their industry. The survey covered 305 companies in 32 industry groups. PepsiCo was labeled the sixth most admired corporation overall, rising from a seventh place finish in 1989. In particular, PepsiCo was ranked high in value as a long-term investment, innovativeness, wise use of corporate assets, quality of management, and quality of products/services offered. PepsiCo's rise is dramatic when compared with its place in past *Fortune* rankings:

EXHIBIT 4
PepsiCo, Inc.—Number of Units Worldwide (1989)

Year	KFC	Pizza Hut	Taco Bell	Total
1984.....	6,175	4,208	1,833	12,216
1985.....	6,396	4,482	2,173	13,051
1986.....	6,575	5,017	2,409	14,001
1987.....	7,522	5,394	2,696	15,612
1988.....	7,761	5,707	2,878	16,346
1989.....	7,948	6,205	3,067	17,220
Five-Year Compounded Annual Growth Rate				
	5.2%	8.1%	10.8%	7.1%

	PepsiCo Ranking
1990	6
1989	7
1988	14
1987	24
1986	25

FAST-FOOD INDUSTRY

U.S. Quick-Service Market

19   According to the National Restaurant Association (NRA), 1989 food-service sales topped $227.2 billion for the approximately 400,000 restaurants and other food outlets making up the U.S. restaurant industry. Fast-food sales reached $65.5 billion. The NRA estimates that sales of the over 86,000 fast-food restaurants will grow by 7.4 percent to approximately $70.4 billion in the United States in 1990. The U.S. restaurant industry as a whole is projected to grow by 6 percent. Approximately 50 percent of the growth in the fast-food segment will come from new unit openings. Another 40 percent will result from higher prices, while the remaining growth will come from improved volume at existing outlets.

20   The 1989 ranking of the leading U.S. fast-food chains, as compiled by Standard & Poor's, is presented in Exhibit 1. Most striking is the dominance of McDonald's, whose U.S. sales exceeded $12 billion in 1989. McDonald's sales accounted for 18 percent of total U.S. fast-food sales in 1989, despite the fact that it accounts for under 10 percent of the industry's total outlets. The 1989 U.S. sales for the PepsiCo system, which includes KFC, Pizza Hut, and Taco Bell, reached $7.9 billion, or 12 percent of U.S. fast-food sales. The PepsiCo system totals 14,127 restaurants, or 16.4 percent of all fast-food restaurants in the United States. While McDonald's holds the No. 1 spot in the hamburger segment, PepsiCo holds the leading market share in the chicken (KFC), Mexican (Taco Bell), and pizza (Pizza Hut) segments.

EXHIBIT 5
U.S. Fast-Food Sales by Business Segment (in millions)

Business Segment	1987	1988	1989
Hamburgers and roast beef	$27,257	$30,386	$33,880
Steak	9,811	10,724	11,954
Pizza	8,126	9,087	10,225
Chicken	4,822	5,345	5,912
Mexican	3,079	3,317	3,673
Seafood	1,480	1,666	1,841
Pancakes and waffles	1,309	1,435	1,553
Sandwiches and other	956	1,185	1,386
Total fast-food sales	$56,840	$63,145	$70,424

Sources: U.S. Dept. of Commerce, Restaurant Business Magazine,
S&P's *Industry Surveys.*

Major Business Segments

21   Eight major business segments make up the fast-food segment of the food-service industry (Exhibit 5 shows sales for each of these segments for the years 1987 through 1989, as compiled by the U.S. Department of Commerce). Hamburgers, hot dogs, and roast beef represent the largest segment of the U.S. market, reaching $33.9 billion in sales in 1989. This is about three times as large as sales in the nearest segment. The largest competitors are McDonald's, Burger King, Hardee's, and Wendy's. McDonald's market share within this segment is 35 percent, compared to a 15 percent share for Burger King, its nearest competitor.

22   The second largest fast-food segment is steak, which is largely dominated by Denny's and Big Boy (these restaurant chains also serve hamburgers, though they are not included in the hamburger segment in the Department of Commerce data). Denny's was acquired by TW Services in 1987, which in turn was acquired by an investment group in early 1990. Big Boy was acquired by Elias Brothers Restaurants from the Marriott Corporation in 1987. Other large franchises within the steak category are Sizzler International, Ponderosa, and Bonanza. Ponderosa and Bonanza were both recently acquired by Metromedia Company, a private investment group.

23   The pizza segment, the third-largest fast-food segment, is the industry's fastest growing. Pizza Hut dominates this segment, with Domino's Pizza and Caesar's Pizza following close behind. Domino's strategy has largely targeted the home delivery market, while Caesar's has concentrated mainly on take-out sales. Pizza Hut, while traditionally a dine-in restaurant concept, successfully has implemented a home delivery and take-out system. By doing so, it has been able to successfully maintain its leading position within the industry.

24   Kentucky Fried Chicken, more than any other business segment leader, has succeeded in dominating its business segment, accounting for over 50 percent of total sales within the chicken segment in 1989. KFC's nearest competitors are Church's Fried Chicken and Popeyes Famous Fried Chicken. Other chicken chains include Bojangles, Chick-fil-a, and Grandy's.

Industry Consolidation

25   Although the restaurant industry has outpaced the overall economy in recent years, indications are that the U.S. market is slowly becoming saturated. According to the U.S. Bureau of Labor, monthly sales of U.S. eating and drinking establishments were up only 1.1 to 3.8 percent from those of the prior year in the last last half of 1989. Following a period of rapid expansion and intense restaurant building in the United States during the 1970s and 1980s, the fast-food industry apparently has begun to consolidate. In January 1990, Grand Metropolitan, a British company, purchased Pillsbury Company for $5.7 billion. Included in the purchase was Pillsbury's Burger King chain. Grand Met already has begun to strengthen the franchise by upgrading existing restaurants and has eliminated several levels of management to cut costs. This should give Burger King a long-needed boost in improving its position against McDonald's, its largest competitor in the U.S. market. In 1988, Grand Met purchased Weinerwald, a West German chicken chain, and the Spaghetti Factory, a Swiss chain.

26   Within the chicken segment, a number of acquisitions have intensified competition behind Kentucky Fried Chicken. In particular, the second-largest chicken segment restaurant chain, Church's, was acquired by Al Copeland Enterprises in 1989 for $392 million. Copeland also owns Popeyes Famous Fried Chicken, the third-largest chicken chain. Following the Church's acquisition, Copeland immediately converted 303 of Church's 1,368 restaurants into Popeyes franchises, bringing the Popeyes restaurant system to a total of 1,030. This made Popeyes the second-largest chicken chain in the United States. Several hundred Church's units were scheduled to be sold to raise cash to pay for the Church's acquisition. Although the Church's acquisition enlarged the competitive base controlled by Copeland, the Copeland restaurant system still is dwarfed by KFC's 4,997 U.S. restaurants.

27   Perhaps more important to Kentucky Fried Chicken was Hardee's acquisition of 600 Roy Rogers restaurants from Marriott Corporation in early 1990. Hardee's immediately began to convert these restaurants to Hardee's units and has introduced "Roy Rogers" fried chicken to its menu. This could significantly impact KFC sales in the future, once Hardee's has introduced fried chicken in all of its 3,327 restaurants. While Hardee's is unlikely to destroy the customer loyalty that KFC has long enjoyed, it is likely to take sales away from KFC because its widened menu selection may appeal to families that must satisfy the eating preferences of different family members.

28   The impact of these and other recent mergers and acquisitions on the industry may be powerful; the top 10 restaurant chains now control over 50 percent of all fast-food sales in the United States. The consolidation of a number of these firms within larger, financially more powerful firms should give these restaurant chains the financial and managerial resources to outgrow their smaller competitors.

Demographic Trends

29   Intense marketing by the leading fast-food chains likely will continue to stimulate demand for fast food in the United States during the 1990s. However, a number of demographic and societal changes are likely to impact the future demand for fast food in different directions. One such change is the rise in single-person households, which have steadily increased from 17 percent of all U.S. households in 1970 to approximately 25 percent today. In addition, disposable household income should continue to increase, mainly because more women are working than ever before. According to Standard & Poor's *Industry Surveys*, Americans spent 38 percent of their food dollars at restaurants in 1988, up 25 percent from 1970. Most of this increase came from increased consumption, while the balance came mainly from higher prices. The National Restaurant Association estimates that Americans ate out on average 3.7 times per week and spent an average of $3.52 per meal in 1988.

30   In addition to these demographic trends, a number of societal changes also may impact future demand for fast food. For example, microwave ovens now have been introduced into approximately 70

percent of all U.S. homes. This already has resulted in a significant shift in the types of products sold in supermarkets and convenience stores, which have introduced a variety of products that can be quickly and easily prepared in microwaves. In addition, the aging of America's baby boomers may change the frequency with which people patronize more upscale restaurants. Last, birth rates are projected to rise in the 1990s. This is likely to have an impact on whether families eat out or stay home. Therefore, these various demographic and societal trends are likely to impact the future demand for fast food in different ways.

International Quick-Service Market

31   Because of the aggressive pace of new restaurant construction in the United States during the 1970s and 1980s, future growth resulting from new restaurant construction in the United States may be limited. In any case, the cost of finding prime locations is rising—increasing the pressure on restaurant chains to increase per store sales to cover higher initial investment costs. One alternative to continued investment in the U.S. market is expansion into international markets, which offer large customer bases and comparatively little competition. However, few U.S. restaurant chains have yet defined aggressive strategies for penetrating international markets.

32   Two restaurant chains that have established successful international strategies are McDonald's and Kentucky Fried Chicken. While McDonald's has the most restaurants in the U.S. market, Kentucky Fried Chicken operates the greatest number of units outside of the United States, opening its 3,000th restaurant abroad in 1989. However, in terms of sales, McDonald's remains the world's largest restaurant chain. In 1989, McDonald's foreign sales were $5.3 billion, approximately twice that of KFC, which had foreign sales of $2.4 billion. In early 1990, McDonald's was operating 2,900 restaurants in 52 countries.

33   Exhibit 6 shows *Hotels and Restaurants International's* 1990 list of the world's 20 largest fast-food restaurant chains. Several important observations may be made from these data. First, 16 of the 20 largest restaurant chains are headquartered in the United States. Only two non-U.S. companies appear in the largest 15 restaurant chains. This may be partially explained by the fact that U.S. firms account for over 25 percent of the world's foreign direct investment. As a result, U.S. firms have historically been more likely to invest assets abroad. However, while both Kentucky Fried Chicken and McDonald's both have close to 3,000 units abroad, no other restaurant chain, U.S. or foreign, has more than 700 units outside of the United States. In fact, most chains have fewer than 100 foreign units and operate in less than 10 countries.

34   There are a number of possible explanations for the relative scarcity of fast-food restaurant chains outside the United States. First, the United States represents the largest consumer market in the world, accounting for almost one fourth of the world's GNP. Therefore, the United States traditionally has been the strategic focus of the largest restaurant chains. In addition, Americans have been quicker to accept the fast-food concept. Many other cultures have strong culinary traditions, which have not been easy to break down. The Europeans, for example, have long histories of frequenting more mid-scale restaurants, where they may spend several hours in a formal setting enjoying native dishes and beverages. While Kentucky Fried Chicken again is building restaurants in Germany, it previously failed to penetrate the German market because Germans were not accustomed to take-out food or to ordering food over the counter. McDonald's has had greater success penetrating the German market because it has made a number of changes in its menu and operating procedures to better appeal to German culture. For example, German beer is served in all of McDonald's German restaurants. KFC has had more success in Asia, where chicken is a traditional dish.

35   Aside from cultural factors, international business carries risks not present in the U.S. market. Long distances between headquarters and foreign franchises often make it difficult to control the quality of individual franchises. Large distances also can cause servicing and support problems. Transportation and other resource costs also may be higher than in the domestic market. In addition, time,

EXHIBIT 6
The World's 20 Largest Fast-Food Chains (1989)

Franchise	Location	Units	Countries
1 McDonald's	Oakbrook, IL	11,162	52
2 Kentucky Fried Chicken	Louisville, KY	7,948	58
3 Burger King	Miami, FL	6,041	34
4 Subway Sandwiches	Milford, CT	4,000	5
5 Wendy's	Dublin, OH	3,755	23
6 Hardee's	Rocky Mount, NC	3,291	9
7 Taco Bell	Irvine, CA	3,125	9
8 Kozo Sushi	Osaka, Japan	2,347	3
9 Arby's	Atlanta, GA	2,224	8
10 Long John Silvers	Lexington, KY	1,500	3
11 Church's Fried Chicken	Jefferson, LA	1,111	9
12 Big Boy	Warren, MI	1,000	3
13 Popeyes	Jefferson, LA	750	6
14 Loteria	Tokyo, Japan	702	3
15 A&W Restaurants	Livonia, MI	599	9
16 Taco Time	Eugene, OR	321	7
17 Country Kitchen	Minneapolis, MN	265	2
18 White Castle	Columbus, OH	244	2
19 Wimpy	London, England	220	21
20 Flunch	Villeneuve d'Ascq., France	118	3

Source: *Hotels and Restaurants International,* May 1990

cultural, and language differences can increase communication and operational problems. Therefore, it is reasonable to expect U.S. restaurant chains to expand domestically as long as they can reasonably achieve corporate profit and growth objectives. However, as the U.S. market becomes more saturated, and companies gain additional expertise in international business, we should expect more companies to turn to profitable international markets as a means of expanding store bases and of increasing sales, profits, and market share.

KENTUCKY FRIED CHICKEN CORPORATION

Management

36   One of PepsiCo's greatest challenges when it acquired Kentucky Fried Chicken in 1986 was how to mold two distinct corporate cultures. When R. J. Reynolds acquired KFC in 1982, it realized that it knew very little about the fast-food business. Therefore, it relied on existing KFC management to continue managing the company. As a result, there was little need for mixing the cultures of the two

companies. However, one of PepsiCo's major concerns when considering the purchase of KFC was whether it had the management skills required to successfully operate KFC using PepsiCo managers. PepsiCo already had acquired considerable experience managing fast-food businesses through its Pizza Hut and Taco Bell operations. Therefore, it was anxious to pursue strategic changes within KFC that would improve performance. However, replacing KFC with PepsiCo managers easily could cause conflicts between managers in both companies, who were accustomed to different operating procedures and working conditions.

37   PepsiCo's corporate culture long has been based heavily on a "fast-track" New York approach to management. It hires the country's top business and engineering graduates and promotes them based on performance. As a result, top performers expect to move up through the ranks quickly and to be paid well for their efforts. However, the competitive environment often results in intense rivalries among young managers. If one fails to perform, there is always another top performer waiting in the wings. As a result, employee loyalty sometimes is lost and turnover tends to be higher than in other companies.

38   The corporate culture at Kentucky Fried Chicken in 1986 contrasted sharply with that at PepsiCo. KFC's culture was built largely on Colonel Sanders' laid-back approach to management. As well, employees enjoyed relatively good employment stability and security. Over the years, a strong loyalty had been created among KFC employees and franchisees, mainly because of the efforts of Colonel Sanders and to provide for his employees' benefits, pensions, and other nonincome needs. In addition, the southern environment of Louisville resulted in a friendly, relaxed atmosphere at KFC's corporate offices. This corporate culture was left essentially unchanged during the Heublein years.

39   When PepsiCo acquired KFC, it began to restructure the KFC organization, replacing most of KFC's top managers with its own. By the summer of 1990, all of KFC's top positions were occupied by PepsiCo executives. In July 1989, KFC's president and chief executive officer, Richard P. Mayer, left KFC to become president of General Foods USA. Mayer had been at KFC since 1977, when KFC was still owned by Heublein. PepsiCo replaced Mayer with John Cranor III, the former president of Pepsi-Cola East, a Pepsi-Cola unit. In November 1989, Martin Redgrave moved from PepsiCo to become KFC's new chief financial officer. In the summer of 1990, Bill McDonald, a Pizza Hut and Frito Lay marketing executive, was named senior vice president of marketing. Two months before, PepsiCo had named Kyle Craig, a former Pillsbury executive, as president of KFC's USA operations.

40   Most of PepsiCo's initial management changes in 1987 focused on KFC's corporate offices and USA operations. In 1988, attention was turned to KFC's international division. During 1988, PepsiCo replaced KFC International's top managers with its own. First, it lured Don Pierce away from Burger King and made Pierce president of KFC International. However, Pierce left KFC in early 1990 to become president of Pentagram Corporation, a restaurant operation in Hawaii. Pierce commented that he wished to change jobs partly to decrease the amount of time he spent traveling. PepsiCo replaced Pierce with Allan Huston, who was formerly senior vice president of operations at Pizza Hut. In late 1988, PepsiCo also brought in Robert Briggs, former director of finance at Pepsi-Cola International, as vice president of international finance. (See Exhibit 7 for current organizational chart.)

41   An example of the type of conflict faced by PepsiCo in attempting to implement changes within KFC occurred in August 1989. A month after becoming president and chief executive officer, Cranor addressed KFC's franchisees in Louisville to explain the details of a new franchisee contract. This was the first contract change in 13 years. The new contract gave PepsiCo management greater power to take over weak franchises, to relocate new stores, and to make changes in existing restaurants. In addition, existing stores would no longer be protected from competition from new KFC restaurants. The contract also gave management to right to raise royalty fees on existing restaurants as contracts came up for renewal. After Cranor finished his address, there was an uproar among the attending franchisees, who jumped to their feet to protest the changes. The franchisees long had been accustomed to relatively little interference from management in their day-to-day operations. This type of interference, of course, was a strong part of PepsiCo's philosophy of demanding change.

EXHIBIT 7
KFC Organizational Chart

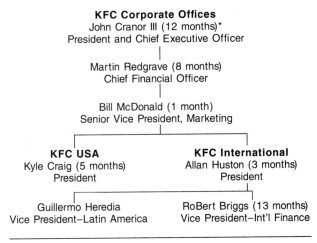

KFC Corporate Offices
John Cranor III (12 months)*
President and Chief Executive Officer

Martin Redgrave (8 months)
Chief Financial Officer

Bill McDonald (1 month)
Senior Vice President, Marketing

KFC USA	**KFC International**
Kyle Craig (5 months)	Allan Huston (3 months)
President	President

Guillermo Heredia
Vice President–Latin America

RoBert Briggs (13 months)
Vice President–Int'l Finance

*Number of months with KFC as of August 1, 1990.

Operating Results

42   KFC's recent operating results are shown in Exhibit 8. In 1989, worldwide sales, which represent sales of both company-owned and franchised restaurants, reached $5.4 billion. Since 1984, worldwide sales have grown by a compounded annual growth rate of 13.2 percent. This is significantly higher than the 5–7 percent annual growth rate of all U.S. fast-food chains. KFC's market share reached 51 percent of the $5.9 billion U.S. market in 1989. KFC's 1989 corporate sales, which include company-owned restaurants and royalties from franchised units, reached $1.3 billion, up 10 percent from 1988 sales of $1.2 billion. New restaurant construction represented 60 percent of this increase in sales, with the balance resulting mainly from increased pricing.

43   Despite KFC's continued dominance of its industry segment, it experienced a 14 percent decline in worldwide profits in 1989 to $100 million, down from $117 million in 1988. This resulted mainly from lower volumes in U.S. stores, partially the result of higher pricing undertaken in 1989. As well, intense competition within the U.S. market continues to affect sales. In contrast to the U.S. market, KFC continues to profit from its international units. In particular, international sales in 1989 were strongest in Australia, New Zealand, and Canada, where additional units, increased prices, and volume increases helped to significantly increase profits over 1988.

Business Level Strategies

Marketing

44   As KFC entered 1990, it focused its marketing strategy on three issues: pricing, new product introductions, and improved distribution. Pricing was of special significance. In 1989, KFC had undertaken a series of price increases, partially to offset higher chicken costs. However, higher prices had cut into sales by the fourth quarter of 1989. In an interview with *Nation's Restaurant News* in February 1990, Smith Barney analyst Joseph Doyle estimated that 3 percent of the 5 percent decline in KFC's fourth quarter 1990 sales came from price hikes. The unexpected decline in KFC sales

EXHIBIT 8
KFC Operating Results

	Worldwide Sales ($b)	KFC Corp.* Sales ($b)	KFC Corp.* Profit ($m)	Percent
1984	$ 2.9			
1985	3.1			
1986	3.5			
1987	4.1	$1.1	$ 90.0	8.3%
1988	5.0	1.2	116.5	9.6
1989	5.4	1.3	100.0	7.5
CAGR%	13.2%			

*KFC corporate figures include company stores and franchisee fees. Data prior to 1987 consolidated with RJReynolds.
Sources: PepsiCo annual reports for 1986, 1987, 1988, and 1989.

demonstrated the importance consumers placed on price and perceived value. As a result, KFC entered 1990 determined to create a better consumer image regarding the value of its products. In early 1990, KFC lowered prices on a number of menu items to make them more competitive. In fact, some prices were planned to be rolled back to 1979 levels. In addition, a number of promotions were planned to offer customers special pricing in double buckets of chicken and other food combinations.

45   In addition to pricing issues, much of the competitive pressure currently being felt by KFC is the result of KFC's traditional slowness in introducing new products to its menu. The popularity of its original-recipe fried chicken allowed KFC to expand through most of the 1980s without significant competition from other chicken competitors. As a result, new product introductions were never an important part of KFC strategy. However, the introduction of chicken sandwiches by hamburger chains has changed the competitive makeup of KFC's competitors. Most important, McDonald's introduced its McChicken sandwich in the U.S. market in 1989 while KFC was still testing its new sandwich. KFC introduced its chicken sandwich several months later. By beating KFC into the market, McDonald's was able to develop a strong consumer awareness for its sandwich. As a result, it will be extremely costly for KFC to develop consumer awareness for its own chicken sandwich. The increased popularity of healthier foods also is creating a need for new products. To capitalize on this trend, KFC now is testing grilled chicken on the bone in Louisville and Las Vegas. A grilled chicken fillet sandwich also is being tested and two new products—"Hot Wings," a spicy chicken wing, and "Hot & Spicy Chicken"—were introduced in early 1990.

46   A third marketing strategy of increasing importance is distribution. KFC traditionally has catered to the take-out and dine-in market. However, the successful implementation of home delivery systems by such pizza chains as Domino's and Pizza Hut has created a new outlet for fast-food sales. Most of the growth in the pizza segment during the last three years has come from home delivery. In early 1990, KFC began testing home delivery in Louisville, Columbus, and several Chicago suburbs. Other distribution channels that offer significant growth opportunities are shopping malls and other high-traffic areas, which have not traditionally been exploited by fast-food chains. Increasingly, shopping malls are developing food areas where several fast-food restaurant chains compete against each other. Universities, hospitals, and corporate parks also offer opportunities for KFC and other chains to improve distribution.

Operating Efficiencies

47   While marketing strategies traditionally improve a firm's profit picture indirectly through increased sales, the improved operating efficiencies can directly impact operating profits. As pressure builds to limit price increases in the U.S. market, restaurant chains will be forced to find ways of reducing overhead and other operating costs to improve profit margins. In 1989, KFC reorganized its U.S. operations to eliminate overhead costs and to increase efficiency. Included in this reorganization was a revision of KFC's crew training programs and operating standards. A renewed emphasis has been placed on improving customer service, on cleaner stores, on faster and friendlier service, and on continued high-quality products. In 1987, computer-controlled fryers were introduced to improve quality and to reduce costs. Computer fryers cook at even temperature and result in less waste of oil and product. In addition, less labor is needed to monitor cooking.

Restaurant Expansion and International Operations

48   While marketing and operating strategies can improve sales and profitability in existing outlets, an important part of success in the quick-service industry is investment growth. Much of the success of the top 10 competitors within the industry during the 1980s can be found in aggressive building strategies. In particular, a restaurant chain often is able to discourage competition by being the first to build in a low-populated area that can only support a single fast-food chain. On the other hand, it is equally important to beat a competitor into more-populated areas, where location is of prime importance.

49   Internationally, KFC opened its 3,000th restaurant outside the United States in 1989. KFC is now the largest quick-service restaurant and the only major chicken system in the world. While U.S. operations showed a decline in operating profits in 1989 as the result of declining customer counts and higher chicken and labor costs, KFC's international operations continued to improve on all criteria. In the future, KFC's international operations will be called on to provide an increasing percentage of KFC's overall sales and profit growth as the U.S. market continues to become saturated.

MEXICO

50   KFC was one of the first restaurant chains to recognize the importance of international markets. By 1971, KFC already was operating in 48 countries. In Latin America, KFC now operates subsidiaries in Mexico and Puerto Rico, and it was operating 94 franchises in 19 countries in the Caribbean at the end of 1989. In addition, KFC plans to open new units in several South American countries in the near future. In the summer of 1990, a franchise was opened in Chile, increasing the number of countries in which KFC operates to 59. Other countries considered to be promising markets are Argentina and Brazil, whose large populations and market sizes offer significant opportunities for growth.

Franchising

51   In Mexico, KFC traditionally has relied on the operation of company-owned stores. At the end of 1989, KFC was operating 55 restaurants, all company-owned (see Exhibit 9). While franchising is popular in the United States, it is still virtually unknown in Mexico. Until the end of 1989, franchises were difficult to operate, because of government restrictions on the payment of royalties and lack of legal protection for the transfer of technology and trade secrets. As a result, it has been more advantageous to operate company-owned stores, which allow KFC to maximize control over assets and technology. However, a new franchise law was passed in 1989, opening the way for franchising in Mexico. The new legislation eliminates much of the discretionary power of the Secretariat of Industry

EXHIBIT 9
Fast-Food Industry in Mexico

	1989 Units	Market Share
KFC	57	9.5%
McDonald's	81	1.3
Burger Boy	48	8.0
Pollo Loco	110	18.3
Church's	13	2.2
Pizza Hut	19	3.2
VIPs	52	8.7
Sanborn's	41	6.8
Other	252	42.0
Total	600	100.0%

and Commerce to regulate foreign franchising in Mexico and allows parties of a franchising agreement to establish their own terms and conditions. KFC planned to use franchising to drive future growth in Mexico and planned to open its first franchises in 1990.

52   At the end of 1989, KFC was operating restaurants in three regions: Mexico City, Guadalajara, and Monterrey. By limiting operations to these three regions, KFC has been able to better coordinate operations and minimize costs of distribution to individual restaurants. With the passing of new franchise legislation, however, KFC now should be able to more easily expand its store base to other regions, where responsibility for management will be handled by individual franchisees. Arby's, McDonald's, and Baskin Robbins already had signed new franchise agreements by July 1990. This increased the pressure on KFC to quickly expand its own franchises in Mexico, or risk losing market share, most importantly to McDonald's.

Economic and Political Environment

53   Many factors make Mexico a potentially profitable location for U.S. direct investment and trade. Mexico's population of 85 million people is approximately one third as large as the United States. This represents a large market for U.S. goods. Because of its geographical proximity to the United States, transportation costs from the Unites States are minimal. This increases the competitiveness of U.S. goods in comparison with European and Asian goods, which must be transported at substantial cost across the Atlantic or Pacific oceans. The United States is, in fact, Mexico's largest trading partner. Almost 75 percent of Mexico's imports come from the United States, while 72 percent of Mexico's export's are to the U.S. market (see Exhibit 10). In addition, low wage rates make Mexico an attractive location for production. By producing in Mexico, U.S. firms may reduce labor costs and increase the cost competitiveness of their goods in world markets.

54   Despite the importance of the U.S. market to Mexico, Mexico still represents a small percentage of overall U.S. trade and investment. U.S. exports to Canada and Asia, where economic growth has outpaced growth in Mexico, have increased more quickly. Canada is the largest importer of U.S. goods. Japan is the largest exporter of goods to the United States, with Canada close behind. While the value of Mexico's exports to the United States has increased during the last two decades, mainly

EXHIBIT 10
Major Trading Partners—1988

	Total Exports (%)	Total Imports (%)
U.S.A.	72.9%	74.9%
Japan	4.9	6.4
West Germany	1.3	3.5
France	1.8	2.0
Other	19.1	13.2

Source: *Business International,* 1990.

because of the rise in the price of oil, Mexico still represents a small percentage of overall U.S. trade. U.S. investment in Mexico also has been small, mainly because of government restrictions on foreign investment. Instead, most U.S. foreign investment has been in Europe, Canada, and Asia.

55 The lack of U.S. investment in and trade with Mexico during this century is mainly the result of Mexico's long history of restricting trade and foreign direct investment in Mexico. In particular, the Institutional Revolutionary Party (PRI), which came to power in Mexico during the 1930s, traditionally has pursued protectionist economic policies to shield its people and economy from foreign firms and goods. Industries have been predominately government-owned or controlled, and production has been pursued for the domestic market only. High tariffs and other trade barriers have restricted imports into Mexico, and foreign ownership of assets in Mexico has been largely prohibited or heavily restricted.

56 In addition, a dictatorial and entrenched government bureaucracy, corrupt labor unions, and a long tradition of anti-Americanism among many government officials and intellectuals has reduced the motivation of U.S. firms for investing in Mexico. As well, the 1982 nationalization of Mexico's banks resulted in higher real interest rates and destroyed investor confidence. Since then, the Mexican government has battled high inflation, high interest rates, labor unrest, and lost consumer purchasing power (see Exhibit 11). Total foreign debt, which stood at $95.1 billion at the end of 1989, remains a problem.

57 Investor confidence in Mexico, however, has improved since December 1988, when Carlos Salinas de Gortari was elected president of Mexico. Salinas has since embarked on an ambitious restructuring of the Mexican economy. In particular, Salinas has initiated policies to strengthen the free market components of the economy. Top marginal tax rates were lowered to 36 percent in 1990, down from 60 percent in 1986, and new legislation has eliminated many restrictions on foreign investment. Foreign firms now are allowed to buy up to 100 percent equity in many Mexican firms. Previously, foreign ownership of Mexican firms was limited to 49 percent. Many government-owned companies have been sold to private investors to eliminate government bureaucracy and improve efficiency. Government spending has been reduced, and a program of price and wage controls has been implemented. In addition, many tariff and nontrade barriers have been eliminated, paving the way for increased trade with the United States.

Import Controls

58 Prior to 1989, Mexico levied high tariffs on most imported goods. In addition, many other goods were subjected to quotas, licensing requirements, and other nontariff trade barriers. In 1986, Mexico joined the General Agreement on Tariffs and Trade (GATT), a world trade organization designed to

EXHIBIT 11
Economic Data for Mexico

	1986	1987	1988	1989
Population (millions)	79.6	81.2	83.3	85.0
GDP (billion pesos)	77.8	193.0	398.0	500.0^e
Real GDP growth (%)	(3.6)	1.6	1.4	2.9
Exchange rate (av.) pesos/US$	611.8	1,378.2	2,273.1	2,453.5
Inflation (%)	86.2	131.8	114.2	20.0
Current account (US$ billions)	(1.7)	3.9	(2.4)	(5.4)
Reserves (excl. gold US$ billions)	5.7	12.5	5.3	7.3
External debt (US$ billions)	100.9	109.3	100.4	95.1
Debt service ratio (%)	50.7	37.3	43.1	—

e means estimated.
Source: *Business International,* 1990.

eliminate barriers to trade among member nations. As a member of GATT, Mexico is obligated to apply its system of tariffs to all member nations equally. As a result of its membership in GATT, Mexico has since dropped tariff rates on a variety of imported goods. In addition, import license requirements have been dropped for all but 300 imported items.

Privatization

59 The privatization of government-owned companies has come to symbolize the restructuring of Mexico's economy. Over 700 government-owned companies have been sold, including Mexicana and AeroMexico, the two largest airline companies in Mexico. On May 14, 1990, legislation was passed to privatize all banks. However, 400 companies remain under government ownership. These represent 90 percent of the assets owned by the state at the start of 1988. Therefore, the sale of government-owned companies, in terms of asset value, has been small. In addition, certain strategic industries, such as the steel, electricity, and petroleum industries, by law are protected by government ownership. As a result, additional privatization of government-owned enterprises may be limited.

Price, Wages, and Foreign Exchange

60 A two-tiered exchange rate system has been in force in Mexico since December 1982. Under this system, a controlled rate is used for imports, foreign debt payments, and conversion of export proceeds. A free market rate is used for other transactions. In January 1988, the Mexican government announced the Pact for Stabilization and Economic Growth (PECE), which replaced the government's December 1987 regulation on prices and wages. The PECE was designed to limit increases in prices and wages, as well as drastic changes in value of the peso against the dollar. On January 1, 1989, Salinas announced that the peso would be allowed to depreciate against the dollar by 1 peso per day. This applied to exports, imports, foreign debt, and royalty payments. The result has been a grossly overvalued peso, which has lowered the price of imports. This led to an increase in imports of over

23 percent in 1989. At the same time, Mexican exports have become less cost competitive on world markets.

61   While the PECE has slowed the rate of inflation and lowered interest rates, it also has resulted in lost purchasing power, because wage increases have failed to keep up with inflation. This has increased labor unrest. Once price and wage controls are eliminated, it is possible that inflation will increase rapidly, as merchants and workers attempt to regain losses sustained under the PECE. As well, once the peso is allowed to float freely against the dollar, it is likely to devalue rapidly. This will increase import prices and inflation. This could have a devastating effect on consumer confidence in the economy and in the Salinas government.

Labor Problems

62   One of KFC's primary concerns is the stability of Mexico's labor markets. Labor is relatively plentiful and cheap in Mexico, though much of the work force is still relatively unskilled. While KFC benefits from lower labor costs, the problems of labor unrest, job retention, absenteeism, and punctuality continue to be significant. A good part of the problem with absenteeism and punctuality is cultural. However, problems with worker retention and labor unrest are mainly the result of workers' frustration over the loss of their purchasing power due to inflation and government controls on wage increases. *Business Latin America* estimated that purchasing power fell by 35 percent in Mexico between January 1988 and June 1990. Though absenteeism is on the decline due to job security fears, it is still high at approximately 8 to 14 percent of the labor force. Turnover also continues to be a problem. Turnover of production line personnel currently is running at 5 to 12 percent per month. Therefore, employee screening and internal training continue to be important issues for foreign firms investing in Mexico.

RISKS AND OPPORTUNITIES

63   Managers in KFC Mexico were hopeful that the government's new economic policies would bring inflation under control and promote growth in Mexico's economy. They also hoped that greater economic stability would help to eliminate much of the the labor unrest that has plagued Mexico during the last several years. Of greatest concern to Guillermo Heredia, KFC's vice president of Latin America, was KFC's market share in Mexico. Heredia expected McDonald's and Arby's to begin aggressive building programs in Mexico, since both had signed franchise agreements in early 1990. If KFC failed to grow at least as quickly as these and other competitors, it could easily lose its No. 1 market share in Mexico. In fact, KFC planned to counter McDonald's by expanding its franchise base in Mexico and relying less heavily on company-owned restaurants as it had in the past. However, this strategy had significant risk. The franchising law was new. As a result, KFC could only hope that its technology and trade secrets would be protected under the new law, which has not yet been tested in the courts.

64   In addition to the risks surrounding the new franchise law, KFC worried that the Mexican government might be unable to correct the severe problems in Mexico's economy. In particular, once price and wage controls are eliminated, inflation again could become a problem, as businesses and workers attempt to recover lost profits and purchasing power sustained under the government's austerity program. It also was questionable whether the PRI would maintain its power in the future. The PRI faces serious challenges from the opposition Party of the Democratic Revolution (PRD) in 1991 elections for the senate and the chamber of deputies. If the PRI were to lose power to the PRD in the near future, the PRD, which favors more government control in the economy, could overturn the more free market policies recently implemented by the PRI.

65   KFC's alternative, one favored by many at PepsiCo, was to approach investment in Mexico more conservatively, until greater economic and political stability could be achieved. Instead, resources could be directed at other investment areas with less risk, such as Japan, Australia, China, and Europe. However, PepsiCo's commitments to these other markets were unlikely to be affected by its investment decisions in Mexico, because PepsiCo's large annual cash flows could satisfy the investment needs of KFC's other international subsidiaries, regardless of its investments in Mexico. However, the danger in taking a conservative approach in Mexico was the potential loss of market share in a large market where Kentucky Fried Chicken enjoyed enormous popularity among its customers.

B STRATEGY IMPLEMENTATION

PULSE ENGINEERING

1   David Flowers, chairman and chief executive officer of Pulse Engineering, Inc., hung up the telephone after talking to yet another newspaper reporter about the prospect of a North American Free Trade Agreement (NAFTA). The controversy over "maquiladoras," in-bond assembly plants mostly located in northern Mexico, was heating up. The economic recession during the 1992 U.S. presidential election campaign, and the ongoing NAFTA negotiations, including the United States, Canada, and Mexico, led to a lot of interest in Pulse's Mexican factories. U.S. labor union leaders complained about the flight of U.S. industry offshore, and the AFL–CIO recently joined forces with environmental groups to raise the alarm about industrial pollution along the U.S.–Mexican border. Many observers pointed to maquiladoras as examples or precursors of NAFTA, while others announced the "maquiladoras will cease to exist" with free trade. As a result, the media was always looking for conflict and controversy between the critics and corporate leaders. Dave Flowers only wished there was as much interest in the company-operated neighborhood health clinic in Tijuana. He also wondered about the long-term relative labor cost advantage of Mexico, given the increasing demand for workers there.

THE COMPANY

2   Pulse is headquartered in San Diego, California, the largest U.S. city on the Mexican border; half of the population along the 2,000-mile U.S.–Mexican border resides in San Diego and Tijuana, Baja California. Pulse opened its first Mexican facility in 1967 and additional facilities in 1979 and 1984.

3   Pulse Engineering, Inc., designs, manufactures, and markets electronic components and modules for the leading manufacturers of local area network (LAN), data processing, and telecommunication equipment. Pulse transformers are miniature magnetic components used for coupling, control, isolation, and impedance matching in LANs and computers. For example, Pulse transformers isolate interface circuits within LAN equipment and intelligent terminals. New applications were being driven by integrated services digital networks and engineering standards. Pulse delay lines are signal devices used to manage the timing of high-frequency electrical impulses in IBM PS/2 personal computer memory systems and controller circuits.

This case was written by Professor Stephen Jenner of California State University.

4   Sales in 1991 were approximately $72 million, with profits of $5.7 million. Pulse was the market leader in three of its four product lines. The company was differentiated by its direct sales force and technical staff who worked closely with the design engineers for its top customers; approximately half of its products were designed for specific applications. Over 5,000 other customers worldwide were serviced by foreign manufacturers' representatives or through catalog sales.

BUILDING A SUSTAINABLE LABOR COST ADVANTAGE

5   Although most people in the United States are just now learning about maquiladoras, they are neither new nor unique to Mexico. For decades, multinational corporations, as well as small to medium-size companies, increasingly looked offshore in their sourcing strategies. The global phenomenon of "production sharing" is the decentralization and internationalization of the production process, in which raw materials and components produced in an industrialized country are further processed or assembled in a developing nation for export back to the country of origin, or to other export markets. To a large extent, this is possible due to technological advances in transportation and communications, which reduce the cost and time required to move goods and information around the world, allowing companies to take advantage of large differences in wage rates. Although production sharing is possible at great distances, there are important advantages of geographical proximity, which lowers transportation costs and lead times and allows managers and technicians to travel back and forth quickly to offshore plants to control day-to-day operations or to solve problems. The company also had offshore manufacturing facilities in Ireland, Hong Kong, and the People's Republic of China (PRC). (See Exhibit 1.)

6   Maquiladoras most often made use of U.S. Tariff Item 9802, which reduces duty in the case of production sharing. When in-bond products return to the U.S. market, U.S. Customs calculated a small duty based only on the value added in Mexico. This policy dates back to the 1930s and is based on the idea that it makes no sense to impose an import tax on U.S.-made components. Some maquiladoras took advantage of trade benefits to less developed countries under the General Agreement on Tariffs and Trade (GATT).

7   Companies paid no duty if their product qualified for special treatment under the Generalized System of Preferences (GSP) under GATT; generally speaking, this duty-free import required 35 percent content from the less-developed country. Mexico's competitive position as a location for offshore production relative to Taiwan, South Korea, and Singapore improved when those three Asian countries no longer were considered less-developed countries and lost their GSP status. The exchange rate was another positive factor in comparing Mexico with Asian countries. (See graph of wages for manufacturing workers in Asia and Mexico, in Exhibit 2.)

8   In Europe, German, French, Dutch, and British companies had similar production sharing or "Outward Processing Relief Arrangements" with factories in Yugoslavia, Hungary, Romania, and Poland, although European firms had not used production sharing nearly as much as U.S. firms, except for textiles and apparel. European countries had stronger labor unions and offered more protection to domestic producers, tariffs were higher, and the administrative procedures were more complex. However, the reasons for European production sharing were similar: gaining significant cost reductions by relocating labor-intensive processes of production to low-wage-rate countries, and overcoming growing competition from low-cost suppliers in East Asia and other developing countries.

9   In the case of the United States and Mexico, the maquiladora program was created in 1965 as a response to the end of the U.S. "Bracero Program," which facilitated the employment of Mexican farm workers north of the border. Maquiladoras also sought to replace Asian sources for U.S. manufacturers, bringing benefits to the local economies of U.S.–Mexican border states. However, critics of the maquiladora program argue that, with the exception of generating foreign exchange, the program failed to achieve its original objectives. Most of the workers were young Mexican women entering

EXHIBIT 1
Pulse Facilities Review, February 1992

Location/Size	Products	Charter
San Diego, CA 50,000 sq. ft.	R&D all products.	Corporate offices. Engineering. Marketing. Finance. Quality. Warehousing.
Wesson, MS 45,000 sq. ft.	EMI filters.	Custom products. More than 10 amps. Industrial filters. Military filters.
Tijuana—Pul, S.A. 60,000 sq. ft.	Network modules. Pulse transformers. Power magnetics. Prototypes—all products.	Custom products. Preproduction. Higher complexity. Larger size.
Chihuahua—PEDC 46,000 sq. ft.	Pulse transformers. Network modules. Power magnetics.	Longer runs. Standard process.
Ireland 58,500 sq. ft	Delay lines. Thick film. Network modules.	European market. Mechanized products. Capital Intensive. Product development.
Hong Kong–Pel 13,000 sq. ft.	Network modules. Power magnetics. Pulse transformers. Delay lines.	Far East market. Low-cost materials. Coordinate PRC
China, PRC 1 25,000 sq. ft.	Power magnetics. Delay lines. Network modules.	Lowest-cost labor. Long runners. Standard processes.
China, PRC 2	Power magnetics.	Lowest-cost labor. Long runners. Standard processes.
China, PRC 3 36,000 sq. ft.	Network modules. Pulse transformers.	Lowest-cost labor. Long runners. Standard processes.

the labor force for the first time, so there was little reduction in unemployment or underemployment. Only 2 percent of other inputs than labor were of Mexican origin, and there was little transfer of technology since most of the production carried out in Mexico was unskilled assembly work. Recently, critics in the United States and Mexico attacked the twin problems of occupational safety and health and of environmental pollution from hazardous waste.

10   In terms of host country controls, the maquiladoras enjoyed special treatment by Mexico. Until 1989, the Mexican foreign investment regulations required corporations to have at least 51 percent Mexican ownership, with the exception of maquiladoras. Historically, there were also high tariff barriers and import licensing requirements designed to protect domestic industry and minimize sales of foreign goods and services in Mexico. However, in the special case of maquiladoras, U.S.–based companies (some of them subsidiaries of Japanese multinationals) were allowed to bring equipment, raw materials, and components into Mexico after posting a small bond with Mexican Customs as a

EXHIBIT 2

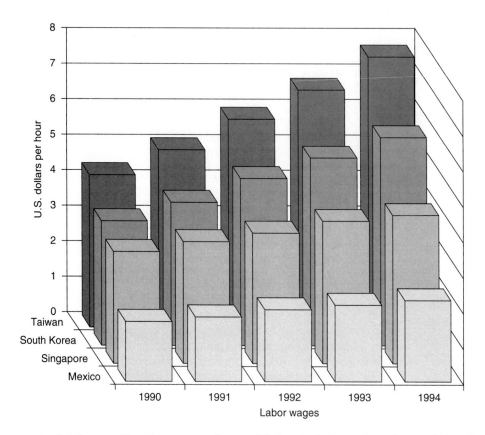

guarantee that these would not be permanent imports. Mexico also had controls on the repatriation of foreign exchange, which required foreign corporations to maintain at least an equilibrium. The Mexican tax code also was changing, seeking to impose higher taxes on maquiladora assets (2 percent per year) and foreign managers and technicians (20 percent income tax withholding).

NAFTA AND THE MAQUILADORAS

11 Because the U.S. economy was 25 times bigger than Mexico's in 1991, the gradual elimination of tariff and nontariff barriers between the two countries would have only a small impact on trade flows and U.S. employment. The results of a study released in March 1992 by the Institute for International Economics concluded that NAFTA would improve the U.S. overall annual trade balance by $10 billion, and turn the U.S. trade balance with Mexico from a $2 billion deficit in 1990 to a $9 billion surplus in 1995, because of sharp increases in exports of pharmaceuticals, high-grade steel, construction equipment, and industrial chemicals. According to the study, by 1996 the United States would add 130,000 new jobs even after subtracting 112,000 jobs eliminated by Mexican imports; Mexico would gain 600,000 jobs; and 700,000 Mexican agricultural laborers would migrate into cities.

12   The most important driving forces for NAFTA were President Bush's desire to reward the Mexican president, Carlos Salinas, for his "right think" economic policies, and Salinas's own need to attract

foreign investment. Carlos Salinas was hand-picked by his predecessor in the ruling Mexican political party, which dominated Mexico since its revolution in 1910. Salinas earned a PhD in Economics at Harvard University and became president of Mexico in 1988 at the age of 39. He made a number of successful and bold moves, including the privatization of many government-owned enterprises, the reduction of tariffs and import licensing requirements, and a dramatic drop in inflation. Mexico opposed a free trade agreement with the United States for many years, but that changed when Salinas traveled to Europe in January of 1990 seeking foreign investment. European investors were much more interested in Central European countries than in Mexico, as were many big Japanese investors.

13 One of the biggest impacts of NAFTA would be a perception by foreign investors that there would be less political risk in Mexico (i.e., a lower probability of forced expropriation). Even without NAFTA, Mexico's stock market attracted massive investments in 1990–92 as it outperformed the rest of the world. That money parked in the Mexican stock market was expected to be converted into longer-term equity investments in high-growth Mexican companies. The growth of the Mexican economy benefitted the United States most of all, since 70 percent of Mexican imports came from the United States.

14 President Salinas appeared on the "MacNeil-Lehrer News Hour" on U.S. Public Television in 1990 arguing that NAFTA would reduce the migration of Mexicans into the United States; either invest in Mexico so Mexicans could stay home and work, or they would move north looking for jobs in the United States, he argued. However, some experts on immigration from Mexico argued that, since one of the industries that would attract foreign investment under NAFTA was agriculture, the poor Mexican farmers displaced from their tiny communal farms called "ejidos" would most likely come to the United States. These arguments suggested that, in the short-term, there would be an increase in the flow of people, but that, in the long term, Mexicans would be more likely to stay in their own country.

15 Protection of the environment was emerging as a high priority socially, and NAFTA was the first trade negotiation ever to address this issue. It was expected that Mexico would have to make major improvements in the control of industrial pollution to obtain the benefits of freer trade with its neighbors to the north. Maquiladoras were increasingly being audited by the Mexican version of the U.S. Environmental Protection Agency, SEDUE, and there were more frequent reports of plant closures for violations. However, only a minority of maquiladoras were confirmed to be in compliance with regulations on air emissions, water discharges, and proper disposal of hazardous waste, and SEDUE struggled to clean up Mexico City and control almost 2,000 maquiladoras, as well as all of Mexican industry, with a budget of less than $10 million. In April of 1992, the Mexican government abolished SEDUE and transferred its responsibilities to the Ministry of Public Health.

16 Like many other U.S. businesses, many companies with maquiladoras looked forward to more sales in Mexico under NAFTA. With a rapidly growing population of 85 million, each Mexican purchased U.S. goods worth $300 per year, compared to $400 per person per year in Japan, a country with 10 times the per capita income.

17 Many U.S. managers were eager to take market share from Mexican domestic producers who were used to being protected from international competition. Some maquiladoras planned to make low end products not only for Mexico but also for other Latin American markets. Although Mexican regulations allowed maquiladoras to sell up to 50 percent of their output in Mexico, there were restrictions: production to be sold in Mexico had to be over and above production for export, and companies were not allowed to take foreign exchange earnings out of Mexico unless they were offset by inflows. Maquiladora managers were also hopeful that Mexico and the United States would work together to simplify import/export procedures.

18 One of the most important issues in the NAFTA negotiations involved "Rules of Origin." In the case of the U.S.–Canadian Free Trade Agreement negotiated in 1988, companies could claim the benefits of reduced duty only if the value of materials originating in North America was used or consumed in the production of the goods, plus the direct cost assembly performed equaled or exceeded

50 percent of the value of the goods when exported. If applied to Mexico, these rules of origin would require many maquiladoras, particularly Japanese and South Korean television manufacturers in Tijuana, to switch away from Asian sources of components. It was unclear whether they would choose to find new suppliers in the United States, Canada, or Mexico, or encourage their Asian suppliers to relocate their factories to Mexico, creating a "second wave" of supplier maquiladoras.

19   Maquiladoras also would likely be affected by the anticipated increase in the demand for Mexican labor under NAFTA, which in turn would lead to higher wages and more employee turnover. Mexican taxes were also in a state of flux, evidenced by the change in 1991 to a nationwide 10 percent value added tax, known in Mexico as "IVA"; previously, the general level of IVA was 15 percent, but only 6 percent on many goods and services in northern border states. Businesses also expected changes in government fees and further reductions in duties.

20   Finally, NAFTA was expected to lead to more technology transfer, and improvements in performance of Mexican workers, technicians, and managers with increased investments in training.

21   Most companies were looking for increased productivity as well as higher world-class levels of quality, such as the new European standards known as ISO 9000.

OVERCOMING HIGH EMPLOYEE TURNOVER IN MAQUILADORAS

22   Compared to other plants, Pulse's Tijuana maquiladora (called "PulSA" from Pulsa S.A. for "Sociedad Anonima" or "Pulse, Inc." in Spanish) had an alarmingly high rate of employee turnover. Dave Flowers believed that during the 15 years prior to 1982, the year of the massive Mexican peso devaluation, the 3 percent monthly employee turnover was due to internal causes only. Since 1982, monthly turnover had been averaging around 7 percent, with the increase due to external causes, such as a lack of housing and the impact of the peso devaluation and high inflation in Mexico. Management consultants estimated that the average cost per worker of turnover was approximately $300, including the cost of recruiting and training replacements, learning curves, and additional supervision for inexperienced workers. Turnover in maquiladoras could be as high as 15 percent per month.

23   The majority of maquiladora workers were young women; 90 percent of PulSA's workers were female, and roughly one half of these women were mothers with children under the age of 5 years.

24   To understand the reasons for high employee turnover, many maquiladoras relied on exit interviews. However, Dave Flowers doubted the validity of the results. About half of the time, the workers simply failed to show up at the plant, perhaps leaving in search of better pay and benefits. Those interviewed tended to say what they thought the company wanted to hear, such as, "I'm leaving so that I can stay home and take care of my children," or "I'm moving back to the interior." Some lied about being students returning to their studies at the end of summer.

25   By Mexican law, companies with over 100 employees were required to have an on-site clinic with a doctor. The Maquiladora Decree of 1989 also required that new or expanding maquiladoras be located in an industrial zone. PulSA was not in an industrial park but in a setting where the vast majority of the workers live in the local community called "Colonia Libertad." Located very close to the U.S. border and the San Ysidro border crossing, the world's busiest, the neighborhood was a major staging area for the nightly dash of undocumented workers who risked injury and arrest to seek employment in the United States. One of the key strategies in the industry for reducing employee turnover was to locate the plant in a residential area. For young Mexican workers living in poor neighborhoods without transportation services, getting to and from work was a major problem. There were no private housing programs financed by maquiladoras, but they were required to pay a 5 percent payroll tax for a federal housing program known as INFONAVIT.

26   The Mexican government was concerned about ecology and the environment and did not want to be an "industrial trash can" for U.S. industries. Some of the things the government was concerned about were industrial air emissions, hazardous solvents used in electronic assembly processes,

potential spills of hazardous waste, and contamination of water and sewage systems. The Mexican government was looking harder at companies coming into the maquiladora program, and those companies already there, to make sure that they were not creating pollution problems. Flowers considered good relations with the Mexican government to be crucial.

PROJECT CONCERN AND THE VOLUNTEER TRAINING PROGRAM

27   Working with Project Concern International, an organization devoted to ensuring the survival of children at risk in Mexico and in many other countries, Pulse developed an innovative program for the company's Tijuana maquiladora. A health clinic staffed by 22 volunteer women workers opened to the 2,000 residents of Colonia Libertad in October of 1990. Services could be provided to as many as 10,000 young mothers and their infants each year, regardless of their ability to pay. One of the key subjects covered in the training provided by Project Concern was the prevention of common diseases, such as dehydration and diarrhea, the No. 1 killer in Third-World countries, which claims 5 million people each year.

28   In addition to taking care of PulSA's work force at the plant, clinic volunteers also visited the employees' homes to help with some basic health training on infant malnutrition and dehydration, among other topics. PulSA management was not concerned about too much response, even though they were operating in a very needy country. The possibility that PulSA's clinic might become a community hospital swamped with people lined up around the block was not a concern; in fact, there were plans to distribute a flyer in the surrounding neighborhoods, starting with 100 houses.

29   According to Flowers, the basic criteria for a maquiladora entering into such a program are as follows:

30   1. They should have medical people already employed in the company, not necessarily doctors, but certainly registered nurses. That is your internal base and the part of the force that drives the program forward.
2. They need a place to train, a training room.
3. They should be willing to commit certain resources.
4. The top person has to support it. If not, it will just fizzle. There are too many other day-to-day priorities that keep plant managers from focusing on this kind of thing, get those shipments out, get the yields up, let's see higher productivity. We get complaints from our supervisors, not all of them, a few. They say, "I can't spare that person off of my production line; I won't make my production goals if you take her away." So there had to be negotiations and compromises. We said we'll adjust your goals a little bit, but it is very important that we do this.

THE PROBLEM OF MAINTAINING INTEREST

31   The participation of PulSA clinic workers in a vaccination program against measles helped to keep their interest and to maintain momentum. These 20 women volunteers gave up their Saturday to vaccinate 600 people, and Flowers wrote a congratulatory letter and put it on the maquiladora bulletin board. Training for the clinic volunteers consisted of a three phase process. Phase 1 focused on determining the interest level of the employees in the program, starting with a survey to determine how many employees had children five years old and younger, since that was the target population of the program. Almost half of the employees had children in that age range in their home, not necessarily their own children. Since the survey results and the focus of the program were compatible, PulSA went ahead with a one-hour introductory program with all employees in the plant. From there they solicited volunteers for a more intensive program.

32   Phase 2 consisted of 18 hours of training: six days times three hours per day. Seventy employees signed up, and the level of interest that was sustained through that training period enabled PulSA to go forward with phase 3.

33   Phase 3 required a lot more commitment, not only from the employees but also on the company's part. The group was narrowed to about 25 people on the basis of the following selection criteria:

34   1. Level of interest expressed and participation in the second phase of the training.
        2. Ability to grasp some of the techniques being taught in class.
        3. Longevity with the company.
        4. How good of an employee they were from a citizenship perspective.
        5. Eighty percent would come from Colonia Libertad and 20 percent from other communities in Tijuana to mirror the demographics of the population in the plant.

TRAINING COSTS

35   PulSA's clinic charged the equivalent of $0.50 just as a token so people could say that they'd paid something. The company felt that providing services as a gift would hurt people's self-esteem and undermine community ownership of the program. "Where people are paying for services when they can afford to pay, that helps create income for the clinic, it helps move them one step closer to self-sufficiency," said Flowers.

36   He estimated the total cost to be a little over $10,000 per program site per year, not including community support. Pulse spent $1,400 for equipment and provided the furnishings and facilities.

37   A significant component of the clinic cost was an opportunity cost of the production lost while the workers were off the line. Workers participated during working hours; for example, during phase 1, 100 percent of the people received one hour of training. During phase 2, 70 people participated for six days for three hours per day, and phase 3 involved 25 workers for three hours per week. Phases 1 and 2 were conducted entirely on company time; PulSA decided that they didn't need to give their own time to show their level of dedication, since most had already participated in the vaccination program.

38   To convince other maquiladoras to copy the PulSA clinic, Flowers felt that employee costs should be expressed in terms of a percentage of the total payroll expense. For example, 2 percent of one week's total payroll, 0.2 percent of 10 week's payroll, and 0.08 percent of a year's payroll. According to Flowers, "If you say the payroll is a $1.70 per hour and you have to take 700 or 1,000 people off of the line for one hour, all of a sudden you've dropped $1,600 or $1,700, just to indoctrinate, and people start looking at it as a big number. The reason I like the percentage better is that maybe the plant only has 300 employees but could still afford the program. Another criterion is probably a minimum plant size because of the economics, unless it's an industrial park clinic, in which case the cost is spread over all the maquiladoras in the park. If it's a single dedicated maquiladora, they need to be a certain size or the cost per employee gets so high they really can't consider it."

39   The clinic also required space. For example, in a 10,000-square-foot facility, a 1,200-square-foot clinic takes up 12 percent of the plant; however, in a 50,000-square-foot plant, the same 1,200 square feet represents only 3 percent of the total plant space.

RESULTS

40   After a year of operation, the clinic had a client base of 400 children with medical records and regular checkups. Over 1,500 Mexican children were vaccinated by PulSA volunteers working Saturdays on their own time, and the Mexican Ministry of Health provided the medication at no charge. Employee

turnover at the maquiladora was down by 40 percent, and Flowers described employee attitudes as "very positive." A typical comment about the company's clinic was that "no one has ever done anything that they didn't have to before."

41   Pulse received a national award for the maquiladora clinic along with a tremendous amount of publicity. Reflecting on this innovative program, Dave Flowers realized that it took a lot longer to complete the training than he had planned, and that none of the other maquiladoras had chosen to imitate the idea of a neighborhood clinic. Perhaps the training should be accelerated; instead of one training session three hours per week, there should be two sessions per week of three hours each. The training period was nine hours per month, once per week for three weeks, and then one week off. Normal community health workers were trained by Project Concern for 18 months. PulSA's training lasted 15 months, but he felt that most maquiladora operators did not have the patience for even a one-year program.

42   Another question lurked in the background. If the Pulsa Tijuana clinic was such a good idea economically, and in terms of multinational corporate social responsibility, why not establish clinics at other Pulse plants in China, Hong Kong, and Ireland?

CASE 17

APPLE COMPUTER, INC.

1   Apple Computer was founded in April 1976 by two college dropouts, Steven Wozniak and Steven Jobs, who at the ages of 26 and 21, respectively, wanted to bring computing power to a more personal level. Wozniak developed a kit, called the Apple I and, and with Jobs' help, sold the kit to other enthusiasts. Wozniak's goal was to build a computer for himself, but Jobs' vision was to package and sell the kit to others. Jobs enlisted the aid of prominent people, such as Nolan Bushnell, founder of Atari; Don Valentine, a venture capitalist; Regis McKenna, owner of a Silicon Valley advertising agency; and A. C. "Mike" Markkula, Jr., a returned marketing executive from Intel, in order to design a more marketable product. The Apple II computer was created shortly thereafter, and demand for the product outside the small computer expert market was strong.

2   Seeing the potential for success, Markkula invested $250,000 in the company and became a partner and chairman of Apple. He set up a business plan for Apple that included $500 million in sales after 10 years. This goal was reached in only half that time (see Exhibit 1 for sales information). An additional $3 million in capital was raised, and Apple moved its headquarters from Jobs' garage to Cupertino, California.

3   Jobs' "one person—one computer" philosophy gave Apple direction in bringing the power of the computer to a personal level. He wanted to take Apple, its products, and its people and change the world "one computer at a time." Apple had a strong soul from the very beginning.

4   Mike Scott, a friend of Markkula, joined Apple as president in 1977 and became an important driving force in the early years. Scott brought discipline and structure to Apple and, along with Markkula's marketing and planning, transformed its dreams into a working company. In addition, Apple's board of directors played an important and active role in the company's success. The board provided experience to complement Apple's youth.

5   Apple incorporated many of Hewlett-Packard's management styles into its organization. HP was a model company for many startups like Apple. These styles emphasized the importance of each employee. Quality was stressed, and a family atmosphere was created that provided incentives, such as profit sharing and job security, to loyal employees. Management by wandering around was used by officials to motivate the employees. HP's more structured styles were disregarded by Apple as being too conventional and unproductive. Apple's codes of conduct formed its Apple "values," which, when combined with its vision, unified the work force.

6   In the fall of 1980, Scott reorganized the company by product lines. The divisions were comprised of the highly successful Apple II, a new powerful computer called *Lisa,* the peripheral products (i.e., disk drives and printers), manufacturing, sales, and service. Before this time, Apple was structured into three divisions: hardware, software, and manufacturing. Jobs wanted to lead the Lisa group, but Scott did not allow it because he believed that Jobs would not make a good manager. In December, Apple went public and issued 4.6 million shares of common stock at $22 per share. Every share was purchased within minutes (see Exhibit 2 for stock price information). By this time, Apple had over 1,000 employees.

This case was prepared by Neil H. Snyder, the Ralph A. Beeton Professor of Free Enterprise, University of Virginia; Russell Teasley, University of South Carolina; and David McDonald, David Mele, Craig Micheals, and Robert Mohan, University of Virginia.

EXHIBIT 1
Net Revenues

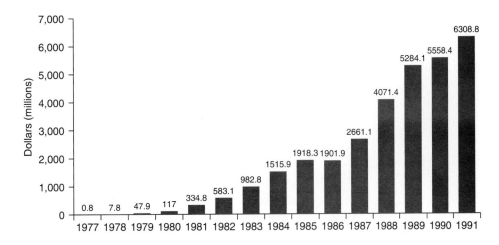

7   In 1981, Jobs replaced Markkula as chairman, Markkula became president and Scott was appointed vice chairman. In August 1981, International Business Machines introduced the IBM Personal Computer. Since the introduction of the IBM PC, Apple has stressed its belief in the fundamental difference between an IBM computer and an Apple, which is that IBM created machines it felt would meet the needs of users, while Apple created machines with the needs of the user in mind. IBM, however, did legitimize the personal computer industry in the business world. Businesses have been using IBM products for decades and felt comfortable with purchasing an IBM computer. Apple was viewed as a company without strength to succeed in the market. Apple countered this argument by distinguishing itself from IBM by emphasizing its feeling that there are people who use computers, and there are people who use Apple computers.

8   Soon after the Lisa division was created, some employees were dissatisfied with its progress in fulfilling Apple's vision and decided to design a new computer, the Macintosh. Apple gave the group minimal resources to operate, and Jobs became its leader. These underdogs banded together like pirates to create a machine that everyone would love and want to use.

9   In the coming years, friction developed between the divisions and separate subcultures formed within Apple. The Apple II Division felt left out, despite the fact that it supplied most of Apple's products. The Lisa group received most of the funding and became too big and bureaucratic to make a great machine to lead Apple into the future. The Macintosh Division was formed to realign Apple with its original visions, but received little respect.

10   By 1983, the Lisa computer was plagued with problems, the Macintosh group was at war with the Lisa group, and the new Apple III machine failed. However, due to the tremendous success of the Apple II computer, these problems were not addressed by management. Apple was not only competing with IBM and over 100 other manufacturers but with itself as well. Few people paid attention to the mounting rivalry forming between the divisions and their leaders.

11   In April 1983, John Sculley, former president of Pepsi-Cola, was elected Apple's president and chief executive officer. Markkula stepped down and became vice chairman. Apple had entered the Fortune 500 list at 411, highlighting its incredible growth rate. Sculley saw great promise for Apple and wanted to build on the creativity of its employees and to guide Apple in maturing.

12   Sculley and Jobs formed an immediate bond. Sculley had the business sense and experience while Jobs had the vision and a never-ending supply of drive and energy. Because Jobs was chairman,

EXHIBIT 2
Apple Computer, Inc., Stock Prices

	Yearly High, Low, and Close		
Year	Yearly High	Yearly Low	Yearly Close
1981	$17.250	$ 7.125	$11.063
1982	16.938	5.375	14.938
1983	31.375	8.625	12.188
1984	16.625	10.875	14.563
1985	15.313	7.125	11.000
1986	21.875	10.875	20.250
1987	59.250	20.438	42.000
1988	47.250	36.125	40.250
1989	49.625	33.750	35.250
1990	47.750	24.250	43.000
1991	73.250	40.250	50.000

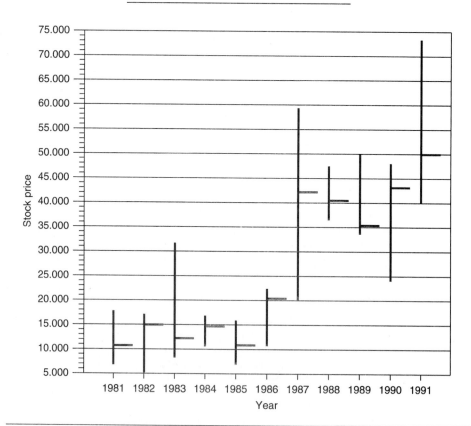

Macintosh leader, and Sculley's friend, his power and influence increased. Both believed that a manager's role is to promote creativity and provide direction, not just goals. Accountability was stressed more than responsibility, which gave employees more freedom to act.

13   Further restructuring took place, and Apple organized itself into two independent divisions, the Apple II Division, and the Macintosh Division. Each division contained engineering, manufacturing, and marketing groups, while corporate employees were responsible for sales, distribution, finance, and human resources.

14   The Macintosh was introduced in 1984 to millions of Super Bowl viewers through its "1984" commercial, which depicted the Macintosh as the young, personal, and powerful alternative to IBM's "totalitarian" products. Macintosh sales reached 50,000 within 74 days, while it took IBM seven and a half months to sell its first 50,000 personal computers. To manufacture the Macintosh, Apple built a highly automated plant, utilizing modern production techniques, such as robotics and just-in-time parts usage. But problems developed as conflicts broke out between Jobs and his workers.

15   Several problems plagued Apple in 1985, including:

A failure to deliver the Macintosh Office, which would have given Apple much-needed leverage in the business market.

Excess inventories.

A major reorganization, which reduced the number of employees by 20 percent.

Its first quarterly loss due to the reorganization, and the resignation of Wozniak.

16   Sculley's power was being questioned as Jobs' control increased. Sculley believed Jobs could not continue to run the Macintosh Division and asked if Jobs would step down. A power struggle ensued, and, with the backing of the board, Sculley won. Jobs resigned from Apple in September 1985 and formed his own company.

17   In late-1985, Sculley was credited with successfully guiding Apple through a devastating period that affected the entire industry. Apple was in a stronger position than most other companies, because it owned the hardware and system software for its products. Apple had to look into the future for new products and restore its spirit of innovation. The best way for Apple to predict the future was to invent it. Sculley repositioned Apple and "opened" the Macintosh by allowing it to connect with other machines, including ones from IBM and Digital.

18   Sculley proclaimed that "the bottom line here is that we are becoming more market-driven and more customer-oriented, which are extremely important steps for us to take as the industry becomes more competitive. Apple is growing up."[1] With this maturation, Apple had to modify some of its philosophies. "One person—one computer" evolved into a "networking" idea, in which the power lies in the ability for computers and uses to connect, communicate, and share ideas. Apple could no longer rely solely on its original visions. It had to focus on selling machines, creating technology to meet future needs of users, and incorporating more conventional management styles to ensure profitability and success.

19   Apple appealed to computer hackers and to the education market because its employees were hackers just finishing school. It failed to attract the business market for the same reasons it succeeded in other areas. The workers did not have any experience in the business world, but Sculley had the business knowledge. Unfortunately, by targeting the corporate market with high-priced machines, Sculley alienated many consumers, schools, and small businesses.

20   In 1988, Apple restructured and created four independent operating units: Apple USA, Apple Europe, Apple Pacific, and Apple Products. Apple USA and Apple Products fought and caused both to lose contact with the market.

---

[1] John Sculley, *Odyssey* (New York: Harper & Row, 1987).

21   In January of 1990, Michael Spindler was named chief operating officer and brought to Apple a new sense of reality and direction. Sculley focused on research and development, while Spindler controlled sales, marketing, manufacturing, and corporate communications. Teamwork, budgets, and deadlines, but not politics, were stressed. Sculley admitted that, prior to Spindler, "if there was a major failing, it was that the organization was confused about where we were going."[2]

22   Spindler oversaw the introduction of three low-cost Macintosh computers in October of 1990. Although they have been selling very well, the lower prices significantly decreased Apple's margins and forced Apple to focus on volume selling. Before, Apple had a gross margin of over 54 percent, one of the highest in the industry. Successfully implementing a low margin strategy will require a different orientation at Apple.

23   By 1991, unit sales at Apple increased 85 percent, while gross margins dropped below 49 percent. To compensate for lost margins, Apple announced a reorganization strategy to reduce operating expenses, which included a 10 percent reduction in the work force. An agreement signed with IBM in the summer of 1991 signified one of the most important events in Apple's history. It called for a joint venture that will combine IBM's expertise in hardware with Apple's superior system software abilities to produce a new type of computer system that will use discrete, interchangeable "objects" that, in different combinations, form sophisticated applications that run the computer.

24   Sculley, Spindler, and the rest of Apple still share the soul of Apple's beginnings. Sculley has stated that, "in 1991, we're going to catch up. In 1993, Apple will be in a position to be shaping the industry, much as we were in the '80s."[3]

25   The appendix provides information on Apple's executive management team and board of directors.

MARKETING STRATEGIES

26   At its inception, Apple believed in the revolutionary power of the microcomputer. It still believes that the best computers are the ones the users cannot see. These "invisible computers" adapt to the needs of users in an intuitive way and avoid forcing users to remember arcane commands. Apple marketed the first successful computer, the Apple II line, and gained recognition for its commitment to the educational market. Forgoing a simple software enhancement for IBM machines, Apple used its software strengths in challenging the IBM PC with the Macintosh. The Macintosh's most distinctive difference was its system software. By combining a graphical user interface (GUI) with a mouse and pull-down menus to represent complex commands, such as file maintenance, Apple attempted to demonstrate its advantages over IBM to end users.

27   Unfortunately, the Mac's ease of use made it look like a toy, and Apple struggled to persuade the important corporate market of its power. In addition, enamored with the technical brilliance of the Mac, Steven Jobs disdained simple connectivity to industry standard hardware, such as pre-existing mainframes or non-Apple printers. Desperate to succeed in the business market, Apple focused on desktop publishing, creating a niche that capitalized on its GUI strength and PC weaknesses. IBM's stable reputation as a customer-oriented, business-solutions company, though, reassured most companies of IBM's longevity and utility, and most businesses continued to use IBM PCs. Although Apple gained a loyal following, its antibusiness image lost it many potential business clients.

28   Because Apple never achieved high-volume sales, software developers complained that, without a large market for their products, it was becoming too costly to develop Macintosh software. Also, developers complained that Claris, Apple's software subsidiary, was receiving an unfair advantage in

---

[2] Barbara Buell, "Apple: New Team, New Strategy," *Business Week,* October 15, 1990, p. 89.

[3] Barbara Buell, "The Second Comeback at Apple," *Business Week,* January 28, 1991, p. 68.

terms of learning about new Macintosh hardware and system software changes before its competitors. These pressures, along with a desire to become more "mainstream," forced Apple to adopt a high-volume approach and promise to spin off Claris. The high-volume broad-appeal approach was instituted, but Claris continues to be part of Apple for strategic importance and is starting to develop software for other platforms.

29   Jobs' removal and Sculley's ascent at Apple signaled change, and Sculley moderated Apple's strategy and rhetoric, embarking upon a campaign to raise credibility and to emphasize an evolutionary approach for the Macintosh after its revolutionary beginnings. Sculley's support of total quality management (TQM) techniques, like design for manufacturability (DFM) and cross-functional design teams, allowed Apple to meet developer demands and produce higher-quality Macs at lower cost. Flexible, lean integrating teams were assigned specific tasks that had to be completed on time.

30   Free to work without significant managerial oversight, these teams included members from engineering, marketing, and manufacturing. Immediate feedback on feasibility, cost, manufacturability, and response to customer needs was available from each team member. With its worldwide organization independently serving Europe, Asia, and America, Apple triumphed with the design and production of a low-cost line in October 1990, with the Mac Classic, LC, and IIsi, and again in October 1991 with high-end machines (Quadra 700 and 900), a more powerful Classic (Classic II), and notebook computers (PowerBook 100, 140, and 170).

31   Cost reduction and quality improvement are achieved through the use of standard components and the avoidance of fasteners in the design phase. Maximizing standard parts at Apple allowed volume-discount buying and greater manufacturing flexibility, since many components can be used in different models. Moreover, such purchasing fostered long-term supplier relationships—new chip designs from Motorola have been quickly incorporated into the Mac line—permitting Apple to provide higher levels of customer support rapidly. Further, careful design minimized superfluous attachments and lengthy corrective measures.

32   Since 1987, Apple has emphasized the connectivity of Macs, from DEC VAXs to IBMs. Also, the joint agreement with IBM will allow both companies to achieve synergistic growth for fostering new innovations. Both Apple and IBM are concerned about Microsoft's clout, and the agreement is meant to lessen Microsoft's dominance over the industry's direction. While increasing corporate acceptance for Apple, this agreement has caused an identity crisis within Apple. Also, there are risks involved with joining forces with a much larger competitor, such as IBM. Apple may avoid some hazards by having similar agreements with other companies, like the one it formed with Sony. Unable to enter the laptop-portable market competitively in 1989, Apple has worked with Sony in developing its new PowerBook line of notebooks. Similar plans for a palmtop knowledge navigator and a CD-based game machine are being planned by Apple and Sony.

MARKETING SEGMENTS

33   Apple refocused its efforts on six distinct market segments, with each one being very important in terms of future success. The segments were:

34   1. Large business.
      2. Small business.
      3. K–12 education.
      4. Higher education.
      5. Government.
      6. Personal.

EXHIBIT 3
Research and Development Spending

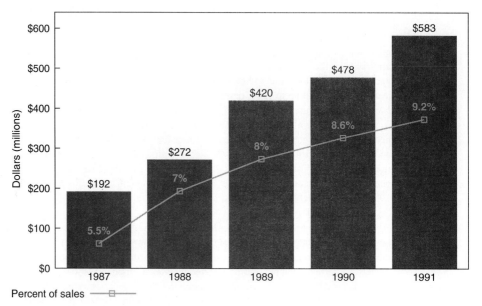

Percent of sales ──□──

Research and Development Target Areas
System software
Hardware: CPUs and peripherals
Networking and communications
Worldwide product localization
Manufacturing enhancements
Advantage technology

Source: Apple Computer, Inc.

RESEARCH AND DEVELOPMENT

35   Apple progressively spent more money on research and development from 1987 to 1991 (see Exhibit 3 for R&D expenditures). Due in part to expanding competition and the dynamism inherent to the industry, Apple constantly must redesign its machines to incorporate new technologies, processors, and ideas. Apple's main research areas include system software, central processing units (CPU) and peripherals, networking and related communications, and worldwide product localization and enhancements. For example, the recently released Quadra line uses the latest Motorola CPU, the 68040, and advanced video for better display, while the Classic II comes from a new, enhanced, low-cost production facility.

36   See Exhibit 4 for pictures of current Macintosh computers.

INDUSTRY AND COMPETITION

37   The personal computer industry made its debut in grand scale with the introduction of the IBM PC in 1981. For most of the past 10 years, IBM has dominated the market with its pioneering technology,

EXHIBIT 4
Some Macintosh Models

Fredrik D. Bodin/Offshoot.

intense advertising, and commitment to broad-scale production. However, the market share gap between the "Big Blue Giant" (IBM) and the rest of the industry competitors has been narrowing considerably in recent years. The PC industry is currently in a state of flux, and the future should prove to be one of dramatic innovations and intense competition.

38   In the 1990s, leading in PCs means leading in computers. In their myriad forms, from $500 clones to $2,000 laptops and $25,000 network hubs, PCs dominate the computer industry. With annual worldwide sales of about $93 billion, PCs now dwarf all other computer markets. Mainframes, for example, bring in only $50 billion annually, including sales of software, diskdrives, and other peripherals. In 1990, IBM led all other PC firms with revenues of $9.6 billion, up 15 percent from 1989 (see Exhibits 5 and 6 for industry sales information). Apple Computers ranked second, with revenues of $3.8 billion, an 8 percent increase from 1989. Compaq placed a close third, with $3.5 billion in revenues, which represented an impressive 25 percent gain from 1989. The next four, in order of annual revenue, were: Unisys, Commodore, Intel, and Tandy. Hewlett-Packard, which had been gaining ground in the late 80s, fell to ninth place with revenues of $625 million, a 27 percent fall from 1989.

EXHIBIT 5
Top 10 Computer Companies Total 1990 Revenue

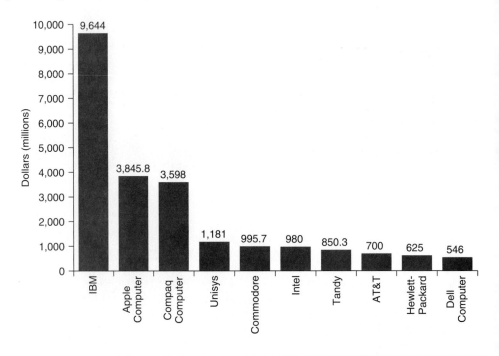

EXHIBIT 6
Top 10 Computer Companies, Percent Change in Revenue 1989–90

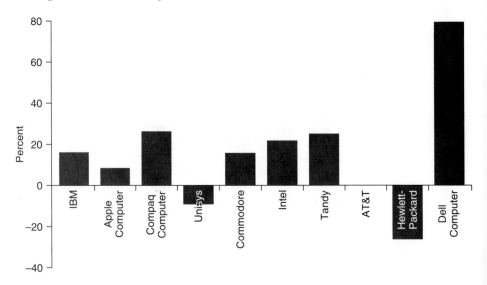

39 These rankings, however, are sure to change in the near future. The PC industry, if it is to continue its tremendous growth, will need to reinvent itself. The glue that has held the business together for the last 10 years, the standard that IBM set with the introduction of its first PC, is coming unstuck. From the moment it was introduced on August 12, 1981, the $1,565 IBM personal computer established the rules of the game. Following IBM's lead, clone makers made the PC standard universal from Texas to Tokyo. Apple succeeded, starting with its Lisa in 1983, and then with the Macintosh in 1984, by defining itself as the alternative to the IBM standard.

40 Now, however, the industry needs a new model: To read handwriting, understand the human voice, manage digitized images and sounds, and take on the big computing jobs that mainframes and mini-computers still do, tomorrow's PCs need a more advanced foundation. Neither the IBM PC standard nor the more user-friendly Apple Macintosh design appears capable of all this. This is why Apple and IBM announced their plan to jointly develop a new PC design that can effectively supplant the original IBM standard as well as Apple's current design. Their agreement, if successful, will produce new computers using powerful RISC (reduced instruction-set computing) chips and a radically new form of operation-system software. In an effort to make technology more proprietary, IBM wants to shake the pack of clone makers that have plagued it so much in the past.

41 Clones were the unintended outcome when IBM chairman John R. Opel approved a crash pro-gram to get into personal computers in 1979. He dispatched a team of 13 engineers to Boca Raton, Florida, to come up with a computer that could halt the advance of such companies as Apple, Com-modore, and Tandy. Opel was particularly alarmed by the stunning progress of Apple. By 1980, Steve Jobs' startup had grown to a $117 million company. Apple's rainbow logos were beginning to appear in the big corporations where IBM's mainframes ruled. The team in Boca Raton was given one year to come up with an answer to the Apple II. To meet the deadline, the team broke the IBM rules and turned to outside suppliers for key hardware and software. In the process, IBM inadvertently played kingmaker. Intel got the microchip order, and tiny Microsoft, then a five-year-old startup, was selected to provide the machine's programming language and operating system. By the mid-1980s, the young kings were taking control of the PC kingdom. Intel and Microsoft, more than IBM or any of its clones, began to determine how PC technology progressed and, to a large extent, how much PCs would cost.

42 IBM, in effect, lost control. Instead of taking their pricing cues from IBM, as minicomputer and mainframe makers had always done, the PC clone makers slashed prices to as much as 30 percent below IBM's. To try to shore up sales, IBM in 1987 went after the clones with PS/2, a more clone-proof design that uses the proprietary MicroChannel architecture. But the clone makers continued to build sales and market share by improving on the older standard. As IBM's share dropped, from 27 percent in 1985 to 16.5 percent in 1990, the company began to compete on price. In the first half of 1991, IBM cut the price of its PS/2 by 25 percent.

43 Apple is feeling the pinch from clone makers as well. It has successfully repulsed all efforts to clone the proprietary Macintosh design. This helped the company pile up earnings, but also left it isolated in a market that preferred a standard, such as the IBM design, which limited its share of the market to about 12 percent in 1990. In an effort to build market share, Apple came out with a less-expensive computer late last year, the $999 Macintosh Classic. The strategy worked, but also backfired. It is estimated that Apple will finish 1991 with a 19 percent share of PC shipments, but profits have plum-meted. Not only are the Classics themselves less profitable but they also have cannibalized sales of Apple's higher-margin computers.

44 These developments are what convinced IBM and Apple to initiate their startling alliance. If they can develop a new standard, they hope to regain industry leadership and restore the type of profit margins that go to the standard-setters. They plan to develop computers based on IBM's own RISC microprocessors and on Apple's innovative work in software. The intended result will be desktop com-puters with far better software than the PCs of the 1980s. But these new teammates are by no means guaranteed the leadership slot in the coming PC era. Because the desktop computer market has become so vast, many computer makers are fighting for the role. Workstation makers, such as Sun Microsystems and Hewlett-Packard, already sell high-powered machines much like the PCs envisioned by IBM and Apple. Companies, such as Digital Equipment and Compaq, which blossomed by cloning the PC, also are determined to stay on top by helping to forge the next industry standard. In addition, nearly every U.S. PC maker has lined up a Japanese ally to supply critical technologies for making laptop and notebook computers.

45   Much of the current PC battle is being fought over software. Future operating systems, which provide PCs with their basic instructions, must be able to manage handwriting, video, graphics, voice, and text. It is not clear which company will provide such an operating system. Microsoft, for example, is trying to engineer these capabilities into its existing Windows graphic program. Windows now is sold as an add-on to give PCs and clones running Microsoft's 10-year-old MS-DOS operating system a look and feel similar to Apple's Macintosh. In 1992, Microsoft plans to supplant MS-DOS with NT (New Technology), a new operating system that will let PC owners do many things at once and will make use of RISC microprocessors feasible.

46   IBM and Apple are taking an even bolder approach. Instead of upgrading the old operating system technology, as Microsoft is doing with NT, IBM and Apple are counting on a whole new approach. They are developing what is known as object-oriented programming, a method that involves building programs from interchangeable blocks of prefabricated computer codes called *objects*. Object programming will help computers accommodate new multimedia technology and allow ordinary office workers to create customer programs.

47   These new advances are sorely needed in the PC industry. Just four years ago, the industry's annual growth rate was nearly 37 percent. In 1991, however, it is estimated that worldwide sales will have grown only 15 percent. In the United States, growth is expected to be only 8 percent in 1991, with some analysts predicting no growth at all. The recession may be partly to blame for the sluggish growth. But, after consuming 75 million IBM compatible PCs, the U.S. market might be approaching saturation. Without new customers, or compelling new uses that require updated hardware, the PC industry risks becoming largely a low-margin replacement business. If the PC industry hopes to experience a resurgence in sales growth, PC makers must fulfill their promises to provide new technology that will make PCs easier to use and software simpler to learn. Apple and IBM, as experienced standard-setters, appear poised and ready to do just that in the near future. They will, however, be faced with fierce competition along the way.

FINANCIALS

48   Exhibits 7, 8, 9, and 10 provide financial information on Apple.

49   In 1990, demand for Apple's older entry-level products softened. Though the Macintosh Plus and Macintosh SE continued to enjoy significant performance advantages over competitive computers, sales of these two products to large and small businesses slowed due to increased price competition. Sales of the long-established Apple II continued to decline in 1990, with many customers asking for lower-priced products and color support. The financial performance of Apple as a result of the changing demands, strong demand for high-performance products, countered by softer demand for older entry-level products, was a little disappointing for Apple executives.

50   Even with these minor problems, Apple's financials still look very strong. While computer industry growth slowed in the United States, Apple's international sales grew 23 percent during 1990, to account for 42 percent of net revenues, up from 36 percent the previous year. Apple's sales grew 5 percent in 1990, to $5.6 billion, up from $5.3 billion. Operating income rose 12 percent from 1989, to $712 million, because of reductions in the cost of components used to manufacture their computers. Net income for the year was $474.9 million, a 5 percent increase over 1989. This included $48 mil-

EXHIBIT 7

APPLE COMPUTER, INC.,
Income Statement
(in millions except earnings per share)

	1992	1991	1990	1989	1988	1987	1986
Results of Operations							
Net sales:							
Domestic	$3,885,042	$3,484,533	$3,241,061	$3,401,462	$2,766,328	$1,940,369	$1,411,812
International	3,201,500	2,824,316	2,317,374	1,882,551	1,305,045	720,699	490,086
Total net sales	7,086,542	6,308,849	5,558,435	5,284,013	4,071,373	2,661,068	1,901,898
Costs and expenses:							
Cost of sales	3,991,337	3,314,118	2,606,223	2,694,823	1,990,879	1,296,220	891,112
Research and development (R&D)	602,135	583,046	478,019	420,083	272,512	191,554	127,758
Selling, general and administrative (SG&A) . . .	1,687,262	1,740,293	1,728,508	1,534,794	1,187,644	801,856	609,497
Restructuring costs and other	—	224,043	33,673	—	—	—	—
	6,280,734	5,861,500	4,846,423	4,649,700	3,451,035	2,289,630	1,628,367
Operating income	805,808	447,349	712,012	634,313	620,338	371,438	273,531
Interest and other income, net	49,634	52,395	66,505	110,009	35,823	38,930	36,187
Income before income taxes. . .	855,442	499,744	778,517	744,322	656,161	410,368	309,718
Provision for income taxes	325,069	189,903	303,622	290,289	255,903	192,872	155,755
Net income	$ 530,373	$ 309,841	$ 474,895	$ 454,033	$ 400,258	$ 217,496	$ 153,963
Retained earnings	$1,904.52	$1,492,02	$1,310.27	$1,170.47	$777.19	$572.53	$467.01
Earnings per share	$4.33	$2.58	$3.77	$3.53	$3.08	$1.65	$1.20

lion, or $0.37 per share, from the sale of common stock holdings of Adobe Systems, Inc. Earnings per share rose 7 percent to $3.77 per share.

51   The balance sheet remained among the strongest in the industry, with almost $1 billion in cash and no long-term debt. In 1990, $188 million was added to cash balances, and 14 million shares of common stock were repurchased. Return on equity was a strong 32 percent, also among the best in the industry.

52   On the negative side, the total debt to total assets ratio doubled from 2.07 to 4.12 in 1990, while total debt to equity almost tripled from 3.82 to 8.48. The current and quick ratios dropped slightly, and such performance ratios as sales to average cash and equivalents, average accounts receivable turnover, sales to average working capital, sales to average net fixed assets, and average asset turnover all dipped slightly in 1990 from their 1989 levels. On the positive side, net cash flow from operations almost doubled, from $507.35 million in 1988 to 963.87 million in 1990, aided by decreases in the amount of accounts receivable and inventory held.

EXHIBIT 8

APPLE COMPUTER, INC.
Balance Sheet
(in millions)

	1992	1991	1990	1989	1988	1987	1986
Assets							
Cash & equivalents	$1,435.50	$ 892.72	$ 997.09	$ 808.95	$ 545.72	$ 565.09	$ 576.22
Receivables.............	1,087.19	907.16	761.87	792.82	638.82	405.64	263.13
Inventories	580.10	671.66	355.47	475.38	461.47	225.75	108.68
Other current assets.......	455.61	392.07	288.89	217.28	136.89	110.94	92.91
Total current assets......	3,558.40	2,863.61	2,403.33	2,294.43	1,782.90	1,307.43	1,040.93
Gross prop., plant, & equip...............	1,135.64	1,036.01	844.87	643.37	420.34	289.13	222.04
Accumulated depreciation	673.43	588.04	446.71	309.15	212.99	158.70	114.72
Net prop., plant, & equip...............	462.21	447.98	398.17	334.23	207.36	130.43	107.32
Other assets	203.08	182.01	174.22	115.24	91.74	40.07	11.88
Total assets	4,223.69	3,493.60	2,975.71	2,743.90	2,082.09	1,477.93	1,160.13
Liabilities & Net Worth							
Short-term debt	184.46	148.57	122.63	56.75	127.87	0	0
Accounts payable.........	426.94	357.08	340.58	334.16	314.67	205.93	118.05
Taxes payable	78.38	14.86	33.24	85.79	62.47	20.24	14.65
Other current liab.	735.74	696.54	530.61	418.55	322.09	252.51	195.83
Total current liab.	1,425.52	1,217.05	1,027.06	895.24	827.09	478.68	328.54
Long-term debt	0.00	0.00	0.00	0.00	0.00	0.00	0.00
Deferred taxes	610.80	509.87	501.83	362.91	251.57	162.77	137.51
Total liabilities..........	2,036.32	1,726.92	1,528.89	1,258.15	1,078.66	641.44	466.04
Common stock (net)	282.31	278.87	136.56	315.28	226.24	236.96	N.A.
Shareholder's equity	2,187.37	1,766.68	1,446.82	1,485.75	1,003.43	836.49	694.09
Total liab. & net worth	4,223.69	3,493.60	2,975.71	2,743.90	2,082.09	1,477.93	1,160.13

WHAT'S NEXT?

53   Apple still controls the direction of its Macintosh computers in both hardware and system software design, unlike IBM and IBM compatible manufacturers who are at the mercy of Microsoft, the leading operating software developer. However, by defining itself as a proprietary hardware manufacturer, Apple missed the opportunity to increase its influence and power in the larger personal computer industry. If Apple "opened" itself, by allowing Macintosh clones and designing a Macintosh-like system software for IBM machines, it would not be forced to let its main rival Microsoft dominate the industry.

EXHIBIT 9

APPLE COMPUTER, INC.
Ratio Analysis

	1990	1989	1988	1987	1986
Total debt to total assets	4.12	2.07	6.14	0.00	0.00
Total debt to equity	8.48	3.82	12.74	0.00	0.00
Current ratio	2.34	2.56	2.16	2.73	3.17
Quick ratio.	1.71	1.79	1.43	2.03	2.55
Cash & equiv. to cur. assets	0.97	0.90	0.66	1.18	1.75
Sales to avg. cash & equiv.	6.16	7.80	7.33	4.66	4.17
Avg. accounts rec. turnover	7.15	7.38	7.80	7.96	7.87
Avg. Inv. Turnover (COGS)	5.79	5.49	5.57	7.33	6.10
Avg. Inv. Turnover (sales)	13.38	11.28	11.85	15.91	13.80
Sales to avg. working cap.	4.01	4.49	4.56	3.45	3.07
Sales to avg. net fxd. assets	15.18	19.51	24.11	22.39	19.23
Avg. asset turnover	1.94	2.19	2.29	2.02	1.81

54   August 21, 1991, marked the 10th anniversary of the IBM PC, a machine that gave credibility to the personal computer industry. For the past few years, IBM has been unable to command a large share of the personal computer market, because of a dramatic increase in the number inexpensive clones on the market, and in its dependence on Microsoft for critical system software. From 1985 to 1990, IBM's market share dropped from 27 percent to 16.5 percent. IBM has been looking for a strategic partner to help rejuvenate and lead the personal computer industry as it rapidly matures in its present condition. Meanwhile, Apple has been searching for help in making the Macintosh more attractive to the business market.

55   On October 2, 1991, Apple and IBM announced the details of a joint agreement, in which the two companies will work together on designing new personal computers and products based on an "open systems" design. The four major points of the agreement are outlined in Exhibit 11.

56   Both Apple and IBM will benefit from this agreement. Apple will be able to increase the Macintosh's connectivity and have a partner to help in developing and marketing new technologies. IBM will receive acceptance for its RISC technology, benefit from Apple's expertise in software, and be able to reduce its reliance on Microsoft. This agreement will not stop Apple and IBM from being direct competitors in the market. In addition, most of the products resulting from the agreement will be available for licensing by other companies.

57   With this agreement, Apple and IBM have strengthened the trend in the computer industry toward viewing hardware as a commodity. With new microprocessors, object-oriented applications, and cross-platform system software, computer companies will rely more on their software divisions for a competitive advantage.

58   How Apple will change in adapting to industry trends and its agreement with IBM is still uncertain. The change will not only affect the company's product but its organization, employees, and customers as well.

59   "These agreements are the foundation for a renaissance," said John Sculley. "We're dramatically expanding customers' choice while lowering their risks when buying computers. We're making open

EXHIBIT 10

APPLE COMPUTER, INC.
Statement of Cash Flows
(in millions)

	1990	1989	1988	1987	1986
Operations					
Income	$474.90	$454.03	$400.26	$217.50	$153.96
+Depr., depl., & amort.	202.69	124.80	77.68	70.52	51.08
+Deferred taxes	138.92	111.34	88.80	25.26	47.24
+Loss (gain) on sale of PP&E	2.19	(73.9)	2.10	2.30	N.A.
+Dec. (inc.) in accts. rec.	30.96	(154.01)	233.18	N.A.	N.A.
+Dec. (inc.) in inventory	119.9	(13.91)	235.72	N.A.	N.A.
+Inc. (dec.) in accr. inc. tax	(52.55)	23.33	42.22	N.A.	N.A.
+Net chg. in other assets & liab.	46.87	35.66	152.27	N.A.	N.A.
Net cash flow: operations	963.87	507.35	294.44	N.A.	N.A.
Investing					
+Chg. in ST investments	(251.76)	(197.29)	0.30	N.A.	N.A.
−Capital expenditures	224.31	238.99	144	86.13	66.63
+Other investing activities	(97.47)	33.21	(42.10)	N.A.	N.A.
Net cash flow: investing	(573.53)	(403.08)	(186.10)	N.A.	N.A.
Financing					
−Purch. of common & pfd. stock	569.56	12.87	299.43	154.14	54.51
−Cash dividends	53.78	50.31	39.65	15.23	0.00
+Changes in current debt	65.88	(71.12)	127.87	0.00	0.00
+Other financing activities	103.51	95.97	83.49	N.A.	N.A.
Net cash flow: financing	(453.95)	(38.33)	(127.71)	N.A.	N.A.
Inc. (dec.) in cash & equiv.	(63.62)	65.94	(19.38)	(11.12)	239.2

systems even more powerful and easier to use. And we're building new foundation technologies that will be a framework for innovation across a vast array of industries."[4]

60   John Akers, chairman of IBM, said: "The second decade of personal computing begins today [October 2]. Increasingly, systems software and semiconductor technology are defining where essential value is added to computers. With this alliance, Apple and IBM are drawing on their strengths and those of Motorola to continue setting the pace for our customers."[5]

61   Apple is in the process of inventing its future. The question is whether it will be as successful as its past.

---

[4] Apple Computer, Inc., press release, October 2, 1991.

[5] Ibid.

EXHIBIT 11
Major Points of the Apple-IBM Agreement*

I. Networking

Starting as early as 1992, Apple and IBM computers in the same office will be able to share software and other information and equipment, thanks to new networking products and cross-licensing agreements. The agreement will provide Apple with an entrance into the corporate environment that has, for the most part, ignored the Macintosh. Products will be tested at an IBM lab in Research Triangle, North Carolina.

II. Microprocessors

About 300 IBM and Motorola employees will combine to create a chip called the *PowerPC*. The chip will use the speedy RISC—reduced instruction-set computing—technology. The processor will be derived from IBM's RS/6000 chip technology and will be used in Apple and IBM workstations. It is scheduled to be available to all computer makers in 1993 or 1994.

III. Software

Apple and IBM will form a jointly owned software company, Taligent, that will design an object-oriented operating system. The system is expected to be completed by the mid-1990s and will be used in future Apple and IBM products, as well as be made available to other manufacturers for licensing.

By 1994, Apple and IBM will introduce a new Unix-based open-systems operating environment, PowerOpen, which will be used on either company's RISC computers. PowerOpen will be derived from AIX, IBM's version of Unix; the Macintosh interface; and the PowerPC architecture. This environment will enable a computer to run both Macintosh and AIX applications.

IV. Multimedia

IBM and Apple will form a jointly owned company, Kaleida, to develop multimedia standards and software. The technologies resulting from this venture will be licensed to other developers. Multimedia provides personal computers with graphic, sound, video, and animation capabilities. The first products are expected to be completed by 1993.

---

* Requires approval by the Federal Trade Commission. Approval is expected by the end of 1991.
Sources: Apple Computer, Inc.; *Business Week*, October 7, 1991; and *MacWeek*, October 8, 1991.

APPENDIX

Apple's Executive Management Team: 1991

John Sculley—Chairman, Chief Executive Officer, and Chief Technology Officer

John Sculley joined Apple Computer, Inc., as chief executive officer in April 1983 and was elected chairman of the board in January 1986. He became chief technology officer in 1990. Sculley has led Apple to a top position in the personal computer industry, focusing on technology for business and education. In fiscal 1990, Apple's 13th anniversary year, worldwide revenue reached $5.55 billion.

Prior to joining Apple, Sculley was president and chief executive officer of Pepsi-Cola Company for five years. During that time, he led Pepsi to the top market share position in the United States, as measured by the A. C. Nielsen Company.

He is the recipient of numerous awards, including Advertising Man of the Year by both *Advertising Age* and *Adweek* magazines, the Joseph E. Wharton Business–Statesman Leadership Award from the Wharton Business School, and UCLA's Anderson Graduate School of Management Exemplary Leadership in Management Award. Most recently, he was chosen CEO of the Decade for Marketing by the Financial News Network.

Sculley was selected by General Secretary Mikhail Gorbachev of the Soviet Union to serve on the board of the International Foundation for the Survival and Development of Humanity, an East-West cooperative effort on the human rights, education, arms reduction, energy, and the environment. In addition, he is chairman of the National Center on Education and the Economy (NCEE), which has prepared a follow-up study to the Carnegie Foundation's "A Nation Prepared," titled "To Secure Our Future." Sculley presented this report to President George Bush in January 1989. The recommendations of the most recent NCEE report, "America's Choice: high skills or low wages!" has become the model for school reform in several states throughout the country.

He currently serves on the SEI Board, the Center for Advanced Studies and Management, and on the Board of Overseers, both at the Wharton School, and is on the advisory board of Scholastic's *Agenda* magazine. In addition, he serves on the board of trustees at Brown University and also has served on the board of advisors at the Graduate School of Business at Stanford University. He is the author of the best-selling autobiography, *Odyssey,* which recollects his personal journey with Apple, high technology, and education. He is a frequent guest on network television and radio, speaking on technology, education, and preparing America for the 21st century.

Sculley graduated from Brown University in 1961, where he studied architectural design. He earned a master's degree in business administration in 1963 from the Wharton School at the University of Pennsylvania. He has received honorary doctorate degrees from the University of Rhode Island, Johns Hopkins University, and Babson College. Sculley was born April 6, 1939, in New York City.

Michael H. Spindler—President and Chief Operating Officer

Michael H. Spindler has played a key role in putting the word *global* in Apple Computer's corporate vocabulary. In 1990, after heading Apple's European operations, Spindler became the company's president and chief operating officer. He oversees all of Apple's international operations, which include Apple USA, Europe, and Pacific. And he's responsible for product development for the company's core Macintosh business, which covers both hardware and system software. He also directs Apple's Manufacturing and Enterprise System divisions.

Spindler joined Apple in 1980 as marketing manager for European operations, where he achieved a succession of higher profile positions, including general manager of European sales and marketing, 1983–85; vice president in charge of Apple's international marketing and sales division, 1985–87; and president of Apple Europe, 1987–90. Under his leadership, sales for Apple's European division tripled.

Prior to Apple, Spindler was European marketing manager for Intel Corporation, spent eight years in a similar position with Digital Equipment Corporation, and worked at Schlumberger, Ltd., and at Siemans AG. Spindler, a German national, was born in December 1942.

Ian W. Diery—Senior Vice President and President, Apple Computer, Inc.

His travels for Apple Computer have convinced Ian Diery that some of the most fertile ground in the global market actually can be found close to his native homeland in the Pacific region. Diery spends half his time traveling in his roles as president, Apple Pacific, and senior vice president, Apple Computer, Inc. He's responsible for the marketing, sales, and support efforts in Australia, Canada, Japan, the Far East, and Latin America. "The appeal of Apple's products reaches into the far corners of the globe, traversing traditional geographic and economic borders," Diery says. "The cultural, political, and economic diversity of the Pacific region, combined with the growing influence of Japan and Asia on world economies, makes the area an exciting and challenging marketplace for the 1990s," he says. "Japan has been an incredibly successful market," Diery says. Apple Japan's revenues have doubled each year since 1988. And the first MacWorld Tokyo, held in February 1991, attracted 60,000 attendees—making it the largest MacWorld ever.

Apple draws on a large federation of relationships—third-party developers, user groups, consultants, and a loyal customer base—to strengthen its Pacific business plan. "Although there are increased competitive pressures, the unique nature of Apple's products continues to differentiate our products from others," says Diery, who joined Apple in 1989. "Macintosh is an excellent international platform because it can be easily localized for non-Roman languages. At a time when computing is increasingly complex, Apple products provide easier access to a variety of computing environments." Diery sees a special opportunity for Apple in personalizing computing environments and believes the company is well-positioned to take advantage of the opportunities in his far-flung region. "The key to our success is the ability of Apple employees to motivate and support the development of relationships with customers and business partners," he says.

Diery, a native of Sydney, Australia, worked in the field office equipment distribution until 1977, when he joined Wang Laboratories. During his 11-year career with Wang, he headed European and U.S. operations, rising to executive vice president, Worldwide Field Operations.

At home in Woodside, California, Diery, born in October 1949, is an active rugby player and an avid equestrian. In his leisure time, he also enjoys reading history and playing golf.

Albert A. Eisenstat—Secretary and Executive Vice President

In the dawning days of the computer industry, Albert A. Eisenstat was making practical business decisions while others concentrated solely on awakening the computer's technical potential. Today, as Apple Computer's executive vice president for corporate development as well as corporate secretary, Eisenstat continues to balance the technical and business sides of a company he has come to know well since 1980.

"Apple's challenge has always been to retain those things which make this a great work environment, but still bring about more disciplined methods in decision making," he says. "We're learning to be more accountable. And we're opening up to learning from our mistakes. That type of thinking is more prevalent in the company."

Through 11 years at Apple and varied experiences in his career, Eisenstat has come to enjoy the intellectual challenge of making well-reasoned decisions in a fast-paced competitive industry. In fact, he believes competition and technical advances have given customers better value for their money in personal computing products.

Eisenstat, born in April 1930, graduated from the Wharton School of Finance of the University of Pennsylvania in 1952 with a bachelor of science degree in economics. Following air force service in Europe, he earned his law degree from New York University in 1960.

As both a lawyer and a certified public accountant, Eisenstat has served stints as Apple's general counsel and chief financial officer. The law group reports to him today. He also spends time on special projects, including acquisitions and licensing considerations. He often visits the Soviet Union in efforts to open a distribution channel for Macintosh computers.

Computers were still relatively new in 1967, when Eisenstat left a professional partnership to co-found United Data Centers (UDC), Inc., which expanded to a national network of computer data centers, providing batch and remote batch data processing businesses. UDC was sold to Tymshare, a national computer time-sharing company, in 1974. Eisenstat then moved to California as Tymshare's vice president and general counsel.

He returned to New York in 1979 as senior vice president and general counsel of Bradford National Corporation, a large financial transaction processing company. Then, it was back to California for the job with Apple in 1980.

Eisenstat makes his home in Atherton, California, with is wife and two children. In his spare time he likes to ski, scuba dive, play tennis, and enjoy a large music collection.

Joseph A. Graziano—Executive Vice President and Chief Financial Officer

Apple Computer is known for having one of the healthiest balance sheets of any company in the world. With $1 billion in cash, Apple routinely is named as one of the strongest performers in the industry. It's Joseph A. Graziano's job to help make Apple a beacon of financial stability in an industry known more for unpredictability.

As Apple's executive vice president and chief financial officer, Graziano is a key member of the company's executive management team and a major player in developing a financial plan that charts long-term business and financial strategies. He believes the best financial plans are developed from the bottom up so a variety of Apple employees contribute to the plan and are committed to making it happen.

"The financial plan supporting Apple's high volume and market share goals is based on a good understanding of the market environment and customer needs," says Graziano. "As CFO, my role is to integrate the financial activities around the company to support Apple's business plan."

Graziano, a 1965 graduate of Massachusetts' Merrimack College, worked from 1981–85 as Apple's chief financial officer and saw the company's annual revenues grow from $300 million to $2 billion. He was drawn back to Apple after a two-year sabbatical, 1985–87, and two years as chief financial officer at Sun Microsystems, 1987–89. Previously, he worked at ROLM Corporation, 1976–81, holding the position of company treasurer, and in accounting positions with other technology companies in Silicon Valley.

Today, Graziano monitors business indicators to understand what is happening with markets, customers, and competitors, and to help Apple react quickly. He remains alert to trends and messages in Apple's financial operations by looking well beyond the quarterly performance. "We do have a better job of planning and anticipating a rapidly changing economy, and assess some of our activities to ensure they are linked to corporate goals," he says.

Graziano, born November 1944, spends his spare time at home with his wife in Saratoga, California.

Sören Olsson—Senior Vice President and President, Apple Europe

Sören Olsson, president of Apple Computer Europe, Inc., joined Apple Computer in 1984. He is responsible for Apple's marketing, sales, and support operations in Apple's European subsidiaries and distribution representation throughout Europe, Africa, and the Middle East. In his position he reports directly to Michael Spindler, chief operating officer.

Prior to his current position, Olsson was Apple's vice president, area general manager for Europe North, which includes Norway, Denmark, Finland, Iceland, Germany, Austria, and Eastern Europe. He directed Apple Sweden since its founding in 1984, making it one of the most successful markets in Europe.

Before joining Apple, he worked for Hewlett-Packard for 15 years. He began as sales engineer for the Computer Group, moving through several positions in Sweden until he became country manager for the Computer Group. His last position at Hewlett-Packard was as regional sales manager for North Europe based in Amsterdam, the Netherlands.

Olsson, 44, is a Swedish national and holds degrees in chemical engineering and in business administration.

Robert L. Puette—President, Apple USA

Robert L. Puette arrived at Apple Computer in 1990 with a reputation for straight shooting, business savvy, and a game plan that would rival any football coach's playbook. That game plan emerged as a vision, which Puette, president, Apple USA, put in action to strengthen the operations he oversees— sales, marketing, support, and distribution.

"We want to be more than just a sales organization," says Puette. "We want to be the best supplier to our customers, the best partner to our dealers, resellers, and third-party trainers, and the best employer for our people."

For Puette, who played football while earning his bachelor of science degree in industrial engineering from Northwestern University in 1964, the sports analogy is appropriate. "In football, you have to study the opposing team and know the moves of every player," he says. "It's the same in business. We have to understand the strengths and weaknesses of our competition and of ourselves to stay ahead of the game."

Apple, he says, has strengths that no other personal computing company can match. "One of the unique things about Apple is that we own the operating system, the user interface, and the hardware," he says. "This integration adds value and puts Apple in the position to do something truly distinctive in personal computing."

Puette, born in February 1942, joined Apple after 24 years with Hewlett-Packard, Inc., where he led the startup and development of HP's worldwide personal computer division. His most recent position at HP was general manager, Personal Computer Group, 1987–90.

Puette earned a master of science degree in operations research from Stanford University, in 1965. In his spare time, he enjoys the outdoors, especially water sports, with his wife and four children.

Puette serves as chairman of the industrial advisory board for the San Jose State engineering department, and on the industrial advisory board for Northwestern's engineering school. In addition, he serves on the board of advisors for the Applied Technology Institute for Microelectronics, and on the board of directors of Cisco Systems.

Kevin Sullivan—Senior Vice President, Human Resources

Named to senior vice president for human resources in 1987, Sullivan reports directly to Apple Chairman and CEO John Sculley. He is the member of Apple's executive staff responsible for supporting the company's business objectives through the company's worldwide human resource functions: employee relations, compensation, benefits, staffing, and in-house communications.

"We play an integral part in implementing the company's business direction," says Sullivan, whose team is involved in the early stages of business planning. "The human resources group is a business parnter made up of people who know how to build management teams and staff organizations that make the strategy work and get the job done."

In his job, Sullivan often draws on many years of experience with Digital Equipment Corporation, where he held senior personnel management positions responsible for domestic and international human resource activities. He served as European personnel manager, corporation compensation/benefits manager, U.S. field personnel manager, and most recently, before joining Apple, corporate personnel manager and a member of Digital's personnel management committee.

Sullivan earned his bachelor of arts degree in political studies from Columbia University in New York City and a master's degree in American studies from Wesleyan University in Middletown, Connecticut.

Born in May 1941, Sullivan spends leisure time at home with his wife in Palo Alto, California.

Source: Apple Computer, Inc.

Salaries and Stock Ownership Information

Current shares outstanding: **117,959,416.**
Total number of shareholders: **34,352.**
Shares held by officers and directors: **10,450,958 (9% of total).**

Salaries of key executives:
John Sculley—chairman, chief executive officer, and chief technology officer: **$2,198,866.**
Michael H. Spindler—president and chief operating officer: **$1,081,469.**
Ian W. Diery—senior vice president and president, Apple Computer, Inc.: **$792,923.**
Joseph A. Graziano—executive vice president and chief financial officer: **$1,292,913.**

Source: Apple Computer, Inc.

Apple's Organizational Structure

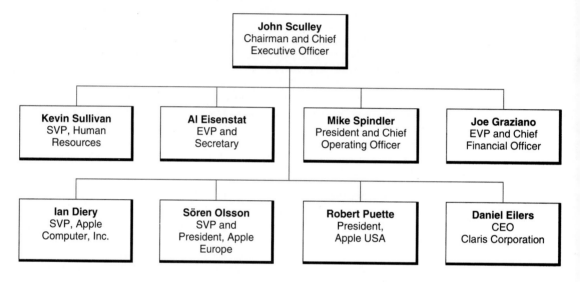

Members of Apple's Board of Directors

Peter O. Crisp
General partner, Venrock Associates
Venture capital investments

Albert A. Eisenstat
Senior vice president and secretary
Apple Computer, Inc.

A.C. Markkula, Jr.
Chairman, ACM Aviation, Inc.
Private flight service

Arthur Rock
Principal, Arthur Rock & Co.
Venture capital investments

John Rollwagen
Chairman and chief executive officer
Cray Research, Inc.

John Sculley
Chairman, chief executive officer and chief technology officer
Apple Computer, Inc.

Michael Spindler
President and chief operating officer
Apple Computer, Inc.
Bernard Goldstein
Partner
Broadview Associates

Source: Apple Computer, Inc.

REFERENCES

Apple Computer, Inc., annual reports.

Apple Computer, Inc., press releases.

Buell, Barbara. "Apple: New Team, New Strategy." *Business Week,* October 15, 1990, pp. 87–96.

—————. "The Second Comeback at Apple." *Business Week,* January 28, 1991. p. 68.

Dworetzky, Tom. "Automated Apple Orchard." *Discover,* September 1984, pp. 80–81.

Hafner, Katherine. "Apple's Comeback." *Business Week,* January 19, 1987, pp. 84–89.

Kawasaki, Guy. *The Macintosh Way.* Glenview, Ill.: Scott, Foresman, 1990.

Moran, Brian. "John Sculley Marketing Methods Bring Apple Back." *Advertising Age,* December 31, 1984, pp. 1, 22–23.

O'Reilly, Brian. "Apple Finally Invades the Office." *Fortune,* November 9, 1987, pp. 52–64.

Patterson, William Pat. "John Sculley Markets a Revolution." *Industry Week,* October 3, 1988, pp. 43–45.

Rapport, Andrew S. "The Computerless Computer Company." *Harvard Business Review,* July–August 1991, pp. 69–80.

Rose, Frank. *West of Eden: The End of Innocence at Apple Computer.* New York: Penguin Books, 1989.

Sculley, John. *Odyssey.* New York: Harper & Row, 1987.

Wise, Deborah. "Apple's New Crusade." *Business Week,* November 26, 1984, pp. 146–56.

CASE 18

NORDSTROM, INC.

1   Wallin and Nordstrom, a shoe store, opened its doors in 1901. During the early part of the century business flourished and, in 1923, a second store was opened. After half a century of increased shoe sales, Wallin and Nordstrom expanded into apparel. Today the company's name is Nordstrom. In 1991, the company had 69 stores with sales of $2,89 billion and a net income of $115.8 million.[1]

2   The retail apparel industry changed dramatically in the early 1990s. R. H. Macy's, the industry's leading retailer, filed for bankruptcy protection in 1992. Alexander's, a major New York retailer, also was seeking bankruptcy protection in early 1992.[2] On the other hand, The Gap, a San Francisco–based specialty retailer, posted $2.5 billion in sales and $100 million in earnings in 1991.[3]

3   Nordstrom had survived and prospered in this turbulent environment. To remain in this position in the 1990s the company had to answer many strategic questions: What customers did it want to serve and what products would these customers want? How could Nordstrom improve its customer services? How quickly and how far could Nordstrom expand and still maintain its formula for success?

THE INDUSTRY AND COMPETITIVE MARKET

The Retail Wearing Apparel Industry

4   The retail industry involves the selling of goods, in a retail store location, to the ultimate consumer for personal or household consumption. A segment of the retail industry, the retail wearing apparel industry, consists of companies that sell clothing, accessories, and shoes to women, men, and children through retail stores.

5   Companies operating within the retail wearing apparel industry are involved in sourcing (finding manufacturers to produce goods), buying, shipping and storing, unpacking and ticketing, promoting and advertising, and selling.

6   Companies in the retail wearing apparel industry sell merchandise through several types of outlets. Department stores sell a wide variety of moderately to high-priced merchandise. Specialty stores sell specific types of merchandise and target specific groups of customers. Mass merchandisers sell a wide variety of goods, at prices lower than most department stores. Discount stores sell fashionable apparel at lower prices than department stores. Catalog retailers sell their merchandise through mail order. Off-price stores sell quality fashionable merchandise at discount prices. Boutiques and small shops sell various types of apparel in many price ranges, with inventory levels varying widely from store to store.

This case was prepared by Professor Robert J. Mockler of St. John's University.

[1] Karen J. Sack, "Nordstrom, Inc.," Standard & Poor's Corp., October 2, 1991, pp. 4793–794.

[2] Edward R. Silverman, "Supplier Trouble for Alexander's," *Newsday*, March 7, 1992(A), and idem, "Macy's Cutbacks Coming," *Newsday*, March 8, 1992(B), p. 7.

[3] Rissell Mitchell, "Inside the Gap," *Business Week*, March 9, 1992, pp. 58–64.

EXHIBIT 1
Sales of Retail Stores by Kind of Business, 1990 and 1989 (millions of dollars)

Kind of Business	1990	1989	Percent Change
Retail trade, total.	$1,826,293	$1,747,804	+4.5%
Total (excluding automotive group)	1,441,204	1,363,653	+5.7
Durable goods stores, total	661,594	652,739	+1.4
Building materials, hardware, garden supply, and mobile home dealers	95,132	92,700	+2.6
Building materials, supply, hardware stores	82,117	79,612	+3.1
Building materials and supply stores	69,703	67,045	+4.0
Hardware stores	12,414	12,576	−1.2
Automotive dealers	385,089	384,151	+0.2
Motor vehicle and miscellaneous automotive dealers	352,892	353,765	−0.2
Motor vehicle dealers	334,859	335,278	−0.1
Motor vehicle dealers (franchised)	312,983	309,714	+1.1
Auto and home supply stores	32,197	30,386	+6.0
Furniture, home furnishing, and equipment stores	91,937	91,493	+0.5
Furniture and home furnishing stores	50,420	51,082	−1.3
Furniture stores.	27,436	29,720	−7.7
Floor covering stores	12,979	12,136	+6.9
Household appliance, radio, and TV	32,561	32,387	+0.5
Household appliance stores	9,071	9,462	−4.1
Radio and television stores	23,490	22,925	+2.5
Sporting good stores and bicycle shops	13,936	13,531	+3.0
Book stores	7,356	6,492	+13.3
Jewelry stores.	14,667	14,049	+4.4
Nondurable goods store, total	164,699	1,095,065	+6.4
General merchandise group stores	212,140	204,387	+3.8
Dept. stores, excl. leased depts.	169,681	164,358	+3.2
Dept. stores, incl. leased depts.	175,684	169,506	+3.6

7   The 1987 stock market crash caused a slowing of sales, earnings, and return on sales for major retail companies. As a result, 1987 sales only marginally surpassed 1986 sales.[4] Exhibit 1 shows apparel retail store sales for 1989 and 1990. Apparel sales are included in two categories: general merchandise stores and apparel and accessory stores.

---

[4] Lisa Marsh, "Analysis of Retail Performances for Fiscal 1988," *Women's Wear Daily*, August 24, 1989, pp. 4–5.

EXHIBIT 1 (concluded)

Kind of Business	1990	1989	Percent Change
Conventional dept. stores (incl. leased depts.)	$ 53,149	$ 52,844	+0.6
Discount dept. stores (incl. leased depts.)	84,494	78,744	+7.3
National chain dept. stores (incl. leased depts.)	38,041	37,918	+0.3
Variety stores	7,410	7,356	+0.7
Miscellaneous general mdse. stores	35,049	32,673	+7.3
Food stores.	371,580	349,120	+6.4
Grocery stores	348,243	328,075	+6.1
Meat, fish (seafood) markets	6,517	6,709	−2.9
Retail bakeries	6,745	5,753	+17.2
Gasoline service stations	130,200	117,791	+10.5
Apparel and accessory stores	94,455	91,426	+3.3
Men's & boys clothing, furnishings	8,976	9,548	−6.0
Women's cloth., spec. stores, furriers.	33,450	32,637	+2.5
Women's ready-to-wear stores	30,194	29,260	+3.2
Family clothing stores.	27,407	25,768	+6.4
Shoe stores	17,839	17,163	+3.9
Eating and drinking places	186,162	175,344	+6.2
Eating places	173,086	163,645	+5.8
Restaurants, lunchrooms, cafeterias	93,809	89,076	+5.3
Refreshment places	76,893	71,189	+6.5
Drinking places (alcoholic bev.)	13,076	11,699	+11.8
Drug and proprietary stores.	69,169	62,495	+10.7
Liquor stores.	21,618	20,033	+7.9
Nonstore retailers.	48,285	45,247	+6.7
Mail-order houses (department store merchandise)	4,669	4,676	−0.1
Other mail order	26,172	24,173	+8.3
Miscellaneous shopping goods stores	65,938	64,025	+3.0

8   As illustrated in Exhibit 1, sales in the apparel and accessory category increased only 3.3 percent from 1989 to 1990, compared to a 3.8 percent increase in the general merchandise category. Consumer spending on clothing continued to rise in 1990, although the approximately 1.0 percent increase recorded was considerably less than the 4.8 percent increase recorded from 1988 to 1989.[5] Many factors contributed to this slow growth: the lack of fashion direction in women's apparel, consumer resistance to higher prices, and rapid overexpansion by retailers.

---

[5] U.S. Department of Commerce, "Apparel," *U.S. Industrial Outlook 1991*, pp. 34-1–34-7.

9   Retailers, nonetheless, planned to open as many stores in 1992 as they had in 1991, with one exception: stores were expected to be even larger. With this strategy, stores were attempting to maximize sales, raise market share, and capitalize on the concept of one-stop shopping. However, many analysts believed that this was not the answer to the problems plaguing the retail industry. The main problem, according to a study conducted by Smith Barney Harris Upham, a New York investment firm, was that the growth rate of sales per store had slowed in the last decade and so size did not matter. The report showed that, in 1987, dollar sales per store grew at an average annual rate of 3 percent between 1948 and 1977. Since 1977, the average annual growth rate of sales growth has slowed to six tenths of 1 percent. In one analyst's opinion, the answer to the retail industry's problems was increased efficiency. One suggested solution was using technology more effectively to automate backroom operations and to allow customers to serve themselves.[6]

10   During 1991 and 1992, an increasing number of retailers, including Macy's, filed for bankruptcy protection. Another popular retailer, the Oklahoma–based Street's, closed its doors after the 1991 Christmas selling season. Street's, which operated 10 stores, had been in operation since the 1930s, but heavy competition from outlets, such as Dillard's Department Stores, The Limited, Inc., and Wal-Mart Stores, forced the 51-year-old chain to shut down.[7]

11   Other retailers who filed for bankruptcy between 1988 and 1992 included Federated Department Stores (1990), Allied Stores (1990), Carter Hawley Hale (1991), Revco Department Stores (1988), Ames Department Stores (1990), and Hills Department Stores (1991).[8]

12   Mergers, acquisitions, and corporate restructuring were also on the rise during the early 1990s. As earning potential lessened, companies acquired or merged with other companies. This trend in the retail wearing apparel industry was expected to continue.[9]

13   Retail square footage increased dramatically during this period. In 1990, 15 square feet of retail space existed for every woman, man, and child in the country. This growth surpassed consumer population growth and created a buyer's market. Retail apparel stores were attempting to gain market share by expanding geographically. Malls especially were becoming overcrowded with specialty department stores, resulting in market saturation in many areas.

Customers

14   The retail wearing apparel industry has a wide range of customers. For purposes of this study, these customers can be grouped according to sex and age, as shown in Exhibit 2.

15   Women, who accounted for more than 75 percent of the apparel market in 1990, spent money on themselves as well as on other family members. As shown in Exhibit 1, retail apparel stores' 1989 sales of women's apparel and accessories were $61.9 billion. This number increased to $63.6 billion in 1990, a 2.8 percent increase. These figures included sales of new merchandise as well as items held in inventory. The sales of this segment reportedly increased by approximately the same margin for the following year.[10] The value of merchandise shipped from manufacturers to retail apparel outlets for major category items, such as blouses, dresses, suits, and coats, was $14.3 billion in 1990. Two thirds of all retail apparel sales for 1989 and 1990 were purchases by women of shoes, accessories, and apparel for women.

16   As shown in Exhibit 2, 18-year-old to 34-year-old women accounted for 20 percent of sales in the U.S. apparel market in 1990. This group responded quickly to changes and trends within the wearing

---

[6] Isadore Barmash, "Down the Scale with the Major Chains," *The New York Times*, Business Section, February 2, 1992, p. 5.

[7] Kevin Helliker, "Final Markdown," *The Wall Street Journal*, December 4, 1991, pp. A1, A6.

[8] Floyd Norris, "Win or Lose, Buyouts Do It Big," *The New York Times*, January 28, 1992, pp. D1, D8.

[9] Ibid.

[10] U.S. Department of Commerce, "Retail Trade: 1990," *Current Business Report*, 1992, pp. 1–29.

EXHIBIT 2
Retail Industry Customer Segment, 1990

Customer	Percent of Apparel Market Sales
Women:	
18–34	20%
35–54	35
55 & over . . .	30
Total	85
Men	10
Children	5
Total	100%

Source: Gary Levin, "Boomers Leave a Challenge," *Ad Age*, July 1991, pp. 1 and 14.

apparel industry and frequented stores that responded likewise. Retailers like The Limited had grown rapidly and became very profitable by targeting this group.[11] However, this group was expected to shrink 11 percent (to 62.4 million) by the year 2000.[12] Even so, this category was expected to continue to be especially important because its members' habits were not formed.[13] Another group characteristic is that these women prefer fashions that are contemporary, rather than traditional. They wish to purchase contemporary styles at outlets that are known for selling such merchandise, often returning to these outlets for repeat purchases.

17   Another trend that had developed was the dramatic increase in the number of women in the work force. This group, the 35–54 age group, accounted for 35 percent of sales in the overall apparel market and was expected to become the most important demographic group in this industry. This segment, unlike the 18 to 34-year-old segment, was expected to grow during the 1990s. Members of this age group are more likely to spend a large proportion of their disposable income on wearable apparel.[14] Individuals in this group spent an average of $2,000 on apparel in 1991. Members of this group sought reasonably priced clothing that was sophisticated and career oriented.[15]

18   The fastest-growing population segment is the over-55 age category. This group made about 30 percent of apparel purchases in 1990. As a whole, this group was at its peak spending capabilities and was expected to be a strong market for many types of career, casual, and active wear apparel. This group had been know to spend $13 billion on apparel in a single year.[16]

19   A special market, known as the large-size market, was an increasingly important segment of the women's market. In 1990, more than $10 billion was spent on apparel by the 40 million American

---

[11] Rita Koselka, "Fading into History," *Forbes*, August 19, 1991, pp. 70, 71.

[12] Scott Donston, "Media Reassess as Boomers Age," *Ad Age*, July 1991, p. 12.

[13] Gary Levin, "Boomers Leave a Challenge," *Ad Age*, July 1991, pp. 1, 14.

[14] U.S. Dept. of Commerce, 1992.

[15] U.S. Dept. of Commerce, 1991.

[16] U.S. Dept. of Commerce, 1992.

women wearing size 14 or larger. This was expected to continue to be a lucrative market since demand was high but supply was low. "This is a great market to be in because customers' appreciation is so high," said Susie Phillips, vice president of marketing at Lane Bryant. Large-size women faced extremely limited choices in selection, quality, and fashion in the past, so opportunities existed in select or diverse lines of large-size apparel.[17]

20   Petite women, those under 5′5″ tall, also found it difficult to purchase apparel that fit. Petite customers frequently encountered ill-fitting sleeve and hem lengths. This segment at times was ignored because of the belief that these customers could alter the clothes to fit. However, this was costly. The popular catalog merchandiser Clifford & Wills was one of several marketers to offer a select group of merchandise that could be purchased in petite sizes at the same cost as the similar regular-size items.[18]

21   Historically, women have spent more than any other demographic group on wearable apparel, and they were considered to be the No. 1 target of apparel merchants. Women favored department stores, discounters, and factory outlets for apparel, although specialty stores seemed to be gaining in popularity in the late 1980s. Women tended to purchase apparel that was moderately priced and had a designer look. Stores that offered designer-look quality apparel at low prices were the most suitable for their shopping needs.[19]

22   Men accounted for only a small portion of retail apparel industry sales, about 10 percent. Men's dollar sales totaled only $8.9 billion in 1990. In general, men devoted less time to shopping. When they did find time, such chain stores at The Gap were the most popular for sportswear items, such as shirts, sweaters, and trousers, according to 47 percent of the men interviewed in a nationwide fashion study. Department stores were the preferred sales outlet for suits and business attire by 37 percent of those interviewed.[20] Men also shopped more often at stores that were conveniently located.

23   The children's market accounted for the smallest portion of retail sales within the apparel industry in 1990: 5 percent of the market. This segment's customers were under the age of 18 and for the most part relied on other family members to purchase or fund their apparel. The industry generally divides this category, based on sex, and combines market data with that for men and women.

Products

24   The ranges of products offered in the retail wearing apparel industry were vast. Items included outerwear products (blouses, jackets, and trousers), accessories (belts, hats, and scarves), and shoes. Retailers offered all of these products at various prices and in many types, styles, colors, and sizes for men, women, and children. Exhibit 3 lists several merchandise categories and their values in 1988, 1989, and 1990.

Price

25   Price was determined by many factors: the cost of labor and shipping; the fabrics used to make a garment; the length of time it took to produce a garment; and the fashion or style of the garment. In 1991, sales of higher-priced fashions slowed and sales of moderately priced products rose as demand increased for reasonably priced apparel. Shoppers spent the largest amounts on inexpensive apparel in 1991.[21] Major retailers, such as Wal-Mart, were planning on cutting out middlemen. These retailers wanted to deal directly with the manufacturer instead of a wholesale broker or merchandise represen-

---

[17] Muriel Adams, "Large (Size) and Growing," *Stores*, May 1988, pp. 33–52.

[18] Clifford & Wills Spring Catalog, 1992.

[19] Georgia Lee, "Lower Prices Key at Atlanta Show," *Women's Wear Daily*, February 12, 1992, p. 8.

[20] "Upfront: Salon International, Mode Masculine," *Stores*, March 1991, p. 14.

[21] "Retail Apparel Industry," *Value Line*, February 28, 1991, pp. 1601–711.

EXHIBIT 3
Value of Apparel Shipments from Wholesalers to Retailers, 1990
Select Merchandise Categories (in millions except percent)

				Percent Change	
Item	1988	1989	1990	1988–89	1989–90
Industry Data					
Value of shipments	$15,101	$15,468	$15,288	2.4%	−1.2%
Men's/boys' suits/coats	3,169	3,102	3,137	−2.1	1.1
Men's and boys' shirts	4,031	4,170	4,101	3.4	−1.7
Men's and boys' neckwear	500	502	501	0.4	−0.2
Men's/boys' trousers	5,767	6,061	5,915	5.1	−2.4
Men's/boys' work clothing	1,633	1,633	1,634	0.0	0.1
Value of shipments	14,315	14,288	14,307	−0.2	0.1
Women's/misses' blouses	3,573	3,810	3,691	6.6	−3.1
Women's/misses' dresses	6,037	5,771	5,908	−4.4	2.4
Women's suits/coats	4,705	4,707	4,708	0.0	0.0
Value of shipments	3,884	3,921	3,904	1.0	−0.4
Women's/child's underwear	2,621	2,716	2,669	3.6	−1.7
Bras & allied garments	1,263	1,205	1,235	−4.6	2.5

Source: Information obtained from U.S. Department of Commerce, "Apparel," *U.S. Industrial Outlook 1991*, pp. 34-1 and 34-7.

tative. The 2 to 3 percent saved on wholesalers' commissions would result in savings for the consumer since this amount normally would be added to the price of a retailer's merchandise.[22]

Type of Style of Clothing

26   The type of clothing offered by the apparel industry included accessories, shoes, outerwear, and undergarments. As shown in Exhibit 3, shipments of men's/boys' trousers, the No. 1 men's category for 1990, were valued at $5.915 billion. Men's/boys' neckwear, the smallest men's category, was valued at $501 million in 1990. Sales in all men's categories except suits/coats and work clothing declined from 1989 to 1990. Under the women's category, women's/girls' dresses, the No. 1 category in 1990, were at $5.195 billion, an increase of 2.4 percent from 1989. The value of shipments in the women's/girls' suits/coats category did not change from 1989 to 1990.[23]

27   Styles of apparel included casual, traditional/classical, and contemporary. Casual apparel, such items as denim jeans, knit stirrup pants, and sweaters, was worn as leisure clothing by all age categories. These items usually were not worn to the office or at a formal affair. Casual clothing appeared to be gaining popularity in the early 1990s. Classical or traditional apparel was simple and sophisticated clothing worn for formal occasions. Traditional-style apparel usually was designed with standard colors and patterns, to enable the customer to use the items for more than one season. Classical items included traditional silhouettes, such as A-line skirts and button-up blouses and shirts, in basic colors

[22] Barmash, "Down the Scale."

[23] U.S. Dept. of Commerce, 1991.

such as black, navy, and beige. These items also included beaded cocktail dresses and elegant evening wear with special details, such as jeweled buttons. Contemporary clothing was unique and original in design. Fabrics usually featured bright colors and abstract patterns.

Inventory Management

28   Advances in technology can benefit retailers of wearing apparel in terms of inventory management. Technology permits tracking the sales of popular sizes and styles and allows for fast reordering. Two types of technology that aid in the inventory management process are bar coding and EDI (electronic data interchange).

29   Bar coding uses various symbols to identify vendor item markings, price, department, and style number. This system has led to automated replenishment of merchandise, improved merchandise information, and speedier check-outs.[24] In 1991, J. C. Penney had converted 40,000 point-of-sale registers to bar-code scanners to decrease supplier response time for reorders.

30   Electronic data interchange is a computerized system that records inventory, as well as items and styles sold. When the need arises, a reorder can be placed automatically by the EDI computer system. An added benefit of this system is decreased inventory costs.[25]

Advertising and promotion

31   Advertising and promotion were an integral part of operations for an apparel retailer. The target market dictated the method of advertising or promotions, or both, used by the retailer. Firms developed positioning strategies and strategies aimed at specific market segments, since retailers who know their clientele can choose the medium that best suits their products. Magazines such as *Vogue*, for example, are geared toward the designer market. Therefore, it is very unlikely that a discount retailer would advertise there.

32   A study of media involvement conducted by Audits & Surveys, Inc., for the Magazine Publishers of America Association found that in 16 of 19 areas of interest, print was the prime media source for working women, young adults, and the affluent. The study also indicated that 60 percent of newspaper readers were professionals with annual incomes of $60,000 or more.[26] Readers found printed advertisements to be far more responsive to their needs and interests than television. Sixty-three percent of men and 64 percent of women believed that print was the medium that best suited their personal needs. Only 29 percent of men and 28 percent of women had the same feelings about television advertising.[27] A Time/Seagram study concluded that as little as four weeks of advertisement exposure in print could increase a product's use by 75 percent and its purchases by nearly 300 percent.[28]

33   Television ranked second to newspapers, with a 21 percent share of overall advertising revenues. Television advertising involved four different areas: network, national, local, and cable. Local advertising spots were used primarily by retailers, such as department stores. Due to the intense competition among department stores, it was necessary for them to reach the local population to inform it of upcoming sales or promotions.[29]

---

[24] Gary Robins, "Auto ID," *Stores*, September 1988(A), pp. 1–16.

[25] Gary Robins, "EDI: Closing the Loop," *Stores*, April 1988(C), pp. 53–62.

[26] Schwartz and Kraft, "Managing Consumer Diversity: The 1991 American Demographic Conference," *American Demographics*, August 1991, pp. 22 (6).

[27] Ibid.

[28] Ibid.

[29] Kurtz Boone, *Contemporary Marketing*, 5th ed., 1989, pp. 404–25.

Customer Service

34   In the 1990s, department stores were realizing what specialty stores had practiced all along: good customer service was important to success in the retail apparel industry. Personalized attention was being stressed in both types of stores to lessen the focus on the increasing prices of apparel. This was especially important due to the increase in the older population, which demands this type of service and attention.

35   Many department stores had problems implementing good customer service programs, possibly due to their lack of experienced and trained personnel. In contrast, specialty stores had a definite competitive edge. These smaller stores offered personalized and specialized services, such as phoning customers when a new item arrived.

Specialization

36   Companies in the retail wearing apparel industry once strove to be all things to all people. The increasing cost of catering to diverse customers, however, led many companies to specialize by product or market segment.[30] Many department stores even subdivided into miniboutiques to capture a variety of market segments. According to some industry authorities, specialization and market segmentation strategies soon will replace population growth as a means to boost sales. The strategy of serving a broad customer base is no longer viable: specialty stores now dominate virtually every category in retailing.[31]

Competitors

37   The retail wearing apparel industry was in the maturity stage of its life cycle in 1992. Both the number of customers and the amount of money they were spending on apparel were slowing. In addition, a large number of firms were competing in the same market. The increase in the number of stores selling apparel had caused the supply of goods to exceed demand in an already saturated market. Competition in this industry came from a variety of sources, including department stores, specialty stores, mass merchandisers, catalog retailers, discount stores, and off-price stores, as well as numerous boutiques and small shops. Exhibit 4 lists the top retailers within each of these segments.

Department Stores

38   Department stores sell a wide variety of merchandise, including apparel, accessories, and cosmetics, in a convenient shopping atmosphere. Department Stores carry a wide range of merchandise and cater to customers' many needs. However, department stores did not achieve the same levels as specialty stores in terms of ambiance and customer service, nor did they compete with off-price chains that carried designer clothes at lower prices.[32] Department stores' sales totaled more than $70 billion in 1990. The top five department stores and their sales volumes in 1990 are shown in Exhibit 4.[33]

39   To improve sales, many department stores targeted their merchandise at higher-income customers. Also, many stores developed the store within a store format, dividing apparel departments into separate sections based on design and fashion.

---

[30] Penny Gill, "Moderate Sportswear: Moderately Optimistic," *Stores*, January 1989, pp. 19–32.

[31] Karen J. Sack, "Retailing: An Industry at the Crossroads," Standard & Poor's *Industry Surveys*, December 22, 1988, pp. 61–63.

[32] Karen J. Sack, "Retailing: A Basic Analysis," Standard & Poor's *Industry Surveys*, April 20, 1989, pp. 75–112.

[33] "Top 100 Department Stores," *Stores*, July 1991, pp. 31–43.

EXHIBIT 4
Retail Apparel Industry 1990 Major Outlets Ranking

	Sales Volume (in billions)
Department Stores	
J. C. Penney	$14.60
Marvin's	4.10
Dillard's	3.60
Macy's Northeast	3.10
Nordstrom	2.89
Specialty Stores	
The Limited	$5.5
Marshalls	2.2
T. J. Maxx	2.0
Gap, Inc.	2.0
Mass Merchandisers	
Wal-Mart	$3.26
Kmart	3.21
Sears	3.20
Catalog Retailers	
Best Products	$2.30
Lands' End, Inc.	1.40
CML	0.74
Luria & Sons	0.33
Discount Stores	
Rose's Stores	$2.0
Dollar General	1.2
Jamesway Corp.	1.1
Off-Price Stores	
Ross Stores	$1.65
Burlington Coat Factory	1.62
Dress Barn	0.60
Syms Corp.	0.45

Specialty Stores

40   Specialty stores offered ambiance, strong fashion statements, and good customer service. They took advantage of the growing segmentation of the mass market by targeting merchandise at distinct market segments. Specialty stores carried apparel that was targeted mainly at upscale customers.

41   Specialty stores usually were distinguished from competitors by merchandise selection and presentation. They often offered a unique type of quality merchandise. Total 1990 sales were more than $35 billion—an increase of 7.3 percent from the previous year. The top four apparel specialty outlets and their sales volumes in 1990 are shown in Exhibit 4.[34]

Mass Merchandisers

42   Mass merchandisers offered customers a wider variety of goods, increased convenience, and lower prices than most department stores. The wearing apparel sold in mass-merchandise stores was generally less fashionable and usually of lower quality than that sold in other types of apparel stores. Unlike specialty and department stores, mass merchandisers were not known throughout the industry as leaders in service. Total sales for this segment were $85.5 billion in 1990. The top three mass merchandisers and their sales volumes in 1990 are listed in Exhibit 4.[35]

Catalog Retailers

43   Catalog retailers were a growing force in the retail wearing apparel industry. The number of mail-order catalog retailers has exploded since 1980, aided primarily by the low start-up costs associated with them. In an effort to compete directly with catalog retailers, many department stores increased catalog mailing in the 1980s. However, the saturated market and increased postal rates have caused many department stores to discontinue their catalogs.

44   Catalog retailers took advantage of demographic changes affecting the retail industry. These changes included the two-income family, rising disposable incomes, customers' limited shopping time, the increased use of credit cards, and Americans' fondness for dialing toll-free numbers. In 1990, total mail-order sales volume was $200.7 billion, a 9.49 percent increase from 1989.[36] The top four catalog retailers and their sales volumes for 1990 are listed in Exhibit 4.[37]

Discount Stores

45   Discount stores offered lower prices and more convenience than mass merchandisers and off-price stores. However, one problem was that consumers sometimes perceived lower prices to mean lower quality and less service. Discount stores were shifting their attention away from selling a broad assortment of goods to selling large selections of targeted products, such as lower-priced apparel. Total discount store sales for 1990 were $85.5 billion, a 7.3 percent increase from 1989. The top discount stores and their sales volumes in 1990 are listed in Exhibit 4.[38]

Off-Price Stores

46   This type of apparel store attracted the price-conscious and fashion-conscious customer. They carried designer fashions at lower prices than department or specialty stores. The major disadvantage of off-price stores was a lack of available capital to invest in their stores. Total sales for 1990 were over $5 billion. The top four off-price stores and their sales volumes for 1990 are listed in Exhibit 4.[39]

---

[34] "Top 100 Specialty Stores," *Stores*, August 1991, pp. 25–41.

[35] "Top 100 Department Stores," 1991.

[36] "Mail Orders Top 250+," *Direct Marketing*," July 1991, pp. 30–49.

[37] "Retail Apparel Industry."

[38] Ibid.

[39] Ibid.

EXHIBIT 5
Percentage of 1990 Nordstrom's Sales by Merchandise Category

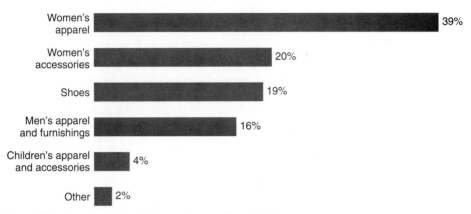

Source: Information obtained from Nordstrom, Inc., annual report, 1990.

THE COMPANY

History of the Company

47   In early 1992, Nordstrom, Inc., operated 69 retail stores. The stores were located mainly in the north-western and western regions of the country, with the exception of its newest stores, which were located in Virginia, Washington, D.C., and New Jersey.

48   During World War I, business was slow and it was difficult to sell shoes, the company's original product. Wallin and Nordstrom worked very hard to keep the business flourishing. In 1923, the newly found postwar prosperity caused business to boom. During this time, Wallin and Nordstrom opened their second store. They were dedicated to keeping the business a family-run business, with each partner employing family members. In 1928, John W. Nordstrom sold his share of the partnership to his three sons, who had started with the company as stock boys.

49   Nordstrom continued to prosper throughout the decades, first increasing the size and locations of stores and then expanding the product line to include wearing apparel and accessories.[40]

Products

50   Nordstrom began as a retailer of high-quality, good-value shoes in a wide variety of styles and sizes for men, women, and children. In 1992, Nordstrom still was dedicated to selling quality merchandise at a good value. However, in addition to shoes, products now included women's, men's, and children's wearing apparel and accessories. The company sold a limited number of styles considered classic, rather than trendy, since Nordstrom targeted customers who preferred traditional apparel. Nordstrom aimed at broad customer appeal and based its stores' inventories on geographic location. Exhibit 5 shows Nordstrom's sales by major merchandise category.

---

[40] Nordstrom, Inc., annual report, 1988.

Customers

51   Nordstrom offered high-priced items for customers with above-average incomes. It targeted customers who were unwilling to purchase from fashion-forward apparel and carried only classic merchandise. Nordstrom's stores were equipped with large traditional designer areas, as well as departments that offered such basic items as blue jeans.

52   Nordstrom entered existing population centers, rather than blazing new trails. It served mainly upwardly mobile markets. For example, Nordstrom's new store in Paramus, New Jersey, was located in an upscale neighborhood. This store included the standard valet parking and piano music that Nordstrom insisted its customers wanted.

53   Decisions regarding Nordstrom's merchandise purchases were made by regional buyers. The theory was that individual buyers knew the actual needs of their customers and were experienced enough to select appropriate needs. New stores opening in East Coast areas were expected to be geared toward career-oriented individuals. Therefore, a new Washington, D.C., store was expected to offer a selection including more than ladies' suits.[41] Nordstrom was convinced that customers wanted wearable fashions at good values, and it targeted merchandise buys accordingly.[42]

Customer Service

54   The basic philosophy of the Nordstrom organization was to provide superior customer service, selection, quality, and value. Customer service has been a distinguishing characteristic for Nordstrom, Inc., throughout its history. For Nordstrom, customer service did not stop with a cheerful smile and an available salesperson. Its stores were known for their elaborate attempts to please their customers. Many Nordstrom stores did not play recorded music but provided live piano music. Coat-checking services were available so customers were not burdened with carrying extra loads while shopping.[43]

55   In an age of incompetent and elusive sales service, shopping had become a chore for most customers. Nordstrom, with its legendary reputation for customer service, had an edge over its competition. Its commitment and dedication to customer service had built a strong base of loyal customers in an age when store loyalty was a thing of the past.[44]

56   Nordstrom provided sales training sessions and motivational seminars for its staff. Salespeople were expected to make merchandise suggestions to customers, ring up sales, and assist customers with returns and exchanges. Nordstrom employed more floor staff people than any other store chain. Sales staff also were expected to call loyal customers and thank them for their patronage, as well as send personal notes to alert them about new lines and special incentive sales. Nordstrom's experienced sales staff even went to new stores to train new customer-service personnel.[45]

57   The strong dedication to customer service did not always have good results. Many salespeople felt too much pressure to sell and to "put on a happy face" at all times. They were expected to follow a dress code, resulting in a loss of individuality for some employees. This caused some problems and, in 1991, Nordstrom was accused of unfair labor practices. Employees reported that they were not being compensated for overtime and extra duties performed. The state of Washington Department of Labor and Industries issued an order against Nordstrom, directing it to change its practices. Also, a

---

[41] Nordstrom, Inc., annual report, 1990.

[42] Ibid.

[43] Francine Schwadel, "Nordstrom's Push East Will Test Its Renown for the Best Service," *The Wall Street Journal*, August 1, 1989, p. A1 (col. 6), p. A4 (col. 4).

[44] Ibid.

[45] Ibid.

EXHIBIT 6
Square Footage by Market Area at End of 1990

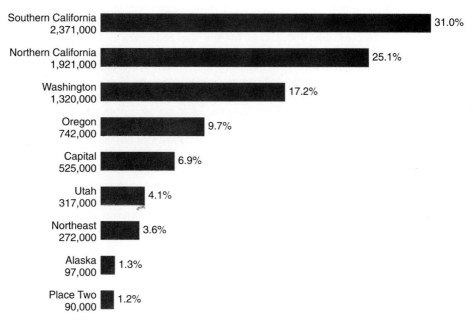

Southern California 2,371,000	31.0%
Northern California 1,921,000	25.1%
Washington 1,320,000	17.2%
Oregon 742,000	9.7%
Capital 525,000	6.9%
Utah 317,000	4.1%
Northeast 272,000	3.6%
Alaska 97,000	1.3%
Place Two 90,000	1.2%

Source: Information obtained from Nordstrom, Inc., annual report, 1990.

lawsuit was filed on behalf of the employees, seeking damages. These lawsuits were pending in early 1992.[46]

58   Nordstrom's excessive expansion also may cause customer-service problems in the future. Only a limited number of the employees were willing to relocate and train future employees at new locations.[47] As a result, Nordstrom may find it difficult to maintain standards.

Expansion

59   Nordstrom, Inc., has undergone many expansions since the company's earliest days. John W. Nordstrom, the founder of Nordstrom, Inc., started the expansion in the early part of the century when he and his partner opened their second shoe store in 1923. In 1961, Nordstrom owned and operated eight shoe stores and had 600 employees. Gross sales were $12 million that year. This success led Nordstrom to expand its business to include wearing apparel, so the company bought an existing chain store and offered a full range of apparel to appeal to customers' needs.

60   Nordstrom's first expansion outside the Pacific Northwest was into southern California in 1978 and, by 1990, its stores were located in six states. Exhibit 6 shows the geographic concentration of Nordstrom stores in 1990.

61   When Nordstrom opened a new store in Sacramento in 1980, the crowds were so overwhelming that the company was forced to request merchandise shipments from its other California stores to meet

---

[46] Charlen-Marmer Soloman, "Nightmare at Nordstrom," *Personnel Journal*, September 1992, pp. 76–83.

[47] Schwadel, "Nordstrom's Push East."

customer demand. Rather than predicting customer needs in this geographic area, Nordstrom executives decided to put everything in the store and let customers decide what should be stocked.[48]

62   The drive to expand nationally was largely due to the fact that Nordstrom had been successful in all of its store openings. This success drove company executives to try their expertise in picking locations on a national level.[49] At first, Nordstrom stores were located only in the northwestern and western regions of the United States. In 1988, it opened its first East Coast store in McLean, Virginia. This suburban Washington, D.C., store was an instant success. Due to Nordstrom's decentralized management structure, the apparel buyers for this store were able to test the market prior to the store's opening and choose merchandise they felt would be successful in that area of the country. This method of buying was successful and sales for the store's first year were in excess of $100 million.[50]

63   In the third quarter of 1989, another East Coast store opened in the Pentagon area of Washington, D.C. Again, the store was stocked with the traditional apparel deemed appropriate for Nordstrom's upwardly mobile, affluent customers. Also, trained staff members were transferred to the Washington, D.C., area to train new employees in the Nordstrom philosophy of selling and customer service. Long-term success was predicted for this store, which was located directly above the Metroliner train service. This location was expected to serve customers who stopped and shopped on a whim, as well as tourists visiting Washington, D.C.[51]

64   By 1992, Nordstrom had built four stores in the eastern United States and had opened 12 clearance stores, called Nordstrom Rack, in Washington State, Oregon, California, and Maryland. Nordstrom also leased shoe departments in stores in Hawaii.[52]

Management Structure

65   Nordstrom, Inc., has continued to be a family-owned and operated business. In 1992, 40 percent of the company's stock was owned by Nordstrom family members. Two brothers, John and Jim, and a cousin, Bruce, were co-chairs of the company. Another cousin, Jack McMillan, was president, and a friend of the family held the position of senior vice president. These top five executives shared decision-making power: all had equal votes concerning policy and store location, and each member was allowed to veto any decision, at any time. Each executive oversaw and operated a different segment of the company.[53]

66   The family ownership of the business was said to have had an extraordinary stabilizing effect on the company during times of industry turbulence, caused by the increase of mergers and acquisitions in the retail wearing apparel industry and the revolving door ownership in many companies.[54] Most decisions regarding the daily operations of the stores were made at the local store level, because Nordstrom had a decentralized management structure. Corporate executives did not offer much direction in this area but, rather, allowed regional and store managers decision-making control.

67   The decentralization of buying operations could cause problems. Some buyers could become overzealous when shopping for their stores, causing an overabundance of merchandise in inventory. This, in turn, could cause a large number of unnecessary markdowns. This was the case during the second

---

[48]   Steve Ginsberg, "Nordstrom's Sacramento Store Has Robust Start," *Women's Wear Daily*, October 24, 1989(B), p. 16.

[49]   Richard W. Stevenson, "Watch Out Macy's, Here Comes Nordstrom," *The New York Times Magazine*, August 27, 1989, pp. 34–40.

[50]   Pete Born, "Macy's, Nordstrom: Pentagon Faceoff," *Women's Wear Daily*, September 28, 1989, p. 11.

[51]   Schwadel, "Nordstrom's Push East."

[52]   Nordstrom annual report, 1990.

[53]   Nordstrom annual report, 1988.

[54]   Schwadel, "Nordstrom's Push East."

EXHIBIT 7

Nordstrom, Inc.
Income Statement 1987–1990
Years Ended January 31
(in thousands)

	1988	1989	1990	1991
Net sales	$1,920,231	$2,327,946	$2,671,114	$2,893,904
Operating expenses:				
Cost of sales	1,300,720	1,563,832	1,829,383	2,000,250
Selling and administrative	477,488	582,973	669,159	747,770
Total operating expenses	1,778,208	2,146,805	2,498,542	2,748,020
Operating income (loss)	142,023	181,141	172,572	145,884
Other income (expenses):				
Service charge income	53,662	57,268	55,958	84,660
Interest expense	(32,952)	(39,977)	(49,121)	(52,228)
Total other income (expenses)	20,710	17,291	6,837	32,432
Earnings before interest and taxes	162,733	198,432	179,409	178,316
Provision (credit) for income taxes				
Income (loss) before minority interest	162,733	198,432	179,409	178,316
Minority interest in income (loss)				
Income from continuing operations	162,733	198,432	179,409	178,316
Taxes	70,000	75,000	64,500	62,500
Net income (loss)	$ 92,733	$ 123,432	$ 114,909	$ 115,816

Sources: Adapted from Nordstrom, Inc., 1989 and 1990 annual reports.

quarter of 1989, when more markdowns occurred than were predicted.[55] Although it is a family-oriented business, with future executives in the Nordstrom family currently working their way upward (three store managers, three buyers, and one management trainer), there are still great opportunities for other dedicated employees. Nordstrom always has promoted from within its organization.[56]

Communications

68   Nordstrom relied on electronic mail for intercompany communications. Because the firm was a specialty retailer with an unusually large number of buyers (900 versus 60 to 100 at regular department stores) and vendors (27,000), its lines of communication needed to be constantly flowing to obtain the latest information. In the spring of 1992, Nordstrom, in conjunction with MCI Communications Corporation, planned to set up what it called V.I.P. Express (vendor information partnership) using a

[55] Michael Schiffman, "Nordstrom, Inc.," *Value Line*, September 1, 1989, p. 1651.

[56] Schwadel, "Nordstrom's Push East."

EXHIBIT 7   (continued)

Nordstrom, Inc.
Balance Sheet 1987–1990
Year Ended January 31
(in thousands)

	1988	1989	1990	1991
Consolidated Balance Sheet				
Assets				
Current assets:				
Cash and equivalents	$ 4,949	$ 16,058	$ 33,051	$ 24,662
Accounts receivable net	404,615	481,580	536,274	575,508
Inventories	312,696	403,795	419,976	448,344
Prepaid expenses	7,922	22,553	21,847	41,865
Total current assets	730,182	923,986	1,011,148	1,090,379
Property, plant, and equipment, net	502,661	594,038	691,937	806,191
Investments in unconsolidated affiliates				
Intangible assets (net)				
Other noncurrent assets	1,424	3,679	4,335	6,019
Total noncurrent assets	504,085	597,717	696,272	812,210
Total assets	$1,234,267	$1,521,703	$1,707,420	$1,902,589
Liabilities and Stockholders' Equity				
Accrued income taxes	$ 17,085	$ 20,990	$ 12,491	$ 24,268
Notes payable	88,795	95,903	102,573	149,506
Accounts payable	166,524	190,755	195,338	204,266
Accrued expenses, salaries, and taxes	101,204	120,821	151,687	163,365
Current portion of long-term debt	21,091	19,696	27,799	10,430
Total current liabilities	394,699	448,165	489,888	551,835
Long-term debt	215,300	356,471	418,533	457,718
Obligations under capitalized leases	23,952	23,049	22,080	21,024
Deferred taxes	67,107	54,077	43,669	45,602
Other noncurrent liabilities	—	—	—	—
Total noncurrent liabilities	306,359	433,597	484,282	524,344
Total liabilities	$ 701,058	$ 881,762	$ 974,170	$1,076,179

product called *Lotus Express*. Nordstrom intended to connect its five-year-old internal e-mail system via a proprietary gateway to MCI's forward network and then to MCI Mail. In the summer of 1991, 40 of Nordstrom's vendors were put on a pilot system and another 2,000 were expected to be on the voluntary system by the end of the following year.[57]

---

[57] Tom McCusker, "The Message Is Integration," *Datamation*, August 15, 1991, pp. 31–32.

EXHIBIT 7   (concluded)

	1988	1989	1990	1991
Stockholders' Equity				
Preferred stock:				
Common stock:				
Paid-in capital	$ 146,317	$ 147,629	$ 148,857	$ 150,699
Retained earnings	386,892	492,312	584,393	675,711
Total stockholders' equity	$ 533,209	$ 639,981	$ 733,250	$ 826,410
Less: treasury stock (520,000 shares) at cost	533,209	639,941	733,250	826,410
Total stockholders' equity	533,209	639,941	733,250	826,410
Total liabilities & equity	$1,234,267	$1,521,703	$1,707,420	$1,902,589

Sources: Adapted from Nordstrom, Inc., 1989 and 1990 annual reports.

Financial

69   Nordstrom was expected to borrow external capital to continue its expansion. Between 1988 and 1991, Nordstrom spent $328.9 million on expansion and improvements and planned to spend another $500.0 million over the following three years. As seen in Exhibit 7, Nordstrom Stores, Inc., consolidated balance sheet for 1990–91, Nordstrom should be able to handle the increased debt needed for its expansion.[58]

70   Steadily increasing sales had reached $2.9 billion by the end of 1991, a substantial difference from the $10,000 earned in 1901, the year Nordstrom opened its first store. Exhibit 8 shows Nordstrom's sales in millions for 1981 through 1990, while Exhibit 9 shows net earnings for the same 10–year period.

Toward the Future

71   In early 1992, Nordstrom management was considering strategic alternatives for the company's future. Nordstrom had a reputation among industry members and customers for providing outstanding customer service and quality apparel. In a saturated industry where consumers were spending less on wearing apparel, Nordstrom was looking for ways to expand the company.

72   Some Nordstrom executives argued that the company should enter markets in other regions of the United States. These executives argued that the affluent Nordstrom customer bought traditional-style apparel and was looking for a conveniently located outlet. These executives wanted to search upscale markets because they knew this was where to find the Nordstrom customer. They believed that, if they approached their expansion efforts in this fashion, they would obtain more customers, as indicated by past efforts. For example, a study showed that 23 percent of the residents of Riverside and Monroe Valley, cities that attracted affluent and upwardly mobile population segments, shopped in other areas. This study also indicated these residents would prefer shopping at more convenient locations, thus representing potential Nordstrom markets.

---

[58] Schiffman, "Nordstrom, Inc."

EXHIBIT 8
Nordstrom Stores, Inc., Net Sales, 1981–1990

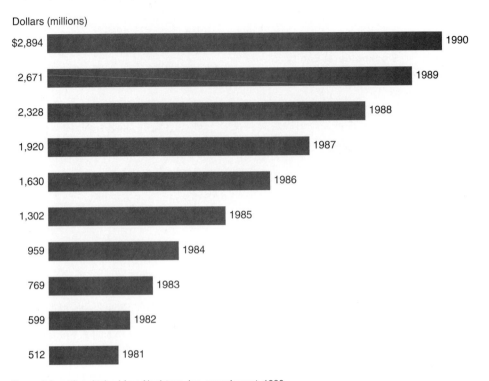

Dollars (millions)

Year	Dollars (millions)
1990	$2,894
1989	2,671
1988	2,328
1987	1,920
1986	1,630
1985	1,302
1984	959
1983	769
1982	599
1981	512

Source: Information obtained from Nordstrom, Inc., annual report, 1990.

73   However, other managers believed this approach was not justifiable during those times. They wanted to put plans for expansion on hold until there were definite signs of an economic recovery and a long-term increase in consumer spending. They felt that, since company earnings had declined over the past years and stock had dropped 13.5 points, it would be unwise for the company to expand. These executives felt customers were balking at Nordstrom's moderate to high prices. They believed customers were not just waiting for an economic recovery before spending, rather that the trend toward lower prices was a long-term trend which would cause these customers to turn to Nordstrom's competitors. In view of this debate, Nordstrom was considering the above alternatives as well as many other strategies and their long-term effects on the company.

EXHIBIT 9
Nordstrom Stores, Inc. Net Earnings 1981–1990

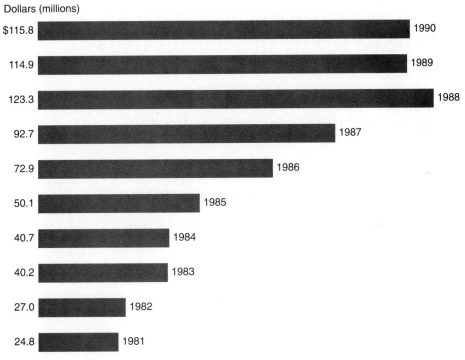

Dollars (millions)

	Dollars
1990	$115.8
1989	114.9
1988	123.3
1987	92.7
1986	72.9
1985	50.1
1984	40.7
1983	40.2
1982	27.0
1981	24.8

Source: Information obtained from Nordstrom, Inc., annual report, 1990.

Case 19

Reebok International, Inc.: The First 12 Years of a Rapidly Growing Company

The Athletic Footwear Industry of the 1980s

1   The athletic footwear industry is unique in that it is market driven instead of product driven. The firm that stays on top is the firm that can predict the fickle shoe market first and then come up with products that will create markets, instead of selling preconceived products to whatever market exists. The industry is virtually controlled by fads, which is a major problem. The development, introduction, and longevity of fads are not known and are nearly impossible to predict. Athletic shoe firms must be able to react quickly to create product variations that will satisfy fad-hungry customers.

2   Another unique characteristic is that the shoe business is similar to show business or the entertainment business, in that what is flashy and "hot" is what sells. L. A. Gear is a typical example of this "Hollywood image." This company became a major contender by selling shoes adorned with bright neon trim, buckles, and rhinestones. Its shoes are advertised by tanned, buxom blondes who suggest sex and southern California sun. Due to the shoe business environment, companies in this industry hire executives from the entertainment industry.

3   The major firms in the athletic shoe industry contract for the manufacture of their products in Asia where labor and raw materials are inexpensive. Hence, the industry is so structured that basically every company that decides to enter the market does so on an international level.

4   Americans lace up 200 million pairs of brand-name athletic shoes a year. The market will reach $9 billion in retail sales in 1989, up 15 percent from 1988. An increase in demand is the expected trend. The athletic shoe industry has grown so rapidly that many of the firms have diversified into sports attire emblazoned with brand names. However, there does not appear to be a universally applicable strategy for growth and diversification. Each of the major contenders in the market has pursued its own unique paths, with both successes and failures.

5   Today's athletic shoe models are a precise mixture of fashion and technology. Athletic shoe manufacturers not only have had to design an appealing, fashionable, and unique shoe but also have had to create some sort of competitive distinction that would add to the perceived performance aspect of the athletic shoes. Air-cylinder suspension systems, anatomically molded ankle collars, outrigger soles, and adjustable support straps are just a few of the technological "advances" in the athletic shoe industry.

6   Specifically, Nike Air is a running shoe with pockets of compressed gas in the soles to provide cushioning. This shoe became a hot seller when transparent plastic windows were added to show the air cells. Reebok has challenged Nike Air with its Energy Return System (ERS), which has an arrangement of cylinders in the soles made of a synthetic material called Hytrel, which compresses on impact to provide extra spring. A new engineering leap taken by both Nike and Reebok is the development of athletic shoes with inflatable sides and collars for extra support.

This case was prepared by J. Carl Clamp, Distinguished Lecturer in Management, University of South Carolina. Professor Clamp was assisted by Deborah H. Francis, Patricia M. Harmon, and Reginald W. Belcher in the preparation of this case.

7   As new product lines and technological advances are introduced, the sale of all athletic shoes probably will increase. Reebok and Nike are the top two firms in the industry. Both utilize research and development and try to research consumer preferences almost before consumers realize that they have a preference!

EARLY YEARS OF REEBOK

8   Reebok was started in the 1890s by Joseph William Foster of Bolton, England. Foster was seeking a way to enhance his performance in long-distance track events by improving his equipment. He eventually developed the concept of putting spikes on the soles of track shoes. This idea was so popular that by 1895 Foster was in business for himself, making handmade shoes for runners. J. W. Foster and Sons soon gained renown in Great Britain. By the 1950s, the company also had developed an international clientele in Europe and North America and had expanded into the manufacture of rugby footwear.

9   In 1958, Reebok International was created as a companion company by two of the founder's grandsons, Joseph and Jeffrey Foster. Reebok International later made its first acquisition by absorbing J. W. Foster and Sons. The original Bolton factory continues to produce handmade specialty running shoes; however, Reebok International, Ltd., has grown into a diversified athletic apparel and shoe company with its products distributed in 28 countries.

MODERN REEBOK AND PAUL FIREMAN

10   In 1979, Paul Fireman, a camping and fishing goods distributor in Brockton, Massachusetts, spotted Reebok shoes at a British trade show. Fireman was so impressed with the shoe that he acquired an exclusive North American license from Reebok International, Ltd., and called his operation Reebok U.S.A., Ltd.

11   Fireman quickly introduced three styles of running shoes for men. Costing over $60, these shoes were the most expensive on the U.S. market. However, he had little luck penetrating the market and, in 1981, "borrowed" $77,500 in cash from Pentland Industries PLC, a British wholesaler of footwear, clothing, and consumer products. In exchange, Pentland received 56 percent of the common stock of Reebok U.S.A. Pentland and Fireman agreed neither party would sell its stock to third parties.

12   After a shaky start, demand for the running shoes eventually exceeded the capacity at the Bolton plant. At this time a decision was made by Fireman and Pentland to contract with a South Korean firm to manufacture the shoes, with Pentland both financing and monitoring the operation. Simultaneously, a more extensive marketing effort in the United States was being organized by Paul Fireman.

13   By 1981, sales exceeded $1.5 million, which was considered a respectable level for a new entry into a tough market. Paul Fireman was not satisfied and began planning an introduction into the women's shoe market that would not only place Reebok among the industry leaders but also would revolutionize the athletic and leisure segments of the shoe industry. In 1982, Reebok U.S.A. introduced the first women's aerobic shoe. This market had been untapped by any other shoe manufacturer. The first aerobic shoes, called Freestyle and Energizer, were introduced in September of 1982.

14   The initial reception for these shoes was cold, with practically no sales for three months. In the fourth month after introduction, the shoes suddenly sold out. Sales rose to $3.5 million in 1982, and, in 1983, sales exploded to $12.8 million. Reebok was able to lure buyers from more conventional casual shoes, such as Bass, by offering a shoe that was as stylish as it was comfortable. By 1985, Reebok had increased its sales to an amazing $307 million.

15   Not satisfied with the stunning success of the aerobic shoes, Reebok decided to enter the market for tennis shoes that was dominated by Adidas and Nike. After a few months of testing, Reebok

entered that market in January 1984 with the Phase I tennis shoe for men and women. The Phase I was designed to be lighter and more comfortable than its competitors and proved to be very successful. The Phase I was followed by the Newport Classic and the ACT 600, which were costlier shoes aimed at the more serious tennis player, and the CLT, which was designed for children.

16   In July 1985, Reebok International and Reebok U.S.A., Ltd., Inc., merged and became known as Reebok International, Ltd., incorporated in Massachusetts. The company then went public with an offering of 4 million shares of common stock priced at $6 per share to finance Reebok's expansion in the United States and in overseas markets. During 1986, the stock rose from $8 per share to $35 per share.

17   Effective January 1, 1986, Reebok agreed to an exclusive arrangement for a Pentland subsidiary to oversee the inspection and shipment of finished goods from Reebok's contract manufacturers in South Korea, Taiwan, and Hong Kong. Reebok pays the subsidiary an annual fee for its services equal to 4 percent of the first $100 million of purchases in the three nations covered by the agreement, 3 percent of the second $100 million, 2 percent of the third $100 million, and 1 percent of purchases over $300 million. Under this arrangement, Reebok paid $13,533,000 to the Pentland subsidiary in 1987.

18   In 1986, Reebok introduced a basketball shoe that generated $72 million in sales in 1986, or 8.6 percent of its 1986 total sales. In 1987, Fireman predicted that Reebok would become the leading manufacturer of basketball shoes by the year's end.

19   At the May 23, 1986, meeting of the board of directors, Paul Fireman was elected chairman of the board, a previously vacant position, and reelected president and CEO of Reebok International, Ltd. Fireman then set about restructuring the organization by creating three divisions. James Barclay was named president of the Reebok Footwear Division; Douglas Arbetman was named president of the Apparel Division; and Joseph W. Foster was named president of the Reebok International Division, which was responsible for developing and servicing markets outside the United States for apparel and footwear.

20   Reebok's first entry into the apparel market was a failure, because there were major problems concerning quality and distribution. The president of the Apparel Division, Douglas Arbetman, replaced the entire design and sales staff in 1987. During this year, net sales were $47 million; however, the organization needed to support this level of sales had not yet been developed and this division recorded a $10 million loss. During 1987, the Apparel Division reduced its product line to focus on what it does best and to avoid more operational problems.

21   In 1987, Paul Fireman set the goal of becoming a $2 billion multinational firm by the year 1990. His three-pronged corporate strategy included (1) acquisitions, (2) internal development, and (3) international expansion. In the area of acquisitions, he only wanted companies with upscale products, not ones that could be sold in discount stores, thus avoiding a cheap image. Reebok heavily emphasized consumer research, which has resulted in a continuous expansion of its product line. Reebok was in a good position for international expansion, since the British corporation Pentland retained 32 percent of Reebok. According to Pentland, it reduced its original 56 percent investment in Reebok to use its money elsewhere. Furthermore, the chairman of Pentland, R. Stephen Rubin, characterized Pentland as "family-controlled" and stated that Reebok—a public corporation—grew so much that it was like "the tail wagging the dog."

22   Reebok expanded into Italy through its ties with the Italian apparel company Ellesse.[1] Through acquisitions of distributors, Reebok expanded into Canada and France. In Germany, where Reebok competed against the well-entrenched Adidas, Puma, and others, Reebok built its own distribution network.

23   In late 1989, Reebok introduced The Pump, priced at $170. *The Wall Street Journal* reported on December 20, that the price "is a bit steep, but it's different" and people will buy it! One retailer com-

---

[1] This connection is explained in the Acquisition section of this case.

mented that "The Pump is blowing off the shelves" and that he expected to sell 100,000 pairs from November 15 (the introduction date) to January 15, which equates to about $17 million in retail sales or $8.5 million wholesale. In addition, *Business Week* in its January 8, 1990, issue picked The Pump as one of the best new products of 1989. Consumer perception has been the key to such fantastic performances.

24   Reebok is determined to be No. 1 by announcing a new campaign entitled "Reebok wide world of technology." In 1990, it introduced two new shoes. One, called the Hexalite, is made of the same lightweight material as that used for the skin of aircraft wings. Another shoe, called the Energaire, will be designed with two air pockets under the heel and toe connected by a tube. Both will be introduced as walking shoes and are designed to take pressure off the back and help with posture control.

ACQUISITIONS

25   In 1986, Reebok decided to diversify its shoe lines to avoid becoming too dependent on a few lines of sneakers. Paul Fireman, believing that walking would be the next exercise craze, sought to acquire Stride-Rite Corporation, a maker of casual shoes, for $280 million, but was rebuffed.

26   In October 1986, Reebok acquired Rockport Company, a manufacturer of high-performance walking and casual footwear, for $118 million in cash. At the time of the purchase, Rockport was operating at only an 8.4 percent operating profit margin. However, Rockport had sustained a 43 percent annual growth rate for the five years prior to the purchase by Reebok and had posted sales of $64.5 million in 1985, with the expectations of passing the $100 million mark in 1986.

27   In one week after the purchase of Rockport, Reebok's share price rose 13 percent to $24 per share. The owner of Rockport, Bruce R. Katz, was retained to continue running the operation. Rockport sales for 1986 were $93 million, a 35 percent increase from 1985. Sales were $152 million in 1987 and $171 million in 1988, making Rockport the most dominant name in the walking shoe industry.

28   After buying Rockport, Reebok still had $20 million in cash and virtually no debt; therefore, Fireman continued to shop for more acquisitions. In April 1987, he purchased Avia Group International, Ltd., an Oregon-based athletic shoe company with 1986 sales of $70.3 million and net profit of $4.3 million, for $180 million. Reebok paid only $16.35 per share, or seven times book value, despite Avia's prevailing market price of $28 per share prior to acquisition. Another interesting facet of the Avia acquisition is the fact that Reebok let Avia remain an independent subsidiary pursuing its own strategies, including aggressive competition with Reebok brands.

29   The acquisition of Avia effectively combined two of the fastest-growing athletic footwear makers in the country. The purchase of Avia boosted Reebok's share of the $2.7 billion shoe market to 34.2 percent and also gave Reebok a new customer—the serious athlete. This was a customer who also favored Nike products. John Haran, the publisher of *Sports Ink,* in industry newsletter, estimated that 80 percent of Reeboks were sold for street wear, while Avias were worn almost exclusively for sports. Avia's net sales increased from $70.3 million in 1986 to over $153 million in 1987, for an increase of 118 percent.

30   In May 1987, Reebok's subsidiary, Rockport Company, acquired the John A. Frye Company, makers of high-quality leather boots. The operations of the Frye Company were consolidated into the Rockport Company with Stanley Kravitz, the former CEO and president of Frye, named the president of Rockport, while Bruce Katz was elevated to chairman. Frye boots are a popular higher-priced boot targeted to style-conscious consumers, but its contribution to overall sales and profits has been negligible.

31   To bolster its shaky Apparel Division, Reebok agreed in September 1987 to purchase Ellesse International S.p.A., an Italian upscale sportswear manufacturer, for $64 million. In December of the same year, however, the agreement was modified and Reebok only purchased Ellesse U.S.A. and its trademarks in the United States and Canada for $25 million. These were markets where Reebok felt that it could make the most money. Sales for Ellesse alone contributed $33 million to total sales for 1988. The Apparel Division posted 1988 sales of $45 million.

32   In August 1987, seeking to boost its overseas sales beyond Italy and Britain, Reebok acquired distributors in Canada and France. Reebok used Ellesse as a distributor in Italy and had its own distribution networks in Britain and Germany.

33   In August 1989, Reebok reached an agreement with CML Group, Inc., a recreational equipment and sportswear company, to purchase CML's Boston Whaler unit for $42 million. Boston Whaler manufactures power boats for the United States Coast Guard and for active recreational use. Its sales for the 1987–88 fiscal year were $66 million. The acquisition of Boston Whaler appears to be an odd move for Reebok. However, Reebok had been looking for acquisitions both inside and outside the footwear and sportswear industries. Reebok characterizes itself as a "marketing-type company," dealing mainly in sporting goods and leisure products with an upper-scale image. Given these beliefs, the philosophy behind the Boston Whaler acquisition is more clear. Furthermore, Boston Whaler will be Reebok's first significant manufacturing operation. How successful this obviously new and different venture will be for Reebok remains to be seen.

THE COMPETITIVE ARENA

34   Since Reebok has diversified into so many different shoe lines, it has a large number of competitors with whom to contend. In the aerobic shoe market, its main competitor remains Nike. Reebok was clearly the leader in this segment in 1986 and, with the acquisition of Avia, had a virtual monopoly throughout 1987. However, Reebok's share of the athletic shoe market fell to 28 percent in 1988, down from 32 percent two years ago. Despite the fact that Avia posted sales of $201 million in 1988, Nike had begun to make serious inroads into Reebok's market share and threatened to regain the No. 1 position in the athletic shoe segment.

35   Reebok also faces competition in the casual shoe market. Its major competitors are L. A. Gear, Converse, and Stride-Rite. These three companies produce shoes that are trendy and fashionable, even flashy!

36   Basketball footwear is just the opposite of the casual shoe market. In this market, Reebok faces a number of competitors, including Nike, Adidas, Puma, Avia, and Converse. The leaders in this segment are Converse and Nike, each of whom sold over $150 million of basketball shoes in 1986. These figures are compared to $72 million for Reebok, or 8.6 percent of its total sales in 1986.

37   Reebok also faces strong competition from Nike, Adidas, Converse,and Puma in the tennis shoe segment. Reebok sold $174.7 million worth of tennis shoes in 1986, or 21 percent of its total footwear sales. Reebok is the leader in this market with a 43 percent share, Nike is No. 2 at 38 percent, Converse is third with 8 percent, while Puma is fourth at 7 percent. The remaining sales are divided among Avia, Fila, Turntec, and others.

38   In the running shoe market, Nike and Reebok are the leaders. Sales totaled $66.4 million, or 7.9 percent of Reebok's total sales, in 1986. As mentioned earlier, Rockport is the most dominant name in the walking shoe industry. Reebok's current position in the apparel industry is not strong.

MAJOR COMPETITORS

Nike, Inc.

39   Nike, Inc., is Reebok's prime competitor in the area of athletic footwear. Nike was founded in 1972 when Philip Knight struck a deal with Nisso Iwai American Corporation (NIAC) of Japan to manufacture his lightweight running shoes. From 1972 through 1984, Nike was the leader in the athletic

footwear and sports apparel industries, perhaps emulating the source of its name Nike, the Greek goddess of victory! Early marketing efforts were centered on running shoes. The jogging craze that characterized this period helped ensure Nike's remarkable success. However, beginning in 1984, the athletic shoe market began to fragment. The new trend became aerobics, and jogging lost its popularity. As a result, Nike's sales stagnated and from 1986 to 1987, revenues fell by $191,865,000.

40   By the end of 1986, CEO Phillip Knight realized that Nike's past strategy of creating "stars," products with potential for high market share and high growth, was no longer effective in the wake of Reebok. Knight developed a long-term strategy that he believed would restore Nike as the industry's leader. The plan reasserted the company's original aims of quality, innovation, performance, and authenticity. As a result, Nike positioned itself closer to the market and mounted a new aggressive advertising campaign. New technology was developed, including the Nike Air shoes and cross-training shoes, which helped Nike implement its new strategic plan.

41   Despite these efforts, Nike's revenues declined during 1987 and market share dropped from 28 to 20 percent. However, 1988 was a highly successful year for Nike, Inc. Nike posted sales of $1.2 billion, a 37 percent increase over the 1987 sales of $877 million. The company regained some of its lost market share and currently ran close to Reebok. In fact, Nike regained the No. 1 position from Reebok by year-end 1989.

42   In the past, Nike had not been very successful in its attempts at diversification. It had focused primarily on the marketing of athletic footwear and apparel and had little activity outside these areas. For the future, Nike plans to continue aiming at the high end of the market. Currently, 69 percent of its sales are in the higher-price categories. Nike plans to capture additional market share by introducing a shoe designed and priced to compete with Reebok in the fashion-conscious women's market. In July 1989, Nike introduced Side 1, a shoe aimed at teenage females. Nike also acquired Cole-Haan, a manufacturer of men's upscale dress and casual shoes, in an attempt to integrate Cole-Haan's superior styling with Nike's technological prowess. A new casual shoe will be introduced in the spring of 1990. Overall, Nike, Inc., is confident that it can maintain its current market share and take shares away from its competitors in the future.

Converse, Inc.

43   Converse, Inc., competes with Reebok mainly in the area of men's athletic footwear. The company manufacturers both canvas and leather sneakers. Converse, Inc., originally the Converse Rubber Shoe Company, was founded by Marquis M. Converse. In 1917, he introduced the first sneaker designed for basketball. This shoe became know as the Chuck Taylor and has remained essentially unchanged since 1936.

44   Converse was very successful until leather sneakers hit the market. By the end of the 1970s, the company's sales had fallen substantially. In its first 64 years of existence, Converse had changed hands three times. In 1972, it was bought by Eltra Corporation, and industrial manufacturer of electrical and typesetting equipment. Seven years later, Allied Corporation bought Eltra, a purchase that included Converse, whose sales had dropped to a low of $119 million. After sales rose to $170 million in 1982, chairman Richard Loynd and a group of Converse executives executed a leveraged buyout of Converse from Allied. Loynd's aggressive management style led Converse in a major turnaround, aided by the proceeds of a public offering in 1983. By 1984, sales had risen to $266 million, despite the company's shrunken market share. The company's activewear clothing line accounted for $10 million of the total sales.

45   During 1985, the momentum Converse had gained was halted by fierce competition from Reebok and Nike. Sales dropped 17 percent to $220 million. In 1986, Converse was acquired in a friendly deal by Interco, Inc., a major manufacturer and retailer of furniture and footwear. Interco owned the Florsheim Shoe Company and obviously saw the acquisition of Converse as a significant broadening of its footwear product lines.

46   In an effort to regain some past market share, Converse, Inc., doubled its expenditures in research and advertising since being bought by Interco. During and since 1986, the company has taken advantage of the fashion popularity of its original sneakers, the Chuck Taylors and the Jack Purcells. In 1987, it sold a record number 13.5 million pairs of the original and very fashionable Chuck Taylors. Sales hit a record high of $318.8 million.

47   Currently, Converse is making efforts to become competitive in the areas of high-tech and women's athletic footwear. In 1988, Converse introduced a line of high-performance athletic shoes with a patented sole construction. It also enlisted NBA basketball stars Magic Johnson and Larry Bird as spokesmen. Despite these efforts, Converse remained a distant third behind Reebok and Nike in terms of market share in 1988. This move seems essential to the long-run success of the company, which cannot rely solely on the faddish popularity of its canvas sneakers. But it is supported by its parent Interco, a $2 billion company with strong experience in promoting name brand products. Interco's ability to continue its support of Converse in the near future is highly questionable, due to its very speculative $2.6 billion recapitalization in 1988, which left it leveraged "to the eyeballs" in feeble junk bonds with punitive interest rates. Further, Richard Loynd was pulled from running Converse to become CEO of Interco in an attempt to salvage the company.

L. A. Gear

48   L. A. Gear competes with Reebok in the area of women's athletic footwear. Producing a leather aerobic and athletic-style leisure shoe, L. A. Gear targets the more fashion-conscious female consumers. The company was founded by its chairman, Robert Y. Greenberg, in 1983. Since 1986, it has climbed from 15th to 3rd among sneaker manufacturers, surpassing even Converse. L. A. Gear can attribute its success to identifying an unserved market niche—women's and girl's very fashionable athletic shoes. Furthermore, the advertising campaign is very effective in promoting the "splashy" image of the shoes.

49   Currently, L. A. Gear is attempting to enter the men's basketball and running shoe market. This segment comprises 60 percent of the total athletic shoe market. However, this move may prove to be very difficult, given the company's current image. Men tend to ignore fashion and focus more on the construction and technology of athletic shoes. L. A. Gear's image is one of a fashion shoe manufacturer, and it may find it difficult to be taken seriously by the hard-core athletes it hopes to target. Chairman Greenberg has signed ex-NBA star Kareem Abdul-Jabbar as spokesman for the new men's shoe line. Whether the endorsement will help gain acceptance for the line remains to be seen. L. A. Gear also is diversifying into apparel and related products. Specifically, it plans to market jeans and wristwatches, which mesh more easily with the corporate image. To enhance its international sales and strengthen its new focus on sports shoes, L. A. Gear at year-end 1989 announced an agreement with Asics Corporation—a Tokyo-based marketer of sports shoes with worldwide sales of $1 billion—to market and distribute its products in Japan.

50   L. A. Gear has enjoyed increasing sales consistently since its 1985 level of $11 million. In 1986 and 1987, sales skyrocketed to $36.2 million and $70.5 million, respectively. Its market share was 4.7 percent in 1988 with sales of $224 million. In March 1987, the company began expanding its foreign operations. By the end of 1989, L. A. Gear expected international sales to reach $60 million. In September 1989, L. A. Gear's stock hit a 52-week high of $41.50. Also, it signed pop star Michael Jackson as another spokesman. Chairman Greenberg expected this move to boost sales even further. Salomon Brothers expected L. A. Gear to outperform the market as a whole.

51   However, on November 15, 1989, L. A. Gear announced that it was the target of a Massachusetts federal grand jury probe into the possible underpayment of duties on shoe imports from Taiwan. Shortly thereafter, Elliott Horowitz resigned as chief financial officer after a conflict with Greenberg over his $4.5 million total compensation in 1989 and his denial of selling 70,400 shares of L. A. Gear stock one week before the announcement of the probe. As a consequence, L. A. Gear stock plummeted from a high of \$46$^7/_8$ to a low of \$22$^1/_2$ before year-end 1989.

Stride-Rite

52   Stride-Rite competes with Reebok in the area of children's shoes and adult leisure shoes. Stride-Rite has been for many years the leading manufacturer of high-quality shoes mainly for children from six months to 12 years old. It markets shoes under the brand names of Stride-Rite, Keds, Zips, and Sperry Top-sider. Its products are sold directly to independent retailers, department stores, and sporting goods stores. In addition, it operates a chain of 173 specialty stores, each called Stride-Rite Bootery.

53   In 1987, Michael W. Rayden was named president and chief operating officer, with Arnold Hiatt remaining CEO and chairman of the board. Rayden said he would take Stride-Rite from mainly manufacturing to marketing and specialty retailing. However, in November 1989, former president and COO Ronald J. Jackson returned to Stride-Rite in the position of president and CEO. With Jackson's appointment, Rayden promptly resigned and Hiatt remained as chairman. According to Stride-Rite, Jackson was chosen because of his successful turnaround of Kenner Parker Toys and the belief that he "can direct Stride-Rite into the next level of growth that it needs to get to."

54   The company dropped its Pro-Keds line of men's athletic footwear, realizing that it could not compete with Reebok and Nike. Stride-Rite is concentrating in the market area of children's shoes. One of the company's biggest assets is its venerable brand name and its huge customer base of 14,000 wholesale outlets and 173 retail stores, owned and leased. By 1987, the company had moved nearly all of its production facilities overseas to lower production cost without sacrificing quality. That same year, Stride-Rite had sales of \$300 million. The recent resurgence in popularity of the canvas Keds sneakers has helped boost revenues. In 1988, Keds sneakers accounted for \$150 million of the company's total sales of \$378.8 million.

55   Another strategic move is the introduction of a sportswear line for children. The clothes will be marketed under the Keds brand name. Currently in the planning stages are lines of women's accessories and sportswear. The dynamic nature of this industry has made Stride-Rite a recent target for a hostile takeover.

56   Another strategy that Stride-Rite is pursuing is the market for children from three to six years old, where its market share is only 4 percent. For the new year, it is mounting an aggressive advertising campaign, including its first television commercials. In the age range from infants to two years old, Stride-Rite commands a healthy 12 percent of the market. It faces the problem of overcoming its image as a baby shoe manufacturer. Also, there are distribution problems in that the shoes are only sold in Stride-Rite stores. In today's market, parents can buy competitive sneakers for both themselves and their children at many stores.

MOST RECENT PERFORMANCE OF REEBOK

57   The growth of Reebok has been phenomenal! As depicted in Figure 1, revenues increased from a paltry \$12.8 million in 1983 to more than \$1.8 billion in 1989. During the same period, net income (shown in Figure 2) soared from \$600,000 to a high of \$165.2 million in 1987. The resurgence of Nike forced a drop in 1988 to \$137 million, but 1989 shows a turnaround in net income to the level of \$175 million.

58   In its January 11, 1988, survey of the 100 largest public U.S. companies, *Forbes* reported that Reebok enjoyed the highest five-year growth rates in revenues and net income of all companies surveyed for the period 1983–87. *Forbes* also rated Reebok first in return on net worth during the same period. Normally this category favors highly leveraged companies; however, Reebok has consistently operated with minimal long-term debt, breaking that pattern only in 1988, as shown in Table. 1.

FIGURE 1
Reebok Revenues, 1983–1991

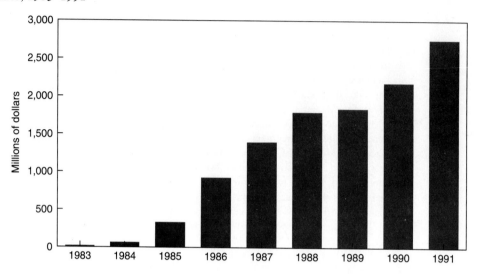

FIGURE 2
Reebok Net Income, 1983–1991

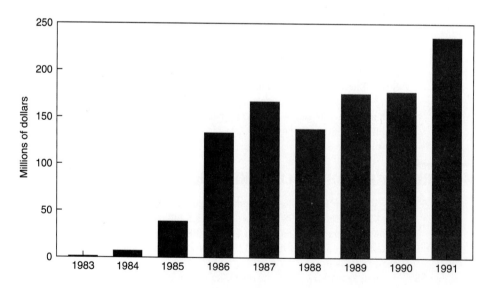

TABLE 1
Reebok, Inc., Selected Financial Data (dollars in millions)

	Years Ended December 31								
	1991	1990	1989	1988	1987	1986	1985	1984	1983
Revenues	$2,734.47	$2,159.24	$1,822.09	$1,785.90	$1,389.90	$919.40	$307.00	$66.00	$12.80
Earnings before taxes	389.89	294.84	290.78	230.50	306.00	261.00	78.10	12.10	1.20
Net income	234.71	176.61	175.00	137.00	165.20	132.10	38.90	6.10	0.67
Cash	84.72	227.14	171.42	99.30	60.17	66.00	7.90	0.99	0.24
Accounts receivable	425.66	391.29	289.36	276.20	204.67	120.00	73.70	15.80	2.90
Inventory	436.58	367.23	276.91	301.90	240.80	122.50	62.70	18.30	3.47
Deferred taxes	45.97	31.67	34.85	26.20	19.50	5.50	0.00	0.00	0.00
Prepaid expenses	34.20	12.33	11.74	9.90	10.80	2.30	0.28	0.18	0.06
Total current assets	1,027.12	1,029.66	784.28	713.60	536.00	316.80	144.30	35.30	7.20
Total current liabilities	424.48	293.78	202.98	255.80	268.00	140.80	58.80	31.00	6.80
Long-term debt	170.40	105.75	110.30	110.00	10.57	0.00	0.69	0.71	0.10
Common stock & paid-in capital	504.23	282.62	276.48	267.70	265.00	120.00	43.60	0.17	N.A.
Retained earnings	913.00	707.34	564.99	424.00	320.80	177.90	45.70	6.70	N.A.
Net worth	823.54	996.73	844.30	690.70	584.80	297.60	88.70	6.80	0.80
Current ratio	2.42	3.50	3.86	2.79	2.00	2.25	2.45	1.14	1.06
Quick ratio	1.20	2.11	2.27	1.47	0.99	1.32	1.39	0.54	0.46
Inventory turnover	6.80	6.70	6.30	6.58	7.65	9.93	7.58	6.06	7.38
Receivables turnover	6.69	6.34	6.44	7.43	8.56	9.49	6.86	7.06	8.83
Asset turnover	2.66	2.10	2.32	2.50	2.59	2.90	2.13	1.87	1.78
Long-term debt/equity	0.21	0.11	0.13	0.16	0.02	0.00	0.01	0.10	0.13
Total debt/equity	0.72	0.40	0.37	0.53	0.48	0.47	0.67	4.66	8.62
Gross profit margin	14.26%	13.65%	15.96%	12.91%	22.02%	28.39%	25.44%	18.33%	9.37%
Net profit margin	8.58%	9.60%	9.60%	7.67%	11.89%	14.37%	12.67%	9.24%	5.23%
Return on net worth	28.50%	17.72%	20.73%	19.83%	28.25%	44.39%	43.86%	89.71%	83.75%
Return on assets	22.85%	17.15%	22.31%	19.20%	30.82%	41.70%	26.96%	17.28%	9.31%

59   With essentially no manufacturing facilities, Reebok has enjoyed a high level of liquidity with its current ratios exceeding 2.0. Such a high level of performance is reflected in an increase in earnings per share from $0.01 in 1983 to $1.53 in 1989, and a movement in common stock prices from an adjusted $5.00 in 1985—its first public offering—to a high of $25.00 in 1987. Virtually all indicators of performance for Reebok in recent years show strongly positive results, as summarized in Table 1.

60   Reebok is attempting to boost its overseas sales. Company insiders believe that offshore sales could provide up to 50 percent of revenues by 1992, up from less than 5 percent in 1987. Sales rose by 85 percent to 13 million pairs of shoes in 1988. Reebok stated that this is the equivalent of about $350 million in wholesale revenue.

TOP MANAGEMENT OF REEBOK

61   Paul Fireman was the first chairman, president, and CEO of Reebok International, Ltd. Originally a camping and fishing goods distributor, Fireman discovered Reeboks at a trade show in Britain in 1979. Since that time, he has built Reebok into a $2 billion-plus company. Fireman was an entrepreneur and, by maintaining that spirit in his company, Paul Fireman has become an American success story.

62   Joseph Labonte was named president and chief operating officer of Reebok International, Ltd., in March 1987. Labonte assumed operations management from Fireman, who remained chairman and chief executive officer. Previously, Labonte had been the president and chief operating officer of 20th-Century Fox and had helped produce the movies *Star Wars* and *Chariots of Fire*. From 1979 through 1983, he oversaw acquisitions and ran the businesses Fox acquired, including soft-drink bottling, television stations, and resort properties. Labonte had never been active in the filmmaking operations. When Marvin Davis acquired Fox, Labonte was directed to spin off most of the nonfilm acquisitions he had previously made. After completing this task, he quit Fox and started a closely held investment and financial advisory company, Vantage Group, Inc. Mr. Labonte's hiring came at the time of increased acquisition activity by Reebok.

63   Frank. J. O'Connell was named to the newly created post of president of Reebok Brands in February 1988 to oversee the footwear and apparel divisions of Reebok in North America. Prior to joining Reebok, O'Connell had been the chief executive officer of HBO Video, Inc., a unit of Time, Inc. Mr. O'Connell succeeded Paul Fireman, who had been serving as the interim president of the division since October 1987.

64   In January 1988, Reebok began to search for someone to fill the position of chief marketing officer. In September 1988, the search ended when Mark R. Goldston was hired. Goldston, who was 33 years old, formerly headed the U.S.A. division of Fabergé, Inc. He resigned that post under pressure at the beginning of September. Goldston is highly regarded in the cosmetics industry for turning around the personal care product lines at Fabergé and previously at Revlon. He was the creator of both the Brut and Charlie media campaigns. It was hoped that he will be able to revitalize the Reebok products with the same success.

65   In August 1988, Reebok hired Heyward Kendall ("Kim") Kelley to the position of senior vice president of sales for Reebok Brands. Kelley will be responsible for sales of athletic footwear throughout North America, as well as the overall sales strategies for Reebok Brands footwear products in the United States and Canada. Formerly, Kelley had been the vice president of sales and channel marketing for PepsiCo.

66   The rationale for hiring these particular men to four executive positions is threefold. First, all had managerial experience in multibillion-dollar concerns. Second, all had experience in the heavy marketing and advertising of consumer brand names. Third, none of them have had any experience in the footwear industry, but all had specific areas of expertise. Fireman believed that the talents that these men brought with them to Reebok would help the company achieve the $2 billion sales level by the end of the decade.

67   Despite Fireman's hopes, Joseph Labonte and Mark Goldston both resigned from Reebok in October and August of 1989, respectively. Sources say that their resignations came as a result of their management styles conflicting with those of Fireman. Labonte and Goldston were considered "hard-charging and abrasive" by other Reebok employees. As a consequence, Fireman again has assumed the positions of chairman, president, and CEO of Reebok.

68   Fireman's initial "reorganization" to handle Labonte and Goldston's departure was to create a key group of executives that were corporate vice presidents while also serving as more independent "presidents" of separate product divisions. They included:

69   John Duerden, senior vice president and president, Reebok Dividion.

Bill Dragon, vice president and president, AVIA Group International.

Bill Ryan, vice president and president, Boston Whaler, Inc.

Bob Slattery, vice president and president, the Rockport Company.

Marilyn Tam, vice president and president, Apparel Products Division.

70   Each of these separate businesses or divisions represented distinct product areas, or the "remnants," of formerly independent companies that Reebok had acquired during its rapid-growth phase in the early 1980s. Exhibit 1 shows Reebok's impact worldwide.

71   By 1992, Fireman remained in the position of chairman, president, and chief executive officer. A move from a somewhat decentralized to a more centralized organization was suggested by Reebok's 1991 annual report. In that report, the above key executives had been reorganized with several key managers reporting to John Duerden, rather than to Paul Fireman. That report listed the following operating corporate officers:

72   John Duerden, senior vice president and president, and CEO, Reebok Brands Division Worldwide.

Robert Meers, vice president and president, U.S. Operations, Reebok Brands Division Worldwide.

Bob Slattery, vice president and president, the Rockport Company.

Marilyn Tam, vice president and president, Apparel Products Division.

EXHIBIT 1
Reebok Operations by Geographic Areas (amounts in thousands)

	1991	1990	1989	1988	1987
Sales:					
United States	$1,882,646	$1,655,101	$1,584,153	$1,586,609	$1,310,345
United Kingdom...	380,108	226,757	34,315⎫	106,019⎫	48,014
Europe	295,546	156,471	82,879⎭		
Other countries ...	176,174	120,914	120,745	93,307	30,837
Total sales	$2,734,474	$2,159,243	$1,822,092	$1,785,935	$1,389,196
Net income:					
United States	$ 139,731	$ 136,307	$ 158,982	$ 83,290	$ 126,505
United Kingdom...	59,737	32,762	6,150⎫	45,929⎫	35,936
Europe	17,901	5,777	1,367⎭		
Other countries ...	17,342	1,760	8,499	7,783	2,759
Total income	$ 234,711	$ 176,606	$ 174,998	$ 137,002	$ 165,200
Identifiable assets:					
United States	$1,018,547	$1,153,897	$ 980,913	$ 858,239	$ 732,427
United Kingdom...	165,367	153,048	104,728⎫	155,296⎫	96,034
Europe	105,273	54,429	23,421⎭		
Other countries ...	141,634	41,851	57,305	49,914	39,905
Total assets	$1,430,821	$1,403,225	$1,166,367	$1,063,449	$ 868,366

Note: One major customer accounted for 11.3 percent, 11.5 percent, 12.6 percent, 12.2 percent, and 12.8 percent of total sales for 1991, 1990, 1989, 1988, and 1987, respectively.

CASE 20

Coping with Success: The Boeing Company

Introduction

1 As the 1990s began, senior management of the Boeing Company was confronted with a number of strategic challenges. These challenges were complicated by several changes in Boeing's operating environments, both inside and outside the firm. Boeing management had to identify these changes and options to prepare for them. The 1980s had ended on a note of unprecedented success for the company. However, several issues facing management in early 1990 had to be addressed in a way that positioned the company for continued growth and profitability well into the 21st century. These issues included:

2 1. The company's $84 billion order backlog.
  2. The maintenance of a stable and satisfied work force.
  3. The decision to enter into a joint venture with the Japanese to develop a new jetliner.
  4. The threat posed by competitors, most notably the European government-subsidized Airbus Industries.
  5. The decline in the defense market as a result of cutbacks in the U.S. military budget.
  6. Rapid changes in the structure of the U.S. and international airline industries.

Boeing's History

3 Early in the history of Boeing, the company followed a pattern: gambling vast sums of money to develop new models and then waiting for the market to adopt the new Boeing offerings. In 1960, the company's second commercial jetliner, the three-engine, 145-seat 727, was launched despite strong internal opposition. Although its first two years were marked by poor sales and skepticism among buyers, the 727 became a best-selling and profitable plane with over 1,800 units sold. In 1968, despite poor market conditions, Boeing introduced the 737, a 110-seat, twin-engine, short-range plane. The 737 was expanded to three different models and became the best-selling plane in the history of commercial aviation.

4 In the late 1960s, Boeing risked over $1 billion, more than the entire net worth of the firm at the time, to build a new plant to produce the first jumbo jet, the 747. The plane was introduced while the aerospace industry was in a depression and, in its early stages, the 747 program almost drove Boeing into bankruptcy. However, the company and the 747 survived and the plane went on to become the industry leader in the wide-body, long-range market. The later-introduced 747-400 was Boeing's top of the line, carrying up to 400 passengers, flying for 16 hours nonstop with a range of 8,500 nautical miles, and requiring only a two-person crew, instead of the usual three-person crew.

5 In the late 1970s, Boeing put up $3 billion, almost double the company's net worth, to develop two twin-engine models simultaneously: the narrow-body, 186-seat 757, designed for medium-range trips

This case was prepared by Robert Letovsky and Debra Murphy, Assistant Professors of Business, Saint Michael's College.

of 500 to 1,200 miles; and the wide-body, 261-seat 767, designed for long-range trips of up to 4,700 miles. Boeing began taking orders for the planes in 1980, but, by late 1982, had not received a single order for the 767 and had only a few orders for the 757. However, as the recession ended, air travel increased and both the 757 and 767 were successes.

6   In January 1986, Boeing purchased de Havilland from the Canadian government. The purchase of de Havilland rounded out Boeing's offerings to include short-, mid-, and long-range commercial aircraft in multiple models. By offering airlines a "family" of jetliners, Boeing could offer cost savings to its customers through interchangeability of parts, common control and operating systems, and reduction in cross-training requirements for ground and in-flight personnel.

7   Boeing had had only three chief executives since its founding in 1945 until 1990. William A. Allen, a lawyer by training, ran the company from 1945 until 1969 and brought Boeing into "the jet age." While the company established itself as a pioneer under Allen, the final years under his management were characterized by sloppy internal controls and declining efficiency. In 1969, Allen was succeeded by an engineer, Thornton A. Wilson (known as "T").

8   Wilson immediately set about to improve productivity at the company. He first targeted Boeing's work force, cutting two thirds, or 95,000 people, including both managers and production workers, from the payroll. Wilson then zeroed in on the production process. He formed a new subsidiary, Boeing Computer Services, which set up a management and control system to catalog every part and every employee in the company. The subsidiary succeeded with dramatic results. As one senior engineer described, "In the difficult days of the late '60s and early '70s, we could have as many as 6,000 parts shortages in a single week. . . . Now, you just pull out a card, put it in the computer, and you can tell exactly what a guy should be doing at that time and what part he needs. Instead of 1,600 shortages a day, we now have about 12."[1]

9   The impact of Wilson's measures was evident. In 1969, it took 25,000 workers to turn out seven 747s per month. By 1981, the same number of planes could be produced by only 11,000. Wilson also insisted that each Boeing plane be designed to generate new versions of itself to meet customers' different needs. While this philosophy added to the design costs of new Boeing models, it gave the company a powerful competitive edge. As Wilson observed, "A new version of an old product line is hard to beat with an entirely new aircraft. You have to have a 20 percent improvement [in the new model]. The cost of engineering and tooling is more on the new plane, and meanwhile the old version is being improved, too."[2]

10   In 1986, Wilson was succeeded by Frank Shrontz, a 30-year Boeing veteran who had joined the company after obtaining a law degree from the University of Idaho and an M.B.A. from the Harvard Business School. Shrontz's background was primarily in negotiating sales contracts for the commercial aircraft division. While he wanted to continue Boeing's advances in aerospace electronics and computer systems, Shrontz shared his predecessor's commitment to the development and support of commercial aircraft.

11   Boeing's product support included seven major parts centers with 15 million spare parts in inventory, a group of engineers called "Reagan's Raiders" that traveled internationally to repair planes, and field representatives in over 100 cities in 50 countries to advise customers.

12   In 1990, to maintain this commitment to customer service and product quality, Boeing reorganized under Shrontz's direction to be a quality-driven company, not a schedule-driven one. (See Exhibit 1 for Boeing's organization chart.) Design-build teams were organized to get a customer's requirements prior to designing the plane. As well, discussion with suppliers was occurring to improve parts deliveries for the Boeing aircraft. Boeing management was striving for continued customer faith in the Boeing Company name and aircraft.

---

[1] Elizabeth Bailey, "Boeing's $23 Billion Bonanza," *Management Today*, January 1981, p. 43.

[2] Walter Guzzardi, "The U.S. Business Hall of Fame," *Fortune*, March 13, 1989, p. 131.

EXHIBIT 1
Organizational Chart as of December 31, 1989

F. A. Shrontz
Chairman of the Board and Chief Executive Officer

Boeing Commercial Airplane Group	Boeing Defense and Space Group	Boeing Computer Services	Boeing Support Services	Boeing Canada de Havilland Div.	ARGO Systems Inc.
Renton, WA	Kent, WA	Belleville, WA	Seattle, WA	Toronto, Ont.	Sunnyvale, CA
D. D. Thornton President	**B. D. Pinick** President	**M. R. Hallman** President	**W. E. Alder** Vice President and General Manager	**R. B. Woodard** President	**B. B. May** Chairman & CEO

Source: The Boeing Company 1989 annual report.

709

AIRCRAFT INDUSTRY

13   By the late 1980s, the commercial aircraft industry had entered an unprecedented boom period. Between 1985 and 1988, airlines and leasing companies ordered a record 3,500 planes. In the United States, deliveries of commercial aircraft rose 20 percent in 1989 to a record $15.1 billion with outstanding orders of over $89 billion. Industry experts estimated total worldwide demand at 7,600 aircraft, or over $500 billion by the year 2000.

14   There were several reasons for this surge in demand for new aircraft. Air travel was experiencing record growth through the 1990s, and the number of passengers was expected to double by the year 2000. In addition to increased passenger travel, world trade increased in the mid-1980s, which required more cargo aircraft. The market for freighter aircraft from 1990 to 2005 was estimated at approximately $35 billion. Another reason for the increased demand of aircraft was the aging of planes around the world, with some 40 percent of the 6,200 planes in operation scheduled for retirement by the year 2005. In the United States, approximately 43 percent of all commercial jets were over 20 years old. Additionally, aircraft were coming under new FAA guidelines for noise control, and new aircraft were up to 30 percent quieter than older planes. The economics of operating more efficiently also led to increased demand for new aircraft that could carry more passengers and that could fly longer hours without refueling stops.

15   The commercial aircraft industry was dominated by three companies, with about 93 percent of the market. Boeing Commercial Airplane Company was the largest, with about 56 percent of the market. Airbus Industries moved into second place in the late 1980s, with 20 percent of the market. McDonnell Douglas Corporation lost its position to Airbus and was in third place, with a 17 percent market share. The other 7 percent was split between British Aerospace and Fokker, which built small-end aircraft.

16   For many ears, U.S. firms dominated the aircraft industry. This domination began to dwindle in the 1980s and was expected to further decline as government-supported Airbus and other companies in countries like Japan began to expand their technological capabilities. The U.S. military and NASA previously had tested and prototyped many of the aircraft technologies in use until 1990, but they were experiencing budget cutbacks. Development of a new plane ran anywhere from $2 billion to $4 billion and took up to 14 years. To break even, 600 units of a model had to be sold, and cash flow was negative for the first five years of a new model's life.

MCDONNELL DOUGLAS

17   As of mid-1990, McDonnell Douglas Corporation was the largest defense contractor in the United States, with almost $9 billion in outstanding military contracts. However, McDonnell's military business, which accounted for over half of its sales and most of its profits, was in jeopardy. Funding for three of the company's leading defense products was scheduled to expire by the end of 1991. Company president Bill Ross expressed the firm's determination when he said: "We were the No. 1 defense contractor in 1980 when the Pentagon budget was $150 billion and I intend to be the No. 1 defense contractor if it goes back to $150 billion. . . . We're going to be a preferred supplier for the Defense Department. . . . If there is such a thing these days."[3]

18   McDonnell Douglas had three commercial offerings. The short to medium-range twin-engine MD80 was an updated version of the DC9, first introduced in the mid-1960s. The company began production of the MD80 in 1980, and, by mid-1990, had delivered almost 750 units of the model,

---

[3] Andy Pasztor and Rick Wartzman, "Winners and Losers: As Defense Industry Shrinks, Suppliers Face Widely Varying Fates," *The Wall Street Journal*, May 24, 1990, p. 47.

with another 450 on order. First offered in 1989, the 158-seat, two-engine MD90 was designed to compete against the Airbus A320. Its main appeal to carriers was its fuel efficiency and low noise level. Initial market response on the MD90 was positive. McDonnell Douglas planned to deliver its first three-engine MD11 jet in late 1990. The MD11 was designed to carry 325 passengers up to 7,000 nautical miles and to operate with just a two-man crew. The MD11 was positioned to compete against the 350-seat A340. McDonnell Douglas's 1989 annual report proudly noted that the MD11 had won almost three times as many orders in 1989 as its Airbus rival. However, the company also admitted that the MD11's share of the total wide-body market was low, due in part to the ability of its competitors to offer a wider choice of models to buyers.

19   By mid-1990, the firm had a backlog of orders for almost 600 MD80/90 and MD11 planes, and production at its Long Beach, California, plant was booked well into the 1990s. The backlog of orders for the company's jets had quadrupled from just under $5 billion in 1985 to over $20 billion in 1989. However, the total sales figures masked the problems at McDonnell Douglas's transport aircraft business, which included not only the MD11 and MD80 programs but also two major military transport programs. In 1989, the division lost $222 million, compared to a profit of $127 million in 1988. In the first quarter of 1990, McDonnell continued to lose money on its transport business. Management blamed the losses on the increased costs from excessive demand on its civilian and military transport programs.

20   Other problems—besides keeping up with demand—included the bloated cost structure and poor productivity at its jetliner plant in Long Beach. In 1990, in an attempt to reduce costs, the company laid off just under half of its plant's payroll. However, it was unclear whether McDonnell Douglas would see significant profits on its transport planes even after these cuts.

21   The success or failure of McDonnell's efforts to earn money in its transport business had implications for the overall jetliner industry. The airlines always had been anxious to see as much competition for Boeing as possible, but the success of Airbus was primarily at the expense of McDonnell Douglas. In 1980, even before the MD11 program formally began, Delta Airlines planned to give McDonnell a $3 billion order for 60 of the planes to ensure the company's continued involvement in the jetliner business. (The deal ultimately broke down and the order was given to Boeing after McDonnell Douglas demanded substantial progress payments from Delta as the planes were being built.) Now, with Airbus doing relatively well, it was not certain that any buyer would bail McDonnell out simply to prevent a Boeing monopoly.

AIRBUS

22   In the early days of the jet age, American dominance of the commercial aircraft market was almost total. European manufacturers were unable to build sales in the American or Third World markets. Finally, in 1970, the Europeans pooled their resources and Airbus Industries was born as a French-based "Groupement d'Interet Economique" (GIE), a unique cross between a joint venture and a corporation. The partners were Aerospatiale of France (38 percent share), Messerschmitt-Blohm of Germany (38 percent), British Aerospace (20 percent), and CASA of Spain (4 percent). Each of these firms received substantial financial support from its respective government. By adopting the GIE legal format, Airbus itself was not responsible for its debts and was not required to file public financial statements. This meant that the four governments could funnel money into Airbus through the four partner companies without having to disclose any of the amounts publicly.

23   The American plane makers concluded, in the words of Boeing commercial airplane group's president Dean Thornton, that "it [Airbus] was just another European scheme to give people jobs."[4]

---

[4] Edwin Kiester, Jr., "Suddenly, It's Airbus," *Business Month*, January 1988, p. 19.

American commercial aircraft manufacturers' complacency was reinforced by the perception that European-made planes had a reputation for poor quality and slipshod maintenance.

24   The first Airbus offering was the A300, a twin-engine, 375-seater designed for medium-range routes; it first flew in 1974. Initial sales were to European government-owned carriers, primarily Air France and Lufthansa, the West German national airline. However, the A300 offered fuel savings, due to its reliance on only two engines, and labor savings, since it could be operated by a two-man crew, which made it attractive to airlines in the Middle East and Far East—and Airbus quickly broke out of the European market. As Boeing's Thornton noted, "They whipped us on deals a couple of times that we wouldn't have expected to lose, and that got our attention."[5]

25   In 1982, Airbus introduced the A310, a twin-engine, 250-seat jet, designed for short and medium runs. Together the A300 and A310 were intended to compete directly against Boeing's 767 and 757 models. By mid-1983, 17 airlines had ordered a total of about 100 A310s.

26   Initially, Airbus suffered from two weaknesses, compared to its American rivals. First, it lacked the wide range of products like Boeing, so it could not offer airlines a "family" of planes to serve a variety of needs. A second weakness of the Airbus group was that it had not cracked the lucrative U.S. market. By 1986, Airbus moved to deal with these weaknesses by offering a number of new models.

27   The most significant of these new models was the 150-seat, single-aisle A320 designed for short- to mid-range routes. The A320 was the first commercial jet to offer "fly-by-wire" technology, where the plane relied almost exclusively on computers to execute pilot commands. Airbus engineers calculated that this new technology led to a 10 percent fuel saving, enhanced safety, and smooth flying. By 1988, Airbus had received orders, options, and commitments from airlines, including from North American carriers, for over 500 of the A320, making it the fastest-selling new plane in aviation history. These sales generally came at the expense of the Boeing 737.

28   To compete with Boeing's "family" of jet offerings, especially in the medium- and long-range markets, in 1988 Airbus introduced the 330-seat, twin-engine A330 and the four-engine, 260- to 295-seat A340. The A330 was designed for distances up to 5,200 nautical miles, and its nearest Boeing competitor would be the smaller 767. The A340 was meant for long distances up to 7,000 nautical miles and for smaller designations that could not justify the use of a 747. By the end of 1989, Airbus had orders for almost 200 of the A330 and approximately 100 of the A340.

29   From its inception in 1970, Airbus had never shown a profit. Estimates of the losses accumulated by the company between 1970 and 1988 varied between $10 billion and $15 billion (U.S.), but this was before incurring most of the costs of developing the A330 and A340 models. According to Boeing, the losses also reflected Airbus's practice of buying market share by underpricing its planes. For example, Boeing calculated in 1988 that Airbus had to sell 600 A320s at $32 million each to break even on the program by the late 1990s, but Airbus was charging only $25 million per plane at the time. Additionally, the fall in the value of the U.S. dollar against major European currencies prohibited Airbus from realizing profits. Although its planes were sold in U.S. dollars, production costs were incurred in European currencies.

30   Given its legal status as a GIE, Airbus never made public the exact amount received from its various member governments. However, the original plan was that the monies received from the member governments were to be repaid from a percentage of each Airbus plane sold. In reality, as of 1989, the French government had received less than 15 percent of the funds it had advanced to Airbus; and the British and German governments had received practically nothing.

31   There were indications that some, if not all, of the European governments involved in Airbus were concerned about the continued subsidization of large losses by the plane maker. In early 1988, as Airbus geared up for the A330 and A340 programs, both British Aerospace and Aerospatiale were given only 60 percent of what they had requested from their respective governments to cover their share of Airbus costs. Boeing raised the issue of alleged subsidies received by Airbus with the U.S. government.

---

[5] Ibid.

Beginning in 1986, the U.S. government held several rounds of negotiations with European trade representatives to try to resolve the issue, but no progress was made.

32   To cut costs, Airbus explored possible collaboration with an American plane maker that would reduce development costs, add a second production facility, and allow Airbus to incur some of its production costs in U.S. funds, rather than in European currencies. A joint venture with an American manufacturer offered Airbus another important potential benefit. It might have diffused some of the tension between Europe and the United States over the subsidization of Airbus. Thus, beginning in 1983, Airbus held talks with McDonnell Douglas. Despite the appeal on paper of a joint venture, however, the 1980s ended with talks between the two firms at a standstill.

33   On June 26, 1988, a new A320 crashed at the Paris Air Show, resulting in the deaths of three passengers. A French government inquiry blamed the pilot; but doubts were raised about the impartiality of the inquiry, given the French government's financial stake in the success of the A320. In February of 1989, another A320 crashed in Bangalore, India, killing 93 passengers. Industry experts began to express doubts about the plane's advanced control systems. However, these concerns did not have an immediate impact on sales or on the overall reputation of the A320. As explained by a spokesperson for Northwest, the carrier's problems with the craft were normal "teething" problems typical of a new plane, and an official of the FAA called them "bugs" that were to be expected.

AIRLINE INDUSTRY

34   In 1938, Congress passed the Civil Aeronautics Act that regulated the airline industry with respect to fares, routes, mergers, and practices. This act was repealed in 1978, with the Airline Deregulation Act. After deregulation, the airline industry became a price-driven industry. Discounted tickets, frequent-flyer programs, special promotional fares for business people or families with children, and coupons were some examples of marketing efforts to attract passengers.

35   Fares in the 1980s rose more slowly than the consumer price index, on average. When adjusted for inflation, air fares actually declined 21 percent in the 10 years following deregulation. The Federal Trade Commission estimated that passengers had saved $100 billion in the first 10 years of deregulation. However, industry representatives insisted that to achieve satisfactory service, number and routes of flights, safety, and ultramodern planes, higher fares were necessary in the future.

36   By the end of the decade, higher fares and fewer discounts, in fact, were becoming a reality. Airlines were restricting the discount fares, increasing the number of miles of frequent-flyer programs, and using sophisticated computer-scheduling programs that listed the prime carriers' connecting flights first and increased fares automatically as usage increased.

37   Deregulation led to an industry that resembled an oligopoly. Competitive price wars resulted in takeovers of the least-healthy airlines. More than 90 percent of the U.S. market was controlled by just eight airlines: American, United, Delta, Northwest, USAir, Texas Air, TWA, and Pan Am.

38   With the gradual increase in fares and an increase in the number of miles flown, industry profits began to rise, hitting a record $2.8 billion in 1988. Profits were high in the first half of 1989 until price wars again reduced the gains. Cargo shipping also became a lucrative market for the airlines. Cargo traditionally had been a sideline for most major carriers, representing only 10 to 15 percent of revenues, but this was rising in the 1980s. Additionally, improved finances had been made possible by reduced fuel and labor costs. Fuel prices dropped from $1.05 per gallon in 1981 to about $0.58 per gallon in 1989, accounting for only 15 percent of the operating expenses, instead of about 33 percent.

39   The growth of the airline industry, not only domestically but internationally, was expected to continue through the 1990s. Domestic and Pacific rim flights were expected to experience double-digit growth in the 1990s, with deregulation and with the impact of the boom in Asian economies. As well, European markets were anticipating deregulation by the mid 1990s. Thus, carriers in Europe were privatizing, enhancing their routes and efficiency, and improving their computer reservation systems.

AIRCRAFT LEASING

40   Because of the cost of a new aircraft, airlines were reluctant (and sometimes unable) to purchase new planes, although new planes were necessary to their continued growth. During the 1980s, aircraft leasing grew for the airlines as an alternative to purchasing aircraft. Two major leasing companies, International Lease Finance Corporation (ILFC) and GPA Group, Limited, placed some of the largest orders ever with the aircraft companies.

41   In May 1988, ILFC ordered $5 billion of aircraft from Boeing and Airbus, a total of 130 aircraft, with an option on 40 more. In March 1989, Ireland's GPA Group, Limited, placed a $17 billion order for 308 new planes with Boeing, McDonnell Douglas, and Airbus. "Airlines no longer feel that it is necessary to own aircraft for the purpose of having access to operate their business, a business whose nature is essentially the transport of passengers and cargo from one place to another," chief operating officer of GPA James King stated.[6] Leasing companies were changing the nature of the markets for aircraft manufacturers.

42   One major concern for airlines was the safety of the aircraft. Any accidents got wide media attention.

AIRLINE SAFETY

43   Domestically in the United States, 300 fatal and nonfatal accidents, or 33 annually, were reported in the nine years prior to deregulation. Only 180 accidents were reported in the first nine years after deregulation, an average of 20 per year, and fatalities declined 57 percent per million miles traveled. It was estimated that the chance of dying in a plane accident was barely one in 500,000 departures in 1988. However, it was widely recognized that the public's perceptions of danger had increased, and that these perceptions could take on a reality of their own.

44   In the 1980s, there were some well-publicized accidents of Boeing jets, but it was not surprising that the Boeing aircraft would be involved in more accidents than other aircraft since about 55 percent of the world's commercial jet market was made by Boeing. Only one, however, was attributable to Boeing error. In 1985, a JAL 747 crashed into a mountainside killing 520 passengers. The accident was blamed on faulty repair work done by Boeing staff.

45   There was also growing public concern in the late 1980s that the megacarriers had taken on so much debt that not enough money was available for proper maintenance or for retiring older aircraft. The average age of the U.S. fleet was about 13 years, and the world fleet's average was 12 years. Aircraft were kept in service longer because of the cost of new planes. Boeing's biggest plane, the 747-400 could cost up to $120 million per plane. In contrast, rebuilding early models of the 727, 737, and 747 cost an average of about $600,000 per plane.

46   Additionally, Boeing had an $84 billion backlog of orders, and the reliability of the planes being produced was questioned. A source leaked to the press a letter from JAL's president Susumu Yamaji to Boeing's CEO Frank Shrontz questioning the safety and quality of new Boeing jets delivered to JAL. With this publicity came other complaints from All Nippon Airways, American Airlines, and British Airways on the poor workmanship and defects in the 747s. Boeing management did admit that perhaps they had underestimated the challenges of building the 747-400. However, the airlines, the FAA, and Boeing pointed out that none of the production problems had caused an accident, and these questions were not having a negative impact on Boeing's financial status.

---

[6] Bruce W. Fraser, "Aircraft Leasing Loans to New Heights," *Christian Science Monitor*, April 29, 1989.

BOEING'S FINANCIAL STATUS

47 Boeing announced at its stockholders annual meeting in May 1990 that its stock would be split 3–2 for a second year in a row. Net income rose 87 percent during the first quarter of 1990 and sales rose 60 percent to $6.4 billion. Dean D. Thornton, president of the Boeing Commercial Airplane Group, noted that production was at 31 planes per month and was being increased in 1990 to 34 planes per month. By mid-1991, Thornton expected production of 38 jets per month (twenty-one 737s, seven 757s, five 767s, and five 747s), and, by 1992, the rate could be 41 jets per month. Thornton also indicated that by mid-1990, Boeing hoped to launch the 777. To introduce the new jet, Boeing management was negotiating firm orders with managements from eight airlines. Boeing's overall margins were only about 3.5 percent in 1988, under that of Airbus and McDonnell Douglas, which were both about 5.1 percent. Margins were expected to improve in the coming years, but probably not to the 1978 high of 9.4 percent. As one analyst put it, "They're [Boeing] earning grocery store margins on a high-tech product."[7] (For detailed financial information on Boeing, see Exhibits 2 and 3.)

48 In the 1980s, Boeing was looking for ways to maintain its product innovation with fewer resources. Since government funds for development were not readily available, Boeing considered possible collaboration with other international firms.

BOEING'S JOINT VENTURES WITH THE JAPANESE

49 As the 1990s began, the aging of air fleets around the world opened new opportunities for plane manufacturers. One opportunity lay in the replacement of large "trijet" (three-engine) planes introduced in the 1970s, like the McDonnell Douglas DC10. To fill this need, Airbus introduced in 1988 the A330, and McDonnell Douglas's offering in this segment was the MD11 trijet. The closest direct Boeing competitive offering, as of 1988, was the 767.

50 In early 1989, in an attempt to capture a leading share of the trijet replacement market, Boeing offered to airlines considering the A330 or the MD11 a new twin-jet wide-body called the *767-X* (to be called the *777* once production began). With initial delivery targeted for 1995, the plane originally was intended to carry between 350 and 375 passengers over 4,300 nautical miles. Boeing found an interest in the marketplace for the 777. However, development costs for the new plane were estimated at about $4 billion, and manpower needs were substantial. One option for Boeing was to subcontract as much of the work as possible to outside firms.

51 Since the mid-1970s, Boeing bought components from several Japanese suppliers; and, in the 1970s, Aeritalia of Italy and Japan Commercial Aircraft Corporation (JCAC) of Japan became "risk-sharing subcontractors" to Boeing for the 767 program. In return for covering up to 15 percent of the development costs of the 767, the two foreign firms were guaranteed a certain share of the work. However, had the 767 been a failure, Aeritalia and the JCAC would have lost their investment in the development costs and the production facilities for 767 components. By early 1990, Boeing considered offering a large share of the 777 project to its Japanese suppliers. The three Japanese firms that were partners in JCAC, Mitsubishi Heavy Industries, Limited, Kawasaki Heavy Industries, Limited, and Fuji Heavy Industries, Limited, proposed contributions of 21 percent of the $4 billion development costs for the new twin jet. In return, the Japanese wanted to participate in the development, assembly, final integration, and marketing of the 777.

52 The Japanese offer was attractive to Boeing. Boeing's experience with its three Japanese suppliers was favorable. According to Lawrence Clarkson, Boeing's senior vice president of government and international affairs, "They [the Japanese] are very reliable; they're very competitive. They do the work

---

[7] Stewart Toy and John Templeman, "Planemakers Have It So Good, It's Bad," *Business Week*, May 8, 1989, p. 36.

EXHIBIT 2
Selected Financial Data 1986–1989 (dollars in millions)

	Year Ended December 31			
	1989	**1988**	**1987**	**1986**
Revenues:				
Commercial transportation products & services	$ 14,305	$ 11,369	$ 9,827	$ 9,820
Military transportation products & related systems	3,962	3,668	3,979	4,882
Missiles and space	1,467	1,457	1,063	1,126
Other industries	542	468	636	616
Operating revenues	20,276	16,962	15,505	16,444
Corporate income, principally interest	347	378	308	304
Total revenues	$ 20,623	$ 17,340	$ 15,813	$ 16,748
Operating profit:				
Commercial transportation products & services	$ 1,165	$ 585	$ 352	$ 411
Military transportation products & related systems	(559)	(95)	60	367
Missiles and space	85	124	119	55
Other industries	26	(28)	(34)	(9)
Operating profit	717	586	497	824
Corporate income	347	378	308	304
Corporate expense	(142)	(144)	(147)	(100)
Earnings before taxes	$ 922	$ 820	$ 658	$ 1,028
Research and development expensed	$ 754	$ 751	$ 824	$ 757
General & administrative expensed	1,012	880	793	606
Additions to plant & equipment	1,362	690	738	795
Salaries & wages	6,082	5,404	5,028	4,374
Average employment	$159,200	$147,300	$136,100	$118,500

well, they deliver on time, and they do it for a price nobody else can beat."[8] Additionally, by the end of the 1980s, the Japanese market was one of Boeing's biggest, with 1988 being one third to one half of all orders for 747s from Japan. Finally, Boeing officials noted discussions between the Japanese manufacturer's and its rival Airbus. As Boeing CEO Frank Shrontz conceded, "Our view is that if we don't work with them someone else will."[9]

53   Boeing already had aborted an earlier joint venture with its Japanese suppliers. During the 1980s, Boeing and the Japanese firms negotiated extensively over joint development and production of a revolutionary, fuel-efficient, 150-seat plane called the *7J7*. In mid-1987, though, Boeing announced that the 7J7 project was being postponed indefinitely, due to weak market interest, reduced fuel costs, and disagreement among potential customers over the jet's optimum size.

---

[8] John Davies, "Boeing Clarifies Japanese 7X7 Role," *The Journal of Commerce*, April 24, 1990, p. 32.

[9] Kenneth Labich, "Boeing Battles to Stay on Top," *Fortune*, September 28, 1987, p. 70

EXHIBIT 2 (concluded)

	Year Ended December 31			
	1989	1988	1987	1986
Identifiable assets at December 31:				
Commercial transportation products & services.........	$ 6,675	$ 4,558	$ 5,170	$ 3,533
Military transportation products & related systems.......	3,367	2,923	2,846	2,285
Missiles and space...............................	911	684	548	434
Other industries................................	329	319	362	364
Total..	11,282	8,484	8,926	6,616
Corporate......................................	1,996	4,124	3,640	4,294
Consolidated assets.........................	$13,278	$12,608	$12,566	$10,910
Depreciation:				
Commercial transportation products & services.........	$ 242	$ 243	$ 218	$ 200
Military transportation products & related systems.......	208	188	170	136
Missiles and space...............................	$ 72	52	42	34
Capital expenditures, net:				
Commercial transportation products & services.........	$ 612	$ 326	$ 286	$ 332
Military transportation products & related systems.......	506	241	316	356
Missiles and space...............................	$ 155	$ 62	$ 72	$ 82
Firm backlog:				
Commercial....................................	$73,974	$46,676	$26,963	$20,084
U.S. government	6,589	6,925	6,241	6,304
Total..	$80,563	$53,601	$33,204	$26,388

Sources: The Boeing Company, 1987, 1988, 1989 Annual Reports.

54   Despite the compelling reasons for a joint venture with the Japanese on the 777, there was concern in the United States. Many observers worried that the partnership would result in transfers of knowledge to the Japanese, allowing them to become a serious rival to American leadership in the commercial jetliner business. Drawing a parallel between the jetliner business and the auto business, Joel Pitcoff, chief of research at Ford, said that, if his company had entered into an early partnership with the Japanese similar to Boeing's proposed deal, "It would have accelerated the Japanese seizure of market share and sped up the departure of jobs from the state of Michigan. . . . If the Japanese want to be partners, they're already convinced in their own minds that they know how to make it cheaper and better."[10]

55   Echoing these fears, David Cole, director of the University of Michigan's office for the study of automotive transportation, said, "The [U.S.] aerospace industry may be a little more cautious about the Japanese and have a little better management techniques than the auto industry, but they're very

---

[10] John Davies, "Detroit Automakers Warn Boeing on Deal with Japan," *The Journal of Commerce*, November 8, 1989, p. 34.

EXHIBIT 3
Consolidated Statement of Financial Position, 1986–1990 (dollars in millions)

	Mar. 31, 1990	Dec. 31, 1989	Dec. 31, 1988	Dec. 31, 1987	Dec. 31, 1986
Assets					
Cash & certificates of deposit	$ 2,344	$ 1,208	$ 3,544	$ 2,197	$ 2,825
Short-term investments at cost which approximates market	555	655	419	1,238	1,347
Accounts receivable	1,870	1,809	1,559	1,546	1,114
Current portion of customer financing	40	46	92	823	87
Inventories	14,524	15,089	11,484	8,802	6,845
Less advances & progress billings	(10,412)	(10,147)	(8,537)	(5,293)	(3,740)
Total current assets	$ 8,921	$ 8,660	$ 8,561	$ 9,313	$ 8,478
Customer financing.	843	822	1,039	392	195
Property, plant, & equip. at cost	7,927	7,590	6,385	5,813	5,156
Less accumulated depreciation	(4,217)	(4,109)	(3,682)	(3,259)	(2,875)
Investments & other assets	317	315	305	307	114
	$13,791	$13,278	$12,608	$12,566	$11,068
Liabilities and Stockholders' Equity					
Accounts payable & other liab.	$ 4,934	$ 4,932	$ 4,697	$ 4,434	$ 3,291
Advances & progress billings in excess of related costs.	1,583	1,445	1,304	846	791
Federal taxes on income	413	291	697	1,773	1,563
Current portion long-term debt	5	5	7	14	14
	$ 6,935	$ 6,673	$ 6,705	$ 7,067	$ 5,659
Long-term debt	286	275	251	256	263
Deferred taxes on income	175	174	205	189	219
Deferred investment credit	22	25	43	67	101
Stockholders' equity:*					
Common shares issued at stated value— 349,277,961 shares	1,740	1,736	1,341	1,335	1,338
Retained earnings	4,685	4,452	4,137	3,760	3,497
Less treasury shares, at cost 1990—3,117,899	(52)	(57)	(74)	(108)	(9)
Total stockholders' equity	$ 6,373	$ 6,131	$ 5,404	$ 4,987	$ 4,826
	$13,791	$13,278	$12,608	$12,566	$11,068

*Number of shares data restated for 3-for-2 stock split approved April 1990.
Sources: The Boeing Company, 1987, 1988, 1989 Annual Reports; March 31, 1990, Form 10-Q.

much the same, and they could find themselves in very deep competitive trouble very quickly."[11] A spokesperson for the International Association of Machinists and Aerospace Workers, the largest union at Boeing, expressed similar concerns, warning that technology transfers to the Japanese would simply mean fewer jobs for Americans.

56 Boeing officials did little to calm these worries. In a speech given in late 1989, Philip Condit, head of Boeing's New Airplanes Division, said, ". . . technology transfer inevitably raises the question of whether we are providing information which might be used by a future competitor or competitors. . . . The answer is yes, . . . we are stimulating potential competitors."[12] Condit believed it was impossible for Boeing to shut off access to important technology or to prevent new entrants to the jetliner business, so it was probably better that the suppliers in question worked with Boeing, rather than with the competition.

57 From the Japanese perspective, the Japanese Ministry of International Trade and Industry (MITI) had targeted the civilian jetliner industry for penetration by Japanese firms. MITI had set a target of 10 percent Japanese market share by the year 2000 and was prepared to commit substantial amounts of government money to help Japanese firms become competitive. According to one European magazine:

58 . . . first-hand experience of how to build a wide-body passenger jet like the 767X (i.e., the 777) would be of great help . . . if they play their cards right, Mitsubishi, Kawasaki, and Fuji . . . could turn themselves into the leading component suppliers to the world's aircraft builders. . . . They would aim to turn this into design and manufacturing leadership in such areas as hydraulic systems, control surfaces. . . . With computers and cars, Japanese manufacturers got a foot in the global market by first building a strong component industry at home. Later, they filled market gaps abroad that American and European firms had overlooked with high-quality, low-priced products. Japan is betting it can pull off a similar trick with aircraft.[13]

59 There was also some question about how Boeing could take on the development and production of one more aircraft, given current demands for its products.

BOEING'S BACKLOG

60 Boeing's success in its commercial passenger and freight aircraft was generating lengthy production backlogs. (See Exhibit 3.) At the end of 1989, Boeing had an $84 billion backlog and some airlines were already placing orders for delivery in the year 2000. Even with these production and delivery delays, Boeing was receiving record orders.

61 One of the Boeing aircraft in high demand was the 747-400 introduced in late 1989. The new model could fly over 8,500 miles, allowing carriers to offer nonstop service between points as far apart as New York and Seoul or London and Tokyo with up to 400 passengers. The freight version of the 747-400 could carry 23 10-foot-high containers, 2 more than 747-200 freighter. Another popular model was the "combi" jet, which carried a mix of cargo and passengers on the main deck.

62 When Boeing delayed delivery of its 747-400s in 1989, it was the first time in 20 years Boeing missed a delivery deadline. "We overcommitted," said Thornton.[14] These delays made some customers angry. Jurgen Weber, chief operations officer at Lufthansa, noted, "The whole fleet program will have

---

[11] John Davies, "Will Boeing Ventures with Japan Cost Jobs?" *The Journal of Commerce*, November 8, 1989, p. 12A.

[12] John Davies, "Boeing Executive Defends Deals with Foreign Aerospace Firms," *The Journal of Commerce*, March 15, 1990, p. 2B.

[13] "The Sincerest Form of Flattery," *The Economist*, November 11, 1989, p. 80.

[14] Seth Payne and Todd Vogel, "Trying Times at Boeing," *Business Week*, March 13, 1989, p. 35.

to be reworked, but we can never fully close all the gaps this year."[15] In July 1989, Lord John King, chairman of British Airways, announced at a predelivery press conference that he was seeking financial compensation for a three-month-late delivery of nineteen 747-400 planes.

63   Because of late delivery penalties, the 747-400 was expected to contribute only about 20 percent gross margin, versus the 30 percent on earlier 747 models. Each 747-400 delivery contributed only about $0.10 per share to annual earnings, versus the expected $0.13.

64   With the new 747-400, Boeing took on more than it realized. The jet was designed with 175 miles of electrical wiring and several million parts. New technology required complex computers and wiring. Boeing offered its customers a choice of three engines, each requiring FAA approval. Boeing's expected delivery schedules were faster than suppliers could meet. Additionally, labor problems added to the delivery delays. About 3,000 new employees were hired at the Everett, Washington, plant near Seattle from January 1987 to April 1988, making employee training difficult. A 48-day strike in the fall of 1989 added to the production slowdown. With continued growth for new passenger and cargo aircraft anticipated, Boeing announced in March 1990 a 10-year plan to expand its Everett facility by 4 million square feet for additional manufacturing, office, and warehouse space.

65   While Boeing was sending new 747-400s to customers as quickly as production capacity permitted, it was impossible to meet the full demand. In late 1990, Boeing resumed a service it had previously offered in the 1970s: converting used 747 passenger planes to all-cargo models. The process, which involved removing seats, replacing floors, and reinforcing sides, was expected to take between three and four months per plane and cost about $20 million for each plane. This was considerably cheaper than either a new 747-400 freighter priced at $120 million each or a used 747 freighter that sold for $60–$75 million each. Boeing planned to do the conversion work at its Wichita, Kansas, facility, which had been used for military aircraft production. Given the limited space, prospective clients were expected to go on a two-year waiting list before their planes could be converted to the all-cargo configuration.

66   As mentioned, labor problems added to the delays in production and would need to be resolved as Boeing continued to expand.

LABOR RELATIONS AT BOEING

67   In the 1983 and 1986 labor negotiations, the Boeing Company management convinced labor to take bonuses instead of wage increases because of poor sales and profits. However, in 1989 negotiations, labor indicated that it wanted a share of profits on the record order backlog.

68   On October 3, 1989, 85 percent of the International Association of Machinists (IAM) members at Boeing voted to strike. About 57,800 workers—primarily from the Everett, Washington, commercial jet production facility—walked off the job on October 4. The IAM strike was centered on both wage increases and overtime issues. Employees were routinely working 12-hour days with no days off for weeks at a time. Many outsiders and insiders felt these hours were impacting not only the employees' lives but also the quality of production. During the strike, which lasted 48 days, nonunion workers and managers finished 11 planes for delivery, versus the prestrike production of 28 aircraft per month.

69   Boeing management and labor were in deadlock, but on November 19, 1989, both sides accepted a proposal designed by a federal mediator. The agreement was approved by 81.4 percent of the union vote, and, on November 22, IAM workers returned to the Boeing production lines. The final agreement improved wages and reduced mandatory overtime hours.

70   The strike resulted in Boeing deliveries being more than 30 planes behind schedule. It also led to a 55.7 percent decline in earnings for the fourth quarter. Frank Shrontz, Boeing's CEO, was

---

[15] John Davies, "BA Chairman Wants Settlement for Late Delivery of Boeing 747s," *The Journal of Commerce*, July 28, 1987.

quoted as saying that the strike also had a severe impact on Boeing's cash and short-term investment position.

71   On January 18, 1990, Boeing announced that, despite a record backlog of orders, the work force would be cut by 5,000 workers, or just less than 5 percent of the 159,200 workers, within the next six months. Many workers hired to correct production problems were no longer needed. Boeing management believed production could be improved by greater efficiency and fewer workers.

72   Demand for new passenger and freight planes and for cargo conversions was high. However, analysts noted that this could slow if the airline industry growth slumped, if older planes were not retired as early, or if an economic downturn caused airlines to stop ordering or to cancel orders. Moreover, the military and space business was still incurring major losses.

THE DEFENSE INDUSTRY AT BOEING

73   Boeing was primarily a military aircraft producer until the mid-1960s, when the civilian work became the majority of Boeing's sales. The company developed and built the bombers that formed the backbone of the U.S. strategic bombing campaign in WWII. In 1954, Boeing rolled out the B-52, a massive four-engine jet bomber designed for carrying nuclear bombs to targets in the Soviet Union. Boeing introduced the Airborne Warning and Control System (AWACS), a sophisticated air-defense tracking system carried in a converted 707 airframe in the early 1980s. The AWACS became the leader in the airborne surveillance field and was adopted by the United States and several key allied nations. In addition to its military activities, Boeing was involved in America's space program, working closely with both the National Aeronautics and Space Administration (NASA) and the U.S. Air Force on a variety of projects.

74   Beginning in the mid-1980s, a number of developments altered the environment for Boeing and other prime defense contractors. First, the Communist regimes in Eastern Europe collapsed and negotiations to reduce both nuclear and nonnuclear forces on both sides intensified between the United States and the Soviet Union. Second, efforts to reduce the U.S. government deficit hit the defense industry. By 1990, the Pentagon announced that new equipment spending would fall by more than 50 percent, and over half a million layoffs were expected in the U.S. defense industry. Boeing had several major contracts with the Pentagon that were in jeopardy of being cut by Congress.

75   Additionally, there were episodes of wasteful procurement by the Pentagon. While the dollar amounts usually were small, these episodes eroded the public support for the defense buildup. Boeing was not immune to these embarrassing incidents. In one incident, as part of a large order for components of the AWACS plane, Boeing charged the Air Force $1,118.26 for a plastic stool cap that outside experts insisted should never have sold for more than $10.00. While admitting that the price charged was high, Boeing blamed government imposed regulations for the unfortunate "cost growth."

76   The high-profile cases of overcharging on parts and components, coupled with the intense pressure on the Pentagon's budget, meant that defense contractors had to conform to increasingly strict terms and conditions in military contracts. Cost control was mandatory. On January 2, 1990, Boeing combined its defense, space, and electronics operations by creating the Boeing Defense and Space Group—to "streamline operations, reduce costs, and provide better management focus to improve performance."[16] In 1989, as a result of various technical problems, Boeing posted a $474 million loss on defense and space programs. This compared with a modest $29 million profit in 1988 and a $179 million profit in 1987. In mid-1990, Boeing officials admitted that the company's defense and space business would sustain "a significant 1990 operating loss, which was blamed on continued cost and schedule problems and technical difficulties."[17]

---

[16] Boeing 1989 Annual Report, p. 19.

[17] "Boeing's Net Nearly Doubles to $387 Million," *The Wall Street Journal*, July 28, 1990.

77   Despite the uncertainty surrounding the defense industry as the 1980s drew to a close, certain military products—like electronics, computer equipment, and training and communications—were lucrative. Another market investigated by defense contractors was the war on drugs. This market seemed attractive, since the equipment needed for these operations—helicopters, radar planes, and tracking equipment—required few modifications from the products sold to the U.S. military. However, the total market for drug interdiction equipment was small, estimated in early 1990 at only about $1 billion, compared with the Pentagon's postcutback annual spending of up to $120 billion.

78   The ultimate strategy for defense contractors as they entered the 1990s was to diversify into non-defense or commercial areas. Boeing noted in its 1989 Annual Report, "Boeing is protected from excessive dependence on any one program or aspect of the defense budget."[18] However, many experts insisted that firms specializing in military equipment were incapable of producing commercially successful products. One of the country's leading industrial engineering experts and chairman of the National Commission for Economic Conversion and Disarmament, Seymour Melman of Columbia University, pointed to Boeing helicopter division's attempt to move from military helicopter production to the manufacture of subway cars and electric trolleys for mass transportation:

79   It failed. The reason it failed is because Boeing did nothing but operate by methods that were well accepted on the military side, in the standard Pentagon fashion called concurrency. . . . [T]hey did the design, testing, evaluation, and production all at the same time instead of dealing with each of these operations sequentially. As a result, the items they produced and delivered to customers were not properly tested. . . . There was a parade of lawsuits and then Boeing abandoned the whole affair.[19]

80   Professor Melman estimated that it would require at least two years for a defense contractor to redesign its military-related facilities to handle commercial work and another two years to retrain managers, engineers, and production staff, especially in the areas of cost minimization.

CONCLUSION

81   Concentration in the U.S. and international airline industries was continuing, and Boeing faced fewer but larger buyers. The order backlog was proving to be a serious problem. How to reduce the backlog, improve deliveries, and maintain customer goodwill remained some of the main challenges facing Boeing. The company's Japanese suppliers were pressing for an answer on their proposed joint venture, especially in light of the Japanese government's goal of promoting airliner production in Japan. Airbus continued to make inroads in the marketplace and was heavily promoting its new "family" of jetliners. In light of continued cutbacks at the Pentagon, Boeing forecast substantial losses on defense sales in 1990. These were known issues, but still unforeseen political and economic developments in the world also could impact Boeing's future success.

82   How to prepare for these changes and deal with these issues remained the key challenge facing Boeing management. This was expressed by CEO Frank Shrontz:

83   Our long-range mission is to be the number-one aerospace company in the world, and among the premier industrial firms, as measured by quality, profitability, and growth. To realize that mission, we are committed to making steady, incremental improvements in the way we design, build, and support our products. We are examining every aspect of our internal processes—from manufacturing to business systems—to look for better ways to get the job done. Our overriding goal in all these continuous improvement efforts is to meet the requirements and expectations of our customers—on whom the company's success ultimately depends.[20]

---

[18] Ibid., p. 30.

[19] Joel Kurtzman, "Civvies for the American Economy," *The New York Times*, June 3, 1990, p. 12.

[20] Boeing 1990 Annual Report, p. 3.

CASE 21

ORBITAL SCIENCES CORPORATION

INTRODUCTION

1   David Thompson, chairman of the board, president, and chief executive officer of Orbital Sciences Corporation, considered the casewriter's question. What would the significant growth that Orbital continued to experience mean for his management of the company? Would the way that he dealt with Orbital people and that they interacted with each other change? If so, were these changes for the good?

2   David had many reasons to be pleased with his organization. Orbital's stock price continued to exhibit an upward trend as Orbital was awarded new contracts. The recent push to hire new employees to meet the needs of the new contracts revealed that Orbital still was seen as a premier place to work. The move to bring existing products from development to production was going well, and the development of newer products was meeting expectations. Was worrying about growth really necessary?

ORBITAL'S BUSINESS

3   Orbital Science Corporation is in the business of providing high-technology space products and services for defense, scientific, commercial, and environmental uses. Existing and planned products and services include orbital and suborbital rockets, orbit transfer vehicles, spacecraft systems, space payloads and experiments, space support products, and satellite services. Founded in 1982 by three graduates of Harvard Business School's MBA program, Orbital has experienced rapid growth. Today, Orbital is a unique, glamorous firm with an important position in a number of space-oriented, dynamic, and promising markets.

HISTORY[1]

4   David Thompson, one of Orbital's cofounders, had a history of interest in space. As a kid, he liked rockets and invented games and experiments with hundreds of small rockets he set off in his back yard. As a young adult, he attended the Massachusetts Institute of Technology, majoring in aeronautics and astronautics. After graduating from the California Institute of Technology with a master's degree in aeronautics, he worked for NASA as a project manager. It was there that the idea of Orbital Sciences Corporation was born.

This case was prepared by Eileen A. Hogan of the School of Business Administration at George Mason University. Development of this case was made possible by a grant from the Funds for Excellence Program of the State Council of Higher Education for Virginia.

[1] Much of the information in this section was taken from Nancy O. Perry, "Shooting for the Stars," *Harvard Business School Bulletin,* June 1989.

5   What I found in working for NASA was an enormous amount of technology that had been developed by the government for a small number of large corporations. The technology worked OK in those programs, but that was about it. It really wasn't being used in many other areas where it could be.

6   It occurred to me that perhaps a private company would be more effective than either a government agency or a large aerospace company that viewed space as a sort of a sideline to its primary business of building defense systems or commercial aircraft. NASA was interested in its traditional mission, which was to explore space, and while they didn't spend money in a frivolous way, they really didn't have the sort of approach that would lead them to drive down costs.

7   I decided I needed to learn a lot about business in a hurry, and it seemed to me that the most efficient way to do that was to go to business school.[2]

8   Entering the Harvard Business School in 1979, David met Scott Webster and Bruce Ferguson, who were to become cofounders of Orbital Sciences Corporation. These three, along with other students, undertook a creative marketing strategy (CMS) study to identify commercial opportunities in space, looking at the potential of the market, financial feasibility, and overall risk. The study won a national prize from the Space Foundation, an organization that encouraged academic research and private-sector programs in space enterprise. This study formed the basis for the future business to be called Orbital Sciences Corporation.

9   Having learned that they worked together well as a team, David, Scott, and Bruce continued to work on developing the idea of commercial space development as each went into jobs after graduating from business school. Fortuitously, 1982 saw the beginning of Reagan's tenure in office. On July 4, 1982, the Reagan Administration announced its space policy, including its goal to "expand private sector investment and involvement in civil space and space-related activities."[3] Having already conducted extensive research into the market for space services and products, and the technology of small space ventures, David, Scott, and Bruce were in an ideal position to respond.

10   The nature of space development was changing at that time. Since the beginning of space exploration until the beginning of the space shuttle missions, satellites and other payloads had been delivered into orbit by huge, powerful, nonreusable rockets. A major advantage of the space shuttle was that it was reusable. When the shuttle was declared fully operational in 1983, government funding of expendable launch vehicles ended.

11   At the same time, the nature of satellites themselves was changing. For a number of reasons, satellites were becoming heavier. Further, their uses were changing, so the need to be placed in very high geosynchronous orbits was becoming more frequent.

12   Orbital's first attempt to land a contract responded to a portion of these changes. NASA saw the need for the development of a rocket to boost large satellites that had been deployed from the shuttle into higher orbits. David, Scott, and Bruce bid this contract, but had to face disappointment when NASA decided to keep the development of this rocket in-house.

13   However, as part of their work in developing this proposal, they had succeeded in soliciting some capital from an outside investor. Using this money, they pursued a contract to build a similar device that could boost medium-sized satellites after their release from the shuttle or a ground-based rocket. Dr. Jack W. Wild, then director of Upper Stages at NASA, recalled the presentation:

14   Thompson made his presentation—and blew their socks off. Each one of my guys did a 180-degree turn. We signed the memorandum of understanding one week later.[4]

---

[2] David Thompson, quoted in Perry, pp. 4–5.

[3] Quoted in Perry, p. 5.

[4] Quoted in Perry, p. 7.

15   According to the agreement, the three entrepreneurs had six weeks to come through with some significant support:

16   In that time, the entrepreneurs had to achieve what seemed the impossible: find an aerospace contractor to work with them on the engineering, manufacturing, and testing aspects of the project; persuade NASA to make a stronger commitment to OSC; and secure a significant amount of venture capital financing. Resigning from their respective jobs, Thompson, Ferguson, and Webster methodically tackled these objectives, first winning the agreement of aerospace contractor Martin Marietta to a fixed-price contract, and then using that extra leverage to secure NASA's approval to develop the Transfer Orbit Stage (TOS®).[5]

17   Simultaneously, the three were able to raise $1.8 million from venture capital firms. They also needed an estimated $50 million to develop the TOS. How they rose to the challenge of raising that money is the subject of a Harvard Business School case study.[6] All of this was accomplished with no guarantee from NASA that it would purchase any of these vehicles.

18   Early in 1986, Orbital received its first order: for two TOSs, from NASA. The launches were planned for 1991 and 1992. Four weeks later, the space shuttle *Challenger* exploded.

19   Many small companies involved in space development work disappeared or performed poorly in the wake of the *Challenger* disaster and of other space accidents in 1986. Orbital, however, did well. Its two contracts gave it four years of predictable payments; in fact, 1986 was Orbital's first profitable year. Orbital employed 25 people in 1986.

ORBITAL'S SECOND PRODUCT

20   Orbital recognized that future opportunities to produce TOSs had been damaged, however, and that it needed a second product to remain a viable firm. In early 1987, Orbital's vice president of engineering, Dr. Antonio Elias, came up with the idea of using a small booster launched from an aircraft to deploy satellites. Such a rocket would have several advantages. First, being launched from an aircraft gives the booster a higher start. Second, such a rocket is boosted horizontally, rather than vertically; and horizontal is the direction a rocket needs to gain orbit. Third, higher altitude also meant less aerodynamic stress would be placed on the vehicle. Fourth, the lower air pressure at high altitude would increase rocket motor efficiency.[7]

21   Elias's idea was met with much skepticism by Orbital's founders. "I told him it was an absolutely crazy idea," said Thompson.[8] One major difficulty associated with the idea was that air-launched rockets drop for long distances before developing enough thrust to gain altitude. Thompson suggested adding a delta wing to the rocket to alleviate this problem. With this, the concept for the *Pegasus* rocket was born.

22   Early in 1988, Orbital agreed to a joint venture with Hercules Aerospace Company to develop *Pegasus.* Enabled by this agreement, Orbital acquired an Arizona firm engaged in the development and manufacture of suborbital rockets in 1989.

---

[5] Perry, p. 7.

[6] James J. Turner and William A. Sahlman, "Orbital Sciences Corporation (A)," Harvard Business School Case #9–386–175, Rev. January 1989.

[7] "Spacesaver: The OSC/Hercules Pegasus Small Launch Vehicle May Herald a Whole New Era in 'Microspace' Technology," Advertiser Sponsored Market Supplement to *Aviation Week and Space Technology,* September 3, 1990, pp. S3–S10.

[8] Quoted in Perry, p. 10.

23   *Pegasus* made its first flight in 1990. *Pegasus* looks like a foot torpedo with a delta wing. On April 5, a *Pegasus* rocket dropped from under the wing of a leased B-52 at 43,000 feet. It descended 350 feet before its booster ignited, then its three stages caused it to climb rapidly to 315 nautical miles. There, it successfully deployed a navy communications satellite and a NASA science payload into low Earth orbit.

GROWTH AT ORBITAL SCIENCES

24   In 1987, Orbital employed 42 people; in 1988, with the acquisition of Space Data Systems in Arizona, Orbital's population totaled 440, including 240 engineers and 140 technicians and assemblers.[9]

25   In its early years, people came to work for Orbital for a variety of reasons. First, Orbital attracted some individuals who were interested in space: people who watched "Star Trek" on TV at home at night and who followed developments in space as a hobby. These individuals often came to Orbital because it represented the state of the art in space development.

26   Others came to Orbital for its excitement and its opportunities and challenge. Barbara Zadina, who joined Orbital in 1988 as manager of government and external relations, came to Orbital because it constituted a group of young people who were actually going to get together and try to build a rocket. She knew of Orbital from some contact with the space community through her husband, an aeronautical engineer. The feeling she got was of an organization with a mission. To Barbara, working at Orbital was like "the group in college building the float for the homecoming parade. You were going to work all day and all night to make something happen."[10]

27   Coming from a government background, she had been frustrated by work in which she did something and passed it on, where it disappeared. At Orbital, results and feedback were immediate. She felt part of a tightly knit team in which what she did would be recognized. "Everything you do is totally depended on by everyone else, and if you let them down you know it. You're a link in the chain, and every single link counts."[11]

28   Working at Orbital was a test. "It's a challenge to see if you're as good as you think you are, that you can hold up your link."[12] Challenge also resulted from the small size of the company, coupled with the doubt people had that the company's goal was really attainable. Part of the joy of working at Orbital was your co-workers. Said Barbara:

29   This is an organization where 99 percent of the people are really hot. You can often go to an organization and find two or three people who are really bright and are great at what they do; here, everyone is bright, and you can learn from them. Here, you perform to the level of the people around you. It's like when you play tennis with someone good, you play better. Being here is almost like going back to school.[13]

30   The early years at Orbital were characterized by an informal, family atmosphere. Everyone knew everyone else. One Friday a month, executives brought lunches—maybe pizza—for all employees, and everyone had a good time eating and chatting.

31   Stress was high at Orbital. People were hired because they were expected to perform at a very high level. Co-workers looked to each other for excellence and continual challenge. Long hours were typical; 60 hours per week were not uncommon, with 80 usual around launch times. Saturdays often saw

---

[9] Perry, p. 10.

[10] Personal interview, June 8, 1991.

[11] Ibid.

[12] Ibid.

[13] Ibid.

almost all employees in corporate headquarters, it looking like a normal business day except for everyone wearing shorts. In fact, Saturday offered a distinct advantage over the other working days: the phones didn't ring.

32   Recognizing that stress was high, David and the other executives tried to do what they could to help out. They instituted "casual day," allowing people to wear casual clothes to work one day a week. Softball teams were formed in spring and summer. Friday night family get-togethers were sometimes planned. This last device might have been particularly useful, as the stress Orbital placed on employees might have been even harder on families—they weren't part of the excitement of Orbital, but waited at home for their spouses and parents.

33   Barbara described the way work got done as "organized chaos." An organization chart had been drawn up a couple of years ago, but after some attempts to keep it up to date, it had fallen into disuse. Basically, job titles didn't matter. Everybody did whatever they could of what the situation required. For example, several months ago, Orbital put on a presentation of its final design of the *Taurus* rocket at a nearby hotel for 300 people from government, other companies, and customers. Two days before the conference, the software that was to produce the name tags for attenders and Orbital's personnel quit working at 11:00 at night. To the rescue came the Orbital's chief engineer, who might otherwise have been working on spacecraft design, to work on the software.

34   People tended to rely on those who had been around the company for a long time to know what to do. People who had been around, be they technicians or executives, had a historical sense of the company and its mission.

35   For most of its work, Orbital organized its engineers and technicians into relatively small project teams. For example, the *Pegasus* team never exceeded 35 people, many of them young for space project engineers. Teams were self-sufficient; team members had to be able to write their own software. The small team size and self-reliance resulted in groups that could move quickly in accomplishing tasks at high standards.[14]

LEADERSHIP

36   David Thompson was the most visible leadership force at Orbital's headquarters in Fairfax, Virginia. Scott Webster, described as the most flamboyant of the three, had taken over management of the Space Data Division in Arizona. Bruce Ferguson, quiet and thoughtful, concerned himself with financial and legal aspects of operating the business. All three made unique and necessary contributions to the business. There was no hierarchy among the three.

37   David has been described as Orbital's driving force.[15] Thirty-eight years old in 1991, he struck subordinates as open, dynamic, and sincere. Many of the persons who originally came to Orbital were drawn by his personality.

38   David was a hands-on manager. He got involved in everything: brochures, press releases, all proposals. Typically, his input included editorial comments as well as feedback on content, plus suggested changes.

39   David's management style was characterized by "managing by walking around." Typically, 5:00 in the afternoon would find him in the halls and offices of corporate headquarters, asking employees how it was going, what they were doing, what they were working on. He was interested in what they answered and remembered their responses. He visited orientation sessions for new employees and explained his open-door policy: "If you ever have a question you can't get answered; if you ever have a good idea; if you ever want to talk, my door is open. I'd love to talk to you."

---

[14] "Spacesaver," p. S5.

[15] Ibid.

ORBITAL IN 1991

40   In 1989, Orbital grew to 520 employees. By the end of 1990, Orbital had grown from its three founders to 706 employees. And 1990 saw the producing of over $100 million in revenues; total assets stood at $91 million. Appendix A summarizes performance and growth. Orbital experienced small losses in 1988, 1989, and 1990 (Appendix A). In 1990, the loss was attributed to adjustments in long-term contracts.

41   In 1991, Orbital now operated a manufacturing and development subsidiary for suborbital rockets in Arizona; corporate headquarters, including some engineering staff, in Fairfax, Virginia; and another engineering facility located by Dulles Airport.

PRODUCTS AND SERVICES

42   Orbital's products and services fall into seven categories: space-launch vehicles, including *Pegasus* and a new venture called *Taurus*; suborbital-launch vehicles; orbit transfer vehicles; spacecraft systems; space payloads and experiments; space support products; and satellite services.

43   Space-launch vehicles represent the portion of Orbital's business that received the most publicity in 1990. *Pegasus,* whose innovative design proved successful on its first launch in April of 1990, is designed to place 500-pound to 1,000-pound payloads in a wide range of low-altitude orbits. *Pegasus* offers significant performance and cost advantages to its potential buyers. First, the use of an aircraft for launching eliminates the cost of an extra booster stage and launch pad. Second, poor weather conditions are less likely to interfere with *Pegasus* launches. Third, *Pegasus* conceivably can be launched from any jet-class airport.

44   In addition to *Pegasus*'s first launch in 1990, the Department of Defense has contracted with Orbital for four additional *Pegasus* flights. With that backlog, Orbital is now managing *Pegasus*'s transition from development to production.

45   Orbital's second space-launch vehicle incorporates the core technology used in developing *Pegasus* to develop *Taurus*, a ground-launched vehicle capable of deploying payloads of up to 3,000 pounds to low-Earth orbits and 800 pounds to geosynchronous orbits. *Taurus*'s first launch is scheduled for 1992 under contract to the Department of Defense, which has options for four additional launches.

46   Orbital's Space Data Division in Arizona is the major industrial supplier of suborbital-launch vehicles in the United States. Boosters range from extremely small to over 60 feet in length, and they place payloads in a variety of trajectories up to 500 miles. Orbital conducted six launches of suborbital vehicles for five customers in 1990, and has more than 50 such launches under contract with government, commercial, and educational customers.

47   Orbital's first project, the transfer orbit vehicle (TOS), continues to provide a potential vehicle to transfer payloads upward from low Earth orbits. The first two TOS vehicles are now nearing completion. Missions are now scheduled for 1992. Follow-up opportunities are being explored.

48   Orbital is exploring the possibilities of marketing a multipurpose small satellite platform. Such a device would contain guidance and control, power supply, and communication and data systems for both its launch vehicle and its payload. This eliminates duplication between satellite and launch vehicle, eliminating some costs and allowing the launching of heavier payloads. This platform, called *PegaStar,* is now in the development phase, and it has been selected for two contracts with NASA and the U.S. Air Force. Orbital also expects to use *PegaStar* in many of its own activities.

49   Orbital has utilized its experience in space systems design and production to produce a variety of special purpose high-tech payloads for use in space missions. For example, Orbital has provided pointing and tracking systems for instruments carried by the space shuttle.

50   Orbital develops and manufactures a number of support products for space systems. For example, Orbital supplies devices for studying the Earth's upper atmosphere for meteorological or environmental purposes. Other products include tracking and communication devices.

51   During 1990, Orbital pursued the idea of combining its core products into complete systems. For example, *Pegasus* and *Taurus* rockets might be used in conjunction with *PegaStar* spacecraft and other hardware to provide complete mobile satellite communications systems or complete environmental monitoring systems.

INDUSTRY

52   Historically, the space industry has been highly concentrated in the hands of major defense contractors. Typically, these contractors handled high-budget, long time frame, extremely complex systems. Orbital represents a revolution in the business of space: toward relatively cheap, flexible, quick-response systems to handle a wide variety of potential customers' needs.

53   Following Orbital's lead have come a number of new competitors, to join the few small space companies that survived the late 1980s. Large established companies with space interests also are attempting to enter the new market for small space systems.

54   A significant portion of that market—that supported by defense budgets—may be shrinking. However, that loss may be more than offset by the entry of new customers now able to afford space technology.

ORBITAL'S BUSINESS STRATEGY

55   David Thompson likens the changes occurring in the space industry to those that occurred in the computer industry following the introduction of the first microcomputers in the late 1970s. Before the advent of microcomputers, few could afford the processing power contained in large clumsy mainframes. Microcomputers made processing power financially feasible for a much larger group of consumers. David believes that a similar revolution is occurring in the space business. Says David:

56   We might properly adopt the term *microspace* to describe spaceborne systems that exhibit a level of affordability and ease of use that makes them attractive to a much larger and more diverse customer base. Often, these same characteristics allow them to be designed and produced in larger quantities by a more heterogeneous industry than has been the case in the past. In this vision of microspace, ownership and use of space systems will involve many nontraditional customers: first time users among Federal and state Government agencies, much larger numbers of private businesses and academic institutions and, eventually, a nontrivial fraction of the population of individual consumers.[16]

57   Given this definition of their market and business, Orbital follows three basic business strategies. First, it targets high-growth niches in the space market that demand innovative, lower-cost products and services. These niches may be fostered by technological advances that allow lower cost products and services, as well as increased cost consciousness by customers.

58   Second, Orbital attempts to control costs through synergies between its product lines and building on its own past development and production experiences. Third, Orbital sees opportunity in combining its own products to create viable end-to-end space systems.

---

[16] David W. Thompson, "The Advent of Microspace Systems," brochure published by Orbital Sciences Corporation, Fairfax, Va., p. 2.

59   Orbital is committed to maintaining its rapid growth. Between January and April of 1991, Orbital landed five contracts worth $140 million.[17] This has resulted in a significant push to hire the new employees needed to fulfill the obligations.

60   David sees the future growth of the company to be a combination of public and private business. In 1988, 80 percent of Orbital's revenues derived from government contracts. While David believes that this portion of the market will continue to grow, he believes that more rapid growth will occur in the commercial side. In 1989, he predicted that within three to four years Orbital's revenues would reflect a 50 to 60 percent commercial proportion.[18]

61   David sees a bright future for the business. He sees a growing market for personal, mobile communications systems that operate worldwide. He sees satellites providing navigation information for railroads, ships, and trucks. He sees the possibility of using space for manufacturing in conditions of weightlessness and high vacuum. Further in the future lies another dream: carrying passengers into space.[19]

CHANGES AT ORBITAL

62   One major change at Orbital in 1991 was the major and rapid staffing-up effort that had been taking place in the last six months. With five major contracts landed in the last four months, many new engineers and other technical personnel have been brought on board. The manager of engineering is now spending 50 percent of his time interviewing, with attention to hiring those persons who will be middle managers for Orbital in 10 years when the company is much larger.

63   Working at Orbital is changing. In the past, everyone knew everyone else; now, when one walked the halls, employees frequently saw other employees they didn't know. Some senior employees noted that new employees often took off work at 5:00. Barbara Zadina recalled talking with the president of Orbital's Space Systems Division two days previously: "It'll never be the same," he said. "Those days are gone. But it was a great time!"[20]

64   Changes were less evident at corporate headquarters than in other locations, because corporate staff hadn't increased at the same pace as the engineering groups. Still, the corporation could no longer provide lunches on Fridays, and the atmosphere was subtly different.

CONCERNS FOR THE FUTURE

65   David took a few moments from his hectic schedule to contemplate his organization. Would Orbital be able to handle the challenges of the next few years?

66   One issue that concerned him was the changing atmosphere at Orbital. He no longer remembered all Orbital's employees, despite his efforts to meet everyone at orientation sessions. Were the new employees less excited about working on Orbital's projects, as some of his more senior people seemed to think?

67   David also projected an increase in the size of his corporate headquarters staff in the next few years. Would he be able to stay as closely involved with the work as he liked?

68   With both these changes, how could he assure himself that Orbital was operating as it should?

---

[17] Stan Hinden, "Orbital's Stock Flies to New Highs on Air Force Wings," *Washington Post,* April 22, 1991.

[18] Perry, p. 11.

[19] Perry, p. 11.

[20] Quoted by Barbara Zadina, personal interview, June 8, 1991.

APPENDIX A

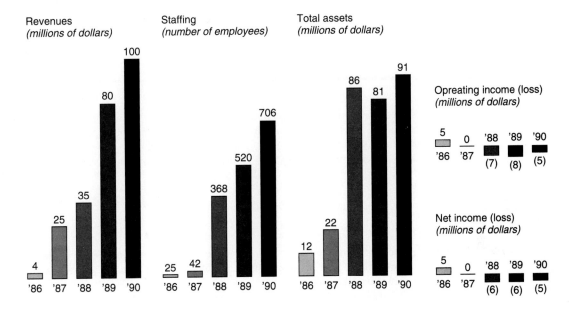

Revenues
(millions of dollars)

Staffing
(number of employees)

Total assets
(millions of dollars)

Opreating income (loss)
(millions of dollars)

Net income (loss)
(millions of dollars)

CASE 22

SYSTEMS CENTER, INC.

1   In 1991, SCI's director of international agent operations, Gillian Parrillo, was assigned the task of deciding whether to allow SCI's marketing in Italy to be handled by a well-connected and productive agent or by an overseas subsidiary already partly established and promised to some of SCI's current customers. Parrillo reflected on the company's history and international successes in helping her decide.

COMPANY BACKGROUND

2   Systems Center, Inc. (SCI), was founded in Reston, Virginia, in 1981 to design, develop, market, and support software products for IBM and compatible mainframe computers running the virtual memory (VM) operating environment.

3   By 1988, SCI's mainstay business was its systems software, which enabled a programmer to automatically control and manage the resources of a computer system. Such software was in contrast to applications software, which assisted the user directly by performing specific tasks, such as reconciling accounts receivable, preparing graphics, or providing computer-aided instruction. Most software manufacturers focused on the production of application software, since this sector of the market grew in concert with the rapidly developing personal computer market.

4   As software services became more comprehensive and sophisticated, the efficiency of user operations and integrity of data were of paramount importance. SCI offered an integrated set of software products that assisted data center managers of VM operating systems in administering and protecting system resources, while streamlining data center operations. The software package included an operating foundation, or basic product, that served as the link for additional modules or products. The addition of such products enhanced the software's basic capabilities. Focusing on providing services specifically for VM operating systems proved to be a very successful niche for SCI.

5   The company continued to pursue a niche strategy, with respect to market development, and experienced little competition in its chosen markets. Through the decade, SCI achieved tremendous growth by penetrating markets worldwide. The company's revenues increased from $400,000 in 1981 to over $66 million in 1989. International sales quadrupled in four years, from $4.1 million in 1985 to $16.0 million in 1989, and, in 1990, were projected to reach 50 percent of the total revenue base. SCI's product quality and highly rated service were instrumental in the growth of the company's export business. Exhibit 1 gives a three-year financial summary of SCI and provides details of the company's financial strength.

6   SCI received national acclaim for its accomplishments as an exporter. In 1990, SCI earned the U.S. Department of Commerce's President "E" Award for exporting, in recognition of a decade of success in international trade. The President's "E" Award is the nation's most prestigious export achievement honor. Created in 1961 by an executive order of President John F. Kennedy, it is designed to give

This case was prepared by John A. Pearce II of the School of Business Administration at George Mason University with the assistance of Kelly S. Nix. Development of this case was made possible by a grant from the Funds for Excellence Program of the State Council of Higher Education for Virginia. This case is distributed by the North American Case Research Association.

EXHIBIT 1

SYSTEMS CENTER, INC.
Consolidated Statements of Income

	Year Ended December 31		
	1989	1988	1987
Net revenues:			
Software products	$45,873,733	$36,776,558	$25,484,508
Product support & enhancements	20,363,789	14,906,242	10,511,846
Total net revenue	66,237,522	51,682,800	35,996,354
Operating expenses:			
Sales and marketing	26,937,500	19,793,948	14,198,655
Research, development, & support	18,153,633	12,479,483	9,366,419
General and administrative	8,763,353	10,026,401	7,677,185
Total operating expenses	53,854,536	42,299,832	31,242,259
Income from operations	12,382,986	9,382,968	4,754,095
Interest income	1,408,128	1,026,884	728,252
Interest expense	(113,858)	(115,697)	(15,099)
Income before income taxes, extraordinary item, & cumulative effect of accounting change	13,677,256	10,254,155	5,467,248
Provision for income taxes	(3,692,859)	(3,265,717)	(1,663,949)
Income before extraordinary item and cumulative effect of accounting change	9,984,397	6,988,438	3,803,299
Extraordinary item-utilization of net operating loss carryforward	—	420,072	203,751
Cumulative effect of change in method of accounting for income taxes	639,586	—	—
Net income	$10,623,983	$ 7,408,510	$ 4,007,050
Earnings per share:			
Income before extraordinary item and cumulative effect of accounting change	$1.25	$0.92	$0.51
Extraordinary item-utilization of net operating loss carryforward	—	0.06	0.03
Cumulative effect of change in method of accounting for income taxes	0.08	—	—
Net income	1.33	—	—
Weighted average shares and common equivalent shares outstanding	8,000,000	7,564,000	7,453,000

special recognition to those outstanding companies and individuals who excelled in the effort to increase United States exports. The "E" award, which stands for excellence, expansion, effort, and exports, symbolized the finest in American commerce, and was a reflection of the ever increasing importance of the global marketplace.

7   Also in 1990, SCI faced a pivotal strategic decision—should marketing for its trade in Italy be handled by the overseas subsidiary or an independent agency. While each option involved financial opportunities and risks, cultural and ethical considerations were complicating influences on the ultimate decision.

THE COMPUTER SOFTWARE INDUSTRY

8   In the 1980s, the computer industry underwent a dynamic evolution. While the cost of computer equipment continued to decrease, labor costs were ever-increasing worldwide. Equally critical to the transformation of the computer industry was the expanded role of software. Originally, the term *software* applied to the computer programs that instruct the computer to perform a specific, useful task. However, as the computer industry became more sophisticated, software began to include not only the properly customized programs, but also training services, reference manuals, troubleshooters, and even the repairman who made physical repairs to the computer. In essence, software included all of the means necessary for providing the continuous changes that kept the computer system productive.

9   Historically, large computer manufacturers were the sole suppliers of software services, combining their hardware and software with a package price. Often, the software was custom-made to meet the individual requirements of a client. However, as the capabilities of software expanded, the cost of providing service became too expensive to hide in the declining price of hardware. Consequently, software sales were taken from under the hardware umbrella so higher prices could be charged and greater profits made. This dramatic shift was pivotal in reshaping the industry, because it opened the door for thousands of small, independent software suppliers to enter the market.

10   As the software industry developed, most of the large computer equipment manufacturers decided not to become actively involved in the development of software for their systems. Hardware equipment and software services increasingly were viewed as separate entities, requiring entirely different strategic postures. Some equipment conglomerates, such as IBM, helped their programmers set up independent software houses and then proceeded to pass contracts to them when hardware sales were made. Other programmers were not so fortunate and simply found themselves out of a job.

11   The dramatic growth in the number of software firms caused intense competition. Firms that had relied primarily on a single product for revenue now attempted to decrease their risks of program obsolescence and vulnerability to competitors by increasing the number of software packages offered. Their expansions into broader product lines and into specific product niches often were accomplished through merger and acquisition, sometimes on an international scale.

FOREIGN EXPANSION: THE NEED FOR SUBSIDIARIES OR AGENTS

12   SCI had entered the export marketplace in 1982 through the sale of its products to multinational companies. Although the software was purchased in the United States, multinational companies installed these products in both their U.S. and overseas operations. Dedicated to providing superior support to its clients, SCI began to recruit international agents to provide technical support to these clients on a local basis.

13   Typically, businesses in the software industry used agents for international marketing and sales. These agents were independent businesses that often represented several competing computer companies. They were not employees of the software companies but operated on a contract basis. The contracts specified pricing for the product, credit and financial policies, promotional services, and payment, and outlined the commission agreement. All of SCI's agents were paid 50 percent commissions on product sales.

14   The independent agents provided low capitalization cost and a low-risk means of penetrating international markets. They did not take title of the goods but simply obtained orders for SCI's products. However, they did provide their personal contacts, distribution channels, promotional campaigns, and their unique knowledge of the local markets.

15   Nevertheless, persuading agents to give sales emphasis to particular software was a challenging task. Agents had their own business agendas, preferring software providers who offered special technical support, marketing promotions, and profit margins of each of the multiple product lines that they carried. Agents were reluctant to concentrate on a single company's product line, out of concern that the company in question could experience a takeover, financial difficulty, or product obsolescence. Thus, providing better overall service and practical sales assistance became SCI management's priorities, as they attempted to build a marketing network by enticing agents to spend time selling SCI products.

16   In 1986, SCI opened its first subsidiary in the United Kingdom (U.K.) when it purchased the regional agent's portion of VM software products. The decision to make the direct investment resulted from problems that SCI had identified within the U.K. territory. The agent had not committed the time and money necessary to attend SCI training seminars, and, as a result, SCI experienced difficulty in providing consistent support to its overseas customers. The potential for the U.K.'s customer base had increased tremendously. This growth made it difficult for the agent to simultaneously service existing clients and pursue new ones.

17   SCI's direct subsidiaries were controlled by the U.S.-based parent company, and they existed to devote the time, effort, and manpower necessary to provide consistent selling and technical support for SCI's products. Improved cash flow expanded the start-up and additional overhead costs of these subsidiaries. Subsequently, subsidiaries were opened in Germany, France, and Sweden.

18   As revenues, territories, and the number of subsidiaries grew, SCI separated the management of its direct foreign sales from that of its international agent operations. Subsidiaries were operated as profit centers responsible for both the costs and profits associated with their respective operation, while agent operations were handled solely as revenue centers.

19   SCI employed foreign nationals to run its overseas operations. International communications were complex and likely to be misunderstood by U.S. personnel. Foreign nationals avoided the problems that resulted from language barriers, and they brought to negotiations both a unique understanding of their national market and an extensive list of local contacts. Local management played an important role in employee morale as well, because many subsidiary employees preferred to work for someone from their own country. Finally, since company workers who transferred to subsidiaries usually expected to be there only a few years, local nationals often provided the continuity required for the completion of long-term objectives.

20   In 1988, SCI opened sales offices in Holland and Belgium. Much like the situation that had preceded the company's first subsidiary opening in the U.K., the agent responsible for sales in Holland and Belgium abandoned his operation in these two areas and offered SCI the opportunity to assume them. SCI decided that it would be more advantageous to maintain the existing operations than to locate and train a new agent. However, because the company already had three subsidiaries in Europe, it determined that no additional benefits would be gained, either to European customers or SCI, in establishing another. Therefore, SCI decided to allow sales personnel to operate these offices, with support from the United Kingdom subsidiary. The 1990 organization chart in Exhibit 2 reflects the structural division.

21   The decision to open a sales office, as opposed to creating a new subsidiary or soliciting a new agent, was based on the perceived size and estimated return of a given market, versus the cost of establishing a subsidiary. If the market and the potential warranted additional sales support, and the estimated return outweighed the potential costs, then a new subsidiary or sales office was established. Once the decision to open a subsidiary or sales office was made, and the agent agreements for that territory dissolved, the Direct European Sales Division took over management.

EXHIBIT 2
Systems Center Organization Chart

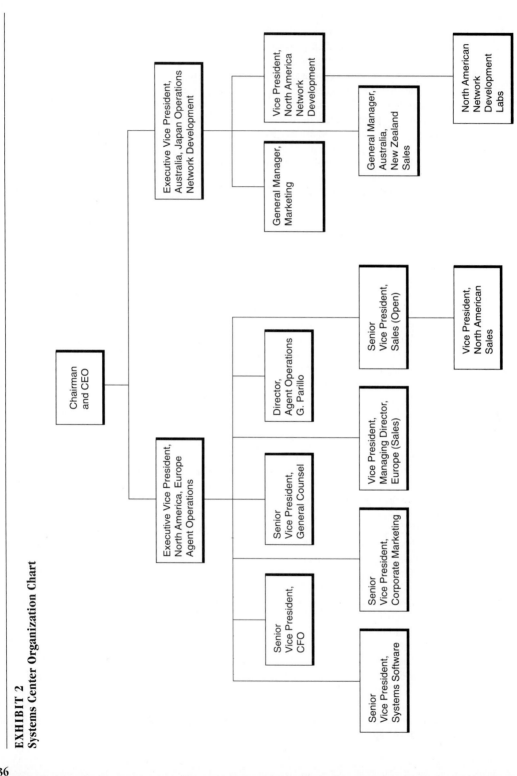

EXHIBIT 3
Systems Center, Inc.
Organizational Profitability Analysis, 1989

	Direct Sales Representatives		European Agents
	N. American	European Subsidiaries	
Sales reps	56	37	N.A.
New licenses sales/rep	$494,000	$468,000	N.A.
Total in sales org.	112	169	19
New licenses sales/person	$247,000	$102,000	$185,000
Total net/revenue sales/person*	$445,000	$173,000	$237,000†
Commission base	12–15%	12–15%	50%

*Commission was subtracted from gross revenue/sales to arrive at a normalized net revenue/sales figure.
†This figure represents sales per person in the international agent operations department.
N.A. means not available.

22   Due to escalating overhead costs, the performance of foreign subsidiaries and sales offices was not as profitable as anticipated in 1989. The foreign direct sales facilities were too new and grew too fast for the company to control costs in the short run. However, analysis of the problem was ongoing, and SCI was confident that the direct sales operation would be competitive, once corrective action was implemented. Exhibit 3 provides profitability statistics for SCI's European agents and the company's direct sales representatives in the United States and in Europe.

THE ITALIAN MARKET

23   SCI estimated the market potential of VM software in Italy to be 3.2 percent of the company's worldwide sales. However, 1989 actuals found that the two Italian agents had underperformed, achieving only 2.8 percent. Due to their marginal performance, SCI decided to sever its relationship with the agents and establish its fourth European subsidiary in Italy. SCI thought that sales representatives working for a subsidiary would have a greater chance at realizing SCI's full market potential, and it set the date of April 1, 1990, for the opening of the new subsidiary.

24   The transition from independent agents to company subsidiary was a normal progression in the life cycle of the software industry firm. Most software companies penetrated the international market through the use of agent operations. However, as the market grew and a solid revenue base was established, most firms, desiring greater control over product sales and service, opened direct subsidiaries or foreign sales offices.

25   In early 1990, Gillian Parrillo, director of SCI's international agent operations, contacted the independent agents in Italy and informed them of the company's decision. The company's customer base also was notified of the change. The agents were to continue selling the VM product line until the new subsidiary opened. All communications stressed that the new sales arrangement was necessary to better meet customer needs.

26   At the same time, SCI entered into an 18-month lease agreement in Italy, thereby securing a location for their operation. They hired and trained a general manager and a business manager to support the venture, and they extended offers to a technical manager and a secretary.

PRODUCT EXPANSION

27 Throughout the 1980s, the computer industry experienced rapid change and innovation. As a result, the playing field was littered with the remains of both small and large firms that failed to predict or respond correctly to shifting market demands. SCI remained an active competitor because of its growth through the development and acquisition of quality products.

28 In 1988, the company expanded its product line by acquiring network administration products to aid in the movement of data between different types of hardware processors. With these expansions, SCI offered a total of 26 computer software products in three different product lines and further lessened the company's risk against product obsolescence.

29 In 1989 and early 1990, VM sales continued to grow. However, SCI's executives felt that most of their market territories were near saturation. SCI's VM penetration in some markets ran as high as 70 percent, leaving little room for growth in the VM product line. Industrywide, sales of VM software were projected to decline annually at a rate of 5 to 8 percent as the market reached maturity.

30 In a major strategic initiative designed to sustain the company's growth pattern, SCI acquired an Australian company, Software Developments International (SDI), and with it worldwide marketing rights for its innovative products from Cincom Systems in 1990. SDI produced a software product line called Net/Master, which provided network and systems management for large IBM mainframes. The product's unique capabilities allow it to manage, from a central location, networks of multiple vendors' mainframes connected to a system. Net/Master was recognized as the premier software for mainframe computer networking in the industry. The acquisition included the worldwide marketing rights for the product line, in addition to the company that manufactured the network software.

31 The acquisition provided two added benefits to SCI's international operations: market leverage and superior agents. IBM's NetView was Net/Master's main competition. NetView achieved greater sales in the United States, but Net/Master performed better in Europe and Asia. Net/Master's superior performance in markets outside the United States was attributed to the quality of the product and the expertise of the independent sales agents. Under the terms of the sales agreement, the independent agents representing Net/Master were to continue selling the product for SCI. The acquisition gave SCI an additional 21 agents, increasing its total to 40. The agents' knowledge of national markets had tremendous influence in local communities. In addition, the agents had a keen understanding of the Net/Master product, and they were able to provide continuing technical service to customers, both before and after the sales.

32 The acquisition agreement required SCI to honor the existing agent agreements with all of the Net/Master agents through 1990. However, it was understood by all parties involved that the Net/Master agents' relationship with SCI would be reevaluated at the end of the year, and every effort would be made to consolidate the agents at that time. It was Parrillo's responsibility to evaluate and integrate the Net/Master agents into SCI's agent operations.

33 Parrillo decided that, except in countries where SCI had an existing subsidiary or sales office territory, she would incorporate new agents into SCI's existing agent distribution channel. In some cases, Net/Master agents already carried the VM software product line. In these situations, she made no changes in the distribution system, and operations continued as before. In other cases, when the two products were carried by different agents in the same territory, she found the consolidation to be quite complicated. She would either allow the agents to continue selling independent of one another or, if one of the two was performing poorly, she would discontinue SCI's relationship with the underachiever and allow the remaining agent to sell both products.

34 In situations where Net/Master territories overlapped those of already existing SCI subsidiaries or sales offices, she terminated agent agreements. She reasoned that to carry both a subsidiary/sales office and an agent in the same territory would not be cost effective. Additionally, agents often had an established clientele base for a variety of software vendors, and hiring them exclusively for SCI was

not an option. The following is a list of the locations of agent operations after consolidation was completed:

Latin America	Southern Europe/Middle East	Asia Pacific
Mexico	Spain	Singapore
Central America	Portugal	Hong Kong
Venezuela	Turkey	Taiwan
Brazil	Greece	Korea
Ecuador	Yugoslavia	Philippines
Argentina	Finland	Indonesia
Peru	Israel	Thailand
Colombia	Saudi Arabia	Malaysia
Chile		Australia

35   The pending Italian subsidiary offered an entirely unique situation. When Parrillo analyzed the Net/Master agent's sales history, she concluded that the Italian agent's performance was outstanding. This agent was the product line's best salesman, in terms of both profit and volume. His sales represented 30 percent of SCI's total worldwide Net/Master revenue from agent sales.

36   With such a strong performance record, Parrillo was hesitant to terminate the Italian agent's sales agreement. Since the Italian subsidiary had not yet opened, it was unclear to both Parrillo and to the director of European subsidiaries and direct sales exactly to whom the territory should be assigned.

PRODUCT PERFORMANCE

37   In 1989, new license revenue of the independent agents, which was the revenue attributable to new customers, was $1.3 million. In 1990, with the addition of the Net/Master product line, new license revenue was projected to reach $4.8 million. VM software sales were to account for approximately $1.90 million, while Net/Master sales were projected at $1.86 million. The remaining $1.04 million was attributed to some of SCI's smaller products.

38   As of January 1, 1990, SCI's international agent operations had 187 Net/Master installations within agent territories. SCI analysts estimated that as many as 30,000 to 35,000 mainframe systems were in use around the world. Each system was a potential customer for the Net/Master product line. Given these projections, sales of the Net/Master line were expected to grow at a rate of 30 to 35 percent annually.

39   The initial sale price for both the VM software and Net/Master products ranged from $20,000 to $25,000. Once the initial setup for either product line had been purchased, additional modules could be added to enhance the software capabilities. Only a few such modules were available for the VM product line, but customers using the Net/Master products could purchase up to $150,000 worth of additional modules.

THE DECISION

40   An exchange between Parrillo and her boss highlighted key issues in the pending decision. His main concern: "We have already made a substantial investment in personnel and office setup. In addition, the escape clause built into the employment contracts of the two managers, already hired for the subsidiary, obligates SCI to pay $200,000 in compensation should their contracts be terminated."

"Those are important issues," Parrillo responded; "on the other hand, the offers extended to the technical manager and secretary have not yet been accepted, and SCI has no obligation to either individual. However, we are committed to paying $150,000 in rental fees on the 18-month office lease."

41   Parrillo was concerned about the effect that canceling the subsidiary operation would have on the company's reputation within the Italian business community. Italian culture was based on pride, honor, and commitment, and the fact that SCI had entered into a legally binding contract could not be taken lightly. Parrillo was certain that the cancellation of the contract would be closely examined within Italian business circles from an ethical standpoint.

42   Even if the Italian market could best be served through the current Net/Master agent, the potential for an adverse effect on future sales had to be considered. The two managers hired for the subsidiary had been selected for their standing and connections within the Italian market. If SCI closed the Italian subsidiary, the corporate reputation would be at stake. Given the managers' influence within the business community, future Net/Master sales could be severely threatened by a perception that SCI was an unfair and unethical company.

43   Even though there were valid reasons why plans for the Italian subsidiary should move forward, the arguments for utilizing the existing Net/Master agent in that market were equally compelling. His expertise and knowledge of the Net/Master product line, as well as his familiarity with the Italian market, were evident by his extraordinary sales record. Since Net/Master product sales in Italy were projected to reach 5.4 percent of the company's worldwide sales in 1990, or approximately $5.7 million, Parrillo had to weigh the importance of continuing the company relationship with a proven Net/Master agent.

44   To further cloud the situation, a certain amount of office politics came into play, because both the agent and the subsidiary management team offered specific sales projections in support of their respective recommendations. The director of subsidiary sales projected a 379 percent increase in sales for the following year, should the subsidiary be allowed to service the territory. Parrillo felt that this figure was extremely inflated and impossible to achieve, with sales representatives who had no prior experience selling the Net/Master product line. Parrillo felt that, should the Net/Master agent be retained, a 25 percent increase in sales was realistic. Exhibit 4 is a copy of correspondence from Parrillo to the senior vice president of North American/European sales and international agent operations concerning the Italian sales projections for both subsidiary and agent operations for 1990.

45   Parrillo also considered the possibility of having the agent continue selling the Net/Master line, while the new subsidiary took control of the VM software products. However, such an arrangement would be cost ineffective, due to the duplication of services and resources.

46   As a final consideration, Parrillo could not overlook the effect that any change in plans might have on SCI's customer base. There were already over 100 Net/Master clients in Italy, and each relationship had been established through the current Italian Net/Master agent. Her decision was not simply an economic one. The decision to be made would require the evaluation of economic, ethical, and behavioral aspects of the situation, to determine the one best way to serve the rapidly growing Italian market.

EXHIBIT 4
Parrillo Memorandum

M E M O R A N D U M

To: The Senior VP of North American/European Sales and
      International Agent Operations
From: Gillian Parrillo
Re: 1990 Italian Budget

Below you will find my proposal for a revenue budget for Italy. The numbers are 284% below Stuart's budgets, respectively, but I think that you can see in the analysis that follows that those budgeted numbers have no reasonable basis. While a subsidiary office has historically done better than its predecessor agency, a 379 percent year-over-year increase is not a justified expectation.

Comparative Growth Analysis

	1989 Actual	Subsidiary 1990 Budget	Percent Increase over 1989	Agency 1990 Budget	Percent Increase over 1989
New licenses	$795,000	$3,806,000	379%	$990,400	25%
Yearly renewals	364,500	724,600	99	630,667	73

I don't believe that any SCI venture, domestic or international, has experienced a 379 percent increase year to year. My belief is that a case was being built for opening a subsidiary, and perhaps an overly aggressive projection was used.

CASE 23

BASF'S PROPOSED PAINT PLANT: A COMMUNITY'S REACTION

INTRODUCTION

1   In early 1988, BASF Corporation, a member of the international German-based BASF Group, released plans for a five-year $2 billion capital expansion program. BASF Corporation is one of the larg-
est chemical companies in North America. In 1988, net sales equalled $5 billion while net income
amounted to $149 million. Nearly 22,000 people are employed by the four divisions of BASF Corpo-
ration. Its diversified product mix includes the following: basic, intermediate, and specialty chemicals,
colorants, dispersions, fiber raw materials, fibers, automotive coatings, printing inks, urethane specialties and chemicals, plastics, advanced composite materials, antifreezes, crop protection products,
pharmeceuticals, vitamins, fragrances, and audio, video, and computer recording media.

2   On March 10, 1988, BASF officials announced that the company intended to build a manufacturing facility somewhere in the American Midwest. Three cities were selected as finalists: Terre Haute,
Indiana (located in Vigo County); Evansville, Indiana; and Portsmouth, Ohio. Terre Haute's drawing
card was an undeveloped county industrial park comprised of 1,476 acres of land. Terre Haute has a
population of roughly 57,483 and is located in the west central part of Indiana. As a community, Terre
Haute was in dire need of expanded employment opportunities, since several major companies had
exited the area over the past decade. Statistics published by the local chamber of commerce showed
that, between 1970–1987, the community suffered a net loss of 6,062 jobs. However, data published
by the local Democratic Party reported that 4,125 new jobs had been created in the community between 1986–91. During this same time span, new capital investment amounted to $729.5 million.

3   On March 28, 1988, the Vigo County commissioners signed a licensing agreement with BASF, allowing the company to inspect and conduct soil tests at the county's industrial park located south of
Terre Haute. Approximately a month later, BASF released more precise information, regarding the nature of the plant facility. Tentative plans called for a $150 million automotive paint plant that would
employ approximately 500 local people. This projected economic infusion encouraged city and county government officials to court BASF Corporation. In mid-June, an entourage of local government
officials and business leaders visited a BASF plant in Gainsville, Ohio. On July 6, 1988, BASF
announced that the soil tests at the industrial park were positive and that the company was initiating
procedures to "option" land at the Vigo County industrial park. Further discussion between company
and county government officials revealed that a small 30 acre parcel of land within the industrial park
was still owned by the federal government. BASF stressed that the company would need this 30 acres
to develop its plant operations. The Vigo County commissioners eventually purchased this acreage
from the General Services Administration to accommodate BASF.

This case was prepared by Professor Max E. Douglas of Indiana State University

EXHIBIT 1
Summary of Jim Shank's Concerns about the Environmental
Impact of BASF's Incinerator/Landfill Proposal

1. BASF would be exempt from local property taxes on its waste disposal operations; hence, Vigo County taxpayers would, in effect, be subsidizing the BASF toxic waste operation.

2. Vigo County would be importing, processing, and storing toxic wastes from other BASF plants whose host communities are allowed to enjoy the economic benefits of higher payroll and corporate property tax contributions while suffering none of the dangers associated with BASF effluents.

3. Initially it is projected that BASF would process 36 million pounds of hazardous waste annually. Transportation of these toxic wastes into Vigo County by truck or railroad will create a great risk, because of the deadly danger of accidental spills.

4. Independent environmental experts seemingly agree that toxic waste incineration can be a health hazard, particularly since the county's prevailing wind direction would carry emissions over large and unpredictable parts of the community.

5. Infusion of toxic substances into the underground water supply is also a probability, because the clay and plastic barriers used in the dump site will eventually leak.

6. BASF's toxic waste operation would adversely affect the county's attractiveness to other industry. Environmental disasters associated with toxic waste disposal—such as Hooker Chemical's Love Canal, Valsicol Chemical's Marshall, Illinois, plant, and Union Carbide's Bhopal, India, factory—have left some communities environmentally crippled.

Source: Personal letter received by the author, November 10, 1988.

CONTROVERSY DEVELOPS

4   On August 10, 1988, Jack Wehman, Midwest venture director for BASF, announced that the company planned to build a hazardous waste incinerator and establish a landfill in addition to building its paint manufacturing plant. The proposed incinerator and landfill would handle on-site wastes and imported wastes trucked to the site from other BASF plants. Following this news release, Evansville mayor Frank McDonald indicated that his city would no longer pursue the BASF plant. Terre Haute mayor Pete Chalos and Portsmouth mayor Roger Bussey indicated that their communities were still positive about the BASF plant regardless of the implications of the incinerator and landfill.

5   In contrast to the favorable reception of the August 10 BASF announcement by Terre Haute's mayor and other BASF supporters, a local community action group, Citizens for a Clean County (CCC), organized to begin an anti-BASF campaign. The initial purpose of the CCC was to stop BASF from building the waste treatment facility on the site and from importing waste to the incinerator/landfill. The CCC eventually became the primary opponent to BASF, although other BASF adversaries expressed their opposition to the importation of toxic wastes. For example, one local entrepreneur, Jim Shanks, mailed out 8,000 letters and petitions to Vigo County residents living in the southern and eastern parts of the county, enlisting their opposition to BASF. A summary of his concerns regarding the environmental impact of BASF's incinerator/landfill proposal is shown in Exhibit 1.

6   In reaction to the growing anti-BASF sentiment, BASF Corporation hired Fleishman Hilliard, a St. Louis opinion research firm, to conduct community focus groups to solicit views about the proposed automotive paint plant, hazardous waste incinerator, and landfill. In addition, BASF launched a letter-writing campaign to reach local citizens, intended to help defuse controversy over the proposed paint plant and waste management facility. In these letters, BASF officials stressed the economic benefits of the plant to the community and BASF's concern for the environmental impact of its proposed facility. A summary of these benefits/concerns is provided in Exhibit 2.

EXHIBIT 2
**Summary of Benefits to Vigo County Accruing from the Proposed Location
of BASF's Paint Plant Facility**

1. Economic Advantages:
   (a) Immediate capital investment of $150 million in community compounded by future plant construction.
   (b) Five hundred skilled jobs with at least 400 hired locally; these assignments will be quality jobs with competitive wages. BASF will offer a comprehensive employee benefits program.
   (c) Building of paint facility will create 3,500 new on-site/off-site construction jobs.
   (d) One thousand new jobs will be created in the initial plant and operations.
   (e) Estimated spill-over of tens of millions of dollars into all sectors of the economy.
   (f) A significantly expanded tax base that will benefit all public supported institutions such as schools, libraries, etcetera.
   (g) Infrastructure of community will be enhanced by improved road systems, utilities, and airport expansion.

2. Environmental Advantages:
   (a) About 200 acres in the southwest corner of the site would be maintained as a wildlife preserve in concert with BASF's positive attitude towards environmental quality.
   (b) Less than 25 acres will be required for permanent storage of BASF wastes over the next 25 years. Based on projected new technology, BASF estimates that a maximum of 50 acres will be used for waste storage over the next century.
   (c) BASF will treat and dispose *only* BASF wastes. BASF is not a commercial waste treatment company and will not become one.
   (d) BASF will build a high-tech incinerator system to treat certain waste materials. Gases from incineration process will be cleaned in a five-step purification process before discharge. Incineration produces *no* odors and poses *no* health hazards.
   (e) Incineration system has *no* liquid discharges, only clean gases and disposable ash. Volume of waste is reduced by 90 percent and the toxic nature of the waste is destroyed.
   (f) BASF will *not* burn or dispose of PCBs or radioactive wastes; no dioxin will be handled.
   (g) BASF plans to construct and monitor an *above-ground* hazardous waste landfill for disposal of certain solid wastes, including ash.
   (h) No liquids will be placed in the landfill. The active use area will be shielded by a portable roof, preventing rain and snow from entering the storage cells.
   (i) Contamination of ground water will be prevented by the use of natural and synthetic barriers.
   (j) BASF will temporarily import wastes from other BASF plants until the plant site is totally developed. As more plants come on line, the processing of outside BASF wastes will diminish.
   (k) BASF estimates that 20 truckloads of raw materials, finished products, and waste materials will move along Indiana Route 41. Proper training and modern equipment will ensure safe transportation.

Sources: Personal letters received by the author on November 21, 1988; December 7, 1988; and December 28, 1988.

ECONOMIC DEVELOPMENT PLAN STIRS PUBLIC DEBATE

7   While this controversy was dominating the community news, local governmental officials continued to pursue a plan for economic development of the industrial park. The Vigo County council created the Vigo County Redevelopment Commission to oversee development of the 1,506 acre industrial park. The county redevelopment commission hired the Terre Haute department of redevelopment to draw up a detailed economic development plan for the industrial park. The existence of an economic development plan for the park was a prerequisite for federal funds to underwrite the development of

infrastructure, such as sewer and water lines. The final economic development plan proposal called for $6 million in improvements to the property to make it suitable for industrial development. On November 28, 1988, the Vigo County Redevelopment Commission declared that the industrial park was an economic development and tax allocation area, despite opposition from area residents. Following this official declaration, the redevelopment commission submitted the proposed economic development plan to the Vigo County Area Planning Commission. The area planning commission was charged with determining whether the proposed economic development plan conformed with the comprehensive land usage plan for the entire county. On December 7, 1988, a public meeting at a local high school was conducted by the area planning commission. Despite much opposition from the audience, the economic development plan was approved by *this* commission 11–3.

8   Following this vote of approval by the area planning commission, the redevelopment commission scheduled public hearings on the industrial park economic development plan. Some 30 hours of testimony were heard over three days. Spearheading the anti-BASF forces was the Citizens for a Clean Community. Members of the CCC hired outside consultants to speak at the hearings.

9   One spokesperson, Hugh Kaufman, an employee of the Environmental Protection Agency, expressed concerns about the BASF incineration/hazardous waste landfill proposal. According to Kaufman, hazardous waste facilities inhibit industrial and economic growth, rather than promote it. Costs and burdens fall on local governments, which may have additional liabilities if waste from incinerators enters public water and sewage systems. Kaufman further stressed that increased industrial traffic and repairs, chemical spills, and the expanded need for continual training of emergency response teams add additional concerns and costs for taxpayers.

10   Environmental issues raised by Hugh Kaufman have become a priority concern of the Chemical Manufacturers' Association. In 1985, the CMA started a Community Awareness and Response Program to encourage chemical companies to reexamine their emergency response programs. As part of these programs, an emergency planning committee is formed to determine the roles of various community groups, to evaluate risks, to develop and test crisis management plans, and to educate the public. These plans require that the targeted company share material safety data sheets to inform the citizenry about the chemicals the company uses. Community groups, physicians, and sundry emergency responders (fire departments, Red Cross) are normally key participants in this type of response program.

11   Another environmentalist, John Blair, gave testimony during the marathon hearings. Blair was being paid $125 per diem by the Oil, Chemical, and Atomic Workers local in Giesmar, Louisiana, to help promote opposition to the BASF plant. OCAW had been engaged in a bitter four-year lock-out with BASF at the Geismar plant. Blair said evidence suggests that BASF often acts in an immoral fashion. He claimed that BASF's real intentions were to locate a hazardous treatment plant, using the paint plant as a carrot. Blair further charged that the economic development plan under consideration had no enforcement provisions. Blair claimed that Terre Haute would become a "national sacrifice zone" if it began accepting hazardous waste from other areas.

12   In addition to the above "expert" testimony, several citizens presented personal position statements. One opponent, Eva Kor, a supervivor of Nazi Germany's World War II Auschwitz concentration camp, claimed that BASF was one of three companies formed out of the ashes of the German company I. G. Farben. Kor claimed that Farben used slave labor from the Auschwitz camp until "they were used up." She opposed BASF locating in Terre Haute and suggested a referendum be held to resolve the issue. Harold Cox, CCC member, reported that more than one half of the polled respondents in a local survey opposed a hazardous waste facility. Although in the minority, BASF supporters cited the tremendous economic boost that the company would provide for the community. In addition, BASF advocates labeled the CCC as a biased group more interested in protecting their property values than in stopping the importation of toxic waste. Nevertheless, the majority of statements presented during the 30 hours of public hearings conducted by the Vigo County Redevelopment Commission demonstrated opposition to the establishment of an incinerator and landfill adjacent to the automotive

paint plant as well as the importation of hazardous wastes from other BASF plants for disposal in Terre Haute.

13   Subsequent to the public hearings, the redevelopment commission reviewed all written testimony regarding the economic development plan. On January 19, 1989, the redevelopment commission conducted its final session to determine the fate of the proposed plan for the industrial park. One of the commissioners, Linda Burger, expressed concern that this plan would allow the importation of several truckloads of hazardous wastes into the community. Ms. Burger indicated further concern about the high cancer rates that already existed in Vigo County. Burger proposed an amendment to the economic development plan that would ban importation of toxic wastes into Vigo County. The amendment was rejected 3–2. The economic development plan finally was approved 4–1.

LEGAL ACTION TAKEN

14   Shortly following the approval of the economic development plan by the redevelopment commission, the CCC and 16 other people living near the industrial park filed a legal petition for judicial review against the redevelopment commission, the Vigo County commissioners, and Vigo County. The petition made the following charges:

15   1. The Economic Development Plan was adopted by using impermissible procedures alleged to be (*a*) inadequate notice of when the Redevelopment Commission would meet; (*b*) holding meetings in rooms too small to accommodate interested parties; (*c*) curtailment of public comment.

          2. The Redevelopment Commission was wrong to meet during regular business hours because that precluded some people from attending.

          3. Four out of five Commission members had conflicts of interest.

          4. The Economic Development Plan jeopardized the public health, safety, and welfare of the community.

16   Coinciding with the filing of the legal petition, by the CCC et al., was the public introduction of a BASF visitation team. The team consisted of employees from various areas of the company, such as human resources, operations, and plant safety. BASF provided biographical sketches of each member and indicated that they were sent to discuss the quality of work life at BASF and to share their experiences with the environmental safety of BASF at other plant locations. Jack Wehman, Midwest venture director for BASF, indicated that the presence of this team did not mean BASF had decided on Terre Haute. That decision, according to Wehman, depended on the outcome of the litigation over the industrial park. Wehman stressed that the visitation team's purpose was to gather and disseminate information pertaining to the proposed paint plant.

17   Shortly following CCC's legal petition and the arrival of BASF's visitation team, the mayor of Terre Haute, Pete Chalos, expressed displeasure that a legal petition had been filed to overturn the economic development plan for the county industrial park. Mayor Chalos stated:

18   I think that there are some people on the loose here that want to take us back 20 years and put Terre Haute in the position of being called an injunction city. I certainly hope cooler heads and wiser people take a leading role in making sure BASF comes here.

19   During March 1989, the litigation and personal charges filed to reject the approved economic development plan intensified. On March 1, the coalition of the CCC and local property owners filed an amended court petition claiming that the adoption of the economic development plan by the redevelopment commission on January 19, 1989, should be canceled because county commissioners failed to adopt an ordinance establishing the redevelopment commission. Hugh Kaufman, an EPA employee, charged that the purchase of the 30-acre tract of land for the Vigo County industrial park from the GSA was fraudulent. Kaufman contended that the GSA should have determined the environmental impact of potential development before selling federal land. He further implied that a new impact study

should have been conducted, rather than relying on the original assessment covering the 1,476 acres sold to Vigo County in 1986. County government officials responded that they had followed appropriate legal advice in purchasing the additional 30 acres for $50,000 at a public auction held on August 19, 1988.

ECONOMIC DEVELOPMENT PLAN DECLARED NULL AND VOID

20   By mid-March 1989, Judge Frank Nardi conducted a pretrial conference in an attempt to resolve questions and issues raised by the plaintiffs. Judge Nardi indicated he would review all evidence about the way the Vigo County redevelopment commission was formed and the procedures used to reach its decision. Following federal court hearings, Judge Nardi gave the CCC and Vigo County adequate time to file written briefs. The core of the plaintiffs' position was as follows: the economic development plan was written especially for BASF, was adopted in violation of certain aspects of state law, and was approved by government officials without giving proper consideration to all factors, including environmental impact issues. The defendants (county officials) testified that plaintiffs were given full rein during public hearings and that the plan was a reasonable one, designed with BASF in mind, seeking economic development by attracting not only BASF but other industry as well to the industrial park. Defendants also contended that monitoring the environment was a state and federal responsibility, and that the incineration of waste from other BASF plants was permissible as part of the industrial park. On July 1, 1989, Judge Nardi ruled that the economic development plan approved by the redevelopment commission was null and void. Nardi cited the following reasons:

21   1. Questions of propriety regarding payments and alliances that suggested possible conflicts of interest among the commissioners: Judge Nardi concluded that Commissioner Harland had a conflict of interest because his son owned acreage that BASF would have to purchase for easement purposes at an estimated cost of between $350,000–$400,000. Business diaries subpoenaed from BASF also supported Judge Nardi's conclusions regarding other possible improprieties.

22   2. Prejudgement of the decision before the Vigo County Redevelopment Commission was formed: County government officials allegedly "packed" the Redevelopment Commission with advocates of the BASF location project and formed an unethical alliance with the company to stifle public opposiion. R. Marc Elliot, Director of the Terre Haute Redevelopment Department and primary "author" of the Economic Development Plan, testified that meetings with BASF officials were held as the plan was taking shape.

23   As a result of these findings, the economic development plan was remanded to the Vigo County commissioners for further action.

MEANWHILE BACK AT THE RANCH

24   While Judge Nardi was analyzing the data contesting the approval of the economic development plan (approximately April 1 to July 1, 1989) another controversy was brewing. BASF opponents expressed concern that the company had not produced a complete list of chemicals that would be imported, burned, and buried at its selected Midwest facility. Company officials indicated that the amount of waste handled, if Vigo County is selected, would be srictly limited by the redevelopment plan. BASF stressed that it would act responsibly and show concern for the short-run and long-run impact on the environment. BASF officials reassured the community that no third-party wastes would be imported. It was also pointed out that BASF was following common corporate practice, in that partial lists seldom were released. According to BASF management, most large companies do not release lists of chemicals until they apply for a state permit for incineration operations.

25   Unfortunately for BASF officials, their responses were jaded by an analysis of data conducted by a local Indiana State University chemistry professor, Dr. John Corrigan. A reporter of the *Sullivan Daily Times* (a local community newspaper 30 miles south of Terre Haute) asked Professor Corrigan to analyze some unpublished BASF documents. Data revealed that BASF intended to incinerate up to 152 chemicals—waste residues from 30 plants in 14 states in 1991–92. Corrigan reported that metals for incineration included cadmium, chromium, lead, and barium, among others; these chemicals cannot be destroyed or rendered harmless by incineration. BASF officials responded that the data were not current and were subject to revision. Jack Wehman, Midwest venture director for BASF, responded to the community concern by saying that, following Judge Nardi's decision, BASF would begin the permitting process and make a full disclosure of chemicals to be disposed of at the Vigo County facility. The controversy over the chemical list at this point remain unresolved. A major factor contributing to the impasse was the ruling by U.S. District Court Judge Nardi declaring the economic development plan null and void.

A Proposal to Sell Industrial Park Land

26   Subsequent to Judge Nardi's ruling declaring the economic development plan for the industrial park null and void, controversy continued about the possible sale of industrial park land to BASF. A joint meeting of the Vigo County commissioners, seven county councilmen, and the five members of the redevelopment commission resulted in a consensus not to appeal Judge Nardi's disallowance of the economic development plan. County commissioners expressed concern that deed restrictions might have to accompany the sale of industrial park acreage to protect the environment. Special concern about importation of hazardous waste was expressed. John Scott, president of the commission, indicated he was worried that BASF had not yet published a list of what wastes would be imported.

27   On July 15, 1989, anti-BASF groups met with county commissioners to share their views about the future of the industrial park. Harold Cox, representative of the CCC, said that a new economic development plan should be written to attract a wider spectrum of potential buyers. It was stressed that Vigo County needs to market to industries that do not present environmental health risks. The commissioners responded that they welcomed ideas for marketing land but emphasized that the industrial park was still for sale, although no specific time frame had been established to offer the property for public bid. About a month after this meeting, the Vigo County commissioners sought legal advice regarding the disposal of the industrial park. The commissioners also stated that public hearings would be conducted. BASF opponents hoped that the new hearings would result in a plan that would restrict ecologically unsound activities while promoting safe economic development of the industrial park.

BASF Modifies Plans

28   On August 31, 1989, BASF Midwest venture director Jack Wehman announced that his corporation was scaling down its plans for an industrial plant in Vigo County. He stated:

29   Our new plan calls for the construction of a stand-alone automotive plant with the necessary waste-management facilities for only the paint plant. This means that the waste-management facility will handle only the waste from the site's paint plant. These are on-site generated wastes.

30   Wehman further explained that the waste-management operations would include a waste-water treatment facility, an incinerator system, and a landfill for the incinerated ash, all of which would dispose of on-site wastes. These revisions would require only 200–300 acres of land and about 300 local employees at a cost of roughly $100 million. Wehman further projected that these 300 local employees would complement 100 "imported" workers, each earning about $10.15 per hour, or about

$8.4 million in annual income. In addition, Wehman estimated that the 2,000 construction workers employed for the two-year project would generate about $40 million per year in payroll. Wehman concluded by stressing the need to negotiate sale of needed land in the park within the next six weeks so the plant could be operational by the end of 1992.

31   The Vigo County commissioners reacted favorably to BASF's revised plan and indicated that selling appropriate acreage with a clear title within six weeks seemed feasible. At this point, the commissioners stated that public hearings on the sale of the land seemed unnecessary, especially since wastes would not be imported into the community.

32   Many community members, however, still questioned the integrity of BASF's proposed revision. A member of one anti-BASF coalition, Mothers Against Toxic Chemical Hazards, indicated that opposition to BASF continued because the revision still proposed a toxic waste incinerator and landfill for the site. Harold Cox, president of the CCC, stated that the proposed landfill was not allowed according to Vigo County's comprehensive land use plan. Other opponents voiced concern that the industrial park had not been appropriately marketed. BASF adversaries stressed the previous "bait and switch" tactics, in which the company initially announced plans for a paint plant and later added the hazardous waste facilities to its agenda. A staunch critic of BASF opponents was Terre Haute City mayor Pete Chalos. Mr. Chalos criticized environmental groups that previously had said they would accept BASF if toxic waste was not imported. Mayor Chalos indicated he had studied BASF's new proposal and was optimistic that the county commissioners would accommodate BASF.

33   Two days after announcing its revised plan for the paint plant operations, BASF released two bound volumes of printed material, explaining in detail the list of chemicals that could be treated and disposed of at its midwestern paint plant. BASF officials assured the community that all of the tested materials would be handled by using procedures that protected the safety, health, and environmental welfare of the citizens.

BASF's Bid for Industrial Park Land Approved by County

34   On October 27, 1989, approximately six seeks following its announced plant revision, BASF submitted a bid of $500,000 for 296.7 acres of industrial park land. Jack Wehman expressed hope for a successful culmination of the sale and stated that his company would begin a skills inventory of the local work force. The skills inventory was quite successful—1,836 people completed the surveys. BASF officials emphasized that the survey wasn't a job application; it was a tool to give BASF an idea of what skills local people have and what training would be needed.

35   At first it appeared that BASF was on the road to Terre Haute. But on November 2, 1989, four local anti-BASF groups united to form the Terre Haute Environmental Rights Coalition (TERC). TERC's attorney, Mike Kendall, wrote a letter to the county attorney, Robert Wright, advising him that the terms of the BASF bid for the 296 acres of industrial park were extremely biased in favor of the company. Kendall said the county should reject the conditions of the BASF offer; Kendall reinforced TERC's opposition by stating that they would take whatever legal steps were necessary to prevent the sale.

36   Controversy heightened because BASF filed an amendment to its original bid that had substantial changes regarding its property rights at the industrial park if the sale was consummated. TERC's legal counsel indicated that BASF's amended bid may have violated the public bid law and expressed concern that the substantive changes made by the amendment may be a de facto new bid. Kendall also pointed out that the original bid was the only one available to the public between October 30 and November 14.

37   On November 20, 1989, a public hearing on the BASF bid proposal sparked heated debate. Several BASF officials made presentations of the company plans and fielded questions from the public and county officials. TERC's attorney, Mike Kendall, stated the following summary position:

38   We are not against having a facility such as the one described per se, but BASF's revised bid is not enough. We question the legality of negotiating a revised bid and the granting of easements which the BASF facility would require. County Commissioners do not have authority to accept an amended bid except one that raises the price and then only after certain other notice provisions have been complied with.

39   Other BASF adversaries continued to remind county officials that the industrial park never had been properly marketed and that no such plan existed. Advocates of BASF stressed that the Vigo County area was in desperate need of jobs.

40   Despite the threats of TERC and other sundry opponents, on November 22, 1989, the Vigo County commissioners and Vigo County council voted unanimously to accept BASF's bid for 296.7 acres of land in the industrial park. Selected parts of the sale order were as follows:

41   1. The Board of Commissioners finds that the county has no other need for the real estate; Vigo County has severe economic stagnation; the use of real estate for industrial development would help alleviate problems of unemployment and economic stagnation; the soil conditions of the real estate are appropriate for the manufacturing facility, incinerator, and landfill.

42   2. The Commissioners are satisfied that the proposed facility will not threaten the health of local residents as long as the incinerator and landfill are operated in accordance with federal, state, and local laws, ordinances, regulations, and rulings.

43   A few days after Vigo County approved the sale of land to BASF, the company announced formation of a Community Awareness Panel to provide information to the Vigo County region about BASF's plans and actions. Jack Wehman reported that the panel would meet monthly to discuss such topics as plant facilities, environmental standards, safety and emergency procedures, employment training, and social commitments. Wehman claimed that the awareness panel was a balanced representation of the community, except that anti-BASF people declined to serve. Two prominent leaders of the CCC, Harold Cox and John Strecker, rebutted Wehman's comments, stating that they had not been asked to serve. Cox pointed out that the makeup of the awareness panel was skewed in favor of BASF.

TERC FILES LAWSUIT

44   On April 10, 1990, the Terre Haute Environmental Rights Coalition filed a lawsuit in U.S. district court charging the following:

45   1. The Government Services Administration violated the National Environmental Policy Act by selling land to Vigo County without requiring an environmental impact study before each of two land sales to the county. TERC requested that the sales be declared null and void and that the title to the industrial park land revert back to the U.S. government. The suit also requested that the GSA be required to conduct an environmental impact study in light of the intended use of the land—e.g., a hazardous waste landfill and incinerator.

46   2. TERC also filed a motion for an injunction stopping the county from selling the 296 acres to BASF until the lawsuit is resolved.

47   TERC legal counsel, Mike Kendall, also stated that the lawsuits would be filed against county officials for failing to disclose the true use of the property to the GSA—a violation of the Racketeer Influenced and Corrupt Organizations Act. In response to the charge that GSA was negligent in failing to conduct an environmental impact study, assistant U.S. attorney Sue Bailey filed a motion to dismiss the TERC lawsuit, based on the position that the action taken by the federal government was several years old and that the property no longer belonged to the federal government. Jack Wehman, Midwest venture director for BASF, issued a position statement:

48   The frivolous filing of two federal lawsuits against the county and federal government by the Environmental Rights Coalition brings into question whether this group is concerned about the health and economic welfare of the citizens of Vigo County. BASF is not a defendant in either of the two lawsuits but, as a partner in the economic development of the community, we are disappointed in these self-serving delaying tactics. BASF is steadfast in its interest to invest more than $100 million in an automotive plant facility which will bring new jobs to Vigo County. BASF remains confident that the county and federal attorneys will resolve this matter to the satisfaction of the great majority of Vigo County residents.

49   Continued debate followed TERC's legal action. A countersuit was eventually filed by Vigo County commissioners charging that TERC's complaint was "frivolous, unreasonable, and groundless." The countersuit further claimed that members of TERC were negligently and maliciously interfering with a contractual relationship simply to fulfill a goal of stopping the sale of land to BASF. TERC responded with the following position statement:

50   Some local government officials put all the public's marbles in one basket with BASF for less than 300 jobs. Instead of going after BASF, the commissioners should have spent the last two years enticing good corporate citizens with sound environmental records that would have provided hundreds of additional jobs. Having evaded the requirement for an environmental impact study and faced with a fickle BASF, the Vigo County commissioners are in danger of being left with an empty plot of land, legal fees, and no jobs for our people.

51   In response to this legal impasse, Jack Wehman stated in mid-June 1990 that, if the federal lawsuit wasn't settled by September 1, 1990, BASF might locate elsewhere. Wehman stressed that BASF must get its plant on line by the end of 1992.

BASF Breaks Off Courtship

52   On September 4, 1990, Jack Wehman announced that BASF corporate officials in Germany had decided that the corporation would no longer consider land at the Vigo County industrial park as an option for its automotive plant. A big stumbling block to the marriage of BASF and Vigo County was the unresolved litigation filed by TERC, claiming that the original sale of federal land by the GSA to Vigo County failed to comply with environmental regulations. Reactions in the community ranged from bitter disappointment to jubilation. City and county officials faced the dilemma of developing a new marketing plan for the industrial park to attract new companies and create jobs. BASF executives wondered what they could have done to avoid the confrontation and how their plant-siting strategy should be changed in the future. TERC's legal counsel, Michael Kendall, stressed that BASF's decision was not an issue about a group of people who allegedly kept a company out of Vigo County but about a victory for environmental integrity.

Bibliography and References

"A Company at Work." *BASF Corporation*, January 1, 1989, 35 pages.

"An Economic Development Plan for the Vigo County Industrial Park." Vigo County Redevelopment Commission, November 1988, 21 pages.

Annual report. BASF Corporation, 1988, 28 pages.

"BASF Corporation: Proposed Midwest Facility for Terre Haute." BASF Corporation, 1988, 9 pages.

"BASF Corporation: Proposed Midwest Facility for Terre Haute." BASF Corporation, January 1989, 10 pages.

"BASF Pulls Out of Wabash Valley." *Terre Haute Tribune Star*, September 10, 1990, p. A 1.

Cox, Harold, and Pat Duffy. "Court Rules Against Plan." *CCC Newsletter* 1, no. 3 (Fall 1989), p. 1.

"GSA Disputes Kaufman's Claim." *Terre Haute Tribune Star*, March 14, 1989, p. A 3.

Halladay, John. "Testimony Ends in BASF Lawsuit." *Terre Haute Tribune Star*, March 24, 1989, p. A 1.

————. "Development-Environmental Tie Possible." *Terre Haute Tribune Star*, July 13, 1989, p. A 1.

————. "Officials Schedule New Hearings on Industrial Park." *Terre Haute Tribune Star*, August 26, 1989, p. A 1.

"Hazard Waste Incinerators." *Greenpeace*, 1987, 4 pages.

"Hazardous Waste Incineration: Questions and Answers." U.S. Environmental Protection Agency, April 5, 1988, 53 pages.

Igo, Becky. "Chalos Says BASF Loss Could Hurt." *Terre Haute Tribune Star*, June 20, 1990, p. A 3.

————. "BASF Foes Call County's Legal Retaliation Intimidation." *Terre Haute Tribune Star*, June 26, 1990, p. A 3.

LeBar, Gregg. "Chemical Industry: Regulatory Crunch Coming." *Occupational Hazards*, November 1988, pp. 36–39.

Loughlin, Sue. "Several Foes Remain Opposed to BASF's Plans." *Terre Haute Tribune Star*, August 31, 1989, p. A 1.

"Mayor Restates He Wants Both Central Soya, BASF." *Terre Haute Tribune Star*, January 31, 1989, p. A 3.

Porter, Kelley. "BASF's Chemicals List Still Not Complete." *Terre Haute Tribune Star*, April 7, 1989, p. A 1.

————. "Prof More Worried Now after Studying Incineration Data." *Terre Haute Tribune Star*, June 26, 1989, p. A 3.

————. "Judge Voids Economic Plan; Cites Conflicts." *Terre Haute Tribune Star*, July 1, 1989, p. A 1.

————. "BASF Scales Back Its Plant Plans." *Terre Haute Tribune Star*, August 31, 1989, p. A 1.

————. "BASF Releases Chemical List in Continued Spirit of Sharing Facts." *Terre Haute Tribune Star*, September 2, 1989, p. A 1.

Walters, Gordon. "BASF Submits $500,000 Bid for Industrial Land." *Terre Haute Tribune Star*, October 28, 1989, p. A 1.

————. "Environmentalists Form Anti-BASF Coalition." *Terre Haute Tribune Star*, November 3, 1989, p. A 1.

————. "Coalition Promises to Sue Commissioners." *Terre Haute Tribune Star*, November 21, 1989, p. A 1.

————. "County Approves Offer to Sell Land to BASF." *Terre Haute Tribune Star*, November 23, 1989, p. A 1.

CASE 24

THE MERGER OF FEDERAL EXPRESS AND THE FLYING TIGERS LINE

1   It was January 1990. Thomas R. Oliver, senior vice president of International Operations for Federal Express Corporation, was on his way to meet with the members of his "Tigerclaws" Committee. The operational merger of Flying Tigers with Federal Express was supposed to be concluded last August. Yet, anticipated and unanticipated problems kept surfacing. International operations were draining financial resources, and there were other problems that had to be immediately resolved.

2   Several days ago, Mr. Oliver met with Mr. Fred Smith, the company founder and CEO, and was assigned the job of heading a special task force, whose purpose was to direct the Flying Tigers' merger efforts and resolve the resulting problems. Mr. Oliver requested, and got, representatives of senior executives from every department of the company to form what he named the Tigerclaws Committee (see Exhibit 1). This committee had the power to cut across departmental bureaucratic lines. It had the resources of all the departments behind it to reach fast-track solutions to any problems in existence. Even with such commitments, Mr. Oliver realized what a formidable task he and his committee were facing.

EXPRESS AND FREIGHT FORWARDING INDUSTRIES

3   In 1990, sending documents or packages by priority mail was viewed as a necessary convenience, rather than a luxury. The domestic market was led by Federal Express Corporation with 53 percent of the market, followed by United Parcel Service at 19 percent. The U.S. Postal Service had 3–4 percent of the market (Curry, 1989). The overnight letter traffic was characterized by slow growth because of the increased use of facsimile machines.

4   The increasing competition between express delivery services and the traditional air freight industry was changing the face of international cargo transportation. Many independent freight carriers complained that big couriers and integrated carriers were poaching on their market niches. Others ignored the competition, believing that the more personalized relationships provided by the traditional air freight companies would keep clients coming back. Still, such companies as Federal Express were having a big effect on the air freight industry. Express couriers were building their nondocument business by 25 to 30 percent a year. Proprietary consolidation and expedited treatment at customs had been the major factors influencing this growth rate. In an effort to move deeper into the cargo sector, some express companies were marketing themselves as providers of third-party logistics services (Strugatch, 1990).

A case study by Howard S. Tu, Fogelman College of Business and Economics, Memphis State University, and Sherry E. Sullivan, Bowling Green State University.

EXHIBIT 1
Representatives on the Tigerclaws Committee

Departments that are represented:
  Memphis SuperHub
  Business Application
  Airfreight Systems
  Q.A. Audits
  Planning and Administration
  International Clearance
  Communications
  Ramp Plans/Program
  Hub Operations
  Personnel Services
  International Operations
  Central Support Services
  Customer Support
  COSMOS/Pulsar System Division
  COO/Quality Improvement

Express Service in the United States

5   Federal Express, United Parcel Service (UPS), Airborne Express, and the U.S. Postal Service were quickly introducing services that promised to translate the fundamentals of speed and information into a powerful competitive edge. They were stressing good service at lower costs. For example, UPS had started offering discounts to its bigger customers and shippers that shipped over 250 pieces weekly. In addition, UPS was building an $80 million computer and telecommunications center to provide support for all operations worldwide. Airborne's chief advantage was that it operated its own airport and had begun operating a "commerce park" around its hub in Wilmington, Ohio.

Europe

6   The international document and parcel express delivery business was one of the fastest-growing sectors in Europe. Its scope was anticipated to grow even faster when most European customs barriers were removed in 1992. Although the express business would become more important in the single European market, none of the four principle players in Europe was European. DHL, Federal Express, and UPS were United States companies while TNT was Australian. Europe was not expected to produce a challenger because the "Big Four" were buying smaller rivals at such a fast pace that the odds seemed to be heavily against a comparable competitor emerging (Arthur, 1989).

Pacific Rim

7   The Asia-Pacific air express market was expanding by 20 to 30 percent annually, and the world's major air express and air freight companies had launched massive infrastructure buildups to take advantage of this growth. Industry leader DHL strengthened its access to air service by agreeing to eventually sell 57.5 percent of the equity of its international operation to Japan Air Lines, Lufthansa, and Nissho Iwai trading company. TNT Skypak's strength was in providing niche services, and its ability to tap into the emerging Asian-East European route with its European air hub. Two new U.S. entrants, Federal Express and UPS, were engaged in an undeclared price war. Willing to lose millions of dollars annually to carve out a greater market share, Federal Express already had captured

about 10 percent of Pacific express business and 15 percent of freight. UPS's strategy was to control costs and to offer no-frills service at low rates. All four companies were seeking to expand the proportion of parcels, which could yield about twice the profits of express documents business (Guyot, 1990).

Major Airlines

8 Since the common adaptation of wide body jets, major international airlines had extra cargo space in their planes. Japan Air Lines and Lufthansa were two of the worldwide players, with most national airlines providing regional services.

9 Airlines were expanding and automating their cargo services to meet the challenges presented by fast-growing integrated carriers. Two strategies were being employed: (1) the development of new products to fill the gap between the demand for next-day service and traditional air cargo service and (2) computerization of internal passenger and cargo operations (McKenna, 1989b).

THE MERGING ORGANIZATIONS

Federal Express Corporation

10 Frederick W. Smith, founder of Federal Express Corporation, went to Yale University, where he was awarded a now infamous C on an economics paper that outlined his idea for an overnight delivery service (Foust, 1989). After college and military service, Smith began selling corporate jets in Little Rock, Arkansas. In 1973, he tapped his $4 million inheritance, rounded up $70 million in venture capital, and launched Federal Express, testing his college paper's thesis. The company turned profitable after three years.

11 Federal Express always had taken pride in its people-oriented approach and its emphasis on service to its customers. Mr. Smith believed that, in the service industry, it is the employees that make the business (Smith, 1991). The philosophy of Smith and his managing staff was manifested in many ways, including: (1) extensive orientation programs, (2) training and communications programs, (3) promotion of employees from within, and (4) a tuition reimbursement program. Federal Express's "open door policy" for the expression of employee concerns also illustrated the commitment of top management to resolve problems (Trunick, 1989).

12 As to services, Federal Express stressed the importance of on-time delivery and established a 100 percent on-time delivery goal. It has achieved a record 95 percent on-time delivery. In 1990, Federal Express was one of the five U.S. firms to win the Malcolm Baldrige National Quality Award. This award was given by the U.S. government to promote quality awareness and to recognize the quality achievements of U.S. companies.

13 Frederick W. Smith had a vision for the overnight express delivery business. Although Federal Express was the No. 1 express firm in the United States, Mr. Smith firmly believed that globalization was the future for the express business (*Journal of Business Strategy*, 1988). From 1986 to 1988, Federal struggled to become a major player in international deliveries. The company ran head on into entrenched overseas rivals, such as DHL, and onerous foreign regulations (Foust, 1989).

14 Frustrated with the legal processes in negotiating for landing rights that were restricted by bilateral aviation treaties (*Journal of Business Strategy*, 1988), Mr. Smith reversed his promise to build only from within and started on a series of acquisitions. From 1987 to 1988, Federal purchased 15 minor delivery companies, mostly in Europe. In December 1988, Mr. Smith announced the merger of Tiger International, Inc., best known for its Flying Tigers airfreight service. On paper, the merger of Federal Express and Tiger International seems to be a marriage made in heaven. As one Federal Express executive pointed out: "If we lay a route map of Flying Tigers over that of Federal Express, there is almost a perfect match. There are only one or two minor overlaps. The Flying Tigers' routes are all over the world, with highest concentration in the Pacific rim countries, while the Federal Express's routes are mostly in domestic U.S.A." As a result of the merger, Federal Express's world routes were completed. For example, the acquisition of Flying Tigers brought with it the unrestricted cargo landing rights at three Japanese airports that Federal Express had been unsuccessful in acquiring for the last three years (Calonius, 1990).

15   One high-level Federal Express employee commented that the merger brought other benefits besides routes. He said: "We got a level of expertise with the people we brought in and a number of years of experiences in the company in handling air freight. . . . You have to look at this acquisition also as a defensive move. If we hadn't bought Flying Tigers, UPS might have bought Flying Tigers."

Tiger International, Inc.

16   Tiger International, Inc., better known for The Flying Tigers Line., Inc., freight service, or Flying Tigers, was founded 40 years ago by Robert Prescott. Over the years, the company became modestly profitable. But in 1977, Smith won his crusade for air-cargo deregulation over the strident objection of Tiger founder, the late Robert Prescott. Heightened competition, troubled acquisitions, and steep labor costs led to big losses at Tigers. In 1986, Stephen M. Wolf, the former chairman of Republic Airline, Inc., came on board at Tigers and managed to get all employees, including those represented by unions, to accept wage cuts. As Tigers rebounded financially, it was ripe to be taken over by one of the major delivery service companies. In 1988, Federal Express announced the acquisition of Tigers to the pleasure of some and dismay of others. At the announcement, some Tigers' employees shouted "TGIF—Thank God It's Federal" or "It's purple [Federal Express] not brown [UPS]—thank goodness." In contrast, Robert Sigafoos, who wrote a corporate history of Federal Express, commented that "Prescott must be turning over in his grave" (Foust, 1989).

17   Flying Tigers always had a distinctive culture, one that partly developed from the military image of its founders. Tigers' employees stressed "Tiger Spirit" or teamwork. Since Mr. Wolf took over as the chairman and CEO at an extremely difficult time, the general orientation of Flying Tigers was to keep the company flying.

18   In October 1980, Flying Tigers purchased Seaboard World Line. One long-time Tiger, who had witnessed the Seaboard merger, remarked: "There was no job protection. Everyone was not offered a job. There were wholesale layoffs. There was no monetary compensation paid to any of the Seaboard employees. If you were moving with the company, it did not pay your moving expenses." Continued cost-cutting was required to enable Tigers' turnaround.

The Merger

19   Federal Express announced the acquisition of Flying Tigers in December 1988. However, because of government regulations, the actual operational merging of the two companies did not occur until August 1989.

20   One top-level Federal Express executive, with considerable expertise in mergers, described the process in the following way: "I think that after any merger you go through three phases. You come in and you have euphoria. Everybody's happy. The second phase is the transition phase. In that phase, the primary qualification that every employee must have is sadomasochistic tendencies, because you kill yourself going through it. . . . And then you start coming out of that into the regeneration and regrowth phase, where you clean up all this hazy area without knowing exactly what you are going to do or thinking this works and trying it out. . . . In the meantime, going through all that turmoil creates a number of problems. . . . People's morale starts to dip. People start to question all the leadership.

You start to see the company reorganizing, you know, trying to figure out, well, what's the best thing to do here or there or whatever and, all of a sudden, all of the confidence that ever existed in the whole world starts to diminish."

21   Although the two companies were supposed to now become one, problems from the merger kept surfacing. Some of these problems were to be anticipated with the merger of two companies of these sizes. However, many problems, as detailed in the next section, were not anticipated and had become very costly to the company.

Human Resource Management Problems

22   Unions   Federal Express traditionally had been a nonunion shop, while the Flying Tigers' employees were predominately unionized. During the merger, the National Mediation Board could not determine a majority among the pilots at Federal Express and Flying Tigers. The board requires a majority to decide the union status at any firm. Because a majority could not be determined, the mediation board decided to allow the temporary mix of union and nonunion employees until the fall of 1989, when elections would determine if there would be union representation. The ruling had created ambiguities in employee status and raised some important financial and legal issues for Federal Express, unions, and employees (Ott, 1989).

23   An executive in the international division described Federal Express's feelings on unions: "They [Flying Tigers] had a lot of unions. Tigers was a traditional company . . . and we [Federal Express] don't dislike unions. . . . Our feelings about unions is [sic] that if you get a union, you deserve it, because you have not managed your business well. We would like to think that we could keep that old family [feeling]. We realize that we can't keep the old family. It's very difficult to keep the family spirit corporatewide [after a merger]."

24   Job Offers   The employees of Federal Express believed that Federal Express was a great place to work, mainly because of its people-oriented policies. Because of this belief, most of the managers thought that the Flying Tigers' employees would "welcome the merger with open arms." A communications official said: "We tried to position Federal Express as a great place to work, a wonderful place to be—cutting edge technology, a great aircraft fleet, a great employee group, good management—all those types of things."

25   Flying Tigers had a rich and long history. Tiger employees prided themselves on their team spirit and their willingness to take pay cuts for the good of The Flying Tiger Line, Inc., during the lean years. Employees proudly displayed items with the Tiger logo on them.

26   A long-time Tiger employee and member of one of the premerger Tiger committees, remarked on the job offers: "For the employees, it [the merger] was a spectrum, we've got all of them on a line. Up in front, we've got those employees for whom the merger was the best thing that ever happened to them. In the back, you've got the employees where it was the worst thing that ever happened— because of personal things, they decided to leave the company. And then there's the group of employees in the middle, which really composed the majority of Flying Tigers' employees, that it really didn't matter one way or the other since they never moved. All they did was change their uniforms from Friday to Monday. They're basically doing the same jobs in the same locations." A member of his family and many friends refused to accept a job with Federal Express. He explained their refusal, by saying: "Because [Federal Express] were taking the name away. You were taking the history of the Flying Tiger line away . . . because we were a small company, we were like a close-knit family." Another middle-level former Tiger said, "Although a lot of merger information was provided to people at headquarters in L.A., people at other locations, like Boston, received less information." She said that some Tigers refused the job offer for the following reason: "They left, I think, just because of the the the attitude that . . . you're taking Flying Tigers away and I don't want to go with you." Some Tigers hoped that Federal Express would permit them to keep the Flying Tiger name or change the company name to Federal Tigers.

27 **Differences in Culture** A Federal Express executive on the Tigerclaws Committee commented on cultural differences by saying: "The difference was astounding. Absolutely astounding. Federal Express's employees, typically, they seem to be younger, we're all in uniforms, enthusiastic about the company. You can walk around Federal Express and everybody can tell you what the corporate philosophy is. . . . I remember standing in the Los Angeles airport facility. . . . it's typical Federal Express. And you go over to the Tiger facility and here are all of these much older guys standing around. None of them in any type of uniform, clothes were all over the mat, there was [sic] no apparent standards, whatsoever. You know, kicking some of the packages, tossing them, throwing. It was just . . . just terrible. I couldn't believe it. But, that was part of the way they did business. They referred to a lot of the cargo that they carried as big, ugly freight. And to us . . . we go around thinking every customer's package is the most important thing we carry."

28 A former Tiger employee shared her perspective on the differences: "Most of the employees that you dealt with you had known for a lot of years. We used to work together side by side very closely for 20 years. And this company, Federal Express, isn't even 20 years old. You walk into a meeting or classroom or something . . . Federal Express people are introducing themselves to other Federal Express people. Tiger people found that really hard to believe—that you didn't know everybody at Federal Express."

29 **Job Assignments** During the announcement of the merger, Mr. Smith made a job offer to all the employees of Flying Tigers. Almost 90 percent of the 6,600 former Tiger employees took the offer. In a two-week period, from July 15 to 31, over 4,000 new jobs were to be created and Tiger employees transferred to these jobs. Many employees had to be relocated, because the old Tiger hub in Columbus, Ohio, was phased out, and primarily only freight and maintenance personnel were kept at the hub in Los Angeles. Some job placements were troublesome, because the human resource department had difficulty obtaining job descriptions and pay scales from Flying Tigers. During the haste, there were quite a number of mismatches of jobs and employees.

30 **Expectations** One of Federal Express's personnel officers remarked: "I was concerned about being able to meet employees' expectations. A lot of times people coming in from outside of Federal Express have this—I mean its a great place, but they have this picture that it's a fairy tale place, and that there aren't any real problems and that everybody gets their own way. So I was concerned about the expectations that people bought, both positive and negative. How are we going to make people feel real good about the company?

31 To help former Flying Tigers' employees determine whether to accept Federal Express's job offers, Federal Express provided the employees with detailed information about the company. Video tapes introducing Federal Express and explaining the benefits of working for the company were mailed to the homes of Tiger employees. Additionally, many Tiger employees were flown into Federal Express's headquarters in Memphis and given the "grand tour." "Express Teams," groups of four to five employees, visited Flying Tigers' locations and gave them previews of what it was like to work for Federal Express.

32 Regarding expectations, one long-time Tiger remarked: "There's still a lot of unhappy people in Memphis that came out of L.A., because I think they expected an awful lot. They had the option of saying no to a job and being out on the street looking for something else, or they could come to Memphis and have Federal Express be their employer. And there are a lot of people that still take offense at the fact that Federal Express bought Flying Tigers. But those people have an attitude that they have to deal with." Another former Tiger remarked: "And I honestly thought that by going from a small company to a large company, I was just going to be another number. But . . . it's also their attention to people. All of the hype and promotion they did before T-day [merger day] to Flying Tiger people that they were people oriented. . . . we really didn't [know] what that meant and what it would mean to us individually until we became employees."

Operational Management Problems

33 *Operational Procedures* Although Flying Tigers had operational policies and procedures for handling international freight, these were not being used after the official date of the operational merger. Because Federal Express was not in the traditional cargo business, it did not have such a manual. Coupled with the inexperience of most Federal Express's managers at the ports of entry, many international cargo shipments were being moved before going through U.S. customs. Federal Express was fined on several occasions for such violations. Because of the lack of operational procedures, top managers could not hold anyone responsible for these mistakes.

34 One executive on the Tigerclaws Committee made this comment about operations: "We tend to think we invented the express business. We're the best at it, and, no matter what someone else has done, what their history might have taught them, we know we do it better than they know it. And we went into this merger process kind of 'big-dogging-it,' in my opinion. That's one reason Tigerclaws was formed. That Federal Express people said 'No, no, no, don't bother to tell us how you used to do things because this is how we do things, so we'll show you the Federal Express way of doing it.' That didn't go over great. You know, you can imagine, you know these people had be in the Flying Tiger business for all these years saying, 'Look, we know the freight business, we know the international business, and Fed Ex people you don't. We do know better than you do.'"

35 Similarly, a former Tiger employee remarked: "It's a whole different concept and there's still a lot of people within the company that don't fully understand the two concepts. I, myself, don't fully understand the express concept . . . if there's freight left over, that's OK because we'll move it out tomorrow. That's not Federal Express's philosophy . . . it's like the difference between driving a Volkswagen and a Cadillac. I mean there are differences and you need to get used to them."

36 *Computer Systems* Federal Express developed the Cosmos II Positive Tracking System. The system, one of the most famous examples of strategic information systems, was honored as the 1990 Computerworld Smithsonian Award winner in the transportation category. The key component of the system was SuperTracker, a hand-held computer. It could accept data from key entry, bar-code scanning, or electronic coupling and withstand rough treatment in warehouses and trucks. The system was designed to track and handle high-quantity movement of small packages (Margolis, 1990).

37 Flying Tigers used the KIAC system. This system was designed to handle large-volume cargoes with limited consignments. Unfortunately, these two systems were not 100% compatible and currently both systems were being used by Federal Express with limited communication between the two systems.

38 *Maintenance of the Tiger Fleet and Equipment* Federal Express discovered after the merger that most of Flying Tigers' planes were poorly maintained. Most of these planes would require considerable upgrading or face retirement.

39 Also, there were differences in equipment requirements. One Federal Express executive remarked: "[The hubs] had to deal with this stuff, packages that were used to flowing along 300 and 500 feet per minute; now they have a skid that might weigh thousands of pounds. You need a forklift. We didn't use forklifts. There might be a forklift here or there for equipment engines, but it was not used to move pallets of freight around. So, all these costs, as you know, whether it was lease or buy, these things mount up. I mean, through all aspects of the company, they can say sure, we planned for that. . . . There are always surprises."

EXHIBIT 2

Federal Express Corporation and Subsidiaries
Consolidated Balance Sheets (in thousands)

	May 31,		
	1987	1988	1989
Assets			
Current assets:			
Cash, including short-term investments of $500, $500, and $79,645	$ 21,685	$ 54,945	$ 157,308
Receivables	399,333	491,324	767,278
Spare parts, supplies and fuel	39,933	48,798	83,563
Prepaid expenses and others	46,529	34,938	91,131
	507,480	630,005	1,099,280
Property and equipment, at cost			
Flight equipment	1,138,875	1,301,978	2,313,082
Package handling and ground support equipment	587,430	755,585	934,426
Computer and electronic equipment	321,651	438,527	553,204
Other	664,096	853,019	1,100,657
	2,712,052	3,349,109	4,901,369
Less accumulated depreciation and amortization	850,620	1,117,234	1,469,555
Net property and equipment	1,861,432	2,231,875	3,431,814
Other assets	130,599	146,669	761,528
	$2,499,511	$3,008,549	$5,293,422

Marketing Problems

40 **Products**   Federal Express moved pieces of 150 pounds or less, primarily with smaller transports. Flying Tigers' forte was heavy cargo and it used primarily Boeing 747 freighter aircrafts (McKenna, 1989a). A Federal Express executive remarked: "[For] 20-year [Tiger] people who sold nothing but freight and [for them] going and talking about time-sensitive stuff is difficult. It's quick. It's overnight. It's don't make a mistake. Whereas, our people who are used to doing things quickly. I mean, they often used to hear the phrase about their freight grew hair on it. I mean the stuff would sit around . . . it's a cheap price but you move it when you've got the space. Well, we're not used to that. At the end of the day, we go into a station and we want that place empty. Move it. Why? Because that's what your customers want."

41 **Customer Relations**   Many of the Flying Tigers' customers, including UPS, are competitors of Federal Express. Previously, they paid Flying Tigers to carry packages to countries where they had no landing rights. Freight forwarders, companies that transport cargo to and from airports, made up a good portion of Flying Tigers' customer base. Because Federal Express handled local logistics for its operations, international freight forwarders complained that Federal Express would take away their

EXHIBIT 2   (concluded)

	May 31,		
	1987	1988	1989
Liabilities and stockholders' investment			
Current liabilities:			
Current portion of long-term debt......................	$60,393	$69,138	69,249
Accounts payable	192,877	199,328	298,502
Accrued expenses...................................	250,455	303,586	621,345
Total current liabilities	503,725	572,052	1,089,096
Long-term debt, less current portion	744,914	838,730	2,138,940
Deferred income taxes and other	171,952	267,088	571,862
Commitments and contingencies			
Common Stockholders' Investment:			
Common Stock, $.10 par value; 1,000,000,000 shares authorized, 52,862,124 shares issued	5,163	5,286	5,286
Additional paid-in capital	571,071	623,057	625,828
Retained earnings....................................	536,386	726,036	901,429
	1,112,620	1,254,379	1,532,543
Less: Treasury stock at cost	0	0	26,619
Less deferred compensation related to stock plan	33,700	23,700	12,400
Total common stockholders' investment	1,078,920	1,330,679	1,493,524
	$2,499,511	$3,008,549	$5,293,422

Source: Federal Express Corporation 1989 Annual Report

business. Federal Express compromised by guaranteeing that it will use its own couriers and custom-clearing services for pieces weighing less than 150 pounds. Forwarders will get the business for anything heavier than 150 pounds. However, freight forwarders were still suspicious and Federal Express had been losing heavy freight business since the merger (Calonius, 1990).

Financial problems

42   Federal Express's nine-month loss from overseas operations doubled to more than $200 million. Financial statements are presented in the exhibits for both Federal Express and Flying Tigers. The poor showing caused Federal Express to report its first-ever quarterly operating loss. Since then its stock had slipped 16 percent. With $2.4 billion in debt and with heated competition at home from United Parcel Service of America, Inc., and Airborne Freight Corporation, Federal Express could not continue to hemorrhage overseas without damaging its domestic operation. Standard & Poor's and Moody's have lowered its long-term debt rating. The international business "doesn't have a lot of time to return to profitability," warned David C. Anderson, Federal Express's chief financial officer (Pearl, 1991).

EXHIBIT 3

Federal Express Corporation and Subsidiaries
Selected Consolidated Financial Data
(in thousands, except per share amounts and Other Operating Data)

	Years Ended May 31,		
	1989	1988	1987
Operating Results			
Revenues	$5,166,967	$3,882,817	$3,178,308
Operating Expenses	4,742,532	3,503,365	2,813,565
Operating income	424,435	379,452	364,743
Other income (expense)	(126,103)	(77,124)	(52,858)
Income before income taxes	298,332	302,328	311,885
Income taxes	131,881	114,612	144,933
Income from continuing operations	166,451	187,716	166,952
Loss from discontinued operations	—	—	(232,523)
Cumulative effect of change in accounting for income taxes	18,100	—	—
Net Income (loss)	$ 184,551	$ 187,716	$ (65,571)
Earnings per share			
Earnings (loss) per share:			
Continuing operations	$ 3.18	$ 3.56	$ 3.21
Discontinued operations	—	—	(4.48)
Cumulative effect of change in accounting for income taxes	.35	—	—
Net earnings (loss) per share	$ 3.53	$ 3.56	$ (1.27)
Average shares outstanding	52,272	52,670	51,905
Financial Position			
Current assets	$1,100,080	$ 630,005	$ 507,480
Property and equipment, net	3,431,814	2,231,875	1,861,432
Total assets	5,293,422	3,008,549	2,499,511
Current liabilities	1,089,096	572,052	503,725
Long-term debt	2,138,940	838,730	744,914
Common stockholders' investment	1,493,524	1,330,679	1,078,920

43   One high-level Federal Express executive and member of the Tigerclaws Committee described the financial situation as follows: "That all of a sudden you hit this brick wall and you have to make decisions now on what we [are] going to do. And when you start making these decisions, you're taking your eye off other balls that you're watching out there. And, you know, we spend a lot of time debating how we're going to do this express product . . . how we're going to keep all this revenue because we couldn't afford to lose it. You could not physically shut down enough business to get out of the air freight side and still be profitable on the express side. The increments of capacity were too excessive. So you had to figure out how you were going to evolve this . . . I mean, it came painfully."

EXHIBIT 3 (concluded)

| | Years Ended May 31, | | |
	1989	1988	1987
Other Operating Data			
Express package:			
Average daily package volume	1,059,882	877,543	704,392
Average pounds per package	5.4	5.3	5.1
Average revenue per pound	$ 3.04	$ 3.10	$ 3.33
Average revenue per package	$ 16.28	$ 16.32	$ 16.97
Heavyweight:			
Shipments	430,130	—	—
Average pounds per shipment	794	—	—
Average revenue per shipment	$ 843	$ —	$ —
Average number of employees	58,136	48,556	41,047
Aircraft fleet at end of year:			
Boeing 747s	21	—	—
McDonnell Douglas DC-10s	24	21	19
McDonnell Douglas DC-8s	6	—	—
Boeing 737s	—	—	—
Boeing 727s	106	68	60
Cessna 208s	147	109	66
Fokker F-27s	7	5	—
Dassault Falcons	—	—	—
Vehicle fleet at end of year	28,900	21,000	18,700

SUMMARY

44 Since 1985, Federal Express's international business had lost approximately $74 million and given company executives a lifetime supply of headaches (Foust, 1989). To improve Federal Express's competitive position with its overseas rivals and overcome the foreign regulations regarding landing rights, Frederick Smith announced, in December 1988, the acquisition of Tiger International, Inc. Although the combined companies would have $2.1 billion in debt, Flying Tigers was expected to provide Federal Express with desperately needed international delivery routes. The Tiger acquisition would allow Federal Express to use its own planes for overseas package delivery where Federal Express used to contract other carriers. In addition, Tigers' sizable long-range fleet could be used to achieve dominance in the international heavy-freight business that Federal Express had yet to crack.

45 Suppose you were in Thomas Oliver's shoes and were the head of the Tigerclaws Committee. What are the major problems and opportunities facing Federal Express? What should be the priorities of the Tigerclaws Committee? How will you solve or reduce the problems and exploit the opportunities?

EXHIBIT 4

THE FLYING TIGER LINE, INC., AND SUBSIDIARIES
Consolidated Balance Sheets
(in thousands)

	December 31, 1987	December 31, 1988
Assets		
Current Assets:		
Cash, including certificates of deposit	$ 47,699	$ 59,178
Short-term interest bearing investments at cost, which approximates market value	200,315	186,581
Cash and short-term interest-bearing investments	248,014	245,759
Receivables, net	142,740	150,307
Inventories	16,974	19,612
Prepaid expenses and others	19,323	21,035
Total current assets	427,051	436,713
Property and Equipment		
Equipment used in flight operations	813,282	863,929
Buildings and leasehold improvements	45,356	46,410
Other equipment	78,262	82,487
Equipment and facilities acquisition in process	186	11,239
	937,086	1,004,065
Less accumulated depreciation and amortization	486,664	548,586
	450,422	455,479
Other assets		
Deposits, deferred charges and investments	47,709	38,268
Cost in excess of fair value of net assets of an acquired business, net	41,181	39,437
	88,890	77,723
Total assets	$966,363	$ 969,915

REFERENCES

Arthur, Charles. 1989. "The War in the Air." *Business [U.K.]*, November, pp. 60–66.

Calonius, Erik. 1990. "Federal Express Battle Overseas." *Fortune* 122, no. 14 (December 3), p. 137–40.

Curry, Gloria M. 1989. "Package Delivery Service: The Options Are Plentiful." *Office* 110, no. 2 (August), pp. 60–62.

Foust, Dean. 1989. "Mr. Smith Goes Global." *Business Week,* February 13, pp. 66–72.

Guyot, Erik. 1990. "Air Courier Fight for Pacific Business." *Asian Finance [Hong Kong]* 16, no. 7 (July 15), pp. 22–23.

"Federal Express Spreads Its Wings." *Journal of Business Strategy* 9, no. 4 (July/August 1988), pp. 15–20.

Margolis, Neil. 1990. "High Tech Gets It There on Time." *Computer World* 24, no. 27 (July 2), p. 77.

EXHIBIT 4 **(concluded)**

	December 31,	
	1987	**1988**
Liabilities and Stockholders' equity		
Current liabilities:		
Current portion of long-term obligations	$ 33,719	$ 30,481
Accounts payable and accrued liabilities	184,771	186,628
Total current liabilities	218,490	217,109
Long-term obligations		
Notes payable and equipment obligations	255,393	220,181
Capital lease obligations	217,806	207,839
	473,199	428,020
Commitments and Contingencies		
Stockholders' Equity		
Common Stock, $1 par value		
Authorized—30,000,000 shares		
Outstanding—18,189,504 shares	18,189	18,189
Additional paid-in capital	213,025	174,438
Retained earnings	50,284	44,194
	281,498	236,821
Amounts due from Parent and Affiliates, net	74,946	—
Total stockholders' equity less amounts due from Parent and Affiliates.	206,552	236,821
Total liabilities and stockholders' equity	$966,363	$ 969,915

Source: Flying Tiger, Inc., 1988 Annual Report

McKenna, James T. 1989a. "Federal Express/Tiger Merger Would Reshape Cargo Industry." *Aviation Week & Space Technology* 130, no. 1 (January 2), p. 106.

McKenna, James T. 1989b. "Airline Boosts International Cargo Services to Protect Market Shares." *Aviation Week & Space Technology* 131, no. 21 (November 20), pp. 124–25.

Ott, James. 1989. "Board Decision Muddle Rules on Union Role after Merger." *Aviation Week & Space Technology* 131, no. 9, (August 28), p. 68.

Pearl, Daniel. 1991. "Innocents Abroad: Federal Express Finds Its Pioneering Formula Falls Flat Overseas." *The Wall Street Journal,* April 15, p. A1, col. 6.

Smith, Frederick W. 1991. "Empowering Employee." *Small Business Reports* 16, no. 1 (January), pp. 15–20.

Strugatch, Warren. 1990. "Air Cargo Report: Reliability Is the Buzzword." *Global Trade* 110, no. 4 (April) pp. 48–51.

Trunick, Perry A. 1989. "Leadership and People Distinguish Federal Express." *Transportation & Distribution* 30, no. 13 (December) pp. 18–22.

"A Tiger's Eye View." *World Wide* 1, no. 5 (1989).

EXHIBIT 5

THE FLYING TIGER LINE, INC., AND SUBSIDIARIES
Consolidated Statements of Operations
(in thousands)

	For the Year Ended December 31,		
	1986	1987	1988
Operating Revenues			
Scheduled freight operations	$ 884,639	$ 964,811	$1,099,708
Commercial charters.	46,682	45,018	45,386
Military Airlift Command	113,528	155,841	142,297
Rentals, service sales and other	29,487	26,010	22,234
	1,074,336	1,191,680	1,309,625
Operating Expenses			
Flying operations:			
Fuel and oil	183,710	186,539	211,728
All other	166,303	196,314	186,363
Ground operations	321,742	320,164	364,452
Maintenance	131,305	133,119	159,136
Sales, advertising and publicity	94,731	92,821	125,930
General and administrative	49,796	53,947	55,151
Depreciation and amortization	54,509	55,557	58,433
	1,004,096	1,038,461	1,161,343
Income from Operations	70,240	153,219	148,282
Other Income (expenses)			
Interest expense.	(61,334)	(58,881)	(48,798)
Interest income	6,996	11,812	18,117
Foreign exchange gains (losses), net	(27,256)	1,519	864
Other income	2,252	757	3,021
Other expense.	(9,543)	(1,816)	(4,080)
	(88,885)	(46,609)	(30,876)
Income (loss) before taxes	(18,645)	106,610	117,406
Income tax provision			
Current	—	22,184	21,800
Deferred.	—	2,716	21,200
	—	24,900	43,000
Net income (loss)	$ (18,645)	$ 81,710	$ 74,406

CASE 25

HAZLETON LABORATORIES CORPORATION IN 1991

INTRODUCTION

1   The recent growth of Hazleton Laboratories Corporation (HLC), a globally disbursed and complex firm, was so phenomenal that, in 1990, the company underwent a second major organizational restructuring in two years. However, because the explosive growth in sales from $87 million in 1986 to $170 million in 1990 was forecasted to continue, Hazleton's CEO Donald Nielson wondered about the need for still further organizational restructuring to meet the needs of the company's expanded international marketplace.

OVERVIEW

2   Hazleton Laboratories Corporation was founded in 1968. Headquartered in Herndon, Virginia, a suburb of Washington, D.C., the company's mission was to provide the highest quality in scientific services and products to organizations engaged in life sciences research. This area of research focused on products, processes, and diseases affecting man and the environment. The company grew to become one of the world's largest providers of biological and chemical research services and a major supplier of laboratory animals. A description of Hazleton's major facilities as of 1990 is provided in Table 1.

3   Hazleton's clients included research institutes; manufacturers of pharmaceuticals, chemicals, food, cosmetics, and biotechnology; other industrial companies; scientific research labs; and government agencies. The company employed 2,600 scientists, technicians, and administrative personnel who conducted operations in the United States, England, France, Japan, and West Germany. Although Hazleton was not a household name, thousands of popular consumer products were developed or tested by the company, particularly in the areas of cosmetic and drugs (prescription and over the counter). Moreover, many processed foods were tested or had their contents labeled by Hazleton.

4   In addition to research, product development, and testing, Hazleton also provided regulatory affairs consulting services. All industries served by Hazleton must meet regulatory and testing requirements before their products were distributed to the public. The Environmental Protection Agency (EPA), Food and Drug Administration (FDA), European Economic Community (EEC), and Organization for Economic Cooperation and Development (OECD) were just some of the agencies that require compliance with their regulations prior to releasing products. Because of the high impact nature of their work, more than 100 scientific papers were written, published, and presented worldwide by Hazleton's researchers each year.

This case was prepared by Professor John A. Pearce II of George Mason University and Sherry S. Chaples. Development of this case was sponsored by a Funds for Excellence grant from the State Council of Higher Education for Virginia.

TABLE 1
Hazleton Facilities

The following discussion elaborates the services and products of each of Hazleton's North American, European, and Japanese locations.

Washington, D.C.

The suburbs of Washington, D.C., were the sites of three units of Hazleton Laboratories America (HLA). The majority of the laboratory facilities and the operational and scientific management were located in Vienna, Virginia, with additional animal laboratory facilities in Rockville, Maryland, and additional laboratory facilities in Kensington, Maryland. The Washington facilities had approximately 700 personnel and 340,000 square feet of laboratory and administrative space.

All Hazleton laboratories had their dossiers accepted by the Japanese ministry of agriculture, forestry, and fisheries, and after inspection of its toxicology program by the Japanese ministry of health and welfare, the Washington laboratories were awarded an "A" rating. The immunotoxicology capabilities of the staff, coupled with the experience and facilities dedicated to primate toxicology, provided support to investigate the toxicology needs of biotechnology. The Washington laboratories served as the North American center for inhalation toxicology studies conducted by Hazleton. In addition, the laboratories participated in the National Toxicology Program for over 15 years and support basic research of investigators at the National Cancer Institute.

Due to HLA–Washington's location, it had ready access to the regulatory agencies. Coupled with its interaction with Hazleton's regulatory affairs personnel, this allowed them to provide total toxicology services to their clients. In addition to the offices in Washington, the Regulatory Affairs Division had offices in Harrogate, England; Paris, France; and Tokyo, Japan.

Vienna, Virginia

The Virginia facility was the original Hazleton toxicology laboratory. This laboratory, accredited by the Toxicology Laboratory Accreditation Board, was one of the first contract laboratories to automate the collection of study data. Its Immunochemistry Division provided biotechnological and chemistry services especially in the areas of development and testing.

Rockville, Maryland

Hazleton acquired this facility from Litton Bionetics, Inc., in September 1985. The laboratory's 100-person staff provided safety evaluation and toxicology studies to governmental and commercial clients since the early 1960s. The labs were housed in an 88,000-square-foot, state-of-the-art building specifically designed as a dual-corridor barrier facility operation. They also had participated for many years in the National Toxicology Program. The labs also supported basic research by investigators at the National Cancer Institute.

The Rockville Laboratories became an extension of the Vienna campus, adding needed capacity for both commercial and governmental clients. This division also provided specialized support in the field of inhalation toxicology.

Kensington, Maryland

This facility, which was acquired in 1985 from Litton Bionetics, became the Molecular Toxicology Division of Hazleton. Recognized as a world leader in molecular toxicology, the division had a staff of 80, occupying about 24,000 square feet of laboratory space. Laboratory operations consisted of both testing and research programs. In addition, the labs conducted studies that monitored human populations for genetic effects and others that analyzed possible effects on the immune system. Sponsors of their ongoing research programs included government agencies, private foundations, and associations, as well as selected research programs funded by the company. The capability in biotechnology services also was established at this location, and this capability fast became a major growth area for the corporation.

(continued)

TABLE 1 (*continued*)

Madison, Wisconsin

The Hazleton Laboratory in Madison, Wisconsin, was located on a 26-acre site and provided services to its clients in the areas of chemistry, toxicology, and clinical sciences. Over 700 scientists and associated personnel worked in the 250,000 square feet of laboratory and office space to support the testing needs of the food, pharmaceutical, and chemical industries. This facility served industry in various chemical, toxicology, and biomedical disciplines since the company was founded.

The Chemistry Division at this location provided analytical testing services that included the determination of nutrient content of foods and feeds, identification of hazardous compounds in the environment, studies of metabolism and of the environmental fate of compounds, and of the migration of packaging components into foodstuffs.

The Madison Toxicology Division provided a full range of preclinical toxicology services that included all phases of classical toxicity testing. These tests were run in all the standard laboratory species, as well as in chickens, ducks, quail, and domestic livestock.

The resources included more than 75,000 square feet of animal and support facilities. Animal surgery capabilities within this group enabled the staff to conduct studies that required specialized surgical procedures. Additional facilities were available that allowed them to conduct domestic livestock programs in a variety of species, with specialization in dairy cattle studies.

Hazleton's clinical sciences provided clinical evaluation services in the areas of drug and personal care product development, OTC and consumer product evaluation, dental research, and biological and analytical chemistry testing services. Hazleton operated clinical facilities in the United States and in United Kingdom.

West Palm Beach, Florida

The Clinical Research Unit in West Palm Beach. Florida, was composed of 24 individual subject rooms, sample collection rooms, and a laboratory with state-of-the-art equipment to process samples for analysis.

Hazleton's West Palm Beach facility provided OTC product testing services for evaluating the safety and efficacy of cosmetic and proprietary products and the advertising claim substantiation of a product.

The Florida clinic also conducted dental studies and studies of the dermatological and health care products, such as sunscreen lotions, shampoos, cosmetics, and antiperspirants.

Denver, Pennsylvania

Hazleton Research Products (HRP) operated in five locations in the United States. Its headquarters and small animal breeding facilities were located in Denver, Pennsylvania. Its other facilities were located in Cumberland, Virginia; Reston, Virginia; Alice, Texas; and Kalamazoo, Michigan.

HRP was engaged in the breeding, importation, and sale of animals used exclusively for research. The animals were used to study the products of pharmaceutical and biotechnology and often were the final step in testing before compounds were introduced into human beings. This lab also was equipped to provide a variety of special services for client's research needs, including blood typing, ophthalmic testing, clinical chemistry, hematology, pathologic support services, and provides anti-sera production.

(*continued*)

DESCRIPTION OF HLC'S ACTIVITIES

5   Hazleton Laboratories Corporation was divided into five major types of activities that provided the various services and products needed to meet the needs of its clients. These activities were: toxicology, chemistry, human clinicals, animal products, and regulatory affairs.

TABLE 1   (continued)

Harrogate, England

Headquarters of Hazleton Europe were at Harrogate in Yorkshire, England. The Harrogate laboratories employed over 400 scientists and support staff, who provided a full array of toxicology and chemistry services in a 180,000-square-foot facility. Their pharmaceutical and agrichemical company clients employed this facility to meet the requirements for registration of candidate materials anywhere in the world.

The metabolism staff worked with a fully computerized laboratory data capture and management system. Staff at the Madison, Wisconsin, laboratories was involved since the system had applicability at both sites.

In toxicology, the Harrogate laboratory was the European center for all inhalation toxicology studies conducted by Hazleton. This laboratory specialized in nose-only exposure for the international toxicology market.

Chemistry and metabolism capabilities in Harrogate mirrored those of the Madison, Wisconsin, laboratories and regular cross-transfer of technology assists both units. Multinational clients took advantage of similar support on both sides of the Atlantic.

Leeds, England

The Hazleton Medical Research Unit was located at Springfield House, Leeds, adjacent to both the university medical school and general infirmary. This 48-bed facility opened in May 1986 and conducted studies in healthy volunteers, including safety and tolerance, drug metabolism studies, drug interactions, and postmarketing product support.

Support services also were offered in conjunction with the studies they conducted and on a "stand alone" basis to clients who are conducting their own clinical trials. Shipment of biotechnological products and other samples from single and multicenters was organized by Hazleton from any location in the world. Analysis of samples, coupled with data transmission where required, provided facility extension to Hazleton's clients.

Lyon, France

Hazleton France offered capabilities in toxicology and chemistry to domestic and international clients from the outskirts of France's second-largest city, Lyon. Hazleton France had an internationally trained staff of 120 scientific, technical, and administrative personnel, who operated more than 88,000 square feet of laboratory and support facilities. This facility grew due to its strategic location and its international focus of the industry. Hazleton France was also the Hazleton center for acute toxicology.

Munster, West Germany

Hazleton Deutschland was located in Munster, West Germany, home of one of Germany's largest universities. Acquired in 1980, this laboratory was recognized worldwide as a leader in the field of primate reproduction studies. Clients from Europe, North America, and Japan used Hazleton Deutschland for those types of specialized research efforts.

The laboratory staff of 65 scientists and technicians operated in 40,000 square feet of modern laboratory space. The animal areas consisted of 26 primate rooms and 32 small-animal rooms, which accommodated over 1,000 primates and up to 15,000 rodents.

Hazleton Deutschland served as the central laboratory for the performance of all primate reproduction studies in Hazleton. Technical links were maintained between this laboratory and other

(continued)

Toxicology

6   Toxicology was concerned with the effects of daily exposure to potentially poisonous materials on humans in the home, workplace, and environment. In the toxicology laboratories, a battery of specialized tests was administered to various species of laboratory animals.

TABLE 1   (concluded)

Hazleton facilities. This ensured that their clients benefited from shared technology development and scientific input.

Tokyo, Japan

Japan was a major market for Hazleton services and products, because of Japan's large pharmaceutical and chemical industries that served those markets worldwide. Requirements for Hazleton's services by Japanese clients reached then-record levels in 1985 and caused Hazleton to open this liaison office in Tokyo. Staffed by Hazleton employees, Nippon Hazleton coordinated with Japanese clients the services of all Hazleton laboratory facilities. This provided Hazleton's Japanese clients direct access to their services and also facilitates communications in English or Japanese.

Other services provided by Nippon Hazleton included:

(*a*) On-site assistance in protocol development and regulatory affairs.
(*b*) Assistance to offshore clients serving the Japanese market.
(*c*) Expeditious coordination of communication between Hazleton Laboratories and Japanese clients.
(*d*) Professional representation of Hazleton Laboratories in other Far East nations.

Paris, France

The Paris office reported to the Lyon, France, office. It operated similarly to Tokyo, in that it was also a liaison office that provided access to Hazleton's services worldwide.

---

7   Professionals from a variety of disciplines were utilized to conduct the experiments and analyze the results. These tests lasted a few hours or continued throughout the animal's entire lifetime and revealed such findings as developmental and reproductive malformations, tumors, lethality, irritations, or other undesirable effects. Hazleton Laboratories established industry standards for excellence in toxicology studies. It was the first independent contract laboratory whose procedures were accredited by the Toxicology Laboratory Accreditation Board.

8   The areas of focus within this division included: acute, subchronic, chronic, oncogenicity, reproduction, inhalation, contract pathology, genetics, in vitro teratology, and immunotoxicology.

Chemistry

9   Chemistry determined the composition and chemical properties of various substances. This set of activities offered a wide range of in-house and contract services, such as formulations, metabolism, nutritional, pesticides, pharmaceutical, pharmacokinetics, and trace analysis. Hazleton's chemists verified the purity of test substances and determined their stability and concentration in the food and water of test animals, analyzed animal tissue or cultures after they were tested in other departments, provided government and industry with an understanding of the chemical behavior and residual environmental effects of particular products, and provided testing or analysis of how organisms were protected from disease.

Human Clinicals

10   Human clinicals conducted clinical investigations that analyzed the blood and urine of people that participated in studies conducted at Hazleton's facilities. Physicians, nurses, technicians, and medical assistants worked with pharmaceutical companies and regulatory agencies to determine the safety and

effectiveness of new drugs and nutritional programs. A diverse population of human volunteers was carefully monitored to assess such effects as product efficacy, photosensitivity, and phytotoxic reactions.

11   This set of activities offered a wide range of services, including design and implementation of test protocols, data reduction and statistical analysis, and substantiation of advertising claims.

Animal Products

12   Animal products bred purpose-bred mongrels and beagles, rabbits, guinea pigs, and primates for laboratory use. The division also imported primates from various parts of the world. These animals are used primarily by the pharmaceutical, chemical, and agricultural industries for testing new drugs or chemicals before approval for marketing. In addition to offering animals for research, Hazleton was equipped to provide a variety of special services, which include anti-sera production, blood typing, ophthalmic testing, clinical chemistry, hematology, and pathology support services. Hazleton's laboratory units were the largest client for Hazleton's animal products.

Regulatory Affairs and Quality Assurance

13   Because all of the industries served by Hazleton were required to meet some type of regulatory requirement before they could market their products, Hazleton's regulatory affairs and quality assurance operations complemented the company's emphasis on providing its clients with a product development package. This package enabled Hazleton's clients to be served from product inception, through market release, to maintaining its marketability. Hazleton personnel provided knowledge of national and international regulations, as well as skills in such areas as strategy design, petition preparation, and liaison assistance and counsel with regulatory agencies. Hazleton took great pride in maintaining constant contact with such agencies around the world as EPA, FDA, EEC, OECD; in designing test standards; and in helping to develop guidelines for regulatory approval.

THE MULTIDISCIPLINED NATURE OF HAZLETON

14   Most of Hazleton's laboratories were multidisciplined—that is, when testing was completed in one area of activity, the services of another area of activity often were required to complete the analysis. Toxicology, one such discipline, usually referred to animal testing, and ultimately, to human testing. Animals were administered a compound to determine whether it caused a toxic reaction. If the compound did not cause adverse reactions, or if the toxic level was at a very high dose level, the compound then could be tested on humans. Toxicology was, therefore, safety testing, not efficacy testing. Hazleton conducted toxicology in five locations, two in the United States and three in Europe. Each toxicology laboratory housed several thousand rats and mice and several hundred dogs, primates, and rabbits.

15   The compounds were administered in a variety of ways: injection, inhalation, capsule, oral interbation, oral gavaging, or mixing the dose directly in the feed or water. Testing usually began with short-term studies that demonstrated at which dose level a significant reaction began. Dose levels then were decreased until no effect appeared. At this dose level, the animals were monitored for long-term effects. The animal then was sacrificed and a total necropsy was performed. Such tissues as the heart, lungs, liver, kidneys, and pituitary glands were removed and examined.

16   For manufacturers of pesticides, Hazleton conducted residue studies. The pesticide was sprayed on crops, which then were harvested, taken to the laboratory, ground up, and tested for pesticide level. The testing was crucial because, if the pesticide level reached a critical level, the crops could not be sold.

17   Finally, in the chemistry labs, Hazleton obtained samples of blood or urine from animals or human beings and conducted analytical profiles. Metabolism chemistry involved measuring the air and performing tests on excreta and urine to determine what happened to the compound once it got into the system of the animal or human. Environmental chemistry involved obtaining samples of effluent in waste soil and liquids and performing content analyses. Nutritional chemistry involved testing for and establishing safe levels of chemicals in food products for the majority of the largest companies in the United States. Different foods were analyzed and labeled according to the FDA regulations.

18   The chemistry laboratories resembled traditional chemistry laboratories, while both the animal and human clinics resembled hospitals. In the human clinic there were even cardiac care centers where a patient's heartbeat could be monitored by doctors and nurses on a 24-hour basis.

HISTORY OF THE COMPANY

19   Under the direction of Donald Nielson, the company president since 1968, Hazleton acquired numerous companies, facilities, and product lines within the life sciences industries. In fact, in its 22-year history, the company successfully had completed 20 corporate mergers. Most notable was its acquisition of Raltech Laboratories in 1982, which expanded Hazleton's United States operations by 50 percent.

20   In April 1987, HLC was acquired by Corning, Inc., in an exchange of stock. Top executives at Hazleton cited the following reason for the merger: Hazleton's growth plans for the future required additional capital and greater expertise in international business operations; and these growth factors could be supplied by Corning. The merger also would provide Hazleton shareholders with an investment in a larger and more diversified enterprise, as well as expanding the laboratory science business of both companies. Additionally, this merger demonstrated Corning's commitment to a growth strategy in a technology-based industry, devoid of Japanese competition, in which they could quickly become a world leader—laboratory services.

21   Following the finalization of the merger, Hazleton became a subsidiary of Corning, with Hazleton's common stockholders receiving approximately one-half share of Corning for each share of Hazleton common stock. Although Hazleton was to benefit from Corning's technology and financial resources, Hazleton continued to operate as an independent subsidiary. Corning's confidence in Hazleton's management, philosophy, and policies was evidenced by Hazleton's continued self-management, with Donald Nielson as CEO and all his top managers, who averaged 15 years of experience, remaining in key positions.

STRATEGY, STRUCTURE, AND THE FUTURE OF HAZLETON

22   In a presentation to the top management team in September 1989, Nielson stated that to ensure the growth of the company an organizational restructuring was required that was compatible with the firm's principles (as provided in Figure 1) and its successful strategy. He stated:

23   The strategy dictates that we think globally, we act locally and globally; we cultivate fewer, but larger clients; we provide more services to each client; we have a closer relationship with each client; we develop new and creative information systems to track the progress of multiple studies, in multiple line disciplines which may be performed at multiple sites; and that we concentrate on clients not markets.

24   To accomplish the above requires some changes in the way we operate. Over the next few years we need to bring all of Hazleton together so we act and think as one unit and our clients worldwide can be comfortable that any Hazleton unit will meet their requirements. The client needs to become more assured that dealing with Hazleton will positively assist in accomplishing their worldwide development requirements.

FIGURE 1
Hazleton Labs' Business Principles

In January 1989, Donald Nielson established and distributed the following business principles, which were still in effect at the end of this case:

Business

To provide superior scientific services and products that add value to organizations engaged in life sciences research.

Mission

To help clients bring to market safe and effective new products and to maintain the marketability of existing products.

To serve clients by providing services and products that may be needed to meet their own internal research or regulatory requirements, or both.

To provide superior scientific services and products as quickly and economically as possible, commensurate with high quality and regulatory compliance.

Strategy

To develop and sell worldwide those scientific services and products needed by the industries we serve to move their new products from the basic research stage through to the regulatory approval stage. Hazleton will also provide those scientific services necessary to keep existing products from falling out of compliance.

Goals

To provide superior services and products to those clients we have the privilege of serving.

To provide all employees with the opportunity to grow and develop to their full potential in a safe and attractive working environment.

To provide our shareholders with an above-average rate of return on their investment.

To be a good neighbor.

---

25   We intend to gain a competitive advantage by stressing quality in everything we do, and by developing a true compound development capability through mega-sites.

ORGANIZATIONAL STRUCTURE

26   Growth during the first 20 years of the life of the company centered on an acquisition strategy, whereas from 1985 to 1990 the strategy shifted to concentrated growth and a global focus. The major challenge that the company faced was the design and activation of an appropriate organizational structure to accompany its recently adopted corporate strategy.

Pre-1989 Structure

27   Figure 2 presents the Hazleton organizational structure prior to 1989. At that time, the company was an organization of fairly independent entities that operated under the direction of a centralized management team, which felt the need for little communication or coordination among locations. Each

FIGURE 2
Pre-1989 HLC Organizational Chart

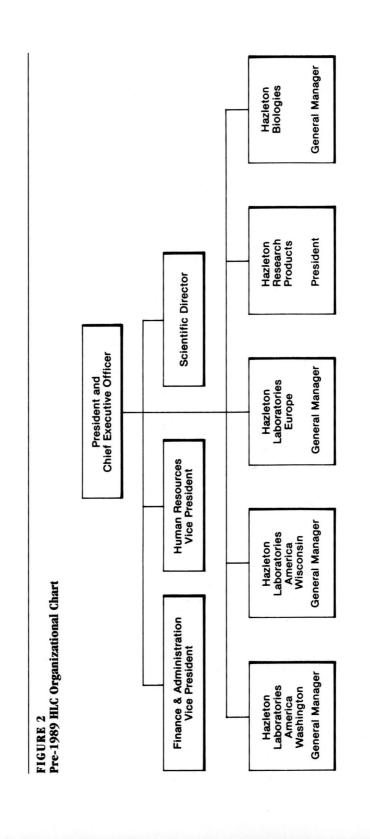

location had an established client base and operated almost exclusively to satisfy its individual performance objectives.

28 Over a period of a few years in the mid-1980s, the marketplace forced the company to accept a global organization toward marketing, production, and customer service or risk its market position. A key impetus for change was Hazleton's need for coordinated efforts on large-scale contracts that it had been awarded. These multimillion-dollar contracts demanded the inputs from several labs. Thus, while globalization had been a long-range goal of the company, competitive market conditions forced an unanticipated rapid acceleration of Hazleton's growth plans. Realizing the need for organizational changes to reflect its dynamically evolving strategy, a new structure was created in 1989.

1989 Structure

29 Figure 3 illustrates the structure as it was redesigned in 1989. This modified matrix format was the company's first attempt to incorporate a global focus into its operations.

30 The operating units or labs were still independent. However, functional SBUs were created in an attempt to coordinate the functional areas of the company. Each location's general manager was responsible for costs, profits, lab utilization, and contract acquisition.

31 Under this arrangement, the company experienced problems with its organizational structure, most notably in three areas. First, coordination between facilities was lacking. When one location did not have the facilities to accommodate all phases of a contract, the general manager needed to contact other labs individually to negotiate an allocation of the work. Also, if a lab was contacted by a client for specific work and the lab did not have the needed capability or capacity, the search for an appropriate location would be necessary. This process of matching resources with client needs was complicated further if the job was highly varied, thus requiring the use of multiple Hazleton facilities.

32 Second, the functional SBUs did not work well, especially in the area of toxicology. There was no coordination between the two vice presidents handling this functional area. As a result, there was little consistency on a companywide basis. The company did learn, however, that a global functional area, as operated in chemistry, worked much better. For example, through the amalgamation of chemistry, HLC was able to condense the time for bringing a compound to market, thereby substantially reducing costs.

33 Third, the managerial role conflict was substantial under the modified matrix structure. The general managers were too busy managing their lab operations to fully carry out their functional duties. With local issues taking precedence, the net result was that GMs were attempting to keep their labs full at the expense of attention to company's global goals.

1990 Structure

34 In an announcement in November 1989, Nielson presented a reorganization of the company for 1990, in a further effort to integrate communication elements into the structure and to split the functional responsibilities from lab responsibilities. Figure 4 shows the relationships between the company's revised organizational chart and the functions carried out at each location.

35 The new structure established a vice president for marketing and business development, who was responsible for global marketing strategy, literature, and coordinating major programs. Reporting to him was the regulatory affairs department, which addressed changing global conditions. Two directors of development (pharmachemicals and food, and chemicals and agrichemicals) were responsible for monitoring and responding to industry needs. R&D spending, new compounds in development, and new client requirements were just some of the areas they oversaw.

36 Also directly reporting to the vice president of marketing and business development were the key client executives. These executives were assigned to large clients and were responsible for the

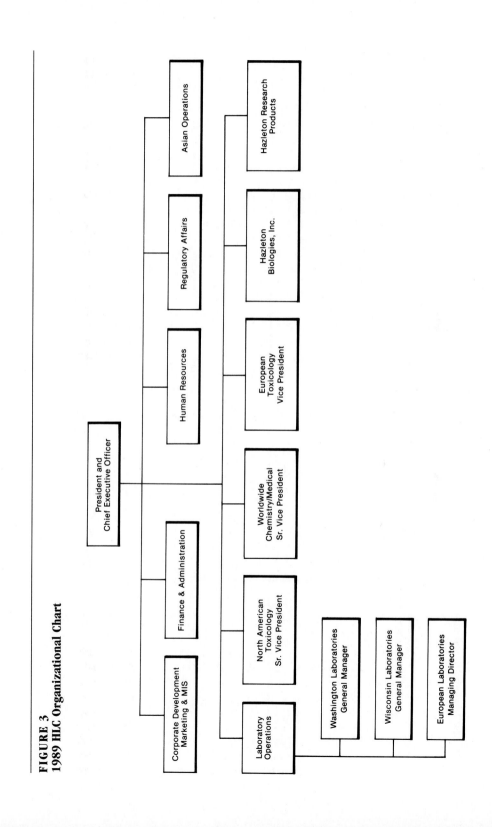

FIGURE 3
1989 HLC Organizational Chart

FIGURE 4
1990 HLC Organizational Chart

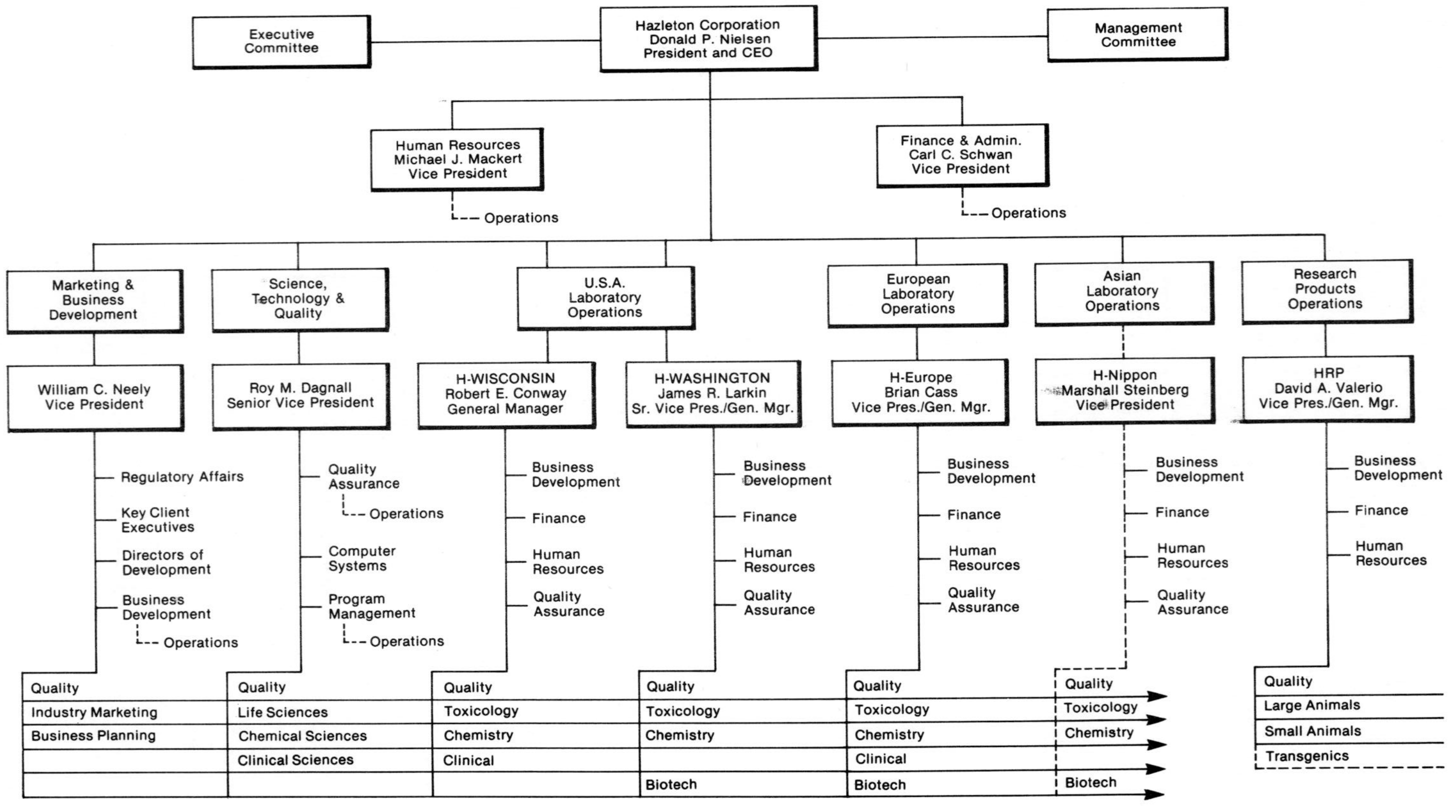

clients' programs within Hazleton. In addition, they had dotted-line reporting responsibility to the labs where the programs were being conducted. These client executives were not physically located at headquarters.

37   The other newly established global functional division was the Science, Technology, and Quality Division. The vice president who headed the division was responsible for ensuring that the best available technology was being employed everywhere in the corporation. Such technology enabled the company to maximize productivity and standardize reporting. Like the vice president of marketing and business development, the VP of science, technology, and quality had global and across-boundaries authority and responsibility, yet lacked line manager authority.

38   The general managers of the laboratories also faced changes in their responsibilities—they were no longer fully independent managers. Those general managers who had succeeded in large part due to an entrepreneurial style were faced with culture shock when their power to negotiate client projects placements was removed. On the other hand, they recognized the need for greater interdependency among the company's labs. They knew that Nielsen's intent was not trying to decrease entrepreneurial spirit but to add the global dimension.

39   Under the general managers, each lab was operated as a profit center. Eventually, the labs were expected to be treated as factories or production centers—and measured on the efficiency of their production facilities. However, half of the GM's bonus was based on the achievement of the corporate goals. This was done to convince the GMs that they needed to be concerned with more than the profitability of their own operations.

40   In addition to overseeing operations, the GMs assisted in the selling function, which was done more inside the lab than outside. The business development person went out and called on a client, but the customer did not generally do business until he or she visited the lab. The general manager was a critical sales agent in such initial visits.

41   The organizational chart reflected other, more subtle, changes as well. For example, as of 1990, there were business development representatives at each location. They reported directly to the lab general manager, with dotted-line responsibility to the vice president of marketing and business development. Since approximately 85 percent of business was still locally obtained, capturing business for their own lab was the primary responsibility of the business development representatives. However, the company established a bonus program, which provided incentives for the business development people to find or to develop clients that utilized labs beyond their home labs.

42   The final responsibility for placement of work was to be handled differently. If clients had a preference for a particular lab, the company attempted to accommodate their requests. If they could not place the work where the clients wanted, Hazleton would try to convince the clients to do it at another location so the work could be started immediately. The clients had the option to wait until their first preference lab (or even specific scientist) had open time periods. In general, however, placement problems stemming from individual client preferences seldom arose, since major program clients typically required and expected multisite lab capability.

43   The major difficulties with work placement occurred when a specific lab did not have the functional capability to carry out a particular stage of a study or when the lab was being fully utilized. Then the business development executive, who was responsible for deciding work placement, contacted other labs by telephone to determine companywide utilization levels. The company was working on a computer network system to facilitate this process. Essentially, then, the marketing and business development executives decided where such overflow work was placed.

44   Nielson experienced some resistance from his management team to these changes in authority and responsibility. Interpersonal conflicts among the new functional vice presidents and the general managers were a particular problem. There were also heightened sensitivities over coordination and communication needs, since information flowed from the study director to the program manager to the key client executives to the client, or the reverse. Nielsen tried to resolve the disputes by stressing the need for more centralization and focus on the company's global market goals.

45   Although not shown in the chart, reorganization also was used to reinforce the importance of a global company focus, the Incentive Compensation Plan changed over the years, as reflected in the following table:

	Percent of Bonus tied to	
Year	Corporate Goals	Local Goals
For general managers:		
1987. . . .	0	100
1988. . . .	25	75
1989. . . .	50	50
1990. . . .	50	50
For business development executives and scientists:		
1988. . . .	0	100
1989. . . .	25	75
1990. . . .	25	75

ORGANIZATIONAL ISSUES

46   Hazleton's organizational structure was becoming more centralized. However, the company remained complex as a result of the number of services and products it provided, in combination with its span of worldwide locations. Hazleton was considering what the next step should be to restructure the company so it could accomplish its global mission and goals.

47   A new organizational structure, if there was one, would need to address a number of specific issues:

   a. Was more centralization necessary? Specifically, how should the company coordinate information and the receipt of contracts from its multiple entry points (i.e., business development, client executives, and multiple scientists all working with the same client)?

   b. With the movement toward a more global focus in serving the world market, was the 1990 structure best? Or should the company be set up by markets served (e.g., drug companies, agricultural chemical companies)?

   c. Should each facility become specialized in one functional or subfunctional area?

   d. Some key client executives and industry specialists were also business development executives. Thus, reporting lines were sometimes confusing. How could this problem be eliminated?

   e. Since the primary selling function was removed from the general manager's responsibilities, GMs could claim that the business development managers or key client executives were not doing the job of keeping the labs fully utilized. Would the GMs be justified in this claim?

   f. Should the marketing and business development personnel continue to be the people to assign work? Or should the power revert back to the originating lab?

   g. Should marketing and sales become a centralized function (with a single entry point to the company) or should they continue to be conducted at the individual lab level?

   h. Who should be the point of contact for status reporting and answering customers' questions? As of 1990, clients were contacting company officials at multiple levels (the lab that obtained the contract, the lab doing the work in question, and the GM). Also, when one location could not handle a particular job and the job was placed at another lab, which lab should be ultimately responsible for this client and who should the client contact for contract updates?

    i. Who should be responsible for the companywide utilization rates of all labs?

    j. Who should be responsible (key client executive, program manager, and so on) when one lab of a multiple location study failed in its task?

    k. To what extent would any proposed change extinguish the entrepreneurial spirit of the location or the firm as a whole?

    l. Would it be better to continue an incremental structure change policy or to incorporate all changes into the structure at one time?

48   In essence, the challenge for the corporation is to answer the question: What are the best organizational structure and coordinating mechanisms for Hazleton Laboratories Corporation?

CASE 26

BEN & JERRY'S HOMEMADE ICE CREAM, INC.

1   One evening in early 1991, company founders Ben Cohen and Jerry Greenfield sat at a local pub trading stories of the early years at Ben & Jerry's Homemade Ice Cream, Inc. In regretful voices they
questioned the virtually overnight success of their company and the changes that had come about in
their once "weird, free-spirited" adventure. Middle management alienation, more-structured outside
managers, and lack of corporate direction threatened Ben & Jerry's original mission, and they wondered if they really could be a big business with a "weird and fun" mentality. Inwardly, both Ben and
Jerry questioned their changing role within the company, their ability to provide a corporate vision,
and, ultimately, whether they should sell out and pursue less-structured ventures.

HISTORY

2   Ben & Jerry's Homemade Ice Cream, Inc., makes Ben & Jerry's super premium ice cream, ice cream
novelties, and Ben & Jerry's Light super premium ice milk. The first "scoop shop" opened on May
5, 1978, in a renovated gas station in Burlington, Vermont. Two lifelong best friends, Ben Cohen and
Jerry Greenfield, invested $12,000 of their own capital and borrowed an additional $4,000 to launch
their entrepreneurial venture. Initially, the only equipment used amounted to an old-fashioned rock salt
ice cream maker. And the owners' ice cream expertise consisted of a $5 correspondence course in ice
cream making from Penn State.

3   Despite these meager beginnings, the company quickly developed a reputation for making chunky,
delicious, unusual flavors made solely from Vermont milk and cream. Local popularity gave way to
larger markets, and, by 1980, they were delivering Ben & Jerry's ice cream to grocery stores and restaurants. *Time Magazine* discovered the company in 1981 and hailed it as the "best ice cream in the
world," helping the company's further expansion.

4   In 1985, Ben & Jerry's moved its corporate headquarters and ice cream factory from Burlington
to Waterbury, Vermont. This new 43,000 square foot facility possessed a production capacity of
400,000 gallons of ice cream per month. A similar facility came on line in 1988 in Springfield, Vermont, to expand product lines into ice cream novelties and Peace Pops.

BEN & JERRY'S UNIQUE BUSINESS PHILOSOPHY

5   Cohen and Greenfield, both products of the 1960s and 1970s, approached business from a unique
perspective. They transformed their personal free-spirited lifestyles into a business adventure. Ben &
Jerry's is dedicated to the creation and demonstration of this new corporate concept of linked prosperity. The corporate mission consists of three interrelated parts:

This case was prepared by Neil H. Snyder, Beeton Professor of Free Enterprise, University of Virginia. Professor Snyder was assisted by Angela Clontz, Bill Deakyne, Johnna Duncan, and Michael Chung of the University of Virginia and George H. Tompson,
University of South Carolina, in the preparation of this case.

6   *Product Mission.*   To make, distribute, and sell the finest quality, all-natural ice cream and related products in a wide variety of innovative flavors made from Vermont dairy products.

7   *Social Mission.*   To operate the company in a way that actively recognizes the central role that business plays in the solitude of society by initiating innovative ways to improve the quality of life of a broad community—local, national, and international.

8   *Economic Mission.*   To operate the company on a sound financial basis of profitable growth, increasing value for our shareholders, and creating career opportunities and financial rewards for our employees.

9   Ben Cohen comments on the Ben & Jerry's approach to corporate operations:

10   It is our objective to run Ben & Jerry's for long-term financial and social gain. We continue to refuse to run our business to make the short term quarterly numbers look good. We are becoming more comfortable and adept at functioning with a two-part bottom line, where our company's success is measured by both our financial and our social performance.

11   This dedication to dual success measures goes beyond lip service. The company's annual report consists of both a financial audit as well as a social audit. By interrelating financial and social performance, the company believes it further improves its financial performance—and it has. Ben & Jerry's has saved millions of dollars in public relations and marketing expenses by providing the media with publicity-generating noteworthy "stunts." Furthermore, Cohen and Greenfield share deep and sincere respect for all individuals and the community. Through Ben & Jerry's, they exercise their belief that business and government have a dual responsibility to devote resources to solve the problems of our society, especially concerning the environment, children, the family, the handicapped, and peace issues.

THE BEN & JERRY'S FOUNDATION, INC.

12   To aid in carrying out this corporate mission, the company established The Ben & Jerry's Foundation, Inc., in September 1985, with Jerry as chairman. Jerry believes the charity foundation seeks to "empower people to take action and to feel effective in their communities and in their lives." The foundation receives 7.5 percent of Ben & Jerry's pretax earnings, which, in 1989, amounted to $288,971 appropriated among 78 groups.

1 PERCENT FOR PEACE

13   Through the foundation, Ben & Jerry's is heavily involved in "1 Percent for Peace," which seeks to redirect 1 percent of the U.S. defense budget toward building understanding between the nations of the world. In 1989, the company contributed $35,433 to the peace movement through earnings from its new "Peace Pop" product.

SOCIAL CONCERNS

International Expansion

14   In line with the company's and the foundation's goals, Ben & Jerry's plans to open a "scoop shop" in the former Soviet Union. The goals of this project are to (1) demonstrate a model of small-scale private enterprise in the old Soviet Union and (2) to use business resources to further peace through understanding between the dissolved Soviet Union and the United States. All profits from the venture will fund citizen exchange programs between the United States and the 15 independent nations of the former Soviet Union.

Bovine Growth Hormone

15   A current concern is the use of bovine growth hormone (BGH) which is a controversial new bio-engineered hormone designed to increase milk production in dairy cattle. The company voiced its opposition to the drug on 6 million of its ice cream cartons, emphasizing the threat the drug poses for small or family-owned dairy farmers.

People Encouraging People

16   Ben & Jerry's dedicated a store franchise worth $21,000 to People Encouraging People. This non-profit program offers community support to mentally ill people and other emotionally handicapped individuals.

Social Mission through Suppliers

17   Ben & Jerry's also seeks suppliers who share enlightened views on the role of business in the community of the world. With over 300 regular suppliers, the company seeks to spread its social mission. For example, Greystone Bakery, which supplies the brownies for the Chocolate Fudge Brownie flavor ice cream, employs homeless and economically at-risk people. In addition, St. Albans Cooperative Creamery is the company's sole supplier of milk and cream, receiving 23 percent of Ben & Jerry's annual payments to vendors. This farmer-owned Vermont cooperative is a successful model of dairy farmers sharing in the profits derived through joint marketing and illustrates Ben & Jerry's commitment to Vermont's farmers.

ENVIRONMENTAL CONCERNS

18   Ben & Jerry's takes several steps to be environmentally aware and safe. In 1989, the company created the position of manager of environmental development to analyze the corporate environmental practices and develop alternatives and solutions to current practices.

19   Recycling efforts remain a major thrust of waste concerns for Ben & Jerry's. Approximately 60 percent of office paper is recycled, and all packaging materials are recyclable. In addition, the company works in combination with Vermont Republic Industries, which employs physically and emotionally handicapped people to recycle plastic ice cream pails.

20   Other environmental steps include Ben & Jerry's construction of a water treatment plant in 1989 as well as energy conservation within the manufacturing process.

21   Most notably, Ben & Jerry's developed a special product, Rain Forest Crunch, to call attention to the destruction of South America's rain forests and to work for their preservation. The product contains Brazil and cashew nuts purchased from Cultural Survival, a human rights organization, which is using the profits to set up cooperative Brazil nut processing plants owned and operated by indigenous forest peoples. Introduced in 1989, 40 percent of Rain Forest Crunch's profits are donated to such preservation groups.

KEY MANAGEMENT

22   *Ben Cohen,* chairman of the board at 40, is far from the typical business executive. He dropped out of Colgate College and entered Skidmore, where he studied pottery and jewelry. Feeling too restrained, he entered Skidmore's "University without Walls" program, an unstructured college degree program, but again quit school never to return. Ben is a self-professed "hippie" whose free spirit led him through various activities before co-founding Ben & Jerry's.

23   *Jerry Greenfield,* 38 and head of Ben & Jerry's Foundation, is another free spirit. He studied pre-medicine at Oberlin College but was unable to gain acceptance to medical school. He drifted about for several years before teaming with Ben on their venture.

24   *Fred Lager,* fondly called "Chico," was hired in 1982 and is the chief executive officer. A University of Southern California MBA, he is described as the company's fiscal soul, the balance to Ben Cohen. Under his direction the company has slashed costs, boosted production, and drastically improved earnings to its current level of $2.05 million.

25   Both Ben and Jerry now spend most of their time travelling and doing marketing promotions for the company, leaving Fred to handle operations.

EMPLOYEES AND WORK ENVIRONMENT

26   Ben & Jerry's views its 250 employees as valuable resources. The company supports its people and the community by hiring the handicapped and providing free therapy sessions—including anonymous drug and alcohol counseling—to any employee who needs it. Employees are actively involved in developing, integrating, and carrying out the company's goals. The company holds monthly staff meetings where all employees—owners, managers, and line workers—congregate over refreshments to discuss projects, performances, changes, and overall "fun" in the workplace.

27   Ben & Jerry's is the antithesis of the typical corporate culture. Fun and a laid-back atmosphere are valued at Ben & Jerry's, where the young and dedicated employees dress casually, know each other, and promote "weird" behavior. Furthermore, the company uses a 5-to-1 salary ratio, which limits the top salary to five times that of the lowest-paid employee. Top salary in 1988 amounted to approximately $89,000.

BEN & JERRY'S MARKETING

28   Ben & Jerry's marketing strategy focuses on innovative, non-traditional methods of promotion and totals to 5 percent of annual sales. By emphasizing its all-natural, high quality ingredients, and "down home Vermont" image on all packaging, sales material, and promotional campaigns, Ben & Jerry's differentiates itself from competitors. Ben Cohen and Jerry Greenfield are also very prominent in defining the products' image. These two "real people" appear on all packaging and make personal appearances to further the company's social mission.

29   Ben & Jerry's has avoided traditional mass media and opted for less costly and more creative means of obtaining publicity. Innovative techniques provide unpaid newspaper, magazine, radio, and television news coverage. For example, Ben & Jerry's sponsors many community events; the Newport Folk Festival, in Newport, Rhode Island; the new Museum of American Folk Art, in New York City; and various charity concerts. Preparations for a Ben & Jerry's scoop shop in the former Soviet Union also have provided free publicity while furthering the corporate mission.

30   In addition, Ben & Jerry's conducts guided tours of its ice cream production facility in Waterbury. In 1989, approximately 167,000 people visited the plant, making it one of Vermont's prime tourist attractions.

FRANCHISE PROGRAM

31   In addition to sales through grocery stores and restaurants, Ben & Jerry's has expanded its store ownership beyond its original scoop shops beginnings. Additional stores have been added in Golchester, Williston, Montpelier, and Waterbury to enhance both sales, community presence, and name recognition. Ben & Jerry's also has over 80 licensed franchises (scoop shops) in California, Connecticut, the District of Columbia, Florida, Georgia, Illinois, Indiana, Maine, Maryland, Massachusetts, New Hampshire, New Jersey, New York, North Carolina, Ohio, Pennsylvania, Rhode Island, Virginia, Canada, and Israel. Franchises cost $25,000 initially, with a yearly advertising fee of 4 percent of sales.

DISTRIBUTION

32   Distribution is critical to the ice cream industry and especially to a small business like Ben & Jerry's, which is entering new and geographically diverse markets. The company primarily uses independent regional ice cream distributors in New England and Florida, and Dreyer's Grand Ice Cream, Inc., handles markets outside these areas. In addition, Ben & Jerry's owns six trucks that distribute products in the Vermont and upstate New York region.

THE ICE CREAM INDUSTRY AND COMPETITION

33   The ice cream industry ranges from super premium to black label ice cream products and has wholesale factory shipments of approximately $500 million per year. Ben & Jerry's competes in the highly competitive super premium ice cream and frozen dessert market. From 1982 to 1985 this segment grew 25 to 30 percent annually, yet growth has since slowed to approximately 15 percent.

34   The principal players are the Häagen-Dazs Company, Inc., Frusen Glädjé, Steve's Homemade Ice Cream, Dreyer's Grand Ice Cream, Inc., and Ben & Jerry's. Häagen-Dazs, the super premium industry leader, is owned by the Pillsbury Company, which is now a subsidiary of Grand Metropolitan, PLC, a British food and liquor conglomerate. Häagen-Dazs also has developed its own line of "chunky" flavors in response to market demand.

35   Frusen Glädjé is owned by Kraft, Inc., a subsidiary of Philip Morris Companies, a tobacco and food conglomerate. Both Grand Metropolitan and Philip Morris are huge, diversified corporations with resources far beyond those of Ben & Jerry's.

36   Steve's, run by aggressive and streetwise marketer Richard Smith, is the most similar to Ben & Jerry's in its product offerings. Steve's has also recently acquired a majority interest in American Glace, a manufacturer of fat and cholesterol-free frozen desserts.

37   Dreyer's, with over 1,000 people, manufactures and distributes a line of premium quality ice cream and sherbet products sold to supermarkets, convenience stores, restaurants, and ice cream parlors.

38   Ben & Jerry's has also recently marketed its Ben & Jerry's Light, which is all-natural and with one third less fat and less cholesterol than normal ice cream. Significant promotion and sales dollars have been invested since its 1989 introduction to gain market share from competition, such as Steve's Ice Milk and frozen yogurt. In addition, Monsanto, another highly diversified corporation, plans to market its own light frozen dessert, Simple Pleasures, using its Simplesse fat substitute.

EXHIBIT 1
Market Players

	Total Assets (000s)	1989 Sales (000s)	ROS
Ben and Jerry's Homemade, Inc.	$ 28,139	$ 58,463	3.5
Dreyer's Grand Ice Cream, Inc.	139,408	227,286	4.6
Steve's Homemade Ice Cream, Inc.	21,304	33,429	4.3
International Yogurt Company	3,464	4,864	−18.7
Tofruzen, Inc.	2,001	1,165	−81.5
Larry's Ice Cream, Inc.	1,986	2,176	−35.3

Ben and Jerry's Ownership Distribution

Type of Investor	Number	Percentage
Institutions	17	11.63%
5% owners	2	30.81
Insiders	4	21.52

39 Further competition comes from the ice cream novelty segment, which includes Dove Bars, Snickers Ice Cream Bars, and other frozen desserts.

40 Given this wide product offering, shelf space remains limited, and expanding franchises in malls and cities leads to more intensified competition. Ben & Jerry's continued sales growth is attributed to geographic market expansion combined with market penetration in the New England segment. Currently, Ben & Jerry's is the best-selling super premium ice cream in New England, but this market remains highly competitive as well.

41 Exhibit 1 shows the major players in the ice cream industry, along with their total assets, sales, and return on sales for the 1989 fiscal year.

FINANCIAL PERFORMANCE

Industry Position

42 In the food processing industry, Ben & Jerry's ranks 11th in earnings per share growth, at 25.4 percent. Its sales growth of 56.1 percent over the last four years places the company 9th in the industry, while return on equity of 15.3 percent ranks 38th.

Capital Structure

43 Ben & Jerry's is a publicly traded company with 8,887 shareholders and 2,614,000 shares outstanding. During the early years, much of the company's growth was financed through debt. Ben & Jerry's has been working to decrease its long-term debt and now has a debt to equity ratio of 72 percent and a long-term debt to capitalization of 33 percent. As of December 1989, the stock sold for $15.00, with a price to earnings ratio of 17.63, with no dividends paid due to a bank loan covenant. Ownership proportions are given in Exhibit 1.

EXHIBIT 2
Percentage Increase in Earnings and Sales, 1986–89

	1986	1987	1988	1989
Sales	102%	59%	49%	22%
Earnings	84	42	11	26

Liquidity

44 Despite its substantial debt, Ben & Jerry's covers its financing costs with a quick ratio of 1.27 and a current ratio of 2.24. Recent cash expenditures have been primarily financed through cash flows generated from operations.

Sales

45 Sales growth doubled each year from 1980 to 1986 and grew an average of 50 percent per year from 1986 to 1988, reaching nearly $20 million. From 1988 to 1989, sales increased 23 percent to nearly $58.5 million. Several factors contributed to this improvement. Unit sales volume rose 18 percent, price per unit rose 7 percent, and better franchise management improved profitability. Sales remain decidedly seasonal, peaking in the summer and bottoming in the winter. Exhibit 2 shows Ben & Jerry's increases in earnings and sales for 1986 to 1989.

Cost of Goods Sold

46 Higher dairy ingredients costs and increased manufacturing costs contributed to a 23 percent increase in costs from 1988 to 1989. The ingredient costs are forecasted to subside and are heavily controlled by supply and demand conditions. The manufacturing expenses, however, will remain and adversely impact the operating margin into the future.

Earnings

47 Ben & Jerry's earnings growth remains impressive, totaling $551,000 in 1985 and then growing 84 percent to just over $1 million in 1986. Since then, net income has grown an average of 28 percent per year to over $2 million in 1989. In addition, earnings per share has grown to $0.78 per share as shares outstanding has remained relatively constant since 1986.

48   Exhibit 3 shows Ben & Jerry's financial highlights for 1985 to 1989. Exhibit 4 shows the firm's distribution percentages for 1989. Exhibit 5 presents Ben & Jerry's financial ratios. Exhibit 6 shows Ben & Jerry's income statements for 1988–89 and pro forma statements for 1990–95. The firm's balance sheet for 1989 is presented in Exhibit 7.

MID-GROWTH CONCERNS

49 In late 1982, bewildered by the company's success and impending structure, Jerry left the company. He felt unable and unwilling to be a "businessman," but he did return in 1985 to head the foundation.

EXHIBIT 3
Ben and Jerry's Five-Year Financial Highlights from 1986 to 1990
(in thousands except per share data)

	Year Ended				
	1990	1989	1988	1987	1986
Net sales.	$77,024	$58,464	$47,561	$31,838	$19,954
Cost of sales	54,203	41,660	33,935	22,673	14,144
Gross profit	22,821	16,804	13,627	9,185	5,810
S&A expenses	17,639	13,009	10,655	6,774	4,101
Operating income	5,182	3,795	2,972	2,391	1,709
Other income	(709)	(362)	(274)	305	208
Income before income taxes	4,473	3,433	2,698	2,696	1,917
Income taxes	1,864	1,380	1,079	1,251	901
Net income	2,609	$ 2,053	$ 1,628	$ 1,445	$ 1,016
Net income per common share	1.00	0.79	0.63	0.56	0.40
Avg common shares outstanding. . . .	2,614	2,599	2,579	2,572	2,565

Balance Sheet Data

	1990	1989	1988	1987	1986
Working capital	8,202	$ 5,829	$ 5,614	$ 3,902	$ 3,678
Total assets	34,299	28,139	26,307	20,160	12,805
Long-term debt.	8,948	9,328	9,670	8,330	2,442

EXHIBIT 4
Ben and Jerry's Distribution
Percent of Net Sales for the Fiscal Year Ended

	December 1989
Wholesale sales to distributors	90.3%
Wholesale sales to franchisees	3.8
Retail sales at company-owned parlors	5.9
Total	100%

50   By this time, Fred Lager had transformed Ben & Jerry's from a small operation to a multimillion-dollar enterprise that had doubled in size each year through 1986. Ben Cohen, too, felt uneasy about this rapid growth and pursued options to sell the company. Ben disliked the negative aspects of a large bureaucracy and felt that he could no longer exercise hands-on management. The growth of Ben & Jerry's, however, enhanced his and the company's ability to follow its social mission to benefit the

EXHIBIT 5
Ben and Jerry's
Financial Ratios

	1987	1988	1989	1990
Quick ratio	1.98	1.43	1.27	.61
Current ratio	2.78	2.19	2.24	1.99
LT debt to equity	0.92	0.89	0.72	.58
Interest coverage	22.24	4.48	5.33	5.96
Inventory turnover	19.91	15.42	14.63	7.63
ROE	15.6%	14.4%	15.3%	16.2%
ROA	7.2%	6.2%	7.3%	7.6%
Net profit margin	4.5%	3.4%	3.5%	3.4%

community. For this reason he decided against selling the company, took it public (initially only offering shares to Vermonters), and pursued growth in hopes of redistributing the wealth throughout the community.

51   Ben and Fred realized that by growing they would confront further competition, so they aggressively moved into eight new markets, including Atlanta and Los Angeles, in only nine months. This move pushed sales up 40 percent and sent the company scurrying to hire more people and to find new facilities to meet demand.

Growth Repercussions

52   Ben & Jerry's rapid growth brought many and often unwanted changes to the old corporate culture. The weird, family atmosphere fell prey to controls, departments, and memos. Flexibility declined as more and more approvals stalled product introductions. No longer did the employees know each other, celebrate employee birthdays, and feel connected. One five-year employee and shift supervisor explained: "It's hard to feel you're a part of a big family if you don't know the brothers and sisters."

53   The forces that had sent Ben & Jerry's into the spotlight as a lean and nimble enterprise had fallen out of balance. Ben described how once small tasks had become unmanageable for the understaffed company:

54   We didn't have good systems or standard operating systems. So every time we had to do something that was pretty much a repetitive process, it would get started from the beginning—instead of just pulling out the procedure and following it. Eventually we'd get the job done, but it took a whole lot more energy.

55   Flexibility limitations in the areas of distribution and ingredients due to Ben & Jerry's social selectivity also placed pressure on the company's ability to meet demand. Facilities produced at nearly full capacity, without plans for added plants in the near future. Employees found themselves spending time putting out small fires in various areas as growth placed stress on all of the company's internal operations.

Middle Management Discontent

56   By 1986, management and line workers alike complained of confusion over corporate objectives. Ben and Jerry called for heightened social contributions, yet remained uneasy about further growth.

EXHIBIT 6
Ben and Jerry's Pro Forma Income Statement
Income Statement 1987–1989

	Actual					Pro Forma		
	1988	1989	1990	1991	1992	1993	1994	1995
Growth rate	49%	22%	31%	20%	15%	15%	15%	15%
Net sales	$47,561,416	$58,463,864	$77,024,037	$84,187,964	$96,816,159	$111,338,583	$128,039,370	$147,245,275
Cost of sales	$33,934,736	$41,659,596	$54,202,387	$59,989,818	$68,988,291	$79,536,535	$91,667,015	$105,617,067
Gross profit	$13,626,680	$16,804,268	$22,821,650	$24,198,146	$27,827,868	$32,002,048	$36,802,355	$42,322,708
Administrative exp.	$10,654,747	$13,008,951	$17,639,357	$18,732,889	$21,542,823	$24,774,246	$28,490,383	$32,763,941
Operating income	$2,971,933	$3,795,317	$5,182,293	$5,465,256	$6,285,045	$7,227,802	$8,311,972	$9,558,768
Other income:								
Interest income	$355,352	$227,331	$296,329	$327,357	$376,460	$432,929	$497,869	$572,549
Interest expense	$(775,533)	$(792,566)	$(868,736)	$(1,141,295)	$(1,312,489)	$(1,509,363)	$(1,735,767)	$(1,996,132)
Other	$145,839	$203,643	$(136,578)	$293,246	$337,233	$387,818	$445,990	$512,889
	$(274,342)	$(361,592)	$(708,985)	$(520,692)	$(598,796)	$(688,616)	$(791,908)	$(910,694)
Income bef. taxes	$2,697,591	$3,433,725	$4,473,308	$4,944,564	$5,686,249	$6,539,186	$7,520,064	$8,648,073
Income taxes	$1,079,187	$1,380,412	$1,864,063	$1,987,793	$2,285,962	$2,628,857	$3,023,185	$3,476,663
Net income	$1,618,404	$2,053,313	$2,609,245	$2,836,771	$3,280,286	$3,790,329	$4,376,879	$5,051,410
Aver. common shares	2,578,701	2,599,194	2,614,474	2,600,000	2,600,112	2,601,126	2,601,126	2,601,126
EPS	0.63	0.79	1.00	1.09	1.26	1.46	1.68	1.94
Market share	9.51%	11.69%	14.03%	16.84%	19.36%	22.27%	25.61%	29.45%

EXHIBIT 7

BEN AND JERRY'S HOMEMADE, INC.
Balance Sheet

	1989	1990
Assets		
Current assets		
Cash	$ 2,393,313	$ 796,190
Accounts receivable	3,669,878	5,044,445
Income taxes refundable	58,119	–0–
Inventories.....................	3,996,550	10,083,142
Prepaid expenses........................	190,289	117,926
Deferred income taxes	204,000	400,000
Total current assets......................	10,512,149	16,441,703
Property, plant, and equipment................	21,704,132	24,164,320
Less accumulated depreciation................	4,666,904	6,864,881
Other assets	589,641	558,223
Total assets.............................	$28,139,018	$34,299,375
Liabilities and Stockholders' Equity		
Current liabilities		
Current capital leases	$ 329,393	$ 355,562
Accounts payable.........................	2,777,655	5,219,474
Accrued payroll	454,201	426,215
Accrued expenses	745,510	1,993,857
Franchise deposits	376,000	244,900
Total current liabilities	4,682,759	8,240,008
Long-term debt	$ 9,327,867	$ 8,947,967
Deferred income taxes	723,000	1,010,000
Stockholders' equity	900	900
Class A common stock	67,261	68,765
Class B common stock	19,209	17,922
Additional paid-in capital.....................	6,386,671	6,474,015
Retained earnings	6,960,493	9,569,738
Class A treasury stock	(29,142)	(29,940)
Total stockholders' equity	13,405,392	16,101,400
Total liabilities and stockholders' equity	$28,139,018	$34,299,375

Growth continued, almost magically, leaving the management team fragmented about the true direction of the company. No longer were the employees 100 percent behind the company's social mission or content with such a "weird and free spirited" approach to business. Furthermore, managers' discontent with the 5-to-1 salary limitation became more vocal as responsibility widened with sales growth. The internal organization needed restructuring and more support services to satisfy the added products and markets.

57   The growing competition and the slowed growth in the super premium market heightened the need for a cohesive, lean, and efficient Ben & Jerry's organization. Ben and Jerry fretted over the erosion of their corporate culture and wondered if they could somehow reinstill their values despite the explosive growth. Many at the company, however, questioned whether Ben and Jerry could provide the corporate vision and leadership necessary for prosperity through the 1990s.

CASE 27

FIRST VIRGINIA BANKS–COMMITTEE STRUCTURE

INTRODUCTION

1   Paul Geithner, president of First Virginia Banks, Inc., considered the casewriter's question. For the last few years, First Virginia Bank had been experiencing excellent performance, measured by return on assets and return on equity, while other banks floundered. What had First Virginia done to account for this performance?

BACKGROUND

2   First Virginia Banks is the oldest registered bank holding company in Virginia, and is the sixth largest banking organization headquartered in Virginia. First Virginia Banks holds about 8 percent of the state's domestic deposits and 12 percent of its banking offices. Assets at the end of the first quarter of 1991 totaled $5.5 billion.

3   First Virginia Banks is a multibank company with 308 branches representing 21 member banks located in Virginia, Maryland, and Tennessee. Most of these branches—259 offices of 16 banks—operate in Virginia, covering areas that include 85 percent of the total population of the state. First Virginia concentrates its business in the areas of northern Virginia, Richmond, Norfolk, and Richmond. First Virginia Banks also includes mortgage banking and insurance affiliates in six states.

4   First Virginia Banks had a reputation for being a "tightly run and hard-working group."[1] First Virginia has always been conservative in its policies, traditional in its practices, and cautious in its decision making. It has preferred to make its money with a consumer orientation, not with dependence on investments. Its style has been to be detail oriented, rather than flashy or trendy.

5   First Virginia's philosophy has caused it to be labeled a "tortoise among hares"[2] The early 1980s saw deregulation of the savings and loan industry, with resulting increase in competition in the financial services industry. In these years, First Virginia Banks was labeled "doomed to failure" for refusing to adopt the liberal loan policies of its competitors. Robert Zalokar, chief executive officer and chairman of the board of First Virginia Banks, was perceived as "old-fashioned, stubborn, even stupid for passing up the big-bucks real estate deals that had catapulted other Washington area banks to the big time."[3] Zalokar and the rest of First Virginia's executives resisted pressure to conform; only 3 percent of First Virginia's loan portfolio is in real estate development, compared to Sovran Bank's 11 percent

---

This case was prepared by Eileen A. Hogan of the School of Business Administration at George Mason University. Development of this case was made possible by a grant from the Funds for Excellence Program of the State Council of Higher Education for Virginia.

[1] Paul Geithner, quoted in Charlotte Crystal, "First Virginia Shines in Troubled Times," *Richmond New Leader,* November 12, 1990, p. 1.

[2] Joel Glenn Brenner, "Banking on a Slower Approach," *Washington Post,* November 5, 1990.

[3] Ibid.

and Signet Bank's 17 percent. Seventy-six percent of First Virginia Banks' loan portfolio is in loans to individuals, compared to 42 percent at much more typical Sovran Bank.

INDUSTRY

6   In 1990, nearly every bank in the Washington, D.C., area was experiencing serious problems due to the collapse of commercial real estate loans. The area was experiencing an extremely high commercial office vacancy rate, as a result of overbuilding. Real estate values plummeted. The largest company in the area, Maryland National Corporation, reported a $242 million loss in the first three quarters of 1990, blamed on problems associated with real estate loans. According to Zalokar, "There's an end to every party. I've been waiting for the end of this one for years."[4]

7   As a result of current financial problems in the industry, banking came under increased scrutiny by the federal government. Crackdowns included forcing banks to reclassify loans that were nonperforming or not paying interest and to increase monetary reserves for bad loans.

PERFORMANCE

8   Appendix A summarizes First Virginia's 1990 performance, compared to other Virginia banks, other southern banks, and national banks. Appendix B gives highlights of First Virginia's 1989 and 1990 results.

9   Contrary to the dire predictions of financial industry analysts a few years ago, First Virginia Banks now finds itself a top performer. First Virginia's return on assets has been consistently among the highest in the nation; in 1990 it stood at 1.39 percent. This compares very favorably with its competition: Central Fidelity came in at 1.05 percent, Crestar at 0.70 percent, Sovran at 0.60 percent, Signet at 0.37 percent, while Dominion reported a loss of 0.11 percent.[5] First Virginia's net interest margin, which measures the difference between interest charged and interest paid, was over 5 percent, while most of its competition was closer to 4 percent. In addition, First Virginia's reserves are substantial, and it has been ranked No. 1 in asset quality ranking among southeastern banks.

10   On September 30, 1990, Dominion Bankshares Mortgage Company reported that 4.19 percent of its loans were nonperforming. Signet Bank reported 3.08 percent. First Virginia Banks reported 0.82 percent.

FIRST VIRGINIA'S PHILOSOPHY

11   First Virginia's philosophy has always been to adopt a slow and steady course. It has pursued small, less-risky loans to consumers and businesses and shied away from risky loans to real estate developers. First Virginia "specializes" in auto loans, credit card business, home equity loans, home mortgages, and business loans; these categories make up around 70 percent of its loan portfolio. It avoids loans outside its trade areas, brokered loans, and loans that finance risky or speculative ventures. Consistent with this philosophy, the interest rates that First Virginia pays to depositors are on the medium to low end of the scale. First Virginia relies on strong, lasting relationships with its customers and on its reputation for stability and security for its continued success.

---

[4] Robert Zalokar, quoted in Brenner.

[5] Ibid.

12   First Virginia extends its philosophy to its technology strategy: it has avoided the leading edge, never pursuing technology for technology's sake. However, First Virginia learns from the mistakes of others—"We let some others get in first, take the hit, and find out the flaws," said Zalokar[6]—and has installed efficient and effective systems for processing and delivering information.

13   Basically, First Virginia's philosophy has reflected an intention to stay the course. Say Zalokar, "We stick religiously to our knitting. What the hell do we know about the market in Louisiana?"[7] This old-fashioned, risk-averse attitude has always set First Virginia apart from most of its competition.

TOP MANAGEMENT AT FIRST VIRGINIA BANK

14   Robert Zalokar, chairman of the board and chief executive officer of First Virginia Banks, clearly had much to do with its philosophy and operation. He joined First Virginia Banks in 1955 after working for the Federal Deposit Insurance Corporation for five years. He became president of the corporation in 1978 and took over as CEO in 1985. He is described as softspoken, conservative, personable, and hard-nosed.

15   Paul H. Geithner, Jr., president and chief administrative officer, came from outside the banking business. He joined First Virginia in 1968, became a vice president in 1969, senior vice president in 1974, and assistant to the chairman and president in 1978. In 1985, he took on the additional title of chief administrative officer. Geithner is a no-nonsense kind of person, direct and to the point, as well as very articulate.

16   Despite Geithner's having come to First Virginia Banks from outside, however, First Virginia is characterized by promotions from within. The top-management team has worked together for many years, to the point where each knows what's expected and knows if ideas will fly or not. For example, of the five regional executive officers, four have been with First Virginia over 20 years, while the last came to the bank 8 years ago. Every regional executive officer has run at least one bank and most have run three to five of varying sizes.

17   Hiring from outside is accomplished, although rarely, when special circumstances warrant the addition of specific expertise. In the case of the regional executive officer brought in eight years ago, First Virginia identified a need for a top-flight commercial lending officer and attracted this candidate from another bank. In certain departments, such as data processing, First Virginia hires regularly at advanced levels to obtain specific expertise. For the most part, however, people at First Virginia grow with the company.

ORGANIZATION STRUCTURE

18   On paper, First Virginia Banks, Inc., appears as 21 independent banks, each with its own board of directors, beneath the holding company. In reality, First Virginia is much more centralized than this facade would indicate.

19   First Virginia attempts to balance the right amounts of centralization and decentralization. Centralization provides significant advantages, in that the small banks that make up First Virginia can utilize the expertise of highly trained professional experts and pooled staff—resources that small banks would normally not have access to. On the other hand, First Virginia recognizes the need for local authority to respond to particular conditions and situations.

---

[6] Robert M. Garsson, "Sticking Close to Home," *American Banker,* October 21, 1990.

[7] Ibid.

20   The organization's policy on lending is stated in its annual report:

21   The general credit approval philosophy of the Corporation is that most commercial loans, lines of credit, and loans secured by real estate should be approved by an appropriate loan committee consisting of the banks' most experienced lenders. We believe that the committee system promotes consistency in loan pricing and credit standards, provides a training ground for junior loan officers, and enables the member banks to benefit from the shared experience and knowledge of their senior officers.

COMMITTEE STRUCTURE

22   First Virginia employs a very strong committee structure to oversee decisions by decentralized operations. Officers are given strict limits to authority. Within prescribed limits, officers do indeed make their own decisions—but according to guidelines, procedures, and rules. Even then, major decisions are reviewed after the fact by assigned committees. Decisions outside of prescribed limits are taken to high-level committees.

23   For example, lending officers are kept on short leashes. Lending officers have a maximum of $100,000 local authority.[8] Each individual lending officer is assigned a review limit, which varies, based on experience, track record, and the size of the branch.

24   An extensive procedures manual, described by Geithner as "a little on the cumbersome side," includes great detail on First Virginia's policies for making every possible type of loan. For each type of loan, it includes definition of terms ("Here's what you're talking about"), examples, necessary forms (with samples filled out), and detailed decision criteria ("Here's what you have to think about as you decide whether to make this loan"). Geithner, joking, quoted an old saying: "It's a system designed by geniuses for execution by idiots." In fact, it represented a training tool for new lending officers and a checklist for experienced ones.

25   First Virginia's loan procedures manual was first written in 1974 and is constantly updated with changes in laws and regulations. However, the basic philosophy behind the manual remains unchanged: conservative lending through crystal-clear guidelines.

26   While each bank has the authority to make loans up to its legal limit, every loan decision over an individual's review limit is reviewed by a corporate committee. Zalokar and Geithner meet with each regional executive officer once a month for the better part of a day to review all loans over the limit. Says Geithner:

27   We are not taking any authority away from the local banks but we are going to be a Monday morning quarterback . . . [we might] say that was a good loan, or don't let any more like that happen, or yes, that wasn't a bad loan, but we think you need more collateral or we think you should restructure it this way or that way . . .

28   Lending officers generally make the strongly recommended changes at the next administrative opportunity.

29   In addition to this review, these top-level executive committees also review other situations that many people might consider mundane. For example, every single nonperforming loan over $25,000 is reviewed monthly. The committee reviews what's happened, who's doing what about it, and why it happened. A similar committee structure exists for credit review.

30   A committee also makes decisions about branch expansion. A bank president might have an idea about where a new branch might be located. He or she and the regional executive officer would prepare a presentation to a committee including Zalokar, Geithner, First Virginia's full-time real estate expert, and the head of engineering and construction. Typically, the committee will discuss the issue

---

[8] Crystal, "First Virginia Shines."

for a half day, perhaps deciding its a good idea, possibly going back and forth in disagreement, possibly agreeing it is a bad idea. If the committee goes ahead, the actual planning of the office becomes the purview of the real estate department for various negotiations, etcetera, within the limits prescribed by the committee.

31   Generally, Geithner described the decision process used in deciding on where to put new branches as not all seat of the pants, but somewhat less than highly sophisticated. Says Geithner:

32   Go out and look at a shopping center in a growing area. If there's a Giant on one corner, a People's Drug store on another, a dry cleaner on the third, it doesn't take any genius to figure out you've got a good location. It's 90 percent common sense."

33   First Virginia also uses a committee structure within banks. Every bank has a loan committee. In a small bank, this typically would include the president, the person responsible for the branch system, the chief lending officer, and various branch managers brought in on a rotating basis. At times, these branch managers contribute to meetings; at others, they listen. Branch managers also attend corporate lending committee meetings.

34   Each member bank's loan committee is responsible for monitoring the lending activities of the individual loan officers. The committee reviews every loan approved by an individual lending officer exceeding $25,000, as well as all significant nonperforming and delinquent loans, at least monthly.

ORGANIZATIONAL CULTURE

35   Officers of the bank don't need to spend a lot of time looking into whether they should consider issues or ideas. "We just know there are certain parameters beyond which we won't go," says Geithner.

36   Officers learn what these parameters are through their experience with various committees—through a process of osmosis. In visiting and in participating on committees, individuals get to see what their cohorts are doing. Cross-fertilization of ideas occurs and, often, morale is helped.

37   Major corporate policy changes occur through a process of involvement by top levels of management. For example, should Geithner decide that something needs to be changed, the topic would be discussed informally and perhaps formally in committees, written up, and distributed. Managers then would be given two weeks to comment. Opinions would be considered, and a decision made. Through this involvement process, managers become committed to corporate policy changes.

PEOPLE MANAGEMENT AT FIRST VIRGINIA

38   First Virginia's management of its people reflects a concern for fairness and for the satisfaction of its employees. This is particularly apparent in its policies for handling acquisitions of other banks or for the merging of banks. First Virginia's 21 member banks are a result of mergers of over 50 independent banks. The strains of merging, as well as the pressures of cost cutting, have been blamed for human resource problems in many banks.

39   Geithner described First Virginia's solution to the need to eliminate positions as "gentle." First Virginia has even been criticized for perhaps too much leniency in handling these potential problems. But one of its proudest boasts is that, of the 53 banks First Virginia has taken over, only four chief executive officers did not remain with First Virginia, and these four left voluntarily. Geithner believes that this has helped create a positive climate at First Virginia.

40   Caring extends not only to top management but to all levels. Whenever jobs are eliminated, a sincere attempt is made to find jobs for everyone. Some factors make this task particularly easy. First, when First Virginia acquires other banks it tends to acquire smaller banks—its acquisitions have

ranged from $4 million to $200 million. The task of absorbing a small redundant workforce is clearly more manageable than a large one.

41 Second, First Virginia's acquisitions generally have tended to be of banks that cover new geographic areas. This usually results in little overlap between existing First Virginia branches and the branches of its acquisition, meaning that fewer branches need to be combined.

42 When First Virginia acquires another bank, First Virginia adopts a soft approach in introducing its management policies. Management does expect that, within a period of a few years, the newly acquired bank will be operating within First Virginia's rules and meeting First Virginia's performance targets. However, First Virginia typically goes to its new acquisition with a "sales pitch." Geithner tells of one such sales pitch presentation, where an individual from the acquirer suggested impatiently, "Why not cut all the —— and tell us what the rules are?" Geithner's response was that First Virginia wants to win the war, not the battle. First Virginia management is sometimes willing to back off, but not too much, in the interest of the long run.

43 And the management does listen and appreciate input; it's not its style to say, "Just because we own the joint you're going to do it." Geithner believes this style has paid off—in ways that are hard to quantify—by keeping most of the people in acquired organizations happy with their treatment.

BRANCH MANAGEMENT AT FIRST VIRGINIA

44 A typical branch manager is a person hired into First Virginia with a bachelor's degree straight out of college. Degrees in economics or accounting are preferred but not essential. Hires go through a six- to nine-month training program in which they rotate through various positions in the bank. For example, potential branch managers work in the collections department for three to four weeks; this often weeds out a number of people.

45 After nine months or so, an individual will be assigned to be an assistant branch manager. After holding this position for about a year, the person might be made a branch manager of a small branch. First Virginia defines three sizes of branches; individuals are promoted up as branch managers of branches of increasing size.

46 After being branch manager of a large bank, an individual might either be promoted into a position of zone manager, sort of a "super branch manager" overseeing several branch managers, or the individual might take a promotion into a staff job at corporate headquarters, for example, in bank operations. From zone manager, an individual might become the No. 2 person at a small bank, directly underneath the president of that bank, with the next logical step being president.

REWARD SYSTEMS

47 First Virginia operates a companywide profit-sharing plan for all employees. Although this represents a minor portion of the bonus package of middle and top-level managers, this mitigates potentially harmful overcompetitive tendencies.

48 Geithner attributes part of the success of First Virginia to a lack of corporate politics, backbiting, and, in general, a distinct lack of unhealthy competition. How has this occurred? Basically, it's not tolerated by top management. In addition, managers receive considerable bonuses based on unit performance. A considerable amount of First Virginia's products and services are uniform, so individual managers cannot do anything really different from their peers. However, bank presidents are responsible for things they can control: deposits, loan quality and production, business development, and day-to-day personnel administration. Each manager is expected to produce; he or she can't adjust rates

but can exercise considerable judgment hustling business. The bonus system creates incentive to do just that.

49   Problems sometimes arise when factors outside the control of the unit manager affect performance negatively. For example, a branch might not make a certain minimum earnings target if it is located in a one-company town and the company goes under. The executive committee that determines bonuses might take exceptional circumstances like these into account. On the other hand, more general economic conditions, such as problems in the coal mining areas of Virginia in the last few years, are less likely to be accepted as an excuse.

50   Bonuses also are available for operations center employees. For example, every employee receives a bonus of $2 for every credit card application they account for. First Virginia's philosophy is to try to provide as many incentives as possible for as many people as possible.

51   Bonuses are available for bank tellers for cross-selling. Over 20 percent of First Virginia's employees are retail tellers. First Virginia experiences a considerable amount of turnover in this position, which is typical for the industry. It is a particular problem in some parts of Virginia, where the teller population tends to be persons completing or returning to school or who are military dependents. Turnover is expensive for First Virginia Banks because it puts each new teller through a week-long special training class, a process that exceeds the training offered by most competitive banks. Often, tellers trained at First Virginia Banks end up working for other banks. "We train half the tellers in the business," kids Geithner.

PRESENT AND FUTURE AT FIRST VIRGINIA

52   In economic conditions that are tough for banking in general, First Virginia has felt and will continue to feel the pinch. It has engaged in various cost-control activities: creating regional backroom operations centers in Roanoke, Richmond, and the northern Virginia area; and by centralizing data processing, investments, accounting, and corporate real estate activities to cut down on duplicating effort and to save money. Efforts will continue to control expenses.

53   Some financial analysts feel that First Virginia is merely late in having to deal with the problems of the current recession. Jeffrey Saut, director of research at a brokerage firm based in Richmond, Virginia, believes that "as the recession deepens, you will see an increase in defaults on installment loans and credit card loans. Consumer loans will not be so great six months from now."[9] First Virginia officials believe that their risk is spread broadly enough that any decline will be minor.

54   For the future, First Virginia is exploring new options, such as offering discount brokerage to its customers. Also under consideration is the possibility of expanding its existing insurance and mortgage banking activities through the acquisition of agencies already serving the bank's markets.

55   Cautious plans are in place to continue expanding its banking activities: in 1990, First Virginia Banks acquired Clifton Trust and opened five new branches. First Virginia plans to continue to branch into high-growth areas and explore additional acquisitions, including possible bargains in the savings and loan industry. Of particular attraction are branches that would fill gaps in the existing market coverage or which could be combined with an existing branch.

56   Paul Geithner sat back to relax. He was certain that First Virginia's conservative philosophy was a direct cause of its current success. He was certain that continuing to travel that road would bring it future success. Yet, how would First Virginia respond when its competitors got back on their financial feet, began operating liberally again, and succeeded in wooing business away from First Virginia?

---

[9] Ibid.

APPENDIX A

First Virginia Banks, Inc., Comparative Performance, 1990

	First Virginia	Average			First Virginia's Rank	
		Six largest banking companies headquartered in Virginia (1)	Southern Region Peer Group 42 banking companies (3)	National Peer Group 28 banking companies (2)	Six largest banking companies headquartered in Virginia (1)	National Peer Group 28 banking companies (2)
Earnings						
Earned on assets (ROA): Net income divided by average total assets	1.25%	0.72%	0.64%	0.81%	1	3
Earned on equity (ROE): Net income divided by average total shareholders' equity	13.59	9.76*	10.29	12.57	2	8
Net interest Margin: Net interest income (tax equivalent) divided by average earning assets	5.15	4.41	4.34	4.39	1	N.T.
Capital Strength						
Equity capital ratio: Total average shareholders' equity divided by total average assets	9.24	6.62	6.60	6.94	1	2
Tier 1 risk-based or "core" capital ratio: Common stock, surplus, and retained earnings, less goodwill (100%) and other intangible assets in excess of 25% of Tier 1 capital	14.05	8.50	8.37	8.84	1	N.T.

	Average				First Virginia's Rank	
	First Virginia	Six largest banking companies headquartered in Virginia (1)	Southern Region Peer Group 42 banking companies (3)	National Peer Group 28 banking companies (2)	Six largest banking companies headquartered in Virginia (1)	National Peer Group 28 banking companies (2)
Asset Quality						
Net charge-offs ratio: Net charge-offs divided by average loans	0.31	0.77	0.87	0.75	1	3
Reserve to nonperforming loans: Year-end reserve divided by year-end nonperforming loans	1.19	0.79	1.04	1.17	1	5
Nonperforming assets to loans: Nonaccrual loans plus reduced rate loans plus other real estate owned divided by year-end loans plus other real estate owned	1.07	2.93	2.56	2.28	1	5

(1) Six largest banking companies headquartered in Virginia are C&S/Sovran, Signet, Crestar, Dominion, Central Fidelity, and First Virginia.

(2) *National Peer Group*—28 banking organizations in the United States with assets from $5 billion to $10 billion.

(3) *Regional Peer Group*—42 banking organizations with assets of $2 billion or more located in the South.

N.T. means not tabulated.

*Excludes Dominion, which reported loss.

Source: Keefe, Bruyette & Woods, Inc.,—Year-end 1990 Report on Comparative Performance and Analysis of Major Banking Organizations from "Keefe Bankbook 1991."

APPENDIX B

Highlights (in thousands except per share data)

	1990	1989	Percent of Change
Earnings			
Net interest income	$ 236,556	$ 228,455	+4%
Net income.	65,111	67,374	−3
Per share of common stock:			
Net income	3.05	3.20	−5
Dividends paid.	1.26	1.18	+7
At Year-End			
Assets.	$5,384,147	$5,123,964	+5
Deposits	4,715,882	4,426,663	+7
Loans	3,390,486	3,294,770	+3
Investment securities	1,286,781	1,069,082	+20
Stockholders' equity	497,687	454,599	+9
Shares of common stock	21,339	21,042	+1
Book value per share of common stock	23.27	21.55	+8
Banks	21	22	−5
Banking offices.	307	298	+3
Stockholder accounts.	19,762	19,856	−
Employees (full-time equivalent).	4,509	4,482	+1
Average Balances			
Assets.	$5,197,386	$4,846,656	+7
Deposits	4,545,499	4,219,299	+8
Loans	3,398,486	3,277,044	+4
Investment securities	1,188,649	987,742	+20
Stockholders' equity	478,946	433,375	+11
Shares of common stock	21,351	21,055	+1
Key Ratios			
Earnings:			
Return on average assets	1.25%	1.39%	
Return on average equity	13.59	15.55	
Net interest margin	5.15	5.36	
Capital strength:			
Stockholders' equity to total assets at year-end . . .	9.24	8.87	
Primary capital at year-end	9.98	9.59	
Asset quality:			
Net charge-offs to average loans	0.31	0.31	
Nonperforming assets to year-end loans	1.07	0.50	
Allowance for loan losses to year-end loans	1.28	1.23	

CASE 28

GENERAL MILLS, INC.: A FOOD COMPANY OR A DIVERSIFIED CONGLOMERATE?

PART 1: FOOD . . . AND MUCH MORE

1   Long before the merger manias of the 1960s, '70s, or '80s, the decision makers of General Mills struggled with the questions of diversification. For the management of General Mills, the relevant questions about diversification, mergers, and acquisitions were not *if* questions but *when and how* questions. Indeed, the company itself was created through the 1928 merger of four major groups: the Washburn-Crosby Company, a Minneapolis-based miller; the Sperry Company, headquartered in San Francisco; the Kell Mills of Oklahoma and Texas; and the Larrowe Milling Company of Detroit.

2   The merger was the brainchild of James Ford Bell of Washburn-Crosby. The consolidation of the first three companies created a nationwide system for distributing the company's primary product, milled flour, which was sold both to consumers and commercial bakers. Bell recognized some of the limitations to growth the flour milling companies faced, and he diversified through the inclusion of Larrowe. Later known as Larro, this company transformed the by-products of the flour milling process into high-grade formula feed for animals. With a daily capacity of 81,700 barrels of flour, 5,950 tons of commercial feed, and 720,000 pounds of other cereal products, the new corporation—comprised of 27 operating companies spread across 16 states—fulfilled Bell's dream of becoming the world's largest miller.

3   The new company soon developed certain distinctive characteristics that continue to exert an influence on its corporate culture—notably a predisposition toward decentralization, an emphasis on marketing, and a commitment to quality and service. Even though the newly combined companies recognized the economic benefits they gained through the merger, each insisted on remaining autonomous and continued to operate as a separate profit center. By pooling their combined assets, General Mills as an entity could borrow at rates below those available to the individual units. Corporate headquarters in Minneapolis provided the subsidiaries with national advertising, merchandising, and administrative support. Each unit was headed by a president from the original company who was responsible for that unit's ultimate performance.

4   As the company grew, the difficulty of coordinating the units' activities also grew, as did the inefficiencies created by duplications of services and product lines. Only in 1937 were the subsidiary companies formally dissolved and the authority of the parent company reluctantly recognized. Even then the operating divisions remained largely autonomous, but there was increased emphasis on corporate goals and how each unit contributed to the company's overall strategy. Although the company frequently had to relearn the hard lessons of adequately coordinating divisional efforts, this early experience in tolerating decentralization, while also achieving companywide goals, proved valuable for General Mills in later years.

This case was prepared by J. Carl Clamp, Distinguished Lecturer in Management, University of South Carolina. Professor Clamp was assisted by George H. Tompson, Susan Ivey, Patricia Harmon, and Reginald Belcher in the preparation of this case.

Innovation and Marketing

5 Merchandising, or marketing, was one area where the benefits of cooperation were readily apparent. As the company moved into the 1930s, Bell, who was president of the new company, and his management team searched for new lines of branded specialties that would supplement the company's staple products. An alert company salesman suggested one such product—a baking mix. On a train trip he noticed that the dining cars always served hot biscuits, even late at night. He asked how the cook managed such a feat and learned that the secret was in premixing some of the ingredients. He passed the idea along to General Mills, and soon the company introduced its first convenience product —the perennial best-seller, Bisquick, the nation's first all-purpose baking mix.

6 This desire to develop such new branded products led to the early establishment of an outstanding corporate research and development function within General Mills. Not only were efforts directed toward the formulation of new products themselves but major attention also was paid to the design, engineering, and eventual manufacture by General Mills of sophisticated equipment to produce the new products. By retaining such expertise within the company, management properly concluded that competitors would lag behind General Mills in new product development. The proprietary processes that made the products unique would remain under the company's control and would preserve General Mills' competitive advantage.

7 Another product's beginnings were even less auspicious than those of Bisquick. A Minneapolis diet theorist, searching for ways to make bran palatable to his clients who wanted to lose weight, noticed that thin round wafers formed when he accidentally spilled gruel on a hot griddle. He took his discovery to General Mills, and George Cormack, Washburn-Crosby's head miller, developed a process for producing the flakes. An employee's wife suggested the name Wheaties and General Mills began production. The new cereal met with some resistance from company salesmen, who felt they already had enough wares to peddle, and initial sales were modest.

8 Sales in the Minneapolis area, however, received a boost from a revolutionary form of advertising—the first singing commercial. Radio was then a relatively new communications medium and some viewed the company's expenditure of $24 for a weekly half-hour program as an extravagant experiment in reaching consumers. Nevertheless, the experiment was successful; when company directors examined Wheaties' sagging 1929 sales of only 53,000 cases nationwide, they found that 30,000 of those cases were sold in the area reached by the radio program.

9 Rather than abandon the product, the company decided to promote it nationally through the newly created Columbia Broadcasting System. Soon the singing commercial was joined by another radio first. The "Skippy Program," based on a then popular comic strip, was the first effort to market cold cereal directly to the end user, the American child. Later the company developed its own program for young listeners, the long-running "Jack Armstrong, the All-American Boy." The company also marketed Wheaties to women through soap operas, such as "Betty and Bob," and to attract the men in the radio audience, the company sponsored broadcasts of baseball games. The company's confidence in this three-pronged radio advertising approach to marketing a marginally successful product was well justified. While experts once had estimated sales of 1.5 million cases annually to be the maximum for Wheaties, actual sales in the late 1930s more than tripled that figure.

10 The company did not neglect the more traditional forms of advertising for the product. The enduring slogan—"Wheaties, Breakfast of Champions"—first appeared on a billboard at a company-sponsored baseball game. With modifications, this theme has survived into the 1990s as a series of athletes (including Bob Matthias, Bruce Jenner, Mary Lou Retton, and Pete Rose) has promoted the product. The company displayed its marketing knack again when it repackaged the theme in 1983 in a effort to shore up Wheaties' sales. To appeal to adults, the company developed its "What the Big Boys Eat" advertising campaign. Commenting on the ads' effectiveness in reaching women, one company official summarized consumers' letters: "I've never seen the work 'hunk' spelled out so many times in my life." This successful "new" campaign also featured the return of an old tactic:

the company purchased radio advertisements during the morning drive time, when many consumers are in their cars commuting to work. The ability to combine innovative and traditional marketing methods effectively and to develop successful products remains a company strong point.

11   A third company tradition that began early in General Mills' history is an emphasis on corporate responsibility, quality, and service. From the company's inception, Bell and his managers insisted that it should provide value and services to customers. General Mills' products have long featured a "money-back guarantee," and all consumer letters to the company receive a personal reply.

Nutrition and "Betty Crocker"

12   Of course, this attention to consumers often has been linked to promoting the company's products. Indeed, the policy of replying to customer letters was responsible for the creation of another company hallmark—Betty Crocker. As part of a promotional campaign for Gold Medal Flour, the company featured a puzzle contest, which turned out not to be much of a puzzle. More than 30,000 correct solutions were mailed in, and many homemakers also enclosed requests for recipes. Company officials felt these should be answered and created Betty Crocker as a composite "super-homemaker" character, complete with name, distinctive signature, and even a portrait, to write the replies. A staff of nutritionists developed and tested the recipes, which were mailed to consumers and later distributed through the Betty Crocker cookbooks and Betty Crocker radio cooking lessons.

13   While General Mills products were featured in many Betty Crocker recipes, they were also a vehicle for improving American's eating habits. During the Great Depression of the 1930s, Betty Crocker emphasized the role of nutrition in health and offered advice to housewives struggling to feed families on restricted budgets. During World War II, the company developed Betty Crocker materials that helped homemakers deal with rationing and also explained the role of "home defense" in the war effort. A 1940s poll showed that Mrs. Crocker was the second-most recognized American woman—only Eleanor Roosevelt, the First Lady, was better known. Although she has undergone a number of adjustments to update her image. Betty Crocker remains a well-recognized symbol of quality in packaged foods.

14   General Mills also has promoted a significant number of nutrition education efforts that did not directly involve its products. It has funded studies on child nutrition and worked closely with government and educational officials to develop and distribute education materials based on the results of such studies. It was an early sponsor of the Four-H program, a federal effort to teach rural youngsters agronomy and home economics.

15   The company also took a more direct approach to improving American nutrition through specific research and development efforts. For instance, General Mills was the first miller to enrich all of its flours. Company scientists were the first to synthesize vitamin D, and the company subsequently donated the patent for the process (and its proceeds) to the University of Wisconsin.

16   The company has not overlooked public service in other areas than nutrition. The General Mills Foundation, established as a means of smoothing the company's ability to make philanthropic contributions in both more and less profitable years, supports a broad range of projects. The company consistently ranks as one of the nation's most generous corporate givers and encourages employees to donate their time and expertise to programs that benefit their communities. Corporate responsibility, like decentralization and marketing skills, has been a constant factor in General Mills' corporate culture.

World War II and Its Impact

17   Although the company was barely a year old when the Great Depression began, it weathered the 1930s well, becoming 1 of only 18 firms on the New York Stock Exchange that survived the decade without any decrease in dividend payments. The 1940s began with their own challenges to the nation and to General Mills. While some of the company's wartime contributions were predictable, given its

major lines of business, others were not. General Mills produced a steady stream of flour, vitamin concentrates, dehydrated eggs and soups, and ready-to-eat breakfast cereals. Mundane products were sometimes transformed for use in the war effort. For example, the company produced sandbags instead of flour bags and converted granular flour into alcohol for use in smokeless gun powder. But the company also began to produce completely new items. For example, General Mills used its mechanical engineering expertise (developed to protect proprietary food-processing secrets, such as the puff-gun process used to produce Cheerios) in unexpected ways. The company manufactured gun sights, fire control devices, torpedo indicators, and torpedo guidance systems. One such system was the "jitter-bug" torpedo, which lulled its targets into complacency with an apparently off-course pattern that was corrected at the last moment with a figure-eight or a swerve to score a hit. The world's largest flour miller thus demonstrated that it understood how to produce more than just breakfast cereals.

18   As the war ended, the company found itself facing a dilemma: its three peacetime lines (flour, packaged foods, and animal feeds) all had enjoyed surges in sales, but future growth appeared somewhat limited. Fundamental changes in American society were affecting the nation's eating and buying habits. Women began entering the labor force in greater numbers and had less time to cook, housewives no longer baked fresh bread daily, per capita consumption of flour products was declining, and consumers clamored for new products after the years of wartime spending restrictions. General Mills' managers wanted to take advantage of such changes and, in a break with long-standing traditions, issued long-term debt and sold new preferred stock to obtain funds for modernizing and diversifying the company. Research and development efforts intensified and the company sought growth in three areas—mechanical products, specialty chemicals, and processed foods.

19   General Mills' mechanical engineering department had demonstrated its capabilities during the war, and Arthur D. (Art) Hyde, director of manufacturing and later vice president for research, wanted to build on this wartime base. The tall, husky Hyde was fortified with a Columbia University degree in mechanical engineering. As the only company officer with an engineering background, he was able to present his ideas with little challenge from other officers who lacked such technical expertise. Hyde maintained contacts with the Washington defense establishment from whom the company obtained contracts for producing an astounding array of equipment. Its newly established aeronautical research laboratories, for example, began Operation Skyhook—the design of upper-atmosphere weather balloons. The enormous balloon envelopes were fabricated in a three-block-long building in St. Paul (a relic from the 19th century St. Paul World's Fair). The company used the expertise it developed in manufacturing torpedo guidance systems to produce the Hounddog, a heat-seeking missile with a unique guidance system. Out of the same background came the development and manufacture of the Alvin II, a two-man deep-submersible submarine still in use.

20   But General Mills' mechanical engineers did not intend to ignore consumer products, either. Hyde, hoping to capitalize upon the pent-up demand that developed during World War II, pushed for the development of electric appliances. In 1946, the company introduced the Betty Crocker line of electric irons, toaster ovens, pressure cookers, and mixers.

21   General Mills sought new uses for its expertise in developing specialty chemical products as well. The company had entered the soybean industry in 1942 and, after the war, continued to produce soybean meal for feeds along with soybean oil for use in a variety of protective coatings. The company commercialized the production of polyamide resins for use in coating and packaging materials. Wheat starch was transformed into a textile finisher, a commercial baking aid, glutamic acid hydrochloride, and monosodium glutamate. General Mills became a major processor of guar gum for use in such products as cosmetics, pharmaceuticals, ice cream mixes, beer, cheese spreads, and rubber latex. The company also became a supplier of fatty acids for industrial uses as diverse as the manufacture of soap, synthetic rubber, chocolate candy, and cosmetics.

22   General Mills' research ultimately led to the development of new processed-food products. Company scientists isolated soy proteins and began to develop them for use in such products as Bacos. Its wartime experience with dehydrated foods led to the introduction of a broad line of new products.

The company answered the consumers' demands for increased convenience by introducing Betty Crocker cake and pie mixes and instant mashed potato products, as well as by producing conceptually new breakfast cereals.

Charles H. Bell and Problems of Growth

23   By 1953, packaged foods accounted for 18 percent of General Mills' sales, as opposed to 9 percent in 1938. Flour dropped from 74 percent of sales to only 52 percent while chemical and mechanical products, in contrast, grew from 0 percent in 1938 to 11 percent of 1953 sales. General Mills as a whole enjoyed enormous growth—the Food Division alone generated pretax profits that were four and one half times greater than those of the entire company in 1938. To deal with this growth, president Charles H. (Charlie) Bell (a son of founder James Ford Bell) reorganized the company into seven operating divisions.

24   Bell also began to realize that growth sometimes masked lack-of-fit problems in the company's diversification efforts. The appliances line, for example, faced direct competition from General Electric and Westinghouse. Although the company understood how to sell Betty Crocker cake mixes, it never quite mastered the selling of electric mixers and toaster ovens and the need for nationwide service facilities to honor warranties on such products. Accordingly, General Mills sold its home appliance business in 1954 to McGraw Electric of Chicago. After the sale, the Mechanical Division turned its attention to other projects, such as the manufacture of electronic components and the acquisition of the Magnaflux Corporation, the leading manufacturer of branded nondestructive materials-testing devices.

25   The 1950s also were marked by the poor performance of General Mills' first diversification venture, the Animal Feed Division. Although farmers recognized the quality of Larro feeds, the number of farms was declining and the agriculture industry's widely fluctuating profits made Larro's earnings stream unstable. General Mills attempted to enter the consumer market with Surechamp dog food and 3 Little Kittens cat food. But individual buyers did not share the farmers' brand-name recognition for Larro, and the company proved unable to transform its highly enriched, growth-promoting commercial feeds into products that were palatable to household pets. In 1961, the Animal Feed Division lost $5.5 million on sales of $50 million.

26   Growth in other areas also slowed—General Mills' sales grew at a compound annual rate of only 2.2 percent between 1956 and 1960, while profit margins fell. Competitors who had concentrated primarily on food products, in contrast, enjoyed healthier growth rates—4.5 percent for General Foods and 6.9 percent for H. J. Heinz. The company's diversification strategy clearly needed modification and, in 1959, Charlie Bell, a good marketer but not a tough manager, recruited his World War II commanding officer, four-star Air Force general Edward W. (Ed) Rawlings, to get the company back on track.

The "Rawlings' Earthquake"

27   After a year as financial vice president and later head of consumer foods, Rawlings took over the presidency and Bell became chairman. In moves that insiders dubbed the "Rawlings' Earthquake," the retired general shook up top corporate management, reorganized the company into smaller operating units, restructured the sales force, recruited key specialized talent from other companies, installed a $1.5 million Data and Communications Center to manage a companywide information system, and created the first corporate planning and development unit to coordinate new product development. As part of his corporate overhaul, Rawlings (now CEO) quickly sold the ailing feed business. Sales dropped 6.5 percent in six months, but corporate profits soared by 49 percent. Later the company also sold its highly profitable but misfitted Magnaflux Division to Champion Sparkplug. Rawlings described his objective as "[the] concentration of our corporate strength in areas of maximum profit

potential, rather than deploying our resources over too wide an area, with the danger of overcommitment in those with low profit potential."

28 New ventures reflected Rawlings' insistence that General Mills focus more attention on taking advantage of its distinctive competencies by concentrating on new packaged food products. The company bought Morton Foods and the Tom Huston Peanut Company (regional snack-food vendors), pursued international food sales through acquiring interests in European companies, and negotiated joint ventures and licensing agreements with Japanese and later Korean food producers.

29 The new planning and control system ensured that the flood of new products (over 100 in the two years between 1961 and 1963) was consistent with the company's redefined objectives. A new vice president of research, Dr. William B. (Bill) Reynolds, commented on the changes: "Sure, the lab used to turn out plenty of new products. But many times it operated on its own. A lot of effort was wasted and a lot of people tripped over each other." New products, now focused on consumers' desires, included casserole mixes, Wondra flour, "adult" cereals, such as Total, and new snack foods with longer shelf lives, such as Bugles and Whistles. Processed foods soon accounted for more than half the company's sales.

McFarland and Focused Diversification

30 During the latter half of the 1960s, General Mills' managers decided the time was right to pursue more rapid growth in other areas through a more narrowly focused diversification strategy and an aggressive acquisition program. James P. (Jim) McFarland, a long-time company veteran who replaced Rawlings as president, expressed the broad strategy: "Take our unusual talents—our marketing ability —and move the company into any area where we could serve customer needs and make ourselves the product leader." He also pointed out the need to achieve a careful balance between businesses that were capital intensive and those which provided cash flows. This new strategy led the company into five seemingly disparate areas of operations: (1) food products, (2) restaurants, (3) toys, games, and crafts, (4) specialty retailing, and (5) fashion apparel and accessories. The areas were unified, however, by their potential for higher profit margins, by the common markets they served, and by their capacity for being marketed as branded consumer products.

31 In expanding its processed foods operations General Mills not only developed products internally but also searched for promising acquisitions. Morton's, a pickle as well as a snack-food company; Gorton's, a frozen seafood processor, and Donruss, a bubble-gum maker, all joined the General Mills fold.

32 Such acquisitions also attracted increased Federal Trade Commission scrutiny. The resulting antitrust charges, combined with the low profit margins common in the food processing industry, spurred General Mills' search for opportunities outside the food area.

33 The move from food products into restaurants seemed a logical development. As consumers searched for convenience, as incomes climbed, and when more women entered the work force, away-from-home eating increased. General Mills decided to avoid entering the fast-food segment of the industry, however, and chose instead to concentrate on medium-priced, family-oriented, full-service dining concepts. The company purchased the three-unit Red Lobster restaurant chain, opened a group of Betty Crocker pie shops, and tested the Union Jack Fish 'n' Chip Shoppes as an outlet for Gorton's fish products.

34 The move into toys, games, and crafts seemed a logical way to use General Mills' expertise at marketing products to children and their parents. The company acquired Kenner (maker of the $6 Million Dollar Man), Parker Brothers (maker of Monopoly, Clue, and Risk), Fundimensions (maker of Lionel model trains), and LeeWards (a mail-order needlework and home-decorating supply chain). The same rationale of familiar markets led to the company's entry into the specialty retailing and fashion and accessories areas with the acquisitions of The Talbots (mail-order retailer of high-quality women's clothing), Eddie Bauer (mail-order retailer of outdoor apparel), David Crystal (maker of Izod/Lacoste sportshirts and women's dresses), and Kimberly Knitwear (maker of women's sportswear).

35   This new diversification strategy was directed by a group of young, aggressive executives. Part of the "baby boom" themselves, they shared its values and were eager to make their mark on the company by moving into new markets. Bright, well-educated MBAs, they sometimes encountered unexpected problems. Henry Porter, Jr., the company's 34-year-old vice president and treasurer, nonplussed one New York bank when he showed up to negotiate a multimillion-dollar bank loan. The bank checked with Minneapolis to see if they were talking to the right person, and Porter's 38-year-old boss—Louis F. (Bo) Polk—assured them they were indeed. Another young policymaker was 38-year-old Craig Nalen, who was largely responsible for the "Fun Division's" move into toys and games. When questioned about the company's involvement and the social value of such products, he seriously replied: "The family that plays together stays together."

36   The mood of the whiz kids also infected company veterans. Venture teams, charged with identifying and developing new products in all five areas of operations, originally were designed to provide a challenge for bright young MBAs. But such positions rapidly became coveted assignments for seasoned managers as well. The teams were so successful that by 1976 one quarter of the company's sales came from products that had not existed five years earlier.

37   Financial results of the new strategies were mixed. Sales increased rapidly, but initially led to lower profit margins and a decline in earnings per share growth. McFarland defended the moves as necessary for long-term growth, and security analysts, who reacted favorably to the changes, seemed to share his assessment. The company successfully weathered the price controls and recession of the early 1970s and, by 1976, profit margins reached 3.3 percent, well above the industry average of 2.2 percent. General Mills, credited by the chairman of a rival company with having "the best overall management in the industry," achieved a 17.9 percent annual sales growth from 1971–76, a 10.8 percent growth in earnings, and a 16.6 percent return on equity.

The Controlled Growth of Bob Kinney

38   E. Robert (Bob) Kinney, former president of Gorton's, took over as General Mills' chairman in 1977. Described by the retiring McFarland as having "good, gutsy Maine business sense," Kinney continued the company's basic direction, but he aimed at achieving "controlled growth and high profit margin."

39   He sold the company's only remaining nonconsumer business, the multinational Specialty Chemical Division, and used the proceeds to buy companies that met his targets for growth. These included Ship 'N Shore, the nation's largest manufacturer of mid-priced women's blouses, and Foot-Joy, a well-respected maker of gloves, golf shoes, and other sports footwear. Monet, maker of high-quality costume jewelry distributed through department stores nationwide, and Wallpapers to Go, a home-decorating products chain, joined The Talbots, Eddie Bauer, Dunbar Furniture, Kittinger Furniture, Pennsylvania House Furniture, and LeeWards in the company's Specialty Retailing Division. Kinney described these companies' common characteristic as low-ticket, high-turnover items with a top market position. Kinney summarized their appeal for General Mills: "We like cash-generating businesses because it's nice to fund our growth with cash rolloff, rather than having to go to debt markets all the time."

40   The company's strategy of consumer-focused diversification appeared to be paying off by 1978–79. Dividends (General Mills was one of only eight NYSE firms that still could boast that its dividends had never been reduced) had a five-year compound annual growth rate of 14.2 percent, while earnings per share from continuing operations grew at 14.3 percent annually over the same period. But this bright financial picture included some problem clouds as well. Sales of apparel and accessories grew at 20.7 percent, but operating profits plunged 48.6 percent to only $20 million. The costs associated with selling Kimberly Knitwear ($20 million) contributed to the decline, as did the $16.6 million pretax loss at Ship 'N Shore. General Mills responded to the Ship 'N Shore losses, which it blamed on management blunders and lax controls, by "paying for the surgery" of overhauling management. Troubles also appeared in toys and games. Even though sales reached $610 million (a 23.8 percent increase fueled primarily by demand for Kenner's Star Wars and Strawberry Shortcake toys), operating profits slumped 4.8 percent as the result of an $8.9 million writeoff associated with the Riviton construction toy's recall.

41   Overall, however, performance was strong and managers gave the company's marketing skills much of the credit. The Proctor & Gamble brand manager system had been adopted in the late 1960s after P&G stole market share from General Mills' products, most notably when P&G's Duncan Hines displaced Betty Crocker as the leading cake mix seller. General Mills' brand managers frequently were responsible for profitable product innovations. F. Caleb (Cal) Blodgett, who later became vice chairman, was one such innovative brand manager. While watching 6-by-300-foot sheets of granola cereal roll out of an oven only to be crumbled, Blodgett became intrigued by an alternative. He suggested cutting the sheets, thus creating the lucrative Nature Valley Granola Bar and moving General Mills into the profitable, fast-growing health-food snack market.

42   Another product manager who later became director of marketing, Steven Rothschild, attacked a similar market via a new product acquisition. He persuaded General Mills to buy a small Michigan company that held a license from SODIMA, a French dairy cooperative, to manufacture Yoplait yogurt. General Mills' marketing for the product emphasized its French origins and included the sponsorship of such European-style sports events as bicycle racing and hot-air ballooning. Ads pointed to France's reputation as the nation of culinary connoisseurs and, by 1985, the once little-known brand finished a strong second in the $880 million U.S. yogurt market. Sales had grown at a five-year annual compound rate of over 30 percent.

Atwater and Preparation for the 1990s

43   Another former brand manager, H. Brewster (Bruce) Atwater, took over as chairman and CEO in 1981. He inherited a company where 45 percent of the past 10 years' growth had come from new products and services developed internally. General Mills continued to enjoy strong performances from its traditional products as well. Thirteen product lines all over 25 years old tripled in volume between 1971 and 1980. Cheerios, for example, continued to reign as the nation's leading cold cereal in sales dollars.

44   Sales also received a boost from acquisitions. Although General Mills acquired over 40 companies between 1967 and 1979, the total cost was only around $335 million plus 3.5 million common shares. These same companies contributed almost $2 billion to 1980 sales. As *Forbes* put it, General Mills was buying "concepts, not assets." Over the years, General Mills' decentralized management style helped acclimatize some of the smaller, more entrepreneurial acquisitions into the larger company. By 1981, however, soaring interest rates and the poor performance of some units led General Mills to institute tighter managerial and financial controls. In 1982, General Mills was voted one of the nation's 10 best-managed companies in a *Fortune* survey.

45   By 1984, however, the earlier problems in toys and fashions reappeared in more disturbing form. Although food earnings were up, losses associated with apparel and toys as well as reduced earnings at the Red Lobster chain of restaurants caused overall earnings to fall for the first time in 22 years, as shown in Exhibit 1. Ironically, some of the problems were the results of earlier successes.

46   Parker Brothers, a late entrant in the markets for both electronic toys and video games, experienced phenomenal sales surges. Video games sales presented an even more exaggerated peak-and-valley pattern for sales: 1981 and 1982 sales hit $125 million, but 1983 ended in a loss as the market evaporated. In 1980, for example, Merlin became the year's best-selling toy and propelled game sales to $60 million, but sales quickly declined.

47   Izod experienced a prolonged version of the same phenomenon. Its line of alligator-marked sportswear, developed by Rene LaCoste in 1933 and produced by David Crystal since 1969, became *de rigueur* for aspiring preppies in the early 1980s. Sales nearly doubled between 1979 and 1982 and Izod was hard pressed to meet demand. Managers failed to keep up with shifts in consumer tastes,

EXHIBIT 1
Financial Data for Years Ended May 31 (amounts in millions of dollars except per share data)

	1985	1984	1983	1982
Sales:				
Consumer foods.	$2,771.3	$2,713.4	$2,792.6	$2,707.4
Restaurants.	1,140.1	1,079.7	984.5	839.4
Toys	1,368.9[1]	782.7	728.3	654.8
Fashion		587.4	616.3	657.3
Specialty retailing & other	373.8	437.6	429.1	453.2
Total	5,654.1[2]	5,600.8	5,550.8	5,312.1
Costs and expenses:				
Costs of sales	2,474.8	3,165.9	3,123.3	3,081.6
Selling, general & administrative[7]	1,368.1	1,849.4	1,831.6	1,635.5
Depreciation & amortization.	110.4	133.1	127.5	113.2
Interest	60.2	61.4	58.7	75.1
Total	4,013.5[3]	5,209.8	5,141.1	4,905.4
Earnings before taxes.	195.9[4]	398.7[5]	409.7	406.7
Taxes.	(80.5)	(165.3)	(164.6)	(181.2)
Net earnings (loss)	$ (72.9)[8]	$ 233.4	$ 245.1	$ 225.5
Per share data:				
Earnings (loss) per share	$ (1.63)	$ 4.98	$ 4.89	$ 4.46
Dividends per share	2.24	2.04	1.84	1.64
Stock price range:				
Low	47¾	41⅝	38⅝	32⅝
High.	60⅝	57⅛	57¾	42⅛
Average common shares outstanding	44.7	46.9	50.1	50.6

[1] Includes sales of Fashion Segment.
[2] Includes sales from discontinued operations—Toys and Fashions in 1985, Specialty Chemicals in 1978.
[3] Excludes costs and expenses from discontinued operations.
[4] Excludes losses from discontinued operations.
[5] Includes gain from redeployment.
[6] Includes $5.2 million gain on disposal of specialty chemicals.
[7] Includes employee retirement, where applicable.
[8] Includes loss from discontinued operations of $188.3 million and redeployment loss of $75.8 million.

however, and the company's increased investments in facilities and inventories made it harder to change in response to the market. General Mills' managers, attuned to long product planning, development, and introduction cycles, were unable to compete effectively in industries that required almost overnight responses to rapidly changing market conditions.

48   To stem losses, General Mills again tightened controls, sometimes with disastrous results. The toy divisions found themselves dumping products in May—an off-season in an industry where 60 percent of sales occur in the November–December holiday season—in a futile attempt to shore up balance

1981	1980	1979	1978	1977	1976
$2,514.6	$2,218.8	$2,062.4	$1,861.6	$1,735.3	$1,633.0
704.0	525.7	436.3	354.9	240.9	180.7
674.3	647.0	583.9	492.3	403.2	347.6
580.5	422.5	360.4	298.1	411.5	379.8
379.0	356.3	302.0	236.1	118.5	103.9
4,852.4	4,170.3	3,745.0	3,243.0	2,909.4	2,645.0
2,936.9	2,578.5	2,347.7	2,015.3	1,797.5	1,663.9
1,384.0	1,145.5	1,021.3	894.6	807.9	704.5
99.5	81.1	73.3	58.6	48.1	46.7
57.6	48.6	38.8	29.3	26.7	29.4
4,478.0	3,853.7	3,481.1	2,997.8	2,680.2	2,444.5
374.4	316.6	263.9	260.4	229.2	200.5
(177.8)	(146.6)	(116.9)	(124.6)	(112.2)	(100.0)
$ 196.6	$ 170.0	$ 147.0	$ 135.8[6]	$ 117.0	$ 100.5
$ 3.90	$ 3.37	$ 2.92	$ 2.72	$ 2.36	$ 2.04
1.44	1.28	1.12	0.97	0.79	0.66
23⅜	19	24	26¼	26½	23⅜
35¾	28¼	34⅛	31½	34⅞	34⅛
50.4	50.5	50.4	49.9	49.6	49.2

sheet results in time for General Mills' May 31 fiscal year ending. The parent company's increasing involvement often demoralized managers in the poorly performing units. New recruits, brought in to spice up sales, sometimes alienated seasoned managers. Some charged that General Mills' headquarters became too involved in product detail decisions. A Parker Brothers' marketing manager, for example, recalled what became a "never-ending procession to General Mills. We started to think we were in the presentation business, rather than the toy business."

49   In early 1985, General Mills once again revised its diversification strategy and put its fashion and toy divisions up for sale. Wall Street and the financial community welcomed the news—the company's stock jumped 32 percent after the announcement. The Casa Gallardo Mexican and Darryl's restaurant chains were sold, as was Foot-Joy, but potential buyers for other units proved skittish. In early spring, the company announced plans to spin off the toy and fashion divisions to shareholders in a tax-free transaction. General Mills wrote off $188 million in assets in preparation for the spinoff and incurred a redeployment loss of $75.8 million. While this produced the company's first year of negative earn-

ings per share, pre-tax earnings from continuing operations remained strong at $271.7 million. In addition to the financial restructuring, management changes in the affected units also began. On November 7, 1985, Crystal Brands and Kenner Parker Toys became independent companies owned by General Mills' shareholders. Managers of the new businesses felt that, unhampered by General Mills' bureaucracy and somewhat conservative corporate culture, they would be in a better position to respond effectively to market changes.

50   Changes also occurred in the mainstream at General Mills, now comprised only of the processed foods, restaurants, and specialty retailing divisions, but with the strong balance sheet shown in Exhibit 2. A major management reorganization designed to shift control to younger executives was announced in November 1985. The restructuring reflected the company's new focus on growth in its $3 billion consumer foods group, which was split into two divisions: one for established lines (cereals, baking mixes, etc.) and one for "major growth opportunities" (in seafood, snacks, yogurt, etc.). Management announced plans to expand the Red Lobster chain at a rate of 25 units annually through 1990, to expand its Olive Garden (Italian) chain, and to acquire a Chinese restaurant chain. Changes in the specialty retailing division included sale of the We Are Sportswear chain and plans for new retail outlets for The Talbots and Eddie Bauer.

51   With the fashion and toy spinoffs and the restructuring of its remaining divisions, General Mills seems to have refocused its diversification strategy yet again. Once more the company is pinning its hopes for growth on the consumer. Stepped-up product introductions, expanded restaurants, and increased retail distributions are seen as the way to achieve the company's new target rate of 6 percent real annual growth. From flour to animal feeds to defense contracts to Star Wars toys, General Mills has learned some hard lessons about the difficulties of managing widely diversified businesses. At the same time, the redirected leaner General Mills has become less attractive as grist for someone else's diversification mill. (Two of General Mills' competitors, Nabisco and General Foods, had been acquired recently—by R. J. Reynolds and Philip Morris, respectively—and *Business Week* had noted that branded consumer products companies were "hot" takeover targets.) Atwater, with 27 years of marketing experience in consumer products, noted: "We're substantially less vulnerable than we would have been had we not done all the streamlining. . . . I feel more comfortable about where we're going than I have for a long time." By pursuing a narrower range of activities, the company hopes to regain its momentum. Earnings for the first two quarters of 1986 rose 13 percent on a sales increase of 6 percent, but only time will tell if the nation's first diversified food company has finally developed the right formula or if history will repeat itself yet again.

PART 2: FOOD . . . AND LITTLE MORE

52   The 1986 fiscal year was an excellent one for General Mills, with sales of continuing operations increasing 7 percent to $4.59 billion. Consumer Foods, General Mills' largest business, led the company with an operating profit increase of 15.9 percent to $307.9 million. The restaurants' business showed a moderate increase of 2.7 percent in operating profit to $88.3 million. The company's last remaining nonfood business, Specialty Retailing, achieved exceptional growth in sales of 26.9 percent to $474.3 million and showed an operating profit of $26.6 million, contrasted with a small loss in 1985. These results were a direct benefit of the major restructuring efforts of the company announced in 1985.

53   The objectives of this 1985 restructuring plan were to achieve a mix of businesses that would provide a combination of high returns, good growth, and substantial reinvestment opportunities, all with reasonable stability in earnings streams. During 1986, General Mills sold its Pennsylvania House and Kittinger furniture operations to Chicago Pacific Corporation and its Casa Gallardo and Darryl's restaurants to W. R. Grace & Company by the end of the third quarter.

54   By the end of fiscal 1986, General Mills had achieved a mixture of businesses it characterized as "exceptionally strong." The company had 44 percent of its sales in high return and growing core businesses, comprised of Big G cereals, Red Lobster restaurants, and The Talbots clothing. It had 37 percent of its sales in high-return established businesses, including Betty Crocker desserts, Bisquick, Gold Medal flour, and Helper dinner mixes. Last, it had 19 percent of its sales in growth opportunities. The growth opportunities included Yoplait yogurt, fruit snacks, Gorton's frozen seafood, Red Lobster International, The Olive Garden, and Leeann Chin's restaurants. The company's strategy targeted continual innovation and preemptive marketing efforts to gain a leading market share for all of its products. Chairman and CEO Bruce Atwater stated in the second quarterly report for 1986 that "the changes were designed to provide strong leadership for General Mills' current and future needs." The company's financial objectives have remained the same. General Mills aims for a minimum return on average equity of 19 percent, a strong balance sheet with an "A" bond rating, and annual increases in dividends. Also, earnings per share growth over a five-year period is targeted at an average of 6 percentage points or more *above* inflation.

55   Another significant action during 1986 was the adoption of anti-takeover measures by General Mills. This poison pill plan was ratified by the board of directors on February 24, 1986. It includes a distribution of rights to the shareholders to purchase shares of cumulative preferred stock upon the occurrence of certain events. The plan will go into effect if a prospective bidder accumulates 20 percent of General Mills common stock or makes an offer to acquire at least 30 percent. According to the company, this measure was taken in light of the current hostile takeover environment in the food industry and not due to any specific threats.

Excellent Performance and Heavy Investment

56   General Mills showed continued improved performance during the 1987 fiscal year. Sales increased 15 percent to $5.19 billion, with over three quarters of the gain resulting from physical volume increases and expansion of the restaurant and retail businesses. Consumer Foods' sales rose 13 percent to $3.45 billion and operating profit rose 30 percent. The restaurants' sales increased by 19 percent to $1.2 billion and operating profit grew by 9 percent. Specialty retailing again achieved excellent growth, with sales increasing 28 percent to $490.3 million and operating profit increasing 165 percent. Results for 1987 more than met the company's financial objectives. For the future, General Mills then added one additional objective—a sustained minimum after-tax return on sales of 5 percent.

57   During 1987, General Mills formulated a planned investment program of $1.6 billion to be executed over the next three years. It planned to invest $800 million in its core businesses for a state-of-the art cereal production plant, 60 to 70 new Red Lobster restaurants in the United States, and a near doubling of The Talbots' retail store base. Approximately $200 million is to be spent on established businesses that do not require major new investment. The rest of the money will be spent on promising new growth opportunities, such as additional Olive Garden restaurants, additional Eddie Bauer retail stores, and new capacity for new food products.

1988—Transformation Completed

58   General Mills achieved record financial results for fiscal year 1988. Sales of continuing operations reached $5.18 billion, an increase of 10 percent. Consumer Foods experienced a gain of 9 percent in sales and 11 percent in operating profits. The restaurants' business had good performance from Red Lobster and The Olive Garden, but the poorly performing Leeann Chin's Chinese restaurants were sold.

59   In May 1988, the transformation of General Mills that began in 1976 continued remarkably. General Mills sold all of its specialty retailing businesses, including Talbots and Eddie Bauer.

EXHIBIT 2
Balance Sheet, Years Ended May 31 (dollars in millions)

	1985	1984	1983
Assets			
Current assets:			
Cash & short-term investments.	$ 66.8	$ 66.0	$ 58.0
Receivables, net	284.5	550.6	468.3
Discontinued operations, net	517.5	18.4	1.0
Inventories	377.7	661.7	632.8
Investments in tax leases	—	49.6	159.1
Prepaid expenses.	40.1	43.6	38.9
Total current assets.	1,286.6	1,389.9	1,358.1
Noncurrent assets:			
Land, buildings, & equipment	1,486.0	1,829.2	1,765.0
Less accumulated depreciation	(530.0)	(599.8)	(567.5)
Net land, buildings, & equipment	956.0	1,229.4	1,197.5
Other assets	420.0	238.8	388.3
Total assets	$2,662.6	$2,858.1	$2,943.9
Liabilities and Stockholders' Equity			
Current liabilities:			
Accounts payable.	$ 360.8	$ 477.8	$ 410.1
Current portion of long-term debt	59.4	60.3	17.5
Notes payable	379.8	251.0	401.9
Other	257.2	356.3	293.0
Total current liabilities	1,057.2	1,145.4	1,122.5
Noncurrent liabilities:			
Long-term debt	449.5	362.6	464.0
Deferred taxes.	29.8	76.5	88.5
Deferred taxes—tax leases	60.8		
Other	42.0	49.0	41.5
Total noncurrent liabilities	582.1	488.1	594.0
Total liabilities	1,639.3	1,633.5	1,716.5
Total stockholders' equity	1,023.3	1,224.6	1,227.4
Total liabilities and stockholders' equity	$2,662.6	$2,858.1	$2,943.9

Specialty retailing only accounted for 10 percent of total sales and 6 percent of net earnings, and the company could not identify any expandable concepts for the businesses. These two factors in combination with the opportunity to realize high selling prices led the board of directors in January 1988 to authorize exploration of the sale of these businesses. Talbots was sold for $325 million

1982	1981	1980	1979	1978	1977	1976
$ 33.4	$ 39.1	$ 39.1	$ 97.0	$ 19.9	$ 22.3	$ 81.8
408.6	391.4	374.2	313.4	297.6	231.6	216.0
—	—	—	—	—	—	—
660.6	611.4	543.1	501.8	440.2	425.8	353.7
124.9	—	—	—	—	—	—
31.5	34.0	29.6	24.2	30.7	33.7	21.3
1,259.0	1,075.9	986.0	936.4	788.4	713.4	672.8
1,552.1	1,368.6	1,123.8	975.0	886.7	829.1	739.3
(498.0)	(448.1)	(376.3)	(331.3)	(299.7)	(289.0)	(267.8)
1,054.1	920.6	747.5	643.7	587.0	540.1	471.5
388.6	304.8	278.9	255.1	237.3	193.8	183.9
$2,701.7	$2,301.3	$2,012.4	$1,835.2	$1,612.7	$1,447.3	$1,328.2
$ 333.1	$ 322.8	$ 235.3	$ 318.7	$ 302.4	$ 277.9	$ 241.3
20.0	17.7	7.8	10.2	6.7	3.4	4.4
409.2	155.5	83.2	44.0	59.0	27.7	24.1
286.0	260.1	243.4	121.9	135.2	106.2	107.9
1,048.3	756.1	569.7	494.8	503.3	415.2	377.7
331.9	348.6	377.5	384.8	259.9	276.1	281.8
46.0	38.2	25.0	22.4	11.1	14.9	11.2
43.3	26.4	19.5	17.0	23.3	10.9	17.3
421.2	413.2	422.0	424.2	294.3	301.9	310.3
1,469.5	1,169.3	991.7	919.0	797.6	717.1	688.0
1,232.2	1,132.0	1,020.7	916.2	815.1	730.2	640.2
$2,701.7	$2,301.3	$2,012.4	$1,835.2	$1,612.7	$1,447.3	$1,328.2

to JUSCO Company, Ltd., one of Japan's largest retailers, and Eddie Bauer was sold to Spiegel, Inc., for $260 million.

60   The sale of the specialty retailing businesses was the culmination of the company's streamlining efforts. General Mills' basic strategy is to remain only in the most attractive segments of those busi-

nesses where its management is competitively superior and where its marketing position is strong. This strategy emphasizes internal growth, but it does not exclude selected acquisitions.

61   The change in corporate structure had begun in 1976 when the company's sales were $2.6 billion. By fiscal 1988, sales had grown to $5.2 billion. General Mills had decreased its investment in volatile, low-return businesses from 30 percent in 1976 to 2 percent in 1988. Also, the company's investment in businesses with good growth potential increased by 36 percent to 64 percent.

62   Another significant event of 1988 was General Mills' increased marketing efforts in the oatmeal market. The company introduced quick and instant oatmeal under the Total brand name. It is trying to reach the goal of becoming the premier breakfast food company and also increase its penetration of the adult cereal market. Since 8 percent of all breakfasts in America contain hot cereal, there is good potential in this area. General Mills' marketing effort will emphasize Total's nutrition image and count on Total's loyal customer base.

63   General Mills became the leading marketer of consumer foods and one of the nation's largest operators of full-service restaurants. Its ongoing goal is to develop new products and services that consumers recognize as better than competitive offerings. It is committed to financial results that place it in the top quartile of all major companies *and* to good corporate citizenship. During 1988, General Mills added again another financial objective of providing annual increases in dividends that will achieve and maintain approximately a 50 percent payout rate.

1989—Emphasis on Internal Growth and Joint Ventures

64   Fiscal 1989 was another successful year for General Mills. Sales increased 13 percent to $5.62 billion and operating profits rose 10 percent to $580.1 million. (See Exhibit 1—Financial Data and Exhibit 2—Balance Sheet.) The company credits the gains to aggressive internal growth measures. The company completed the disposition of its specialty retailing businesses in the first quarter of 1989, leaving General Mills in just two separate markets, consumer foods and restaurants, down from 13 in the 1970s. Consumer Foods' sales and operating profits grew 9 percent and 7 percent to $4.0 billion and $452.4 million, respectively. The restaurants' business showed a sales increase of 24 percent to $1.62 billion and operating profits increased 23 percent to $127.7 million. To emphasize its confidence about its continued success, General Mills' management increased two of its financial objectives. First, the target five-year growth rate for earnings per share was raised from 6 to 7 percent. Second, the target for the minimum after-tax return on sales was increased from 5.0 to 5.5 percent.

65   On November 30, 1989, General Mills signed a joint venture agreement with Nestlé S.A., the world's No. 1 food company. This strategic alliance plans to develop a major breakfast cereal business in Europe to be called Cereal Partners Worldwide. Combining the cereal expertise and technology of General Mills with the local marketing expertise and massive sales distribution systems of Nestlé, the venture will attempt to gain a leading share of the growing European cereal market. Currently, the market is about $1.6 billion, but it is estimated to increase to about $6.5 billion by the year 2000. General Mills, the world's No. 2 cereal company, decided to enter into this joint venture because management felt that entering the European market alone would be too risky. The CEO of Cereal Partners Worldwide will be General Mills' Charles W. Gaillard, who served as general manager of Big G Cereals from 1979 until 1988. Concurrently, the company is working with the Calbee Company, a Japanese firm, to test market Cheerios and Golden Graham cereals in Tokyo.

66   General Mills then explored the possibility of selling its O-Cel-O Division, which is the leading marketer and producer of cellulose sponges in the United States. This division was the last remaining operation competing in markets unrelated to foods and restaurants. In recent years, O-Cel-O has achieved very profitable record sales of approximately $45 million. However, selling this division would be in line with the company's emphasis on its two core businesses. The O-Cel-O Division and its assets were sold to 3M in 1991.

The Battle of the Cereals

67   General Mills' Big G cereal business has been stealing market share from Kellogg in recent years. Its market share has risen from 21 percent in 1979 to 27 percent in 1989. Kellogg has dominated the cereal market since the company was started in 1906. Most of Big G's gains lately have been the result of the oat bran craze that has swept the United States. Forty percent of Big G's cereals are made from oats, which put it in an excellent position to take advantage of the new consumer preference. Kellogg only has 20 percent of its cereals made from oats and has been slow to respond to the market change. Kellogg's share of the cereal market eroded to an estimated 39.8 percent by year-end 1989 from 42 percent in 1987. During 1989, Kellogg experienced a significant turnover in its management. Horst W. Schroeder, the president and heir-apparent to the position of CEO, resigned unexpectedly in September. Schroeder left after less than one year. *The Wall Street Journal* reported that Schroeder's management style conflicted with that of Kellogg. Further, his top management had talked of attaining more than 50 percent of the market by 1992.

68   In the short 12 months from July 1988 to July 1989, Big G's Cheerios gained 3.1 percentage points in market share, rising from 6.8 to 9.9 percent. This gain translates into huge amounts of revenue for General Mills because a single market share percentage point equals about $66 million of revenue. By the end of 1989, Cheerios had replaced Kellogg's Frosted Flakes as the most popular cereal in America. General Mills also was fortunate in that the company had planned a big marketing push for its Cheerios and Total cereals before the oat bran craze hit, so it was able to react immediately.

69   General Mills also had a major problem in 1989. In the spring of 1989, the company introduced a new bran cereal called Benefit, containing psyllium. It was an attempt to capitalize further on the consumer demand for bran by incorporating psyllium, a soluble fiber cited in studies as having cholesterol-reducing abilities. However, the new cereal turned into a problem child for the company. The Food and Drug Administration questioned the amount of psyllium that humans could safely consume. The FDA stated that too much of the fiber could potentially have harmful intestinal effects on humans. Initially, General Mills thought it could overcome the FDA report by altering the packaging and marketing efforts for Benefit cereal. In November of 1989, the cholesterol-reducing claim was dropped from the packaging and advertisements. However, General Mills finally decided to simply remove the cereal from the market on January 4, 1990, because it saw that it could not overcome the controversy.

The Early 1990s

70   The early 1990s have been successful ones for General Mills. Companywide sales have increased almost 10 percent each year and after-tax earnings are up 75 percent in just four years. Big G's ready-to-eat cereal dollar market share has risen from 25 percent in 1989 to 29 percent in 1992. This gain is the result of increased sales in its established cereal lines and the success of its new cereals, Apple Cinnamon Cheerios and Total Raisin Bran. However, results were constrained by lack of production capacity until one new plant came on line in mid-1992.

71   Big G's strategy is to keep its old cereal brands vital and to introduce new cereals that taste good and are nutritious. The Cheerios and Wheaties brands of cereal have remained among the top 10 cereals during the early 1990s. General Mills plans to continue its marketing of the athletic heritage and whole grain goodness of Wheaties. Accordingly, it has signed NBA superstar Michael Jordan as a spokesperson for Wheaties. Wheaties and Cheerios were chosen by McDonald's to be sold as part of the breakfast menu beginning in April of 1990. General Mills also has been very successful in its efforts to introduce new cereals. Four of the eight remaining new brands introduced since 1990 achieved market shares of 1 percent more in 1992. New brands will contribute 27 percent of the company's 1993 sales. The Cheerios and Total cereal families account for nearly one half of General Mills' cereal business. General Mills consistently has been taking market share from Kellogg in recent years.

TABLE 1
1992 Cereal Market Growth

Market	1992 Market Retail Sales ($MM)	Growth vs '91	1992 $ Share
U.S. retail	$8,000	+ 8%	29%
U.S. foodservice	375*	+ 5	26
Canada	595	+ 4	15
United Kingdom	1,400	+ 7	14
France	320	+26	14
Spain	160	+43	10
Portugal	35	+76	45
Italy	85	+11	NM

* Distributor sales.

Of the approximately 200 brands of cereal sold today, only 30 have a market share of 1 percent or more and 12 of those cereals are Big G brands. Only the future will tell if General Mills will be able to sustain this growth.

72   The restaurants' businesses also have been performing well in the 1990s. The Olive Garden's sales grew by 165 percent and operating profits more than 400 percent between 1990 and 1992. This reflects steadily improving margins and continued rapid expansion. The Olive Garden is currently the fastest-growing dinnerhouse chain in the United States.

73   In its history, Red Lobster has never shown an annual decline in sales per unit and only one year of lower earnings. And 1990 does not appear to be an exception. The success of Red Lobster is due to the company's efforts to keep the concept fresh and to respond quickly to changing consumer preferences. General Mills plans to realize increasing profitability from recent investments to accelerate the growth of both restaurant chains. Total sales reached $2.54 billion in 1992, up from $1.6 billion in 1989.

74   Red Lobster International also recorded modest gains in sales and operating profits since 1989, attributing 1992 declines to a weak Canadian economy and a new 7 percent food tax. At year-end, there were 70 restaurants in operation in the Toronto, Montreal, Ottawa, and London markets. Red Lobster Japan, a joint venture with a leading Japanese retailer, opened 4 new restaurants for a 1992 year-end total of 50. The emphasis on international restaurant expansion has been outmatched by a renewed emphasis on international food operations, other than cereals, particularly in France, Belgium, Spain, Portugal, and the Netherlands.

75   General Mills recognized that it could not neglect the rest of the world in its quest for growth. Uncharacteristically, it took an "unorthodoxed" approach to expand overseas: joint ventures. It jumped quickly into the $3.5 European cereal market by forming a joint venture with Nestlé—Cereal Partners Worldwide (CPW). CPW dropped most of the feeble Nestlé cereal brands, replacing them with Cheerios and Golden Grahams, and reformulated the Nestlé brands. The venture also quickly bought the Rank Hovis McDougall cereal unit, giving it an immediate 15 percent market share in Great Britain as well as a springboard for the Continent. General Mills' CPW joint venture with Nestlé achieved impressive sales gains in 1991–92, supported by the European cereal market growth shown in Table 1. And in August 1992, General Mills and PepsiCo, Inc., received the European Commis-

TABLE 2
Strong Market Positions

Business: 1989	FY 1989 Sales ($MM)	1989 Retail $ Market Share	Market Position
Consumer foods:			
Big G RTE Cereals	$1,340	25%	2
Betty Crocker Desserts	420	42	1
Family Flour & Bisquick	270	55	1
Yoplait Yogurt	200	21	2
Gorton's Frozen Seafood	190	25	1
Helper Dinners	170	65	1
Fruit Snacks	100	39	2
Pop Secret Microwave Popcorn	80	21	2
Restaurants:			
Red Lobster USA	1,220	24	1
The Olive Garden	300	8	1

sion's approval to combine their European snack-food businesses into a joint venture that combines Bugles and Frito-Lay products, making the venture the largest snack-food marketer in the $17 billion European market.

76   Despite its divestiture of Leeann Chin's, General Mills began market testing for a new Chinese dinnerhouse chain called China Coast in 1990 in Orlando, Florida. Testing for The Olive Garden began in Orlando, also, and took five years. General Mills is being cautious with this venture, because it does not want another failure like the Leeann Chin's venture. Entering the Chinese restaurant business is very hard, because so many of the restaurants are family owned and have cheap labor rates. Between 1990 and 1992, the Orlando China Coast recorded steady sales growth and General Mills has opened two more restaurants in 1993 to further test the concept.

77   In 1989, *Fortune* again rated General Mills near the top of its Fortune 500 ratings. Overall, General Mills ranked 85th in sales. In profits, the company was 63rd and, in market value, 57th. General Mills ranked extremely high in return on assets and return on average equity at 25th and 13th, respectively.

78   General Mills' overall performance in the 1990s has been significantly impacted by the major restructuring efforts effected in 1985. The company has moved from 13 separate industries in the 1970s to two—consumer foods and restaurants. General Mills' business structure has been strengthened by disposing of what it deemed nonstrategic, highly cyclical, or slower growth/low return businesses.

79   In 1992, earnings per share from continuing operations was more than 2.7 times the 1986 level. Return on sales has steadily increased to 6.5 percent in 1992 from 3.6 percent in 1985. Significant growth also was experienced in return on equity, increasing from 12 percent in 1985 to 41 percent in 1992. General Mills' share price has more than tripled and dividend growth has accelerated almost 250 percent since 1986. The net result is a business structure that management considers to have "unusually strong growth characteristics" for their industries (note Tables 2 and 3). This growth is further noted in Tables 4, 5, and 6. Commenting on this growth posture, company spokeswoman Kristen Wenker had this to say in June 1993:

80   While General Mills remains committed to strong growth consistent with what we have achieved in the last 5+ years, we no longer choose to classify our businesses like we did in the 1989 Annual Report

TABLE 2 (concluded)

Business: 1992	1992 Sales ($MM)	1992 Retail $ Share	Market Position
Consumer foods:			
Big G Cereals	$2,010	29%	1
Betty Crocker Desserts	430	43	1
Helper Dinner Mixes	295	78	1
Fruit Snacks	195	54	1
Family Flour	180	41	2
Yoplait Yogurt	175	19	2
Pop Secret Microwave Popcorn	165	35	2
Gorton's Frozen Seafood	150	23	2
Restaurants:			
Red Lobster USA	1,530	26	1
The Olive Garden USA	807	16	1

TABLE 3
General Mills' Business Structure

Business Type: 1989	Percent 1989 Sales	Projected 5-year "Real" Growth Rate
Good growth/high return (Big G, Red Lobster)	47%	6%
High growth/low return (The Olive Garden, etc.)	22	15
Lower growth/high return (Gold Medal, Betty Crocker, etc.)	31	3
Total	100%	7%

(Table 3). Rather, General Mills has chosen to focus intensely on two basic lines of business—consumer foods and casual dining restaurants—which we see as having dynamic growth possibilities for years to come. General Mills further chooses to compete in consumer food products or restaurant concepts where we are or can be the market leader in broad market segments with strong, long-term growth potential. Several of our consumer products that have been around for some time as well as selective "niche" additions are well positioned to do this; benefiting among other things from increasingly health conscious, convenience-demanding consumers and substantial international expansion opportunities. On the restaurant side, we like the casual dining segment of the restaurant industry. This segment provides the format of preference for people 40-to-60 years old. The aging "baby boomers" (40 million+) combined with a generally fragmented industry segment bode well for the future growth of the casual dining segment and General Mills' prospects with Red Lobster and The Olive Garden when compared to segments like fast food.

TABLE 4
Seven-Year Financial Summary: General Mills (in millions except per share and employee data)

	May 31, 1992	May 26, 1991	May 27, 1990	May 28, 1989	May 29, 1988	May 31, 1987	May 25, 1986
Financial Results							
Earnings (loss) per share[1]	$ 2.99	$ 2.87	$ 2.32	$ 2.53	$ 1.63	$ 1.25	$ 1.03
Return on average equity	39.9%	49.2%	49.5%	60.0%	41.1%	31.4%	21.5%
Dividends per share[1]	1.48	1.28	1.10	0.94	0.80	0.625	0.565
Sales[2]	7,777.8	7,153.2	6,448.3	5,620.6	5,178.8	5,189.3	4,586.6
Consumer foods	5,233.8	4,939.7	4,520.3	3,998.7	3,667.5	3,450.0	3,060.0
Restaurants	2,544.0	2,213.5	1,928.0	1,621.9	1,312.1	1,250.0	1,050.0
Toys	—	—	—	—	—	—	—
Fashion	—	—	—	—	—	—	—
Specialty retail and other	—	—	—	—	199.2	490.3	474.3
Costs and expenses:							
Cost of sales[2]	4,123.2	3,722.1	3,485.1	3,114.8	2,847.8	2,834.0	2,563.9
Selling, general and administrative[2]	2,504.5	2,386.0	2,138.0	1,808.5	1,710.5	1,757.5	1,547.2
Depreciation and amortization[2]	247.4	218.4	180.1	152.3	140.0	131.7	113.1
Interest[2,3]	58.2	61.1	32.4	27.5	37.7	32.9	38.8
Earnings before income taxes[2]	844.5	765.6	612.7	517.5	442.8	433.2	323.6
Net earnings (loss)	495.6	472.7	381.4	414.3[5]	283.1	222.0	183.5
Net earnings (loss) as a percent of sales	6.4%	6.6%	5.9%	7.4%	5.5%	4.3%	4.0%
Weighted average number of common shares[1]	165.7	164.5	164.4	163.9	174.0	177.5	178.5
Taxes (income, payroll, property, etc.) per share[1,2]	3.09	2.77	2.29	1.98	1.66	1.80	1.33
Financial Position							
Total assets	4,305.0	3,901.8	3,289.5	2,888.1	2,671.9	2,280.4	2,086.2
Land, buildings, and equipment, net	2,648.6	2,241.3	1,934.5	1,588.1	1,376.4	1,249.5	1,084.9
Working capital at year end	(337.1)	(190.1)	(263.1)	(197.1)	(205.5)	(57.1)	41.6
Long-term debt, excluding current portion	920.5	879.0	688.5	536.3	361.5	285.5	458.3
Stockholders' equity	1,370.9	1,113.5	809.7	731.9	648.5	730.4	682.5
Stockholders' equity per share[1]	8.28	6.74	4.96	4.54	3.88	4.14	3.81

TABLE 4   (concluded)

	May 31, 1992	May 26, 1991	May 27, 1990	May 28, 1989	May 29, 1988	May 31, 1987	May 25, 1986
Receivables	291.9	306.3	258.7	254.6	230.0	236.7	220.0
Inventory	487.2	493.6	394.4	370.1	423.5	388.6	350.9
Total Current Assets	1,034.6	1,082.3	910.1	841.3	985.9	940.9	811.9
Total Current Liabilities	1,371.7	1,272.4	1,173.2	1,038.4	1,191.4	923.0	772.6
Total Liabilities	2,934.1	2,788.3	2,479.8	2,156.2	2,023.4	1,625.0	1,403.7
Other Statistics							
Cash provided by operations[2]	$ 790.4	$ 548.6	$ 657.1	$ 527.3	$ 329.9	$ 442.9	$ 466.5
Total dividends	245.2	210.6	180.8	154.4	139.3	110.8	100.9
Gross capital expenditures[4]	695.3	554.6	540.0	442.4	410.7	329.1	244.9
Research and development[2]	62.1	57.0	48.2	41.2	40.7	38.3	41.7
Advertising media expenditures[2]	426.8	419.6	394.6	336.5	345.9	330.0	317.0
Wages, salaries and employee benefits[2]	1,398.5	1,331.6	1,171.5	987.1	911.3	958.6	895.8
Number of employees[2]	111,501	108,077	97,238	83,837	74,453	65,619	62,056
Accumulated LIFO reserve	67.0	75.9	71.4	65.5	53.0	51.5	45.8
Common stock price range[1]	75$\frac{7}{8}$	60$\frac{7}{8}$	39$\frac{5}{8}$	33$\frac{7}{8}$	31	28	20
	54$\frac{1}{4}$	37$\frac{7}{8}$	31$\frac{3}{8}$	22$\frac{3}{8}$	20$\frac{3}{8}$	18$\frac{1}{2}$	13

[1] Years prior to fiscal 1991 have been adjusted for the two-for-one stock splits in November 1990 and 1986.

[2] Includes continuing operations only; years prior to fiscal 1989 include the discontinued cafeteria-style restaurant and frozen novelties operations; years prior to fiscal 1988 include the discontinued specialty retailing apparel operations; years prior to fiscal 1987 include the discontinued furniture operations; and years prior to fiscal 1985 include the discontinued toy, fashion, and specialty retailing nonapparel operations.

[3] Interest expense is net of interest income; amounts for years prior to fiscal 1986 are interest expense only with interest income included in selling, general, and administrative expenses.

[4] Includes capital expenditures of continuing operations and discontinued operations through the date disposition was authorized.

[5] Includes after-tax discontinued operations income of $169.0 million and cumulative effect of accounting change charge of $70.0 million.

TABLE 5
Five-Year Business Segment Information (in millions)

	Consumer Foods	Restaurants	Unallocated Corporate Items*	Consolidated Total
Sales				
1992	$5,233.8	$2,544.0		$7,777.8
1991	4,939.7	2,213.5		7,153.2
1990	4,520.3	1,928.0		6,448.3
1989	3,998.7	1,621.9		5,620.6
1988	3,667.5	1,312.1		4,979.6
Operating Profits				
1992	744.3[1]	190.8	$ (90.6)	844.5
1991	689.5[2]	172.2	(96.1)	765.6
1990	533.9	154.2	(75.4)	612.7
1989	452.4	127.7	(62.6)	517.5
1988	421.2	104.0	(54.8)	470.4
Identifiable Assets[3]				
1992	2,481.2	1,419.3	404.5	4,305.0
1991	2,189.2	1,256.4	456.2	3,901.8
1990	1,834.2	1,038.2	417.1	3,289.5
1989	1,571.6	862.2	454.3	2,888.1
1988	1,391.6	736.0	545.7	2,673.3
Capital Expenditures				
1992	397.1	297.0	1.2	695.3
1991	277.6	273.0	4.0	554.6
1990	298.2	239.1	2.7	540.0
1989	254.1	182.9	5.4	442.4
1988	184.2	157.3	69.2	410.7
Depreciation Expense				
1992	140.3	99.4	2.3	242.0
1991	131.7	79.7	2.0	213.4
1990	110.2	64.2	1.7	176.1
1989	96.0	51.3	1.5	148.8
1988	85.7	41.7	1.4	128.8

* Corporate expenses reported here include net interest expense and general corporate expenses. Corporate capital expenditures include capital expenditures of discontinued operations through the date disposition was authorized.

[1] Consumer foods operating profits include a net gain of $17.5 million (U.S.A. $20.5 million loss; foreign $38.0 million gain) for unusual items described in note three.

[2] Consumer foods operating profits include a net gain of $48.2 million (U.S.A. $20.9 million; foreign $27.3 million) for unusual items.

[3] Identifiable assets for our segments consist mainly of receivables, inventories, prepaid expenses, net land, buildings and equipment, intangible assets and investments and miscellaneous assets. Corporate identifiable assets consist mainly of cash, cash equivalents, time deposits, deferred income taxes, marketable investments and net assets of discontinued operations.

TABLE 6
Five-Year Geographic Segment Information (in millions)

	U.S.A.	Foreign	Unallocated Corporate Items*	Consolidated Total
Sales				
1992	$7,039.6	$738.2		$7,777.8
1991	6,376.8	776.4		7,153.2
1990	5,796.1	652.2		6,448.3
1989	5,071.2	549.4		5,620.6
1988	4,474.5	505.1		4,979.6
Operating Profits				
1992	896.3[1]	38.8[1]	$ (90.6)	844.5
1991	805.8[2]	55.9[2]	(96.1)	765.6
1990	655.9	32.2	(75.4)	612.7
1989	543.0	37.1	(62.6)	517.5
1988	494.1	31.1	(54.8)	470.4
Identifiable Assets[3]				
1992	3,462.2	448.3	404.5	4,305.0
1991	3,001.5	444.1	456.2	3,901.8
1990	2,543.3	329.1	417.1	3,289.5
1989	2,181.1	252.7	454.3	2,888.1
1988	1,903.2	224.4	545.7	2,673.3

* Corporate expenses reported here include net interest expense and general corporate expenses. Corporate capital expenditures include capital expenditures of discontinued operations through the date disposition was authorized.

[1] Consumer foods operating profits include a net gain of $17.5 million (U.S.A. $20.5 million loss; foreign $38.0 million gain) for unusual items described in note three.

[2] Consumer foods operating profits include a net gain of $48.2 million (U.S.A. $20.9 million; foreign $27.3 million) for unusual items.

[3] Identifiable assets for our segments consist mainly of receivables, inventories, prepaid expenses, net land, buildings and equipment, intangible assets and investments and miscellaneous assets. Corporate identifiable assets consist mainly of cash, cash equivalents, time deposits, deferred income taxes, marketable investments and net assets of discontinued operations.

C STRATEGIC CONTROL

AIR MAX, INC.

1   During the spring of 1991, Vernice and Ross Gandy and Jimmy Suggs, three friends, decided to investigate the possibility of forming a jointly owned manufacturing business. It was to be located in the general vicinity of their homes, had to be a product they understood, and must be financed with their own capital. Air Max, Inc. (AMI), began operations in August 1991 as a manufacturer of commercial and industrial venturi-style fans. After evaluating several sites in Florence and Columbia, South Carolina, the three co-founders rented a 3,700-square-foot assembly, storage, and office facility in a small multi-user building in Cayce, South Carolina. The site was in an industrial park centrally located to suppliers with adequate transportation facilities.

2   AMI produced the Air Max Cyclone fan, which utilized a venturi design. The founders based their hopes of profitability on the perceived potential of what they thought was a unique product. The venturi design principle is a method of compressing incoming air to create a more powerful and efficient air flow. They believed the Air Max Cyclone fan would do the work of three to six standard fans. Although the founders were sure their product was unique and would be more cost effective than standard fans, they were not as clear about how they could create product awareness and stimulate demand.

3   The key question for AMI was how to develop and implement a marketing plan that would accomplish the established sales and profit goals. When the company began operations, the owners had neither identified the competitive structure of the fan industry nor fully explored the uses to which the venturi-style fan could be applied. The owners estimated about 2,500 companies manufactured various types of fans and approximately 15 of these firms made venturi-style fans. The only clearly defined source of competition was a small local firm where Ross Gandy previously had been employed. The AMI founders began their marketing effort by persuading several regional distributors of industrial equipment to sell AMI fans. However, based on the experience of their local competitor, they still were considering direct selling efforts as well. In the first eight months of operation, AMI tried several marketing approaches, ranging from direct mailings to face-to-face customer calling. Their efforts achieved only modest results. Although AMI received some favorable responses, which resulted in a few initial orders for fans, the founders believed they needed to implement a well-planned marketing scheme to achieve profitability and then to sustain growth.

This case was prepared by Amy Vernberg Beekman and Frank S. Lockwood, University of South Carolina College of Business Administration.

THE FAN INDUSTRY

General Industry Conditions

4   The fan industry was a mature industry in 1991. One example of the longevity of the industry was seen in the founding dates of the three industry associations that comprised the Air Movement and Control Association (AMCA): National Association of Fan Manufacturers (1917); Industrial Unit Heater Association (1927); and Power Fan Manufacturers Association (1939).

5   The different types of products manufactured by firms in the industry "had remained steady for decades," according to Randy Fite of Dillon Supply Company, a Columbia, South Carolina, industrial machinery and supply company. Further, firms in the industry manufactured very similar product lines. Gregory Prose, a mechanical engineer with Hoffman & Hoffman, Inc., a regional firm that specialized in heating, ventilation, and air-conditioning systems (HVAC), described the differences between the products of like kind and uses as being only "different types and grades of paint, different thicknesses of metal comprising the fans and fan housings, different types of motors, such as foreign, enclosed, and open-cased, as well as differences in the quality of assembling the units." He further elaborated that most buyers "want a fan that will be durable and put forth the amount of air power claimed in the specifications."

6   Capital barriers to entry in the fan industry were not high. However, a new firm would be entering a mature market with fairly homogeneous products and well-established competition. A company needed to have low costs or a high-quality product to be able to compete.

7   Another feature of the industry, which represented another potential nonfinancial barrier to entry, was that channels of distribution were well established. A partial listing of the channels of distribution included direct selling by the companies themselves, through telemarketing and face-to-face customer calling; direct mailings; trade shows; manufacturers representatives; industrial distribution organizations, such as W. W. Grainger, Dillon Supply, Baker Brothers, or Graybar; and retail outlets, such as Sears, Wal-Mart, and other chains. According to those interviewed for this case, existing firms had well-developed channels of distribution or long-term satisfactory relationships with distributors. Because of the maturity of the industry, the profit margins for both selling and manufacturing parts of the industry were well established. In 1991, margins were as follows:[1]

	Manufacturers (%)	Distributors (%)
Gross profit margin	41.8%	39.8%
Operating profit margin	2.8	2.9
Net profit margin (before taxes)	1.4	1.9

An Industry Development: The Venturi Principle

8   An Italian physicist, G. B. Venturi, was credited with the discovery of the venturi principle during the 1820s, but this technology had just started to be utilized in fans in the 1980s. The concept of the venturi used a short tube that was tapered in the middle to simultaneously create an increased velocity of air flow and a corresponding decrease in its pressure. This structure resulted in a stream of air that was somewhat "compressed" and had a greater effective range than conventional fans. Ross Gandy, of AMI, compared the venturi design to that of "the full choke position of a shotgun."

9   According to Ross, the venturi design of the Air Max Cyclone comprised an "intake venturi, a main linear body, and the exhaust venturi." The purpose of the intake venturi was to increase the velocity of the air flow by compressing it into the smaller diameter of the main linear body. The purpose of the exhaust venturi was to reduce the exit pressure, which further increased the strength and distance of

---

[1] *Robert Morris Associates Annual Statement Studies*, 1991–1992.

air flow. As a result, "the venturi principle allows the air to be thrown 100 feet or more, enabling the venturi fan to do the work of three to six conventional fans."

Market Segmentation

10   The fan industry was composed of several markets. General categories included HVAC systems and components, industrial and commercial grade fans and blowers, and fan products for office and home use. General economic conditions affected each segment of the market differently. A downward trend in economic conditions, which restricted new construction of plant and office buildings, negatively affected the demand for HVAC systems. The industrial/commercial and the household/office segments, however, seemed less influenced by overall economic conditions. One positive aspect of an economic downturn on these two segments was the increased use of portable fans, rather than installing new or upgraded HVAC systems.

11   Another factor affecting demand for industrial/commercial and consumer/office fans was climate. Fans were utilized more in warmer climates and in areas of the country that had multiple seasons, and their use increased during the warmer months. Thomas Smith, a sales engineer with the Patterson Fan Company in Columbia, South Carolina, said, "There was definitely a seasonal factor which made summer a better part of the year than the winter [to sell fans]."

12   A general trend in the fan market that applied to both large and portable uses of fan equipment was a growing concern regarding environmental conditions. Air pollution, air purification, and filtering systems were becoming more prevalent. Also, employers in facilities with high ambient temperatures, who were concerned about maintaining reasonable temperatures at work stations, used portable fans as a supplement to installed HVAC systems, especially in warehouses and in heavy manufacturing plants.

13   An analysis of the products AMI manufactured was compared to several of the Standard Industrial Classification (SIC) code definitions. The SIC code 3564 entitled, "Industrial and Commercial Fans and Blowers and Air Purification Equipment," provided the best fit for AMI and the fan industry.[2]

14   This SIC code definition of the fan industry was broad and included such products as air and dust collection and air purification equipment; these products were not manufactured by AMI. However, other SIC codes were even less applicable. For example, SIC 3634, which was referenced in the definition of SIC 3564, covered primarily household products, which AMI did not manufacture at all. Additionally, SIC 5084, which included competitors of AMI, also incorporated firms manufacturing or selling a wide variety of industrial machines and equipment. Therefore, the segment of the fan industry described by SIC 3564 was used as the best approximation of the industry in which AMI competed.

The Size and Structure of SIC Code 3564

15   Industry information for SIC code 3564 indicated that 163 firms had sales of $1 million or more in 1990. No information was available, however, for firms with sales of less than that amount. Total sales for those 163 firms totaled $3.4 billion.[3] A possible source for information on the whole fan industry was the AMCA, whose members included firms that manufactured "air moving and control

---

[2] *Standard Industrial Classification Manual, 1987*, p. 213. A complete definition for this SIC code is:

> Establishments primarily engaged in manufacturing industrial and commercial blowers, industrial and commercial exhaust and ventilating fans, and attic fans, or in manufacturing dust collection and other air purification equipment for heating, ventilating, and air-conditioning (HVAC) systems or for industrial gas cleaning systems. Establishments primarily engaged in manufacturing air-conditioning units are classified in Industry 3585; those manufacturing free air-circulating fans for use on desks, pedestals, or wall brackets as well as household window-type fans and roll-abouts, and kitchen and household ventilating and exhaust electric fans, except attic, are classified in Industry 3634.

[3] *Ward's Business Directory of U.S. Private and Public Companies*, 1992, pp. 475–76.

TABLE 1
Sales for SIC 3564

	Firms	1991 Total Sales*	1991 Average Sales*	Avg. No. Emplys.
Sales of eight largest.	8	$1,346	$168	1,613
Sales of $40 to $50 million	8	428	48	450
Sales of $30 to $40 million	18	573	32	383
Sales of $20 to $30 million	15	347	23	206
Sales of $10 to $20 million	26	352	14	144
Sales of $5 to $10 million	37	252	7	68
Sales of $1 to $5 million	40	102	3	26
Total	152	$3,400	$ 22	222

*Dollar figures in millions

TABLE 2
Summary Data for the Eight Largest Firms in SIC 3564

	1991 Annual Sales*	Emplys.	State
Air and Water Technologies, Inc.	$ 611	3,900	NJ
American Air Filter.	254	4,800	KY
Cooper Industries (Indust. Mach. Div.)	140	1,400	IL
Environmental Elements Corp.	95	300	MD
Farr Corp.	65	700	CA
Tompkins Industries (Lau Division)	65	700	OH
Greenheck Fan Corporation	60	600	WI
Proctor & Schwartz	56	500	PA
Total	$1,346	12,900	
Average (for top eight firms)	$ 168	1,613	

*Dollar figures in millions.

equipment used in systems for ventilation, heating, and cooling."[4] It listed 190 members but would not provide information regarding sales. Therefore, the information available about the 163 firms with sales over $1 million was reviewed to assess competitive conditions in the fan industry.

16   Analysis of the 163 members of SIC 3564 showed that 11 of the 163 listed firms were parent organizations for subsidiaries that also were listed in the industry compilation.[5] The data for these parent organizations were eliminated to avoid double counting, leaving 152 firms to be analyzed. Of these

---

[4] *Trade, Business, and Commercial Organizations*, p. 1845.

[5] *Ward's Business Directory of U.S. Private and Public Companies, 1992*, pp. 475–76.

EXHIBIT 1
Regional Distribution for SIC 3564

	Firms	Total Sales	Average Sales	Total Employ.	Average Employ.
Northeastern Region					
Connecticut	7	$ 6,500,000	$ 928,571	650	93
Delaware	—	—	—	—	—
Maine	—	—	—	—	—
Maryland	2	9,900,000	4,950,000	350	175
Massachusetts	2	3,200,000	1,600,000	300	150
New Hampshire	—	—	—	—	—
New Jersey	8	67,800,000	8,475,000	4,600	575
New York	13	17,200,000	1,323,077	2,400	185
Pennsylvania	11	20,300,000	1,845,455	2,250	205
Rhode Island	—	—	—	—	—
Vermont	—	—	—	—	—
Total	43	$ 124,900,000	$ 2,904,651	10,550	245
Midwestern Region					
Illinois	14	$ 38,000,000	$ 2,714,286	4,100	293
Indiana	8	9,500,000	1,187,500	1,050	131
Iowa	—	—	—	—	—
Michigan	7	5,400,000	771,429	600	86
Minnesota	7	11,500,000	1,642,857	1,050	150
Missouri	5	10,800,000	2,160,000	250	50
Ohio	12	24,200,000	2,016,667	2,650	221
Wisconsin	4	9,300,000	2,325,000	1,100	275
Total	57	$ 108,700,000	$ 1,907,018	10,800	189

152 companies, approximately half had annual sales of less than $10 million (Table 1). Most of those companies had 50 or fewer employees. A summary of the eight largest firms, as of 1991, is listed in Table 2. A geographic breakdown (Exhibit 1) of the industry showed that older industrial states in the Northeast and Midwest contained the largest number of firms in the industry. The Southeast and Southwest regions, however, represented firms with the largest sales volumes. The Northwest region was only nominally represented in numbers of firms and sales.

Regional Competition

17   AMI's competition consisted of local distributors and manufacturers. Some distributors included local outlets of W. W. Grainger, Inc., the country's largest distributor of industrial equipment and manufacturer of its own line of fans, Dayton Fans; Graybar Electric; McMaster Carr; Dillon Supply; and Baker Brothers Supply. Grainger, Graybar, and McMaster Carr sold competing brands of venturi-

EXHIBIT 1   (continued)

	Firms	Total Sales	Average Sales	Total Employ.	Average Employ.
Southeastern Region					
Alabama	1	$ 1,400,000	$ 1,400,000	125	125
Arkansas	2	5,000,000	2,500,000	250	125
Florida	6	89,000,000	14,833,333	1,400	233
Georgia	1	7,000,000	7,000,000	100	100
Kentucky	2	99,000,000	49,500,000	350	175
Louisiana	—	—	—	—	—
Mississippi	1	7,000,000	7,000,000	100	100
North Carolina	7	199,000,000	28,428,571	1,950	279
South Carolina	1	3,000,000	3,000,000	25	25
Tennessee	2	23,000,000	11,500,000	300	150
Virginia	3	54,000,000	18,000,000	500	167
West Virginia	—	—	—	—	—
Total	26	$ 487,400,000	$28,746,154	5,100	196
Southwestern Region					
Arizona	—	—	—	—	—
California	15	$ 199,000,000	$13,266,667	2,000	133
Colorado	1	1,000,000	1,000,000	5	5
Hawaii	—	—	—	—	—
Kansas	1	16,000,000	16,000,000	15	15
Nevada	—	—	—	—	—
New Mexico	1	8,000,000	8,000,000	10	10
Oklahoma	1	50,000,000	50,000,000	500	500
Texas	5	65,000,000	13,000,000	1,600	320
Utah	—	—	—	—	—
Total	24	$ 339,000,000	$14,125,000	4,130	172

design fans while Dillon and Baker Brothers sold the Air Max Cyclone. See Exhibit 2 for a summary of the features and prices of the competing venturi fans.

18   Competition from manufacturers of venturi-style fans included Coppus, Patton, and Patterson Fans. The Coppus fan was an extremely heavy-duty and high-priced fan that did not compete with AMI's fan. Patton fans also were higher priced. Patterson Fan Company, located in Columbia, South Carolina, was AMI's biggest competitor. Patterson Fan Company was also Ross Gandy's former employer. Patterson Fan Company, a subsidiary of a parent company owned by Vance Patterson and his father, has been in business since 1989. The parent company sold a flat roof sprinkling system that was intended to cool the roof-top temperature. The lower temperature in the building's interior ceiling area would reduce the load on the air-conditioning system and the cost of air-conditioning a

EXHIBIT 1 (concluded)

	Firms	Total Sales	Average Sales	Total Employ.	Average Employ.
Northwestern Region					
Alaska	—	—	—	—	—
Idaho	—	—	—	—	—
Montana	—	—	—	—	—
Nebraska	—	—	—	—	—
North Dakota	—	—	—	—	—
Oregon	—	—	—	—	—
South Dakota	—	—	—	—	—
Washington	2	$ 5,000,000	$2,500,000	50	25
Wyoming	—	—	—	—	—
Total	2	$ 5,000,000	$2,500,000	50	25
National totals	152	$1,065,000,000	$7,006,579	30,630	202

building. The owner of Patterson Fan, Vance Patterson, and the sales engineer, Thomas Smith, said, "developing a fan which would further lower the interior temperature was a natural progression." At its inception, Patterson Fan was a small operation and most of its employees were members of the local volunteer fire department. When Ross became the first production manager in 1990, Patterson had 10 production employees. In 1991, the company sold 3,000 units and had $1.2 million in sales. Patterson used in-house telemarketing exclusively and felt its greatest competition came from the Dayton line of fans sold by W. W. Grainger. Patterson increased the promotion of its fans in early winter and continued through most of the summer, and then reduced marketing efforts in the fall. A summary of the Patterson, Patton, and Coppus fan features and prices are included in Exhibit 2.

THE COMPANY REPORT

The Origins

19   Three people, who had been friends for 10 years, Jimmy Suggs, Vernice Gandy, and Ross Gandy, established Air Max, Inc., in July 1991. The startup of a company was something they had thought about and discussed during most of this friendship. Earlier, Jimmy and Ross once started an art business, Arts Unlimited, in which Jimmy sold Ross's art. They also had been in a part-time band together and even produced a cassette tape, with proceeds going to a hurricane relief fund. Vernice had been the band manager. In 1991, however, a good product idea and changes in each of their personal circumstances created the opportunity for collaboration. Each had gained experience in a variety of industries and each brought different sets of skills to AMI.

20   Jimmy Suggs was the marketing manager for AMI. He was previously employed by the Sumter, South Carolina, plant of Interlake Packaging as an industrial engineer, working with customers and as Interlake's salesman in the customer service department. Although he contributed marketing skills to AMI, Jimmy also had experience as a project engineer at Interlake. Prior to working at Interlake,

EXHIBIT 2
Competitor Analysis

	Blade size	Motor size	Motor type	Wgt.	Price	Performance	Features
Graybar Electric Co.							
Portable Industrial Mancooler (belt-drive)	36″	1/2 HP 2 SPD	Open	N.A.	$ 592.80	N.A.	Deep Spun Venturi 4″ wheels OSHA Intake/Exhaust
Portable Industrial Mancooler (belt-drive)	48″	1 HP 1 SPD	Open	N.A.	$ 792.00	N.A.	Deep Spun Venturi 4″ wheels OSHA Intake Exhaust
Economy Portable Industrial Mancooler (belt-drive)	36″	1/2 HP 2 SPD	Open	N.A.	$ 396.00	N.A.	Deep Spun Venturi 4″ wheels OSHA Intake/Exhaust
Economy Portable Industrial Mancooler (belt-drive)	48″	1 HP 1 SPD	Open	N.A.	$ 651.60	N.A.	Deep Spun Venturi 4″ wheels OSHA Intake/Exhaust
Patton Industrial							
Man Cooler Direct Drive Fan	24″	1/2 HP	Enclosed	120 lbs.	$1,443.00	N.A.	Low Stand—4″ Wheels UL listed 14 gauge steel
W. W. Grainger, Inc.							
Agricultural Duty Direct-Drive Mobile Circulator	36″	1/2 HP	Enclosed	110 lbs.	$ 455.00 $ 109.60	N.A.	8-ft. power cord & handle storage Optional tilting kit OSHA Intake/Exhaust UL listed
High-Volume Mobile Air Circulator (square design)	36″	1/2 HP 2 SPD	Open	148 lbs.	$ 504.15	HS-110 ft. LS-73 ft.	10-ft. power cord Deep Venturi design OSHA Intake/Exhaust Hard rubber casters UL listed
High-Volume Mobile Air Circulator (square design)	48″	3/4 HP 2 SPD	Open	242 lbs.	$ 810.60	HS-85 ft. LS-85 ft.	10-ft. power cord Deep Venturi design OSHA Intake/Exhaust UL listed
High-Volume Direct-Drive Mobile Circulator (round design)	36″	1/2 HP	Enclosed	110 lbs.	$ 395.25	92 ft.	10-ft. power cord & handle storage OSHA Intake/Exhaust 20 gauge steel housing UL listed 7″ wheels

Jimmy had worked for Federal Mogul as an industrial engineer, and in a heavy metal manufacturing company, Hannaco Knives & Saws, which made saw blades and knives. In 1990, Interlake packaging was sold to a firm in Toronto, Ontario. Jimmy went to Canada to assist in the transition but, after five months, decided to come back to South Carolina. Unemployed and without any promising job leads, he saw starting his own company as a viable alternative to finding a job.

21   Vernice Gandy was the president of AMI. Her prior experience in two startup companies and in contract administration at Gould/ITE Imperial Corporation had developed administrative and financial management skills. In 1980, Vernice and her former husband both worked in the Gould Switch Gear Division in Atlanta, Georgia. She was in government contract negotiation and he was the plant

---

EXHIBIT 2 (concluded)

	Blade size	Motor size	Motor type	Wgt.	Price	Performance	Features
Coppus Engineering							
Double-Duty Heat Killer Man Fan	24″	3/4 HP	N.A.	147 lbs.	$1,949.00	N.A.	Selective blade angle adjustment
Patterson Fan Company							
Portable Stroller	14″	1/2 HP	Open	N.A.	$359.00	N.A.	OSHA Intake/Exhaust
Portable Stroller	18″	1/2 HP	Open	N.A.	$401.00	N.A.	OSHA Intake/Exhaust
Portable Stroller	22″	1/2 HP	Open	N.A.	$450.00	N.A.	OSHA Intake/Exhaust
Greenskeeper	22″	1/2 HP	Enclosed	N.A.	$677.00	N.A.	OSHA Intake/Exhaust Oscillator, Pole & Bracket
McMaster-Carr							
Breeze Maker Belt-Driven Fan	24″	1/3 HP	Enclosed	N.A.	$616.91	N.A.	OSHA Intake/Exhaust 8″ wheels
Breeze Maker Belt-Driven Fan	36″	1/2 HP	Enclosed	N.A.	$727.41	N.A.	OSHA Intake/Exhaust 8″ wheels
Breeze-or-Blast Adjustable Vane Fan	24″	1 HP	Enclosed	N.A.	$2,642.57	N.A.	OSHA Intake/Exhaust Self-locking wheels
Air Max, Inc.							
Porta-Zaust Direct Drive Fan	22″	1/2 HP	Enclosed	N.A.	$375.00	100 ft.	OSHA Intake/Exhaust 16 gauge steel Rust-Oleum paint
Greenskeeper Direct Drive Fan	22″	1/2 HP	Enclosed	N.A.	$580.00	100 ft.	OSHA Intake/Exhaust 16 gauge steel Rust-Oleum paint Oscillator, Pole & Bracket

N.A. means not available

manager. When the division was sold in 1980, they left Gould to form their own switch gear manufacturing company, Electro Marine Industries. Utilizing their prior government contacts, they succeeded in getting large ($2–$3 million) navy contracts for electrical switching gear.

22   Vernice and her ex-husband started a second company in 1984, H&R Metal, which manufactured metal trays for batteries. Although 1984 and 1985 national budget cuts in defense spending negatively affected Electro Marine, and contributed to its filing for bankruptcy protection in 1986, H&R Metal continued to grow. From 1984 to 1991, H&R Metal grew to $3.8 million in sales and from 13 to 65 employees. In 1991, however, subject to the terms of the divorce, Vernice sold her portion of H&R Metal to her former husband. Because she was unemployed after the divorce, the prospect of starting another new company was attractive to Vernice.

23   Ross Gandy, the third partner, was AMI's manufacturing manager. He provided the basic idea for AMI, the venturi-type fan. Ross's manufacturing background came from his experience at H&R Metal, Federal Mogul, and Talon Zipper Company. In each of those jobs, Ross had been in a supervisory or a foreman position. Immediately before starting AMI, Ross was the production manager at Patterson Fan Company, AMI's local competition. At Patterson Fan, he became familiar with the venturi-style fan. He was impressed with the concept but felt design improvements could be made. He eventually left Patterson Fan because he was frustrated by his inability to convince the owners of

Patterson to implement changes. Immediately after quitting, Ross had no plans to start a fan company. After discussions with Vernice, to whom he was now married, and with Jimmy, he became convinced he could make a higher-quality fan that could be sold at a lower price. All three agreed that the concept was promising and the timing was right.

24   To explore the viability of the idea, Ross, Vernice, and Jimmy called potential suppliers to obtain some feedback on the prospect of entering the fan market. At the request of suppliers, Ross drew the plans for the proposed venturi-style fan. He presented his design to several suppliers, including MagneTek, the motor supplier, and the suppliers of the venturi drum, finger guards, and blades. He also received input from the engineers at the blade supplier on specification development to increase efficiency. Ross characterized the suppliers as "eager" to help and as a major factor contributing to the decision to proceed in manufacturing a venturi-style fan.

25   Once Ross, Vernice, and Jimmy reached a decision to form AMI, they immediately began to plan. Ross was designated as manufacturing manager, Vernice as the financial manager, and Jimmy as the marketing manager. However, each took an active role in all aspects of AMI's future operations. They had intended to begin operations in April 1991 but, due to various delays, did not actually receive parts and begin producing fans until August 1991.

Strategy and Implementation

26   AMI's strategy was to make a higher-quality product and price it below that charged by Patterson Fan Company. The managers intended to "let Patterson spend the money to develop the market, then they would follow behind with their higher-quality, lower-cost fan." The claim of having a higher-quality product was based on the superior components that were standard on all AMI fans. First, AMI's totally enclosed MagneTek motor was more functional and dependable than the exposed motors on Patterson fans. The fully enclosed motor was usable in dirty and wet conditions, which gave the Air Max Cyclone a broader range of uses than a fan without a similar-type motor. Second, to increase durability, AMI used stronger hardware (bolts) and a thicker gauge steel than Patterson. Third, AMI included the federal OSHA-approved intake and exhaust finger guards to improve safety on all models, items not included in the Patterson fan. And, as a final distinguishing feature, AMI primed the metal on each fan and used a higher-quality paint, Rust-oleum™. These quality additions not only increased the fan's longevity but also were required for some applications, such as in poultry houses. AMI produced fans in two sizes, 16 inch and 22 inch, and offered a variety of ancillary products, such as an oscillator, stroller,and pedestal. An oscillator is a motor that swings the fan from side to side. A stroller is a wheel and handle attachment that makes the fan portable. The pedestal is a pole that extends the height of the fan by six or eight feet. See Exhibit 3 for a complete price list and Exhibits 4 and 5 for product information.

27   The other main feature of AMI's strategy was to keep prices below those of their competitors. To do so, AMI had to operate with little overhead, few marketing costs, and a slimmer profit margin. Jimmy stated the goal was not to make as much money as they could in the beginning, but to develop a long-term growth strategy that focused on gaining market share by producing a quality product at the most competitive price. Operations were conducted in the warehouse section that adjoined AMI's modest offices. Jimmy and Ross provided the labor to produce the Air Max Cyclone and ancillary products. This process consisted of a welding step to construct the fan tube, then assembling the fan, motor, and mountings and painting the fans in a spray booth. Jimmy estimated they had the capacity to manufacture about 100 fans a month. The initial business plan established a sales goal of 100 fans per month in 1992.

28   They hoped to achieve this goal by taking sales away from Patterson as well as by developing additional uses and customers for their venturi-style fan. As a result of lower operating costs, AMI could charge consistently lower prices than Patterson. For example, for one model of the oscillating fan, the Greenskeeper, Patterson charged $700 while AMI charged $580.

EXHIBIT 3

AIR MAX INCORPORATED

AIR MAX CYCLONE

PRICE LIST

DESCRIPTION	P/N	PRICE
22" Fan only	CY22	$375.00
22" Mister Fan	MS22	425.00
22" Exhaust Fan	EX22	305.00
22" Ventilation Fan	VT22	390.00
22" Pedestal Fan	PS22	432.00
16" Fan Only	CY16	330.00
16" Mister Fan	MS16	375.00
16" Exhaust Fan	EX16	270.00
16" Ventilation Fan	VT16	345.00
16" Pedestal Fan	PS16	380.00
Wall Bracket	WM01	40.00
Ceiling/Beam Mount	CM01	30.00
22" Stroller	ST22	70.00
16" Stroller	ST16	70.00
Oscillator	OS01	120.00
Truck-Bay Mount	TB01	35.00
3Phase Motor adder	MT3P	78.00
2Speed Motor adder	MT2S	75.00
Explosion Proof Motor adder	MTEX	215.00

Modifications and Quantities in excess of ten quoted separately

EXHIBIT 4

AIR MAX INCORPORATED
1149 - D Walter Price Drive
Cayce, SC 29033
803-739-9739

AIR MAX CYCLONE
Maximum Air Movement
Maximum Quality

The unique design of the Air Max Cyclone utilizes the Venturi principle to compress the air into a 22" diameter column, and propel this air column up to **100 FEET** away much like a nozzle on a water hose. Each Cyclone can replace **two or three** standard industrial fans and provide more air movement throughout a building. Standard industrial fans throw air an average of twenty to thirty feet from the fan while the air from the Cyclone can be felt seventy to one-hundred feet away.

APPLICATIONS:
- Employee "spot cooling"
- Eliminate floor moisture
- Emergency Ventilation for smoke or fumes
- Ventilation for dust laden areas
- Equipment Cooling
- Drying paint
- Cool or warm air circulation
- Room or building exhaust
- Truck bay cooling
- Greenhouse air flow and misting
- Poultry and livestock cooling
- Manhole ventilation

Options:
Ceiling mount - No power cord to trip on, no storage problems.
Wall mount - Frees floor space
Stroller - Provides portability
Mister - .08-.33 at 50 psi
Explosion - Proof motor
Single or 3 - phase motor

STANDARD FEATURES:
16 Ga. spun steel construction
1/2 Hp. totally enclosed motor
115V, 1725 RPM, 6612 CFM
4-blade balanced aluminum propeller
OSHA approved guards
Industrial Gray RUST-OLEUM® Paint

EXHIBIT 4   (concluded)

FAN ONLY

Wall Mount - Frees floor space

Stroller - Provides portability

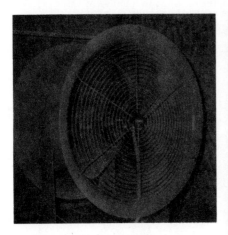

"MISTER" FOR GREENHOUSES AND POULTRY AND LIVESTOCK BARNS

PEDASTAL FANS

EXHAUST FANS

VENTILATION SYSTEMS

WARRANTY--A.M.I. warrants this equipment to be free from defects in materials and workmanship for one year from the date of shipment. Any units or parts which prove to be defective and are reported during the warranty period will be repaired or replaced, exclusive of labor, at our option when returned to our plant, freight prepaid. Damage due to heat, chemical, abrasive, improper installation or operation or lack of normal maintenance shall not constitute defect, and are not covered by the warranty. The motor is warranted by the motor manufacturer for one year. If the motor becomes defective during the warranty period, call the factory for instructions for return. A.M.I. is not responsible for installation, removal, or re-installation or any consequential damages.

DISTRIBUTED BY:

AIR MAX INCORPORATED
1149 - D Walter Price Drive
Cayce, SC 29033

803-739-9739

PROTECTED WITH RUST-OLEUM COATINGS

MagneTek

ENCLOSED MOTORS

EXHIBIT 5

-AIR MAX INCORPORATED
1149 - D Walter Price Drive
Cayce, SC 29033
803-739-9739

AIR MAX "GREENS KEEPER"
Maximum Air Movement
Maximum Quality

The Air Max Greens Keeper fan is a must for maintaining healthy greens, providing air circulation to quickly evaporate excess moisture and standing water. The powerful venturi design pushes a high volume of air over 100', and when equipped with an oscillator will cover a huge area. This power enables the Greens Keeper to be positioned out of the way, and it's Forest Green color blends nicely with foilage.

USES:
Evaporate Moisture to:
    Reduce Fungus Growth
    Develop Healthier Root System
    Reduce Rot
    Keep Green Cool
Control Mosquitoes And Gnats
Control Dead Leaf Buildup

Mounting Options
    Pole - Painted steel
    Tree - Bracket
    Portable Stroller
Optional Oscillator For Greater Coverage
OSHA Approved Finger Guards
6612 CFM Air Movement
Quiet Operation
Affordable Price
Physical Characteristics
    Diameter - 29"
    Depth - 18"
    22" Balanced Aluminum Blade
    Motor - 1/2 HP,115V,1725RPM
        3Ph Available
        Totally Enclosed

PROTECTED WITH RUST-OLEUM COATINGS

MagneTek MOTOR

Fan placement up to sixty feet away

WARRANTY--A.M.I. warrants this equipment to be free from defects in materials and workmanship for one year from the date of shipment. Any units or parts which prove to be defective and are reported during the warranty period will be repaired or replaced, exclusive of labor, at our option when returned to our plant, freight prepaid. Damage due to heat, chemical, abrasive, improper installation or operation or lack of normal maintenance shall not constitute defect, and are not covered by the warranty. The motor is warranted by the motor manufacturer for one year. If the motor becomes defective during the warranty period, call the factory for instructions for return. A.M.I. is not responsible for installation, removal, or re-installation or any consequential damages

EXHIBIT 5   (concluded)

AIR MAX INCORPORATED

AIR MAX GREENS KEEPER
PRICE LIST

DESCRIPTION	P/N	PRICE
22" Fan only	GK22	$400.00
Trunk Mount Bracket*	TM01	40.00
Pole Mount*	PM22	60.00
Stroller	ST22	70.00
Oscillator	OS01	120.00
3Phase Motor adder	MT3P	78.00
2Speed Motor adder	MT2S	75.00

*Can be equipped with oscillator

Modifications and Quantities in excess of ten quoted separately.

Standard Configurations:

Pole Mounted Fan	460.00
Pole Mounted, Oscillator Fan	580.00
Trunk Mounted Fan	440.00
Trunk Mounted, Oscillator Fan	560.00
Stroller Mounted Fan (for portability)	470.00

Marketing Efforts

29   AMI's marketing strategy also had been patterned somewhat after Patterson. Patterson did all of its own marketing and sales; it primarily relied on cold-calling and telemarketing. To increase awareness about the venturi principle, Patterson produced a video on the applications of the venturi-style fan and sent out demonstration models for a 10-day trial period. Patterson also attended various industrial and trade shows.

30   AMI tried similar marketing practices. The managers prepared some promotional information sheets (Exhibit 4). Jimmy made some cold calls and implemented a direct mail campaign. There were some favorable responses. In the fall of 1991, AMI conducted a mailing program directed at Arizona-based manufacturing firms. It picked Arizona to test the direct mailing concept because of the warm climate. Based on that mailing, an aluminum manufacturer placed an initial order for 10 fans and a subsequent order for 15 more.

31   Jimmy also mass mailed information on AMI to golf courses in North and South Carolina (Exhibit 5). Golf course greens planted with bent grass must be keep dry to prevent rotting. Consequently, the powerful venturi-style fan mounted on a pedestal would be useful in drying the greens. Although Patterson was doing the same thing, AMI did not originally plan to target this market. After receiving a few requests for information from golf courses, however, Jimmy decided to pursue that avenue.

32   Shortly after the mailing, Jimmy followed up with visits mainly in the area of Myrtle Beach, South Carolina. Unfortunately, Patterson already had visited some of the same courses and had sold them fans. AMI did get some promising leads, however, and the application was well received by greens keepers. To tailor the fan to the golfing environment, AMI painted the fan green and named it the "Greenskeeper." Similarly, AMI specifically targeted fire departments that could use the fan for ventilation or cooling purposes (Exhibit 6). AMI painted those fans red and labeled them the "Porto-Zaust."

33   Like Patterson, AMI also sent demonstration models to potential customers. Of the 11 fans sent out, 7 were returned. Jimmy was not pleased with the results and did not plan to utilize this marketing method except in response to specific requests from customers or distributors. With AMI's limited inventory, he preferred to keep the fans on hand.

34   Other marketing efforts of AMI included joining a couple of associations, obtaining lists of trade show participants, establishing relationships with distributors, and setting up volume discounts. Early in 1992, AMI joined the South Carolina Golf Course Superintendents Association. Through this membership, AMI learned of a national greens keeper association meeting, where approximately 20,000 members attended. Although AMI did not send a representative, Vernice sent away for the list of participants to direct mail AMI's marketing material. To further increase its exposure and chance for referrals, AMI also joined an HVAC association and placed advertisements in the *Thomas Register*. Additionally, AMI gained approval as a qualified supplier on the national United States government bidders' list.

35   AMI also sought to establish relationships with industrial equipment distributors. Initially, AMI obtained names of some distributors from MagneTek Motors, the supplier of the motor used in the Air Max Cyclone. These contacts resulted in AMI developing relationships with two distributors, Dillon Supply and Baker Brothers. Both distributors conducted business primarily in the southeastern United States. AMI also contacted W. W. Grainger because, at the time, W. W. Grainger did not sell a venturi-style fan. Shortly thereafter, Grainger's Dayton Fan Division started manufacturing and distributing one. AMI's discount policy for distributors that stocked their products was to discount 20 percent on orders for 10 or more units. A 15 percent discount was given on orders for 10 or more units to nonstocking distributors. In late 1991, AMI also hired a sales representative in Atlanta.

EXHIBIT 6

AIR MAX INCORPORATED
1149 - D Walter Price Drive
Cayce, SC 29033

803-739-9739

AIR MAX "PORTA-ZAUST"
Maximum Air Movement
Maximum Quality

The Air Max "Porta-Zaust" fan is designed and built for use as a portable smoke and fume exhausting device, or fresh air supplier. The powerful venturi design pushes a high volume of air over 100 feet and moves over 6,000 cubic feet of air per minute. This is equivalent to exhausting a 25' x 30' room in one minute. Durably built of 16 guage steel with a 115v totally enclosed motor, the "Porta-Zaust" fan is a must for every fire department, hospital and maintenance shop.

STANDARD FEATURES:
Exhaust Smoke
Exhaust Fumes
Supply Fresh Air
Evaporate Moisture
Cool Equipment
Cool Personnel
Air Movement

APPLICATIONS:
OSHA Approved Finger Guards
6612 CFM Air Movement
Quiet Operation
Affordable Price
Physical Characteristics
    Diameter - 29"
    Depth - 18"
    22" Balanced Aluminum Blade
    Motor - 1/2 HP,115V,1725RPM
        3Ph Available
        Totally Enclosed

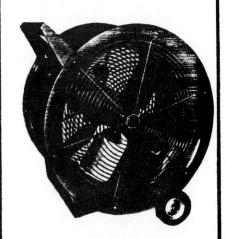

22" Model - $425.00
(Also available in 16" Model at $375.00)

WARRANTY—A.M.I. warrants this equipment to be free from defects in materials and workmanship for one year from the date of shipment. Any units or parts which prove to be defective and are reported during the warranty period will be repaired or replaced, exclusive of labor, at our option when returned to our plant, freight prepaid. Damage due to heat, chemical, abrasive, improper installation or operation or lack of normal maintenance shall not constitute defect, and are not covered by the warranty. The motor is warranted by the motor manufacturer for one year. If the motor becomes defective during the warranty period, call the factory for instructions for return. A.M.I. is not responsible for installation, removal, or re-installation or any consequential damages.

PROTECTED
WITH
RUST-OLEUM
COATINGS

MagneTek
MOTORS

Operating Structure and Financial Performance

36 In establishing AMI, Jimmy, Vernice, and Ross utilized a holding company strategy to protect themselves from financial liability. Kane Enterprises, Inc., a South Carolina holding company, was established on July 19, 1991. Each principal received a pro rata portion of the 1,000 shares of authorized and issued common stock. Kane Enterprises, Inc., formed Air Max, Inc., on July 19, 1991, for the purpose of manufacturing high-quality, high-velocity, venturi-style fans. The holding company owned 100 percent of AMI.

37 AMI was structured to be certified as a woman-owned or operated business. To be certified as such, a woman must be the president or controlling officer, actively involved in the business, and owning 51 percent of the company. This was accomplished by naming Vernice as chairperson of the board of directors as well as president and chief operating officer of both corporations. Ross was vice president and secretary and Jimmy became vice president and treasurer. Certification as a woman-owned or operated business qualified AMI for benefits available for being based on minority ownership status, such as priority in government-sponsored purchasing programs.[6] Initially, the principals loaned AMI $36,000 ($12,000 apiece) and agreed to defer their salaries until the beginning of 1992, the date they had forecasted sales revenue to be sufficient to begin compensating themselves.

38 To begin operations, AMI rented a 3,700-square-foot facility and leased a welding machine and steel bending equipment. All other manufacturing and office equipment was owned by the principals or purchased by AMI. Initial funds were used to acquire materials to produce test and demonstration models of the 22-inch fans. They designed marketing material and wrote and tested customer assembly instructions. AMI established credit with suppliers, such as MagneTek Motors, and began production. Policies for accounts receivable were established at 30 days net FOB and accounts payable at 45 days. Demonstration models were shipped and sales calling began.

39 The initial goal of AMI was to generate sales of 100 units per month by the end of 1991. The basic 16-inch and 22-inch fans were aggressively priced at $330 and $375, respectively (see Exhibit 3 for a complete price list and Exhibit 2 for a comparison of other venturi-style fan prices). Actual sales results showed that, despite competitive pricing, the sales goal was overly ambitious. By January 1992, actual sales volume was at a rate of 15 to 20 units per month and, by the end of March 1992, total sales since operations began (July 1991–March 1992) had reached $27,000. Based on the lowest-priced model, this represents sales of approximately 81 fans. Gross sales for 1992 were $25,482 with a net loss of $14,193, after adding back in accrued but not paid salaries of $15,000 (Exhibit 7). In March 1992, AMI revised its sales forecasts to 50 units per month. The managers felt that this was a reasonable goal with the summer months around the corner. AMI had the operational capacity to manufacture 75 to 80 fans per month, and the facility and equipment to handle production and shipping of 200 units per month.

40 By the end of April, however, most of the sales revenue and the initial $36,000 had been invested in inventory or used to pay expenses. To date, the principals had not received any compensation. Inventory on hand included enough materials to produce 100 of the 22-inch fans and 50 of the 16-inch models. However, motors that cost $55 each had not been purchased yet. Additional capital or sales were needed to buy motors and to continue operations.

41 Vernice estimated that a monthly sales volume of $25,000 from 50 units ($500 per unit) would be required to sustain operations, increase marketing efforts, repay the initial loans made to AMI by the principals, and pay salaries to the principals. A pro forma analysis (Exhibit 8) assumed a sales volume of 50 units per month at a sales price of $500 per fan. Payment for each fan sold was received in the month following the sale and payment for materials also was assumed to be made in the following

---

[6] The Office of Minority Business Enterprise (OMBE) was established by Executive Order 11458 in 1969 to coordinate and promote programs helping minority enterprises. These programs include the establishment of the National Minority Purchasing Councils designed to encourage corporations to buy from minorities. The Small Business Administration (SBA) also supports minority businesses by providing funding.

EXHIBIT 7
3/31/92 YTD Income Statement

	AMI		SIC Code 3564
Gross sales	$25,482	100.00%	
Cost of goods sold	14,888	58.43	
Gross profit	$10,594	41.57%	41.8%
G&A expenses:			
Salaries	$15,000	58.87%	
Advertising	3,921	15.39	
Professional fees	2,040	8.01	
Dues and subscriptions	,381	1.50	
Rent	5,535	21.72	
Build. repair & maint.	1,126	4.42	
Telephone	2,180	8.56	
Insurance	4,206	16.51	
Office supplies	3,976	15.60	
Other	1,422	5.58	
Total expenses	39,787	156.14	39.1
Operating profit/loss	($29,193)	−114.56%	2.8%

month. Total direct costs to produce each fan were assumed to be $242. This cost included $18 in labor costs, $119 for materials, and approximately $105 in selling costs. Based on a $500 selling price, that left $258 per fan to cover general and administrative costs ($203 per fan), equipment costs ($9 per fan), and service debt ($42 per fan). Net income for the year based on these figures would be $2,600 ($4 per fan).

42   The March 1992 balance sheet and a 12-month pro forma balance sheet were compared to industry statistics from a Dun & Bradstreet survey of 146 firms found in SIC 3546 (Exhibit 9). The March 1992 balance sheet reflected a company with 78 percent of total assets, consisting of accounts receivable and inventory. Compared to industry standards, inventory was too high and accounts payable and owner's equity were out of line. The 12-month pro forma balance sheet based on Vernice's projections presented a much improved picture, which compared favorably with the D&B industry statistics, except that accounts receivable would still be too high.

THE FUTURE

43   In April 1992, AMI expected sales to increase as warmer temperatures signaled the beginning of "fan season." Prior to April, most 1992 sales had been orders from existing customers. Jimmy, Vernice, and Ross hoped that some of their marketing efforts had been successful in attracting new customers who were just waiting until summer arrived to make purchases. They also hoped that AMI fans had been sufficiently differentiated from regular fans to justify the customer's added expenditure for a venturi-style fan. And, for those possible customers already aware of the venturi-style fan benefits, they

EXHIBIT 8
Pro Forma Analysis
Assumptions:
    Price per unit $500
    Monthly production 50

	April	May	June	July	Aug.
Beginning cash balance	$ 3,000	$ 1,355	$ 4,110	$ 3,865	$ 4,170
Cash infusion					
Debt outstanding	$36,000	$36,000	$36,000	$34,000	$32,000
Revenue:					
Sold (# units)	50	50	50	50	50
Shipped (# units)	50	50	50	50	50
Payment rcvd (# units)	50	50	50	50	50
Price per unit	$ 500	$ 500	$ 500	$ 500	$ 500
Gross revenue	$25,000	$25,000	$25,000	$25,000	$25,000
Direct expenses:					
Labor Costs:					
Production (# units)	50	50	50	50	50
Cost per unit	$ 18	$ 18	$ 18	$ 18	$ 18
Total labor costs	$ 900	$ 900	$ 900	$ 900	$ 900
Material costs:					
Parts ordered (# units)	50	50	50	50	50
Parts on hand (# units)	100	110	110	110	110
Production (# units)	40	50	50	50	50
Cost per unit	$ 119	$ 119	$ 119	$ 119	$ 119
Total material costs	$ 5,950	$ 5,950	$ 5,950	$ 5,950	$ 5,950
Selling costs:					
Advertising	$ 1,600	$ 500	$ 500	$ 0	$ 0
Commissions/discounts	$ 2,500	$ 2,500	$ 2,500	$ 2,500	$ 2,500
Postage	$ 250	$ 250	$ 150	$ 150	$ 150
Telephone/utilities	$ 200	$ 200	$ 200	$ 200	$ 200
Sales material	$ 1,500	$ 500	$ 200	$ 100	$ 100
Marketing salary	$ 1,000	$ 1,000	$ 2,000	$ 2,000	$ 2,000
Total selling costs	$ 7,050	$ 4,950	$ 5,550	$ 4,950	$ 4,950
Total direct costs	$13,900	$11,800	$12,400	$11,800	$11,800
(Direct cost per fan)	$ 278	$ 236	$ 248	$ 236	$ 236

Sept.	Oct.	Nov.	Dec.	Jan.	Feb.	Mar.	Total
$ 3,925	$ 4,280	$ 4,485	$ 4,440	$ 4,895	$ 5,350	$ 5,705	
$30,000	$28,000	$26,000	$24,000	$22,000	$20,000	$18,000	
50	50	50	50	50	50	50	600
50	50	50	50	50	50	50	600
50	50	50	50	50	50	50	600
$ 500	$ 500	$ 500	$ 500	$ 500	$ 500	$ 500	
$25,000	$25,000	$25,000	$25,000	$25,000	$25,000	$25,000	$300,000
50	50	50	50	50	50	50	600
$ 18	$ 18	$ 18	$ 18	$ 18	$ 18	$ 18	
$ 900	$ 900	$ 900	$ 900	$ 900	$ 900	$ 900	$ 10,800
50	50	50	50	50	50	50	600
110	110	110	110	110	110	110	
50	50	50	50	50	50	50	590
$ 119	$ 119	$ 119	$ 119	$ 119	$ 119	$ 119	
$ 5,950	$ 5,950	$ 5,950	$ 5,950	$ 5,950	$ 5,950	$ 5,950	$ 71,400
$ 0	$ 200	$ 100	$ 0	$ 0	$ 100	$ 500	$ 3,500
$ 2,500	$ 2,500	$ 2,500	$ 2,500	$ 2,500	$ 2,500	$ 2,500	$ 30,000
$ 150	$ 100	$ 100	$ 100	$ 100	$ 100	$ 100	$ 1,700
$ 200	$ 200	$ 200	$ 200	$ 200	$ 200	$ 200	$ 2,400
$ 100	$ 100	$ 500	$ 100	$ 100	$ 100	$ 100	$ 3,500
$ 2,000	$ 2,000	$ 2,000	$ 2,000	$ 2,000	$ 2,000	$ 2,000	$ 22,000
$ 4,950	$ 5,100	$ 5,400	$ 4,900	$ 4,900	$ 5,000	$ 5,400	$ 63,100
$11,800	$11,950	$12,250	$11,750	$11,750	$11,850	$12,250	$145,300
$ 236	$ 239	$ 245	$ 235	$ 235	$ 237	$ 245	

EXHIBIT 8 (concluded)

	April	May	June	July	Aug.
General & Admin. Costs:					
Administrative salary	$ 7,500	$ 7,500	$ 7,500	$ 7,500	$ 7,500
FICA/FUTA/SUTA	$ 565	$ 565	$ 565	$ 565	$ 565
Deposits	$ 1,250	$ 0	$ 0	$ 0	$ 0
Telephone/Utilities	$ 200	$ 200	$ 200	$ 200	$ 200
Key Man Insurance	$ 250	$ 250	$ 250	$ 250	$ 250
Group Health Insurance	$ 535	$ 535	$ 535	$ 535	$ 535
Office supplies	$ 100	$ 50	$ 50	$ 100	$ 50
Postage	$ 250	$ 250	$ 150	$ 150	$ 150
Professional Fees	$ 1,000	$ 0	$ 0	$ 0	$ 600
Rent	$ 650	$ 650	$ 650	$ 650	$ 650
Total G&A Costs	$12,300	$10,000	$ 9,900	$ 9,950	$10,500
Equipment Costs:					
Maintenance	$ 200	$ 200	$ 200	$ 200	$ 200
Purchase	$ 0	$ 0	$ 0	$ 0	$ 0
Rental	$ 145	$ 145	$ 145	$ 145	$ 145
Supplies	$ 100	$ 100	$ 100	$ 100	$ 100
Total Equipment Costs	$ 445	$ 445	$ 445	$ 445	$ 445
Total Operating costs	$26,645	$22,245	$22,745	$22,195	$22,745
(Total Cost Per Fan)	$ 533	$ 445	$ 455	$ 444	$ 455
Net Operating Revenue	$ (1,645)	$ 2,755	$ 2,255	$ 2,805	$ 2,255
Debt Service:					
Interest	$ 0	$ 0	$ 500	$ 500	$ 500
Principal Payments	$ 0	$ 0	$ 2,000	$ 2,000	$ 2,000
Debt Service	$ 0	$ 0	$ 2,500	$ 2,500	$ 2,500
Net Income	$ (1,645)	$ 2,755	$ (245)	$ 305	$ (245)
Ending Cash Balance	$ 1,355	$ 4,110	$ 3,865	$ 4,170	$ 3,925

hoped they had distinguished their fan from the Patterson fans and those of national distributors, such as W. W. Grainger and Graybar.

44   Financial issues, however, were of primary concern. Should AMI continue to operate with the expectation that orders would increase, or should they seek out additional sources of capital and aggressively attack the market? If they decided on the latter option, several crucial decisions had to be made. First, should AMI expand the product line to include a less-seasonal product to carry the company through the slow months? Second, which market should they target? Among the numerous potential uses for the venturi-style fans, on what specific applications should AMI focus? Or should AMI forget targeting any segment at all and rely instead on a broad marketing approach?

Sept.	Oct.	Nov.	Dec.	Jan.	Feb.	Mar.	Total
$ 7,500	$ 7,500	$ 7,500	$ 7,500	$ 7,500	$ 7,500	$ 7,500	$ 90,000
$ 565	$ 565	$ 565	$ 565	$ 565	$ 565	$ 565	$ 6,780
$ 0	$ 0	$ 0	$ 0	$ 0	$ 0	$ 0	$ 1,250
$ 200	$ 200	$ 200	$ 200	$ 200	$ 200	$ 200	$ 2,400
$ 250	$ 250	$ 250	$ 250	$ 250	$ 250	$ 250	$ 3,000
$ 535	$ 535	$ 535	$ 535	$ 535	$ 535	$ 535	$ 6,420
$ 50	$ 100	$ 50	$ 50	$ 50	$ 50	$ 50	$ 750
$ 150	$ 100	$ 100	$ 100	$ 100	$ 100	$ 100	$ 1,700
$ 0	$ 0	$ 0	$ 0	$ 0	$ 0	$ 0	$ 1,600
$ 650	$ 650	$ 650	$ 650	$ 650	$ 650	$ 650	$ 7,800
$ 9,900	$ 9,900	$ 9,850	$ 9,850	$ 9,850	$ 9,850	$ 9,850	$121,700
$ 200	$ 200	$ 200	$ 200	$ 200	$ 200	$ 200	$ 2,400
$ 0	$ 0	$ 0	$ 0	$ 0	$ 0	$ 0	$ 0
$ 145	$ 145	$ 145	$ 145	$ 145	$ 145	$ 145	$ 1,740
$ 100	$ 100	$ 100	$ 100	$ 100	$ 100	$ 100	$ 1,200
$ 445	$ 445	$ 445	$ 445	$ 445	$ 445	$ 445	$ 5,340
$22,145	$22,295	$22,545	$22,045	$22,045	$22,145	$22,545	$272,340
$ 443	$ 446	$ 451	$ 441	$ 441	$ 443	$ 451	
$ 2,855	$ 2,705	$ 2,455	$ 2,955	$ 2,955	$ 2,855	$ 2,455	$ 27,660
$ 500	$ 500	$ 500	$ 500	$ 500	$ 500	$ 500	$ 5,000
$ 2,000	$ 2,000	$ 2,000	$ 2,000	$ 2,000	$ 2,000	$ 2,000	$ 20,000
$ 2,500	$ 2,500	$ 2,500	$ 2,500	$ 2,500	$ 2,500	$ 2,500	$ 25,000
$ 355	$ 205	$ (45)	$ 455	$ 455	$ 355	$ (45)	$ 2,660
$ 4,280	$ 4,485	$ 4,440	$ 4,895	$ 5,350	$ 5,705	$ 5,660	$ 2,660

45   A second factor to consider, regardless of the selected market, was how to differentiate the venturi-style fan from conventional fans and the AMI fan from competing venturi-style fans. Although AMI printed marketing fliers tailored for mass mailings and had several handouts describing fan specifications and general information, the company had not assembled a promotional "package" of AMI products. Was this a necessary item? If not, what other methods should be considered in promoting the AMI product?

46   A final consideration for Jimmy, Vernice, and Ross was what selling methods to use. Although two distributors had agreed to sell AMI fans, neither had generated any sales by the end of March 1992. Would direct sales be more effective? Increasing telemarketing efforts was a possibility. AMI also had

EXHIBIT 9
Comparative Balance Sheets

	03/31/92	Percent (%)	12-Month Pro Forma	%	Dun & Brad. 146 Firm Avg.	Percent (%)
Assets						
Current assets:						
Cash	$ (151)	−1%	$ 2,660	7%	$ 120,904	12%
Accounts receivable	7,507	35	25,000	65	312,334	31
Notes receivable	0	0	0	0	13,098	1
Inventory	9,233	44	5,950	16	223,672	22
Other current assets	1,250	6	1,250	3	57,505	7
Total current assets	17,839	84	34,860	91	737,513	73
Equip. & fixed assets	3,319	16	3,319	9	157,512	16
Other noncurr. assets	0	0	0	0	112,843	11
Total assets	$21,158	100%	$38,179	100%	$1,007,868	100%
Liabilities						
Current liabilities:						
Accounts payable	$35,351	167%	$ 8,450	22%	$ 151,167	15%
Bank loans	0	0	0	0	0	0
Notes payable	0	0	0	0	73,550	7
Other current liab.	15,000	71	0	0	127,956	13
Total current liab.	50,351	238	8,450	22	352,673	35
Other L/T liabilities	0	0	0	0	129,971	13
Deferred credits	0	0	0	0	1,008	0
Total liabilities	50,351	238	8,450	22	483,652	48
Owners' equity	(29,193)	−138	29,729	78	524,216	52
Total liabilities & equity	$21,158	100%	$38,179	100%	$1,007,868	100%

considered hiring or contracting with a manufacturer's representative or hiring additional sales representatives but did not know if it could afford either.

47   Jimmy Suggs, Vernice Gandy, and Ross Gandy knew they had a good product. Now, they needed
to decide how to convince potential customers of the same thing.

CASE 30

HEARTWARE INTERNATIONAL CORPORATION: A MEDICAL EQUIPMENT COMPANY "BORN INTERNATIONAL"

INTRODUCTION

1   In May 1990, Mr. Gerald Seery, chief executive and founder of Heartware International Corporation (Heartware), a two-year-old multinational venture headquartered in Atlanta, was looking toward the future. He had recently sent a fax that captured his thoughts to Dr. Pedro Cortez,* in Aagst, Belgium. Dr. Cortez was one of the two developers of the medical equipment that inspired Heartware's formation. That fax read:

2   Date: May 30, 1990
To: Pedro Cortez
From: Gerald Seery

Without repeating myself too much, this past year has been both challenging and greatly frustrating. I believe we all anticipated making further advances than we have.

3   Certainly, I am able to report several positive developments. . . . FDA approval, some early sales, and establishing Heartware as an organization. But as every businessman knows, every business needs cash, cash, cash. For Heartware, that cash has been tough to come by.

4   I remain a believer, however. I have spoken with my wife, Tricia, and our investors about refocusing attention of Heartware onto the European market. They have a number of questions. In general, they feel that we should capitalize on the opportunity where it makes the most sense. Obviously, the United States offers a very large market for our products. However, we should exploit the position of leadership we currently enjoy in the international markets.

5   The key to building upon our early success will be the availability of money. Having expended all that I can afford (and then some), Heartware will be able to expand quickly only with additional capital infusion. This can come from several sources: sales; private investors; venture capital; and a partner. Pedro, I am committed to making this happen. If we can get through these early months, I know we can build Heartware into a company with great products and a sound future.

6   Heartware entered into the international arena at start-up. Its headquarters and investors were located in the United States. Human resources were in the United States and the Netherlands. Product development and technical support originated in the Netherlands. Early sales came from the United States, United Kingdom (U.K.), Italy, Spain, and Brazil. The company set up distributorships in the United States, U.K., Saudi Arabia, South Africa, and Turkey. Although start-ups headquartered in the United States that begin multinationally (sometimes called *global start-ups*) are unusual, Mr. Seery's involvement in such a venture was not surprising. However, Mr. Seery's dedication to international business was evident when, in the summer of 1990, he said:

This case was prepared by Benjamin M. Oviatt, Georgia State University; Patricia P. McDougall, Georgia Instititute of Technology; and Mark Simon and Rodney C. Shrader, Georgia State University. It recently appeared in *Entrepreneurship: Theory and Practice*.
*Names that are disguised are marked with an asterisk the first time they appear.

7 If all of a sudden someone said, "Here's a chunk of money for your company and for all you've done," and asked, "Now what will you do?" I would definitely do something international. It's in my blood. Atlanta has the Olympics coming up in 1996; so I'd get involved in that. I would love to help smaller and mid-size companies expand overseas, because I think it's a great opportunity and because I could help them overcome that fear factor. It opens up a world that they don't know about.

THE FOUNDER'S BACKGROUND

8 Acquaintances described Heartware's founder as a friendly, humorous, and personable man. He was born in 1956, raised in Long Island, New York, and traced his international interest to childhood. He had been fascinated by stories about the uncle he was named after who worked overseas. During the summer between his junior and senior years in high school, Mr. Seery traveled to Spain on a student exchange program and studied Spanish with students from England, France, Ireland, and Italy. His international interests were expanded at the Catholic University of America in Washington, D.C., where he earned a BA in international economics. He went on in 1980 to earn an MBA with a specialty in marketing from Columbia University.

9 Mr. Seery's international exposure continued after graduation. Six months after taking his first job, he completed the management development program in a large chemical company in Philadelphia and was transferred to the international sales department. There he learned the nuts and bolts of international business, including letters of credit, financing, and shipping. In just one and a half years with the chemical company, Mr. Seery generated sales of $7 million.

10 In 1982, Mr. Seery changed jobs but continued in international sales as product manager for a New Jersey medical supply company. In this job he gained familiarity with medical devices through managing a product line that produced $5 million in revenue annually. Mr. Seery also developed a program to bring doctors from other nations to the United States to introduce them to the company and its products. In 1984, he assumed a position as senior product manager for a dental supply company in New York, where for the next two years he managed the worldwide marketing of a product line that produced $10 million in revenue annually.

11 For the five years prior to founding his own company in 1988, Mr. Seery was director of international marketing and sales for Hospicath* Corporation, a small medical device company in New Jersey. Under his leadership, annual domestic sales increased from $5.6 million in 1986 to $9.3 million in 1988, and international sales increased by more than 40 percent. Mr. Seery managed a network of exclusive distributors in Europe, Canada, and Japan; and, during his tenure with Hospicath, he traveled to Western Europe five or six times a year for two to three weeks at a time. On these trips he met with salespeople and distributors, called on hospitals, and met cardiologists in several European countries. On one of these trips Mr. Seery was introduced to the technology on which he founded Heartware.

ELECTROPHYSIOLOGY LAB AND MAPPING SYSTEM

12 During a September 1987 trip to Europe, Hospicath's Dutch distributor introduced Mr. Seery to Dr. Pedro Cortez, a Spanish cardiologist who held both an MD and a PhD. Dr. Cortez was employed as a director of the Hospital of Maastricht, located in Maastricht, the Netherlands. The Netherlands was well regarded in the medical community for its pioneering role in cardiology. At the time of Mr. Seery's trip, Dr. Cortez and Mr. Jan van der Swoort,* chairman of the engineering department at the University of Limburg in Maastricht, were actively seeking a commercial outlet for the electrophysiology lab and mapping system they had jointly developed.

13   Electrophysiology (EP) is the study of the electrical signals of the heart, and Dr. Cortez's equipment was used for the diagnosis and treatment of irregular heartbeats (cardiac arrhythmias). General EP studies[1] were used to diagnose the type of arrhythmia. The most standard approach was that a catheter (thin plastic tube) was inserted into a blood vessel at the groin and fed into the heart. Wires were fed through the catheter so that twelve electrode leads at the end of the wires touched the heart. A cardiologist then used a cardiac stimulator to deliver a series of electric signals to the heart. This procedure was known as pacing the heart. The cardiologist studied the resulting pattern of the heartbeat in order to better understand the nature of the arrhythmia.

14   Mapping studies were special EP studies performed in a hospital operating room, because the studies required that the chest cavity be surgically opened so electrodes could be moved to various positions on the heart's surface. This procedure generated a detailed map of the heart's electrical activity. A general EP study often preceded mapping.

15   Growing use of EP led Dr. Cortez and Mr. van der Swoort to invest roughly four years in the mid 1980s in the development of their EP system. By 1987, when Mr. Seery was introduced to the system, it was already in use at the Hospital of Maastricht. Their system was the only computerized system in the world and was owned and managed by the University of Limburg's instrumentation and engineering department. The full $125,000 EP lab and mapping system (EP system) is described in Exhibit 1. It could be sold in its entirety to perform both types of studies or it could be sold in subsystems— the EP Lab subsystem to perform general EP studies and the mapping subsystem to perform mapping studies. Separate components could be sold for incorporation into a hospital's existing system.

HEARTWARE FOUNDED

16   Mr. Seery was especially interested in the university's EP products because he had already directed the launch of an EP product line for Hospicath. That product line produced $1.1 million in sales over a two-year period. Upon returning from Europe to the United States, Mr. Seery proposed that Hospicath acquire all of the university's products. Hospicath's president began immediately to work with Dr. Cortez and Mr. van der Swoort to further develop the catheter and to incorporate it into Hospicath's product line. He decided to further investigate the university's EP system.

17   In February 1988, Hospicath sent an engineer to Maastricht with Mr. Seery to examine the EP system, and they recommended acquisition and further development of the system. However, the president of Hospicath decided not to pursue capital equipment product lines and to concentrate instead on disposable products like the cardiac catheter.

18   Frustrated by the president's response, Mr. Seery began to explore the possibility of forming his own company to acquire and market the EP system. During 1988, while still working at Hospicath, Mr. Seery took steps to form Heartware. He solicited funds, prepared a submission for the Food and Drug Administration (FDA), and negotiated with the university.

19   Because FDA approval was of such vital importance in the U.S. medical products market, Mr. Seery began to seek approval in April 1988, several months before he acquired the product rights. Medical products without FDA approval could not be marketed in the United States, and investors and potential partners usually were not interested in a company whose product may have been months or even years away from market. The FDA required that medical devices be proven safe and effective. If the product was comparable to others already on the market, it had to be proven equivalent to or better than the others. On September 10, 1988, Heartware contracted the services of Medsys, Inc., a consulting firm that specialized in submitting medical equipment proposals to the FDA. For a fee of $5,000 over the next seven months, Medsys prepared Heartware's submission with help from Mr.

---

[1] Often the prefex "general" is dropped.

EXHIBIT 1
Components of the EP Lab and Mapping System

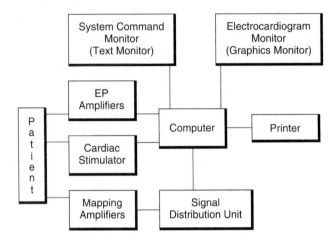

Computer: All the modular parts of the EP lab and mapping system were connected to the personal computer, which served as the heart of the system.

Cardiac Stimulator: The programmable cardiac stimulator (price: $25,000) delivered electrical signals to the heart.

Amplifiers and Signal Distribution Unit: The amplifiers and the signal distribution unit transformed electrical signals received from the heart into a form that could be interpreted by the computer and output to the printer or monitor. Although other components were used for both EP studies and mapping studies, the amplifiers were specially designed for one or the other type study. Each amplifier was priced at $25,000.

Output Devices: One color monitor displayed a menu of command options for running the system, while the other displayed output about the patient's heart. The printer produced hard copy of this output.

EP Lab Subsystem and Mapping Subsystem: The EP lab subsystem (price: $100,000) contained all system components except the mapping amplifiers and was only used to perform general EP studies. Similarly, the mapping subsystem (price: $100,000), contained all components except the EP Lab amplifiers.

Supplementary Products Developed by Dr. Cortez

Belt Electrode: The belt electrode (price: $2,500) used for the mapping procedure contained 21 electrodes and was wrapped around the surface of the heart, enabling information from 21 locations on the heart to be simultaneously relayed to the mapping system.

Cardiac Catheter: The cardiac catheter (price: $100) could be used with the EP Lab in general EP studies or in conjunction with other cardiac care products on the market.

Seery. This submission included a product instruction book, sample advertisements, quality control procedures, results from general EP and mapping studies, manufacturing procedures, and charts comparing Heartware's product to similar products already being sold in the United States.

20   Heartware International Corporation was incorporated in the state of New Jersey on October 28, 1988. The following week, the founder opened a corporate suite in New York City, although he continued his employment with Hospicath. Mr. Seery resigned from Hospicath on April 30, 1989, after which he devoted his full energies to Heartware.

21   During spring of 1989, Mr. Seery's wife, Ms. Patricia Browne, developed Heartware's business plan as a class assignment at New York University Graduate School of Business. By mid-summer,

Ms. Browne assumed a part-time position as Heartware's chief financial officer with a deferred salary. Before joining Heartware, Ms. Browne had founded a financial consulting firm, which she managed for three years, and she had nearly 10 years' experience as corporate controller and accountant. Ms. Browne held a BA in economics/accounting from Catholic University and an MBA in finance from New York University.

22   Initial funding for Heartware came from Mr. Seery and his wife, who provided $185,000 from savings, personal debt, and loans against their home equity. In May of 1989, Heartware's founder sent a summary of the company's five-year plan to more than a dozen private individuals. Within five weeks, four close relatives invested a total of $85,000.

HEARTWARE'S CONTRACT WITH THE UNIVERSITY

23   Heartware acquired exclusive worldwide rights to market the EP system and belt electrodes on May 4, 1989. Under the agreement with the university, Heartware would be credited with all sales of the EP system regardless of whether Heartware or the university generated the sales lead. All price quotations outstanding at the time of the agreement were included. The university would provide assembly, inspection, and testing of all systems ordered for about 50 percent of the list price of the system. Mr. Seery expected that this percentage would decrease dramatically when the sales level made mass production possible.

24   In exchange for the above services, Heartware was to make an initial payment of 50,000 Dutch guilders (Dfl)[2] followed by 10 quarterly payments of 50,000 Dfl. Rights to the product would revert to the university if Heartware failed to meet its obligations.

25   Mr. van der Swoort was to be Mr. Seery's point of contact at the university. Separate agreements were drawn up for Mr. van der Swoort and Dr. Cortez. They would receive royalties from Heartware on units sold in exchange for providing assistance with sales demonstrations, installations, and service calls. Heartware's founder counted on Mr. van der Swoort to service and support all European customers. In addition to the royalties received, Mr. van der Swoort received about $400 a month for providing general support, such as answering inquiries. To Mr. Seery, the spirit of the contract implied that the university would provide technical support to further the development and sales of the EP system to the mutual benefit of both Heartware and the university.

26   Dr. Cortez had an international reputation as a leader in the field of electrophysiology, which Mr. Seery counted on to help sell the system. Because product and company credibility were crucial in the medical equipment industry, Dr. Cortez was retained in a consultant capacity as a medical advisor to the company.

Products Launched

27   On May 4–6, 1989, Mr. Seery set up a display in Toronto, Canada, at the annual meeting of the North American Society of Pacing and Electrophysiology (NASPE), the professional association of almost all electrophysiologists. Approximately 1,500 doctors, nurses, technicians, and engineers attended the meeting that year, and nearly 75 percent of the 800 cardiologists in attendance had a specialty in electophysiology. Heartware's products generated significant interest among NASPE members, and Mr. Seery made several important contacts at the meeting.

28   Heartware's founder felt that launching the company at this NASPE meeting was crucial due to the very broad exposure the meeting would bring. However, Mr. Seery acknowledged that the product

---

[2] On May 4, 1989, the date the contract was signed, 2.132 Dfl were the equivalent of 1 U.S. dollar.

could use aesthetic improvements, design alterations to facilitate mass production, and FDA approval for the U.S. market, and he did not want to wait a full year for the next NASPE meeting.

THE EP MARKET

29   In the late 1980s, EP was still a relatively new field. EP techniques were used in clinical diagnosis beginning about 1980. However, EP was not widely used in the medical community until about 1986. In 1989, 1,300 coronary care units were functioning in the United States and treated 390,000 patients. Approximately 10 percent of those patients required pacing to return the heart to a normal rhythm. Use of EP was closely tied to the amount of government reimbursement for EP procedures. On October 1, 1989, the reimbursement rate rose from $2,700 to $8,100, which greatly increased the profit potential for cardiology departments.

30   Mr. Seery anticipated that heartware could take advantage of expansion in the EP market.[3] Growth in the market was expected to come from several sources. An EP study was the preferred diagnostic test in candidates for sudden cardiac death. However, in the late 1980s, less than 10 percent of patients who were at significant risk actually underwent the test. One of the major reasons for this low usage was a shortage of cardiologists trained in EP. However, EP represented an attractive specialty and the number of physicians in this area was growing rapidly.

31   The EP market was segmented into two primary areas: systems designed to perform general EP studies in EP laboratories within hospitals, and systems for performing mapping studies in operating rooms. EP labs offered the best growth potential. The bulk of this growth was expected to be generated by the expansion of cardiology departments into EP technology. By the end of 1989, 400 EP labs in the United States had an installed base of EP equipment. These labs were not expected to purchase replacement systems in the near future. However, these labs were potential customers for add-on components, such as Heartware's cardiac stimulator. It was expected that 400 additional hospitals would add EP programs to their cardiology departments between 1990 and 1994. Equipment sales during that time period were expected to be about $45 million.

32   Heartware's mapping system would be sold in the surgical market. By the end of 1989, 80 U.S. hospitals performed arrhythmia surgery and another 80 were expected to expand into such surgery by 1994.

33   Heartware's initial product line consisted of the EP lab and mapping system and belt electrodes, and Mr. Seery planned to later add cardiac catheters. The company expected to subcontract catheter production until 1992 or 1993, at which point Heartware would build its own production facilities. The market for cardiac catheters was growing. Hospitals were expected to purchase new catheters at an increasing rate because the resterilization and reuse of catheters increased infection control problems and hospital liability for malfunctioning products. In 1989, EP catheter sales totaled about $6.5 million. Had hospitals used new catheters for each procedure, rather than sterilizing and reusing some, the 1989 market would have been about $15 million. The expected market in 1994 was $35 million.

34   The number of hospitals using EP was expected to increase most quickly in the United States, because health care delivery abroad had greater financial limitations. In the international market, about 80 hospitals in Western Europe, South America, Canada and Japan used EP. Although smaller, the international market presented several advantages over the U.S. market. First, with the notable exception of Japan, governmental regulations abroad tended to be less stringent than FDA regulations in the United States. Second, the smaller market size and slower growth resulted in less competition. Third, appearance and design features that did not enhance the performance of medical products were not as important outside the United States.

---

[3] The statistics and market estimates in this section are from Heartware's business plan.

EXHIBIT 2
Heartware's Major Competitors

Most competitors were headquartered in the United States, and less than 20 percent of their sales were generated overseas.

Bard Electrophysiology

Parent:	C.R. Bard, Inc. (A medical supply company with $100 million annual revenue.)
Annual sales:	Approximately $11 million.
Main product:	Cardiac catheters.
EP product:	$100,000 cardiac mapping system.
Product advantage:	Bard's system excelled Heartware's in graphics capability by producing a picture of the heart with shading to indicate the intensity of electrical activity.
Product drawbacks:	Bard's system was not portable and its components could not be used for general EP studies. Foreign doctors were unwilling to pay for added graphics capability.
Competitive advantages:	Bard dominated the catheter market, offered a full product line and extensive service, and had a large distribution system and established training programs. Bard derived a significant competitive advantage from the fact that many cardiologists received their initial EP training on Bard equipment. Later, when these cardiologists were in the position of ordering equipment for their own practices or of giving advice about such a purchase, they were inclined to order the familiar brand.
Research & development:	Developing a general EP lab system.

Biomedical Business Instrumentation (BBI)

EP product:	EP system that needed FDA approval.
Drawbacks:	Product had not been commercially marketed or produced.
Other:	Founded in 1986 by two Canadian engineers. In 1989, BBI was considering signing a joint venture agreement with another more established Canadian medical firm.

HEARTWARE'S MARKET POSITION

35   In 1989, several companies competed in the EP market. Exhibit 2 discusses Heartware's major competitors. Heartware's EP system offered several advantages over the noncomputerized systems that dominated the market in the late 1980s. These advantages are summarized in Exhibit 3.

EXPLORING STRATEGIC PARTNERSHIPS

36   Mr. Seery spent much of his time seeking "strategtic partnerships" with established medical device companies that might want to add Heartware's products to their current product lines. Mr. Seery envisioned an agreement in which another company would receive an equity interest in Heartware in return for that company's financial, marketing, and technical support. Mr. Seery hoped such an

EXHIBIT 2   (concluded)

Bloom Associates

Annual sales:	Approximately $3 million.
EP product:	Noncomputerized general EP system and mapping system.
Product advantages:	Lower cost than Heartware's systems.
Product drawbacks:	Bloom's systems were slower and stored information on paper, rather than on disk.
Other:	The firm was for sale for $10 million.

Digital Cardiovascular Incorporated (DCI)

EP product:	$20,000, computer-controlled stimulator for use in EP studies.
Product drawbacks:	Stimulator could not store or record output. DCI marketed its stimulator through Medtronic, Inc., the leading manufacturer of cardiac pacemakers. As of 1989, Medtronic was emphasizing pacemaker products, not DCI's stimulator.

Electrophysiology Company (EPCO)

Annual sales:	Approximately $5 million.
Research & development:	EPCO's mapping system prototype needed FDA approval, and the firm was developing a general EP system.

agreement later might lead the partner to buy Heartware and provide him and other investors a valuable return on their investment. With basically only one product, Mr. Seery expected that Heartware would exhaust its market in five years. Thus, his goal was to ally with a company that offered multiple products.

37   Heartware's CEO contacted dozens of companies of all sizes throughout the United States, Australia, and Japan, sent them a condensed version of Heartware's business plan, and later contacted them by phone. This led to extensive dialogue in some cases; however, most companies were only casually interested in Heartware's products.

38   Negotiations progressed the furthest Electrophysiology Company (EPCO),* a U.S. company that specialized in equipment associated with arrhythmia detection and treatment. At the 1989 NASPE meeting, Mr. Seery had discussed Heartware and its products with a cardiologist who recommended he contact EPCO. That cardiologist also told EPCO's officers about Heartware. The day after Mr. Seery returned to New York from Toronto, Epco's president called Mr. Seery to express interest in Heartware.

39   Over the next several months, Heartware's founder and EPCO representatives met three times and communicated frequently via telephone and fax machine. They discussed the possibility of EPCO investing in Heartware in return for equity in the company. Mr. Seery anticipated EPCO eventually would buy out Heartware and hire him as a consultant or manager. Between negotiations with EPCO, consultations with lawyers, flights to EPCO's home office, and product demonstrations for EPCO, much of Mr. Seery's time and resources were consumed. During this period he concentrated on these negotiations and greatly curtailed efforts with other companies.

40   In July 1989, Mr. Seery sent EPCO a two-page summary of the general terms that they had agreed upon to date. A few days later, EPCO sent Mr. Seery a letter of intent, but did not mention his letter regarding terms of agreement. On July 20, 1989, Mr. Seery sent a letter to Heartware's stockholders with the following details:

EXHIBIT 3
Heartware's Product Advantages

Computerization of the EP system allowed electrical signals from the heart to be displayed or saved in a variety of ways. Certain time segments (e.g., critical episodes) could be marked for later analysis, the scale of output could be changed, or readings from different parts of the heart could be emphasized or deemphasized. This clarified relevant information, led to easier analysis, decreased the chance of error, and decreased the amount of time needed after the study to diagnose the arrhythmia.

Heartware's computerized cardiac stimulator was the only one that could constantly monitor the patient's condition by measuring and reporting beat-to-beat time intervals.

Computerization allowed preprogrammed pacing protocols (ordered series of electrical signals sent to the heart by the stimulator) to be used instead of manually delivering individual signals. Pacing protocols could be stored on disk for quick retrieval, thus drastically reducing the time required to deliver protocols and potential errors.

Computerization allowed the hospital to permanently store output on disk instead of paper, significantly simplifying storage. A single general EP study could last up to four hours, generating a stack of printed output between four and six inches tall.

Heartware's mapping system could simultaneously obtain and display information about a heart's electrical patterns, reducing the time required in surgery by approximately 30 to 40 minutes.

In about 60 percent of the mapping studies, even more time could be saved when the belt electrodes were used. The conventional method of obtaining signals to map the heart involved the use of only two to four electrodes, which were moved from one small area of the heart to another, taking between 20 to 30 minutes to locate the problem site. Because the belt electrode contained 21 leads that were in direct contact with the heart, the time needed to locate a problem site could be reduced to under a minute.

41   "We have negotiated with several firms over the past several months. Our efforts have focused most recently on concluding an agreement with EPCO. EPCO has a proven technology in the field of electrophysiology. They are seeking to expand their product line. Heartware's EP System is an attractive opportunity for EPCO.

42   "Consequently, we have concluded an agreement under which EPCO would invest up to $350,000 in Heartware, in exchange for an equity position of up to 35 percent. At the 30-month point, EPCO could exercise its option to purchase the remaining equity of Heartware for $750,000.

43   "While a final agreement has not been concluded, we are confident of the respective commitment each party has to closing the deal. We believe that the current shareholders of Heartware are well served by this agreement."

44   In addition to the compensation described above, Mr. Seery also negotiated with EPCO to receive an "earnout" over four years. An earnout is a series of payments, usually made over several years, based upon some measure of the company's performance, such as profits or sales.

FDA ASKS FOR CLARIFICATION

45   Mr. Seery's negotiations to obtain strategic partners, investments, and sales continued to be blocked by the EP system's lack of FDA approval. After having reviewed Heartware's submission, the FDA responded on July 8, 1989, by asking for further clarification of a few issues. With the help of Medsys's consulting services, Mr. Seery responded to these questions. The issues that needed to be clarified were all relatively minor, and all indications were that FDA approval would be forthcoming. However, the FDA would have another 90 days before it was required to respond to Heartware's clarifications.

FURTHER NEGOTIATIONS WITH EPCO

46   In August 1989, negotiations with EPCO intensified. Mr. Seery shipped equipment from The Netherlands at Heartware's expense to conduct a demonstration in Atlanta for EPCO's chairman. An engineer from the University of Limburg flew to Atlanta to conduct the demonstration, and Mr. Seery flew from New York.

47   During the demonstration, Mr. Seery stood in the hallway of the hospital. On one pay phone he spoke to his attorney in Boston; on another he spoke simultaneously to EPCO's president. Mr. Seery recalled the incident as follows:

48   The president of EPCO said that the final hitch was FDA approval. I said, "We agreed to this back in June. This agreement is not subject to FDA approval." He agreed. Right then and there he agreed with me that the deal was not subject to FDA approval. I said, "Do we have a deal?" He said, "Yes, we have a deal." I hung up the phones and walked back into the clinical lab where the chairman was. I said, "I just got off the phone and we've got a deal." He shook my hand and said, "Ah, that's great. And of course it's subject to FDA approval." I said, "No. We just agreed that it's not." He said, "Yes it is." I blew up.

49   Because the chairman knew cash was tight, he said, "I'll tell you what we'll do. We'll give you a working capital loan for $50,000 to carry you until the FDA approval." We expected FDA approval to come in September or October, so we weren't that far away, and I had every expectation we would get it. With $50,000 working capital, that could work. He told me to call him later to solidify this $50,000 commitment. By then of course the deal was subject to this and that and some other things. A few days later the $50,000 working capital loan was for one year at some percent interest rate, and the collateral was the technology, and they weren't required to sign the deal even if the FDA approved. They had about 10 days after approval to decide whether they wanted it or not.

50   After consulting with his attorney about the deal, Mr. Seery decided not to go through with it.

ANOTHER MAJOR PUSH FOR FUNDING

51   When negotiations with EPCO broke down, Mr. Seery responded with what he called a frantic effort to make new contacts.

52   I probably sent out letters to and called everybody who was anybody who knew somebody who may have once invested, and I wrote off letters and made phone calls to just about every major medical company who might have an interest. I felt that it was only a matter of time before competitors would develop EP technology as sophisticated as the EP Lab.

53   In addition to reinitiating contacts with possible strategic partners and private investors, Mr. Seery began to actively pursue the venture capital market.

FDA APPROVAL

54   On October 2, 1989, less than six months after Heartware's initial submission, Mr. Seery received a letter from the FDA stating that Heartware's EP system was approved for the U.S. market. Within days of receiving the FDA's letter, Mr. Seery called EPCO once again to tell them Heartware had received FDA approval and to ask if a new deal was possible. He recalled that phone conversation as follows:

55   They said, "Same terms?" And I said, "No, we now have FDA approval." That was the last I talked to them for a while. They had no interest in revisiting it because they were now advancing their own system. Not that they didn't have it to start with. I don't want you to think they just took what we had, but they saw our technology and possibly benefited from it. In my heart of hearts, I don't think they wanted to deal. They wanted the information.

SALES

56 As Mr. Seery's efforts to strike an agreement with EPCO seemed to come to a dead end, Heartware began to generate orders. When Mr. Seery acquired rights to the EP system, he also acquired rights to all outstanding quotations made by the university. One quote was to Dr. Jacob Atie, a Brazilian doctor, who had worked on the EP system as a graduate student at the University of Maastricht. He later decided to buy amplifiers for a mapping system. On October 30, 1989, Heartware's CEO received the following fax from Jan van der Swoort in Holland:

57 Date: 30 Oktober 1989
To: Gerry Seery
From: Jan van der Swoort
Subj: Orders and safety regulations

1. Congratulations! You got your first order. Today I got a visit from Dr. Atie and Dr. Cruz. They will finance the system with their personal means. They asked me to inform you about the order. I put it on the fax. I informed them that I needed a deposit of 25 percent for the University in order to start working on the system. Then I have to ask the Financial Department to send them an invoice for this deposit. Now in order not to confuse the Financial Department it makes sense that you order the University to prepare this system and that the invoice should be sent directly to these doctors. The difference between the invoice and the agreed compensation for the University will be credited to the installments or otherwise.

58 Heartware's second sale occurred the following day and also stemmed from an outstanding quotation to a former Brazilian graduate student at the university. During 1989, three hospitals, the two in Brazil and one in Spain, ordered amplifiers to add to existing EP systems. The sales totaled $66,000. Because these orders were not shipped until May 1990, Heartware received no cash in 1989 and the sales appear on the 1990 income statement. Heartware's only revenue in 1989 was $6,900 from the sale of three belt electrodes. In most cases, customers paid the university directly in Dutch guilders and the university credited the amount Heartware owed for the technology.

MOVE TO ATLANTA, GEORGIA

59 In December 1989, Mr. Seery relocated Heartware's headquarters to Atlanta. He knew that Heartware would be operating on a tight budget and felt that Atlanta's lower cost of living relative to New York would increase the business's chance for success. Atlanta offered several additional advantages. Mr. Seery already had established a relationship with a cardiology group there. He also planned to apply for entry into the Advanced Technology Development Center (ATDC) headquartered at and administered by the Georgia Institute of Technology.

60 The ATDC was a technology business development center and acted to promote high-technology start-ups (an incubator). The center was created in 1980 by the state of Georgia to help high-technology entrepreneurs by providing technical and business assistance. The Technology Business Center, an arm of ATDC, offers office space, shared secretarial service, and shared office equipment to its tenants. The sharing of services and assets gives young firms access to many resources that might otherwise have been prohibitively expensive.

61 The technological benefits were as important to Mr. Seery as the other services provided, because Heartware had not yet been able to employ an in-house engineering staff. ATDC members have access to the resources of all public universities within Georgia. Most important, Heartware also benefited from its proximity to other high-tech firms. A firm located at ATDC that specialized in engineering development work was helpful to Heartware by suggesting minor product improvements on a limited, informal basis at no charge.

62   After arrival in Atlanta, Patricia Browne accepted the position of controller at Turner Broadcasting System. She continued to serve as Heartware's CFO.

HEARTWARE'S RELATIONSHIP WITH THE UNIVERSITY OF LIMBURG

63   Although ATDC offered some technical assistance, most technological support and product improvement came from the University of Limburg. The system was sound in terms of performance. However, it was not particularly attractive in terms of design and aesthetics. Further product design work also was needed before the system could be manufactured efficiently.

64   Demonstrations for potential customers and distributors often were held at the University of Limburg. Mr. van der Swoort attended shows like NASPE with Mr. Seery. Mr. Seery, customers, and potential customers contacted Mr. van der Swoort when they had questions about the system's capabilities, service, or installation.

65   Heartware's founder felt his relationship with the two codevelopers was quite favorable, although not problem free. In addition to contractual issues that needed clarifying, confusion about sales or payments often arose. The following fax sent by Mr. Seery to Mr. van der Swoort is an example of some of the confusion that arose as a result of what Heartware's CEO called a "3,000 mile umbilical cord":

66   Based upon your first phone call, I thought the doctors were ready to place an immediate order during their visit to you. Now it appears that a great deal of time will go by either before they place an order or accept delivery of the systems.

67   Because of my initial impression, I compromised significantly on the price, recognizing the potential value of an immediate order and the fact that the University had already provided quotations to these doctors. Now the quotations from Heartware are being interpreted by others as applying to their situation.

68   I am in a very difficult situation. We cannot increase the quotations that are outstanding despite the longer delivery date. And how am I to modify the quotation to the new doctor to more accurately reflect the value of the product? Heartware cannot survive unless we price our products at a rate which yields a reasonable return.

69   Mr. Seery also felt that differences in cultural perceptions may have caused difficulty. Mr. van der Swoort seemed to believe that Americans and their firms were wealthy and, therefore, could afford to pay higher fees and royalties to him. Mr. Seery tried to correct that impression, especially as it pertained to start-up ventures, but the issue was a constant thorn in their relationship. According to the founder: "When Heartware *could not* afford to do something, the developer interpreted this to mean that we *did not want* to do something."

70   Nevertheless, Mr. van der Swoort continually upgraded the software for the EP system. Even though Heartware had the most technologically advanced system on the market, Mr. Seery feared that competitors could easily catch up. No other company had FDA approval on a computer-based EP system, but both Bard and EPCO had functioning prototypes. For competitors, the stimulator represented the primary hurdle in obtaining FDA approval. Mr. Seery felt that, "if you're a decent engineer, you can put a stimulator together." Time was the main issue. He anticipated that a competitor would need six months to develop a stimulator compatible with a computerized EP system and another year or more to obtain FDA approval.

71   To lessen dependence on the university, Heartware's founder wanted in-house ability to continuously improve products. He felt confident, given his contacts in the industry, that he would have no difficulty finding qualified candidates to fill the position of technical director. However, poor cash flow delayed his plans.

72   In February 1990, another problem developed, and Heartware's relationship with the university and the hospital changed. Dr. Cortez announced his intention to leave the hospital in May and to move into private practice in Belgium. His future role in Heartware was unclear.

EXPANDING SALES

73 Heartware's ability to hire additional staff depended heavily on securing more capital and increasing sales. In total, during Heartware's first 19 months of business, the company had sold $83,000 worth of products and had another $60,000 in orders. Exhibits 4 and 5 provide the financial statements as of June 1990.

74 All sales had been a function of Mr. Seery's personal efforts or contacts made by the university. While no single pattern was evident in the way sales evolved, many of the orders came through the university from former students. To prepare for the future, Heartware's founder also began to develop a network of distributors. Most of these distributorships arose from contacts Mr. Seery had made in previous business deals. Mr. Seery's association with distributors was informal.

CONTINUED PURSUIT OF FUNDING AND PARTNERSHIPS

75 During spring of 1990, fund raising proceeded much slower than Heartware's founder anticipated. He was unable to raise funds beyond the $270,000 invested by family members. Most of those funds had been spent to acquire the technology, travel to Europe, display and demonstrate the product, and seek FDA approval. Mr. Seery anticipated that further development and sales of the EP system would require an additional $1 million.

76 When Mr. Seery contacted venture capitalists, some told him their companies did not invest in ventures that required less than about $3 million. Others expressed reluctance because Heartware had no track record, was too dependent on one product, was too high-tech, or did not have a well-rounded management team.

77 Negotiations with potential strategic partners progressed further than negotiations with venture capitalists. However, none had yet come to fruition. Companies approached about partnerships gave various reasons for not forming an alliance. Some were not interested because the EP system required too large a capital investment for too small a market niche. Others indicated that the EP system was not a good fit with their current product lines. Negotiations with several companies continued.

ESOPHAGEAL EP TECHNOLOGY

78 During this period, Mr. Seery also began to explore an opportunity to extend Heartware's product line into esophageal EP technology. This technology took advantage of the fact that the heart and part of the esophagus are very close together. Thus, a specially designed catheter could be placed down the esophagus along with leads from a cardiac stimulator for sending electrical signals to the atria of the heart. The distance from the esophagus to the ventricles was significantly greater; therefore, such a system only could be used to diagnose and treat atrial arrhythmias.

79 Atrial arrhythmias were relatively less life-threatening than ventricular arrhythmias and could be treated fairly quickly without a hospital stay. Once an atrial arrhythmia was diagnosed, an esophageal EP system often could be used to pace the heart out of the arrhythmia. Thus, esophageal pacing was less invasive to the body and could be performed in an increased number of locations, without a cardiologist, in a decreased amount of time.

80 The procedure's speed and mobility often made esophageal treatment an ideal method for stimulating the heart in emergency situations, such as in coronary care units. In contrast to a general EP study, a patient did not need to be disconnected from all other support systems and moved to another location.

EXHIBIT 4

HEARTWARE INTERNATIONAL
Income Statement
for Period Ended 06/30/90

	6 Months	Ratio
Sales revenue:		
Amplifiers and signal distribution unit	$ 53,263.30	69.9%
Electrodes.	21,919.05	28.8
Miscellaneous income	1,000.00	1.3
Total sales revenue	76,182.35	100.0
Distributor commissions:		
Distributor commissions.	405.00	0.5
Royalties.	2,889.50	3.8
Net sales revenue	72,887.85	95.7
Cost of sales:		
Amplifiers & signal distribution unit	39,728.80	52.1
Electrodes.	12,030.75	15.8
Other cost of sales.	5.00	0.0
Gross profit	$ 21,123.30	27.7%
Operating expenses:		
Employment	$ 2,617,12	3.4%
Marketing and sales	3,995.12	5.2
Travel and entertainment	5,490.35	7.2
Professional fees	2,045.00	2.7
General and administrative	6,032.97	7.9
Depreciation	802.26	1.1
Amortization expense	15,000.00	19.7
Total operating expenses	35,942.82	47.2
Income before interest and tax	(14,819.52)	(19.5)
Interest	8,521.41	11.2
Net income before tax	(23,340.93)	(30.6)
Income tax.	25.00	0.0
Income after tax	$(23,365.93)	(30.7)%

81   Before 1988, esophageal diagnosis and treatment had been used primarily on a clinical basis, with the results recorded in scientific journals. Medical equipment could be sold on a "clinical use basis" prior to FDA approval. Clinical-use sales allowed for a system to be evaluated to obtain FDA acceptance; however, no marketing was allowed, only a limited quantity could be sold, and the product only could be sold at or below cost. Although esophageal technology became more routinely used in

EXHIBIT 5

HEARTWARE INTERNATIONAL
General Ledger
Balance Sheet
as of 06/30/90

Assets

Current assets:

Cash and marketable securities.	$ 2,919.41	
Accounts receivable	5,025.00	
Total current assets		$ 7,944.41

Fixed assets:

Furniture and equipment.	8,022.66	
Accumulated depreciation	(1,604.53)	
Total fixed assets		6,418.13

Noncurrent assets:

System license	150,000.00	
Accumulated amortization.	(30,000.00)	
System license, net	120,000.00	
Deposits.	604.45	
Total noncurrent assets		120,604.45
Total assets		$134,966.99

Liabilities

Current liabilities:

Accounts payable	$ 1,758.84	
Payable to officers	33,364.20	
Interest payable	4,529.05	
Total current liabilities		$ 39,652.09

Long-term liabilities:

License payable	88,042.69	
Total long-term liabilities		88,042.69
Total liabilities		$127,694.78

Shareholders' Equity

Common stock	2,000.00	
Paid-in capital	103,000.00	
Retained earnings.	(74,361.86)	
Current earnings.	(23,365.93)	
Total shareholders' equity		7,272.21
Total liabilities and shareholders' equity		$134,966.99

coronary care units and emergency rooms after 1988, it was still considered a fairly recent development in 1990.

82   While Mr. Seery had been employed by Hospicath, it had been approached about the possibility of acquiring an esophageal EP product developed at an American university. But the company had deferred its decision, never telling the developer "yes" or "no." Mr. Seery's interest in the technology had been keen, however, and his interest continued after he founded Heartware.

83   Mr. Seery projected that each of the 1,300 U.S. coronary care units would install a minimum of two esophageal systems between 1990 and 1995, generating a market of $10 million for the period. In 1990, over 5,300 emergency rooms were providing care in the United States. Mr. Seery estimated this segment of the market would generate sales of $35 million in esophageal products for the period between 1990 and 1995. Other possible market segments included field response teams (ambulances and paramedics) and general practitioners. Hospitals with EP systems also could use an esophageal system to screen a patient. If the arrhythmia was located in the atria, a general EP study might not be needed.

84   Few companies marketed esophageal products. Mr. Seery only knew of one Italian company marketing an esophageal system in Europe and one small U.S.-based medical device company marketing a system in the United States.

85   Acquisition of the esophageal stimulator also would potentially lead to the sale of esophageal catheters. Each stimulator sold would generate sales of 15 to 20 catheters per year. The esophageal catheter market was expected to total $40 million between 1990 and 2000.

HEARTWARE ACQUIRES ESOPHAGEAL TECHNOLOGY

86   In March 1990, knowing that negotiations were not progressing between Hospicath and the developer of the esophageal stimulator, Mr. Seery decided to approach the developer about acquiring the rights for Heartware. The two agreed that Heartware would pay 10 to 15 percent in royalties to the developer on any units sold (no fixed payments) and in exchange would receive the product rights. Although schematics were given to Mr. Seery, no formal agreement was signed because Heartware did not have funding available to develop and promote the product.

87   Prior to this agreement, the developer already had sold two dozen stimulators on a clinical-use basis. However, Mr. Seery realized that he would need assistance to further develop the product. He believed that until he could hire in-house technical expertise, the system's developer would provide support. The system still required FDA approval, clinical evaluations, and a new casing. Additionally, the system had to be redesigned to simplify manufacture. The founder estimated that $250,000 would be needed to complete the development process and to cover management expenses. Another year and a half would be needed before the product was ready to market commercially in the United States. Initially, to limit expenses, Mr. Seery planned to concentrate sales efforts for the esophageal product in the U.S. market. He felt that was feasible because the United States contained many outlets and almost no competition.

88   Heartware's CEO planned to target the domestic distributors of cardiology products as sources of capital. Ideally, he hoped to raise the needed $250,000 in lots of $25,000. Mr. Seery believed that if distributors invested in the product they would also actively promote it. Distributors would be offered 15 to 20 percent commissions to generate sales, collect receivables, and maintain inventory. The product was expected to sell for about $7,000. Mr. Seery anticipated exhibiting the esophageal system at the next NASPE meeting in 1990.

89   Mr. Seery also planned to sell esophageal catheters and started to investigate manufacturers who would make catheters under Heartware's label. He anticipated that the selling price per esophageal catheter would be $100. Hospicath was the only company selling esophageal catheters.

NEWS FROM THE UNIVERSITY OF LIMBURG

90   On Mr. Seery's way to work on May 1, 1990, he was contemplating the strategic direction his company should take. When he arrived at the office, the following fax from an attorney at the University of Limburg awaited him:

91   From: Ben van Werscht
      To: Mr. Gerry Seery

      Dear Mr. Seery,

92   I have a painful message for you. The Head of the Instrumental Department, Mr. Jan van der Swoort, has been suspended from duty. I will take duty from him and in this capacity I would like to settle some things with you.

93   As we both know there is a contract between Heartware Corporation and the University of Limburg for the Cortez Electrophysiology System. So far Mr. van der Swoort settled this business, but I have no sound judgment on the administration yet.

94   It is important for me to get answers on the following questions: What is the general rule of conduct when a new system is ordered? Who fixes the price? Who is taking care of product liability, etc.?

95   News of Mr. van der Swoort's suspension from the university, coming from an attorney and accompanied by a question about product liability, led Mr. Seery to wonder if the system had failed and a patient had died. However, a letter soon arrived from Mr. van der Swoort explaining that his suspension was due to budget problems and internal politics. Mr. Seery promptly arranged a trip to Holland to meet Mr. van der Swoort, get an explanation of events, and reevaluate Heartware's relationship with the University of Limburg.

96   Mr. van Werscht became the main contact between Heartware and the university, but Mr. Seery felt the attorney was more concerned with enforcing the strict letter of their contract than abiding by the spirit of the agreement worked out between Mr. Seery and the product's developers. University support and interest waned in the further development of the EP system's hardware and software.

HEARTWARE'S OPTIONS

97   With technical support no longer coming from the university, Mr. Seery began to explore alternatives. He continued to contact U.S. companies with technical infrastructures already in place that might be interested in a partnership. Mr. Seery identified several small U.S. firms that had the ability to upgrade the technology and the willingness to do so on a contract basis; but Heartware lacked the operating cash to pay for their services. Another alternative was to add a full-time technical expert to Heartware's payroll; however, Mr. Seery did not feel comfortable bringing someone on board until Heartware had a solid capital base.

98   On several occasions the founder had examined the possibility of moving his home and Heartware's headquarters to Europe. From there he could better manage relations with the university, Dr. Cortez, and Mr. van der Swoort. Both the Netherlands and Belgium were considered as possible locations. Heartware's products were receiving recognition and sales in Europe, and competition was hardly an issue there. Investors in Europe consistently presented the warmest responses to Heartware's business plan. By spring 1990, Mr. Seery was spending approximately one fourth of his time overseas. The main obstacle to making the move was the need for a steady cash flow to support Mr. Seery and his family while the company got off the ground. A major disadvantage to a European headquarters would be that less attention would be given to the larger U.S. market where Heartware had the most advanced system with FDA approval.

99   If the company did not move to Europe, another option that Heartware's CEO considered was to begin concentrating exclusively on marketing the esophageal technology in the United States. If Mr. Seery focused on the esophageal technology, he would have to essentially abandon Heartware's relationship with the University of Limburg since the start-up did not have enough resources to invest in both directions.

100   A final alternative was simply to go out of business. Resources already were stretched, and the other options would risk additional capital. To Mr. Seery, no option was clearly superior.

CASE 31

CINCINNATI MILACRON

1   The decade of the 1980s was supposed to have been one of high earnings recovery and the realization of new growth and market plans for Cincinnati Milacron (CM). Industry analysts and "the Mill's" top management team believed it had all the requisites for success. It was the largest machine tool company in the United States, and it could afford to develop and market the new technologies needed for the factories of the future. CM had a diversified customer base and was not dependent on the capital investment swings and fortunes of just one industry. It also had a strong reputation in plastics molding equipment, and plastics were rapidly replacing metals in many applications. Most important, the company had especially bright prospects for its newly developed "cutting edge" line of robots and computer-controlled manufacturing systems.

2   The period's realities were much more harsh. Instead of obtaining high earnings, Cincinnati Milacron operated in the red over the years of 1981–1991 and lost $80.0 and $100.2 millions, respectively, in 1987 and 1991. After starting the decade as America's largest machine tool company, it ended it as merely "one of America's largest" after turning its top managers over in 1988 and eliminating the jobs of almost half of its employees. Moreover, Milacron found itself outclassed and outmaneuvered in its high-tech diversifications into robots, lasers, and semiconductor wafers, which were supposed to protect it from the fearsome competitive strength of Japan's machine tool companies. The robotics industry, which was expected to amount to $4 billion in American sales by 1990, never took off and the company's profits and market responsiveness were hampered by production inefficiencies, rigid assembly techniques, and a slow, cumbersome management system. After suffering high losses on the robotics line, it was sold in April 1990 to the Swedish–Swiss manufacturer Asea Brown Boveri after failing to find a manufacturing partner for its excellently designed equipment.

3   As 1992 begins, Cincinnati Milacron's new strategy is to return to its core business of standard machine tools. While this strategy pits the firm squarely against the mainly Japanese competition it attempted to avoid in the first place, Daniel J. Meyer, the company's chief executive officer, says this is the correct path to follow because "we had more confidence in machine tools." More important for the company's long-term fortunes, "We have a 107-year reputation in manufacturing, and the opportunity for success is still there, based on the history we have. We're not going to lose."

MACHINE TOOLS AND THE MACHINE TOOL INDUSTRY

4   The machine tool industry (SIC 3541) consists of metal-cutting and metal-forming power machinery. It is the business that makes the machines that makes the machines of industry, because almost all manufacturing processes require these tools. A nation's manufacturing capabilities are highly dependent on the quantity and quality of its machine tools. Accordingly, this industry is of strategic importance to a country's ability to compete internationally. The major users of machine tools are the auto industry (roughly 20 to 40 percent of annual sales orders), the oil and gas industry, and the makers of

This case was prepared by Joseph Wolfe, Management and Marketing Department, College of Business Administration, University of Tulsa.

EXHIBIT 1
Major Categories and Manufacturers of Metal-Working Machinery and Tools

Machine Tools

As a general class, machine tools are power-driven metal-working devices that shape or form metal by use of cutting, sawing, pressing, pounding, or electrical discharges.

Within this general class are two types of machine tools, classified by their operating method—metal-cutting and metal-forming machines. Metal-cutting machines shape metal by cutting away the material not wanted in the final product. This carving can be accomplished by any of the following methods alone or in combination:

1. *Turnings.* These machines turn or spin the object being shaped against a cutting edge. Examples of these types of machines are lathes, automatic bar machines, and screw machines.
2. *Boring.* Machines that cut circles or cylindrical shapes into metal from either a horizontal or vertical plane.
3. *Planing and shaping.* Machines that shear metal in continuous strokes.
4. *Drilling.* Smaller-diameter holes that are pierced through the metal by a continuous rotating action.
5. *Grinding and honing.* Shaping the metal through the use of abrasives.

Metal-forming machines operate through the actions of forging, shearing, hammering, extruding (stretching), bending, die casting, or pressing. The automobile industry is the largest market for these types of machines. As plastics, ceramics, and exotic materials have begun to be used more frequently in cars and other products, these tools have been modified or applied to those applications. America's largest manufacturers of machine tools are Cross & Trecker, Cincinnati Milacron, Giddings & Lewis, Industrial Automation Systems (Litton Industries), and Ingersoll Milling Machine.

Automatic, Numerically Controlled Machine Tools

Numerically controlled (NC) machine tools use some type of medium to control the tool being used. This degree of automation eliminates human mistakes, lowers labor costs, and allows the machine to easily switch jobs. Three kinds of NC tools are currently available:

1. *Conventional NC system.* Also known as hard-wired NC tools, the functions of these machines are precoded into a fixed and unalterable routine or activity sequence.
2. *Computerized numerical control (CNC) system.* Also known as soft-wired NCs, a small computer is used to control the machine tool's functions. A set of programs controlling those functions are stored in the computer's memory, and these programs can be called upon by the machine's operator when desired. While conventional NC systems are still the major sellers in this market, CNCs have been rapidly increasing their market shares through the availability of low-cost, free-standing minicomputers in the late 1960s.

---

farm and industrial machinery, appliances, aircraft, and electronic equipment. Exhibit 1 describes the various machine tools manufactured by this industry as well as citing America's major machine tool suppliers. Exhibit 2 displays the value of domestic and foreign machine tool shipments by major category.

5   While firms using metals and plastics as part of their manufacturing processes are the consumers of machine tools, the basic demand for them is derived from a number of production-related factors. Machine tools can alter a factory's production levels, are capital intensive, and affect the skill levels and number of machinists needed to operate them. Therefore, the demand for machine tools is dependent on (1) the sales expectations for the products the tools support and (2) the supply and cost of skilled labor. The role of sales expectations and projected factory utilization rates can be seen in Exhibit 3. When capacity utilization rates begin to raise above the 85 percent mark, the demand for machine tools tends to rise. This relationship is somewhat delayed, however, depending on the complexity of the machinery being produced and labor-capital substitution considerations. The historical

EXHIBIT 1 (concluded)

3. *Direct numerical control (DNC).* In this system a main computer simultaneously controls the actions and functions of a number of machine tools. Rather than using punched cards, paper or magnetic tape to control the machine's actions, jobs and routines are called and corrected through the use of a display screen.

The principle manufacturers of these types of machines are General Electric, Allen-Bradley (Rockwell International), and Fanuc of Japan. Cincinnati Milacron, Cross & Trecker, Monarch Machine Tool, Giddings & Lewis, and Ex-Cell-O Corporation (Textron, Inc.) are also major players in this industry's segment.

Expendables and Accessories

These are products or supplies employed during the metal-working process. These are taps, dies, twist drills, chucks, gauges, reamers, and jigs. Because these products wear out in proportion to their use, the demand for these products is closely tied to industry's level of activity. National Twist Drill, Acme-Cleveland, and Vermont American are the largest manufacturers of twist drills, while the major manufacturers of taps, dies, and gauges are United-Greenfield, TRW Geometric Tools (TRW, Inc.), and Ex-Cell-O Corporation.

Hand Tools and Mechanics' Precision Tools

Hand tools can employ either human or electrical/mechanical energy to accomplish their task. Hand tools are pliers, hammers, screw drivers, tool boxes, and interchangeable socket wrenches. These are primarily manufactured by Snap-On Tools, Stanley Works, McDonough Company, and Triangle Corporation. Power-driven hand tools are of two power types—portable pneumatic tools and portable electric tools. The pneumatic, air-driven tools, which include drills, screw drivers, nut setters, ratchet wrenches, hoists, grinders, sanders, polishers, and shipping and riveting hammers, usually are made to customer specifications and are sold to mass production assemblers. America's largest manufacturer of these types of tools is Chicago Pneumatic Tools followed by Ingersoll-Rand and Thor Power Tool (Stewart-Warner).

Portable electric tools are used for both metal and woodworking and for home maintenance purposes. Professional electric tools include electric drills, saws, sanders, polishers, hammers, lawn and garden tools, and chain saws. Black & Decker is the largest producer of these types of tools. Other manufacturers are Rockwell International, McGraw-Edison (Cooper Industries), and Ingersoll-Rand.

When accomplishing their tasks, mechanics employ various measuring devices. These hand-operated devices include micrometers, steel rules, combination squares, calipers, verniers, and protractors. Among many manufacturers in the United States the largest are Brown & Sharpe, L. S. Starrett, and the Triangle Corporation.

Sources: "Machinery Outlook," *Standard & Poor's Industry Surveys: Steel and Heavy Machinery* 158, no. 30, sect. 1 (August 9, 1990), p. 28; and various *Value Line* Machine Tool Industry overviews, 1980 to 1991.

lag between orders and shipments graphed in Exhibit 4 shows it ranges from five to six business quarters. When Detroit's car manufacturers planned for the production of their redesigned transmissions and engines for the 1991 and 1992 model years, the machine tools for them were ordered in late-1987 and nearly all of 1988. The lag, however, between orders and shipments is much shorter for standard, commodity-like machine tools. These are sold "off-the-shelf" from inventories, with no customizing and little manufacturer's service or support.

6   In the short-term, weakened labor unions or an ample supply of machinists may cause manufacturers to delay purchasing labor-saving machine tools. Weak labor unions have difficulty protesting the labor replacement and skill-lowering aspects of programmed machine tools, while an ample supply of skilled machinists tends to dampen the worker's demands for higher wages. Moreover, in the long term, labor is a variable cost and can be adjusted to different plant production levels. Once new machine tools are purchased they become fixed expenses which must be covered regardless of the

EXHIBIT 2
Shipments of Complete Machine Tools (in hundred thousands)

Tool Type	1981	1982	1983	1984	1985	1986	1987	1988	1989	1990	1991
Metal-cutting:											
Domestic	3,550	2,599	1,200	1,484	1,538	1,885	1,499	1,400	2,059	1,772	1,543
Foreign	551	296	172	123	194	206	178	174	299	298	344
Total	4,102	2,985	1,372	1,607	1,732	1,891	1,677	1,567	2,359	2,070	1,888
Metal-forming:											
Domestic	824	600	430	608	744	621	538	702	704	761	546
Foreign	167	110	43	71	60	67	109	122	133	134	202
Total	991	710	474	679	804	688	647	825	837	894	748

Source: *The Economic Handbook of the Machine Tool Industry,* National Machine Tool Builder's Association (The Association for Manufacturing Technology), various years.

EXHIBIT 3
Quarterly Machine Tool Shipments and Net New Orders

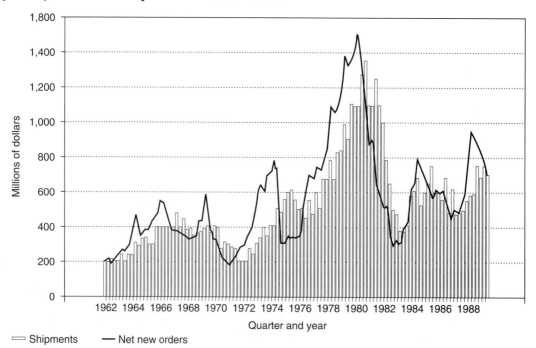

Source: The Association for Manufacturing Technology, for various years.

EXHIBIT 4
Machine Tool Orders versus Factory Operating Rates

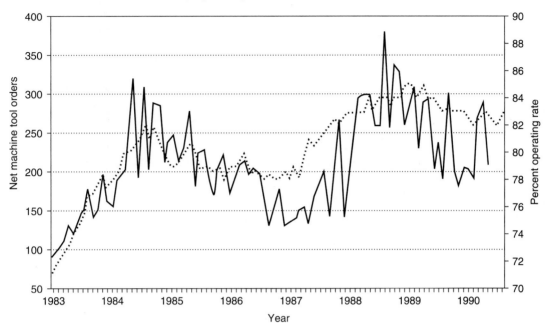

Machine tool orders ······ Operating rate

Sources: Federal Reserve Board and the Association for Manufacturing Technology.

factory's utilization rate. Producers are reluctant to commit to these fixed obligations unless there is a guarantee these expenses can be recovered in a reasonable amount of time. If in doubt many will wait regarding fixed expenses until the future is more certain.

CHANGING INDUSTRY STRUCTURE

7   America's machine tool industry has traditionally been fractionalized and craft-related. Companies often were founded on a single good idea. One such idea by one firm and one man led to the wire electrical discharge machine segment, which currently has sales of $700 million per year. Victor Harding's job during World War II was to remove broken bits of metal left in the grooves of newly threaded pieces. By rigging a spark-producing copper electrode to his machine, he found the sparks eroded the metal, thereby loosening waste material. Because his employer was not interested in his innovation, Harding started his own company and, by the mid-1960s, his Elox Corporation was selling an entire line of "electron drills."

8   Product and entrepreneurial patterns such as this resulted in an industry comprised of a large number of small firms producing a few particular machine tools. It was a highly segmented industry and its manufacturers had limited economies of scale. Despite this fractionalized nature, America's producers were the world's leaders, because they possessed the most advanced technology and almost one third of the world's sales.

9   In the late 1970s, however, the introduction of NC and CNC machine tools began to change the industry's economics. The new technologies of electronics and computers were added to the machine tool manufacturer's production matrix. Higher capital investments, new skills, and plant retooling expenses had to be financed, and those operating on a small scale were unable to do so. Also coming into play were learning curve effects associated with high-technology electronics. Being basically small single-line producers, many firms could not upgrade or acquire these skills or capture these learning curve effects. To stay in business, many gravitated toward the market's lower and technologically simpler end, comprising standard machine tool products.

10   For many American companies this was a disastrous strategy. Japan's machine tool firms had just come on the domestic scene and they were pursuing the same market niche. Many U.S. firms were quickly overwhelmed by that country's superior lower-priced products. By the mid-1980s, Japan had captured 80 percent of new sales in the American NC lathe and machining center market, after only having entered it in 1976. The fate of Victor Harding's Elox Corporation is an example in miniature. It is now a small-time player in the segment it created, as over 80 percent of America's market in wire electrical discharge machines has been captured by the Japanese firms of Mitsubishi, Fujitsu Fanuc, Sodick, and Hitachi.

11   On the international scene, America's machine tool firms experienced similar problems during this period. Japan's share of world exports of machine tools grew from 3.5 percent in 1970 to 15.0 percent in 1983, while America's share fell from 11.7 to 4.8 percent.

JAPAN'S MACHINE TOOL INDUSTRY POLICY

12   How did this sweep of the American machine tool industry come about? What did the Japanese do to overwhelm an industry that had the United States as its leading participant?

13   As part of its economic revival in the 1950s, the Japanese government's policies have been guided by "developmental capitalism." Under this system the state works hand-in-hand with private enterprise to further the nation's economic development. Through its Ministry of International Trade and Industry (MITI), various "vision" statements are intermittently authored. These statements generally specify the strategies and the industries to be targeted for special emphasis. As early as 1956, MITI recognized the strategic value of the machine tool industry by passing the Extraordinary Measures Law for the Promotion of Specified Machinery Industries.

14   Teeth were soon put into MITI's vision for Japan's machine tool industry. To obtain rationalization and economic efficiency within the domestic industry itself, it recommended the following:

15   1. Japanese domestic firms would stop manufacturing any product line whose Japanese market share was less than 5 percent; or
        2. Firms would stop manufacturing any product line that was less then 20 percent of the firm's total production. Once rationalization was achieved within the industry, then;
        3. All machine tool firms would concentrate on NC tools. This machine tool type should account for over 50 percent of the industry's total output by 1980.

16   After having accomplished rationalization within its own industry by the early 1970s, new policies were adopted to promote overseas sales, with the United States being a prime target. Exhibit 5 summarizes these policies and actions, while Exhibit 6 summarizes the competitive strategies employed by Japan's machine tool companies.

17   As the Japanese have succeeded in the United States, via the relatively safe strategy of exporting their machines into the country, they now are establishing deeper roots and greater equity commitments on American soil. These roots and commitments have taken the following form:

EXHIBIT 5
MITI's Policies and Maneuvers for the Machine Tool Industry

Policy	Maneuvers
Industry structure	Rationalization of the machine tool industry through forced or encouraged mergers, the divestment of extraneous or nonstrategic product lines, and the achievement of economies of scale.
Product line	Concentration on NC machine tools. This type to be at least 50 percent of all output by 1980. Certain companies would specialize in particular products. Export cartels created to facilitate joint export activities. Government research funds and tax credits provided for joint research in earmarked technologies. All activities coordinated by a machine tool industry association.
Customer financing	Small businesses receive loans and special depreciation allowances made to firms purchasing machine tools. Leasing of Japanese-made robots subsidized by Japan Robot Leasing Authority.
Exports	Export cartel set floor prices on NC lathes and machining centers exported to United States, Canada, and the EEC. Expenses shared regarding exporting, market research, and international marketing information.

Source: Adapted from Ravi Sarathy, "The Interplay of Industrial Policy and International Strategy: Japan's Machine Tool Industry," *California Management Review*, Spring 1989, pp. 138–41.

18   *Joint ventures*—Fujitsu Fanuc, Ltd.–General Motors; Okuma Machinery Works, Ltd.–DeVlieg; Toyoda–Bendix; Toshiba–Cross & Trecker; Yokogawa Electric Manufacturing–Gould; Dijet Industrial–Kennametal.

United States subsidiary operations—U.S. Mazak, a subsidiary of Yamazaki; Mori Seiki, OSG Manufacturing, Sonoike Manufacturing, Hitachi.

Acquisition—Makino acquired LeBlond.

19   These strategies and commitments have been so effective that about 30 percent of America's machine tool capacity is now provided by the Japanese firms of Mazak Corporation, LeBlond Makino Machine Tool Company, and Okuma Machinery Works, Ltd. This presence will be even greater in the early 1990s. In July 1990, Mitsubishi Heavy Industries America, Inc., opened a plant in Hopkinsville, Kentucky, to make horizontal and vertical machining centers and NC lathes. Mazak completed a $55 million expansion of its Florence, Kentucky, plant in March 1990, and this raises its monthly capacity from 80–85 units to 100–120 units.

CURRENT INDUSTRY CONDITIONS

20   The composite results for a number of benchmark American machine tool companies indicates the difficulties they experienced in the 1980s. Exhibit 7 shows combined losses from 1987 to 1991 for Acme-Cleveland, Brown & Sharpe, Cincinnati Milacron, Cross & Trecker, Gleason Works, and the Monarch Machine Tool Company. Future profits are expected to be relatively low. The health of today's firms appears to be partially related to their past strategies. As described in Exhibit 8, some companies attempted to diversify away from the extremely competitive machine tool industry, while others tried to apply their core strengths to exotic applications. During the past decade, about half of

EXHIBIT 6
Japanese Machine Tool Competitive Strategy

Strategy	Implementation
Company cost structure	Lower the company's manufacturing cost structure through high-volume production of standardized products in capital-intensive factories. From 1975–86, Japan's major machine tool manufacturers reduced their labor expenses from 25.0 to 12.2 percent and general overhead from 16.2 to 14.2 percent of sales. This was accomplished by heavy capital investment per employee. Capital stock increased from ¥2.15 million in 1975 to ¥6.19 million by 1986, resulting in greater productivity. Sales per employee were ¥9.83 million in 1975 and they increased to ¥34.76 million by 1986.
Product/market niches	Sell standardized, off-the-shelf machine tools to small and medium-sized firms. Designed small, cheaper, and lower-performance CNC lathes for Japan's own medium and smaller-sized firms. These standard products were subsequently widely distributed in the United States through independent dealers, rather than through company-controlled sales engineers who were only needed for custom-fitted machine tool applications.
R&D	Efforts aimed at simplifying the product and making it easier to manufacture and be produced in large volumes via assembly-line techniques.
Pricing	Sell the product for less. By 1982, Japan's prices were lower by 19 percent on 25 hp horizontal spindles, 39 percent for 50 hp horizontal spindles, 32 percent for vertical spindle lathes, and 44 percent for horizontal spindles with a y-axis of over 40 inches. Machining centers were 30 to 41 percent lower in price.
Delivery and distribution	Standardized, off-the-shelf products easier to warehouse and deliver during boom times. Import penetration tends to increase when domestic order backlogs exceed 9.5 months. Japan's products immediately were available from stockpiled warehouses and they made large inroads. Heavy use of distributors, rather than direct customer sales.
Foreign direct investment	Obtain an American manufacturing presence through either transplants, acquisitions, or joint ventures. The American firm LeBlond was acquired by Makino, allowing it to manufacture machining centers in the United States with Japanese parts. Mori Seiki, OSG Manufacturing, Sonoike Manufacturing, and Hitachi have created American subsidiaries. Joint ventures have been established between General Motors and Fanuc, Okuma with DeVlieg, Toyoda and Bendix, Toshiba and Cross & Trecker, Gould and Yokogawa Electric Manufacturing, and Dijet Industrial with Kennametal.

Source: Adapted from Ravi Sarathy, "The Interplay of Industrial Policy and International Strategy: Japan's Machine Tool Industry," *California Management Review*, Spring 1989, pp. 149–53.

America's machine tool companies went out of business and a large number of consolidations occurred. Despite the resulting greater industry concentration, the average U.S. tool firm has less than $3 million in annual sales and fewer than 25 employees. It can be expected that more casualties will be experienced in the 1990s.

21   Industry observers have cited two sets of factors that could improve the industry's prospects. The first set of factors is historical and demographic in nature. A historically weakening dollar has made

EXHIBIT 7
Composite Machine Tool Industry Results (in hundred thousands)

	1987	1988	1989	1990	1991	1992*	1994–96*
Sales	1,882.8	1,944.2	1,945.5	1,933.4	1,400.0	1,550.0	2,050.0
Operating profit	90.4	108.9	118.7	97.7	70.0	116.3	225.5
Depreciation	80.5	71.9	58.7	59.1	50.0	50.0	75.0
Net profit	−111.2	−26.2	−6.3	−34.5	−80.0	30.0	95.0

* Estimated by *Value Line.*
Note: Composite companies have changed for various years due to mergers and acquisitions. Firms included have been Acme-Cleveland, Brown & Sharpe, Cincinnati Milacron, Cross & Trecker, Gleason Works, and Monarch Machine Tool Company.
Source: Theresa Brophy, "Machine Tool Industry," *Value Line Industrial Survey,* May 17, 1991, p. 1336, and November 15, 1991, p. 1335.

American goods more price competitive with foreign goods. This generally could give American manufacturers an incentive to increase their capacity, and for the machine tool manufacturers themselves it means American-built machine tools will continue to be price competitive with those built overseas. Regarding demographics, America's aging population and declining birth rate translate into a shortage of industrial skilled labor. This shortage of skilled labor can be compensated by "smarter" machine tools, which also have the advantage of being depreciated.

22   The second set of factors is competitive in nature. American firms are under continuing pressure to lower costs and raise quality. Efficient and accurate machine tools are at least a partial solution. Much of America's manufacturing equipment is more than 20 years old and needs replacement. Due to inefficiencies in the face of foreign competition, these factories must retool to survive. Improvements in computer and manufacturing technology also are occurring more rapidly, and these could force an industry's remaining firms to use these technologies as competitive weapons. Computer prices have fallen drastically, thus lowering the costs of various CNC and DNC units. This means factories can now adopt "cutting edge" technology at a lower cost.

23   Many U.S. companies are finally realizing they must modernize if they are to succeed. Caterpillar, Inc., will have spent about $3.4 billion from 1986 to 1992 to build its new automated "Plant with a Future." When completed, it will produce more heavy duty equipment than ever but with 3.0 million square feet less manufacturing space. Pressures for modernization should also increase when Europe completes its unification plans in 1992 and Japan completes its current capital improvement program. Additional markets will be opening with the emergence of Eastern and Central Europe as invigorated customers. In June 1990, the coordinating committee on Multilateral Export Controls, of which the United States is a major partner, agreed to ease its 41-year-old embargo on the sale of machine tools to the Eastern bloc countries.

24   Because America's automobile manufacturers are the machine tool industry's single largest customer, trends and experiences in that industry are extremely important. Japan's superiority in engine design and transmissions may force Detroit to retool plants even though the Motor City's sales prospects and capacity utilization rates for the mid-1990s are not that bright. Japan has taken the lead in producing multivalve engines and electronically controlled transmissions. The engines boost performance without increasing pollution or diminishing fuel economy, and electronically controlled five-speed automatic transmissions provide better fuel economy and smoother gearshifts. Regardless of what the Japanese do, the U.S. government is redefining its automobile emission standards and Detroit probably will want to invest in new drive train programs for the 1993 and 1994 models.

25   Detroit's automobile manufacturers currently have excess capacity, so they probably will not build new plants but, instead, will attempt to make given capacity more efficient. Ford has indicated it has

EXHIBIT 8
Company Profiles

Cross & Trecker. In the 1980s, Cross & Trecker emphasized the machine tool market's more specialized end. This did not work out well. Companies pursuing this strategy take all the risks of designing customized tools, but this does not guarantee their ultimate sale. This strategy has the attendant problems of estimating expenses and, therefore, many contracts are underpriced and unprofitable. Cross & Trecker had to suspend its first dividend in 1986, and in 1987 took a large charge against earnings to consolidate operations and write down old equipment and inventories. Dislocations caused by its corporate restructuring hampered sales in 1989, and it has been struggling for a number of years. Giddings & Lewis will finalize its acquisition of this company in fall 1991.

Giddings & Lewis. The AMCA International Corporation acquired this company in 1982. After losing $6.1 and $138.1 million in 1986 and 1987 it was sold off in July 1989. Giddings & Lewis quickly earned a profit of $17.1 million in 1989 after increasing its revenues 38 percent in one year. By August 1990, the company had no long-term debt and it generated cash in excess of capital spending and normal needs. Giddings has been very successful with large yet flexible integrated manufacturing systems selling for up to $30 million each. Chairman William J. Fife, Jr., vows: "We're not going into competition with the Japanese. [They] move low-end machine tools by the truckload. We're going to stay away from truckload sales." As one of America's most profitable machine tool companies, it will be the industry's largest firm after it completes its acquisition of Cross & Trecker.

Gleason Works. In the mid-1980s, Gleason attempted to capitalize on its dominance of the bevel gear grinding industry. It soon lost money marketing a complex differential for sports cars. It subsequently has retrenched to its gear making specialty. As of May 1991, its new line of simplified computer-controlled gear production machinery is generating relatively healthy company earnings. Gleason also has begun to reduce design and manufacturing costs by using standardized parts. The company is basically a niche manufacturer; it dominates the worldwide market for bevel gear making machinery. Its sales are concentrated in the automobile industry.

Monarch Machine Tool. This venerable company was established in Sidney, Ohio, in 1909. It produces highly computerized yet standardized lathes and machining centers in antiquated plants in Sidney and Cortland, New York. Monarch was very profitable in the early 1980s, when it earned as much as $19 million on sales of $139 million in 1981. Losses occurred shortly thereafter. To save money, management stopped all "unnecessary" spending, including dividends, research and development, and new shop floor machinery. Only old, used equipment was purchased, which pushed further back Monarch's already outdated manufacturing operations. The company has relatively little exposure to the auto industry, and CEO Robert Siewert says they will focus on customer service. "We haven't done business that way in the past. It was forced upon us by the Japanese. It was our way of staying in this business."

Newell Company and **Stanley Works.** Along with Vermont American, these companies cater to the relatively healthy do-it-yourself and equipment maintenance markets. In late-1991, the Newell Company announced its intentions of buying up to 15 percent of Stanley Works' common stock, with the later aim of making a complete acquisition.

Norton. This company is a high-tech materials and grinding wheel manufacturer. It began to benefit from a cost reduction program it launched in 1986. In the late-1980s, Norton restructured itself, and it has been carried by profits from its nonmachine tool operations.

---

about 20 percent more capacity than it needs. Instead, it will spend about $600 million to retool and "prep" its Van Dyke plant in Sterling Heights, Michigan, to produce four- and five-speed automatic front-wheel-drive transmissions for cars and light trucks.

26   While many are hoping for a rosy future for the machine tool industry, a number of unsettling factors remain. The dollar must remain weak, if mere price competitiveness is to be employed by the

American machine tool manufacturers. Moreover, neither the weak dollar nor the trade restrictions the American government has placed on foreign machine tool manufacturers have kept the Japanese manufacturers from making serious inroads into the U.S. machine tool market. Regarding the capital-labor substitution effects associated with the installation of labor-saving machine tools, there are other less expensive and more flexible ways to increase a factory's efficiency. Quality circles and just-in-time methods can increase efficiency, and these methods can be quickly turned on or off depending on the company's needs for efficiency.

27   Closer to home, within the American automobile industry itself, the Japanese have begun to produce and assemble their cars in transplants. When this is done, the tendency has been to employ their own country's machine tool equipment in their factories, rather than purchasing American machine tools. The Japanese nameplates of Honda, Toyota, Nissan, Mazda, Mitsubishi, and others garnered a 31 percent share of America's 1991 automobile sales, and this was an 11 percent increase over their 1990 share. To circumvent the import restrictions that have been placed on them, more and more of these cars are being manufactured in the United States. While an opportunity exists for American machine tools to be used in Japan's transplants, sales to them have been difficult. Most Japanese manufacturers are part owners of the machine tool companies they use. They find it financially and culturally beneficial to continue these relationships, regardless of the comparative quality or cost of the tools themselves.

28   Strategies for handling the foreign competition, especially the Japanese, with the most efficient manufacturing facilities in the world, are varied. Some companies emphasize the "Made in America" label, while others emphasize service which may be a disguised method of taking advantage of foreign producer's unfamiliarity with American customs, values, and decision-making methods. The standardized products segment, where service is not of great importance, has all but been surrendered to the Japanese. American companies have tended to concentrate on the highly sophisticated CNC machines priced from $300,000 to $2 million. As noted by Henry Mamlok, president of Jacobson Tool & Manufacturing Corporation, "The Japanese are awfully hard to beat in the commodity end of the business. We focus on customized tools made to fill a special need with prices up to $500,000 or so."

29   Some companies have emphasized a niching strategy. Harvey Rohmiller of the Lodge & Shipley Division of Manuflex Corporation says:

30   To be successful, American companies—even the small ones—have to get better at defining their markets more narrowly and deciding what products will fit that market. Twenty years ago, a company like ours was manufacturing-driven. We'd produce a new tool with the confidence it would soon have wide appeal. With so much more engineering and technology in the industry today, the stakes are higher and we've all had to become market-driven.

31   Then there is the last group of companies. They feel their fortunes are tied to the degree they can capitalize on whatever eventualities occur with their product's major users. Accordingly, they are attempting to hold on and keep their options open.

CINCINNATI MILACRON

32   Within the machine tool industry, CM currently manufactures and sells industrial process equipment and systems. These products are gathered into three groups, with independent profit accountability:

33   *Machine Tool Group.* Machine tools, composites processing equipment, advanced manufacturing systems, and electronic controls. The machine tool product lines include vertical and horizontal machining centers, turning centers, aerospace profilers and routers, bridge and portal mills, die and mold-making machines, horizontal boring machines, grinding machines, and special machines.

EXHIBIT 9
Diversifications, Acquisitions, and Divestitures

Diversifications	Acquisitions	Divestitures, Plant Closings, and Liquidations
Pre-1976—Small business systems	1983—Purchased a line of injection molding machines from Emhart Corporation's Farrel Rochester Division.	1978—Liquidated its German machine tool manufacturing subsidiary at a loss of $3.6 million.
1976—Computer controlled industrial robots		
1978—Silicon wafers and circuit board composite material	1984—Purchased LK Tool Company, Ltd., of England, a manufacturer of coordinate measuring machines.	1982—$10 million write-down on the closing of a British machine tool plant.
1986—Plastic packaging film		
1987—Expert systems software and PC-based shop floor management software	1986—Purchased Laser Machines Corporation of Indianapolis, Indiana.	1988—Sold metals fabrication division to Cast-Fab Technologies, Inc.
	1986—Purchased Sano Design and Machine Company, Inc., a manufacturer of plastic packaging films.	1989—Semiconductor materials business sold to a subsidiary of Japan's Osaka Titanium Company, Ltd.
	1988—Purchased Chesapeake Laser Systems, Inc., as a complement to the LK Tool Company.	1990—Sold all laser operations to The 600 Group, PLC, for a $4.5 million loss.
	1989—Acquired a line of plastics extrusion blow molding machines from the Bemis Company's Hayssen Manufacturing Company.	1990—Sold entire robot line to Asea Brown Boveri for a $1.7 million loss.
	1990—Bought SL Abrasives, Inc., a grinding wheel manufacturer.	1990—Closed Vlaardingen, Holland, machine tool plant.
	1990—Acquired from Pratt & Whitney its die and mold product line.	1991—Took a $75.1 million charge against earnings to sell most of its grinding machine products. An additional write-down of about $15 million was taken on the value of its measurement equipment in preparation for its sale.

Plastics Machinery Group. Reaction injection molding machines, systems for extrusion, blow molding and blown film, auxiliary equipment, and contract services.

Industrial Products Group. Cimcool metalworking fluids, precision grinding wheels, and LK measurement and inspection systems.

34 This product array is far different, however, from the one pursued just 10 years before and came about after much soul-searching and upheaval. In late-February 1991, Milacron's management explained the rationale for its newest strategy:

35 For several decades in the post-World War II era, Milacron's strategy was diversification and we brought to market new manufacturing technologies in many fields: electronics, plastics, robotics, laser, and flexible manufacturing systems, to name only a few. Certain new product lines, such as plastics machinery, were highly successful. However, the widely predicted large markets for other technologies never evolved. So, for the 1990s, we have honed a new strategy. We are channeling and focusing all Milacron's creativity, innovation, and entrepreneurial spirit directly into our core businesses, which are products and services for the metalworking and the plastics processing industries.

36 Today, global markets for machine tools and plastics machinery are large and growing steadily. Annual worldwide sales of machine tools have doubled since the mid-1980s and now exceed $40 billion. The

EXHIBIT 10
Net Profits for Cincinnati Milacron versus Benchmark Machine Tool Companies

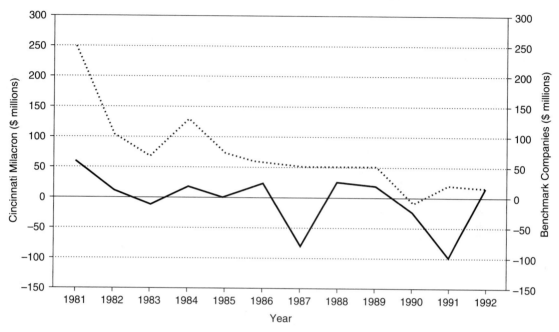

world market for plastics processing machinery, although smaller, is growing even faster. It is currently approaching $8 billion, with a real growth rate higher than the GNP. These are the primary markets Milacron is targeting in the 1990s.

37   In the late 1970s and early 1980s, facing record-high demand for capital equipment, [with] fierce foreign competition and the overvalued dollar, Milacron and other U.S. machine tool builders moved away from producing *standard* machine tool products (i.e., basic machining centers and turning centers). Instead, we concentrated on highly engineered and custom-designed machines and systems for automotive, aerospace, and other important industries. The standard machine business, however, offers excellent economies of scale in manufacturing and the benefits of a broad marketing network. So now Milacron is going back after the standard machine tool market, not only in the United States but throughout the world. And we're doing it by building cost-competitive all-metric machines with world-class quality and features.

38   In pursuing its original diversification strategy, the company jettisoned its original stodgy name of the Cincinnati Milling Machine Company and became the space-age sounding company called Cincinnati Milacron. Donald Shively, who would later be passed over for the company's top spot because he was too much a machine tool man, recalled, "The board decided we were beating a dead horse with machine tools, so the decision was made to more or less abdicate the standard line." Exhibit 9 lists the various diversifications and acquisitions the company made as it implemented this strategy. The exhibit also lists the ultimate disposition of many of those activities.

39   As the 1980s proceeded, management took solace that it often did not perform as badly as other firms in the machine tool industry. In 1981, Milacron's orders did not fall as much as the industry's, because of its strong position in the less cyclical special machine tool market, rather than

EXHIBIT 11
Cincinnati Milacron Sales, Expenses, and Earnings (in hundred thousands)

	1981	1982	1983	1984	1985	1986	1987	1988	1989	1990	1991	1992*
Sales	$934.4	$759.7	$559.0	$660.5	$732.2	$850.0	$828.0	$857.8	$850.6	$837.7	$754.0	$865.0
Cost of goods sold	691.5	569.8	458.4	535.0	549.2	595.0	612.7	637.3	625.3	647.5	649.8	617.7
Gross profit	242.9	189.9	100.6	125.5	183.0	255.0	215.3	220.5	225.4	190.2	104.2	247.3
General administration	142.4	121.6	57.6	48.4	115.3	163.5	229.7	135.3	152.5	156.4	150.5	152.0
R&D	22.4	35.7	30.2	36.3	36.6	40.0	35.6	35.2	31.5	34.3	30.9	35.5
Depreciation	17.3	20.4	23.1	26.0	29.6	28.3	30.0	25.0	22.9	23.7	23.0	22.0
Profit before taxes	60.8	12.2	−10.3	14.8	1.5	23.3	−80.0	25.0	18.5	−24.3	−100.2	37.8
Taxes	25.4	6.5	0.0	4.1	0.0	6.9	0.0	10.7	8.8	−11.6	0.0	20.8
Profit after taxes	35.4	5.7	−10.3	10.7	1.5	16.4	−80.0	14.3	9.7	−12.7	−100.2	17.0

* Estimated from *Value Line* data.
Source: Reconstructed from annual August *Value Line* reports.

in commodity-type tools. Additionally, the company was able to offer attractive credit terms to its customers through its financial subsidiary, and it also benefitted from close ties to its customers through its direct marketing channels. A year later, management stated "although our operating results were down for the year, it should be kept in mind that Milacron performed better than many capital goods companies; and while the size of our markets declined, we gained share in our major product lines." In 1990, the company observed that orders for the American machine tool industry had declined 27 percent while its own orders declined only 14 percent. Exhibit 10 plots Cincinnati Milacron's net profits versus those obtained by its major competitors for the years 1981 to 1992. Exhibit 11 reports the company's overall profits and expenses for the same period.

40 To provide better guidance, top management enunciated various goals and predictions for the firm during the mid-1980s. In 1985, James A. D. Geier, then-chairman and CEO, forecast Milicron's sales would surpass $1 billion before 1990 and that plastics machinery revenues would be more than $300 million by that year. To provide a level of financial comfort, management's goal for 1989 was to produce a total capital ratio in the low- to mid-30s. In December 1986, this ratio was 43 percent and it was deemed inappropriate.

41 More important, asset usage was to be realigned according to the schedule shown in Exhibit 12. Between 1980 to 1985, the company closed five plants and reduced its machine tool work force by 46 percent. In 1981, 65.7 percent of its assets were dedicated to machine tools, and this had been cut back 21.0 percent by 1985. Still, there was too much capacity in this money-losing line. In 1986, operations were discontinued in one of its Cincinnati plants, in the robot plant in Greenville, South Carolina, and at its turning center in Wilmington, Ohio. Overall, over 200 pieces of equipment were taken out of production that year. Exhibits 13 and 14, respectively, show Milacron's capital expenses and asset maneuvers from 1985 to 1991 and the recent operating results of its two latest divestitures.

42 In carrying out its reallocations Cincinnati Milacron established the following new investment or new product criteria in 1985:

43 1. The investment or product had to provide now, or provide by 1990, at least $100 million in revenues and good profits.
2. They exist in a product area where Milicron already has a leadership position.
3. They are sold on the basis of technology and service, rather than on price alone.

EXHIBIT 12
Actual and Targeted Percent of Assets Employed by Product Division

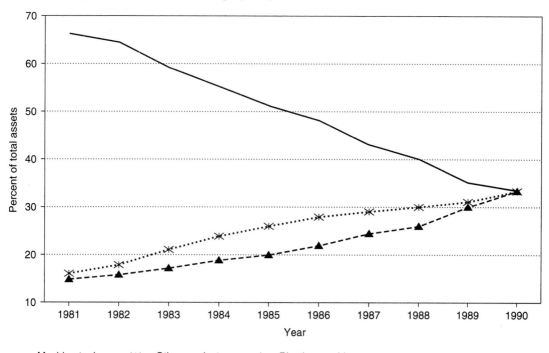

——— Machine tools   ··✕·· Other products   –▲– Plastics machinery

Note: Actual assets dedicated from 1981–85 and targeted proportions for 1986–90.

44   Accordingly, the product areas to be emphasized would be process plastics, flexible manufacturing cells and systems, special machinery for advanced applications, automation for advanced composites, metrology and inspection systems, and silicon epitaxial wafers.

45   With a firmer grasp on the products to be pursued the company turned next to rationalizing its production facilities. This was spelled out in its most ambitious and comprehensive reorganization plan approved by the Board February 16, 1988. A number of "focus factories" were created. These factories were to operate as independent business units with full profit and loss responsibility. Each was dedicated to manufacturing and marketing similar or complementary product lines. This reorganization's goal was a reduction of the company's burdensome and over-centralized bureaucracy and faster responsiveness to changes in the market place. The following "focus factories" were created at this time and they were to be fully operational by mid-1989:

46   1. Robots—Factory in Greenwood, South Carolina, with support functions being moved from Cincinnati to Greenwood. Liaison with the American automobile industry would be continued through its technical center in Detroit.
  2. Aerospace and special-purpose machines—Cincinnati, Ohio.
  3. Turning centers—Wilmington, Ohio.
  4. Machining centers—Fountain Inn, South Carolina, and Birmingham, England.
  5. Grinding machines—Worchester, Massachusetts.
  6. Service parts—Cincinnati, Ohio.

EXHIBIT 13
Asset Changes and R&D Activities (in hundred thousands)

	1991*	1990	1989	1988	1987	1986	1985
Capital expenditures:							
Machine tools	$15.0	$16.1	$17.0	$ 9.9	$ 8.0	$11.8	$ 9.2
Plastics machinery	12.0	14.0	14.0	4.7	3.4	10.6	11.6
Industrial products	3.0	4.0	2.6	6.9	4.3	6.9	23.6
Total	$30.0	$34.1	$33.6	$21.5	$15.7	$29.3	$44.4
Write-downs, reorganization charges, and liquidation losses:							
Machine tools	$90.0	$34.0			$54.0		$46.3
Plastics machinery							
Industrial products			$ 4.5		24.0		
Headquarters					5.0		27.2
Total	$90.0	$34.0	$ 4.5		$83.0		74.4
Research and development	$37.0	$34.4	$31.4	$35.3	$35.6	$39.6	$36.8

* Projected by management.

EXHIBIT 14
Operating Performance of Industrial Robots and Laser Machines (in thousands)

	1990	1989	1988
Sales:			
Industrial robots	$31,182	$30,527	$38,697
Laser machines	—	3,180	7,036
	31,182	33,707	45,733
Net loss from operations:			
Industrial robots	−441	−588	−911
Laser machines	—	−2,313	−1,459
	441	−2,901	−2,370
Net loss on sale of assets	−1,700	−4,474	—

Source: 1990 company 10-K.

7. Plastics machinery—Most products produced in Afton, Ohio, with the systems for extrusion, reheat blow molding, and thermoforming moved to a plant in Cincinnati, Ohio.

47   In early 1990, Milacron had created a specific process for developing new products. Initially called *team engineering* but now termed *Wolfpack Projects,* the idea is to create world-class products de-

signed simultaneously for marketability and "manufacturability." The anticipated outcomes from creating new product development teams were a shortened product development cycle, lower product manufacturing costs, improved machine tool performance and quality, and increased market share. Top management also spelled out the process for creating a Wolfpack Project:

48   1. Create a team of personnel relevant to the production, sale, and service of a product. The team members typically would come from the departments of design engineering, production, marketing, purchasing, cost analysis, manufacturing engineering, assembly, and inventory control.

49   2. Analyze and conduct market research on all competitive products. The features, design, materials, electronics, and performance of all products are studied, as well as citing the reasons why the competitive products are succeeding or failing.

50   3. Apply the principles of "simultaneous" or "concurrent" engineering to work with potential customers and suppliers. To be approved for commercialization, a Wolfpack Project's product must demonstrate that it can *(a)* capture significant new market share in existing or new markets and *(b)* provide at least a 30 percent manufacturing cost savings over the product it would replace in the line. Through concurrent engineering, the company will create products that fill a place in the market and are easier and less costly to manufacture.

51   As of February 1991, the Wolfpack program had slashed Milacron's manufacturing costs on standard machine tools by as much as 40 percent. About 20 percent of its standard tools can match the foreign competition's prices and quality. Overall manufacturing costs have been reduced about 30 percent by using fewer and standard off-the-shelf parts in the product's assembly. The typical newly designed tool has about two thirds of its parts outsourced, where before it was less than half. The results are also lower warranty and installation costs.

52   Management already has introduced a new line of simplified plastics injection-molding machines and is the country's lowest-cost producer of these tools. The *Vista* line has been very successful, and additional products have made it the broadest line available from an American manufacturer. In 1988, the plastics operation was increased by 100,000 square feet, with a capital infusion of $4.7 million; in 1989, an additional $14.5 million was budgeted, with about 70 percent of that amount going into a 78,000-square-foot expansion of its Mt. Orab, Ohio, plastics parts plant. While management is pleased with the results it has obtained through Wolfpack programs, it does not believe their outcomes will be fully realized until the mid-1990s. On this basis, top management is optimistic about the company's future.

53   Management also believes that problems caused by its past reorganization efforts and by production "bugs" are over. In 1985, sales of $17.8 million were lost on machine tools alone. The tools scheduled for shipment used new designs, innovative software, and higher precision and performance standards, resulting in longer than anticipated production times. Sales for that year had to be delayed until early 1986. The company also experienced serious bottlenecks in making grinding machine shipments in November 1989. These bottlenecks caused lost sales through cancellations. It also did not allow the company to obtain part of the $45 million per year savings it had projected from its most recent reorganization effort. Additional bottlenecks occurred in February 1990 as production and equipment were shifted between plants to create its numerous "focus factories."

1992 AND BEYOND

54   As part of its new strategy to make competitively priced $100,000 standard machine tools, Cincinnati Milacron points with pride to its Cincinnati-based "incubator" demonstration plant. The factory makes the company's Talon computer-controlled turning centers and uses the most efficient production and management techniques available. It employs just-in-time parts deliveries; the Talons use only 16 outside vendors, and they need 60 percent fewer parts. More important, they can be made for

40 percent less. C. William Murray, Milacron's division manager for standard machine tools, says, however, that it might take five years for the techniques used in this 19-person plant to spread to the company's other plants and employees. Others are more pessimistic about this and other company actions.

55   Manufacturers in the Cincinnati area have noticed that Milacron is losing key people and that morale has sagged badly in recent months. Based on the number of résumés and job inquiries, many of the "Mill's" middle managers fear they may lose their jobs in another reorganization move, or that they may be pushed onto the shop floor. Cincinnati Milacron's recently retired chief technical officer, Richard C. Messinger, says, "They've got the basic technology and capability, but they have had a problem in that it's very difficult to change the culture and direction of that kind of organization."

56   It has also been noted that, of its 27 current Wolfpack projects, several are actually imported products and that many of its "American-made" tools use almost 50 percent foreign parts. To Jack Addy, an independent Detroit machine tool distributor, this makes Milicron's "Made in the U.S.A." label a fraud. He says the company is "importing just like the Japanese, and what they're importing are not good machines."

57   The quality of the company's new products also may suffer in the long term. To save money, Milacron has not increased its engineering staff, which would be needed to implement future plant efficiencies like those found in the "incubator" plant, and it is spending only 4.1 percent of sales on research and development. Leading firms, such as Giddings & Lewis, spend about 10 percent on similar efforts. As an additional money-saving move, the company has retreated from its promise to its distributors to spend $250 million on machine tools over the next five years.

58   Given that plastics machinery has been a highlight of the company's operations, it takes pride in noting that it has helped lower Japan's market share in plastics machinery. That country's sales have fallen 20 percent since 1987 to about 50 percent of the American market. By cutting prices on the Vista line, Milacron was able to win back the business of General Motors and the Toyota Motor Corporation of America. Financial analysts, however, are pessimistic about Cincinnati Milacron's near-term and long-term prospects. Both Moody's Investors Service and Standard & Poor's downgraded Milacron's debt in early October 1991. In making its judgment on the firm's financial security, Standard & Poor's particularly noted the company's debt level of 55 to 60 percent of total capital and questioned the wisdom of the new strategy being pursued by the company. As observed by David Sutliff, an S. G. Warburg & Company analyst, "I give them credit for giving it the old college try, but I don't think it's too smart. They're going into the most competitive sector again, where the Japanese sell tools like cookies."

APPENDIX

Operating Margins by Product Group (in millions of dollars)

Product Group	1981	1982	1983	1984	1985	1986	1987	1988	1989	1990	1991
Machine tools	$ 83.1	$42.8	$−14.5	$−8.1	$−30.0	$11.0	$−47.9	$20.2	$−7.6	$4.3	$−2.2
Plastics machines	11.5	−8.6	0.0	20.8	17.7	26.3	25.5	30.9	35.0	18.0	8.3
Industrial products	9.5	−5.1	−7.4	4.0	5.0	26.3	−12.0	19.1	18.7	16.7	13.0
Total	$104.1	$26.1	$−21.9	$16.8	$−7.3	$63.5	$−34.4	$70.2	$46.1	$39.0	$19.0

Source: Various *Value Line* reports.

Cincinnati Milacron Quarterly Income Statements (in thousands)

	6/15/91	3/23/91	10/6/90	6/16/90
Net sales	$173,069	$181,054	$233,959	$204,804
Cost of goods	136,571	143,840	177,702	159,233
Gross profit	36,498	37,214	56,257	45,571
R&D expenditures	N.A.	N.A.	N.A.	N.A.
Selling, general, and administration	36,946	37,465	48,430	36,643
Income before depreciation and amortization	−448	−251	7,827	8,928
Depreciation and amortization	N.A.	N.A.	N.A.	N.A.
Nonoperating income	853	−131	1,217	810
Interest expense	4,389	4,452	5,830	4,916
Income before taxes	−3,984	−4,834	3,214	4,822
Provision for income taxes	541	1,078	1,155	1,708
Net income before extra items	−4,525	−5,912	2,059	3,114
Extra items and discontinued operations	N.A.	N.A.	−515	N.A.
Net income	−4,525	−5,912	1,544	3,114

N.A. means not available.
Source: Company 10-K.

Cincinnati Milacron Quarterly Balance Sheets as of 6/15/91 and 3/23/91 (in thousands)

	6/15/91	3/23/91
Assets		
Cash	$ 15,031	$ 15,780
Receivables	171,124	181,347
Inventories	229,074	231,282
Raw materials	9,394	9,401
Work in progress	173,406	169,708
Finished goods	46,274	52,173
Other current assets	11,638	14,183
Total current assets	426,867	442,592
Property, plant, & equipment	428,397	440,688
Accumulated depreciation	282,010	283,069
Net property & equipment	146,387	157,619
Deposits and other assets	43,758	44,285
Total assets	617,012	644,496
Liabilities		
Notes payable	8,255	9,452
Accounts payable	42,139	54,479
Accrued expenses	95,644	90,778
Income taxes	7,177	10,713
Other current liabilities	45,496	41,607
Total current liabilities	198,711	207,029
Deferred charges	7,852	8,408
Long-term debt	156,960	157,148
Other long-term liabilities	38,901	40,887
Total liabilities	402,424	413,472
Preferred stock	N.A.	N.A.
Common stock net	173,654	173,642
Capital surplus	N.A.	N.A.
Retained earnings	48,436	57,945
Other liabilities	− 7,502	− 563
Shareholder equity	214,588	231,024
Total liabilities and net worth	617,012	644,496

N.A. means not available.
Source: Company 10-K.

Cincinnati Milacron Quarterly Balance Sheets as of 10/6/90 and 6/16/90 (in thousands)

	10/6/90	6/16/90
Assets		
Cash	$ 22,607	$ 16,810
Receivables.	185,377	191,752
Inventories.	292,501	269,458
Raw materials	8,737	8,750
Work in progress	229,594	215,516
Finished goods	54,170	45,192
Other current assets.	16,028	12,918
Total current assets	516,513	490,938
Property, plant, & equipment	435,087	422,567
Accumulated depreciation	283,041	273,047
Net property & equipment	152,046	149,520
Deposits and other assets	44,494	43,486
Total assets	713,053	683,944
Liabilities		
Notes payable	12,972	36,446
Accounts payable	57,987	55,126
Accrued expenses	85,013	101,796
Income taxes	8,826	N.A.
Other current liabilities	48,083	46,996
Total current liabilities	212,881	240,364
Deferred charges	13,214	13,329
Long-term debt	162,297	162,169
Other long-term liabilities.	41,116	41,969
Total liabilities	429,508	457,558
Preferred stock.	N.A.	N.A.
Common stock net	N.A.	N.A.
Capital surplus.	173,174	121,892
Retained earnings	105,271	108,717
Other liabilities.	5,100	− 4,223
Shareholder equity	283,545	226,386
Total liabilities and net worth	713,053	683,944

N.A. means not available.
Source: Company 10-K.

CASE 32

CIRCUIT CITY

INTRODUCTION

1   When *Forbes* magazine listed five-year performance figures on 1,012 companies for its 1988 report on American industry, four-year-old Virginia-based Circuit City, with 138 stores in the Atlantic Coast states and California, made the list: 1st in stock appreciation, 21st in growth, 40th in profitability.

2   Yet just three years later, Anne M. Collier, Financial Relations Manager for Circuit City, had cause for concern. Figures for the fiscal year ending February 28, 1991, showed that the company had experienced a 96 percent drop in net earnings. A Financial Accounting Standards Board (FASB) ruling was forcing the company to take a huge overtime write-off on top of an earnings decrease of 18 percent for the year. How should Collier present the information in the annual report? What strategic redirections faced Circuit City as consequences of these unprecedented reversals?

3   Contributing to Collier's concerns were recessionary effects of the economy, increased competition, conservative consumer spending due to the Gulf War, slumping industry sales, cannibalization among Circuit City's own stores, and increasing selling, general, and administrative expenses.

4   Richard Sharp, President and CEO of Circuit City, has assigned to Collier the responsibility to recommend solutions to him. Collier explained, "I came to Circuit City in 1989 as the manager of investor relations, reporting to the treasurer who, in turn, reported to the senior vice president and to the chief financial officer. However, in October 1990, the month before the FASB ruling, the treasurer left and our organizational structure was so changed that I moved to a new corporate planning department as Manager Of Financial Relations. I then reported directly to Richard Sharp."

5   One immediate concern for Collier was how to prepare news releases on the information about the FASB impact without negatively affecting the company's stock price. In doing so, she also had to keep in mind that the earnings of some of Circuit City's competition, notably big L.A. competitor Good Guys, would not show an impact of the FASB ruling, because it pertained only to sales from warranties sold by the company; Good Guys' warranties were sold through a third party. Further, the results of the second major L.A. competitor, Silo, were not reported separately, because it was a subsidiary of Britain's Dixons Group.

BACKGROUND

6   Circuit City was founded in 1949 by Samuel S. Wurtzel as Wards, a small TV and home appliance company. It went public in 1961. Beginning in 1970, the company operated the audio department for 30 Zodys discount stores in Los Angeles. In 1975, the company put half of its net worth of $2 million toward opening a new type of store. In 1984, "Wards" became Circuit City and Alan L. Wurtzel, Sam's son, built a Circuit City marketing concept around the new store type known as the *superstore*.

This case was prepared by Professor John A. Pearce II of the School of Business Administration at George Mason University with the assistance of Mary Ellen Bock. Development of this case was made possible by a grant from the Funds for Excellence Program of the State Council of Higher Education for Virginia.

7   The superstore concept consisted of a new merchandise mix, and a new image reflected in its high-tech efficiency and consumer-oriented service. In fact, Collier knew Sharp was keenly aware of the need to choreograph the look with the service. "Circuit City views retailing as part theater," Sharp had said. The superstore mix included not only traditional consumer electronic products, such as stereos and VCRs, but also major appliances, such as refrigerators and washing machines. This mix brought in more female consumers who, at that time, were not traditionally the decision makers on consumer electronics purchases. Women were attracted to Circuit City because they were the purchasers of household appliances. With the VCR and microwave popularity, the superstore mix helped fuel a healthy growth period for Circuit City.

8   In 1985, the superstores were 32,000 to 40,000-square-foot buildings with red and gray hi-tech exterior. Their 37-foot, red tiled towers were designed to grab the attention of passing motorists. Coupled with the company's "selection and service" advertisements, this eye-catching building helped set the stage for interesting the consumer in exploring Circuit City. What consumers found was a broad product mix and a company with an emphasis on hi-tech service, as reflected in its advertising slogan: "Welcome to Circuit City, where service is state of the art."

9   Collier was aware that this image was an important part of the Circuit City concept. Richard L. Sharp, who became president and CEO after Alan Wurtzel stepped down, said, "For all the marketing dollars spent by manufacturers to establish product differences, I think of Circuit City as a commodity business." As evidence, Sharp said that many competitor consumer electronics stores quickly followed Circuit City's switch to the superstore format. To distinguish its superstore from the competitors', Circuit City had offered something different. That difference was its image.

10   The Circuit City image included a consumer orientation to which consumers responded favorably. From FY1983 to FY1990, the company enjoyed a sales growth record of consistency and strength. Exhibit 1 shows the company's market share lead among its top competitors from FY1987 to FY1991. It is notable that, while competitors' sales either stalled, as in the cases of Crazy Eddie and Leo's, or declined, as in the cases of Audio Video Affiliates, Fretter, and Highland, Circuit City sales grew an average of 31.9 percent per year. However, sliding in the back door was L.A. competitor Good Guys, growing an average of 34.5 percent, 50 percent in the 1991 results.

11   Then, in FY1991, with essentially the same mix and image, financial performance took an unexpected turn. In the third quarter of FY1991, from September 1 to November 30, 1990, the company's stock suffered a further decline—from a 52-week high of $28 to $10 3/8 per share. In the third quarter, the company's net income had fallen 83 percent from the previous year's $14.6 million to $2.5 million.

POSSIBLE CONTRIBUTORS TO DECLINE

12   In varying degrees, Collier felt four factors contributed to Circuit City's situation:

13   1. A bulletin issued in late 1990 by the Financial Accounting Standards Board (FASB), titled "Accounting for Separately Priced Extended Warranty and Product Maintenance Contracts," required a change in the way Circuit City recognized revenue from the sale of extended service warranties.

14   2. The nation's economic growth had slowed, fueled by the threat of a war in the Gulf after the invasion of Kuwait by Saddam Hussein. The industry's sales were also down because of a lack of new products to interest the public; therefore, competition increased among electronics retailers for decreasing consumer dollars.

15   3. Circuit City's same-store sales had declined more than the industry's, due to both tough credit policies and the possible cannibalistic effects of its own growth in number of stores.

16   4. Costs for selling, general, and administrative expenses increased, as did interest expenses.

17   Collier had this to say about the situation: "When the [FASB] ruling was made, a number of things happened: Monthly sales for October 1990 were down, same store sales declined 7 percent, and two strong competitors entered our largest market—Los Angeles."

EXHIBIT 1
Circuit City and Competitors Sales from FY1987 to FY1991 (in thousands)

Company Name	FY1991	FY1990	FY1989	FY1988	FY1987
Audio/Video Affiliates	$ 163,653	$ 143,660	$ 194,776	$ 211,156	$ 227,787
Best Buy Co., Inc.	664,823	512,850	560,674	439,040	239,496
Circuit City Stores, Inc.	2,366,901	2,096,588	1,721,497	1,350,425	1,010,692
Crazy Eddie, Inc.	—	—	253,398	315,539	352,523
Dixons Group (1)	892,700	2,902,492	2,728,500	2,864,500	1,864,600
Fretter, Inc.	217,351	224,681	231,183	250,280	272,568
Good Guys, Inc.	293,967	195,015	149,369	120,239	89,473
Highland Superstores	860,786	919,774	910,747	753,446	656,456
Intertan (2)	694,565	656,257	570,202	478,355	410,310
Newmark & Lewis, Inc.	293,835	245,543	238,143	242,367	213,530
Leo's Industries	—	82,743	65,855	72,565	60,081

Notes:
(1) Dixons Group owns Circuit City competitor, Silo.
   FY1991 sales for Silo are shown (includes 25 Federated stores).
   Figures for other years are for total Dixons Group's sales.
(2) The Tandy Group.
Source: Compustat, 1993.

EXHIBIT 2
Quarterly Financial Data

Fiscal 1991

(Amounts in thousands) Fiscal 1991	May 31, 1990	Aug. 31, 1990	Nov. 30, 1990	Feb. 28, 1991
Net sales and operating revenues	$490,143	$550,548	$585,041	$741,169
Gross profit	139,823	162,341	164,478	223,079
Net earnings.	10,511	16,935	2,531	26,674
Earnings per common share	0.23	0.36	0.05	0.58

Fiscal 1990

(Amounts in thousands) Fiscal 1990	May 31, 1989	Aug. 31, 1989	Nov. 30, 1989	Feb. 28, 1990
Net sales and operating revenues	$407,996	$471,591	$525,886	$691,115
Gross profit	117,538	138,136	155,195	208,217
Net earnings.	10,735	16,852	14,600	35,913
Earnings per common share	0.23	0.37	0.32	0.78

Source: Circuit City annual report, 1991, p. 31.

FASB RULING

18   On November 6, 1990, the Financial Accounting Standards Board issued a new guideline on revenue recognition for sales made on extended service warranties (ESW). The rule paced the rate at which companies could claim the revenue from ESW sales to match more closely the terms of the contract. When a sale was made on an electronics product, a warranty that extended the life of the manufacturer's warranty by two to five years was commonly sold with it. The ESW profit margin, or the selling price of the warranty less the actual costs incurred in fulfilling warranty obligations, was an important source of profit for Circuit City. In fact, the gross margins on Circuit City's electronic products and appliances were about 25 percent, while the gross margins on the warranties sold were close to 70 percent.

19   With the FASB ruling came the restriction that revenues received from warranty sales had to be allocated over the entire lifetime of the warranty and not recognized in total at the time of sale. For example, if the company sold 300 three-year extended warranties at $100 apiece, it recognized revenue of $30,000 and profit of $21,000 (70 percent of the $100 $\times$ 300). With the new ruling, the company could only recognize that portion of the warranties that would be expiring in that year (i.e., one third of $21,000, or only $7,000, could be recognized as profit in the year).

20   In addition, Collier had to consider the fact that past earnings and revenue figures had included revenue from warranty sales. Further, warranty sales occurred with approximately 70 percent of all transactions. In FY1991, the accounting for extended warranties effected a $9.8 million reduction in earnings. Also, there occurred a cumulative effect, for adjustments to warranties sold in previous years whose maturities had not been reached, amounting to $53.5 million. Collier could recommend that Circuit City either deduct this as a lump sum from FY1991 earnings (taking the "big hit") or allocate it over several years. In either case, she felt that she had to show it was the "slowdown in the national economy, increased competition, and widespread promotional pricing" that had the major impact on Circuit City's bottom line.

21   Collier was concerned that taking the big hit might exacerbate a skiddish stock price situation. On the other hand, such a bold move would enable Circuit City to start fresh.

ECONOMY SLOWS AND INDUSTRY PRODUCTS AGE

22   The effects of the general national economic slowdown of 1990 were compounded in the consumer electronics industry by the lack of new electronic products to interest the consumer as powerfully as had some 1980s blockbusters. In the 1980s, the industry had grown because of the introduction of microwave ovens, personal computers, and video cassette recorders (VCRs). In fact, the Electronics Industries Association reported that consumer electronics' sales increased from $9.4 billion in 1979 to $31.6 billion in 1989 as a result of the success of these products.

23   In particular, the incredible sales growth of the 1980s in the consumer electronics industry was due to the success of the VCR. From 1980 to 1987, total factory VCR sales rose from $621 million to a peak of $5 billion. Throughout this sales period, there were growing sales of complementary goods, including TVs and cameras, which postponed the effects of the industrywide levelling of VCR sales in 1987.

24   As Exhibit 3 shows, from 1987 to 1991 industry sales slowed and declined. The exhibit shows the dollar value throughout the period of all products and services sold in the household audio and video equipment and in the appliances industries in constant 1987 dollars to remove the effect of inflation. There was an obvious slowing in the growth rate of all products and a decline in sales of the household appliances.

EXHIBIT 3
Values of All Products and Services Sold in Household Appliances and Household Audio and Video Equipment (in thousands)

Industry Data	1987	1988	1989	1990	1991
Household cooking equipment	$3,396	$3,709	$3,780	$3,522	$3,310
Household refrigerators	3,519	3,744	3,850	3,877	3,760
Household laundry equipment	3,035	3,154	3,225	3,199	3,071
Household audio & video	5,911	6,538	6,798	7,002	7,212

Note: Value of all products and services sold in the industry in constant 1987 dollars to remove inflation effects.
Source: *U.S. Industrial Outlook 1991*—Household Consumer Durables, *Household Appliance*, p. 38–8; *Consumer Electronics*, p. 38–12.

EXHIBIT 4
Circuit City Sales by Merchandise Categories

	Fiscal				
	1987	1988	1989	1990	1991
TV	25%	25%	24%	24%	24%
VCR	27	25	23	23	22
Audio	21	22	22	22	22
Other electronics	9	10	11	12	14
Appliances	18	18	20	19	18
Total	100%	100%	100%	100%	100%

Source: Circuit City annual report, 1991, p. 18.

25   These high-ticket items were a big part of Circuit City's mix. In FY1987, VCR sales provided 27 percent of Circuit City's revenues, with individual units selling for $200 to $1,000 each. Likewise, television set purchases represented a quarter of the revenues. The makeup of Circuit City's FY1987–91 sales are shown in Exhibit 4. By FY1991, the VCR and TV mix had changed from 27 and 25 percent to 22 and 24 percent, respectively, reflecting the slowing VCR sales. In the industry, color TV sales for 1990 failed to set a record for the first time since 1980.

26   In the first half of FY1991, Collier noticed that, despite a marketing emphasis on Circuit City's higher quality merchandise, Circuit City was unable to increase its gross margin by more than 0.1 percent to 29.6 percent. In fact, from FY1987 to mid-FY1991, the part of Circuit City's mix that showed the most improvement was the "Other Electronics" category, such as telephones, calculators, and electronic toys. That category increased steadily as a portion of sales for Circuit City from 9 to 14 percent, corresponding to a drop in VCR revenues from 27 percent of sales to 22 percent. Unfortunately, "the shift in consumer purchases," Sharp noted, "was to lower-priced and less-profitable selections."

27   Industry executives maintained the industry's trouble was that the overall economy was moving at such a slow rate that, even if a new product with VCR sales level potential came on the market, consumer confidence was so low because of unemployment and a high cost of living that sales projections would remain at low levels.

COMPETITION

28   With no new product to push sales after the VCR market had leveled off in 1987, the consumer electronics market was stagnant and tied primarily to replacement sales. Since Circuit City had to battle for sales against consumer electronic stores and superstores, as well as against such discounters as Best Products, and department stores like Sears and Montgomery Wards, competition was a major factor in determining profitability. Indeed, discount suppliers of consumer electronics were fighting to regain a major portion of their customer base that had been siphoned off in the mid-1980s by electronic superstores, including those of Circuit City.

29   Although many consumer electronic retailers had suffered setbacks during the industry shakeout in the late 1980s, Circuit City had avoided external displays of difficulties. Circuit City's overriding strength was its dominance in important consumer electronic markets, such as Atlanta and Los Angeles. In fact, the Los Angeles market, the second largest consumer electronics market in the United States, was the source of over $2 billion of annual sales for the industry.

30   When Circuit City entered the Los Angeles market in 1985, the dominant competitor then using a "superstore" format was Federated Group, although its stores did not carry major appliances. Federated was the local leader in consumer electronics sales, with 8 percent of the Los Angeles market.

31   Circuit City faced competition on a second front from Sears, in part because both firms' sales mix included high-ticket consumer staples, such as appliances, in addition to traditional consumer electronics products. Despite its stiff competition, Circuit City executives predicted that, by the spring of 1986, Circuit City would have annual sales in Los Angeles of $150 million from a 10 percent share of the southern California consumer electronics and appliances market.

32   By 1986, Circuit City had opened 15 stores in the Los Angeles–Orange County area. Circuit City's sales from the L.A. market for FY1986 met the company's prediction. This volume constituted 26 percent of Circuit City's total sales for that year.

33   By the end of 1986, Circuit City had become the No. 1 consumer electronics retailer in the Los Angeles market. For FY1987, after a year in the Los Angeles market, Circuit City's overall sales were $1.01 billion. In contrast, Federated sales had started to slide due to the Circuit City attack on its market share. By 1989, Federated had been purchased and "discontinued" by Atari.

34   Sears suffered from the Circuit City attack as well. The figures below illustrate Circuit City's lead share in L.A. For example, television sales, traditionally the strongest selling consumer electronics product, show that by 1990 Sears' Los Angeles market share had garnered only a little over 5 percent, while Circuit City enjoyed a huge lead at 29 percent. However, when the L.A. market later experienced a new influx of heavy competition, Collier noted that Circuit City's market share suffered.

Los Angeles TV Sales, 7/89–6/90

Competitor	TV Sales
Circuit City	28.8%
Sears	5.4
Broadway	4.5
Price Club	3.6
Montgomery Ward	3.5

35   Collier pointed out that Circuit City had maintained an unchallenged lead until FY1991, at which time a couple of new competitors decided they, too, wanted a piece of the second-largest consumer electronics market in the country. The Good Guys and Silo chains each opened groups of stores just in time for the 1990 Christmas season.

36   The entry of Silo and Good Guys worried Circuit City. Collier noted that the margins were already pressed and, with the Gulf War, the economic forecasts were pessimistic. She said, "We view Silo as a comparable superstore-type competitor and Good Guys as a strong consumer electronics-only competitor, since Good Guys does not carry appliances. But our main competitor for appliances had been Sears and its popular Kenmore line. Further, Sears has repair center strengths to compete without repair center and warranties."

37   Good Guys and Silo confronted not only Circuit City and Sears but also a slowing economy and other smaller consumer electronics retailers and discounters that had survived the 1985 entry of Circuit City. It appeared that prosperity for the three big chains—Circuit City, Silo, and Good Guys—depended on stealing sales from department stores and from the remaining small local retailers.

38   Silo's move to Los Angeles began when it took over 25 Federated leases in January 1990. During September, October, and November 1990 it opened 15 Los Angeles superstores, averaging selling space of 17,000 square feet. It further publicly committed to opening 30 more superstores in Los Angeles by 1993.

39   As noted by Collier, Good Guys, a considerably smaller (5,800 square feet) consumer electronics store carried audio, video, and personal electronic merchandise on the higher end of the scale, but no appliances. Good Guys opened six stores in Los Angeles from July to November 1990 and planned six more in 1991 to compete with Circuit City's 26 stores.

40   Competition intensified among consumer electronic outlets and department stores, because of the concentration on price/item promotions of products that were increasingly seen as commodities. Department stores tried to arrest the outflow of customers from their electronic departments to the superstores by retaliating with their own consumer electronic specialty stores. In fact, Montgomery Wards' "Electric Avenue" stores (332 units) and Sears' "Brand Central" stores (820 units) became significant industry players across the country.

41   These specialty stores were located either within essentially traditional department store locations or as free-standing units. In either case, they enjoyed the costing advantages and customer accepted images of the large department store chains. Additionally, since they had added national brands, their merchandise became increasingly similar to Circuit City's.

COMPARABLE STORE SALES DECLINES

42   Competing successfully in the consumer electronics industry meant matching prices and advertising efficiently. Circuit City's advertising stressed not only low prices but the lowest prices around, or it would refund twice the difference. With an annual advertising budget of $131.2 million, or approximately 6 percent of total sales, Circuit City was No. 81 among the top advertisers in the nation in 1990, and the fourth-largest buyer of local television advertising.

43   Circuit City's advertising was intended to remind those customers who entered the consumer electronics marketplace on a sporadic basis that Circuit City offered the lowest prices and specific other nonprice benefits, notably the service. The effectiveness of this message was measured in terms of "same store" sales or of sales of stores open more than one year. Although new stores had the advantage of novelty, the most efficient technology, and new opening "sales" to draw consumers, the newcomer advantages generally wore off after a year, at which time the store was expected to prosper because of advertising promotion and consumers' past experiences with the store.

44   A decline in same store sales was the third factor influencing the drop in Circuit City's FY1991 earnings. Continued growth in same store sales was counted on to offset the costs of expansion and intensive storing that were part of Circuit City's 1991 plan. Additionally, same store sales were considered to be a prime indicator of the health of the business. The company's official explanation for the decline in its same store sales was that industry sales were down. However, credit had been tightened by Circuit City, and the company had partially cannibalized its traditional markets by increasing the number of stores it had in key cities, through its practice of intensive storing. Collier expressed the consensus of Circuit City's top management that the cannibalization had had a minimal impact on same store sales.

45   In FY1987, same store sales for the industry (sometimes called *comparable store sales*) increased 8 percent over FY1986. However, Circuit City's same store sales increased 18 percent. The company continued to show a growth in its same store sales through FY1990, albeit small at 2 percent. On the other hand, in 1990 the industry suffered its first same store sales decline in several years.

46   In FY1991, the industry's same store sales dropped once more, this time by only 1 percent. Unfortunately, Circuit City's FY1991 decline over FY1990 was at 3 percent, primarily due to a whopping 12 percent sales decline in the last half of FY1991, with 7 percent of that decline occurring in quarter four. Again, Circuit City executives felt that the company's disappointing results were a result of the slowdown in the national economy, increased competition, and widespread promotional pricing.

TIGHTENED CREDIT

47   Responding to the consequences of a weakened economy, Circuit City tightened the credit extended to its customers. The company had used a third-party (private label) credit card provider to make credit available to its customers who required financing of purchases. Through Circuit City's point of sale information system, the company was able to check credit lines and process credit card transactions as well as track and coordinate inventory shipments from suppliers to warehouses to the consumer. By early FY1991, Circuit City decided that its third-party credit card program, which accounted for about 27 percent of the company's total revenue, was losing sales because the provider was too conservative in its credit standards.

48   As a consequence, in September FY1991, Circuit City established a customer credit program that was administered entirely by the company's newly established national credit card bank subsidiary. The receivables were sold by Circuit City to a third nonaffiliated party, with Circuit City as the agent of collection. For FY1991, Circuit City sold $125 million of credit card receivables, of which $111 million was the outstanding balance on the annual report date of February 28, 1991. Of the total receivables, Circuit City's loss exposure was $23 million. The company's total commitments to credit card customers were $426 million on unused credit lines. Exhibit 5 shows the change in receivables over the FY1987–1991 period.

EXPANSION-INTENSIVE STORING

49   Circuit City increased its number of superstores by 32 units during FY1991. Total company retail units increased by 36. The difference in store count was due to the net increase in its smaller, mall-based store format called "Impulse" stores and in the upgrading or removal of older and smaller Circuit City electronics-only retail outlets. Exhibit 6 provides a breakdown of the company's store mix for the FY1987–FY1991.

50   As expressed by Collier, Circuit City's strategic plan for growth involved two thrusts:

1. An expansion into new markets to increase revenues and national market share.
2. The opening of additional stores in existing markets to retain market share leads. The theory behind "intensive storing" was that dominance in a particular market allowed the company to operate more efficiently than could its local competitors.

51   By 1990, industry analysts predicted that Circuit City would be hard pressed to achieve the 4 to 5 percent same store sales gains required to protect its 6 percent pretax margins and still absorb the costs associated with the opening of a planned 35 new stores for FY1991. However, in FY1991,

EXHIBIT 5

Consolidated Balance Sheets
(amounts in thousands)

Assets

Current assets:

Cash and cash equivalents	$ 25,241	$ 91,712
Accounts and notes receivable	26,631	9,721
Merchandise inventory	389,818	331,244
Prepaid and other current assets	8,720	9,531
Total current assets	450,410	442,208
Property and equipment, net	355,452	250,006
Deferred income taxes	50,865	6,460
Other assets	17,336	14,981
Total assets	$874,063	$713,655

Liabilities and Stockholders' Equity

Current liabilities:

Current installments of long-term debt	$ 2,065	$ 2,038
Accounts payable	207,462	165,545
Accrued expenses and other current liabilities	35,394	31,837
Accrued income taxes	16,119	22,823
Total current liabilities	261,040	222,243
Long-term debt	94,350	93,882
Deferred revenue and other liabilities	151,806	38,244
Total liabilities	507,196	354,369

Stockholders' equity:

Common stock of $1 par value	46,340	45,860
Capital in excess of par value	25,775	17,454
Retained earnings	294,752	259,972
Total stockholders' equity	366,867	359,286
Total liabilities and stockholders' equity	$874,063	$713,655

Source: Circuit City annual report, 1991, p. 23.

Circuit City's total sales rose 14 percent, reflecting the success of Circuit City's strategy to gain market share by entering new markets. Unfortunately, in that same year, Circuit City also experienced a same store sales decline of 3 percent.

52   Although Circuit City successfully increased its market share by opening stores in new metropolitan markets, intensive storing seemed to rob some of its established stores of revenues. Ironically, until FY1991, the company enjoyed success through these paired strategies, especially where the existing competitors were small local companies that lacked a large national base from which to draw resource support when competition intensified.

EXHIBIT 6
Circuit City Store Mix

	Retail Units at Fiscal Year-End				
	1987	1988	1989	1990	1991
Superstore	53	76	96	125	157
Circuit City	34	29	23	20	14
Impulse	—	—	3	4	14
Total	87	105	122	149	185

Source: Circuit City annual report, 1991, p. 18

EXHIBIT 7
Store Openings—New Markets

Fiscal Year	Store Openings	Growth in Same Store Sales	Total No. Outlets
1986	Jacksonville, Montgomery, Huntsville, Atlanta, Los Angeles	—	69 (net)*
1987	Columbus, Birmingham, Mobile, Pensacola, Bakersfield, Fresno, Santa Barbara	18%	87
1988	San Francisco, Oakland, Sacramento	8%	105
1989	—	7%	122
1990	Miami, Tampa, Philadelphia, San Diego, Phoenix	2%	149
1991	Cincinnati, St. Louis	−3%	185

* Closed 30 Zody's in Los Angeles and 12 Lafayettes in New York.

53   In fact, Circuit City increased its total number of stores by an average of 22 percent each year over the FY1986–1991 period. Circuit City's expansion plans and "intensive storing" (essentially a Circuit City in every city of a market area) started in earnest with the 1986 Los Angeles expansion. Exhibit 7 tracks the company's expansion into new markets over the five years leading up to FY1991, and Exhibit 8 compares that expansion with its total market penetration by FY1991.

54   Simultaneous with the Los Angeles market entry was a New York market exit and a concentration on filling out the company's presence in three geographic areas, namely the Mid-Atlantic, Southern, and West Coast regions. These regions were centered around warehouses so the stores could be efficiently serviced.

55   The three warehouse centers were in Richmond, Virginia; Atlanta, Georgia; and City of Industry, California. Richmond's Mid-Atlantic division was the original company stronghold, developed through intensive storing. Likewise, four Atlanta openings had spawned a Southern division. In FY1986 and FY1987, the company had expanded to new markets in this region; specifically, stores were opened in Jacksonville and Pensacola, Florida; in Montgomery, Huntsville, Birmingham, and Mobile, Alabama; and in Columbus, Georgia.

EXHIBIT 8
Circuit City Markets by Fiscal Year 1991

○ Circuit City markets
◇ Impulse markets
△ Mechanized distribution centers
□ Product service centers

Source: Circuit City annual report, 1991.

56   The company established a West Coast division centered on its success in the Los Angeles area. During FY1987, new markets were entered in Bakersfield, Fresno, and Santa Barbara, California. By the beginning of FY1988, intensive storing put the Los Angeles area store at 19. The company then turned to new markets. It entered the San Francisco area by opening eight superstores in two months in addition to entering the Oakland and Sacramento markets.

57   During FY1990, new market stores appeared in Miami, Tampa, Philadelphia, San Diego, and Pheonix to round out and further expand the company's three regions. Meanwhile, the Mid-Atlantic stores were systematically upgraded to the newer superstore model, including 8 of the 14 outlets in the Washington, D.C., area. For FY1990, Circuit City had a total of 149 stores.

58   During FY1991, the company entered Cincinnati and St. Louis and intensively stored in Philadelphia, Atlanta, Tampa, Miami, Orlando, San Francisco, Los Angeles, San Diego, and Phoenix. This brought total store count to 185 for FY1991. Collier explained that, although New York was an important market, one in which the company had not totally abandoned hope, it was not easily accessible and, therefore, not as lucrative a market as some others. In fact, Richard Sharp estimated that $26 billion of annual industry sales were recorded in other areas not served by Circuit City.

59   Since Circuit City chose to put more stores in its existing markets, competition occurred among its own stores as well as between its stores and their local competitors. In FY1989, the company experienced a decline in sales per selling square foot. Superstores were particularly hard hit:

Dollar Sales per Square Foot

	Fiscal Year				
	1987	**1988**	**1989**	**1990**	**1991**
Superstores	$1,237	$1,309	$1,361	$1,288	$1,141
Total company	1,464	1,488	1,441	1,345	1,186

60   Although Circuit City stores had enjoyed annual gains per selling square foot of as much as 6 percent only four years earlier in FY1988, in FY1991 they experienced a decline per square foot of 11 percent; in other words, sales per square foot dropped over the four-year period by 17 percent. Still, Collier defended the company's commitment to intensive storing and new market expansion by asserting that the strategy enabled it to maintain a lead share in existing markets and to acquire a lead share in new markets.

HIGHER COSTS

61   Earnings for FY1991 were affected by higher selling, general, and administrative expenses (SG&A) and by a higher interest expense. Exhibit 9 shows that SG&A increased 1.8 percent in 1991 to 24.8 percent of net sales and operating revenues. Additionally, start-up costs to establish the credit card bank subsidiary increased expenses. Circuit City invested $20 million to begin the credit program that improved credit availability for its customers.

62   Fixed assets increased 42 percent in FY1991 over FY1990 (Exhibit 5). Most of this increase was due to the new retail units and distribution facilities. The company's capital expenditures for FY1991 were $159.7 million—an increase of $48.8 million over FY1990 and an increase of $77.8 million over FY1989. The company was able to fund $53.2 million of its capital expenditures for FY1991 with net cash from operating activities, with the balance coming from seasonal lines of credit.

THE FUTURE OF CIRCUIT CITY

63   A major aspect of Circuit City's continuing strategy was a mall-based approach for new store placement. These 3,000-square-foot Impulse stores included over 1,000 personal and gift electronics and numbered 14 units nationally at the end of FY1991. Collier indicated the purpose of the Impulse stores was to compete within the malls; these stores were being placed in malls or so near they benefited from the drive-and-walk-by traffic of the malls. Collier said the company did not expect the Impulse stores to compete with the mall department stores (i.e., Sears and Montgomery Ward's Brand Central and Electric Avenue consumer electronics). Each mall shop was expected to generate $1 million in sales annually. The company expected to open 50 Impulse stores in the 1992FY, in an effort to turn the disadvantage of a slumping economy into a plus by taking advantage of the buyer's market in real estate.

64   In addition to markets that the company entered and dominated, untapped markets offered huge potential opportunities. For example, a high-profile but still untapped geographic market was the once attempted New York market, with an annual estimated market of $3 billion. But as Collier had noted, the current challenges of competing in that area outweighed the advantages in her mind, especially while more accessible markets remained as yet untapped. These markets were scattered nationwide, with potential for Circuit City in various formats of superstores, mall-based stores, scaled-down superstores, and their original small electronics-only stores. One specific attempt to seize an opportunity involved a plan to enter three major Texas markets with 13 superstores.

EXHIBIT 9
Selected Financial Data (amounts in thousands, except per share data)

	1991	1990	1989	1988	1987
Net sales and operating revenues	$2,366,901	$2,096,588	$1,721,497	$1,350,425	$1,010,692
Net earnings	3,151	78,100	69,475	50,400	35,300
Net earnings per common share— primary and fully diluted	0.07	1.70	1.52	1.12	0.79
Total assets	874,063	713,655	587,481	433,241	361,617
Long-term debt	94,350	93,882	94,674	96,676	101,149
Deferred revenue and other liabilities	151,806	38,244	27,040	18,934	13,035
Cash dividends per share paid on common stock	0.095	0.075	0.055	0.0375	0.029

Source: Circuit City annual report, 1991, p. 16.

65   Circuit City's optimistic plans for growth, including a 16.2 percent increase in superstores in FY1992, projected the company's confidence that its financial performance in FY1991 was reversible. Circuit City confidently expected another growth-generating product that would have consumers out spending again, even though such a new product was unidentified. Collier insisted that she felt the FY1991 results would prove to be a reflection of the general economy, and of L.A. competition and the Gulf War impact, if evaluators ignored the obvious impact of the FASB ruling. She decided that the presentation of the FY1991 results would have to incorporate a certain stoicism, if not optimism, that none of these negative forces would continue to be of lasting competitive disadvantage to Circuit City. Most important, she decided that the presentation would need to address the FASB rules without upsetting stock prices further. Collier knew, however, that the presentations would have to be very carefully crafted, since, in the view of competitors, Wall Street, and industry analysts, many of the challenges to Circuit City's success were real and sustainable.

CASE 33

MICROSOFT CORPORATION

1   Microsoft began in 1975 in the midst of great excitement and anticipation among American back-room computer hobbyists, who began to foresee the advent of microcomputers made possible by the development of the microprocessor. Until then, computers were very large, usually filling an entire room, and, thus, computer enthusiasts were forced to buy expensive computer time on mainframes. But microprocessor technology was rapidly advancing, and pockets of young computer enthusiasts watched eagerly, waiting for the pivotal breakthrough that would launch a revolution.

2   Shortly after INTEL announced development of the 8080 chip in 1974, the December issue of *Popular Mechanics* featured the Altair, the world's first minicomputer, produced by a small company called MITS (Micro Instrumentation and Telemetry Systems). Finding practical applications for the Altair was extremely difficult, though, because it required the user to be technically proficient with programming in machine language, a skill only the most gifted possessed.

3   One week after reading the article on the Altair, two 19-year-old computer buffs, Paul Allen and Bill Gates, called MITS and claimed to have written a program that would allow the Altair to be programmed in BASIC, a programming language that had been used on larger computers. Two months later, in February 1975, they successfully demonstrated their program at a MITS laboratory in Albuquerque. In July 1975, Gates and Allen formed a partnership called Microsoft (short for microcomputer software) with the intent of developing computer languages for the Altair and other microcomputers that were sure to follow. Microsoft's first contract was to develop BASIC for the Altair.

MS-DOS

4   In 1980, IBM covertly decided to enter the burgeoning microcomputer industry. At this time, IBM contacted Microsoft and asked if it could write a BASIC program to reside in the permanent memory of an 8-bit computer. IBM also asked Microsoft to furnish languages for the machine to include FORTRAN, Pascal, and COBOL. To do this, Microsoft had to gain access to operating system software. While BASIC had its own operating system embedded within itself, the other languages worked off CP/M, which was then the dominant operating system in the industry and was produced by Digital Research. Both Gates and IBM representatives approached Digital Research about supplying CP/M as the operating system for the IBM machines, but Digital balked because IBM insisted on extremely restrictive contract provisions. Gates was disappointed. He had hoped to gain access to Digital's CP/M for the 8086 chip, which was then in development. Then, Microsoft could have adapted their languages to the emergent operating system.

5   Until then, Digital Research had developed operating systems and Microsoft had focused on programming languages, and both had respected the other's domain. A year earlier, Digital Research had violated this implied understanding by adding languages to its catalog. Microsoft's relationship with Digital Research was disintegrating.

This case was prepared by George W. Danforth, Robert N. McGrath, and Gary J. Castrogiovanni, Louisiana State University Department of Management, College of Business Administration.

6   Bill Gates decided on a bold move. He told IBM that Microsoft could not only supply the languages for the IBM machine but also the operating system. IBM, now tiffed with the inflexibility of Digital Research, accepted.

7   Microsoft's contract to supply the IBM operating system started a battle with Digital Research over which company would supply the dominant operating system in the industry. Many proponents of CP/M argued that, as the industry standard, CP/M was best for linking existing languages, applications software, and hardware. Nonetheless, less than a year following the announcement of the IBM PC, numerous microcomputer manufacturers signed contracts with Microsoft to include MS-DOS (the Microsoft operating system) as their hardware's resident operating system. If a major player like IBM was entering the market, it was highly likely that application software programmers would write programs that were compatible with the IBM system. If a manufacturer's machine could not run popular applications programs, customers would not buy it.

8   In 1983, Lotus released what was to be the most popular applications software ever produced, an electronic spreadsheet program called Lotus 1-2-3. Lotus 1-2-3 was written for and operated only under MS-DOS. Largely due to the phenomenal demand for 1-2-3, MS-DOS was used by over 80 percent of all users in 1984. By 1986, half of Microsoft's annual revenues of $61 million came from the sale of MS-DOS.

9   Although Microsoft had made short thrift of Digital Research in the MS-DOS versus CP/M battle, there is little doubt that its remarkable success was due to MS-DOS's affiliation with the IBM name. CP/M was by all standards an excellent operating system, and nearly all software and hardware were tuned into it. It was the quick and powerful emergence of the IBM PC that catapulted MS-DOS and Microsoft into success. The IBM PC quickly became the industry standard machine, forcing other manufacturers to make machines that were compatible with the IBM system. And 99 percent of IBM compatibles carried MS-DOS as their operating system.

10   Digital Research learned a costly lesson. Whether a company produced hardware, operating systems, languages, or applications software, its product had to be positioned so as to be included in the dominant configuration of these products. Customers bought hardware that was capable of running certain programs, and, likewise, bought software that would run on the particular machine they owned. Understanding this interdependence between microcomputers and various types of software was the key to positioning both hardware and software in the market. Holding a commanding position in operating systems software, Microsoft turned its attention to applications software.

THE ELECTRONIC SPREADSHEET

11   In the early 1980s, many computer companies did not believe that microcomputers held significant potential for business applications. Then, the appearance of the first electronic spreadsheet, called *VisiCalc,* met a specific and powerful business need. Previously, managers interested in calculating the solutions to complex problems were forced to either spend hours using a calculator or to get company computer personnel to write a specific program for the company mainframe. VisiCalc enabled managers to define their model and run countless alternative solutions. Initially, the program could be run only on an Apple II (and this was a primary determinant of the Apple II's success). It was later adapted to run on the IBM PC. Another spreadsheet program, SuperCalc, was developed by Sorcim to run on CP/M systems. There was little doubt that the advent of spreadsheets heralded a boom in hardware and software sales to businesses.

12   When Gates and Allen decided to enter the applications software market in 1980, the spreadsheet was a logical starting point. Because there was no hardware standard at the time, Microsoft's strategy was to develop a spreadsheet that could be ported to as many different machines as possible. The two dominant spreadsheet programs were limited in this respect. VisiCalc could not run under the CP/M operating system, and SuperCalc could operate only on Apple IIs. Gates decided to develop a spread-

sheet that was ported to all the operating systems on the market, including CP/M, Apply DOS, Unix, and, of course, MS-DOS.

13   While Microsoft was developing its spreadsheet, dubbed Multiplan, IBM placed great pressure on Microsoft to ensure that the new spreadsheet could run on its limited 64K PC models. Gates acquiesced to the computer giant, sacrificing many design attributes to keep in the good graces of Microsoft's primary customer.

14   When released in late 1982, Multiplan met with some initial success but then was quickly eclipsed by Lotus 1-2-3 in 1983. Unlike Multiplan, 1-2-3 was aimed at 256K machines and reflected the richness of capability that the increased RAM afforded.

15   Microsoft had made a costly mistake. By agreeing to IBM's request that Multiplan be operable on 64K machines, Microsoft had been blind to the growing demand for more powerful high-end machines and their associated software. Interesting, IBM's sales of 256K PCs skyrocketed that year. IBM felt that 1-2-3 had done for the IBM PC what VisiCalc had done for the Apple II.

16   However, the Multiplan project was not a complete loss. Although 1-2-3 had taken firm control of the U.S. spreadsheet market, accounting for 80 percent of all sales in 1986, Microsoft had adeptly positioned Multiplan in Europe. In 1982, Microsoft began to adapt Multiplan to each of the European languages. In addition, Gates decided to open subsidiaries in each of the firm's three major European markets—England, France, and Germany. Multiplan's ability to run on many different systems proved to be a great advantage. Unlike the U.S. market, IBM PCs and compatibles did not dominate in Europe. Apple controlled 50 percent of the market and Commodore 30 percent.

17   When IBM arrived in Europe in 1984, its PC included Multiplan, rather than Lotus 1-2-3. By the time Lotus brought 1-2-3 to Europe in 1985, it was too late. In 1987, while Lotus 1-2-3 held 80 percent of the American spreadsheet market to Multiplan's 6 percent, Multiplan dominated the European market, accounting for 60 percent in Germany and 90 percent in France.

18   Because Multiplan was so successful overseas, Microsoft continued to distribute it. But Bill Gates would not forget why the package had failed in the United States and 1-2-3 had succeeded, instead.

WORD PROCESSING

19   In 1983, Microsoft launched its offensive on a second front, word processing. At that time, WordStar, developed by MicroPro, was the most popular word processing software. The Microsoft designers believed they could best WordStar by including in their program a number of additional characteristics. Microsoft Word would be the first word processing software that displayed boldface type, underlining, italics, subscripts, and superscripts on the screen. In addition, the screen could be divided into windows, allowing the user to work with more than one text at a time. Instead of requiring the user to format each text individually, Word would offer style sheets that stored formats created by the user for repeated use. Lastly, Word would be capable of printing out in any of the fonts available in the state-of-the-art laser printers.

20   Word was introduced to the U.S. market in a novel way. Demonstration copies, which would do everything but save or print files, were sent out at great expense to the 100,000 subscribers of *PC World* in its November 1983 special edition. Although many newspapers lauded the unique and imaginative marketing technique employed by Microsoft, Word was greeted with a marginal response. The word processing program, although extremely powerful, proved to be too complex for the average user. Subsequent improved versions in 1984 and 1985 steadily increased sales; however, Microsoft was again beat out, this time by a small software publisher called WordPerfect.

21   WordPerfect was jointly founded by a computer science professor and his student in 1979. The company's only employees were a group of students that helped with distribution tasks. Yet the fledgling enterprise was able to differentiate its program through a heavy emphasis on service. WordPerfect

provided free telephone support to customers and followed up every inquiry until the customer was satisfied.

22   While Microsoft spent millions promoting Word, WordPerfect avoided sophisticated promotional campaigns, building a loyal following by word of mouth. Microsoft was at a loss about how to respond to WordPerfect's ingenious grassroots campaign. WordPerfect's sales grew steadily and quickly. In 1986, it became the top-selling word processing software. Info Corp listed the top-selling word processing programs for 1986 as follows:

23

1.	WordPerfect	31%
2.	WordStar	16
3.	IBM VisiOn	13
4.	pfs:Write and Multimate	12
5.	Word	11

24   Word was losing out to WordPerfect and others for a very different reason that Multiplan had lost to Lotus 1-2-3. Multiplan failed in the United States because Microsoft was coerced by IBM to gauge the program for IBM's low-end machines. Word was losing because Microsoft in its zeal to create the most powerful word processing program available had failed to consider the full array of user needs.

25   Just as the success of Multiplan was resurrected by turning to the European market, so, too, would Word fare better there. When Word arrived in France in 1984 with mixed reviews, WordStar, and Textor, produced by a French company, were already well positioned. Gates and his European staff decided on a three-prong penetration strategy. First, to encourage distributors to sell Word, Microsoft France provided distributors with free training and a free copy of Word. Second, Microsoft arranged to have all retailer demonstrations of Hewlett-Packard's new LaserJet printer performed using Word. Last, Microsoft France convinced many printer manufacturers to promote Word, because of its ability to port to sophisticated high-end multifont printers. Michael Lacombe, CEO of Microsoft France, explained:

26   When a client would go to a retailer and ask to see how Word worked with a printer, in 95 percent of the cases the distributor would not be able to answer the question. We visited all the printer manufacturers and sold them on the idea of a Microsoft Word binder with several pages of printing samples.

27   As a result of this aggressive marketing effort, Word began making inroads into the French market in 1985. After a much refined Word 3.0 was released in April 1986, sales of Word rose fast. In 1987, it was the highest-selling word processing software in France, with sales of 28,700 copies, compared to 10,300 for IBM VisiOn, 7,000 for Textor, 3,800 for WordPerfect, and 3,300 for WordStar.

28   While Microsoft had again created a phenomenal success in Europe with a program that had been unsuccessful in the United States, the great improvements made in the 3.0 version of Word also substantially increased its U.S. market share. In this version, the previous problems experienced by users in learning Word were solved by what was then an ingenious solution. Included with all 3.0 versions of Word was a step-by-step on-line tutorial that replaced the traditional user's manual. U.S. sales of Word climbed substantially. By 1989, Word's sales had reached 650,000, compared to 937,000 for WordPerfect. Although Word was by many standards a superior product, WordPerfect had firmly established itself as the word processing software of choice for PC users. Once customers learned and grew comfortable with a program, it often was difficult and costly for them to switch.

29   While Microsoft was having difficulty capturing market share with its earlier versions of Word in 1984 and 1985, it was working feverishly on a Word program for the Apple Macintosh computer, which was the only substantial challenger to the IBM standard. When Word for the MAC was released in 1985 there were no other word processing programs available for the Macintosh except Apple's own software called MacWrite which was included with the sale of each machine. Although Word for the MAC had some bugs, it began to gather a following among Macintosh users. When the 3.0 version was released in 1986, it was a tremendous success. By 1988, with annual sales of 250,000 copies, it was second only to the PC versions of WordPerfect and Word. WordPerfect released its own version

for the Macintosh in 1988, but it was too late. As WordPerfect had beaten Microsoft to the U.S. PC market, so had Microsoft preempted WordPerfect in the Macintosh market. When Word version 4.0 was released in 1989, 100,000 copies were sold immediately, confirming Word's preeminence with the Macintosh.

GRAPHICAL USER INTERFACES

30 Although the IBM PC was the best-selling microcomputer in the industry and was copied by a great number of other manufacturers, the Apple Macintosh surpassed all others in user friendliness due to Apple's unique work with graphical user interfaces. While users of IBM PCs and compatibles had to interact with their machines using learned text commands, such as *erase,* the Macintosh user employed a mouse to connect icons or simple images on the screen. For instance, instead of typing the command *erase,* the MAC user could use a mouse to point to a file icon and pull it to an icon of a trash can. Both Gates and Apple co-founder Steve Jobs believed that the future of microcomputing was in graphical interface technology, because it made computers extremely user-friendly, opening up the world of computers to the most unsophisticated user.

31 In 1981, Apple asked Microsoft to write applications programs for the Macintosh, realizing that the availability of the high-demand software could determine the success of the Macintosh, just as the popularity of VisiCalc had launched the Apple II. Microsoft and Apple began a close collaboration aimed at designing an optimum match between the Macintosh configuration and Microsoft's applications programs. The agreement specified that Microsoft versions of Multiplan, Chart, and File would be shipped with each Macintosh machine, and that Microsoft could not publish software with a graphical user interface until one year after the Macintosh was released, or December 1983 at the latest.

32 In the following years, Microsoft enjoyed tremendous success with its Macintosh applications programs. In addition to Word for the MAC, Microsoft's new spreadsheet program, Excel, sold at a rapid rate, beating out Lotus's new integrated software called Jazz. In 1986, Microsoft sold 160,000 copies of Excel to MAC users, compared to 10,000 copies of Lotus's Jazz. By 1989, Lotus had decided to stay away from the Macintosh market altogether. Microsoft's success with Macintosh users made it the No. 1 developer of applications software for the first time. The key lesson learned from Microsoft's experience in the Macintosh market was that Microsoft's primary competitive advantage was in graphical user interfaces. Because it was clear that the PC market would inevitably move toward graphical interface technology, Microsoft appeared to be in a commanding position to expand its influence in the development of software for that market.

WINDOWS

33 Windows was Microsoft's attempt to change MS-DOS into a graphical user interface. Although IBM had been successful in setting its hardware and operating system (MS-DOS) as industry standards, no such standardization applied to PC applications software. Each applications program written for the PC was unique in the method demanded to modify or print a file. In addition, the popular PC applications programs communicated with printers differently. Different printers demanded different intermediary programs, called *drivers,* to enable printers to receive data from applications. Consequently, when a customer bought a copy of a particular applications software, she or he often received as many as a dozen diskettes, only one of which carried the applications program. The extra diskettes contained drivers to adapt the program to various printers.

34 To address this problem, Microsoft decided in 1981 to develop a program that would act as a layer between the operating system and applications software, interpreting the particular communications

requirements of the printer and monitor being used. The second purpose of this program would be to place a graphical interface over MS-DOS that would standardize the appearance of applications, so they would share common commands for such actions as modifying texts or printing files.

35   While Microsoft was working on its graphical interface, dubbed *Windows,* other companies began to develop their own versions. VisiCorp, for example, released VisiOn in 1983. More perturbing, however, was that some industry analysts were speculating IBM was working on its own version of a graphical interface. In the past, powerful IBM had largely looked to Microsoft to develop the software for its PC; however, Gates suspected that IBM wanted to grab a piece of the highly lucrative software market for itself. Past dealings with Big Blue proved that the computer giant was intent on expanding its control to include standardization of the entire computer configuration to include not only hardware but also software. When IBM announced in 1983 that it was releasing TopView, a graphical interface to rest on top of DOS, it was a clear signal that IBM was no longer content to remain in the domain of hardware. This action by IBM, although disturbing to Microsoft, was not at all surprising. The computer industry in general was characterized by Machiavellian moves and countermoves. While companies often were dependent on others to develop and position their products into a dominant or advantageous hardware-software configuration, collaborative efforts and contracts usually were characterized by ulterior motives and covert countervailing thrusts.

36   Recognizing that IBM was attempting to squeeze Microsoft out of future software sales, Gates acted quickly. He contacted the manufacturers of IBM compatible computers and tried to persuade them to follow Microsoft's lead with Windows and, thus, isolate IBM. A large group of IBM compatible manufacturers did not want IBM to further monopolize standards and were amenable to waiting for Microsoft's version of Windows, rather than following IBM's lead by including TopView with its machines. Although being competitors, many software companies also pledged their support to Microsoft Windows. The support of Lotus was particularly appreciated because it was the primary supplier of applications software for the PC and compatibles. It was apparent that the companies did not relish the thought of a stronger, more influential IBM and were willing to accept Microsoft's lead to prevent it. The software publishers also were confident that Microsoft would create an interface environment into which they could easily port their applications programs. IBM, on the other hand, had released a version of TopView configured in such a way that, if successful, would give Big Blue a significant advantage in the development of future applications.

37   Gates's success in this effort would prove critical to the success of Windows. He had never hesitated to play hardball in the past with larger, more powerful companies. While some criticized Gates as an opportunist, others saw him as an astute and resolute visionary.

38   The Windows project was characterized by lengthy and embarrassing delays. Although Gates announced the imminent release of Windows in 1983, it did not hit the market until November of 1985. Over 20 software publishers had to delay their Windows ported applications software. By 1985, most of these companies had put all Windows associated software projects on hold. Nevertheless, shortly after its introduction, Windows was a great success. After sales exceeded 1 million copies of Windows, the 2.0 version was released in 1987. This version offered a user interface that was very similar to that of the Macintosh. When Microsoft released its PC version of Excel that same year, Windows's credibility increased even more, and PC manufacturers began positioning their machines against Apple's Macintosh.

THE APPLE LAWSUIT

39   On March 17, 1988, Apple announced that it was suing Microsoft over Windows 2.03 and Hewlett-Packard over New Wave, its graphical interface environment. What made the announcement particularly unsavory to Gates was that he had just seen the CEO of Apple, John Sculley, and no mention was made of it. Apple announced the news of the suit to the press before notifying Microsoft.

40   Apple argued that it had spent millions creating a distinctive visual interface, which had become the Macintosh's distinguishing feature, and that Microsoft had illegally copied the "look and feel" of their Macintosh. Microsoft countered that its 1985 contract with Apple granted it license to use the visual interface already included in six Microsoft programs, and that this license implicitly covered the 1987 version, Windows 2.03. In July of 1989, Judge Schwarzer dropped 179 of the 189 items that Apple had argued were copyright violations. The 10 remaining items were related to the use of certain icons and overlapping windows in Windows 2.03. In February of 1990, Judge Walker of the Federal District Court of San Francisco took over the case. He previously had ruled against Xerox in its suit against Apple over the same copyrights. In March 1990, Walker ruled that the portions of 2.03 under debate were not covered by the 1985 agreement between Apple and Microsoft. As of late 1991, the case was still in litigation.

A DISTINCTIVE ORGANIZATION

41   Computer programming is an activity dominated by the young. It is also an extremely intense activity that demands absolute focused concentration on the part of the programmer for extended periods. The software industry can be characterized as competition between groups of minds. It is an utterly innovative industry, in which relatively little resources are spent on anything but the support of the imaginative process.

42   Finding its genesis in the early days of Microsoft, when Gates and Allen and a small coterie of programmers literally worked and slept at work for weeks at a time under incredible pressure, the Microsoft culture has gelled into its present and unique form. The working atmosphere at Microsoft counterbalances the intensity of activity with an offbeat emphasis on an unstructured and informal environment. Working hours are extraordinarily flexible. Dress and appearance are extremely casual. Many programmers work in bare feet. It is not unknown for a team of programmers working on an intense project to take a break at 3:00 A.M. and spend 30 minutes making considerable racket with their electric guitars and synthesizers.

43   The present Microsoft complex in Redmond, Washington, looks more like a college campus than the headquarters of a Fortune 500 company. It can be almost surrealistic. Most of the 5,200 employees have offices with windows. The courtyards adjoining the principal structures often are rife with the activity of employees juggling, riding unicycles, or playing various musical instruments.

44   Microsoft employs many people from foreign countries, giving the company grounds an international flavor. Some of these employees work on the many foreign translations of Microsoft's software. Others are simply many of the best programmers in the world that Microsoft attracts to its fold.

45   Microsoft hires the very best and hardest working programmers and then allows them wide discretion in their work. When hiring, Microsoft cares little about a candidate's formal education or experience. After all, neither Bill Gates nor Paul Allen ever graduated from college. No matter how lofty an applicant's credentials appear to be, the applicant is not hired until she or he has been thoroughly questioned on programming knowledge and skills. Charles Simonyi, chief architect of the developers groups for Multiplan, Word, and Excel, insisted for some time on personally interviewing each applicant. He explained:

46   There are a lot of formulas for making a good candidate into a good programmer. We hire talented people. I don't know how they got their talent and I don't care. But they are talented. From then on, there is a hell of a lot the environment can do.

47   Microsoft employees earn relatively modest salaries, compared to the rest of the industry. Bill Gates himself has never earned more than $175,000 in salary per year. (He is, however, a billionaire due to his 35 percent share of Microsoft stock.) Employee turnover is about 8 percent, well below the industry standard.

48   Microsoft is loosely structured. Programmers usually are assigned to small project teams. Gates explains, "It takes a small team to do it right. When we started Excel, we had five people working on it, including myself. We have seven people working on it today."

49   Communications at Microsoft are open. Everyone is tied together in a vast electronic network, and anyone can send a message to anyone else via electronic mail regardless of relative status.

50   One of the keys to Microsoft's success is that it attracts the finest programmers in the industry and creates an environment that not only pleases and retains employees but is also conducive to high computer programming productivity. No amount of financial might can make a software company successful. There are no apparent economies of scale to be realized. The primary asset that determines success or failure of a software company is the creativity and performance of its people.

POSITIONING FOR THE '90S

51   In 1987, Microsoft began collaborating with IBM on the development of a new operating system, called *OS/2,* and a new, more powerful graphical interface named *Presentation Manager.* In late 1989, IBM released OS/2 version 1.2 for IBM PCs. Microsoft released OS/2 version 1.21 for IBM compatible machines in mid-1990. Sales of OS/2 have been far lower than hoped.

52   Many industry observers consider OS/2 the inevitable replacement of DOS; however, DOS version 5.0 was released in 1991, fueling speculation and confusion about what direction Microsoft was leading the industry. In fact, IBM appears to believe it was double-crossed. When the introduction of OS/2 went poorly, Microsoft continued to upgrade and push MS-DOS and Windows, at the expense of OS/2 and Presentation Manager. IBM since has taken over the majority of the development on OS/2 and distanced itself from Microsoft.

53   In June of 1991, IBM and Apple began a joint venture to develop an entirely new PC standard, in which they will control the rights to the operating system and the microprocessor. This cooperation between the two largest microcomputer manufacturers could have a tremendous impact on the software industry. If IBM and Apple are successful in developing and controlling a new industry standard operating system, Microsoft would lose its preeminent position in the industry. Right now, nearly all applications programs written are ported through Microsoft's MS-DOS/Windows environment, enabling Microsoft to determine the direction and makeup of future computer applications. If the IBM–Apple initiative proves successful, Microsoft could be placed in the unfamiliar position of following another company's lead for the first time in its history.

54   The IBM–Apple venture is not a sure bet, though. The advanced technology they are working on is extraordinarily complex, and the risks are high for both companies. John Sculley, CEO of Apple, has said: "This is something only Apple and IBM could pull off. Still, it's a big gamble, and we're betting our whole company on it." Another concern is that the radically different cultures of the two manufacturers and their historical disdain for one another may make progress difficult.

55   In addition, Microsoft still holds significant sway over the applications development efforts of other software companies. Over time, customers have made significant investments in hardware and software that operate in the MS-DOS/Windows environment. It is questionable whether software publishers or customers would make wholesale changes so readily. Bill Gates comments:

56   Sure, we're being attacked on all sides, but that's nothing new. Customers will vote on all of this. I think ours will thank us for preserving their current investment in PCs, while improving that technology. That has always been our strategy.

APPENDIX

Five-Year Summary of Microsoft's Financial Performance (dollars in thousands)

Date	Sales	Net Income	EPS
1990	$1,183,446	$279,186	2.34
1989	803,530	170,538	1.52
1988	590,827	123,908	1.11
1987	345,890	71,878	0.65
1986	197,514	39,254	0.39
Growth rate (%)	56.4%	63.3%	56.5%

Source: *Compact Disclosure* (Information Database), Disclosure, Inc.

Microsoft's Earnings per Share Growth (actual and future estimates)
Microsoft versus Industry

	EPS Growth Rates				
	Last 5 Yrs. Actual (%)	91/92 (%)	92/93 (%)	Next 5 Years. (%)	P/E on 92 EPS (%)
Microsoft	51.8%	35.1%	23.8%	27.7%	26.5%
Industry	9.3	30.6	25.7	20.4	21.3
S&P 500	6.5	1.7	17.5	7.8	17.7
Microsoft/industry	5.6	1.1	0.9	1.4	1.2
Microsoft/S&P 500	8.0	21.1	1.4	3.5	1.5

Source: *Compact Disclosure* (Information Database), Disclosure Inc.

REFERENCES

"The Future of the PC." *Fortune,* August 26, 1991, pp. 40–49.

"How Bill Gates Keeps the Magic Going." *Fortune,* June 18, 1990, pp. 82–89.

"IBM, Apple in Pact to Control Desktop Standard." *Computerworld,* July 8, 1991, pp. 1, 102–03.

Ichbiah, D., and S. Knepper, *The Making of Microsoft.* Rocklin, Calif.: Prima Publishing; 1991.

"It's Grab Your Partner Time for Software Makers." *Business Week,* February 8, 1988, pp. 86–88.

"PCs: What the Future Holds." *Business Week,* August 12, 1991, pp. 58–64.

"Redrawing the Map: Will IBM/Apple Alliance Shift the Balance of Power." *InfoWorld,* July 22, 1991, pp. 44–436.

"Software: The New Driving Force." *Business Week,* February 27, 1984, pp. 74–98.

CASE 34

XEROX CORPORATION LOOKS TO THE FUTURE AND SEES ONLY QUALITY

COMPANY BACKGROUND

1   The organization now known as Xerox Corporation was incorporated on April 18, 1906, under the name Haloid Company. In 1958, the name was changed to Haloid Xerox Incorporated, and the present name was selected three years later.

2   Xerox is a multinational corporation divided into four segments. Document processing is the primary activity, but Xerox also provides insurance, third-party financing, and investment banking services. Xerox Corporation dominates the Western Hemisphere, while Rank Xerox, Ltd., operates and distributes in Europe, Africa, and most of Asia. Fuji Xerox, launched in 1962, covers the Pacific nations.

3   Originally, Xerox dominated the market for document processing. But by 1970, the Japanese were rapidly overtaking the industry with lower-cost products. Xerox was not worried: low cost mean low quality. All of American industry in the 1970s was reacting similarly to world competition—so assured were they of their superior quality and technology, they were untouchable.

4   American products were considered luxury, state of the art, and of superior quality to any foreign competitor. The Japanese in particular posed no threat, because their products were seen as cheap, unreliable, and of laughable quality.

5   After World War II, as Japan struggled to rise out of their destruction to home and economy, it was a joke in the United States when the label "Made in Japan" was noticed. With the help of Dr. William Edwards Deming (an American, ironically), Japan's production philosophies and quality turned around. By the 1970s, Japan was "catching up." Costs were still low, but the product no longer was inconsequential in terms of quality.

6   In 1970, Xerox all but monopolized the almost $2 billion copier industry. As shown in Exhibit 1, by 1977, although the industry market quadrupled, Japanese market share dramatically increased, IBM made a significant impact, and Xerox's share was drastically reduced. In 1974, the Japanese introduced the cheap and efficient plain paper copiers, while Xerox continued using coated paper. From 1975 to 1978, Japanese firms, such as Ricoh, Canon, and Konishiroku (not including Fuji Xerox), gained 25 percent of the world market for slow copiers.

7   Not only were competitors producing faster but the toner (liquid ink) that the Japanese were using was less expensive than Xerox's dry power, and the parts used were less complex, mass produced, more reliable, and easier to fix. In addition, aggressive advertising and pricing by the Japanese allowed them to sell, rather than lease, their copiers, which released tied-up capital. Xerox was being outproduced and underpriced.

8   It was in 1979 that Xerox finally rallied and began to make the changes necessary for survival. Although Xerox stood at 36 in the Fortune 500 listings early in 1979, such managers as

This case was prepared by Neil H. Snyder, the Ralph A. Beeton Professor of Free Enterprise, University of Virginia; Katherine Lilley, McIntire School, University of Virginia; and Deborah Francis, University of South Carolina.

EXHIBIT 1
International Copier Market

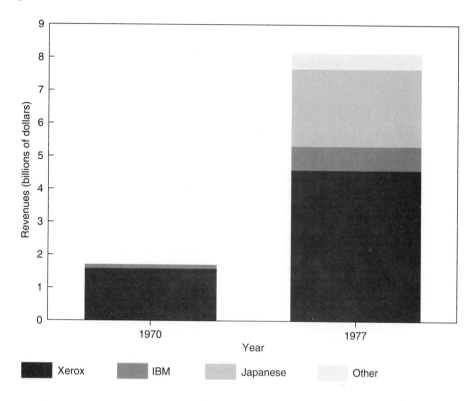

then-chairman and CEO C. Peter McColough had the foresight to see that they had to do better than simply relax to stay ahead of competitors.[1]

9   David Kearns, elected president and CEO in 1982, took the risk, bent the rules, and used creativity to make the necessary changes at Xerox. Kearns's total quality strategy gave Xerox employees the tools they needed to compete in the global market.

XEROX LOOKS TO QUALITY IMPROVEMENT

10   When CEO David Kearns decided that Xerox was ready for significant changes, the corporate attitude concerning quality was the first thing to be scrutinized. As he had learned, "the better the quality, the lower the overall costs." This massive cultural change would be accomplished through extensive training. In 1983, Xerox implemented a "Quality through Leadership" program that had three objectives:

11   To improve profits as reflected in higher return on assets.

To improve customer satisfaction.

To improve market share.

[1] Joseph F. McKenna, "The Great Expetations of David Kearns," *Industry Week*, June 17, 1991, p. 34.

12   Kearns at first believed all three of these goals to be of equal importance, and he did not want to overshadow the others. Soon, however, conflicts became unavoidable. To increase the return on assets, employees would try to cut costs. These actions sometimes would be at the expense of customer satisfaction and, hence, the market share would decline. At this time it was necessary to prioritize these goals; customer satisfaction became No. 1.

13   The "QTL" program cost an estimated $125 million and 4 million man hours of work. It produced a 40 percent increase in customer satisfaction and a 60 percent decrease in complaints. It involved every level of the company from top to bottom. The orientation phase of the program took six months to complete. It took four years of training to reach the entire organization with the QTL message. Each supervisor learned from his supervisor, then trained and inspected his direct reports. Managers become coaches and a team approach was adopted.

14   After promoting its "Leadership through Quality" campaign, employees made it known that they were aware that promotions were based on criteria not related to quality. The "Role Model Manager" concept was then created.[2] New criteria were developed to guide promotion decisions, based on leadership characteristics fundamental to the total quality concept.

15   By 1989, 75 percent of Xerox workers participated in this drive for perfect quality, on more than 7,000 quality improvement teams. Spending for training was increased to 2.5 to 3.0 percent of annual revenues.[3]

16   TQC became the buzzword at Xerox—total quality control. This "has nothing to do with checking quality as your products roll off the assembly line," says Kearns. "It is empowering employees to take responsibility for quality."[4] Allowing the responsibility to be shifted to lower levels is of prime importance in reducing costs, especially for the largest supplier of cut-sheet paper in the world. In 1989, Xerox produced 600,000 tons of paper.

17   To attain quality in every area, role models were chosen: L.L. Bean for distribution, American Express for collection, and American Hospital Supply Corporation on automated inventory control. These companies were selected as the most outstanding in these respective areas. Xerox investigated how these companies achieved their success and established goals for its employees as well as methods for acheiving them. This process is known as competitive benchmarking which is "the continuous process of measuring products, services, and practices against the company's toughest competitors or those companies renowned as industry leaders."[5] Benchmarking is a direct setting process and the means by which practices required to achieve new goals are discovered. It forces a continual focus on the environment. Xerox was one of the earliest U.S. proponents of benchmarking and institutionalized the practice in its organization.

18   Finally, Kearns realized that quality begins with suppliers. It is important to include suppliers in the quality program, and it is difficult to monitor 5,000 suppliers, so Xerox cut its base of vendors to 300 to gain more control over the quality of inputs and to reduce costs.

Quality Costs

19   Three different types of costs are involved in product production, and there are trade-offs within these types as methods vary. The goal of management is to reduce total costs, and it is most effective to do this by improving quality from the start.

---

[2] G. M. Herrington, "The Catch-22 of Total Quality Management," *Across the Board*, September 1991.

[3] M. Katherine Glover, "The Quest for Excellence," *Business America*, November 20, 1989, pp. 2–11.

[4] David Kearns, "Quality in Copiers, Computers, and Floor Cleaning," *Management Review*, February 1989, pp. 61–63.

[5] R. C. Camp, "Learning from the Best Leads to Superior Performance," *Journal of Business Strategy*. 13, no. 3 (1992), pp. 3–6.

20   1. *Prevention costs.* When defect-free products are demanded, prevention costs escalate. Each worker must be certain that each task is done perfectly the first time. The cost of this quality and perfection is prevention cost.

21   2. *Appraisal costs.* As the number of defects approaches zero, there becomes no necessity to inspect. The cost of inspectors and other ways of detecting defects drops to nothing.

22   3. *Internal and external failure costs.* Internal failure costs are experienced when defects are noted before shipping. External costs occur when flaws are not detected until after shipping. Both are reduced to zero when perfect quality is attained.

23   As the quality improves, prevention costs escalate, but the decline in appraisal costs and internal and external failure costs more than offset this increased expense. It is much cheaper to do it right the first time. As Dr. Deming had told the Japanese in 1946, and later told David Kearns, the closer a company comes to producing with zero defects the less money is necessary for quality control.

24   Production techniques were examined to determine ways to eliminate defects from the beginning, with the focus on producing products with no defects, as opposed to the earlier focus of simply catching all of the products below certain standards as they came off the assembly line. Suppliers were included in this drive. Xerox cut its supplier base to have more control over supply quality, and it became more demanding in terms of specifications.

25   The focus on producing no defects at each step in the production process reduces costs considerably. The cost to repair a mistake, or a defect, increases geometrically as the defective product moves away from the point of defect in the assembly or production process. For example, it may take only a few seconds of time and a few cents to correct a mistake while a product is in the production process. Once the defective product leaves the plant and gets into the hands of the final consumer, it may cost weeks of time and thousands of dollars to correct the same mistake.

26   If production operations are of perfect quality, there is no need for quality control, recalls, rejections, or repairs on machines necessitated by production faults. It is, therefore, very cost effective to use TQM as a philosophy about how to do business.

27   Through this focus on costs, manufacturing costs were reduced by more than 20 percent (despite inflation), the time needed to bring a new product to market was reduced by 60 percent, and quality improved. These improvements were possible without any factories being closed or any of the manufacturing being moved offshore.[6]

HARD WORK IS REWARDED

28   The changes at Xerox implemented by Kearns were far-reaching. They included reorganizing the research and development staff and the marketing force, with the objective of viewing new products as systems. McColough was the first to describe Xerox as an information company, as opposed to a copier company. Xerox was one of the first companies to conclude that the "Industrial Age" is over and the "Information Age" has begun.

29   With this definition, "myopic marketing" was avoided, and Xerox began to develop its electronic "Office of the Future." This atmosphere included an office communications network and a new word processing system. The Ethernet network was similar to IBM's System Network architecture in that it connected many offices that were in one building, or in a group of buildings, but unlike IBM, Xerox's system did not need a mainframe. Working with Digital Equipment Corporation, a leader in the field, this high technology was soon installed in the White House and in Congress.

---

[6] Paul Allaire, and Norman Rickard, "Quality and Participation at Xerox," *Journal for Quality and Participation*, March 1989, pp. 24–26.

30   Although Xerox was still big in the upper end of the industry, management began to concentrate more on the lower end. Steps were taken to begin marketing in China and India, two of the biggest untapped plain paper copier markets. By working closely with Fuji Xerox, Xerox Corporation was able to learn more efficient and less costly ways of producing a more reliable product.[7]

31   By 1988, Xerox's management decided to undertake an extensive strategic review. The results of this endeavor led to savings of $60 million in the first year,[8] and the winning of the Malcolm Baldrige National Quality Award in 1989.

32   A decade after the implementation of these changes, the results are astounding. Customer satisfaction, the return on assets ratio, and market share are steadily rising.

33   The rise in customer satisfaction is due primarily to the increased involvement of employees, who now are directly responsible for keeping customers happy. As one executive says, "Employees are closest to the customer," so they would know best how to please the customer. Employees also are promised more job security. After the heavy layoffs in 1981 and 1982, Xerox agreed to abide by a no-layoff policy in 1983. Management stuck by this, even through the difficult years of 1983 and 1984.

34   Employees were included in more management decisions. Line workers and others, closer to the action, were invited to add their input concerning ways to improve production and service through quality improvement teams. By working with them instead of fighting them, union leadership was committed to the company's excellence. More money was spent on training employees.

35   In 1990, Xerox introduced a "Total Satisfaction Guarantee," where instead of monetary refunds, the products are replaced. Revenues neared $18 million, with a net income of $243 million. Fuji Xerox was named the No. 1 Japanese business in terms of future growth. This same subsidiary also was awarded the prestigious Deming award.

36   By better utilizing assets, including the employees, Xerox was able to increase its return on assets by threefold from 1982 to 1990, as shown in Exhibit 2. With a smaller number of more closely monitored suppliers, the number of defect-free products rose to 99.95 percent; but, although they received the highest honor for a quality company, David Kearns was not happy—they had not yet reached 100 percent defect-free.

37   The increased market share evidenced in Exhibit 3 reflects the response of the marketplace to Xerox's quality management decisions. It took a while for the turnaround to take place—results were not immediate. Most of the key decisions were made in 1979, yet the upward swing did not become apparent until five years later. This is due partially to the sharp recession in the early 80s—the economy was at its worst in 1984. For Xerox, the return on assets was at an all-time low, as was the market share. In only two years, Xerox was able to double both figures.

38   Exhibits 4 and 5 show balance sheet and income statement data for Xerox as a background picture of Xerox's financial situation during this time.

THE BALDRIGE AWARD[9]

39   The Malcolm Baldrige National Quality Award was named after the U.S. Secretary of Commerce who served from 1981–87, Robert Mosbacher. During his tenure in office, he made tremendous strides in improving the efficiency and effectiveness of the United States government. He stated:

40   Quality is the key to increasing our exports around the world and to a strong economy that assures job growth.

---

[7] Subrata N. Chakravarty, "Xerox—Back on the Road to Success," *Forbes*, July 7, 1980, pp. 40–42.

[8] 1990 Moody's Industrial Manual, pp. 4381–89.

[9] Unless otherwise specified, the information contained in this section was obtained from the "1991 Application Guidelines," produced by the Foundation for the Malcolm Baldrige National Quality Award.

EXHIBIT 2
Return on Assets

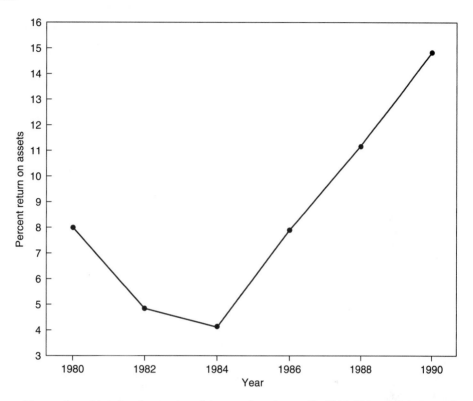

41   Ideas such as this led to the creation of the award on August 20, 1987. This public/private effort is financially supported by the Foundation for the Malcolm Baldrige National Quality Award. The basis for this venture was the belief that through improved quality, more open management/employee relations, and better treatment of the customer, American corporations can stand up to foreign competition with less costs and better products.

42   To qualify for the Malcolm Baldrige award, a company must be outstanding in these areas:

43   Leadership.

Information and analysis.

Planning.

Human resource utilization.

Quality assurance.

Quality results.

Customer satisfaction.

44   **Leadership**   In a company seeking a quality award, leadership must be exhibited not as an authoritarian style management but as a two-way system. Upper management must delegate much authority and decision making to line supervisors. Input from workers must be solicited. Leaders should be open to opinions and changes, keeping goals in sight but being flexible enough to adapt to

EXHIBIT 3
Market Share

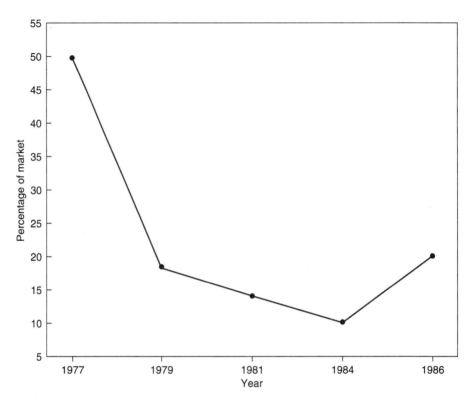

environmental changes within or outside of the company. Public responsibility as exhibited by senior executives also plays a crucial role in determining the quality of leadership. **100 pts.**

45 Information and Analysis   This area examines the breadth and depth of the data collected and utilized by the corporation. Impressive benchmarks should have been set in terms of quality planning, evaluation, and improvement. Analysis techniques are scrutinized. **70 pts.**

46 Planning   To successfully compete in this area, a company must have mapped out, in some depth, both short-term and long-term management strategies. These plans must realize company goals, but they also must be flexible enough to change with unforeseen occurrences. **60 pts.**

47 Human Resource Utilization   Management must utilize the work force to maximize its potential. Employees should feel involved in the company, and that they have contributed to making the company successful. All should be trained in quality production. Recognition and praise should be given often, on an equal basis. Morale should be maintained at a high level. **150 pts.**

48 Quality Assurance   Tracing a product from its development through manufacturing, a company must be able to show how quality was assured in each stage. Each product should have been developed to meet key quality requirements, and it should have been constructed with the highest-quality materials from suppliers. Continual assessment and improvements must be made. **140 pts.**

EXHIBIT 4
Xerox Corporation Balance Sheet 1980–1990 (in millions)

	1980	1982	1984	1986	1988	1990
Current assets	$ 130	$ 606	$ 784	$11,882	$16,478	$19,004
Investments	4,924	4,421	5,974	5,489	7,960	10,479
Land, buildings, and equipment	2,460	2,641	2,779	1,679	1,958	2,012
Total assets	$7,514	$7,668	$9,537	$19,050	$26,396	$31,495
Current liabilities	$2,085	$2,306	$2,451	$5,252	$9,318	$12,595
Long-term debt	898	850	1,614	3,443	5,356	7,108
Preferred stock	0	0	442	442	296	1,081
Common stock	3,630	3,724	4,101	4,687	5,371	5,051
Other liabilities	901	788	929	5,226	6,055	5,660
Total liabilities and equity	$7,514	$7,668	$9,537	$19,050	$26,396	$31,495

EXHIBIT 5
Xerox Corporation Income Statement, 1980–1990 (in thousands)

	1980	1982	1984	1986	1988	1990
Revenues:						
Sales, rentals, and service	$7,886	$8,258	$8,792	$9,420	$11,152	$12,692
Financing income	3	39	68	3,443	3,663	4,390
Other income	143	162	142	324	536	891
Total revenues	8,032	8,459	9,002	13,187	16,177	17,973
Research and development expenses	419	548	561	650	794	848
Income from continuing operations	545	357	376	460	347	605
Net income	$ 565	$ 424	$ 291	$ 465	$ 388	$ 243

49   **Quality Results** This category relies heavily on the activity of a firm's key competitors. Industry trends in quality improvement and levels must be assessed, along with the achievements of the industry's world leaders. After summarizing these trends and levels for business processes, operations, and support services, supplier quality must be discussed. For a product to be of superior quality, it must begin with superior materials. **180 pts.**

50   **Customer Satisfaction** Customer expectations are examined, as are corporate relationships with the customers. Information gained from these relationships, as well as complaints submitted, should be analyzed and utilized by management to improve quality. Customer satisfaction is compared with that of others in the industry. **300 pts.**

51   As shown in Exhibit 6, a perfect quality score would add up to **1000 points.**

EXHIBIT 6
1991 Examination Categories and Items
Malcolm Baldrige National Quality Award

1991 Examination Categories/Items		Maximum Points	
1.0	Leadership:		
1.1	Senior executive leadership	40	
1.2	Quality values	15	
1.3	Management for quality.	25	
1.4	Public responsibility	20	**100**
2.0	Information and analysis:		
2.1	Scope and management of quality data and information	20	
2.2	Competitive comparisons and benchmarks	30	
2.3	Analysis of quality data and information	20	**70**
3.0	Strategic quality planning:		
3.1	Strategic quality planning process	35	
3.2	Quality goals and plans	25	**60**
4.0	Human resource utilization:		
4.1	Human resource management	20	
4.2	Employee involvement.	40	
4.3	Quality education and training	40	
4.4	Employee recognition and performance measurement	25	
4.5	Employee well-being and morale	25	**150**

52   The Malcolm Baldrige award application is both lengthy and expensive. The applying company must submit proof of eligibility plus $50. There is a $3,000 application fee included for manufacturing companies and services to apply, and $1,000 for small businesses. Fees are requisite so the Malcolm Baldrige Foundation may become self-supporting financially.

53   After the fees, an extensive written document must be submitted, detailing how the company excels in each of the above-mentioned areas. The report consists of a two-page overview and up to 75 pages of text for manufacturing and service, and up to 50 pages for small business. Any supplemental sections can be up to 50 pages. The criteria for preparing the document is stringent. With this, a corporation must submit the application form, a site listing form, and a descriptor's form.

54   In the words of Robert Mosbacher:

> The winners of this award have made quality improvement a way of life. Quality is their bottom line, and that kind of can-do attitude makes for world-class products and services.

55   The Baldrige award promotes:

Awareness of quality as an increasingly important element in competitiveness.

Understanding of the requirements for quality excellence.

The sharing of information on successful quality strategies and on the benefits derived from implementation of these strategies.

EXHIBIT 6 **(concluded)**

1991 Examination Categories/Items		Maximum Points
5.0	Quality assurance of products and services:	
5.1	Design and introduction of quality products and services	35
5.2	Process quality control	20
5.3	Continuous improvement of processes	20
5.4	Quality assessment	15
5.5	Documentation	10
5.6	Business process and support service quality	20
5.7	Supplier quality	20 **140**
6.0	Quality results	
6.1	Product and service quality results	90
6.2	Business process, operational, and support service quality results	50
6.3	Supplier quality results	40 **180**
7.0	Customer satisfaction	
7.1	Determining customer requirements and expectations	30
7.2	Customer relationship management	50
7.3	Customer service standards	20
7.4	Commitment to customers	15
7.5	Complaint resolution for quality improvement	25
7.6	Determining customer satisfaction	20
7.7	Customer satisfaction results	70
7.8	Customer satisfaction comparison	70 **300**
Total points		**1,000**

56   The success of this award is due to a partnership between the federal government and the private sector. The board of examiners, which reviews the applications, consists of volunteer quality experts from industries, professional and trade associations, universities, health care organizations, and government agencies. Expenses are covered mostly by application fees, with the remainder paid by the foundation.

57   Although it is executives of large companies who serve as trustees for the foundation, the award was created and continues to be managed by a government unit, the National Institute of Standards and Technology (NIST). NIST is an agency of the Department of Commerce's Technology Administration. Other duties of this agency include aiding U.S. industries through research and improving public health and safety.

58   Three dimensions exist for evaluation. The "approach" is the way in which the company attempts to reach its goals. "Deployment" assesses the thoroughness of the approach in all areas of the company. "Results" measures the consequences of all actions (i.e., the effectiveness of the quality program).

EXHIBIT 7
Malcolm Baldrige National Quality Improvement Act of 1987, Public Law 100–107

The Findings and Purposes Section of Public Law 100–107 states that:

1. The leadership of the United States in product and process quality has been challenged strongly (and sometimes successfully) by foreign competition, and our Nation's productivity growth has improved less than our competitors' over the last two decades.

2. American business and industry are beginning to understand that poor quality costs companies as much as 20 percent of sales revenues nationally and that improved quality of goods and services goes hand in hand with improved productivity, lower costs, and increased profitability.

3. Strategic planning for quality and quality improvement programs, through a commitment to excellence in manufacturing and services, are becoming more and more essential to the well-being of our Nation's economy and our ability to compete effectively in the global marketplace.

4. Improved management understanding of the factory floor, worker involvement in quality, and greater emphasis on statistical process control can lead to dramatic improvements in the cost and quality of manufactured products.

5. The concept of quality improvement is directly applicable to small companies as well as large, to service industries as well as manufacturing, and to the public sector as well as private enterprise.

6. In order to be successful, quality improvement programs must be management-led and customer-oriented, and this may require fundamental changes in the way companies and agencies do business.

7. Several major industrial nations have successfully coupled rigorous private-sector quality audits with national awards giving special recognition to those enterprises the audits identify as the very best.

8. A national quality award program of the kind in the United States would help improve quality and productivity by:

   A. helping to stimulate American companies to improve quality and productivity for the pride of recognition while obtaining a competitive edge through increased profits;

   B. recognizing the achievements of those companies that improve the quality of their goods and services and providing an example to others;

   C. establishing guidelines and criteria that can be used by business, industrial, governmental, and other organizations in evaluating their own quality improvement efforts; and

   D. providing specific guidance for other American organizations that wish to learn how to manage for high quality by making available detailed information on how winning organizations were able to change their cultures and achieve eminence.

CASE 35

IBM: Is This an Ethical Issue or Just Good, Aggressive Accounting?

1   To all outward appearances, International Business Machines Corporation ran into trouble with startling speed. Even its harshest critics were stunned by its nearly $5 billion of losses in 1992, its first layoffs in half a century, and an unprecedented purge of top executives. By early 1993, its stock had lost more than $70 billion in market value since it peaked in 1987. And the crisis sparked a once-unthinkable move: IBM turned to an outsider, Louis V. Gerstner, to rescue it.

2   Now, considerable evidence suggests that IBM may have helped delay its day of reckoning with some surprisingly aggressive accounting moves. The moves didn't violate any laws or cause the company's fundamental business problems. Some, though not all, of the moves were fully disclosed to the public.

3   But some finance experts say that, just as IBM's business started to sour, its accounting became markedly less conservative. "Since the mid-1980s, IBM has been borrowing from the future to bolster today's profits," says Thornton O'glove, a frequently critical San Francisco accounting expert and former publisher of the *Quality of Earnings* newsletter.

Booking Sales Quickly

4   Although IBM doesn't dispute any of the facts about the accounting changes, it takes strong issue with the conclusion by some experts that it was stretching to make its numbers look better, while pushing possible bad news into the future.

5   The evidence of the aggressive accounting comes on several fronts:

6   IBM's former chief outside auditor, Price Waterhouse's Donald Chandler, wrote IBM a blistering 20-point memo in November 1988 suggesting that the company was reporting revenue that it might never get. For example, he criticized IBM for booking revenue when its products were shipped to dealers who could return them and sometimes even to its own warehouses—a far more aggressive approach than many companies take.

7   For more than 10 years, IBM has quietly turned to Merrill Lynch & Company and others to execute a rare financial maneuver that propped up the results of IBM's big leasing business. The maneuver allowed IBM to book immediately all the revenue from a long-term computer lease—even though the actual dollars would flow in only over the life of the lease. That didn't break any accounting rules, but some accountants term it an end-run that most blue-chip companies would avoid. Mr. Chandler called the revenue booster "troubling indeed" and urged IBM to take "immediate action" to use the maneuver less—advice that IBM ignored.

8   Footnotes in IBM's annual reports disclose that, in 1984, it adopted more liberal accounting for its huge investments in equipment and for its retirement plan. The changes—a bit like removing a car's shock absorbers—enabled IBM to push the cost of its investments into the future. While similar to moves at many other companies, they may have increased IBM's profits more than many investors

Prepared by John Logan, University of South Carolina; Sandra Logan, Newberry College; and Richard Robinson, University of South Carolina. This case is an edited version of the article, "Softer Numbers," which appeared in *The Wall Street Journal*, April 7, 1993, pp. A1, A8.

realize. Although IBM disclosed details of the changes, it never said how much they lifted earnings—and still refuses to do so.

Policies Defended

9   IBM strongly defends all its accounting moves and says all the changes were made for prudent business reasons. In a 22-page response to questions, it writes: "When our accounting policies and practices are compared with others in our industry or other major corporations, they cannot be shown, even with perfect hindsight, to be other than thoughtful and prudent."

10   IBM calls the Chandler memo part of the normal give-and-take between a company and an auditor with a flair for peppery language. The company says it improved its procedures in response to some of his concerns but hasn't changed its general accounting philosophy and many of the practices at issue.

11   Mr. Chandler, who retired last year, at first declined to comment when reached at home. Later, in a statement released by IBM, he said his work with the company was "totally open and frank." Of his specific criticisms, he cautioned, "It's absolutely vital that they not be taken out of context." He said every "significant" matter he raised was "satisfactorily resolved" and noted that he consistently blessed IBM's financial statements with clean audit opinions.

12   Questions about IBM's accounting could be awkward for the wounded computer giant. IBM long enjoyed a reputation as the epitome of financial conservatism, with triple-A-rated debt and the bluest of blue-chip stocks. A pioneer in mandating rigorous workplace ethics, IBM requires all employees to swear that they have read a 28-page "Business Conduct Guidelines" manual that warns them against "not only reporting information inaccurately, but also organizing it in a way that is intended to mislead or misinform."

13   Since 1985, IBM has openly discussed its business troubles—but always with an upbeat tone and never foreshadowing the full dimensions of last year's staggering loss. Meanwhile, in the late 1980s, IBM's executives got enormous raises and bonuses, partly pegged to its earnings, and sanguine investors loaded up on its stock. In early 1993, the stock languished at $52 a share, down from a 52-week high of $100 and a 1987 peak of $175 a share.

14   The questions about IBM's accounting fall into three broad areas:

WHEN IS A SALE A SALE?

15   As competition in the computer market heated up over the past decade, IBM's sales force dreamed up new gimmicks: free upgrades; stretched-out payment plans; a "try and buy" plan with no initial payment; "price protection" refunds if prices later drop. And at IBM's Armonk, New York, headquarters, accountants struggled to keep up with all the twists and turns of its sales deals. Their basic question: How much money should be recorded as revenue in IBM's financial reports?

16   In an interview in late 1992, Daniel Gough, a former IBM accounting manager, said he and his colleagues were under pressure to make more liberal interpretations of IBM's sales policies. "It amazed me to see how aggressive IBM became to help bolster a revenue stream that was slowing down significantly," he said. Mr. Gough conceded that he left IBM last year unhappily, because he didn't approve of its accounting policies; an IBM spokesman declines to comment on why Mr. Gough left. But Mr. Gough's concern was echoed in the 1988 memo by Price Waterhouse's Mr. Chandler.

17   In his memo to Michael Van Vranken, then IBM's controller, Mr. Chandler detailed the practices that upset him and his team of accountants. Mr. Chandler's fundamental complaint: that IBM was rushing to record revenue on its books as soon as it shipped a product, even for sales with escape hatches that could reduce the revenue IBM ultimately received.

18   For example, Mr. Chandler wrote that IBM's computer shipments to dealers "are recorded as sales at time of shipment," even though the dealers have the right to return the computers. He worried that some revenue from such shipments would be "difficult to defend at very best." In some cases, he found, IBM was recording revenue when it shipped products merely to its own warehouses. "This seems clearly inappropriate," he wrote.

19   IBM defends its continuing practice of booking revenue as soon as it ships a product, and says it makes allowances for returns. "The earnings process is substantially complete upon shipment," IBM contends, adding, "Price Waterhouse was, and continues to be, in full agreement." Price Waterhouse's current lead partner for auditing IBM, Kenneth Doyle, says IBM's terms with dealers weren't as lenient as Mr. Chandler believed.

20   However, IBM's approach "can lead to many revenue-booking abuses, particularly in the computer business," says Paul Regan, a leading expert on revenue issues at the Hemming Morse accounting firm in San Francisco. He offers a more conservative standard for when the "earnings process" is complete: when the products "are functioning properly in keeping with the sales agreement—and that can take a long time."

21   IBM isn't the only company that books revenue upon shipment. But many of its high-tech rivals are more conservative.

22   "We just don't put it on the floor, then say we can book it," says a spokesman for Amdahl Corporation, IBM's leading rival in mainframe computers. "It has to be turned over by outfield engineering group. They have to check the machine out, and make sure it's up and running. That's the point we actually take credit for the revenue."

23   A middle-ground approach is used by Xerox Corporation. It books revenue from its small copiers immediately upon shipment; but, with its bigger machines, it waits until "everyone says, 'Wow, it's better than sliced bread,'" a spokesman says.

24   IBM concedes that it sometimes books revenue when it ships a product to its own warehouses—for "temporary in-transit storage" en route to a customer. But it says it does so only when "installation at the customer" is "expected within 30 days." In part because of the Chandler memo, IBM says it cut that period from 45 days previously. Joseph Martin, IBM's assistant controller in charge of accounting practices, says the warehouse shipments involve only small sums with a negligible effect on earnings.

25   Mr. Chandler also found "very troubling" IBM's handling of "price protection"—its term for assuring customers that, if it later cut prices, they would owe only the reduced price. He said IBM was booking full revenue as soon as it shipped its products, despite "ample evidence" that it would later cut prices and thus receive less money. IBM says Mr. Chandler wasn't giving it enough credit for its broad allowance for "revenue adjustments," which was "based on historical experience and was applied to all revenue."

THE LEASING GAME

26   In 1982, IBM asked Merrill Lynch to perform a rare, inventive piece of financial surgery that directly affected its profits, though few shareholders or analysts ever heard of it. Experts say that, in the arcane area of lease financing, IBM exploited accounting rules in a troubling way.

27   When companies lease out equipment, they can account for it as an "operating" or a "sales-type" lease. An operating lease is conservative; revenues go on the books as they actually flow in each year. A sales-type lease is more liberal; all the revenue that will ever come in is recorded in the first year.

28   To restrain revenue-hungry companies, the Financial Accounting Standards Board has extensive rules, running more than 100 pages, about sales-type leases. IBM's accountants zeroed in on a formula in paragraph 7D: Add up all the lease payments, plus the value of the computer when the lease expires. If the total is 90 percent of the computer's value today, the lease can be considered a sales-type one.

29   In the hotly competitive market, IBM was offering terms that didn't add up to the 90 percent mark. Merrill's solution: It sold IBM "7D insurance," guaranteeing a certain value of the computer at the end of the lease—enough to push IBM over 90 percent. "Helping IBM keep the accounting proper for these leases was a simple matter, and we were able to provide this service for them," says Frederick Butler, a former Merrill director of lease financing. "Without this guarantee, these leases would be just under the [90 percent] line and would have to be taken as operating leases." Mr. Butler says Merrill didn't offer the service to any other company. Asked later for further information about the arrangement, a Merrill spokesman declined to comment.

30   IBM says it also had a second reason for seeking 7D insurance: The value of the products it leases out might plunge by the time the leases ended, so it hired Merrill to "spread" that risk. But IBM's Mr. Martin concedes that IBM also wanted the immediate revenue that sales-type leases would bring. "That's one answer," he says.

31   IBM says its deal with Merrill lasted until 1990. Today, IBM uses an offshore 7D insurer it won't identify. Price Waterhouse's Mr. Doyle won't say how much IBM revenue is affected by 7D insurance, but he calls it "not material"—accounting parlance for 5 percent of revenue or less.

32   Some accounting experts call 7D insurance a surprising tactic for a conservative company. "Structuring a lease to violate the spirit of the accounting rule . . . is weaseling, hokey, and totally inappropriate for a company of IBM's stature," says Howard Schilit, an associate professor of accounting at American University in Washington, D.C.

33   The experts also note great danger in recording a lease's entire revenue up front: What if it never materializes? That has become increasingly likely in the computer industry, where the breakneck pace of change has customers constantly switching to ever-cheaper machines.

34   "Converting operating leases into [sales-type] leases in a very aggressive way can create a lot of problems for a lessor down the road," says Dan Jozefov, vice president and controller of Mitsui-Nevitt Capital Corporation, a San Francisco leasing firm. If the cash flow doesn't come in, he adds, "the company will eventually have to take a hit against profits."

35   Did IBM book sales-type lease revenue that never materialized? Mr. Doyle says such reversals "were not material to IBM's finances." He adds that 7D insurance is "acceptable accounting, and it was thoroughly reviewed before it was implemented. The company evidenced prudence in the way that it was reviewed, and it didn't get out of control."

36   IBM isn't the only company to take out 7D insurance. Howard Chickering, president of a U.S. West, Inc., leasing unit called R.V.I. Guaranty Company, says his firm sells 7D insurance—but not to companies such as IBM, whose product prices fall so unpredictably. "We wouldn't touch the computer business," he says.

37   IBM's former outside auditor, Mr. Chandler, also sounded the alarm about IBM's aggressive push to sales-type leases. He noted that some of these transactions "rarely qualify" as sales-type leases without the help of a third party, such as Merrill. He urged IBM to act quickly to "bring down reliance" on 7D insurance.

TAKING OFF SHOCK ABSORBERS

38   In hindsight, 1984 was almost precisely when the computer-industry dynamics began to turn against IBM. The personal computer boom was just starting to erode the role of IBM's mighty mainframes in office work. IBM's return on equity hit a peak of 26.5 percent that year—before plunging to 9.6 percent by 1989 and disappearing amid losses in 1991 and 1992.

39   Footnotes in IBM's 1984 annual report show that it began overhauling its accounting tactics to spread the costs of factories and other investments far into the future, instead of recording them in the short term. IBM also reduced the estimated cost of its retirement plans, which then would take a smaller chunk out of each year's earnings. The accounting changes themselves were standard practice at many companies and hardly a secret; IBM's annual report disclosed them.

40   But in hindsight, IBM's critics say the changes were more evidence that IBM was imprudently shifting away from its traditional conservatism. Confident that mainframe computers would again yield enormous profits, IBM chose to defer more costs into the future, the critics suggest.

41   Mr. O'glove, the auditing expert, calculates that in 1984 the accounting changes were responsible for 26 percent of IBM's profit gain. That year profits surged by $1.73 a share, to $10.77; so that 26 percent amounts to 45 cents a share. In 1985, earnings fell 10 cents a share, but without the accounting changes, Mr. O'glove says, they would have dropped 86 cents a share.

42   "It was just the beginning of the slide that many other financial analysts missed in the mid- and late-1980s because they continued to believe IBM was following conservative accounting as it did in the early part of the decade," he says.

43   Although IBM has never specified how much the accounting changes affected its earnings, it says Mr. O'glove's numbers are "way off." It also cites a 1985 accountants' survey showing that 70 percent of U.S. companies were spreading investment costs into the future, just as IBM did. And as for lowering its retirement-plan costs, IBM says its financial advisers predicted that the plans' invested assets would start earning a higher return—and, thus, the cost to the company would drop. "We strongly disagree that our actions were anything but appropriate," IBM says. What do you think? Is this an ethical issue or just good, aggressive accounting?

CASE INDEX

SUBJECT INDEX

VGM's
CAREERS
ENCYCLOPEDIA

VGM's
CAREERS
ENCYCLOPEDIA

Third Edition

The Editors of VGM Career Horizons

VGM Career Horizons
a division of *NTC Publishing Group*
Lincolnwood, Illinois USA

Library of Congress Cataloging-in-Publication Data

VGM's careers encyclopedia / the editors of VGM Career Horizons.—
  3rd ed.
       p.   cm.
  Includes index.
  ISBN 0-8442-8692-3 (hardcover) : $39.95
  1. Vocational guidance—United States.   2. United States-
-Occupations.   I. VGM Career Horizons (Firm)
HF5382.5.U5C337   1991
331.7'02'0973—dc20   90-50726
                                                         CIP

Published by VGM Career Horizons, a division of NTC Publishing Group.
© 1991 by NTC Publishing Group, 4255 West Touhy Avenue,
Lincolnwood (Chicago), Illinois 60646-1975 U.S.A.

1 2 3 4 5 6 7 8 9 AG 9 8 7 6 5 4 3 2 1

Foreword

VGM Career Horizons is pleased to bring you this third edition of *VGM's Careers Encyclopedia*. Thoroughly revised, expanded, and updated, we feel this comprehensive and timely publication offers a wealth of career information in one source that will be extremely useful to students, parents, and guidance counselors.

Since the publication of the first edition in 1980, there have been many changes in America's job marketplace. The nation's economy continues to shift from one of manufacturing to an economy based on services. The number and types of jobs available, as well as the salaries commanded by each, have changed considerably. We have incorporated all this new information into the third edition, blending the updated material into the A-to-Z descriptions of 200 different careers.

We hope that *VGM's Careers Encyclopedia* serves you well and provides you with the career information that you seek. If it helps you or someone you know to pursue a career that is fulfilling, enjoyable, and rewarding, then the book has successfully served its purpose.

The Editors
VGM Career Horizons

Contents

CONTENTS

ACCOUNTANT

The job

Accountants prepare and analyze the financial reports that furnish up-to-date information for businesses, government agencies, and other organizations. The data they provide influence just about every business and government decision since the financial condition of an organization is an ever-present ingredient of any decision. There are also many opportunities for part-time work, especially with small businesses.

There are four major accounting fields: public, management, government, and internal auditing. About one-third of all accountants are *public accountants* who work for a number of clients; they work for themselves or for an accounting firm. Public accountants often specialize in one phase of accounting, such as auditing or taxes. Many also function as management consultants, advising clients on accounting systems and equipment.

Certified public accountants (CPAs) must hold a certificate issued by the state board of accountancy. To obtain certification they usually must have at least two years of public accounting experience and pass the CPA examination prepared by the American Institute of Certified Public Accountants. Most successful CPA candidates also have a college degree.

Most accountants are management accountants, employed by a single company to handle the company's financial records. Some management accountants function as *internal auditors*. Auditing entails reviewing financial records and reports to judge their reliability. The internal auditor's evaluation of the financial systems and management control procedures of a company enables the company to function efficiently and economically.

In some companies a management accountant may function as a credit manager, handling the company's accounts receivable and making decisions on extending credit to customers. (See the separate job description for credit manager.)

Government accountants maintain and examine the financial records of government agencies and audit the records of businesses and individuals whose financial activities are subject to government regulations. These accountants are employed by federal, state, and local government agencies.

Beginners in accounting usually start as ledger accountants, junior internal auditors, or as trainees for technical accounting positions. Junior public accountants usually assist with auditing work for several clients.

Related jobs are appraiser, loan officer, and internal revenue agent.

Places of employment and working conditions

All business, industrial, and government organizations use the services of accountants. Accountants work for the corner deli operator as well as for AT&T; for the smallest municipal government as well as for the government of the United States. They work throughout the country with the heaviest concentration of job opportunities in large urban areas, where many public accounting firms and central offices of large businesses are located, such as Chicago, Los Angeles, New York City, and Washington, D.C.

Accountants have desk jobs and usually work no more than 40 hours a week. Those employed by accounting firms carry heavy work loads during tax season, roughly from early December to May. Accountants employed by national firms may travel extensively to conduct audits and perform other services for their clients or employers.

Qualifications, education, and training

If you want to be an accountant, you need an aptitude for mathematics. In addition, you must be neat, accurate, able to work with little supervision, and able to handle responsibility.

Training in accounting is available at business schools and correspondence schools as well as at colleges and universities. However, most large public accounting and business firms require beginning accountants and internal auditors to have at least a bachelor's degree in accounting or in a closely related field. Many employers prefer a master's degree. Many companies also require familiarity with computer technology. The federal government requires four years of college with at least 24 semester hours of accounting or an equivalent combination of college and work experience.

Work experience is important and can help an applicant get a job after graduation. Therefore, many colleges provide students with an opportunity to gain experience through internship programs while still in school.

Accountants who wish to advance professionally must continue studying accounting throughout their careers. Seminars and courses are offered by many employers and professional associations. More and more accountants are studying computer operation and programming in addition to accounting subjects.

In the field of internal auditing, the designation certified internal auditor (CIA) is awarded by The Institute of Internal Auditors to those who have two years' experience and complete a four-part examination. Candidates for this designation must also have a bachelor's degree from an accredited college or university.

Nearly all states are requiring both CPAs and licensed public accountants to complete continuing education courses for license renewal.

Potential and advancement

There are about 963,000 accountants in the United States; about 300,000 are CPAs and about 15,000 are CIAs. The demand for skilled accountants is expected to increase over the next decade as business and government agencies continue to grow in size and complexity. Internal auditing is a specialty field that is growing rapidly.

There will be job opportunities for accountants without college degrees especially in small businesses and accounting and tax preparation firms. CPAs should have a wider range of job opportunities than other accountants. A master's degree is an asset for those competing for jobs with prestigious firms.

Accountants may advance to such jobs as chief plant accountant, chief cost accountant, budget director, or manager of internal auditing. Some achieve

3

corporate-level positions such as controller, treasurer, financial vice-president, or president.

Public accountants can advance from beginner through intermediate-level positions in one or two years to senior positions in another few years as they gain experience and handle more complex accounts. In large accounting firms, they often become supervisors, managers, or partners. Some transfer to executive positions in private firms or open their own public accounting offices. Entry-level accountants employed by the federal government are usually promoted within two years.

Income

Annual salaries for beginning public accountants in public accounting firms average $22,100. Those with more experience who are not owners or partners of their firms average $26,600 per year, but some have annual salaries of more than $38,000. Owners and partners of firms earn considerably more.

Starting salaries for management accountants in private industry average $22,200 a year, and those with more experience earn average annual salaries of $33,500, with some of the most experienced earning over $75,000. Chief accountants who direct the accounting program of a company earn between $38,000 to more than $97,000 a year, depending on the size of the accounting staff and the scope of their authority.

Trainee internal auditors average $23,500 a year; internal auditors earn an average of $32,900 per year. Some of the most experienced internal auditors have average annual salaries of more than $47,000.

In the federal government, junior accountants and auditors begin at about $15,700 a year; those with superior academic records can begin as high as $19,500. A beginner with a master's degree or two years of professional experience starts at about $23,900 a year.

Additional sources of information

American Institute of Certified Public Accountants
1211 Avenue of the Americas
New York, NY 10036-8775

American Society of Women Accountants
35 East Wacker Drive
Suite 2250
Chicago, IL 60601

The Institute of Internal Auditors
249 Maitland Avenue
Altamonte Springs, FL 32701-4201

National Association of Accountants
10 Paragon Drive
Montvale, NJ 07645

National Society of Public Accountants and the
Accreditation Council for Accountancy
1010 North Fairfax Street
Alexandria, VA 22314

ACTOR

The job

Probably the most famous people in today's society are the leading actors who perform in motion pictures and stage plays and on television and radio. Through these mediums, actors entertain their audiences using facial and verbal communication and body motion to bring characters to life creatively.

Only a very few actors achieve great fame and popularity and become stars. More become fairly well known and play important supporting roles. Most, however, struggle to find employment and accept small acting roles in order to gain experience and earn a reputation in the field; these actors often face periods of unemployment and are forced to supplement their incomes by working at other jobs, such as waiters or salespeople.

Actors usually begin their careers in shorter roles, or bit parts. As they gain experience, they may move on to supporting roles and then a few move on to the principal parts.

Some actors work as extras, who rarely have any lines. They appear as people walking by or in crowd scenes.

Places of employment and working conditions

Most actors working in motion pictures are employed in Hollywood and New York City. Film studios are also located in Florida, Texas, and in other parts of the United States. Television actors find the most opportunities at the headquarters for the major networks—New York City and Los Angeles. Stage actors work in New York City and other large cities.

Acting can be a very stressful career. Acting jobs are usually temporary, and many actors find themselves unemployed frequently. Those who have the talent, persistence, and stamina to find acting jobs must often travel, work long hours, and work evenings. The work itself is at times tedious—memorizing lines and repetitious rehearsals. Motion picture actors sometimes film on location in places with uncomfortable climates.

Qualifications, education, and training

It is a good idea for those who aspire to acting careers to get involved in as much amateur theater as possible—high school and college plays and local theater groups.

While some people enter the acting field and achieve success without formal training and experience, such things are usually necessary. Dramatic arts schools in New York and Los Angeles and many colleges and universities throughout the United States that have bachelor's- and master's-degree programs in dramatic and theater arts offer formal training. Having formal training in singing and dancing may provide opportunities for employment.

Actors need a great deal of talent, confidence, persistence, the ability to portray a convincing character, and, often, an attractive physical appearance.

Potential and advancement

Employment opportunities for actors are expected to increase rapidly as the number of theatrical and motion picture productions increases and as audiences continue to demand live theater productions. But there will be a great deal of competition for jobs—many more people are trying to find acting jobs than there are jobs available.

Actors develop the necessary creative skills and experience they need by taking advantage of amateur acting opportunities. They then move on to local and regional theater, which may help them find opportunities in New York City, Hollywood, and Los Angeles. Modeling experience is sometimes helpful.

Income

Several unions represent workers in the different branches of the acting field and negotiate salaries. The Actors' Equity Association represents stage actors; actors in motion pictures, television, commercials, and films are represented by the Screen Actors Guild and the Screen Extras Guild; and actors in television and radio are represented by the American Federation of Television and Radio Artists.

Actors in Broadway productions earn a minimum weekly salary of $800. Those working in off-Broadway productions earn a minimum of $280 to $505 a week, depending on the size of the theater. Actors working in traveling shows are paid an additional $73.50 per day.

Motion picture and television actors earn a minimum of $398 a day, and extras are paid $93 a day. Television actors often earn residuals for reruns.

Those few actors who achieve stardom receive salaries many times the size of the minimum.

Additional sources of information

Actors' Equity Association
165 West 46th Street
New York, NY 10036

Theatre Communications Group, Inc.
355 Lexington Avenue
New York, NY 10017

ACTUARY

The job

Actuaries are, for the most part, mathematicians. They assemble and analyze statistics on probabilities of death, illness, injury, disability, unemployment, retirement, and property losses to design insurance and pension plans and set up the premium structure for the policies.

For example, statistics on auto accidents are gathered and analyzed by actuaries employed by a company selling auto insurance. The actuaries then base the premiums for their company's policies on the accident statistics for

7

different groups of policyholders. They consider age, miles driven annually, and geographic location, among other things.

Since the insurance company is assuming a risk, the premium rates developed by company actuaries must enable the company to pay all claims and expenses and must be adequate to provide the company with a reasonable profit for assuming that risk. To function effectively, actuaries must keep up-to-date on general economic and social trends and on any legislative developments that might affect insurance practices.

Actuaries provide information to executives in their company's investments, group underwriting, and pension planning departments; they prepare material for policyholders and government requirements; and they may be called on to testify before public agencies on proposed legislation on insurance practices.

Actuaries employed by the federal government usually work on a specific insurance or pension program such as Social Security. Those in state government positions regulate insurance companies, supervise state pension programs, and work in the unemployment insurance and workers' compensation programs.

Consulting actuaries set up pension and welfare plans for private companies, unions, and government agencies. Some consulting actuaries evaluate pension plans and certify their solvency in compliance with the Employee Retirement Income Security Act of 1974.

Life insurance companies employ the most actuaries; others work for property and liability companies. Large companies may employ as many as 100 actuaries; many smaller companies use the services of consulting firms or rating bureaus. Other actuaries work for private organizations that administer independent pension or welfare plans or for federal and state agencies.

Beginning actuaries often rotate among various jobs within a company's actuarial operation to become familiar with its different phases. In the process, they gain a broad knowledge of insurance and related fields.

Only about 10 percent of all actuaries are women. This is due to women having traditionally avoided mathematics majors in college and will probably change as more female high school and college students are encouraged to study math.

Related jobs are mathematician, statistician, accountant, and claim representative.

Places of employment and working conditions

Many actuaries work in Boston, Chicago, Hartford, New York City, and Philadelphia in insurance company headquarters.

Actuaries have desk jobs and usually work at least 40 hours a week. Occasional overtime is necessary.

Qualifications, education, and training

A strong background in mathematics is necessary for anyone interested in a career as an actuary.

Only about 30 colleges and universities offer a degree in actuarial science. However, a bachelor's degree with a major in mathematics, statistics, or business administration is also a good educational background for an actuary. Courses in insurance law, economics, and accounting are valuable.

Some companies will also accept an applicant who has a degree in engineering, economics, or business administration if courses in calculus, probability, and statistics have been included.

Of equal importance to a strong mathematics background are the examination programs offered by professional actuarial societies to prospective actuaries. Examinations are given twice a year, and extensive home study is required to pass the more advanced ones. Completion of one or more of these examinations while still in school helps students to evaluate their potential as actuaries; those who pass one or more examinations usually have better employment opportunities and receive higher starting salaries. Actuaries are encouraged to complete an entire series of examinations as soon as possible in their careers to achieve full professional status. This usually takes from five to ten years.

Associate membership in their respective professional societies is awarded to actuaries after successful completion of five examinations in the life insurance or pension series or seven examinations in the casualty series. Full membership is awarded, along with the title "fellow," upon completion of an entire series.

Consulting pension actuaries who service private pension plans and certify the plans' solvency must be enrolled and licensed by the Joint Board for the Enrollment of Actuaries, which stipulates the experience, education, and examination requirements.

Potential and advancement

There are about 16,000 persons employed as actuaries in the United States. Employment in this field is expected to grow rapidly through the year 2000 with job opportunities best for college graduates who have passed at least two actuarial examinations while still in school. More actuaries will be required as the complexity and number of insurance policies and pension plans increase. Even though the field is expected to have substantial growth, the large number of new graduates with degrees in actuarial science, mathematics, and statistics will mean increased competition for available job openings.

Advancement within the field depends on job performance, experience, and the number of actuarial examinations completed successfully. Actuaries can be promoted to assistant, associate, and chief actuary within their company. Because they have a broad knowledge of insurance and its related fields, actuaries are often selected for administrative positions in other company departments such as underwriting, accounting, or data processing. Many actuaries advance to top executive positions, where they help determine company policy.

Income

Recent college graduates just beginning their careers earn about $22,000 to $26,000 a year if they have not passed any actuarial examinations. Those who have completed the first exam receive between $24,000 and $28,000, and those who have passed the second exam average between $26,000 and $30,000, depending on geographic location. Earnings increase with experience and advancement in the examination program, with many companies giving merit increases for each examination successfully completed.

Actuaries who become associates average between $35,000 and $48,000 a year; those who become fellows average between $47,000 and $57,000. Top actuarial executives receive salaries of $55,000 to $100,000 a year and higher.

Additional sources of information

American Society of Pension Actuaries
2029 K Street, NW
Fourth Floor
Washington, DC 20006

Casualty Actuarial Society
One Penn Plaza
250 West 34th Street
New York, NY 10119

National Association of Insurance Women
1847 East 15th Street
P.O. Box 4410
Tulsa, OK 74159

Society of Actuaries
475 North Martingale Road
Schaumburg, IL 60173

ADVERTISING ACCOUNT EXECUTIVE

The job

Each of an advertising agency's clients is assigned to an account executive who is responsible for handling everything concerning the client's advertising campaign. The account executive must know the client's product and marketing plans and the agency's resources for successfully carrying out the client's requirements. Together they plan the advertising campaign and create its components.

The account executive studies a client's company and its sales, its present public image, and its advertising requirements and budget. In developing an advertising campaign to suit the client's needs, the account executive calls upon all the resources of the agency artists and designers, copywriters, media buyers, production staff, and market researchers.

The account executive then has the job of selling the client on the planned advertising campaign. Considerable time may be spent changing and reworking the plan before the client grants approval. As the advertising campaign progresses, the account executive keeps track of sales figures and may further alter the campaign to achieve the results the client wants.

The job of an account executive can sometimes be glamorous—they get to wine and dine the clients and sometimes go on location to oversee the production of commercials or other material for a client—but it also carries with it a great deal of responsibility. The account executive must ensure that artists, copywriters, and production people meet schedules and must act as liaison between the agency and the client, keeping costs within the client's budget.

In some large agencies, account executives report to an *account supervisor*, but in most agencies they are supervised by top management or owners of the agency. In small agencies, the owners of the firm often function as account executives and may even do some of the creative work, such as copywriting.

Places of employment and working conditions

Advertising agencies exist in many cities, but the heaviest concentrations are in New York City, Los Angeles, and Chicago. "Madison Avenue" is, of course, the term applied to the many large and prestigious agencies in New York City. Other rapidly growing advertising centers are Atlanta, Houston, Dallas, and Detroit.

Pressures are extreme and working hours are long and unpredictable. Advertising is a very competitive field, and there is very little job security. The loss of a large account can mean the firing or the laying off of everyone who worked on the account, including the account executive.

Qualifications, education, and training

Job experience in sales, advertising, or market research is valuable, but you also need at least a bachelor's degree to become an advertising account executive. A major in advertising, marketing, business administration, or liberal arts is preferred, and some large agencies prefer a master's degree in business administration.

Training programs for account executives are offered by some agencies.

Potential and advancement

The employment outlook for the advertising field is good, and job opportunities should continue to grow in the 1990s. The advertising field is strongly affected by general business conditions, however, since most firms expand or contract their advertising budgets according to how their own sales are affected by economic conditions. Entry-level jobs and trainee positions usually have an overabundance of applicants, but experienced account executives with a proven track record will continue to be in demand.

Skilled and experienced account executives can advance to the highest positions in an agency. In a large agency, they can become account supervisors of one or more accounts, advance to the executive suite, become partners in the firm, or open their own agencies. Some leave their agency jobs to become advertising managers for former clients.

Income

Trainees start at around $20,000 to $31,000, depending on education and the size of the agency. Account supervisors average between $41,500 and $51,900, again, depending on the size of the agency. Account executives average from $30,100 in smaller agencies to $36,100 or higher in large agencies.

Additional sources of information

American Advertising Federation
1225 Connecticut Avenue
Washington, DC 20036

American Association of Advertising Associations
666 Third Avenue
New York, NY 10021

Business/Professional Advertising Association
205 East 42nd Street
New York, NY 10017

ADVERTISING MANAGER

The job

In many companies the amount of advertising done to place the company's product or service before the public requires the time and talents of a full-time advertising manager. Working in close cooperation with the marketing department, or as part of the marketing department, the advertising manager develops advertising appropriate to the consumers the company wants to attract.

In some companies the advertising manager is the only one on the staff, creating the art and written copy and placing it in newspapers, magazines, and radio or television as well. Other advertising managers supervise a staff that may include artists, copywriters, production and research workers, and media buyers. The department may turn out display ads, point-of-sale and direct mail advertising, a company product catalogue, and trade show displays. In such advertising departments, the advertising manager is responsible for the administration of a large budget, coordinates the activities of the department to meet deadlines and schedules, places the company's advertising in the appropriate media vehicles, and handles the day-to-day administration of the department.

In a company that uses the services of an advertising agency for all or part of its advertising, the advertising manager represents the company in its dealings with the agency. Depending on the extent of the manager's authority, he or she might select the advertising agency, supervise the handling of the account by the agency, supply market research information, apportion the advertising budget, and approve the final advertising campaign. In some companies, top management has the final approval of the advertising campaign and budget.

Regardless of whether the advertising manager works with an advertising agency or supervises an in-house advertising department, and regardless of the size of the company or the budget it allows for advertising, the advertising manager is expected to produce visible results in the form of increased sales volume of the company's product or service.

Places of employment and working conditions

Advertising managers work in all areas of the country, with the most job opportunities in large metropolitan areas.

Advertising managers work under considerable pressure. They generally work long hours and are required to successfully coordinate the ideas, personalities, and talents of a variety of people—from top management to the creative staff of the advertising department.

Qualifications, education, and training

Success in advertising depends on imagination, creativity, a knowledge of what motivates consumers, and the ability to function as part of a team. An advertising manager must also have supervisory ability, budgeting experience, and a solid grounding in all areas of advertising.

The first step is a must—a college degree. The most useful degrees are liberal arts, business administration, or marketing.

After graduation, beginners in this field usually start in one of the specialty arts of advertising such as art, copywriting, research, production, or media buying in either an advertising department or advertising agency to gain as much experience as possible. Experience in several different specialties provides the best training for a prospective advertising manager.

Potential and advancement

As with all top management positions, there is competition for the top spot in an advertising department. The job outlook is good for the future because a slight growth is expected in the number of company advertising departments. The best jobs will go to those with education, experience, and proven abilities in advertising.

Advertising managers are already in top positions. They advance by moving to larger companies or to advertising agencies where they will have greater responsibilities and more challenging work. Some open their own advertising agencies.

Income

Salaries vary depending on location, sales volume, and size of company. Most are in the $23,700 to $52,500 range. In general, salaries for advertising managers are higher in consumer product firms than in industrial firms.

Many advertising managers also receive bonuses or company stock for effective advertising campaigns and participate in profit-sharing plans.

Additional sources of information

American Advertising Federation
1225 Connecticut Avenue
Washington, DC 20036

Association of National Advertisers
155 East 44th Street
New York, NY 10017

Business/Professional Advertising Association
205 East 42nd Street
New York, NY 10017

ADVERTISING SALESPERSON

The job

The money necessary to finance the activities of radio and television stations and most of the publication costs of newspapers and magazines comes from the sale of time or space to clients who wish to advertise a product or service.

Advertising salespeople sell directly to clients or to advertising agencies that represent the clients. Technically, the sales worker is selling broadcasting time segments on the stations or space in the publications, but actually what is being sold is the station's programming or a publication's content and the amount and type of audience that each attracts.

Newspapers get a portion of the dollars spent on advertising—almost 13 percent. Advertising salespeople in this field work both locally and as *national sales representatives*. There are three principal categories of newspaper advertising: general, retail, and classified. General, also known as national, advertising is the advertising of products and services marketed nationally or regionally through local retail outlets. This type of newspaper advertising is usually handled by independent national sales representatives who deal with national advertisers and their advertising agencies. They usually represent a number of local newspapers.

Retail advertising is local advertising. Salespeople handling this type of newspaper advertising may also provide some of the copywriting and layout required or provide advice on an ad content and design. Classified advertising is sold by outside salespersons who call on auto dealers, real estate brokers, and other regular advertisers and by inside salespeople who handle walk-in or telephone classified advertising. *Retail* and *classified advertising salespeople* keep close track of clients and often provide pick-up service for advertising copy, handle changes in ads, and suggest advertising approaches.

On small newspapers, advertising may be sold by all members of the staff, or the paper may employ a part-time advertising salesperson.

Even more advertising dollars—about 16 percent—are spent on magazine advertising. Magazines use national sales representatives even more than newspapers since most magazines have a wider, often national, distribution. Local and regional magazines employ more local salespeople.

Radio stations employ *radio advertising salespeople* to sell air time to local businesses and use national sales representatives on a commission basis to sell local time to national and regional advertisers. The radio advertising salesperson sells radio time in the form of entire programs or portions of programs or spot announcements. He or she must know not only the type of audience that listens to a particular station but also the time of day that a very specific segment of the audience is most likely to be listening. Radio advertising salespeople must be well versed in the latest market research analysis of their local marketing areas and must be prepared to advise a client on the best advertising approach for the money.

At small radio stations, everyone may sell advertising, or the station manager may handle all advertising. Larger stations employ several salespeople, and those in large marketing areas may have large sales staffs.

The largest advertising medium by far is television. The typical television station in a major city employs six to eight *television advertising salespeople* to call on local businesses. A great deal of television advertising time is also sold by national sales representatives who have branch offices in major cities. These "sales reps" sell most television advertising and act as the go-between for local stations and the national advertisers.

Network salespeople work for the national television and radio networks and sell network time to national advertisers. They handle accounts worth hundreds of thousands of dollars.

Places of employment and working conditions

Advertising sales jobs can be found in all communities, with the most opportunities in large metropolitan areas. National sales representatives are concentrated in cities such as Chicago, Los Angeles, and New York.

Advertising sales is a combination of office, telephone, and leg work. The salespeople work long hours. It is often necessary to spend a great deal of time on a particular account, including the preparation of sales presentations and cost estimates.

Qualifications, education, and training

The personal qualities of a good salesperson include aggressiveness, enthusiasm, perseverance, and the ability to get along with people.

Sales experience of any kind is valuable, and experience in selling advertising is especially helpful.

Although a college degree is not required by all employers, large metropolitan newspapers, mass-circulation and trade magazines, major radio and television stations, networks, and national sales representative firms require a bachelor's degree in marketing or journalism. Some require a major in advertising.

Potential and advancement

The future for magazine, newspaper, radio, and television advertising is very good. Media sales will continue to grow and provide many opportunities.

Beginners will find the best opportunities with small local newspapers and magazines and small radio and television stations where they can gain valuable experience. There will continue to be opportunities for part-time work with small newspapers and small or local radio and television stations.

Newspaper advertising salespeople can advance to positions such as general advertising manager, retail advertising manager, classified advertising manager, or advertising director.

Radio advertising salespeople can advance to sales manager positions where they would be involved developing sales plans as well as policies and programming.

In television, advertising salespeople can advance to regional, national, and general sales manager positions. The top-level positions in television station management are very often filled by former general sales managers.

Income

Advertising salespeople work on a commission basis, and the amount of their earnings is governed by their own ability and ambition. Some employers provide a base salary plus a commission. Commission rates vary but are usually between 10 and 15 percent.

Sales managers on large magazines earn $31,000 to $50,000 a year. Newspaper space salespeople earn from $21,000 to $48,000.

Radio advertising salespeople average about $24,000 a year with much higher earnings for network salespeople.

Earnings of television national sales representatives are better than sales earnings in just about any other industry. Beginners can earn $25,000 to $37,000 in their first year, and earnings of experienced national salespeople often approach six figures. They also take part in company stock or profit-sharing plans.

On a local level, television advertising salespeople earn between $15,000 and $45,000 a year. Beginners can earn $14,000 to $20,000 a year; more experienced salespeople earn between $25,000 and $32,000. Top local television salespeople earn between $36,000 and $47,000. In the largest cities, these figures are even higher.

In all advertising sales fields the median income is about $28,000 a year, with men earning $30,000 annually and women, around $22,000.

Additional sources of information

American Newspaper Publishers Association
Box 17407
Dulles International Airport
Washington, DC 20041

International Newspaper Advertising and Marketing Executives, Inc.
P.O. Box 17210
Washington, DC 20041

National Association of Broadcasters
1771 N Street, NW
Washington, DC 20036

Radio Advertising Bureau
304 Park Avenue, South
New York, NY 10010

Television Bureau of Advertising
477 Madison Avenue
New York, NY 10022

ADVERTISING WORKER

The job

For the thousands of people working in advertising, job satisfaction may come from having their work appear in print or on television or radio.

The work of a number of people with special talents goes into every advertising campaign, and the end result, when the campaign is successful, can make a great difference in the sales figures of a product or service.

Artists, designers, and layout artists create the visual aspects of advertising in magazine and newspaper ads, television commercials, and product packaging. They select photographs, draw illustrations, and decide on the colors and style of type to be used. They also prepare samples of art work for account executives who are planning advertising campaigns with clients and prospective clients.

Copywriters provide the words. A copywriter usually works closely with the account executive to produce just what the client wants to say about his or her product or service. The work of the copywriter is an integral part of almost all advertising but is especially important in radio where words are the only vehicle for the advertiser's message.

Production managers arrange for the actual filming, recording, or printing of the completed advertisement. They must be able to produce the finished product on time and within the budget allocated by the client. They normally deal with models, actors, and photographers.

Media buyers are specialists who are well informed on costs and audiences of the various media. They work with account executives to decide on how to reach the largest and most appropriate consumer audience for a client's product or service. Working within the client's budget, they buy advertising time on radio or television and advertising space in newspapers and magazines. In some agencies, the functions are separated into *time buyers* and *space buyers*.

About 100,000 people are employed in advertising agencies, and two or three times that number work in the advertising departments of commercial and industrial firms, retail stores, and newspapers and magazines. Printing companies, package design firms, sign companies, and mail order catalogues also employ persons with advertising skills.

Beginners in advertising usually start as assistants in research, production, or media buying. Those with writing ability usually start as *junior copywriters*.

Related jobs are advertising account executive, advertising manager, advertising salesperson, and marketing researcher.

Places of employment and working conditions

About half of all advertising workers are employed in the New York City and Chicago areas, but opportunities exist in most cities.

All advertising workers function under a great deal of pressure. The usual 35- to 40-hour workweek often includes overtime because of deadlines, the demands of clients, and production schedules.

Although advertising agencies are considered the most glamorous places to work, there may be little job security in an agency. If an agency loses a big account, all the people who worked on the account, including the account executive, may lose their jobs.

Qualifications, education, and training

Creativity and a knowledge of what motivates consumers are the keys to success in advertising.

Successful advertising workers also have imagination, a flair for language, and the ability to sell ideas. They must get along well with people, be able to function as part of a team, enjoy challenge and variety, and thrive on excitement and competition.

High school courses in art and writing are valuable as are experience in selling advertising for a school newspaper or a summer job at a radio station or newspaper office. Any education or professional experience in marketing, art, writing, journalism, or business and marketing research is valuable.

There are no specific educational requirements in the advertising field, but most employers prefer college graduates; they will accept a degree in almost any field. Some have a preference for a liberal arts background with majors in art, literature, and social sciences; others want applicants with degrees in marketing, business, or journalism. There are, however, more than 100 colleges and universities in the United States that offer majors in advertising.

When seeking a position in advertising, certain job applicants are expected to provide samples of their work. A beginning artist should supply a portfolio of drawings; a writer should supply samples of written work. Experienced advertising workers include samples of the work they have handled for previous employers.

Potential and advancement

About 300,000 persons work in the advertising field, one-third of them in advertising agencies. This is a popular field with stiff competition for entry-level jobs and for jobs with the best companies. Job opportunities should increase steadily, but, since the amount of money spent on advertising is strongly affected by general business conditions, they may be better in some years than in others. Local television, radio, and newspapers are expected to increase their share of total advertising, while magazines, direct mail, and national newspapers are declining and will provide fewer job opportunities.

Opportunities for advancement usually exist within each specialty area. An artist or designer can become an art director; a copywriter can be promoted to copy chief. Advancement to management is possible from any of the specialties, and experienced advertising workers sometimes open their own advertising agencies.

Income

Entry-level jobs pay $15,000 to $22,000 a year, with top starting salaries going to outstanding liberal arts graduates. Junior layout artists earn about $15,000 to $19,000; junior copywriters about $18,000 to $23,000.

Average salaries for experienced advertising workers include: senior layout artists, $30,000; art directors, $30,000; executive art directors, $39,000; production managers, $31,000; senior copywriters, $41,000. Media space or time buyers average from $19,000 to $24,000; media directors, $80,000. Highly experienced buyers earn more.

Top executive officers in advertising earn from $80,000 to $120,000 or more annually.

Additional sources of information

American Advertising Federation
1225 Connecticut Avenue
Washington, DC 20036

American Association of Advertising Agencies
666 Third Avenue
New York, NY 10021

AEROSPACE ENGINEER

The job

The design, development, testing, and production of commercial and military aircraft, missiles, and spacecraft are the duties of aerospace engineers. Their work is important to commercial aviation, national defense, and the space program.

Aerospace engineers often specialize in one area such as structural design, instrumentation and communication, or production methods. They may also specialize in one type of product such as helicopters, passenger planes, or rockets.

Two-thirds of the aerospace engineers are employed by aircraft, aircraft parts, guided missile, and space vehicle manufacturers. The National Aeronautics and Space Administration and the Department of Defense provide over one out of ten jobs. A few aerospace engineers work for commercial airlines and consulting firms.

Places of employment and working conditions

The aerospace industry is concentrated in California, Texas, Washington, and states with large aerospace manufacturers.

Qualifications, education, and training

The ability to think analytically, a capacity for details, and the ability to work as part of a team are all necessary. Good communication skills are important.

Mathematics and the sciences must be emphasized in high school. A bachelor's degree in engineering is the minimum requirement in this field. In a typical curriculum, the first two years are spent in the study of basic sciences such as physics and chemistry and mathematics, introductory engineering, and some liberal arts courses. The remaining years are usually devoted to specialized engineering courses.

Engineering programs can last from four to six years. Those that require five or six years to complete may award a master's degree or may provide a cooperative plan of study plus practical work experience with a nearby industry.

Because of rapid changes in technology, many aerospace engineers continue their education throughout their careers. A graduate degree is necessary for most teaching and research positions and for many management jobs. Some persons obtain graduate degrees in business administration.

All states require licensing of engineers whose work may affect life, health, or property or who offer their services to the public. Those who are licensed, about one-third of all engineers, are called registered engineers. Requirements for licensing include graduation from an accredited engineering school, four years of experience, and an examination.

Potential and advancement

There are about 78,000 aerospace engineers. Employment in this field is expected to grow about as fast as the average for all occupations through the year 2000. A large proportion of aerospace engineering jobs are defense related, so employment opportunities with the federal government will be limited unless there is an increase in defense and space exploration spending. However, faster growth for this field is expected in the civilian sector as present airliners are replaced with quieter and more fuel-efficient aircraft and demands increase for spacecraft, helicopters, and business aircraft.

Income

Starting salaries for engineering graduates with a bachelor's degree average about $29,200 a year in private industry. Starting offers for those with a master's degree average $34,600 a year and for those with a Ph.D., $46,600. Senior engineers working in private industry with management responsibilities earn an annual average salary of about $87,900.

The average yearly salary for engineers employed by the federal government is about $42,300.

Additional sources of information

Accreditation Board for Engineering and Technology
345 East 47th Street
New York, NY 10017

American Institute of Aeronautics and Astronautics, Inc.
AIAA Student Programs
The Aerospace Center
370 L'Enfant Promenade, SW
Washington, DC 20024

American Society for Engineering Education
11 Dupont Circle
Suite 200
Washington, DC 20036

Junior Engineering Technical Society (JETS)
1420 King Street
Suite 405
Alexandria, VA 22314

National Society of Professional Engineers
1420 King Street
Alexandria, VA 22314

Society of Women Engineers
345 East 47th Street
Room 305
New York, NY 10017

AGRICULTURAL COOPERATIVE EXTENSION SERVICE WORKER

The job

Extension agents, as they are usually called, are employed jointly by state land-grant universities and the U.S. Department of Agriculture. They conduct educational programs for rural residents in agriculture, home economics, youth activities, and community resource development. Agents usually specialize in one of these areas, and most of them are employed at the county level.

Extension agents usually work with groups of people. An agent for youth activities conducts 4-H meetings and organizes recreational activities such as camping. One whose specialty is home economics would present programs and information on nutrition, food preparation and preservation, child care, and home furnishings. In community resource development, an extension agent would help local community leaders to plan public projects such as water supply and sewage systems, recreational programs, libraries, and schools. Agricultural science extension agents conduct seminars for local farmers and provide advice to individual farmers who have specific problems.

Extension agents use every available communication method to reach as large an audience as possible. They write for local newspapers, appear on local radio and television stations, and sometimes produce films covering specialized subjects.

Some extension agents are employed at the state level at land-grant universities where they coordinate the work of the county agents. State extension agents often conduct research and may spend part of their time teaching classes at the university.

County extension service workers also work in home economics, child care, and health services.

Places of employment and working conditions

Extension agents work in rural areas throughout the United States.

Most extension service offices are located in small communities, a fact that appeals to people who do not wish to work in the city. Extension agents lead a very busy, active life and, depending on specialty area, may spend a great deal of time outdoors. Many meetings and seminars are presented in the evening for the convenience of the participants.

Qualifications, education, and training

Extension workers must have the ability to work with people and an interest in farm life.

A bachelor's degree in an appropriate specialty is the basic requirement for extension service agents. Some training in communication skills and teaching techniques is extremely valuable also. Agents usually receive specific training in extension work in a preinduction training program and may improve their skills through regular in-service training programs.

In most states, specialists and state-level or multicounty agents must have a graduate degree, sometimes a Ph.D.

Potential and advancement

There are about 15,000 cooperative extension workers. The number of workers will grow very slowly through the year 2000 to between 16,000 and 17,000.

Agents at the county level can advance to positions as state specialists. State specialists can then be promoted to administrative positions in the state extension service. Some workers with the necessary advanced degrees advance to staff positions at a college or university.

Income

Salaries vary by locality and depend on the education and experience of the worker. Starting salaries range from $11,500 to $16,500 a year, and workers with experience average about $21,000 a year.

Additional sources of information

Extension Service
U.S. Department of Agriculture
Washington, DC 20250

AGRICULTURAL ENGINEER

The job

Agricultural engineers design and develop a variety of products and services for farmers, ranchers, and the agricultural industry.

Agricultural engineers may design the most effective layout for a farm including placement of barns and irrigation systems; others design specific buildings such as dairy barns. Utility companies employ agricultural engineers to develop electrical power systems for farms and food processing companies. Manufacturers of farm equipment and machinery employ them in design and development as well as in sales.

The federal government employs agricultural engineers in soil and water management projects and as cooperative extension service agents, most of them in the Department of Agriculture.

Places of employment and working conditions

Agricultural engineers work mainly in rural areas, and their work is often done out-of-doors.

Qualifications, education, and training

The ability to think analytically, a capacity for details, and the ability to work as part of a team are all necessary. Good communication skills are important.

Mathematics and the sciences must be emphasized in high school.

A bachelor's degree in engineering is the minimum requirement in this field. In a typical curriculum, the first two years are spent in the study of basic sciences such as physics and chemistry and mathematics, introductory engineering, and some liberal arts courses. The remaining years are usually devoted to specialized engineering courses.

Engineering programs can last from four to six years. Those requiring five or six years to complete may award a master's degree or may provide a cooperative plan of study plus practical work experience with a nearby industry.

Because of rapid changes in technology, many agricultural engineers continue their education throughout their careers. A graduate degree is necessary for most teaching and research positions and for many management jobs. Some persons obtain graduate degrees in business administration or in an agricultural field such as soil science or forestry.

All states require licensing of engineers whose work may affect life, health, or property or who offer their services to the public. Those who are licensed, about one-third of all engineers, are called registered engineers. Requirements for licensing include graduation from an accredited engineering school, four years of experience, and an examination.

Potential and advancement

There are only about 8,000 agricultural engineers, and the field is not expected to grow significantly because of poor economic conditions among farmers. But increasing population means a growing demand for agricultural products and an increasing demand for conservation of resources such as soil and water.

Income

Starting salaries in private industry average about $25,700 a year for those with a bachelor's degree. Agricultural engineers with a master's degree earn about $26,000 to $35,000 a year, and those with a Ph.D. earn about $42,000 to $50,000 a year.

Additional sources of information

Accreditation Board for Engineering and Technology
345 East 47th Street
New York, NY 10017

American Society of Agricultural Engineers
2950 Niles Road
St. Joseph, MI 49085-9659

American Society for Engineering Education
11 Dupont Circle
Suite 200
Washington, DC 20036

Junior Engineering Technical Society (JETS)
1420 King Street
Suite 405
Alexandria, VA 22314

National Society of Professional Engineers
1420 King Street
Alexandria, VA 22314

Society of Women Engineers
345 East 47th Street
Room 305
New York, NY 10017

AIR-CONDITIONING, REFRIGERATION, AND HEATING MECHANIC

The job

These skilled workers install, maintain, and repair a large variety of complicated equipment and machinery. They usually specialize in one area of the
field but often work in several. About one out of seven is self-employed.

Air-conditioning and refrigeration mechanics install and repair equipment that
ranges in size from small (a window air conditioner) to very large (a central
air-conditioning system for a large building or the refrigeration system for a
frozen food processor). Following blueprints and design specifications, they
put the components of a system into place—connecting duct work, refrigerant
lines, piping, and electrical power. They are busiest in the spring and summer
months.

Furnace installers install oil, gas, and electrical heating units. They install fuel supply lines, air ducts, pumps, and other components and connect electrical wiring and controls. Most furnace installers, as well as air-conditioning and refrigeration mechanics, are employed by cooling and heating equipment dealers and contractors.

Oil burner mechanics keep oil-fueled heating systems in good operating condition. They are busiest in the fall and winter months. Most of them are employed by fuel oil dealers.

Gas burner mechanics have duties similar to oil burner mechanics. In addition, they also repair stoves, clothes dryers, and hot water heaters that use gas as their fuel. Their busiest seasons are also fall and winter, and most of them are employed by gas utility companies.

Employers try to provide a full workweek year-round, usually by servicing both air-conditioning and heating equipment or by providing inspection and repair services during off-season months. Reduced hours or layoffs may occur during slow periods, however.

Related jobs are appliance repairer, electrician, plumber, and pipefitter.

Places of employment and working conditions

Air-conditioning and refrigeration mechanics and furnace installers work in all parts of the country. Oil burner mechanics are concentrated in areas that use oil as a major heating fuel, which means that more than half of them work in Illinois, Massachusetts, Michigan, New Jersey, New York, and Pennsylvania. About half of all gas burner mechanics work in California, Illinois, Michigan, Ohio, and Texas, where gas is a major heating fuel.

Most air-conditioning, refrigeration, and heating mechanics work a 40-hour week with overtime and irregular hours during peak seasons. Layoffs or shortened workweeks may occur during slow months.

When installing new equipment, mechanics often work at great heights; much of their work is also done in awkward or cramped positions. They are subject to hazards such as electrical shock, burns, and muscle strain from handling heavy equipment.

Qualifications, education, and training

Good physical condition is an absolute necessity in this field since agility and strength are often required for installation and repair work. Mechanical aptitude is also important.

A high school background that includes shop classes and courses in mechanical drawing or blueprint reading, mathematics, physics, or electronics is helpful.

Most air-conditioning, refrigeration, and heating mechanics acquire their skills through on-the-job training; some enter a formal apprenticeship. In either method, training lasts three to five years. Apprentices must also have related classroom instruction in mathematics, blueprint reading, and basic construction and engineering concepts.

Courses lasting two or three years are offered by vocational and technical schools and are often taught by personnel from local firms and organizations, such as the Air Conditioning and Refrigeration Institute or the Petroleum Marketing Education Foundation.

Potential and advancement

There are about 225,000 mechanics in this field at the present time. Employment is expected to increase about as fast as the average for all occupations through the year 2000. Many jobs will be created by economic growth; as new residential, commercial, and industrial structures are built, mechanics will be needed to repair and install climate control systems. Mechanics will also be in demand to replace climate control systems in existing buildings with more modern energy-saving systems. The overall outlook for opportunities in this field are good, but job availability is closely related to trends in the construction industry.

Income

Average weekly earnings for mechanics who are wage and salary workers are about $414.

Apprentices usually begin at about 50 percent of the wage rate paid to experienced mechanics. Their earnings increase as they gain experience and improve their skills.

Additional sources of information

Associated Builders and Contractors
729 15th Street, NW
Washington, DC 20005

National Association of Home Builders
Home Builders Institute
15th and M Streets, NW
Washington, DC 20005

National Association of Plumbing, Heating, and Cooling Contractors
P.O. Box 6808
Falls Church, VA 22046

AIRPLANE MECHANIC

The job

Airplane mechanics perform scheduled maintenance, make repairs, and complete inspections required by the Federal Aviation Administration (FAA).

Many airplane mechanics specialize in either repair work or scheduled maintenance. They specialize further and are licensed as *powerplant mechanics*, who work on the engine; *airframe mechanics*, who work on the wings, landing gear, and structural parts of the plane; or *aircraft inspectors*. Some mechanics specialize in one type of plane or in one section of a plane such as the electrical system.

In the course of their work, airplane mechanics take engines apart; replace worn parts; use x-ray and magnetic inspection equipment; repair sheet metal surfaces; check for rust, distortion, or cracks in wings and fuselages; check electrical connections; repair and replace gauges; and then test all work after completion.

Over three-fifths of all airplane mechanics work for airlines; about one-fifth work for the federal government as civilian mechanics at military air bases. The remainder are employed in general aviation including those who work for airports in small repair shops and for companies that own and operate their own planes.

Mechanics employed by most major airlines belong to either the International Association of Machinists and Aerospace Workers or the Transport Workers Union of America. Some belong to the International Brotherhood of Teamsters, Chauffeurs, Warehousemen and Helpers of America.

Places of employment and working conditions

Airplane mechanics in general aviation work in every part of the country, as do civilians employed by the federal government at military bases. Most airline mechanics work near large cities at airports where the airlines have installations.

Mechanics usually work in hangars or other indoor areas; where repairs must be made quickly, however, they may work outdoors. Work areas are often noisy, and mechanics do a lot of standing, bending, stooping, and climbing.

Qualifications, education, and training

Physical strength, ability, good eyesight and eye-hand coordination, and mechanical aptitude are necessary.

High school courses in mathematics, physics, chemistry, and mechanical drawing are good preparation for this field. Automotive repair or other mechanical work is helpful.

A few airplane mechanics learn through on-the-job training, but most acquire their skills in two-year training programs at FAA-approved trade schools. Those who receive their training in the armed forces attend a shorter trade-school program to familiarize themselves with material specific to civilian aircraft. These schools do not, however, guarantee either a job or an FAA certificate.

Most mechanics who work on civilian aircraft are certificated by the FAA. Applicants for all certificates must pass written and oral tests, give a practical demonstration of their ability to do the work authorized by the particular certificate, and fulfill the experience requirements.

At least 18 months of work experience is required for an airframe, powerplant, or repairman's certificate and 30 months for a combination airframe/powerplant certificate. To obtain an inspector's authorization, a mechanic must first hold a combination certificate for at least three years. Uncertified mechanics must work under the supervision of certified mechanics.

Potential and advancement

There are about 124,000 airplane mechanics. On the whole, this job field is expected to grow steadily. In general aviation, job opportunities should be good. Although pay is often lower, many openings occur as more experienced mechanics move up to the top jobs with private companies or airlines. Competition is keen for airline jobs since the pay scale is high. Federal job opportunities will fluctuate with changes in defense spending.

Advancement to supervisory positions depends on experience and certificates held. Some airplane mechanics advance to executive positions or inspector positions with the FAA. Some open their own maintenance facilities for aircraft.

Income

Airline mechanics average about $26,000 a year. They usually receive the added benefit of reduced airfares for themselves and their family.

Earnings of general aviation mechanics vary greatly depending on the employer and the size of the airport.

Additional sources of information

Aviation Maintenance Foundation
P.O. Box 2826
Redmond, WA 98073

Professional Aviation Maintenance Association
500 Northwest Plaza
Suite 401
St. Ann, MO 63074

AIRPLANE PILOT

The job

Pilots work in facilities from tiny country airfields to the huge international complexes located near large cities. They work as crop dusters, power line inspectors, aerial photographers, charter pilots, or flight instructors. Many work for federal, state, and local governments, and a rapidly growing number work for businesses that own and operate their own company aircraft.

Except on the smallest aircraft, two pilots are usually needed. The more experienced pilot (called *captain* by the airlines) is in command and supervises all other crew members on board. A copilot assists in communicating with air traffic controllers and monitoring instruments in addition to assisting with flying the plane. Most larger airliners carry a third pilot in the cockpit, a flight engineer, who aids the pilots by monitoring and operating instruments, making minor in-flight repairs, and monitoring other traffic.

Before takeoff, the pilot plans the flight carefully, using information on weather en route and at destination. Once decisions are made on route, altitude, and speed, the pilot files the flight plan and notifies air traffic control so that the flight can be coordinated with other air traffic. Pilots also check the plane thoroughly before each flight—testing engines, controls, and instruments.

Takeoff and landing are the most difficult parts of a flight and require close cooperation between pilot and copilot. Once in the air, the flight is relatively easy unless the weather is bad. Pilots steer the plane along the planned route, maintain radio contact with air traffic control stations along the route, and keep close watch on instruments and fuel gauges. In bad weather, pilots can request information on changes in route or altitude from air traffic controllers as they search for better flying conditions. If visibility is poor, pilots must depend on instruments to fly safely over mountains or other obstacles and to land completely "blind" at their destination.

When a flight is over, pilots must file a complete record of the flight with the airline or other employer and with the Federal Aviation Administration (FAA).

Most airline pilots are members of the Air Line Pilots Association, International; one major airline's pilots are members of the Allied Pilots Association.

Places of employment and working conditions

Most pilots work out of the larger airports located in major population centers such as Los Angeles, San Francisco, New York City, Dallas-Fort Worth, Chicago, Miami, and Atlanta.

The mental stress of flying can be tiring, especially for a pilot who is responsible for the safety of passengers and crew.

By law, airline pilots cannot fly more than 100 hours a month or more than 1,000 hours a year; they actually fly an average of 80 hours a month and work an additional 120 hours a month performing nonflying duties. Since most flights involve layovers away from their assigned base, much of the pilots' free time is spent away from home. While pilots are on layover, airlines provide pilots with hotel accommodations and living expense allowances. Pilots with little seniority get the less desirable night and early morning flights.

Pilots employed by other than major airlines often work odd hours and have irregular schedules, perhaps flying 30 hours one month and 90 hours the next. Other nonflying duties add to their work schedule in many instances. Airline pilots have the advantage of large support staffs that handle almost all nonflying duties, but business pilots often make minor plane repairs, schedule and supervise aircraft maintenance, oversee refueling, and load passengers and baggage for proper balance and safety.

Qualifications, education, and training

The FAA regulates the licensing of pilots at all levels of competence and experience. There are about 600 FAA-certified civilian flying schools, including some colleges and universities that offer degree credit for pilot training.

Flying can be learned in either military or civilian flying schools, but service in the armed forces provides an additional opportunity to gain substantial experience on jet aircraft. Airlines and many businesses prefer to hire applicants with this experience.

All pilots who are paid to transport passengers or cargo must have a commercial pilot's license in addition to a pilot's license. The license is issued by the FAA, and to qualify pilots must be at least 18 years old and have at least 250 hours of flight experience. In addition, they must pass a strict physical examination and have 20/20 vision with or without glasses, good hearing, and no physical handicaps that would prevent quick reactions. Applicants for a commercial license must also pass a written examination covering principles of safe flight, navigation, and FAA regulations and demonstrate their flying ability to FAA examiners.

Pilots who want to fly in all types of weather must be licensed by the FAA for instrument flying. To qualify for this license, pilots must have 40 hours of experience flying by instruments, pass a written examination, and demonstrate their ability to fly by instruments.

There are additional FAA requirements for airline pilots. They must pass written and flight examinations to earn a flight engineer's license. Airline captains must also have an airline transport pilot's license. Applicants for this license must be at least 23 years old and have a minimum of 1,500 hours of flying experience, including night and instrument flying.

All licenses are valid so long as a pilot can pass the required physical examinations and the periodic tests of flying skills required by government regulations.

Pilots who apply for airline jobs must be high school graduates. Most airlines also require at least two years of college and prefer to hire those who are college graduates. Airlines give all applicants psychological tests to assess their ability to make the quick decisions and accurate judgments that are part of an airline pilot's job. All new airline pilots receive several weeks of intensive training including classroom instruction and simulator experience before assignment to a flight, usually as flight engineer. Airlines prefer to hire applicants who already have a flight engineer's license but will sometimes train those who have only a commercial license.

Companies other than airlines usually do not require as much experience or formal education, but a commercial license is necessary. Most companies prefer to hire pilots who have experience in the type of plane they will be flying for the company and will generally start them as copilots.

Potential and advancement

There are about 83,000 civilian pilots; about nine out of ten of them work for major airlines. An expected shortage of pilots and projected growth in airline passenger and cargo traffic is creating a great demand for pilots. Employment of pilots will increase much faster than the average for all occupations through the year 2000. These opportunities are available for several reasons. Many pilots who were hired during the last major boom in the airline industry during the 1960s will soon be facing mandatory retirement. The military, once a major supplier of airline pilots, is now offering benefits and financial incentives to retain its pilots. The best opportunities will be for college graduates who have experience flying jet aircraft and have a commercial pilot's license and a flight engineer's license.

Advancement for pilots is generally limited to other flying jobs. As they gain experience and accumulate flying time, they may become flying instructors, fly charter planes, or work for small air transportation firms such as air taxi companies. Some pilots advance to jobs with large companies where they can progress from copilot to pilot and occasionally to chief pilot in charge of aircraft scheduling, maintenance, and flight procedures.

For airline pilots, advancement depends on seniority as established by union contract provisions. It takes two to seven years for a flight engineer to advance to copilot, five to fifteen years to advance from copilot to captain. Choice of the more desirable routes also depends on seniority.

A few specially trained pilots become evaluators, or "check pilots," who test pilots and copilots at least twice a year by flying with them and evaluating their proficiency.

Income

Airline pilots' salaries are among the highest in the nation. The average annual salary for airline pilots is $80,000; for flight engineers, $42,000; for copilots, $65,000; and for captains, $107,000. Earnings depend on type, size, and speed of planes and number of hours and miles flown, with extra pay for night and international flights. In addition, pilots and their families usually are entitled to reduced airfares on their own and other airlines.

Generally, pilots working outside the airlines have lower salaries.

Additional sources of information

For information about job opportunities in companies other than airlines, consult the classified sections of aviation trade magazines or apply to companies that operate aircraft at local airports.

For information on requirements for airline pilots, contact:

Air Line Pilots Association
1625 Massachusetts Avenue, NW
Washington, DC 20036

Air Transport Association of America
1709 New York Avenue, NW
Washington, DC 20006

AIRPORT MANAGER

The job

Whether it is a small local airport or an elaborate complex handling international flights, there has to be an airport manager in charge. An airport manager is responsible for the efficient day-to-day operation of the airport including provisions for aircraft maintenance and fuel, condition and safety of runways and other facilities, budget and personnel, negotiation of leases with airport tenants such as airlines and terminal concessionaires, enforcement of airport and government regulations, record keeping, and public relations.

An airport manager must be familiar with state and federal regulations pertaining to airports and must strive to maintain good relations with local communities. An important part of the job is making local businesses and industries aware of the services available at the airport. In an airport operated by a local government agency, the airport manager may be responsible for reporting to a variety of boards or committees.

At a small installation, the owner-operator may handle all duties, while at a large airport the manager, or director, is assisted by a number of specialists, each of whom is responsible for specific areas of airport operation.

An *assistant airport director* assists the director or manager with administrative responsibilities and may be in charge of public relations, maintenance, personnel, or tenant relations. An *engineer* handles maintenance of runways, terminal buildings, hangars, and grounds. The engineer oversees new construction, handles real estate and zoning matters, and administers Federal Aid to Airports programs.

An important position at all but the smallest airports is that of *fixed based operator (FBO)*. At owner-operated airports, the manager may fulfill this function personally, but at other airports it is handled by a retail firm employing from one or two people to several hundred. The FBO provides (sells) general aviation products and/or services at an airport. This can include aircraft repair services, flight training, aircraft sales, fuel and spare parts, air taxi service, and charter flights.

Places of employment and working conditions

Airport managers are employed throughout the United States in airports of all sizes. The most job opportunities are in California, Florida, Illinois, Indiana, Michigan, Missouri, New York, Ohio, Pennsylvania, and Texas.

In a small airport, the manager usually works long hours, many of them outdoors. At large facilities, the manager usually works regular hours, in an office, but is on call for emergency situations. Managers do some traveling in the course of their work as they negotiate with airport tenants, such as airlines, or when they appear before state and federal regulatory agencies. Community activities and meetings usually require some evening hours.

Qualifications, education, and training

Leadership qualities, tact, initiative, good judgment, and the ability to get along with people are important qualities. Managers of airports with airline service usually need a college degree in airport management, business or public administration, or aeronautical or civil engineering. Colleges and universities that offer these degrees sometimes offer flight training as well.

At smaller airports, experience as a fixed base operator or superintendent of maintenance plus a pilot's license are often sufficient for the position of airport manager.

Potential and advancement

There are approximately 13,000 airports of various sizes in the United States. Substantial growth is expected in this field as existing airports are enlarged and new ones built to handle increased passenger travel, air cargo tonnage, and general aviation activity.

The present heavy air traffic at major airports, which creates takeoff and landing delays, is expected to lead to the construction of a network of smaller satellite airports to service general aviation aircraft and helicopters that will ferry passengers to and from the major airports. Both airport managers and fixed based operators will be in demand for these new facilities.

Advancement in this field usually takes the form of moving to a larger airport with more complex responsibilities. Some airport managers move up to state or federal positions in regulatory agencies.

Income

Earnings range from about $18,000 at a small general aviation airport to over $63,000 at a major international airport.

Additional sources of information

Airport Operators Council International
1700 K Street, NW
Washington, DC 20036

Office of General Aviation
Federal Aviation Administration
Washington, DC 20591

AIR TRAFFIC CONTROLLER

The job

The safe and efficient operation of the nation's airways and airports is the responsibility of air traffic controllers. They coordinate all flight activities to prevent accidents. Some regulate airport traffic; others regulate planes in flight between airports.

Airport traffic controllers monitor all planes in and around an airport. Planes that are not visible from the control tower are monitored on a radar screen. When the airport is busy, controllers fit the planes into a holding pattern with other planes waiting to land. The controller must keep track of all planes in the holding pattern while guiding them in for landings and instructing other planes for takeoffs.

After a plane departs the airport, the airport traffic controller notifies the appropriate *enroute controller*. There are 24 enroute control centers in the United States where enroute controllers work in teams of two or three. Each team is assigned a specific amount of airspace along one of the designated routes generally flown by all airplanes.

Before taking off, each pilot files a flight plan that is sent by teletype to the appropriate control center. When a plane enters a team's airspace, one member of the team will communicate with the pilot by radio and monitor the flight path on radar. This controller will provide information on weather, nearby planes, and other hazards and can approve and monitor such things as altitude changes.

All civilian air traffic controllers work for the Federal Aviation Administration (FAA), most of them at major airports and air traffic control centers located near large cities. Military and naval air installations use their own personnel as air traffic controllers, and many civilian controllers acquire their skills during military service.

There are very few women air traffic controllers. Aviation has always been a male-dominated field, and many air traffic controllers come from the ranks of civilian and military pilots, navigators, and controllers. As more women become pilots, they will have the required experience and background to move into jobs as air traffic controllers.

Places of employment and working conditions

Air traffic controllers work at civilian and military installations throughout the country, but most of them work at main airports and air traffic control centers near large cities.

Because control towers and centers operate around the clock, seven days a week, controllers work night and weekend shifts on a rotating basis. They work under great stress because they usually have several planes under their control at one time. They must make quick decisions that affect the safety of many people.

Qualifications, education, and training

Potential controllers need a decisive personality, since they must make quick decisions; and they should be articulate, since instruction to pilots must be given quickly and clearly. A quick and retentive memory is a must as is the ability to work under pressure and to function calmly in an emergency.

Air traffic controller trainees are selected through the federal civil service system. Applicants must be under 31 years of age, in excellent health, and have vision correctable to 20/20. They must pass a written examination that measures their ability to learn and their aptitude for the work. In addition, applicants must have three years of general work experience or four years of college or a combination of both. Applicants with experience as military controllers, pilots, or navigators can improve their test rating by scoring well on the occupational knowledge portion of the examination. Passing a drug screening test is also a requirement for applicants.

Trainees receive 11 to 13 weeks of intensive on-the-job training combined with formal training. They learn the fundamentals of the airway system, federal aviation regulations, aircraft performance characteristics, and the use of controller equipment. Their training also includes practice on simulators at the FAA Academy in Oklahoma City.

After training, it usually takes several years of progressively more responsible work experience to become a fully qualified controller.

A yearly physical examination is required of all controllers, and they must pass a job performance examination twice a year. Drug screening is also a condition of continued employment.

Potential and advancement

There are about 24,000 air traffic controllers.

Competition for air traffic controller jobs will be stiff through the year 2000; the number of applicants is expected to exceed the number of openings. Employment in this field is expected to grow about as fast as the average for all occupations through the year 2000. The need for air traffic controllers during the 1990s will be reduced because of the introduction of a new air traffic control system that will involve the use of a computer radar network; this network will perform many of the tasks now performed by air traffic controllers.

Controllers can advance by transferring to different locations and larger airports. In installations with a number of air traffic controllers, experienced controllers can advance to supervisory positions. Some advance to management jobs in air traffic control or to administrative jobs in the FAA.

Income

The average salary for controllers is about $38,200. Trainees earn about $19,500 a year. Air traffic controllers receive overtime pay or equal time off for any hours worked over 40 hours per week.

Depending on length of service, controllers receive 13 to 26 days of paid vacation and 13 days of paid sick leave each year; they also receive life insurance, health benefits, and a retirement program. Because of the stress of this occupation, the retirement program is more liberal than for other federal employees.

Additional sources of information

A pamphlet on air traffic controllers is available from any U.S. Office of Personnel Management Job Information Center. To find the telephone number of your local Job Information Center, look in your telephone book under U.S. Government, Office of Personnel Management. If there is no listing in your telephone book, dial the toll-free number 800-555-1212 and request the number of the Office of Personnel Management Job Information Center in your area.

APPLIANCE REPAIRER

The job

Appliance repairers service the many laborsaving appliances in use in just about every home today. These include stoves and ovens, washing machines and dryers, dishwashers, refrigerators and freezers, and small appliances. Appliance repairers usually specialize in one or two of these items.

Large appliances are usually serviced in the customers' homes, while small appliances or parts from large appliances may be taken back to a repair shop by the appliance repairer.

Most appliance repairers work in independent appliance stores and repair shops. Others work for service centers operated by appliance manufacturers, department stores, and utility companies. Every community also has its share of appliance repairers who conduct their own small independent businesses.

In addition to servicing appliances, the repairer sometimes gives instruction in the correct use and care of an appliance; prepares estimates of repair costs; keeps records of service, parts, and working time on each job; and may be responsible for collecting payment for completed work.

Related jobs are air-conditioning, refrigeration, and heating mechanic; television and radio service technician; business machine service technician.

Places of employment and working conditions

Appliance repairers work in just about every community with the highest concentrations in highly populated areas.

Those who work in repair shops usually work in quiet, well-lighted areas. Repairers who work on the customers' premises must sometimes work in cramped or dusty areas and often spend several hours a day in travel. Repairers are subject to electrical hazards and muscle strain from moving large appliances.

Independent appliance repairers must supply their own tools, equipment, truck, and parts inventory.

Qualifications, education, and training

Anyone interested in this field should have mechanical aptitude and manual dexterity. The ability to work independently is important, and a pleasant personality is an asset when dealing with customers.

High school shop classes in electricity are helpful as are mechanical drawing and mechanics.

Some appliance repairers acquire their skills in other jobs and then transfer into appliance repair. Although formal training in appliance repair is available from some vocational and technical schools and community colleges, additional on-the-job training is also necessary to become fully qualified.

In companies that repair major appliances, trainees start as helpers and accompany experienced repairers as they make house calls. Those who work in repair shops learn basic skills by repairing and rebuilding increasingly more complicated appliances or parts. Trainees receive supplementary training by attending one- and two-week courses conducted by appliance manufacturers. Some large companies, such as department store chains, have formal training programs that include shop classes and home study courses.

Experienced appliance repairers attend manufacturers' training courses periodically to keep up with the changes in the field.

Potential and advancement

There are about 79,000 appliance repairers. Most work in retail trade establishments such as department stores, household appliance stores, and dealers that sell or service appliances and power tools. Other employers are gas and electric utility companies, wholesalers, and electrical repair shops. About one out of ten repairers is self-employed.

Little or no change is expected in the employment of appliance repairers through the year 2000. Although the number of appliances used is expected to increase with the number of households, advanced technology will reduce the need for repairs.

Appliance repairers who work in large shops or for service centers may be promoted to supervisor or service manager. A few may advance to management positions such as regional service manager or parts manager for appliance manufacturers.

Income

Earnings of appliance repairers vary according to skill level, geographic location, and the type of equipment serviced. For experienced repairers, average yearly salaries range from $15,000 to $24,000. Trainees earn less and more experienced repairers earn more. In general, repairers earning the highest salaries are those who work for large firms or service gas appliances.

Additional sources of information

Local appliance repair shops, appliance dealers, chain stores, and utility companies can provide information about job opportunities. Local technical and vocational schools can provide information on courses available.

Other information about training programs or work opportunities is also available from:

Appliance Service News
P.O. Box 789
Lombard, IL 60148

ARCHITECT

The job

An architect designs buildings and other structures—anything from a private home to a large office building or an entire city's redevelopment.

The architect must oversee all phases of the project from initial idea to completed structure. He or she must solve complex technical problems while retaining artistic design and must be able to function in a highly competitive atmosphere.

After discussing ideas, needs, and concepts with the client, the architect prepares preliminary drawings and then detailed plans for the project including the plumbing, electrical, and heating systems. He or she must specify materials that comply with local building regulations and must stay within the client's budget.

All through this process, the architect may have to make changes at the request of the client. Once plans are ready and approved, the architect may help the client select a contractor and will continue to check the work while it is in progress to ensure that all design specifications are being carried out. The architect's responsibility does not end until the structure is completed and has successfully passed all required inspections.

Architects can work in salaried positions for architectural firms or they can go into private practice. Those who decide to open their own businesses usually begin their careers with a few years in salaried positions to accumulate experience.

Most architects are employed by architectural firms, building contractors, and community planning and redevelopment authorities. A few architects work for government agencies such as the Department of Defense, Housing and Urban Development, and the General Services Administration.

Only about 10 percent of all architects are women, but about 22 percent of the new degrees being awarded in architecture now go to women. Because this is a field where part-time practice is possible and since architects often work from their homes, the field has advantages for people with family responsibilities. There is, however, a wide salary inequality between men and women in architecture.

Related fields are building contractor, urban planner, landscape architect.

Places of employment and working conditions

Architects are employed throughout the country, in towns and cities of all sizes. A large proportion of all architectural work, however, is concentrated in Boston, Chicago, Los Angeles, New York City, Philadelphia, San Francisco, and Washington, D.C.

Architects generally work in comfortable offices and spend much of their time advising clients, developing reports and drawings, and working with other architects and engineers. They sometimes must put in overtime to meet deadlines. Once building is under way, they spend a great deal of time outdoors inspecting the progress of construction.

Qualifications, education, and training

Architecture requires a wide variety of technical, artistic, and social skills. Anyone planning a career in this field should be able to work independently, have a capacity for solving technical problems, and be artistic. Good business skills are also helpful.

High school students interested in architecture should take courses in mathematics, physics, and art. Summer jobs with architects or building contractors can provide useful experience.

There are several types of degrees granted in architecture. Most architecture degrees are from five-year bachelor of architecture programs intended for students continuing their education after high school. Another type of bachelor of architecture program requires three to four years and is for students with a prior degree in another discipline. There are also two master of architecture programs; these require two years for students with undergraduate degrees in

47

architecture or a related area and three to four years for students with a degree in another discipline. Courses typically include architectural theory, design, graphics, engineering, urban planning, English, mathematics, chemistry, sociology, economics, and a foreign language.

Although many architects work without a license, all states require that a licensed architect take the final legal responsibility for a completed project. To qualify for the licensing examination, the applicant must have a bachelor's degree plus three years of experience in an architect's office and pass all sections of the Architect Registration Examination.

Potential and advancement

There are approximately 86,000 architects at present, most of them in large cities. Prospects for employment in architecture are expected to be good through the year 2000, but opportunities depend upon the number of degrees being granted and the rise and fall of the building market. Competition is expected to be keen for jobs with the most prestigious firms. Most openings will occur in architectural firms, but some jobs will also be available in government agencies and in colleges and universities.

New graduates usually begin as assistants in architectural firms. Their tasks include helping in the preparation of architectural documents or drawings, researching building codes and materials, and writing specifications. Experienced architects may be promoted to supervisory or management positions in large firms. Some may become partners in firms, while others set up their own firms.

Income

Salaries for experienced architects average about $32,000 a year. The top 10 percent earn more than $51,700, and the bottom 10 percent earn less than $19,500.

Architects in private practice usually go through a period with high expenses and low income. Once a practice is established, partners earn much more than their salaried employees, but income will fluctuate with the cyclical changes in the construction industry.

Additional sources of information

The American Institute of Architects
1735 New York Avenue, NW
Washington, DC 20006

The Association of Collegiate Schools of Architecture, Inc.
1735 New York Avenue, NW
Washington, DC 20006

The National Council of Architectural Registration Boards
1735 New York Avenue, NW
Suite 700
Washington, DC 20006

ATHLETE, PROFESSIONAL

The job

One of the most difficult aspects of the move from amateur or college sports to the world of professional sports for many players is the change in attitude from sports as a game to sports as big business. The drive to get to the top and the constant pressure to stay there can prove disillusioning to some players.

Athletes who reach the professional teams usually developed their interest in sports at an early age. By the time they reach high school, they have usually already decided on a particular sport as their favorite or the one they are best at playing.

Professional teams recruit most of their players from among the top-notch college players. A few are hired from industrial and business leagues, the military, and from minor and semipro teams. On rare occasions, an exceptional player is hired right out of high school.

Women as professional athletes have appeared mostly in golf. Women also play professional tennis and basketball and are securing a limited number of positions as professional jockeys. Although there are some regional women's softball leagues, they have never developed into a money-making professional status.

49

Places of employment and working conditions

In general, many professional athletes face the possibility of being traded or dropped, and older players are constantly pressured by talented newcomers. Injuries are always a danger, and, for the most part, the active playing years are limited to the early 20s through the mid-30s. Only golfers play longer.

Travel is a constant necessity during the playing season with very little time off for personal life and family. Rigorous training schedules, the need to be in top physical form, and the strict training rules and curfews of some coaches are a hardship for some players.

In baseball, spring training starts in February or March. The playing schedule of one or two games a day with occasional travel days lasts until October.

Football players report to training camp in July for eight or nine weeks. Fourteen weekly games make up the playing season, and bowl games can extend the season into January.

Basketball training starts in September or October. Three or four games a week, for a total of 82 to 84 games, make up the regular season with a possible 4 to 21 postseason games.

Professional hockey players train in September and play from October to May. Soccer season is traditionally from April through August, but an indoor season from January to March is becoming popular in the United States.

Golfers manage to play a major part of the year because they follow the sun. Tennis players participate in tournaments year-round.

Qualifications, education, and training

Competitiveness, top playing skills, physical stamina, strength, good eyesight and hearing, self-discipline, and the ability to work as part of a team are all necessary for a professional athlete. Quick reflexes, concentration, timing, and speed are also necessary in most sports.

High school athletic training is very important. Good coaching at this level develops basic skills and physical condition and introduces the player to the regimen of exercise, dieting, practice, and training that will be necessary throughout a professional career. Good coaching in high school also increases the player's chances for a college scholarship.

Although a college education is not required to play professionally, college does offer some unique advantages. College-level coaching refines and upgrades the skills developed in high school. There is greater emphasis on technique and application of skills. College games usually reach a wider audience including scouts from professional teams.

The biggest advantage of a college education is the opportunity to prepare for an alternative lifetime career. Not every talented player reaches the professional teams, and even those who do have a limited playing career. Not everyone gets to be a coach or a celebrity who earns a lifetime living as a result of sports fame.

Potential and advancement

Only a very few make it to the top professional teams. Even those who do can play for only a limited time. Athletes who have college training can move into fields such as radio, television, and journalism after they retire. Others open restaurants or sporting goods stores or work for community recreation departments.

Other opportunities exist in local amateur, semipro, and industrial leagues. Talented college players may fill openings for coaching positions in small colleges or secondary schools, some of which require teaching certification.

Professional athletes may also move into coaching and management positions after their professional playing careers end.

Income

Well-publicized three- and five-year contracts of several million dollars or more, earned by a few superstars, are few and far between. However, many athletes are well paid. Salaries range from $18,000 to well over $1 million a year.

Salaries in individual sports vary a great deal. Athletes earn their income by participating in tournaments and meets. Usually only the top players in sports such as golfing, boxing, and horse racing earn high salaries.

Many professional athletes earn additional income through endorsements and personal appearances. Many also have businesses that they operate during off-season months.

Additional sources of information

National Association of Professional Baseball Leagues
P.O. Box A
St. Petersburg, FL 33731

National Basketball Association
645 5th Avenue
New York, NY 10022

National Football League
410 Park Avenue
New York, NY 10022

ATHLETIC COACH

The job

A coach must be a leader who can draw out the talent of each individual player and, at the same time, mold the players into an effective team. A good coach uses sports as a means of developing the personal qualities as well as the physical abilities of the athletes he or she coaches.

Most athletic coaches are employed in secondary schools where they are regular members of the faculty. They usually teach physical education classes and some classroom subjects and may coach several different sports.

Athletic coaches are also employed by colleges, professional teams, and, in a few instances, by elementary schools. Colleges, professional teams, and large high schools employ one or more assistant coaches as well as a head coach.

A coach is usually an experienced player in the sport he or she coaches. The coach must be able to teach the finer points of the sport, direct the physical training of the team members, judge abilities and personalities, plan game strategy and playing schedules, and, in some instances, function as a substitute parent. In addition, a coach should be able to administer first aid in emergency situations.

New laws that require equality for women in school sports programs have resulted in a substantial increase in athletic programs and scholarships for women athletes. Because high school sports for girls has grown especially fast in the past few years, the need for qualified women coaches should remain high for some time.

Places of employment and working conditions

Athletic coaches work throughout the country with the most job opportunities in metropolitan areas large enough to support a number of secondary schools.

Working conditions vary depending on the employer. In a sports-minded community, a coach will usually have modern equipment and a liberal budget; in other areas, a tight budget and poor facilities. During the sports season, a coach's life can be hectic, but this is offset by the fact that coaches have the summer months free.

Qualifications, education, and training

Coaches need physical stamina and good health and, of course, must possess athletic ability. They should like to work with young people and possess qualities of honesty and fair play.

High school courses should include English, public speaking, biology, and sports. Volunteer work or a part-time job at a summer camp or community center can provide valuable experience.

In college, a physical education major plus experience in competitive sports at the varsity level are considered the minimum requirement. A graduate of a small college who has varsity experience will find it easier to get a job than the physical education major from a big university who lacks varsity experience.

Most states require high school coaches to be certified teachers and some require them to be certified coaches. Coaches who wish to maximize their job opportunities usually have at least one additional area besides coaching in which they can receive certification, since budget restrictions in some schools require that the athletic coach be able to fill a teaching position as well.

Potential and advancement

Over 100,000 athletic coaches are employed in the United States. The demand for qualified coaches should increase in the next decade because of population growth and the increase in athletic opportunities for girls and women.

Coaches usually advance by moving to larger schools or colleges as they build a reputation for turning out winning teams. In large schools, a coach can be promoted to athletic director or move into educational administration as a school principal or superintendent. As they reach the end of their peak physical years, some coaches prefer to move into related fields such as sportswriting, physical rehabilitation, or sporting goods sales. Some become managers or owners of health centers or summer camps.

Income

High school and college coaches earn salaries ranging from about $20,000 to $44,000 a year. Many coaches earn extra salaries for their coaching responsibilities, depending on the sport and the amount of time involved. Top colleges pay their coaches $60,000 a year or more. Top professional coaches earn up to $300,000 a year.

Additional sources of information

American Alliance for Health, Physical Education, and Recreation
1900 Association Drive
Reston, VA 22091

National High School Athletic Coaches Association
P.O. Box 1808
Ocala, FL 32678

AUTOMOTIVE MECHANIC

The job

One of the disadvantages of automobile ownership is that cars require maintenance and, sometimes, repairs to keep them operating. Automotive mechanics are workers who have the skills to provide repair and maintenance service for cars and light trucks, such as vans and pickups, with gasoline engines.

Mechanics' first task is to diagnose the vehicle's problem. They first discuss the symptoms with the owner or with the worker who wrote the repair order. Then they may test-drive the vehicle or use testing equipment such as engine analyzers, spark plug testers, or compression gauges to determine the problem.

Once mechanics have determined what the problem is, they make any repairs or adjustments that are necessary. They sometimes have to replace damaged parts.

Automotive mechanics also provide regular maintenance service. This includes inspecting, lubricating, and adjusting the engine and other parts and replacing parts that are damaged.

In large automotive repair shops, mechanics often specialize in the types of repairs they perform such as automatic transmissions, air conditioning, front-end alignment, brakes, and radiators.

Places of employment and working conditions

Automotive mechanics work for automotive dealers, independent automotive repair shops, and gasoline service stations. Other employers are automotive repair centers at department, automotive, and home supply stores; taxicab and auto leasing companies; and federal, state, and local governments.

Automotive mechanics usually work indoors, and some repair shops are drafty and noisy. Mechanics often have to work with dirty, greasy parts in awkward positions. They are sometimes subject to minor injuries.

Mechanics usually work 40 hours a week, but self-employed mechanics may work more.

Qualifications, education, and training

While some automotive mechanics learn their skills on the job, the increasing complexity and sophistication of automotive technology is making it necessary for mechanics to complete a formal training program after graduating from high school.

Training programs are offered in high schools, community colleges, and public and private vocational and technical schools. Trade and technical school programs usually last six months to a year, and community college programs are spread out over two years. The course is made up of a combination of hands-on practice and classroom instruction.

Some automobile manufacturers and their participating dealers also offer training programs. They sponsor associate's degree programs at community colleges throughout the country. Because these programs combine classroom instruction with actual work experience, they usually take four years to complete.

Beginners usually start as trainee mechanics, helpers, lubrication workers, or service station attendants and develop and learn skills by working with experienced mechanics. It usually takes one to two years to become a journeyman service mechanic except for those who graduate from the better formal mechanic training programs; they often achieve this level after a few months. To become knowledgeable and experienced with all types of repairs takes another one to two years. Difficult specialties may take another one or two years of training and experience.

Automotive mechanics continue to receive training throughout their careers. They are sometimes sent by their employers to factory training centers to learn to repair new models or receive special training.

Potential and advancement

There are currently about 771,000 automotive mechanics. Employment opportunities should be good for graduates of formal training programs. Workers without formal training will face competition for entry-level jobs.

Experienced mechanics may advance to supervisory or managerial positions. Some mechanics advance by opening their own shops.

Income

The most skilled, experienced automotive mechanics earn hourly wages of $17.40; those who are less skilled and perform routine repairs, $12.40; and those who are only semiskilled, $8.70.

Additional sources of information

Automotive Service Association, Inc.
P.O. Box 929
Bedford, TX 76021-0929

Automotive Service Industry Association
444 North Michigan Avenue
Chicago, IL 60611

National Automotive Technicians Education Foundation
13505 Dulles Technology Drive
Herndon, VA 22071-3415

B

BANK OFFICER

The job

Bank officers are responsible for carrying out the policy set by the board of directors of the bank and for overseeing the day-to-day operations of all the banking departments. A thorough knowledge of business and economics is necessary plus expertise in the specialized banking area for which each officer is responsible.

Bank officers and their responsibilities include: *loan officer*, who evaluates the credit and collateral of individuals and businesses applying for loans; *trust officer*, who administers estates and trusts, manages property, invests funds for customers, and provides financial counseling; *operations officer*, who plans and coordinates procedures and systems; *branch manager*, who is responsible for all functions of a branch office; *international officer*, who handles financial dealings abroad or for foreign customers; and *cashier*, who is responsible for all bank property. Other officers handle auditing, personnel administration, public relations, and operations research. In small banks there may be only a few officers, each of whom handles several functions or departments.

A related job is credit manager.

Places of employment and working conditions

Bank officers are employed in towns and cities of all sizes throughout the country.

Bank officers are usually involved in the civic and business affairs of their communities and are often called upon to serve as directors of local companies and community organizations. This can entail evenings spent away from home attending meetings and functions related to these positions.

Qualifications, education, and training

The ability to inspire confidence in others is a necessary characteristic of a successful bank officer. Officers should also display tact and good judgment in dealing with customers and employees. The ability to work independently and to analyze information is also important.

High school students interested in banking should study mathematics and take any available courses in economics.

Potential bank officers usually start their careers at a bank by entering the bank's management training program after graduation from college. Occasionally, outstanding clerks and tellers work their way up the ladder through promotions and are also accepted into these training programs, but the usual background is a college degree.

The ideal preparation for the banking officer has been described as a bachelor's degree in social science along with a master of business administration degree. A business administration degree with a major in finance or a liberal arts degree with courses in accounting, economics, commercial law, political science, and statistics are also good college backgrounds.

Potential and advancement

Employment is expected to increase substantially. Banking is one of the fastest-growing industries in the economy; expanding bank services and the increased use of computers will continue to require trained personnel in all areas of banking.

It usually takes many years of experience to advance to senior officer and management positions. Experience in several banking departments, as well as continuing education in management-sponsored courses, can aid and accelerate promotion.

Income

Income varies, with banks in large cities paying more than those in small towns.

Management trainees usually earn about $19,000 a year. Those with an M.B.A. degree can command starting salaries of $27,000 a year. Senior bank officers earn annual salaries of $60,000 or more.

Additional sources of information

American Bankers Association
Bank Personnel Division
1120 Connecticut Avenue, NW
Washington, DC 20036

Board of Governors
The Federal Reserve System
Personnel Department
Washington, DC 20551

Federal Deposit Insurance Corporation
Director of Personnel
550 17th Street, NW
Washington, DC 20429

National Association of Bank Women, Inc.
National Office
500 North Michigan Avenue
Suite 1400
Chicago, IL 60611

National Bankers Association
122 C Street, NW
Suite 240
Washington, DC 20001

BANK TELLER

The job

Bank tellers are the most visible employees of a bank and should project an efficient, pleasant, and dependable image, both for themselves and for their employer. Tellers cash checks, handle deposits and withdrawals, sell savings bonds and travelers' checks, keep records, and handle paperwork. In the course of this work, they must be thorough and accurate in checking identification, verifying accounts and money amounts, and counting out money to customers. At the end of their working day, all transactions must balance.

Some opportunities for part-time teller work exist in larger banks. These extra tellers are used during peak banking hours and on peak banking days.

Places of employment and working conditions

Bank tellers work in all areas of the country, in communities of all sizes.

In small banks, tellers usually perform a variety of duties, while in large banks they work in one specialty area. Boredom can be a problem in some of the clerical functions, and some bank tellers object to the close supervision that is part of their working atmosphere.

Tellers stand on their feet during much of their workday; anyone who does not like to be confined to a small space might find the teller cages of some banks unpleasant.

Qualifications, education, and training

Personal qualities of honesty and integrity are necessary for a job in banking. A fondness for working with numbers, attention to detail, and the ability to work as part of a closely supervised team are essential. Tellers should have a pleasant personality and like to work with people.

A high school diploma is adequate preparation for entry-level jobs, especially if the applicant has had courses in typing, bookkeeping, office machine operation, and business arithmetic.

Tellers receive anywhere from a few days to three weeks or more of training and spend some time observing an experienced teller before handling any work on their own.

Bank training courses are available to all bank employees throughout their working years. Employees who avail themselves of these courses can advance by gaining new skills. The successful completion of specific banking courses can lead to promotion.

Potential and advancement

There are about 522,000 bank tellers. The increased use of automatic teller machines and other electronic equipment will result in relatively slow employment growth in the number of bank tellers needed through the year 2000. In general, there will be slow employment growth in commercial, stock, and mutual savings banks and loan associations, the major employers of tellers. However, there should be good opportunities for qualified applicants. Part-time tellers are in demand for busy periods, and the banking industry traditionally has a large turnover.

Income

The banking industry has traditionally paid lower salaries than many other industries, and this trend has not changed in recent years.

Important factors determining salaries are range of responsibilities, experience, length of service, and the location and size of the bank. The median annual salary for full-time bank tellers is $12,800, with the lowest 10 percent earning about $9,200 and the top 10 percent earning $20,300.

Additional sources of information

American Bankers Association
1120 Connecticut Avenue, NW
Washington, DC 20036

American League of Financial Institutions
1709 New York Avenue, NW
Suite 201
Washington, DC 20006

BIOCHEMIST

The job

Biochemists study the chemical composition and behavior of living things and the effects of food, drugs, hormones, and other chemicals on various organisms. Their work is essential to a better understanding of health, growth, reproduction, and heredity in human beings and to progress in the fields of medicine, nutrition, and agriculture.

Most biochemists are involved in basic research; those engaged in applied research use the results of basic research to solve practical problems. For example, basic research into how an organism forms a hormone has been used to synthesize and produce hormones on a mass scale.

Laboratory research can involve weighing, filtering, distilling, and culturing specimens or the operation of electron microscopes and centrifuges. Biochemists sometimes design new laboratory apparatus or develop new techniques to carry out specific research projects.

About half of all biochemists are employed in colleges and universities, where they combine their research work with teaching positions. Other job opportunity fields for biochemists are the drug, insecticide, and cosmetic industries and nonprofit research foundations and government agencies in the areas of health and agriculture.

Places of employment and working conditions

Biochemists are employed in all regions of the country, mainly in areas where chemical, food, and drug industries and colleges and universities are located.

Laboratory work can involve the handling of dangerous or unpleasant substances. Biochemists involved in research projects may work irregular or extended hours during certain phases of a project.

Qualifications, education, and training

Keen powers of observation, a curious mind, patience and perseverance, mechanical aptitude, and good communication skills are among the abilities necessary for the biochemist. Anyone planning a career in this field should be able to work either independently or as part of a team.

An advanced degree is the minimum required, even for many beginning jobs in this field. The prospective biochemist should begin with an undergraduate degree in chemistry, biology, or biochemistry, which will also involve courses in mathematics and physics.

A Ph.D. degree is almost mandatory for anyone who hopes to do significant biochemical research or advance to management and administrative levels. This degree requires extensive original research and the writing of a thesis.

Potential and advancement

Job prospects in the next ten years are expected to be very good, as a result of efforts to cure major diseases, concern for the safety of food and drug products, and public awareness of environmental and pollution problems. Biochemists will also be needed in the drug manufacturing industry, in hospitals and health centers, in colleges and universities, and in federal regulatory agencies.

Beginners in biochemistry jobs usually start work as technicians or assistants doing testing and analysis. They may advance, through increased experience and education, to positions that involve planning and supervising research. Positions in administration and management can be achieved by those with experience and advanced degrees, but many prefer to remain in the laboratory—doing biochemical research.

Income

Salaries for experienced biochemists in industry average $25,000 to $42,000 a year for those with a bachelor's degree or master's degree and $39,000 to $61,000 with a Ph.D.

Biochemists employed by colleges and universities receive salaries comparable to other faculty members, with average salaries much lower than in industry.

Additional sources of information

American Society for Biochemistry and Molecular Biology
9650 Rockville Pike
Bethesda, MD 20814

BIOMEDICAL ENGINEER

The job

Biomedical engineers apply engineering principles to medical and health-related problems.

Most engineers in this field are involved in research. They work with life scientists, chemists, and members of the medical profession to design and develop medical devices such as artificial hearts, pacemakers, dialysis machines, and lasers for surgery. Others work for private industry in the development, design, and sales of medical instruments and devices.

Biomedical engineers with computer expertise adapt computers to medical needs and design and build systems to modernize laboratory and clinical procedures. Some work for the National Aeronautics and Space Administration developing life support and medical monitoring systems for astronauts.

Places of employment and working conditions

Some phases of this work may be unpleasant when working with certain illnesses or medical conditions.

Qualifications, education, and training

The ability to think analytically, a capacity for details, and the ability to work as part of a team are all necessary. Good communication skills are important.

Mathematics and the sciences must be emphasized in high school. A bachelor's degree in engineering is the minimum requirement in this field. In a typical curriculum, the first two years are spent in the study of basic sciences such as physics and chemistry and mathematics, introductory engineering, and some liberal arts courses. The remaining years are usually devoted to specialized engineering courses. For this field that means a sound background in mechanical, electrical, industrial, or chemical engineering plus additional specialized biomedical training.

Engineering programs can last from four to six years. Those that require five or six years to complete may award a master's degree or may provide a cooperative plan of study plus practical work experience with a nearby industry.

All states require licensing of engineers whose work may affect life, health, or property or who offer their services to the public. Those who are licensed, about one-third of all engineers, are called registered engineers. Requirements for licensing include graduation from an accredited engineering school, four years of experience, and an examination.

Potential and advancement

There are only about 4,000 biomedical engineers. Substantial growth is expected, but, since the field is relatively small, few actual job openings will occur. Those with advanced degrees will have the best job opportunities.

Income

Starting salaries in private industry average $25,000 a year with a master's degree and $32,000 or more with a Ph.D.

Additional sources of information

Accreditation Board for Engineering and Technology
345 East 47th Street
New York, NY 10017

Alliance for Engineering in Medicine and Biology
1101 Connecticut Avenue, NW
Suite 700
Washington, DC 20036

American Society for Engineering Education
11 Dupont Circle, NW
Suite 200
Washington, DC 20036

Biomedical Engineering Society
P.O. Box 2399
Culver City, CA 90230

Junior Engineering Technical Society (JETS)
1420 King Street
Suite 405
Alexandria, VA 22314

National Society of Professional Engineers
1420 King Street
Alexandria, VA 22314

Society of Women Engineers
345 East 47th Street
Room 305
New York, NY 10017

BROADCAST TECHNICIAN

The job

The operation and maintenance of the electronic equipment used to record and transmit radio and television programs is the responsibility of broadcast technicians, also called broadcast engineers.

In small stations, broadcast technicians perform a variety of duties. In large stations and in networks, technicians are more specialized. They may perform any or all of the following functions.

Transmitter technicians monitor and log (keep records of) outgoing signals and are responsible for transmitter operation. *Maintenance technicians* set up, maintain, and repair the broadcasting equipment. *Audio control technicians* regulate sound; *video control technicians* regulate the quality of television pictures; and *lighting technicians* direct the lighting. *Recording technicians* operate and maintain sound recording equipment, while *video recording technicians* operate and maintain video tape recording equipment. When programs originate outside of a radio or television station, *field technicians* set up and operate the broadcasting equipment.

Radio stations usually employ only a few broadcast technicians, three to ten, depending on the size and broadcasting schedule of the station. Television broadcasting is more complex, and television stations usually employ between 10 and 30 technicians in addition to supervisory personnel.

Related jobs are drafters, engineering and science technicians, and surveyors.

Places of employment and working conditions

Broadcast technicians are employed in all areas of the United States, especially in large metropolitan areas. The highest paid and most specialized jobs are in Los Angeles, New York City, Chicago, and Washington, D.C., where most network programs originate.

In large stations, broadcast technicians work a 40-hour week. In smaller stations, the workweek is usually longer. In stations that broadcast 24 hours a day, seven days a week, some weekend, evening, and holiday work is necessary. Network technicians covering an important event often have to work continuously and under great pressure until the event is over.

Qualifications, education, and training

Manual dexterity, good eyesight and hearing, reliability, and the ability to work as part of a team are all requisites for anyone interested in this field.

High school should include algebra, trigonometry, physics, and electrical shop. Electronics courses can also provide valuable background.

Many technical schools and colleges offer special courses for broadcast technicians.

Anyone who operates a transmitter in a television station must have a restricted radiotelephone operator permit, according to federal law. No examination is required to obtain one. While some states require anyone working with a microwave to have a general radiotelephone operator license, there is no Federal Communications Commission requirement.

A college degree in engineering is becoming necessary for many supervisory and executive positions in broadcasting.

Potential and advancement

There will be strong competition for broadcast technician jobs in major metropolitan areas, where the number of broadcast technicians exceeds the number of openings. There is better potential for entry-level positions in small cities and towns.

Employment of broadcast technicians is expected to decline through the year 2000. Any job openings that are likely to occur will be to replace technicians who retire or transfer to other occupations. The increasing use of automated equipment will eliminate the need for broadcast technicians in some jobs.

One potential area of growth is in nonbroadcast organizations that use video for employee communications, training, and marketing and promotion.

Income

In general, television stations pay higher salaries than radio stations. Commercial broadcasting pays more than educational broadcasting. Stations in large cities pay more than stations in smaller cities and towns.

Average earnings for technicians at radio stations are $21,600 a year. At television stations, chief technicians earn between $12,000 and $44,800 a year; maintenance technicians earn between $21,500 and $36,000; and chief engineers earn between $34,800 and $61,500.

Additional sources of information

Corporation for Public Broadcasting
1111 16th Street, NW
Washington, DC 20036

Federal Communications Commission
1919 M Street, NW
Washington, DC 20554

National Association of Broadcasters
1771 N Street, NW
Washington, DC 20036

BUILDING CONTRACTOR

The job

A building contractor, or *builder*, is responsible for the actual erection of a structure. The contractor is hired at an agreed-upon fee to handle all phases of building. Working within the client's budget, the contractor orders all materials, schedules work, and hires all necessary labor. The contractor usually assigns specific parts of the construction to subcontractors such as electricians and plumbers.

Places of employment and working conditions

Building contractors work in all areas of the country, in communities of all sizes and in urban areas.

The building contractor has all the headaches—bad weather that delays construction, materials that don't arrive on time, security at the building site, subcontractors that don't complete their work on schedule and hold up subsequent construction steps, labor problems, cost overruns. For small contractors, a few of these problems on a single job can put them out of business.

For further information

Building contractors usually start out in one of the building trades. See the job descriptions for *carpenter; electrician; air-conditioning, refrigeration, and heating mechanic; plumber and pipefitter* for specific information on training, potential, and income.

BUILDING OR PROPERTY MANAGER

The job

A building or property manager is responsible for overseeing the day-to-day happenings of a building with multiple tenants such as office buildings, apartment houses, or shopping centers.

A building or property manager is a combination administrator, rental agent, accountant, public relations expert, purchasing agent, and maintenance person. The manager may simply have an office on the premises, or he or she may live there in an apartment supplied by the owners of the building.

In a single building with only a handful of tenants, the manager handles everything with the help of a small clerical and maintenance staff. In large units, the manager supervises a large staff that handles the details of maintenance, security, leases and rent collection, accounting, and other matters.

One of the most important duties of a building manager is securing tenants for the facility. That involves showing available units to prospective tenants, arranging leases, and providing renovations to suit commercial tenants. Each of these activities is of prime importance to the profitable operation of the building. The reputation of the building manager and staff for competence and service may influence the prospective tenant's decision to move into a building.

Most building managers are employed by real estate and development firms, banks or trust companies, or insurance companies that own investment property. Government agencies employ building managers in subsidized public housing projects. Some building managers are self-employed.

A beginner in this field usually works under the supervision of an experienced manager. To gain experience, the beginner might be given responsibility for a small building or hired as a resident supervisor or maintenance manager.

A related job is real estate agent/broker.

Places of employment and working conditions

Building and property managers work in offices, but they often spend a great deal of time away from their desks visiting the properties that they manage. They confer with various members of the maintenance staff and tenants.

Building managers must recognize that tenants can sometimes be demanding, troublesome, and unreasonable, and the building manager is on call at all times for emergencies and problems.

Qualifications, education, and training

Reliability, good judgment, tact, and diplomacy are all necessary. A building manager must also have initiative and a well-developed sales ability.

High school preparation should include business courses and the development of communication skills.

A college education is becoming more and more important in this field. A background in accounting, law, finance, management, government, or economics is helpful; a business degree with a major in real estate is ideal. Junior and community colleges offer two-year programs leading to an associate degree, which is also acceptable to many employers.

Various professional and trade organizations involved in the real estate field offer short-term formal training programs. A number of organizations also offer certification programs; certification is granted to those who complete training programs, meet job experience standards, and pass written examinations.

Potential and advancement

There are about 225,000 building and property managers. Large metropolitan areas, retirement and resort communities, and industrial areas all provide numerous job opportunities. Growth in the demand for office buildings, retail establishments, and apartments and houses should create a demand for building and property managers through the 1990s. Those with bachelor's degrees in business administration and related fields should have the best opportunities.

Income

Earnings vary greatly depending on geographic area, size of buildings, and level of responsibility. Beginners earn about $225 a week, sometimes with living facilities provided.

Experienced managers earn from $16,000 to $42,000 a year or more. Owners of management firms earn as much as $100,000 to $135,000.

On-site apartment managers earn an average of $28,000 a year; property managers responsible for multiple apartment properties earn an average of $55,100 a year; those responsible for office buildings earn an average of $67,100 a year; and managers of shopping centers earn an average of $60,800 a year.

Additional sources of information

American Industrial Real Estate Association
Sheraton Grande Office Center
345 South Figueroa
Suite M-1
Los Angeles, CA 90071

Building Owners and Managers Institute International
1521 Ritchie Highway
Arnold, MD 21012

Institute of Real Estate Management
430 North Michigan Avenue
Chicago, IL 60611

BUSINESS MACHINE SERVICE TECHNICIAN

The job

Maintenance and repair of business and office machines is the work of business machine service technicians. Most of these technicians work for business machine manufacturers and dealers or repair shops; a few work for large organizations that have enough machines to employ an in-house, full-time technician.

The majority of business machine service technicians work on typewriters, calculators and adding machines, and copiers and duplicating equipment. A few repair and service dictating machines; the remainder service accounting-bookkeeping machines, cash registers, and postage and mailing equipment.

Technicians usually specialize in one type of business machine, such as typewriters or copiers. Those who work for a manufacturer or dealer probably service only the brand produced or sold by their employer.

Related jobs are appliance repairer, computer service technician, communications equipment mechanic, and television and radio service technician.

Places of employment and working conditions

Business machine service technicians work in communities of all sizes throughout the country. Even small communities have at least one repair shop or self-employed technician.

Servicing business machines is cleaner work than most mechanical jobs, and business machine service technicians usually wear business clothes. There are no slow periods since business machines must be serviced regardless of slack economic periods.

Qualifications, education, and training

Mechanical ability, manual dexterity, good eyesight and hearing, and the ability to work without supervision are required for this work. Since these technicians work directly with the customer, they must also be pleasant and tactful.

High school classes in electrical shop, mechanical drawing, mathematics, and physics are helpful.

There are no specific educational requirements for this field, but many employers prefer some technical training in electricity or electronics. Courses are available at trade and technical schools and junior and community colleges. Training received in the armed forces is also valuable.

Trainees who are hired by a manufacturer or dealer attend a training program sponsored by the manufacturer. Such programs last from several weeks to several months and are followed by one to three years of on-the-job training. Training offered by independent repair shops is less formal but basically the same.

All business machine service technicians keep up with technological changes by attending frequent training seminars sponsored by manufacturers when new machines are developed. Many companies also provide tuition assistance for technicians who take additional work-related courses in colleges or technical schools.

Potential and advancement

There are about 57,000 business machine service technicians, and the field is expanding. Job opportunities will be especially good for those with some training in electronics. Since electronic business machines are becoming more and more popular, in a few years, an electronics background will be essential for all business machine service technicians.

Advancement to positions such as service manager or supervisor is possible for experienced technicians. Some open their own repair business or go into business machine sales.

Income

The median annual salary for business machine service technicians is about $25,300. The middle 50 percent earn between $20,000 and $33,000, and the lowest 10 percent, probably trainees, earn less than $15,900 a year. The top 10 percent earn $40,500 a year.

Additional sources of information

Local offices of firms that sell and service business machines can provide information on job opportunities and training.

C

CARPENTER

The job

Carpenters are the largest group of building trade workers in the United States and are employed in almost every type of construction activity. Carpentry is divided into rough and finish work, and a skilled carpenter is able to do both.

Rough work includes erecting the wood framework in buildings, including subfloors, partitions, and floor joists; installing the heavy timbers used in the building of docks and railroad trestles; erecting scaffolds and temporary buildings at construction sites; and making the chutes for pouring concrete and the forms to enclose the concrete while it hardens. Rough work must be completed before finish work can begin.

Installing molding, wood paneling, cabinets, windows and doors, and hardware, as well as building stairs and laying floors, is finish work. In some construction jobs, finish work may also include installing wallboard and floor coverings such as linoleum or asphalt tile.

In small communities and rural areas, carpenters often install glass and insulation and do the painting; in large metropolitan areas, carpenters tend to specialize in just one phase of carpentry.

Carpenters work from blueprints or from instructions given by supervisors and must use materials and building techniques that conform to local building codes. They use hand tools such as hammers, saws, chisels, and planes (which each carpenter usually provides for him- or herself), as well as portable power saws, drills, and rivet guns (which are usually supplied by the builder or contractor).

Most carpenters work for contractors and builders who construct new buildings or renovate and remodel older structures; many are self-employed or combine wage employment with a part-time business of their own. Some are employed by government agencies, manufacturing firms, and other large organizations.

A large proportion of carpenters belong to the United Brotherhood of Carpenters and Joiners of America.

Slowly but surely, women are beginning to enter this field—currently about 2 percent of all carpenters are women. One major attraction is the high hourly wage, which is more than twice that paid in the clerical and health fields where so many women work. Women carpenters often face resentment and sometimes discrimination in this traditionally male field, but affirmative action programs and equal employment opportunity regulations are helping smooth the way. A woman interested in carpentry as a career should make sure she acquires the best technical skills possible in high school if she expects to be considered for acceptance into an apprenticeship program.

Places of employment and working conditions

Carpenters work throughout the country in communities of all sizes and in rural areas.

A carpenter's work is always active and sometimes strenuous, depending on whether it is rough or finish work. Prolonged standing, climbing, and squatting are necessary, and there is danger of injury from falls, sharp or rough materials, and the use of sharp tools and power equipment.

Qualifications, education, and training

Manual dexterity is an extremely important qualification as is the ability to solve mathematical problems quickly and accurately. Anyone interested in carpentry as a career should also be in good physical condition, have a good sense of balance, and be unafraid of working on high structures.

Although a large number of workers in this field have acquired their skills by working as carpenters' helpers or for contractors who provide some training, the best training is obtained in a formal apprenticeship program. Carpenters with such training are in greater demand, command better pay, and have greater opportunities for advancement.

Apprenticeship applicants generally must be at least 17 years old and meet local requirements. Courses in carpentry shop, mechanical drawing, and general mathematics are helpful. Applicants are usually given an aptitude test to assess their suitability for carpentry work.

An apprenticeship consists of three to four years of on-the-job training supplemented by related classroom instruction. The classroom instruction includes drafting, blueprint reading, mathematics for layout work, and the use of woodworking machines to familiarize the apprentice with the materials, tools, and principles of carpentry.

Most apprenticeship programs are sponsored and supervised by a joint committee of local contractors and builders and representatives of the local chapter of the carpenters' union. The committee determines the number of carpenters the local job market can support and establishes the minimum standards of education, training, and experience. If specialization by local contractors is extensive, the committee sometimes rotates apprentices among several employers to provide training in all areas of carpentry.

Potential and advancement

There are about 1,106,000 carpenters in the United States, one-third of whom are self-employed. Job opportunities should be plentiful over the next decade as population growth adds to the demand for housing and other structures. The construction industry is very sensitive to the national economy, however, and the number of job openings can fluctuate greatly from year to year.

Carpenters have greater opportunity for advancement to general supervisory positions than other construction workers because they are involved in the entire construction process. For this same reason, carpenters often become building contractors.

For women in this field, the best areas for job opportunities are in the building trade groups and in companies being formed by women to create jobs for women in the building trades.

Income

For carpenters who are not self-employed, median weekly earnings are $381. Those in the middle of the salary range earn between $282 and $516 per week.

Those at the top of the salary range earn more than $676 a week, while those at the bottom earn less than $215.

Carpenters' earnings may be affected at times by bad weather that causes them to lose work time or availability of jobs.

Additional sources of information

Associated Builders and Contractors, Inc.
729 15th Street, NW
Washington, DC 20005

Associated General Contractors of America, Inc.
1957 E Street, NW
Washington, DC 20006

National Association of Women in Construction
327 South Adams Street
Fort Worth, TX 76104

United Brotherhood of Carpenters and Joiners of America
101 Constitution Avenue, NW
Washington, DC 20005

CARTOONIST

The job

Cartoonists are specialized artists who use small drawings to illustrate ideas, concepts, text, customers' products, or humorous situations. Many cartoonists are free-lancers and may work for a number of clients. Often, their work is syndicated and appears in a number of publications. A cartoonist may specialize in one of a number of areas.

A *political* or *editorial cartoonist* uses his or her skill to focus attention on political issues and personalities of the day, local issues, or other community activities and personalities. Political cartoons are not always humorous—many are sad and some almost brutal. The political cartoonists, the fewest in number of all cartoonists, usually have a broad background in history, politics, literature, and human behavior as well as artistic talent.

Sports cartoonists use their talents to depict sports figures and situations. They usually work for newspapers and must have an eye for physical action and a knowledge of the fine points of various sports.

Commercial or *advertising cartoonists* work in the field of advertising. This is a rapidly growing field and one that offers many opportunities to beginners. Most cities have at least one art studio that supplies drawings for local businesses and industries to use in their ads; larger cities have a number of such studios. Experienced commercial cartoonists are also employed by advertising agencies, advertising departments of large industries and businesses, educational publishers, and many federal and state agencies.

Comic strip cartoonists combine writing and drawing techniques to produce a small story in cartoon form. In longer, continuous comic strips or comic books, where a more complex story line is used, the cartoonist often works in conjunction with a writer.

Magazine cartoonists usually work on a free-lance basis by submitting humorous cartoons to magazines. Some specialize in a particular topic such as industrial safety or sales and submit their work to trade magazines.

Caricaturists are basically very talented portrait artists who exaggerate and distort to portray the qualities of a personality in terms of physical characteristics. Caricature is more subtle, and usually less kind, than political cartooning.

Motion picture cartoonists draw a series of pictures, or frames, each one differing only slightly from the preceding one. When reproduced on film and projected, the cartoon characters appear to move. More than any other cartoonists, motion picture cartoonists work as part of a team. Some cartoonists draw and paint in the background; others make rough sketches of the main points of the story. Animators fill in these sequences by preparing the detailed drawings of every movement.

One of the newest fields is that of *television cartoonist*. These cartoonists usually have a solid background in several phases of cartooning—especially advertising and animation—and a working knowledge of television production techniques and requirements.

Places of employment and working conditions

Job opportunities are everywhere, especially for a beginner. Boston, Chicago, Los Angeles, and New York City provide many jobs in the newspaper and publishing fields, while most motion picture cartoonists, animators, and television cartoonists work in Los Angeles or New York City.

Most cartoonists work regular schedules of 35 to 40 hours a week. Comic strip and editorial cartoonists must meet deadlines. Free-lance cartoonists set their own hours.

Qualifications, education, and training

Artistic talent and a sense of humor are the prime requisites. Creativity, imagination, an understanding of human nature, manual dexterity, good color vision, and perseverance are also necessary.

Sometimes talent alone is enough, but a solid foundation provided by formal art training is the best preparation. This training can begin in high school. An aspiring cartoonist should take any available art courses and should follow an academic program as preparation for college or art school. Any opportunity to draw for school or local publications or to make posters for community events can provide valuable experience.

Most art schools provide a few courses in cartooning plus comprehensive training in commercial art; a few offer special programs in cartooning. These are Chouinard Art Institute (Los Angeles), Corcoran School of Art (Washington, D.C.), Chicago Academy of Fine Arts (Chicago), and Cartoonists and Illustrators School (New York City).

Some accredited home study courses provide art training, but these should be checked out thoroughly before a person decides to enroll.

Walt Disney Studios offers a limited number of apprenticeships to artists who have completed two or three years of formal art training. Some large art studios also have apprenticeship programs.

The accumulation of a portfolio should start as early as possible. Samples of a cartoonist's work are always the best way to impress an employer or a school with the quality of his or her work and imagination.

Potential and advancement

This is a growing field with many job opportunities for those with talent and training. Competition is keen, but beginners with persistence will find opportunities, especially for free-lance work or in small art studios. The biggest money is in syndication, but this is the toughest field to break into.

Income

Salaries for cartoonists vary widely depending on the location and type of their work. Earnings range from $200 to $1,500 a week. Syndicated artists working on commission earn much more. Free-lance cartoonists earn from $50 to $1,200 or more for a single cartoon, depending on their talent and reputation.

Additional sources of information

Association of American Editorial Cartoonists
242 West 18th Street
Ohio State University
Columbus, OH 43210

Cartoonists Guild
11 West 20th Street
New York, NY 10003

National Cartoonists Society
9 Ebony Court
Brooklyn, NY 11229

CERAMIC ENGINEER

The job

Ceramic engineers work not only with ceramics (as in pottery) but with all nonmetallic, inorganic materials that require high temperatures in their processing. Thus these engineers work on such diverse products as glassware, heat-resistant metals, electronic components, and nuclear reactors. They also design and supervise construction of plants and equipment used in the manufacture of these products.

Ceramic engineers normally specialize in one or more ceramic products—whiteware (porcelain and china or high-voltage electrical insulators); structural materials such as brick and tile; electronic ceramics, glass, or fuel elements for atomic energy, to name a few. Most are employed in the stone, clay, and glass industries. Others work in industries that use ceramic products including the iron and steel, electrical equipment, aerospace, and chemical industries.

Places of employment and working conditions

Ceramic engineers are employed in all areas of the country. Their work locations vary from laboratories to factory production areas, depending on the product and the industry.

Qualifications, education, and training

The ability to think analytically, a capacity for details, and the ability to work as part of a team are all necessary. Good communication skills are important for the ceramic engineer.

Mathematics and the sciences must be emphasized in high school.

A bachelor's degree in engineering is the minimum requirement in this field. In a typical curriculum, the first two years are spent in the study of basic sciences such as physics and chemistry and mathematics, introductory engineering, and some liberal arts courses. The remaining years are usually devoted to specialized engineering courses. Engineering programs can last from four to six years. Those requiring five or six years to complete may award a master's degree or may provide a cooperative plan of study plus practical work experience with a nearby industry.

Because of rapid changes in technology, many ceramic engineers continue their education throughout their careers. A graduate degree is necessary for most teaching and research positions and for many management jobs. Some persons obtain graduate degrees in business administration.

Engineering graduates usually work under the supervision of an experienced engineer or in a company training program until they become acquainted with the requirements of a particular company.

All states require licensing of engineers whose work may affect life, health, or property or who offer their services to the public. Those who are licensed, about one-third of all engineers, are called registered engineers. Requirements include graduation from an accredited engineering school, four years of experience, and an examination.

Potential and advancement

Job opportunities in this field are expected to increase substantially through the year 2000. Nuclear energy, electronics, defense, medical science, pollution control, energy, and conservation will all offer increasing job opportunities for ceramic engineers.

Income

Starting salaries in private industry average $24,000 a year for beginning ceramic engineers. Experienced ceramic engineers earn annual salaries of about $48,000, and those who are highly qualified earn $80,000 and more.

Additional sources of information

Accreditation Board for Engineering and Technology
345 East 47th Street
New York, NY 10017

American Ceramic Society
757 Brooksedge Plaza Drive
Westerville, OH 43081

American Society for Engineering Education
11 Dupont Circle
Suite 200
Washington, DC 20036

Junior Engineering Technical Society (JETS)
1420 King Street
Suite 405
Alexandria, VA 22314

National Society of Professional Engineers
1420 King Street
Alexandria, VA 22314

Society of Women Engineers
345 East 47th Street
Room 305
New York, NY 10017

CHEF

The job

The preparation of food for public consumption in restaurants, schools, hospitals, hotels, and numerous other establishments is the work of chefs and cooks.

Cooks vary from the short-order cook in a small restaurant serving only a few easily prepared dishes to a highly trained specialist in a large institution or expensive restaurant. These large facilities employ a number of cooks and assistant cooks who specialize in one type of food such as pastry or sauces.

In a kitchen that employs a number of cooks, a head cook—or *chef*—coordinates the activities of the entire staff and may him- or herself cook certain foods. The chef is also responsible for planning menus and ordering food supplies.

Places of employment and working conditions

Cooks and chefs are employed throughout the country in communities of all sizes.

Many kitchens are spacious and pleasant, with air conditioning and the latest appliances. In older buildings or in small restaurants, conditions are not always as pleasant. All cooks and chefs must stand most of the time, lift heavy pots and kettles, and work near hot ovens and stoves. They are also subject to burns and cuts from sharp implements.

Qualifications, education, and training

Cleanliness, a keen sense of taste and smell, and physical stamina are important qualities for a cook or chef. They must also work well as part of a team.

High school or vocational school courses in business arithmetic and food preparation are helpful; part-time or summer work in a fast food restaurant can be valuable.

Although many cooks acquire their skills through on-the-job training, larger institutions and the better hotels and restaurants prefer to hire those with more formal training.

Some professional associations and trade unions offer apprenticeship programs in cooperation with local employers and junior colleges, and a few large hotels and restaurants have their own training programs. Colleges and universities offer courses in commercial food preparation as part of their hotel management curriculum; the armed forces are also a good source of training in this field. Courses and training programs vary in length from a few months to several years. Students study basic food preparation, care of kitchen equipment, food storage, menu planning, and food purchasing.

Most states require cooks and chefs to have health certificates indicating that they are free from contagious diseases.

Potential and advancement

Employment opportunities for cooks and chefs are expected to be plentiful through the year 2000. Small restaurants, school cafeterias, and other places serving simple foods will offer the best opportunities for beginners.

There are several reasons for this expected employment growth. Food and beverage sales and employment in eating and drinking establishments are associated with the general growth of the economy. Increased business activity results in workers' lunches and entertainment of clients. Population growth, rising family and personal incomes, and more leisure time will allow more people to dine out more. Also, as more women join the work force, families will eat out for convenience.

Employment in restaurants is expected to grow rapidly, but employment of institutional chefs and cooks will not grow as rapidly. Their employment is concentrated in the educational sector, and the growth of the student population is expected to be modest. However, there will be many opportunities in institutions associated with the elderly due to the growth in the number of elderly people.

Advancement in this field usually takes the form of moving to larger foodservice facilities or restaurants. Some chefs gradually advance to supervisory or management positions in hotels, clubs, or the more elegant restaurants. Others open their own restaurants or catering businesses.

Income

Assistant cooks earn from $4.50 to $5.50 an hour; cooks earn from about $3.90 to $7.65 an hour.

Chefs earn about $5.00 to $6.75 an hour, with those in the best restaurants earning much more. Several chefs with national reputations earn over $40,000 a year.

Additional sources of information

American Culinary Federation
Educational Institute
P.O. Box 3466
St. Augustine, FL 32084

Culinary Institute of America
P.O. Box 53
Hyde Park, NY 12538

The Educational Foundation of the National Restaurant Association
250 South Wacker Drive
Suite 1400
Chicago, IL 60606

CHEMICAL ENGINEER

The job

The duties of chemical engineers entail a working knowledge of chemistry, physics, and mechanical and electrical engineering.

Chemical engineers design chemical plants, manufacturing equipment, and production methods; they develop processes for such things as removing chemical contaminants from waste materials.

This is one of the most complex and diverse areas of engineering. Chemical engineers often specialize in a particular operation such as oxidation or polymerization. Others specialize in plastics or rubber or in a field such as pollution control.

Most chemical engineers work in manufacturing firms primarily in chemicals, petroleum, and related industries. A number of them work in the nuclear energy field.

Places of employment and working conditions

Chemical engineers may be subject to hazards that occur when working with dangerous chemicals. They work in many different parts of the country.

Qualifications, education, and training

The ability to think analytically, a capacity for details, and the ability to work as part of a team are all necessary. Good communication skills are important for anyone who holds chemical engineering as a career goal.

Mathematics and the sciences must be emphasized as much as possible in high school.

A bachelor's degree in engineering is the minimum requirement in this field. In a typical curriculum, the first two years are spent in the study of basic sciences such as physics and chemistry and mathematics, introductory engineering, and some liberal arts courses. The remaining years are usually devoted to specialized engineering courses. Engineering programs can last from four to six years. Those requiring five or six years to complete may award a master's degree or may provide a plan of study plus a work experience with a nearby industry.

Because of rapid changes in technology, many engineers continue their education throughout their careers. A graduate degree is necessary for most teaching and research positions and for many management jobs. Some chemical engineers obtain graduate degrees in business administration.

Graduates usually work under the supervision of an experienced chemical engineer or in a company training program until they become acquainted with the requirements of a particular company.

All states require licensing of engineers whose work may affect life, health, or property or who offer their services to the public. Those who are licensed, about one-third of all engineers, are called registered engineers. Requirements for licensing include graduation from an accredited engineering school, four years of experience, and an examination.

Potential and advancement

There are about 49,000 chemical engineers. Job opportunities should be good through the year 2000, especially in the fields of pharmaceuticals, biotechnology, and materials science.

Income

Starting salaries for chemical engineers with a bachelor's degree average about $31,000 a year in private industry. Starting offers for those with a master's degree average $34,600 a year and for those with a Ph.D., $46,600. Senior engineers working in private industry with management responsibilities earn an annual average salary of about $87,900.

The average yearly salary for engineers employed by the federal government is about $42,300.

Additional sources of information

Accreditation Board for Engineering and Technology
345 East 47th Street
New York, NY 10017

American Institute of Chemical Engineers
345 East 47th Street
New York, NY 10017

American Society for Engineering Education
11 Dupont Circle
Suite 200
Washington, DC 20036

Junior Engineering Technical Society (JETS)
1420 King Street
Suite 405
Alexandria, VA 22314

National Society of Professional Engineers
1420 King Street
Alexandria, VA 22314

Society of Women Engineers
345 East 47th Street
Room 305
New York, NY 10017

CHEMIST

The job

Chemists perform laboratory research to gain new knowledge about the substances that make up our world. Knowledge gained in basic research is then put to practical use and applied to the development of new products. For example, basic research on the uniting of small molecules to form larger ones (polymerization) led to the development of products made from synthetic rubber and plastic.

Many chemists work in industrial production and inspection, where they must coordinate their efforts with a manufacturing operation. They give directions for the carrying out of a manufacturing process and then take periodic samples to check that process. Others work as marketing sales representatives because of the technical knowledge needed to market certain products. Chemists also work as college teachers and researchers and as consultants.

Chemists often specialize in one of the subfields of chemistry. *Analytical chemists* study the structure, composition, and natures of substances. *Organic chemists* study all elements made from carbon compounds, which include vast areas of modern industry. The development of plastics and many other synthetics is a result of the work of organic chemists. *Inorganic chemists* study compounds other than carbon and are involved in the development of such things as solid-state electronic components. *Physical chemists* study energy transformation and are engaged in finding new and better energy sources.

More than half of all chemists work in the chemical, food, petroleum, paper, electrical, and scientific instrument industries. About 19,000 work in colleges and universities. Chemists also work for government agencies, primarily in health and agriculture.

Related jobs are chemical engineer, agricultural scientist, and biological scientist.

Places of employment and working conditions

Although chemists work in all parts of the country, the largest concentrations are in New York, New Jersey, California, Pennsylvania, Ohio, and Illinois.

Chemists usually work in modern facilities in laboratories, classrooms, and offices. In certain industries, hazards are present in the handling of explosive or otherwise dangerous materials, but safety regulations in these industries are very strict.

Qualifications, education, and training

The student who plans a career as a chemist should enjoy performing experiments and building things and should have a genuine liking for math and science. A wide range of abilities is necessary, including perseverance, concentration on detail, good eye-hand coordination, and the ability to work independently.

High school students looking forward to a career in chemistry should take as many math and science courses as possible and develop good laboratory skills. Foreign language courses can also prove valuable.

Many colleges and universities offer a bachelor's degree in chemistry. Courses include analytical, organic and inorganic, and physical chemistry, as well as mathematics and physics.

A master's degree in chemistry, usually requiring extensive, independent research, is offered by several hundred colleges and universities. Independent research is required for master's and Ph.D. degrees.

Potential and advancement

About 80,000 people are presently employed as chemists. The outlook for employment is good primarily because of the development of new products by private industry. In addition, problems of pollution, energy, and health care must be addressed by chemists in both government agencies and private industry. Employment of chemists in crime detection work is also expected to increase on local, state, and federal levels.

Little growth is expected in college and university positions, and competition for existing teaching jobs is expected to be very strong. Candidates for advanced degrees may secure teaching or research positions while completing their studies, but these positions are usually at the assistant or instructor level.

In all areas, advanced degrees will continue to be the key to administrative and managerial positions. College professors, chemists doing basic research, and those employed in the top administrative positions in both industry and teaching will need a Ph.D. degree to achieve these levels.

Income

Salaries for chemists vary according to experience, education, and place of employment. Entry-level starting salaries in private industry average $26,000 with a bachelor's degree, $31,600 with a master's degree, and $41,300 with a Ph.D.

Experienced chemists with comparable degrees average $35,400, $41,000, and $50,000, respectively.

Federal government starting salaries range from about $15,700 with a bachelor's degree to about $34,600 with a Ph.D.

Additional sources of information

American Chemical Society
Career Services
1155 16th Street, NW
Washington, DC 20036

Chemical Manufacturers Association
2501 M Street, NW
Washington, DC 20037

CHILDCARE WORKER

The job

Childcare workers look after children whose parents work outside their homes or cannot be with them for some reason. Job duties vary depending on the age of the children. Infants must be fed, diapered, calmed, and played with. Pre-school children must also be given this basic care plus activities that will stimulate them physically, emotionally, and socially.

Childcare workers begin their workdays by greeting children at the door and helping them take off coats, hats, and mittens. They plan activities that will provide both physical and mental exercise such as outdoor and indoor games, drawing and coloring, singing, and reading.

Childcare workers are also responsible for the child's physical welfare. They provide healthy meals and snacks and make sure that the children have appropriate rest time.

Childcare workers may be employed by a daycare center, or they may be self-employed and work in their own homes.

Places of employment and working conditions

Childcare workers may work in their homes, churches, schools, workplaces where employers provide care for employees' children, or buildings used for childcare.

Childcare workers have an active and hectic day. They often have to work long hours to accommodate parents' work schedules. The job can be physically tiring—workers spend a lot of time standing, walking, bending, stooping, and lifting. Sometimes children can be difficult to deal with, and childcare workers must provide firm discipline.

Qualifications, education, and training

Childcare workers must enjoy working with children. They need to be patient and have a lot of energy.

There are no specific education requirements for entry-level positions or for childcare workers who are self-employed. Most employers prefer to hire high school graduates.

Some jobs do require some type of education. Colleges offer degree programs in childcare, early childhood education, child and family studies, and pre-elementary education.

One valuable credential for childcare workers is certification from the Child Development Associate (CDA) program. Participants must be at least 18 years old and have some childcare experience and formal classroom training. Instructors help workers improve their childcare skills, assess their abilities and performance, and determine whether they qualify for certification. The program is offered in local schools and colleges.

Potential and advancement

There are 670,000 childcare workers, and many of them work part-time. Opportunities are expected to be good through the year 2000. Even though the number of children under the age of five is expected to decrease, the number of children who need daycare will increase because of the many women who work outside their homes.

Childcare workers may advance as they gain experience and additional training. In large childcare centers, they may become supervisors or administrators. Some childcare workers advance by starting their own businesses.

Income

Median annual earnings for full-time childcare workers are $9,724. Many entry-level workers are paid minimum wage—$4.25 an hour as of April 1, 1991.

Additional sources of information

CDA National Credentialing Program
1718 Connecticut Avenue, NW
Suite 500
Washington, DC 20009

National Child Care Association
920 Green Street, NW
Washington, DC 20037

CHIROPRACTOR

The job

Chiropractors treat patients by manual manipulations (called adjustments) of parts of the body, especially the spinal column. This system of treatment is based on the theory that pressure on nerves that pass from the spinal cord to different parts of the body interferes with nerve impulses and their functioning, causing disorders in parts of the body. By means of certain manipulations of the vertebrae, the chiropractor seeks to relieve the pressure on specific nerves and thus remove the cause of a specific ailment.

Most chiropractors also employ x-rays to aid in locating the source of an ailment. They use supplementary treatment with water, light, or heat therapy and may prescribe diet, exercise, and rest. Drugs and surgery are not used in this system of treatment.

Newly licensed chiropractors often start their careers by working in salaried positions—as assistants to established practitioners or in chiropractic clinics.

Since a chiropractic practice can be conducted on a part-time basis, it is a good field for people with family responsibilities.

Places of employment and working conditions

Chiropractors often locate in small communities, with about half of all chiropractors practicing in cities of 50,000 or less. California, Oregon, Colorado, Wyoming, Arizona, and New Mexico have the most chiropractors.

Most chiropractors are in private practice, which allows them to schedule their own working hours. Evening and weekend hours are sometimes necessary to accommodate their patients.

Qualifications, education, and training

Manual dexterity rather than strength is necessary for a chiropractor. A keen sense of observation, an ability to deal with people, and a sympathetic manner with the sick are also important.

High school courses in science are important, and the two years of college required before entrance into chiropractic school must include chemistry, biology, and physics.

There are 14 chiropractic colleges that are accredited by the Council on Chiropractic Education; three others are working towards accreditation. The four-year course of study emphasizes courses in manipulation and spinal adjustment, but most schools also offer a broad curriculum that includes basic and clinical sciences.

The first two years of study include classroom and laboratory work in anatomy, physiology, and biochemistry. The last two years are devoted to practical experience in college clinics. The degree of D.C. (doctor of chiropractic) is awarded upon completion of the course.

All chiropractors must be licensed to practice. In addition to a state board examination, licensing requirements usually include two years of college and the successful completion of an accredited four-year chiropractic course, as described above. Some states also require a basic science examination.

Potential and advancement

There are about 36,000 practicing chiropractors. This number will increase because the profession is gaining greater public acceptance. Enrollment in chiropractic colleges has increased in recent years. New chiropractors may find it increasingly difficult to establish a practice in areas where other practitioners are located; the best opportunities will be in areas with few established chiropractors.

Income

As in any type of independent practice, earnings are relatively low in the beginning. Experienced chiropractors earn about $64,000 a year, with many earning considerably more.

Additional sources of information

American Chiropractic Association
1701 Clarendon Boulevard
Arlington, VA 22209

Council on Chiropractic Education
4401 Westown Parkway
Suite 120
West Des Moines, IA 50265

CIA WORKER

The job

The Central Intelligence Agency (CIA) gathers and analyzes information from all over the world that might affect the interests of the United States. This information is used by the government's senior policy makers as they make decisions on U. S. policy concerning many issues and areas.

In addition to employing those who gather information, the CIA employs intelligence analysts, economists, geographers, and other specialists in science and technology to provide additional information on foreign countries and governments. Career fields within the CIA include computer sciences, economics, engineering (especially mechanical, electrical/electronic, aerospace, nuclear, and civil engineering), foreign area studies, languages, mathematics, photographic interpretation, the physical sciences, psychology, and library science.

The CIA career development program provides orientation, training, opportunities for growth, and advancement in specialty fields as well as in general intelligence work.

A full range of clerical positions is also available with the Central Intelligence Agency, including some overseas assignments.

Places of employment and working conditions

Most CIA employees work in the Washington, D.C., area, but some positions require foreign travel or assignment for varying lengths of time. Overseas tours of duty are optional for clerical personnel and usually last for a two-year period.

The usual workweek is 40 hours, but this may vary depending on specialty field and area of assignment.

Qualifications, education, and training

General qualifications for anyone interested in working for the CIA include good character, intelligence and resourcefulness, willingness to accept responsibility, and a strong motivation for public service. Applicants should be willing to serve overseas if necessary and be aware that their work must often remain anonymous. U. S. citizenship is required.

An undergraduate or graduate degree in an appropriate field is necessary; related work experience is a plus. Some colleges and universities take part in a cooperative education program with the CIA. Interested undergraduates who are majoring in engineering, physics, mathematics, computer science, business administration, or accounting may spend part of their time in a cooperative work program.

The CIA also has a summer intern program available to a limited number of graduate students. Students in economics, geography, political science, history, linguistics, international relations, or the specific areas of China, Southeast Asia, Latin America, Africa, the Middle East, and the Soviet Union may participate. Foreign language ability is useful, but not essential, for this program.

Applicants for clerical positions must meet the basic requirement for specific jobs and must complete an aptitude test.

A background security investigation will be completed on all accepted applicants before assignment to duty. Because this investigation takes time, applicants should apply well in advance of the time they wish to start working.

Potential and advancement

Although the CIA employs a wide variety of people in many fields, active recruitment of specific specialties varies from year to year. For example, current needs for foreign language specialists are Russian, Eastern European, Middle

Eastern, and Asian. Information on current job opportunities in other fields is available from the CIA; see listings at the end of this article.

The CIA offers advancement opportunities to all employees. Formal and on-the-job training is available during early and midcareer stages, and professional-level training is given not only within the CIA but also at other government training establishments and at local colleges and universities. The CIA has its own highly regarded Language Learning Center for employees who wish to study a foreign language.

For clerical employees, the CIA's Office of Training offers courses in administrative procedures, writing, employee development, and supervision and management. Off-campus courses are offered by some local universities and specialized schools at the CIA headquarters building; tuition costs for approved job-related courses are paid by the CIA. Foreign language training is provided for those who are to serve overseas.

Income

Employees of the CIA are paid according to the federal General Schedule (GS) pay scale.

Starting salaries are approximately $19,000 a year—depending on qualifications. Starting salaries for clerical workers are about $13,200 a year.

Those on overseas assignments receive regular government allowances including transportation and housing.

Benefits include 13 to 26 vacation days per year, depending on years of service; 13 paid sick-leave days; and nine paid holidays.

Additional sources of information

If you are in college, see your placement officer and request an interview with the CIA representative who visits your campus from time to time or whose regional office may be situated nearby.

Write to the Director of Personnel, Central Intelligence Agency, P.O. Box 12727, Arlington, VA 22209-8727. Enclose a resume of your education and experience and ask for preliminary application forms.

Visit the CIA Recruitment Office, Ames Center Building, 1820 North Fort Myer Drive, Arlington (Rosslyn), Virginia. No appointment is necessary for an interview during weekday business hours. Employment inquiries may be made by telephoning (703) 351-2028.

CITY MANAGER

The job

A city manager, usually appointed by the elected officials of a community, administers and coordinates the day-to-day activities of the community. The city manager oversees such functions as tax collection and disbursement, law enforcement, public works, budget preparation, studies of current problems, and planning for future needs. In a small city, the manager handles all functions; in a larger city, the manager usually has a number of assistants, each of whom manages a department.

City managers and their assistants supervise city employees, coordinate city programs, greet visitors, answer correspondence, prepare reports, represent the city at public hearings and meetings, analyze work procedures, and prepare budgets.

Most city managers work for small cities (under 25,000) that have a council-manager type of government. The council, which is elected, hires the manager who is then responsible for running the city as well as for hiring a staff. In cities with a mayor-council type of government, the mayor hires the city manager as his or her top administrative assistant.

A few managers work for counties and for metropolitan and regional planning bodies.

Most city managers begin as management assistants in one of the city departments such as finance, public works, or planning. Experience in several different departments is valuable and can provide a well-rounded background.

There are few women in this field, but this is a new and growing profession with room for people with training in a variety of disciplines that relate to the functions and problems of urban life.

Places of employment and working conditions

City managers are employed in cities of all sizes, but job opportunities are greatest in the eastern states.

Working conditions for a city manager are usually those of an office position with considerable public contact. More than 40 hours a week is usually required, and emergency situations and public meetings frequently involve evening and weekend work.

Qualifications, education, and training

Persons planning a career in city management must be dedicated to public service and willing to work as part of a team. They should have self-confidence, be able to analyze problems and suggest solutions, and should function well under stress. Tact and the ability to communicate well are very important.

A graduate degree is presently required even for most entry-level positions in this field. An undergraduate degree in a field such as engineering, recreation, social work, or political science should be followed by a master's degree in public or municipal administration or business administration.

Requirements in some of the 185 colleges and universities that offer advanced degrees in this field include an internship of six months to a year, in which the candidate must work in a city manager's office to gain experience.

Potential and advancement

More than 5,000 persons are presently employed as city managers and assistants, and the field is growing. However, job competition is expected to be very strong over the next few years, due to an increase in the number of graduates in this field.

Recent computerized management techniques for taxes, traffic control, and utility billing will create openings for those trained in finance, while increasing emphasis on broad solutions to urban social problems will result in job opportunities for those with a strong public administration background. In addition, the council-manager system of government is the fastest growing type of government in the country, and the move is toward professional, rather than elected, city management.

Generally, one begins as an assistant to a city manager or department head with promotions leading to greater responsibility. A city manager will probably work in several different types and sizes of cities in his or her career, which will further broaden the person's experience and promotion potential.

Income

Salaries for city managers depend on education, experience, job responsibility, and the size of the employing city. Salaries are generally high, ranging from $42,559 per year in cities of 5,000 to $84,591 in cities of 100,000 or more and more than $109,000 a year in cities of 500,000. Those who work as assistants earn $29,578 to $72,130 in cities of comparable size.

Benefits usually include travel expenses, and a car is often provided for official business.

Additional sources of information

The International City Management Association
1120 G Street
Suite 300
Washington, DC 20005

CIVIL ENGINEER

The job

This is the oldest branch of the engineering profession. Civil engineers design and supervise construction of buildings, roads, harbors, airports, dams, tunnels and bridges, and water supply and sewage systems.

Specialties within civil engineering include structural, hydraulic, environmental (sanitary), transportation, geotechnical, and soil mechanics. Many civil engineers are in supervisory or administrative positions. They may supervise a construction site or administer a large municipal project such as highway or airport construction.

Most civil engineers work for construction companies or for federal, state, and local government agencies. Others work for public utilities, railroads, architectural firms, and engineering consulting firms.

Places of employment and working conditions

Civil engineers work in all parts of the country, usually in or near major industrial and commercial centers. Some work for American firms in foreign countries.

A great deal of the civil engineer's time is spent outdoors. They sometimes work in remote areas and may have to move from place to place as they work on different projects.

Qualifications, education, and training

The ability to think analytically, a capacity for details, and the ability to work as part of a team are all necessary. Good communication skills are important.

Mathematics and the sciences must be emphasized in high school.

A bachelor's degree in engineering is the minimum requirement in this field. In a typical curriculum, the first two years are spent in the study of basic sciences such as physics and chemistry and mathematics, introductory engineering, and some liberal arts courses. The remaining years are usually devoted to specialized engineering courses. Engineering programs can last from four to six years. Those requiring five or six years to complete may award a master's degree or may provide a cooperative plan of study plus practical work experience in a nearby industry.

Because of rapid changes in technology, many engineers continue their education throughout their careers. A graduate degree is necessary for most teaching and research positions and for many management jobs. Some persons obtain graduate degrees in business administration.

Engineering graduates usually work under the supervision of an experienced engineer or in a company training program until they become acquainted with the requirements of a particular company or industry.

All states require licensing of engineers whose work may affect life, health, or property or who offer their services to the public. Those who are licensed, about one-third of all engineers, are called registered engineers. Requirements include graduation from an accredited engineering school, four years of experience, and a written examination.

Potential and advancement

There are about 186,000 civil engineers. Job opportunities in this field will increase somewhat because population growth will create an increasing demand for housing, transportation, power generating plants, and other energy sources.

Income

Starting salaries for civil engineers with a bachelor's degree average about $25,600 a year in private industry. Starting offers for those with a master's degree average $34,600 a year and for those with a Ph.D., $46,600. Senior engineers working in private industry with management responsibilities earn an average annual salary of about $87,900.

The average yearly salary for engineers employed by the federal government is about $42,300.

Additional sources of information

Accreditation Board for Engineering and Technology
345 East 47th Street
New York, NY 10017

American Society of Civil Engineers
345 East 47th Street
New York, NY 10017

American Society for Engineering Education
11 Dupont Circle
Suite 200
Washington, DC 20036

Junior Engineering Technical Society (JETS)
1420 King Street
Suite 405
Alexandria, VA 22314

National Society of Professional Engineers
1420 King Street
Alexandria, VA 22314

Society of Women Engineers
345 East 47th Street
Room 305
New York, NY 10017

CIVIL SERVICE WORKER, FEDERAL

The job

The federal government is the largest single employer in the United States. Some 3 million civilian workers are employed in a full range of occupational and professional fields plus some that are unique to the federal government such as postal worker, foreign service officer, and internal revenue agent.

The federal government employs general clerical workers and postal clerks and mail carriers. Many civilians are employed in engineering and related fields, most in the U.S. Department of Defense. Many accounting workers, including professional accountants, are employed throughout the federal government, with the largest concentrations in the Department of Defense, the Treasury Department, and the General Accounting Office.

Federal civilian employees also work in hospitals or other health care facilities and public health activities. Most are employed by the Veterans Administration, the Department of Defense, the Department of Education, or the Department of Health and Human Services.

In the departments of the Treasury, Justice, and Agriculture, the federal government employs workers in the field of law as well as in investigation and inspection.

Other federal employees work in the fields of social science, biological and agricultural science, physical science, and mathematics.

The federal government also employs many blue-collar workers, most in the Department of Defense. Skilled craft workers in all fields and mobile equipment operators and mechanics make up a large segment of these jobs.

Places of employment and working conditions

Federal employees work throughout the country, in Washington, D.C., in U.S. territories, and foreign countries.

Most federal employees work a 40-hour, five-day week; for extra hours worked, they receive overtime pay or compensatory time off.

Working conditions vary depending on the job.

Qualifications, education, and training

The federal government usually has the same educational and experience requirements as private employers. Jobs requiring licensing, however, may have different requirements at the federal level. Check this section under each individual job description for detailed information.

Almost all federal jobs are under a merit system of one kind or another. The U.S. Civil Service Commission covers 60 percent of all federal jobs. Most of those not governed by the Civil Service requirements are covered by separate merit systems within a specific agency such as the Foreign Service of the State Department or the Federal Bureau of Investigation.

An applicant for a federal job must fulfill the minimum age, training, and experience requirements for a particular job and usually must take the appropriate competitive examination. Applicants are notified as to their eligibility or ineligibility and rating, and eligible applicants are listed according to their test scores. Job openings are filled as they occur from the three top positions on a list. Persons not chosen for immediate job openings remain on the list for a period of time and may be selected for subsequent job openings.

Potential and advancement

The federal government employs about three million people. On the whole, federal employment will rise very little, but the job outlook varies depending on the field.

Advancement opportunities for each individual job follow the same patterns as in the private sector. The top positions in many agencies, however, are filled by presidential or congressional appointments.

Income

About one-quarter of all federal civilian workers are paid according to the coordinated Federal Wage System. Under this system, wage rates for craft, service, and manual workers vary by locality since their hourly wage rates are based on prevailing rates paid by local private employers.

The Postal Service Schedule actually consists of several rate schedules that cover different types and levels of postal workers such as production, supervisory, technical or clerical workers, rural carriers, and postal executives. Pay schedules, except for executives, include periodic "step" increases, and most postal workers receive cost-of-living adjustments.

Over half of all federal workers are paid under the General Pay Schedule, where jobs are graded according to difficulty of duties, knowledge, education, skills, and experience required and level of responsibility. Each of the 18 grades has an entrance and maximum pay range, and employees receive within-grade pay increases for acceptable work at stipulated time periods. Within-grade increases may also be given in recognition of superior work.

Some examples of grade levels and pay ranges follow.

Graduates of two-year colleges and technical schools with no related work experience would probably begin at GS-4 level with a starting salary of $13,200 a year.

Professional and administrative employees enter at GS-5 or GS-7, depending on their academic record. The GS-5 pay level starts at $15,300 a year; the GS-7 level starts at $19,000.

Those with a master's degree or equivalent education or experience usually enter at the GS-11 level, where pay starts at $31,000 a year.

Federal employees receive 13 days of annual leave (vacation) during each year of their first three years of employment, 20 days per year until 15 years of employment, and 26 days per year after that. Other benefits include nine paid holidays, a contributory retirement system, optional participation in group life and health insurance programs which are partly paid by the government, and government-provided training and educational programs.

Additional sources of information

State employment service offices have information on some federal job openings.

The U.S. Civil Service Commission has 62 area offices and over 100 Federal Job Information Centers in various cities throughout the country. These offices announce and conduct examinations for federal jobs; they can be located under the "U.S. Government" listing in most telephone books. Job openings and local test and interview schedules are sometimes also listed in the help-wanted sections of local newspapers.

Applicants can also obtain information from the individual agency in which they are interested.

CIVIL SERVICE WORKER, MUNICIPAL AND STATE

The job

Government employees make up a significant portion of every state's work force. State governments employ about 4 million workers, and local governments employ 10 million. The range of job opportunities includes just about every occupational and professional field.

Many government employees provide educational services, including instructional personnel and administrative and support services personnel. Most of these work in elementary and secondary schools administered by local governments; the remainder work for state governments, usually at college, university, and technical school levels.

State and local governments also employ workers in some phase of health care. This includes a full range of health care professionals such as physicians, nurses, dentists, and technical personnel.

Other persons work in general governmental control and finance activities including those employed in the administration of justice, tax collection, and general administration. Police and fire protection is supplied by law enforcement officers and support personnel and firefighters. Most of the police and practically all of the firefighters are employed by local governments.

Some government employees work in street and highway construction and maintenance. This includes civil engineers and surveyors, operators of construction machinery and equipment, truck drivers, carpenters, construction laborers, and highway toll collectors.

Places of employment and working conditions

Nearly three-quarters of the workers in this category are employed at the local community level. Those who work for state governments are located throughout the state, with most clerical and administrative facilities located at the state capital.

Working conditions vary depending on the job.

Qualifications, education, and training

State and local governments usually require the same educational and professional backgrounds as private employers.

Just about all state jobs and a majority of local government jobs are filled through some type of formal civil service test or examination. Most jobs are ranked by grade with each grade level having specific educational and experience requirements and pay ranges.

Qualified applicants are notified of testing dates; the test grades (plus a score for relevant circumstances such as area of residence or veteran's preference) then determine an applicant's position on the civil service list for that position. As openings occur, they are filled from the top of the list.

Potential and advancement

Over 14 million persons are employed by state and local governments. Employment opportunities are expected to increase substantially because of population increases and the trend toward providing more social services at taxpayers' expense.

Advancement to jobs at higher grade levels for state and municipal workers is usually through civil service examinations. Promotion to other positions is also possible, but the promoted worker is usually required to pass the appropriate examination at a later date.

Income

Government pay scales are usually comparable to those in the private sector.

Additional sources of information

Anyone interested in working for a state or local government should contact the appropriate agency or departments for job information and examination dates. The local office of the state employment service can also provide job information and will usually supply a list of current openings including requirements, pay scale, and examination dates.

CLAIM REPRESENTATIVE

The job

Claim representatives, including both claim adjusters and claim examiners, investigate claims for insurance companies, negotiate settlements with policyholders, and authorize payment of claims.

Claim adjusters work for property-liability (casualty) insurance companies and usually specialize in specific types of claims such as fire, marine, or automobile. They determine whether their company is liable (that is, whether the customer's claim is a valid one covered by the customer's policy) and recommend the amount of settlement. In the course of investigating a claim, adjusters consider physical evidence, testimony of witnesses, and any applicable reports. They strive to protect their company from false or inflated claims and at the same time settle valid claims quickly and fairly. In some companies, adjusters submit their findings to *claim examiners* who review them and authorize payment.

In states with no-fault auto insurance, adjusters do not have to establish responsibility for a loss but must decide the amount of the loss. Many auto insurance companies employ special inside adjusters who settle smaller claims by mail or telephone or at special drive-in centers where claims are settled immediately.

Most claim adjusters work for insurance companies, but some work for independent firms that contract their services to insurance companies for a fee. These firms vary in size from local firms employing two or three adjusters to large national organizations with hundreds of adjustment specialists.

A few adjusters represent the insured rather than the insurance company. These public adjusters are retained by banks, financial organizations, and other businesses to negotiate settlements with insurance companies.

In life insurance companies, claim examiners are the equivalent of claim adjusters. In the course of settling a claim, an examiner might correspond with policyholders or their families, consult medical specialists, calculate benefit payments, and review claim applications for completeness. Questionable claims or those exceeding a specified amount would be even more thoroughly investigated by the examiner.

Claim examiners also maintain records of settled claims and prepare reports for company data processing departments. More experienced examiners serve on company committees, survey claim settlement procedures, and work to improve the efficiency of claim handling departments.

Related jobs are actuary, insurance agent and broker, and underwriter.

Places of employment and working conditions

Claim adjusters work in all sections of the United States, in cities and towns of all sizes. Claim examiners, on the other hand, work in home offices of insurance companies, most of which are located in and around Boston, Chicago, Dallas, New York City, Philadelphia, and San Francisco.

Adjusters make their own schedules, doing whatever is necessary to dispose of a claim promptly and fairly. Since most firms provide 24-hour claim service, adjusters are on call all the time and may work some weekends and evenings. They may be called to the site of an accident, fire, or burglary or the scene of a riot or hurricane. They must be physically fit since they spend much of their day traveling, climbing stairs, and actively investigating claims. Much of their time is spent out-of-doors—this is not a desk job.

Claim examiners, by contrast, do have desk jobs. Their usual workweek is 40 hours, but they may work longer hours during peak loads or when quarterly and annual reports are prepared. They may travel occasionally in the course of their investigations and are sometimes called upon to testify in court regarding contested claims.

Qualifications, education, and training

Claim representatives should be able to communicate tactfully and effectively. They need a good memory and should enjoy working with details. Some knowledge of computers is helpful because they are being used more and more for recordkeeping. Claim examiners must also be familiar with medical and legal terms, insurance laws and regulations, and have mathematical skills.

Insurance companies prefer to hire college graduates for positions as claim representatives but will sometimes hire those with specialized experience, for example, automobile repair experience for automobile claims adjuster positions. Because of the complexity of insurance regulations and claim procedures, however, claim representatives without a college degree may advance more slowly than those with two years or more of college.

Many large insurance companies provide on-the-job training combined with home-study courses for the newly hired claim adjusters and claim examiners. Throughout their careers, claim representatives continue to take a variety of courses and programs designed to certify them in many different areas of the profession.

Licensing of adjusters is required in most states. Requirements vary, but applicants usually must be 20 or 21 years of age and a resident of the state, complete an approved training course in insurance or loss adjusting, provide character references, pass a written examination, and file a surety bond (a bond guaranteeing performance of a contract or obligation).

Potential and advancement

About 144,000 persons are employed as claim representatives. While all indications point to continued growth of the insurance industry and a continued need for claim representatives, persons trying to enter the field will have an advantage if they have certain specialized skills. The growing trend toward drive-in claim centers and claim handling by telephone will probably reduce the demand for automobile adjusters but increase the demand for inside adjusters. Those who specialize in workers' compensation, product liability, and other types of complex business insurance will be more in demand than ever. Job opportunities for claim examiners are becoming more numerous in property-liability companies than in life insurance companies, where computers are processing more and more of the routine claims and group policy claims.

Claim representatives are promoted as they gain experience and complete courses and training programs. Those who demonstrate unusual ability or administrative skills may become department supervisors or may advance to management jobs. Some qualified adjusters, however, prefer to broaden their knowledge by transferring to other departments such as underwriting or sales.

Income

Earnings of claim representatives vary a great deal. Inside adjusters, those who contact claimants by telephone or mail to get information, earn an annual average salary between $22,300 and $26,700, depending on the level of their experience. Outside adjusters, workers who handle more complex cases and actually investigate claims, earn, on average, a yearly salary of between $24,800 and $33,200, depending on the level of their experience. Adjusters are often provided with a company car or reimbursed for using their own cars for business purposes.

Claim examiners earn an average yearly salary of between $33,600 and $47,100, depending on the level of their experience and responsibilities.

Additional sources of information

American Council of Life Insurance
1001 Pennsylvania Avenue, NW
Washington, DC 20004

American Mutual Insurance Alliance
20 North Wacker Drive
Chicago, IL 60606

Insurance Information Institute
110 William Street
New York, NY 10038

National Association of Independent Insurers
Public Relations Department
2600 River Road
Des Plaines, IL 60018

National Association of Public Adjusters
300 Water Street
Baltimore, MD 21202

COMMUNICATIONS EQUIPMENT MECHANIC

The job

The installation, maintenance, and repair of communications equipment are the responsibility of communications equipment mechanics. This equipment includes telephone, telegraph, wireless, FAX, and cable equipment as well as radio, television, and radar broadcasting equipment. (Broadcast technicians, who are equipment operators, are covered in another job description under that title.)

Communications equipment mechanics are employed by communications systems, manufacturers of communications equipment, airlines, police and fire departments, government agencies, and radio and television studios.

Communications equipment mechanics have various duties and specialties.

Central office equipment installers handle the installation of switchboards, dialing equipment, and other equipment in the central office of a telephone company. *Station installers* and *repairpersons* install and service telephone equipment in homes, offices, businesses, and telephone booths and maintain outside facilities. *PBX installers* and *repairpersons* work on private switchboard equipment. *Linepersons* and *cable splicers* install and maintain aerial and underground wires and cables.

Radio and telephone technical operators set up and adjust overseas radio-telephone communication equipment. They contact foreign terminals and make mutually agreed-upon adjustments in transmitting power, frequency, and speech levels.

In radio and television studios, a *construction technician* installs broadcasting equipment, assembles and wires units of technical equipment, and assists in testing the equipment.

Radar technicians install and service radar equipment.

Related jobs are broadcast technician, television and radio service technician, business machine service technician, and computer service technician.

Places of employment and working conditions

Positions for communications technicians are available throughout the United States and in many locations overseas.

Because most communications systems operate 24 hours a day, seven days a week, most communications equipment mechanics work shifts, weekends, and holidays. They are also usually required to be on 24-hour call to take care of equipment failure emergencies.

Mechanics usually work in comfortable surroundings, but, depending on the job, they may have to stand for long periods, climb, reach, stoop, and lift light objects. They must be careful to avoid electrical shocks. Workers who wear headsets may suffer hearing loss from acoustic shock, a high-pitched, shrill noise produced by some headsets.

Qualifications, education, and training

Mechanical aptitude, manual dexterity, normal eyesight and hearing, physical stamina, and the ability to work as part of a team are necessary.

High school should include courses in mathematics, physics, and electrical shop. Hobbies that deal with electronics and communication equipment are helpful.

In the past, trainees were hired from both inside and outside the company, but with the deregulation of the American Telephone and Telegraph Company (AT&T) in 1984, a new practice has emerged. Large companies are reducing the size of their own training programs and seeking employees with previous work experience who have already learned the skills necessary for doing the job. These workers often come from smaller companies or the armed forces.

Companies' second preference is to hire people who have an associate's degree or postsecondary vocational school training in telecommunications technology, electronics, computer maintenance, or related subjects.

If there are no available applicants with these credentials, some companies will promote from within and provide training. The trend, however, is to reduce company costs by phasing out internal training programs.

Many telephone companies are replacing traditional classroom training programs with modular training programs, in which employees work at their own pace using entry tests, videotapes, movies, computer terminals, and programmed workbooks.

Some smaller companies are still hiring high school graduates with little or no specialized experience or training. These employees may receive some formal training, but they primarily gain skills through on-the-job training.

Potential and advancement

There are about 113,000 communications equipment mechanics. Job opportunities for these workers are expected to decline through the year 2000 because of the computerization of this type of equipment. This new technology and equipment will require fewer maintenance and repair workers because they have fewer moving parts and are more reliable. Computerized equipment also allows more centralized maintenance at control centers. Job openings in this field will result only as workers leave the labor force or transfer to other occupations.

Income

Earnings for communications equipment mechanics vary greatly depending on the size and location of the employer. Specific information can be obtained from local telephone companies.

Most communications equipment mechanics are members of the Communications Workers of America or the International Brotherhood of Electrical Workers. For these workers, wage rates, increases, and the time needed to advance in the job are determined by union contracts. Union contracts also require extra pay for work beyond the normal eight hours a day or five days a week and for all work on Sundays and holidays. Contracts also provide for additional pay for night work; paid vacations; paid sick leave; group life, medical, and dental insurance; and several other employee benefits.

Additional sources of information

Local telephone and telegraph companies and radio and television stations can provide information on job requirements.

Also, more information on the telephone industry and career opportunities in it is available in *Phonefacts* and *Is It for You? A Career in the Telephone Industry*. Request copies from:

United States Telephone Association
900 19th Street, NW
Suite 800
Washington, DC 20006

COMPUTER PROGRAMMER

The job

Computer programmers write detailed instructions, called programs, that list the orderly steps a computer must follow to solve a problem. Once programming is completed, the programmer runs a sample of the data to make sure the program is correct and will produce the desired information. This is called debugging. If there are any errors, the program must be changed and rechecked until it produces the correct results. The final step is the preparation of an instruction sheet for the computer operator who will run the program.

A simple program can be written and debugged in a few days. Those that use many data files or complex mathematical formulas may require a year or more of work. On such large projects, several programmers work together under the supervision of an experienced programmer.

Programmers usually work from problem descriptions prepared by *systems analysts* who have examined the problem and determined the next steps necessary to solve it. In organizations that do not employ systems analysts, employees called *programmer-analysts* handle both functions. An *applications programmer* then writes detailed instructions for programming the data. Applications programmers usually specialize in business or scientific work.

A *systems programmer* is a specialist who maintains the general instructions (software) that control the operation of the entire computer system.

Beginners in this field spend several months working under supervision before they begin to handle all aspects of the job.

Most programmers are employed by manufacturing firms, banks, insurance companies, data processing services, utilities, and government agencies. Systems programmers usually work in research organizations, computer manufacturing firms, and large computer centers.

A related job is systems analyst.

Places of employment and working conditions

Programmers are employed in all areas of the country.

Most programmers work a 40-hour week, but their hours are not always 9:00 to 5:00. They may occasionally work on weekends or at other odd hours to have access to the computer when it is not needed for scheduled work.

Qualifications, education, and training

Patience, persistence, and accuracy are necessary characteristics for a programmer. Ingenuity, imagination, and the ability to think logically are also important.

High school experience should include as many mathematics courses as possible.

There are no standard training requirements for programmers. Depending on the work to be done, an employer may require only some special courses in computer programming; a college education; or a graduate degree in computer science, mathematics, or engineering.

Computer programming courses are offered by vocational and technical schools, colleges and universities, and junior colleges. Home-study courses are also available, and a few high schools offer some training in programming.

Scientific organizations require college training; some require advanced degrees in computer science, mathematics, engineering, or the physical sciences.

Because of rapidly changing technologies, programmers take periodic training courses offered by employers, software vendors, and computer manufacturers. Like physicians, they must keep constantly abreast of the latest developments in their field. These courses also aid in advancement and promotion.

Potential and advancement

There are about 519,000 computer programmers. This is a rapidly growing field because of the expanding use of computers. Simpler programming needs will be increasingly handled by improved software so that programmers with only the most basic training will not find as many job openings as in the recent past. A strong demand will continue, however, for college graduates with a major in computer science or a related field. Graduates of two-year programs should find ample job openings in business applications.

There are many opportunities for advancement in this field. In large organizations, programmers may be promoted to lead programmers with supervisory responsibilities. Both applications programmers and systems programmers can be promoted to systems analyst positions.

Income

Programmers earn an average of $30,600 a year. Those in the middle of the salary range earn between $22,100 and $39,900 annually; those at the top of the salary range earn more than $49,500; and those at the bottom of the salary range earn less than $16,700.

Programmers who work in the South and West earn more than those who work in the Northeast and Midwest.

Additional sources of information

American Federation of Information Processing Societies
1899 Preston White Drive
Reston, VA 22091

Association for Computing Machinery
11 West 42nd Street
Third Floor
New York, NY 10036

Data Processing Management Association
505 Busse Highway
Park Ridge, IL 60068

COMPUTER SERVICE TECHNICIAN

The job

Computer systems perform a wide variety of tasks in business and industry. Keeping the systems in working order is the responsibility of computer service technicians.

Computer service technicians not only do repair work but also provide regular scheduled maintenance checks to prevent emergency breakdowns of equipment. Some computer technicians install new equipment, while others design and develop maintenance and repair schedules and manuals. Some technicians specialize in a particular computer model or system or in a certain type of repair.

Most computer service technicians are employed by the manufacturers of computer equipment or by firms that contract to provide maintenance service to a manufacturer's customers. A few are employed directly by organizations that have large computer installations.

Related jobs are appliance repairer, business machine service technician, communications equipment mechanic, and television and radio service technician.

Places of employment and working conditions

Computer service technicians work throughout the country. Most work in large cities, where computer equipment is concentrated.

The normal workweek is 40 hours, but large amounts of overtime are standard. Many service technicians work rotating shifts or are on call 24 hours a day because many businesses run their computers around-the-clock.

Qualifications, education, and training

Mechanical aptitude, manual dexterity, good eyesight and color vision, normal hearing, patience, and the ability to work without supervision are necessary. Because technicians work directly with customers, they must get along well with people.

A high school student interested in this field should take courses in mathematics, physics, and electrical shop. Hobbies that involve electronics, such as ham radio operation or building stereo equipment, are helpful.

Employers usually prefer to hire trainees with one or two years of technical training in electronics or electrical engineering. Technical and vocational schools, junior colleges, and the armed forces provide this training.

Trainees usually receive training from their employer for three to six months and then complete six months to two years of on-the-job training. Because of constant technological changes in the field, all technicians normally take periodic training courses as new equipment is developed.

Experienced technicians may take advanced courses for specialization in particular systems or repairs. Some technicians study computer programming and systems analysis to broaden their knowledge of computer operation.

117

Potential and advancement

There are about 71,000 computer service technicians, and the field is expanding rapidly. Since most people in the computer field are relatively young, few jobs openings will occur because of death or retirement; almost all openings will result from the rising demand for computers.

Experienced technicians may advance to supervisory positions or may become specialists or troubleshooters who diagnose difficult problems. Some transfer into sales. Others open their own repair shops.

Income

Median annual earnings for computer service technicians are about $26,700. Those in the middle of the salary range earn between $20,000 and $33,300 a year. Those at the bottom of the salary range, mainly trainees, earn less than $15,900 a year, and those at the top of the salary range earn $40,500.

Additional sources of information

Manufacturers of computers can provide information on job opportunities and training programs.

CONTROLLER

The job

The briefest and broadest definition of a controller (or the comptroller) is the key financial executive who controls, analyzes, and interprets the financial results and records of a company or an organization.

The *treasurer*, on the other hand, is responsible for the receipt, custody, and properly organized disbursement of an organization's or company's funds.

Some organizations also have a *vice-president of finance* who has overall financial responsibility and reports to the chief executive officer—president or chairman of the board—of the company.

A company may have one or all of these financial officers or may combine all three into one executive-level position with any of the above titles. This job description will be confined to the usual duties of a controller in an organization that has a separate treasurer position.

The controller is responsible for the design of a company's accounting system(s), the preparation of budgets and financial forecasts, internal auditing of company operations and records, controls of company funds kept by the treasurer, establishment and administration of tax policies and procedures, and preparation of reports to government agencies. Since an organization's financial operations involve the accumulation, interpretation, and storage of vast amounts of detailed information, a controller is very often in charge of the company's computerized data processing operation, too.

Places of employment and working conditions

Controllers are employed throughout the country. They work for government agencies, businesses, industry, nonprofit organizations, hospitals, and other institutions of all sizes.

As with many top-level jobs, controllers often work long hours under great pressure. Peak work loads occur when tax reports and stockholders' reports are prepared.

Qualifications, education, and training

A controller needs more than facility with mathematics and the ability to do accurate work. At this level of responsibility, good judgment, planning ability, administrative and management skills, ability to motivate other people, and communication skills must be combined with expertise in cost accounting, budgeting, taxes, and other specialized areas.

A college background in finance, accounting, economics, mathematics, or business administration is usually the basic education for this field. The majority of people who reach this level have a master's degree in business administration or a CPA (certified public accountant) certificate (see *accountant* job description for information on CPA requirements).

Potential and advancement

The career paths to the post of controller are varied. Cost analysis and accounting, budgeting, tax auditing, financial analysis, planning and programming, credit collections, systems and procedures, and data processing are all training grounds for executive-level financial positions.

Once the top management level has been reached, the usual method of advancement for a controller is to transfer to a larger organization where the responsibilities are greater and more complex. Some advance by moving from a top financial position in a large organization to the chief executive post in a smaller one.

Income

Salaries for controllers depend on the size of the organization and its location and are generally higher in larger institutions and cities. The median annual salary is $32,800, with the lowest 10 percent of controllers earning $17,500 or less and the highest 10 percent earning over $52,000. Many controllers receive bonuses, which vary according to the size of the firm.

Additional sources of information

Financial Executives Institute
Academic Relations Committee
P.O. Box 1938
Morristown, NJ 07962-1938

CORRECTIONS OFFICER

The job

Corrections officers, more commonly known as prison guards, are responsible for the daily activities of prisoners. They guard prisoners both inside and outside the prison. They explain prison rules to inmates and listen to their complaints and needs.

Inside the prison, corrections officers escort inmates to their daily activities, such as meals, classes, work, and chapel. If a prisoner is sick, the corrections officer sees that he or she gets to the hospital. Corrections officers oversee recreational activities and make sure that all bars, gates, doors, and windows are secure so that prisoners cannot escape. They must count the prisoners at certain times during the day and report any that are missing. Corrections officers must intervene in the case of a fight, disturbance, or escape attempt. They must also make sure prisoners do not have any forbidden articles.

Some corrections officers oversee prisoners outside the boundaries of the prison. They escort prisoners to and from jobs and on court-ordered trips and return escapees and parole violators.

Places of employment and working conditions

Most corrections officers work in state and county correctional institutions. Some work in federal prisons.

Corrections officers usually work a 40-hour week. Since prisons must be guarded around the clock, some guards work nights, evenings, and weekends.

Corrections officers may find themselves in dangerous situations at times. They must be able to remain calm and make good decisions quickly.

Qualifications, education, and training

Corrections officers must be U.S. citizens and, in most states, at least 21 years old.

A high school education is necessary or preferred for most jobs. Some two-year colleges offer programs in correctional science.

Most states test applicants on their ability to read and follow directions. Other states give a civil service examination. Some states require a psychological examination, and all require a physical exam.

All beginning officers must go through a training program lasting from one to six months. Trainees learn modern correctional methods, personal defense, physical restraint of prisoners, and the use of guns.

Potential and advancement

The job outlook for corrections officers is very good through the year 2000. Opportunities will result from the expansion of existing prisons and the construction of new ones.

As they gain additional training, experience, and education, corrections officers advance in rank and salary. They move from corrections officer to sergeant to lieutenant to corrections captain to deputy keeper. Titles for ranks may vary from institution to institution.

Income

Pay scales vary by rank and by the branch of government that is the employer. Corrections officers working for the federal government earn an average of about $20,000 a year. State corrections officers earn an average of about $17,000 annually; county corrections officers, from $15,000 to $20,000.

Additional sources of information

American Correctional Association
4321 Hartwick Road
College Park, MD 20740

National Council on Crime and Delinquency
77 Maiden Lane
San Francisco, CA 94108

COSMETOLOGIST

The job

An attractive personal appearance is important to many people. Cosmetologists, also called hairstylists or beauticians, help people look good and feel better about themselves.

Cosmetologists cut, shampoo, and style hair. They advise clients on suitable hairstyles and teach them how to care for their hair. Sometimes cosmetologists straighten or permanent wave a client's hair. They are also trained to either lighten or darken hair color. Other job duties include giving manicures and scalp and facial treatments; providing makeup analysis for women; and cleaning and styling wigs and hairpieces.

Cosmetologists also make appointments and keep records of their clients' hair care preferences. They must keep their work areas clean and sell hair products and other supplies.

Some cosmetologists own their own businesses and have managerial responsibilities.

Places of employment and working conditions

Cosmetologists work in all cities and towns, but opportunities are greatest in the most populated cities and states. Cosmetologists who set fashion trends usually work in New York City or Los Angeles.

Most full-time cosmetologists work 40 hours a week, sometimes during evenings and weekends. They spend a great deal of time on their feet.

Qualifications, education, and training

Cosmetologists should be creative. They must enjoy dealing with people and have skill in working with their hands.

All states require cosmetologists to be licensed. Most states require a person to have graduated from a state-licensed cosmetology school, pass a physical exam, and be at least 16 years old. Some states require graduation from high school while others require only an eighth-grade education.

Cosmetology training is offered in both public and private vocational schools. Daytime courses take six months to one year for completion; night courses take longer. Programs include classroom study, demonstrations, and hands-on experience.

Students take the state licensing exam after graduating from a cosmetology program. The exam usually consists of a written portion and an oral test.

Potential and advancement

There are about 649,000 cosmetologists, and the field should continue to grow through the year 2000. Population growth, higher incomes, the rising number of working women, and expansion of the beauty salon industry will result in many job opportunities.

Cosmetologists advance as they gain experience and their number of clients grows. Some are promoted into management positions or open their own salons. Some teach in cosmetology schools. Others advance by becoming sales representatives for cosmetology firms. Cosmetologists can also become examiners for state cosmetology boards.

Income

Median weekly earnings for wage and salary cosmetologists who work full-time are about $235. Earnings usually include a base salary, commissions, and tips.

Additional sources of information

National Association of Accredited Cosmetology Schools, Inc.
5201 Leesburg Pike
Falls Church, VA 22041

National Cosmetology Association, Inc.
3510 Olive Street
St. Louis, MO 63103

CREDIT INVESTIGATOR

The job

The work of a credit investigator varies greatly, depending on the employer and the size of the organization.

In a local department store extending credit in the form of a charge account or for the purchase of a home appliance, the credit investigator will probably be a clerical employee who calls the applicant's employer to verify employment and earnings and the local credit bureau to ascertain the applicant's credit rating.

In a bank or savings and loan association, the credit department is large and is usually called a loan department. Credit investigators in this setting do more in-depth analysis of a credit applicant's finances and require more information than a retail store credit department because the amounts of bank loans are usually much larger. In the case of business loans, huge sums of money may be involved. The credit investigation would probably include acquisition and analysis of a firm's records including financial statements, inventory records, details of operation, and other information.

Manufacturers, wholesalers, and distributors who extend credit to their customers also employ credit investigators. Because the sums of money involved are often very large, the credit investigation is a thorough one and often as detailed as a bank's investigation.

Additional information relative to this occupational field is contained in the job description for *credit manager*.

CREDIT MANAGER

The job

When either a business or an individual requests credit, the financial background of the requestor is investigated by the lender. Final acceptance or rejection of an application for credit is the responsibility of a credit manager.

In extending credit to a business (commercial credit), the credit manager or an assistant analyzes financial reports submitted by the applicant, checks the firm's credit record, and checks with banks or other institutions that handle the firm's accounts.

In extending credit to individuals (consumer credit), credit managers must rely on personal interviews, credit bureau reports, and the applicant's bank to provide relevant information.

In large companies, credit managers analyze the information gathered by application clerks or credit investigators and that provided in financial reports. In small companies, credit managers do much of the information gathering themselves and may also be involved in collecting delinquent accounts. In some large organizations, executive-level credit managers formulate company credit policies and establish credit department procedures.

Some credit managers are employed in wholesale and retail trade; others work for manufacturing firms and financial institutions.

Beginners in this field usually gain experience as management trainees. They learn to deal with credit bureaus, banks, and other businesses and receive a thorough grounding in the company's credit procedures and policies.

Related jobs are accountant, bank officer, and economist.

Places of employment and working conditions

Credit managers work in all areas of the country in communities of all sizes. Most job opportunities are in urban areas having many financial and business firms.

This is an office job and usually consists of a 35- to 40-hour week. In some businesses, there may be seasonal peak work loads that require overtime.

Qualifications, education, and training

The ability to analyze and draw conclusions, a pleasant personality, and communication skills are necessary for this career.

High school courses in business, bookkeeping, and public speaking are helpful. Summer or part-time jobs in business offices or credit agencies provide valuable experience.

Even though some employers will promote high school graduates to the position of credit manager if they have substantial experience in credit collection or processing of credit information, a college degree is becoming increasingly important, even for entry-level jobs in credit management. A bachelor's degree in business administration, economics, accounting, or liberal arts with a business or accounting major is the preferred educational background.

Some professional organizations in the credit and finance field offer formal training programs that include home-study courses, college courses, or other special instruction. These programs aid beginners who are developing their skills and help experienced credit managers keep abreast of new developments.

Potential and advancement

Good employment opportunities are expected in this field through the year 2000 as the volume of credit in the economy continues to grow. The number of real estate, retail sales, and other transactions requiring credit will increase rapidly, creating a demand for credit workers. Many other job openings will result from workers leaving this field or the work force.

Advancement is limited in small and medium-sized companies, but, in large companies, credit managers can advance to top executive positions.

Income

Credit investigators earn average annual salaries ranging from about $11,000 to $25,000. Credit managers earn median annual salaries of $32,800.

Additional sources of information

International Credit Association
Education Department
Box 27357
St. Louis, MO 63141-1757

CRIMINOLOGIST

The job

The field of criminology broadly covers all those who work in law enforcement, criminal courts, prisons and other correctional institutions, and counseling and rehabilitation programs for offenders. Many jobs in these categories are covered elsewhere in this book. This job description, however, focuses on the term *criminologist* as it applies to those who are involved in the scientific investigation of crime through analysis of evidence.

The scientific gathering, investigation, and evaluation of evidence is known as criminalistics, and those who work in this field are called *forensic scientists*. These technical experts, including specially trained police officers and detectives, carefully search victims, vehicles, and scenes of crimes. They take photographs, make sketches, lift fingerprints, make casts of footprints and tire tracks, and gather samples of any other relevant materials.

Once the evidence has been gathered, scientists and technicians trained in various natural sciences analyze it along with reports from medical examiners and pathologists. Other specialists interview victims to prepare composite pictures or psychological profiles of the criminal. Those who specialize in firearms and ballistics conduct tests that identify weapons used in specific crimes.

Forensic specialists also include handwriting experts, fingerprint and voiceprint specialists, polygraphy (lie detector) examiners, and odontologists (teeth and bite-mark specialists).

Almost all the people in this field work for federal, state, or local law enforcement and investigative agencies. Municipal and state police departments all have investigative responsibilities that include the processing of evidence. Some employ civilian scientists and technicians, but many utilize specially trained police officers in police crime laboratories.

The federal government employs forensic scientists in a number of agencies including the Federal Bureau of Investigation and the Secret Service.

Related jobs are chemist, medical laboratory technologist, biochemist, and police officer.

Places of employment and working conditions

Forensic scientists may be on call at all hours and may be required to work out-of-doors or in unpleasant conditions when gathering evidence.

Qualifications, education, and training

Personal traits of curiosity, ability to work with detail, patience, and good eyesight and color vision are necessary.

High school should include mathematics and science courses.

College training depends on the specialty field selected. A degree in chemistry, biology, electronics, or whatever related field is appropriate should be obtained. Course work in forensic science is offered by some colleges and by law enforcement training programs and police departments.

Potential and advancement

There are relatively few positions for criminologists. The number of available positions in the future will depend on the amount of public funding for crime prevention.

Income

Beginning criminologists earn from about $20,000 to $22,000 a year. Those who are experienced earn from about $34,000 to $43,000.

Additional sources of information

American Society of Criminology
1314 Kinnear Road
Suite 212
Columbus, OH 43212

Federal Bureau of Investigation
U.S. Department of Justice
Washington, DC 20535

D

DANCER

The job

Professional dancers perform classical ballet, modern dance, and other forms of dance; work in opera, musical comedy, movies, and television; and teach dancing. Some specially trained dance teachers also use dance therapy in working with the mentally ill.

Dancers who perform lead a very demanding life with little job security. Shows can close unexpectedly, and movie and television assignments are of short duration. Unemployment rates are high, and even highly qualified dancers find it difficult to obtain year-round work. Dancers who are part of an established dance company or who are in a long-running hit show have the most stable performing life. Many dancers take part-time jobs to support themselves between dancing assignments, and those who are qualified to teach often combine teaching and performing.

Dancers who teach full-time have the most stable working life. Those who teach at colleges and universities have the same schedule as other faculty members. Others teach in private studios, professional dancing schools, and dance companies. Those who work for dance companies also travel with the group when it goes on tour.

Dancers who create dance routines or new ballets are called *choreographers*. They usually have experience as performers and can continue their careers as choreographers long after their active performing years. *Dance directors* train dancers in new routines or productions.

Dancers who perform usually are members of one of the unions affiliated with the Associated Actors and Artists of America (AFL-CIO).

Places of employment and working conditions

New York city is *the* city for performing dancers. Other cities that provide substantial numbers of job opportunities are Atlanta, Boston, Philadelphia, Cleveland, Dallas, Miami, Cincinnati, Chicago, Milwaukee, Pittsburgh, Houston, Salt Lake City, Seattle, and Washington, D.C.

Just about every town and city has at least one dancing school that employs teachers. Job openings for dancing teachers also exist in colleges and universities and in secondary schools, dance companies, and private studios.

A dancer's life is one of rigorous practice and self-discipline, with strict dieting a constant factor. Performances are scheduled on evenings and weekends, and lessons and practice take up daytime hours, leaving little time for personal life. Heavy travel schedules and the unstable nature of show business can drain a performer's physical and emotional strength. The physical demands of this career mean that a dancer's active performing career is usually over by his or her late thirties.

Qualifications, education, and training

Good health and physical stamina are absolutely essential for a dancer. Body build and height should be average with good feet and normal arches. Agility, grace, creativity, and a feeling for music are also necessary. Dancers should also be able to take direction and function as part of a group.

Selection of a good professional dance school is very important. Serious training for a dancer begins before the age of 12. In ballet, training must begin even earlier, at about age 7. Most dancers are ready for professional auditions by age 17 or 18, but training never ends. Ten to 12 lessons a week and many hours of practice make up the life of a dancer, even when performing with a dance company or in a show.

Because of the strenuous training schedule, a dancer's general education may suffer. Some dancers solve this problem by taking correspondence courses. In addition to dancing, professional dancing schools usually teach music, literature, and history to aid students in dramatic interpretation of the dance.

An alternative to professional school training is a college or university degree in dance. About 250 schools confer degrees in dance. Bachelor's and master's degrees are usually offered in the departments of physical education, music, theater, or fine arts. A college degree is usually necessary for teaching at the college or university level but is not required for teaching in a professional school or dance studio where performing experience is preferred. College-trained dancers who wait to begin a performing career until graduation from college may find themselves at a disadvantage when competing with beginners of 17 or 18.

Potential and advancement

There are about 11,000 dancers performing on stage, screen, and television, and many others are involved in teaching. This is a field where qualified applicants always exceed the number of job openings. Increased employment opportunities exist in teaching dance.

Income

Basic agreements between unions and producers specify minimum wages, working hours, and other employment conditions, but individual contracts signed by each dancer with a producer may be favorable.

The minimum weekly salary for new dancers in ballet and modern productions is $445. The basic rate paid to new performers for single performances is $198 per performance and $140 per rehearsal. Dancers on tour receive an additional allowance for room and board. Dancers on television earn a minimum of $536 to $573 for a one-hour show.

The normal workweek for a dancer under a union contract is 30 hours (6 hours per day maximum) of rehearsals and performances. Extra compensation is paid for any additional hours worked.

Dancers who teach earn salaries that vary with location, prestige of the school or dance company for which they work, and personal reputation of the teacher. At colleges and universities, dance teachers earn the same salaries as other faculty members.

Additional sources of information

American Dance Guild
33 West 21st Street
Third Floor
New York, NY 10010

National Dance Association
1900 Association Drive
Reston, VA 22091

DENTAL ASSISTANT

The job

Dental assistants work with dentists and oral hygienists as they examine and treat patients. They are usually employed in private dental offices and often combine office duties, such as making appointments, maintaining patient records, and billing, with chairside assisting.

Dental assistants prepare instruments and materials for treatment procedures, process dental x-ray films, sterilize instruments, prepare plaster casts of teeth from impressions taken by the dentists, and sometimes provide oral health instructions to patients. In some states, they are permitted to apply medications to teeth and gums, remove excess filling materials from surfaces of teeth, and fit rubber isolation dams on individual teeth before treatment by the dentist.

Dental assistants are also employed in dental schools, hospital dental departments, state and local public health departments, and private clinics. The federal government employs them in the Public Health Service, the Veterans Administration, and the armed forces.

Most dental assistants are women. Opportunities for part-time work are numerous, making this a good field for people with family responsibilities.

A related job is dental hygienist.

Places of employment and working conditions

Dental assistants are employed in communities of all sizes with the most job opportunities in large metropolitan areas.

A 40-hour workweek is usual for full-time dental assistants, but this includes some evening and Saturday hours in most dental offices.

Qualifications, education, and training

Neatness and the ability to help people relax are important personal qualities.

High school courses in biology, chemistry, health, typing, and office practices are helpful.

Most dental assistants acquire their skills on the job. Office skills often provide entry into a dental office where a beginner handles appointments, acts as receptionist, and performs routine clerical and record-keeping chores. Dental assisting skills are then acquired over a period of time.

An increasing number of dental assistants are acquiring their training in formal programs at junior and community colleges and vocational and technical schools. Most of these programs require one year or less to complete. Two-year programs include some liberal arts courses and offer an associate's degree upon completion. Some private schools offer four- to six-month courses in dental assisting, but these are not accredited by the Commission on Dental Accreditation. Dental assistants who receive their training in the armed forces usually qualify for civilian jobs.

Graduates of accredited programs may receive professional recognition by completing an examination given by the Dental Assisting National Board. They are then designated as certified dental assistants.

Potential and advancement

There are about 166,000 people working as dental assistants; one-third work part-time. Job opportunities should be excellent for the future, especially for graduates of formal training programs.

Dental assistants in large dental offices or clinics are sometimes promoted to supervisory positions. Some advance by fulfilling the educational requirements necessary to become dental hygienists. Others teach in or administer dental assisting education programs.

Income

Salaries vary widely from community to community and depend on training and experience, job responsibilities and duties, and size of dental practice.

The average income for full-time dental assistants is about $267 a week.

Additional sources of information

American Dental Assistants Association
919 North Michigan Avenue
Suite 3400
Chicago, IL 60611

Dental Assisting National Board, Inc.
216 East Ontario Street
Chicago, IL 60611

DENTAL HYGIENIST

The job

Dental hygienists are involved in both clinical dental work and education with specific responsibilities governed by the state in which the hygienist is employed.

Working as part of a dental health team under the supervision of a dentist, a dental hygienist may clean and polish a patient's teeth, removing deposits and stains at the same time; apply medication for the prevention of tooth decay; take and develop x-rays; make model impressions of teeth for study; take medical and dental histories; and provide instruction for patient self-care, diet, and nutrition. In some states, pain control and restorative procedures may also be performed by dental hygienists.

Some dental hygienists work in school systems where they examine students' teeth, assist dentists in determining necessary dental treatment, and report their findings to parents. They give instruction in proper mouth care and develop classroom or assembly programs on oral health.

Most dental hygienists are employed in private dental offices; many are employed part-time.

Other employers are public health agencies, industrial plants, clinics and hospitals, dental hygienist schools, the federal government, and the U.S. armed forces (those with a bachelor's degree are commissioned officers). A few dental hygienists are involved in research projects.

Places of employment and working conditions

Dental hygienists work in communities of all sizes.

They usually work a 35- to 40-hour workweek; those employed by a dentist in private practice usually have some weekend and evening hours. Dental hygienists are required to stand for a good part of the working day.

Certain health protection procedures are important for anyone working in this field. These include regular medical checkups and strict adherence to established procedures for disinfection and use of x-ray equipment.

Qualifications, education, and training

An enjoyment of people and the ability to put a patient at ease are strong assets. Manual dexterity is necessary. Good health, personal cleanliness and neatness, and stamina are very important.

High school courses recommended for anyone interested in a career in this field include biology, chemistry, health, and mathematics.

Requirements for admission to dental hygienist schools vary. Some hygienist schools that offer a bachelor's degree require one or two prior years of college.

There are 197 programs in dental hygiene in the United States that are accredited by the Commission on Dental Accreditation. Students in dental hygienist programs study anatomy, physiology, chemistry, pharmacology, nutrition, tissue structure, gum diseases, dental materials, and clinical dental hygiene. Liberal arts courses are also part of the program. Most programs grant an associate's degree with some schools awarding a bachelor's degree. Several schools offer master's degree programs in dental hygiene or related fields.

Licensing is required for all dental hygienists; all states require graduation from an accredited dental hygienist school as well as written and clinical examination. To pass the clinical examination, the applicant for licensing is tested on proficiency in performing dental hygiene procedures. Most states will accept a passing grade on the written examination given by the American Dental Association Joint Commission on National Dental Examinations as part of the licensing requirement.

Potential and advancement

About 91,000 persons work as dental hygienists.

This is a field where current job openings outnumber qualified graduates, and the employment outlook for potential dental hygienists is excellent. An expanding population, increased participation in dental insurance plans, more group practice by dentists, and dental care programs for children will all contribute to a still greater demand for trained dental hygienists in the future. There will also be many opportunities for dental hygienists who desire part-time work and for those willing to work in rural areas.

Income

Dental hygienists working in private dental offices are paid on an hourly, daily, salary, or commission basis.

According to the American Dental Hygienists' Association, half of all hygienists earn between $15,000 and $25,000 a year. Their average hourly pay is $14.61.

Additional sources of information

Division of Dentistry
Public Health Service
U.S. Department of Health and Human Services
9000 Rockville Pike
Bethesda, MD 20014

Division of Professional Development
American Dental Hygienists' Association
444 North Michigan Avenue
Suite 3400
Chicago, IL 60611

DENTIST

The job

Graduates of approved dental schools are entitled to use the designations D.D.S. (doctor of dental surgery) or D.M.D. (doctor of dental medicine).

Most dentists are general practitioners who provide many types of dental care. They examine teeth and mouth tissues to diagnose and treat any diseases or abnormalities of the teeth, gums, supporting bones, and surrounding tissues. They extract teeth, fill cavities, design and insert dentures and inlays, and perform surgery. The dentist, or someone on his or her staff, takes dental and medical histories, cleans teeth, and provides instructions on proper diet and cleanliness to preserve dental health.

About 20 percent of all dentists are specialists. The two largest fields are made up of *orthodontists*, who straighten teeth, and *oral surgeons*, who operate on the mouth and jaws. Other specialties are pediatric dentistry (dentistry for children), periodontics (treatment of the gums), prosthodontics (artificial teeth and dentures), endodontics (root canal therapy), oral pathology (diseases of the mouth), and public health dentistry.

Close to 2,000 civilian dentists are employed by the federal government. These dentists work in hospitals and clinics of the Veterans Administration or in the U.S. Public Health Service.

Places of employment and working conditions

Almost 90 percent of dentists work in private practice, which includes a wide variety of work settings and payment systems. Of the dentists who work outside private practice, half are researchers, teachers, or administrators in dental schools. Others work in hospitals and clinics. The federal government employs about 2,000 dentists, primarily in the hospitals and clinics of the Veterans Administration and the U.S. Public Health Service.

Most dentists' offices are open five days a week, and some dentists work weekend and evening hours to accommodate their patients' needs. Dentists usually work about 40 hours a week, with those who are just starting up working fewer hours until their practice grows.

Qualifications, education, and training

Students interested in dentistry as a career should possess a high degree of manual dexterity and scientific ability and have good visual memory and excellent judgment of space and shape.

High school courses should include biology, chemistry, health, and mathematics.

Dental education is very expensive because of the length of time required to earn a dental degree. From three to four years of predental college work in the sciences and humanities is required by dental schools with most successful applicants having a bachelor's or master's degree. Since competition for admission is stiff, dental schools give considerable weight to the amount of predental education and to college grades. Schools also require personal interviews and recommendations as well as completion of the admission testing program used by all dental schools. In addition, state-supported dental schools usually give preference to residents of the state.

Dental school training lasts four academic years after college or, in some dental colleges, three calendar years. The first two years consist of classroom instruction and laboratory work in anatomy, microbiology, biochemistry, physiology, clinical sciences, and preclinical technique. The remainder of the training period is spent in actual treatment of patients.

A license to practice is required by all states and the District of Columbia. Requirements include a degree from a dental school approved by the Commission on Dental Accreditation and written and practical examinations. A passing grade on the written examination given by the National Board of Dental Examiners is accepted by most states as fulfilling part of the licensing requirements; 20 states will grant a license without examination to dentists already licensed by another state.

In 15 states, dentists who wish to specialize must have two or three years of graduate training and, in some cases, pass an additional state examination. In the remaining states, a licensed dentist may engage in general or specialized dentistry. In these states, the additional education is also necessary to specialize; however, specialists are regulated by the state dental profession rather than by state licensing.

Potential and advancement

There are about 142,000 active dentists, 90 percent of them in private practice. The demand for dentists is expected to grow because of population growth, increased awareness of the necessity of dental health, and the expansion of prepaid dental insurance benefits to employees in many industries.

Income

Dentists setting up a new practice can look forward to a few lean years in the beginning. As the practice grows, income will rise rapidly with average yearly earnings around $70,000.

A practice can usually be developed most quickly in small towns where there is less competition from established dentists. Over the long run, however, earnings of dentists in urban areas are higher than earnings in small towns. Specialists generally earn much more than general practitioners, whatever the location, averaging about $100,000 a year.

Additional sources of information

American Association of Dental Schools
1625 Massachusetts Avenue, NW
Washington, DC 20036

American Dental Association
Council on Dental Education
211 East Chicago Avenue
Chicago, IL 60611

Division of Dentistry
Public Health Service
U.S. Department of Health and Human Services
9000 Rockville Pike
Bethesda, MD 20014

DIETICIAN

The job

Dieticians plan nutritious and appetizing meals, supervise the preparation and service of food, and manage the purchasing and accounting for their department. Others are involved in research and education.

More than half of all dieticians are employed in hospitals, nursing homes, and other health care facilities. Colleges, universities, school systems, restaurants and cafeterias, large companies that provide food service for their employees, and food processors and manufacturers also employ dieticians.

Some serve as commissioned officers in the armed forces. The federal government also employs dieticians in Veterans Administration hospitals and in the U.S. Public Health Service.

Clinical dieticians form the largest group of dieticians. They plan the diets and supervise the service of meals to meet the various nutritional needs of patients in hospitals, nursing homes, and clinics. They confer with doctors and instruct patients and their families on diet requirements and food preparation.

Management dieticians are responsible for large-scale meal planning and preparation. They purchase food, equipment, and supplies; enforce safety and sanitary regulations; and train and direct food service and supervisory workers. If they are directors of a dietetic department, they may also have budgeting responsibilities, coordinate dietetic service activities with other departments, and set department policy. In a small institution, the duties of administrative and clinical dieticians are usually combined into one position.

Research dieticians evaluate the dietary requirements of specific groups such as the elderly, space travelers, or those with a chronic disease. They also do research in food management and service systems and equipment. *Dietetic educators* teach in medical, dental, and nursing schools.

Nutritionists provide counseling in proper nutrition practices. They work in food industries, educational and health facilities, agricultural agencies, welfare agencies, and community health programs.

Places of employment and working conditions

Dieticians are employed throughout the country with most job opportunities in large metropolitan areas and in areas with large colleges and universities.

Most dieticians work a 40-hour week, but this usually includes some weekend hours. There are many part-time opportunities for dieticians.

Qualifications, education, and training

Anyone interested in this career field should have scientific aptitude, organizational and administrative ability, and the ability to work well with people.

High school courses should include biology, chemistry, home economics, mathematics, and some business courses, if possible.

A bachelor's degree in the home economics department with a major in foods and nutrition or institutional management is the basic requirement for a dietician. Almost 260 schools offer undergraduate programs in the field.

A 9- to 12-month internship or a preprofessional practice program should also be completed by any dietician who wants professional recognition. These programs consist primarily of clinical experience under the direction of a qualified dietician. Some colleges and universities have coordinated undergraduate programs that enable students to complete both the clinical and bachelor's degree requirements in four years.

Vocational and technical schools as well as junior colleges also offer training in dietetic services. Students who complete these training courses can work as dietetic assistants or technicians and usually find ample job opportunities.

The American Dietetic Association registers dieticians who meet their established qualifications. The designation RD (registered dietician) is an acknowledgment of a dietician's competence and professional status.

Potential and advancement

About 40,000 people work as dieticians. Job opportunities, both full- and part-time, should be plentiful through the year 2000.

Dieticians usually advance by moving to larger institutions. In a large institution, they may advance to director of the dietetic department. Some advance by entering some area of clinical specialization. Others become consultants or opt for careers in business and management. Advancement in research and teaching positions usually requires a graduate degree.

Income

Beginners in this field earn about $21,800 a year. Experienced dieticians earn about $29,500 a year.

Additional sources of information

The American Dietetic Association
216 West Jackson Boulevard
Suite 800
Chicago, IL 60606-6995

DRAFTER

The job

Drafters prepare detailed drawings from rough sketches, specifications, and calculations made by engineers, architects, designers, and scientists. Work completed by a drafter usually includes a detailed view of the object from all sizes, specifications for materials to be used, and procedures to be followed. Any other information necessary to carry out the job is also included by the drafter.

Drafters usually specialize in a particular field, such as mechanical, electronic, structural, architectural, electrical, or aeronautical drafting. They are classified according to the work they do and their level of responsibility. *Senior drafters* translate preliminary drawings and plans into design layouts—scale drawings of the object to be built. *Detailers* draw each part shown on the layout giving dimensions, materials, and other information. *Checkers* examine drawings and specifications for errors. Supervised by experienced drafters, *tracers* make minor corrections and trace drawings for reproduction on paper or plastic film. Beginners usually start as tracers or junior drafters and work their way up through checker and detailer positions.

About 95 percent of all drafters work in private industry. Engineering and architectural firms employ about one-third; another one-third work for fabricated metals, electrical equipment, machinery, and construction firms. Over 13,000 drafters work for federal, state, and local government agencies. The U.S. Department of Defense is the main federal employer; state and local governments employ drafters mainly in highway and public works departments.

Places of employment and working conditions

Drafters work in all areas of the country with the largest concentrations in industrialized areas.

Working areas are usually pleasant, but drafters do very detailed work at drawing boards or computer terminals and must often sit for long periods of time.

Qualifications, education, and training

Drafters need good eyesight, manual dexterity, and drawing ability and must be able to do accurate, detailed work. They must have the ability to work as part of a team. In some specialized fields, artistic ability is also necessary.

High school courses should include mechanical drawing, science, computers, and mathematics. Shop skills are also helpful.

Drafting skills may be acquired in several ways. Vocational and technical high schools provide enough training for entry-level jobs at companies with on-the-job training programs. Technical institutes, junior and community colleges, and extension divisions of universities provide training for full-time and evening students. The armed forces also train drafters.

Due to the increasing use of computer-aided design (CAD) systems, persons trained in electronic drafting will have the best prospects for employment.

Potential and advancement

There are about 319,000 drafters, and the field is expected to grow through the year 2000. Increased use of CAD equipment may offset some of this growth.

Experienced drafters can advance to senior drafter and supervisory positions. Some drafters become independent designers or continue their education to transfer to engineering or architectural positions.

Income

In private industry, experienced drafters earn between $17,900 to $30,900 a year; senior drafters average about $32,600.

Additional sources of information

American Design Drafting Association
5522 Norbeck Road
Rockville, MD 20853

International Federation of Professional and Technical Engineers
8701 Georgia Avenue
Suite 701
Silver Spring, MD 20910

E

ECONOMIST

The job

Economists study and analyze the relationship between the supply and demand of goods and services and how they are produced, distributed, and consumed.

Over three-fifths of all economists work in private industry such as manufacturing firms, banks, insurance companies, securities and investment firms, and management consulting firms. They provide information to management that affects decisions on marketing and pricing of company products, long- and short-term economic forecasts, and the effect of government policies on business.

Many economists are employed by colleges and universities where they teach or are engaged in research and writing. These economists are often called upon to act as consultants to business firms and government agencies.

Economists employed in government prepare studies to assess economic conditions and the need for changes in government policies. They usually work in the fields of agriculture, forestry, business, finance, labor, transportation, and international trade and development.

A related job is credit manager.

Places of employment and working conditions

Economists work in all large cities and in university towns. The largest concentrations are in the New York City, Washington, D.C., and Chicago metropolitan areas.

Qualifications, education, and training

Anyone interested in this career field should be able to work accurately and in detail since economics entails careful analysis of data. Good communications skills are also necessary.

High school should include as many mathematics courses as possible.

A college major in economics is the basic preparation for a career in economics. Students should also study political science, psychology, sociology, finance, business law, and international relations. A bachelor's degree is sufficient for many beginning research, administrative, management trainee, and sales jobs. However, graduate school is increasingly necessary for advancement.

Graduate training in a specialty area such as advanced economic theory, labor economics, or international economics is necessary for college teaching positions. The larger colleges and universities require a Ph.D.

Potential and advancement

There are about 36,000 economists in the United States. Growth in the economics field is expected to be faster than the average for all occupations through the year 2000. Most opportunities will occur as workers transfer to other occupations or leave the labor force for some reason.

The best opportunities will be in manufacturing, financial services, advertising agencies, research organizations, and consulting firms. Nonprofit organizations and trade associations will provide other opportunities. No significant change is expected in the employment of economists in the federal government, and employment of economists in state and local government is expected to grow slowly.

Advancement in this field usually requires advanced degrees.

Income

Average annual earnings for economists are about $35,000. The lowest-paid economists earn under $21,000 a year, while the highest paid earn over $52,000.

Additional sources of information

American Economic Association
1313 21st Avenue, South
Nashville, TN 37212

National Association of Business Economists
28349 Chagrin Boulevard
Suite 201
Cleveland, OH 44122

EDITOR, BOOK PUBLISHING

The job

An editor has two basic functions: to work with the author in the preparation of the author's work for publication and to prepare the manuscript for the various phases of the production process. Because no one person could handle all the editorial details involved in publication, specific areas of responsibility are usually assigned to individual members of an editorial staff.

The *editor-in-chief*, sometimes called executive editor, manages the editorial department, organizes the editorial staff, sets the budget, and makes key decisions on editorial policy. Editors function within the financial and policy goals of the publisher and editor-in-chief. They work with authors, agents, and other publishers; develop authors and manuscripts; and prepare contracts. Editors have titles in accordance with their seniority. After the editor-in-chief and executive editor, *senior editors* have the most seniority, followed by *full editors, associate editors, and assistant editors.*

In some publishing houses, there is an added distinction between *acquisitions editors* and *production editors* or *project editors*. Acquisitions editors scout for manuscripts and read and evaluate submissions. Production or project editors edit the manuscript and work with production and art department personnel to turn the manuscript into a finished book.

A *managing editor* coordinates all editorial functions on each project and acts as a traffic manager, seeing that all production schedules are met. A *copy editor* does a careful reading of the manuscript with attention to grammar, spelling, and punctuation as well as to coherence, arrangement, and accuracy. The copy editor marks all necessary directions for the typesetter and may query (question) the author on any material that is not clear.

Editorial assistants handle incoming manuscripts, give a first reading to unsolicited ones, return rejected manuscripts, and handle clerical duties.

An important job in the editorial and production processes is that of the *proofreader*, who checks material after it has been set into type. The proofreader checks the typeset copy against the copyedited manuscript to make sure that the typesetter has set the material exactly as indicated. The proofreader is expected to catch any mistakes in spelling, design specifications, or other printer's errors, as well as any errors of grammar or discrepancies overlooked by the copy editor. Although proofreading is a specialty in itself, most editors have done their share of it at some point in their careers.

Although in the past men have generally held the higher-paid, executive editorial positions and women have performed the lower-level editorial functions, this situation is changing. Now, women compete with men for top management positions and generally earn equal, or near equal, salaries.

Places of employment and working conditions

Every city has some job opportunities for editors. The biggest publishing center is New York City, followed by Philadelphia, Boston, Chicago, Los Angeles, San Francisco, and Washington, D.C. Most college communities also provide a number of job openings in this field.

The usual workweek is 40 hours, but production deadlines and large work loads frequently make overtime necessary.

Qualifications, education, and training

The ability to work with people, tact, an ability to recognize not only what is well written but also what will sell, attention to detail, good judgment, and excellent communication skills are necessary.

High school courses in English are very important, but a student interested in this field should also get a well-rounded education to prepare for college. Typing is a must, and computers and word processing skills are becoming increasingly important.

Liberal arts with a major in English or a bachelor's degree in journalism is the usual preparation for this field. Textbook, scientific, and technical publishers usually require a background in specific subject areas as well as proficiency in English.

Potential and advancement

There are about 6,000 book publishers that employ editors. Since there is always an overabundance of English and journalism majors seeking jobs in this field, the best job prospects are with small publishers, especially for beginners.

Promotion up through various editorial positions occurs as an editor gains experience, but advancement in this field very often takes the form of moving to a larger company.

Income

The publishing field is not a well-paid field on the whole. Salaries are low compared to other fields that require comparable education and experience.

Beginning editorial positions pay $13,000 to $18,000 a year. Associate editors earn from $18,500 to $26,000.

Full editors earn $23,000 and up; a few earn as much as $40,000 a year. Some executive editors earn $53,000 to $68,000 yearly.

Additional sources of information

Association of American Publishers, Inc.
220 East 23rd Street
New York, NY 10010

EDITOR, NEWSPAPER AND MAGAZINE

The job

The editorial positions and responsibilities on a newspaper differ in many respects from those in book publishing; those in magazine publishing cover aspects of both publishing fields.

The editor or *editor-in-chief* of a magazine or newspaper sets general editorial policy in accordance with the wishes of the publisher, who may also be the editor. The editor may write some or all of the editorials and may be involved to varying degrees in the daily operation of the paper or magazine.

A *managing editor* directs and supervises the day-to-day operation of the publication. On a newspaper, the managing editor usually has the responsibility of selecting the news stories that will receive top play. Some newspapers and magazines also have an *executive editor* whose responsibilities lie between those of the editor and the managing editor, taking some of the work load from each job.

On a newspaper, the *city editor* directs local and area news coverage. He or she schedules reporters and assigns the news stories they are to cover. The city editor also supervises the rewrite staff. The *wire editor* handles the national and foreign news. On some papers, a *news editor* rather than the managing editor decides on the final mix of local, national, and foreign news and on which stories will receive top play. Weekly news magazines also have foreign and news editors.

The *makeup editor* on a newspaper or magazine is responsible for page layout. On a newspaper, the makeup editor must be able to work swiftly to meet deadlines and may have to remake pages at the last minute when late-breaking news bumps previously positioned stories.

Both magazines and newspapers employ *copy editors*, or *copyreaders*, who prepare all material for typesetting. They correct grammar, spelling, and punctuation; check names, dates, and other facts; and write headlines to go with each item or article. Some copy editors also handle page layout and photo editing. On a daily newspaper, all of this must be done quickly to meet production deadlines.

Various special editorial positions may include women's editor, sports editor, financial editor, food editor, and many others. These editors have responsibility for news and features in their specialty area and sometimes supervise large staffs.

Women are being hired by newspapers and magazines in growing numbers. Once relegated to handling the women's pages and food sections, women now handle politics, economics, sports, and other topics on an equal footing with men.

Places of employment and working conditions

Large metropolitan areas provide the most opportunities for newspaper and magazine editors, but opportunities exist throughout the country in communities of all sizes.

Constant deadline pressure is a fact of life for newspaper editors and, to a lesser extent, magazine editors. For newspaper and news magazine editors, personal plans must often be subordinated to the demands of the job. The pace and pressure can be physically and emotionally wearing.

Although the workweek is supposed to be about 40 hours, very often this is not the case, since important news stories can mean longer hours and irregular schedules. Those who work on morning papers usually work evening hours.

Qualifications, education, and training

A newspaper or magazine editor needs a sense of what is important and interesting to the reader. An excellent command of the English language, management skills, good judgment, and the ability to motivate people are necessary skills.

A broad high school curriculum with emphasis on the development of communication skills is important. Experience on school publications or as a stringer (covering local events such as sports for several newspapers) can provide valuable background. Typing is a must, although word processors have replaced typewriters in the newsroom and editorial office.

College is very important for anyone interested in working as an editor. A liberal arts degree or degree in journalism is the usual preparation, with employers about evenly divided on which they prefer.

Potential and advancement

There are about 13,000 newspapers in the United States, as well as 1,200 consumer magazines, 2,500 business publications, and 8,000 house organs (internal publications of a business) that employ editors. Competition for all editorial jobs on large newspapers and magazines is the norm; publications in smaller communities and in areas away from large metropolitan areas offer the best employment opportunities. Beginners will find the best opportunities on small magazines and weekly newspapers where they can accumulate experience in a variety of editorial functions.

Promotion in this field is usually up through the ranks, with many editors starting as reporters, feature writers, and rewriters. Advancement also takes the form of movement to larger publications or larger cities.

Income

Salaries for newspaper employees vary greatly, depending on the level of experience and the size of the paper.

Beginners earn a median starting salary of $13,900.

Salaries are higher for employees of newspapers that have a contract with The Newspaper Guild, the union for newspaper employees. Reporters working for daily newspapers that have contracts with the guild have annual starting salaries ranging from about $9,400 to $47,000; the majority start at between $15,600 and $23,400. Experienced reporters average about $31,200.

Additional sources of information

American Newspaper Publishers Association
The Newspaper Center
Box 17407
Dulles International Airport
Washington, D.C. 20041

ELECTRICAL/ELECTRONICS ENGINEER

The job

Electrical and electronics engineering is the largest branch of engineering. These engineers design and develop electrical and electronic equipment and products. They may work in power generation and transmission; machinery controls; lighting and wiring for buildings, automobiles, and aircraft; computers; radar; communications equipment; missile guidance systems; or consumer goods such as television sets and appliances.

Engineers in this field usually specialize in a major area such as communications, computers, or power distribution equipment or in a subdivision such as aviation electronic systems. Many are involved in research, development, and design of new products; others in manufacturing and sales.

The main employers of electrical engineers are companies that manufacture electrical and electronic equipment, aircraft and parts, business machines, and professional and scientific equipment. Telephone, telegraph, and electric light and power companies also employ many electrical engineers. Others work for construction firms, engineering consulting firms, and government agencies. A number of them work in the field of nuclear energy.

Places of employment and working conditions

Engineers are employed in all areas of the country, in towns and cities of all sizes as well as rural areas, with some specialties concentrated in certain areas.

Qualifications, education, and training

The ability to think analytically, a capacity for detail, and the ability to work as part of a team are all necessary. Good communications skills are important.

Mathematics and the sciences must be emphasized in high school.

A bachelor's degree in engineering is the minimum requirement in this field. In a typical curriculum, the first two years are spent in the study of basic sciences such as physics and chemistry and mathematics, introductory engineering, and some liberal arts courses. The remaining years are usually devoted to specialized engineering courses. Engineering programs can last from four to six years. Those requiring five or six years to complete may award a master's degree or may provide a cooperative plan of study plus practical work experience with a nearby industry.

Because of rapid changes in technology, many engineers continue their education throughout their careers. A graduate degree is necessary for most teaching and research positions and for many management jobs. Some persons obtain graduate degrees in business administration.

Engineering graduates usually work under the supervision of an experienced engineer or in a company training program until they become acquainted with the requirements of a particular company or industry.

All states require licensing of engineers whose work may affect life, health, or property or who offer their services to the public. Those who are licensed, about one-third of all engineers, are called registered engineers. Requirements include graduation from an accredited engineering school, four years of experience, and a written examination.

Potential and advancement

There are about 439,000 electrical engineers. Increased demand for computers, communications, and military electronics is expected to provide ample job opportunities for electrical engineers through the year 2000. A sharp rise or fall in government spending for defense could change this picture in either direction.

Income

Starting annual salaries in private industry average $29,200 with a bachelor's degree; $34,600 with a master's degree; and $46,600 or more with a Ph.D.

Additional sources of information

Accreditation Board for Engineering and Technology
345 East 47th Street
New York, NY 10017

American Society for Engineering Education
11 Dupont Circle
Suite 200
Washington, DC 20036

Institute of Electrical and Electronics Engineers
United States Activities Board
1828 L Street, NW
Suite 1202
Washington, DC 20036

Junior Engineering Technical Society (JETS)
1420 King Street
Suite 405
Alexandria, VA 22314

National Society of Professional Engineers
1420 King Street
Alexandria, VA 22314

Society of Women Engineers
345 East 47th Street
Room 305
New York, NY 10017

ELECTRICIAN

The job

The installation and maintenance of electrical systems and equipment is handled by electricians. They follow National Electrical Code specifications and any state and local electrical codes. Observance of safety practices is very important in this field, and electricians often use protective equipment and clothing.

Construction electricians, following blueprints and specifications, install wiring systems in newly constructed or renovated homes, offices, and factories. They also install electrical machinery, electronic equipment and controls, and signal and communications systems. Most construction electricians are employed by electrical contractors; some are self-employed.

Maintenance electricians maintain the electrical systems installed by construction electricians and usually work in factories or other large buildings such as office buildings and apartment houses. They also install new electrical equipment and keep lighting systems, generators, and transformers in good working order. Maintenance electricians spend much of their time doing preventative maintenance, inspecting equipment to locate and correct problems before breakdown can occur. More than half of all maintenance electricians are employed in manufacturing industries. Others are employed by public utilities, mines, and railroads and by federal, state, and local governments.

Electricians usually furnish their own hand tools (screwdrivers, pliers, knives, hacksaws), while employers furnish heavier tools (pipe threaders, conduit benders) and most test meters and power tools.

Most construction electricians are members of the International Brotherhood of Electrical Workers.

Places of employment and working conditions

Electricians are employed throughout the country, but the greatest numbers are in industrialized and urban areas. The heavily industrialized states such as

California, New York, Pennsylvania, Illinois, and Ohio employ many maintenance electricians.

Electricians do not need great physical strength, but they must be in good physical condition since they must stand for long periods and often work in cramped spaces. Because they usually work indoors, they are not exposed to bad weather as much as other workers in the building trades; however, they do risk injury from falls, electrical shock, and falling objects. Maintenance electricians work near high voltage industrial equipment and are exposed to noise and the grease and oil of machinery.

Qualifications, education, and training

Electricians need at least average physical strength, agility, and dexterity. Good color vision is important since electrical wires are often identified by color.

High school or vocational school courses in electricity, electronics, mechanical drawing, science, and electrical shop are a good background for someone interested in becoming an electrician. Because completion of a formal apprenticeship program is considered the best way to become an electrician, this trade has a higher percentage of apprenticeship-trained workers than most other construction trades. A local union-management commission sponsors and supervises each program. Those who complete an apprenticeship program can usually qualify as either a construction or maintenance electrician.

Applicants for apprenticeship should be in good health and at least 18 years of age. Most programs require a high school or vocational school diploma and one year of algebra. Most programs last four years and include up to 8,000 hours of comprehensive on-the-job training as well as 150 hours per year of classroom instruction. Classroom courses include blueprint reading, electrical theory, electronics, mathematics, and safety and first-aid training.

Some people learn the trade informally by working as electricians' helpers in construction or maintenance jobs. They can gain additional knowledge through trade schools, correspondence courses, or through special training in the armed forces. This method, however, often takes longer than a formal apprenticeship program.

In most areas electricians must be licensed. The examination for licensing requires a thorough knowledge of the craft and of state and local building codes.

Potential and advancement

There are approximately 542,000 electricians. Job opportunities for electricians are expected to be good through the year 2000. They will be needed to install and repair electrical devices and wiring in homes, factories, offices, and other building structures. New technologies and types of electrical equipment should keep electricians in demand.

Employment of electricians is subject to shifts in the economy, geographic area, and the cyclical nature of construction work. Construction electricians may find that they will experience periods of unemployment between construction projects and during times when the weather does not allow construction work. Maintenance electricians working for industries that are sensitive to shifts in the economy, such as the automotive, may be laid off during recessions.

Experienced construction electricians can be promoted to supervisory jobs or become estimators for contractors. Many start their own contracting businesses. Maintenance electricians can become supervisors and occasionally advance to jobs such as plant electrical superintendent or plant maintenance superintendent.

Income

Electricians who are not self-employed earn a weekly average of $478. Those at the low end of the pay scale earn less than $254, and those at the high end of the pay scale earn more than $740.

Electricians working in the West and Midwest generally earn more than those living in the South and Northeast.

Apprentices usually have beginning salaries that are 35 to 50 percent of those paid to experienced electricians, depending on their level of experience.

Additional sources of information

International Association of Machinists and Aerospace Workers
1300 Connecticut Avenue
Washington, DC 20036

International Brotherhood of Electrical Workers
1125 15th Street, NW
Washington, DC 20005

International Union of Electronic, Electrical, Salaried, Machine, and
   Furniture Workers
1126 16th Street, NW
Washington, DC 20036

National Electrical Contractors Association
7315 Wisconsin Avenue
Bethesda, MD 20814

United Steelworkers of America
5 Gateway Center
Pittsburgh, PA 15222

EMERGENCY MEDICAL TECHNICIAN

The job

Emergency medical technicians, or EMTs, are usually the first caregivers to arrive on the scene of a medical emergency. Their ability to provide medical care quickly and accurately may save a victim's life.

Upon arrival at the scene, EMTs must assess the situation and decide which emergency services must be given first. They must determine the victim's condition as well as whether he or she has any preexisting medical conditions, such as epilepsy or diabetes, that will affect the type of treatment given. Some of the medical treatments EMTs are trained to give include opening airways, restoring breathing, controlling bleeding, treatment for shock, administering oxygen, assisting in childbirth, and treating and resuscitating heart attack victims.

Sometimes when a situation is very serious, EMTs must report directly to the hospital by radio, transmitting vital signs and other information, so that the hospital can then provide instructions for treatment.

Another difficulty EMTs sometimes face is that they must free trapped victims, as in a car accident or a collapsed building. They must somehow free the victim while making sure that he or she is not injured further.

If victims must be transported to the hospital, EMTs put them on stretchers, carry them to the ambulance, and place them inside, making sure that the stretcher is secure. One EMT drives the ambulance while the other stays with the victim and continues medical treatment. After the ambulance arrives at the hospital, the EMTs help get the victim into the emergency room and inform the physicians and nurses of their observations and the treatment they have given.

It is also EMTs' responsibility to make sure that the ambulance is properly equipped and maintained. They must see that any supplies that have been used are either replaced or cleaned and sterilized and check the equipment to ensure that it is working properly. They also must see that the ambulance is in good working condition.

There are three classifications for EMTs: EMT-ambulance (EMT-A), EMT-intermediate, and EMT-paramedic. EMT-As are basic EMTs. EMT-intermediates and EMT-paramedics have received more training and are capable of giving additional types of medical treatment. A fourth level—EMT-defibrillator (EMT-D)—is emerging. These EMTs are trained in using electrical defibrillation to resuscitate heart attack victims.

Places of employment and working conditions

EMTs are employed by private ambulance services; hospitals; and municipal police, fire, and rescue squad departments.

EMTs work inside and outside, sometimes in poor weather conditions. EMTs' services are needed 24 hours a day, so they are often required to work evenings, weekends, and holidays. This job is physically strenuous—it involves a great deal of lifting. There is also much pressure in this field—EMTs must make life-and-death decisions as part of their regular job.

Qualifications, education, and training

EMTs must be physically strong and healthy. They must be able to make good decisions quickly in stressful situations. They should be emotionally stable and have leadership abilities. EMTs should have a neat and clean appearance and a pleasant personality.

EMTs are required to undergo instruction in emergency medical care techniques. The U.S. Department of Transportation has designed a national standard training program. The course is 110 hours long and trains EMT-As in basic life support techniques. It is offered in all 50 states, the District of Columbia, and the Virgin Islands. The course is offered by police, fire, and health departments; hospitals; and medical schools, colleges, and universities.

Those taking the course learn how to deal with emergencies such as bleeding, fractures, oxygen administration, airway obstruction, cardiac arrest, and emergency childbirth.

After completing this course, students may take a two-day course in removing trapped victims and a five-day course in driving emergency vehicles.

To become an EMT-intermediate, EMT-As must take additional courses and learn more medical procedures. EMT-paramedics have completed a nine-month training program to achieve their designation.

Applicants to EMT training courses must be at least 18 years old, have a high school diploma or its equivalent, and a valid driver's license.

The National Registry of Emergency Medical Technicians registers EMT-paramedics who meet its standards. While registration is not a requirement, it does give greater credibility to EMTs who have earned it.

All 50 states have certification procedures.

Potential and advancement

There are currently 76,000 EMTs. There will be some growth in employment of EMTs through the year 2000. The rapid growth in the number of senior citizens and developments in the field of emergency medicine will create a demand for EMTs. However, the high cost of training and equipping EMTs may lessen opportunities. The best job prospects will be with municipal governments and private ambulance services.

EMTs who have advanced through the ranks to become EMT-paramedics must leave fieldwork to advance any further. They may become field supervisor, operations supervisor, operations manager, administrative director, and then executive director.

Another advancement route for EMTs is to become instructors, but this usually requires a bachelor's degree in education.

Other EMTs leave the field altogether, becoming sales representatives for emergency medical equipment manufacturers. Others become police officers or firefighters. By getting more education, some are able to move into clinical or management careers in health or related fields.

Income

Earnings for EMTs depend on the level of their experience and training, the type of employer they have, and their geographical area.

Average starting salaries for EMT-As are $16,960 a year; for EMT-intermediates, $17,130; and EMT-paramedics, $22,510.

Additional sources of information

National Association of Emergency Medical Technicians
9140 Ward Parkway
Kansas City, MO 64114

National Registry of Emergency Medical Technicians
P. O. Box 29233
Columbus, OH 43229

EMPLOYMENT COUNSELOR

The job

Employment counselors, also called vocational counselors, help jobseekers who have difficulties finding jobs. They provide services to experienced workers who have been displaced by automation or who are unhappy in their present jobs and to returning veterans, school dropouts, handicapped and older workers, ex-prisoners, and those with minimal job skills.

In-depth interviews with jobseekers, aptitude tests, and other background information help the counselor evaluate the capabilities of each person. The counselor then helps the jobseeker develop a vocational plan and a job goal that will be implemented using whatever remedial action is necessary. This could include education or retraining, physical rehabilitation or psychological counseling, specific work experience, or development of appropriate work skills. Once the jobseeker obtains a position, the counselor usually provides follow-up counseling for a period of time.

Counselors must be familiar with the local labor market and with the job-related resources of the community. Some employment counselors contact local employers and keep abreast of job openings within local industries to refer jobseekers to specific jobs.

Most employment counselors work for state employment centers or community agencies. Others work for private agencies, prisons, training schools, and mental hospitals. The federal government employs employment counselors in the Veterans Administration and the Bureau of Indian Affairs.

Places of employment and working conditions

Employment counselors work throughout the country in communities of all sizes.

Counselors usually work a 40-hour week. Those in community agencies may work overtime or some evening and weekend hours.

Qualifications, education, and training

Anyone interested in this field should have a strong interest in helping others, should be able to work independently and keep detailed records, and should possess patience.

Graduate work beyond a bachelor's degree or equivalent counseling-related experience is necessary for even entry-level jobs in employment counseling. Undergraduate work should include courses in psychology and sociology; graduate work includes actual counseling experience under the supervision of an instructor.

Employment counselors working for state and local government agencies must fulfill local civil service requirements, which include specific education and experience requirements and a written examination.

Potential and advancement

The employment outlook for employment counselors should be good through the year 2000, especially in private business. Employment opportunities in federal and state agencies will depend on the availability of government funding.

Employment counselors in federal and state agencies may advance to supervisor or administrative positions. Those working in private business may move into personnel and management positions.

Income

Earnings vary widely for employment counselors. Counselors with their own private practices have the highest earnings. Salaries in state agencies vary from state to state. Beginning salaries start at $14,000 a year. In business, the average salary for experienced employment counselors is $27,000 a year.

In private nonprofit organizations, the average starting salary is about $14,000; experienced workers average $19,000.

Additional sources of information

American Association for Counseling and Development
5999 Stevenson Avenue
Alexandria, VA 22304

National Employment Counselors Association
5999 Stevenson Avenue
Alexandria, VA 22304

ENGINEER

The job

Engineers apply the theories and principles of science and mathematics to practical technical problems. This is one of the largest professions in the country.

Most engineers specialize in one of the 25 major branches of engineering. Within these branches there are numerous subdivisions, and engineers may further specialize in one industry, such as motor vehicles, or one field of technology, such as propulsion or guidance systems. This job description provides an overall picture of engineering as a career. Information on 12 major branches of this profession appears elsewhere in this book.

In general, engineers in a particular field may be involved in research, design, and development; production and operation; maintenance; time and cost estimation; sales and technical assistance; or administration and management. Engineers usually work as part of a team and, regardless of specialty, may apply their knowledge across several fields. For example, an electrical engineer can work in the medical field, in computers, missile guidance systems, or electric power distribution. An agricultural engineer may design farm equipment, manage water resources, or work in soil conservation.

While more than half of all engineers work for manufacturing industries, a little over 35 percent work in nonmanufacturing industries such as construction, public utilities, engineering and architectural services, and business and consulting services.

Federal, state, and local government agencies employ about 13 percent of all engineers. Federally employed engineers work mainly for the Department of Defense, Interior, Agriculture, Transportation, Energy, and NASA. In state and local governments, engineers usually work for highway and public works departments.

Some engineers teach and do research.

Related jobs are mathematician, engineering and science technician, and architect.

Places of employment and working conditions

Engineers are employed in all areas of the country, in towns and cities of all sizes as well as rural areas, with some specialties concentrated in certain areas.

Most engineers work indoors, but some, depending on specialty, work outdoors or at remote locations.

Qualifications, education, and training

The ability to think analytically, a capacity for detail, and the ability to work as part of a team are all necessary. Good communication skills are important.

Mathematics and the sciences must be emphasized in high school.

A bachelor's degree in engineering is the minimum requirement in this field. In a typical curriculum, the first two years are spent in the study of basic sciences such as physics and chemistry and mathematics, introductory engineering, and some liberal arts courses. The remaining years are usually devoted to specialized engineering courses. Engineering programs can last from four to six years. Those requiring five or six years to complete may award a master's degree or may provide a cooperative plan of study plus practical work experience with a nearby industry.

Because of rapid changes in technology, many engineers continue their education throughout their careers. A graduate degree is necessary for most teaching and research positions and for many management jobs. Some specialties such as nuclear engineering are taught only at the graduate level. Some persons obtain graduate degrees in business administration or in a field such as law (for patent attorneys).

Engineering graduates usually work under the supervision of an experienced engineer or in a company training program until they become acquainted with the requirements of a particular company or industry.

All states require licensing of engineers whose work may affect life, health, or property or who offer their services to the public. Those who are licensed, about one-third of all engineers, are called registered engineers. Requirements include graduation from an accredited engineering school, four years of experience, and a written examination.

Potential and advancement

There are approximately 1.4 million engineers. The employment outlook for engineers is good for the foreseeable future with some specialties more in demand than others. The field will continue to grow while the number of degrees granted in engineering is expected to decline.

Experienced engineers may advance to administrative and management positions. Many of the highest-level executives in private industry started their careers as engineers.

Income

Starting salaries in private industry average $29,200 a year with a bachelor's degree; $34,600 with a master's degree; and $46,600 or more with a Ph.D. Starting salaries for civil engineers average slightly less, chemical engineers slightly more.

Additional sources of information

Accreditation Board for Engineering and Technology
345 East 47th Street
New York, NY 10017

American Society for Engineering Education
11 Dupont Circle
Suite 200
Washington, DC 20036

Junior Engineering Technical Society (JETS)
1420 King Street
Suite 405
Alexandria, VA 22314

National Society of Professional Engineers
1420 King Street
Alexandria, VA 22314

Society of Women Engineers
345 East 47th Street
Room 305
New York, NY 10017

ENVIRONMENTALIST

The job

Pollution is one of the major problems of modern society. Environmentalists are workers who find ways to control and prevent water, air, and land pollution. They must keep in mind the needs of the environment as well the economic needs of industries.

There are several areas of specialization for environmentalists: land conservation, acid rain, toxic waste removal and disposal, wildlife preservation, and groundwater contamination. Environmentalists do research, perform environmental impact studies, and develop systems to monitor pollution. Some work with community groups and leaders to solve environmental problems in a particular area. They may attend public meetings or appear before legislative committees or in court.

Some environmentalists work as consultants. They are hired by the government or a private company to study a problem and then advise their employer on how best to deal with it in order to protect the environment and not suffer financial loss.

Other environmentalists work with members of Congress and state legislatures to see that laws are written and passed that protect the environment.

Places of employment and working conditions

Environmentalists may work for the federal government, usually in the Environmental Protection Agency (EPA) or the Department of the Interior. Others work for state and local governments. Employers hiring environmentalists also include environmental consulting firms, nonprofit environmental organizations, chemical and oil companies, and mining companies.

Environmentalists work both indoors, in an office, and outdoors. They often have to travel to problem sites to perform research and studies. Their work hours may be irregular.

Qualifications, education, and training

Environmentalists must be able to work well with people. They should be good communicators and have an interest in the outdoors and science.

Environmentalists usually must have a bachelor's degree in one of the environmental or natural sciences. Some have degrees in engineering or political science. Most environmentalists continue to take courses in order to stay aware of the latest developments in the field.

Potential and advancement

Environmentalists will be in demand through the year 2000. Because of current awareness of environmental problems and the subsequent laws that are being passed that regulate environmental quality, companies will need the advice of experts in the field. This should result in very good opportunities for environmentalists.

Environmentalists usually begin as researchers or interns. They advance by becoming project directors or managers. Those with experience often become consultants.

Income

Salaries for beginning environmentalists average about $17,000 to $21,000 a year. Experienced environmentalists earn between $31,000 and $42,000 or more annually.

Additional sources of information

Association of Environmental Scientists and Administrators
3433 Southwest McNary Parkway
Lake Oswego, OR 97035

National Association of Environmental Professionals
P.O. Box 9400
Washington, DC 20016

F

FARMER

The job

Farmers today are businesspeople. They buy seed, fertilizer, and equipment; plant only a few crops or even one crop; follow scientific production methods; and sell all they grow or raise.

The dwindling supply and high cost of available farmland, plus the cost of the equipment necessary to run a farm using today's agricultural technology, are leading to an increase in some alternative styles of farming. And farmers in areas with long winters often take jobs in nearby cities during the cold months, working their farms through the spring, summer, and fall.

Tenant farmers rent their land from farm owners, usually in return for a percentage of the crop. Some owners also supply machinery, seed, and fertilizer.

Large corporate and partnership farms are usually operated by *farm managers* who handle all the day-to-day responsibilities as well as decisions on what crops to plant.

Firms that supply seed, feed, fertilizer, and farm equipment also attract experienced farmers to work as salespeople and dealers for their products. Some farmers use their accumulated knowledge in other areas related to farming such as farm insurance, banking and credit, real estate sales, and appraisals.

Related jobs are agricultural engineer, soil scientist, range manager.

Places of employment and working conditions

Some farming is done in just about every county in the United States. The eastern and southern states have smaller farms than the midwestern and western states. Many of the larger or corporate farms employ many laborers.

The workweek for a farmer during the planting, growing, and harvesting seasons is often six or seven days and much longer than eight hours a day. Farmers who raise livestock and poultry have a more even work schedule year-round, but their work is always seven days a week since animals must be cared for every day.

Farmers face constant financial risk due to the uncertainties of weather, which can ruin a crop and eliminate an entire year's income.

Qualifications, education, and training

To successfully run a modern farm, a farmer needs managerial and business skills, mechanical ability, physical stamina, patience, and a love of working outdoors.

Probably the best background is growing up on a farm or working for a farmer. Organizations such as the 4-H clubs and Future Farmers of America provide valuable preparation for young people interested in farming.

The complexities of modern scientific farming make formal training in a two- or four-year agricultural college almost a necessity. Most such colleges offer majors in areas such as dairy science, crop science, agricultural economics, horticulture, and animal science, plus special course work in the products produced in the area in which the college is located.

Colleges that offer degrees in agricultural engineering sometimes offer degrees or course work in mechanized agriculture. These programs provide broad basic agricultural training, practical application of farm machinery and equipment to agricultural production, and economics and management courses.

Potential and advancement

There are about 1,272,000 people employed as farmers or farm managers. While the rapidly increasing world population demands more food and fiber, the employment of farmers is expected to decrease through the year 2000, but at a slower rate than in the past for several reasons. The high productivity of the very efficient agricultural sector is expected to meet domestic and export needs. Also, the trend is toward fewer and larger farms. Another reason for the decreasing employment of farmers is the great expense of purchasing and operating a farm.

Because farms are increasing in size and becoming more complex to operate, there will be a need for farm managers, workers who run farms and oversee tenant farmers in the owners' absence.

Income

Earnings for farmers vary from year to year. Weather conditions, which are for the most part unpredictable, determine the amount and quality of farm products and, thus, their price. A farm that achieves a large profit one year might show a loss the next.

Farm managers earn from $15,000 to $30,000 a year, depending on size or number of farms managed.

Additional sources of information

American Farm Bureau Federation
225 Touhy Avenue
Park Ridge, IL 60068

Higher Education Program
Cooperative State Research Service
U.S. Department of Agriculture
14th and Independence Avenue, SW
Washington, DC 20250

National FFA Organization
Box 15160
5632 Mt. Vernon Memorial Highway
Alexandria, VA 22309

FASHION DESIGNER

The job

Fashion and clothing designers create new styles or adjust and change existing styles. They may work in men's, women's, or children's clothing design.

Designers work with sketches or directly with fabric in creating a design. They must understand color, fabrics, production processes, and costs as well as the public's tastes and preferences. Many designers work on one type of apparel such as sports clothes or evening wear.

People who want a career in designing often take any job they can in the fashion field to get a start. The field is popular and always has more new talent than it can adequately support.

Places of employment and working conditions

New York City is the center of the fashion industry; Los Angeles is an important swimsuit and casual clothes fashion center, and other cities produce limited fashion trends.

Fashion is a hectic and fast-paced field with seasonal peaks that often require long hours.

Qualifications, education, and training

Fashion designers must have a flair for clothes, a sense of style, a keen sense of color, and the ability to turn their ideas into reality.

High school courses in art, merchandising, and business are helpful. Sewing experience is important.

Apparel firms prefer to hire designers with formal training, and they often recruit designers from colleges and schools that provide specialized training in fashion design. They seek workers who are knowledgeable about textiles, fabrics, ornamentation, and trends in the fashion world. A few designers work their way up through the ranks from tailoring or cutting jobs.

Beginners should be prepared to serve as sample makers or assistant designers or even work in clerical jobs for their first few years.

Potential and advancement

Fashion is a crowded, popular, and often cut-throat career field. There are always many more eager jobseekers than there are job openings, and there will be stiff competition for all designer positions.

Income

Average annual earnings for experienced, full-time designers are about $26,400 a year. Those at the bottom of the salary range earn annual salaries of less than $11,300, and those at the top of the salary range earn more than $47,000.

Additional sources of information

American Apparel Manufacturers Association
2500 Wilson Boulevard
Suite 301
Arlington, VA 22201

American Fur Industry
363 Seventh Avenue
9th Floor
New York, NY 10001

FBI SPECIAL AGENT

The job

Special agents for the Federal Bureau of Investigation (FBI) investigate violations of federal laws in connection with bank robberies, kidnappings, white-color crime, thefts of government property, organized crime, espionage, and sabotage. The FBI, which is part of the U.S. Department of Justice, has jurisdiction over many different federal investigative matters. Special agents, therefore, may be assigned to any type of case, although those with specialized training usually work on cases related to their background. Agents with an accounting background, for example, may investigate white-color crimes such as bank embezzlements or fraudulent bankruptcies or land deals.

Because the FBI is a fact-gathering agency, its special agents function strictly as investigators, collecting evidence in cases in which the U.S. government is, or may be, an interested party. In their casework, special agents conduct interviews, examine records, observe the activities of suspects, and participate in raids. Because the FBI's work is highly confidential, special agents may not disclose any of the information gathered in the course of their official duties to unauthorized persons, including members of their families. Frequently, agents must testify in court about cases that they investigate.

Although they usually work alone on most assignments, two agents or more are assigned to work together when performing potentially dangerous duties such as arrests and raids. Agents communicate with their supervisors by radio or telephone as the circumstances dictate.

Places of employment and working conditions

Most agents are assigned to the FBI's 59 field offices located throughout the nation and in Puerto Rico. They work in cities where field office headquarters are located or in resident agencies (suboffices) established under field office supervision to provide prompt and efficient handling of investigative matters arising throughout the field office territory. Some agents are assigned to the Bureau headquarters in Washington, D.C., which supervises all FBI activities.

Special agents are subject to call 24 hours a day and must be available for assignment at all times. Their duties call for some travel, for they are assigned wherever they are needed in the United States or Puerto Rico. They frequently work longer than the customary 40-hour week.

Qualifications, education, and training

To be considered for appointment as an FBI special agent, an applicant usually must be a graduate of a state-accredited law school; a college graduate with a major in accounting, engineering, or computer science; or be fluent in a foreign language.

Applicants for the position of FBI special agent must be citizens of the United States; between 23 and 35 years old; and willing to serve anywhere in the United States and Puerto Rico. They must be capable of strenuous physical exertion and have excellent hearing and vision, normal color perception, and no physical defects that would prevent their using firearms or participating in dangerous assignments. All applicants must pass a rigid physical examination as well as written and oral examinations testing their aptitude for meeting the public and conducting investigations. All of the tests except the physical examinations are given by the FBI at its facilities. Background and character investigations are made of all applicants. Appointments are made on a probationary basis and become permanent after one year of satisfactory service.

Each newly appointed special agent is given about 15 weeks of training at the FBI Academy at the U.S. Marine Corps base in Quantico, Virginia, before assignment to a field office. During this period, agents receive intensive training in defensive tactics and the use of firearms. In addition, they are thoroughly schooled in federal criminal law and procedures, FBI rules and regulations, fingerprinting, and investigative work. After assignment to a field office, the new agent usually works closely with an experienced agent for about two weeks before handling any assignments independently.

Potential and advancement

The jurisdiction of the FBI has expanded greatly over the years. Although it is impossible to forecast personnel requirements, employment may be expected to increase with growing FBI responsibilities.

The FBI provides a career service and its rate of turnover is traditionally low. Nevertheless, the FBI is always interested in applications from qualified persons who would like to be considered for the position of special agent.

All administrative and supervisory jobs are filled from within the ranks by selection of those agents who have demonstrated the ability to assume more responsibility.

Income

The entrance salary for FBI special agents is about $26,300 a year. Experienced agents start at around $41,000 a year, and supervisory agents start at around $48,600.

Additional sources of information

FBI
Applicant Recruiting Office
1900 Half Street, SW
Washington, DC 20535

FIREFIGHTER

The job

Firefighters must be prepared to respond to a fire and handle any emergency that arises. This is dangerous work that requires courage and expert training.

Firefighting requires organization and teamwork. Each firefighter at the scene of a fire has specific duties assigned by a company officer; but each must also be ready to perform any of the duties—such as connecting hoses to hydrants, positioning ladders, or operating pumps—at any time, because duties change in the course of a fire. Firefighters may also be called on to rescue people or to administer first aid.

Between fires, firefighters spend their time cleaning and maintaining equipment, carrying out practice drills, and maintaining their living quarters. They also take part in fire prevention activities such as building inspections and educational programs for schools and civic groups.

Ninety percent of all firefighters work for municipal fire departments. The remainder work on federal and state installations or in private firefighting companies.

Most firefighters are members of the International Association of Firefighters (AFL-CIO).

Places of employment and working conditions

In some cities, firefighters are on duty for 24 hours and then off for 48 hours. In other cities, they work a 10-hour day shift or a 14-hour night shift, with shifts rotated frequently. The average workweek varies from 42 to 52 hours, but some firefighters work as many as 84 hours a week. These duty hours usually include free time which can be used for personal interests or study.

Firefighters face the risk of injury or death in the course of their work and must work outdoors in all kinds of conditions and weather.

Qualifications, education, and training

A firefighter must have courage, mental alertness, physical stamina, mechanical aptitude, and a sense of public service. Initiative, good judgment, and dependability are essential. Because firefighters live together as well as work together, they should be able to get along with others.

Applicants for municipal firefighting jobs may have to pass a written test and medical examination that includes a test that screens for drug use and tests of strength, physical stamina, and agility. They must meet other local regulations as to height and weight, have a high school education or equivalent, and be at least 18 years old. Experience as a volunteer firefighter or firefighting training received in the armed forces improve the applicant's chances for appointment to a job, and some communities also give extra credit to veterans of the armed forces.

Begineers are usually trained at the city's fire school for several weeks and are then assigned to a fire company for a probationary period.

Fire departments frequently conduct training programs to help firefighters upgrade their skills, and many colleges offer courses such as fire engineering and fire science that are helpful to firefighters. Experienced firefighters also continue to study to prepare for promotional examinations.

Potential and advancement

There are about 291,000 firefighters. Employment of firefighters is expected to grow slowly through the year 2000. Although there is a great need for firefighters as the population continues to grow, local government spending will limit the number of available jobs. Also, turnover of firefighting jobs is relatively low.

Opportunities for promotions are good in most fire departments. Promotion to lieutenant, captain, battalion chief, assistant chief, deputy chief, and finally chief depend on written examination, seniority, and rating by supervisors.

Income

Beginning salaries average about $19,700 a year. Earnings vary for firefighters with experience depending on city size and region of the country. Average earnings range from $23,200 in the smallest cities to $31,400 in the largest cities and from $21,500 in the South to $29,300 in the West. Firefighters in supervisory positions may earn significantly more.

Most fire departments provide allowances to pay for protective clothing such as helmets, boots, and rubber coats, and many also provide dress uniforms.

Firefighters are usually covered by liberal pension plans that often provide retirement at half pay at age 50 after 25 years of service or at any age if disabled in the line of duty. Generous sick leave and compensation are usually provided for any firefighter injured in the line of duty.

Additional sources of information

Information is available from local civil service commission offices or fire departments.

International Association of Fire Chiefs
1329 18th Street, NW
Washington, DC 20036

National Fire Protection Association
Batterymarch Park
Quincy, MA 02269

FLIGHT ATTENDANT

The job

Few jobs appear as glamorous as that of a flight attendant. The lure of travel and the opportunity to meet all kinds of people appeal to those interested in this field.

Formerly called stewardesses and stewards, flight attendants are aboard almost every commercial passenger plane to look after passenger safety and comfort. Airliners usually carry from one to ten flight attendants, depending on the number of seats and the proportion of economy to first-class passengers. (The Boeing 747 carries up to 16 flight attendants.) Federal Aviation Administration safety regulations require at least one attendant for every 50 seats.

Before each flight, attendants check supplies such as food, beverages, blankets, reading material, first-aid kits, and emergency equipment. During flight, they instruct passengers in the use of emergency equipment; check seat belts before takeoff or landing; and help care for small children, the elderly, and the handicapped. They also distribute reading material and serve food and beverages.

The main reason planes carry flight attendants is to provide assistance to passengers in the event of an emergency. A calm and reassuring manner is very important, whether the emergency is a sick passenger or an emergency landing. Flight attendants are trained to handle many situations including evacuation of the plane.

Most flight attendants are members of either the Transport Workers Union of America or the Association of Flight Attendants.

This has always been a traditionally female career, and women still predominate. But the number of male flight attendants is increasing, and the entrance of men into this job has prompted the name change from stewardess (and steward) to flight attendant.

Places of employment and working conditions

Over one-half of all flight attendants work out of Chicago, Dallas, Los Angeles, Miami, New York City, and San Francisco. The remainder are assigned to other cities where airlines maintain facilities.

Since airlines operate around-the-clock for 365 days a year, flight attendants must be prepared to work nights, weekends, and holidays. They usually fly 75 to 85 hours a month with about 75 to 85 additional hours of ground duties. Their workweek is not divided into neat segments, and because of scheduling and limitations on flying time, many have 11 or 12 days or more off each month. As much as one-third of their time may be spent away from their home base. Airlines provide hotel accommodations and meal allowances for these periods.

Flight attendants are on their feet during most of a flight. Poor weather can cause difficulties as can sick or frightened passengers. Flight attendants are expected to be pleasant and efficient under all circumstances and with even the most difficult passengers.

Qualifications, education, and training

Anyone considering this career field should be poised and tactful, enjoy working with people, and be able to talk comfortably with strangers. Excellent health is a must as is good vision (Contact lenses and eyeglasses are acceptable on most airlines, however.) Airlines also have height and weight requirements, and all flight attendants must be at least 19 to 21 years old and have a high school diploma.

Airlines give preference to applicants with several years of college, nurse's training, or experience in dealing with the public. Fluency in a foreign language is required on international airlines.

Large airlines provide about four to six weeks of training in their own schools. Some also provide transportation to the training center and an allowance while training. Instruction includes emergency procedures, evacuation of a plane, operation of emergency equipment, first aid, flight regulations and duties, and company operations and policies. On international airlines, flight attendants also study passport and customs regulations. Practice flights complete the training. After assignment to a home base, new flight attendants begin their careers by "filling in" on extra flights or replacing attendants who are sick or on vacation.

Potential and advancement

There are about 88,000 flight attendants working for airlines in the United States. Employment of flight attendants is expected to grow as increases in population and income increase the use of air transportation. Air travel, however, is sensitive to the ups and downs of the economy, and job opportunities may vary from year to year. Even though employment of flight attendants is expected to grow, there will be stiff competition for jobs; the number of applicants is expected to exceed the number of job openings.

Opportunities for advancement are limited to choice of flight assignment and home base, which flight attendants are entitled to as they accumulate seniority. A few attendants do advance to positions as flight service instructors, customer service directors, or recruiting representatives.

Income

Salaries for beginners average about $12,600 a year. Flight attendants with six years of flying experience earn about $21,500 a year, while some senior flight attendants earn as much as $38,000 a year. Flight attendants earn compensation for overtime and night and international flights.

An attractive fringe benefit is the reduced airfare for flight attendants and their families, on their own and most other airlines.

Additional sources of information

Information about job opportunities and requirements for a particular airline may be obtained in writing to the personnel manager of the company. Addresses are available from:

Air Transport Association of America
1709 New York Avenue, NW
Washington, DC 20006

FLORAL DESIGNER

The job

Floral designers, also called *florists*, combine a knowledge of flowers and plants with design techniques to produce floral and plant gifts and decorations.

Just about all floral designers work in retail flower shops, many of which are small and employ only a few people. Many of the shops are owner operated.

Floral designers must know the seasonal availability and lasting qualities of many flowers and have a sense of form, color harmony, and depth. They prepare bouquets, corsages, funeral pieces, dried flower arrangements, and decorations for weddings, parties, and other events.

Places of employment and working conditions

Flower shops are located throughout the country with at least one in nearly every city and town.

Floral designers stand during much of their workday. Work areas are kept cool and humid to preserve the flowers, and designers are subject to sudden temperature changes when entering or leaving refrigerated storage areas.

A 40-hour workweek is usual, but this often includes Saturday hours. Floral designers work very long hours around certain holidays such as Valentine's Day and Mother's Day.

Qualifications, education, and training

Good color vision and manual dexterity are necessary for a floral designer. Business and selling skills are important for those who operate their own shops.

High school courses in business arithmetic and bookkeeping are helpful. Part-time or summer jobs in a plant nursery or flower shop can provide valuable experience.

Many floral designers acquire their skills through on-the-job training. They work under the guidance of an experienced floral designer for about two years to become fully qualified.

The trend in recent years, however, is toward more formal training. Adult education programs and flower shops offer courses in flower arranging, while junior colleges and commercial floral design schools offer wider training. The longer programs provide training in basic horticulture, flower marketing, and flower shop management as well as floral design. Such training is especially useful for floral designers who intend to open their own shops.

Potential and advancement

The field is expected to grow as the population increases. Ups and downs in the economy may cause temporary slow periods, but over the long run the outlook is good.

Income

In large flower shops, flower designers may advance to shop manager or to design supervisor. Others advance by opening their own shops. A new flower shop in an area with many other florists faces stiff competition and must establish a reputation by efficient operation and outstanding work if the business is to succeed. Floral designers who can provide such workers are always in demand.

Floral designers receive relatively low pay. Beginners earn about $9,600 a year. Designers with one to three years of experience earn $11,500, and designers with over three years of experience earn an average of $13,800 a year. Managers of floral shops earn an average of about $17,400 a year. Some floral designers report average earnings of more than $31,200.

The earnings of shop owners vary greatly depending mainly on locality and the size of the community being served.

Additional sources of information

Society of American Florists
1601 Duke Street
Alexandria, VA 22314

FORESTER

The job

The forest lands of the United States—whether publicly or privately owned—must be carefully and efficiently managed if they are to survive. It is the work of the professional forester to develop, manage, and protect forest lands and their resources of timber, water, wildlife, forage, and recreation areas. If properly protected and managed, these resources can be utilized repeatedly without being destroyed.

Foresters often specialize in one type of work such as timber management, outdoor recreation, or forest economics. In these capacities, they might plan and supervise the planting and cutting of trees or devote themselves to watershed management, wildlife protection, disease and insect control, fire prevention, or the development and supervision of recreation areas.

About one-fourth of all foresters work for private industries such as pulp and paper, lumber, logging, and milling companies. The federal government employs about half of all foresters, most of them in the Forest Service of the Department of Agriculture. Others do research, teach at the college and university level, or work as consultants. State and local governments also employ foresters.

Related jobs are environmentalist, soil scientist, soil conservationist.

Places of employment and working conditions

Foresters are employed in just about every state, but the largest numbers are employed in the heavily forested areas of the Northwest, Northeast, and South.

Foresters, especially beginners, spend a great deal of time outdoors in all kinds of weather and often at remote locations. During emergencies such as fires and rescue missions, they may work long hours under difficult and dangerous conditions.

Qualifications, education, and training

Anyone interested in forestry as a career should be physically hardy, enjoy working outdoors, and be willing to work in remote areas.

A bachelor's degree with a major in forestry is the minimum requirement, but employers prefer to hire applicants with advanced degrees. About 50 colleges offer degrees in forestry, most of them accredited by the Society of American Foresters. Scientific and technical forestry subjects, liberal arts, and communication skills are emphasized along with courses in forest economics and business administration. All schools encourage work experience in forestry or conservation, and many of the colleges require at least one summer at a college-operated field camp.

Potential and advancement

About 27,000 persons are employed as foresters. Employment opportunities are expected to grow slowly due to the government's budget restrictions—the government is a major employer of foresters. The job outlook, however, is better than in the past because of an expected wave in retirements and recent declines in the number of graduates in forestry. Job opportunities will probably be greatest with private industry to improve forest, logging, and range management practices and to increase output and profitability.

Advancement in this field depends on experience with federally employed foresters able to advance through supervisory positions to regional forest supervisors or to top administrative positions. In private industry, experienced foresters may advance to top managerial positions within a company.

Income

Starting salaries for federally employed foresters vary: those having a master's degree or equivalent experience receive about $23,800 a year; Ph.D.s start at $28,900 to $34,600; with a bachelor's degree, the salary is about $15,700. Salaries in state and local governments and in private industry are generally lower.

Additional sources of information

American Forestry Association
P.O. Box 2000
Washington, DC 20013

Society of American Foresters
5400 Grosvenor Lane
Bethesda, MD 20814

U.S. Forest Service
U.S. Department of Agriculture
P.O. Box 96090
Washington, DC 20090-6090

FORESTRY TECHNICIAN

The job

Forestry technicians assist foresters in the care and management of forest lands and their resources. They estimate timber production, inspect for insect damage, supervise surveying and road-building crews, work in flood control and water quality programs, supervise firefighting crews, supervise planting and reforestation programs, and maintain forest areas for hunting, camping, and other recreational uses.

About half of all forestry technicians work for private logging, lumber, paper, mining, and railroad companies. The federal government employs about an equal number. Many of the technicians employed by the federal and state governments work during summer only or during the spring and fall fire seasons.

A related job is landscape architect.

Places of employment and working conditions

Forestry technicians work throughout the country in just about every state.

Outdoor work in all kinds of weather is the norm for this job field. In emergencies such as forest fires and floods, the working hours are very long and the work can be dangerous. In many areas, the work is seasonal.

Qualifications, education, and training

Good physical condition, stamina, love of the outdoors, and ability to work with or without supervision and to work with a variety of people are all necessary for a forestry technician.

High school should include as many science courses as possible.

Some technicians acquire their training through experience on firefighting crews, in recreation work, or in tree nurseries. Because this is a very competi-

185

tive job field, however, those with specialized training in forestry have better opportunities for full-time employment.

One- and two-year courses for forestry technicians are available in technical institutes, junior colleges, and colleges and universities. Subjects studied include mathematics, biology and botany, land surveying, tree identification, aerial photography interpretation, and timber harvesting.

Potential and advancement

This field is expected to grow steadily, but applicants will continue to exceed job openings due to the popularity of the work. Private industry will continue to provide the bulk of the full-time positions.

Income

Salaries range from $16,000 to $18,300 a year. Experienced forestry technicians may earn over $20,000 a year.

Additional sources of information

American Forestry Association
P.O. Box 2000
Washington, DC 20013

Society of American Foresters
5400 Grosvenor Lane
Bethesda, MD 20814

U.S. Forest Service
U.S. Department of Agriculture
P.O. Box 96090
Washington, DC 20090-6090

FUNERAL DIRECTOR

The job

While this job field does not appeal to everyone, persons involved in funeral directing take great pride in the fact that they provide efficient and appropriate service to their customers. Probably more than in any other job situation, personal qualities of tact, compassion, and the ability to deal with people under difficult circumstances come into play. A funeral director arranges for the transportation of the deceased to the funeral home, obtains information for the death certificate and obituary notices, and arranges all details of the funeral and burial as decided upon by the family of the deceased. The funeral director must be familiar with the funeral and burial customs of many faiths, ethnic groups, and fraternal organizations. Even after the funeral, the funeral director assists the family in handling Social Security insurance and veteran's claims.

An *embalmer* prepares the body for viewing and burial. Embalming is a sanitary, cosmetic, and preservative process and is required by law in some areas. The body is washed with germicidal soap, blood is replaced with embalming fluid, cosmetics are applied to provide a natural appearance or to restore disfigured features, and the body is placed in the casket.

In small funeral homes, the duties of funeral director and embalmer may be handled by one person; in large funeral homes, an embalming staff of one or more embalmers plus several apprentices may be employed. Embalmers are also employed by hospitals and morgues.

In most funeral homes, one of the funeral directors is also the owner. The staff may consist of from one to twenty or more funeral directors, embalmers, and apprentices. In some communities it is customary for a prospective embalmer or funeral director to obtain a promise of employment from a local funeral home before starting mortuary training.

Places of employment and working conditions

There is at least one funeral home in every community in the United States, so job opportunities are everywhere.

In smaller funeral homes, working hours may vary, but in larger homes employees work eight hours a day, five or six days a week. Shift work is sometimes necessary since funeral home hours include evenings.

Embalmers occasionally come into contact with contagious diseases but are not likely to become ill because of strict observance of sanitary procedures.

Qualification, education, and training

High school courses in biology, chemistry, and public speaking are helpful, and a part-time or summer job at a funeral home can provide exposure to the profession for anyone considering the field.

There are over 30 mortuary science programs that are accredited by the American Board of Funeral Service Education. They usually take from nine months to three years to complete. A few colleges also offer four-year programs in mortuary science.

A period of apprenticeship must be completed under the guidance of an experienced funeral director or embalmer. Depending on state regulations, this apprenticeship consists of from one to three years and may be served during or after mortuary school.

All states require embalmers to be licensed, and most states also require funeral directors to be licensed.

State board licensing examinations vary but usually consist of written and oral tests as well as a demonstration of skills. Other state licensing standards usually require the applicant to be 21 years old, have a high school diploma or its equivalent, and a complete a mortuary science program and an apprenticeship.

Some states issue a single license to funeral directors and embalmers. In states that have separate licensing and apprenticeship requirements for the two positions, most people in the field obtain both licenses. Some states will accept the credentials of those licensed by another state without further examination.

Potential and advancement

Employment opportunities in this field are good through the year 2000 because the number of jobs available is greater than the number of graduates from mortuary science programs.

Advancement opportunities are best in large funeral homes where higher-paying positions exist such as general manager or personnel manager. Directors and embalmers who accumulate enough money and experience often establish their own businesses.

Income

Funeral directors earn starting salaries of about $19,493 to $25,343 a year. Owners of funeral homes can earn up to $60,000 or more annually.

Additional sources of information

Information on licensing requirements is available from the appropriate state office of occupational licensing.

American Board of Funeral Service Education
23 Crestwood Road
Cumberland, ME 04021

National Funeral Directors Association
11121 West Oklahoma Avenue
Milwaukee, WI 53227

G

GEOGRAPHER

The job

Geographers study and analyze the distribution of land forms; climate; soils, vegetation; and mineral, water, and human resources. These studies help to explain the patterns of human settlement.

Many geographers are employed by colleges and universities. The federal government also employs many geographers for mapping, intelligence work, and remote sensing interpretation. State and local governments employ geographers on planning and development commissions.

Textbook and map publishers; travel agencies; manufacturing firms; real estate developers; and insurance, communications, and transportation companies employ geographers. Those with additional training in another discipline such as economics, sociology, or urban planning have a wider range of job opportunities and can work in many other fields.

Cartographers design and construct maps and charts. They also conduct research in surveying and mapping procedures. They work with aerial photographs and analyze data from remote sensing equipment on satellites.

Places of employment and working conditions

Geographers are employed throughout the country and on foreign assignment as well. The largest single concentration of geographers is in the Washington, D.C., area.

Fieldwork sometimes entails assignment to remote areas and less developed regions of the world. A geographer should be prepared for the physical and social hardships such relocation may require.

Qualifications, education, and training

Anyone interested in this field should enjoy reading, studying, and research and be able to work independently. Good communication skills are also necessary.

High school should include as many mathematics and science courses as possible.

A bachelor's degree with a major in geography is the first step for a would-be geographer. Course work should also include some specialty fields such as cartography, aerial photography, or statistical analysis.

Advanced degrees are required for most teaching positions and for advancement in business and government; a Ph.D. is necessary for the top jobs. Mathematics, statistics, and computer science are of increasing importance in graduate studies; students interested in foreign regional geography are usually required to take a foreign language as well.

Potential and advancement

In general, this field will grow, but some areas will offer more job opportunities than others. No growth is expected in college and university teaching positions. The federal government will employ a growing number of geographers and cartographers as will state and local governments. Private industry will provide the largest increase in job openings in this field. There will also be a demand for geographers who specialize in geographic information systems (GIS), which combines computer graphics, artificial intelligence, and high-speed communication to store, retrieve, manipulate, and map geographic data. Persons with only a bachelor's degree will face competition for jobs.

Advancement in this field depends on experience and additional education.

Income

Geographers with a bachelor's degree start at about $15,500 to $18,500 a year. An experienced cartographer employed by the federal government can earn over $32,000 annually.

A beginning instructor of geography at a four-year college earns about $22,000 for the academic year.

Additional sources of information

Association of American Geographers
1710 16th Street, NW
Washington, DC 20009

GEOLOGIST

The job

By examining surface rocks and rock samples drilled from beneath the surface, geologists study the structure, composition, and history of the earth's crust. Their work is important in the search for mineral resources and oil and in the study of predicting earthquakes. Geologists are also employed to advise on the construction of buildings, dams, and highways.

Geologists study plant and animal fossils as well as minerals and rocks. Some specialize in the study of the ocean floor or the composition of other plants. *Vulcanologists* study active and inactive volcanoes and lava flows. *Mineralogists* analyze and classify minerals and precious stones.

About two-fifths of all geologists work in private industry mainly for petroleum and mining companies. The federal government employs over 6,000 geologists in the U.S. Geological Survey, the Bureau of Mines, and the Bureau of Reclamation. State and local governments employ geologists in highway construction and survey work.

Colleges and universities, nonprofit research institutions, and museums also employ geologists.

Related jobs are geophysicist, meteorologist, and oceanographer.

Places of employment and working conditions

Five states account for most jobs in geology: Texas, California, Louisiana, Colorado, and Oklahoma. Other areas with large oil and mineral deposits also provide job opportunities. American companies often send their geologists to overseas locations for varying periods of time.

Much of the work done by geologists is out-of-doors, often at remote locations. Geologists also cover many miles on foot. Those involved in mining often work underground; geologists in petroleum research often work on offshore oil rigs.

Qualifications, education, and training

Curiosity, analytical thinking, and physical stamina are all necessary for a geologist.

High school work should include as much science and mathematics as possible.

A bachelor's degree in geology or a related field is the basic preparation and is adequate for some entry-level jobs. Teaching and research positions require advanced degrees with specialization in one particular branch of geology.

Potential and advancement

About 34,000 people work as geologists. This is a growing field, and job opportunities will increase steadily as exploration activities for new sources of oil and gas increase. There will also be opportunities in environmental protection.

Those with advanced degrees will have the most job opportunities and the best chances for promotion.

Income

Beginners with a bachelor's degree earn about $21,200 a year. Managers earn annual salaries of about $50,000.

The federal government pays beginners from $15,738 to $19,493 a year for those with a bachelor's degree; $19,493 to $23,846 for those with a master's degree; and $28,852 to $34,580 for those with a Ph.D. The average annual salary for all geologists employed by the federal government is about $40,200 a year.

Additional sources of information

American Geological Institute
4220 King Street
Alexandria, VA 22302

Geological Society of America
P.O. Box 9140
3300 Penrose Place
Boulder, CO 80301

GEOPHYSICIST

The job

In general terms, geophysicists study the earth—its composition and physical aspects and its electric, magnetic, and gravitational fields. They usually specialize in one of three general phases of the science—solid earth, fluid earth, or upper atmosphere—and some also study other planets.

Solid earth geophysicists search for oil and mineral deposits, map the earth's surface, and study earthquakes. This field includes *exploration geophysicists*, who use seismic prospecting techniques (sound waves) to locate oil and mineral deposits; *seismologists*, who study the earth's interior and earth vibrations caused by earthquakes and human-engineered explosions, explore for oil and minerals, and provide information for use in constructing bridges, dams, and large buildings (by determining where bedrock is located in relation to the surface); and *geologists*, who study the size, shape, and gravitational field of the earth and other planets and whose principal task is the precise measurement of the earth's surface.

Hydrologists are concerned with the fluid earth. They study the distribution, circulation, and physical properties of underground and surface waters including glaciers, snow, and permafrost. Those who are concerned with water supplies, irrigation, flood control, and soil erosion study rainfall and its rate of infiltration into the soil. *Oceanographers* are also sometimes classified as geophysical scientists.

Geophysicists who study the earth's atmosphere and electric and magnetic fields and compare them with other planets include *geomagneticians*, who study the earth's magnetic field; *paleomagneticians*, who study rocks and lava flows to learn about past magnetic fields; and *planetologists,* who study the composition and atmosphere of the moon, planets, and other bodies in the solar system. They gather data from geophysical instruments placed on interplanetary space probes or from equipment used by astronauts during the Apollo missions. *Meteorologists* sometimes are also classified as geophysical scientists.

Most geophysicists work in private industry chiefly for petroleum and natural gas companies. Others are in mining, exploration, and consulting firms or in research institutes. A few are independent consultants doing geophysical prospecting on a fee or contract basis.

A number of geophysicists work for the federal government mainly in the U.S. Geological Survey, the National Oceanic and Atmospheric Administration, and the Department of Defense. Other employers are colleges and universities, state governments, and research institutions. Some geophysicists are also employed by American firms overseas.

New geophysicists usually begin their careers doing field mapping or exploration. Some assist senior geophysicists in research work.

Places of employment and working conditions

In the United States, many geophysicists are employed in southwestern and western states and along the Gulf Coast where large oil and natural gas fields are located.

Many geophysicists work outdoors and must be willing to travel for extended periods. Some work at research stations in remote areas or aboard ships and aircraft. When not in the field, geophysicists work in modern, well-equipped laboratories and offices.

Qualifications, education, and training

Geophysicists should be curious, analytical, and able to communicate effectively and should like to work as part of a team.

High school courses should include as many science courses as possible and mathematics.

A bachelor's degree in geophysics or in a geophysical specialty is acceptable for most beginning jobs. A bachelor's degree in a related field of science or engineering is also adequate, provided courses in geophysics, physics, geology, mathematics, chemistry, and engineering have been included.

About 75 colleges and universities award a bachelor's degree in geophysics. Other training programs offered include geophysical technology, geophysical engineering, engineering geology, petroleum geology, and geodesy.

More than 60 universities grant master's and Ph.D. degrees in geophysics. Geophysicists doing research or supervising exploration should have graduate training in geophysics or a related science, and those planning to do basic research or teach at the college level need a Ph.D. degree.

Potential and advancement

About 12,000 people work as geophysicists; employment opportunities are expected to grow some through the year 2000. The number of qualified geophysicists will fall short of requirements if present trends continue. As known deposits of petroleum and other minerals are depleted, petroleum and mining companies will need increasing numbers of geophysicists to find less accessible fuel and mineral deposits. In addition, geophysicists with advanced training will be needed to research alternate energy sources such as geothermal power (use of steam from the earth's interior) and to study solar and cosmic radiation and radioactivity. Federal agencies are also expected to hire more geophysicists for research and development in the earth sciences, energy research, and environmental protection.

Geophysicists with experience can advance to jobs such as project leader or program manager. Some achieve management positions or go into research.

Income

Geophysicists earn relatively high salaries. The average starting salary for graduates with a bachelor's degree is $21,200 a year. Those working as managers or supervisors earn about $53,000 a year.

The federal government pays geophysicists with a bachelor's degree a starting salary of between $15,738 to $19,493 depending on their college records. Those with a master's degree start at $19,493 to $23,846 a year; with a Ph.D. degree, from $28,852 to $34,580. The average salary for all geophysicists employed by the federal government is about $43,900 a year.

Additional sources of information

American Geophysical Union
2000 Florida Avenue, NW
Washington, DC 20009

Society of Exploration Geophysicists
P.O. Box 70240
Tulsa, OK 74170

GRAPHIC DESIGNER

The job

The field of commercial art includes not only *illustrators* but a variety of other art and graphic specialists who contribute to the final ad or design. For this reason, the title "graphic designer" has gradually replaced the term "commercial artist."

In a small firm or art department, an *art director*, assisted by a few trainees, might perform all or most of the work. In a large office, however, the art director would develop the artistic theme or idea and supervise the preparation of the material by the various graphic specialists in the department.

The *sketch artist*, also called a *renderer*, prepares a rough drawing of any pictures required. A *layout artist* arranges the illustrations or photographs, plans the typography (typeset material), and selects colors. Once the art director, sketch artist, and layout artist agree on the composition and layout, other graphic artists complete the detail work.

Letterers use a variety of methods and materials to insert headlines and other words. They may hand letter with pen and ink or apply prepared set or photo lettering. *Mechanical artists* prepare mechanicals—illustrations with all of the elements, in exact size, pasted in place as they are to appear. This is a very precise part of the artwork. *Pasteup artists* do more routine work; this position is often filled by a beginner.

Many commercial artists work as free-lance illustrators, some in addition to a regular salaried position. They provide sketches and other graphic specialties to advertising agencies, magazines and newspapers, medical or other technical book publishers, and greeting-card manufacturers.

Most people in this field work as salaried staff artists for advertising agencies or departments, commercial art studios, printing and publishing firms, textile companies, photographic studios, television and motion picture studios, and department stores. The federal government employs several thousand commercial artists mainly in the Department of Defense.

Others work for architectural firms and toy manufacturers and in the fashion industry, industrial designing, and theater set and costume designing.

Places of employment and working conditions

Opportunities exist in all parts of the country, but the majority are in large cities such as Boston, Chicago, Los Angeles, New York City, and San Francisco.

The workweek for salaried artists and designers is usually 40 hours. They sometimes put in additional hours, often under considerable pressure, to meet deadlines.

Qualifications, education, and training

Artistic talent, imagination and style, manual dexterity and the ability to work with great precision, and the ability to transform ideas into visual concepts are all necessary for anyone interested in this field.

Prospective graphic designers should tailor their high school work to the requirements of the art school or college they wish to attend. Any training in art is valuable, and students should begin to accumulate a portfolio of their work, since art schools and colleges usually require a sample of the applicant's work as well as an aptitude test.

Art schools, trade schools, junior colleges, and universities offer two- and four-year courses in commercial art or graphic design; some offer fine arts with some course work in commercial art. Art directors especially need a broad background in art plus experience and training in business, photography, typography, and printing production methods.

The continued accumulation of a portfolio representative of the artist's talents and abilities is necessary for employment. Free-lance artists especially must be prepared to display their work for prospective clients.

Potential and advancement

There are about 216,000 people working in this field. Competition for all jobs is normal, and beginners with little specialized training or experience face the stiffest competition. Beginners are usually willing to take any design job they can get just to get into the field and gain some experience.

Some jobs will be more in demand than others. Most new jobs will be in advertising agencies and graphic art studios. This field is also very sensitive to changes in general economic conditions.

Advancement in commercial art usually depends on specialization in either the mechanical elements of graphic design (letterers and mechanical and layout artists) or the pictorial elements (sketch artists, illustrators).

Income

Average annual earnings for graphic designers who are full-time employees are about $20,000 a year. The top 10 percent earn more than $37,000 a year, and the bottom 10 percent earn less than $12,000.

Earnings for free-lance graphic designers vary widely.

Additional sources of information

American Institute of Graphic Artists
1059 3rd Avenue
New York, NY 10021

GUARD

The job

Valuable properties need to be protected from theft, fire, vandalism, and trespassers. It is the duty of guards, sometimes called security officers, to maintain the security of properties and prevent any of these damaging situations.

Guards have a variety of different duties depending on the type, size, and location of their employer. Most guards usually make their rounds on foot, but some who watch over larger properties may patrol by car or motor scooter. Very large organizations may have a managing security officer who oversees a guard force.

Some guards are responsible for the protection of records, merchandise, money, equipment, and, in museums and other public buildings, art and exhibits. Other guards must keep unauthorized people from going where they are not supposed to go; usually this is the case when the employer is trying to maintain the security of new products, computer codes, or defense secrets. At airports, railroad stations, and public events, guards must make sure that order is maintained and watch for people who might try to cause trouble. Guards are also needed to protect money and valuable items while they are being transported in armored cars. Bodyguards are hired to protect people who may be at risk of injury, kidnapping, or invasion of privacy.

Guards usually wear uniforms and carry nightsticks and sometimes guns. Other equipment they use for carrying out their duties are computers, flashlights, two-way radios, and watch clocks.

Places of employment and working conditions

Guards work throughout the country, but most work in urban areas. Organizations employing guards include security firms and guard agencies; banks; building management companies; hotels; hospitals; retail stores; restaurants and bars; schools, colleges, and universities; and federal, state, and local governments.

Guards work both indoors and outdoors. Those who work outdoors must carry out patrols in all types of weather. While the work is usually routine, guards may find themselves in dangerous situations when either they or the property they protect is threatened. Many guards have to work alone at night and have very little contact with people. They are also sometimes required to work weekends and holidays.

Qualifications, education, and training

There are very few formal requirements for becoming a guard. Most employers prefer to hire high school graduates, and some prefer to hire workers with experience in the military police or in local and state police departments. Some jobs require a driver's license.

Applicants should be honest and responsible and have good character references and good health. Employers check for police records and often require applicants to take polygraph and drug screening tests.

Guards who work for contract security agencies are required to be licensed or registered in most states. To become registered, they must be at least 18 years old; have no convictions for perjury or violence; pass an exam; and complete training in property rights, emergency procedures, and seizure of suspected criminals. Very few states have licensing requirements for in-house guards.

Training varies for guards. Most guards receive some training before they begin their jobs and then get more instruction on the job. Employers with very complex security systems may give more extensive formal training.

Potential and advancement

There are currently about 795,000 guards. Job opportunities for guards should be plentiful through the year 2000 as concern about crime, vandalism, and terrorism increases. There will be more competition for in-house positions because they usually offer higher pay, better benefits, and more opportunities for training and advancement.

Advancement for guards is limited. Some workers with guard experience take training and move on to police work. Guards with some college education may advance to jobs that involve administrative tasks or preventing espionage and sabotage. Some guards advance by owning their own contract security agencies.

Income

Earnings for guards vary by type of employer. The average hourly wage for guards is $5.71. Guards in public utilities and transportation earn an average of $11.28 an hour; in banking, finance, and real estate, $7.82; in retail trade, $6.43; and in service industries, $5.04. In-house guards who are union members often earn more.

Additional sources of information

More information about employment as a guard can be obtained from local employers and the state employment service office. Registration and licensing information is offered by state licensing commissions or police departments.

GUIDANCE COUNSELOR

The job

Although their services are used in a wide variety of ways, the main function of school guidance counselors is to assist individual students with their problems, whether the problems are educational, social, or personal. To accomplish this, the counselors work closely with the school staff, parents, and the community.

Most guidance counselors are employed in secondary schools where they assist students in making career choices and work with them in selecting courses and meeting college requirements. Counselors also test and assess a student's abilities. A counselor's involvement in social problems includes work with drug and alcohol abuse, criminal behavior, and pregnancy. A student's personal problems can also require that the counselor help the student find a job or obtain medical or psychiatric help. In some schools, guidance counselors also teach some classes or supervise extracurricular activities.

The number of counselors in elementary schools is growing. At this educational level, counselors concentrate on the early detection of learning and personality problems because treatment and counseling can be most effective if started at an early age.

Most guidance counselors work in school buildings. A typical workday might include individual counseling sessions, meetings with small groups, or large meetings with students, parents, and community groups. Counselors may also be required to meet with law enforcement officers or agencies and with parents—sometimes in emotionally charged or unpleasant situations.

Places of employment and working conditions

Guidance counselors work in all areas of the United States in communities and schools of all sizes.

This is an active job, not always limited to an office atmosphere. There can be unpleasant and highly emotional confrontations from time to time, and a counselor must be careful not to become overinvolved in the lives and problems of the individual students.

Qualifications and training

A sincere desire to help young people is the most important characteristic for potential guidance counselors. The ability to work not only with students but with all members of the educational team is also essential. Guidance counselors should also have a thorough background in the study of human behavior.

Most guidance counselors come from the teaching profession, and most states require teacher certification as well as counseling certification for school counselors. College courses leading to teacher certification with additional courses in psychology and sociology are the best preparation.

One or two years of additional study are usually necessary to obtain the master's degree needed for counseling certification. Graduate courses usually include student appraisal, individual and group counseling, career information services, professional relations, ethics, statistics, and research. Depending on the state, from one to five years of teaching experience are also required.

Some states allow other types of education and experience and requirements have been changing rapidly in recent years. A prospective counselor should check with the appropriate state department of education before selecting a graduate program.

Potential and advancement

About 82,000 people work full-time as guidance counselors. Employment opportunities for school guidance counselors should be favorable through the year 2000. Renewed emphasis on quality education has encouraged expanded counseling programs. Many schools will expand existing programs and initiate new ones in the coming years.

School counselors may advance to supervisory positions or administrative posts in larger schools or school districts. With additional education and experience, they can become educational psychologists or college counselors, positions that require a Ph.D.

Income

School counselors usually earn more than classroom teachers in the same school. Salaries average about $34,200 a year, with increases usually granted for additional education and experience. Some counselors supplement their income with work for government, private, or industrial counseling units.

Additional sources of information

American School Counselor Association
5999 Stevenson Avenue
Alexandria, VA 22304

H

HEALTH SERVICES MANAGER

The job

The exact title may vary from institution to institution, but the responsibilities are the same—to plan, organize, coordinate, and supervise the delivery of health care. There are two types of health services managers: generalists, who manage or help to manage an entire facility; and health specialists, who manage specific clinical departments or services found only in the health industry.

The top administrator must staff the hospital with both medical and non-medical personnel; provide all aspects of patient care services; purchase supplies and equipment; plan space allocations; and arrange for housekeeping items such as laundry, security, and maintenance. The administrator must also provide and work within a budget; act as liaison between the directors of the hospital and the medical staff; keep up with developments in the health care field including government regulations; handle hospital community relations; and sometimes act as a fund raiser.

In large facilities, the administrator has a staff of assistants with expertise in a variety of fields, but, in small and medium-sized institutions, the administrator is responsible for all of them.

Health specialists manage the daily operations of individual, specialized departments such as surgery, rehabilitation therapy, nursing, and medical records. These workers have more narrowly defined responsibilities than generalists. They also receive more specialized training and experience in their field.

In addition to working in hospitals, health services managers are employed by nursing homes and extended-care facilities, community health centers, mental health centers, outreach clinics, city or county health departments, and health maintenance organizations (HMOs). Others are employed as advisors and specialists by insurance companies, government regulatory agencies, and professional standards organizations such as the American Cancer Society and the American Heart Association. Some serve as commissioned officers in the medical service and hospitals of the various armed forces or work for the U.S. Public Health Service or Veterans Administration.

Depending on the size of the institution, a new graduate might start as an administrative assistant, an assistant administrator, a specialist in a specific management area, a department head, or an assistant department head. In a small health care facility, the new graduate would start in a position with broad responsibilities, while in a large hospital the position might be narrow in scope with rotating work in several departments necessary to gain broad experience.

Places of employment and working conditions

Health services managers work throughout the country in hospitals and health care facilities of all sizes.

Health services managers put in long hours. They are on call at all times for emergency situations that affect the functioning of the institutions. They have very heavy work loads and are constantly under a great deal of pressure.

Qualifications, education, and training

Health services managers should have health and vitality, maturity, sound judgment, tact, patience, the ability to motivate others, good communication skills, and sensitivity for people.

Good grades in high school are important. Courses should include English, science, mathematics, business, public speaking, and social studies. Volunteer work or a part-time job in a hospital is helpful.

Preparation for this career includes the completion of an academic program in health administration that leads to a bachelor's, master's, or Ph.D. degree. The various levels of degree programs offer different levels of career preparation. Most health care organizations prefer to hire administrators with at least a master's degree in health administration, hospital administration, public health, or business administration. Usually, larger organizations require more academic preparation for their administrative positions.

The administrators of nursing homes must be licensed. Licensing requirements vary from state to state, but all require a specific level of education and experience.

Potential and advancement

There are about 177,000 people working is some phase of health care administration. Significant growth is projected for this field through the year 2000 as the increasing number of people 85 years old and over create a greater demand for health services.

The most opportunities will be in hospitals as well as in hospital subsidiaries that provide services such as ambulatory surgery, alcohol and drug abuse rehabilitation, hospice facilities, or home health care. There will also be many opportunities in physicians' offices, outpatient care facilities, health and allied services, and nursing and long-term care facilities.

In spite of the tremendous growth in this field, there will be keen competition for upper-level management jobs in hospitals.

Health services managers advance as they move into higher paying positions with more responsibilities. They also may advance by transferring to another health care facility or organization.

Income

Average earnings for all health services managers are $30,524 per year. Those at the low end of the salary range earn less than $15,704, while those at the high end earn an annual average of more than $50,800. Salaries vary depending on the manager's level of experience and expertise, the type and size of health facility, the geographic location, and the type of ownership.

Additional sources of information

American College of Health Care Administrators
8120 Woodmont Avenue
Suite 200
Bethesda, MD 20814

American College of Healthcare Executives
840 North Lake Shore Drive
Chicago, IL 60611

Association of University Programs in Health Administration
1911 Fort Myer Drive
Suite 503
Arlington, VA 22209

HISTORIAN

The job

The description and analysis of events of the past through writing, teaching, and research is the work of historians. Historians usually specialize in the history of an era—ancient, medieval, or modern—or in a specific country or area. They may also specialize in the history of a field such as economics, the labor movement, architecture, or business.

In the United States, many historians specialize in the social or political history of either the United States or modern Europe. The fields of African, Latin American, Asian, and Near Eastern history are becoming popular as well.

Most historians are employed in colleges and universities where they lecture, write, and do research in addition to teaching. Historians are also employed by libraries, museums, research organizations, historical societies, publishing firms, large corporations, and state and local government agencies.

The federal government employs historians primarily in the National Archives, Smithsonian Institution, and the Departments of Defense, Interior, and State.

Archivists collect historical objects and documents, prepare historical exhibits, and edit and classify historical materials for use in research and other activities. They are employed by museums, special libraries, and historical societies.

Places of employment and working conditions

Historians are employed in just about every college and university, and most cities have at least one museum. Those who work for the federal government work mostly in Washington, D.C.

Qualifications, education, and training

Anyone interested in this field should have an interest in reading, studying, and research and should have the ability and desire to write papers and reports. A historian needs analytical skills and should be able to work both independently or as part of a group.

High school should include as many social science courses as possible. Summer or part-time jobs in museums or libraries are helpful.

Although a bachelor's degree with a major in history is sufficient for a few entry-level jobs, almost all jobs in this field require advanced degrees. A master's degree is the minimum requirement for college instructors, with a Ph.D. necessary for a professorship and administrative positions.

History curriculums vary, but all provide training in the basic skills of research methods, writing, and speaking, which are needed by historians. Also important are training in archival work and quantitative methods of analysis, including statistical and computer techniques.

Potential and advancement

Competition will continue to be stiff for all job openings in this field since there will soon be thousands more Ph.D.s in the history field than there will be jobs for them to fill. Most openings will occur to replace those who retire or leave the field. Those graduating from prestigious universities and those well trained in quantitative methods of historical research will have the best job opportunities.

Historians with a master's degree will find teaching positions in community and junior colleges or high schools, but these jobs may also require state teaching certification.

Those with only a bachelor's degree will find very limited opportunities, but their major in history can be an excellent background for a career in journalism, politics, and other fields or for continuing education in law, business administration, or other related disciplines.

Income

The average annual starting salary for professional historians is $26,000. Archivists begin at an average of $24,000 a year.

The starting salary for historians employed by the federal government averages about $18,500 a year.

Many professional historians supplement their income by consulting, writing, and lecturing.

Additional sources of information

American Historical Association
400 A Street, SE
Washington, DC 20003

National Trust for Historic Preservation
1785 Massachusetts Avenue, NW
Washington, DC 20036

Organization of American Historians
112 North Bryan Street
Bloomington, IN 47401

HOME ECONOMIST

The job

The comfort and well-being of the family and the products, services, and practices that affect them are the concern of home economists. Some have a broad knowledge of the whole professional field, while others specialize in consumer affairs, housing, home management, home furnishings and equipment, food and nutrition, clothing and textiles, or child development and family relations.

Many home economists teach. Those who teach in secondary schools provide instruction in foods and nutrition, child development, clothing selection and care, sewing, consumer education, and other homemaking subjects. Others teach in adult education programs and present material on improving family relations and homemaking skills; some teach the handicapped and the disadvantaged. College teachers often combine research and teaching duties.

Home economists who are employed by private business firms and trade associations do research, test products, and prepare advertising and instructional materials. Some study consumer needs and advise manufacturers on products to fill those needs.

The federal government employs home economists in the U.S. Department of Agriculture to research the buying and spending habits of families in all socioeconomic groups and to develop budget guides for them. Federal, state, and local governments, as well as private agencies, employ home economists in social welfare programs to instruct clients in homemaking skills and family living.

Some home economists work as cooperative extension service agents and provide adult education programs for rural communities and farmers. They also provide youth programs such as 4-H clubs and train and supervise volunteer leaders for these programs.

Most home economists are women, although a growing number of men have entered the field in recent years.

Related jobs are agricultural cooperative extension service worker, dietician.

Places of employment and working conditions

A 40-hour workweek is the norm in this field, but those in teaching positions usually work some evening hours.

Qualifications, education, and training

Leadership, poise, communication skills, the ability to work with people of many cultures and levels of income, and an interest in the welfare of the family are necessary for this work.

High school courses should include English, home economics, health, mathematics, chemistry, and the social sciences. Part-time or summer jobs in children's camps or day nurseries provide valuable experience.

A bachelor's degree in home economics qualifies graduates for most entry-level positions. A master's degree or Ph.D. is required for college teaching, some research and supervisory positions, extension service specialists, and most jobs in nutrition.

Students who intend to teach at the secondary level must complete courses required for teaching certification. Those who intend to specialize in a particular area of home economics need the appropriate advanced courses: chemistry and nutrition for work in foods and nutrition; science and statistics for research work; journalism for advertising and public relations; art and design for clothing and textiles.

Potential and advancement

Job competition for home economics teachers will be stiff through the year 2000. There will be many more qualified home economics teachers than openings. The best opportunities will be for college-level and adult education teachers and for those who work with the disabled.

Concern over product quality and environmental issues will bring about a slight increase in job opportunities for home economists who work in research. The best jobs will go to those with advanced degrees or experience.

Home economics teachers advance by becoming head of the home economics department in their school or by overseeing the home economics program of an entire school system. Research home economists advance by becoming the head of a department or team. They can also become administrators or executives in government agencies.

Income

Starting salaries for home economics teachers who teach in secondary schools are between $17,000 and $23,500 a year. Average salaries for experienced teachers are about $24,000 to $30,000 a year. Those who teach at the college level receive average annual salaries that range from $20,000 to $32,000.

Home economists who work for the federal government have starting salaries of about $15,000 to $19,000 a year. Those with experience earn annual salaries of about $19,500 to $28,000 or more.

Additional sources of information

American Home Economics Association
2010 Massachusetts Avenue, NW
Washington, DC 20036

HOTEL/MOTEL MANAGER

The job

The manager of a hotel or motel is responsible for the profitable operation of the facility and for the comfort and satisfaction of the guests.

The manager is responsible for setting room rates and credit policies, the operation of the kitchen and dining rooms, and the housekeeping, accounting, and maintenance departments. In a large hotel or motel, the manager may have several assistants who manage some parts of the operation while, in small facilities, the manager may handle all aspects of the business personally including front-desk clerical work such as taking reservations. This is especially true in owner-operated facilities.

Hotels and motels that have a restaurant and/or cocktail lounge usually employ a *restaurant manager* or *food and beverage manager* to oversee these functions since this is usually an important part of the hotel's business.

A number of all hotel and motel managers are self-employed. Others work for large hotel and motel chains.

Places of employment and working conditions

Managers and their families very often live in the hotel or motel they manage, and they are on call at all times. Owner-operators often work very long hours.

Qualifications, education, and training

Initiative, self-discipline, and a knack for organization are necessary in this field. Summer or part-time work in a hotel, motel, or restaurant is helpful.

Although small hotels, motels, and restaurants do not have specific educational requirements, they do require experience for manager positions. Some employers, especially in larger facilities, require a bachelor's degree in hotel and restaurant administration.

Training is also available at many junior and community colleges, technical institutes, vocational and trade schools, and other academic institutions.

Some large hotels have on-the-job management programs in which trainees rotate among various departments to acquire a thorough knowledge of the hotel's operation.

Potential and advancement

There are about 96,000 hotel and motel managers holding wage and salary jobs. The field is expected to grow faster than the average through the year 2000 due to the growth in business travel and increased domestic and foreign tourism.

Assistant managers can advance to manager positions, but they often advance by moving to a larger hotel. Hotel and motel chains usually provide better opportunities for advancement than independent hotels since employees can transfer to another hotel in the chain or to the central office.

Income

Salaries of hotel and motel managers and assistants depend on the size, location, and sales volume of the facility.

Annual salaries of assistant managers average about $30,000, with those working in larger hotels averaging about $40,000 and those working in small hotels averaging about $23,000.

General managers earn an annual average of about $37,800 in large hotels to $22,600 in small hotels.

Additional sources of information

The American Hotel and Motel Association
1201 New York Avenue, NW
Washington, DC 20005

Council on Hotel, Restaurant, and Institutional Education
1200 17th Street, NW
Washington, DC 20036-3097

The Educational Institute of the American
    Hotel and Motel Association
P.O. Box 1240
East Lansing, MI 48826

I

IMPORT/EXPORT WORKER

The job

The buying and selling of raw materials and finished products between U.S. companies and companies in foreign countries are typically handled by import and export workers. Some workers handle both importing and exporting materials; others specialize in one or the other.

Import and export workers may work for firms that do only importing, only exporting, or both. Some work in the foreign trade divisions of large companies.

An *export manager* is responsible for overall management of a company's exporting activities. He or she supervises the activities of sales workers called *foreign representatives* who live and work abroad. These foreign representatives may work in a single country or travel between several countries in the course of servicing the company's customers. They also keep the company informed of any foreign political or economic conditions that might affect business. Orders from foreign customers are processed by *export sales managers*, who draw up contracts and arrange shipping details, and *export credit managers*, who review the customer's financial status and arrange credit terms.

For importing functions, a company usually employs a *support manager* to handle the purchase of foreign goods or raw materials. He or she supervises the work of *buyers*, who live and work abroad.

Companies that do not employ their own import and export workers may utilize the services of *export brokers*, who sell the companies' goods abroad for a commission, or *import merchants*, who sell products from foreign countries in this country. A company may also sell its goods to an *export commissionhouse broker*. These brokers are speculators who buy domestic goods outright and then sell them in foreign countries.

Related jobs are sales manager, wholesaler, translator, interpreter.

Places of employment and working conditions

Most import and export workers are employed in the United States. The few overseas positions usually go to those with many years of experience or a special area of expertise.

Workers employed in the United States usually work a 35- to 40-hour week; in foreign countries they are expected to adapt to local working conditions and hours. They may be exposed to extremes in climate and living conditions and may have to spend a great deal of time traveling.

Qualifications, education, and training

Ability to work with detail, administrative talents, diplomacy, and tactfulness are necessary. Those in sales need aggressiveness and the ability to get along with people as well as adaptability for living in foreign cultures. Knowledge of a foreign language is also usually required.

Most employers require a college degree. Some will accept a liberal arts degree, but most prefer specific areas such as law, engineering, or accounting. An advanced degree in business administration is necessary for some positions.

Many employers provide training for new employees. This usually includes classroom and on-the-job training that covers U.S. laws governing foreign trade and the practices of foreign countries.

Potential and advancement

Job opportunities in this field are expected to increase through the year 2000. Population growth and expanding foreign trade will account for a number of new job openings.

Import and export workers can advance to management and executive positions. Buyers and foreign representatives sometimes advance by going into business for themselves as export brokers or import merchants.

Income

Beginners earn starting salaries of about $16,000 a year.

Experienced workers in management-level positions average from $23,000 to $35,000, sometimes much more.

Import and export workers stationed overseas receive overseas incentive allowances.

Additional sources of information

American Association of Exporters and Importers
11 West 42d Street
New York, NY 10036

International Group
Chamber of Commerce of the United States
1615 H Street, NW
Washington, DC 20062

National Foreign Trade Council
100 East 42d Street
New York, NY 10017

INDUSTRIAL DESIGNER

The job

Industrial designers develop new styles and designs for products ranging from pencil sharpeners and dishwashers to automobiles. Some specialize in package design or the creation of trademarks; others plan the entire layout of commercial buildings such as supermarkets.

Industrial designers combine artistic talent with knowledge of materials and production methods. Teamwork is necessary in this field, and input from many people goes into a finished product. Working closely with engineers, production personnel, and sales and marketing experts, industrial designers thoroughly research a product. They prepare detailed drawings, then a scale model of a new design. After approval of a design, a full-scale working model is built and tested before production begins.

Most industrial designers work for large manufacturing firms where they fill day-to-day design needs and work on long-range planning of new products or for design consulting firms that service a number of industrial companies. Some do free-lance work or work for architectural and interior design firms. A few teach in colleges and universities or art schools.

Places of employment and working conditions

Industrial designers work for manufacturing firms in all parts of the United States. Industrial design consultants work mainly in New York City, Chicago, Los Angeles, and San Francisco.

A five-day, 35- to 40-hour week is usual with occasional overtime necessary to meet deadlines.

Qualifications, education, and training

Creativity, artistic talent and drawing skills, the ability to see familiar objects in new ways, and communication skills are necessary. An industrial designer must be able to design to meet the needs and tastes of the public, not just to suit his or her artistic ideas.

High school should include courses in art, mechanical drawing, and mathematics.

Four- to five-year programs in industrial design are offered by art schools, technical schools, and colleges and universities. Most large manufacturing firms require a bachelor's degree in industrial design.

Some schools require the submission of samples of artistic ability before acceptance into their industrial design programs. After graduation, job applicants are expected to show a portfolio of their work to demonstrate their creativity and design ability.

Potential and advancement

This is a relatively small field with only limited growth expected in the foreseeable future. Job opportunities will be best for college graduates with degrees in industrial design.

Industrial designers may be promoted to supervisory positions with major responsibility for design of a specific product or group of products. Those with an established reputation sometimes start their own consulting firms.

Income

Beginners in this field earn about $18,000 to $21,000 a year. Experienced designers earn from $29,000 to $34,000, depending on their talent and the size of the firm.

Additional sources of information

Industrial Designers Society of America
1142 East Walker Road
Great Falls, VA 22066

INDUSTRIAL ENGINEER

The job

Industrial engineers are concerned with people and methods while other engineers may usually be concerned with a product or process. Industrial engineers determine the most efficient and effective way for a company to use the basic components of production—people, machines, and materials.

Industrial engineers develop management control systems for financial planning and cost analysis, design production planning and control systems, design time study and quality control programs, and survey possible plant locations for the best combination of raw materials, transportation, labor supply, and taxes.

About 80 percent of all industrial engineers are employed by manufacturing industries, but, because their skills can be used in almost any type of company, industrial engineers work in many industries that don't employ other types of engineers. They may work for insurance companies, banks, hospitals, retail organizations, and other large business firms as well as more traditional engineering employers such as construction companies, mining firms, and utility companies.

Related jobs are office manager, interior designer, systems analyst.

Places of employment and working conditions

Industrial engineers work in all parts of the country and are concentrated in industrialized and commercial areas.

This is a physically active engineering specialty involving daily visits to departments within the plants, offices, and grounds of the employer as well as travel to possible plant locations.

Qualifications, education, and training

The ability to think analytically, a capacity for detail, and the ability to work as part of a team are all necessary. Good communication skills are important.

Mathematics and the sciences must be emphasized in high school.

A bachelor's degree in engineering is the minimum requirement in this field. In a typical curriculum, the first two years are spent in the study of basic sciences such as physics and chemistry and mathematics, introductory engineering, and some liberal arts courses. The remaining years are usually devoted to specialized engineering courses. Engineering programs can last from four to six years. Those that require five or six years to complete may award a master's degree or may provide a cooperative plan of study plus practical work experience with a nearby industry.

Because of rapid changes in technology, many engineers continue their education throughout their careers. A graduate degree is necessary for most teaching and research positions and for many management jobs. Some persons obtain graduate degrees in business administration.

Engineering graduates usually work under the supervision of an experienced engineer or in a company training program until they become acquainted with the requirements of a particular company or industry.

All states require licensing of engineers whose work may affect life, health, or property or who offer their services to the public. Those who are licensed, about one-third of all engineers, are called registered engineers. Requirements include graduation from an accredited engineering school, four years of experience, and a written examination.

Potential and advancement

There are about 132,000 industrial engineers. Job opportunities in this field are expected to increase substantially through the year 2000 because of the increased complexity and expanding use of automated processes and increased recognition of the importance of scientific management and safety engineering in reducing costs and increasing productivity.

Income

Starting annual salaries in private industry average $29,200 with a bachelor's degree; $34,600 with a master's degree; and $46,600 or more with a Ph.D. Experienced engineers average $45,777 in private industry.

Additional sources of information

Accreditation Board for Engineering and Technology
345 East 47th Street
New York, NY 10017

American Society for Engineering Education
11 Dupont Circle
Suite 200
Washington, DC 20036

Institute of Industrial Engineers, Inc.
25 Technology Park/Atlanta
Norcross, GA 30092

Junior Engineering Technical Society (JETS)
1420 King Street
Suite 405
Alexandria, VA 22314

National Society of Professional Engineers
1420 King Street
Alexandria, VA 22314

Society of Women Engineers
345 East 47th Street
Room 305
New York, NY 10017

INSURANCE AGENT AND BROKER

The job

Insurance agents and brokers sell insurance policies to individuals and businesses to protect against financial losses and to provide for future financial needs. They sell one or more of the three basic types of insurance: life, property-liability (casualty), and health.

An *agent* may be either the employer of an insurance company or an independent representative of one or more insurance companies. A *broker* is not under contract to a specific insurance company or companies but places policies directly with whichever company can best serve the needs of a client. Both agents and brokers spend the largest part of their time discussing insurance needs with prospective customers and designing insurance programs to fill each customer's individual needs.

Life insurance agents and brokers (life underwriters) sell policies that provide payment to survivors (beneficiaries) when the policyholder dies. A life policy can also be designed to provide retirement income, educational funds for surviving children, or other benefits.

Casualty insurance agents and brokers sell policies that protect against financial losses from such things as fire, theft, and automobile accidents. They also sell commercial and industrial insurance such as workers' compensation, product liability, and medical malpractice.

Health insurance policies offer protection against the cost of hospital and medical care as well as loss of income due to illness or injury and are sold by both life and casualty agents and brokers.

More and more agents and brokers are becoming multiline agents, offering both life and property-liability policies to their clients. Some agents and brokers also sell securities such as mutual funds and variable annuities or combine a real estate business with insurance selling. Successful insurance agents or brokers are highly self-motivated. Anyone interested in this work as a career should be aware that many beginners leave the field because they are unable to establish a large enough clientele. For those who succeed, the financial rewards are usually very good.

Recognizing that the professional working woman represents a new market, the insurance industry has recently been designing insurance programs to meet her special needs. The need for women insurance agents and brokers to service these new clients has expanded, and some insurance companies are actively recruiting women for their sales forces. While some companies hire only college graduates, others are interested in women with experience in sales, business, and finance.

Related jobs are actuary, claim representative, underwriter.

Places of employment and working conditions

Insurance agents and brokers are employed throughout the country, in all locations and communities, but the largest number work in or near large population centers.

Agents and brokers are free to schedule their own working hours but often work evenings and weekends for the convenience of their clients. In addition, hours devoted to paper work and continuing education often add up to much more than 40 hours a week.

Agents and brokers usually pay their own automobile and travel expenses. If they own and operate their own agency, they also pay clerical salaries, office rental, and operating expenses out of their own incomes.

Qualifications, education, and training

Agents and brokers should be enthusiastic, self-confident, and able to communicate effectively. They need initiative and sales ability to build a clientele and must be able to work without supervision.

Many insurance companies prefer a college degree (in almost any field) but will hire high school graduates with proven ability or other potential. Courses in accounting, economics, finance, business law, and insurance subjects are the most useful, whether the agent works for an insurance company or is self-employed.

New agents receive training at the agency where they will work or at the home office of the insurance company for which they work. Much of this training involves home study courses.

All states require agents and most brokers to be licensed. In most states, this takes the form of a written examination covering state insurance laws. Insurance companies often sponsor classes to prepare their new agents for the licensing exam, while other new agents study on their own. Some trade and correspondence schools offer courses for insurance agents.

Agents and brokers who wish to succeed in this field are constantly studying to increase their skills. They take college courses and attend educational programs sponsored by their own company or by insurance organizations.

The Life Underwriter Training Council awards a diploma in life insurance marketing after successful completion of the council's two-year life program. The council also sponsors a program in health insurance. Experienced agents and brokers earn the chartered life underwriter (CLU) designation by passing a series of examinations given by the American College of Bryn Mawr, Pennsylvania. Property-lability agents receive the chartered property casualty underwriter (CPCU) designation in the same way from the American Institute for Property and Liability Underwriters.

Potential and advancement

There are approximately 423,000 full-time insurance agents and brokers with many more working part-time.

Employment of insurance agents and brokers is expected to grow through the next decade. Although sales volume should increase rapidly as a larger proportion of the population enters the period of peak earnings and family responsibilities, the employment of agents and brokers will not necessarily grow as rapidly as sales volume. This is due to the fact that more policies will be sold to groups and by multiline agents and because more of an agent's time-consuming paper work will be done by computer, releasing agents to spend more time in actual selling and client contact.

Promotion to positions such as sales manager in a local office or to management positions in a home office or agency is open to agents with exceptional sales ability and leadership. However, many agents who have a good client base prefer to remain in sales with some establishing their own independent agencies or brokerage firms.

Income

Insurance agents and brokers usually work on a commission basis. Beginners are often provided with a moderate salary for about six months until they complete their training and begin to build a clientele.

Average annual earnings for insurance agents and brokers is about $25,000. Those at the bottom of the pay scale earn $13,900 or less, while those at the top of the pay scale earn over $52,000. Earnings usually increase rapidly as an agent gains experience.

Additional sources of information

General occupational information about insurance agents and brokers is available from the home office of many insurance companies. Information on state licensing requirements may be obtained from the department of insurance at any state capital. Additional sources are:

American Society of Chartered Life Underwriters (CLU) and
  Chartered Financial Consultants (ChFC)
270 Bryn Mawr Avenue
Bryn Mawr, PA 19010

Independent Insurance Agents of America
100 Church Street
19th Floor
New York, NY 10007

National Association of Professional Insurance Agents
400 North Washington Street
Alexandria, VA 22314

INTERIOR DESIGNER

The job

Interior designers plan and supervise the design and arrangement of building interiors and furnishings. Some work on private residences; others specialize in large commercial and public buildings.

An interior designer considers the purpose of the area and the client's budget and taste. Sketches are prepared for the client's approval, and changes are made as required. In some cases, plans and sketches must be prepared several times before a client is satisfied. Once the plans and the cost are approved, the designer shops for and buys furnishings and accessories; supervises the work of painters, carpet layers, and others; and makes sure furnishings are delivered and properly arranged.

Designers who specialize in nonresidential work, such as entire office buildings, or public buildings, such as libraries or hospitals, plan the complete layout of the interior, working with the architect. In some instances, they design the furnishings and arrange for their manufacture.

Most interior designers work for large design firms that provide design services to a number of clients. Others work for large department or furniture stores, furniture and textile manufacturers, and antique dealers. A few have permanent jobs with hotel and restaurant chains.

A few interior designers design stage sets for motion pictures and television or work for home furnishing magazines.

Places of employment and working conditions

Interior designers work throughout the country, usually in larger communities.

Interior designers usually work in comfortable, pleasant studios or stores. Their work may require some travel to visit homes, buildings being constructed, and warehouses. The workweek is usually long in this field, and the hours are often irregular.

Qualifications, education, and training

Artistic talent, color sense, good taste, imagination, and the ability to work well with people are all necessary.

High school courses should include art and business skills. Part-time or summer jobs in a home furnishings department or store are helpful.

Formal training in interior design is necessary for all the better jobs with architectural firms, well-established design firms, department and furniture stores, and other major employers. Programs are available at professional schools of interior design (three-year programs); colleges and universities, which award a bachelor's degree; or in graduate programs leading to a master's degree or Ph.D. Courses in sales and business subjects are also valuable.

Regardless of education, beginners almost always go through a training period with the company that hires them. They may function as shoppers, stockroom assistants, salesworkers, assistant decorators, or junior designers. This trainee period lasts from one to five years.

After several years of experience as a designer, including supervisory experience, an interior designer who has had formal training may become a member of the American Society of Interior Design, which is recognized as a mark of achievement in this field.

Potential and advancement

Even though growth is expected in this field, its popularity means competition for just about all job openings. The field is also affected by ups and downs in the economy.

After considerable experience, designers may advance to supervisory positions. Some open their own businesses.

Income

Beginners may be paid anywhere from minimum wage plus commission to salaries of $15,000 to $19,000 a year.

Experienced interior designers may work on commission, salary plus commission, or straight salary. They have annual salaries ranging from $25,000 to $75,000 a year. Good designers with an established reputation can earn well over $85,000 a year.

Additional sources of information

American Society of Interior Design
1430 Broadway
New York, NY 10018-3399

INTERNAL REVENUE AGENT

The job

Internal revenue agents examine and audit the financial records of individuals, businesses, and other organizations to determine their correct federal income tax liability.

In district offices throughout the country, agents audit income tax returns, handle investigations, and provide information and assistance to the public on questions concerning income taxes.

A rapidly expanding career field within the Internal Revenue Service is computerized information processing. Job openings for mathematicians, statisticians, computer programmers, systems analysts, economists, and other computer specialists are increasing steadily.

Places of employment and working conditions

Internal revenue agents work throughout the country as well as in Washington, D.C.

Agents usually work a normal 40-hour workweek with occasional overtime during peak work loads. Agents involved in auditing and investigative work may spend some time in travel.

Qualifications, education, and training

Aptitude for mathematics, ability to do detailed work accurately and to work independently, patience, tact, and ability to get along with people are important for this job.

In high school, a college preparatory course with plenty of mathematics should be followed.

A college degree is required for all internal revenue agents. A degree in accounting or law or a liberal arts degree with some study of accounting and directly related subjects has been the traditional background for agents. Degrees in computer-related specialties are now also accepted.

Most new agents are hired by district offices through local college recruitment programs. Applicants must pass a civil service examination before being hired. (See job description for *civil service worker, federal.*)

Potential and advancement

Requirements have remained stable in recent years with increases in work load being handled with the aid of computers. The number of interested applicants and the available job openings have just about matched. The employment outlook is good.

Opportunities for advancement are numerous in the Internal Revenue Service. Agents may be promoted to supervisory and management positions in district and regional offices and to top-level positions in Washington.

Income

Internal revenue personnel are paid according to the federal General Schedule (GS) salary scale.

Beginning salaries range from $17,000 to $22,000 a year, depending on education and college grades. Within-grade increases and promotion are rapid, for the most part.

Experienced agents in the Internal Revenue Service earn from $30,000 to $38,000 a year.

Additional sources of information

Contact the Internal Revenue Service district office in your locality.

INTERPRETER

The job

Oral interpretation is needed whenever a difference in language creates a barrier between people of different cultures. Interpreters can be found escorting foreign visitors and businesspeople, interpreting highly technical speeches and discussions at international medical or scientific meetings, or appearing in a courtroom when the proceedings involve persons who do not speak or understand English.

There are two basic types of interpretation: simultaneous and consecutive. In simultaneous interpretation, the interpreter translates what is being said in one language as the speaker continues to speak in another. This requires both fluency and speed on the part of the interpreter and is made possible by the use of electronic equipment that allows the transmission of simultaneous speeches. Simultaneous interpretation is preferred for conferences and meetings. Conference interpreters often work in a glass-enclosed booth using earphones and a microphone. Those attending the conference can tune into their preferred language by turning a dial or pushing a button.

In consecutive interpretation, the speaker and the interpreter take turns speaking. In addition to having fluency in the language, a consecutive interpreter must also have a good memory and usually takes notes to give a full and accurate translation. This method is very time-consuming but is the usual method with person-to-person interpretation.

The United Nations (UN) employs full-time interpreters. Full-time staff interpreters are also employed by the Organization of American States, the International Monetary Fund, the Pan American Health Organization, and the World Bank. The U.S. Department of State and the U.S. Department of Justice are the major employers of full-time interpreters in the federal government.

Free-lance interpreters usually work on short-term contracts, although some assignments can be of longer duration. The greatest number of free-lance interpreters work under contract for the U.S. Department of State and the Agency of International Development, serving as escort interpreters for foreign visitors to the United States. The next largest group of free-lance interpreters works in the conference field.

A related job is translator.

Places of employment and working conditions

This is a relatively small job field with the largest concentration of interpreters in New York City and Washington, D.C.

The conditions under which interpreters work vary widely. Free-lance interpreters have little job security because of the fluctuations in demand for their service. Free-lance assignments can last from a few days for a typical conference to several weeks on some escort assignments. Although interpreters do not necessarily work long hours, they often work irregular hours, with escort interpreters often required to do a great deal of traveling.

Qualifications, education, and training

Anyone interested in becoming an interpreter should be an articulate speaker and have good hearing. This work requires quickness, accuracy, tact, and emotional stamina to deal with the tensions of the job. Interpreters must be dependable as to the honesty of their interpretations and have a sense of responsibility as to the confidentiality of their work.

A complete command of two languages or more is the usual requirement for an interpreter. Interpreters at the UN must know at least three of the six official UN languages: Arabic, Chinese, English, French, Russian, and Spanish.

An extensive and up-to-date working vocabulary and ease in making the transition from one language structure to another are necessary as well as the ability to instantly call to mind appropriate words or idioms of the language.

Many individuals may qualify on the basis of their own foreign backgrounds, and the experience of living abroad is also very important. Interpreters should be generally well informed and, in the case of conference interpretation, be well grounded in technical subjects such as medicine or scientific and industrial technology.

Interpreters who speak Portuguese, Japanese, and German are also widely in demand in the United States.

Although there is no standard requirement for entry into this profession, a university education generally is essential. In the United Sates, two schools offer special programs for interpreters. Foreign language proficiency is an entry requirement in both.

Applicants to Georgetown University School of Languages and Linguistics in Washington, D.C., must qualify on the basis of an entrance examination and previous studies at the university level; they usually hold a bachelor's degree and often a master's degree. The school awards a certificate of proficiency as a conference interpreter upon successful completion of a one- or two-year course of study. The certificate is recognized by the International Association of Conference Interpreters.

The Department of Translation and Interpretation at the Monterey Institute of Foreign Studies in Monterey, California, offers a two-year graduate program leading to a master's degree in intercultural communication and a graduate certificate in either translation, translation/interpretation, or conference interpretation. School entrance requirements include a bachelor's degree, an aptitude test, fluency in English plus one other language if studying translation, or two other languages for the interpretation field. After two semesters of basic courses in translating and interpreting, applicants must pass a qualifying examination for entrance into the translation or interpretation programs.

Potential and advancement

There are about 1,000 interpreters working full-time in the United States. Many others do some interpretation work in the course of their jobs. Secretaries with foreign-language abilities are in demand by companies with foreign subsidiaries or customers.

Only highly qualified applicants will find jobs in this field. There is stiff competition for the very limited number of job openings, and the number of openings is not expected to increase through the year 2000. Some openings will occur, however, to replace those who retire, die, or leave the field for other reasons. In the past, any increase in the demand for full-time interpreters has been slight and usually temporary and has been met by the existing pool of free-lance interpreters.

Income

Beginning salaries for full-time interpreters are around $20,000 a year. Experienced interpreters earn annual salaries ranging from about $30,000 to

$35,000 a year. Some high-level interpreters working for the federal government earn $60,000 and over a year.

Free-lance interpreters are paid on a daily basis, with conference interpreters earning about $300 a day and free-lance escort interpreters receiving $100 a day.

Additional sources of information

The American Association of Language Specialists
1000 Connecticut Avenue, NW
Suite 9
Washington, DC 20036

Department of Translation and Interpretation
Monterey Institute of Foreign Studies
P.O. Box 1978
Monterey, CA 93940

Division of Interpretation and Translation
School of Languages and Linguistics
Georgetown University
Washington, DC 20057

Language Services Division
U.S. Department of State
Washington, DC 20520

Secretariat Recruitment Service
United Nations
New York, NY 10017

INVESTMENT MANAGER

The job

An investment manager's function is to manage a company's or an institution's investments. Investment decisions involve such things as what to buy in the way of securities, property for investment, or other items; or what and when to sell existing holdings for maximum return on investment.

Also called financial analysts and securities analysts, these investment specialists work for banks (where they are usually officers), insurance companies, brokerage firms, and pension plan investment firms and mutual funds. They may function as trustees for institutions or individuals with large holdings or for colleges that have endowment funds to manage. Some use their expertise as financial journalists, analyzing the market for financial publications, newspapers, and magazines. (For a detailed description of the work of people involved in this field see the job description for *market analyst*.)

Places of employment and working conditions

Investment managers work in all parts of the country but are concentrated in Boston, Chicago, New York City, and San Francisco.

The work is very time consuming since investment specialists must read constantly—newspapers, annual reports, trade publications—to keep abreast of developments and changes in the market.

Qualifications, education, and training

Facility in mathematics; ability to digest, analyze, and interpret large amounts of material; an inquiring mind; and good communication skills are important in this field.

A college degree in economics, political science, business administration, finance, or marketing is preferred in the investment field. Engineering or law, especially if combined with graduate work in business administration, can also provide an excellent background. Training in mathematics, statistics, and computers is becoming increasingly important.

The mark of professionalism in this field is the chartered financial analyst (CFA) degree, which is comparable to the certified public accountant (CPA) for an accountant. To earn it, the applicant must fulfill the membership requirements of one of the financial analyst societies and complete three examination programs. Five or more years of experience as a financial analyst are necessary before the third examination can be taken.

Potential and advancement

Job opportunities will be good into the year 2000 for those with the appropriate degrees and experience.

Since this is already a high-level position in most organizations, further advancement for an investment manager would usually take the form of moving to a larger institution or organization if he or she has achieved a reputation for accurate analysis and wise management of investments.

Income

Investment managers who work in banking or for large institutions such as colleges earn up to $50,000 or more a year.

The range for all top-level analysts in this field is about $25,000 to $65,000. Some with excellent reputations earn considerably more.

Additional sources of information

The Institute of Chartered Financial Analysts
P.O. Box 3668
Charlottesville, VA 22903

New York Stock Exchange
11 Wall Street
New York, NY 10005

Securities Industry Association
120 Broadway
New York, NY 10271

J

JANITOR

The job

Janitors, or building custodians, clean and maintain many types of buildings, including offices, hotels, stores, homes, apartments, and hospitals.

Janitors have a variety of duties, depending on their employer and the extent of their responsibilities. Some janitors are responsible only for cleaning while others have maintenance responsibilities as well. Some typical janitorial duties include mopping floors, vacuuming carpets, emptying garbage cans, dusting, cleaning bathrooms, making beds, and dusting furniture. Light maintenance work may include changing light bulbs, painting, carpentry, and repairing leaky faucets.

Janitors use tools and cleaning equipment to perform their tasks.

Places of employment and working conditions

Janitors are employed throughout the United States.

Most janitors work in the evenings when buildings are empty. Some janitors work during the day, especially in schools, hotels, and hospitals.

Janitors usually work indoors, but they sometimes have to work outdoors to shovel sidewalks and mow lawns. Some tasks a janitor may be required to perform are dirty and unpleasant. Janitors spend most of their working hours on their feet and may have to move heavy objects or cleaning equipment.

Many janitors are employed part-time.

Qualifications, education, and training

There are no formal educational requirements for janitors. Janitors do need to know simple arithmetic and must be able to follow directions.

Most janitors receive on-the-job training. Beginners usually work with a more experienced person to learn efficient methods of performing tasks.

Potential and advancement

Janitors and cleaners hold about 2.9 million jobs. There are expected to be good opportunities in this field through the year 2000.

Advancement opportunities for janitors are generally limited. Where there are large maintenance staffs, some janitors may become supervisors. Others advance by owning their own cleaning business.

Income

Janitors earn an average of $245 a week. Those in the middle of the salary range earn between $185 and $325; those at the bottom earn less than $145, and those at the top earn more than $425.

Additional sources of information

Building Service Contractors Association International
10201 Lee Highway
Suite 225
Fairfax, VA 22030

L

LABOR RELATIONS SPECIALIST

The job

The field of labor relations covers the relationship between the management of a company and the company's unionized employees. Since more and more government employees are becoming unionized, specialists in the field of labor relations are now employed in government agencies as well as in private industry.

The day-to-day administration of the provisions of a union contract is usually the responsibility of a company's personnel department or, in a large company, the industrial relations department. In a small or medium-sized company, the personnel manager might handle union matters as part of his or her responsibilities, but in a large company one or more labor relations specialists are employed. Their responsibilities include handling grievances, preparing for collective bargaining sessions, and participating in contract negotiations. In some companies, labor relations specialists are also involved in accident prevention and industrial safety programs.

A labor relations specialist must stay abreast of developments in labor law and wages and benefits in local companies and within the industry and must provide constant liaison between the company and union officials. An effective labor relations specialist must be able to work with union representatives in an atmosphere of mutual respect and cooperation.

In companies, usually large ones, that have both union and nonunion employees, labor relations and the personnel department are part of the industrial relations department functions.

Labor relations specialists employed by government agencies perform much the same duties as those employed in private industry.

Labor unions do not employ many professionally trained labor relations specialists. At the company and local level, elected union officials handle all union-management matters. At national and international union headquarters, however, research and education staffs usually include specialists with degrees in industrial and labor relations, economics, or law.

Related jobs are personnel manager and employment counselor.

Places of employment and working conditions

Labor relations specialists work throughout the United States, with the largest concentrations in heavily industrialized areas.

A 40-hour workweek is usual in this field, but longer hours may be necessary during contract negotiations or periods of labor problems.

Qualifications, education, and training

The ability to see opposing viewpoints is important for a labor relations specialist. Integrity, a sense of fairness, and the ability to work with people of many educational levels and social backgrounds are necessary qualities. Communication skills are a major requirement.

High school courses should include social studies, English, and any courses or extracurricular activities available in public speaking and debating.

Most labor relations specialists begin their careers in personnel work and move into labor relations as they gain experience. (Educational requirements for personnel workers are listed under the personnel manager job description.) Those who enter the field of labor relations directly are usually graduates of master's degree programs in industrial or labor relations or have a law degree with course work in industrial relations. Courses in labor law, collective bargaining, labor economics and history, and industrial psychology should be included in either undergraduate or graduate study.

Potential and advancement

There are about 252,000 people working as labor relations specialists. Substantial growth is expected in this field, with the most job opportunities in private business as employers try to provide effective training and employee relations programs for a rapidly growing work force. In spite of this projected growth in the field, there will be competition for available job openings since there are many qualified workers and college graduates with degrees in labor relations.

Advancement often takes the form of moving to a larger company. Others advance by moving from middle-level positions in large companies to top-level positions in smaller companies.

Labor relations specialists who gain substantial experience and establish a widely known reputation sometimes work as federal mediators. Their services are made available to companies or industries that have arrived at a stalemate in contract negotiations with a union.

Income

The average annual salary for labor relations specialists is $29,000, with the top 10 percent earning over $52,000 and the bottom 10 percent earning less than $15,700.

Additional sources of information

American Arbitration Association
140 West 51st Street
New York, NY 10020

American Society for Personnel Administration
606 North Washington Street
Alexandria, VA 22314

International Personnel Management Association
1617 Duke Street
Alexandria, VA 22314

LANDSCAPE ARCHITECT

The job

Landscape architects design the outdoor areas of commercial buildings and private homes, public parks and playgrounds, real estate developments, airports, shopping centers, hotels and resorts, and public housing. Their work not only beautifies these areas but helps them to function efficiently as well.

A landscape architect prepares detailed maps and plans showing all existing and planned features and, once the plans are approved, may accept bids from landscape contractors on the work to be done. In addition to planning the placement of trees, shrubs, and walkways, the landscape architect supervises any necessary grading, construction, and planting.

Most landscape architects are self-employed or work for architectural, landscape architectural, or engineering firms. State and local government agencies employ landscape architects for forest management; water storage; public housing, city planning, and urban renewal projects; highways, parks, and recreation areas. The federal government employs them in the Departments of Agriculture, Defense, and Interior. A few are employed by landscape contractors.

Beginners in this field are given simple drafting assignments, working their way up by preparing specifications and construction details and other aspects of project design. It is usually two or three years before they are allowed to handle a design through all stages of development.

Related jobs are environmentalist, farmer, floral designer, forester, forestry technician, urban planner, nursery worker, and architect.

Places of employment and working conditions

Landscape architects work throughout the United States, but most job opportunities exist in areas with favorable weather conditions, such as Florida, California, and Texas.

Salaried employees in this field usually work a 40-hour week; self-employed landscape architects often work much longer hours. Although a great many of an architect's hours are spent outdoors, a substantial number of hours are spent indoors in planning and mapping activities.

Qualifications, education, and training

Creative ability, appreciation of nature, talent in art and design, and the ability to work in detail are important. Business ability is necessary for those who intend to open their own landscape architectural firms.

High school should include courses in biology, botany, art, mathematics, and mechanical drawing. Summer jobs for landscaping contractors or plant nurseries provide good experience.

Forty-seven colleges offer bachelor's degree programs in landscape architecture that are approved by the American Society of Landscape Architects. Bachelor-degree programs take four or five years to complete.

A license is required in 41 states for the independent practice of landscape architecture. Requirements include a degree from an accredited school of landscape architecture, one to four years of experience, and a passing grade on a uniform national licensing examination.

Potential and advancement

There are about 19,000 practicing professional landscape architects. The outlook is for rapid growth in this field through the year 2000, although any periods of downturn in the construction industry could cause temporary slow periods. City and regional planning programs, interest in environmental protection, and the growth of transportation systems and recreational areas will contribute to the demand for qualified landscape architects, as will the general growth in population.

Landscape architects usually advance by moving to a larger firm, by becoming associates in their firm, or by opening their own businesses.

Income

Beginning landscape architects earn about $18,000 a year. Workers with master's degrees start at about $27,000.

Experienced landscape architects earn an average of about $37,000 a year.

Additional sources of information

American Society of Landscape Architects
4401 Connecticut Avenue, NW
Washington, DC 20008

LAWYER

The job

The basic work of a lawyer involves interpreting the law and applying it to the needs of a particular case or client.

Lawyers, also called attorneys, who have a general practice handle a variety of legal matters—making wills, settling estates, preparing property deeds, and drawing up contracts. Others specialize in criminal, corporate, labor, tax, real estate, or international law.

About four-fifths of all lawyers are in private practice, either alone or in a law firm. Business firms employ lawyers as salaried in-house counselors to handle company legal matters. The federal government employs lawyers in the Department of Justice and other regulatory agencies; state and local governments employ even more. Some lawyers teach full- or part-time in law schools.

Many people with legal training do not practice law but instead use their legal knowledge as a background for careers in financial analysis, insurance claim adjusting, tax collection, or management consulting. Others work as parole officers or law enforcement officers. Many elected public officials also have a background in law.

Places of employment and working conditions

Lawyers are needed in every community and by businesses and government agencies throughout the country.

Lawyers often work long hours and are under considerable pressure when a case is being tried. Those in private practice, however, can determine their own hours and caseloads and are usually able to work past the usual retirement age.

Qualifications, education, and training

Assertiveness, an interest in people and ideas, the ability to inspire trust and confidence, and top-notch debating and writing skills are necessary for this field. A successful lawyer must be able to research and analyze a case and to think conceptually and logically.

High school courses that develop language and verbal skills are important. Typing, American history, civics and government, and any training in debating, public speaking, or acting will prove useful.

At least seven years of full-time study beyond high school are necessary to obtain a law degree. This study includes four years of college and three years of law school. About one-eighth of all graduates attend law school on a part-time basis, taking four years or longer to complete the work.

Although there is no specific "prelaw" college program, the best undergraduate training is one that gives the student a broad educational background while developing the writing, speaking, and thinking skills necessary for a legal career. Majors in the social sciences, natural sciences, and humanities are suitable and should include courses in economics, philosophy, logic, history, and government. Good grades are very important.

Most law schools test an applicant's aptitude for the study of law by requiring the applicant to take the Law School Admission Test (LSAT). Competition for admission to law school is intense. At one point in the mid-1970s, the ratio of applicants to available openings was ten to one. Although this has slowed to some extent, stiff competition for entrance into law school will remain for the foreseeable future, particularly for the more prestigious law schools.

Students should attend a law school that is approved by the American Bar Association (ABA) or by an individual state. ABA approval indicates that the school meets the minimum standards of education necessary for practice in any state; state-approved law schools that lack ABA approval prepare graduates for practice in that particular state only. A few states recognize the study of law done entirely in a law office or a combination of law office and law school study. California will accept the study of law by correspondence course, if all other qualifications are met. Several states require the registration and approval of law students by the state board of law examiners before they enter law school or during the early years of legal study.

The first part of law school is devoted to the study of fundamental courses such as constitutional law, contracts, property law, and judicial procedure. Specialized courses in such fields as tax, labor, or corporate law are also offered. The second part of law school consists of practical training through participation in school-sponsored legal aid activities, courtroom practice in the school's practice court under the supervision of experienced lawyers, and through writing on legal issues for the school's law journal.

Upon successful completion of law school, graduates usually receive the degree of doctor of laws (J.D.) or bachelor of laws (L.L.B.). Those who intend to teach, do research, or specialize usually continue with advanced study.

All states require a lawyer to be admitted to the state bar before practicing law. Requirements include a written examination, at least three years of college, and graduation from an ABA- or state-approved law school.

Potential and advancement

There are about 582,000 lawyers practicing in the United States. Although this field is expected to grow steadily, a rapid increase in the number of law school graduates in recent years has created keen competition for available jobs. This situation will probably continue. Graduates of prestigious law schools and those who rank high in their graduating class will have the best chance of securing salaried positions with law firms, corporations, and government agencies and as law clerks (research assistants) for judges. Lawyers who wish to establish a new practice will find the best opportunities in small towns and in expanding suburban areas.

Lawyers advance from positions as law clerks to experienced lawyers through progressively more responsible work. Many establish their own practice. After years of experience, some lawyers become judges.

Income

Lawyers who establish their own practice usually earn little more than expenses during the first few years, but their income increases rapidly as the practice develops. Private practitioners who are partners in a law firm generally earn more than those who practice alone.

Lawyers starting in salaried positions earn about $34,000 a year. Starting salaries with the federal government are $23,800 or $28,900.

Additional sources of information

Association of American Law Schools
One Dupont Circle, NW
Suite 370
Washington, DC 20036

Information Services
American Bar Association
750 North Lake Shore Drive
Chicago, IL 60611

LIBRARIAN

The job

Librarians select and organize books and other publications and materials and assist readers in their use. Their work is divided into two areas: librarians in user services deal directly with the public, helping them to find the information and materials they need; those in technical services order, classify, and catalog materials and do not usually deal with the public. A librarian in a small or medium-sized library does both types of work.

Librarians are usually classified by the type of library in which they work—public, school, college and university, or special library.

Public librarians work in community libraries and provide a full range of library services for the citizens of the community. Depending on the budget and size of the community, the library staff may include acquisition librarians who purchase books and other materials and help users find what they need, reference librarians who help with specific questions and suggest information sources, and extension or outreach librarians who staff bookmobiles. Children's librarians and adult services librarians may be in charge of services for those particular age groups.

School librarians in elementary and secondary schools instruct students in the use of school library facilities, work with teachers to provide materials that interest students and supplement their classroom work, sometimes participate in team-teaching activities, and develop audio-visual programs.

College and university librarians provide services to students, faculty members, and researchers. Some operate documentation centers that record, store, and retrieve specialized information for university research projects or work in a special field such as law, medicine, or music.

Special librarians work in libraries maintained by government agencies and by commercial and business firms. They build and arrange the organization's information resources and provide materials and services covering subjects of special interest or use to the organization. They may be called upon to conduct a literature search or compile a bibliography on a specific subject.

Information science specialists work in much the same way as special librarians, but they have a more extensive technical and scientific background and greater knowledge of new information-handling techniques. They condense complicated information into readable form and interpret and analyze data

245

for highly specialized clientele. They develop classification systems, prepare coding and programming techniques for computer information storage and retrieval, and develop microfilm technology.

Most librarians work in school and academic libraries. Others work in special and public libraries.

Because many opportunities for part-time work exist in public libraries and because elementary and secondary school librarians work a nine-month year, this is a good job opportunity field for people with family responsibilities.

Places of employment and working conditions

Librarians work in communities of all sizes.

A typical workweek is 35 to 40 hours. In public libraries and college and university libraries, this usually includes some evening and weekend work.

Qualifications, education, and training

Intellectual curiosity and an interest in helping others are necessary characteristics for a librarian. A knack for organization and a retentive memory are very important.

High school should include courses and activities that develop verbal and language skills in a broad college preparatory program.

A liberal arts degree with a major in the social sciences, the arts, or literature, including course work in library science and a reading knowledge of at least one foreign language, is required for entrance into a graduate program in library science. The one- or two-year program leads to a master of library science degree (M.L.S.). Those who intend to work as special librarians or information science specialists usually earn a bachelor's degree in their specialty plus a master's or Ph.D. degree in library or information science.

Both undergraduate and graduate programs offer course work in such library specialties as data processing fundamentals and computer languages and the use and development of audio-visual materials. Librarians who intend to work as public school librarians must also complete teaching certification requirements in most states.

A Ph.D. degree is usually necessary for administrative positions in large public library systems and in college and university libraries.

Potential and advancement

There are about 143,000 professional librarians. Slow growth for employment in this field is projected through the year 2000. Limited budgets and slow population growth will lessen the demand for public librarians, and declining enrollments in schools and colleges will result in slow employment. Those trained as information science specialists will be in demand because of the expanding use of computers to store and retrieve information.

Experienced librarians with graduate training can advance to administrative positions. Those who acquire specialized training can advance to special librarian positions or to specialized libraries in government agencies or businesses.

Income

Salaries for librarians depend on individual qualifications and the type, size, and location of the library.

Starting salaries average $23,491 a year for all librarians. They range from $21,531 in public libraries to $25,183 in school libraries. College and university librarians earn an average of $22,454 a year to start, and in special libraries, starting salaries average $25,190 a year.

Additional sources of information

American Library Association
50 East Huron Street
Chicago, IL 60611

American Society for Information Science
1424 16th Street, NW
Suite 404
Washington, DC 20036

Office of Educational Research and Improvement
　Library Programs
Library Development Staff
U.S. Department of Education
555 New Jersey Avenue, NW
Room 402
Washington, DC 20202-1430

Special Libraries Association
1700 18th Street, NW
Washington, DC 20009

LIFE SCIENTIST

The job

From the smallest living cell to the largest animals and plants, life scientists study living organisms and their life processes. Life scientists usually work in one of three broad areas: agriculture, biology, or medicine.

About two-fifths of all life scientists are involved in research and development—doing basic research or applying it in medicine, increasing agricultural yields, and improving the environment. Others hold management and administrative positions in zoos and botanical gardens and in programs dealing with the testing of foods and drugs. Some work in technical sales and service jobs for industrial firms or work as consultants to business and government.

Some life scientists call themselves *biologists,* but the usual method of classification is according to type of organism studied or the specific activity performed. *Botanists* deal with plants—studying, classifying, and developing cures for plant disease. *Agronomists* work with food crops to increase yields, to control disease, pests, and weeds, and to prevent soil erosion. *Horticulturists* are concerned with orchard and garden plants such as fruit and nut trees, vegetables, and flowers.

Zoologists, who study animal life, have titles that reflect the group they study: *ornithologists* study birds, *entomologists* study insects, and *mammalogists* study mammals. *Animal husbandry specialists* are involved in breeding, feeding, and controlling disease in domestic animals. *Embryologists* study the development of animals from fertilized egg through the birth or hatching process.

Microbiologists investigate the growth and characteristics of microscopic organisms such as bacteria, viruses, and molds. *Medical microbiologists* study the relationship between bacteria and disease and the effects of antibiotics on bacteria.

Pathologists study the effect of diseases, parasites, insects, or drugs on human cells and tissue. *Pharmacologists* test the effect of drugs, gases, poisons, and other substances on animals and use the results of their research to develop new or improved drugs and medicines.

Anatomists, ecologists, geneticists, and *nutritionists* are also life scientists. Many of these life scientists are employed in colleges and universities usually in medical schools and state agricultural colleges. Some of these professionals are employed by the federal government, almost all of them in the Department of Agriculture. The remainder are employed by private industry in drug, food products, and agricultural-related industries.

Related jobs are biochemist, environmentalist, oceanographer, soil scientist, and veterinarian.

Places of employment and working conditions

Life scientists work throughout the United States, with the largest concentrations in metropolitan areas.

Most life scientists work in laboratories; some jobs, however, require outdoor work and strenuous physical labor. Working hours may be irregular in some specialties due to the nature of the research or activity under way.

Qualifications, education, and training

The ability to work independently and to function as part of a team is necessary for a career in the life sciences. Good communication skills are also necessary. Physical stamina is necessary in some of the specialty areas that require outdoor work.

High school courses should include as much science and mathematics as possible.

Almost all liberal arts programs include a biology major, and life science students should also include chemistry and physics courses. Some colleges offer bachelor's degrees in specific life sciences; many state universities offer programs in agricultural specialties. A bachelor's degree is adequate preparation for testing and inspection jobs and for advanced technician jobs in the medical field. With courses in education, it is also adequate background for high school teaching positions.

An advanced degree is required for most jobs in the life sciences. A master's degree is sufficient for some jobs in applied research and college teaching, but a Ph.D. is required for most teaching positions at the college level, for independent research, and for many administration jobs. A health-science degree is necessary for some jobs in the medical field.

Requirements for advanced degrees usually include field work and laboratory research.

Potential and advancement

There are approximately 57,000 life scientists in the United States. An additional 50,000 hold faculty positions in colleges and universities.

Job opportunities in the life sciences will increase, but some fields will be better than others. The most growth will be in private industry, in genetic and biotechnical research, in efforts to clean up and preserve the environment, and in health-related research. There will be slow growth in the employment of life scientists in the federal government.

Advancement in this field depends on experience and is usually limited to those with advanced degrees.

Income

In private industry, beginners with a bachelor's degree earn an average of $20,400 a year.

Life scientists who have an M.D. degree earn more than other life scientists but not as much as physicians in private practice.

Additional sources of information

American Institute of Biological Sciences
Office of Career Services
730 11th Street, NW
Washington, DC 20001-4584

American Physiological Society
Membership Services Department
9650 Rockville Pike
Bethesda, MD 20814

American Society for Microbiology
Office of Education and Professional Recognition
1913 I Street, NW
Washington, DC 20006

LOBBYIST

The job

Lobbying is an effort by an interested person or organization to influence legislation. On one hand, lobbying provides information relative to the target legislation and lets the legislator know the feelings of a particular group of constituents. On the other hand, lobbying may also have the negative reputation of applying pressure.

Lobbyists may take the form of individual citizens who write to members of Congress or state legislators about a particular matter. Groups of citizens who band together in demonstrations, telephone campaigns, or other efforts to influence lawmakers and regulatory agencies are also lobbying.

At the professional level, there are full-time officials of powerful organizations and industries who are paid to present their employer's side of a controversial question to the appropriate congressperson or committee. Their titles may signify legislative liaison or public relations duties, but their actual work is lobbying. There are some professional lobbyists who represent several clients simultaneously.

Some of the most effective lobbyists are former congresspersons, state legislators, and other administrative officials who are no longer active politically but who know their way around state capitals or federal agencies.

The most active lobbying groups at all levels are those from business, labor, farming, education, churches, and citizens' groups.

Places of employment and working conditions

Lobbyists operate at all levels of government in all parts of the country.

Although some lobbyists are involved in "wining and dining activities," a lot of hard work accompanies the more glamorous activities. Long hours are normal, and it is often necessary to work irregular hours to get to see important congresspersons and state officials.

Qualifications, education, and training

Personal integrity, good judgment, persistence, resourcefulness, patience, tact, an ability to get along with people, good communication skills, and physical stamina are necessary.

There are no specific educational requirements for a lobbyist. Training or experience in a particular field of interest, which provides a thorough background, plus a knowledge of how the government works and which people can make a difference are what make an effective lobbyist.

Potential and advancement

So long as there is legislation being considered, there will be lobbyists employed to influence the legislators. Active participation in a professional or political organization can provide opportunities for lobbying, and membership in nationally active groups can lead to federal-level lobbying.

Income

Earnings of lobbyists are difficult to establish. Many people are unpaid lobbyists who work for organizations or causes in which they have an interest. Others, although registered lobbyists, earn the bulk of their income in some other line of work. An example is public relations directors for large organizations who spend most of their time in that function but also represent their companies' interest as lobbyists on a particular piece of pending legislation.

Additional sources of information

American Association of Political Consultants
1211 Connecticut Avenue, NW
Washington, DC 20036

M

MACHINIST

The job

Machinists are skilled metal workers who know the working properties of a variety of metals and use this knowledge to turn a block of metal into a precisely machined part. In addition to making metal parts for automobiles, machines, and other equipment, machinists also repair or make new parts for factory machinery.

Machinists work from blueprints or written specifications and use a variety of machine tools, precision instruments such as micrometers, and hand tools.

All factories employ machinists to handle repairs and maintenance on equipment and machinery. Others are employed in industries that manufacture large numbers of metal parts such as the auto industry. Independent machine shops of all sizes employ many machinists; the federal government employs many more in navy yards and other installations.

Machinists are usually union members, with most of them belonging to either the International Association of Machinists and Aerospace Workers, the International Union, United Automobile, Aerospace and Agricultural Implement Workers of America; the International Union of Electrical, Radio, and Machine Workers; the International Brotherhood of Electrical Workers; or the United Steelworkers of America. A related job is tool-and-die maker.

Places of employment and working conditions

Machinists work in all parts of the United States but mainly in large industrial areas such as Boston, Chicago, New York City, Philadelphia, San Francisco, and Houston.

Machinists work in well-lighted areas, but the work is often noisy and can be tedious and repetitious. They use grease and oil in the course of their work and often stand most of the day. Finger, hand, and eye injuries are possible from flying metal particles, and safety rules usually require the use of specially fitted eyeglasses, protective aprons, and short-sleeve shirts.

Qualifications, education, and training

Anyone who wants to be a machinist should be mechanically inclined and temperamentally suited to doing work that requires concentration, precision, and physical effort. A machinist must also be able to work independently.

High school or vocational courses should include mathematics, physics, and machine shop classes, if possible.

A formal apprenticeship is the best training for all-around machinist. Some companies offer shorter courses for machinists who will work on single-purpose machines; and some machinists do learn through on-the-job training. But those who complete a formal apprenticeship program usually have the best opportunities for advancement since they are capable of handling a wider variety of jobs.

A typical apprentice program consists of shop training and related classroom instruction in blueprint reading, mechanical drawing, and shop mathematics.

Some companies require experienced machinists to take additional courses in mathematics and electronics, at company expense, so that they qualify to service and operate numerically controlled (computerized) machine tools.

Potential and advancement

There are about 397,000 machinists, and the field is expected to grow slowly through the year 2000. Population growth will increase the demand for machined goods, but this demand will be increasingly met by imported products. Other factors decreasing the demand for machinists are improvements in metalworking technology and the growing substitution of nonmetal parts for metal parts.

Advancement in this field is to supervisory positions. With additional training, machinists can also become tool-and-die makers or instrument makers. Some experienced machinists open their own machine shops or take technical jobs in machine tooling and programming.

Income

Average weekly earnings for machinists are $435. Most earn between $331 and $538, with the bottom 10 percent earning less than $246 and the top 10 percent earning more than $663.

Additional sources of information

International Association of Machinists and Aerospace Workers
1300 Connecticut Avenue, NW
Washington, DC 20036

International Union of Electronic, Electrical, Salaried, Machine,
    and Furniture Workers
1126 16th Street, NW
Washington, DC 20036

International Union, United Automobile, Aerospace and Agricultural
    Implement Workers of America
Skilled Trades Department
8000 East Jefferson Avenue
Detroit, MI 48214

The National Machine Tool Builders
7901 Westpark Drive
McLean, VA 22102

The National Tooling and Machining Association
9300 Livingston Road
Fort Washington, MD 20744

MANAGEMENT CONSULTANT

The job

Management consultants help managers analyze the management and operating problems of an individual organization. They recommend solutions to problems concerning the objectives, policies, and functions of the organization. They may also help with implementation of any recommended programs.

About half of all management consultants are self-employed. The rest work for general management consulting and accounting firms; and for federal, state, and local governments.

Businesses and industries of all kinds use the services of management consultants as do government agencies, nonprofit organizations, and institutions such as hospitals.

Related jobs are systems analyst, operations research analyst, industrial engineer, and office manager.

Places of employment and working conditions

Management consultants are employed in all areas of the country. Some jobs may involve temporary overseas assignment if multinational corporations are involved.

Management consultants work long hours. A 50-hour week is a short week; most consultants work even more hours. Travel plays a large part in the consultant's work; some estimates say 20 to 35 percent of a consultant's time is taken up in traveling to a client's location or between different locations of a client's organization.

Qualifications, education, and training

An analytical mind, good judgment, objectivity, tact, good communication skills, and the ability to work as part of a team are necessary.

High school should provide a solid college preparatory course with emphasis on mathematics, social sciences, and communication skills.

A college degree in engineering, business administration, accounting, or other related fields should be followed by graduate study in business administration or public administration.

A number of professional societies offer examinations leading to various certifications in this field. Some of them are certified management consultant

(CMC), certified management accountant, registered professional engineer, and certified data processor.

Potential and advancement

There are about 130,000 people engaged in management consulting. This field is expected to grow rapidly through the year 2000 as companies strive to improve their performance. Even if the growth rate is slower than anticipated, there will be plenty of job opportunities for qualified management consultants.

Management consultants can advance to positions as project directors and, with extensive experience, may become associates or partners in their firm. Some advance by going into business for themselves or take a high-level job with a large corporation.

Income

The income of management consultants varies so greatly that the figures are difficult to estimate. Those who are wage and salary workers earn an average annual income of about $34,900.

Additional sources of information

The Institute of Management Consultants, Inc.
230 Park Avenue
Suite 544
New York, NY 10169

MANUFACTURER'S SALES REPRESENTATIVE

The job

Most manufacturing firms sell their products to businesses, other industrial firms, and retail outlets through their own sales representatives. Familiarly known as *sales reps* or *manufacturer's reps,* these sales workers are thoroughly familiar with their employer's product and often provide advice and technical expertise to the customers they service.

When the product sold is highly technical, such as computers or industrial equipment, a manufacturer usually employs engineers or other technically trained people for sales. These *sales engineers* or *technical sales workers* may design systems for the client, supervise installation of equipment, and provide training for the client's employees who will use the new equipment or material.

Most manufacturer's sales representatives work in the wholesale trade. Others are employed in manufacturing and mining.

Related jobs are sales manager, engineer, and wholesaler.

Places of employment and working conditions

Some sales reps work out of local or regional offices, which keeps them fairly close to home. Others cover large territories and do a great deal of traveling. Since they almost always work on commission, successful sales reps spend as much time as possible calling on customers during business hours and do any necessary traveling evenings and weekends.

Qualifications, education, and training

Selling skills, assertiveness, a pleasant personality, physical stamina, and the ability to get along with all kinds of people are necessary for this job.

A college preparatory course should be followed in high school. Part-time or summer job experience in selling is valuable experience.

A college degree is becoming increasingly important for those who wish to work as a manufacturer's sales representative. Manufacturers of nontechnical products often prefer a liberal arts, business administration, or marketing degree. Other employers have special educational requirements. Pharmaceutical retailers (drug sales workers) sometimes need training at a college of pharmacy; chemical manufacturers often require a degree in chemistry; a computer manufacturer might hire only electronic engineers for its sales positions.

Regardless of the field, employers usually provide a training period of up to two years for new employees. Some training programs consist of classroom instruction plus on-the-job training in a branch office under the supervision of a field sales manager. In other programs, trainees are rotated through a number of jobs and departments to learn all phases of production, installation, and service of the employer's product before being assigned to a sales territory.

Potential and advancement

There are about 1,883,000 manufacturer's sales representatives. The employment outlook for this field is good through the year 2000, as the demand for more and more technical products will increase the demand for technically trained sales workers. Employers are expected to be very selective, however, and those with solid educational backgrounds will get the choice jobs.

Experienced and hard-working people in this field can advance to branch manager and district manager positions and to executive-level positions such as sales manager. Many of the top-level corporate positions in industry are filled by people who started out in sales positions.

Income

Manufacturer's sales representatives may be paid in a number of ways—a salary (usually for trainees), salary plus commission, or straight commission. Many companies also provide bonuses based on sales performance.

Earnings for sales reps average about $28,000 a year. The highest starting salaries are paid by manufacturers of electrical and electronics equipment, construction materials and goods, food products, rubber goods, and scientific and precision instruments.

Additional sources of information

Manufacturers' Agents National Association
23016 Mill Creek Road
P.O. Box 3467
Laguna Hills, CA 92654

National Association of Wholesaler-Distributors
1725 K Street, NW
Washington, DC 20006

Sales and Marketing Executives International
Statler Office Tower, #458
Cleveland, OH 44115

MARKET ANALYST

The job

The decision to buy, hold, or sell securities is sometimes made through utilizing the knowledge of the individual buyer or seller, but most individuals consult their stockbroker for advice. The stockbroker, in turn, depends on the expertise of the research department of his or her firm to provide the necessary information. These experts are called market analysts or securities analysts.

In addition to being employed in brokerage houses, market analysts and securities analysts are also employed by investment banking firms, bank trust departments, insurance companies, pension and mutual funds, investment advisory firms, and institutions such as colleges that have endowment funds to manage. All these organizations expect the same thing: expert advice that will help them to invest wisely with the best return on their money.

Market analysts evaluate the market as a whole. They study information on changes in the gross national product, cost of living, personal income, rate of employment, construction starts, fiscal plans of the federal government, growth and inflation rates, balance of payments, market trends, and indexes of common stocks. They also monitor events that might produce a psychological reaction in the market: international crisis, war, political activity, or a tragedy large enough to cause the market to change direction. Market analysts also keep an eye on business and industry developments and actions of the Federal Reserve to loosen or tighten credit.

Securities analysts study and analyze individual companies or industries, relating knowledge of the current and future state of the economy to predict the future performance of the company or industry. Analysts may specialize in a specific area such as companies involved in energy production or the aircraft manufacturing industry. The analyst studies all available material on an individual company including annual reports and details of company management and sometimes travels to the company to take a closer look in person.

An investor who has an investment portfolio containing a number of different securities needs advice not only on the individual securities but also on the makeup of the entire portfolio. A *portfolio analyst* has the broad general knowledge to give advice on the market and its relationship to the objectives of the investor. The accumulation of a balanced portfolio can then be accomplished.

Those analysts who deal in securities actually combine elements of all of these three areas within the scope of their work. But, in organizations that employ large numbers of researchers, the jobs are often separate.

Related jobs are actuary, economist, insurance agent and broker, investment manager, statistician, and securities sales worker (stockbroker).

Places of employment and working conditions

Analysts work in all parts of the country but are concentrated in Boston, Chicago, New York City, and San Francisco. Major brokerage houses have branch offices in about 800 cities.

Analysts find their work fascinating but time consuming. They must read constantly—newspapers, annual reports, trade publications—to keep abreast of developments and changes in the market. Their advancement depends on the reputation they achieve for accurate analysis and predictions. They are sometimes required to make decisions quickly on securities worth thousands, or even millions, of dollars.

Qualifications, education, and training

The ability to interpret and analyze large amounts of material, an inquiring mind, and facility in mathematics are absolutely necessary. Good communication skills are important.

A high school background with plenty of mathematics and preparation for college are essential. Some type of selling experience is usually necessary.

A college degree is required by just about all employers. Economics, political science, and business administration are the preferred degrees. Engineering, law, finance, and marketing, especially when combined with graduate work in business administration, are also accepted. The growing use of computers in this field requires the addition to research staffs of those trained in mathematics and statistics.

The mark of professionalism among analysts is the chartered financial analyst (CFA) degree, comparable to the CPA for an accountant. To earn this degree, an analyst must fulfill the membership requirements of one of the financial analysts societies in the United States and complete three examination programs. Analysts must have five or more years of experience before taking the third examination.

Potential and advancement

Job opportunities in this field will be good through the year 2000 for those with appropriate degrees and some knowledge of computers. However, opportunities fluctuate along with the ups and downs in the economy.

In the securities field, research departments are considered the best springboard to advancement since analysts acquire in-depth knowledge of the economy and the market. Within research, the career path is usually junior analyst; analyst, sometimes in a specialty field; then senior analyst. Advancement to management positions in branch offices is also possible.

Income

Beginning analysts with an MBA earn $22,000 a year; experienced analysts, about $35,000.

Senior analysts who acquire a reputation can earn over $100,000 a year.

Additional sources of information

The Institute of Chartered Financial Analysts
P.O. Box 3668
Charlottesville, VA 22903

Securities Industry Association
120 Broadway
New York, NY 10271

MARKETING MANAGER

The job

In order for a company to stay in business, it must be able to sell its goods or services at a profit. It is the responsibility of the marketing manager to coordinate and oversee the workers and strategies that will enable a company to identify potential customers and sell its goods or services to them successfully.

Marketing managers develop a business's marketing strategy. They work closely with product development managers and market research managers to determine the demand for the business's goods or services and to identify competitors and customers. These strategies are then developed based on researchers' findings regarding the best markets for the goods or services by geographic region, age, income, and life-style.

Marketing managers are also responsible for setting prices that will allow the business to make a profit while at the same time dominating the market for its particular goods or services.

By working with sales and product development managers, marketing managers follow sales trends and come up with ideas for new products.

Marketing managers also work closely with advertising and publicity departments to see that the business's products are promoted adequately to attract customers.

Places of employment and working conditions

Marketing managers can be found working in nearly every industry.

Marketing managers are considered to be among top management and face a great deal of pressure. They often work long hours, including evenings and weekends. They often have to travel to attend meetings and meet with customers.

Qualifications, education, and training

Marketing managers must be creative, aggressive, responsible, and hard working. Usually marketing managers have been promoted from other positions where they have gained experience, decision-making skills, and leadership ability.

Educational backgrounds for marketing managers vary, but most employers require a college degree in either liberal arts or business administration with an emphasis on marketing. Highly technical industries, such as computer and electronics manufacturing, often require a degree in engineering or science.

Some large firms have management training programs. Others offer continuing education opportunities either in-house or at local colleges and universities. Often companies encourage their employees to attend seminars and conferences given by professional organizations by paying their costs.

Potential and advancement

Growing competition between foreign and domestic companies for control of their markets will result in many opportunities for marketing managers. Open positions will also occur as some managers are promoted to top executive positions and others leave the work force.

Some industries will offer better opportunities than others. Faster growth is expected in data processing services, ratio and television broadcasting, and motor vehicles. Growth will be slower in educational services and some manufacturing industries.

Income

The median salary for marketing managers is $36,500 a year. Those earning the lowest salaries earn $19,200 or less, and those earning the highest salaries earn $52,000 or more. Many marketing managers with experience and higher levels of responsibility earn annual salaries between $75,000 and $100,000.

Additional sources of information

American Marketing Association
250 South Wacker Drive
Chicago, IL 60606

Sales and Marketing Executives, International
458 Statler Office Tower
Cleveland, OH 44115

MARKETING RESEARCHER

The job

Marketing researchers plan and design research projects, conduct interviews and other fact-gathering operations, and tabulate and analyze the resulting material.

The information a marketing researcher provides may help a company to decide on brand names, product and packaging design, company locations, and the type of advertising to use.

A *marketing research director* designs a research project after studying a company's sales records, its competitors, and the consumer market that uses the type of product or service the company offers. He or she then calls on members of the marketing research staff to implement the project.

A *statistician* will determine a sample group of consumers to be studied. A *senior analyst* or *project director* might design a questionnaire or a mail or telephone survey for field interviewers to use. *Coders and tabulators* synthesize the results, which are reviewed by a *research analyst* who studies the results and makes recommendations based on the findings.

Advertising researchers specialize in studying the effects of advertising. They pretest commercials, test-market new products, and analyze the appropriateness of the various media (radio, television, newspapers, magazines, or direct mail) for a particular product or advertiser. Beginners in this field start by coding and tabulating data. They move on to interviewing and writing reports and may move up to jobs as research assistants as they gain experience.

Many opportunities for part-time work exist in marketing research. Coding, tabulating, interviewing, and making telephone surveys are jobs for which research organizations often hire people who can work odd hours or during peak workloads. High school and college students and homemakers will find this a good field for summer jobs or for weekend or evening work.

Related jobs are advertising account executive, advertising manager, advertising worker, mathematician, statistician, and psychologist.

Places of employment and working conditions

Most market researchers are employed by manufacturers, advertising agencies, and market research firms. The largest corporations are in Chicago and New York City, but job opportunities exist in almost every large city.

The usual workweek is 40 hours, but those conducting interviews and surveys are likely to have evening and weekend work. Market researchers often work under pressure and may be called upon to work overtime to meet deadlines. Although this is basically an office job, travel is a necessary part of the work in the information-gathering stages. The travel may be local or far afield depending on the scope and design of the research project.

Qualification, education, and training

Assertiveness, analyzing skills, and communication skills are very important.

High school courses should include English, mathematics, and public speaking. Summer or part-time jobs coding or taking surveys are good experience.

A college degree is required for just about all of the full-time jobs in marketing research. A bachelor's degree in liberal arts, business administration, marketing, economics, or mathematics is necessary for most trainee positions. Courses in English, marketing economics, statistics, psychology, sociology, and political science should be included. A knowledge of data processing is of increasing importance as the use of computers for sales forecasting, distribution, and cost analysis is growing.

Advanced degrees are becoming more and more important for jobs beyond the entry level and for promotion. Job applicants with a combination background—for example, a bachelor's degree in statistics and a master's degree in marketing or business administration—have a good chance of being hired at the management level right out of college. Industrial marketing firms prefer those with a bachelor's degree in a related field, such as engineering, plus a master's degree in a marketing-related field.

Potential and advancement

There are about 22,000 marketing researchers and thousands more who work part-time taking surveys and interviewing consumers. Job opportunities will be good in this field, as the growth in population and continued emphasis on advertising will result in more marketing jobs. Those with advanced degrees in marketing will be the most in demand.

Promotion is slower in this field than in most others requiring similar training; the pay scale for beginners, however, is better than that in many fields. Once a marketing research worker reaches the research assistant level, promotion is possible to junior analyst, then to senior analyst or project director. Top jobs, such as marketing research director, are few and require many years of experience plus good management skills.

Many experienced marketing researchers go into business for themselves doing independent marketing surveys or acting as marketing consultants.

Income

College graduates starting in a training program earn about $21,500 a year. Experienced analysts earn an average of $35,000 a year.

Additional sources of information

American Marketing Association
250 South Wacker Drive
Chicago, IL 60606

Marketing Research Association
111 East Wacker Drive
Suite 600
Chicago, IL 60601

MATHEMATICIAN

The job

The work of mathematicians falls into two sometimes overlapping categories—applied and theoretical mathematics.

Theoretical, or pure, mathematicians develop new principles and seek new relationships between existing principles of mathematics. This basic knowledge is the foundation for much of the work in the second category, applied mathematics. In this area, mathematical theories are used to develop theories and techniques for solving practical problems in business, government, and the natural and social sciences. Mathematicians may work in statistics, actuarial jobs, computer programming, economics, or systems analysis.

Many mathematicians, usually theoretical mathematicians, work in colleges where they teach or do research. Mathematicians are found in the private sector in the aerospace, communications, machinery, and electrical equipment industries. The Department of Defense and National Aeronautics and Space Administration employ most of those who work for the federal government.

Related jobs are economist, marketing researcher, statistician, actuary.

Places of employment and working conditions

Mathematicians can be found working in government agencies, private firms, and as faculty members at colleges and universities. Some mathematicians work alone, and some work as members of research teams.

While those working for government agencies and private firms usually have structured work schedules, they may face deadlines, overtime work, and travel to seminars or conferences. College faculty have more flexible schedules, with their time devoted to teaching, research, consulting, and administrative responsibilities.

Qualifications, education, and training

Mathematicians need good reasoning ability and persistence in solving problems. In applied mathematics especially, they should be able to communicate effectively with nonmathematicians in the discussion and solution of practical problems.

A prospective mathematician should take as many mathematics courses as possible while still in high school and should obtain a bachelor's degree that includes courses in analytical geometry, calculus, differential equations, probability and statistics, mathematics analysis, and modern algebra.

Most positions in research or in university teaching require an advanced degree, frequently a Ph.D. Private industry and the government also prefer those with advanced degrees.

For work in applied mathematics, a background in a specialty field such as engineering, economics, or statistics is also necessary. This can be accomplished by including a minor in one of these fields while in college. In modern industry, knowledge of computer programming also is essential since most complex problems are now solved with the aid of computers.

Nearly 500 colleges and universities offer a master's degree program in mathematics and about 220 also offer a Ph.D. program. Candidates for graduate degrees in mathematics concentrate on a specific field such as algebra, geometry, or mathematical analyses and conduct research in addition to taking advanced courses.

Potential and advancement

There are nearly 50,000 mathematicians in the United States, and over 30,000 of those hold mathematics faculty positions in colleges and universities.

Employment of mathematicians is expected to grow through the year 2000, with the best opportunities for those with a Ph.D. Holders of a doctorate in applied mathematics will be in greater demand in industry than those who specialize in theoretical mathematics. However, theoretical mathematicians with a Ph.D. should find many opportunities for teaching and research jobs in colleges and universities.

Mathematicians with a master's degree will face competition for research and teaching jobs, but there will be many opportunities in applied mathematics fields. Holders of a bachelor's degree with some experience in computer science will have good opportunities in computerized data processing activities. Those who fulfill the necessary requirements may become high school mathematics teachers.

Income

Average annual salaries for mathematicians start at $27,500 for those with a bachelor's degree; $29,600 for holders of a master's degree; and $40,700 for Ph.D.s.

Experienced mathematicians earn average salaries ranging from $35,300 to $64,900 a year.

College and university teachers are paid at the same rate as other faculty members; salaries tend to be lower than in private industry or government.

Additional sources of information

American Mathematical Society
P.O. Box 6248
Providence, RI 02940

Mathematical Association of America
1529 18th Street, NW
Washington, DC 20036

Society for Industrial and Applied Mathematics
1400 Architects Building
117 South 17th Street
Philadelphia, PA 19103

MECHANICAL ENGINEER

The job

The production, transmission, and use of power is the concern of mechanical engineers. They design and develop power-producing machines such as internal combustion engines and rocket engines and power-using machines such as refrigeration systems, printing presses, and steel rolling mills.

The specific work of mechanical engineers varies greatly from industry to industry because of the wide application possibilities of their skills and training; many specialties within the field have developed as a result. These include motor vehicles, energy conversion systems, heating, and machines for specialized industries, to name a few. Many mechanical engineers are involved in research and testing while others work mainly in production and maintenance. Some utilize their training as a background for technical sales.

Over three-fifths of all mechanical engineers are employed in manufacturing, mainly in the electrical equipment, transportation equipment, primary and fabricated metals, and machinery industries. Others work for engineering consulting firms, government agencies, and educational institutions.

Places of employment and working conditions

Mechanical engineers work in all parts of the country with the heaviest concentrations in industrialized areas.

Qualifications, education, and training

The ability to think analytically, a capacity for detail, and the ability to work as part of a team are all necessary. Good communication skills are important.

Mathematics and the sciences must be emphasized in high school.

A bachelor's degree in engineering is the minimum requirement in this field. In a typical curriculum, the first two years are spent in the study of basic sciences such as physics and chemistry and mathematics, introductory engineering, and some liberal arts courses. The remaining years are usually devoted to specialized engineering courses. Engineering programs can last from four to six years. Those that require five or six years to complete may award a master's degree or may provide a cooperative plan of study plus practical work experience in a nearby industry.

Because of rapid changes in technology, many engineers continue their education throughout their careers. A graduate degree is necessary for most teaching and research positions and for many management jobs. Some specialties such as nuclear engineering are taught only at the graduate level. Some persons obtain graduate degrees in business administration.

Engineering graduates usually work under the supervision of an experienced engineer or in a company training program until they become acquainted with the requirements of a particular company or industry.

All states require licensing of engineers whose work may affect life, health, or property or who offer their services to the public. Those who are licensed, about one-third of all engineers, are called registered engineers. Requirements include graduation from an accredited engineering school, four years of experience, and a written examination.

Potential and advancement

There are about 225,000 mechanical engineers. An increase in the demand for mechanical engineers—as a result of growth in the industrial machinery and machine tools field and the push to develop alternative energy sources—means ample job opportunities in this field through the year 2000.

Income

Starting annual salaries in private industry average $29,200 for mechanical engineers with a bachelor's degree; $34,600 for those with a master's degree; and $46,600 for those with a Ph.D.

Experienced engineers average $45,777 a year in private industry.

Additional sources of information

Accreditation Board for Engineering and Technology
345 East 47th Street
New York, NY 10017

American Society for Engineering Education
11 Dupont Circle
Suite 200
Washington, DC 20036

The American Society of Mechanical Engineers
34 East 47th Street
New York, NY 10017

Junior Engineering Technical Society (JETS)
1420 King Street
Suite 405
Alexandria, VA 22314

National Society of Professional Engineers
1420 King Street
Alexandria, VA 22314

Society of Women Engineers
345 East 47th Street
Room 305
New York, NY 10017

MEDICAL ASSISTANT

The job

Medical assistants perform administrative tasks and work with patients, helping doctors keep their practices running efficiently.

Medical assistants' duties vary from office to office, depending on the size of the medical practice. In smaller practices, they have a wider range of responsibilities, often performing both administrative and clinical tasks. In larger practices, they may specialize in a particular area.

Laws regarding the procedures medical assistants are permitted to perform vary from state to state, but some of the more common clinical tasks they are allowed to do include taking and recording medical histories and vital signs; explaining treatments to patients; preparing patients for examination; and assisting in examinations.

After an examination, medical assistants may collect laboratory specimens and perform basic laboratory tests; dispose of contaminated supplies; and sterilize medical instruments.

Some of the administrative duties medical assistants often have include answering telephones, greeting patients, recording and filing medical records, filling out insurance forms, scheduling appointments, arranging for hospital admission and laboratory tests, and taking care of billing and bookkeeping.

Some medical assistants specialize in a certain branch of medicine such as podiatry or ophthalmology.

Places of employment and working conditions

Most medical assistants work in doctors' offices; some work in the offices of optometrists, podiatrists, and chiropractors. Others work in hospitals.

Medical assistants usually have a 40-hour workweek, which may include some weekend and evening hours.

Qualifications, education, and training

Medical assistants spend a great deal of time working with people, so they must be neat, pleasant, and courteous. They must be able to listen and follow doctors' instructions closely and also listen to patients' needs.

There are no formal education requirements for medical assistants, and many receive their training on the job. However, formal programs in medical assisting are offered at secondary and postsecondary levels in technical high schools, vocational schools, community and junior colleges, and universities. Most doctors prefer to hire medical assistants with formal training.

Two agencies accredit medical assisting programs: the American Medical Association's Committee on Allied Health Education and Accreditation (CAHEA) and the Accrediting Bureau of Health Education Schools (ABHES). These programs usually include course work in biological sciences and medical terminology and typing, transcription, recordkeeping, accounting, and insurance processing.

There are no general licensing requirements for medical assistants, but some states require passing a test or completing a course for medical assistants who perform certain procedures such as taking x-rays, drawing blood, or giving injections.

Several associations certify or register medical assistants who meet their requirements. Employers often prefer to hire those who are certified and have experience.

Potential and advancement

There are about 149,000 medical assistants. Job opportunities should be very good through the year 2000 due to the increasing demands for medical care.

Opportunities will be excellent for those with formal training, experience, or both. Those who are certified and have computer and word processing skills will have even greater advantages when seeking employment.

Medical assistants may advance by becoming office managers. Others become consultants for medical office management or for the medical insurance industry. Some work for hospitals as ward clerks, medical record clerks, phlebotomists, and EKG technicians. Others sometimes get further education and become nurses or work in some field of medical technology.

Income

Earnings for medical assistants vary widely depending on the worker's credentials and level of experience, the size and location of the employer, and the number of hours worked. A survey by CAHEA shows that starting salaries for graduates of medical assisting programs it accredits average about $13,000.

273

Additional sources of information

The American Association of Medical Assistants
20 North Wacker Drive
Suite 1575
Chicago, IL 60606

Registered Medical Assistants of American Medical Technologists
710 Higgins Road
Park Ridge, IL 60068

MEDICAL LABORATORY TECHNOLOGIST

The job

Medical laboratory work often appeals to people who would like to work in the medical field but who are not necessarily interested in direct care of patients. Those who work in medical laboratories are involved in the analysis of blood, tissue samples, and body fluids. They use precision instruments, equipment, chemicals, and other materials to detect and diagnose diseases. In some instances, such as blood tests, they also gather the specimens to be analyzed.

The work of medical laboratory technologists is done under the direction of a pathologist (a physician who specializes in the causes and nature of disease) or other physician or scientist who specializes in clinical chemistry, microbiology, or other biological sciences.

Medical technologists, who have four years of training, usually perform a wide variety of tests in small laboratories; those in large laboratories usually specialize in a single area such as parasitology, blood banking, or hematology (study of blood cells). Some do research, develop laboratory techniques, or perform supervisory and administrative duties.

Medical laboratory technicians, who have two years of training, have much the same testing duties but do not have the in-depth knowledge of the technologists. Technicians may also specialize in a particular field but are not usually involved in administrative work.

Medical laboratory assistants have about one year of formal training. They assist the technologist and technicians in some routine tests and are generally responsible for the care and sterilization of laboratory equipment, including glassware and instruments, and do some recordkeeping.

Most technologists, technicians, and laboratory assistants work in hospital laboratories. Others work in physicians' offices, independent laboratories, blood banks, public health agencies and clinics, pharmaceutical firms, and research institutions. The federal government employs them in the U.S. Public Health Service, the armed forces, and Department of Veterans Affairs.

Places of employment and working conditions

Work in this field is available in all areas of the country, with the largest concentrations in the larger cities.

Medical laboratory personnel work a 40-hour week with night and weekend shifts if they are employed in a hospital. Laboratories are usually clean and well lighted and contain a variety of testing equipment and materials. Although unpleasant odors are sometimes present and the work involves the processing of specimens of many kinds of diseased tissue, few hazards exist because of careful attention to safety and sterilization procedures.

Qualifications, education, and training

A strong interest in science and the medical field is essential. Manual dexterity, good eyesight, and normal color vision are necessary. One must also show attention to detail, accuracy, the ability to work under pressure, and the desire to take responsibility for one's own work.

High school students interested in this field should take courses in science and mathematics and should select a training program carefully.

Medical technologists must have a college degree and complete a specialized program in medical technology. This specialized training is offered by hospitals and schools in programs accredited by either the Committee on Allied Health Education and Accreditation (CAHEA) in cooperation with the National Accrediting Agency for Clinical Laboratory Sciences (NAACLS) or the Accrediting Bureau of Health Education Schools (ABHES). The programs are usually affiliated with a college or university. A few training programs require a bachelor's degree for entry; others require only three years of college and award a bachelor's degree at the completion of the training program. Those who wish to specialize must complete an additional 12 months of study with extensive lab work.

Advanced degrees in this field are offered by many universities and are a plus for anyone interested in teaching, research, or administration.

Technicians may receive training in two-year educational programs in junior colleges, in two-year courses at four-year colleges and universities, in vocational and technical schools, or in the armed forces.

Medical laboratory assistants usually receive on-the-job training. Some hospitals—and junior colleges and vocational schools in conjunction with a hospital—also conduct one-year training programs, some of which are accredited by the ABHES. A high school diploma or equivalency diploma is necessary.

Medical technologists may be certified by the Board of Registry of the American Society of Clinical Pathologists, the American Medical Technologists, the National Certification Agency for Medical Laboratory Personnel, or the Credentialing Commission of the International Society of Clinical Laboratory Technology. These same organizations also certify technicians.

Some states require technologists and technicians to be licensed. This usually takes the form of a written examination. Other states often require registration.

Potential and advancement

There are about 242,000 persons employed as medical laboratory workers. Medical laboratory technology is a good job opportunity field since, like the entire medical field, it is expected to grow steadily due to population growth and the increase in prepaid medical insurance programs. Job opportunities will probably be slightly better for technicians and assistants, because the increasing use of automated lab equipment will allow them to perform tests that previously required technologists. Technologists will be needed for supervisory and administrative positions, however, and will continue to be in demand in laboratories where their level of training is required by state regulations or employer preference.

Advancement depends on education and experience. Assistants can advance to the position of technician or technologist by completing the required education; technicians can advance to supervisory positions or complete the required education for technologists. Advancement to administrative positions is usually limited to technologists.

Income

Salaries in this field vary depending on employer and geographic location; the highest salaries are paid in the larger cities.

Newly graduated medical technologists start at about $20,000 a year; technicians at about $16,800. Experienced medical technologists earn an average of about $29,000 a year.

Additional sources of information

Accrediting Bureau of Health Education Schools
Oak Manor Office
29089 U.S. 20 West
Elkhart, IN 46514

American Medical Technologists
710 Higgins Road
Park Ridge, IL 60068

American Society of Clinical Pathologists
Board of Registry
P.O. Box 12270
Chicago, IL 60612

American Society for Medical Technology
2021 L Street, NW
Washington, DC 20036

International Society for Clinical Laboratory Technology
818 Olive Street
St. Louis, MO 63101

MEDICAL RECORD TECHNICIAN

The job

Medical record technicians are responsible for keeping an accurate permanent file on patients treated by doctors and hospitals.

When patients are undergoing treatment, doctors and hospitals keep records of their medical history, results of physical exams, x-ray and lab test reports, diagnosis and treatments, and doctors' and nurses' notes. Also included is information about the patients' symptoms, the tests undergone, and the response to treatment.

Medical record technicians assemble, organize, and check these records for completeness and accuracy. Often doctors and nurses record their information and observations on computer, and medical record technicians must retrieve them from the hospital's central computer.

After medical record technicians have gathered all of the information, they consult classification manuals and assign codes to the diagnoses and procedures included in the record. They then assign the patient to a diagnosis-related group (DRG), which determines the amount the hospital will be reimbursed by Medicare or other insurance programs that use the DRG system.

The medical records that technicians keep serve several important purposes. They provide important clinical information that helps in patient treatment, research, and training of medical personnel. They also are important for documentation in the case of legal actions and for insurance claims and Medicare reimbursement.

Medical record technicians sometimes analyze data and provide statistics that help hospital administrators and planners keep the hospital running efficiently.

Medical record technicians also sometimes collect and interpret medical records for law firms, insurance companies, government agencies, researchers, and patients.

Qualifications, education, and training

Medical record technicians who have earned the credential *accredited record technician* are generally preferred by employers. To become accredited, medical record technicians must pass a written examination given by the American Medical Record Association (AMRA). The requirement for taking the test is the completion of a two-year associate's degree program accredited by the Committee on Allied Health Education and Accreditation in collaboration with AMRA or the independent study program in medical record technology along with 30 semester hours in prescribed areas.

Medical record technology programs include course work in the biological sciences, medical terminology, medical record science, business management, legal aspects, and introduction to computer data processing.

Potential and advancement

There are about 47,000 medical record technicians, and opportunities should be excellent for those who have completed a formal training program through the year 2000, primarily because of the important role they play in managing health care costs.

There are three major routes for advancement for medical record technicians—teaching, managing, or specializing. Experience technicians who have a master's degree in a related field sometimes go into teaching. They can also advance into the management of a medical record department. Finally, technicians can advance into a specialty such as Medicare coding and tumor registry.

Income

Medical record technicians earn an annual median salary of $17,200, according to the *Hospital and Health Care Report.*

Additional sources of information

American Medical Record Association
875 North Michigan Avenue
John Hancock Center
Suite 1850
Chicago, IL 60611

MEDICAL SECRETARY

The job

Secretaries are the center of communication in an office. The duties they perform keep offices running efficiently. Medical secretaries are specialized secretaries who are employed by physicians or medical scientists.

Medical secretaries transcribe dictation, type letters, and help doctors or medical scientists prepare reports, speeches, and articles.

They also have responsibilities similar to other secretaries. They take shorthand, deal with visitors, keep track of appointments, make travel arrangements, and see that any of the employer's paperwork is taken care of.

Places of employment and working conditions

Medical secretaries are employed throughout the country, in physicians' offices, hospitals, and other types of health agencies.

Working conditions vary, but full-time medical secretaries usually work a 37- to 40-hour week.

Qualifications, education, and training

Medical secretaries must be accurate and neat. They must display discretion and initiative and have a good command of spelling, grammar, punctuation, and vocabulary. They need to know medical terms and be familiar with hospital or laboratory procedures.

High school business courses are valuable and so are college preparatory courses because secretaries should have a good general background. They should take as many English courses as possible.

Secretarial training as part of a college education or at a private business school is preferred by many employers. Training for specialty areas such as medicine can take a year or two.

Well-trained and highly experienced secretaries may qualify for the designation *certified professional secretary* (CPS) by passing a series of examinations given by the National Secretaries Association. This is a mark of achievement in the secretarial field and is recognized as such by many employers.

Potential and advancement

The demand for well-qualified medical secretaries will continue to grow as the demand for medical services increases. Job opportunities should be very good through the year 2000.

Opportunities for advancement depend on the acquisition of new or improved skills and on increasing knowledge of the medical field. Some medical secretaries may become administrative assistants or office managers.

Income

Salaries for medical secretaries vary greatly depending on the level of their skill, experience, and responsibility; the area of the country in which they work; and the type of employer they have.

The average annual salary for all types of secretaries is $21,710, with a range from $17,810 to $29,354. Secretaries working in the West and Midwest earn higher salaries in general than those working in the Northeast and South.

Additional source of information

Professional Secretaries International
301 East Armour Boulevard
Kansas City, MO 64111

METALLURGICAL ENGINEER

The job

Metallurgical engineers develop methods to process and convert metals into usable forms. Other scientists who work in this field are called *metallurgists* or *materials scientists,* but the distinction between scientist and engineer in this field is so small as to be almost nonexistent.

There are three main branches of metallurgy—extractive or chemical, physical, and mechanical. *Extractive metallurgists* are engaged in the processes for extracting metals from ore, refining, and alloying. *Physical metallurgists* work with the nature, structure, and physical properties of metals and alloys to develop methods for converting them into final products. *Mechanical metallurgists* develop methods to work and shape metals. These include casting, forging, rolling, and drawing.

Most metallurgical engineers are employed by the metalworking industries—iron, steel, and nonferrous metals—where they are responsible for specifying, controlling, and testing the quality of the metals during manufacture. Others work in industries that manufacture machinery, electrical equipment, aircraft and aircraft parts, and in mining. Some work in federal agencies such as the Bureau of Mines.

The development of new, lightweight metals for use in communications equipment, computers, and spacecraft is a growing field for metallurgical engineers as are the processing and recycling of industrial waste and the processing of low-grade ores. Problems associated with the use of nuclear energy will also require the expertise of metallurgists and metallurgical engineers.

Places of employment and working conditions

The work settings of metallurgical engineers vary from the laboratory to smelting and mining locations to factory production lines. Some of these operations are located in remote areas.

Qualifications, education, and training

The ability to think analytically, a capacity for detail, and the ability to work as part of a team are all necessary. Good communication skills are important.

Mathematics and the sciences must be emphasized in high school.

A bachelor's degree in engineering is the minimum requirement in this field. In a typical curriculum, the first two years are spent in the study of basic sciences such as physics and chemistry and mathematics, introductory engineering, and some liberal arts courses. The remaining years are usually devoted to specialized engineering courses. Engineering programs can last from four to six years. Those requiring five or six years to complete may award a master's degree or may provide a cooperative plan of study plus practical work experience in a nearby industry.

Because of rapid changes in technology, many engineers continue their education throughout their careers. A graduate degree is necessary for most teaching and research positions and for many management jobs. Some specialties such as nuclear engineering are taught only at the graduate level. Some persons obtain graduate degrees in business administration.

Engineering graduates usually work under the supervision of an experienced engineer or in a company training program until they become acquainted with the requirements of a particular company or industry.

All states require licensing of engineers whose work may affect life, health, or property or who offer their services to the public. Those who are licensed, about one-third of all engineers, are called registered engineers. Requirements include graduation from an accredited engineering school, four years of experience, and a written examination.

Potential and advancement

Substantial growth is expected in this field as the demand for new metals and alloys and new applications for current ones increases. There should be good employment prospects through the year 2000.

Income

Starting annual salaries in private industry average $29,200 for metallurgical engineers with a bachelor's degree; $34,600 for those with a master's degree; and $46,600 for those with a Ph.D.

Experienced engineers average $45,777 a year in private industry.

Additional sources of information

Accreditation Board for Engineering and Technology
345 East 47th Street
New York, NY 10017

American Society for Engineering Education
11 Dupont Circle
Suite 200
Washington, DC 20036

ASM International
Metals Park, OH 44073

Junior Engineering Technical Society (JETS)
1420 King Street
Suite 405
Alexandria, VA 22314

The Minerals, Metals, and Materials Society
420 Commonwealth Drive
Warrendale, PA 15086

National Society of Professional Engineers
1420 King Street
Alexandria, VA 22314

Society of Women Engineers
345 East 47th Street
Room 305
New York, NY 10017

METEOROLOGIST

The job

The study of the atmosphere—its physical characteristics, motions, and processes—is the work of meteorologists. Although the best-known application of this study is in weather forecasting, meteorologists are also engaged in research and problem solving in the fields of air pollution, transportation, agriculture, and industrial operations.

Physical meteorologists study the chemical and electrical properties of the atmosphere as they affect the formation of clouds, rain, and snow. *Climatologists* analyze past data on wind, rainfall, and temperature to determine weather patterns for a given area; this work is important in designing buildings and in planning effective land use. *Operational* or *synoptic meteorologists* study current weather information, such as temperature, humidity, air pressure, and wind velocity, in order to make short- and long-range forecasts.

The largest single employer of civilian meteorologists is the National Oceanic and Atmospheric Administration (NOAA), which employs about 1,800 meteorologists at stations in all parts of the United States.

Some meteorologists work for private industry, including airlines, private weather consulting firms, manufacturers of meteorological instruments, radio and television stations, and the aerospace industry.

Colleges and universities employ about 1,000 meteorologists in teaching and research.

Related jobs are geologist, geophysicist, oceanographer.

Places of employment and working conditions

Meteorologists work in all areas of the United States, but the largest concentrations are in California, Maryland, and the Washington, D.C., area.

Since they continue around the clock, seven days a week, jobs in weather stations entail night and weekend shifts. Some stations are at remote locations and may require the meteorologist to work alone.

Qualifications, education, and training

Curiosity, analytical thinking, and attention to detail are necessary qualities for a meteorologist.

High school should include as many science and mathematics courses as possible.

A bachelor's degree with a major in meteorology or a related field is acceptable for some jobs, but many employers prefer to hire workers with an advanced degree. Teaching positions, research, and many jobs in private industry require advanced degrees.

Potential and advancement

There are about 6,200 civilian meteorologists and several thousand members of the armed forces who do forecasting and meteorological work. Job opportunities for meteorologists should be more plentiful in the next five to ten years than they have been in the past. The National Weather Service plans to increase its employment of meteorologists, and there will be many jobs created in private industry as private weather forecasting and meteorological services come into greater demand. Employment of meteorologists in branches of the federal government other than the National Weather Service is not expected to increase.

Meteorologists with advanced degrees and experience can advance to supervisory and administrative positions.

Income

The federal government pays average starting salaries of $15,738 or $19,493 a year, depending on college grades, to meteorologists with a bachelor's degree; $19,493 or $23,846 to those with a master's; and $28,852 or $34,580 to those with a Ph.D.

The average annual salary for experienced meteorologists employed by the federal government is $40,800.

Additional sources of information

American Geophysical Union
2000 Florida Avenue, NW
Washington, DC 20009

American Meteorological Society
45 Beacon Street
Boston, MA 02108

MINING ENGINEER

The job

Mining engineers frequently specialize in a specific mineral such as coal or copper. They find, extract, and prepare minerals for manufacturing use.

Some mining engineers work with geologists and metallurgical engineers (see appropriate job descriptions) to locate and appraise new ore deposits. Others design and supervise construction of open-pit and underground mines including mine shafts and tunnels or design methods for transporting minerals to processing plants.

Mining engineers engaged in the day-to-day operations of a mine are responsible for mine safety, ventilation, water supply, power and communication, and equipment maintenance. Direction of mineral processing operations, which requires separating the usable ore from dirt, rocks, and other materials, is also usually the responsibility of a mining engineer.

Some mining engineers specialize in the design and development of new mining equipment. An increasing number work on the reclamation of mined land and on air and water pollution problems related to mining.

Most mining engineers work in the mining industry. Others work for mining equipment manufacturers or as independent consultants. Federal and state agencies employ mining engineers on regulatory bodies and as inspectors.

Places of employment and working conditions

Most mining engineers work at the location of the mine, usually near small communities in rural areas. Many find employment opportunities overseas.

The work can be hazardous since at least some time is often spent underground.

Qualifications, education, and training

The ability to think analytically, a capacity for detail, and the ability to work as part of a team are all necessary. Good communication skills are important.

Mathematics and the sciences must be emphasized in high school.

A bachelor's degree in engineering is the minimum requirement in this field. In a typical curriculum, the first two years are spent in the study of basic sciences such as physics and chemistry and mathematics, introductory engineering, and some liberal arts courses. The remaining years are usually devoted to specialized engineering courses. Engineering programs can last from four to six years. Those that require five or six years to complete may award a master's degree or may provide a cooperative plan of study plus practical work experience with a nearby industry.

Because of rapid changes in technology, many engineers continue their education throughout their careers. A graduate degree is necessary for most teaching and research positions and for many management jobs. Some persons obtain graduate degrees in business administration.

Engineering graduates usually work under the supervision of an experienced engineer or in a company training program until they become acquainted with the requirements of a particular company or industry.

All states require licensing of engineers whose work may affect life, health, or property or who offer their services to the public. Those who are licensed, about one-third of all engineers, are called registered engineers. Requirements include graduation from an accredited engineering school, four years of experience, and a written examination.

Potential and advancement

There are about 5,300 mining engineers. Employment opportunities will not be good through the year 2000 because of the low demand for coal, metals, and other minerals. However, if these commodities should come into demand because of the lack of availability and high price of other energy sources, employment opportunities will increase. Other factors that may bring about job growth include technological advancements, enforcement of mine health and safety regulations, more efficient methods of mining and processing ores, and a demand for less widely used ores.

Income

Starting annual salaries in private industry average $29,448 for those with a bachelor's degree; $34,600 for those with a master's degree; and $46,600 for those with a Ph.D.

Experienced engineers earn an average of $42,300 a year.

Additional sources of information

Accreditation Board for Engineering and Technology
345 East 47th Street
New York, NY 10017

American Society for Engineering Education
11 Dupont Circle
Suite 200
Washington, DC 20036

Junior Engineering Technical Society (JETS)
1420 King Street
Suite 405
Alexandria, VA 22314

National Society of Professional Engineers
1420 King Street
Alexandria, VA 22314

The Society of Mining Engineers, Inc.
P.O. Box 625002
Littleton, CO 80127-5002

MINISTER (PROTESTANT)

The job

Protestant ministers lead their congregations in worship services and administer the rites of baptism and holy communion. They perform marriages, conduct funerals, visit the sick, and counsel members of the congregation who seek guidance. Ministers are also usually involved in community activities.

The exact services provided by ministers differ among the different denominations. The greatest number of ministers are affiliated with the five largest denominations—Baptist, United Methodist, Lutheran, Presbyterian, and Episcopal. Some serve small congregations where they provide all services; ministers of large congregations usually have one or more assistants who share duties.

Many ministers serve as chaplains in the armed forces, hospitals, prisons, or colleges and universities. Others teach in seminaries.

Some denominations are now allowing women to enter the ministry in small numbers. Some denominations and some congregations continue to oppose this, so women interested in becoming ministers should seek the counsel of clergy in the denomination of their choice.

Places of employment and working conditions

Ministers work in communities of all sizes. Larger communities may support more than one congregation of a particular denomination. Working hours can be long and are often irregular. Some ministers handle more than one congregation, especially in rural areas, and may spend considerable time in travel.

Qualifications, education, and training

The most important quality for anyone considering the ministry as a calling is a deep religious faith. A minister must also be a model of moral and ethical conduct.

Educational requirements vary, depending on denomination. Bible colleges, Bible institutes, and liberal arts colleges all provide training acceptable to some denominations, but training in a theological seminary is necessary for others.

Potential and advancement

About 429,000 ministers serve Protestants in the United States. Limited growth is expected in this field through the year 2000 because of the increasing costs of operating churches. Employment opportunities will vary among denominations and geographic regions. Most openings will occur to replace ministers who retire or leave the ministry for some reason.

Income

Earnings vary widely, with the average income for Protestant ministers in the $23,000 range. Additional fringe benefits such as housing, a car, and school tuition for dependents bring the average annual salary to about $38,000.

Additional sources of information

Anyone interested in becoming a minister should seek the counsel of a minister within the denomination of his or her choice. Theological schools can provide information on admission requirements.

MODEL

The job

Models demonstrate and sell a wide variety of goods and services. Models display clothes for local fashion shows as well as for high-fashion magazines; those models working in television commercials sell everything from toothpaste to home appliances; and photographers and artists often employ models in the course of their work. Models usually specialize in live or photographic work.

Photographic models are usually hired for an individual assignment. Most model clothes or cosmetics, but they also promote a wide variety of other products as well. In addition to serving for still photography, models may also appear in television commercials, especially if they have some acting ability or training.

Live modeling contains a variety of specialty areas. *Fashion models* usually work before an audience, modeling the creations of a well-known designer at fashion shows. *Showroom* or *fitting models* work in the manufacturer's or distributor's display room where they model the employer's products for prospective retail buyers and work with designers during the fitting stages of new designs.

Informal models work in local department stores and custom shops, at manufacturers' trade shows and exhibits to demonstrate products, and for artists and art schools.

Most models work through a modeling agency to ensure a continuous flow of job assignments.

Places of employment and working conditions

Some modeling jobs are available in almost every community, but Chicago, Detroit, Los Angeles, and especially New York City provide the largest number of modeling jobs. New York City's garment district has hundreds of clothing manufacturers, designers, and wholesalers who employ permanent models to display their products. These models must usually meet certain standard physical requirements because sample clothes must fit the model without alteration. For women this means a height of 5 feet 7 inches to 5 feet 9 1/2 inches and a weight of 110 to 122 pounds. Male models must be 6 feet tall and wear a size-40 suit. Specialty lines, such as teenage clothes or styles for mature women, may have other requirements.

Photographic models must be thinner than other models because the camera adds at least ten pounds to a model's appearance.

Qualifications, education, and training

Distinctive and attractive physical appearance, good health, physical stamina, the ability to withstand the pace and pressure of the field, and competitiveness are all necessary for a successful model.

There are no educational requirements for a model, but any training in acting, dancing, art, or fashion design is valuable for a model.

There are modeling schools in many communities that provide instruction in such things as proper posture, hairstyling and makeup, and how to pose in front of a camera, but these schools do not provide job assignments. Some modeling agencies also provide some training.

Potential and advancement

About 60,000 people work as models full-time in the United States and there are always many more applicants than jobs in this glamorous field. Because most assignments go to experienced models, aspiring models should get as much local experience as possible before trying for a job in the larger cities or agencies.

Modeling can be a stepping-stone to many other careers in the fashion field. Fashion magazines, cosmetic firms, and department stores often hire former models for a variety of positions. Some models become actors or actresses.

Income

A few top models earn as much as $500,000 a year, but most earn considerably less.

Models employed by manufacturers or wholesalers earn between $45 and $75 an hour.

Models who register with an agency pay the agency a commission for each new assignment they receive. Steadily employed models usually earn from $25,000 to $40,000 a year.

Models in television commercials are paid $2,000 to $3,000 for an eight-hour photo session. They may also receive additional income (residuals) if the commercial is used more than once.

Additional sources of information

The Fashion Group
Nine Rockefeller Plaza
17th Floor
New York, NY 10020

Federation of Apparel Manufacturers
450 Seventh Avenue
New York, NY 10001

MUSEUM CURATOR

The job

A museum curator is in charge of a museum or a museum department. The curator is responsible for planning exhibits; acquisition of material within budgetary limitations; development, care, and classification of collections; and laboratory research and field studies including museum-sponsored expeditions.

There are about 5,000 museums of various sizes in the United States. They are maintained by the federal government, state and local governments, nonprofit corporations, colleges and universities, business groups and industries, and private individuals and societies.

Some curators are employed by historical museums. These museums may specialize in the artifacts and memorabilia of a particular period in history; a specific area, industry, or group of people; a single person, such as a president; a sport; or an item, such as toys. They vary in size from small, local museums to large, world-renowned institutions.

The largest in individual size are the natural history museums. Their collections are the most widely diversified, and research and field expeditions form a major part of their programs. They employ *anthropologists* (experts in the study of humanity and its domain through the ages), *botanists* (plant-life specialists), *geologists* (scientists who study structure and materials of the earth), and *zoologists* (specialists in all phases of animal life). Natural history museums also do a great deal of publishing as a result of their research and field studies.

Many museum curators work for art museums, which collect and exhibit art objects of all kinds including paintings, prints, drawings, photographs, sculpture, ceramics, jewelry, textiles, woodwork, and carvings. Some large art museums have schools of art and design.

Curators employed by outdoor museums often oversee complete towns or villages such as Williamsburg, Virginia, or zoological parks or arboretums. A uniquely American idea, the trailside museum, incorporates bird, botanical, or geological walks with animal life. The Petrified Forest in Arizona is such a museum. A related job is historian.

Places of employment and working conditions

Curator positions exist throughout the United States, but most are in the major cities that have the most museums—Boston, Chicago, Los Angeles, New York City, and Washington, D.C.

Working conditions vary greatly depending on size and type of museum and specialty of the curator. Some work closely with the public, others work alone and spend most of their time processing records, and still others may install or restore exhibits and have to climb, stretch, and lift heavy objects.

Qualifications, education, and training

Patience, a logical mind, creative imagination, physical stamina, administrative ability, the ability to work with people, and communication skills are necessary for a museum curator. A curator is also usually a specialist in a particular field, such as art, or in a specific discipline, such as anthropology.

In high school, a college preparatory course should be followed. If the student is already interested in a specific field of museum work, the appropriate courses such as art, history, or science should be emphasized. If possible, the study of one or more languages should begin in high school and continue in college. French, German, Spanish, Italian, Latin, or Greek are recommended.

College courses should be related to the student's field of interest. A bachelor's degree in history, art history, fine arts, anthropology, or one of the natural sciences is the usual first step. Some colleges and universities offer a bachelor's or master's degree in museology.

A master's degree, and in some cases a Ph.D., is necessary for most curator positions.

Many museums, colleges, and universities offer assistantships, fellowships, internships, apprenticeships, summer programs, and certification programs. These programs are usually part of an undergraduate or graduate program, but some are open to other experienced museum employees. Some, especially summer programs, are also open to high school students.

Potential and advancement

There are about 16,000 people engaged as curators throughout the United States. This is a very competitive job field, and thousands of new graduates apply each year for the few available openings. Those with a graduate degree and some part-time or summer experience have the best chance of securing a job.

It takes years of training and experience to achieve the level of curator. One of the drawbacks of this field is the slowness with which advancement occurs, especially in older, established museums.

Income

Salaries in the federal government start at $15,738 a year for those with a bachelor's degree and no experience; $19,493 for those with a bachelor's degree and some experience; $23,846 for those with a master's degree; and $28,852 or $34,580 for those with a doctorate.

Experienced curators working for the federal government earn an average of $38,303 a year.

Additional sources of information

American Association of Museums
1225 I Street, NW
Suite 200
Washington, DC 20005

MUSICIAN

The job

Professional musicians play in symphony orchestras, dance bands, rock groups, and jazz combos and accompany individual performers, musical comedies, and opera performances. Others teach in music conservatories and colleges and universities or give private lessons. Many musicians combine performing careers with teaching or with arranging and composing.

A few musicians specialize in library science for work in music libraries or study psychology for work in music therapy in hospitals. The armed forces also offer many career opportunities for musicians.

Musicians put in many hours of practice and rehearsal in addition to performing. Many find that they are unable to support themselves by music alone and can only pursue it as a part-time career.

Places of employment and working conditions

Musicians work throughout the entire country, but the best opportunities are in large metropolitan areas and in the cities where entertainment and recording activities are concentrated—New York City, Chicago, Los Angeles, Nashville, Miami, and New Orleans.

Musicians normally work evenings and weekends and usually do a lot of traveling. The work is often unsteady, and performers do not usually work for one employer for any length of time.

Qualifications, education, and training

Necessary qualities for a professional musician, in addition to musical talent, are creative ability, poise and stage presence, self-discipline, and physical stamina.

Musicians usually start studying an instrument at an early age with private lessons. Those who perform popular music gain experience by performing in amateur programs, by forming small groups or bands, and by gradually obtaining work with better-known bands as they gain a reputation. Some expand their knowledge and understanding of music by taking some classical training.

Classical musicians study privately, in music conservatories, or in colleges and universities that have strong classical music programs. Auditions are usually required for entrance into these schools or for private lessons with the best teachers.

Music conservatories and colleges and universities offer bachelor's degree programs that include liberal arts courses in addition to musical training. Many schools also offer a bachelor's degree program in music education, which qualifies graduates for state certification in elementary and secondary teaching positions.

College teaching positions usually require advanced degrees, except in the case of very talented musicians.

Potential and advancement

About 229,000 musicians work as performers, with many more employed as teachers. Opportunities in this field are expected to grow slowly through the year 2000. Competition for jobs in this field is always keen, especially for those jobs that offer stable employment.

Income

Music teachers earn salaries comparable to other faculty in the same school.

Earnings of musicians vary widely depending on geographic location and professional reputation. Most jobs are covered by union minimum wage scales.

Additional sources of information

American Federation of Musicians
1501 Broadway
New York, NY 10036

American Music Conference
303 East Wacker Drive
Suite 1214
Chicago, IL 60601

Music Educators National Conference
1902 Association Drive
Reston, VA 22091

National Association of Schools of Music
11250 Roger Bacon Drive
Reston, VA 22091

N

NEWSPAPER REPORTER

The job

Newspaper reporters gather the latest news and write about it. They do research, interview people, attend public events, and do whatever else is necessary to give a complete report of a news event. When deadlines require it, reporters may phone in their information to be transcribed by a rewriter.

General assignment reporters handle all types of news stories; other reporters are assigned to a specialized "beat," such as police stations, the courts, or sports. Reporters with specialized backgrounds may be assigned to write about and analyze the news in such fields as medicine, politics, labor, or education.

On small newspapers, reporters often take their own photographs, do some layout or editorial work, solicit subscriptions and advertising, and perform some general office work.

Some reporters work for national news services where they are usually assigned to a large city or to a particular specialty. *Stringers* work part-time for one or more employers and are paid according to how much of their work is published.

Beginning reporters usually work for small daily or weekly newspapers where they function as general assignment reporters or copy editors. As they gain experience they cover more important news.

A related job is editor, newspaper and magazine.

Places of employment and working conditions

Newspaper reporters work in communities of all sizes. Although the majority of newspapers are in medium-sized towns, most reporters work in cities where each daily newspaper employs many reporters.

Reporters generally work a five-day, 35- to 40-hour week. On morning newspapers, the working hours are from late afternoon to midnight. Coverage of certain news events sometimes requires extended or irregular working hours, and a fast pace and constant deadline pressures are a part of every reporter's working life.

Qualifications, education, and training

Writing skills, curiosity, resourcefulness, an accurate memory, stamina, and the ability to work alone are essential for newspaper reporters.

High school should include as many English courses as possible and typing, social sciences, and experience on school publications, if possible. Summer or part-time jobs on local newspapers also provide valuable experience.

Most newspapers require a news reporter to have a bachelor's degree in either journalism or liberal arts; some require a master's degree. Small newspapers will usually accept less education if the applicant demonstrates exceptional ability or has at least junior college training in the basics of journalism.

Potential and advancement

About 70,000 persons work as newspaper reporters. Employment of newspaper reporters is expected to have average growth through the year 2000, mainly because small-town and suburban daily and weekly newspapers are expected to increase in number. No increase is expected in the number of big-city dailies. There will be a great deal of competition for positions with large city newspapers; the best opportunities for beginning reporters are with small-town and suburban newspapers.

Reporters can advance to editorial or administrative positions or can move on to larger newspapers or press services. Some reporters become columnists, correspondents, editors, or top executives. Others turn to public relations, writing for magazines, or preparing news copy for radio and television.

Income

The average starting salary for reporters whose newspapers have contracts negotiated by The Newspaper Guild ranges from about $13,000 to about $26,000. Experienced reporters' earnings range from about $20,800 to $41,600 a year.

Additional sources of information

American Council on Education for Journalism
School of Journalism
University of Missouri
Columbia, MO 65201

American Newspaper Publishers Association Foundation
The Newspaper Center
Box 17407
Dulles International Airport
Washington, DC 20041

The Dow Jones Newspaper Fund, Inc.
P.O. Box 300
Princeton, NJ 08543-0300

The Newspaper Guild
Research and Information Department
8611 2nd Street, NW
Silver Spring, MD 20910

NURSE, LICENSED PRACTICAL

The job

Licensed practical nurses (LPNs) provide much of the bedside care for patients in hospitals, nursing homes, and extended care facilities. They work under the direction of physicians and registered nurses and perform duties that require technical knowledge but not the professional education and training of a registered nurse. In some areas they are called licensed vocational nurses.

LPNs take and record temperatures and blood pressures, change dressings, administer certain prescribed medicines, bathe patients, care for newborn infants, and perform some special nursing procedures.

Those who work in private homes provide daily nursing care and sometimes prepare meals for the patient as well. LPNs employed in physicians' offices or clinics may perform some clerical chores and handle appointments.

Places of employment and working conditions

Licensed practical nurses work in all areas of the country, most of them in hospitals.

LPNs usually work a 40-hour week, but since patients require 24-hour care, they may work some nights, weekends, and holidays. They spend most of their working hours on their feet and help patients move in bed, stand, or walk. They also experience the stress of working with sick patients and their families.

LPNs face many hazards and difficulties on their jobs. They often come into contact with caustic chemicals, radiation, and infectious diseases. They may also suffer from back injuries and muscle strains when moving patients. The people they take care of may often be confused, angry, or depressed.

Qualifications, education, and training

Anyone interested in working as a practical nurse should have a concern for the sick, be emotionally stable, and have physical stamina. The ability to follow orders and work under close supervision is also necessary.

A high school diploma is not always necessary for enrollment in a training program, although it is usually preferred. One-year, state-approved programs are offered by trade, technical, and vocational schools; high schools; junior colleges; local hospitals; health agencies; and private institutions. Some army training programs are also state-approved.

Applicants for state licensing must complete a program in practical nursing that has been approved by the state board of nursing and must pass a written examination.

Potential and advancement

There are about 626,000 licensed practical nurses. The employment outlook for LPNs is very good through the next decade.

Advancement in this field is limited without formal education or additional training. Training programs in some hospitals help LPNs complete the educational requirements necessary to become registered nurses while they continue to work part-time.

Income

Starting salaries for LPNs working in hospitals average about $15,900 a year. Experienced LPNs average about $21,400 a year.

Additional sources of information

Communications Department
National League for Nursing
350 Hudson Street
New York, NY 10014

National Association for Practical Nurse Education and Service, Inc.
1400 Spring Street
Suite 310
Silver Spring, MD 20910

National Federation of Licensed Practical Nurses, Inc.
P.O. Box 1088
Raleigh, NC 27619

NURSE, REGISTERED

The job

Registered nurses (RNs) play a major role in health care. As part of a health care team, they administer medications and treatments as prescribed by a physician, provide skilled bedside nursing care for the sick and the injured, and work toward the prevention of illness and promotion of good health.

Most nurses are employed in hospitals where they usually work with a group of patients requiring similar care such as a postsurgery floor, the children's area (pediatrics), or the maternity section. Some specialize in operating room work.

Doctors, dentists, and oral surgeons employ nurses in their offices who perform routine laboratory and office work in addition to nursing duties. Industries employ nurses to assist with health examinations, treat minor injuries of employees, and arrange for further medical care if it is necessary. Industrial nurses may also do some recordkeeping and handle claims for medical insurance and workers' compensation.

Community health nurses work with patients in their homes, the schools, public health clinics, and in other community settings. Nurses also teach in nursing schools and conduct continuing education courses for registered and licensed practical nurses.

Private duty nurses are self-employed nurses who provide individual care in hospitals or homes for one patient at a time when the patient needs constant attention. This care may be required for just a short time or for extended periods.

Registered nurses who receive special advanced training may become *nurse practitioners*. They are permitted to perform some services, such as physical examinations, that have traditionally been handled by physicians. Nurse practitioners are an important part of many neighborhood health center staffs.

The federal government employs nurses in Veterans Administration hospitals and clinics, in the U.S. Public Health Service, and as commissioned officers in the armed forces.

Most nurses are women, but young men are entering the field in increasing numbers in recent years.

Places of employment and working conditions

Nurses are usually on their feet most of the day. Those who work in hospitals, nursing homes, or as private duty nurses must be prepared to work evenings, weekends, and holidays.

Nurses need both physical and emotional stamina to cope with the stresses of their jobs. They face the dangers of infectious diseases and the hazards of working with radiation, chemicals, and gases. They also must be careful to avoid back injuries and muscle strains when moving patients.

Qualifications, education, and training

Nurses need the ability to follow orders precisely, use good judgment in emergencies, and cope with human suffering and must have good physical and emotional stamina.

In high school, students should take a college preparation program with an emphasis on science.

There are three types of training for registered nurses. Many hospitals offer three-year diploma programs in their own nursing schools that combine classroom instruction and clinical experience within the hospital. Four-year bachelor-degree programs are available at many colleges. Two-year associate-degree programs are offered by some junior and community colleges. These degree programs are combined with clinical practice in an affiliated hospital or health care facility.

A bachelor's degree is required for administrative or management positions in nursing; research, teaching, and clinical specializations usually require a master's degree.

Potential and advancement

There are about 1,577,000 registered nurses, one-fourth of them working part-time. Future employment opportunities should be excellent for some time due to a current shortage of nurses. Nursing opportunities exist in every community; there are shortages of qualified nurses in many inner-city areas and in some southern states. Employment prospects for nurses with specialized training in fields such as intensive care, geriatrics, and oncology are excellent.

Experienced hospital nurses can advance to head nurse or assistant director or director of nursing services. Many supervisory and management positions require a bachelor's degree, however.

Income

Registered nurses working in hospitals start at average annual salaries of about $23,100. Experienced nurses earn an average of about $32,100, while experienced head nurses average about $40,800. Nurses working in nursing homes have a median annual salary of about $21,300.

Additional sources of information

American Nurses' Association
2420 Pershing Road
Kansas City, MO 64108

Communications Department
National League for Nursing
350 Hudson Street
New York, NY 10014

NURSERY WORKER

The job

Plant nurseries grow and sell trees, flowers, shrubs, and other plants. They may be wholesale or retail operations, garden centers, or mail-order businesses.

Nursery workers perform a variety of special tasks: plant propagation through seeds, cuttings, and root division; preparation of soil in outdoor growing areas; greenhouse management; weed, disease, and insect control; plant breeding; storage and packaging of plants; and business operations.

Nursery workers are also employed by other establishments that use large numbers of plants and trees requiring expert care and maintenance. These include parks and botanical gardens; large estates and institutions, such as schools; industrial and commercial facilities with extensive outdoor areas; and planned residential areas, such as senior citizen retirement communities or public housing.

State and federal government agencies employ nursery workers in agricultural extension services, inspection and law enforcement, and in developmental and administrative positions.

Some specially trained nursery workers are called *plant scientists.* They do research on specific plants or groups of plants, especially food-producing plants, to improve their yield or to find solutions to problems such as insect infestation. Plant scientists also develop new plants.

Related jobs are landscape architect, farmer, range manager, biologist.

Qualification, education, and training

Curiosity about and a love of growing things are a basic qualification for anyone in this field. Good health, average strength, manual dexterity, color perception, a sense of design, and patience are important. Business management skills and sales ability are also valuable.

High school courses in science, social studies, mathematics, mechanical drawing, and art are good preparation for this field. Summer jobs at plant nurseries or with landscape contractors provide valuable experience.

There are no specific educational requirements for nursery workers and many of them acquire their skills through on-the-job training. Many employers, however, prefer some formal training for those who work as managers. Two-year courses in this field are available at junior and community colleges, four-year colleges, and technical and vocational schools.

Nursery workers who are in charge of groundskeeping for large companies usually need at least a bachelor's degree and in some cases an advanced degree. Majors in the biological sciences, landscape architecture, urban planning, and environmental design are recommended.

Research work requires advanced study in a specialty field such as agronomy, entomology, chemistry, soil science, or biology.

Potential and advancement

This is a growing field of employment at all levels. Openings exist in small local nurseries, large retail and wholesale companies, and in basic research. In the future there is expected to be a greater demand for specialists in ornamental nursery stock, agricultural products, and insect and plant disease control.

For the most part, advancement in this field depends on ambition and experience. Many persons start as laborers and then work their way up through jobs as landscape helpers, groundskeepers, greenhouse workers, tree trimmers, or other positions. Supervisory and management positions are available to those who acquire a broad range of experience and knowledge. Many managers advance by opening their own nursery businesses.

Income

Earnings vary widely depending on the size and location of the business and the worker's education and experience.

Beginning nursery workers with a high school education earn between $7,800 and $10,500 a year. Those with an associate's degree start at about $12,500 to $14,700 a year. Part-time workers earn hourly wages between $6 and $8.

Additional sources of information

American Association of Nurserymen, Inc.
1250 Eye Street, NW
Suite 500
Washington, DC 20005

OCCUPATIONAL THERAPIST

The job

This fast-growing field offers personal satisfaction as well as financially rewarding job opportunities. Occupational therapists work with both the physically and emotionally disabled, helping some to return to normal functions and activities and others to make the fullest use of whatever talents they may have.

Occupational therapists plan and direct educational, vocational, and recreational activities; evaluate capabilities and skills; and plan individual therapy programs, often working as part of a medical team. Their clients are all ages and can range from a stroke victim relearning daily routines such as eating, dressing, and using a telephone to an accident victim learning to reuse impaired limbs before returning to work.

To restore mobility and dexterity to hands disabled by injury or disease, occupational therapists teach manual and creative skills through the use of crafts such as weaving, knitting, and leather working. They design games and activities especially for children or make special equipment or splints to aid the disabled patient.

Many part-time positions are available for occupational therapists; some occupational therapists work for more than one employer, traveling between job locations and clients.

In addition to hospital rehabilitation departments, other types of organizations that employ occupational therapists are rehabilitation centers and nursing homes, schools, mental health centers, schools and camps for handicapped children, state health departments and home-care programs, Veterans Administration hospitals and clinics, psychiatric centers, and schools for learning and development disabilities.

Most occupational therapists are women, but the number of men entering the field has been increasing. Because there are many opportunities for part-time work, this is a good field for people with family responsibilities.

Related jobs are physical therapist and respiratory therapist.

Places of employment and working conditions

Occupational therapists usually work a 40-hour week, but this may include weekends and evenings. Those who work for schools have regular school hours.

Therapists spend a lot of time on their feet, and they may be subject to back injuries and muscle strains from lifting and moving patients and equipment. Therapists who give home health care may spend several hours a day driving.

Qualifications, education, and training

Maturity, patience, imagination, manual skills, and the ability to instruct are important as is a sympathetic but objective attitude toward illness and disability.

Anyone considering this career field should have high school science courses, especially biology and chemistry. Courses in health and social studies along with training in crafts are also important. Volunteer work or a summer job in a health care facility can provide valuable exposure to this field.

A bachelor's degree in occupational therapy is required to practice in this field. Thirty-four states, Puerto Rico, and the District of Columbia require a license. Sixty-three colleges and universities offer bachelor's degrees in occupational therapy.

Some schools offer a shorter program leading to certification or to a master's degree in occupational therapy for students who already have a bachelor's degree in another field.

Occupational-therapy students study physical, biological, and behavioral sciences as well as the application of occupational theory and skills. Students also spend from six to nine months working in hospitals or health agencies to gain clinical experience.

Graduates of accredited programs take the certification examination of the American Occupational Therapy Association to become a registered occupational therapist (OTR).

Potential and advancement

There are about 33,000 occupational therapists with approximately 40 percent employed in hospitals. Employment in this field is expected to grow substantially because the public is becoming more interested and more knowledgeable about programs for rehabilitating the disabled. Job opportunities will be excellent on the whole through the year 2000; however, as the increasing number of qualified graduates catches up to the number of available jobs, competition for job openings may develop in some geographic areas.

Advancement in this field is usually to supervisory or administrative positions. Advanced education is necessary for those wishing to teach, do research, or advance to top administration levels.

Income

Beginning therapists employed by hospitals average about $24,000 a year; experienced therapists earn an average of $31,800.

Additional sources of information

American Occupational Therapy Association
P.O. Box 1725
1383 Piccard Drive
Rockville, MD 20850-4375

OCEANOGRAPHER

The job

Using the principles and techniques of natural science, mathematics, and engineering, oceanographers study the movements, physical properties, and plant and animal life of the oceans. They make observations, conduct experiments, and collect specimens at sea that are later analyzed in laboratories. Their work contributes to improving weather forecasting, locating fishing, locating petroleum and mineral resources, and improving national defense.

Most oceanographers specialize in one branch of the science. *Marine biologists* study plant and animal life in the ocean to determine the effects of pollution on marine life. Their work is also important in improving and controlling sport and commercial fishing. *Marine geologists* study underwater mountain ranges, rocks, and sediments of the oceans to locate regions where minerals, oil, and gas may be found. Other oceanographic specialists study the relationship between the sea and the atmosphere and the chemical composition of ocean water and sediments. Others with engineering or electronics training design and build instruments for oceanographic research, lay cables, and supervise underwater construction.

Many oceanographers work for colleges and universities. In addition to holding teaching positions, they take part in research projects sponsored by universities at sea and in facilities along U.S. coasts.

The U.S. Navy and the National Oceanic and Atmospheric Administration employ oceanographers. State fisheries employ a few. An increasing number of oceanographers are being employed by private industry, particularly in aquaculture, chemical firms, construction, and oceanographic equipment manufacturers.

Related jobs are chemist, geologist, geophysicist, life scientist, and meteorologist.

Places of employment and working conditions

Most oceanographers work in the states that border the ocean, such as California, Maryland, and Virginia.

Oceanographers engaged in research that requires sea voyages are often away from home for long periods of time, and they may have to live and work in cramped quarters.

Qualifications, education, and training

Anyone interested in this career field should have curiosity and the patience necessary to collect data and do research.

High school should include as many science and mathematics courses as possible. Hobbies or summer jobs that involve boating or ocean fishing are helpful.

A bachelor's degree with a major in oceanography, chemistry, biology, earth or physical sciences, mathematics, or engineering is the first step for a would-be oceanographer and is sufficient for entry-level jobs such as research assistant.

Graduate training in oceanography or a basic science is required for most jobs in research and training and for all top-level positions; a Ph.D. is required for many. Graduate students usually spend part of their time at sea conducting experiments and learning the techniques of gathering oceanographic information.

Potential and advancement

There are about 3,600 people employed as oceanographers. This is a relatively small field, and there will be competition for any available job 'openings. Those who combine training in other scientific or engineering fields with oceanography will have the best chances for employment.

Oceanographers with advanced degrees and experience can advance to administrative or supervisory positions in research laboratories. They may also advance by becoming directors of surveys or research programs.

Income

Oceanographers employed by colleges and universities receive the same salaries as other faculty members. In addition, they may earn extra income from consulting, lecturing, and writing.

The average yearly salary for experienced oceanographers working for the federal government is about $30,000.

Additional sources of information

American Society of Limnology and Oceanography
Great Lakes Research Division
University of Michigan
Ann Arbor, MI 48109

U.S. Civil Service Commission
Washington Area Office
1900 E Street, NW
Washington, DC 20415

International Oceanographic Foundation
3979 Rickenbacker Causeway
Virginia Key
Miami, FL 33149

OFFICE MANAGER

The job

The title *office manager* brings to mind the secretary or clerk who has worked her or his way up in the office hierarchy to the top supervisory position. While this description is accurate to some degree, the field also includes office management positions that are much more complex and far-reaching.

In a small or medium-sized company, an office manager supervises the day-to-day work of a clerical staff that might include accounting functions such as billing, maintenance of personnel records, payroll, plus all other secretarial and clerical functions. The mail room, telephone switchboard, and duplicating and copier equipment also are part of the office manager's responsibilities. The size and makeup of the office staff varies depending on the company and its requirements.

In a large company, the office manager is responsible for a larger and much more complex office staff, often at multiple locations within the company buildings. With one of many possible titles—director of secretarial support systems, administrative manager, office administrator—a manager at this level is involved in systems analysis and electronic data processing as well as office systems, procedures, and operations.

A rapidly growing specialty within this field is management of a centralized word processing facility within a company in which trained specialists, specific procedures, and the latest in automatic equipment are combined to handle the clerical needs of a variety of departments. Such a *word processing manager* coordinates the word processing services with the needs of the user departments and is responsible for staff levels and training, budgets, and design and implementation of word processing systems.

The number of the clerical workers varies from organization to organization depending on the nature of the organization. The greatest concentrations of clerical workers and the managers necessary to oversee their work are in public administration, insurance, finance, and banking. Other large employers are the wholesale and retail fields and manufacturing firms.

Related jobs are accountant, bank officer, civil service worker (federal, municipal, and state), computer programmer, industrial engineer, personnel manager, secretary, and systems analyst.

Places of employment and working conditions

Although the usual office workweek is 40 hours, office managers often put in extra hours. The responsibilities of planning and organization plus meetings with executives of user departments sometimes add many hours to the daily schedule.

The entire clerical staff may work under a great deal of pressure at times to meet deadlines and handle busy seasons.

Qualifications, education, and training

A successful office manager must have a talent for organization, an analytical mind, and the ability to work with detail. Creativity, resourcefulness, flexibility, self-assurance, tact, and the ability to get along with people are also necessary. Good communication skills and a background that includes clerical skills are solid assets.

A high school student looking forward to a career in office management should include business courses as well as those courses necessary to enter college or a good business school. Work experience in an office in a part-time or summer job is valuable preparation.

A college degree is usually necessary for a person to achieve the top levels in this field. Small businesses that require a degree often prefer a bachelor's degree in accounting, while large companies often prefer a degree in business administration. Some colleges offer a major or minor in office management.

Business schools, trade and technical schools, community colleges, and university extension programs also offer a variety of programs in this field, some leading to a degree. In addition to taking courses in office management, the student should include systems and procedures, data processing, accounting, and personnel management to acquire diversified business training. A number of two- and four-year degree programs offer electives in law or economics and other liberal arts courses to provide a well-rounded education.

Home study programs are also available for office management. The diploma awarded by such programs does not carry the prestige of a college degree, but many people find them convenient for supplementary study in specific areas of business management.

Large corporations often have training programs in office management, but these programs are usually open only to college graduates.

Regardless of educational background, people in this field continue to study throughout their careers. New development in office technology alone would require this. In addition to taking college courses, most office managers attend seminars and conferences sponsored by various professional societies as well as training sessions and workshops presented by office equipment manufacturers.

Potential and advancement

There are about 1,183,000 office managers. Qualified office managers will continue to be in demand through the year 2000. While there will continue to be a place for the skilled clerical worker who advances through the ranks, the growing complexity of the office communications and data processing functions of even small companies will require more comprehensive knowledge and training than is acquired by that route. The best job opportunities will be for those with a college degree and diversified business experience.

Office managers are already at the middle-management level. In companies where the office administration function is a major component of the firm's service, office managers can advance to top-level executive positions.

Income

Salaries of office managers vary widely depending on size of the company and its clerical staff, responsibilities of the manager, and complexity of its operation. The supervisor or manager averages $23,700 annually. The median income for male office managers is $28,600 a year, while female managers earn slightly less than $18,000 annually.

Additional sources of information

American Management Association
135 West 50th Street
New York, NY 10020

Association of Information Systems Professionals
104 Wilmot Road
Suite 201
Deerfield, IL 60015

Administrative Management Society
4622 Street Road
Trevose, PA 19047

OFFICER, U.S. ARMED FORCES

The job

A career as an officer in the army, navy, marines, or Coast Guard may be achieved through different methods: The Reserve Officers Training Corps (ROTC), the service academies, Officer Candidate Schools (OCS), the National Guard State Officer Candidate School, the Uniformed Services University of Health Sciences; and other programs.

Women are eligible to enter almost 90 percent of all military specialties.

Places of employment and working conditions

Members of the U.S. armed forces serve throughout the world. Although some effort is made to allow choice of location at the time of enlistment, assignments are not always to the location of choice.

Officers who receive their training at one of the service academies as well as officers who receive their training and college education through ROTC scholarships are obligated to serve on active duty for a stipulated period of time. Other officers serve various lengths of time on active duty.

Qualifications, education, and training

Leadership qualities are important for anyone interested in a career as an officer. Applicants must be between 18 and 28 years of age (there are a few exceptions), U.S. citizens, and in good physical condition. The service academies require a rigorous physical examination and have specific height, weight, eyesight, color vision, and hearing requirements. The academies also require cadets to remain unmarried until after graduation.

Women applicants to any of the programs cannot have dependents under 18 years of age.

High school courses should include English, science, and mathematics. Extracurricular activities that develop leadership qualities are valuable.

Ninety percent of the officers in the armed forces are college graduates, and it is very difficult to achieve this status without some college education.

ROTC programs are offered at over 150 colleges and universities; some scholarships are available. Most are four-year programs, but there are some two-year programs as well. Candidates must receive a passing grade on the Officers Qualifying Test at the end of the second year of college to continue the program. Information on ROTC programs may be obtained directly from participating colleges or from local recruiting offices of the various services.

Enlisted personnel in the various services may be appointed to Officer Candidate School through classification exams and interviews and grades received on specific aptitude tests and the Officer Candidate Test. Civilian applicants should apply at local recruiting offices where they may take the appropriate examinations. OCS training lasts from 9 to 39 weeks, depending on branch of service and previous military training.

Applicants for West Point, Annapolis, and the Air Force Academy must be appointed by their congressperson. The Coast Guard Academy does not require applicants to be appointed; the Coast Guard recruits through an annual nationwide competition. The army, navy, and air force academies require the College Board Entrance Exam, while the Coast Guard requires the Scholastic Aptitude Test (SAT) or the American College Testing Assessment (ACT). High school guidance counselors can usually provide up-to-date information on requirements at the service academies, or interested students may write to the academies directly.

The Army Nurse Program is open to applicants between the ages of 18 and 24. A four-year program leading to a commission includes two years of college and two years at Walter Reed Army Medical Center. A one- to two-year Army Student Nurse Program is also available at some hospital and university schools of nursing.

The Naval Air Reserve has an 18-month program for naval aviation cadets. Applicants must have completed two years of college and must receive a passing score on the Aviation Qualification Test and the Flight Aptitude Rating Test.

Potential and advancement

The need for qualified officers in all of the services will provide career opportunities for applicants with a wide range of skills, and promotion to higher rank is possible for everyone.

Income

Depending on their pay grade level, officers with less than two years of experience earn monthly salaries ranging between $1,338.90 and $1,903.50. They also receive free room and board (or a housing and subsistence allowance), medical and dental benefits, 30 days' paid vacation a year, a military clothing allowance, military supermarket and department store shopping privileges, and travel opportunities. They may receive retirement benefits after 20 years of service.

Additional sources of information

High school and college guidance counselors and local recruiting offices can provide information on careers in the armed forces. Information is also available from:

United States Military Academy
West Point, NY 10996

United States Naval Academy
Annapolis, MD 21402-5018

U.S. Air Force Academy
Colorado Springs, CO 80901

Naval Reserve Center
Pensacola, FL 32509

U.S. Coast Guard Academy
New London, CT 06320

OPERATING ENGINEER

The job

Operating engineers, who are also called material moving equipment operators, operate all kinds of construction equipment. They are usually classified by the type or capacity of the machines they operate.

Heavy equipment operators are highly skilled in the operation of complex machinery such as cranes. They must accurately judge distances and heights while operating the buttons, levers, and pedals that rotate the crane, raise and lower the boom and loadline, and open and close attachments such as steel-toothed buckets or clamps for lifting materials. At times, operators work without being able to see the pickup or delivery point, depending on hand or flag signals from another worker. When constructing new buildings, they work far above the ground.

The operation of medium-sized construction equipment requires fewer controls and is done at ground level. *Bulldozer operators,* for example, lift and lower the blade and move the bulldozer back and forth over the construction area. Trench excavators, paving machines, and other construction equipment are also in this category.

Lightweight equipment such as an air compressor is the simplest to operate. (An air compressor is a diesel engine that takes in air and forces it through a narrow hose. The resulting pressure is used to run special tools.) The operator makes sure the compressor has fuel and water, adjusts and maintains pressure levels, and makes minor repairs.

Operating engineers often work with helpers called *oilers* who keep the equipment properly lubricated and supplied with fuel.

About 33 percent of all operating engineers work in manufacturing; more than 20 percent work in construction.

Many operating engineers work for contractors in large-scale construction projects such as highways, dams, and airports. Others work for utility companies and business firms that do their own construction; state and local highway and public works departments; and factories and mines using power-driven machinery, hoists, and cranes. Very few operating engineers are self-employed.

The International Union of Operating Engineers is the bargaining unit for many workers in this field.

Places of employment and working conditions

Most operating engineers work outdoors. They work steadily during the warm months but have slow periods in cold months or in bad weather. Operation of medium-sized equipment is physically tiring because of constant movement and the jolting and noise levels of the equipment. Those working on highway construction sometimes work in remote locations.

Qualification, education, and training

Operating engineers need physical stamina, mechanical ability, excellent eyesight and eye-hand coordination, and manual dexterity.

Driver education and automobile mechanics courses in high school are helpful, and experience in operating a tractor or other farm equipment can provide a good background for this work.

A number of private schools offer instruction in the operation of some types of construction equipment, but anyone considering such a school should check with local construction employers for their opinion of the training received by the school's graduates. Not all schools produce suitably trained people.

Most employers prefer to hire operating engineers who have completed a formal apprenticeship program, since they are more thoroughly trained and can operate a variety of equipment. Programs are usually sponsored and supervised by a joint union-management committee; the armed forces also provide apprenticeship programs. An apprenticeship consists of at least three years of on-the-job training plus 144 hours per year of related classroom instruction in hydraulics, engine operation and repair, cable splicing, welding, safety, and first aid.

Apprenticeship applicants usually need a high school or vocational school diploma, but not always. They must be at least 18 years old.

Apprentices start by working as oilers or helpers. They clean, grease, repair and start engines. Within the first year of apprenticeship, they usually begin to perform simple machine operations and progress to more complex operations, always under the supervision of an experienced operating engineer.

Potential and advancement

There are about 1 million operating engineers. Employment of operating engineers is not expected to grow much through the year 2000, but many opportunities will arise as experienced workers transfer to other careers or leave the labor force. Because this field is sensitive to ups and downs in the economy, employment of operating engineers may fluctuate from year to year.

Income

Wage rates vary depending on the machine operated. The median earnings for all operating engineers is about $385 a week. Pay scales are generally higher in metropolitan areas.

Additional sources of information

Associated General Contractors of America, Inc.
1957 E Street, NW
Washington, DC 20006

International Union of Operating Engineers
1125 17th Street, NW
Washington, DC 20036

OPERATIONS RESEARCH ANALYST

The job

An organization or system can usually be operated in several ways, but the best way is not necessarily the most obvious one. Operations research specialists use their knowledge of engineering, mathematics, and economics to decide on the most efficient way to use all available resources to achieve maximum results.

This relatively new field is concerned with the design and operation of worker-machine systems. Using a number of scientific methods of analysis, operations research analysts decide on the best allocation of resources within an organization or system. These resources include such things as time, money, trained people, space, and raw materials.

In another application of operations research techniques, analysts might apply appropriate theories and methods to two possible research projects that are competing for funding. Their analysis could produce information on which project would probably achieve the best results in the shortest time with the available money and other resources.

The applications of operations research are numerous. Originated during World War II to deal with the allocation and tactical employment of available equipment, workers, and materials, operations research is now a standard and growing aspect of management in industry, marketing, capital development, financial planning, government, and exploration activities.

A number of people in this field are engaged in teaching and research. Related jobs are industrial engineer, systems analyst, office manager.

Places of employment and working conditions

While many operations research analysts work in an office setting, many others work in classrooms; out-of-doors; and in laboratories, factories, and hospitals. It is often an active field, with the analyst moving throughout a building or to several different locations to study the operation of a company or system.

Qualifications, education, and training

An analytical mind, resourcefulness, patience, good communication skills, and the ability to get along with people are necessary.

High school should include as much mathematics and science as possible.

A degree in engineering, mathematics, economics, or the physical sciences are all acceptable beginnings for this field since there is no typical operations research program. Graduate study is, however, usually necessary, and a working knowledge of computers should be acquired during undergraduate or graduate education.

Potential and advancement

The demand for competent operations research analysts far exceeds the supply. This trend is expected to continue through the year 2000, providing increasing job opportunities for those who pursue it as a primary career or as an adjunct to another area of specialization.

The potential for advancement in this field is excellent. Experienced analysts can advance to supervisory and management positions in all types of organizations. Because this field provides exposure to the full spectrum of operations within a company or organization, it is becoming recognized as a major training ground for senior management and executive positions.

Many experienced operations research analysts become management consultants, opening their own companies or working for an established management consulting firm.

Income

Experienced operations research analysts within an organization have median earnings from $25,000 to $42,000 a year. Government positions pay an average of $45,000 a year.

Additional sources of information

The Operations Research Society of America
428 East Preston Street
Baltimore, MD 21202

OPHTHALMOLOGIST

The job

Ophthalmologists are also called eye physicians-surgeons. They are qualified physicians and osteopathic physicians who have completed additional specialized training in the treatment of eye diseases and disorders. They treat a full range of eye problems including vision deficiencies, injuries, infections, and other disorders with medicines, therapy, corrective lenses, or surgery. Their job is distinct from that of optometrists and opticians, who are not physicians and treat only vision problems.

Most ophthalmologists are in private practice. Others are employed by hospitals and clinics, medical schools and research foundations, federal and state agencies, and the armed forces.

Related jobs are optometrist, dispensing optician, physician, and osteopathic physician.

Places of employment and working conditions

Ophthalmologists work in all areas of the country. Those who are osteopathic physicians are concentrated in the areas that have osteopathic hospital facilities—mainly in Florida, Michigan, Pennsylvania, New Jersey, Ohio, Texas, and Missouri. The workweek for ophthalmologists is from 35 to 50 hours. Those involved in general patient care are always on call for emergencies.

Qualifications, education, and training

Information on the training and licensing requirements for physicians and osteopathic physicians is contained in the appropriate job description elsewhere in this book.

An additional three to five years of residency in an accredited ophthalmology program must be completed by doctors who wish to specialize in this field. Candidates for the specialty must then pass the certification examination of the American Board of Ophthalmology or the American Osteopathic Board of Ophthalmology.

Potential and advancement

The demand for ophthalmologists will continue to grow as the population grows. Greater interest in eye care, the growing number of senior citizens, and the increase in health insurance plans will all add to the need for qualified practitioners of this medical specialty.

Income

Ophthalmologists who start a private practice face a few lean years until the practice is established. In addition, a sizable investment in specialized equipment is necessary. Earnings during this early period may barely meet expenses.

As a practice grows, earnings usually increase substantially. Average annual earnings for all ophthalmologists are in the $75,000 range with some earning even more. In general, ophthalmologists in private practice earn more than those in salaried positions.

Additional sources of information

American Academy of Ophthalmology
655 Beach Street
P.O. Box 7424
San Francisco, CA 94120

American Medical Association
535 North Dearborn Street
Chicago, IL 60610

OPTICIAN, DISPENSING

The job

Over half the people in the United States use some form of corrective lenses (eyeglasses or contact lenses). These corrective lenses are prepared and fitted by dispensing opticians who are also called ophthalmic dispensers. Working with the prescription received from an ophthalmologist (eye physician) or optometrist, the dispensing optician provides the customer with appropriate eyeglasses. He or she measures the customer's face, aids in the selection of the appropriate frames, directs the work of ophthalmic laboratory technicians who grind the lenses, and fits the completed eyeglasses.

In many states, dispensing opticians also fit contact lenses, which requires even more skill, care, and patience than the preparation and fitting of eyeglasses. Opticians measure the corneas of the customer's eyes and, following the ophthalmologist's or optometrist's prescription, prepare specifications for the contact lens manufacturer. The optician will instruct the customer on how to insert, remove, and care for the contact lenses and will provide follow-up attention during the first few weeks.

Some dispensing opticians specialize in the fitting of artificial eyes and cosmetic shells to cover blemished eyes. Some also do their own lens grinding.

Most dispensing opticians work for retail optical shops or other retail stores with optical departments. Ophthalmologists and optometrists who sell glasses directly to patients also employ dispensing opticians, as do hospitals and eye clinics. A number of dispensing opticians operate their own retail shops and sell other optical goods such as binoculars, magnifying glasses, and sunglasses.

Places of employment and working conditions

Dispensing opticians are located throughout the United States with most employed in large cities and in the more populous states. Working conditions are usually quiet and clean with a workweek of five or six days. Dispensing opticians who own their own businesses usually work longer hours than those employed by retail shops or by ophthalmologists and optometrists.

Qualifications, education, and training

The ability to do precision work is essential for anyone planning a career as a dispensing optician. Patience, tact, and the ability to deal with people are other valuable assets.

Applicants for entry-level jobs in this field need a high school diploma with courses in the basic sciences. High school courses in physics, algebra, geometry, and mechanical drawing are especially valuable.

Most opticians acquire their skills through on-the-job training. A small number of dispensing opticians learn their trade in the armed forces. In addition, large manufacturers of contact lenses offer nondegree courses in lens-fitting.

Forty programs offer a two-year full-time course in optical fabricating and dispensing which leads to an associate's degree; 15 are accredited by the Commission on Opticianry Accreditation. Students learn optical mathematics, optical physics, and the use of precision measuring instruments.

Apprenticeship programs lasting from two to five years are also available. In these programs, the students study optometric technical subjects and basic office management and sales and work directly with patients in the fitting of eyeglasses and contact lenses.

Dispensing opticians must be licensed in at least 22 states. Specific requirements vary from state to state but generally include minimum standards of education and training along with a written or practical examination.

Potential and advancement

About 49,000 persons work as dispensing opticians. Employment opportunities in this field are expected to increase steadily as the population increases. Increased health insurance coverage, Medicare services, and state programs to provide eye care to low-income families—along with current fashion trends, which encourage sales of more than one pair of glasses to individual buyers—will add to the demand for dispensing opticians.

Many dispensing opticians go into business for themselves. Others advance to positions in the management of retail optical stores or become sales representatives for wholesalers or manufacturers of eyeglasses or contact lenses.

Income

Earnings for dispensing opticians vary a great deal. Highest earnings are in those states that require licensure. The average annual earnings for dispensing opticians are $25,000 a year and range from about $15,000 to $30,000.

Additional sources of information

National Academy of Opticianry
10111 Martin Luther King, Jr. Highway
Suite 112
Bowie, MD 20715

Opticians Association of America
10341 Democracy Lane
P.O. Box 10110
Fairfax, VA 22030

OPTOMETRIST

The job

Over half of the U.S. population wear corrective lenses (eyeglasses or contact lenses). Before obtaining lenses, people need an eye examination and a prescription to obtain the correct lenses for their particular eye problem. Optometrists (doctors of optometry) provide the bulk of this care.

In addition to handling vision problems, optometrists also check for disease. When evidence of disease is found, an optometrist refers the patient to the appropriate medical practitioner. Optometrists also check depth and color perception and the ability to focus and coordinate the eyes. They may prescribe corrective eye exercises or other treatments that do not require surgery. Optometrists can utilize medications for diagnosis, while in 23 states they can also treat eye diseases with drugs.

Some optometrists specialize in work with children or the aged or work only with the partially sighted who must wear microscopic or telescopic lenses. Industrial eye-safety programs also are an optometric specialty. A few optometrists are engaged in teaching and research.

Although most optometrists are in private practice, many others are in partnerships or in group practice with other optometrists or with other physicians as part of a health care team. Some work in retail vision chain stores. Many combine private, group, or partnership practice with work in specialized hospitals and eye clinics.

Some optometrists serve as commissioned officers in the armed forces. Others are consultants to engineers specializing in safety or lighting; to educators in remedial reading; and to health advisory committees of federal, state, and local governments.

Places of employment and working conditions

Although most optometrists work in California, Illinois, New York, Pennsylvania, and Ohio, opportunities exist in towns and cities of all sizes.

Most self-employed optometrists can set their own work schedule but often work longer than 40 hours a week. Because the work is not physically strenuous, optometrists can practice past the normal retirement age.

Qualifications, education, and training

Because most optometrists are self-employed, anyone planning on a career in this field needs business ability and self-discipline in addition to the ability to deal effectively with people.

High school preparation should emphasize science, and business courses are also helpful.

The doctor of optometry degree is awarded after successful completion of at least six years of college. The two years of preoptometrical study should include English, mathematics, physics, chemistry, and biology or zoology. Some schools also require psychology, social studies, literature, philosophy, and foreign languages.

Admission to optometry schools is highly competitive. Because the number of qualified applicants exceeds the available places, applicants need superior grades in preoptometric courses to increase their chances of acceptance by one of the 16 schools and colleges of optometry approved by the Council on Optometric Education of the American Optometric Association.

Optometrists who wish to advance in a specialized field of optometry may study for a master's or Ph.D. degree in visual science, physiological optics, neurophysiology, public health, health administration, health information and communication, or health education. Career officers in the armed forces also have an opportunity to work toward advanced degrees and to do research.

Potential and advancement

There are about 37,000 practicing optometrists, many of them in private practice. Employment opportunities are expected to grow steadily through the year 2000. Increasing coverage of optometric services by health insurance, greater recognition of the importance of good vision, and the growing population—especially older people who are most likely to need eyeglasses—should contribute to an increase in the demand for optometrists.

Income

Incomes for optometrists vary greatly depending on location, specialization, and factors such as private or group practice. New optometry graduates average $40,000 in their first year.

Experienced optometrists average about $65,000 a year with those in associate or partnership practices earning substantially more than those in private practice.

Additional sources of information

American Optometric Association
243 North Lindbergh Boulevard
St. Louis, MO 63141

OSTEOPATHIC PHYSICIAN

The job

The dictionary defines osteopathy as "a system of medical practice based on the theory that diseases are due chiefly to a loss of structural integrity in the tissues and that this integrity can be restored by manipulation of the parts, supported by the use of medicines, surgery, proper diet, and other therapy."

Most osteopathic physicians are family doctors engaged in general practice. They see patients at the office or make house calls and treat patients in osteopathic and other private and public hospitals. Some osteopathic physicians specialize in such fields as internal medicine, neurology, psychiatry, ophthalmology, pediatrics, anesthesiology, physical medicine and rehabilitation, dermatology, obstetrics and gynecology, pathology, proctology, radiology, and surgery.

Most osteopathic physicians are in private practice, although a few hold salaried positions in private industry or government agencies. Others hold full-time positions with osteopathic hospitals and colleges where they are engaged in teaching, research, and writing.

Places of employment and working conditions

Most osteopathic physicians practice in states that have osteopathic hospital facilities; over half are in Florida, Michigan, Pennsylvania, New Jersey, Ohio, Texas, and Missouri. Most general practitioners are located in towns and cities having less than 50,000 people; specialists are usually located in larger cities.

Qualifications, education, and training

Anyone interested in becoming an osteopathic physician should have emotional stability, patience, tact, and an interest in and ability to deal effectively with people.

The education requirements for the doctor of osteopathy (D.O.) degree include a minimum of three years of college (although almost all applicants have a bachelor's degree) plus a three- to four-year professional program. The education and training of an osteopathic physician is very expensive due primarily to the length of time involved. Federal and private funds are available for loans, and federal scholarships are available to those who qualify and agree to a minimum of two years of service for the federal government after completion of training.

Undergraduate study must include courses in chemistry, physics, biology, and English, with high grades an important factor in acceptance into the professional programs. In addition to high grades, schools require a good score on the Medical College Admission Test and letters of recommendation. One very important qualification is the applicant's desire to study osteopathy rather than some other field of medicine.

During the first half of the professional program, the student studies basic sciences such as anatomy, physiology, and pathology as well as the principles of osteopathy. The second half of the program consists primarily of clinical experience. After graduation, a 12-month internship is usually completed at one of the osteopathic hospitals approved for internship or residency by the American Osteopathic Association. Those who intend to specialize must complete an additional two to five years of training.

All practicing osteopathic physicians must be licensed. State licensing requirements vary, but all states require graduation from an approved school of osteopathic medicine and a passing grade on a state board examination. Most states require internship at an approved hospital.

Potential and advancement

There are about 53,500 practicing osteopathic physicians in the United States. Population growth, an increase in the number of persons covered by medical insurance, and the establishment of additional osteopathic hospitals will contribute to an increasing demand for osteopathic physicians. The greatest demand will continue to be in states where osteopathic medicine is well known and accepted as a method of treatment.

Opportunities for new practitioners are best in rural areas (many localities lack medical practitioners of any kind), small towns, and suburbs of large cities. The availability of osteopathic hospital facilities should be considered when one is selecting a location for practice.

Income

As is usually the case in any field where setting up an individual practice is the norm, earnings in the first few years are low. Income usually rises substantially once the practice becomes established and, in the case of osteopathic physicians, is very high in comparison with other professionals. Geographic location and the income level of the community are also factors that affect the level of income. The average annual income of general practitioners is $91,500.

Additional sources of information

American Osteopathic Association
Department of Public Relations
142 East Ontario Street
Chicago, IL 60611

American Association of Colleges of Osteopathic Medicine
6110 Executive Boulevard
Suite 405
Rockville, MD 20852

P

PARALEGAL

The job

Lawyers often face a tremendous workload; every legal specialty requires a great deal of research, drafting and filing of documents, and preparation of reports. Many lawyers hire paralegals, or legal assistants, to help them accomplish these tasks.

Paralegals perform many of the same duties as lawyers, but they are prohibited from actually practicing law—accepting clients, setting legal fees, giving legal advice, or presenting a case in court. Paralegals work under the supervision of lawyers because lawyers are ultimately responsible for their work.

Paralegals' responsibilities vary depending on the type and size of their employer. Those working for litigators assist in preparing a case for trial. They may conduct interviews and investigations to determine the facts of a case. They also may research laws, judicial decisions, and any other material that may be relevant to the case. They then must prepare reports telling of their findings so that the lawyer can determine the best strategy for the case. If a lawsuit is filed, the paralegal prepares and files necessary documents with the court, helps formulate legal arguments, and assists the lawyer during the trial.

Paralegals working for lawyers in other specialties, such as corporation law, patent law, and tax law, often draw up documents and prepare tax returns.

Many major corporations employ full-time attorneys to handle their legal affairs. Paralegals assist them in tasks such as preparing financial reports, employee contracts, and employee benefit plans.

Other employers of paralegals are government agencies and community legal service projects.

Paralegals working in large law firms often specialize in some area of the law. The duties of paralegals in small or medium-sized law firms often vary from day to day.

Places of employment and working conditions

Most paralegals work for private law firms. Another large employer is the federal government. Some also work for state and local governments. A small number of paralegals work for corporations such as banks, real estate companies, and insurance companies.

Paralegals working for large law firms often work very long hours and are under a great deal of pressure to meet deadlines. Those working for corporations and the government usually work about 40 hours a week.

Entry-level paralegals often become frustrated with their jobs because of the routine tasks they are assigned. However, as paralegals gain experience, they are often given more responsible, challenging tasks.

Qualifications, education, and training

Paralegals must be able to think logically and communicate effectively in both speaking and writing. They must have good research skills and understand legal terminology.

There are no formal educational requirements, but most employers prefer to hire paralegals with training from a four-year college, law school, community or junior college, business school, or proprietary school.

Most formal paralegal programs take two years to complete, but there are some bachelor's-degree programs that last four years. Another type of program can be completed in a few months if the student already has a bachelor's degree.

The course work in paralegal programs includes subjects such as law and legal research, specialized areas of the law, and legal applications for computers. Some programs offer internships that provide valuable practical experience.

Some employers prefer to provide on-the-job training for experienced legal secretaries or for workers with college education but no legal experience.

The National Association of Legal Assistants offers voluntary certification to paralegals who meet certain requirements of education and experience. Paralegals who meet these requirements then take a two-day examination; if they pass it, they earn the title *certified legal assistant* (CLA).

Potential and advancement

There are about 83,000 paralegals. Much growth is expected in this field through the year 2000, but the number of people entering the field is expected to increase significantly; there will be some competition for jobs.

The largest employers will be private law firms, but there will be more opportunities in many types of companies as they begin to realize that paralegals can perform many of the same functions as lawyers at less pay.

As paralegals gain more experience, they advance by being given more responsible, challenging, and interesting tasks. In firms with large staffs, some paralegals become managers or supervisors.

Income

Salaries for paralegals depend on the level of their education and experience, the type of employer, and the geographic location of the job.

Paralegals earn an average annual salary of about $24,900. Beginning paralegals start at an average of $20,900 a year; those with three to five years of experience earn about $24,200; and paralegals with more than ten years of experience average about $28,500.

Many paralegals also receive annual bonuses.

Additional sources of information

American Association for Paralegal Education
P.O. Box 40244
Overland Park, KS 66204

National Association of Legal Assistants, Inc.
1601 South Main Street
Suite 300
Tulsa, OK 74119

National Paralegal Association
P.O. Box 406
Solebury, PA 18963

PAROLE OFFICER

The job

An offender who has completed a sentence in a prison or jail is usually assigned a parole officer upon release. The exoffender is required to report to the parole officer at specific time intervals, and the parole officer, in turn, provides counseling and assistance during the transition from prison to community life.

The parole officer helps the exoffender find a job or secure job training; arranges for welfare or other public assistance for the family, if necessary; and provides positive support and a helping hand in any way possible to aid the parolee in his or her return to society. The parole officer's main concern is helping the parolee go straight instead of returning to a life of crime.

Probation officers deal with juvenile delinquents and first offenders who are often released by the court, subject to proper supervision, instead of being sentenced to jail or prison. A probation officer may also be involved in the presentencing investigation of a defendant's family, background, education, and any problems contributing to the defendant's offense.

Parole and probation officers are usually employed by state or municipal governments. In the course of their work, they deal with teachers, chaplains, social workers, rehabilitation counselors, local employers, and community organizations. A number of parole and probation officers come from the ranks of police officers.

Perhaps the most important ingredient of the work of a probation officer is the rapport the officer is able to establish with the juvenile offender. The opportunity to discuss problems with an understanding adult can result in the juvenile being put back on the right track. At the same time, the probation officer must be objective enough not to be deceived by lies or false promises of better behavior.

Related jobs are police officer (municipal and state), social worker, corrections officer, rehabilitation counselor.

Places of employment and working conditions

Emotional wear and tear is a factor in the work of parole and probation officers. The frustration of seeing a parolee or a juvenile return to a life of crime in spite of great effort is part of every officer's experience.

In many jobs, the caseload itself can be a hindrance to effective work. Instead of carrying the recommended 30 to 50 cases, many parole and probation officers must keep track of up to 100 assigned cases. This makes is virtually impossible to give each person the attention and help that is usually necessary.

Qualifications, education, and training

Personal characteristics of understanding, objectivity, good judgment, and patience are necessary. Good communication skills and the ability to motivate people are very important.

High school should include the social sciences, English, and history.

People who work in this field need a bachelor's degree in sociology, psychology, criminology, or law. Those who start out as police officers usually acquire additional training in these fields through college courses. Many employers also require one or two years of experience in a correctional institution or other social agency or a master's degree in sociology or psychology.

Potential and advancement

Worker shortages in all areas of law enforcement will increase even more as the population grows. The demand for qualified parole and probation officers will be especially great in large metropolitan areas.

Parole and probation officers are not usually promoted to other positions, but they do advance in salary as they gain experience. Some officers advance by acquiring additional education that qualifies them for positions in other areas of law enforcement.

Income

Beginning probation and parole officers earn about $20,000 to $24,000 a year.

Additional sources of information

American Correctional Association
4321 Hartwick Road
College Park, MD 20740

National Council on Crime and Delinquency
77 Maiden Lane
San Francisco, CA 94108

PERSONNEL MANAGER

The job

Personnel managers conduct and supervise the employment functions of a company. These include recruiting, hiring, and training employees; developing wage and salary scales; administering benefit programs; complying with government labor regulations; and other responsibilities that affect the employees.

In a small company, a personnel manager performs all these functions, usually assisted by one or two workers who help with interviewing and perform clerical duties related to the personnel department. In a large company, the personnel manager supervises a staff of trained personnel workers that includes some or all of the following specialists.

A *personnel recruiter* searches for promising job applicants through advertisements and employment agencies. A recruiter may also travel to college campuses to talk to students who are about to graduate. *Employment interviewers* talk to job applicants, sometimes administer and interpret tests, and may make some final hiring decisions.

Job analysts collect and analyze detailed information on each job within a company to prepare a description of each position. These descriptions include the duties of a particular job and the skills and training necessary to perform the job. Position descriptions are used by *salary and wage administrators* when they develop or revise pay scales for a company. They also use information gathered in surveys of wages paid by other local employers or by other companies within the same industry. Wage and salary administrators also work within government regulations such as minimum wage laws.

Training specialists may supervise or conduct orientation sessions for new employees, prepare training materials and manuals, and handle in-house training programs for employees who wish to upgrade existing skills or gain promotion. In some companies, a training specialist may handle details concerning apprenticeship to management trainee programs.

An *employee benefits supervisor* provides information and counseling to employees regarding the various fringe benefits offered by a company. The supervisor is also in charge of the administration of these programs which may include health, life, and disability insurance and pension plans. Other employee services such as cafeterias, newsletters, and recreational facilities are also covered.

Some companies now employ a special personnel worker to handle all matters pertaining to the government's equal employment opportunity regulations and the company's affirmative action programs.

Personnel workers in federal, state, and local government agencies have the added duties of devising, administering, and scoring the competitive civil service examinations that are administered to all applicants for public employment. Others oversee compliance with state and federal labor laws, health and safety regulations, and equal employment opportunity programs.

Personnel specialists also work for private employment agencies, executive search organizations, and office temporaries agencies. A few work as self-employed management consultants, and others teach at the college and university level.

Related jobs are employment counselor and labor relations specialist.

Job opportunities for personnel specialists and personnel managers exist throughout the country with the largest concentrations in highly industrialized areas.

Qualifications, education, and training

Integrity and fairmindedness are important qualifications for those interested in personnel work because they are often called on to act as the liaison between the company and its employees in the day-to-day administration of company policies. Personnel workers must be able to work with people of many educational levels and must have excellent written and oral communications skills.

In high school, a college preparatory course should include emphasis on English and social studies.

Some personnel workers enter the field as clerical workers in a personnel office and gain experience and expertise in one or more specialty areas over a period of time. In some small and medium-sized companies, they may advance to personnel manager positions on the basis of experience alone, but most employers require a college education even for entry-level jobs in personnel.

People in personnel work come from a variety of college majors. Some employers prefer a well-rounded liberal arts background; others want a business administration degree. A few insist on a degree in personnel administration or in industrial or labor relations. Government agencies prefer applicants who have majored in personnel administration, political science, or public administration. Any courses in the social sciences, behavioral sciences, and economics are valuable.

Graduate study in industrial or labor relations is necessary for some top-level jobs in personnel work.

Potential and advancement

About 442,000 people are employed in the overlapping fields of personnel and labor relations. These fields are expected to grow quickly with the largest growth in the private sector as employers try to provide better training and employee relations programs for the growing work force. Slower growth is expected in labor unions and organizations as well as in the area of public personnel administration.

Income

Personnel managers earn a median annual salary of $34,000, with the lowest 10 percent earning under $15,700 and the highest 10 percent earning over $52,000.

Additional sources of information

American Society for Personnel Administration
606 North Washington Street
Alexandria, VA 22314

American Society for Training and Development
1630 Duke Street
Box 1443
Alexandria, VA 22313

International Personnel Management Association
1617 Duke Street
Alexandria, VA 22314

PETROLEUM ENGINEER

The job

Petroleum engineers are responsible for exploring and drilling for oil and gas and for efficient production. Some concentrate on research and development into methods to increase the proportion of oil recovered from each oil reservoir.

Most petroleum engineers are employed by the major oil companies and by the hundreds of small, independent oil exploration and production companies. Drilling equipment manufacturers and suppliers also employ petroleum engineers. Engineering consulting firms and independent consulting engineers use their services, and federal and state agencies employ petroleum engineers on regulatory boards and as inspectors.

Banks and other financial institutions sometimes employ petroleum engineers to provide information on the economic value of oil and gas properties.

Places of employment and working conditions

Most petroleum engineers work in California, Louisiana, Oklahoma, and Texas. Many work overseas for U.S. companies and foreign governments.

This can be dirty work and is sometimes dangerous. Assignments to offshore oil rigs or remote foreign locations can make family life difficult.

Qualifications, education, and training

The ability to think analytically, a capacity for detail, and the ability to work as part of a team are all necessary. Good communication skills are important.

Mathematics and the sciences must be emphasized in high school.

A bachelor's degree in engineering is the minimum requirement in this field. In a typical curriculum, the first two years are spent in the study of basic sciences such as physics and chemistry and mathematics, introductory engineering, and some liberal arts courses. The remaining years are usually devoted to specialized engineering courses. Engineering programs can last from four to six years. Those requiring five or six years to complete may award a master's degree or may provide a cooperative plan of study plus practical work experience with a nearby industry.

Because of rapid changes in technology, many engineers continue their education throughout their careers. A graduate degree is necessary for most teaching and research positions and for many management jobs.

Engineering graduates usually work under the supervision of an experienced engineer or in a company training program until they become acquainted with the requirements of a particular company or industry.

All states require licensing of engineers whose work may affect life, health, or property or who offer their services to the public. Those who are licensed, about one-third of all engineers, are called registered engineers. Requirements include graduation from an accredited engineering school, four years of experience, and a written examination.

Potential and advancement

There are about 17,000 petroleum engineers, and some employment growth is expected in this field. Demand for increased domestic oil and gas resources means increased exploration and production, which will provide job openings for petroleum engineers.

Income

Starting salaries in private industry average $32,016 a year with a bachelor's degree; $34,600 with a master's degree; and $46,600 or more with a Ph.D.

Experienced engineers average $45,777 in private industry.

Additional sources of information

Accreditation Board for Engineering and Technology
345 East 47th Street
New York, NY 10017

American Society for Engineering Education
11 Dupont Circle
Suite 200
Washington, DC 20036

Junior Engineering Technical Society (JETS)
1420 King Street
Suite 405
Alexandria, VA 22314

National Society of Professional Engineers
1420 King Street
Alexandria, VA 22314

Society of Petroleum Engineers
P.O. Box 833836
Richardson, TX 75083-3836

Society of Women Engineers
345 East 47th Street
Room 305
New York, NY 10017

PHARMACIST

The job

Pharmacists dispense drugs and medicines prescribed by physicians and dentists, advise on the use and proper dosage of prescription and nonprescription medicines, and work in research and marketing positions. Many pharmacists own their own businesses.

The majority of pharmacists work in community pharmacies (drugstores). These range from one-person operations to large retail establishments employing a staff of pharmacists.

Hospitals and clinics employ pharmacists to dispense drugs and medication to patients, advise the medical staff on the selection and effects of drugs, buy medical supplies, and prepare sterile solutions. In some hospitals, they also teach nursing classes.

Pharmaceutical manufacturers employ pharmacists in research and development and in sales positions. Drug wholesalers also employ them as sales and technical representatives.

The federal government employs pharmacists in hospitals and clinics of the Veterans Administration and the U.S. Public Health Service; in the Department of Defense; the Food and Drug Administration; the Department of Health, Education and Welfare; and in the Drug Enforcement Administration. State and local health agencies also employ pharmacists.

Many community and hospital pharmacists also do consulting work for nursing homes and other health facilities that do not employ a full-time pharmacist.

Places of employment and working conditions

Just about every community has a drugstore employing at least one pharmacist. Most job opportunities, however, are in larger cities and densely populated metropolitan areas.

Pharmacists average about a 44-hour workweek; those who also do consulting work average an additional 15 hours a week. Pharmacists in community pharmacies work longer hours—including evenings and weekends—than those employed by hospitals and other health care institutions, pharmaceutical manufacturers, and drug wholesalers. Some community and hospital pharmacies are open around-the-clock; pharmacists employed by them may have to work nights, weekends, and holidays.

Qualifications, education, and training

Prospective pharmacists need an interest in medicine and should have orderliness and accuracy, business ability, honesty, and integrity.

Biology and chemistry courses along with some business courses should be taken in high school.

At least five years of study beyond high school are necessary to earn a degree in pharmacy. A few colleges admit pharmacy students immediately following high school, but most require one or two years of prepharmacy college study in mathematics, basic sciences, humanities, and social sciences.

Seventy-four colleges of pharmacy are accredited by the American Council on Pharmaceutical Education. Most of these schools award a bachelor of science (B.S.) or a bachelor of pharmacy (B.Pharm.) degree upon completion of the required course of study. About one-third of the schools also offer an advanced degree program leading to a doctor of pharmacy (Pharm.D.) degree. A few schools offer only the Pharm.D. degree.

A Pharm.D. degree or a master's or Ph.D. degree in pharmacy or a related field is usually required for research, teaching, and administrative positions.

Pharmacists are usually required to serve an internship under the supervision of a registered pharmacist before they can obtain a license to practice. All states require a license and an applicant must usually have: 1) graduated from an accredited pharmacy college; 2) passed a state board of examination; and 3) had a specified amount of practical experience or internship. Many pharmacists are licensed to practice in more than one state, and most states will grant a license without examination to a qualified pharmacist licensed by another state.

Potential and advancement

About 162,000 people work as pharmacists. Job opportunities are expected to be excellent through the year 2000 as the population becomes older and has more pharmaceutical needs. Shortages may even occur in states with high concentrations of the elderly.

Many pharmacists in salaried positions advance by opening their own community pharmacies. Those employed by chain drugstores may advance to management positions or executive-level jobs within the company. Hospital pharmacists may advance to director of pharmacy service or to other administrative positions.

Pharmacists employed by the pharmaceutical industry have the widest latitude of advancement possibilities because they can advance in management, sales, research, quality control, advertising, production, or packaging. There will be fewer job opportunities, however, with manufacturers than in other areas of pharmacy.

Income

Experienced pharmacists working in chain drugstores earn an average of $41,800 a year; those working in independent drugstores earn an average of $38,200 a year; and hospital pharmacists average $42,600 a year.

Additional sources of information

American Association of Colleges of Pharmacy
1426 Prince Street
Alexandria, VA 22314

American Society of Hospital Pharmacists
4630 Montgomery Avenue
Bethesda, MD 20814

National Association of Boards of Pharmacy
1300 Higgins Road
Suite 103
Park Ridge, IL 60068

PHOTOGRAPHER

The job

A photographer takes pictures as an artistic or commercial occupation. Some specialize in portrait photography; others work as photojournalists or industrial photographers. Photographers with knowledge in a special field may specialize in scientific, medical, or engineering photography. Artists who employ photography as an art form have undergone a surge in recent years.

Portrait photographers take pictures of individuals and groups in studios, at weddings, and at other types of gatherings. Many portrait photographers own their own studios and often begin their careers working part-time. These people should have firm business skills to succeed in their own businesses. They must also have a knack for getting people to relax.

Commercial photographers, many of whom work in advertising, photograph everything from livestock to buildings to manufactured articles. They must be familiar with many different photographic techniques.

Industrial photographers work in industry and handle everything from photographs for the company newspaper or stockholders' report to photographs of the company's products or manufacturing processes. Those who specialize in fields such as science or medicine may use special equipment and techniques such as infrared photography, x-rays, or time-lapse photography.

Photojournalists are newspaper and magazine photographers who must have a "nose for news" in addition to photographic skills. Those who work for nationwide publications or prestigious newspapers are among the highest-paid photographers.

Other specialists include *educational photographers,* who prepare slides, filmstrips, and movies for classroom use; *photomicrographers,* who work with microscopes; and *photogrammetrists,* who specialize in the use of aerial photographs for surveying.

Most photographers work in portrait or commercial studios. The next largest group works as photojournalists. Government agencies and industrial firms employ a significant number, and a few photographers teach in colleges and universities. Nearly half of all photographers are self-employed.

Places of employment and working conditions

Photographers work in all areas of the United States.

Those employed in salaried jobs usually work a 35- to 40-hour, five-day week. Those in business for themselves work longer hours. Press photographers usually have to work some evening and weekend hours to cover news assignments. Free-lance, press, and commercial photographers do a great deal of traveling.

Qualifications, education, and training

Good eyesight and color vision, artistic ability, and manual dexterity are necessary for a photographer. Patience, accuracy, and an ability to work with detail are also important.

There are no formal educational requirements in this field, although a high school education does provide a good general background for a photographer. Many would-be photographers acquire their skills through two or three years of on-the-job training in a commercial studio. Technical training, however, is the best preparation and is usually necessary for industrial, medical, or scientific work.

Photographic training is available in colleges, universities, junior colleges, and art schools. The armed forces also train many photographers. Two-year training courses sometimes offer an associate degree in photography. Some colleges offer a bachelor's degree in photography, and a few offer a master's degree in specialized areas such as photojournalism. Art schools provide useful training in design and composition but do not usually offer technical training in photography.

A background in a particular science, medical, or engineering field is necessary for many specialty areas of photography. Some employers may require a bachelor's degree in a particular field in addition to photographic skills and experience. News photographers may be expected to have a background in journalism.

Potential and advancement

There are about 105,000 photographers, and the field is expected to grow over the next decade. Job opportunities will be best in business and industry and in such fields as medicine where technical training and a specialty background are important. Slow growth is expected for portrait or commercial photographers as well as photojournalists.

Advancement usually depends on experience. Some industrial and scientific photographers may be promoted to supervisory positions; magazine and news photographers may eventually become photography editors or heads of graphic arts departments. Self-employed photographers advance as they build a reputation and receive more lucrative assignments. Photographers in salaried positions may open their own studio or do free-lance work.

Income

Photographers who are experienced earn an average salary between $24,600 and $33,800 a year.

Beginning photographers who work for newspapers that have contracts with The Newspaper Guild earn an average of about $385 a week. Those with experience earn an average of $635 a week.

Experienced photographers with the federal government earn about $25,550 a year.

Self-employed and free-lance photographers sometimes earn more than salaried photographers; they often do not. Their earnings are affected by the number of hours they work, the type of clientele, the quality of their work, and their marketing ability.

Additional sources of information

Associated Photographers International
P.O. Box 2172
Chatsworth, CA 91313

Professional Photographers of America, Inc.
1090 Executive Way
Des Plaines, IL 60018

PHOTOGRAPHIC LABORATORY TECHNICIAN

The job

The development of film, preparation of prints and slides, enlarging and retouching of photographs, and other film processing chores are performed by photographic laboratory technicians. They service both the amateur photographer (in labs that mass-process film) and the professional photographer in independent labs or for individual studios.

All-around *darkroom technicians* can perform all tasks necessary to develop and print film including enlarging and retouching. They can handle black-and-white negative, color negative, or color positive work. Since color work is more difficult than black-and-white, some highly skilled technicians specialize as *color technicians*.

Technicians who work in photography studios often function as assistants to the photographer, setting up lights and cameras. Many future photographers begin this way, dividing their time between processing film and learning photography.

In some labs, technicians may be assisted by helpers or assistants who specialize in just one process such as developing or retouching. In large photo labs with automatic film-processing equipment, darkroom technicians supervise semiskilled workers who handle many individual tasks such as film numbering, chemical mixing, or slide mounting.

Places of employment and working conditions

Photographic laboratory technicians are employed in all parts of the country with most job opportunities in large cities.

Photographic laboratory technicians usually work a 40-hour week. In labs that process film for amateur photographers, the summer months and several weeks after the Christmas season require considerable amounts of overtime. Jobs in this field are not physically strenuous, but many of the semiskilled jobs are repetitious and fast paced; some of the processes can cause eye fatigue.

Qualifications, education, and training

Good eyesight and color vision are necessary as well as manual dexterity.

A high school diploma is not always necessary but can provide a good background. Chemistry and mathematics courses are valuable, and any courses, part-time jobs, or amateur photography and film processing work are helpful.

Most darkroom technicians acquire their skills through on-the-job training, which takes about three years. Others attend trade or technical schools or receive their training in the armed forces.

A few junior and community colleges offer a two-year course in photographic technology leading to an associate degree. College-level training is helpful in securing supervisory and management positions.

Potential and advancement

There are about 67,000 people employed in some phase of photographic laboratory work. This job field is expected to grow significantly in spite of the increasing use of automated processing equipment and self-processing cameras. Job opportunities will be good in business and industry and in independent labs that service photographers in specialty fields.

Income

Earnings for photographic process technicians vary according to the worker's level of skill, experience, and geographic location. Median weekly earnings for full-time workers are about $275.

Additional sources of information

Photo Marketing Association International
3000 Picture Place
Jackson, MI 49201

PHYSICAL THERAPIST

The job

At some point in their treatment, accident and stroke victims, handicapped children, and disabled older persons are usually referred by their doctor to a physical therapist. The therapist will design and carry out a program of testing, exercise, massage, or other therapeutic treatment that will increase strength, restore the range of motion, relieve pain, and improve the condition of muscles and skin.

Physical therapists provide direct patient care and usually do their own evaluation of the patient's needs. The physical therapist works, however, in close cooperation with the physician and any other specialists involved in the care of the patient such as vocational therapists, psychologists, and social workers. In large hospitals and nursing homes, physical therapists may carry out a program designed by the director or assistant director of the physical therapy department rather than develop the program themselves. Some physical therapists specialize in one variety of patient such as children or the elderly or one type of condition such as arthritis, amputations, or paralysis.

Most physical therapists work in hospitals. Nursing homes employ a growing number and also use the services of self-employed therapists. Rehabilitation centers, schools for handicapped children, public health agencies, physicians' offices, and the armed forces all employ physical therapists. Some therapists also work with patients in their own homes or provide instructions to the patient and the patient's family on how to continue therapy at home.

Because this field has so many opportunities for part-time practitioners, it appeals to people with family responsibilities.

Places of employment and working conditions

Physical therapists are employed throughout the country, with the largest number working in cities with large hospitals or medical centers.

Since physical therapy, unlike many other medical procedures, does not have to be provided on a 24-hour basis, most therapists work a 40-hour week. In the case of self-employed and part-time therapists, some evening and weekend work may be required.

Qualifications, education, and training

Patience, tact, emotional stability, and the ability to work with people are important for anyone interested in this field. Manual dexterity and physical stamina are also important.

High school students considering this field should take courses in health, biology, social science, mathematics, and physical education. Part-time or volunteer work in the physical therapy department of a hospital can provide a close look at the work for anyone trying to decide on a career in physical therapy.

349

There are two types of programs for physical therapy training: a four-year bachelor's degree in physical therapy or an entry-level master's degree program.

Physical therapists must be licensed. A degree or certificate from an accredited program and a passing grade on a state board examination completes the requirements for obtaining a license.

Potential and advancement

There are about 68,000 licensed physical therapists. Employment in the field is expected to expand rapidly as the demand grows for more rehabilitative facilities for accident victims, the elderly, and handicapped children. Opportunities for part-time work will also continue to grow.

As the number of new graduates in the field catches up with the number of job openings, job competition will probably develop in large population centers. Job opportunities will continue to be good in suburban and rural areas, however.

Advancement in this field depends on experience and advanced education especially for teaching, research, and administration positions.

Income

Newly graduated physical therapists earn about $25,000 a year. Earnings of experienced therapists average about $33,400.

Additional sources of information

American Physical Therapy Association
1111 North Fairfax Street
Alexandria, VA 22314

PHYSICIAN

The job

Physicians diagnose diseases, treat illnesses and injuries, and are involved in research, rehabilitation, and preventive medicine.

Most physicians specialize in a particular field of medicine such as internal medicine, general surgery, psychiatry, or pediatrics. The fastest growing specialty is family practice, which emphasizes general medicine.

Most new physicians open their own offices or join associate or group practices. Those who enter the armed forces start with the rank of captain in the army or air force or lieutenant in the navy. Other federal positions are in the Veterans Administration; the U.S. Public Health Service; and the Department of Health and Human Services.

Places of employment and working conditions

Just about every community has at least one physician.

The northeastern states have the highest ratios of physicians to population; the southern states have the lowest. Physicians tend to locate in urban areas close to hospital facilities and educational centers; rural areas are often underserved.

Many physicians have long and irregular working hours. Specialists work fewer hours than general practitioners. Physicians do have the option of curtailing their practices as they grow older, thus being able to work at a reduced pace past the normal retirement age.

Qualifications, education, and training

Anyone interested in this field must have a strong desire to serve the sick and injured. He or she must have emotional stability and the ability to make quick decisions in an emergency and be able to relate well to people. The study of medicine is long and expensive and requires a commitment to intense, vigorous training.

High school should include as much mathematics and science as possible, and grades should average "B" or above.

Most medical school applicants have a bachelor's degree, although medical schools will accept three years of premedical college study. Competition or entrance into medical school is fierce. Premedical college grades of "B" or better are usually necessary along with a high grade on the Medical College Admission Test (MCAT). Other relevant factors are the applicant's character, personality, and leadership qualities; letters of recommendation; and, in state-supported medical schools, area of residence.

351

It usually takes four years to complete medical school; students with out-standing ability sometimes complete it in three. A few schools have programs that allow completion of premedical and medical studies in a total of six years.

The first half of medical school is spent in classrooms and laboratories studying medical sciences. The remaining time is spent in clinical work under the supervision of experienced physicians. At completion of medical school, students are awarded a doctor of medicine (M.D.) degree.

After graduation, a three-year hospital residency is usually completed. Those seeking certification in a specialty spend up to five years in advanced residency training; this is followed by two or more years of practice in the specialty before the required specialty board examination is taken.

Physicians who intend to teach or do research must earn a master's or Ph.D. degree in a field such as biochemistry or microbiology.

All physicians must be licensed to practice medicine. Requirements usually include graduation from an accredited medical school, completion of a residency program, and a passing grade on a licensing examination—usually the National Board of Medical Examiners (NBME) test. Applicants who have not taken the NBME test must sit for the Federation Licensing Examination that is accepted by all jurisdictions. Physicians licensed in one state can obtain a license in most other states without further examination.

Graduates of foreign medical schools must pass an examination given by the Educational Commission for Foreign Medical Graduates before they are allowed to serve a residency in the United States.

Potential and advancement

There are about 535,000 professionally active physicians in the United States. Employment opportunities should be very good through the year 2000 due to the growing demands for health care. Anticipated increases in the number of medical graduates of existing and new U.S. medical schools, combined with foreign medical graduates, could cause the supply to exceed the demand. This should encourage more physicians to establish practices in areas that have traditionally lacked sufficient medical services such as rural and inner-city areas. An increase in the supply of new physicians will also mean more competition in some specialty fields. Primary care practitioners, such as family physicians, pediatricians, and internal medicine specialists, will continue to be in demand.

Income

Physicians have the highest average annual earnings of any occupational or professional group—about $132,300 a year.

New physicians setting up their own practice usually have a few very lean years in the beginning, but, once a practice is established, earnings rise rapidly. Physicians in a private practice usually earn more than those in salaried positions, and specialists earn considerably more than general practitioners.

Because practitioners in metropolitan areas have much better incomes than those in rural areas, some rural communities offer a guaranteed annual income to a physician who is willing to practice in their area.

Additional sources of information

American Medical Association
535 North Dearborn Street
Chicago, IL 60610

Association of American Medical Colleges
Publications Department
One Dupont Circle, NW
Suite 200
Washington, DC 20036

PHYSICIAN ASSISTANT

The job

Physician assistants, or PAs, relieve primary care physicians of some of their duties. They are trained to perform such medical procedures as taking medical histories, performing physical examinations, making preliminary diagnoses, prescribing treatments, and suggesting medications and drug therapies. In some states, PAs are permitted to prescribe medication.

PAs also treat minor medical problems such as cuts and burns. They provide pre- and postoperative care and sometimes assist in surgery.

PAs work in several medical specialties, including family practice, internal medicine, general and thoracic surgery, emergency medicine, and pediatrics.

Other titles for PAs include MEDEX, surgeon's assistant, child health associate, and physician associate.

Places of employment and working conditions

PAs work in physicians' offices, hospitals, and clinics. Some work in inner city or rural clinics where a physician comes only once or twice a week. The rest of the week, the PA independently provides health care services after consulting with the supervising physician by telephone.

PAs have varying schedules depending on their work setting. Usually they share the same work hours as their supervising physician. If their employer provides 24-hour medical care, they may be required to work nights, weekends, and holidays.

Qualifications, education, and training

PAs should enjoy working with people. Leadership skills, confidence, and emotional stability are also important qualities.

Almost all states require that PAs complete an accredited formal education program. There are currently over 50 educational programs for physician assistants. Most offer a bachelor's degree; others offer a certificate, an associate's degree, or a master's degree.

Admission requirements for many programs include two years of college and work experience in the health field. A number of programs, however, are doing away with requirements for previous work experience.

PA programs are usually two years long. They are offered by medical schools, schools of allied health, and four-year colleges; a few are sponsored by community colleges or hospitals. Coursework includes classroom instruction and supervised experience in clinical practice.

Most states have laws concerning the qualifications or practice of PAs and require them to pass a certifying exam given only to graduates of accredited programs.

Potential and advancement

There are about 48,000 physician assistants. There should be very good opportunities for physician assistants through the year 2000. The health services industry is expected to expand greatly, and PAs will be in demand to relieve doctors of some of their more routine tasks and assist them in more complex medical and surgical procedures.

PAs sometimes advance by taking additional training that allows them to work in a specialty area such as surgery and emergency medicine. Others earn higher salaries and are given more responsibility as they gain experience and increase their knowledge. PAs, though, are always supervised by doctors.

Income

The average starting salary for physician assistants is about $26,500 a year. Experienced physician assistants earn an average annual salary of about $34,000.

Additional sources of information

American Academy of Physician Assistants
950 North Washington Street
Alexandria, VA 22314

American Medical Association
535 North Dearborn Street
Chicago, IL 60610

PHYSICIST

The job

Physicists develop theories that describe the fundamental forces and laws of nature. Most physicists work in research and development. Their work in recent years has contributed to progress in such fields as nuclear energy, electronics, communications, aerospace, and medical instrumentation.

Physicists usually specialize in one branch of the science—elementary particle physics; nuclear physics; atomic, electron, and molecular physics; physics of condensed matter; optics; acoustics; plasma physics; or the physics of fluids.

About 14,000 physicists teach or do research in colleges and universities. Private industry employs about 30 percent of all physicists mainly in companies manufacturing chemicals, electrical equipment, aircraft, and missiles. About 20 percent of all physicists work for the federal government, most of them in the Departments of Defense and Commerce and in the National Aeronautics and Space Administration.

Places of employment and working conditions

Physicists are employed in all parts of the country with the heaviest concentrations in industrial areas and areas with large college enrollments.

Physicists usually work in offices and laboratories. They have regular working hours.

Qualifications, education, and training

An inquisitive mind, imagination, the ability to think in abstract terms, and mathematical ability are necessary for a physicist.

High school courses in science and mathematics are necessary.

A career in physics usually requires a Ph.D. A bachelor's degree in physics or mathematics is usually the first step followed by a master's degree. Some graduate students are able to work as research assistants while they study for a master's degree and may be hired as instructors while completing the Ph.D. requirements.

Potential and advancement

There are about 32,000 physicists. There should be good job opportunities through the year 2000, particularly for physicists with a Ph.D. Most job openings will occur to replace those who retire or leave the field. Those with only a bachelor's degree in physics may become secondary school teachers if they fulfill state teacher certification requirements.

Physicists advance to more complex tasks as they gain experience and may move up to positions as project leaders or research directors; some advance to top management jobs. Physicists who develop new products often form their own companies.

Income

Salaries for physicists start at about $34,700 a year for those with a master's degree and $42,500 a year for those with a Ph.D.

Additional sources of information

American Institute of Physics
335 East 45th Street
New York, NY 10017

American Physical Society
335 East 45th Street
New York, NY 10017

PLUMBER AND PIPEFITTER

The job

Plumbing and pipefitting are usually considered a single trade with workers specializing in one or the other. Plumbers install, repair, and maintain water, gas, and waste disposal systems in homes, schools, factories, and other buildings; pipefitters install high- and low-pressure pipes that carry hot water, steam, and other liquids and gases used in industrial processes.

Plumbers and pipefitters work from blueprints and use a variety of hand and power tools. They glue, solder, or weld pipe connections to prevent leaks and may have to drill holes in ceilings, floors, or walls or hang steel supports from ceilings to position pipes properly.

Most plumbers and pipefitters work for contractors engaged in new construction. A substantial number of plumbers are self-employed or work for contractors who do repair, alteration, and remodeling work in homes and other buildings. Others are employed by government agencies and public utilities, do maintenance work in industrial and commercial buildings, or work in construction of ships and aircraft. Many pipefitters are employed as maintenance personnel in the petroleum, chemical, and food-processing industries.

Places of employment and working conditions

Plumbers and pipefitters work throughout the country in communities of all sizes. The largest concentrations are in heavily industrialized areas, especially those with petroleum, chemical, or food-processing plants.

357

Plumbers and pipefitters often work in cramped or uncomfortable positions and must stand for long periods of time. They are subject to cuts and burns and risk falls from ladders.

Many plumbers and pipefitters belong to the United Association of Journeymen and Apprentices of the Plumbing and Pipe Fitting Industry of the United States and Canada. Those who are contractors usually belong to the National Association of Plumbing-Heating-Cooling Contractors.

Qualifications, education, and training

Mechanical aptitude and physical stamina are necessary for this job field.

A high school diploma is recommended but is not always required. Vocational or technical school training is usually preferred, and courses in chemistry, general mathematics, mechanical drawing, physics, and shop are useful.

Apprenticeship to experienced workers is considered the best way to learn all aspects of the trade. Apprenticeship programs are usually sponsored by local union-management committees. Applicants must be at least 16 years old and are usually given an aptitude test. Those accepted receive four years of on-the-job training and spend about 144 hours each year in related classroom instruction.

Most communities require plumbers and pipefitters to be licensed. This requires a passing grade on an examination covering knowledge of the trade and of local building and plumbing codes.

Potential and advancement

There are about 396,000 plumbers and pipefitters. Job opportunities in this field are expected to be very good through the year 2000. Work should also be steady because plumbing and pipefitting are less sensitive to the ups and downs in construction activity than most other building areas.

Plumbers and pipefitters can advance to supervisory positions. Many prefer to advance by going into business for themselves.

Income

Plumbers and pipefitters have median weekly earnings of $461. Most earn between $318 and $609 a week.

Apprentices begin at about 50 percent of the wage rate paid to experienced plumbers and pipefitters and earn more as they acquire skills.

Additional sources of information

National Association of Plumbing-Heating-Cooling Contractors
P.O. Box 6808
Falls Church, VA 22046

National Fire Sprinkler Association
P.O. Box 1000
Patterson, NY 12563

United Association of Journeymen and Apprentices of the Plumbing and Pipe
  Fitting Industry of the United States and Canada
P.O. Box 37800
Washington, DC 20013

PODIATRIST

The job

The diagnosis and treatment of diseases and deformities of the feet is the special field of podiatrists. They treat corns, bunions, calluses, ingrown toenails, skin and nail diseases, deformed toes, and arch disabilities. If a person's feet show symptoms of medical disorders that affect other parts of the body (such as arthritis or diabetes), the podiatrist will refer the patient to a medical doctor while continuing to treat the patient's foot problem.

In the course of diagnosis, podiatrists may take x-rays and perform blood tests or other pathological tests. They perform surgery; fit corrective devices; and prescribe drugs, physical therapy, and proper shoes.

Most podiatrists provide all types of foot care, but some specialize in foot surgery, orthopedics (bone, muscle, and joint disorders), children's foot ailments, or foot problems of the elderly.

Some podiatrists purchase established practices or spend their early years in a salaried position while gaining experience and earning the money to set up their own practices. Podiatrists in full-time salaried positions usually work in hospitals, podiatric medical colleges, or for other podiatrists. Public health departments and the Veterans Administration also employ both full- and part-time podiatrists, and some serve as commissioned officers in the armed forces.

Places of employment and working conditions

Podiatrists work in all sections of the country but are usually found in or near one of the seven states that have colleges of podiatric medicine.

Most podiatrists are in private practice, work about 40 hours a week, and set their own schedules. They also spend some hours handling the administration and paperwork of their practice. Podiatrists who work for hospitals or HMOs may be required to work nights or weekends. This is not physically strenuous work, a fact that allows practitioners in private practice to work past normal retirement age.

Qualifications, education, and training

Anyone interested in a career as a podiatrist should have scientific aptitude, manual dexterity, and an ability to work with people.

High school courses in mathematics and science are important preparation.

The degree of doctor of podiatric medicine (D.P.M.) is available after successful completion of at least three years of college and four years of a school of podiatric medicine. Competition for entry in these schools is strong and, although three years of college is the minimum requirement, most successful applicants have a bachelor's degree and an overall grade-point average of "B" or better. College study must include courses in English, chemistry, biology or zoology, physics, and mathematics. All schools of podiatric medicine also require applicants to take the Medical College Admission Test (MCAT).

The first two years in podiatry school are spent in classroom and laboratory study of anatomy, bacteriology, chemistry, pathology, physiology, pharmacology, and other basic sciences. In the final two years, students obtain clinical experience. Additional study and experience are necessary for practice in a specialty.

All podiatrists must be licensed. Requirements include graduation from an accredited college of podiatric medicine and passing grades on written and oral state board proficiency examinations. Many states also require a residency in a hospital or clinic. A majority of states grant licenses without examination to podiatrists licensed by another state.

Potential and advancement

There are about 17,000 practicing podiatrists, most of them located in large cities. Employment in this field is expected to grow, and opportunities for graduates to establish new practices or enter salaried positions should be good through the year 2000.

Increasing population, especially the growing number of older people who need foot care and who are covered by Medicare, will contribute to the demand for podiatrists.

Income

Most newly licensed podiatrists set up their own practices and, as in most new practices, earn a great deal less in the early years than they will after a few years in practice. The average yearly income of all podiatrists is about $90,000.

Additional sources of information

American Association of Colleges of Podiatric Medicine
6110 Executive Bouelvard
Suite 204
Rockville, MD 20852

American Podiatric Medical Association
6110 Executive Boulevard
Suite 204
Rockville, MD 20852

POLICE OFFICER, MUNICIPAL

The job

The duties of a police officer may include law enforcement, crowd and traffic control, criminal investigations, communications, and specialties such as handwriting and fingerprint identification or chemical and microscopic analysis. All police officers are trained in first aid.

In a small community, police officers perform a wide variety of duties, while in a large city they may be assigned to one type, such as patrol, traffic, canine patrol, accident prevention, or mounted and motorcycle patrols. Law enforcement is complex and each police force is tailored to meet the particular problems of its own community. A city of any size that has heavy traffic congestion will need more police assigned to accident prevention and traffic control; a city with a high juvenile crime rate will use more officers in criminal investigation and youth aid services.

361

New police officers usually begin a patrol duty with an experienced officer to become thoroughly familiar with the city and its law enforcement requirements. This probationary period can last from a few months to three years in some communities.

All police officers report to police headquarters at regular intervals by radio or telephone or through police call boxes. They also prepare written reports about their activities and may be called upon to testify in court on cases they handle.

Detectives are plain-clothes police officers whose primary activity is to carry out investigative procedures. They are often assigned to a specific case, such as a murder investigation, or a particular type of case, such as illegal drugs. Detectives gather information and evidence to be used by police and prosecuting attorneys.

Places of employment and working conditions

Police officers work throughout the country in communities of all sizes.

The usual workweek of a police officer is 40 hours, including shift work and weekend and evening hours. Payment for extra hours worked on some police forces takes the form of extra time off. Officers must often work outdoors in all kinds of weather and are subject to call at any time.

Police officers face the constant threat of injury or death in their work. The injury rate for police officers is higher than in many other occupations.

Qualifications, education, and training

A police officer should be honest, have a sense of responsibility and good judgment, and enjoy working with people and serving the public. Good health and physical stamina are also necessary.

High school courses should include English, U.S. history, and civics and government. Physical education and sports are very helpful in developing stamina and agility.

Local civil service regulations govern the appointment of police officers in most communities. Candidates must be at least 21 years old, be U.S. citizens, meet certain height and weight standards, and pass a rigorous physical examination. Character traits and backgrounds are investigated, and a personality test is sometimes administered. Applicants are usually interviewed by a senior police officer and, in some police departments, by a psychiatrist or psychologist.

An applicant's eligibility for appointment depends on his or her performance on a competitive examination. Applicants are listed according to their scores on the examination, and when a police department appoints new police officers, it hires the required number of recruits from the top of the list.

Most police departments require a high school education; a few cities require some college training. More and more police departments are encouraging their officers to continue their education and to study subjects such as sociology, psychology, law enforcement, criminal justice, and foreign languages. These courses are available in junior and community colleges as well as four-year colleges and universities.

New police officers go through a training period. In small communities, this may consist of working with experienced officers. Large cities have more formal training programs that last from several weeks to a few months. Officers receive classroom instruction in constitutional law and civil rights, state and local ordinances, accident investigation, patrol, and traffic control. They learn to use a gun, defend themselves from attack, administer first aid, and deal with emergencies.

Experienced police officers improve their performance, keep up-to-date, and prepare for advancement by taking various training courses given at police department academies and colleges. They study crowd-control techniques, civil defense, the latest legal developments that affect police work, and advances in law enforcement equipment.

In some large cities, high school graduates who are still in their teens may be hired as police cadets or trainees. They function as paid civilian employees and do clerical work while they attend training classes. If they have all the necessary qualifications, they may be appointed to the police force at age 21.

Potential and advancement

There are about 440,000 full-time police officers working in communities throughout the United States. All police departments are funded by local governments and, since police protection is considered essential, law enforcement expenses usually have a high priority in municipal budgets. As the population grows, the demand for police officers will also grow. Applicants with some college training in law enforcement will have the best job opportunities.

Advancement in police work depends on length of service, job performance, and written examinations. In some large departments, promotion may also allow a police officer to specialize in one type of police work, such as communications, traffic control, or working with juveniles.

Income

Entry-level salaries are about $20,600 a year. Police officers receive periodic increases until they reach the maximum pay rate for their rank. Average maximum is about $26,700.

Higher rank brings a higher salary and the same periodic increases until maximum. The average starting rate for sergeants ranges from $17,500 in small communities to $35,300 in larger cities.

Police officers are usually covered by liberal plans that allow them to retire after 20 or 25 years of service at half pay. Most police departments furnish revolvers, nightsticks, handcuffs, and other equipment and provide an allowance for uniforms.

Additional sources of information

Information is available from local police departments and civil service commissions.

POLICE OFFICER, STATE

The job

State police officers, sometimes called state troopers, patrol the highways throughout the United States. They enforce traffic laws, issue traffic tickets to motorists who violate those laws, provide information to travelers, handle traffic control and summon emergency equipment at the scene of an accident or other emergency, sometimes check the weight of commercial vehicles, and conduct driver examinations.

In several areas that do not have a local police force, state police officers may investigate crime. They also help city and county police forces to catch lawbreakers and control civil disturbances.

Some officers are assigned to training assignments in state police schools or to investigate specializations such as fingerprint classification or chemical and microscopic analysis of criminal evidence. A few have administrative duties.

Places of employment and working conditions

State police officers often work irregular hours since police protection is provided 24 hours a day. Sometimes they must work weekends and holidays.

State police officers spend most of their time driving in all kinds of weather. They may be involved in dangerous situations and have to risk their lives in the line of duty.

Qualifications, education, and training

Honesty, a sense of responsibility, and a desire to serve the public are important. Physical strength and agility are necessary, and height, weight, and eyesight standards must be met.

High school courses in English, government or civics, U.S. history, and physics are helpful. Physical education and sports develop stamina and agility. Driver education courses or military police training are also valuable.

State civil-service regulations govern the appointment of state police officers. Applicants must be U.S. citizens at least 21 years old and must usually have a high school education. Applicants must pass a competitive written examination, a rigorous physical examination, and a character and background investigation.

Recruits enter a formal training program that lasts for several months. They study state laws and jurisdictions, patrol, traffic control, and accident investigation. They learn to use firearms, defend themselves from attack, handle an automobile at high speeds, and give first aid.

State police recruits serve a probationary period ranging from six months to three years. After gaining some experience, some officers take advanced training in police science, administration, law enforcement, criminology, or psychology. Courses in these subjects are offered by junior colleges, four-year colleges and universities, and special police training institutions including the National Academy of the Federal Bureau of Investigation.

Some states hire high school graduates who are still in their teens to serve as cadets. They study police work and perform nonenforcement duties such as clerical work. If they qualify, they may be appointed to the state police force when they reach 21.

Potential and advancement

There are about 52,000 state police officers. Job opportunities should be good, although investigative specialties are being increasingly handled by civilian specialists.

Promotion depends on the amount of time spent in a rank and the individual's standing on competitive examinations.

Income

Beginning officers average about $20,600 a year. Salaries for experienced officers average about $26,700.

Additional sources of information

State civil-service commissions or state police headquarters, usually located in each state capital, can provide information to anyone interested in a career as a state police officer.

PRIEST

The job

Roman Catholic priests provide spiritual guidance, perform and administer rites and sacraments, and oversee the education of Catholics in the United States.

There are two main classifications of priests. *Diocesan,* or *secular, priests* generally are assigned to a parish by the bishop of their diocese. They work as individuals to provide complete pastoral services for their congregations and are involved in the elementary and secondary schools of their parish and diocese.

Religious priests are part of a religious order such as the Jesuits or Franciscans. They perform specialized work such as teaching or missionary work, which is assigned to them by their superiors in the order. Those involved in education usually work at the high school, college, or university level.

Places of employment and working conditions

There are Catholic priests in nearly every city and town and in many rural areas. The largest concentrations are in metropolitan areas where large Catholic parishes and educational institutions are located.

Working conditions for priests vary greatly. Those assigned to parishes usually work long and irregular hours. Priests are not permitted to marry, and the absence of a family life is a hardship for some priests.

Qualifications, education, and training

As with all members of the clergy, whatever denomination, a deep religious commitment and a desire to serve others are the most important qualifications for a priest. He must also be a model of moral and ethical conduct.

For young men who decide early in life to become priests, high school seminaries provide a college preparatory program.

Preparation for the priesthood requires eight years of study beyond high school. Seminary colleges provide a liberal arts program stressing philosophy and religion, behavioral sciences, history, and the natural sciences. Four additional years are spent in the study of the rites and teachings of the Catholic church and field work.

Potential and advancement

There are about 54,000 priests in the United States. The need for priests is expected to grow along with the growth in population, but the number of ordained priests has traditionally been insufficient to meet the needs of the church and will probably continue to be insufficient.

Newly ordained diocesan priests usually start out as assistants to pastors of established parishes. As they gain experience, they may advance to posts in larger parishes or be assigned to parishes of their own. Some priests advance to administrative positions within the diocese.

Newly ordained religious priests begin work immediately in the specialty for which they are trained. They may advance to administrative positions within their religious order or in the institutions where they work.

Income

The salaries of diocesan priests vary from diocese to diocese and range from $6,000 to about $9,000 a year. Those assigned to a parish live in the parish rectory where all living expenses are paid by the parish and a car allowance is usually provided. Some dioceses also provide group insurance and retirement benefits.

Priests engaged in other than parish work are usually paid at least a partial salary by the institution that employs them. Housing is sometimes also provided.

Religious priests take a vow of poverty and are supported by their religious orders.

Additional sources of information

Young men interested in entering the priesthood should seek the guidance of their parish priest or contact the diocesan director of vocations.

PRINTING PRESS OPERATOR

The job

The preparation, care, and operation of printing presses are the responsibilities of printing press operators. In a small commercial shop, an operator may run simple equipment and learn through on-the-job training; the operator on a giant newspaper or magazine press is a highly trained and experienced worker with several assistants.

The press operator sets up and adjusts the press, inserts type setups or plates and locks them into place, adjusts ink flow, and loads paper—by hand on a small press, with mechanical assistance on a large one. When printing is complete, the press operator or an assistant cleans the press and may oil it and make minor repairs.

Press operators are usually designated according to the type of press they operate: letterpress, gravure, or offset. Offset press operators are further designated as sheet-fed or web-press operators. (Web-fed presses use paper in giant rolls instead of single sheets.) Companies that switch from sheet-fed to web-fed presses must retrain their entire press crew since the two types of presses are very different. Web-fed presses are very large, operate at faster speeds, and require greater physical effort, monitoring of more variables, and faster decisions than sheet-fed presses.

Most printing press operators work for commercial printing shops and newspaper plants. The remainder work for businesses, manufacturers, and other organizations that have their own in-house printing facilities. This includes many federal, state, and local government agencies.

Places of employment and working conditions

Printing press operators work throughout the country, but employment is greatest in large cities.

Pressrooms are noisy, and press operators are subject to the hazards that go with working around machinery. Many printing companies have two or three shifts, and press operators may be required to do a certain amount of shift work; press operators who work for morning newspapers almost always work night shifts. Press operators often stand for long periods, and some presses require lifting of heavy plates and paper.

Qualifications, education, and training

Mechanical aptitude is important for a press operator. Physical strength is needed for some jobs.

High school courses in chemistry and physics are helpful. Printing shop classes can provide valuable experience.

Some printing press operators acquire their skills through on-the-job training or a combination of training and vocational or technical school courses. Many operators, however, complete a formal apprenticeship program.

An apprenticeship lasts from two to five years depending on the press being learned. In addition to receiving on-the-job instruction, the apprentice must complete related classroom or correspondence-course work.

Potential and advancement

There are about 239,000 printing press operators, and the field is expected to grow through the year 2000. Best opportunities in the future will be for offset, gravure, and flexographic operators.

Advancement usually takes the form of learning to operate a more complex press. In large shops, some press operators move up to supervisory positions.

Income

Earnings for printing press operators depend on the type of press on which they work, the area of the country in which they live, and whether they belong to a union. Surveys by the Printing Industries of America show that the average wage for two-color sheet-fed press operators is $16.98 an hour and for four-color sheet-fed press operators, $18.06 an hour.

Additional sources of information

Education Council of the Graphic Arts Industry
4615 Forbes Avenue
Pittsburgh, PA 15213

Graphic Communications International Union
1900 L Street, NW
Washington, DC 20036

Printing Industries of America, Inc.
1730 North Lynn Street
Arlington, VA 22209

PRODUCER/DIRECTOR OF RADIO, TELEVISION, MOVIES, AND THEATER

The job

These two jobs are often combined in actual practice, but this job description will deal with them as separate positions.

The *producer* is the business head of a production. Anyone with a script and a bankroll can be a producer, it has been said, but the successful ones have much more than that. They have taste and discrimination and the ability to raise money from backers.

A producer must be able to estimate production and operating costs, obtain or provide financing, hire a staff and performers, arrange for rehearsal facilities, and handle all other production details. In the theater and movies, producers take an enormous financial risk; radio and television are more stable fields. On any project, the producer is the boss, since he or she controls the purse strings.

The *director* is the unifying force that brings together the diverse talents involved in a production. To some, the director is the most important element. A well-known director can attract top stars and backers to a production on the strength of his or her reputation. A good director is said to be part psychologist and part disciplinarian in his or her handling of the creative, temperamental, and strong-willed people who make up a production. He or she must have a working knowledge of costume, lighting, and design as well as acting. Most directors have at least some experience as actors themselves. The director's ability to bring out the best in the performers, plus his or her interpretation of the script as a whole, usually means the difference between success or failure for a production.

In television and radio, the director's duties are a little different. The selection and scheduling of programs are also part of the director's organizational and administrative duties because many programs come prepackaged and ready for airing.

In the theater, touring shows employ an *advance director.* Because many shows send only the stars and a few other principal players on tour, remaining roles in the cast are filled by local actors. The advance director arrives ahead of time to select and rehearse the local cast and have the production ready when the stars arrive. This is not a very creative type of directing, since all decisions have been made and the director must prepare the cast to duplicate the performances being given in other cities on the tour.

An important position in any production is that of *stage manager (floor manager* in radio and television), who is, in effect, the "executive in charge of operations." The stage manager sees that everyone gets on stage at the right moment, that lighting crews and stagehands operate on cue. The stage manager assigns dressing rooms, handles emergencies of all types, and is sometimes the understudy for one or more roles in a production. Many stage managers start out as actors and, although stage managing is a demanding specialty in its own right, go on to become directors or producers.

Places of employment and working conditions

There are opportunities for producers and directors in large cities throughout the country, but most are concentrated in Boston, Chicago, Houston, Los Angeles, New York City, Philadelphia, and San Francisco—the prime locations of the movie, television, and theater industries.

As with all aspects of the entertainment field, work is not steady. For a producer or a director, the pressures of putting together a new production are enormous. When the production is not a success, the financial and emotional costs can be staggering.

Qualifications, education, and training

A producer has to have business and administrative ability as well as a grasp of what the public wants in the way of entertainment. A director must have artistic talent and good judgment, emotional and physical stamina, a thorough knowledge of techniques and devices, patience, and assertiveness.

There are no educational requirements for either of these positions. In the case of the director, talent is the most important factor combined with experience gathered through years of practice. Many of today's directors, however, received their basic training at a top drama school or college. Many colleges offer programs in dramatic arts that include course work in directing, production, costume, and other related fields, as well as radio and television courses. One big advantage of formal training is the opportunity it provides for an aspiring director to work in college productions.

Producers with an educational background that combines the arts and business administration skills have an advantage in the modern entertainment field.

Potential and advancement

Many opportunities exist in addition to the glamorous jobs at the top of the entertainment field. Community theaters, summer stock, touring shows, industrial shows, and commercial production companies all require producers and directors. Teaching positions are available in colleges, drama schools, and some secondary schools (many require teacher certification). The trend is toward a good solid educational background combined with experience.

All experience is valuable in this field; nothing is irrelevant. Getting a job in almost any capacity of performing or production is important for the beginner. From there, advancement comes through hard work, talent, and being noticed by the right people. A prop manager can work up to stage manager; an experienced actor can branch out into directing. Whatever the job, advancement to better companies, bigger radio or television stations, and working with well-known stars are the marks of progress.

Income

Producers' earnings vary greatly depending, in movies and the theater, on the success or failure of individual productions. Television and radio are the most stable and dependable fields.

Directors have sporadic earnings. Those working on Broadway earn the most—$20,000 for a five-week rehearsal period. Those in summer stock community theaters and touring shows have a wide range of earnings depending on size and caliber of the productions, on average, $500 to $600 a week.

Radio and television provide full-time salaried positions for directors. Earnings depend on the station's size, with major networks paying the highest salaries.

Producers usually receive a percentage of the show's earnings; some get a set fee.

Additional sources of information

Association of Motion Picture and Television Producers
14144 Ventura Boulevard
Sherman Oaks, CA 91403

Producers Guild of America
400 South Beverly Drive
Beverly Hills, CA 90212

PRODUCTION MANAGER, INDUSTRIAL

The job

Production managers coordinate the activities of production departments of manufacturing firms. They are part of middle management, just below corporate, or top-level management, which sets long-range goals and policies.

Production managers carry out the plans of top management by planning and organizing the actual production of company products. They work closely with industrial designers, purchasing managers, labor relations specialists, industrial traffic managers, and production supervisors. Their responsibilities include materials control (the flow of materials and parts into the plant), production control (efficient production processes), and quality control (testing of finished products).

Places of employment and working conditions

Production managers work throughout the country, with the largest concentrations in heavily industrialized areas.

Hours for production managers are often long and irregular. In addition to their regular duties, they spend a great deal of time on paperwork and meetings and are expected to be available at all times to handle problems and emergencies.

Qualifications, education, and training

Strong leadership qualities and communication skills are necessary as well as the ability to work well under pressure.

High school should include mathematics and science courses. A college degree is necessary for almost all jobs at this level. In some small companies, a production supervisor (foreman) or technical worker may occasionally rise through the ranks to production manager, but they usually acquire some college training along the way.

Some companies will hire liberal arts graduates as production managers, but most employers prefer a bachelor's degree or advanced degree in engineering or business administration. A very effective combination is a bachelor's degree in engineering and a master's degree in business administration.

Some companies have management training programs for new graduates. As a trainee, the employee spends several years, usually in several different departments, gathering experience.

Potential and advancement

Demand for production managers will decrease through the year 2000. Best opportunities will be for college graduates who have accumulated experience in a variety of industrial production areas.

Since this is already a high management level, it takes outstanding performance to be promoted to the corporate level; only a very few get to be vice-president of manufacturing. Most production managers advance by moving to a larger company where the responsibilities are greater and more complex.

Income

Salaries vary greatly from industry to industry and also depend on size of plant. Production managers in large plants earn as much as $60,000 a year and receive bonuses based on performance.

Additional sources of information

American Management Association
135 West 50th Street
New York, NY 10020

American Production and Inventory Control Society
500 West Annandale Road
Falls Church, VA 22046

PSYCHIATRIST

The job

A psychiatrist is a medical doctor (physician) who specializes in the problems of mental illness. Because a psychiatrist is also a physician, he or she is licensed to use a wider variety of treatments—including drugs, hospitalization, somatic (shock) therapy—than others who provide treatment for the mentally ill.

Psychiatrists may specialize as to psychiatric technique and age or type of patients treated.

Most psychiatrists are *psychotherapists* who treat individual patients directly. They sometimes treat patients in groups or in a family group.

This is a technique of verbal therapy and may be supplemented with other treatments such as medication. Some psychiatrists are *psychoanalysts* who specialize in a technique of individual therapy based on the work of Sigmund Freud. Psychiatrists who practice this specialty must themselves undergo psychoanalysis in the course of their training. *Child psychiatrists* specialize in the treatment of children.

Some psychiatrists work exclusively in research, studying such things as the effect of drugs on the brain or the basic sciences of human behavior. Others teach at the college and university level. Research and teaching psychiatrists, however, usually combine their work with a certain amount of direct patient care.

In addition to private practice, psychiatrists work in clinics, general hospitals, and private and public psychiatric hospitals. The federal government employs a number of psychiatrists in the Veterans Administration and the U.S. Public Health Service.

Related jobs are psychologist and rehabilitation counselor.

Places of employment and working conditions

Psychiatrists work in all parts of the country, almost always in large metropolitan areas or near universities and medical schools.

This field can be emotionally wearing on the psychiatrist. The shortage of psychiatrists and the increasing demand for psychiatric services means that many practitioners are overworked and often cannot devote as much time as they would like to each individual patient.

The expense and time involved in securing an education for this field deters some people from pursuing psychiatry as a career.

Qualifications, education, and training

More than in any other field, the personality of the psychiatrist is very important. Emotional stability, patience, the ability to empathize with the patient, and a manner that encourages trust and confidence are absolutely necessary. The psychiatrist must be inquisitive, analytical, and flexible in the treatment of patients and must have great self-awareness of his or her own limitations and biases.

A high school student interested in this field should take a college preparatory course strong in science.

After high school, the training of a psychiatrist takes from 12 to 14 years. (Educational requirements for a physician are detailed under that job description).

After receiving an M.D. degree and completing a one-year medical internship in a hospital approved by the American Medical Association (AMA), a prospective psychiatrist begins a three- to four-year psychiatric specialty program. This program must take place in a hospital approved for this purpose by both the AMA and the American Psychiatric Association.

Training is carried on during a residency program that requires study, research, and clinical practice under the supervision of staff psychiatrists. After completion of the program and two years of experience, a psychiatrist is eligible to take the psychiatry examination of the American Board of Neurology and Psychiatry. Successful applicants then receive a diploma from this specialty board and are considered to be fully qualified psychiatrists.

At this point, a psychiatrist who wishes to specialize in child psychiatry must complete an additional two years of training, usually in a children's psychiatric hospital or clinic. A diploma in child psychiatry is then awarded after successful completion of the required examination.

Psychiatrists must also fulfill state licensing requirements before starting the residency period. Licensing requirements are explained in the job description for physician.

Potential and advancement

Job opportunities are excellent for psychiatrists through the year 2000. Although there is currently an oversupply in some areas of the United States, some predict a shortage, especially in areas such as child psychiatry.

Psychiatrists may advance by building their practices. Some become experts in a certain field of psychiatry. Those employed in psychiatric hospitals may advance to administrative positions, and those who teach in colleges and universities may advance through the academic ranks to become full professors.

Income

During training, psychiatric residents receive a salary and are often provided with living quarters; their average annual earnings are about $22,000.

Experienced psychiatrists' earnings are similar to other physicians'. Their average yearly salary is about $85,000, with some who work in private practice earning about $200,000 or more a year.

Additional sources of information

American Medical Association
535 North Dearborn Street
Chicago, IL 60610

American Psychiatric Association
1400 K Street, NW
Washington, DC 20005

PSYCHOLOGIST

The job

Psychologists study the behavior of individuals and groups to understand and explain their actions. Psychologists gather information through interviews and tests, by studying personal histories, and conducting controlled experiments.

Psychologists may specialize in a wide variety of areas. *Experimental psychologists* study behavior processes by working with human beings as well as rats, monkeys, and pigeons. Their research includes motivation, learning and retention, sensory and perceptual processes, and genetic and neurological factors in human behavior. *Developmental psychologists* study the patterns and causes of behavior change in different age groups. *Personality psychologists* study human nature, individual differences, and the ways in which these differences develop.

Social psychologists examine people's interactions with others and with the social environment. Their studies include group behavior, leadership, and dependency relationships. *Environmental psychologists* study the influence of environments on people; *physiological psychologists* study the relationship of behavior to the biological functions of the body.

Psychologists often combine several of these or other specialty areas in their work. They further specialize in the setting in which they apply their knowledge.

Clinical psychologists work in mental hospitals or clinics or maintain their own practices. They provide individual, family, and group psychotherapy programs. *Counseling psychologists* help people with problems of daily life—personal, social, educational, or vocational. *Educational psychologists* apply their expertise to problems in education while *school psychologists* work with students and diagnose educational problems, help in adjustment to school, and solve learning and social problems.

Others work as *industrial and organizational psychologists* (personnel work), *engineering psychologists* (human-machine systems), and *consumer psychologists* (what motivates consumers).

About 19,000 psychologists work in colleges and universities as teachers, researchers, administrators, or counselors. Most of the rest work in hospitals, clinics, rehabilitation centers, and other health facilities. The remainder work for federal, state, and local government agencies, correctional institutions, research firms, or in private practice.

Related jobs are psychiatrist, rehabilitation counselor, guidance counselor, marriage counselor, and social worker.

Places of employment and working conditions

Psychologists work in communities of all sizes. The largest concentration are in areas with colleges and universities.

Working hours for psychologists are flexible in general. Their specialties, however, determine their schedules. Clinical and counseling psychologists, for example, often work in the evening to accommodate the work and school schedules of their patients.

Qualifications, education, and training

Sensitivity to others and an interest in people are very important as are emotional stability, patience, and tact. Research requires an interest in detail, accuracy, and communication skills.

High school preparation should emphasize science and social science skills.

A bachelor's degree in psychology or a related field such as social work or education is only a first step, because a Ph.D. is the minimum requirement for employment as a psychologist. Those with only a bachelor's degree will be limited to jobs as research or administrative assistants in mental health centers, vocational rehabilitation offices and correctional programs, government, or business. Some may work as secondary school teachers if they complete state certification requirements.

Stiff competition for admission into graduate psychology programs means that only the most highly qualified applicants are accepted. College grades of "B" or higher are necessary.

At least one year of graduate study is necessary to earn a master's degree in psychology. Those with a master's degree qualify to work under the supervision of a psychologist and collect and analyze data and administer and interpret some kinds of psychological tests. They may also qualify for certain counseling positions such as school psychologist.

Three to five years of additional graduate work are required to earn a Ph.D. in psychology. Clinical and counseling psychologists need still another year or more of internship or other supervised experience. Some programs also require competence in a foreign language.

A dissertation based on original research that contributes to psychological knowledge is required of Ph.D. candidates. Another degree in this field is the Psy.D. (doctor of psychology). Acquisition of this degree is based on practical work and examinations rather than a dissertation.

The American Board of Professional Psychology awards diplomas in clinical, clinical neuropsychology, counseling, forensic, industrial and organizational, and school psychology. Candidates must have a Ph.D. or Psy.D., have five years of experience, pass an examination, and provide professional endorsements.

State licensing and certification requirements vary but usually require a Ph.D. or Psy.D., one to two years of professional experience, and a written examination.

Potential and advancement

There are about 104,000 people working as psychologists. Employment in this field is expected to grow, but opportunities will be best for those with doctoral degrees.

Traditional academic specialties such as experimental, physiological, and comparative psychology will provide fewer job opportunities than the applied areas of school, clinical, counseling, health, industrial, and engineering psychology.

Income

Median salaries for experienced psychologists with doctoral degrees are in educational institutions, $42,100; in state and local governments and hospitals and clinics, $40,000; in nonprofit organizations, $34,500; and in business and industry, $60,100.

Additional sources of information

American Psychological Association
Educational Affairs Office
1200 17th Street, NW
Washington, DC 20036

PUBLIC RELATIONS WORKER

The job

Building, maintaining, and promoting the reputation and image of an organization or a public figure constitute the work of public relations specialists. They use their skills in sales promotion, political campaigns, and many other fields.

A large corporation employs public relations workers to present the company in a favorable light to its various audiences—its customers, employees, stockholders, and the community where the company is located. A college or university uses its public relations staff to present an image that will attract students. A government agency explains its work to the public by means of public relations specialists.

Public relations workers also have the opposite duty—to keep their employers aware of the attitudes of their various publics. For example, a public relations specialist working for a manufacturing firm located in a city neighborhood might advise the company that nearby residents blame the company for parking and traffic problems in the area. Resulting company efforts to provide more employee parking facilities or to reschedule deliveries and shipments to off-peak traffic hours would then be well publicized to improve the relations between the company and its nearby public.

In small businesses, one person may handle all public relations functions, including writing press releases and speeches for company officials, placing information with various newspapers or radio stations, representing the employer at public functions, or arranging public appearances for the employer. On a large public relations staff, a *public relations manager* would be assisted by many different specialists, each handling a single phase of publicity. In some companies, public relations functions are combined with advertising or sales promotion work.

Many public relations specialists work for consulting firms that provide services for clients on a fee basis. Others work for nonprofit organizations, advertising agencies, and political candidates. Those who work for government agencies are often called *public information specialists.*

Related jobs are advertising account executive, advertising manager, advertising worker, and newspaper reporter.

Places of employment and working conditions

Public relations specialists are found in organizations of all kinds and in all areas of the country. Public relations consulting firms, however, are concentrated in large metropolitan areas. Over half are located in New York City, Los Angeles, Chicago, and Washington, D.C.

The usual workweek in this field is 35 to 40 hours, but attendance at meetings and community affairs can often mean overtime or evening hours. In some assignments, a public relations specialist may be on call at all times or may be required to travel for extended periods while accompanying a client such as a political candidate or other public figure.

Qualifications, education, and training

Self-confidence, enthusiasm, assertiveness, an outgoing personality, and imagination are necessary characteristics for success in public relations. The ability to motivate people, an understanding of human psychology, and outstanding communications skills are also necessary.

High school courses should emphasize English—especially writing skills. Any courses or extracurricular activities in public speaking or writing for school newspapers are valuable as are summer or part-time jobs for radio or television stations or newspapers.

A college degree in journalism, communications, or public relations is the usual preparation for this field. Some employers prefer a degree in a field related to the firm's business—science, engineering, or finance, for example— plus course work or experience in public relations or communications. Some firms especially seek out college graduates who have work experience in one of the news media, which is how many writers, editors, and newspaper reporters enter the public relations field.

The Public Relations Society of America accredits public relations specialists who have worked in the field for at least five years. Applicants for this professional designation must pass a comprehensive six-hour examination that includes five hours of written and one hour of oral examination.

Job applicants in this field at all levels of experience are expected to present a portfolio of public relations projects on which they have worked.

Potential and advancement

About 91,000 people work in public relations. Because this is a glamorous and popular field, competition for jobs is stiff. Over the long run, job opportunities are expected to increase substantially, but general economic conditions can cause temporary slow periods when companies delay expansion or cut public relations budgets. Job applicants with solid academic backgrounds plus some media experience will have the best job opportunities.

Advancement usually takes the form of handling more demanding and creative assignments or transferring to a larger company. Experienced public relations specialists often start their own consulting firms.

Income

Experienced full-time public relations workers earn a median annual salary of $45,000.

Experienced public relations specialists earn the highest salaries in large organizations with extensive public relations programs. Median annual salaries for various other employers and positions are the federal government, $36,300 a year; social services and nonprofit organizations, $32,000 a year; industrial organizations, $60,000 a year.

Additional sources of information

PR Reporter
P.O. Box 600
Exeter, NH 03833

Public Relations Society of America, Inc.
33 Irving Place
New York, NY 10003

Service Department
Public Relations News
127 East 80th Street
New York, NY 10021

PURCHASING AGENT

The job

Purchasing agents buy the raw materials, products, and services a company needs for its operation. They coordinate their buying schedules with company production schedules so that company funds will not be tied up unnecessarily in materials ordered too soon or in too large a quantity.

In small companies, a *purchasing manager,* assisted by a few purchasing agents and expediters, handles all aspects of buying. Large companies employ many purchasing agents, with each one specializing in one item or in a group of related items.

Beginners in this field function as junior purchasing agents, ordering standard and catalog items until they gain enough experience to handle more difficult assignments.

Over one-fourth of all purchasing agents work in manufacturing industries. Others are employed by government agencies, construction companies, hospitals, and schools.

Related jobs are retail buyer, traffic manager, and production manager.

Places of employment and working conditions

Purchasing agents work in all sections of the country but are concentrated in heavily industrialized areas.

They usually work a standard 40-hour workweek but may have longer hours during peak production periods if they work in a seasonal industry.

Qualifications, education, and training

A purchasing agent must be able to analyze numbers and technical data to make responsible buying decisions. The person must have a good memory for details and be able to work independently.

High school should include mathematics and science; business courses are also helpful.

Small companies sometimes promote clerical workers or technicians into purchasing jobs or hire graduates of two-year colleges. Most companies, however, require at least a bachelor's degree in liberal arts or business administration with course work in purchasing, accounting, economics, and statistics. Companies that produce complex products such as chemicals or machinery may prefer a degree in science or engineering with an advanced degree in business administration.

Regardless of their educational background, beginners usually undergo an initial training period to learn the company's operating and purchasing requirements and procedures. Successful purchasing agents keep up with developments in their field through participation in seminars offered by professional societies and by taking courses at local colleges and universities.

In private industry, the recognized mark of experience and professional competence is the designation certified purchasing manager (CPM) conferred by the National Association of Purchasing Management, Inc. In government agencies, the designation is certified public purchasing officer (CPPO), which is conferred by the National Institute of Governmental Purchasing, Inc. Both have educational and experience standards and require a series of examinations.

Potential and advancement

There are about 458,000 purchasing agents; growth in this field is expected. Job opportunities will be good in the future, especially for those with graduate degrees in business administration or a bachelor's degree in science, engineering, or business administration with some course work in purchasing. Graduates of two-year programs will find the best opportunities with small firms.

Purchasing agents can advance to purchasing manager and to executive positions such as director of purchasing or materials management. Some advance by moving to larger companies with more complex purchasing requirements.

Income

Beginning salaries approximate $21,000 a year.

Experienced purchasing agents average $27,000 to $35,500. Purchasing managers in private industry average about $42,400.

Additional sources of information

National Association of Purchasing Management, Inc.
P.O. Box 22160
Tempe, AZ 85285

National Institute of Governmental Purchasing, Inc.
115 Hillwood Avenue
Falls Church, VA 22046

R

RABBI

The job

Rabbis are the spiritual leaders of their congregations and teachers and interpreters of Jewish law and tradition. They conduct religious services, preside at weddings and funerals, and provide counseling. There are four main types of congregations—Orthodox, Conservative, Reform, and Reconstructionist. Customs and rituals may vary among them, but all congregations preserve the substance of Jewish religious worship.

Rabbis also serve as chaplains in the armed forces, work in the many Jewish social service agencies, and teach in colleges and universities.

Newly ordained rabbis usually begin as leaders of small congregations, assistants to experienced rabbis, or directors of Hillel Foundations on college campuses.

Places of employment and working conditions

Rabbis serve Jewish congregations in communities throughout the country. Those states with large Jewish populations have the highest concentrations of rabbis—New York, California, Pennsylvania, New Jersey, Illinois, Massachusetts, Florida, Maryland, and Washington, D.C.

Depending on the size of the congregation and the number of assistants a rabbi has, his or her working hours can be very long and are often irregular.

Qualifications, education, and training

As do all clergy, rabbis must have a deep religious faith and a desire to serve people. Their ethical and moral conduct must be of the highest order.

Educational requirements vary depending on the branch of Judaism. College is required by most branches as a preparation before entering a seminary. The seminary training lasts from three to five years and includes the study of the Bible and Talmud, Jewish history, pastoral psychology, and public speaking.

Potential and advancement

There are about 2,500 rabbis serving Jews in the United States. Approximately 850 are Orthodox; 800, Conservative; 800, Reform; and 65, Reconstructionist.

There will be good opportunities for rabbis in all branches of the religion, and they will generally be best in nonurban areas, especially in smaller communities in the South, Midwest, and Northwest.

Income

Average annual earnings for rabbis range from $30,000 to $80,000.

Additional sources of information

Anyone considering this vocation should discuss his or her plans with a practicing rabbi. Information is also available from the following:

Hebrew Union College—Jewish Institute of Religion (Reform)
1 West Fourth Street, New York, NY 10012; or 3101 Clifton Avenue,
Cincinnati, OH 45220; or 3077 University Mall, Los Angeles, CA 90007

The Jewish Theological Seminary of America (Conservative)
3080 Broadway
New York, NY 10027

The Rabbi Isaac Elchanan Theological Seminary (Orthodox)
2540 Amsterdam Avenue
New York, NY 10033

Reconstructionist Rabbinical College
Church Road and Greenwood Avenue
Wyncote, PA 19095

RADIO/TELEVISION ANNOUNCER

The job

Radio announcers act as disc jockeys, present the news, do commercials, and present other types of material. They may work from prepared scripts or do ad-lib commentary. In small stations, they may also operate the control board, write commercial and news copy, and sell radio advertising time.

Television announcers and radio announcers at large radio stations usually specialize in a particular field such as sports or news. They use written scripts and may do their own research and writing in some instances.

Some announcers work on a free-lance basis, selling their services for individual assignments to networks, advertising agencies, and independent producers.

Places of employment and working conditions

Radio announcers are employed throughout the country in radio stations of all sizes. Television announcers do not have such a wide distribution but are concentrated in large metropolitan areas where most television studios operate.

Announcers often work irregular hours such as during early-morning commuting time or late at night. In small stations, announcers often put in up to 12 hours a week in overtime. Since many stations operate 24 hours a day, seven days a week, all announcers do their share of evening, weekend, and holiday duty.

Qualifications, education, and training

A pleasant speaking voice, good command of the English language, a dramatic flair, and an interest in sports, music, and current events are necessary in this field.

High school courses should include writing, public speaking, and English. Extracurricular involvement in acting, sports, and music is helpful.

A college liberal arts background is excellent for a radio or television announcer. Some colleges and universities offer courses in the broadcasting field, and students may also gain valuable experience by working on the campus radio station.

A number of private broadcasting schools offer training in announcing, but these should be checked out with local broadcasters and Better Business Bureaus before enrolling.

Potential and advancement

There are about 57,000 announcers employed by radio and television broadcasting stations. The popularity of this field plus its relatively small size mean stiff competition for jobs. The best opportunities for beginners exist in small radio stations; television stations usually hire only experienced announcers.

Announcers usually work in several stations in the course of their careers. As they gain experience, announcers advance by moving to larger stations, to stations in larger cities, or to network jobs. Others advance by getting their own program or by developing a specialty such as sportscasting or news reporting.

Income

Salaries in broadcasting vary widely, depending on whether the work is in television or radio, commercial or public broadcasting, and the size of the market.

Salaries in radio are generally lower than in television. Experienced radio announcers earn an average of about $20,000 a year, with salaries ranging from $11,000 in the smallest markets to $51,000 for on-air personalities, $45,000 for sports reporters, and $39,000 for news announcers in the largest markets.

TV news anchors average $56,000 a year, with salaries ranging from $22,000 in the smallest markets to $204,000 in the largest. Weathercasters average $43,000, and sportscasters average $40,000.

Additional sources of information

Broadcast Education Association
1771 N Street, NW
Washington, DC 20036

National Association of Broadcasters
1771 N Street, NW
Washington, DC 20036

RADIOLOGIC (X-RAY) TECHNOLOGIST

The job

In the medical field, x-ray pictures (radiographs) are taken by radiologic technologists who operate x-ray equipment. They usually work under the supervision of a radiologist—a physician who specializes in the use and interpretation of x-rays.

There are three specialties within the field of radiologic technology; a radiologic technologist works in all three areas.

The most familiar specialty is the use of x-ray pictures to study and diagnose injury or disease to the human body. In this specialty, the technologist positions the patient and exposes and develops the film. During fluoroscopic examinations (watching the internal movements of the body organs on a screen or monitor), the technologist prepares solutions and assists the physician.

The second specialty area is nuclear medicine technology—the application of radioactive material to aid in the diagnosis and treatment of illness or injury. Working under the direct supervision of a radiologist, the technologist prepares solutions containing radioactive materials that will be absorbed by the patient's internal organs and show up on special cameras or scanners. These materials trace the course of a disease by showing the difference between healthy and diseased tissue.

Radiation therapy—the use of radiation-producing machines to provide therapeutic treatments—is the third specialty. Here, the technologist works under the direct supervision of a radiologist, applying the prescribed amount of radiation for a specified length of time.

During all these procedures, the technologist is responsible for the safety and comfort of the patient and must keep accurate and complete records of all treatments. Technologists also schedule appointments and file x-rays and the radiologist's evaluations.

About three-fifths of all radiological technologists work in hospitals. The remainder work in medical laboratories, physicians' and dentists' offices, federal and state health agencies, and public school systems.

Places of employment and working conditions

Radiologic technologists are found in all parts of the country in towns and cities of all sizes. The largest concentrations are in cities with large medical centers and hospitals.

Full-time technologists usually work a 40-hour week. Those employed in hospitals that provide 24-hour emergency coverage have some shift work or may be on call. There are potential radiation hazards in this field, but careful attention to safety procedures and the use of protective clothing and shielding devices provide protection.

Qualifications, education, and training

Anyone considering this career should be in good health, emotionally stable, and able to work with people who are injured or ill. The job also requires patience and attention to detail.

A high school diploma or its equivalent is required for acceptance into an x-ray technology program. Programs approved by the Committee on Allied Health Education and Accreditation are offered by many hospitals, medical schools affiliated with hospitals, colleges and universities, vocational and technical schools, and the armed forces. The programs vary in length from one to four years; a bachelor's degree in radiologic technology is awarded after completion of the four-year course.

These training programs include courses in anatomy, physiology, patient care procedures, physics, radiation protection, film processing, medical terminology and ethics, radiographic positioning and exposure, and department administration.

Although registration with the American Registry of Radiologic Technologists is not required for work in this field, it is an asset in obtaining highly skilled and specialized positions. Twenty-five states require radiologic technologists to be licensed.

Potential and advancement

There are about 132,000 radiological technologists at the present time. Employment in this field, as in all medical fields, is expected to expand rapidly because of the importance of this technology to diagnosing and treating disease.

In large x-ray departments, technologists can advance to supervisory positions or qualify as instructors in x-ray techniques. There is more opportunity for promotion for those having a bachelor's degree.

Income

Starting salaries in hospitals and medical centers average about $18,408 a year. Experienced technologists average about $24,552.

Sick leave, vacation, insurance, and other benefits are usually the same as other employees in the same institution receive.

Additional sources of information

American Society of Radiologic Technologists
15000 Central Avenue, SE
Albuquerque, NM 87123

RANGE MANAGER

The job

Range managers are specialists in grazing management. They plan the optimum combination of animals, size of herds, and conservation of vegetation and soil for maximum production without destroying the ecology of an area. Their work also involves timber production, outdoor recreation, erosion control, and fire prevention.

Most range managers work for the federal government in the Forest Service, Soil Conservation Service, and the Bureau of Land Management. State governments employ range managers in fish and game agencies, land agencies, and extension services.

Private firms that employ range managers include coal and oil companies and large livestock ranches. United Nations agencies and foreign governments also employ American range managers.

Places of employment and working conditions

Most range managers work in the West and in Alaska.

Outdoor work is usual for range managers, and locations are often remote. They sometimes spend long periods away from home.

Qualifications, education, and training

Good physical condition, love of the outdoors, and scientific interest are necessary. Communication skills are also important.

High school should include as many science courses as possible.

Thirty-five colleges and universities offer degree programs in range management or range science; others offer some course work in this field. A degree in a related field such as forestry or agronomy is accepted by some employers. Studies include biology; chemistry; physics; mathematics; plant, animal, and soil sciences; and ecology. Electives in economics, computer science, forestry, wildlife, and recreation are desirable.

Graduate degrees in range management are usually necessary for teaching and research positions.

Potential and advancement

Job opportunities should be more plentiful than in the past because of numerous retirements and fewer graduates in this field. There will be slow growth in this field due to government budget cuts. More range managers will be needed in private industry.

Income

Starting salaries range from $15,700 to $34,600, depending on education and experience.

Experienced range managers earn about $30,000 a year.

Additional sources of information

Bureau of Land Management
Denver Service Center
Federal Center Building 50
Denver, CO 80255

Society for Range Management
1839 York Street
Denver, CO 80206

REAL ESTATE AGENT/BROKER

The job

The sale and rental of residential and commercial properties are handled by real estate agents and brokers. If they belong to the National Board of Realtors, brokers are called realtors; agents are realtor-associates. They also appraise, manage, or develop property. Some combine a real estate business with an insurance agency or law practice.

Real estate brokers employ *real estate salesworkers,* or *agents,* to show and sell properties. Most real estate businesses sell private homes and other residential property. Some specialize in commercial or industrial property or handle farms and undeveloped land.

Before a property can pass from the seller to the buyer, a title search must be made to prove that there is no doubt about the seller's right to sell the property. This abstract of title is performed by an *abstractor* or an abstract company. The abstract is a condensed history of the property which includes current ownership chain of title (ownership); description of the property; and, in chronological order, all transactions that affect the property. These include liens, mortgages, encumbrances, tax assessments, and other liabilities. Abstractors work for real estate firms, title insurance companies, and abstracting companies or may be self-employed.

Agents obtain listings (properties to sell) by signing an agreement with the seller giving the agent and the real estate firm the right to represent the seller in disposing of the property. It is the agent's responsibility to locate a buyer by advertising and showing the property to interested people. If the buyer requests it, the real estate agent may help locate mortgage funds. In cases where the seller's asking price is higher than the buyer is willing to pay, the agent often acts as a negotiator to bring the sale to a successful conclusion. Agents also are present at closing when the property actually changes hands.

A successful real estate agent must be well versed in all local information relative to the type of real estate sold. An agent selling houses must know local

395

tax and utility rates and the availability of schools, shopping facilities, and public transportation. A commercial or industrial property agent must be able to provide information on taxes, marketing facilities, local zoning regulations, the available labor market, and nearby railroad and highway facilities.

Most real estate salespeople are employed in relatively small businesses. Some large real estate firms employ several hundred agents in many branch offices, but five to ten persons is the usual number employed by a single real estate business. Many agents sell real estate on a part-time basis.

Brokers are independent business owners who are responsible for all business matters relating to the firm's function. Some brokers operate a one-person firm, doing all the selling themselves. A related job is real estate appraiser.

Places of employment and working conditions

Real estate agents and brokers work throughout the country in communities of all sizes.

The working hours of real estate agents and brokers are irregular, and evening and weekend hours are the norm. These persons spend a great deal of time on the phone obtaining listings and are also responsible for the paperwork on the sales they handle.

Qualifications, education, and training

A pleasant personality, neat appearance, and tact are necessary qualities for a successful real estate agent. Sales ability along with a good memory for names and faces are very important.

Some real estate brokers prefer to hire college graduates with a degree in real estate or business, but most will hire high school graduates with sales ability.

All states and the District of Columbia require agents and brokers to be licensed.

A college degree is not necessary to obtain a license, but most states require at least 30 hours of classroom instruction. Local colleges, adult education programs, and correspondence schools offer the courses necessary to obtain a license, and many prospective real estate agents hold down a full-time job while studying to be a real estate agent. Many brokers hire real estate students as office assistants or rent collectors while they are preparing for the state licensing exam, but others hire only those who have already obtained a license.

Some colleges and universities offer an associate's or bachelor's degree with a major in real estate; several offer advanced education courses to agents and brokers.

A prospective agent must be 18 years old, a high school graduate, and pass a written test on real estate transactions and state laws regarding the sale of real estate to complete the licensing requirements.

Candidates for a broker's license must complete 90 hours of formal training, have a specified amount (usually one to three years) of real estate selling experience, and pass a more comprehensive exam. Some states waive the experience requirements if the candidate has a bachelor's degree in real estate.

Potential and advancement

There are about 422,000 licensed real estate agents and brokers in the United States. The employment outlook is good, and beginners will find it relatively easy to find a job. But anyone entering real estate should be aware that it is difficult to earn enough to be self-supporting when working on commission.

In large real estate firms, experienced agents can advance to sales manager or general manager. Experienced sales workers often obtain a broker's license and go into business for themselves. Others go into property management or appraising. Many successful agents prefer to continue selling because the financial awards are very good.

Income

When property is sold, the seller pays a percentage to the broker. The agent who sells the property receives part of that fee, usually about 50 percent, as a commission.

Earnings vary, but agents average about $18,000 a year. Experienced brokers earn about $41,000 a year.

Some real estate brokers provide their sales workers with fringe benefits such as life and health insurance.

Additional sources of information

National Association of Realtors
430 North Michigan Avenue
Chicago, IL 60611

REAL ESTATE APPRAISER

The job

A real estate appraiser studies and evaluates information about a property and estimates its market value. A written appraisal is then prepared to document the findings and conclusions.

An appraisal is usually required whenever a property is sold, insured, or assessed for taxation. Mortgage lenders require an appraisal as do federal, state, and local governments when acquiring property for public use. Insurance companies require an appraisal when determining the proper amount of insurance on a property.

An appraiser must be familiar with public records and their location, be able to read blueprints and mechanical drawings, recognize good and bad construction materials, and be up-to-date on building zoning laws and government regulations. Appraisers usually specialize in one type of property such as farms, single-family dwellings, industrial sites, or apartment houses.

Appraisers often enter the field from other jobs in real estate sales or management, but more and more are entering the field directly. Those with a college education have the greatest chance of success. Beginners in appraisals usually start as appraisal assistants or trainees.

Opportunities for beginners exist in local assessors' offices and in federal, state, and city departments. Local independent appraisers also offer part-time and full-time work to beginners and college students studying real estate appraisal.

A related job is real estate agent/broker.

Places of employment and working conditions

Appraisers work in all areas of the country in towns and cities of all sizes wherever property is bought, insured, or taxed.

Much of an appraiser's time is spent away from the office inspecting properties and researching records. Independent appraisers set their own working hours but frequently work evenings and weekends to meet client deadlines. Appraisers who work in salaried positions usually have more regular working hours.

Appraisers spend varying amounts of time in travel if they evaluate property in other areas or in other countries. These appraisers are usually involved in appraising industrial and commercial property or property for investment.

Qualifications, education, and training

An appraiser must have the highest standards of personal integrity and honesty and should possess good communication skills, both written and oral. An appraiser also needs good health and stamina because this is a physically demanding job.

Many private firms, financial institutions, and government agencies will hire only appraisers who have a college degree. Many colleges and universities offer programs in real estate and in real estate appraising. Other relevant courses are economics, finance, business administration, architecture, law, and engineering.

Appraisers may obtain professional recognition by working toward designations awarded by an organization. These designations are awarded by the American Institute of Real Estate Appraisers, the Society of Real Estate Appraisers, and the American Society of Appraisers.

The federal government is requiring that appraisers of most types of real estate be licensed or certified by July 1, 1991. State licensing requirements must meet federal standards, but they are permitted to be more stringent than federal standards. Work experience and a passing score on a written examination are needed for certification.

Potential and advancement

This is a good job opportunity field because there is expected to be an increased demand for home purchases and rental units. However, real estate appraising is affected by the swings in the economy. During times when the economy is weak, the earnings of appraisers decline, and many are forced to leave the occupation.

Income

Beginning real estate appraisers often work on a free-lance basis and are paid by the job. They earn about $20,000 a year. More experienced real estate appraisers earn between $35,000 and $50,000 a year.

Additional sources of information

Contact your local Board of Realtor office or state real estate commission for specific requirements in your area. Information is also available from:

American Institute of Real Estate Appraisers
430 North Michigan Avenue
Chicago, IL 60611

National Association of Realtors
430 North Michigan Avenue
Chicago, IL 60611

RECREATION WORKER

The job

Physical fitness has become very important in today's culture, and people have more leisure time to devote to exercise and sports. There is a wide variety of opportunities and work settings for recreation workers—those who coordinate physical activity and sports programs that meet these needs.

Organized recreation programs can be found in a wide variety of settings: schools, churches, synagogues, nursing homes, corporations, playgrounds, health clubs, and primitive wilderness areas. In each of these settings, recreation workers organize and oversee programs that meet the needs of the people they serve. Different types of activities that recreation workers plan are arts, crafts, fitness, and sports.

Some recreation workers plan activities for vacationers at theme parks and tourist attractions. Others are employed by companies to develop programs for their employees, such as bowling and softball leagues and fitness and exercise programs. Recreation workers are also employed at camps, where they teach campers sports such as swimming, hiking, and horseback riding. Instructing, coaching, and maintaining recreation centers are recreation workers' primary responsibilities.

Places of employment and working conditions

Most jobs for recreation workers are in urban areas, where most people live. Jobs in camping are usually found in heavily populated states.

The average workweek for recreation workers is 35 to 40 hours. Recreation workers often have irregular hours, including nights and weekends. Much of a recreation worker's time is spent outdoors, sometimes in poor weather conditions. Recreation work can be tiring, and recreation workers are subject to injuries.

Qualifications, education, and training

Recreation workers must be enthusiastic, able to motivate people, and sensitive to people's needs.

Educational requirements vary according to the type of job. Part-time, summer jobs usually require only a high school diploma, while supervisory or administrative jobs may require a bachelor's or graduate degree.

About 200 junior and community colleges offer associate's degrees in parks and recreation, and 300 colleges and universities offered bachelor's, master's, and Ph.D. park-and-recreation programs. There is a demand for college graduates with experience in commercial recreation and tourism, and many colleges are offering specializations in these fields.

Usually a college degree and experience is necessary for those advancing to supervisory or administrative positions.

Potential and advancement

There are about 186,000 recreation workers, and many more who work only during the summer. This field is expected to grow through the year 2000 as more people become interested in fitness and health and have the money to purchase recreational services. Also, there is a growing demand for recreational services for senior citizens and people with disabilities.

The best opportunities will be in the commercial recreation industry and in social services. Because of budget cuts, there will be fewer opportunities working for local governments. There is a great deal of competition for full-time positions. Temporary seasonal jobs will offer the best opportunities.

Recreation workers who wish to advance to supervisory or administrative positions should have experience and formal training in recreation as well as college courses in business management, personnel management, and accounting.

Income

Recreation workers employed full-time earn a median annual salary of about $14,300. Camp directors average about $380 a week. Seasonal employees at camps earn an average of between $95 and $175 a week.

Additional sources of information

American Association for Leisure and Recreation
1900 Association Drive
Reston, VA 22091

National Recreation and Park Association
Division of Professional Services
3101 Park Center Drive
Alexandria, VA 22302

YMCA National Office
101 North Wacker Drive
Chicago, IL 60606

REHABILITATION COUNSELOR

The job

Rehabilitation counselors work with mentally, physically, and emotionally disabled persons to help them become self-sufficient and productive. Many counselors specialize in one type of disability, such as the mentally retarded, the mentally ill, or the blind.

In the course of designing an individual rehabilitation program, the counselor may consult doctors, teachers, and family members to determine the client's abilities and the exact nature of the handicap or disability. He or she will, of course, also work closely with the client. Many counselors discuss training and career options with the client, arrange specialized training and specific job-related training, and provide encouragement and emotional support.

An important part of a counselor's work is finding employers who will hire the disabled and the handicapped. Many counselors keep in touch with members of the local business community and try to convince them to provide jobs for the disabled. Once a person is placed in a job, the rehabilitation counselor keeps track of the daily progress of the employee and also confers with the employer about job performance and progress.

The amount of time spent with an individual client depends on the severity of the person's problems and the size of the counselor's case load. Counselors in private organizations can usually spend more time with their clients than those who work for state and local agencies. Less-experienced counselors and counselors who work with the severely disabled usually handle the fewest cases at one time.

Most rehabilitation counselors are employed by state or local rehabilitation agencies. Others work in hospitals or sheltered workshops or are employed by insurance companies and labor unions. The Veterans Administration employs psychologists who act as rehabilitation counselors.

Related jobs are employment counselor, psychologist, and social worker.

Places of employment and working conditions

Rehabilitation counselors work throughout the country with the largest concentrations in metropolitan areas.

A 40-hour workweek is usual, but attendance at community meetings sometimes requires extra hours. A counselor's working hours are not all spent in the office but include trips to prospective employers, training agencies, and client's homes.

The work of a counselor can be emotionally exhausting and sometimes discouraging.

Qualifications, education, and training

Anyone considering this field should have emotional stability, the ability to accept responsibility and to work independently, and the ability to motivate and guide other people. Patience is also a necessary characteristic of a rehabilitation counselor because progress often comes slowly over a long period of time.

High school courses in the social sciences should be a part of a college preparatory course.

A bachelor's degree with a major in education, psychology, guidance, or sociology is the minimum requirement. This is sufficient for only a few entry-level jobs.

Advanced degrees in psychology, vocational counseling, or rehabilitation counseling are necessary for almost all jobs in this field.

Most rehabilitation counselors work for state and local government agencies and are required to pass the appropriate civil service examinations before appointment to a position. Many private organizations require counselors to be certified; this is achieved by passing the examinations administered by the Commission on Rehabilitation Counselor Certification.

Potential and advancement

Employment opportunities are expected to be very good, but, since most job openings are in state and local agencies, the employment picture will depend to a great extent on government funding for such services.

Experienced rehabilitation counselors can advance to supervisory and administrative jobs.

Income

Beginning salaries range from $350 to $500 a week. Rehabilitation counselors at the highest level of experience earn nearly twice that amount.

Additional sources of information

American Rehabilitation Counseling Association
5999 Stevenson Avenue
Alexandria, VA 22304

National Rehabilitation Counseling Association
633 South Washington Street
Alexandria, VA 22314

RESPIRATORY THERAPIST

The job

Respiratory therapists provide treatment for patients with cardiorespiratory problems. Their role is important and the responsibilities are great.

These therapists' work includes giving relief to chronic asthma and emphysema sufferers; emergency care in cases of heart failure, stroke, drowning, and shock; and treatment of acute respiratory symptoms in cases of head injuries, poisoning, and drug abuse. They must respond swiftly and start treatment quickly because brain damage may occur if a patient stops breathing for three to five minutes, and lack of oxygen for more than nine minutes almost invariably results in death.

In addition to respiratory therapists, the field includes *respiratory technicians* and *respiratory assistants.*

Therapists and technicians perform essentially the same duties, with therapists having greater responsiblity for supervision and instruction.

Assistants have little contact with the patients; their duties are usually limited to cleaning, sterilizing, and storing the respiratory equipment used by therapists and technicians.

Respiratory therapists and technicians work as part of a health care team following doctors' instructions. They use special equipment and techniques—respirators, positive-pressure breathing machines, and cardiopulmonary resuscitation (CPR)—to treat patients. They are also responsible for keeping records of materials costs and charges to patients and maintaining and making minor repairs to equipment. All respiratory therapy workers are trained to observe strict safety precautions in the use and testing of respiratory equipment to minimize the danger of fire.

Most respiratory therapists, technicians, and assistants work in hospitals in respiratory, anesthesiology, or pulmonary medicine departments. Others work for nursing homes, ambulance services, and oxygen equipment rental companies.

Places of employment and working conditions

Respiratory therapy workers are employed in hospitals throughout the country in communities of all sizes. The largest number of job opportunities exists in large metropolitan areas that support several hospitals or large medical centers.

Respiratory therapy workers usually work a 40-hour week and may be required to work evenings, nights, or weekends. Respiratory therapists spend much of their working time on their feet and experience a great deal of stress. They must be careful when working with gases, and they run the risk of catching an infectious disease.

Qualifications, education, and training

Anyone interested in entering this field should enjoy working with people and have a patient and understanding manner. The ability to follow instructions and work as a member of a team is important. Manual dexterity and some mechanical ability are necessary in the operation and maintenance of the sometimes complicated respiratory therapy equipment.

High school students interested in this field should take courses in health, biology, mathematics, physics, and bookkeeping.

Formal training in respiratory therapy is necessary for entering the field. There are about 255 institutions that offer programs approved by the Committee on Allied Health Education and Accreditation (CAHEA). All these programs require a high school diploma. Courses vary from two to four years and include both classroom and clinical work. Students study anatomy and physiology, chemistry, physics, microbiology, and mathematics. A bachelor's degree is awarded to those completing a four-year program, with an associate degree awarded from some of the shorter programs.

Some respiratory therapists are *registered respiratory therapists* (RRTs). They obtain this designation by completing an examination of the National Board for Respiratory Care and meeting education and experience requirements.

Respiratory technicians can receive certification as a *certified respiratory therapy technician* (CRTT) if they have completed a CAHEA-approved technician training program and have one year of experience. They must pass a single written examination. All respiratory technicians are certified as CRTTs.

Potential and advancement

There are currently about 56,000 respiratory therapists. The field is growing rapidly. Growth of health care services in general and the expanding use of respiratory therapy and equipment by hospitals, ambulance services, and nursing homes make this a good job opportunity area, as more and more respiratory specialists are hired to release nurses and other personnel from respiratory therapy duties.

Advancement in this field depends on experience and additional education. Respiratory assistants can advance to the technician or therapist level by completing the required courses; technicians can advance by achieving certification or completing education and testing requirements for the therapist level.

Respiratory therapists can be promoted to assistant chief or chief therapist. With graduate study they can qualify for teaching positions.

Income

Starting salary for respiratory therapists in hospitals and medical centers is about $19,632 a year; experienced therapists earn an average of $25,764 a year.

Additional sources of information

American Association for Respiratory Care
11030 Ables Lane
Dallas, TX 75229

The National Board for Respiratory Care, Inc.
11015 West 75th Terrace
Shawnee Mission, KS 66214

RETAIL BUYER

The job

Every item carried in every store has been selected by a retail buyer. The owner of a small retail business functions as a retail buyer when ordering the store's merchandise; but large retail stores or chains of stores employ professionally trained buyers to make decisions and purchases involving thousands, and sometimes millions, of dollars. The difference between a retail buyer and a purchasing agent is in the ultimate use of what they buy. The buyer purchases goods for resale; the purchasing agent buys materials to be used by his or her firm.

This is an exciting, fast-paced, often nerve-wracking job. The buyer must order merchandise that will satisfy the store's customers, sell at a profit, and move on and off the store's shelves within a reasonable time. With clothing and a number of other items, this means seasonally. Buyers must be familiar with manufacturers and distributors, be aware of fashion trends and local customer preferences, and work within the budget allotted for a particular store or department. They must be able to stock the basics as well as take advantage of unexpected good buys or fad items.

Buyers work closely with sales workers to keep up with customer likes and dislikes, and they study and analyze past store sales records and market research reports. They must be aware of the merchandise and prices of competitors and keep track of economic conditions in the area where their customers live.

Some buyers are assisted by junior buyers who handle routine chores such as verifying shipments. Junior buyers may also be involved in sales and often take part in store training programs.

Merchandise managers coordinate all the buying and selling activities of a large store or chain. The merchandise manager decides what merchandise to stock, devises the budget, and assigns different buyers to purchase certain items or lines of goods. Merchandise managers are also involved in sales promotion.

Places of employment and working conditions

About two-thirds of all buyers and merchandise managers work for retail stores. Although buyers are found in all parts of the country, most job opportunities are in cities and large metropolitan areas such as New York City, Chicago, and Dallas.

Buyers often work more than 40 hours a week. Depending on the store's location and the type of merchandise being purchased, a buyer might travel as little as four or five days a month or might spend one-third of his or her working time in travel. Some buying trips are glamorous—to Paris, for example, for a showing of ladies' fashions—while most are routine but fast paced.

Qualifications, education, and training

If you are interested in this field, you must be able to stand the pace and the pressure. You must be a good planner and able to make decisions, have good leadership and communication skills, and be assertive.

Many buyers have worked their way up the ladder from sales or stockroom positions. Others attend junior and four-year colleges that offer degree programs in marketing and purchasing. Many trade schools offer courses in fashion merchandising.

More and more employers are requiring college training, especially those who include buyers in their management of executive training programs. Most employers will accept applications from almost any field of college study and consider courses or experience in merchandising, fashion, sales, or business a plus.

The formal training programs in retail stores usually last several years and include classroom instruction combined with rotating assignments to various jobs and departments. The buyer trainee's first job will probably be as assistant or junior buyer.

Potential and advancement

There are about 207,000 buyers and merchandise managers working for retail firms. Job opportunities in this field will grow slowly through the next decade with most openings occurring to replace those who leave the field. Increasing use of computers for inventory control and reordering merchandise will also limit employment growth in the coming years.

This is a popular career field, and competition for available openings will be keen. College graduates with courses or experience in relevant areas will have the best chance of securing choice positions.

It takes years of experience as a buyer to advance to the position of merchandise manager. A few experienced buyers and merchandise managers can also advance to top executive positions in store or chain management, but these positions are limited by the size and growth of the company.

Income

Salaries depend on the product line purchased, sales volume of the store, and seniority. Discount department stores, mass merchandising firms, and large department store chains offer the highest salaries. Most buyers earn between $17,420 and $35,412 a year.

Buyers often earn large bonuses for exceptional performance and are included in store incentive plans such as profit sharing and stock options.

Additional sources of information

National Retail Merchants Association
100 West 31st Street
New York, NY 10001

RETAIL SALES WORKER

The job

Whether they sell computers, food, furniture, or clothing, retail sales workers' main objective is to convince the customer to purchase their merchandise. They accomplish this by showing how the product works, how it is made, and by making customers aware of the variety of options they have. Retail sales workers who sell more complex products such as computers and software must have special skills and knowledge so that they can answer customers' questions in a clear, helpful manner.

Retail sales workers also make out sales checks; receive payment by cash, check, or charge; and give change and receipts. They are often responsible for the contents of their cash register, and, depending on when they are scheduled to work, they may have to count the money in the cash drawer and separate it from charge slips, coupons, and exchange vouchers. They may have to deposit the money with the cash office.

Retail sales workers must know store procedures on returns and exchanges. They also have to be knowledgeable of the store's security practices.

Some retail stores offer customer services such as gift wrapping; sales workers provide these services. During slow periods, retail sales workers may have to stock shelves or racks, arrange displays, take inventory, or price items.

Places of employment and working conditions

Every town and city has retail stores; jobs are distributed in much the same way as the population.

Most retail sales jobs are part-time, but employees often are scheduled to work during the evening and on weekends. During the Christmas season, hours are usually longer and vacation time is restricted.

Qualifications, education, and training

Retail sales workers must be friendly and courteous, have a neat appearance, be able to communicate well, and enjoy working with people.

There are no formal education requirements for retail sales workers. In small stores, an experienced worker or the manager or owner trains new employees in the store's sales procedures. Large stores often have a formal training program for beginners. Trainees are taught how to perform cash, check, and credit transactions as well as procedures for returns and special orders.

Some workers may be given specialized training if they are selling certain types of products. For example, workers selling appliances may be given instruction on the types of products available and the differences between them.

Potential and advancement

There are currently nearly 4.6 million retail sales workers, and opportunities are expected to be excellent through the year 2000. There is very high turnover in this field, and retail sales are expected to grow.

Adverse economic conditions slow sales and reduce the demand for sales workers. However, because the turnover rate is so high, layoffs are unlikely.

As employees gain experience and achieve sales success, they are often moved into positions with higher potential for earnings. Even though a college education is becoming increasingly important for obtaining managerial or administrative positions, capable workers are still often promoted to these jobs. In small stores, promotion opportunities are limited.

Income

Earnings for retail sales workers vary depending on the type of product they sell. Beginners are usually paid minimum wage.

Some sales workers are paid salary plus commission, and others are paid either by salary or by commission.

Additional sources of information

National Retail Merchants Association
100 West 31st Street
New York, NY 10001

RETAIL STORE MANAGER

The job

The manager of a retail store, whether the store is large or small, has one goal—to operate the store at a profit. To this end the manager applies years of accumulated training and experience.

Retailing is one of few remaining fields where talented and hardworking people can still advance all the way to the top regardless of education. Several career paths are possible including sales work, merchandise and fashion buying, advertising, accounting, and personnel relations. Those who reach the level of store manager usually have experience in several of these areas.

Four major tasks are involved in the operation of a retail store: merchandising (buying and selling), store operations (staffing, shipping, and receiving), accounting, and advertising. In a small store, the manager handles all of these. The manager of a large store might handle one or two of these areas personally and assign assistant managers to supervise the others. In some stores, the manager provides overall supervision and policy making while employing four or more division heads to oversee specific functions. In chain stores, centralized buying and accounting relieves the individual store managers of these two responsibilities.

Related jobs are retail buyer, purchasing agent, wholesaler, advertising manager, and personnel manager.

Places of employment and working conditions

This is a highly competitive field, and the store manager is under constant pressure to increase the store's sales volume. Many managers work 50 or more hours a week.

Managers employed by chain stores may be required to move frequently, especially during their early years with the company.

Qualifications, education, and training

Good judgment, tact, administrative ability, a feeling for what the public wants to buy, good communication skills, and the ability to deal with all types of people are necessary for a store manager.

High school should include mathematics, English, and social sciences; distributive education programs, where available, provide an excellent background. Part-time or summer jobs in retail stores are good experience.

Education requirements in this field vary greatly. Some large stores and many chain stores will accept high school graduates into the management training programs. Many large employers require a college degree in liberal arts, marketing, accounting, or business administration. Top positions in some stores require a master's degree in business administration.

Potential and advancement

Growth in retailing is expected to accompany the growth in population, creating substantial job opportunities through the year 2000. Positions in large independent stores will be the most competitive, but entry-level jobs in retailing will be numerous.

Regardless of educational background and career path within retailing, advancement to the top positions requires years of experience and a record of success at each level. When the store-manager level is achieved, sales volume figures become the deciding factor in the manager's career. Increased sales can mean promotion to field manager or transfer to a more desirable store in a chain store operation or the opportunity to work for a larger independent store.

Income

Trainees earn between $15,000 and $19,500 a year.

Experienced store managers earn from $19,500 to $31,000 or more. Many also receive bonuses or participate in profit-sharing plans, based on store sales volume.

Additional sources of information

National Retail Merchants Association
100 West 31st Street
New York, NY 10001

S

SAFETY ENGINEER

The job

The specific duties of safety engineers (also called occupational safety and health specialists) vary depending on where they work. In general, they are responsible for the safe operation of their employer's facilities and for the physical safety of the employees. They inspect, advise, and train.

In a large manufacturing plant, a safety engineer might develop a comprehensive safety program covering thousands of employees. This would include making a detailed analysis of each job, identifying potential hazards, investigating accidents to determine causes, designing and installing safety equipment, establishing safety training programs, and supervising employee safety committees.

In a trucking company, a safety engineer inspects heavy rigs such as trucks and trailers; checks out drivers for safe driving practices; and studies schedules, routes, loads, and speeds to determine their influence on accidents. In a mining company, a safety engineer inspects underground or open pit areas for compliance with state and federal laws, designs protective equipment and safety devices and programs, and leads rescue activities in emergency situations.

Safety engineers are also concerned with product safety. They work with design engineers to develop products that meet safety standards and monitor manufacturing processes to ensure the safety of the finished product.

Other occupational safety and health specialists work as *fire protection engineers* who safeguard life and property from fire, explosion, and related hazards. Some specialists research the causes of fires and the flammability of different building materials. Others identify hazards and develop protective measures and training programs. They work for fire equipment manufacturers, insurance rating bureaus, and consulting firms. Some are specialists in sprinkler or fire-detection systems.

Industrial hygienists detect and remedy industrial problems that affect the health of workers. They monitor noise levels, dust, vapors, and radioactivity levels. Some work in laboratories and study the effects of various industrial substances on humans and air and water. They work with government regulatory agencies, environmental groups, and labor organizations as well as plant management.

Loss control consultants and *occupational health consultants* work for property-liability insurance companies. The services they provide include inspecting the premises for safety violations and giving advice, designing safety training programs, and designing plant health and medical programs. They also work with the insurance company's underwriters to assess risks and develop premium schedules.

Related jobs are claim representative, engineering and science technician, environmentalist, firefighter, industrial designer, and underwriter.

Places of employment and working conditions

Safety engineers and other occupational and health specialists work throughout the country with the largest concentration in heavily industrialized areas.

These jobs are usually very active and often entail climbing and other strenuous activities in the course of inspections or emergency situations. A great deal of travel is involved for some workers, expecially those who work as consultants for insurance companies.

Qualifications, education, and training

Safety engineers and other safety and health specialists must have good communications skills and be able to motivate people. They should get along well with people and be able to deal with them effectively at all levels—from company president to production line worker. They should be assertive and have good judgment. Good physical condition is important.

A college preparatory course should be taken in high school with emphasis on mathematics and science.

Graduates of two-year colleges are sometimes hired to work as technicians in this field, but most employers require at least a bachelor's degree in science or engineering. Some prefer a more specialized degree in a field such as industrial safety, safety management, or fire protection engineering or graduate work in industrial hygiene, safety engineering, or occupational safety and health engineering.

Technological advancements make continuing education a necessity in this field. Many insurance companies offer training seminars and correspondence courses; the Occupational Safety and Health Administration conducts courses in occupational injury investigation and radiological health hazards.

After having successfully completed examinations and the required years of experience, specialists in occupational health and safety may achieve certification from their respective professional societies. These designations include certified safety professional; certified industrial hygienist; and member, Society of Fire Protection Engineers.

Potential and advancement

Employment of occupational safety and health specialists is expected to grow slowly. Most job openings will occur in manufacturing and industrial firms.

In large companies, advancement to top-level management is possible for experienced occupational safety and health specialists.

Income

Beginning salaries range from $19,000 to $20,000 a year. Experienced workers earn $30,000 to $38,000; corporate-level executives earn $55,000 or more.

Additional sources of information

American Society of Safety Engineers
1800 East Oakton Street
Des Plaines, IL 60016

American Industrial Hygiene Association
475 Wolf Ledges Parkway
Akron, OH 44311

Society of Fire Protection Engineers
60 Batterymarch Street
Boston, MA 02110

SALES MANAGER

The job

The title of sales manager means different things in different companies. In general, a sales manager is responsible for supervising a firm's sales staff.

Depending on a company's size and management structure and the level of responsibility of the sales manager, this could mean only the day-to-day co-ordination of the activities of sales workers, branch managers, and sales training programs; or it could mean a corporate-level position that entails setting company marketing policy and sales goals. The sales manager may be responsible for a staff of five salespeople or for a marketing department employing hundreds of people.

Readers should refer to the separate job descriptions for sales positions that appear throughout this book.

See also *advertising salesperson, engineer, import/export worker, insurance agent and broker, manufacturer's sales representative, office manager, pharmacist, purchasing agent, real estate agent/broker, securities sales worker, travel agent, and wholesaler.*

SCHOOL ADMINISTRATOR

The job

School administrators have the responsibility of running the various schools and school systems in the United States. Their duties depend on whether they work at the state or local level, whether they work in a public or parochial school system or private school, and their area of responsibility.

At the state level, a *superintendent of schools* or *director of education* oversees the functioning of the public school systems and state colleges with the state. The superintendent is responsible for setting and enforcing minimum standards for schools and teachers, administering teacher certification programs, and administering whatever state and federal funds are provided for education.

At the local level, a superintendent of schools is appointed by a local public school board or by a parochial school system to administer an individual school system. The system may consist of just a few schools or many schools. The superintendent hires and supervises all personnel; prepares the school budget; is responsible for physical maintenance of buildings and equipment; makes projections for future needs; and oversees curriculum and textbook decisions, purchasing, public transportation, and many other details. The superintendent's job is often a thankless one—the local school board and citizens, on one hand, trying to keep taxes down and teachers trying to provide the best education possible for the students on the other. It is the superintendent, working to appease both groups, who usually gets the blame for everything.

The superintendent is usually assisted by various other administrators who handle special areas. *Special-subject supervisors* coordinate the activities and curriculum of a specific subject area throughout all the schools in the system. The most common special areas are music, art, remedial reading, physical education, libraries, and business or technical education. *Special-education supervisors* plan and supervise the instruction of handicapped students and, in school systems that provide them, handle programs for gifted students as well.

A *curriculum director* evaluates the subjects and activities included in the curricula of the schools within the school system and makes recommendations to teachers and other administrators.

Within an individual school, the *principal* is responsible for the day-to-day operation of the school. The principal must operate within a budget, be both an educator and a business manager, develop and maintain a good working relationship with teachers and students, handle discipline, and oversee building maintenance.

In a private school, the principal is often called a *headmaster* or *headmistress*. If the school also provides residence facilities for its students, the headmaster has additional responsibilities besides those of a school principal. Living quarters, food, laundry, recreation facilities, and "substitute parent" functions would then be part of the headmaster's duties as well.

Places of employment and working conditions

School administrators function under constant pressure, especially at the highest levels. Frustration is often part of the job, and administrators must face the fact that they are often resented by the very people they work to serve.

Hours for most administrators are long and irregular. Evening meetings and civil functions often push the total up to 50 or 60 hours or more a week.

Qualifications, education, and training

An interest in the development of children, the ability to get along with people, communication and business skills, patience, tact, and good judgment are all necessary.

The first step in this career field is a degree in teaching or education. (See the job descriptions for teachers elsewhere in this book for educational requirements at the elementary, secondary, and college levels.)

Graduate study in educational administration is necessary for most administrative positions. A master's degree is the minimum requirement; top-level positions in large schools or school systems usually require a Ph.D.

Potential and advancement

There are about 320,000 school administrators at the present time. Employment will grow, but there will be stiff competition for all jobs in this field. Those persons who combine the appropriate educational credentials with wide experience will have the best chance of securing the choice jobs at all levels.

Advancement in this field may be from teacher up through the ranks in a single school system or may take the form of moving to a larger school system. Administrators in middle-level positions in large systems often advance by securing top-level positions in small school systems or private schools.

Income

Earnings vary widely depending mainly on the size and location of the school system, level of responsibility, and experience.

The median annual salary for full-time school administrators is $35,000 a year. Those in the middle of the salary range earn between $23,000 and $45,000.

Additional sources of information

American Association of School Administrators
1801 North Moore Street
Arlington, VA 22209

National Education Association
1201 16th Street, NW
Washington, DC 20036

SECRET SERVICE AGENT

The job

The U.S. Secret Service is part of the Department of the Treasury and employs special agents and uniformed officers.

Special agents have both protective and investigative responsibilities. Their primary responsibility is the protection of the president of the United States. They also protect the vice-president, the president-elect and vice-president-elect, a former president and his wife, the widow of a former president until her death or remarriage, minor children of a former president until age 16, major presidential and vice-presidential candidates, and visiting heads of foreign states or foreign governments.

Special agents also work to suppress counterfeiting of U.S. currency and securities and investigate and arrest people involved in forging and cashing government checks, bonds, and securities. All special agents must qualify for both protective and investigative assignments.

The Secret Service Uniformed division employs *uniformed officers* to provide protection for the president and his immediate family while they are in residence at the White House. Previously called the White House Police, their duties have been expanded to include protection of the vice-president and his immediate family, the White House and grounds, the official residence of the vice-president in Washington, D.C., buildings in which presidential offices are located, and foreign diplomatic missions located in the metropolitan Washington, D.C., area or such other areas of U.S. territories and possessions as the president may direct.

Uniformed officers carry out their responsibilities through foot and vehicular patrols, fixed posts, and canine teams.

Treasury security force officers are also a part of the Secret Service Uniformed division. They are responsible for security at the main treasury building and the treasury annex and for security of the office of the secretary of the treasury. They have investigative and special arrest powers in connection with laws violated within the treasury building including forgery and fraudulent negotiation or redemption of government checks, bonds, and securities.

Related jobs are FBI special agent, CIA worker, and police officer.

Places of employment and working conditions

Special agents may be employed at Secret Service headquarters in Washington, D.C., or at one of over 100 field offices and residential agencies throughout the United States. Uniformed officers and treasury security force officers work in Washington, D.C.

Special agents must be willing to work wherever they are assigned and are subject to frequent reassignment. Because the protective responsibilities of the Secret Service go on around the clock, all agents and officers perform some shift work.

Qualifications, education, and training

Each of these three Secret Service jobs has separate physical and educational requirements. All, however, require a comprehensive background investigation and top-secret security clearance.

Applicants for *special agent* appointments must be less than 35 years of age at the time of entrance to duty; be in excellent physical condition and pass a rigorous medical examination; have weight in proportion to height; and distance vision, uncorrected, of 20/20 in one eye and no less than 20/30 in the other.

Applicants must have a bachelor's degree in any major field of study, or three years' experience of which at least two are in criminal investigation, or a comparable combination of experience and education. A passing grade on the Treasury Enforcement Agent Examination, administered by area offices of the United States Civil Service Commission, is a prerequisite for consideration.

Only a limited number of the most qualified applicants reach the interview stage. They are rated on personal appearance, bearing and manner, ability to speak logically and effectively, and ability to adapt easily to a variety of situations. Applicants who achieve appointment must be prepared to wait an extended period of time for a vacancy to occur; it is usually during this period that background investigations are completed.

Once active duty begins, special agents receive general investigative training at the Federal Law Enforcement Training Center in Brunswick, Georgia, and specialized training at Secret Service facilities in Washington, D.C. They study protective techniques, criminal law, investigative procedures and devices, document and handwriting examination and analysis, first aid, use of firearms, and arrest techniques. They also receive on-the-job training. Advanced in-service training programs continue throughout an agent's career.

Uniformed officers must be U.S. citizens, have vision of at least 20/40 in each eye (correctable to 20/20), have weight in proportion to height, and pass a comprehensive physical examination. They must have a high school diploma or equivalent or one year of experience as a police officer in a city of over 500,000 population. Applicants must pass a written examination and an in-depth personal interview and have a valid driver's license.

Uniformed officers undergo a period of training at Secret Service facilities in Beltsville, Maryland, and Brunswick, Georgia. They study legal procedures in law enforcement, first aid, community relations, self-defense, and the use and care of firearms. Additional on-the-job training takes place after assignment.

Potential and advancement

From time to time the service may actively recruit for a specific job category, but, for the most part, job opportunities are limited. The extremely high public interest in this work means that only the most highly qualified applicants are considered for appointment. Even after acceptance, special agents must wait until a vacancy occurs before they begin active service.

Promotion depends on performance and the needs of the Secret Service.

Income

Special agents start at about $15,700 or $19,500 a year. Experienced agents start at $34,600 a year, and supervisory agents start at $41,100.

Additional sources of information

The nearest area office of the U.S. Civil Service Commission can supply information on examination schedules.

United States Secret Service
Personnel Division
1800 G Street, NW
Washington, DC 20223

SECRETARY

The job

A secretary is the center of communication activities in a firm or department. The secretary transmits information from the employer to other members of the firm and to other organizations. Most secretaries type, take shorthand, deal with visitors, keep track of the employer's appointments, make travel arrangements, and, generally, relieve the employer of excess paperwork.

Executive secretaries work for the top executives in a firm. Jobs at this level require top-notch skills and usually some college education. *Social secretaries* arrange social functions, answer personal correspondence, and keep the employer informed about all social activities. Public figures such as politicians, elected officials, celebrities, and others with a busy social life usually employ social secretaries.

Some secretaries have training in specialized areas. *Medical secretaries* study medical terminology to prepare case histories and medical reports. *Legal secretaries* are trained to do some legal research and to help prepare briefs; they are familiar with legal terminology and the format of legal papers. *Technical secretaries* assist engineers and scientists in drafting reports and research proposals. They are acquainted with scientific and mathematical terms and are trained in the use of the technical vocabulary and symbols used in these fields.

Stenographers take dictation and then transcribe their notes on a typewriter or word processor. They do not handle the wide range of duties that a secretary does, although in some offices stenographers handle routine chores such as filing, answering the phone, or operating office machines. Stenographers may also specialize in medical, legal, or technical work; some specialize in a foreign language. *Public stenographers* serve traveling business people or others who have only occasional need for stenographic services. They are usually located in large hotels and busy downtown areas of cities.

Shorthand reporters are specialized stenographers who record all statements made during a proceeding. They record the sessions of state legislatures, the Congress of the United States, meetings and conventions, and out-of-court testimony for attorneys. Their transcription then becomes the official record of the proceeding. Many shorthand reporters work as *court reporters* who take down all statements made during legal proceedings in courts of law.

Places of employment and working conditions

Secretaries and stenographers are employed throughout the country. About one-half of them are employed by educational, health, legal, and business firms and other types of companies that provide services.

Working conditions vary, but full-time secretaries and stenographers usually work a 37- to 40-hour week. Shorthand reporters may work irregular hours and may have to sit for long periods of time while recording an event.

Qualifications, education, and training

Secretaries and stenographers must be accurate and neat. They must display discretion and initiative and have a good command of spelling, grammar, punctuation, and vocabulary. Shorthand reporters must have good hearing and be able to concentrate amid distractions.

High school business courses are valuable and so are college preparatory courses because secretaries and stenographers should have a good general background. In either type of high school preparation, there should be as many English courses as possible.

Secretarial training as part of a college education or at a private business school is preferred by many employers. Training can vary from a few months for basic instruction in shorthand and typing to a year or two for some of the specialty areas such as medicine or law. Shorthand reporters usually complete a two-year program in a shorthand reporting school.

Well-trained and highly experienced secretaries may qualify for the designation *certified professional secretary* (CPS) by passing a series of examinations given by the National Secretaries Association. This is a mark of achievement in the secretarial field and is recognized as such by many employers.

Potential and advancement

There are about 3.4 million people employed in this field.

The demand for qualified secretaries will continue to grow. Stenographers will not be as much in demand in the future, as the increased use of dictation machines and word processing centers will reduce the need for them. Skilled shorthand reporters, however, will be in demand, and competition for entry-level jobs will increase as more people enter this field.

Opportunities for advancement depend on the acquisition of new or improved skills and on increasing knowledge of the employer's firm or field of business. Some private firms and government agencies have their own training facilities to help employees upgrade their skills.

Executive secretaries are sometimes promoted to management positions because of their extensive knowledge of their employer's operation.

Income

Salaries for secretaries vary greatly depending on the level of their skill, experience, and responsibility; the area of the country in which they work; and the type of industry for which they work.

The average annual salary for secretaries is $21,710, with a range from $17,810 to $29,354. Secretaries working in the West and Midwest earn higher salaries in general than those working in the Northeast and the South. Also, secretaries in the transportation and public utilities industries tend to earn the highest salaries, and secretaries in retail trade, finance, real estate, and insurance tend to earn the lowest.

Additional sources of information

Association of Independent Colleges and Schools
One Dupont Circle, NW
Suite 350
Washington, DC 20036

National Shorthand Reporters Association
118 Park Street, SE
Vienna, VA 22180

Professional Secretaries International
301 East Armour Boulevard
Kansas City, MO 64111

SECURITIES SALES WORKER (STOCKBROKER)

The job

When investors buy or sell stocks, bonds, or shares in mutual funds, they use the services of securities sales workers. These workers are also called registered representatives, account executives, or customers' brokers.

Securities sales workers relay the customer's buy or sell orders to the floor of the appropriate securities exchange or to the firm's trading department and notify the customer of the completed transaction and final price. They also provide related services such as financial counseling, the latest stock and bond quotations, and information on financial positions of corporations whose securities are being traded.

Securities sales workers can help a client accumulate a financial portfolio of securities, life insurance, and other investments geared either to long-term goals such as capital growth or income or to short-term goals. Some sales workers specialize in one type of customer such as institutional investors or in certain types of securities such as mutual funds.

Beginners in this field spend much of their time searching for new customers. As they establish a clientele, they spend more time servicing their existing customers and less in seeking new ones.

Securities sales workers are employed by brokerage firms, investment banks, and mutual fund firms. Most work for a few large firms that have offices in cities throughout the country.

Places of employment and working conditions

Securities sales workers are employed in cities throughout the United States, usually in the branch offices of a few large firms whose main offices are usually in New York.

Sales workers usually work in bustling, sometimes noisy offices. Beginners usually put in long hours until they acquire a clientele, and sales workers occasionally meet with clients on evenings or weekends.

427

Many sales workers leave the field each year because they are unable to establish a large enough clientele.

Qualifications, education, and training

Selling skills and ambition are necessary for success as a securities sales worker. A sales worker should also be mature, well groomed, and able to motivate people. Many employers prefer to hire applicants who have had previous experience in sales or management positions.

A college education is preferred by the larger firms. A liberal arts background with training in economics, prelaw, businesss administration, or finance is particularly helpful.

Most employers provide training to new sales workers to help them meet registration requirements. In most firms, the training program lasts at least four months. Trainees working in larger firms often undergo a more extensive period of on-the-job training that lasts up to two years.

Almost all states require securities sales workers to be licensed. Licensing requirements usually include a written examination and the furnishing of a personal bond.

Sales workers must be registered as representatives of the firm for which they work. To qualify, they must pass the General Securities Registered Representative Examination. All states requrie a second examination called the Uniform Securities Agents State Law Examination.

Potential and advancement

There are about 200,000 full-time securities sales workers and many others in other occupations who sell securities.

The demand for securities sales workers fluctuates with the economy, but currently the job outlook is good through the year 2000. There will be a great deal of competition for available jobs, though, because of the potential for high earnings. Job opportunities will be best for those with experience who have achieved success.

Income

Securities sales workers earn commissions on the transactions they handle for clients.

Beginners' salaries average about $28,000 a year.

Earnings of full-time experienced sales workers servicing individual investors average about $71,000 a year. Those servicing institutional investors average about $240,000.

Additional sources of information

Securities Industry Association
120 Broadway
New York, NY 10271

SINGER

The job

Professional singers are employed in every field of music. For every singing star of popular, classical, country and western, and musical comedy music, there are many more who work in choruses; who teach in churches, schools, and music conservatories; and who are employed by commercial advertising firms.

Employment opportunities exist in radio, movies, and television; on the concert stage, in opera, and in musical productions; in nightclubs; in elementary and secondary schools; and in colleges and universities. Many opportunities exist for part-time work in churches.

Anyone considering this field should be aware that few singers are able to secure full-time employment except in teaching. The time necessary for rehearsing and performing leaves little time for other part-time work, and many singers are unable to support themselves with singing alone.

Professional singers usually belong to some branch of the Associated Actors and Artists of America.

Places of employment and working conditions

The most job opportunities for performers are in New York City, Los Angeles, Las Vegas, Miami, New Orleans, and Chicago. Nashville, Tennessee, is one of the major centers of the recording industry and offers many opportunities for musicians of all types.

Singers engaged in a performing career work evenings and weekends and must usually travel a great deal. The work is not steady, and many careers are short because of changes in public taste.

Qualifications, education, and training

In addition to a good voice, a singer needs poise, physical stamina, an attractive appearance and stage presence, perseverance, and determination.

Those persons who wish to pursue a singing career should acquire a broad background in music including piano lessons (for music theory and composition) and dancing lessons, because singers are sometimes required to dance as well. Voice training should not begin until physical maturity is achieved, although young boys sometimes receive some training for church choirs before their voices change.

Singers who intend to perform classical music can take private voice lessons, enroll in a music conservatory, or enroll in the music department of a college or university. Those who attend a conservatory or a college also receive training in such music-related subjects as foreign languages, dramatics, history, and literature. In four-year programs, the student receives a bachelor of arts or science (in music), a bachelor of music, or a bachelor of fine arts degree.

Singers who plan to teach music must also meet state teaching certification requirements, and those who expect to teach at the college level usually need a master's degree or a Ph.D.

In the field of popular music, voice training is an asset but is not always necessary. Many singers in this field start singing with groups or in amateur contests and go on to employment with better-known bands or groups as they gain experience and popularity.

Potential and advancement

This is a field where there will always be many more qualified applicants than there are job openings. Except for a handful of top stars in opera and popular music, the only full-time steady employment for singers will continue to be in teaching positions.

Income

Singing teachers are paid on the same scale as other faculty members in the institution in which they teach.

In an opera chorus, singers earn a base salary of between $600 and $800 a week. Soloists who have earned a reputation for their talent earn about $8,000 a performance.

In television, the minimum rate is $536 for a one-hour show.

Additional sources of information

American Federation of Musicians
1501 Broadway
New York, NY 10036

American Guild of Musical Artists (concert stage and opera singers)
1727 Broadway
New York, NY 10019

Music Educators National Conference
1902 Association Drive
Reston, VA 22091

National Association of Schools of Music
11250 Roger Bacon Drive
Reston, VA 22090

SOCIAL WORKER

The job

Social workers strive to help individuals, families, groups, and communities solve their problems. They also work to increase and improve the community resources available to people.

Depending on the nature of the problem and the time and resources available for solving it, social workers may choose one of three approaches or a combination of them—casework, group work, or community organization.

In casework, social workers interview individuals or families to identify problems. They help people understand and solve their problems by securing appropriate social resources such as financial aid, education, job training, or medical assistance.

In group work, social workers work with people in groups, helping them to understand one another. They plan and conduct activities for children, teenagers, adults, older persons, and other groups in community centers, hospitals, and nursing homes.

In community organizations, social workers coordinate the work of political, civic, religious, and business groups working to combat social problems. They help plan and develop health, housing, welfare, and recreation services.

Many social workers provide direct social services and work for public and voluntary agencies such as state and local departments of public assistance and community welfare and religious organizations. Others work for schools, hospitals, business, and industry. Some social workers are in private practice and provide counseling services on a fee basis.

A related job is rehabilitation counselor.

Places of employment and working conditions

Social workers are employed throughout the United States, usually in urban areas.

Most social workers have a 5-day, 35- to 40-hour workweek. Evening and weekend work are sometimes necessary.

Qualifications, education, and training

A social worker must be sensitive, have concern for the needs of others, be objective and emotionally stable, and be willing to handle responsibility.

A college preparatory course in high school should provide as broad a background as possible. Volunteer work or a part-time or summer job in a community center, camp, or social welfare agency are good experience.

A bachelor's degree in social work (B.S.W.) or a major in sociology or psychology can prepare the student for some positions in this field, but the usual requirement is a master's degree in social work (M.S.W.). Those with only a bachelor's degree have limited promotion opportunities.

The M.S.W. degree is awarded after two years of specialized study and supervised field instruction. A graduate degree plus experience are necessary for supervisory and administrative positions; research work also requires training in social science research methods.

A Ph.D. is usually required for teaching and for top administrative positions.

The National Association of Social Workers (NASW) grants certifications and the title ACSW (Academy of Certified Social Workers) to members who qualify.

Forty-six states require the licensing or registration of social workers. Requirements usually include specified experience plus an examination. Social workers employed by federal, state, and local government agencies are usually required to pass a civil service test before appointment to a position.

Potential and advancement

There are about 385,000 social workers. Job opportunities should continue to be good. It is probable that the number of degrees being awarded in this field will not keep pace with the increasing number of social work positions. Job opportunities will continue to be plentiful in rural areas and small towns.

Advancement in this field depends on experience and advanced education.

Income

Salaries for social workers vary by the type of agency and the geographic region. They are highest in large cities and in states with large urban populations.

Median annual earnings for full-time social workers are $22,000, with the middle 50 percent earning between $18,000 and $28,600 a year. The lowest 10 percent earn less than $12,600 a year, and the highest 10 percent earn over $38,480 a year.

Additional sources of information

Council on Social Work Education
1744 R Street, NW
Washington, DC 20009

National Association of Social Workers
7981 Eastern Avenue
Silver Spring, MD 20910

SOCIOLOGIST

The job

Sociologists study human social behavior by examining the groups that human beings form—families, tribes, and governments and social, religious, and political organizations. Some sociologists study the characteristics of social groups and institutions; others study the way individuals are affected by the groups to which they belong.

Most sociologists are college and university teachers. Others are engaged in research and writing. Those doing research collect information, prepare case studies, and conduct surveys and laboratory experiments. Many research sociologists may apply statistical and computer techniques in their research.

The federal government employs sociologists in the Department of Health and Human Services; Defense; Agriculture; and Interior.

Others work in private industry, social work, and public health.

Places of employment and working conditions

Sociologists work throughout the country but are heavily concentrated in areas with large colleges and universities.

Qualifications, education, and training

Study and research skills are necessary as well as communication skills.

In high school, a college preparatory course with a strong academic program is the best background.

A master's degree with a major in sociology is usually the minimum requirement in this field. A Ph.D. is required for professorship and tenure, for directors of major research projects, and for important administrative positions.

Those with only a bachelor's degree in sociology will be limited to jobs as interviewers, research or administrative assistants, or recreation workers. Some may secure social worker or counselor positions or teach in secondary schools.

Potential and advancement

Job competition will be very stiff as thousands of Ph.D.'s with degrees in sociology are expected to compete for the limited number of job openings through the year 2000. Most job openings will occur to replace those who retire or leave the field.

Advancement in this field depends on experience and obtaining higher degrees.

Income

The median annual salary of sociologists is $41,700. Those working in educational institutions earn a median annual salary of $41,900; in business and industry, $41,200; and in nonprofit organizations, $34,800.

Sociologists with a bachelor's degree earn annual starting salaries of $15,800 or $19,400 with the federal government; those with a master's start at about $23,900; and those with a Ph.D., $28,900 or $34,600. Sociologists working for the federal government average annual earnings of $42,900.

Additional sources of information

The American Sociological Association
1722 N Street, NW
Washington, DC 20036

SOIL CONSERVATIONIST

The job

Soil conservationists provide technical advice to farmers, ranchers, and others on soil and water conservation as well as land erosion.

Most soil conservationists are employed by the federal government in the Department of Agriculture's Soil Conservation Service or in the Department of Interior's Bureau of Land Management. Other soil conservationists work for state and local governments.

Related jobs are soil scientist, range manager, and forester.

Places of employment and working conditions

Soil conservationists work throughout the United States in nearly every county.

Most of their work is done outdoors.

Qualifications, education, and training

A soil conservationist should have good communication skills, an analytical mind, and a liking for outdoor work.

High school courses should include chemistry and biology.

Soil conservationists usually have a bachelor's degree with a major in agronomy (interaction of plants and soils), agricultural education, general agriculture, or related fields of natural resource sciences such as wildlife biology or forestry. Courses in agricultural engineering and cartography (mapmaking) are also helpful.

An advanced degree is usually necessary for college teaching and research positions.

Potential and advancement

Although there will be growth of job opportunities in this field, the relatively small size of the field will mean competition for available openings.

Advancement is limited. Conservationists working at the county level can move up to state positions. They can also move on to similar occupations such as farm or ranch management advisor or land appraiser.

Income

Starting annual salaries with the federal government are $15,700 with a bachelor's degree; $23,800 with a master's degree. Experienced soil conservationists earn an average of $30,000 a year.

Additional sources of information

American Society of Agronomy
677 South Segoe Road
Madison, WI 53711

Soil Conservation Service
U.S. Department of Agriculture
Room 6155
P.O. Box 2890
Washington, DC 20013

SOIL SCIENTIST

The job

Soil scientists study the physical, chemical, biological, and behavioral characteristics of soils. Their work is important to farmers, builders, fertilizer manufacturers, real estate appraisers, and lending institutions.

A large part of soil science has to do with categorizing soils according to a national classification system. Once the soils in an area have been classified, the soil scientist prepares a map that shows soil types throughout the area.

A builder who wants to erect a factory or an apartment building will consult a soil-type map to locate a spot with a secure base of firm soils. Farmers also consult soil-type maps. Some communities require a certified soil scientist to examine the soil and test the drainage capabilities of any building lot that will be used with a septic system.

Some soil scientists conduct research into the chemical and biological properties of soil to determine what crops grow best in which soils. They also test fertilizers and soils to determine ways to improve less productive soils. Soil scientists are also involved in pollution control programs and soil erosion prevention programs.

More than half of all soil scientists are employed by the Soil Conservation Service of the U.S. Department of Agriculture. Others are employed by the state agricultural experiment stations and agricultural colleges. Private institutions and industries that employ soil scientists include fertilizer companies, land appraisal firms, farm management agencies, and lending institutions such as banks and insurance companies.

Related jobs are soil conservationist, farmer, range manager, and forester.

Places of employment and working conditions

Soil scientists work in every state and in most counties of the United States.

They spend much of their time doing fieldwork in a particular area—usually a county. During bad weather they work indoors preparing maps and writing reports. Soil scientists involved in research usually work in greenhouses or small farm fields.

Qualifications, education, and training

An interest in science and agriculture is necessary as well as a liking for outdoor work. Writing skills are also important.

High school courses should include chemistry and biology.

A bachelor's degree with a major in soil science or a closely related field such as agriculture or agronomy (interaction of plants and soils) is necessary. Courses in chemistry and cartography (mapmaking) are also important.

An advanced degree is necessary for many of the better-paying research positions.

Some states require certification of soil scientists who inspect soil conditions prior to building or highway construction. Certification usually entails a written examination plus specified combinations of education and experience.

Potential and advancement

There are about 5,000 soil scientists. Job openings in this rather small field usually occur to replace those who leave the field or retire, although some limited growth will probably occur.

Soil scientists who have been trained in both fieldwork and laboratory research will have the best opportunities for advancement, especially if they have an advanced degree.

Income

Soil scientists start at about $13,500 a year with a bachelor's degree; $16,600 with a master's degree; and $23,000 to $26,500 with a Ph.D.

Additional sources of information

American Society of Agronomy
677 South Segoe Road
Madison, WI 53711

Soil Conservation Service
U.S. Department of Agriculture
Room 6155
P.O. Box 2890
Washington, DC 20013

SPEECH PATHOLOGIST AND AUDIOLOGIST

The job

Speech pathologists and audiologists evaluate speech and hearing disorders and provide treatment. Speech pathologists work with children and adults who have speech, language, and voice disorders because of hearing loss, brain injury, cleft palate, mental retardation, emotional problems, or foreign dialect. Audiologists assess and treat hearing problems. Speech and audiology are so interrelated that expertise in one field requires thorough knowledge of both.

Almost half of all speech pathologists and audiologists work in public schools; colleges and universities employ large numbers in teaching and research. The remainder work in hospitals, clinics, government agencies, industry, and private practice.

Places of employment and working conditions

Speech pathologists and audiologists are employed throughout the country with most of them located in urban areas.

Speech pathologists and audiologists usually work at a desk or table in an office setting. While the job is not physically strenuous, it does require concentration and attention to detail and can be mentally exhausting. Some speech pathologists and audiologists work at several different facilities and spend a lot of time traveling.

Qualifications, education, and training

Patience is an extremely important personal characteristic for anyone who wants to work in this field since progress is usually very slow. The therapist must also be able to encourage and motivate the clients who are often frustrated by the inability to speak properly. Objectivity and the ability to take responsibility and work with detail are also necessary.

High school should include a strong science background.

A bachelor's degree with a major in speech and hearing or in a related field such as education or psychology is the usual preparation for graduate work.

Most jobs in this field require a master's degree. Graduate study includes supervised clinical training as well as advanced study.

The American Speech and Hearing Association confers a certificate of clincal competence (CCC) on those who have a master's degree, complete a

439

one-year internship, and pass a written examination. Certification is usually necessary to advance professionally.

In 37 states, speech pathologists and audiologists must be licensed.

Potential and advancement

There are about 53,000 speech pathologists and audiologists. The field is expected to grow as a result of population growth among those age 75 and older, the trend toward earlier recognition and treatment of hearing and language problems in children, recent laws requiring services for the handicapped, and the expanded coverage of Medicare and Medicaid programs. Any decreases in government-funded programs could change this employment picture.

If present trends continue, the increasing number of degrees being awarded in this field may cause some job competition in large metropolitan areas. Job opportunities will continue to be good in smaller cities and towns.

Those with only a bachelor's degree will find very limited job opportunities; advancement will be possible only for those with graduate degrees.

Income

Starting salaries for speech pathologists and audiologists in hospitals are about $25,000 a year. Experienced speech pathologists in hospitals earn about $33,000, and experienced audiologists earn about $37,000.

Most speech pathologists and audiologists working in schools are classified as teachers and are paid similar salaries.

Additional sources of information

American Speech-Language-Hearing Association
10801 Rockville Pike
Rockville, MD 20852

STATISTICIAN

The job

Statisticians gather and interpret numerical data and apply their knowledge of statistical methods to a particular subject area such as economics, human behavior, natural science, or engineering. They may predict population growth, develop quality-control tests for manufactured products, or help business managers and government officials make decisions and evaluate programs.

Statisticians often obtain information about a group of people or things by surveying a portion of the whole. They decide where to gather the data, determine the size and type of the sample group, and develop the survey questionnaire or reporting form. Statisticians who design experiments prepare mathematical models to test a particular theory. Those in analytical work interpret collected data and prepare tables, charts, and written reports on their findings. Mathematical statisticians use mathematical theory to design and improve statistical methods.

Most statisticians are employed in private industry: in manufacturing, finance, insurance companies, and business service firms. The federal government employs statisticians, primarily in the Departments of Commerce, Education, Health and Human Services, Labor, and Defense. The remaining statisticians are employed by state and local government, colleges and universities, hospitals, and nonprofit organizations.

Related jobs are mathematician, economist, and actuary.

Qualifications, education, and training

Statisticians must have good reasoning ability, persistence, and the ability to apply principles to new types of problems.

High school courses in mathematics are important.

A bachelor's degree with a major in statistics or mathematics is the minimum requirement for this field. A bachelor's degree with a major in a related field such as economics or natural science with a minor in statistics is preferred for some jobs.

Teaching positions and many jobs require graduate work in mathematics or statistics, and courses in computer use and techniques are becoming increasingly important. Economics and business administration courses are also helpful.

Potential and advancement

There are about 15,000 statisticians, and the field is expected to grow substantially. Those who combine training in statistics with knowledge of a field of application will have the best job opportunities.

Opportunities for promotion in this field are best for those with advanced degrees. Experienced statisticians may advance to positions of greater technical responsibility and to supervisory positions.

Income

Statisticians have average annual salaries of about $28,000 to $35,000. Those employed by colleges and universities receive salaries comparable to other faculty members and often earn extra income from outside consulting, research, and writing.

Statisticians with a Ph.D. have a median annual salary of $46,700. Those in business and industry earn a median annual salary of $55,000; in educational institutions, $45,000; and in the federal government, $50,000.

Additional sources of information

American Statistical Association
1429 Duke Street
Alexandria, VA 22314

STUDENT PERSONNEL WORKER

The job

The job of the student personnel worker is to develop and administer programs and services that fulfill the housing, social, cultural, recreational, and personal needs of students on the campuses of colleges and universities. At a major university, a large staff performs these functions; at a small two-year college, one person may be responsible for all student personnel services. The services are organized in a wide variety of ways under titles that may include some or all of the following jobs.

The *dean of students* may be a college vice-president. The duties include advising the president on the changing needs of students, formulating new programs and policies for dealing with problems on the campus, dealing with student participation in decision making, and outlining course offerings. This job can involve the supervision of a large staff.

Admissions officers oversee the process of admitting new students. They process applications, travel as representatives of the college to recruit new students, and help in setting standards for admission. They work closely with financial aid officers and are sometimes connected with the registrar's office, where a *registrar* maintains the academic records of past and present students.

Financial aid officers must keep abreast of all sources of financial aid— grants, loans, scholarships, jobs, and teaching research fellowships. Working closely with the counseling and financial offices, these officers must determine who is eligible for aid and devise aid packages with the available funds.

Career planning and placement counselors assist students in making career decisions, work with representatives of employers who visit the campus for job recruiting, and assist students with the mechanics of job placement such as writing resumes and handling interviews.

Student activities personnel assist student-run organizations and handle the orientation of new students. *College union personnel* may be a separate staff dealing with the food service, maintenance, and finances of student-run facilities.

Student housing officers may live in dormitories and deal with personal counseling as well as dormitory management.

General counselors, usually psychologists, help students with personal problems and handle crisis situations. Some larger colleges also employ special *foreign student counselors.*

Places of employment and working conditions

Work on college campuses usually involves a wide variety of settings. Workers may be found in offices where they counsel students or in larger facilities directing many workers. Employment is usually on a 12-month basis rather than an academic year. Work hours, at least 40 a week, may be irregular.

Qualifications, education, and training

Student personnel workers must be able to work well with a wide variety of people. They should have the emotional stability and patience to deal with sharply conflicting points of view and with unexpected and emergency situations.

Backgrounds vary widely in this field, but a college degree in one of the social sciences is good preparation. The potential student personnel worker should then take a master's degree in some area of student personnel work. For example, psychology provides a foundation for counseling and career planning and placement positions; data processing is an asset in admissions, records, and financial aid work; and a specialty in recreation would be helpful in student activities work.

443

A master's degree in clinical or counseling psychology is usually required for those engaged in counseling. A Ph.D. is necessary for the top student personnel positions and for most such positions at large universities.

Potential and advancement

Job prospects are expected to be quite limited in the coming decade because budgets are being tightened in both public and private institutions. The increase in the number of two-year colleges should, however, result in a certain number of new positions in that academic area.

Advancement in the student personnel field is usually through increased experience and education but is limited for those without a master's degree. Entry-level positions available to those with a master's degree include residence hall director, financial aid counselor, admissions counselor, and assistant to a dean.

Income

Salaries vary greatly in this field depending on the size and location of the institution. Salaries range from about $14,000 a year in small institutions to more than $45,000 annually in very large ones. In small colleges and two-year institutions, salaries for starting workers may be very low.

In many schools, student personnel workers are entitled to insurance, sabbatical leaves, and other benefits on the same basis as the faculty.

Additional sources of information

American Association for Counseling and Development
5999 Stevenson Avenue
Alexandria, VA 22304

SURVEYOR

The job

Surveyors measure construction sites, establish official land boundaries, assist in setting land valuations, and collect information for maps and charts.

Most surveyors serve as leaders of surveying teams; they are in charge of the field party and responsible for the accuracy of its work. They record the information disclosed by the survey, verify the accuracy of the survey data, and prepare the sketches, maps, and reports.

A typical field party consists of the *party chief* and three to six assistants and helpers. *Instrument workers* adjust and operate surveying instruments and compile notes. *Chain workers* use steel tape or surveyor's chain to measure distances between surveying points; they usually work in pairs and may mark measured points with pointed stakes. *Rod workers* use a level rod, range pole, or other equipment to assist instrument workers in determining elevations, distances, and directions. They hold and move the range pole according to hand or voice signals from the instrument worker and remove underbrush from the survey line.

Surveyors often specialize in highway surveys; land surveys to establish boundaries (these are also required for the preparation of maps and legal descriptions for deeds and leases); or topographic surveys to determine elevations, depressions, and contours and the location of roads, rivers, and buildings. Other specialties are mining, pipeline, gravity, and magnetic surveying.

Photogrammetrists measure and interpret photographs to determine various characteristics of natural or artificial features of an area. They apply analytical processes and mathematical techniques to aerial, space, ground, and underwater photographs to prepare detailed maps of areas that are inaccessible or difficult to survey. Control surveys on the ground are then made to determine the accuracy of the maps derived from photogrammetric techniques.

Federal, state, and local government agencies employ about 25 percent of all surveyors. Those who work for state and local governments usually work for highway departments and urban planning and development agencies. Those who work for the federal government are in the U.S. Geological Survey, Bureau of Land Management, Army Corps of Engineers, Forest Service, National Ocean Survey, and Defense Mapping Agency.

Many surveyors work for construction companies, engineering and architectural consulting firms, public utilities, and petroleum and natural gas companies. Others own or work for firms that conduct surveys for a fee.

Places of employment and working conditions

Surveyors work throughout the United States.

Surveying is outdoor work with surveyors often walking long distances or climbing hills carrying equipment and instruments. They usually work an eight-hour, five-day week but may work much longer hours in summer months when conditions are more favorable for surveying.

Qualifications, education, and training

Surveyors should be in good physical condition. They need good eyesight, coordination, and hearing and must have the ability to visualize and understand objects, distances, sizes, and other abstract forms. They also need mathematical ability.

High school courses should include algebra, geometry, trigonometry, drafting, and mechanical drawing.

Surveyors acquire their skills through a combination of on-the-job training and courses in surveying. Technical institutes, vocational schools, and junior colleges offer one-, two-, and three-year programs in surveying.

High school graduates without any training usually start as helpers. If they complete a surveying course and gain experience, they may advance to technician, senior survey technician, party chief, and finally, licensed surveyor.

Photogrammetrists usually need a bachelor's degree in engineering or the physical sciences.

All states require licensing or registration of land surveyors. Registration requirements are very strict because, once registered, surveyors can be held legally responsible for their work. Requirements usually include formal education courses and from five to twelve years of surveying experience.

Potential and advancement

There are about 100,000 surveyors. Job opportunities are expected to grow steadily in this field; extended periods of slow construction activity, however, could cause temporary slow periods.

Advancement in this field depends mainly on accumulating experience.

Income

The federal government pays high school graduates with little or no training or experience starting salaries of about $11,484 a year for entry-level positions. Those with one year of postsecondary training start at $12,531. Those with an associate's degree start as instrument assistants with salaries of about $14,067. Federal surveying technicians earn about $19,535 a year. Depending on their qualifications, land surveyors start at $15,738 or $19,493 a year. The average yearly salary for federal land surveyors is $32,880.

Additional sources of information

American Congress on Surveying and Mapping
210 Little Falls Street
Falls Church, VA 22046

American Society of Photogrammetry and Remote Sending
210 Little Falls Street
Falls Church, VA 22046

SYSTEMS ANALYST

The job

Systems analysts decide what new data need to be collected, the equipment needed to process the data, and the procedure to be followed in using the information within any given computer system. They use various techniques such as cost accounting, sampling, and mathematical model building to analyze a problem and devise a new system to solve it.

Once a system has been developed, the systems analyst prepares charts and diagrams that describe the system's operation in terms that the manager or customer who will use the system can understand. The analyst may also prepare a cost-benefit analysis of the newly developed system. If the system is accepted, the systems analyst then translates the logical requirements of the system into the capabilities of the particular computer machinery (hardware) in use and prepares specifications for programmers to follow. The systems analyst will also work with the programmers to debug (eliminate errors from) a new system.

Because the work is complex and varied, systems analysts specialize in either business or scientific and engineering applications. Some analysts improve systems already in use or adapt existing systems to handle additional types of data. Those involved in research, called *advanced systems designers,* devise new methods of analysis.

447

Most systems analysts are employed by banks, insurance companies, large manufacturing firms, and data processing services. Others work for wholesale and retail businesses and government agencies.

In many industries, all systems analysts begin as computer programmers and are promoted to analyst positions only after gaining experience. In large data processing departments, they may start as junior systems analysts. Many persons enter this occupation after experience in accounting, economics, or business management (for business positions) or engineering (for scientific work).

Places of employment and working conditions

Opportunities for systems analysts exist throughout the entire country.

Systems analysts usually work a normal 40-hour week with occasional evening or weekend work.

Qualifications, education, and training

Systems analysts must be able to think logically, to concentrate, and to handle abstract ideas. They must be able to communicate effectively with technical personnel such as programmers as well as with those who have no computer background.

High school should include as many mathematics courses as possible.

Because job requirements vary so greatly, there is no universally accepted way of preparing for a career as a systems analyst. A background in accounting, business administration, or economics is preferred by employers in business. Courses in computer concepts, systems analysis, and data retrieval techniques are good preparation for any systems analyst.

Many employers require a college degree in computer science, information science, or data processing. Scientifically oriented organizations often require graduate work as well as some combination of computer science and a science or engineering specialty.

Because technological advances in the computer field come so rapidly, systems analysts must continue their technical education throughout their careers. This training usually takes the form of one- and two-week courses offered by employers, computer manufacturers, and software (computer systems) vendors.

The Institute for Certification of Computer Professionals confers the designation of *certified data processor* (CDP) on systems analysts who have five years of experience and who successfully complete a core examination and exams in two specialty areas.

Potential and advancement

There are about 403,000 systems analysts. This job field is expected to grow steadily because of the expanding use of computers. College graduates who have had courses in computer programming, systems analysis, and data processing will have the best opportunities, while those without a degree may face some competition for the available jobs that don't require a degree.

Systems analysts can advance to jobs as lead systems analysts or managers of systems analysis or data processing departments.

Income

Systems analysts who work full-time earn a median yearly salary of about $35,800. The middle 50 percent earn between $27,100 and $45,400. The bottom 10 percent earn less than $19,900 while the top 10 percent earn over $51,600.

Additional sources of information

Association for Systems Management
24587 Bagley Road
Cleveland, OH 44138

Institute for the Certification of Computer Professionals
2200 East Devon Avenue
Suite 268
Des Plaines, IL 60018

T

TEACHER, COLLEGE AND UNIVERSITY

The job

The function of a teacher at the college or university level is to present in-depth analysis of or training in a particular subject.

Depending on the subject matter and grade level of the students, a teacher may conduct large lecture classes for basic courses, lead advanced seminars for only a few students, or work with students in laboratories. Many teachers at this level carry on research projects and act as consultants to business, industry, and government agencies. They are active in professional societies and write for publications in their field. Those who are *department heads* also have supervisory and administrative duties.

There are four academic ranks on college and university faculties: *instructor, assistant professor, associate professor,* and *full professor.* Beginners usually start as instructors. Education and experience govern advancement to higher rank. Many teachers are assisted by part-time assistant instructors, teaching fellows, teaching assistants, and laboratory assistants. These posts are often filled by graduate students working toward advanced degrees.

Over seventy percent of all teachers at this level teach in public colleges and universities. About thirty percent work part-time.

Places of employment and working conditions

One of the advantages college and university teachers have is their flexible schedule. They usually spend 12 to 16 hours a week in classes and set aside 3 to 6 office hours a week to assist students on an individual basis. They may also be required to attend faculty meetings. Otherwise, they are free to schedule study, class preparation, and research as they see fit. During the summer and school holidays, they may teach, do research, travel, write, and participate in other activities.

One of the current problems confronting college and university professors is that budget cutbacks are causing many institutions to replace full-time and permanent positions with part-time and temporary ones. Also, in order to advance, college and university teachers are under a great deal of pressure to publish their research as books and articles, often leaving them less time to teach.

Qualifications, education, and training

A master's degree, which qualifies the teacher for instructor rank, is the minimum requirement for college and university teaching positions.

A year of study beyond the master's degree and a year or two of experience as an instructor are usually necessary for assistant professors. Associate professors frequently need a Ph.D. as well as three years or more of college teaching experience.

For a full professorship, a Ph.D. degree, extensive teaching experience at the college and university level, and published articles and books are usually required. Full professors may achieve tenure after a certain number of years, thus being assured of a teaching position for as long as they choose to remain at the school.

Potential and advancement

There are approximately 846,000 college and university teachers. Due to declining enrollments through the early 1990s, little or no employment growth is expected in this field. However, enrollments are expected to increase by the early 1990s, and conditions should improve then.

Advancement usually depends on advanced study and college teaching experience. Outstanding academic, administrative, or professional work as well as research and publication in a subject can hasten advancement.

Income

Salaries for college and university professors vary by faculty rank, type of institution, and field. In general, faculty in four-year colleges earn more than those teaching in two-year schools.

For a nine- or ten-month academic year, salaries for full-time faculty average $39,410. The average for professors is $50,420; associate professors, $37,530; assistant professors, $31,160; and instructors, $23,660.

Many college and university professors supplement their income by consulting, writing, researching, teaching additional courses, or other employment.

Additional sources of information

Professional societies in the various subject fields will generally provide information on teaching requirements and employment opportunities in their particular field. Other sources of information are:

American Council on Education
One Dupont Circle, NW
Washington, DC 20036

American Federation of Teachers
555 New Jersey Avenue, NW
Washington, DC 20001

American Association of University Professors
1012 14th Street, NW
Suite 500
Washington, DC 20005

TEACHER, KINDERGARTEN AND ELEMENTARY SCHOOL

The job

School teachers at the kindergarten and elementary levels introduce children to the basic concepts of mathematics, language, science, and social studies. They aid children in the development of good study and work habits and help them acquire the skills necessary for further education. They evaluate each child and work with parents to provide whatever help a child may need to develop his or her full potential.

Kindergarten and elementary teachers are also concerned with the social development and health of their students. They work to resolve behavior or personality problems and are alert to health problems or illness. In these early school years, teachers try to give students as much individual attention as possible.

Most teachers at this level teach a single grade and cover all subjects including music, art, and physical education. Recent trends, however, are for specialization in one or two subjects; the teacher then teaches these subjects to several classes or grades. Team teaching, with several teachers sharing responsibility for a group of students, is also popular in some areas.

Teachers have duties outside of the classroom as well. They attend faculty meetings, supervise after-school activities such as glee clubs, and supervise lunch and playground activities.

Most kindergarten and elementary teachers work in public school systems; about one-fifth work in private and parochial schools. During the summer, many teachers teach in summer-school programs or work as camp counselors. Others use the time to secure additional education.

Places of employment and working conditions

Elementary teachers work in every geographic area—in cities and towns of all sizes and in rural areas throughout the United States.

The workweek for elementary teachers is about 36-1/2 hours, but time spent grading papers, preparing lessons, and attending meetings increases the hours to about 46 a week.

At this level, teachers must be active physically. They do a great deal of walking, kneeling, sitting on low stools, chairs, and on the floor. In the lowest grades, they help children with boots and heavy clothing.

Most elementary teachers work a nine-month school year with a three-month summer vacation. Some school districts, however, function year-round; they have eight-week sessions, one week off, and a three-week midwinter break. This type of schedule makes extra employment difficult.

Many states provide for tenure after a certain number of years in a position; while tenure does not guarantee a job, it does provide some security.

Qualifications, education, and training

An enthusiasm for young children is a prime requisite for a kindergarten and elementary teacher. Dependability, good judgment, creativity, and patience are also necessary.

In high school, a broad college preparatory course should be followed.

A bachelor's degree in an approved teacher education program is required. This includes a liberal arts program, education courses, and student-teaching experience.

All states require public school teachers to be certified by the state department of education; some also require private and parochial teachers to be certified. State requirements vary and may include a health certificate, U.S. citizenship, an oath of allegiance, or supplementary graduate education—usually a master's degree or a fifth year of study.

Some school systems sometimes have additional local requirements.

Potential and advancement

There are about 1.4 million elementary school teachers. Rising enrollments through the mid-1990s will make opportunities in this field good. Even though enrollments are expected to drop off slightly after the mid-1990s, teaching opportunities are expected to increase because of the large number of teachers who will reach retirement age and need to be replaced. Job opportunities are expected to be best in the South and the West and in inner cities and rural areas.

Income

Experienced elementary teachers average about $28,900 for a nine- or ten-month year. Teachers working in private schools usually earn less.

Additional sources of information

Information on certification requirements for local school systems is available from individual state departments of education. Other sources are:

American Federation of Teachers
555 New Jersey Avenue, NW
Washington, DC 20001

455

National Education Association
1201 16th Street, NW
Washington, DC 20036

TEACHER, SECONDARY SCHOOL

The job

Teachers at this level, high school, instruct students in specific subject areas such as English, science, or mathematics. They usually teach four or five different classes each day and may teach different areas of their specialty to different grades. For example, a mathematics teacher might teach algebra to two ninth-grade classes, geometry to one tenth-grade class, and have two classes of seniors studying trigonometry.

The teacher must prepare lesson plans and examinations for each class and try to meet the needs of individual students. This could mean arranging tutoring for slower students or providing extra work for fast learners. Secondary school teachers also take students on field trips, attend faculty meetings and workshops, and supervise extracurricular activities such as sports, school plays, and student clubs.

Some teachers, called vocational teachers, train junior and senior high school students in specific job skills such as carpentry, auto mechanics, or distributive education (retail, production, and marketing training). They work with the actual tools of the particular trade.

Places of employment and working conditions

Secondary school teachers work in all parts of the country with job concentrations in the most populated areas.

The average workweek is about 37 hours, but meetings, lesson preparation, and grading papers increase the working hours to about 48 per week. Most teachers work a nine-month school year with a three-month summer vacation. In school systems with a year-round schedule, teachers usually work eight weeks and have one week off with a longer midwinter break.

Many states provide tenure after a certain number of years in a position; this provides teachers with some job security.

Qualifications, education, and training

Secondary school teachers should enjoy working with adolescents, be interested in a specific subject area, and have the ability to motivate people.

A broad high school background with preparation for college is necessary. Courses in the student's specific area of interest should be included.

A bachelor's degree from an approved secondary teaching education program, with course work in the specialty area, is the minimum requirement. Some states require a master's degree or a fifth year of education within a certain time period after beginning employment.

All states require certification, and requirements vary. Recommendations from college instructors, a health certificate, or U.S. citizenship may be required in addition to education and student-teaching practice. Local school systems may have still more requirements.

Teachers who intend to work as nonacademic specialists such as *guidance counselors, school psychologists,* and *reading specialists* need additional special education as well as separate certification in the specialty.

Potential and advancement

There are over one million secondary school teachers. Rising enrollments through the year 2000 will make opportunities in this field good. There will also be more jobs as a large number of teachers reach retirement age and have to be replaced. Job opportunities are expected to be best in the South and West and in inner cities and rural areas.

Income

Experienced teachers average about $30,300 for a nine- or ten-month school year. Salaries are highest in the Mid-Atlantic states and the West.

Additional sources of information

Information on certification for local school systems is available from individual state departments of education. Other sources are:

American Federation of Teachers
555 New Jersey Avenue, NW
Washington, DC 20001

National Education Association
1201 16th Street, NW
Washington, DC 20036

TECHNICAL WRITER

The job

Writers who specialize in preparing scientific and technical material are much in demand. Technical writers may write for the professional members of a special field, detailing new developments and the work of others in the same field. On other assignments, the writer may write for those outside the field—the general public, equipment users, company officers, and stockholders.

Technical writers also prepare operating manuals, catalogs, and instructional materials for manufacturers of scientific equipment. This material is used by company salespeople, technicians who install and maintain the equipment, and the persons who operate the equipment. Writing manuals and training aids for military equipment and weapons is a highly specialized segment of this field.

Research laboratories employ many technical writers who report on the results of research projects. Others write proposals—requests for money or facilities to do research, conduct a project, or develop a prototype of a new product.

Technical writers also write technical books, articles for popular and trade magazines and newspapers, and prepare advertising copy and press releases.

Technical writers are employed by firms in many industries, with the largest numbers working for electronics, aviation, aerospace, weapons, chemical, pharmaceutical, and computer-manufacturing industries. The energy, communications, and computer-software fields are employing increasing numbers of technical writers.

The federal government employs many technical writers in the departments of Interior; Agriculture; Health and Human Services; and the National Aeronautics and Space Administration. The largest federal employer of technical writers, however, is the Department of Defense.

Publishing houses employ substantial numbers of technical writers and *technical editors*. These companies publish business and trade publications and professional journals in engineering, medicine, physics, chemistry, and other sciences. Textbook publishers also employ technical writers and editors.

Many technical writers work as free-lancers, sometimes in addition to holding a full-time technical writing job.

Most people do not enter this field directly from college. They usually spend several years or longer working as technicians, scientists, engineers, research assistants, or teachers before turning to technical writing or editing.

Places of employment and working conditions

Technical writers have interesting work that requires creativity. They must be able to work well with other people, but free-lance writers must have the discipline to work alone and set schedules that will allow them to meet deadlines.

Technical writers usually work between 30 and 40 hours a week. They may be required to work extra hours at times in order to meet deadlines.

Qualifications, education, and training

In addition to having writing skills and scientific or technical knowledge, a technical writer should be logical, accurate, able to work alone or as part of a team, and have disciplined work habits.

High school courses should develop writing skills and must include science and mathematics.

Technical writers come from a variety of educational backgrounds. Some employers prefer a degree in English, journalism, or technical communications plus course work or experience in a specific scientific or technical subject. Others prefer a degree in an appropriate science or in engineering with a minor in journalism or technical communications. A few colleges and universities offer bachelor's and graduate degrees in technical writing.

Many technical writing workshops and seminars, usually intensive one- and two-week courses, are also available at colleges and universities throughout the country.

Potential and advancement

There are over 50,000 technical writers, and the field is expanding. Job opportunities will be best for talented writers with education in a specific scientific or technical field. Opportunities for federal employment have been declining and will probably continue to do so.

Technical writers can move up to technical editor or to supervisory and management positions. Some advance by opening their own firms where they handle technical writing assignments plus industrial publicity and technical advertising.

Income

Starting salaries average about $26,000 a year. Experienced technical writers average between $28,000 and $38,000 a year. Those who become technical editors can earn more than $45,000 a year.

Additional sources of information

Society for Technical Communication, Inc.
815 15th Street, NW
Washington, DC 20005

TELEVISION AND RADIO SERVICE TECHNICIAN

The job

Skilled television and radio service technicians repair many electronic products in addition to radios and television sets. They repair stereo components, tape recorders, intercom and public address systems, closed-circuit television systems, and some medical electronic equipment.

Most of the technicians in this field work in shops and stores that sell or service radios, television sets, and other electronic products. Some work for major manufacturers and service only the products of that manufacturer. About one-quarter of all television and radio service technicians are self-employed.

Related jobs are appliance repairer, electrician, computer service technician, communications equipment mechanic; business machine service technician, and broadcast technician.

Places of employment and working conditions

Television and radio service technicians employed in local service shops or dealer service departments work between 40 and 44 hours a week.

Qualifications, education, and training

Work in this field requires mechanical ability; manual dexterity and good eye-hand coordination; normal hearing, good eyesight, and color vision; and the ability to work with people.

High school courses should include mathematics and physics. Vocational or technical school courses in electronics or hobbies such as amateur ham radio operation are also helpful.

About two years of technical training in electronics plus two to four years of on-the-job experience are usually necessary to become a fully qualified service technician. Training is available from a number of sources including high schools, vocational-technical schools, junior and community colleges, and correspondence schools. The armed forces also offer training.

Some employers provide training through apprenticeship programs. The apprentice works under the supervision of a fully qualified technician who is responsible for the apprentice's work. Such programs usually include home study courses or classroom instruction as well.

Many manufacturers, employers, and trade associations conduct training programs to keep service technicians up-to-date on new models or products. Manufacturers also provide service manuals and other technical material.

Some states require licensing of television and radio technicians, which usually entails a written examination.

Potential and advancement

There are about 44,000 service technicians in this field, and growth in demand for technicians is expected as the population increases. This field is not very sensitive to ups and downs in the economy, so employment is usually steady.

Income

Typical earnings range from $7 to $14 an hour.

Additional sources of information

Electronics Industries Association
2001 Eye Street, NW
Washington, DC 20006

Electronics Technicians Association
604 North Jackson
Greencastle, IN 46135

TOOL-AND-DIE MAKER

The job

The production of the tools, dies, and special guiding and holding devices used by machining workers to mass produce metal parts is the work of tool-and-die makers.

Toolmakers produce and repair jigs and fixtures (devices that hold metal while it is stamped, shaved, or drilled). They also make gauges and other measuring devices for use on machinery-making precision metal parts.

Diemakers construct and repair metal forms (called dies) for use on machinery that stamps out or forges metal parts. They also make metal molds for diecasting and for molding plastics.

Tool-and-die makers usually receive training in the full range of skills needed to perform either job. They are required to have a broader knowledge of machining operations, mathematics, and blueprint reading than workers in related fields. They use a variety of hand and machining tools as well as precision measuring instruments.

Most tool-and-die makers work in plants that produce manufacturing, construction, and farm machinery. Others work in automobile, aircraft, and other transportation equipment industries; small tool-and-die shops; and electrical machinery and fabricated metal industries.

A related job is machinist.

Places of employment and working conditions

Tool-and-die makers work throughout the United States, but job opportunities are best in large industrialized areas. Most work in the Midwest and Northeast, where many metalworking industries are.

Working conditions are those of a factory and can be quite noisy. Tool-and-die makers come into direct contact with grease and oil in the course of their work and may be subject to injuries to hands and eyes caused by flying metal particles. These workers are usually required to wear special protective eyeglasses and to avoid loose clothing that could catch on machinery.

Qualifications, education, and training

Anyone interested in tool-and-die making should have mechanical ability, finger dexterity, and an aptitude for precision work.

High school or vocational school courses should include machine shop classes, mathematics, and physics, if possible.

Some tool-and-die makers learn their skills in vocational schools or through on-the-job training, but the best training is usually obtained in a formal apprenticeship program. Some companies have separate apprenticeship programs for toolmaking and diemaking.

An apprenticeship program combines practical shop training in all phases of tool-and-die making with classroom instruction in mathematics, shop theory, mechanical drawing, tool designing, and blueprint reading. After completion of an apprenticeship, several years of additional experience are usually necessary to qualify for the more difficult tool-and-die projects.

Some experienced machinists become tool-and-die makers without completing a formal tool-and-die apprenticeship. After years of experience and some additional classroom training, skilled machinists and machine tool operators can develop the skills necessary to qualify them as tool-and-die makers.

Potential and advancement

There are about 152,000 tool-and-die makers, and job opportunities will increase somewhat slowly through the year 2000. The use of electrical discharge machines and numerically controlled machines that require fewer special tools, jibs, and fixtures will reduce the need for tool-and-die makers in some industries.

Tool-and-die makers can advance to supervisory positions and, because of their broad knowledge, can change jobs within the machining occupations more easily than less-skilled workers. Some become tool designers; others open their own tool-and-die shops.

Income

Tool-and-die makers are among the highest paid in the machining field. Hourly wage rates vary from $12.50 to $17.63 an hour with the highest rates paid on the West Coast.

Median income for tool-and-die makers is $575 a week.

Additional sources of information

The National Machine Tool Builders
7901 Westpark Drive
McLean, VA 22102

The National Tooling and Machining Association
9300 Livingston Road
Fort Washington, MD 20744

TRAFFIC MANAGER, INDUSTRIAL

The job

The efficient movement of materials into and finished products out of an industrial firm is the responsibility of an industrial traffic manager.

In the course of their work, traffic managers analyze various transportation possibilities—rail, air, truck, or water—and select the method most suited to the company's needs. They select the carrier and the route; prepare necessary shipping documents; handle claims for lost or damaged shipments; consult company officials about purchasing, producing, and scheduling shipments; and sometimes appear before rate-making and government regulatory agencies to represent their company.

Because many aspects of transportation are subject to federal, state, and local government regulations, industrial traffic managers must be well versed in all such regulations and any other legal matters that affect the shipping operations of their company. They must also be informed about advances in transportation technology and the present and future prices and availability of fuels necessary for the company's transportation requirements. Traffic managers often make decisions on or advise top management about the advisability of purchasing versus contracting for railcars or trucking fleets.

Most traffic managers work for manufacturing firms. A substantial number are employed by wholesalers, large retail stores, and chain stores.

Places of employment and working conditions

Industrial traffic managers usually have standard working hours but may put in some extra time on paperwork, meetings, or travel to hearings before state and federal regulatory bodies.

Qualifications, education, and training

The ability to work independently, to analyze technical and numerical data, and to present facts and figures in a logical and convincing manner are all necessary for a traffic manager.

The high school curriculum should include mathematics courses.

Although some traffic managers arrive at their positions through experience only, college training is becoming more and more important in this field. Traffic managers who argue cases before the Interstate Commerce Commission, for instance, must have at least two years of college education.

Some employers prefer to hire graduates of trade or technical schools or two-year college programs in traffic management. Other employers require a college degree with a major or course work in transportation, logistics, physical distribution, business administration, economics, statistics, marketing, computer science, or commercial law.

Potential and advancement

This relatively small field is expected to have steady growth into the year 2000 with first consideration for job openings going to college graduates with a major in traffic management or transportation.

Industrial traffic workers can advance to supervisory positions and to assistant traffic manager and traffic manager positions. Experienced industrial traffic managers very often advance by moving to a larger company where job responsibilities are more complex.

Income

Beginners in traffic management start at about $25,000 a year.

Salaries of experienced industrial traffic managers average about $38,000 a year.

Additional sources of information

American Association of State Highway and Transportation Officials
444 North Capitol
Washington, DC 20001

Institute of Transportation Engineers
525 School Street, SW
Washington, DC 20024

TRANSLATOR

The job

Translators render the written material of one language into written material in another language. Their work differs from that of interpreters who provide *oral* translation.

Most translators work on a free-lance basis. Those employed full-time usually work for literary or technical publishers, banks, or large industrial firms with foreign subsidiaries and customers.

The largest single employer of translators is the U.S. government. Agencies such as the Joint Publications Research Service have in-house translation staffs, while other government agencies contract their translating requirements to commercial translating agencies, which in turn employ free-lancers.

A related job is interpreter.

Places of employment and working conditions

Translators who work for private companies and banks are found in large metropolitan areas such as Chicago and San Francisco. The largest concentrations, however, are in the New York City and Washington, D.C., areas where government and publishing industry requirements provide the most job opportunities.

Working conditions vary from an office setting to the free-lancer's own home. Occasionally, a rush assignment may mean long or irregular working hours, but in-house translators usually work a 37- to 40-hour week. Free-lance translators can set their own schedules. Many work only part-time—some through choice, but many because they cannot secure enough free-lance work to provide a steady income.

Qualifications, education, and training

Translators need a working knowledge of one or more foreign languages. A translator's own foreign background, time spent living abroad, or intensive study of a language at the college or university level provides sufficient preparation for many translating jobs.

A college degree is usually necessary for this type of work. Course work should include foreign languages and writing. Studying abroad can also be a very valuable experience for translators. Those who wish to work in literary translation should study the literature of foreign countries.

Potential and advancement

There are only 1,500 translators working full-time in the United States. Exact numbers are difficult because those employed full-time, as well as those handling only an occasional assignment in conjunction with other work, are all classed as translators. Job opportunities in this field are limited, since any full-time, in-house positions are usually filled from the existing pool of free-lancers.

Advancement in this field usually takes the form of better translating assignments because of experience and reputation. Some translators form their own commercial translating agencies and secure contract work for themselves and their in-house or free-lance staff.

Income

Beginning translators earn about $18,000 a year. Free-lance translators may charge by the word or by the hour. Some free-lance translators earn between $15 and $30 an hour.

Additional sources of information

American Translators Association
109 Croton Avenue
Ossining, NY 10562

Institute of International Education
809 United Nations Plaza
New York, NY 10017

Translators and Interpreters Educational Society
P.O. Box 3027
Stanford, CA 94305

TRAVEL AGENT

The job

Travel agents are specialists who make the best possible travel arrangements to fit the requirements and budgets of individuals or groups traveling anywhere in the world. A travel agent can provide a client with plane tickets and a hotel reservation or can plan a trip down to the last detail—guided tours, rental car, passports and visas, currency exchange rates.

Many services of a travel agency are provided free of charge to the customer with a service fee charged only for complicated travel and lodging arrangements.

Although personal travel experience is part of a successful agent's background, travel agents do not spend most of their time traveling and vacationing. They are usually found behind a desk talking to a customer or completing necessary paperwork or on the phone making airline, ship, or hotel reservations. Agents also speak to social and special interest groups—often presenting slide or movie presentations of vacation tours—or meet with business executives to plan company-sponsored trips and business travel.

Some large companies whose employees do a great deal of traveling employ experienced travel agents in-house to make all the company's travel arrangements.

Places of employment and working conditions

Travel agents work throughout the country, but most job opportunities are in urban areas.

During vacation seasons, travel agents may work under a great deal of pressure. They frequently have to work long hours.

Qualifications, education, and training

A travel agent is basically a sales representative and, as such, should have patience and a pleasant personality, like to deal with the public, and be willing to work with the hard-to-please customer as well as the timid or inexperienced traveler.

Travel experience is another important qualification for a travel agent. This is an asset when applying for a job in this field but can also be acquired during the years of training. Being able to speak from personal experience, an agent can provide more comprehensive advice to clients.

Part-time or summer jobs as a receptionist or reservation clerk in a travel agency or working as an airline ticket clerk can provide valuable experience.

Some travel agents receive on-the-job training, but more formal training is becoming important for travel agents. Many vocational schools offer three- to twelve-week full-time programs as well as evening and Saturday programs. Courses for travel agents are sometimes offered in public adult education classes and in community and four-year colleges. A few colleges offer bachelor's and master's degrees in travel and tourism. Home study courses are also available from either the American Society of Travel Agents or the Institute of Certified Travel Agents.

Three states, Ohio, Hawaii, and California, require registration of travel agents, and Rhode Island requires licensing. In California, travel agents not approved by a corporation are required to be licensed.

Potential and advancement

There are about 142,000 travel agents. The prospect for jobs in this field through the year 2000 is good.

Spending on travel is expected to increase significantly through the year 2000. Rising incomes and increased leisure time mean more people traveling more often than in the past. More efficient planes and the economics of group tour packages have brought even international travel within the budget of more Americans than ever. In addition, increased business travel, much of it international, and an increasing flow of foreign visitors to the United States will add to the demand for travel agents.

The travel industry, however, is sensitive to fluctuations in the economy. The price and availability of gasoline also have an effect on the travel industry because rapidly rising fuel costs could make a significant difference in the price of travel.

Travel agents in larger agencies can be promoted to supervisory or management positions. Some agents advance by opening their own agencies—many travel agents are self-employed.

Income

Salaries of travel agents range from $12,000 a year for beginners to $21,000 for experienced workers. Agency managers earn about $30,000 a year. Standard fringe benefits such as pension plans, insurance, and paid vacations are usually available. Additional benefits in the form of substantially reduced travel rates and an occasional free holiday offered by a hotel or resort help to make this an attractive field.

Earnings of self-employed travel agents depend mainly upon commissions from airlines and other carriers, tour operators, and hotels and resorts. Commissions for domestic travel arrangements, cruises, hotels, sight-seeing tours, and car rentals are about 10 percent; and international travel, 11 percent. Travel agents must receive conference approval before they can receive commissions, however. (Conferences are organizations of shiplines, rail lines, or airlines—such as the International Air Transport Association.) To obtain conference approval, the travel agency must demonstrate that it is in operation, that it is financially sound, and that it employs at least one experienced travel agent who can arrange foreign and domestic travel as well as hotel and resort accommodations. Obtaining conference approval usually takes up to a year or more, which means that self-employed agents make very little money during their first year except for hotel and tour operation commissions. For this reason, working capital of more than $50,000 is usually needed to carry a new agency through a profitless first year.

Additional sources of information

American Society of Travel Agents
1101 King Street
Alexandria, VA 22314

The Institute of Certified Travel Agents
148 London Street
P.O. Box 56
Wellesley, MA 02181

TRUCK DRIVER

The job

The movement of goods throughout the country is the work of truck drivers. Many truck drivers are *owner-operators* who own their own trucks and operate independently by leasing their services and trucks to individual companies.

Local truck drivers move goods from warehouses and terminals to factories, stores, and homes within an area. Their skills include the ability to maneuver a truck through narrow streets and alleys, into tight parking spaces, and up to loading platforms. The work and schedule of a local truck driver varies depending on the product transported. With some products, the driver starts out in the morning with a loaded truck, makes deliveries to a number of locations during the day, and returns at the end of the day. The driver who works for a lumber company, on the other hand, might return to the lumberyard after each large delivery, thus making several round trips each day.

Long-distance truck drivers, also called *over-the-road drivers,* move goods between cities and across the country. They are considered to be the top professional drivers and receive the highest wages of all drivers. These drivers work both day and night with many preferring the night runs when highways and turnpikes are less crowded.

The runs of long-distance truck drivers can include a short turnaround, where they deliver a loaded trailer to a nearby city, pick up another loaded trailer, and return it to home base—all within one day. Other runs take an entire day to complete, and the driver remains away overnight. On longer runs, the driver could be away for a week or longer.

On very long runs, many companies use two drivers. One sleeps in a berth behind the cab while the other drives. On these sleeper runs, the truck keeps moving day and night except for stops to eat or refuel. At the end of a trip, drivers complete reports on the trip and on the condition of the truck; these are required by the U.S. Department of Transportation.

Depending on the product transported, a truck driver may or may not be responsible for unloading the trucks. In deliveries to a warehouse or loading dock at a store or factory, the customer is usually responsible for unloading the truck. In other deliveries, the driver, sometimes with a helper, does the unloading. Drivers hauling cargo that requires special handling always do their own unloading: a gasoline tank truck driver attaches the hoses and pumps the gasoline into the gas station storage tanks; a truck driver transporting new cars drives and positions the cars on the racks and removes them at the final destination.

Most local truck drivers and a few long-distance truck drivers have regularly assigned runs. Drivers with smaller companies are more likely to be assigned regular runs early in their employment. In large companies, drivers usually start on the extra board, where they bid for runs on the basis of seniority.

Most long-distance drivers and some local drivers are members of the Teamsters, Chauffeurs, Warehousemen and Helpers of America. Others who are union members usually belong to the unions that represent the plant employees of the companies for which they work.

Places of employment and working conditions

Every community needs local truck drivers who usually work for businesses that deliver their own products and goods. Most, however, work in and around large communities and manufacturing centers.

Those who specialize in transportating agricultural products or minerals may live in rural areas.

Working conditions are somewhat different for local and long-distance truck drivers. Both must be excellent drivers, but the local truck driver faces a daily schedule that involves the driving strain of heavy city traffic while the long-distance driver must contend with the fatigue of sustained highway driving. Time spent away from home for long-distance truck runs is another drawback.

Local truck drivers often work 48 hours or more a week; night or early morning work is often necessary. The working hours and conditions of long-distance drivers are government regulated. They may not drive more than 60 hours in any seven-day period or drive more than ten hours without at least eight hours off.

Qualifications, education, and training

Reliability, good judgment, and good driving skills are necessary, as are good health and vision.

A high school diploma is not necessary, but some trucking companies prefer it. Driver education courses and shop classes in automotive mechanics are helpful.

Truck drivers usually acquire their skills through experience. They may start as a helper or extra driver on smaller trucks, be given some company training on larger vehicles, and gradually work up to driving the largest trucks. Long-distance truck drivers usually do some local driving before handling long-distance assignments.

A few private and public technical and vocational schools offer truck-driving courses. These courses should be checked out with local trucking companies before enrolling, however, since not all of them offer acceptable training.

By April 1, 1992, truck drivers must have a commercial driving license if they drive vehicles designed to transport at least 26,000 pounds. This is usually obtained by passing a general physical examination, a written examination on driving regulations, and a driving test.

The U.S. Department of Transportation establishes minimum qualifications for long-distance truck drivers who are engaged in interstate commerce. The driver must be at least 21 years old; must pass a physical examination; and must have good hearing, 20/40 vision with or without glasses, normal blood pressure, and normal use of arms and legs. Drivers must also pass a written examination on the motor carrier safety regulations of the U.S. Department of Transportation.

In addition to these requirements, some trucking companies may require a driver to be at least 25 years old, be able to lift heavy objects, and have three to five years of experience. Many employers now also require periodic drug screening tests. Employers usually require a clean driving record as well.

Potential and advancement

There are about 2.6 million truck drivers. Because earnings are high and no formal training is required, truck drivers usually face competition for attractive job openings, even though the field is growing. Opportunities for truck drivers will be favorable, as a growing population means increased movement of goods within every area.

Local truck drivers can advance to long-distance driving and occasionally to positions in scheduling or dispatching. Long-distance truck drivers have limited opportunities for advancement. Some move to positions as safety supervisors or driver supervisors, but the lower starting pay and lack of independence usually do not appeal to them.

Income

Average earnings for truck drivers are about $11.60 an hour.

The earnings of long-distance truck drivers vary depending on miles driven, hours worked, and type of truck. Their earnings range from $20,000 to $50,000 a year.

Additional sources of information

American Trucking Associations, Inc.
2200 Mill Road
Alexandria, VA 22314

U

UNDERWRITER

The job

Because insurance companies assume millions of dollars in risks by transferring the chance of loss from their policyholders to themselves, they employ underwriters to study and select the risks the company will insure. Underwriters analyze insurance applications, medical reports, actuarial studies, and other material. They must use personal judgment in making decisions that could cause their company to lose business or competitors (if they are too conservative) or to pay too many claims (if they are too liberal).

Most underwriters specialize in one of the three basic types of insurance: life, property-liability, or health. Property-liability underwriters also specialize by type of risk: fire, automobile, or workers' compensation, for example. Underwriters correspond with policyholders, insurance agents, and insurance office managers. They sometimes accompany salespeople as they call on customers and may attend meetings with union representatives or union members to explain the provisions of group policies.

Underwriters who specialize in commercial underwriting often evaluate a firm's entire operation before approving its application for insurance. The growing trend toward package underwriting of various types of risks under a single policy requires that the underwriter be familiar with several different lines of insurance, rather than be specialized in just one line.

Beginners work under the close supervision of an experienced underwriter. They progress from evaluating routine applications to handling those that are more complex and have greater face value.

Related jobs are actuary, claim representative, and insurance agent and broker.

Places of employment and working conditions

Most underwriters are employed in the home offices of their companies, which are usually located in and around Boston, Chicago, Dallas, Hartford, New York City, Philadelphia, and San Francisco. Some are also employed in regional offices in other parts of the country.

Underwriting is basically a desk job. The average workweek is 37 hours with occasional overtime required.

Qualifications, education, and training

A career as an underwriter can be very satisfying to someone who likes to work with details and who enjoys relating and evaluating information. Underwriters must be able to make decisions and be able to communicate well. They must often be both imaginative and aggressive when searching out information from outside sources.

High school courses in mathematics are valuable.

Some small insurance companies will hire underwriter trainees without a college degree. Large insurance companies require a college degree, preferably in liberal arts or business administration.

As in all jobs in the insurance industry, great emphasis is placed on the completion of independent study programs throughout an employee's career. Salary increases and tuition costs are often provided by the company on completion of a course. The study programs are available through a number of insurance organizations and professional societies.

Potential and advancement

About 103,000 underwriters work for insurance companies at the present time. The field is expected to grow significantly.

Experienced underwriters can advance to senior or chief underwriter or to underwriting manager if they complete appropriate courses. Some are promoted to supervisory and senior management positions.

Income

Annual earnings for underwriters range from $23,400 to $49,000 depending on their specialty and level of position. Those working in commercial insurance lines generally have higher salaries than their counterparts working in personal lines.

Most insurance companies have liberal employee benefits including life and health insurance and retirement pensions. Paid holidays are more numerous than in most other industries, and vacation policies are generous.

Additional sources of information

Alliance of American Insurers
1501 Woodfield Road
Suite 400 W
Schaumburg, IL 60173

American Council of Life Insurance
1001 Pennsylvania Avenue, NW
Washington, DC 20004

Insurance Information Institute
110 William Street
New York, NY 10038

The National Association of Independent Insurers
Public Relations Department
2600 River Road
Des Plaines, IL 60018

URBAN PLANNER

The job

Urban planners develop plans and programs to provide for the future growth of a community; revitalize run-down areas of a community; and achieve more efficient uses of the community's land, social services, industry, and transportation.

Before preparing plans or programs, urban planners conduct detailed studies of local conditions and current population. After preparing a plan, they develop cost estimates and other relevant materials and aid in the presentation of the program before community officials, planning boards, and citizens' groups.

Most urban planners (also called city planners, community planners, or regional planners) work for city, county, or regional planning agencies. State and federal agencies employ urban planners in the fields of housing, transportation, and environmental protection. Large land developers also employ urban planners, and some teach in colleges and universities.

Many urban planners do consulting work, either part-time in addition to a regular job or full-time for firms that provide planning services to private developers and government agencies.

Related jobs are architect, engineer, and landscape architect.

Places of employment and working conditions

Urban planners are employed throughout the United States in communities of all sizes.

A 40-hour workweek is usual for urban planners, but evening and weekend hours are often necessary for meetings and community activities.

Qualifications, education, and training

The ability to analyze relationships and to visualize plans and designs are necessary for urban planners. They should be able to work well with people and cooperate with those who may have different viewpoints.

High school students interested in this field should take social science and mathematics courses. Part-time or summer jobs in community government offices can be helpful.

Almost all jobs in this field require a master's degree in urban or regional planning, even for entry-level positions. Most graduate programs require two years to complete. Part-time or summer work in a planning office is usually a required part of the advanced degree program.

Urban planners seeking employment with federal, state, or local governments usually must pass civil service examinations before securing a position.

Potential and advancement

There are about 20,000 urban planners at work in the United States. This field is expected to grow through the year 2000, but demand for urban planners will be greater in some regions than others. Demand for urban planners will be higher in states such as Florida and Maine, which have mandated planning, and in rapidly growing areas such as California and northern Virginia. There will also be many opportunities in smaller cities and in older areas, like the Northeast, which are undergoing development and preservation.

Income

Median annual earnings for urban planners range from $34,700 to $50,000 depending on the type of employer and the worker's level of experience.

Additional sources of information

American Planning Association
1776 Massachusetts Avenue, NW
Washington, DC 20036

Association of Collegiate Schools of Planning
Department of Urban Planning
University of Wisconsin
P.O. Box 413
Milwaukee, WI 53201

V

VETERINARIAN

The job

Doctors of veterinary medicine diagnose, treat, and control diseases and injuries of animals. They treat animals in hospitals and clinics and on farms and ranches. They perform surgery and prescribe and administer drugs and vaccines.

While most familiar to the general public are those veterinarians who treat small animals and pets exclusively, others specialize in the health and breeding of cattle, horses, and other farm animals. Veterinarians are also employed by federal and state public health programs where they function as meat and poultry inspectors. Others teach at veterinary colleges; do research on animal foods, diseases, and drugs; or take part in medical research for the treatment of human diseases. Veterinarians are also employed by zoos, large animal farms, horse-racing stables, and drug manufacturers.

In the army, the air force, and the U.S. Public Health Service, veterinarians are commissioned officers. Other federally employed veterinarians work for the Department of Agriculture.

Places of employment and working conditions

Veterinarians are located throughout the country—in rural areas, small towns, cities, and suburban areas.

Working hours are often long and irregular, and those who work primarily with farm animals must work outdoors in all kinds of weather. In the course of their work, all veterinarians are exposed to injury, disease, and infection.

Qualifications, education, and training

A veterinarian needs the ability to get along with animals and should have an interest in science. Physical stamina and a certain amount of strength are also necessary.

High school students interested in this field should emphasize science courses, especially biology. Summer jobs that involve the care of animals can provide valuable experience.

The veterinary degree program (D.V.M. or V.M.D.) requires a minimum of six years of college—at least two years of preveterinary study with emphasis on physical and biological sciences followed by a four-year professional degree program. Most successful applicants complete four years of college before entering the professional program.

There are only 27 accredited colleges of veterinary medicine, many of them state supported. Admission to all of these schools is highly competitive with many more qualified applicants than the schools can accept. Successful applicants need preveterinary college grades of "B" or better, especially in science courses; part-time work or summer job experience working with animals is a plus. State-supported colleges usually give preference to residents of the state and to applicants from nearby states or regional areas.

The course of study in veterinary colleges is rigorous. It consists of classroom work and practical experience in diagnosing and treating animal diseases, surgery, laboratory work in anatomy and biochemistry, and other scientific and medical studies. Veterinarians who intend to teach or do research usually go on to earn a master's degree in pathology, physiology, or bacteriology.

All states and the District of Columbia require veterinarians to be licensed. Licensing requires a doctor of veterinary medicine degree from an accredited college and passing a written state board of proficiency examination. Some states will issue licenses without examination to veterinarians licensed by another state.

Potential and advancement

There are about 46,000 active veterinarians, most of them in private practice. Employment opportunities for veterinarians are excellent primarily because of growth in the population of companion animals—horses, dogs, and other pets—and an increase in veterinary research. The growing emphasis on scientific methods of breeding and raising livestock and poultry as well as an increase in public health and disease control programs will also contribute to the demand for veterinarians.

Income

The incomes of veterinarians in private practice vary greatly depending on type of practice, years of experience, and size and location of community. They usually have higher incomes, however, than veterinarians in salaried positions. The average starting salary for veterinarians is $23,000 a year. More experienced veterinarians' salaries range from $40,000 to $60,000 a year.

Additional sources of information

American Veterinary Medical Association
930 North Meacham Road
Schaumburg, IL 60196

WAITER

The job

As a result of rising personal incomes and increased leisure time, eating out at restaurants has become a very popular form of entertainment. Not only do restaurants serve as entertainment, they have also become a convenience for two-income families. Waiters play a very important role in the operation of the restaurant—often the type of service they provide determines whether the customer will return.

Waiters take orders, serve drinks and food, prepare checks, and accept payments. However, the manner in which they perform these tasks depends on the type of restaurant where they work. In restaurants that serve primarily sandwiches, often called coffee shops, waiters are expected to provide fast, friendly service. In more formal restaurants where gourmet food is served, waiters are expected to be able to make wine suggestions, explain how certain items on the menu are prepared, and prepare salads and other dishes at the table. Waiters at these restaurants work at a slower, more leisurely pace.

Other duties often performed by waiters include showing customers to their tables, setting or clearing tables, or cashiering.

Places of employment and working conditions

Eating establishments are located throughout the country but are most plentiful in large cities and tourist areas. Most waiters work in restaurants, coffee shops, bars, and other retail eating and drinking places. Others work in hotels, bowling alleys, casinos, and country clubs.

Waiters spend most of their working time on their feet and have to carry heavy trays of food, dishes, and glassware. They are under pressure to work quickly and efficiently.

Some waiters work 40 or more hours a week, but most work part-time. They are often scheduled to work evenings, weekends, and holidays.

Qualifications, education, and training

Waiters must be friendly and should enjoy working with people. Other important qualities are a neat appearance, a good memory, and basic math skills.

There are no formal education requirements for waiters. Most employers prefer to hire high school graduates in more formal restaurants, but completing high school is usually not necessary for jobs in coffee shops.

Most waiters receive on-the-job training from more experienced workers.

Potential and advancement

There are almost 2 million waiters, and opportunities should continue to be plentiful through the year 2000. This field has a very high turnover rate, and most openings will occur as workers leave the occupation.

Opportunities for advancement are limited in small restaurants. Most waiters advance by getting jobs in larger restaurants where the potential for earning tips is greater. Some waiters move into management or supervisory positions.

Income

Waiters' earnings are usually made up of tips plus an hourly wage. Median annual earnings for full-time waiters (including tips) is about $4.70 an hour.

Additional sources of information

Council on Hotel, Restaurant, and Institutional Education
1200 17th Street, NW
Washington, DC 20036-3097

The Educational Foundation of the National Restaurant Association
250 South Wacker Drive
Suite 1400
Chicago, IL 60606

WHOLESALER

The job

The wholesaler is a middle link in the distribution chain between the producer of goods and the retail store in which the goods are sold. Because no producer could possibly contact all the retail outlets or industries that use his or her products and no retail store manager has the time to contact all his or her suppliers individually, the wholesaler provides a valuable service to both segments of the marketplace.

The largest number of wholesalers are *merchant wholesalers* who buy merchandise outright, warehouse the merchandise until needed, and then sell to retail outlets. They employ salespeople to call on retail customers, extend credit to customers, and lend money to suppliers in the form of prepaid orders.

The second largest group in wholesaling is *manufacturer's agents*. These are independent businesspeople who contract with a manufacturer to sell a specific product or group of products, usually in a specific geographic area. A manufacturer's agent usually represents several manufacturers and sells to retail stores, local distributors, industrial concerns, and institutions. If the business is large enough, the agent may employ additional sales personnel. An industrial distributor is a wholesaler who handles one or more products of only one manufacturer.

Merchandise brokers may represent either the buyer or seller in a wholesale transaction. The broker, however, does not buy or take direct responsibility for the goods being sold but acts as the agent of either the buyer or seller. Merchandise brokers work mainly in a few fields—food and grocery specialties, fresh fruits and vegetables, piece goods, cotton, grain, livestock, and petroleum products.

Commission merchants usually deal in agricultural products. They take possession of, but not title to, the merchandise. They may store it, transport it, and condition it for market (inspect, weigh, grade) before finding a buyer. They charge a commission for their services as a part of the final selling price.

Auction companies are wholesalers who sell a client's product at a public auction. Most sales of this nature are in tobacco, fresh fruits and vegetables, livestock, floor coverings, furs and skins, jewelry, and furniture.

Related jobs are retail buyer, retail store manager, manufacturer's sales representative, import/export worker, and sales manager.

Places of employment and working conditions

Some wholesalers, especially the largest and best known, are in large cities such as Chicago, Kansas City, Los Angeles, New York, and St. Louis. The others are located throughout the United States, many of them in small cities and towns.

Wholesalers, especially those dealing in perishable or seasonal goods, run the risk of sudden financial loss. They must have a secure financial base to carry them over lean periods or unexpected losses.

Qualifications, education, and training

Good judgment, business and management skills, experience as a buyer or salesperson, and an ability to deal with people are all necessary.

There are no specific education requirements for this field. The largest wholesalers, however, usually require experience or training in business administration, sales and marketing, retailing, or a particular technical area such as electrical products or other industrial fields.

Potential and advancement

The best job opportunities for beginners are with smaller wholesalers, while persons with appropriate college education can often start in management-level positions with large wholesalers.

Income

Income varies greatly depending on the size of the business. Small wholesalers earn from about $12,600 to $57,000 a year; large ones up to $100,000.

Manufacturer's agents average about $23,000 to $67,000 a year; a few earn over $100,000.

Additional sources of information

Manufacturer's Agents' National Association
23016 Mill Creek Road
P.O. Box 3467
Laguna Hills, CA 92653

National-American Wholesale Grocers Association
51 Madison Avenue
New York, NY 10010

National Association of Wholesaler-Distributors
1725 K Street, NW
Washington, DC 20006

WORD PROCESSOR

The job

Modern offices process a great deal of information and data and keep numerous records. Word processors play an important role in maintaining this function.

Word processors use word processing equipment to make copies of reports, letters, and memoranda. They are also responsible for editing, storing, and revising these materials. In large organizations, there is often a word processing center where the typing for several departments is done. Some word processors work throughout the company and come into close contact with other employees.

Word processors often have additional tasks such as answering telephones, filing, and operating copiers and other office machines.

Places of employment and working conditions

Word processors work throughout the country in firms that provide business services, educational institutions, health care facilities, law offices, and government agencies.

Word processors work in offices and must sit for long hours.

Recent studies have shown that there can be physical and mental health hazards for word processors. They may experience musculoskeletal strain, eye problems, and stress. Women may risk pregnancy complications, miscarriages, and birth defects.

Word processors usually work 37 to 40 hours a week. There are a variety of work arrangements for word processors. Many hold temporary jobs or work part-time.

Qualifications, education, and training

Word processors need to have spelling, grammar, and punctuation skills. They should have familiarity with office procedures and different types of standard office equipment. Most employers prefer to hire applicants who are high school graduates.

Word processing can be learned in high schools, community colleges, business schools, home study schools, or by using self-teaching aids.

Potential and advancement

Employment of word processors is expected to decline through the year 2000 due to the productivity that has resulted from the increasing use of automated office equipment. In spite of this decline, there will still be thousands of job openings as workers leave the profession to retire or transfer to other occupations.

Word processing positions are often filled by workers who are beginning their first job. Often these positions serve as steppingstones to higher-paying jobs. Word processors often become secretaries, statistical clerks, or stenographers. They may also become the supervisor in a word processing department.

Income

Word processors earn average annual salaries of $18,148. Salaries tend to be highest in transportation and public utilities and lowest in retail trade, finance, insurance, and real estate. The highest-paying region of the country is the West.

Additional sources of information

For information about job opportunities in word processing, contact the nearest office of the state employment service.

Index

INDEX

American Association of Language Specialists, The, 232

American Association of Museums, 294

American Association of Nurserymen, Inc., 306

American Association of Political Consultants, 252

American Association of School Administrators, 421

American Association of State Highway and Transportation Officials, 466

American Association of University Professors, 453

American Association of Medical Assistants, The, 274

American Bankers Association, 59, 61

American Bar Association (ABA), 243, 244

American Board of Funeral Service Education, 189

American Board of Neurology and Psychiatry, 377

American Board of Ophthalmology, 323

American Ceramic Society, 83

American Chemical Society, 91

American Chiropractic Association, 95

American College of Bryn Mawr, 224

American College of Health Care Administrators, 207

American College of Healthcare Executives, 208

American Congress on Surveying and Mapping, 447

American Correctional Association, 122, 336

American Council of Life Insurance, 110, 477

American Council on Education, 453

American Council on Education for Journalism, 299

American Culinary Federation, 86

American Dance Guild, 132

American Dental Assistants Association, 134

American Dental Association, 139

American Dental Association Joint Commision, 135

American Dental Hygienists' Association, 136

American Design Drafting Association, 143

American Dietetic Association, The, 141

American Economic Association, 147

American Farm Bureau Federation, 171

American Federation of Information Processing Societies, 116

American Federation of Musicians, 296, 431

American Federation of Teachers, 453, 455, 457

American Forestry Association, 184

American Fur Industry, 173

American Geological Institute, 195

American Geophysical Union, 198, 285

American Guild of Musical Artists, 431

American Historical Association, 210

American Home Economics Association, 212

American Hotel and Motel Association, The, 214

American Industrial Hygiene Association, 418

American Industrial Real Estate Association, 71

American Institute for Property and Liability Underwriters, 224

American Institute of Aeronautics and Astronautics, Inc., 24

American Institute of Architects, The, 49

American Institute of Biological Sciences, 250

American Institute of Certified Public Accountants, 1, 4

American Institute of Chemical Engineers, 88

American Institute of Graphic Artists, 200

American Institute of Physics, 357

American Institute of Real Estate Appraisers, 399, 400

American League of Financial Institutions, 61

American Library Association, 247

American Management Association, 314, 375

American Marketing Association, 264, 266

American Mathematical Society, 269

American Medical Association (AMA), 353, 355, 376, 377

American Medical Association's Committee on Allied Health Education and Accreditation (CAHEA), 273

American Medical Record Association (AMRA), 278, 279

American Medical Technologists, 277

American Meteorological Society, 285

American Music Conference, 296

American Mutual Insurance Alliance, 110

American Newspaper Publishers Association, 19, 152, 299

American Nurses' Association, 303

American Occupational Therapy Association, 309

American Optometric Association, 328

American Osteopathic Association, 330

American Osteopathic Board of Ophthalmology, 323

American Physical Society, 357

American Physical Therapy Association, 350

American Physiological Society, 250

American Planning Association, 479

American Podiatric Medical Association, 361

American Production and Inventory Control Society, 375

American Psychiatric Association, 376, 378

American Psychological Association, 381

American Registry of Radiologic Technologists, 392

American Rehabilitation Counseling Association, 404

American School Counselor Association, 204

American Society for Biochemistry and Molecular Biology, 63

American Society for Engineering Education, 24, 29, 65, 83, 88, 102, 154, 165, 221, 271, 283, 288, 340

American Society for Information Science, 247

American Society for Medical Technology, 277

American Society for Microbiology, 250

American Society for Personnel Administration, 239, 338

American Society for Training and Development, 338

American Society of Agricultural Engineers, 29

American Society of Agronomy, 436, 438

American Society of Appraisers, 399